Human Development
across the Life Span 7e

Carol K. Sigelman
The George Washington University

Elizabeth A. Rider
Elizabethtown College

WADSWORTH
CENGAGE Learning

Australia • Brazil • Japan • Korea • Mexico • Singapore • Spain • United Kingdom • United States

**Human Development across the Life Span,
Seventh Edition, International Edition**
Carol K. Sigelman, Elizabeth A. Rider

Senior Editor: Jaime Perkins

Associate Developmental Editor: Nicolas Albert

Assistant Editor: Paige Leeds

Editorial Assistant: Phil Hovanessian

Media Editor: Lauren Keyes

Marketing Manager: Jessica Egbert

Marketing Assistant: Anna Andersen

Marketing Communications Manager: Laura Localio

Content Project Manager: Rita Jaramillo

Design Director: Rob Hugel

Art Director: Vernon Boes

Print Buyer: Karen Hunt

Rights Acquisitions Specialist: Roberta Broyer

Production Service: Megan Greiner,
Graphic World Inc.

Text Designer: Jeanne Calabrese

Photo Researcher: Kim Adams Fox, Roaring Lion
Image Research LLC

Text Researcher: Sarah d'Stair

Copy Editor: Graphic World Inc.

Cover Designer: Jeanne Calabrese

Cover Image: Greg Pease/Getty Images

Compositor: Graphic World Inc.

Library of Congress Control Number: 2011920073

International Edition:
ISBN-13: 978-1-111-34315-6
ISBN-10: 1-111-34315-2

Cengage Learning International Offices

Asia
www.cengageasia.com
tel: (65) 6410 1200

Australia/New Zealand
www.cengage.com.au
tel: (61) 3 9685 4111

Brazil
www.cengage.com.br
tel: (55) 11 3665 9900

India
www.cengage.co.in
tel: (91) 11 4364 1111

Latin America
www.cengage.com.mx
tel: (52) 55 1500 6000

UK/Europe/Middle East/Africa
www.cengage.co.uk
tel: (44) 0 1264 332 424

**Represented in Canada by Nelson
Education, Ltd.**
tel: (416) 752 9100 / (800) 668 0671
www.nelson.com

Cengage Learning is a leading provider of customized learning solutions with office locations around the globe, including Singapore, the United Kingdom, Australia, Mexico, Brazil, and Japan. Locate your local office at:
www.cengage.com/global

For product information: **www.cengage.com/international**

Visit your local office: **www.cengage.com/global**

Visit our corporate website: **www.cengage.com**

AVAILABILITY OF RESOURCES MAY DIFFER BY REGION. Check with your local Cengage Learning representative for details.

Printed in China
2 3 4 5 6 7 14 13 12

To the students who have inspired us

brief contents

contents

3 Biological and Environmental Influences on Development 74

Odilon Dimier/PhotoAlto/Corbis

6 Perceptual Development **184**

© Stuart O'Sullivan/Corbis

9 Intelligence 286

© Indeed/Photodisc/Getty Images

12 Gender and Sexuality 392

© Cindy Karp/*New York Times/Redux*

15 Human Development and the Family 494

© Larry Dale Gordon/The Image Bank/Getty Images

This book is about the development of human beings—from their days as fertilized eggs to their dying days. It highlights regularities as well as differences in development, and it asks fundamental questions about why we humans develop as we do. The field of life-span human development is a dynamic one, and we attempt to keep up with the change in this, the seventh edition of *Human Development across the Life Span*.

This new edition incorporates many exciting changes, yet it retains four core features valued by students and instructors over the years: (1) our unique integrated topical–chronological approach, (2) a presentation that is both research-based and relevant to students, (3) an emphasis on ideas—on the different theoretical perspectives that guide thinking about human development and research—and (4) an in-depth exploration of the all-important nature–nurture issue. In addition, we introduce new topics and controversies in life-span human development, update coverage throughout, and offer new pedagogical features and supplements to enhance the teaching–learning process.

Topical and Chronological Approach

The most distinctive feature of this book is its unique integrated topical–chronological approach. Almost all other life-span development textbooks adopt a chronological or "age–stage" approach, carving the life span into age ranges and describing the prominent characteristics of individuals within each age range. In contrast, we adopt a topical approach for the overall organization of the book blended with a chronological approach within chapters. Each chapter focuses on a domain of development, such as physical growth, cognition, or personality, and traces developmental trends and influences in that domain from infancy to old age. Each chapter also highlights the special qualities of different age groups through major sections on infancy, childhood, adolescence, and adulthood.

Why Topical?

Why have we fought the tide? Like many other instructors, we have typically favored topically organized textbooks when teaching child-, adolescent-, or adult-development courses. As a result, it seemed natural to use that same topical approach in introducing students to the whole life span. Besides, chronologically organized texts often have to repeat themselves as they remind

readers of where development left off in an earlier age period that was covered in a previous chapter.

More important, a topic-by-topic organization conveys the flow of development in each area—the systematic, and often dramatic, transformations that take place as well as the developmental continuities. The topical approach also helps us emphasize the processes behind development.

Finally, a predominantly topical approach is more compatible with a life-span perspective, which views each period of life in relation to what comes before and what is yet to come. In chronologically organized textbooks, many topics are described only in connection with the age group to which they seem most relevant—for example, attachment in relation to infancy, or sexuality in relation to adolescence and adulthood. A topical organization stimulates us to ask intriguing questions we might otherwise not ask, such as these about attachment relationships:

- What do infants' attachments to their parents have in common with, and how do they differ from, attachments between childhood friends or between adult romantic partners?
- Do securely attached infants later have a greater capacity to form and sustain friendships or romantic partnerships than infants whose early social experiences are less favorable?
- What are the consequences at different points in the life span of lacking a close relationship?

Attachments are important throughout the life span, and a topical organization helps make that clear.

Why Chronological?

We also appreciate the strengths of the chronological approach, particularly its ability to portray the whole person in each period of the life span. For this reason, we integrated the age–stage approach with the topical organization, aiming to have the best of both worlds.

Each topical chapter contains major sections on infancy, childhood, adolescence, and adulthood. The existence of these sections is proof that the chapters consider development in each of the domains covered across the whole life span. These age–stage sections call attention to the distinctive qualities of each phase of life and make it easier for students to find material on an age period of particular interest to them. In short, we believe that our integrated topical–chronological approach allows us to convey the flow of life-span development in particular areas and the factors influencing it while highlighting the major physical, cognitive, and psychosocial developments within any particular developmental period.

Adaptability of the Integrated Topical–Chronological Approach

Even though links among chapters are noted throughout the book, instructors who are teaching short courses or who are otherwise pressed for time can omit a chapter without fear of rendering other chapters incomprehensible. For example:

- A cognitively oriented course might omit one or more of the socially oriented chapters (Chapters 11, 12, and 14–17).
- A socially oriented course might omit one or more of the cognitively oriented chapters (Chapters 6–10).

Moreover, this approach gives instructors the flexibility to cover infancy, childhood, and adolescence in the first portion of the course, if they prefer, and to save the material on adulthood for the end.

Research-Oriented and Relevant Coverage

We have worked hard to create a text that is rigorous yet readable—research-oriented yet "real" to students. The seventh edition of *Human Development across the Life Span* tackles complex theoretical controversies and presents the best of both classic and contemporary research from multiple disciplines in a way that is accessible and relevant to students' life experiences and career development.

We believe that it is critical for students to understand how we know what we know about development—to appreciate the research process. With that in mind, we describe illustrative studies and present their data in graphs and tables, and we cite the authors and dates of publication for a large number of books and articles, all fully referenced in the bibliography at the end of the book. Some students may wonder why they are there. It is because we are committed to the value of systematic research, because we are bound to give credit where credit is due, and because we want students and their professors to have the resources they need to pursue their interests in human development during and after the course.

We also appreciate that solid scholarship is of little good to students unless they want to read it, can understand it, and see its relevance. We maintain that even the most complex issues in human development can be made understandable through clear and organized writing. To make the material more "real," we clarify developmental concepts through examples and analogies, connect topics in the text to topics in the news, and highlight the practical implications of research findings. We also incorporate applied material relevant to students' current and future roles as parents, teachers, psychologists, health professionals, and other human service professionals. And we help students see that major theories of human development do not just guide researchers but can help anyone analyze issues that we all face—including such practical matters as raising and educating children, working with troubled adolescents, or coping with Alzheimer's disease or death in the family.

Theoretical Grounding

Theories are critical in any science, telling scientists what to study, how to study it, and how to interpret their findings. We want students to leave the study of life-span human development with more than facts alone; we want them to appreciate the major issues of interest to developmental scientists and how the leading theories in the field have shaped our thinking about development. Most important, we want students to learn to use these theoretical perspectives to guide their thinking and action when they encounter a question about human development outside the course.

With this in mind, we have devoted Chapter 2 to laying out in broad strokes the psychoanalytic, learning, cognitive developmental, and epigenetic systems perspectives on human development, showing what they say, where they stand on key developmental issues, and how they would explain developmental phenomena such as school refusal and teenage pregnancy. We delve deeper into these and other perspectives and show how they have been applied to the study of specific aspects of development in later chapters; see, for example, a treatment of the dynamic systems view of motor development in Chapter 5; a comparison of Jean Piaget's cognitive-developmental and Lev Vygotsky's sociocultural perspectives in Chapter 7; an application of the information-processing perspective in Chapter 8; alternative views of intelligence in Chapter 9; nativist, learning, and interactionist theories of language development in Chapter 10; alternative theories of personality development in Chapter 11; theories of gender role in chapter 12; theories of moral development in Chapter 13; attachment theory in Chapter 14; and family systems theory in Chapter 15.

Nature–Nurture Theme

Finally, we want students to gain a deeper understanding of the nature–nurture issue and of the many interacting forces affecting the developing person. We want students to appreciate that human development is an incredibly complex process that grows out of transactions between a changing person and a changing world and out of dynamic relationships among biological, psychological, and social influences. No contributor to development—a gene, a temperament, a parent, a culture—acts alone and is unaffected by other influences on development.

We introduce the nature–nurture issue in Chapter 1 and give it extended treatment in Chapter 3 on genes and environment. Each subsequent chapter includes one or more illustrations of the intertwined contributions of nature and nurture to development. Along the way, we describe some exciting studies that compare individuals with and without particular genes and with and without particular life experiences to bring home what it means to say that genes and environment interact to influence development— as when genes predisposing an individual to depression combine with stressful life events to produce depression. We also illustrate the many ways in which genes and environment are intertwined and affect one another—for instance, ways in which genetic makeup influences the experiences an individual has, and ways in which experience influences which of an individual's genes are activated or expressed. In this edition, we have expanded coverage not only of genes, hormones, brain functions, and other biological forces in development but also of ways in which ethnicity, social class, community, and the larger cultural context modify development. Most important, we illuminate the complex interrelationships between biological and environmental influences that are at the heart of the developmental process.

The following theme index shows the scope of coverage of the nature–nurture issue in this text:

Nature–Nurture Theme Index

Organization of the Text

Core Concepts: Chapters 1 to 4

The book begins by orienting students to the life-span perspective on human development and to approaches to the scientific study of development (Chapter 1), as well as to the central issues and theoretical perspectives that have dominated the field (Chapter 2). It then explores developmental processes in some depth, examining genetic and environmental influences on development (Chapter 3) and then focusing on prenatal and other early environmental influences (Chapter 4). These chapters establish how both genes and environments contribute to both typical changes and individual differences throughout the life span.

Development of Basic Human Capacities: Chapters 5 to 10

Chapters on the growth and aging of the body and nervous system (Chapter 5) and on the development of sensory and perceptual capacities (Chapter 6) launch our examination of the development of basic human capacities. Chapter 7 covers Jean Piaget's perspective on cognitive development and the quite different perspective offered by Lev Vygotsky; Chapter 8 views memory and problem solving from an information-processing perspective; Chapter 9 highlights the psychometric approach to cognition, exploring individual differences in intelligence and creativity; and Chapter 10 explores language development and the roles of language, cognition, and motivation in educational achievement.

Development of Self in Society: Chapters 11 to 17

The next three chapters concern the development of the self: changes in self-conceptions and personality, including in vocational identity (Chapter 11); in gender roles and sexuality (Chapter 12); and in social cognition and morality (Chapter 13). The self is set more squarely in a social context as we trace life-span changes in attachment relationships (Chapter 14) and in roles and relationships within the family (Chapter 15). Finally, we offer a life-span perspective on developmental problems and disorders (Chapter 16) and examine why people die and how they cope with death (Chapter 17).

Getting the Big Picture

To help students pull together the "big picture" of life-span human development at the end of the course, we remind students of some of the major themes of the book at the end of Chapter 17 and offer a chart inside the back cover that summarizes major developments in each of the seven periods of the life span. Finally, the appendix, Careers in Human Development, lays out possibilities for translating an interest in human development into a career in research, teaching, or professional practice.

New Features in This Edition

In this edition, we have made several changes intended to increase students' active engagement with the material. We have begun chapters with Ask Yourself This boxes that pose questions to guide students' reading, and we have ended each numbered chapter section with Checking Mastery and Making Connections questions to encourage students to test themselves on and think in new ways about the material. We have also created Engagement boxes that challenge students to look at themselves in new ways.

Ask Yourself This

To help students read with a purpose, we pose the major questions addressed in the chapter in a box at the beginning of the chapter.

Checking Mastery Questions

To encourage students to actively check their command of the material as they progress through the chapter, we have posed two to four Checking Mastery questions at the end of each numbered chapter section, the answers to which are online at www.cengagebrain.com.

Making Connections Questions

At the end of each major section, Making Connections questions invite students to reflect on the material—to weigh in on a debate in the field, evaluate the material's implications for public policy, apply the material to a case example, or explore the material's relevance to their own development.

Engagement Boxes

This new feature is a new kind of box that supplements the Exploration and Application boxes we have included in previous editions. Engagement boxes provide opportunities for students to engage actively and personally with the material—to assess their own knowledge, beliefs, traits, and attitudes by completing personality scales, test items, surveys, and short quizzes (see later examples).

Content Updates

As always, the book has been thoroughly updated to convey the most recent discoveries and insights developmentalists have to offer. We take pride in having written a well-researched and well-referenced book that professors and students can use as a resource. We have added some exciting new topics and greatly revised, expanded, and updated coverage of other topics. A sampling:

Chapter 1. Introduction to the Human Life Span

- A fascinating excerpt from Charles Darwin's baby biography of his son
- Introduction of the concept of neuroplasticity and of the increasing role of functional magnetic resonance imaging in studying brain-behavior relationships
- Relationship between the scientific goal of optimizing development and today's emphasis on evidence-based practice in many professions
- Rites of passage from adolescence to adulthood and the issue of when a person is an adult

Chapter 2. Ways to Think about Human Development

- Focus on school refusal as a developmental phenomenon to be explained by the major theories of development
- Illustration of the application of theories to reducing unwanted teenage pregnancy
- More on psychoanalytic theory and learning theory so that primary coverage of these theories is now in Chapter 2
- Reorganized and updated coverage of Gottlieb's epigenetic psychobiological systems theory

Chapter 3. Biological and Environmental Influences on Development

- Engagement box testing for common misconceptions about genetic influences on development
- The latest on fragile X syndrome and its implications for relatives of an affected child
- Early environmental influences on gene expression, including exciting research by Meaney, Champagne, and others on how early parenting of rat pups can affect gene expression and, in turn, later parenting style and ability to cope with stress
- Updates on uses of gene therapy and stem cell therapy to treat genetic disorders

Chapter 4. The Prenatal Period and Birth

- The latest research on prenatal development and teratogens
- New section on sibling adjustment to birth of a new baby
- Engagement box testing knowledge of teratogens
- Effects of diabetes and mercury exposure during pregnancy
- Mother's race/ethnicity and fetal/infant mortality rates
- Exploration box on untangling the effects of nature and nurture in studying effects of a mother's smoking during pregnancy
- Exploration box on why pregnant women might not know they are pregnant

Chapter 5. Physical Development and Health

- Substantial revision and addition of material on health, nutrition, weight issues, and obesity, including discussion of diabetes
- Expanded discussion of celiac disease
- Engagement box allowing students to estimate how their lifestyle choices will affect their life expectancy

Chapter 6. Perceptual Development

- Coverage of attention deficit hyperactivity disorder (ADHD) and an Engagement box on recognizing adult ADHD symptoms
- New material on the chemical senses and adolescence
- Engagement box on supertasters

Chapter 7. Cognitive Development

- Simplified presentation of Piaget's explanation of development and position on nature–nurture
- Engagement box testing students' knowledge of Piaget's stages of cognitive development
- Expanded coverage of scientific thinking, including research by Bullock, Sodian, and Koerber on LOGIC
- Strengthened discussion of postformal thought

Chapter 8. Information Processing and Memory

- Chapter opener on Jill Price, woman with a phenomenal autobiographical memory
- Engagement box on improving your memory
- More on the neural bases of memory

Chapter 9. Intelligence

- Revised coverage of Sternberg's triarchic theory of intelligence
- Expanded coverage of creativity
- Discussion of neuroplasticity

Chapter 10. Language Development and Education

- Reorganized coverage of language development to clarify what must be mastered, when it is mastered, and how it happens
- More on the neurobiological underpinnings of language
- Engagement box on identifying one's motivation style

Chapter 11. The Conceptualization of Self and Personality

- New material on the significance of personality for health, well-being, and development

- Expanded coverage of ageist stereotypes
- More on retirement, including a new graph on labor force participation and an Exploration box on husbands' and wives' experiences of retirement

Chapter 12. Gender and Sexuality

- Clarification of sex versus gender and the relative importance of gender similarities versus differences
- Emphasis on agentic and communal roles rather than masculine or feminine stereotypes
- New Engagement box with the Personal Attributes Questionnaire asking students to self-assess their views of gender types
- New summary table on STDs

Chapter 13. Social Cognitive and Moral Development

- More on infant social cognition, including intriguing evidence that infants understand false beliefs and evaluate other people based on their behavior
- New neuroscience discoveries about areas of the brain involved in social cognition and the role of mirror neurons
- Engagement box with a sample theory-of-mind task suitable for adults
- More on bullying in schools
- New section on religion and spirituality across the life span
- Dual-process model of the roles of rational thought and emotion/intuition in morality

Chapter 14. Human Development and Relationships

- Exploration box on the significance of the hormone oxytocin in intimate relationships
- Engagement box asking students which orientation toward attachment relationships best describes themselves
- Research on how co-rumination about personal problems by adolescent girlfriends may aggravate depression and anxiety symptoms
- Revised coverage of adult romantic relationships, with more on mate selection and the nature of love
- Application box on attachment therapies, including emotion-focused therapy for couples

Chapter 15. Human Development and the Family

- Updates on trends in the American family, including increased births to unmarried women
- Revised coverage of the family life cycle concept and diverse family experiences
- Research on the involvement of unmarried fathers with their children

- Exploration box on the intergenerational transmission of parenting and explanations of why abused children are at risk to become abusive parents

Chapter 16. Human Development and Psychopathology

- Preview of the upcoming revision of the *Diagnostic and Statistical Manual of Mental Disorders, DSM-V*
- More on the distinction between externalizing and internalizing problems in childhood
- Exploration box on child mental health problems in the aftermath of Hurricane Katrina
- A dissonance approach to preventing eating disorders
- New section on substance abuse in adolescence
- Coverage of the Maudsley approach to family therapy for adolescents with eating disorders

Chapter 17. Death and Dying

- The latest on why we age and die, including new research on telomeres and prospects for extending life
- Evidence that some patients in "vegetative states" may have more awareness than we thought
- New data on death-hastening practices around the world
- New Exploration box on secrets to long life among centenarians in Okinawa, Japan
- More on the dual process model of bereavement
- Introduction of the concept of disenfranchised grief

Chapter Organization

The chapters of this book use a consistent format and contain the following:

- A chapter outline that orients students to what lies ahead
- A chapter opener that engages student interest
- An Ask Yourself This box that states key questions to guide chapter reading
- Introductory material that lays out the plan for the chapter and introduces key concepts, theories, and issues relevant to the area of development to be explored
- Developmental sections (in Chapters 5–17) that describe and explain key changes and continuities during four developmental periods: infancy, childhood, adolescence, and adulthood

This edition includes three kinds of boxes, each with a different purpose:

Exploration boxes allow more in-depth investigation of research on a topic (for example, characteristics of the baby boom generation, effects of early experience on gene expression, brain development and adolescent risk taking, aging drivers, language acquisition among deaf children, his and her retirements, parenting in cultural contexts, Hurricane Katrina and mental health, and secrets to a long life).

Application boxes examine how knowledge has been applied to optimize development in a domain of development (for instance, to prevent teenage pregnancy, treat genetic defects, promote healthy babies, improve cognitive functioning, combat the effects of negative stereotypes of aging, treat aggressive youth, strengthen relationships, prevent family violence, treat children with psychological disorders, and support bereaved families).

Engagement boxes provide opportunities for students to engage personally with the material (for example, by deciding where they stand on major issues in development, determining how long they can be expected to live, finding out if they might have characteristics associated with ADHD, completing a "Big Five" personality scale, or determining their orientation toward romantic attachment relationships).

Checking Mastery and Making Connections questions after each major chapter section challenge students to test their understanding of the chapter material and to think about or apply it in new ways.

The Chapter Summary section at the end of each chapter gives an overview of the chapter's main themes to facilitate student learning and review of the material.

The Key Terms section lists the new terms introduced in the chapter in the order in which they were introduced and with the page number on which they were introduced. The terms are printed in boldface, defined when they are first presented in a chapter, and included in the glossary at the end of the book.

The Media Resources section describes selected websites that offer further information about chapter topics and are accessible from the book's website at www.cengagebrain.com. Students are also directed to the other resources available at that site, including Understanding the Data: Exercises on the Web and the online diagnostic study tool CengageNOW.

Supplements

The seventh edition of *Human Development across the Life Span* is accompanied by a better array of supplements prepared for both the instructor and the student to create the best learning environment inside and outside the classroom. All the supplements have been thoroughly revised and updated. Especially noteworthy are the media and Internet-based supplements. We invite instructors and students to examine and take advantage of the teaching and learning tools available.

For the Instructor

Instructor's Manual with Test Bank. Revised by Bradley Caskey, University of Wisconsin, River Falls. This manual contains chapter-specific outlines; a list of print, video, and online resources; and student learning objectives. The manual has a special emphasis on active learning with suggested student activities and projects for each chapter. The test bank, in both print and computerized form, consists of 135 multiple-choice, 20 true-or-false, 20 fill-in-the-blank, and 10 essay questions for each chapter. Questions are marked with the correct answer, main text page reference, and difficulty and are keyed to the Learning Objectives.

Microsoft® PowerPoint® lecture slides with graphics from the text by Pat Lefler of Bluegrass Community and Technical College. These lecture slides contain figures from the text and videos, allowing you to bring together text-specific lecture outlines and art from the text, along with video and animations from the web or your own materials—culminating in a powerful, personalized, media-enhanced presentation.

ExamView® testing software with all the test items from the printed Test Bank in electronic format enables you to create customized tests of up to 250 items in print or online.

ABC® Videos for Life-Span Development. The ABC videos feature short, high-interest clips about current studies and research in psychology. These videos are perfect for discussion starters or to enrich lectures. Some topics include:

- Infant Mental Health
- Fathers and Autism
- Foster Care
- Child and Adult Daycare
- Midlife Memory
- Alzheimer's Test

Contact your sales representative to order.
DVD ISBN-10: 0-495-50315-0; ISBN-13: 978-0-495-50315-6
VHS ISBN-10: 0-495-00328-X; ISBN-13: 978-0-495-00328-1

Wadsworth Developmental Psychology Video Library. Bring developmental psychology concepts to life with videos from Wadsworth's Developmental Psychology Video Library, which includes thought-provoking offerings from Films for Humanities and other excellent educational video sources. This extensive collection illustrates important developmental psychology concepts covered in many life-span courses. Certain adoption conditions apply.

For the Student

Study Guide. Written by coauthor Elizabeth A. Rider of Elizabethtown College, the *Study Guide* is designed to promote active learning through a guided review of the important principles and concepts in the text. The study materials for each chapter include a comprehensive multiple-choice self-test and exercises that challenge students to think about and to apply what they have learned.
ISBN-10: 1-111-35137-6; ISBN-13: 978-1-111-35137-3

Internet-Based Supplements

Psychology CourseMate at www.cengagebrain.com. Access an integrated e-book and chapter-specific learning tools including flashcards, quizzes, videos, Checking Mastery answers, and Understanding the Data exercises.

CengageNOW. Not only is CengageNOW a valuable course-management and time-saving tool for instructors, it *also* offers many features that provide students with efficient ways to study for success in the course. CengageNOW includes diagnostic pre-tests and post-tests, with resulting Personalized Study Plans. For every chapter, students' unique Personalized Study Plans enable them to focus on what they need to learn and select the activities that best match their learning styles. CengageNOW includes an integrated e-book, videos, simulations, and animations—all designed to help students gain a deeper understanding of important concepts. Prompts at the end of each chapter guide students online to CengageNOW.

CengageNOW includes pre-tests and post-tests written by Peter Green of Maryville University. If the textbook does not include an access code card, students can go to www.cengagebrain.com to order an access code.

CengageBrain. At www.cengagebrain.com, students can select from more than 10,000 print and digital study tools, including the option to buy individual e-chapters and e-books. The first e-chapter is free.

WebTutor™ on WebCT™ and Blackboard. This online supplement helps students succeed by taking them into an environment rich with study and mastery tools, communication aids, and additional course content. For students, WebTutor Toolbox™ offers real-time access to a full array of study tools, including flashcards (with audio), practice quizzes, Internet exercises, asynchronous discussion, a whiteboard, and an integrated e-mail system. Instructors can use WebTutor Toolbox™ to offer virtual office hours, to post syllabi, to set up threaded discussions, to track student progress on quizzes, and more. You can customize the content of WebTutor Toolbox™ in any way you choose, including by uploading images and other resources, adding web links, and creating course-specific practice materials.

Acknowledgments

We would like to express our continuing debt to David Shaffer of the University of Georgia for allowing his child development textbook to inform the first and second editions of this book.

Credit for excellent supplementary materials goes to Bradley Caskey, who revised the *Instructor's Manual with Test Bank*, and coauthor Elizabeth Rider, who wrote the *Study Guide* that accompanies this book.

Producing this book required the joint efforts of Wadsworth and Graphic World Publishing Services. We thank our editor, Jaime Perkins, for his capable leadership of the project, and Tali Beesley, our development editor, for her thorough and thoughtful readings of each chapter and special efforts to make this edition the most visually appealing and pedagogically effective edition yet. We thank Megan Greiner at Graphic World for outstanding management of the book's production and Kim Adams for photo research. All of these pros were a joy to work with, and the book is much better because of them. We are grateful, as well, for the able assistance of Rita Jaramillo, production project manager; Vernon Boes, art director; Lauren Keyes, media editor; and Paige Leeds, assistant editor. We also appreciate the strong support of Talia Wise, advertising project manager; Jessica Egbert, marketing manager; and Anna Anderson, marketing assistant.

We remain deeply indebted to sponsoring editors past—to C. Deborah Laughton, who insisted that this project be undertaken, and to Vicki Knight, who skillfully shepherded the first edition through its final stages and oversaw the second edition. Finally, Lee Sigelman is owed a lifetime of gratitude for a life of love, and Corby Rider and Tucker deserve the deepest appreciation for their patience, understanding, and ability to entertain themselves (quietly) while mom works.

Reviewers

We are very grateful to seven "cohorts" of reviewers for the constructive criticism and great suggestions that have helped us make each edition of this book better than the one before:

Barinder Bahvra, *Macomb Community College*
David Beach, *University of Wisconsin–Parkside*
Howard Bierenbaum, *College of William & Mary*
Fredda Blanchard-Fields, *Louisiana State University*
Cheryl Bluestone, *Queensborough Community College*
Tracie Blumentritt, *University of Wisconsin La Crosse*
Denise Ann Bodman, *Arizona State University*
Bob Bornstein, *Miami University–Oxford*
Janet Boseovski, *University of North Carolina at Greensboro*
Kim G. Brenneman, *Eastern Mennonite University*
Donna Brent, *Hartwick College*
Mary Ann Bush, *Western Michigan University*
Elaine H. Cassel, *Lord Fairfax Community College*
Yiwei Chen, *Bowling Green State University*
Shelley Drazen, *Binghamton University (SUNY)*
Michelle R. Dunlap, *Connecticut College*
Marion Eppler, *East Carolina University*
Dan Florell, *Eastern Kentucky University*
James N. Forbes, *Angelo State University*
Claire Ford, *Bridgewater State College*
Carie Forden, *Clarion University*
Jody S. Fournier, *Capital University*
Janet Fritz, *Colorado State University*
Rebecca J. Glover, *University of North Texas*
Cheryl Hale, *Jefferson College*
Charles Harris, *James Madison University*
Karen Hartlep, *California State University at Bakersfield*
Christina Hawkey, *Arizona Western College*
Debra L. Hollister, *Valencia Community College*
Stephen Hoyer, *Pittsburg State University*
Malia Huchendorf, *Normandale Community College*
David P. Hurford, *Pittsburg State University*
Vivian Jenkins, *University of Southern Indiana*
Wayne G. Joosse, *Calvin College*
John Klein, *Castleton State College*
Franz Klutschkowski, *North Central Texas College*
Jim Korcuska, *University of San Diego*
Suzanne Krinsky, *University of Southern Colorado*

Brett Laursen, *Florida Atlantic University*
Sherry Loch, *Paradise Valley Community College*
Becky White Loewy, *San Francisco State University*
Rosanne Lorden, *Eastern Kentucky University*
Nancy Macdonald, *University of South Carolina–Sumter*
Susan Magun-Jackson, *University of Memphis*
Robert F. Marcus, *University of Maryland*
Gabriela A. Martorell, *Portland State University*
Rebecca Kang McGill, *Temple University*
Russell Miars, *Portland State University*
Ann K. Mullis, *Florida State University*
Ronald L. Mullis, *Florida State University*
Bridget C. Murphy-Kelsey, *University of Oklahoma*
Susan L. O'Donnell, *George Fox University*
Shirley M. Ogletree, *Southwest Texas State University*
Jim O'Neill, *Wayne State University*
Rob Palkovitz, *University of Delaware*
Suzanne Pasch, *University of Wisconsin at Milwaukee*
Louise Perry, *Florida Atlantic University*

Sharon Presley, *California State University East Bay*
Mark Rafter, *College of the Canyons*
Lakshmi Raman, *Oakland University*
Marjorie Reed, *Oregon State University*
Elizabeth Rhodes, *Florida International University*
Eileen Rogers, *University of Texas at San Antonio*
Mark Runco, *California State University at Fullerton*
Pamela Schuetze, *Buffalo State College*
Matt Scullin, *West Virginia University*
Lisa Sethre-Hofstad, *Concordia College*
Timothy Shearon, *Albertson College of Idaho*
Luis Terrazas, *California State University at San Marcos*
Polly Trnavsky, *Appalachian State University*
Katherine Van Giffen, *California State University at Long Beach*
Catherine Weir, *Colorado College*
Kyle Weir, *California State University at Fresno*
Ruth Wilson, *Idaho State University*
Robin Yaure, *Penn State Mont Alto*

CAROL K. SIGELMAN is professor of psychology and, until recently, the associate vice president for research and graduate studies and then graduate studies and academic affairs at The George Washington University. She earned her bachelor's degree from Carleton College and a double-major doctorate in English and psychology from George Peabody College for Teachers. She has also been on the faculty at Texas Tech University, Eastern Kentucky University (where she won her college's Outstanding Teacher Award), and the University of Arizona. She has taught courses in child, adolescent, adult, and life-span development and has published research on such topics as the communication skills of individuals with developmental disabilities, the development of stigmatizing reactions to children and adolescents who are different, and children's emerging understandings of diseases and psychological disorders. Through a grant from the National Institute of Child Health and Human Development, she and her colleagues studied children's intuitive theories of AIDS and developed and evaluated a curriculum to correct their misconceptions and convey the facts of HIV infection. With a similar grant from the National Institute on Drug Abuse, she explored children's and adolescents' understandings of the effects of alcohol and drugs on body, brain, and behavior. For fun, she enjoys hiking, biking, discovering good movies, and communing with her cats.

ELIZABETH A. RIDER is professor of psychology and associate academic dean at Elizabethtown College in Pennsylvania. She has also been on the faculty at the University of North Carolina at Asheville. She earned her undergraduate degree from Gettysburg College and her doctorate from Vanderbilt University. She has taught courses on child and life-span development, women and gender issues, applied developmental psychology, and genetic and environmental influences on development. She has published research on children's and adults' spatial perception, orientation, and ability to find their way. Through a grant from the Pennsylvania State System for Higher Education, she studied factors associated with academic success. The second edition of her text on the psychology of women, *Our Voices*, was published by John Wiley & Sons in 2005. When she is not working, her life revolves around her son and a fun-loving springer spaniel.

Introduction to the Human Life Span
CHAPTER

Introduction to the Human Life Span

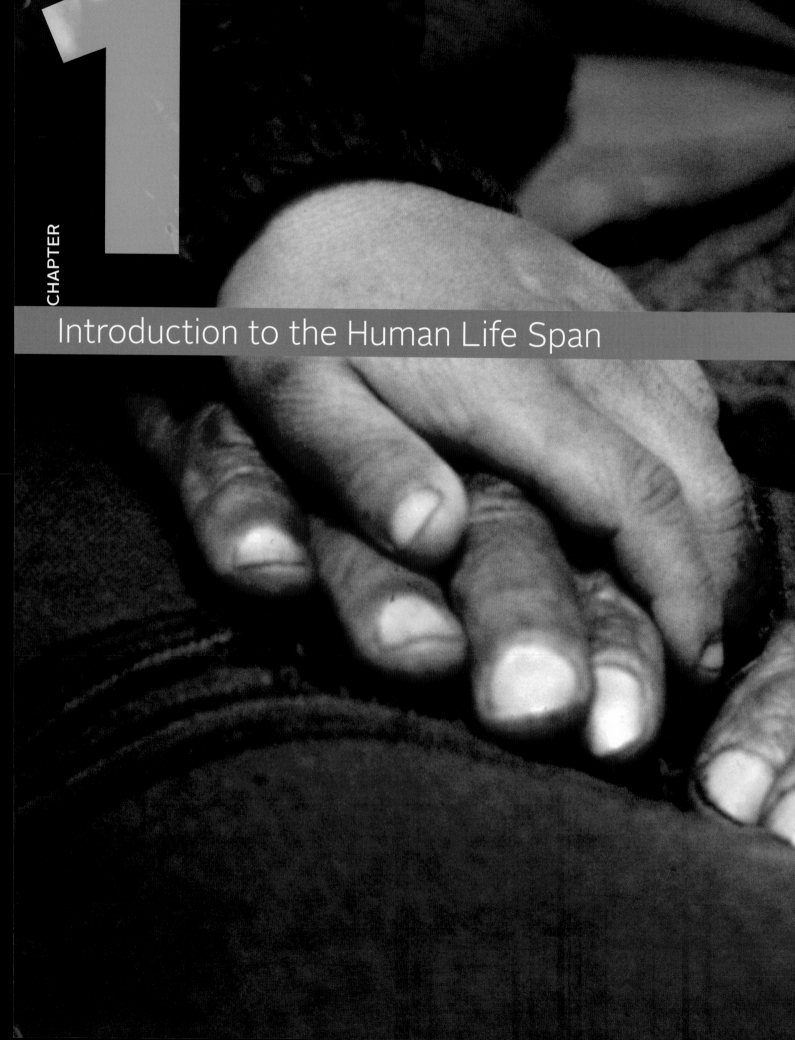

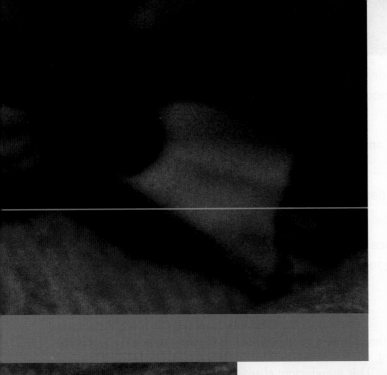

John Tatum thought he might be losing his edge, but he won three gold medals in swimming at the 2009 National Senior Games, competing for the first time in the 90–94 age group and avoiding head-to-head competition with his spry younger brother Brad, who snared five medals in the 85–89 age group (Hallett, 2009). John had always loved sports, from his days swimming in a racially segregated pool as a child to his participation on sports teams as an adult. After retiring, he and his brother joined a senior swim team, swimming at least two hours three times a week, with workouts in between.

John grew up in Washington and remembers playing on the Lincoln Memorial just after it was built in 1922 (Parker, 2008). He attended segregated schools and served in an all-black regiment during World War II. He wanted to be a frogman (a combat diver or swimmer) but was told he could not because he was black, so he became a computer systems analyst with the Navy. He married in 1944 and had six children with his wife, Pearl. Pearl died of pancreatic cancer in 1978, but John coped well with the challenge of caring for her, feeling that he had done all he could (Parker, 2008). He suffered further blows when a daughter and a son both died of cancer in the early 1990s. He knows he's in excellent shape for a 90-year-old but also knows that he won't last forever.

Ask Yourself This

1. What basic concepts and distinctions are needed to understand human development and aging, the life span and its periods, and the nature–nurture issue?

2. How has the science of life-span development evolved, and what are the key elements of the modern life span perspective?

3. What research methods and designs are used to study development, and what are their strengths and limitations?

4. What special challenges do developmental scientists face in studying humans in different ecological contexts and in adhering to standards of ethical research?

John Tatum, left, and his brother Brad at the 2009 National Senior Games.

© Marvin Joseph/The Washington Post/Getty Images

This book is about the development of humans like John Tatum—and you—from conception to death. Like any life, the life of John Tatum raises questions: Was his extraordinary physical fitness at age 90 mainly a matter of good genes, or was it the result of a life of physical activity and hours in the pool? What changes in physical functioning and fitness does aging entail, and are they inevitable? Going in a different direction, how were John and others of his generation affected by growing up black in a society that openly discriminated against them? And what allows some people to cope better than others with negative life events such as the death of a spouse or child?

We address questions like these and more in this book. Among other things, we'll ask how infants perceive the world, how preschool children think, how life events such as divorce affect a child's adjustment and later romantic relationships, why some college students have more trouble than others deciding on a major, whether most adults experience a midlife crisis in which they question what they have done with their lives, and how people typically change physically, mentally, and emotionally as

they age. We will also take on even more fundamental questions: How in the world does a single fertilized egg cell turn into a unique human being like John Tatum? And how can we use knowledge of the genetic and environmental forces that shape development to optimize it?

Do any of these questions intrigue you? Probably so, because we are all developing persons interested in ourselves and the other developing people around us. Most college students want to understand how they and those they know have been affected by their experiences, how they have changed over the years, and where they may be headed. Many students also have practical motivations for learning about human development—for example, a desire to be a good parent or to pursue a career as a psychologist, nurse, teacher, or other human services professional.

This introductory chapter lays the groundwork for the remainder of the book by addressing some basic questions: How should we think about development and the influences on it? What is the science of life-span development? How is development studied? And what are some of the special challenges in studying human development?

1.1 How Should We Think about Development?

We begin by asking what it means to say that humans "develop" or "age" over the life span, how we can conceptualize the life span, and how we can approach the single biggest issue in the study of development, the nature–nurture issue, and understand developing humans in their ever-changing environments.

Defining Development

Development can be defined as systematic changes and continuities in the individual that occur between conception and death, or from "womb to tomb." Development entails many changes; by describing these changes as systematic, we imply that they are orderly, patterned, and relatively enduring—not fleeting and unpredictable like mood swings. Development also involves continuities, ways in which we remain the same or continue to reflect our past selves.

The systematic changes and continuities of interest to students of human development fall into three broad domains:

1. *Physical development.* The growth of the body and its organs, the functioning of physiological systems including the brain, physical signs of aging, changes in motor abilities, and so on.
2. *Cognitive development.* Changes and continuities in perception, language, learning, memory, problem solving, and other mental processes.

3. *Psychosocial development.* Changes and carryover in personal and interpersonal aspects of development, such as motives, emotions, personality traits, interpersonal skills and relationships, and roles played in the family and in the larger society.

Even though developmentalists often specialize in one of these three aspects of development, they appreciate that humans are whole beings and that changes in one area affect the others. The baby who develops the ability to crawl, for example, has new opportunities to develop her mind by exploring kitchen cabinets and to hone her social skills by trailing her parents from room to room. And for John Tatum, introduced at the start of the chapter, exercise through swimming may have helped him retain his cognitive abilities and enriched his social interactions.

How would you portray, in a graph, typical changes from birth to old age? Many people picture tremendous positive gains in capacity from infancy to young adulthood, little change during early adulthood and middle age, and loss of capacities in the later years. This stereotyped view of the life span is largely false, but it also has some truth in it, especially with respect to biological development. Traditionally, biologists have defined **growth** as the physical changes that occur from conception to maturity. We indeed become biologically mature and physically competent during the early part of the life span. **Biological aging** is the deterioration of organisms (including humans) that leads inevitably to their death. Biologically, then, development *does* involve growth in early life, stability in early and middle adulthood, and declines associated with now-accumulated effects of aging in later life.

Many aspects of development do not follow this "gain–stability–loss" model, however. Modern developmental scientists have come to appreciate that developmental change at any age involves both gains and losses. For example, child development is not all about gain; children gain many cognitive abilities as they get older, but they also lose self-esteem and become more prone to depression (Gotlib & Hammen, 2002; Robins et al., 2002). Nor should we associate aging only with loss: Adults aged 60 and older score higher on vocabulary tests than adults aged 18 to 30 (Verhaeghen, 2003); some cognitive abilities and types of knowledge and expertise hold steady or even grow during adulthood (Ackerman, 2008; Alexander, Murphy, & Kulikowich, 2009). At age 68, gerontologist Margaret Cruikshank (2009) conveyed the positives of aging this way: "Decline is thought to be the main theme of aging, and yet for many old age is a time of ripening, of becoming most ourselves" (p. 207).

In addition, people do not always improve or worsen but instead just become different than they were (as when a child who once feared loud noises comes to fear hairy monsters under the bed instead). Development clearly means more than positive growth during infancy, childhood, and adolescence. And **aging** involves more than biological aging (Ryff & Singer, 2009); it refers to a range of physical, cognitive, and psychosocial changes, *positive and negative*, in the mature organism. In short, development involves gains, losses, neutral changes, and continuities in each phase of the life span.

What periods of the life span do these four females, representing four generations of the same family, fall in? What periods of the life span do you distinguish? Table 1.1 provides one answer.

Conceptualizing the Life Span

If you were to divide the human life span into periods, how would you do it?

● **Table 1.1** lists the periods that many of today's developmentalists regard as distinct. You will want to keep them in mind as you read this book, because we will constantly be speaking of infants, preschoolers, school-age children, adolescents, and young, middle-aged, and older adults. Note, however, that the given ages are approximate. Age is only a rough indicator of developmental status. Improvements in the standard of living and health, for example, have meant that today's 65-year-olds are not as "old" physically, cognitively, or psychosocially as 65-year-olds a few decades ago were. There are also huge differences in functioning and personality among individuals of the same age; while some adults are bedridden at age 90, others like John Tatum are out swimming laps and displaying the physical abilities of much younger people.

● TABLE 1.1 AN OVERVIEW OF PERIODS OF THE LIFE SPAN

Period of Life	Age Range
Prenatal period	Conception to birth
Infancy	First 2 years of life (the first month is the neonatal or newborn period)
Preschool period	2 to 5 or 6 years (some prefer to describe as *toddlers* children who have begun to walk and are age 1 to 3)
Middle childhood	6 to about 12 (or until the onset of puberty)
Adolescence	Approximately 12 to 20 (or when the individual becomes relatively independent of parents and begins to assume adult roles)
Early adulthood	20 to 40 years (some distinguish an emerging adulthood period from 18 to 29—see Exploration 1.1)
Middle adulthood	40 to 65 years
Late adulthood	65 years and older (some break out subcategories such as the young-old, old-old, and very old based on differences in functioning)

Each January 15 in Japan, 20-year-olds are officially pronounced adults in a national celebration and enter a new age grade. Young women receive kimonos, young men receive suits, and all are reminded of their responsibilities to society. Young adults also gain the right to drink, smoke, and vote. The modern ceremony grew out of an ancient one in which young samurai became recognized as warriors (Reid, 1993). The age-grading system in Japanese culture clearly marks the beginning of adulthood with this rite of passage.

Despite stereotypes that suggest that old people are alike (that they are all forgetful, frail, socially isolated, and cranky, for example), elderly adults are in fact the most diverse of all age groups in terms of physiological and psychological functioning (Andrews, Clark, & Luszcz, 2002; Nelson & Dannefer, 1992).

Table 1.1 represents only one view of the periods of the life span. Age—like gender, race, and other significant human characteristics—means different things in different societies (Fry, 2009). Each society has its own ways of dividing the life span and of treating the people in different age groups. Each socially defined age group in a society—called an **age grade** or age stratum—is assigned different statuses, roles, privileges, and responsibilities. Segregating children into grades in school based on age is one form of age grading. Just as high schools have "elite" seniors and "lowly" freshmen, whole societies are layered into age grades. We, for example, grant "adults" (18-year-olds by law in the United States) a voting privilege not granted to children. Legal definitions of the boundary between adolescence and adulthood vary, though. In most states in the United States, the legal age for marrying is lower than the legal ages for voting or serving in the military, and the right to drink alcohol is granted last, commonly at age 21 (Settersten, 2005). Similarly, although many of us define age 65 as the boundary between middle age and old age, in fact the ages at which people become eligible for Medicare, Social Security benefits, and "senior discounts" at restaurants and stores differ. And they change as well: The age of eligibility for full Social Security benefits has increased to age 67 for anyone born after 1960.

In certain other cultures, the recognized periods of the life span include a period before birth and an afterlife, or the life span may be pictured as a circle that includes reincarnation or some other way of being "recycled" and born again (Fry, 1985; Kojima, 2003). The St. Lawrence Eskimo simply distinguish between boys and men (or between girls and women), whereas the Arusha people of East Africa devised six socially meaningful age grades for males: youths, junior warriors, senior warriors, junior elders, senior elders, and retired elders (Keith, 1985). We define old age as age 65 or older, based largely on Social Security eligibility, but the !Kung San of Botswana often don't know people's chronological ages and define old age instead in terms of functioning (Rosenberg, 2009). They distinguish between the *na* or "old" (an honorary title meaning big and great granted to all older people starting at around age 50); the "old/dead" (older but still able to function); and the "old to the point of helplessness," who are ailing and need care.

Cultures clearly differ in the importance they attach to age, in the age grades they recognize, and in how they mark the transition from one age grade to another (Fry, 2009). A **rite of passage** is a ritual that marks a person's "passage" from one status to another, usually in reference to the transition from childhood to adulthood. Rites of passage can involve such varied practices as body painting, circumcision, instruction by elders in adult sexual practices, tests of physical prowess, and gala celebrations (see Kottak, 2009; and the photo on this page for Japan's rite of passage for 20-year-olds).

In our society, Jewish youth experience a clear rite of passage when they have their *bar* or *bat mitzvahs*, and 15-year-old Hispanic-American girls in some communities participate in a *quinceañera* (meaning "fifteen years") ceremony to signify that they have become women. Unfortunately, one of the clearest rites of passage for adolescents in our society is a night of binge drinking at age 21. In one study, 4 of 5 college students reported that they drank on their 21st birthday to celebrate; about half of them drank more than they had ever consumed before, 12% of them an extremely dangerous 21 drinks (Rutledge, Park, & Sher, 2008). Perhaps because we lack a clear, society-wide rite of passage like Japan's, adolescents in our society end up less sure than adolescents in many other societies when they are adults.

Once a society has established age grades, it defines what people should and should not do at different points in the life span (Elder & Shanahan, 2006). According to pioneering gerontologist Bernice Neugarten and her colleagues (Neugarten, Moore, & Lowe, 1965), these expectations, or **age norms**, are society's way of telling people how to act their age. In our culture, for example, most people agree that 6-year-olds are too young to date or drink beer but are old enough to attend school. We also tend to agree that adults should think about marrying around age 25 (although in some segments of society earlier or later is better) and should retire around age 65 (Neugarten, Moore, & Lowe, 1965; Settersten, 1998). In less industrialized countries, age norms often call for having children in one's teens and stopping work earlier than 65 in response to illness and disability (Shanahan, 2000).

Why are age norms important? First, they influence people's decisions about how to lead their lives. They are the basis for what Neugarten (1968) called the **social clock**—a person's sense of when things should be done and when he or she is ahead of or behind the schedule dictated by age norms. Prompted by the social clock, for example, an unmarried 30-year-old may feel that he should propose to his girlfriend before she gives up on him, or a childless 35-year-old might fear that she will miss her chance at parenthood unless she has a baby soon. Second, age norms affect how easily people adjust to life transitions. Normal life events such as having children typically tend to affect us more negatively when they occur "off time" than when they occur "on time," at socially appropriate ages (McLanahan & Sorensen, 1985). It can be challenging to experience puberty at either age 8 or age 18 or to become a new parent at 13 or 48. However, age norms in our society have been weakening for some time; it's less clear now what one should be doing at what age and so people do things like marry and retire at a wide range of ages (Settersten & Trauten, 2009).

Although medieval children were pressured to abandon their childish ways as soon as possible and were dressed like miniature adults, it is doubtful that they were really viewed as miniature adults. Still, the modern concept of children as innocents to be nurtured and protected did not begin to take hold until the 17th century.

Photograph © 2005 Museum of Fine Arts, Boston

Subcultural Differences

Age grades, age norms, social clocks, and the meanings of age differ not only from culture to culture but also from subculture to subculture. Our own society is diverse with respect to race; **ethnicity,** or people's classification or affiliation with a group based on common heritage or traditions; and **socioeconomic status (SES),** or standing in society based on such indicators as occupational prestige, education, and income. African American, Hispanic American, Native American, Asian American, and European American individuals sometimes hold different age norms and have different developmental experiences as a result. Within each of these broad racial and ethnic groups, though, there are immense variations associated with such factors as specific national origin, length of time in North America, degree of integration into mainstream society, language usage, and socioeconomic status.

Generally, individuals from lower-income families tend to reach milestones of adulthood such as starting work, marrying, and having children earlier than those from middle-income and upper-income families do (Elder & Shanahan, 2006). For example, Linda Burton (1996a) studied age norms in a low-income African American community and found it was considered appropriate there for a young woman to become a mother at 16 and a grandmother at 34—earlier than in most middle-class communities, white or black. Teenage mothers in this community looked to their own mothers and, especially, their grandmothers to help them care for their children. Burton has also found that children in economically disadvantaged environments like this one are asked to grow up faster than middle-class children; they often assume adultlike responsibilities in the family such as tending siblings and making meals (Burton, 2007). Such age norms may seem unusual from a middle-class perspective; yet it is not at all unusual in many cultures around the world for child care responsibilities to be shared by parents with grandmothers and other relatives or for children to be heavily involved in the work of the family and in sibling care (Rogoff, 2003).

Historical Changes

The meanings of childhood, adolescence, and adulthood also change from historical period to historical period. In Europe and North America, they have changed along these lines:

Childhood. Not until the 17th century in Western cultures did children come to be viewed as distinctly different from adults, as innocents to be protected and nurtured. In medieval Europe (A.D. 500–1500), for example, 6-year-olds were dressed in miniature versions of adult clothing and treated to some extent as "miniature adults" (Ariès, 1962). Although medieval parents surely

Are You an Adult Yet?

What do you regard as the most important criteria to use in defining whether someone is an adult, and how many of them do you believe you have achieved? In a study of this (Nelson et al., 2007), college students and their parents were asked to judge the importance of various criteria of adulthood—for example, being financially independent of parents, avoiding violations such as drunk driving and petty crime, reaching age 21, developing greater consideration for others, accepting responsibility for one's actions. Students and parents agreed that traditional college students are no longer adolescents but are not quite adults either. And although they did not agree perfectly on the importance of different criteria of adulthood, both parents and children emphasized psychological qualities such as accepting responsibility for one's actions.

However adulthood is defined, it is taking youth in our society longer to get there today than in earlier eras. After World War II, adolescents began to attend college in large numbers and to postpone marriage and parenthood, delaying their entry into the adult world even more than

was the case at the beginning of the 20th century (Furstenberg et al., 2004; Keniston, 1970). As a result, Jeffrey Arnett and others now talk about the appearance, at least in developed countries in which youth must spend years getting educated and accumulating wealth in order to make it as adults, of a new period of development called *emerging adulthood* from about age 18 to age 29 (Arnett, 2000; Arnett & Tanner, 2006; Tanner, Arnett, & Leis, 2009). According to Arnett, this is a distinctive phase of life in which youth:

- explore their identities;
- lead unstable lives filled with job changes, new relationships, and moves;
- are self-focused, relatively free of obligations to others, and therefore free to focus on their own psychological needs;
- feel in between—adultlike in some ways but not others; and
- believe they have limitless possibilities ahead (Arnett, 2000; Arnett & Tanner, 2006).

Not everyone agrees that emerging adulthood is a truly distinct period of development. However, most agree that adolescents in our society are taking longer and longer to become adults. Consider this: Frank Furstenberg and his colleagues (2004) found that only 31% of 30-year-old men and 46% of 30-year-old women in the United States surveyed in 2000 had achieved all of what the researchers considered to be the traditional, objective markers of adulthood: completing an education, being financially independent, leaving home, marrying, and having children. Back in 1960, by contrast, 65% of men and 77% of women age 30 had achieved these milestones. Granted, many people today no longer consider marriage and parenthood to be markers of adulthood, as the Nelson et al. (2007) study testifies. Still, progress toward adulthood is occurring more slowly than it used to, lending some support to the concept of a period of emerging adulthood between adolescence and adulthood.

---

recognized that children are different from adults, children were expected to work alongside adults at home, at a shop, or in the fields and to grow up as fast as possible so that they could contribute to the family's survival (Cunningham, 1996; Hanawalt, 2003). (Some observers argue that modern society has been reverting to a medieval view of childhood—asking children to grow up quickly and to cope with such "adult" matters as terrorism, drugs, gun violence, and other social ills (Elkind, 1992; Koops, 2003).)

Adolescence. Not until the late 19th century and early 20th century was **adolescence**—the transitional period between childhood and adulthood that begins with puberty and ends when the individual has acquired adult competencies and responsibilities—recognized as a distinct phase of the life span (Hine, 1999; Kett, 1977). As industrialization advanced, an educated labor force was needed, so laws were passed restricting child labor and making schooling compulsory. By the middle of the 20th century, adolescence had become a distinct life stage in which youths spent their days in school—separated from the adult world and living in their own peer culture (Furstenberg, 2000). Now the transi-

tion period from childhood to adulthood has become so long that some scholars believe we should recognize a new period of the life span called **emerging adulthood,** extending from about age 18 to age 29, when young people are between adolescence and full-fledged adulthood, as discussed in Exploration Box 1.1.

Middle age. Not until the 20th century did our society begin to define a period of middle age between early adulthood and old age in which the nest is emptied of children. This distinct life stage emerged as 20th-century parents began to bear fewer children and live long enough to see their children grow up and leave home (Moen & Wethington, 1999). Sometimes characterized as a time of "crisis," sometimes as a time of hardly any psychological change, middle age is now understood to be a time of good health, peak cognitive functioning, stable relationships, many responsibilities, and high satisfaction for most people (Whitbourne & Willis, 2006).

Old age. Not until the 20th century did our society come to define old age as a period of retirement. There were not many old people in early eras, and they were not as healthy as old people today. In ancient Rome, the average age of death was 20 to 30 years old; in the late 17th century, it was 35 to 40 years (Dublin & Lotka, 1936). These figures, which are *averages*, are low mainly because so many more infants died in the past than now. Still, those lucky enough to make it through early childhood had relatively low odds, by modern standards, of living to be 65 or older. Those who did survive to old age literally worked until they dropped. In the last half of the 20th century, thanks to Social Security, pensions, and other support programs, working adults often retired in their 60s (Schulz & Binstock, 2006).

What is ahead? In the early 21st century, the average **life expectancy** for a newborn—the average number of years a newborn who is born now can be expected to live—is 78 years, compared with 47 years in 1900 (National Center for Health Statistics, 2009). Life expectancy is 81 for a white female, 77 for a black female, 76 for a white male, and 70 for a black male. Although these gaps between women and men and between Whites and African Americans have been narrowing in recent decades, differences between high and low socioeconomic groups have been widening. This may be because people with higher incomes and more education have been quicker to control their smoking, weight, and blood pressure and otherwise adopt healthy lifestyles, as well as because they more often have good health insurance coverage (Congressional Budget Office, 2008). Today's elderly adults generally have fewer chronic diseases and disabilities, and are less affected by the ones they have, than elderly adults of the past (Kinsella, 2009; Satariano, 2006). Yet as more and more people reach older ages, more will have chronic diseases and disabilities and an increasingly large group of elderly people will depend on an increasingly small group of younger, working adults to support them through Social Security, Medicare, and other programs (Wilmoth & Longino, 2006). This "graying of America," and indeed of the world's population, along with societal changes we cannot yet anticipate, will make the aging experience by the end of the 21st century different than it is today.

In sum, age—whether it is 7, 17, or 70—has had different meanings in different historical eras and most likely will mean something different in the 21st century than it did in the 20th. The broader message is clear: *We must view development in its historical, cultural, and subcultural context.* We must bear in mind that each social group settles on its own definitions of the life span, the age grades within it, and the age norms appropriate to each age range, and that each social group experiences development differently. We must also appreciate that it was only in the 17th century that children came to be seen as innocents; in the late 19th century that adolescence emerged as a distinct phase; and in the 20th century that our society recognized emerging adulthood, a middle-aged "empty nest" period, and an old age characterized by retirement. One of the most fascinating challenges in the study of human development is to understand which aspects of development are universal and which differ across social and historical contexts—and why (Norenzayan & Heine, 2005; Shweder et al., 2006).

Framing the Nature–Nurture Issue

Understanding human development means grappling with *the* major issue in the study of human development—the **nature–nurture issue,** or the question of how biological forces and environmental forces act and interact to make us what we are. We raised a nature–nurture question at the start of the chapter by asking whether 90-year-old John Tatum's swimming prowess was mainly attributable to good genes or good training, and we will highlight this central and always fascinating issue throughout this book.

On the *nature* side of the debate are those who emphasize the influence of heredity, universal maturational processes guided by the genes, biologically based predispositions produced by evolution, and biological influences such as hormones and brain growth spurts. To those who emphasize nature, development is largely a process of **maturation,** the biological unfolding of the individual according to a plan contained in the **genes** (the hereditary material passed from parents to child at conception). Just as seeds turn into mature plants through a predictable process, humans "unfold" within the womb (assuming that they receive the necessary nourishment from their environment). Their genetic blueprint then makes it likely that they will walk and utter their first words at about 1 year of age, achieve sexual maturity between 12 and 14, and gray in their 40s and 50s. Maturational changes in the brain contribute to cognitive changes such as increased memory and problem-solving skills and to psychosocial changes such as increased understanding of other people's feelings. Genetically influenced maturational processes guide all of us through many of the same developmental changes at about the same points in our lives. Meanwhile, *individual* hereditary endowment is making each person's development unique.

On the *nurture* side of the nature–nurture debate are those who emphasize change in response to **environment**—all the external physical and social conditions, stimuli, and events that can affect us, from crowded living quarters and polluted air, to social interactions with family members, peers, and teachers, to the neighborhood and broader cultural context in which we develop. We know that the physical environment matters—for example, that exposure to lead in the paint in old buildings can stunt children's intellectual development or that living near a noisy airport can interfere with their progress in learning to read (Evans, 2006). And we will see countless examples in this book of how the social environment—the behavior of other people—shapes development. Rather than seeing maturation as the process driving development, those on the nurture side of the nature–nurture debate emphasize **learning**—the process through which experience (that is, environmental stimuli) brings about relatively permanent changes in thoughts, feelings, or behavior. A certain degree of physical maturation is clearly necessary before a child can dribble a basketball, but careful instruction and long, hard hours of practice are just as clearly required if the child is to excel in basketball. (See ●**Table 1.2** for the terms of the nature–nurture debate.)

If nature is important in development, we would expect all children to achieve similar developmental milestones at similar times because of maturation, and we would expect differences

TABLE 1.2 THE LANGUAGE OF NATURE AND NURTURE

Nature	Nurture
Heredity	Environment
Maturation	Learning
Genes	Experience
Innate or biologically based predispositions	Cultural influences

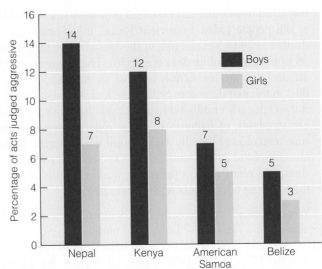

■ **FIGURE 1.1** Aggression among children in four cultures.

SOURCE: Based on means reported in Munroe et al. (2000)

among individuals to be largely caused by differences in their genetic makeup. If nurture is important in development, we would generally expect human development to take a variety of pathways depending on the individual's life experiences.

Let's settle the nature–nurture debate right now: Developmental changes are the products of a complex interplay between nature (genetic endowment, biological influences, and maturation) and nurture (environmental influences, experiences, and learning). It is not nature *or* nurture; it is nature *and* nurture. To make matters more complex, it is nature affecting nurture and nurture affecting nature! For example, biology (nature) provides us with a brain that allows us to learn from our experiences (nurture), experiences that in turn change our brains by altering neural connections. Much of the joy of studying human development comes from trying to understand more precisely how these two forces combine to make us what we are and become.

Ponder this nature–nurture question: In the United States, there is consistent evidence that, on average, boys are more likely than girls to engage in physically aggressive behavior and that men commit more violent crimes than women (Card et al., 2008; Quinsey et al., 2004). Does this sex difference reflect nature (biological differences between the sexes, such as different hormone balances) or nurture (for example, a tendency of parents to tolerate or even encourage aggression in boys but to suppress it in girls)? How might you try to answer this nature–nurture question?

One approach is to find out whether sex differences in physical aggression are evident across cultures. So Robert Munroe and his colleagues (2000) studied aggression among 3- to 9-year-old children in four nonindustrialized societies from diverse parts of the globe: Belize, Kenya, Nepal, and American Samoa. In each society, 24 girls and 24 boys were studied. Residents of the target communities were trained to observe children's social behavior, including their aggressive behavior. Aggressive behavior was defined as assaulting (hitting, kicking, or otherwise attacking someone), horseplay (roughhousing), and symbolic aggression (making insulting or threatening gestures or statements).

As ■ **Figure 1.1** shows, boys exhibited more aggression than girls in all four societies. Overall, about 10% of boys' social behaviors, compared with 6% of girls' behaviors, were aggressive. Munroe and his colleagues speculated that establishing domi-

nance in the peer group gives males an edge in competing for mates and reproducing later in life, suggesting that genes that predispose males to be aggressive may have been built into the human genetic code over the course of evolution (Barash, 2002). Although the evidence is not strong, Munroe's findings suggest that nature or biology could contribute to gender differences in aggression. Evidence that boys are more physically aggressive than girls as early as 17 months of age in our society further supports the nature side of the nature–nurture debate (Baillargeon et al., 2007).

However, significant cultural differences in the amount of aggression—as well as in the size of the gender difference in aggression—were also evident in Munroe's study—and are evident in other studies as well. The two most patrilineal cultures (cultures in which families are organized around male kin groups) were Kenya and Nepal. These proved to be the cultures in which aggressive behavior was most frequent (10–11% of social acts, as opposed to 4–6% in Belize and American Samoa). Moreover, sex differences in aggression were sharpest in these patrilineal cultures. As is often the case when we ask whether nature or nurture is more important in development, these findings, like those of other studies, suggest that both nature and nurture contribute to gender differences in aggression. The findings also make us want to conduct more research, including studies examining specific biological and environmental influences, to understand more fully why males, especially in some cultural contexts, are more physically aggressive than females.

Grasping the Ecology of Development

If we take seriously the concept that human development is shaped by interacting biological and environmental factors, we need a way to conceptualize a changing person in a changing environment. To help you think about this, we will consider an influential conceptual model of development formulated by

Russian-born American psychologist Urie Bronfenbrenner (1917–2005). Bronfenbrenner became disturbed that many early developmental scientists were studying human development out of context, expecting it to be universal and failing to appreciate how much it could vary from culture to culture, from neighborhood to neighborhood, and from home to home. Bronfenbrenner formulated an ecological model to describe how the environment is organized and how it affects development. He later renamed it a **bioecological model** of development to stress how biology and environment interact to produce development (Bronfenbrenner, 1979, 1989; Bronfenbrenner & Morris, 2006).

In Bronfenbrenner's view, the developing person, with his or her genetic makeup and biological and psychological characteristics, is embedded in a series of environmental systems. These systems interact with one another and with the individual over time to influence development. Bronfenbrenner described four environmental systems that influence and are influenced by the developing person, as shown in ■ **Figure 1.2**.

1.   A **microsystem** is an immediate physical and social environment in which the person interacts face-to-face with other people and influences and is affected by them. The primary micro-

system for a firstborn infant is likely to be the family—perhaps infant, mother, and father, all reciprocally influencing one another. The developing child may also experience other microsystems such as a day care center or grandmother's house. We have much evidence that the family environment is an important influence on child development and have come to appreciate the importance of peer groups, schools, and neighborhood environments.

2.   The **mesosystem** consists of the interrelationships or linkages between two or more microsystems. For example, teenagers who experience stressful events such as arguments in the family (one microsystem) report increased problems of poor attendance and difficulty learning at school (a second microsystem) for a couple of days afterward; similarly, problems at school spill over to the family, possibly because adolescents take their bad moods home with them (Flook & Fuligni, 2008). In any developing person, what happens in one microsystem can have implications, good or bad, for what happens in another microsystem.

3.   The **exosystem** consists of linkages involving social settings that individuals do not experience directly but that can still influence their development. For example, children can be affected by how their parents' day at work went or by a

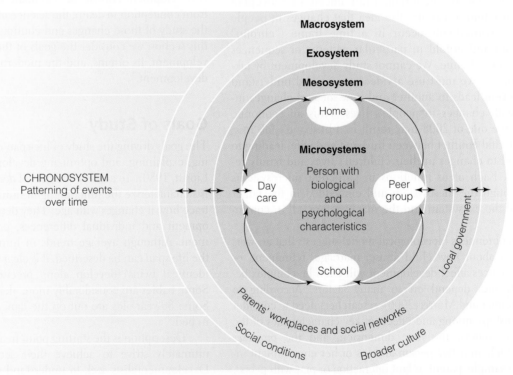

■**FIGURE 1.2** Urie Bronfenbrenner's bioecological model of development pictures environment as a series of nested structures. The microsystem refers to relations between the developing person and her immediate environment, the mesosystem to connections among microsystems, the exosystem to settings that affect but do not contain the individual, the macrosystem to the broader cultural context of development, and the chronosystem to the patterning over time of historical and life events. All these systems influence and are influenced by the developing person. SOURCE: Adapted from Kopp & Krakow (1982)

decision by the local school board to focus instruction almost entirely on getting more children to pass the state reading examination.

4. The **macrosystem** is the larger cultural context in which the microsystem, mesosystem, and exosystem are embedded. **Culture** is often defined as the shared understandings and way of life of a people, including beliefs and practices concerning the nature of humans in different phases of the life span, what children need to be taught to function in society, and how people should lead their lives as adults. Although the United States has a high standard of living, it is not a very family-friendly cultural environment in many ways, as Bronfenbrenner himself often lamented (Bronfenbrenner & Morris, 2006). For example, the United States is one of only 4 countries out of 168 studied by one team of researchers that does not provide paid maternity leave to female employees; the Family and Medical Leave Act provides for 12 weeks of leave, but it is *unpaid* leave and it is not available to workers in small companies (Heymann, Penrose, & Earle, 2006). Nor does the United States do as much as many other nations to ensure that workers can take leave to care for sick children or ailing elders or that children of all income levels have appropriate preschool and after-school programs.

In addition to the microsystems, mesosystems, ecosystems, and macrosystems, Bronfenbrenner introduced the concept of the **chronosystem** to capture the idea that changes in people and their environments occur in a time frame ("chrono" means time) and unfold in particular patterns or sequences over a person's lifetime. We cannot study development by taking still photos; we must use a video camera and understand how one event leads to another and how societal changes intertwine with changes in people's lives. Thus an economic crisis like the one of 2008 may result in a husband's job loss, causing marital conflict between husband and wife, leading to divorce and to changes in their children's lives and family relationships. Each of us functions in particular microsystems linked through the mesosystem and embedded in the larger contexts of the exosystem and the macrosystem, all in continual flux.

Bronfenbrenner's bioecological model suggests that answers to questions about how child abuse, marriage, retirement, or other experiences affect development will often be complex because outcomes depend on so many factors. According to Bronfenbrenner and Morris (2006), researchers need to consider the relationships among and effects of key characteristics of the *person*, the *context*, the *time* dimension, and the *processes* through which an active person and his or her environment interact (for example, parent–infant interaction or play with peers). Nature and nurture cannot be separated easily because they are part of a dynamic system, continually influencing one another. Complex research designs and statistical techniques are needed to assess the many interacting influences on development portrayed in Bronfenbrenner's bioecological model, but progress is being made (Holt, 2009; Sameroff, 2009). It is appropriate, then, that we look next at the science of life-span human development and whether it is up to the challenge.

Checking Mastery

1. How does the concept of aging differ from the concept of biological aging?

2. In Bronfenbrenner's bioecological model, where is "nature" and where is "nurture"? (Consult Figure 1.2.)

Making Connections

1. Many observers believe that age norms for transitions in adult development such as marriage, parenthood, peak career achievement, and retirement are weakening in our society. Do you think such age norms could ever disappear entirely? Why or why not?

2. Applying Bronfenbrenner's bioecological model to yourself, give an example of how each of Bronfenbrenner's four environmental systems may have affected you and your development within the past year.

1.2 What Is the Science of Life-Span Development?

If development consists of systematic changes and continuities from conception to death, the science of development consists of the study of those changes and continuities and their causes. In this section we consider the goals of the science of life-span development, its origins, and the modern life-span perspective on development.

Goals of Study

The goals driving the study of life-span development are describing, explaining, and optimizing development (Baltes, Reese, & Lipsitt, 1980). To achieve the goal of *description*, developmentalists characterize the functioning of humans of different ages and trace how it changes with age. They describe both normal development and individual differences, or variations, in development. Although average trends in human development across the life span can be described, it is clear that no two people (even identical twins) develop along precisely the same pathways. Some babies are considerably more alert and active than others. Some 80-year-olds are out on the dance floor; others are home in bed.

Description is the starting point in any science, but scientists ultimately strive to achieve their second goal, *explanation*. Developmentalists seek to understand why humans develop as they typically do and why some individuals develop differently than others. To do so, developmentalists study the contributions of nature and nurture to development.

The third goal is *optimization* of human development. How can humans be helped to develop in positive directions? How can their capacities be enhanced, how can developmental difficulties be prevented, and how can any developmental problems that emerge be overcome? Pursuing the goal of optimizing devel-

Excerpt from Darwin's Baby Biography

In this excerpt from Charles Darwin's (1877) baby biography, we get a sense of both his powers of observation and his thinking regarding influences on development as he describes the development of anger in his firstborn son. (He had 10 children in all.) He and others of his time favored the nature side of the nature–nurture debate, as you can see from this discussion of sex differences in anger:

Anger.—It was difficult to decide at how early an age anger was felt; on his eighth day he frowned and wrinkled the skin round his eyes before a crying fit, but this may have been due to pain or distress, and not to anger. When about ten weeks old, he was given some rather cold milk and he kept a slight frown on his forehead all the time that he was sucking, so that he looked like a grown-up person made cross from being compelled to do something which he did not like. When nearly four months old, and perhaps much earlier, there could be no doubt, from the manner in which the blood gushed into his whole face and scalp, that he easily got into a violent passion. A small cause sufficed; thus, when a little over seven months old, he screamed with rage because a lemon slipped away and he could not seize it with his hands. When eleven months old, if a wrong plaything was given to him, he would push it away and beat it; I presume that the beating was an instinctive sign of anger, like the snapping of the jaws by a young crocodile just out of the egg, and not that he imagined he could hurt the plaything. When two years and three months old, he became a great adept at throwing books or sticks, &c., at anyone who offended him; and so it was with some of my other sons. On the other hand, I could never see a trace of such aptitude in my infant daughters; and this makes me think that a tendency to throw objects is inherited by boys.

From Darwin, C. A. (1877). A biographical sketch of an infant. *Mind, 2*, 285–294; quotation from pp. 287–288. Available at: Complete Works of Charles Darwin Online, http://darwin-online.org.uk/contents .html#periodicals. Accessed July, 2009.

---

opment might involve evaluating ways to stimulate intellectual growth in preschool programs, to prevent binge drinking among college students, or to support elderly adults after the death of a spouse.

To those who are or aspire to be teachers, psychologists or counselors, nurses or occupational therapists, or other helping professionals, applied research on optimizing development is especially relevant. Today's educators and human service and health professionals are being asked to engage in **evidence-based practice**, grounding what they do in research and ensuring that the curricula and treatments they provide have been demonstrated to be effective. Too often, these professionals go with what their personal experience tells them works rather than using what scientific research says are the most effective approaches (Baker, McFall, & Shoham, 2009). Ensuring that the results of research are implemented faithfully and successfully in real schools and treatment facilities is challenging (McCall, 2009), but we can all probably agree that we would rather see investment in interventions of proven effectiveness than in ones that could be ineffective or even harmful. If you seek a career dedicated to optimizing human development, you might want to consult the appendix of this book for information about career options related to life-span human development.

Early Beginnings

Just as human development has changed through the ages, attempts to understand it have evolved over time (Cairns & Cairns, 2006). Although philosophers have long expressed their views on the nature of humans and the proper methods of raising children, it was not until the late 19th century that the first scientific investigations of development were undertaken. Several scholars began to carefully observe the growth and development of their own children and to publish their findings in the form of **baby biographies**. Perhaps the most influential baby biographer was Charles Darwin (1809–1882), who made daily records of his son's development (Darwin, 1877; see also Dewsbury, 2009, and Exploration Box 1.2 for a sample). Darwin's curiosity about child development stemmed from his interest in evolution. He believed that infants share many characteristics with their nonhuman ancestors and that understanding the development of the embryo and child can offer insights into the evolution of the species. Darwin's evolutionary perspective and studies of the development of embryos strongly influenced early theories of human development, which emphasized universal, biologically based maturational changes (Cairns & Cairns, 2006; Parke et al., 1994).

Baby biographies left much to be desired as works of science, however. Because different baby biographers emphasized different aspects of their children's behavior, baby biographies were difficult to compare. Moreover, parents are not entirely objective observers of their own children, and early baby biographers may have let their assumptions about evolution and development bias their observations. Finally, because each baby biography was based on a single child—often the child of a distinguished family—its findings were not necessarily generalizable to other children.

Although Darwin and other baby biographers deserve credit for creating interest in the study of human development and influencing early views of it, the man most often cited as the founder of developmental psychology is G. Stanley Hall (1846–1924), the first president of the American Psychological

Association. Well aware of the shortcomings of baby biographies, Hall attempted to collect more objective data on large samples of individuals. He developed a now all-too-familiar research tool—the questionnaire—to explore "the contents of children's minds" (Hall, 1891). By asking children questions about every conceivable topic, he discovered that children's understanding of the world grows rapidly during childhood and that the "logic" of young children is often not very logical.

Hall went on to write an influential book, *Adolescence* (1904). Inspired by Darwin's evolutionary theory, Hall drew parallels between adolescence and the turbulent period in the evolution of human society during which barbarism gave way to modern civilization. Adolescence, then, was a tempestuous period of the life span, a time of emotional ups and downs and rapid changes—a time of what Hall called **storm and stress**. Thus, we have Hall to thank for the notion that most teenagers are emotionally unstable—a largely inaccurate notion, as it turns out (Arnett, 1999). Yet as this book will reveal, Hall was right to mark adolescence as a time of dramatic change; substantial changes in the brain and in cognitive and social functioning do take place during this period.

Hall capped his remarkable career by turning his attention to the end of the life span in *Senescence* (1922), an analysis of how society treats (or, really, mistreats) its older members. He deserves credit for recognizing that aging involves more than just decline (Thompson, 2009). Overall, Hall's developmental psychology was limited by modern standards (Shanahan, Erickson, & Bauer, 2005). He was mainly concerned with describing development, whereas today's developmentalists are more concerned with explaining it. His ideas about evolution and its relation to periods of human development were also flawed. Yet he deserves much credit for stimulating scientific research on the entire human life span and for raising many important questions about it.

The Modern Life-Span Perspective

Although a few early pioneers of the study of human development like G. Stanley Hall viewed all phases of the life span as worthy of study, the science of human development began to break into age-group specialty areas during the 20th century. Some researchers focused on infant or child development, others specialized in adolescence, and still others formed the specialization of **gerontology**, the study of aging and old age. In the 1960s and 1970s, however, a true **life-span perspective** on human development began to emerge. In an influential paper, noted developmental psychologist Paul Baltes (1939–2006) laid out seven key assumptions of the life-span perspective (Baltes, 1987; also see Baltes, Lindenberger, & Staudinger, 1998, 2006, for elaborations). These are important themes that you will see echoed throughout this book. They will also give you a good sense of the challenges facing researchers who study human development.

1. **Development is a lifelong process.** Today's developmentalists appreciate that human development is not just "kid stuff," that we change throughout the life span. They also believe that development in any period of life is best seen in the context of the whole life span. For instance, our understanding of adolescent career choices is bound to be richer if we concern ourselves with formative influences in childhood and the implications of such choices for adult career development.

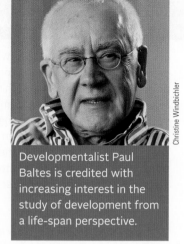

Christine Windbichler

Developmentalist Paul Baltes is credited with increasing interest in the study of development from a life-span perspective.

2. **Development is multidirectional.** To many pioneers of its study, development was a universal process leading in one direction—toward more "mature" functioning. Today's developmentalists recognize that different capacities show different patterns of change over time; for example, some intellectual skills decline faster than others in late adulthood; some don't change much; and some even continue to improve, as we'll see in Chapter 9. Different aspects of human functioning have different trajectories of change.

3. **Development involves both gain and loss.** As we have noted already, development is not just gain in childhood and loss in old age. Rather, gain and loss are intertwined during every phase of the life span. Baltes believed that gain inevitably brings with it loss of some kind, and loss brings gain—that gain and loss occur jointly. Examples? As infants gain command of the sounds of the language they hear spoken, they lose their early ability to "babble" sounds heard in other languages of the world (see Chapter 10); gaining a capacity for logical thought as a school-age child means losing some of the capacity for fanciful, imaginative thinking one had as a preschooler (see Chapter 7); and choosing to hone certain skills in one's career can mean losing command of other skills (see Chapter 11).

4. **Development is characterized by lifelong plasticity. Plasticity** refers to the capacity to change in response to both positive and negative experiences. Developmental scholars have long known that child development can be damaged by a deprived environment and optimized by an enriched one. It is now understood that this plasticity continues into later life—that the aging process is not fixed but rather can be altered considerably depending on the individual's experiences. For example, elderly adults can maintain or regain some of their intellectual abilities and even enhance them with the help of physical exercise like John Tatum's swimming, a mentally and socially active lifestyle, or training designed to improve specific cognitive skills (Hertzog et al., 2009; Willis et al., 2006). Older adults who regularly engage in mentally stimulating activities such as playing chess, playing a musical instrument, and dancing (the dancer not only gets exercise but has to think about the steps) even appear to be less likely than their mentally inactive peers to develop Alzheimer's disease and other forms of dementia (Verghese et al., 2003). Studies of animals tell us such cognitive benefits are rooted in **neuroplasticity**, the brain's remarkable ability to

change in response to experience throughout the life span, as when it recovers from injury or benefits from stimulating learning experiences. It is now clear that physical exercise and mental stimulation can result in changes in neurochemistry, the formation of new connections among neurons, and, remarkably, new neurons in the hippocampus of the brain—even in an aging brain (Doidge, 2007; Hertzog et al., 2009; Pereira et al., 2007; and see Chapter 5).

5. **Development is shaped by its historical–cultural context.** This theme, a big message of Bronfenbrenner's bio-ecological model, is illustrated beautifully by the pioneering work of Glen Elder and his colleagues. They researched how the Great Depression of the 1930s affected the later life courses and development of the era's children and adolescents—work that is now very timely given the many families affected by the economic downturn of 2008 (Elder, 1998; Elder, Liker, & Cross, 1984). A few years after the stock market crashed in 1929, one of three workers was unemployed and many families were tossed into poverty (Rogler, 2002). Although many families survived the Great Depression nicely, this economic crisis proved to be especially difficult for children if their out-of-work and demoralized fathers became less affectionate and less consistent in disciplining them. When this happened, children displayed behavior problems and had low aspirations and poor records in school. They turned into men who had erratic careers and unstable marriages and women who were seen by their own children as ill tempered. Adolescents generally fared better than children did. Less dependent on their parents than children, adolescents were pushed into working to help support their families and developed a strong sense of responsibility from their experience.

We will see many examples of cultural influences on development—effects of Bronfenbrenner's macrosystem—in this book. As societies change, the developmental experience changes. For example, Patricia Greenfield (2009) has shown how the transition from a traditional society (think rural village) to a more modern, urbanized society affects cultural values and learning environments and, in turn, human development. Among other things, children in more modern societies are raised to hold individualistic as opposed to communal values, to be more independent, and to place less emphasis on social responsibility and more on personal satisfaction and achievement. Clearly the trajectories lives take are affected by the historical and cultural context in which we develop.

6. **Development is multiply influenced.** Today's developmental scientists share Urie Bronfenbrenner's belief that human development is the product of many interacting causes—both inside

Viktor Schreckengost, famous for his Art Deco designs, coaches Heather McClellan as she creates a new variant of Schreckengost's Jazz bowl. The plasticity of the human brain is evident even in old age among people like Mr. Schreckengost who remain intellectually active. New neural connections and even new neurons can be formed in response to intellectual stimulation.

© David Joseph/The New York Times/Redux

and outside the person, both biological and environmental. It is the often-unpredictable outcome of ongoing interactions between a changing person and her changing world. Some influences are experienced by all humans at similar ages, others are common to people of a particular generation, and still others are unique to the individual (Baltes, 1987).

7. **Development must be studied by multiple disciplines.** Because human development is influenced by everything from biochemical reactions to historical events, it is impossible for one discipline to have all the answers. A full understanding of human development will come only when many disciplines, each with its own perspectives and tools of study, join forces. Where we once talked of developmental psychology as a field of study, we now talk of *developmental science* (Lerner, 2006). Not only psychologists but also biologists, neuroscientists, historians, economists, sociologists, anthropologists, and many others have something to contribute to our understanding. Some universities have established interdisciplinary human development programs that bring members of different disciplines together to forge more integrated perspectives on development.

Checking Mastery

1. Focusing on the development over childhood of digit span (the ability to remember longer and longer strings of numbers), state a research question that illustrates each of three main goals of the study of life-span development.

2. Which three of the seven assumptions in Baltes's life-span perspective concern the nature–nurture issue?

Making Connections

1. How does the developmental psychology of Paul Baltes improve on the developmental psychology of Charles Darwin?

2. Create examples to show how four of the assumptions of the life-span perspective might apply to John Tatum, the 90-year-old swimmer introduced at the beginning of the chapter.

1.3 How Is Development Studied?

How do developmental scholars gain understanding of the complexities of life-span development? Let us review for you, briefly, some basic concepts of scientific research and then turn to research strategies devised specifically for describing, explaining, and optimizing development (see Creasey, 2006; Teti, 2005). Even if you have no desire to do developmental research yourself, it is important for you to understand how the knowledge of development represented in this book was generated.

The Scientific Method

There is nothing mysterious about the **scientific method**. It is both a method and an attitude—a belief that investigators should allow their systematic observations (or data) to determine the merits of

The launching of the Internet is a good example of an historical change with implications for human development. According to one analysis (Valkenberg & Jochen, 2009), early studies of the impact of the Internet on adolescents suggested that it was isolating them and keeping them from developmentally important social experiences such as interacting with peers. More recent studies are revealing positive effects of time on the Internet. Why? In the 1990s, adolescent Internet users were fewer in number and usually surfed the net or talked to strangers in chat rooms. More recently, many more adolescents are on the Internet and they are networking with their friends by text messaging, visiting social sites like Facebook and Twitter, and so on. As a result, the Internet has become an important vehicle for maintaining and strengthening friendships.

© Yellow Dog Productions/Getty Images

their thinking. For example, for every "expert" who believes that psychological differences between males and females are largely biological in origin, there is likely to be another expert who just as firmly insists that boys and girls differ because they are raised differently. Whom should we believe? It is in the spirit of the scientific method to believe the data—the findings of research. The scientist is willing to abandon a pet theory if the data contradict it. Ultimately, then, the scientific method can help the scientific community and society at large weed out flawed ideas.

The scientific method involves a process of generating ideas and testing them by making observations. Often, preliminary observations provide ideas for a **theory**—a set of concepts and propositions intended to describe and explain certain phenomena. Jean Piaget, for instance, formulated his influential theory of cognitive development by closely observing how French children of different ages responded to items on the Binet IQ test when he worked on the test's development, as well as by watching his own children's development (see Chapters 2 and 7).

Theories generate specific predictions, or **hypotheses**, regarding a particular set of observations. Consider, for example, a theory claiming that psychological differences between the sexes are largely caused by differences in their social environments. Based on this theory, a researcher might hypothesize that if parents grant boys and girls the same freedoms, the two sexes will be similarly independent, whereas if parents let boys do more things than they let girls do, boys will be more independent than girls. Suppose that the study designed to test this hypothesis indicates that boys are more independent than girls no matter how their parents treat them. Then the hypothesis would be disconfirmed by the findings, and the researcher would want to rethink this theory of gender differences. If other hypotheses based on this theory were inconsistent with the facts, the theory would have to be significantly revised or abandoned in favor of a better theory.

This, then, is the heart of the scientific method: theories generate hypotheses, which are tested through observation of behavior, and new observations indicate which theories are worth keeping and which are not (■ **Figure 1.3**). It should be clear that theories are not just speculations, hunches, or unsupported opinions. A good theory should be:

- *Internally consistent.* Its different parts and propositions should hang together and should not generate contradictory hypotheses.
- *Falsifiable.* It can be proved wrong; that is, it can generate testable hypotheses that can be studied and either supported or not supported by data. If a theory is vague or generates contradictory or ambiguous hypotheses, it cannot guide research, cannot be tested, and therefore will not be useful in advancing knowledge.
- *Supported by data.* A good theory should help us better describe, predict, and explain human development; that is, its predictions should be confirmed by research results.

Sample Selection

Any study of development focuses on a particular research **sample** (the group of individuals studied) with the intention of generalizing to a larger **population**, a well-defined group (such

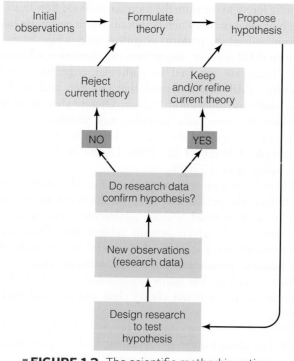

■ **FIGURE 1.3** The scientific method in action.

major methods of data collection used by developmental researchers: verbal reports, behavioral observations, and physiological measurements.

Verbal Reports

Interviews, written questionnaires or surveys, ability and achievement tests, and personality scales all involve asking people questions, either about themselves (self-report measures) or about someone else (for example, child behavior as reported by informants such as parents or teachers). These verbal report measures usually ask the same questions in precisely the same order of everyone so that the responses of different individuals can be directly compared.

Although self-report and other verbal report methods are widely used to study human development, they have shortcomings. First, self-report measures typically cannot be used with infants, young children, cognitively impaired elders, or other individuals who cannot read or understand speech well. Informant surveys, questionnaires, or interviews are often used in these situations instead. Second, because individuals of different ages may not understand questions in the same way, age differences in responses may reflect age differences in comprehension or interpretation rather than age differences in the quality of interest to the researcher. Finally, respondents may try to present themselves (or those they are providing information about) in a positive or socially desirable light.

Behavioral Observations

Naturalistic observation involves observing people in their everyday (that is, natural) surroundings (Pellegrini, 1996). Ongoing behavior is observed in homes, schools, playgrounds, workplaces, nursing homes, or wherever people are going about their lives. Naturalistic observation has been used to study child development more often than adult development, largely because infants and young children often cannot be studied through self-report techniques that demand verbal skills. It is the only data collection technique that can reveal what children or adults do in everyday life.

However, naturalistic observation has its limitations as well. First, some behaviors (for example, heroic efforts to help in emergencies) occur too infrequently and unexpectedly to be observed in this manner. Second, it is difficult to pinpoint the causes of the behavior, or of any developmental trends in the behavior, because in a natural setting many events are usually happening at the same time, any of which may affect behavior. Finally, the presence of an observer can sometimes make people behave differently than they otherwise would. Children may "ham it up" when they have an audience; parents may be on their best behavior. Therefore, researchers sometimes videotape the proceedings from a hidden location or spend time in the setting before they collect their "real" data so that the individuals they are observing become used to their presence and behave more naturally.

To achieve greater control over the conditions under which they gather behavioral data, and to capture rarely occurring events,

as premature infants, American high school students, or Chinese elders) from which the sample is drawn and about which we want to draw conclusions. Although it is advocated more than it is used, the best approach is to study a **random sample** of the population of interest—a sample formed by identifying all members of the larger population and then, by a random means (such as drawing names blindly), selecting a portion of that population to study. Random sampling increases confidence that the sample studied is representative of the larger population of interest and therefore that conclusions based on studying the sample will be true of the whole population.

In practice, developmentalists often draw their samples—sometimes random, sometimes not—from their local communities. Thus, researchers might survey students at a local high school about their drug use but then be unable to make statements about American teenagers in general if, for example, the school is in a suburb where drug-use patterns are different than they might be in an inner-city or rural area. They would certainly be unable to generalize about Kenyan or Brazilian high school students. All researchers must therefore be careful to describe the characteristics of the sample they studied and to avoid overgeneralizing their findings to populations that might be socioeconomically or culturally different from the research sample (Rogoff, 2003).

Data Collection

No matter what aspect of human development we are interested in, we must find appropriate ways to measure what interests us. The methods used to study human development are varied, depending on the age group and aspect of development of interest (Creasey, 2006). Here we will look at some pros and cons of three

Naturalistic observation of young children is done in day care centers, preschools, homes, and other everyday settings. Here, the play of hispanic children in Los Angeles is being observed and coded into categories.

researchers often use **structured observation**; that is, they create special stimuli, tasks, or situations designed to elicit the behavior of interest. To study helping behavior in adults of different ages, for example, researchers might stage an emergency that involves a loud crash and a scream coming from the room next to the one where the research participant is working on cognitive tasks and see if the participant takes action. By exposing all research participants to the same stimuli, this approach increases the investigator's ability to compare the effects of these stimuli on different individuals. Concerns about this method center on whether research participants will behave naturally and whether conclusions based on their behavior in specially designed settings will generalize to their behavior in natural settings.

Physiological Measurements

Finally, developmental scientists sometimes take physiological measurements to assess variables of interest to them; for example, they use electrodes to measure electrical activity in the brain, chart changes in hormone levels in menopausal women, or measure heart rate and other indicators of arousal to assess emotions.

Today, for example, exciting breakthroughs are being made in understanding relationships between brain and behavior through the use of **functional magnetic resonance imaging (fMRI)**, a brain-scanning technique that uses

magnetic forces to measure the increase in blood flow to an area of the brain that occurs when that brain area is active. By having children and adults perform cognitive tasks while lying very still in an fMRI scanner, researchers can determine which parts of the brain are involved in particular cognitive activities. Sometimes fMRI studies reveal that children and adults, or young adults and older adults, rely on different areas of the brain to perform the same tasks, providing new insights into the development and aging of the brain and cognitive functions (see, for example, Church et al., 2008; Dennis & Cabeza, 2008; O'Shaughnessy et al., 2008).

Physiological measurements have the advantage of being hard to fake; the person who tells you she is not angry may be physiologically aroused, and the adolescent who claims not to take drugs may be given away by a blood test. Physiological measurements are also particularly useful in the study of infants because infants cannot tell us verbally what they are thinking or feeling. The main limitation of physiological measurements is that it is not always clear exactly what they are assessing.

These, then, are the most commonly used techniques of collecting data about human development: verbal report measures (interviews, questionnaires, and tests), behavioral observation (both naturalistic and structured), and physiological measures. Exploration Box 1.3 provides an illustration of the use of all three approaches in a study of anger and aggression. Because each method has its limitations, knowledge is advanced the most when *multiple* methods are used to study the same aspect of human development and these different methods lead to similar conclusions.

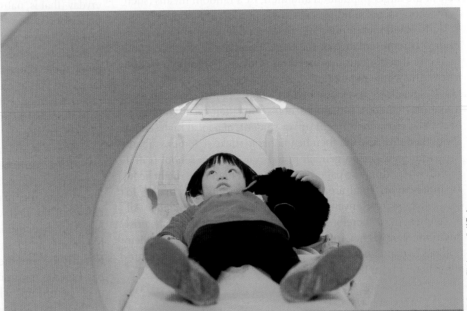

Functional magnetic resonance imaging is increasingly being used to study which parts of the brain are activated when humans of different ages perform various cognitive tasks. Testing children is challenging, however; they may fear entering the tube of the MRI and, once there, may have difficulty staying still as required.

We can illustrate the primary methods of data collection by considering a study by Julie Hubbard and her colleagues (2002) that used all three approaches. Hubbard was interested in the relationship between anger and two styles of aggression in 8-year-olds, as determined by teachers' responses to questions about children's behavior in the classroom: a "hot" kind of aggression in which children hit, pinch, and otherwise abuse other children when provoked, and a cooler, more calculating style of aggression in which children use aggression to get what they want. The researchers hypothesized that aggressive children of the first type would be more likely than aggressive children of the second type to become angry in a laboratory situation in which another child (a confederate of the researchers) cheated shamelessly in a board game about astronauts and won. The researchers needed a way to measure anger. What would you suggest?

Behavioral observation. Hubbard used the structured observation approach by setting up the astronaut game situation, having the confederate cheat to provoke children's anger, and then observing signs of anger in facial expressions and nonverbal behavior. The confederate was carefully trained to behave the same way with each of the 272 participants in the study. Sessions were videotaped; Hubbard then trained graduate and undergraduate students to code second by second whether the participants' facial expressions were angry, sad, happy, or neutral and whether they showed any nonverbal signs of anger (for example, slamming game pieces on the table). Two students coded a subsample of the videotapes to ensure that they could agree upon, or reliably code, facial expressions and nonverbal behavior.

Verbal report. The researchers also had each participant watch a videotape of the game he or she played with the cheating confederate, stopped the tape at each turn in the game, and asked each child, "How angry did you feel now?" The child responded on a four-point scale ranging from 1 (not at all) to 4 (a lot). The researchers used these ratings to calculate for each child an average degree of self-reported anger over the entire game.

Physiological measurements. The researchers collected data on two physiological measures of anger by attaching electrodes to children's hands and chests (after convincing the children that astronauts normally wear sensors when they go into space!). Emotionally aroused people, including angry ones, often have sweaty palms and low skin conductance, or electrical resistance of the skin, as measured by electrodes attached to their hands. Emotional arousal is also given away by a high heart rate, measured through electrodes on the chest.

Using these measures, Hubbard and her colleagues were indeed able to distinguish between children who show "hot" and "cool" types of aggression. As expected, children who engaged in "hot" aggression in the classroom showed more anger during the game than "cool" aggressors, although the difference was more evident in their skin conductance and nonverbal behavior than in their verbal self-reports and heart rates. Because all data collection methods have their weaknesses, and because different measures often yield different results, as in Hubbard's study, use of multiple methods in the same study is a wise research strategy.

The Case Study, Experimental, and Correlational Methods

Once developmental scientists have formulated hypotheses, chosen a sample, and figured out what to measure and how to measure it, they can test their hypotheses. As we have seen, developmental science got its start with baby biographies, and on occasion today's researchers still study the development of individuals through case studies. More often they use the experimental and correlational methods to examine relationships between one variable and another—and, where possible, to establish that one variable causes another.

The Case Study

A **case study** is an in-depth examination of an individual (or a small number of individuals), typically carried out by compiling and analyzing information from a variety of sources, such as observation, testing, and interviewing the person or people who know her. The case study method can provide rich information about the complexities of an individual's development and the influences on it. It is particularly useful in studying people with rare conditions and disorders, when it is simply not possible to assemble a large sample of people to study, and it can be a good source of hypotheses that can be examined further in larger-scale studies. This approach has been used, for example, to explore the origins of multiple personality disorder and to examine the effects of being deprived of human contact early in life. However, it is a limited method. Conclusions based on a single case may not generalize to other individuals, and inferences about what may have caused the person to develop as he or she did are more like speculations than solidly established scientific findings.

The Experimental Method

In an **experiment**, an investigator manipulates or alters some aspect of the environment to see how this affects the behavior of the sample of individuals studied. Consider an experiment conducted by Lynette Friedrich and Aletha Stein (1973) some years ago—one of the first to suggest that watching violence on television could affect the social behavior of preschool children. These researchers divided children in a nursery school into three groups: one group was exposed to violent cartoons such as *Superman* and *Batman* (aggressive treatment condition), another group watched episodes of *Mister Rogers' Neighborhood* portraying many helpful and cooperative acts (prosocial treatment condition), and a third group saw programs featuring circuses and farm scenes with neither aggressive nor altruistic themes (neutral control condition).

The goal of an experiment is to see whether the different treatments that form the **independent variable**—the variable manipulated so that its causal effects can be assessed—have differing effects on the behavior expected to be affected, the **dependent variable** in the experiment. The independent variable in Friedrich and Stein's experiment was the type of television children watched: aggressive, prosocial, or neutral. The dependent variable of interest was aggressive behavior. Any variable represents one specific way of measuring a concept of interest. Friedrich and Stein chose to use a complicated naturalistic observation system to count several types of aggressive actions toward classmates in the nursery school. Behavior was observed before each child spent a month watching daily episodes of one of the three kinds of television programs and was recorded again after that period to see if it had changed. When cause–effect relationships are studied in an experiment, the independent variable is the hypothesized cause and the dependent variable is the effect. Similarly, if researchers were testing drugs to improve memory function in elderly adults with Alzheimer's disease, the type of drug administered (for example, a new drug versus a placebo with no active ingredients) would be the independent variable and performance on a memory task would be the dependent variable.

So, did the number of aggressive behaviors observed "depend on" the independent variable, the type of television watched? It did. Children who watched violent programs became more aggressive than children who watched prosocial or neutral programs—but this was only true of the children in the study who were already relatively aggressive. Thus, this experiment demonstrated a clear cause–effect relationship—although only for some children—between the kind of behavior children watched on television and their own subsequent behavior.

This study has the three critical features shared by any true experiment:

1. *Random assignment of individuals to treatment conditions.* **Random assignment** of participants to different experimental conditions (for example, by drawing names from a jar) is a critical feature of experiments. It helps ensure that the treatment groups are similar in all respects at the outset (in previous tendencies to be aggressive or helpful, in socioeconomic status, and in all other individual characteristics that could affect their aggressive behavior). Only if experimental groups are similar in all respects initially can researchers be confident that differences among groups at the end of the experiment were caused by differences in the experimental treatments they received.

2. *Manipulation of the independent variable.* Investigators must arrange for different groups to have different experiences so that the effects of those experiences can be assessed. If investigators merely compare children who already watch a lot of violent television and children who watch little, they cannot establish that violent television watching *causes* increased aggression.

3. *Experimental control.* In a true experiment with proper **experimental control**, all factors other than the independent variable are controlled or held constant so that they cannot contribute to differences among the treatment groups. Thus, Friedrich and Stein ensured that children in the three treatment conditions were studied in the same environment and treated similarly except for the type of television they watched.

The greatest strength of the experimental method is its ability to establish unambiguously that one thing causes another—that manipulating the independent variable causes a change in the dependent variable. When experiments are properly conducted, they contribute to our ability to *explain* human development and sometimes to *optimize* it.

Does the experimental method have limitations? Absolutely! First, the findings of laboratory experiments do not always hold true in the real world, especially if the situations created in laboratory experiments are artificial and unlike the situations that people encounter in everyday life or if research participants do not act naturally because they know they are being studied. Urie Bronfenbrenner (1979), who was critical of the fact that so many developmental studies are contrived experiments, once charged that developmental psychology had become "the science of the strange behavior of children in strange situations with strange adults" (p. 19). Experiments often show what can cause development but not necessarily what *does* most strongly shape development in natural settings (McCall, 1977).

A second limitation of the experimental method is that it cannot be used to address many significant questions about human development for ethical reasons. How would you conduct a true experiment to determine how older women are affected by their husbands' deaths, for example? You would need to identify a sample of elderly women, randomly assign them to either the experimental group or the control group, and then manipulate the independent variable by killing the husbands of all the mem-

Many studies demonstrate that observational learning of aggression occurs when children watch a lot of violence on television.

Tony Freeman/Photo Edit Inc.

bers of the experimental group! Ethical principles obviously demand that developmentalists use methods other than true experimental ones to study questions about the effect of widowhood—and a host of other important questions about development.

Researchers sometimes study how a program or intervention affects development through a **quasi experiment**—an experiment-like study that evaluates the effects of different treatments but does not randomly assign individuals to treatment groups (see Pitts, Prost, & Winters, 2005). A gerontologist, for example, might conduct a quasi experiment to compare the adjustment of widows who choose to participate in a special support group for widows and those who do not. When individuals are not randomly assigned to treatment groups, however, uncontrolled differences among the groups studied could influence the results (for example, the widows who seek help might be more sociable than those who do not). As a result, the researcher is not able to make strong statements about what caused what, as in a true experiment.

The Correlational Method

Largely because of ethical issues, most developmental research today is correlational rather than experimental. The **correlational method** generally involves determining whether two or more variables are related in a systematic way. Researchers do not randomly assign participants to treatment conditions, manipulate the independent variable, or control other factors, as in an experiment. Instead, researchers take people as they are and attempt to determine whether there are relationships among their experiences, characteristics, and developmental outcomes.

How might a correlational study of the effects of television on children's aggressive behavior differ from Friedrich and Stein's experiment on this topic? In a well-designed correlational study, L. Rowell Huesmann and his colleagues (2003) correlated children's TV viewing between the ages of 6 and 9 with their aggressive behavior as adults 15 years later. A self-report measure of the amount of violent TV watched was created by having children pick their favorites from lists of TV programs and indicate how often they watched each program. The researchers then correlated a violent TV-watching measure with a measure of adult aggressive behavior that combined in one index criminal behavior, traffic violations, spouse abuse, and physical aggression, as well as more indirect forms of aggression such as trying to get other people to dislike someone.

Huesmann and his colleagues were then able to determine the strength of the relationship between these two variables by calculating a **correlation coefficient**—an index of the extent to which individuals' scores on one variable are systematically associated with their scores on another variable. A correlation coefficient (symbolized as r) can range in value from $+1.00$ to -1.00. A positive correlation between TV viewing and aggression would indicate that as the number of hours of TV children watch increases, so does the number of aggressive acts they commit (■ **Figure 1.4, Panel A**). A positive correlation of $r = +0.90$ indicates a stronger, more predictable positive relationship than a smaller positive correlation such as $r = +0.30$. A negative correlation would result if the heaviest TV viewers were consistently the least aggressive children and the lightest viewers were the most aggressive children (**Figure 1.4, Panel B**). A correlation near 0.00 would be obtained if there was no relationship between the two variables—if one cannot predict how aggressive children are based on knowing how much violent TV they watch (**Figure 1.4, Panel C**).

Huesmann's team found the positive relationship they hypothesized between watching violent TV as a child and engaging in aggressive and antisocial behavior as an adult. The correlation was $+0.21$ for men and $+0.19$ for women—not very large but still indicative of a meaningful relationship. People who watched a great deal of violent TV as children, whether male or female, had higher composite aggression scores as adults than did people who watched less violence on television as children. But does this correlational study firmly establish that watching slug fests and shootouts on television causes children to become more aggressive for life? Or can you think of rival explanations for the correlation between watching TV and aggression?

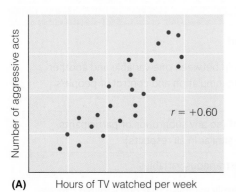

(A) Hours of TV watched per week

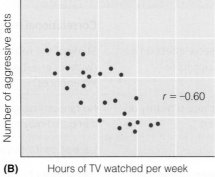

(B) Hours of TV watched per week

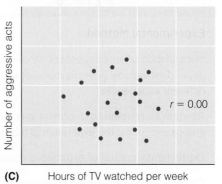

(C) Hours of TV watched per week

■ **FIGURE 1.4** Plots of hypothetical correlations between the amount of TV children watch and the number of aggressive acts they display. Each dot represents a specific child who watches a certain amount of TV (low, medium, or high) and commits a certain number of aggressive acts. Panel A shows a positive correlation between television watching and aggression: the more TV children watch, the more aggressive they are. Panel B shows a negative correlation: the more TV children watch, the less aggressive they are. Finally, Panel C shows zero correlation: the amount of TV watched is unrelated to the amount of aggression displayed.

One rival interpretation in correlational studies is that *the direction of the cause–effect relationship is reversed*. That is, exposure to violent TV may not *cause* children to become aggressive; rather, being aggressive may cause children to seek out blood and gore on TV. However, this problem of determining the directionality of causation was not as bothersome in Huesmann's study as it is in correlational studies that measure both variables of interest at the same time. It is difficult to argue that aggression in adulthood caused violent TV watching in childhood. Moreover, Huesmann collected data on how aggressive children in his sample were during childhood. He was then able to demonstrate that, although highly aggressive children do in fact watch more violent TV than other children, watching violent TV predicts becoming an aggressive adult, even controlling statistically for how aggressive these adults were as children.

A second rival interpretation in correlational studies is that *the association between the two variables is caused by some third variable*. An example of such a third variable might be parental rejection. Some children might have parents who are harsh and rejecting, and they might watch more TV than most children in order to avoid unpleasant interactions with their parents. They may be aggressive because they are angry and upset about being rejected. If so, watching TV did not cause these children to become more aggressive than their peers. Rather, a third variable—parental rejection—may have caused both their aggressive ways and their TV-viewing habits.

Thus, the correlational method has one major limitation: it cannot unambiguously establish a causal relationship between one variable and another the way an experiment can. Correlational studies can *suggest* that a causal relationship exists, however. Indeed, Huesmann's team used complex statistical techniques in which a correlation is corrected for the influence of other variables to show that watching violent television in childhood probably contributed to aggression in adulthood. Several

potential third variables, including parental rejection, low socioeconomic status, and low intelligence quotient (IQ)—all correlated with both watching violent TV and aggression—were ruled out as explanations of the relationship between TV viewing and aggression. Still, despite all their efforts to establish that the direction of the cause–effect relationship is from watching violent TV to aggression rather than vice versa, and to rule out possible third variables that could explain the TV–aggression relationship, Huesmann's team could not establish a definite cause–effect link because of the correlational nature of the study.

Despite this key limitation, the correlational method is extremely valuable. First, as already noted, most important questions can be addressed only through the correlational method because it would be unethical to manipulate people's experiences in experiments. Second, complex correlational studies and statistical analyses allow researchers to learn about how multiple factors operating in the "real world" combine to influence development. We just have to be on the lookout for rival interpretations in explaining correlational relationships. See ●Table 1.3 for a comparison of experimental and correlational methods.

Overall, the understanding of why humans develop as they do is best advanced when the results of different kinds of studies *converge*—when experiments demonstrate a clear cause–effect relationship and correlational studies reveal that the same relationship seems to be operating in everyday life. The results of multiple studies addressing the same question can be synthesized to produce overall conclusions through the research method of **meta-analysis** (Glass, McGaw, & Smith, 1981; Lipsey & Wilson, 2001). A meta-analysis of multiple studies of the link between watching violence on television and aggression showed a reliable relationship between the two (Anderson & Bushman, 2002; Bushman & Anderson, 2001). The magnitude of the correlation is usually between +0.10 and +0.30. That may seem small, but it is larger than the average correlation between calcium intake

●**TABLE 1.3 A COMPARISON OF THE EXPERIMENTAL METHOD AND THE CORRELATIONAL METHOD**

Experimental Method	Correlational Method
Manipulation of an independent variable to observe effect on a dependent variable (investigator exposes participants to different experiences)	Study of the relationship between one variable and another (without investigator manipulation and control of people's experiences)
Random assignment to treatment groups to ensure similarity of groups except for the experimental manipulation	No random assignment (so any subgroups of participants compared may not be similar in all respects)
Experimental control of extraneous variables	Lack of control over extraneous variables
Can establish a cause–effect relationship between independent variable and dependent variable	Can suggest but not firmly establish that one variable causes another
May not be possible for ethical reasons	Can be used to study many important issues that cannot be studied experimentally for ethical reasons
May be artificial (findings from contrived experimental settings may not generalize well to the "real world")	Can study multiple influences operating in natural settings (findings may generalize better to the "real world")

and bone mass or between time spent doing homework and academic achievement (Huesmann & Taylor, 2006). Watching violent programs is related not only to roughhousing on the playground but to the kinds of serious aggression and violence displayed by some juvenile delinquents (Boxer et al., 2009). Moreover, the relationship shows up in studies using the correlational method as well as in studies using the experimental method, and in both laboratory and naturalistic settings (Huesmann & Taylor, 2006; Kirsh, 2006). Much more remains to be learned, though, about the effects of television and other media on human development (see Calvert & Wilson, 2008). For example, the American Academy of Pediatrics has recommended that children younger than 2 not watch television at all, but the fact is that we are not yet sure of the effects of TV on the many infants and toddlers in the United States who receive daily doses of it (Courage & Setliff, 2009).

Developmental Research Designs

Along with the experimental and correlational methods used by all kinds of researchers to study relationships between variables, developmental researchers need specialized research designs to study how people change and remain the same as they get older (Creasey, 2006; Schaie, 2000). To describe development, researchers have relied extensively on two types of research designs: the cross-sectional design and the longitudinal design. A third type of design, the sequential study, has come into use in an attempt to overcome the limitations of the other two techniques. We will consider these three designs and their strengths and weaknesses in turn.

Cross-Sectional Designs

In a **cross-sectional design**, the performances of people of different age groups, or cohorts, are compared. A **cohort** is a group of individuals born at the same time, either in the same year or within a specified span of years (for example, a generation is a cohort). A researcher interested in the development of vocabulary might gather samples of speech from several 2-, 3-, and 4-year-olds; calculate the mean (or average) number of distinct words used per child for each age group; and compare these means to describe how the vocabulary sizes of children age 2, 3, and 4 differ. The cross-sectional study provides information about *age differences*. By seeing how age groups differ, researchers can attempt to draw conclusions about how performance changes with age.

Suppose a team of researchers was interested in whether, as adults get older, their attitudes about the roles of men and women in society typically become more traditional or more liberated and in favor of greater equality between the sexes. Suppose that in 2010 they conducted a cross-sectional study comparing the gender-role attitudes of adults 30, 50, and 70 years old at that time. Suppose that they found that the gender-role attitudes of older adults were more conservative than those of younger adults.

What interests developmental researchers is **age effects**— the relationship between age (a rough proxy for changes brought about by nature and nurture) and a particular aspect of development. **Cohort effects** are the effects of being born as a member of a particular cohort or generation in a particular historical context. People who are in their 70s not only are older than people in their 50s and 30s but belong to a different cohort or generation and have had different formative experiences. The 70-year-olds in our gender-role attitudes study were born in 1940, the 50-year-olds in 1960, and the 30-year-olds in 1980. The cross-sectional study tells how people of different ages (cohorts) differ, but it does not necessarily tell how people normally *change* as they get older. Do 70-year-olds hold more conservative gender-role attitudes than 30-year-olds because people become more conservative as they get older? Or is it because 70-year-olds are members of a cohort raised in a more traditional era and have stuck with the traditional attitudes they learned in their formative years? We cannot tell. *Age effects and cohort effects are confounded, or entangled.* What initially looked like a developmental trend toward greater traditionalism in later life (an age effect) could actually be a cohort effect resulting from differences in the formative experiences of the different generations studied.

Cohort differences are of interest in their own right; they can tell us about the influence of the sociocultural environment on development and about the implications of being part of one generation or another, as suggested by Exploration Box 1.4 on the baby boom generation. However, the presence of cohort effects poses a problem in cross-sectional research whenever the growing-up experiences of the cohorts studied differ. As you will see in Chapter 9, it was once believed, based on cross-sectional studies of performance on intelligence tests, that people experience significant declines in intellectual functioning starting in middle age. Later longitudinal studies suggested that intellectual declines were less steep and, when they did occur, came later in life (Schaie, 2000). The conclusion reached was that the elderly adults in cross-sectional studies probably did not experience steep losses of intellectual abilities during adulthood (a true developmental or age effect); they merely performed less well than younger cohorts because they had received less education in their youth (a cohort effect) and probably always had lower intellectual abilities than younger cohorts as a result.

The second major limitation of the cross-sectional design is that, because each person is observed at only one point, researchers learn nothing about how people change with age. They cannot see, for example, returning to our gender-role example, whether different people show divergent patterns of change in gender-role attitudes over time or whether individuals who are especially liberated in their attitudes as 30-year-olds are also especially liberated at 70. To address issues like these, researchers need longitudinal research.

Despite these problems with the cross-sectional design, it is a very important approach and developmentalists continue to rely heavily on it. It has the great advantage of being quick and easy: researchers can go out this year, sample individuals of different ages, and be done with it. Moreover, cross-sectional studies should yield valid conclusions about age effects if the cohorts studied are likely to have had similar growing-up experiences—as when 3- and 4-year-olds rather than 30- and 40-year-olds are compared. It is when researchers attempt to make inferences

Does it make a difference whether one is part of the Silent Generation (the World War II and Korean War generation born between 1925 and 1946), the **baby boom generation** (the huge cohort born after World War II between 1946 and 1964), Generation X (the small generation, also called the "Me Generation," born between 1964 and 1982), or Generation Y (also called the millennials, the "baby boomlet" generation born from 1982 to the late 1990s and raised on the Internet)? We seem to believe that different cohorts or generations not only have different formative experiences but develop different characters. For example, some surveys suggest that younger generations (Generations X and Y) are less committed to work and more interested in freedom and personal fulfillment than the baby boomers or the silent generation (Fogg, 2008). In truth, we know very little about how the generations differ from each other as groups. Popular books on the subject often present overgeneralized portraits of generations like the millennials based on little solid data. There are undoubtedly more psychological differences within than between generations. Still, understanding how people are affected by the historical–cultural context in which they develop is an important part of the science of life-span

development and genuine cohort differences sometimes emerge in research studies.

The baby boomers have been the focus of extraordinary attention because they are such a large generation and have posed a variety of challenges to society as they have developed. The first wave of baby boomers turned 65 in 2011: George W. and Laura Bush, Bill Clinton, Dolly Parton, Donald Trump, and Cher, not to mention the senior (in more ways than one) author of this book. They were a year old when Howdy Dowdy first appeared on the first home TVs and 17 when John F. Kennedy was assassinated; they grew up fearing nuclear bombs and Russians and listening to rock and roll; and many of them protested the Vietnam War or fought in it (Adler, 2005).

By 2030, when most baby boomers will have retired from work, adults 65 or older will represent not the 13% of the U.S. population they represent today, but more like 20% (Satariano, 2006). They will be healthier, wealthier, and better educated than the cohorts that preceded them, but they will also need a lot of services as more of them attain very old age (Treas & Hill, 2009). As a result, today's policy makers are wondering about whether Social Security and Medicare funds will last, whether there will be enough health and mental health

For baby boomers growing up in the 1950s, sex roles were more traditional than they are now. Fewer women worked outside the home, and more parents dressed and treated girls and boys differently.

professionals trained in geriatrics to go around, and whether more baby boomers will (or perhaps should) continue working and contributing to society rather than retiring in their 60s (Schulz & Binstock, 2006; Treas & Hill, 2009). It will be up to Generations X and Y to work these policy issues through and determine what the experience of aging in America will be like not only for the boomers but for their own generations.

about development over the span of many years that cohort effects in cross-sectional studies can yield a misleading picture of development.

Longitudinal Designs

In a **longitudinal design**, the performance of one cohort of individuals is assessed repeatedly over time. A study of the development of vocabulary would be longitudinal rather than cross-sectional if a researcher identified a group of 2-year-olds, measured their vocabulary sizes, waited a year until they were age 3 and measured their vocabularies again, did the same thing a year later when they were age 4, and then compared the mean scores of these same children at the three ages. In any longitudinal study, whether it covers only a few months in infancy or 50 years, the same individuals are studied as they develop. Thus, the longitudinal design provides information about *age changes* rather than age differences.

Suppose we had designed a longitudinal study of gender-role attitudes by administering a gender-role questionnaire three times to a group of men and women: in 1970 (when these adults were 30), in 1990 (when they were 50), and in 2010 (when they were 70). ▪ **Figure 1.5** compares a cross-sectional and a longitudinal design for studying gender-role attitudes.

Because the longitudinal design traces changes in individuals as they age, it can tell whether most people change in the same direction or whether different individuals travel different developmental paths. It can indicate whether the characteristics and behaviors measured remain consistent over time—for example, whether people who had liberated attitudes at age 30 are still relatively liberated at age 70. And it can tell whether experiences earlier in life predict traits and behaviors later in life. The cross-sectional design can do none of these.

What, then, are the limitations of the longitudinal design? Our hypothetical longitudinal study of gender-role attitudes centered on *one cohort* of individuals: members of the 1940 birth

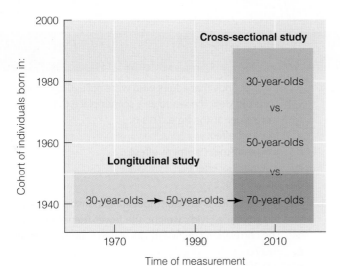

■ **FIGURE 1.5** Cross-sectional and longitudinal studies of development from age 30 to age 70. The longitudinal study involves repeated assessment every 20 years starting in 1970, whereas in the cross-sectional study, the three age groups of interest are compared in 2010.

cohort. These people were raised in an historical context in which gender-role attitudes were traditional and lived through an era in which the women's movement changed many of those attitudes considerably. Their responses in 2010 could easily have become more liberal than their responses in 1970 as a result (whereas in our hypothetical cross-sectional study, older adults today would probably be more conservative than young adults). However, this trend toward liberation might not be because gender-role attitudes *typically* become more liberal as people get older but because major societal changes occurred from one time of measurement to the next during the time frame of this particular study. **Time-of-measurement effects** in developmental research are the effects of historical events and trends occurring when the data are collected (for example, effects of an economic recession, a traumatic event like 9/11, advances in health care, or technological advances such as the introduction of the Internet). Unlike cohort effects, time-of-measurement effects are not unique to a particular cohort; they can affect anyone alive at the time. In the longitudinal study, then, *age effects and time-of-measurement effects are confounded.*

Because of time-of-measurement effects, we may not be able to tell for sure whether the age-related changes observed in a longitudinal study are generalizable to people developing in other sociohistorical contexts. Gender-role attitudes clearly became more liberal in the United States from the 1970s to the 1990s. For example, in 1977, more than half of respondents to a survey said it was more important for a wife to help her husband's career than to have her own; by 1996, only about one in five agreed (Brewster & Padavic, 2000). Perhaps we would obtain different "developmental" trends if we were to conduct a longitudinal study in an era in which traditional gender roles suddenly

became popular again. So, it can be challenging to identify true developmental or age effects—in cross-sectional studies because of cohort effects and in longitudinal studies because of time-of-measurement effects.

The longitudinal design has other disadvantages. One is fairly obvious: this approach is costly and time-consuming, particularly if it is used to trace development over a long span and at many points in time. Second, because knowledge is constantly changing, measurement methods that seemed good at the start of the study may seem dated or incomplete by the end. Third, participants drop out of long-term studies; they may move, lose interest, or, especially in studies of aging, die during the course of the study. The result is a smaller and often less representative sample on which to base conclusions. Finally, there may be effects of repeated testing; sometimes simply taking a test improves performance on that test the next time around.

Are both the cross-sectional and the longitudinal designs hopelessly flawed, then? That would be overstating their weaknesses. Cross-sectional studies are very efficient and informative, especially when the cohorts studied are not widely different in age or formative experiences. Longitudinal studies are extremely valuable for what they can reveal about how people change as they get older—even though it must be recognized that the cohort studied may not develop in precisely the same way that an earlier or later cohort does. Still, in an attempt to overcome the limitations of both cross-sectional and longitudinal designs, developmentalists have devised a more powerful method of describing developmental change: the sequential design.

Sequential Designs: The Best of Both Worlds

A **sequential design** combines the cross-sectional approach and the longitudinal approach in a single study (Schaie, 1994; Schaie & Caskie, 2005). In Chapter 9, you will read about an ambitious and important sequential study of changes in mental abilities during adulthood conducted by K. Warner Schaie and his colleagues (1996, 2005). Adults ranging in age from 22 to 70 and grouped into age groups were tested on a battery of mental ability tests (in a cross-sectional design), and then they were retested every 7 years (to create a longitudinal design). At each testing point a new sample of adults in their 20s to 70s was added to the study and those age groups were then retested. Some of the adults in the study were followed for as long as 45 years. This elaborate study has yielded many insights into intellectual aging. Not only were systematic changes with age in mental abilities identified, but cohort and time-of-measurement effects were revealed, suggesting that intellectual functioning is indeed influenced by the times in which people develop (see also Alwin, 2009).

Sequential designs, by combining the cross-sectional and longitudinal approaches, improve on both. They can tell researchers (1) which age-related trends are truly developmental in nature and reflect how most people, *regardless of cohort*, can be expected to change over time (age effects); (2) which age trends differ from cohort to cohort and suggest that each generation is affected by its distinct growing-up experiences (cohort effects); and (3) which trends suggest that events during a specific period of history similarly affect all cohorts alive at the time (time-of-

For each research example, identify the most appropriate descriptive term. Answers are printed upside down below.

__1. A researcher creates a situation on a school playground in which children are excluded one by one from a group game by the teacher so that their emotional reactions can be studied.
   a. structured observation
   b. case study
   c. experiment
   d. correlational study

__2. A researcher assesses the job satisfaction of a group of managers who are age 30 at the start of the study every 5 years and does similar every-5-years assessments of a second group of managers who are age 30 in 2020.
   a. quasi-experimental
   b. correlational
   c. sequential
   d. cross-sectional

__3. In a comparison of a new program to prepare teenage mothers for childbirth with a standard prenatal preparation program, the independent variable is:
   a. age of mother
   b. type of prenatal preparation program
   c. pain during labor
   d. labor

__4. A researcher finds that adults who were college age when 9/11 occurred view the world as a scarier place than adults who were older at the time. This is:
   a. a cohort effect
   b. a time-of-measurement effect
   c. a sequential effect
   d. an age effect

__5. A researcher finds a small or modest relationship indicating that the greater a child's weight, the fewer friends he or she has. The correlation coefficient calculated is probably around:
   a. +0.70
   b. +0.20
   c. –0.70
   d. –0.20

Answers: 1. a 2. c 3. b 4. a 5. d

---

measurement effects). In short, sequential designs can begin to untangle the effects of age, cohort, and time of measurement. Yet they are extremely complex and expensive. Generally, the study of life-span human development has progressed from early (and sometimes misleading) cross-sectional studies to more long-term longitudinal studies and, increasingly, to more complex sequential studies, especially of adult development (Baltes, Lindenberger, & Staudinger, 2006). See ● Table 1.4 for a summary of the three basic developmental designs.

Now that you have encountered examples of the various data collection methods and research designs used to study development, we challenge you to identify the research examples in Engagement Box 1.1.

Checking Mastery

1. Design an experiment to determine whether test performance is better when students read a chapter all at once or when they read it section by section and have breaks between sections. Make it clear that your experiment has the key features of an experiment and label the independent and dependent variables.

2. You conduct a longitudinal study of the development among college students of confidence in romantic relationships from age 18 to age 22. What would you be able to learn that you could not learn by conducting a cross-sectional study of the same topic?

Making Connections

1. How do you think our knowledge of human development would be different if no scientific studies of development had ever been conducted? What would we know and not know? What would our knowledge be based on?

2. Professor Tunnelvision conducts a study that reveals a correlation of +0.50 between self-esteem and academic achievement (grade point average) among college students. He then argues, based on this finding, that his college should launch a self-esteem–boosting program if it wants its students to gain more from their college experience. Convince the professor that there are at least two rival explanations for this correlation and suggest how he could do research to try to determine which explanation is most correct.

● TABLE 1.4 CROSS-SECTIONAL, LONGITUDINAL, AND SEQUENTIAL DEVELOPMENTAL DESIGNS

	Cross-Sectional Design	Longitudinal Design	Sequential Design
Procedure	Observe people of different cohorts at one point in time	Observe people of one age group repeatedly over time	Combine cross-sectional and longitudinal approaches; observe different cohorts on multiple occasions
Information Gained	Describes age differences	Describes age changes	Describes age differences and age changes
Advantages	Demonstrates age differences in behavior and hints at developmental trends Takes little time to conduct and is inexpensive	Indicates how individuals are alike and different in the way they change over time Can reveal links between early behavior or experiences and later behavior	Helps separate the effects of age, cohort, and time of measurement Indicates whether developmental changes experienced by one generation or cohort are similar to those experienced by other cohorts
Disadvantages	Age trends may reflect cohort effects rather than true developmental change Provides no information about change in individuals over time	Age trends may reflect time of measurement effects during the study rather than true developmental change Relatively time-consuming and expensive Measures may later prove inadequate Participants drop out Participants can be affected by repeated testing	Complex and time-consuming Despite being the strongest method, may leave questions about whether a developmental change can be generalized

1.4 What Special Challenges Do Developmental Scientists Face?

We hope we have convinced you that conducting good research on human development, while very important, is not easy. We conclude this chapter by discussing two additional challenges in the study of human development: being sensitive to cultural and subcultural differences and protecting the rights of research participants.

Conducting Culturally Sensitive Research

Both Bronfenbrenner's bioecological model and Baltes's lifespan perspective emphasize that development is shaped by its cultural context. They imply that we need to study development in a variety of contexts using culturally sensitive research methods and measurements to understand both what is universal and what is culturally specific about human development (Lonner, 2005). Easier said than done!

Developmentalists now appreciate the need to study samples of developing persons from a variety of ecological settings, not just white middle-class America. A particularly important aspect of the ecology of human development is socioeconomic status (SES). We know that low-SES families are often exposed to more stress but have fewer coping resources than higher-income families (Heymann, Penrose, & Earle, 2006). We know too that the developmental experiences and trajectories of children are significantly affected by whether they grow up in poverty or affluence. On average, although there are many exceptions, parents of middle or high socioeconomic status tend to provide more stimulating and supportive home environments for their children than low-SES parents do. The result is higher academic achievement and better adjustment among higher-SES children than among lower-SES children, as well as better health, cognitive functioning, and adjustment in adulthood (Bornstein & Bradley, 2003; Conger & Donnellan, 2007; Luo & Waite, 2005).

Studying different subcultural and cultural groups is also critical. However, ensuring that questionnaire, interview, and test questions and testing and observation procedures are meaningful in a culture, and that they mean the same thing for individuals from different subcultural and cultural groups if comparisons are to be made, can be extremely challenging (Rogoff, 2003). Example: When one organization translated a survey into 63 languages and then had the questions translated back into English, strange things happened: "married or living with a partner" was translated as "married but have a girlfriend," and "American ideas and customs" became "the ideology of America and border guards" (Morin, 2003). When another team sought to conduct a cross-cultural study of caregiver–infant interactions, they faced a dilemma about whether to observe such interactions when the caregiver and infant were alone (typical in American homes) or when the caregiver and infant were in a group (typical in Micronesia). They settled on observing in both social contexts to avoid findings that might be biased toward one cultural group or the other (Sostek et al., 1981).

This Bedouin family bakes bread in their goathair tent. Only cross-cultural research can tell us whether the findings of research conducted in our society hold true in societies very different from ours.

In addition, researchers who study cultural influences on development or racial, ethnic, and socioeconomic differences in development must work hard to keep their own cultural values from biasing their perceptions of other groups. Too often, Western researchers have let **ethnocentrism**—the belief that one's own group and its culture are superior—creep into their research designs, procedures, and measures. And too often, researchers in the United States have judged minority group children and adults according to white middle-class standards, have labeled them "deficient" when they would better be described as "different," and have looked more at their vulnerabilities than at their strengths (Ogbu, 1981; Spencer, 2006). Also too often, researchers have assumed that all African Americans or Asian Americans or Hispanic Americans are alike psychologically, when in fact there is immense diversity within each racial or ethnic group (Helms, Jernigan, & Mascher, 2005). Today's developmentalists appreciate the importance of understanding human development in its ecological context, but actually doing so is a tremendous challenge.

Protecting the Rights of Research Participants

Developmental researchers must also be sensitive to issues involving **research ethics**—the standards of conduct that investigators are ethically bound to honor to protect their research participants from physical or psychological harm (see, for example, Buchanan, Fisher, & Gable, 2009; Kodish, 2005; Pimple, 2008). Recall the study by Hubbard and colleagues (2002) described in Exploration Box 1.3, in which 8-year-olds were deliberately provoked to become angry after witnessing another child cheat them and win a board game unfairly. The researchers recognized that their study raised ethical issues. As a result, they arranged for the following: (1) children's parents observed the session through a one-way mirror so that they could call a halt to it if they thought their child was becoming too upset; (2) so that children would not leave with bad feelings about losing, they played another game with the confederate that was rigged so that they would win; (3) children were debriefed about the real purposes of the study; and (4) children enjoyed snack and play time with the confederate (who was very concerned not to be branded a cheater).

Many ethical issues arise in research. For example, is it ethical to tell children that they performed poorly on a test to create a temporary sense of failure? Is it an invasion of a family's privacy to ask adolescents questions about conversations they have had with their parents about sex? Should a study of how a hormone replacement pill affects menopausal women be halted if it appears that the drug is having harmful effects? If a drug to treat memory loss in elderly adults with Alzheimer's disease appears to be working, should it be withheld from the control group in the study?

Such issues have led the federal government (through the Office for Human Research Protections), the American

Psychological Association, the Society for Research in Child Development, the American Geriatrics Society, and other organizations and agencies to establish guidelines for ethical research with humans. Federal regulations require universities and other organizations that conduct research with humans to have institutional review boards (IRBs) that determine whether proposed research projects conform to ethical standards and to approve projects only if they comply. The federal government has tightened its oversight of research in recent years as a result of past abuses.

Deciding whether a proposed study is on safe ethical ground involves weighing the possible benefits of the research (gains in knowledge and potential benefits to humanity or to the participants) against the potential risks to participants. If the potential benefits greatly outweigh the potential risks, and if there are no other, less risky procedures that could produce these same benefits, the investigation is likely to be viewed as ethical. The investigator's ethical responsibilities boil down to respecting the rights of research participants by (1) allowing them to make informed and uncoerced decisions about taking part in research, (2) debriefing them afterward (especially if they are not told everything in advance or are deceived), (3) protecting them from harm, and (4) treating any information they provide as confidential.

1. *Informed consent.* Researchers generally should inform potential participants of all aspects of the research that might affect their decision to participate so that they can make a voluntary decision based on full knowledge of what the research involves. But are young children or mentally impaired people capable of understanding what they are being asked to do and of giving their *informed* consent? Probably not. Therefore, researchers who study such "vulnerable" populations should obtain informed consent both from the individual (if possible) and from someone who can decide on the individual's behalf—for example, the parent or guardian of a child or the legal representative of a nursing home resident. Investigators also must take care not to pressure anyone to participate and must respect participants' right to refuse to participate, to drop out during the study, and to refuse to have their data used by the investigator.

Researchers face many challenges in deciding when children are old enough to understand what is involved in a study, in communicating the basics of the study as simply and clearly as possible, and in ensuring that children really understand what they have been told (for example, see Burke, Abramovitch, & Zlotkin, 2005; Kodish, 2005). They must take similar care in studying elderly adults, especially those with Alzheimer's disease or other cognitive impairments (Karlawish et al., 2009; Kim et al., 2004). Cultural differences must also be considered; for example, people in non-Western societies may have difficulty understanding the difference between research and medical or psychological treatment and may have different ideas than we do about who should give consent for participation or how best to protect research participants (Molyneux et al., 2005). For this reason, more researchers are now trying to involve community members in the planning and design of their studies (Karlawish et al., 2009; Martin & Lantos, 2005).

2. *Debriefing.* Researchers generally tell participants about the purposes of the study in advance, but in some cases doing so would ruin the study. If you told college students in advance that you were studying moral development and then gave them an opportunity to cheat on a test, do you think anyone would cheat? Instead, you might set up a situation in which students believe they can cheat without being detected and then debrief them afterward, explaining the true purpose of the study. You would also have an obligation to make sure that participants do not leave feeling upset about cheating.

3. *Protection from harm.* Researchers are bound not to harm research participants either physically or psychologically. Infants may cry if they are left in a room with a stranger. Adolescents may be embarrassed if they are asked about their sex lives. Adults who are depressed may experience negative side effects when given experimental antidepressants. Investigators must try to anticipate and prepare to deal with such consequences.

If physical or psychological harm to the participants seems likely, the researcher should consider another way of answering the research question. Federal regulations provide special protection to children; if a research project does not benefit child participants directly, they should be exposed to only minimal levels of risk—not more than the risks of daily life or of undergoing routine physical and psychological tests and examinations (Kodish, 2005). Moreover, if participants of any age become upset or are harmed, the researcher must take steps to undo the damage.

4. *Confidentiality.* Researchers also have an ethical responsibility to keep confidential the information they collect. It would be unacceptable, for example, to tell a child's teacher that the child performed poorly on an intelligence test or to tell an adult's employer that a drinking problem was revealed in an interview. The confidentiality of medical records concerning a person's physical and mental health is now particularly well protected by the Health Insurance Portability and Accountability Act of 1996, or HIPAA (Gostin, 2001). Only if participants give explicit permission to have information about them shared with someone else, or in rare cases if the law requires disclosure of information (such as when a researcher learns that a child is being abused), can that information be passed on.

Clearly, developmental researchers have some serious issues to weigh if they want their research to be not only well designed but also culturally sensitive and ethically responsible. They must make many choices in designing their studies; as a result, all studies have limitations of one sort or another and we are left to piece together the best picture of human development we can from the available (flawed) evidence. Understanding life-span human development would be downright impossible if researchers merely conducted study after study without guiding ideas, however. Theories of human development provide those guiding ideas and are the subject of Chapter 2.

Checking Mastery

1. If researchers do not try to keep ethnocentrism out of their research, what can happen?

2. A researcher deceives research participants into thinking they are in a study of learning when the real purpose is to determine whether they are willing to inflict harm on people who make learning errors if told to do so by an authority figure. What ethical responsibilities does this researcher have?

Making Connections

1. Now that you have your PhD in life-span developmental psychology, you want to interview elderly widows in Japan and in the United States about their emotional reactions to widowhood shortly after the deaths of their husbands. What ethical issues should you consider, and what steps should you take to make your study as ethical as possible?

2. What might you do to make this research as culturally sensitive as possible?

Chapter Summary

1.1. How Should We Think about Development?

- Development is systematic changes and continuities over the life span, involving gains, losses, and neutral changes in physical, cognitive, and psychosocial functioning; it is more than growth in childhood and biological aging in adulthood.

- Development takes place in an historical and cultural context and is influenced by age grades, age norms, and social clocks.

- Concepts of the life span and its distinctive periods have changed over history and differ from culture to culture. Starting in the 17th century, children came to be seen as innocents; in the late 19th century, adolescence emerged as a distinct phase; and only in the 20th century did our society recognize emerging adulthood, a middle-aged "empty nest" period, and an old age characterized by retirement.

- Understanding the nature–nurture issue means understanding the interaction of biology and maturation with environment and learning. The complexities of transactions between people and their environment are captured in Bronfenbrenner's bioecological model, in which the individual, with his or her biological and psychological characteristics, interacts with environmental systems called the microsystem, mesosystem, exosystem, and macrosystem over time (chronosystem).

1.2. What Is the Science of Life-Span Development?

- The study of life-span development, guided by the goals of description, explanation, and optimization, began with the baby biographies written by Charles Darwin and others.

- Through his use of questionnaires and attention to all phases of the life span, including the storm and stress of adolescence, American psychologist G. Stanley Hall came to be regarded as the founder of developmental psychology.

- By adopting the modern life-span perspective on human development set forth by Baltes, we assume that development (1) occurs throughout the life span, (2) can take many different directions, (3) involves gains and interlinked losses at every age, (4) is characterized by plasticity, (5) is affected by its historical and cultural context, (6) is influenced by multiple interacting causal factors, and (7) can best be understood if scholars from multiple disciplines join forces to understand it.

1.3. How Is Development Studied?

- The scientific method involves formulating theories and testing hypotheses derived from them by conducting research with a sample (ideally a random sample) from a larger population; good theories should be internally consistent, falsifiable, and, ultimately, supported by the data.

- Common data collection methods include verbal reports, behavioral observations, and physiological measures.

- The goal of explaining development is best achieved through experiments involving random assignments to conditions, manipulation of the independent variable, and experimental control. Case studies have limited generalizability, and in correlational studies, it is difficult to determine the direction of influence and to rule out the effects of third variables.

- Developmental research designs seek to describe age effects on development. Cross-sectional studies compare different age groups but confound age effects and cohort effects. Longitudinal studies study age change but confound age effects and time-of-measurement effects. Sequential studies combine the cross-sectional and longitudinal approaches.

1.4. What Special Challenges Do Developmental Scientists Face?

- To understand human development in its ecological context, researchers must study humans in a variety of ecological contexts, develop culturally sensitive methods and measures, and keep their own cultural values and ethnocentrism from biasing their conclusions.

- Researchers must adhere to standards of ethical research practice, with attention to ensuring informed consent, debriefing individuals from whom information has been withheld, protecting research participants from harm, and maintaining confidentiality of data.

Checking Mastery Answers

For answers to Checking Mastery questions, visit
www.cengagebrain.com

Key Terms

development **14**
growth **15**
biological aging **15**
aging **15**
age grade **16**
rite of passage **16**
age norms **17**
social clock **17**
ethnicity **17**
socioeconomic status (SES) **17**
adolescence **18**
emerging adulthood **18**
life expectancy **19**
nature–nurture issue **19**
maturation **19**
genes **19**
environment **19**
learning **19**
bioecological model **21**
microsystem **21**
mesosystem **21**
exosystem **21**
macrosystem **22**
culture **22**
chronosystem **22**
evidence-based practice **23**
baby biographies **23**
storm and stress **24**
gerontology **24**
life-span perspective **24**
plasticity **24**
neuroplasticity **24**
scientific method **26**
theory **26**
hypothesis **26**
sample **26**
population **26**
random sample **27**
naturalistic observation **27**
structured observation **28**
functional magnetic resonance imaging (fMRI) **28**
case study **29**
experiment **29**
independent variable **30**
dependent variable **30**
random assignment **30**
experimental control **30**
quasi experiment **31**
correlational method **31**
correlation coefficient **31**
meta-analysis **32**
cross-sectional design **33**
cohort **33**
age effects **33**
cohort effects **33**
baby boom generation **34**
longitudinal design **34**
time-of-measurement effects **35**
sequential design **35**
ethnocentrism **38**
research ethics **38**

Media Resources

Psychology CourseMate

Access an integrated eBook and chapter-specific learning tools including flashcards, quizzes, videos, and more. Go to **www.cengagebrain.com**

American Psychological Association Division 7 (Developmental Psychology)

Division 7 of APA is the official development subgroup. On their website you'll find their mission and history, Division 7 specific resources, and links to journals and other professional organizations. To access, see "web links" in Psychology CourseMate at www.cengagebrain.com

American Psychological Association Ethical Standards

The APA maintains an excellent website describing the ethical principles and code of conduct for psychologists. This code addresses both research and professional standards of behavior. To access, see "web links" in Psychology CourseMate at www.cengagebrain.com

Understanding the DATA: Exercises on the Web

www.cengagebrain.com
For additional insight on the data presented in this chapter, try out the exercises for these figures in Psychology CourseMate at **www.cengagebrain.com**:

Figure 1.1 Aggression Among Children in Four Cultures

CengageNOW

www.cengagebrain.com
Go to www.cengagebrain.com to link to CengageNOW, your online study tool. First take the Pre-Test for this chapter to get your Personalized Study Plan, which will identify topics you need to review and direct you to online resources. Then take the Post-Test to determine what concepts you have mastered and what you still need work on.

Ways to Think about Human Development

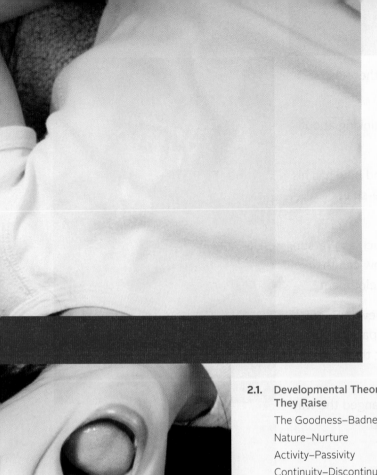

Terrell, age 6, just started first grade last week, all decked out in his new shirt and pants. Now he is begging his mother each morning to let him stay home. He cries and says that he has a terrible stomachache, and a head-ache and a sore foot besides, and is going to throw up any second so please, please, can he stay home. Because his symptoms clear up quickly if he is allowed to stay home, Terrell's problem does not appear to be a physical illness. But what *is* wrong?

© Plush Studios/Bill Reitzel/Blend Images/Corbis

Ask Yourself This

1. What are the main issues addressed by developmental theories (and by our own "theories" of development)?

2. What did Freud's psychoanalytic theory contribute to thinking about development?

3. How did neo-Freudian Erik Erikson differ from Freud, and how has his psychosocial theory shaped thinking about stages of life-span development?

4. What was different about the ways learning theorists such as Watson, Skinner, and Bandura conceived of development, and how can their learning principles help us understand behavior and development?

5. Why is Jean Piaget such a major figure in the study of development, and what does his cognitive developmental theory, compared with other perspectives on cognitive development, say about the development of thinking?

6. How have systems theorists such as Gilbert Gottlieb changed the way developmentalists think about the roles of biological and environmental forces in development?

7. All things considered, what stands on key development issues do these theories take, and how have they informed today's thinking about human development (as well as your own thinking about it)?

© AP Photo/*The Ames Tribune*/Andrew Rullestad

Clara wipes away a tear as she leaves her mother to start the first day of first grade. School refusal (sometimes called school phobia) is quite common among children starting school. Why might they be reluctant to go?

School refusal behavior is a reluctance or refusal to go to school or to remain there, sometimes called school phobia in the past because it often involves intense anxiety (C. A. Kearney, 2008). Did you ever seriously not want to go to school at some point in your educational career? School refusal affects as many as 5% of school-age children at any given time, many more at some point in their development; it is most common among 5- to 7-year-olds like Terrell who are venturing off to school for the first time (Fremont, 2003; Heyne, King, & Tonge, 2004). School refusal can have a number of different causes, involve considerable emotional distress for the child, and can have negative consequences such as academic difficulty, dropping out, and even adjustment problems in adulthood (C. A. Kearney, 2008).

How might we explain a 6-year-old's refusal to go to school from a developmental perspective? What is your explanation? What explanations might the leading theories of human development offer? In this chapter we will illustrate that different theories of human development provide different lenses through which to view developmental phenomena such as school refusal.

2.1 Developmental Theories and the Issues They Raise

As noted in Chapter 1, a theory is a set of ideas proposed to describe and explain certain phenomena—in this book, the phenomena of human development. In science, it is not enough simply to catalog facts without organizing this information around some set of concepts and propositions. Researchers would soon be overwhelmed by trivia and would lack "the big picture." A theory of human development provides needed organization, offering a lens through which researchers can interpret and explain any number of specific facts or observations. A theory also guides the collection of new facts or observations, making clear (1) what is most important to study, (2) what can be hypothesized or predicted about it, and (3) how it should be studied. Because different theorists often have different views on these critical matters, what is learned in any science greatly depends on which theoretical perspectives become dominant, which largely depends on how well they account for the facts.

Where Do You Stand on Major Developmental Issues?

Choose one option for each statement, and write down the corresponding letter or fill it in at the end of the box. See Table 2.4 to compare your results with how the theorists described in this chapter view development.

__1. Biological influences (heredity and maturational forces) and environmental influences (culture, parenting styles, and learning experiences) are thought to contribute to development. Overall,
a. biological factors contribute far more than environmental factors.
b. biological factors contribute somewhat more than environmental factors.
c. biological and environmental factors are equally important.
d. environmental factors contribute somewhat more than biological factors.
e. environmental factors contribute far more than biological factors.

__2. Children are innately
a. mostly bad; they are born with basically negative, selfish impulses.
b. neither good nor bad; they are tabulae rasae (blank slates).
c. both good and bad; they are born with predispositions that are both positive and negative.
d. mostly good; they are born with many positive tendencies.

__3. People are basically
a. active beings who are the prime determiners of their own abilities and traits.
b. passive beings whose characteristics are molded either by social influences (parents, other significant people, and outside events) or by biological changes beyond their control.

__4. Development proceeds
a. through stages so that the individual changes rather abruptly into a different kind of person than she was in an earlier stage.
b. in a variety of ways—some stagelike and some gradual or continuous.
c. continuously—in small increments without abrupt changes or distinct stages.

__5. When you compare the development of different individuals, you see
a. many similarities; children and adults develop along universal paths and experience similar changes at similar ages.
b. many differences; different people often undergo different sequences of change and have widely different timetables of development.

Statement

| 1 | 2 | 3 | 4 | 5 |

Your pattern of choices:

__ __ __ __ __

In this chapter, we examine four major theoretical viewpoints, each with important messages about the nature of human development:

1. The *psychoanalytic* viewpoint developed by Sigmund Freud and revised by Erik Erikson and other neo-Freudians
2. The *learning* perspective developed by such pioneers as Ivan Pavlov, John Watson, B. F. Skinner, and Albert Bandura
3. The *cognitive developmental* viewpoint associated with Jean Piaget
4. The *systems theory* approach, exemplified by Urie Bronfenbrenner (see Chapter 1), Gilbert Gottlieb (this chapter), and Esther Thelen (Chapter 5)

We will be asking as we go whether these theoretical perspectives meet the criteria of good theories introduced in Chapter 1—that is, whether they are internally consistent (coherent), falsifiable (testable), and supported by data (confirmed by research). To further aid in comparing the theories, we outline five key developmental issues on which

theorists—and people in general—often disagree (Miller, 2010; Parke et al., 1994): the goodness–badness of human nature, nature–nurture, activity–passivity, continuity–discontinuity, and universality–context specificity. All of us hold some basic beliefs about human development—for example, about the importance of genes versus good parenting in healthy development. Reading this chapter should make you more aware of your own assumptions about human development and how they compare with those of the major theorists. We therefore invite you to clarify your stands on these issues by completing the questionnaire in Engagement Box 2.1. Table 2.4 at the end of the chapter indicates how the major developmental theorists might answer the questions, so you can compare your assumptions with theirs.

In Exploration boxes throughout this chapter, we imagine some major points each theorist might make about the causes of school refusal. We suggest that you predict what each theorist would say before you read each of these boxes to see whether you can successfully apply each theory to this developmental problem. At the end of the chapter, we'll invite you to apply the different theories to understanding and preventing unwanted teenage pregnancy. It is our hope that when you master the major theories of human development, you will be able to draw on their concepts and propositions to make better sense of—and perhaps to guide in more positive directions—your own and other people's development.

The Goodness–Badness of Human Nature

Are people inherently good, inherently bad, or neither? Well before modern theories of human development were proposed, philosophers of the 17th and 18th centuries were taking stands on the nature of human beings and human development. Thomas Hobbes (1588–1679), for one, portrayed children as inherently selfish and bad and believed that it was society's responsibility to teach them to behave in civilized ways. By contrast, Jean-Jacques Rousseau (1712–1778) argued that children were innately good, that they were born with an intuitive understanding of right and wrong, and that they would develop in positive directions as long as society did not interfere with their natural tendencies (as he felt it often did). In the middle was English philosopher John Locke (1632–1704), who maintained that infants are **tabulae rasae**, or "blank slates," waiting to be written on by their experiences. That is, children were neither innately good nor innately bad but could develop in any direction depending on their experiences.

These different visions of human nature are all represented in one or more theories of development, and they have radically different implications for how to raise children. In teaching children to share, for example, should parents assume that their innate selfish tendencies must be battled at every step, that they are predisposed by nature to be helpful and caring, or that they have the potential to become either selfish beasts or selfless wonders depending on how they are brought up? Evidence that humans have biologically based tendencies, both good and bad, has challenged the Lockean (and quite popular) belief that humans are blank slates and can become anything they are raised to become (Pinker, 2002), but many questions remain about the fundamental nature of human beings and the extent to which human nature can be modified.

Nature–Nurture

Is development primarily the product of nature (biological forces) or nurture (environmental forces)? As you saw in Chapter 1, the nature–nurture issue is the most important and most complex issue in the study of human development. Strong believers in nature (like Rousseau, champion of the innate goodness of children) stress the importance of individual genetic makeup, universal maturational processes guided by genes, biologically based predispositions built into genes over the course of evolution, and other biological influences. They are likely to claim that all normal children achieve the same developmental milestones at similar times because of matura-

tional forces, that major changes in functioning in late adulthood are biologically based, and that differences among children or adults are largely because of differences in genetic makeup and physiology.

By contrast, strong believers in nurture (like Locke, who claimed experience shapes development) would emphasize environment—the range of influences outside the person. Nurture includes influences of the physical environment (crowding, pollution, and the like) as well as the social environment (for example, learning experiences, child-rearing methods, peers, societal trends, and the cultural context in which the person develops). A strong believer in nurture would argue that human development can take many paths depending on the individual's experiences over a lifetime.

Activity–Passivity

The **activity–passivity issue** focuses on the extent to which human beings are active in creating and influencing their own environments and, in the process, in producing their own development, or are passively shaped by forces beyond their control. Some theorists (following in the tradition of Rousseau) believe that humans are curious, active creatures who orchestrate their own development by exploring the world around them and shaping their environments. The girl who asks for dolls at the toy store and the boy who clamors instead for toy machine guns are actively contributing to their own gender-role development. Both the budding scientist who experiments with chemicals in the basement and the sociable adolescent who spends hours text messaging are seeking out and creating a "niche" that suits their emerging traits and abilities—and that further develops those traits in the process (Harris, 2006).

Other theorists (in the tradition of Locke) view humans as passive beings shaped largely by forces beyond their control—usually environmental influences but possibly strong biological forces. From this vantage point, children's academic failings might be blamed on the failure of their parents and teachers to provide them with the right learning experiences, and the problems of socially isolated older adults might be attributed to societal neglect of the elderly rather than to deficiencies within the individual.

Continuity–Discontinuity

Do you believe that humans change gradually, in ways that leave them not so different from the way they were before, or do you believe humans change abruptly and dramatically? One aspect of the **continuity–discontinuity issue** focuses on whether the changes people undergo over the life span are gradual or abrupt. Continuity theorists view human development as a process that occurs in small steps, without sudden changes, as when grade school children gradually gain weight from year to year. In contrast, discontinuity theorists tend to picture the course of development as more like a series of stair steps, each of which elevates the individual to a new (and often more advanced) level of functioning. When an adolescent boy rapidly shoots up 6 inches in

Continuity in development | Discontinuity in development

Little frog Bigger frog | Tadpole Frog
(A) | **(B)**

■**FIGURE 2.1** Is development continuous (A) or discontinuous (B)? That is, do people change quantitatively, becoming different in degree (as shown in Panel A with a size increase), or do they change qualitatively, becoming different in kind (as shown in Panel B, where a tadpole becomes a frog)?

height, gains a bass voice, and grows a beard, the change seems discontinuous.

A second aspect of the continuity–discontinuity issue focuses on whether changes are quantitative or qualitative in nature. Quantitative changes are changes in *degree* and indicate continuity: a person gains more wrinkles, grows taller, knows more vocabulary words, or interacts with friends less frequently. By contrast, qualitative changes are changes in *kind* and suggest discontinuity. They are changes that make the individual fundamentally different in some way (■**Figure 2.1**). The transformations of a caterpillar into a butterfly rather than just a bigger caterpillar, of a nonverbal infant into a speaking toddler, or of a prepubertal child into a sexually mature adolescent are examples of qualitative changes.

So continuity theorists typically hold that developmental changes are gradual and quantitative, whereas discontinuity theorists hold that they are more abrupt and qualitative. Discontinuity theorists often propose that people progress through **developmental stages**. A stage is a distinct phase of development characterized by a particular set of abilities, motives, emotions, or behaviors that form a coherent pattern. Development is said to involve fairly rapid transitions from one stage to another, each stage being qualitatively different from the stage before or the stage after. Thus, the preschool child may be said to have a fundamentally different approach to solving problems than the infant, adolescent, or adult.

Universality–Context Specificity

Finally, developmental theorists often disagree on the **universality–context-specificity issue**—or the extent to which developmental changes are common to all humans (universal) or different across cultures, subcultures, task contexts, and individuals (context specific). Stage theorists typically believe that the stages they propose are universal. For example, a stage theorist might claim that virtually all children enter a new stage in their intellectual development as they enter adolescence or that most adults, sometime around age 40, experience a midlife crisis in which they raise major questions about their lives. From this perspective, development proceeds in certain universal directions.

But other theorists believe that human development is far more varied. Paths of development followed in one culture may be quite different from paths followed in another culture (or subculture, neighborhood, or even performance context). For example, preschool children in the United States sometimes believe that dreams are real but give up this belief as they age. By contrast, children raised in the Atayal culture of Taiwan have been observed to become more and more convinced as they get older that dreams are real, most likely because that is what adults in their culture believe (Kohlberg, 1966b). Within a particular culture, developmental change may also differ from subcultural group to subcultural group, from family to family, and from individual to individual. There seems to be both universality and context specificity in human development. As American poet Mark Van Doren once said, "There are two statements about human beings that are true: that all human beings are alike, and that all are different" (cited in Norenzayan & Heine, 2005, p. 763).

Now that you are familiar with some major issues of human development that different theories resolve in different ways (●**Table 2.1**), we will begin our survey of the theories, starting with Freud's well-known psychoanalytic perspective.

To what extent is human development universal and to what extent is it culture specific? Only cross-cultural research can tell us.

● TABLE 2.1 ISSUES IN HUMAN DEVELOPMENT

Issue	Description
1. Goodness–Badness of Human Nature	Are humans innately good, innately bad, neither (tabulae rasae), or both?
2. Nature–Nurture	Is development primarily the product of genes, biology, and maturation—or of experience, learning, and social influences?
3. Activity–Passivity	Do humans actively shape their own environments and contribute to their own development—or are they passively shaped by forces beyond their control?
4. Continuity–Discontinuity	Do humans change gradually and in quantitative ways—or do they progress through qualitatively different stages and change dramatically into different beings?
5. Universality–Context Specificity	Is development similar from person to person and from culture to culture—or do pathways of development vary considerably depending on the social context?

Checking Mastery

1. If you believe that children are tabulae rasae, what stands do you take on the goodness or badness of human nature and the nature-nurture issues?

2. Stage theorists can disagree about a lot, but they are all likely to take certain stands on the issues of nature–nurture, continuity–discontinuity, and universality–context specificity. What stands?

Making Connections

1. Professor Whitehead has developed a theory of positive aging emphasizing that older adults all over the world are basically similar to younger adults in their psychological needs, that they have great potential to shape their own aging experience by selecting who they want to interact with and how, and that, unless they are thwarted by society, they will generally want to contribute positively to their communities rather than being dependent. What stands on the major issues in human development does Professor Whitehead seem to be taking? Explain why you think so.

2. What stands on the five major issues in human development do you feel your parents took in raising you? Why?

Sigmund Freud's psychoanalytic theory was one of the first, and one of the most influential, theories of how the personality develops from childhood to adulthood.

© Mary Evans Picture Library/Alamy

2.2 Freud: Psychoanalytic Theory

It is difficult to think of a theorist who has had a greater effect on Western thought than Sigmund Freud, the Viennese physician who lived from 1856 to 1939. This revolutionary thinker's **psychoanalytic theory**, which focused on the development and dynamics of the personality, challenged prevailing notions of human nature and human development by proposing that people are driven by motives and emotional conflicts of which they are largely unaware and that they are shaped by their earliest experiences in the family (Hall, 1954; Westen, Gabbard, & Ortigo, 2008). Freud's ideas continue to influence thinking about human development, even though they are far less influential today than they once were.

Instincts and Unconscious Motives

Central to Freudian psychoanalytic theory is the notion that humans have basic biological urges or drives that must be satisfied. Freud viewed the newborn as a "seething cauldron," an inherently selfish creature "driven" by **instincts**, or inborn biological forces that motivate behavior. These biological instincts are the source of the psychic (or mental) energy that fuels human behavior and that is channeled in new directions over the course of human development.

Freud strongly believed in **unconscious motivation**—the power of instincts and other inner forces to influence our behavior without our awareness. A preadolescent girl, for example, may not realize that she is acting in babyish ways in order to regain the security of her mother's love; a teenage boy may not realize that his devotion to body building is a way of channeling his sexual and aggressive urges. You immediately see that Freud's theory emphasizes the nature side of the nature–nurture issue: biological instincts—forces that often provide an unconscious motivation for actions—guide human development. The fact that he viewed these innate forces as selfish and aggressive suggests that he also held a negative view of human nature.

Id, Ego, and Superego

According to Freud (1933), each individual has a fixed amount of psychic energy that can be used to satisfy basic urges or instincts and to grow psychologically. As a child develops, this psychic energy is divided among three components of the personality: the id, the ego, and the superego. At birth, all psychic energy resides in the **id**—the impulsive, irrational, and selfish part of the personality whose mission is to satisfy the instincts. The id seeks immediate gratification, even when biological needs cannot be realistically or appropriately met. If you think about it, young infants do seem to be all id in some ways. When they are hungry or wet, they fuss and cry until their needs are met. They are not known for their patience.

The second component of the personality is the **ego**, the rational side of the individual that tries to find realistic ways of gratifying the instincts. According to Freud (1933), the ego begins to emerge during infancy when psychic energy is diverted from the id to energize cognitive processes such as perception, learning, and problem solving. The hungry toddler may be able to do more than merely cry when she is hungry; she may be able to draw on the resources of the ego to hunt down Dad, lead him to the kitchen, and say "cookie." However, toddlers' egos are still relatively immature; they want what they want *now*. As the ego matures further, children become more capable of postponing their pleasures until a more appropriate time and of devising logical and realistic strategies for meeting their needs.

The third part of the Freudian personality is the **superego**, the individual's internalized moral standards. The superego develops from the ego as 3- to 6-year-old children internalize (take on as their own) the moral standards and values of their parents. Once the superego emerges, children have a parental voice in their heads that keeps them from violating society's rules and makes them feel guilty or ashamed if they do. The superego insists that people find socially acceptable or ethical outlets for the id's undesirable impulses.

Conflict among the id, ego, and superego is inevitable, Freud said. In the mature, healthy personality, a dynamic balance operates: the id communicates its basic needs, the ego restrains the impulsive id long enough to find realistic ways to satisfy these needs, and the superego decides whether the ego's problem-solving strategies are morally acceptable. The ego has a tough job: it must strike a balance between the opposing demands of the id and the superego while accommodating the realities of the environment.

According to Freud (1940/1964), psychological problems often arise when the individual's supply of psychic energy is unevenly distributed among the id, the ego, and the superego. For example, a person diagnosed as an antisocial personality, or sociopath, who routinely lies and cheats to get his way, may have a weak superego, whereas a married woman who cannot undress in front of her husband may have an overly strong superego, perhaps because she was made to feel ashamed about any interest she took in her body as a young girl. Through analysis of the dynamics operating among the three parts of the personality, Freud and his followers attempted to describe and understand individual differences in personality and the origins of psychological disorders.

Psychosexual Development

Freud (1940/1964) maintained that as the child matures biologically, the psychic energy of the sex instinct, which he called **libido**, shifts from one part of the body to another, seeking to gratify different biological needs. In the process, as outlined in ● **Table 2.2**, the child moves through five **psychosexual stages**: oral, anal, phallic, latent, and genital.

Emphasizing the role of nature over that of nurture in development, Freud maintained that inborn biological instincts drive behavior and that biological maturation guides all children through the five psychosexual stages. Yet he also viewed nurture—especially early experiences within the family—as an important contributor to individual differences in adult personality. At each psychosexual stage, the id's impulses and social demands come into conflict. Harsh child-rearing methods—punishing babies for mouthing paychecks and other interesting objects around the house, or toddlers for their toileting accidents, or preschoolers for taking interest in their genitals—can heighten psychic conflicts and the child's anxiety.

The baby in the oral stage of psychosexual development focuses on the mouth as a source of sexual pleasure and can, according to Freud, experience anxiety and need to defend against it if denied oral gratification by not being fed on demand, being weaned too early, being chastised for mouthing objects, and so on. Through **fixation**, arrested development in which part of the libido remains tied to an earlier stage of development, an infant deprived of oral gratification might become "stuck" in the oral stage. He might become a chronic thumb sucker and then a chain smoker and depend too much on other people rather than moving on to the next psychosexual stages. Freud thought too much oral gratification could also pose a problem if it makes it difficult for the child to leave the oral stage. Either way, he believed that how the child copes with the challenges of a stage and what parents do to help or hurt can leave a lasting imprint on the personality.

Similarly, the toddler in the anal stage must cope with new demands from the parents when toilet training begins. Parents who are impatient and punitive as their children learn to delay the gratification of relieving themselves can create high levels of anxiety and a personality that resists demands from authority figures not only to defecate on schedule but to control other impulses (by holding back, as the so-called anal personality does, or by acting out inappropriately). The parent's goal should be to allow some (but not too much) gratification of impulses while

TABLE 2.2 THE STAGE THEORIES OF FREUD AND ERIKSON

Freud's Psychosexual Theory		Erikson's Psychosocial Theory	
Stage (Age Range)	Description	Stage (Age Range)	Description
Oral stage (birth to 1 year)	Libido is focused on the mouth as a source of pleasure. Obtaining oral gratification from a mother figure is critical to later development.	Trust vs. mistrust (birth to 1 year)	Infants must learn to trust their caregivers to meet their needs. Responsive parenting is critical.
Anal stage (1 to 3 years)	Libido is focused on the anus, and toilet training creates conflicts between the child's biological urges and the society's demands.	Autonomy vs. shame and doubt (1 to 3 years)	Children must learn to be autonomous—to assert their wills and do things for themselves—or they will doubt their abilities.
Phallic stage (3 to 6 years)	Libido centers on the genitals. Resolution of the Oedipus or the Electra complex results in identification with the same-sex parent and development of the superego.	Initiative vs. guilt (3 to 6 years)	Preschoolers develop initiative by devising and carrying out bold plans, but they must learn not to impinge on the rights of others.
Latent period (6 to 12 years)	Libido is quiet; psychic energy is invested in schoolwork and play with same-sex friends.	Industry vs. inferiority (6 to 12 years)	Children must master important social and academic skills and keep up with their peers; otherwise, they will feel inferior.
Genital stage (12 years and older)	Puberty reawakens the sexual instincts as youths seek to establish mature sexual relationships and pursue the biological goal of reproduction.	Identity vs. role confusion (12 to 20 years)	Adolescents ask who they are and must establish social and vocational identities; otherwise, they will remain confused about the roles they should play as adults.
		Intimacy vs. isolation (20 to 40 years)	Young adults seek to form a shared identity with another person, but may fear intimacy and experience loneliness and isolation.
		Generativity vs. stagnation (40 to 65 years)	Middle-aged adults must feel that they are producing something that will outlive them, either as parents or as workers; otherwise, they will become stagnant and self-centered.
		Integrity vs. despair (65 years and older)	Older adults must come to view their lives as meaningful to face death without worries and regrets.

helping the child achieve reasonable (but not too much) control over these impulses.

The phallic stage from age 3 to age 6 is an especially treacherous time, according to Freud. Youngsters develop an incestuous desire for the parent of the other sex and must defend against it. A boy experiencing an **Oedipus complex** loves his mother, fears that his father will retaliate by castrating him, and resolves this conflict through **identification** with his father. Identification involves taking on or internalizing the attitudes and behaviors of another person; the Oedipal boy defends against his forbidden

desire for his mother and hostility toward his father by possessing his mother vicariously through his now-admired and less fear-provoking father. Meanwhile, a girl experiencing an **Electra complex** is said to desire her father (and envy the fact that he has a penis, whereas she does not), view her mother as a rival, and ultimately resolve her conflict by identifying with her mother. When boys and girls resolve their emotional conflicts by identifying with the same-sex parent, they incorporate that parent's values into their superego, so the phallic period is critical in moral development.

Freud: Notes on School Refusal

Children who refuse to attend school are sometimes suffering from psychological problems such as anxiety or depression (Elliott, 1999; C. A. Kearney, 2008). More specifically, Terrell's problem, of which he is probably unaware, may not be fear

of school as much as separation anxiety—fear of leaving his mother, originating in an unresolved Oedipal conflict involving his incestuous desire for his mother in the phallic stage of psychosexual development.

We should analyze the mother–son relationship from birth to find the source of this boy's problems. Lack of gratification, or too much gratification, during the oral or anal stages may have contributed to his current difficulty resolving his Oedipal conflict.

During the latency period, sexual urges are tame and 6- to 12-year-olds invest psychic energy in schoolwork and play, but adolescents experience new psychic conflicts as they reach puberty and enter the final stage of psychosexual development, the genital stage. Adolescents may have difficulty accepting their new sexuality, may reexperience conflicting feelings toward their parents that they felt during the phallic stage, and may distance themselves from their parents to defend themselves against these anxiety-producing feelings. During adulthood, people may develop a greater capacity to love and typically satisfy the mature sex instinct by having children. However, Freud believed that psychosexual development stops with adolescence and that the individual remains in the genital stage throughout adulthood.

Defense Mechanisms

To defend itself against anxiety, the ego adopts unconscious coping devices called **defense mechanisms** (Freud, 1940/1964). Some examples (besides identification, which we already discussed) include:

- **Repression**, or removing unacceptable thoughts or traumatic memories from consciousness, as when a young woman who was raped has no memory at all of having been raped (or less drastically, engages in denial, knowing deep down that she was raped but not accepting the reality of it).
- **Regression**, or retreating to an earlier, less traumatic stage of development, as when a preschool girl, threatened by a new baby brother, reverts to infantile behavior and coos like a baby.
- **Projection**, or seeing in others the motives we fear we possess, as when a husband charges his wife with being the one who is jealous and insecure, not he.
- **Reaction formation**, or expressing motives that are just the opposite of one's real motives, as when a woman who unconsciously wants to gratify her sexual urges instead takes up a crusade against pornography.

Defense mechanisms illustrate the importance of unconscious motivations in Freudian theory; we learn these and other defense mechanisms to cope with inner conflicts of which we are largely unaware, deceiving ourselves in order to save ourselves. Defense mechanisms can be healthy in that they allow us to function despite anxiety, but they can also spell trouble for some

people if they involve too much distortion of reality. Moreover, they sap psychic energy and usually do not resolve underlying psychic conflicts, which is why Freud believed that the goal of psychotherapy should be to bring unconscious fantasies, desires, and beliefs to the level of consciousness.

In Exploration Box 2.1, we imagine the notes that Freud might have scribbled down to explain Terrell's school refusal, as described at the start of the chapter. What might you say if you were Freud?

Strengths and Weaknesses

Many developmentalists fault Freud for proposing a theory that is ambiguous, internally inconsistent, difficult to pin down and test, and therefore not easily falsifiable (Fonagy & Target, 2000). Testing hypotheses that require studying unconscious motivations and the workings of the unseen id, ego, and superego has been challenging. Freud himself offered little hard evidence to support his theory. Moreover, when the theory has been tested, many of its specific ideas have not been supported (Crews, 1996; Fisher & Greenberg, 1977). One critic went so far as to call it "a theory in search of some facts" (Macmillan, 1991, p. 548).

To illustrate, Freud initially concluded that many of his patients had been sexually or physically abused during childhood but had repressed memories of their traumatic experiences. Because the idea of rampant incest and sexual abuse was difficult to accept, he later said that children in the phallic stage wished for and fantasized about, but did not actually experience, seduction by their parents (Masson, 1984). There is still controversy about whether Freud meant to deny the reality of incest and other forms of child sexual abuse or to call attention to the importance of fantasy in his later writings (Ahbe-Rappe, 2006). Moreover, it is still debated whether Freud's patients were really sexually abused or whether his therapeutic techniques planted thoughts in their minds and created false memories of abuse. Overall, Freud's claims about the role of sexual fantasy in child development have not received much support (Crews, 1996), although psychologists certainly appreciate that sexual abuse in childhood can contribute to later psychological problems (see Chapter 12).

Although many of Freud's specific ideas have been difficult to test or have not been supported by research when they have been tested, many of his general insights have stood up well and have profoundly influenced theories of human development, personality, and psychotherapy (Fonagy & Target, 2000; Westen et al., 2008). First, Freud called attention to *unconscious processes* underlying human behavior; his fundamental insights in this area are supported by modern psychological and neuropsychological research (Bargh & Morsella, 2008; Westen et al., 2008), and they have profoundly influenced psychotherapy by making the goal to bring unconscious motivations to the surface where they can be confronted and changed. Second, he was one of the first to highlight the importance for later development of *early experiences* in the family. Finally, he emphasized the importance of *emotions* and emotional conflicts in development and the workings of personality. Developmentalists have often slighted emotional development, focusing instead on observable behavior or on rational thought processes.

Checking Mastery

1. Jaime believes that people have both a moral side and a selfish side that work against each other. According to Freud's psychoanalytic theory, what are these "sides" called and when do they arise in development?

2. According to Freud, how do girls relate to their mothers and fathers during the phallic stage of development?

3. What is one thing Freud got right and one thing Freud got wrong?

Making Connections

1. In 2006, a congressman from Florida resigned from office in disgrace after it was revealed that he wrote sexually suggestive e-mails to adolescent males serving as congressional pages. He also chaired the House Caucus on Missing and Exploited children, speaking often on the need to protect children from sexual predators. What might Freud hypothesize about the congressman's personality?

2.3 Erikson: Neo-Freudian Psychoanalytic Theory

Another sign of Freud's immense influence is that he inspired so many disciples and descendants to make their own contributions to the understanding of human development (Bergen, 2008). Among these well-known neo-Freudians were Alfred Adler, who suggested that siblings (and rivalries among siblings) are significant in development; Carl Jung, a pioneer in the study of adult development who claimed that adults experience a midlife crisis and then become freer to express both the "masculine" and the "feminine" sides of their personalities; Karen Horney, who challenged Freud's ideas about sex differences; Harry Stack Sullivan, who argued that close friendships in childhood set the stage for intimate relationships later in life; and Freud's daughter Anna, who developed techniques of psychoanalysis appropriate for children.

Erik Erikson built on Freudian theory and proposed that people experience eight psychosexual crises over their life span.

© Bettmann/Corbis

But the neo-Freudian who most influenced thinking about life-span development was Erik Erikson (1902–1994), whom we will revisit in more detail in Chapter 11. Erikson studied with Anna Freud and emigrated from Germany to the United States when Hitler rose to power (Friedman, 1999). Like Sigmund Freud, Erikson (1963, 1968, 1982) concerned himself with the inner dynamics of personality and proposed that the personality evolves through systematic stages. However, compared with Freud, Erikson:

• Placed less emphasis on sexual urges as the drivers of development and more emphasis on social influences such as peers, teachers, schools, and the broader culture.
• Placed less emphasis on the unconscious, irrational, and selfish id and more on the rational ego and its adaptive powers.
• Held a more positive view of human nature, seeing people as active in their development, largely rational, and able to overcome the effects of harmful early experiences.
• Put more emphasis on development after adolescence.

As one scholar summed it up, Erikson shifted Freudian thought "upward in consciousness, outward to the social world, and forward throughout the complete life span" (Hoare, 2005, p. 19).

Psychosocial Stages

Erikson believed that humans everywhere experience eight major **psychosocial stages**, or conflicts, during their lives. (Erikson's psychosocial stages are matched up with Freud's in Table 2.2.) Whether the conflict of a particular stage is successfully resolved or not, the individual is pushed by both biological maturation and social demands into the next stage. However, the unsuccessful resolution of a conflict will influence how subsequent stages play out.

For example, the first conflict, *trust versus mistrust*, revolves around whether or not infants become able to rely on other people to be responsive to their needs. To develop a sense of trust, infants must be able to count on their primary caregivers to feed them, relieve their discomfort, come when beckoned, and

Erikson: Notes on School Refusal

Like a good Freudian, I would check for unresolved conflicts from earlier stages of development. For example, might Terrell have developed a sense of shame and doubt owing to negative reactions from his parents when he tried to assert himself as a toddler?

I would also focus on his current psychosocial stage, industry versus inferiority. Might Terrell have performed poorly on school tasks during the first week of school and concluded that he is inferior to the other children?

Like Freud, I would also focus on the parent–child relationship, but I would recognize that other relationships count too. Something going on in Terrell's relationships with his peers or teacher, or even something happening in the wider culture, may be upsetting him.

return their smiles and babbles. Whereas Freud focused on the significance of the caregiver's feeding practices, Erikson believed that the caregiver's general responsiveness was critical to later development. If caregivers neglect, reject, or respond inconsistently to infants, infants will mistrust others. A healthy balance between the terms of the conflict must be struck for development to proceed optimally. Trust should outweigh mistrust, but an element of skepticism is also needed: an overindulged infant may become too trusting (a gullible "sucker").

So it goes for the remaining stages of childhood. If all goes well as children confront and resolve each conflict, they will gain a sense of self and develop *autonomy* (rather than shame and doubt about their ability to act independently), develop the *initiative* (as opposed to guilt) that allows them to plan and tackle big projects, and acquire the sense of *industry* (rather than inferiority) that will enable them to master important academic and social skills in school. This growth will position adolescents to successfully resolve the conflict for which Erikson (1968) is best known, *identity versus role confusion*. Erikson characterized adolescence as a time of "identity crisis" in which youth attempt to define who they are (in terms of career, religion, sexual identity, and so on), where they are heading, and how they fit into society. As part of their search, they often change their minds and experiment with new looks, new majors, new relationships, and new group memberships. Erikson should know: He was the tall, blond stepson of a Jewish doctor who wandered all over Europe after high school, trying out a career as an artist and several other possibilities before he ended up studying child psychoanalysis under Anna Freud and finally found his calling in his mid-20s (Friedman, 1999).

Whereas Freud's stages stopped with adolescence, Erikson believed that psychosocial growth continues during the adult years. Successfully resolving the adolescent conflict of identity versus role confusion paves the way for resolving the early adulthood conflict of *intimacy versus isolation* and for becoming ready to participate in a committed, long-term relationship. Successful resolution of the middle-age conflict of *generativity versus stagnation* involves adults gaining a sense that they have produced something that will outlive them, whether by successfully raising children or by contributing something meaningful to the world through work or volunteer activities. Finally, elderly adults who resolve the psychosocial conflict of *integrity versus despair* find a sense of meaning in their lives that will help them face death.

Erikson clearly did not agree with Freud that the personality is essentially "set in stone" during the first 5 years of life. Yet he, like Freud and other psychoanalytic theorists, believed that people progress through systematic stages of development, undergoing similar personality changes at similar ages. Individual differences in personality presumably reflect the different experiences individuals have, both in the family and beyond, as they struggle to cope with the challenges of each life stage. Both biological maturation and demands of the social and cultural environment influence the individual's progress through Erikson's sequence of psychosocial stages. As an illustration, Exploration Box 2.2 shows what Erikson might have said about Terrell's school refusal.

Strengths and Weaknesses

Many people find Erikson's emphasis on our rational, adaptive nature and on an interaction of biological and social influences easier to accept than Freud's emphasis on unconscious, irrational motivations based in biological needs. Erikson also seems to have captured some central developmental issues in his eight stages. He has had an especially great impact on ideas about and research on adolescent identity formation and issues faced during adulthood (see Berzoff, 2008, and Chapter 11). Still, Erikson's theory has many of the same shortcomings as Freud's. It is sometimes vague and difficult to test. And although it provides a useful *description* of human personality development, it does not provide an adequate *explanation* of how this development comes about. Important psychoanalytic theorists such as Erikson continue to shape understanding of human development (Austrian, 2008), but many developmentalists have rejected the psychoanalytic perspective in favor of theories that are more precise and testable.

Checking Mastery

1. What are four major ways in which Erikson differed from Freud?
2. Wanda, at age 40, is depressed. She seems to doubt her ability to assert herself and take charge of situations and she thinks other people will let her down. What Eriksonian stages might have been problematic for her in childhood, and how might her parents have contributed to her current problems?

Making Connections

1. How might Erikson analyze the wayward congressman described in the Section 2.2 Making Connections, and how would his analysis differ from Freud's?

2. Thinking about yourself, your parents, and your grandparents, can you see any evidence that Erikson's conflicts of adolescence and adulthood are relevant in your family?

2.4 Learning Theories

Give me a dozen healthy infants, well formed, and my own specified world to bring them up in, and I'll guarantee to take any one at random and train him to become any type of specialist I might select—doctor, lawyer, artist, merchant, chief, and yes, even beggar-man and thief, regardless of his talents, penchants, tendencies, abilities, vocations, and race of his ancestors. (Watson, 1925, p. 82)

This bold statement—that nurture is everything and that nature, or genetic endowment, counts for nothing—was made by John B. Watson, a strong believer in the importance of learning in human development and a pioneer of learning theory perspectives on human development. Early learning theorists such as Watson and B. F. Skinner emphasized that human behavior changes in direct response to environmental stimuli; later learning theorists such as Albert Bandura grant humans a more active and cognitive role in their own development but still believe that their development can take different directions depending on their experiences. All learning theorists have provided us with some very important and practical tools for understanding how human behavior changes through learning.

Watson: Classical Conditioning

Watson's (1913) **behaviorism** rested on his belief that conclusions about human development and functioning should be based on observations of overt behavior rather than on speculations about unobservable cognitive and emotional processes. Watson rejected psychoanalytic theory and devoted a good deal of effort to trying to explain Freud's fascinating discoveries about humans in terms of basic learning principles (Rilling, 2000). He maintained that learned associations between external stimuli and observable responses are the building blocks of both normal and abnormal human development. Like John Locke, Watson believed that children have no inborn tendencies and that how they turn out depends entirely on the environment in which they grow up and the ways in which their parents and other significant people in their lives treat them.

To make his point, Watson and colleague Rosalie Raynor (1920) set out to demonstrate that fears can be learned—that they are not necessarily inborn, as was commonly thought. They used the principles of **classical conditioning**, a simple form of learning in which a stimulus that initially had no effect on the individual comes to elicit a response through its association with a stimulus that already elicits the response. The Russian physiologist Ivan Pavlov first discovered classical conditioning quite accidentally while studying the digestive systems of dogs. In a famous experiment, Pavlov demonstrated how dogs, who have an innate (unlearned) tendency to salivate at the sight of food, could learn to salivate at the sound of a bell if, during a training period, the bell was regularly sounded just as a dog was given meat powder. Food is an **unconditioned stimulus (UCS)**—that is, an unlearned stimulus—for salivating. Salivating, in turn, is an automatic, unlearned, or **unconditioned response (UCR)** to the presentation of food. No one has to teach dogs to salivate when food is presented to them. By repeatedly pairing the bell with the arrival of food, Pavlov made the bell a **conditioned stimulus (CS)**—that is, a learned stimulus—for what was now a **conditioned response (CR)** of salivation. When Pavlov then presented the bell without the food, the dogs still salivated.

Using these classical conditioning principles, Watson and Raynor presented a gentle white rat to a now-famous infant named Albert, who showed no fear of it. However, every time the rat was presented, Watson would slip behind Albert and bang a steel rod with a hammer. The loud noise served as an unconditioned stimulus (UCS) for fear, an unconditioned response (UCR) to loud noises (since babies are naturally upset by them). During conditioning, the stimuli of the white rat and the loud noise were presented together several times. Afterward, Watson presented the white rat to Albert without banging the steel rod. Albert now whimpered and cried in response to the white rat alone. His behavior had changed as a result of his experience: An initially neutral stimulus, the white rat, had become a conditioned stimulus (CS) for fear, now a conditioned response (CR), as shown in ■ **Figure 2.2**. This learned or conditioned response generalized to other furry items such as a rabbit and a Santa Claus mask. By today's standards, Watson's experiment would be viewed as unethical, but he had made his point: *emotional responses can be learned*. Fortunately, fears learned through classical conditioning can be unlearned if the feared stimulus is paired with a UCS for happy emotions (Jones, 1924).

Classical conditioning is undoubtedly involved when infants learn to love their parents, who at first may be neutral stimuli but who become associated with the positive sensations of receiving milk, being rocked, and being comforted. And classical conditioning helps explain why adults find that certain songs on the radio, scents, or articles of clothing "turn them on." A range of emotional associations and attitudes are acquired through classical conditioning.

According to the learning theory perspective, then, it is a mistake to assume that children advance through a series of distinct stages guided by biological maturation, as Freud, Erikson, and other stage theorists have argued. Instead, learning theorists view development as nothing more than learning. It is a continuous process of behavior change that is context specific and can differ enormously from person to person. Watson's basic view was further advanced by B. F. Skinner.

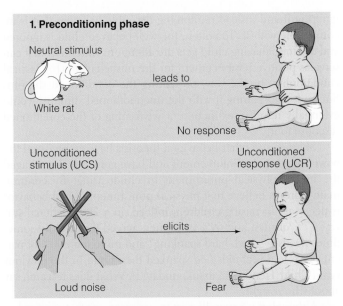

1. Preconditioning phase

Neutral stimulus

White rat → leads to → No response

Unconditioned stimulus (UCS) / Unconditioned response (UCR)

Loud noise → elicits → Fear

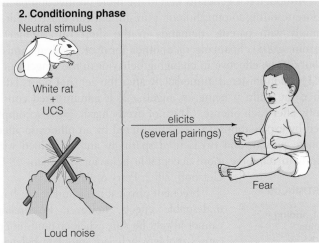

2. Conditioning phase

Neutral stimulus

White rat + UCS

Loud noise → elicits (several pairings) → Fear

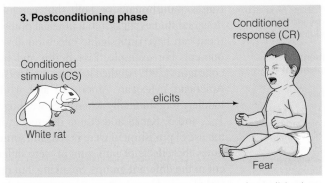

3. Postconditioning phase

Conditioned response (CR)

Conditioned stimulus (CS)

White rat → elicits → Fear

■ **FIGURE 2.2** The three phases of classical conditioning.

Skinner: Operant Conditioning

B. F. Skinner (1905–1990), probably the most famous American psychologist, had a long, distinguished career at Harvard University and a huge impact on approaches to behavior change (Rutherford, 2009). Through his research with animals, Skinner (1953) gained understanding of another important form of learn-

B. F. Skinner's operant conditioning theory emphasized the role of environment in controlling behavior.

ing, **operant conditioning**, in which a learner's behavior becomes either more or less probable depending on the consequences it produces. A learner first behaves in some way and then comes to associate this action with the positive or negative consequences that follow it. The basic principle behind operant conditioning makes sense: People tend to repeat behaviors that have desirable consequences and cut down on behaviors that have undesirable consequences. Through operant conditioning, individuals learn new skills and a range of habits, both good and bad.

In the language of operant conditioning, *reinforcement* occurs when a consequence strengthens a response, or makes it more likely to occur. If a preschool child cleans his room, receives a hug, then cleans his room more frequently thereafter, the hug provided **positive reinforcement** for room cleaning. *Positive* here means that something pleasant or desirable has been added to the situation, and *reinforcement* means that the behavior is strengthened. Thus, a positive reinforcer is a desirable event that, when introduced following a behavior, makes that behavior more probable. (Note that the effect on the child's behavior, not the parent's belief that the child might find a hug reinforcing, defines the consequence as reinforcing.)

Behaviorists have found that it is best to provide continuous positive reinforcement when a new skill or habit is first being learned, reinforcing every occurrence. Then, to maintain the behavior, it is best to shift to a "partial reinforcement schedule" in which only some occurrences of the behavior are reinforced and the pattern of reinforcement is unpredictable. Then the learner is likely to continue performing even if reinforcement stops.

Negative reinforcement (which is *not*, we repeat *not*, a fancy term for punishment) occurs when a behavioral tendency is strengthened because something unpleasant or undesirable is removed from the situation, or is escaped or avoided, after the behavior occurs. Are you familiar with the annoying sounds that go off in cars until you fasten your seat belt? The idea is that your "buckling up" behavior will become a habit through negative reinforcement: buckling your seat belt allows you to escape the unpleasant sound. No candy or hugs follow the action, so negative rather than positive reinforcement makes you likely to buckle your seat belt. Many bad habits develop because they allow people to avoid or escape unpleasant events; they were learned through negative reinforcement. Teenagers may learn to lie to avoid lectures from their parents or to drink because it allows them to escape feelings of anxiety at parties. In each case, a behavior is strengthened through negative reinforcement—through the removal or elimination of something undesirable like a lecture or anxiety.

Contrast reinforcement, whether it is positive or negative, with punishment: Whereas reinforcement increases the strength of the behavior that preceded it, *punishment* decreases the strength of the behavior or weakens it. Two forms of punishment parallel the two forms of reinforcement. **Positive punishment** occurs when an unpleasant stimulus is applied or added to the situation following a behavior (for example, a child is spanked for misbehaving, a cashier is criticized for coming up short of cash at the end of the day). **Negative punishment** occurs when a desirable stimulus is removed following the behavior (a child loses the privilege of watching TV, the amount the cashier was short is deducted from her pay). Both positive and negative punishment decrease the likelihood that the punished behavior will be repeated.

The four possible consequences of a behavior are summarized in ■ **Figure 2.3**. In addition, some behavior has no consequence. Behavior that is ignored, or no longer reinforced, tends to become less frequent through the process of **extinction**. Indeed, a good alternative to punishing a child's misbehavior is ignoring it and instead reinforcing desirable behavior that is incompatible with it. Too often, the well-behaved child is ignored and the misbehaving child gets the attention—attention that can serve as positive reinforcement for the misbehavior. (In classical conditioning, by the way, presenting the conditioned stimulus but no longer pairing it with the unconditioned stimulus would eventually result in extinction or weakening of the conditioned response to it.)

Skinner and other behavioral theorists have emphasized the power of positive reinforcement and have generally discouraged the use of physical punishment in childrearing. By contrast, many parents believe that physical punishment of bad behavior is necessary in raising children; indeed, in a 2004 national survey, 77% of men and 69% of women agreed that a child sometimes needs a "good, hard spanking" and more than 90% of parents of 3- to 4-year-olds *had* spanked their child in the previous year (Child Trends Databank, undated). What does research say about who is right?

Although it is generally best to use more positive approaches before resorting to punishment, punishment can make children comply with parents' demands in the short run (Benjet & Kazdin, 2003). Spanking or another form of physical punishment can be effective in changing behavior in the longer run if it (1) is administered immediately after the act (not hours later, when the child is being an angel), (2) is administered consistently after each offense, (3) is not overly harsh, (4) is accompanied by explanations, (5) is administered by an otherwise affectionate person, and (6) is used sparingly and combined with efforts to reinforce more acceptable behavior (Domjan, 1993; Gershoff, 2002; Perry & Parke, 1975).

Frequent physical punishment can have undesirable effects, however. Researchers cannot always be sure whether punishment causes problem behavior, problem behavior causes punishment, or both, but carefully designed studies suggest that physical punishment can have undesirable effects on development. For example, Lisa Berlin and her colleagues (2009) studied low-income African American, Mexican American, and white toddlers longitudinally when they were ages 1, 2, and 3. Racial and ethnic differences in the use of punishment were noted, and sometimes the effects of punishment were different in the different groups. Spanking, but not verbal punishment, at age 1 was associated with more aggressive behavior at age 2 and lower mental development scores at age 3. Importantly, although fussiness at age 1 predicted more use of spanking and verbal punishment later, the researchers were able to demonstrate that aggression and low mental development at an early age did not predict later use of punishment. Especially worrisome is evidence that punishment may make children resentful and anxious and may breed aggression by teaching them that hit-

	PLEASANT STIMULUS	UNPLEASANT STIMULUS
ADMINISTERED	**Positive reinforcement, adding a pleasant stimulus** (strengthens the behavior) Dad gives in to the whining and lets Moosie play Nintendo, making whining more likely in the future.	**Positive punishment, adding an unpleasant stimulus** (weakens the behavior) Dad calls Moosie a "baby." Moosie does not like this at all and is less likely to whine in the future.
WITHDRAWN	**Negative punishment, withdrawing a pleasant stimulus** (weakens the behavior) Dad confiscates Moosie's favorite Nintendo game to discourage whining in the future.	**Negative reinforcement, withdrawing an unpleasant stimulus** (strengthens the behavior) Dad stops joking with Lulu. Moosie gets very jealous when Dad pays attention to Lulu, so his whining enables him to bring this unpleasant state of affairs to an end.

■ **FIGURE 2.3** Possible consequences of whining behavior. Moosie comes into the TV room and sees his father talking and joking with his sister, Lulu, as the two watch a football game. Soon Moosie begins to whine, louder and louder, that he wants them to turn off the television so he can play Nintendo. If you were Moosie's father, how would you react? Above are four possible consequences of Moosie's behavior. Consider both the type of consequence—whether it is a pleasant or aversive stimulus—and whether it is administered ("added to" the situation) or withdrawn (taken away). Notice that reinforcement, by definition, always strengthens whining behavior, or makes it more likely in the future, whereas punishment weakens it.

ting is an appropriate way to solve problems. The negative effects of physical punishment are especially clear when the child punished is older than 6 years (Benjet & Kazdin, 2003).

In sum, Skinner, like Watson, believed that the course of human development depends on the individual's learning experiences. One boy's aggressive behavior may be reinforced over time because he gets his way with other children and because his parents encourage his "macho" behavior. Another boy may quickly learn that aggression is prohibited and punished. The two may develop in different directions based on their different histories of reinforcement and punishment.

Skinner's operant conditioning principles can help explain many aspects of human development; they are still studied by psychologists and applied in behavioral and, more recently, cognitive behavioral interventions in educational and therapeutic settings (A. J. Kearney, 2008; Mayer et al., 2009). Yet many developmentalists believe that Skinner placed too little emphasis on the role of cognitive processes such as attention, memory, and reflection in learning. Therefore, today's developmental scholars are more attracted to Albert Bandura's cognitive brand of learning theory than to Skinner's operant conditioning approach.

Bandura: Social Cognitive Theory

In his **social cognitive theory** (formerly called social learning theory), Stanford psychologist Albert Bandura (1977, 1986, 1989, 2000, 2006) claims that humans are cognitive beings whose active processing of information plays a critical role in their learning, behavior, and development. Bandura argues that human learning is very different from rat learning because humans have far more sophisticated cognitive capabilities. He agrees with Skinner that operant conditioning is an important type of learning, but he notes that people think about the connections between their behavior and its consequences, anticipate the consequences likely to follow from their behavior, and often are more affected by what they believe will happen than by the consequences they actually encounter. Individuals also reinforce or punish themselves with mental pats on the back and self-criticism, and these cognitions also affect behavior. More generally, Bandura wants his position to be called *social cognitive theory* rather than *social learning theory* for a reason: to distance himself from behavioral learning theories like Watson's and Skinner's and to emphasize that his theory is about the motivating and self-regulating role of cognition in human behavior (Bandura, 1986).

By highlighting observational learning as the most important mechanism through which human behavior changes, Bandura made his cognitive emphasis clear. **Observational learning** is simply learning by observing the behavior of other people (called *models*). By imitating other people, children can learn how to use computers and tackle math problems, as well as how to swear, snack between meals, and smoke. Observational learning is regarded as a more cognitive form of learning than conditioning because learners must pay attention, construct and remember mental representations (images and verbal summaries) of what they saw, retrieve these representations from memory later, and use them to guide behavior.

Albert Bandura's social cognitive theory highlighted the role of cognition in human learning. He is on the faculty at Stanford University.

© Linda A. Cicero/Stanford News Service

In a classic experiment, Bandura (1965) set out to demonstrate that children could learn a response neither elicited by a conditioned stimulus (as in classical conditioning) nor performed and then strengthened by a reinforcer (as in operant conditioning). He had nursery school children watch a short film in which an adult model attacked an inflatable "Bobo" doll: hitting the doll with a mallet while shouting "Sockeroo," throwing rubber balls at the doll while shouting "Bang, bang, bang," and so on. Some children saw the model praised, others saw him punished, and still others saw no consequences follow his violent attack. After the film ended, children were observed in a playroom with the Bobo doll and many of the props the model had used to work Bobo over.

What did the children learn? The children who saw the model rewarded and the children in the no-consequences condition imitated more of the model's aggressive acts than did the children who had seen the model punished. But interestingly, when the children who had seen the model punished were asked to reproduce all of the model's behavior they could remember, it turned out that they had learned just as much as the other children about how to treat a Bobo doll. Apparently, then, through a process termed **latent learning** in which learning occurs but is not evident in behavior, children can learn from observation even though they do not imitate (perform) the learned responses. Whether they will perform what they learn depends partly on **vicarious reinforcement,** a process in which learners become more or less likely to perform a behavior based on whether consequences experienced by the model they observe are reinforcing or punishing.

In Bandura's classic study of observational learning, children who watched an adult model (top row) attack an inflatable Bobo doll imitated many of the actions they observed (bottom two rows). Children who saw the model rewarded and children who saw the model experience no consequences were more likely to imitate aggressive actions than children who saw the model punished for them, but all three experimental groups learned a lot about how to work over a Bobo doll.

Observational learning is a very important form of learning in our society, but it may be even more important in traditional societies (Rogoff et al., 2003). There, children learn not in schools where they are segregated from adults and given formal instruction, but through participation in everyday activities in which they actively observe and listen to their elders, learning skills such as weaving and hunting without the adults intentionally teaching them (Rogoff et al., 2003). In one interesting cross-cultural study (Correa-Chavez & Rogoff, 2009), Mayan children living in Guatemala, especially those whose mothers had had little Western schooling, were much more attentive while their siblings were taught to use a new toy than European American children from the United States were—and learned more as a result. The Mayan children were more used to learning by watching what was going on around them than the European American children, who seemed to look to teachers and parents to arrange learning experiences directed toward them personally.

In recent years, Bandura (2000, 2006) has moved beyond the study of observational learning to emphasize the concept of **human agency**, ways in which people deliberately exercise cognitive control over themselves, their environments, and their lives. From the time they are infants recognizing that they can make things happen in their worlds, people form intentions, foresee what will happen, evaluate and regulate their actions as they pursue plans, and reflect on their functioning. These cognitions play a real causal role in influencing their behavior and that of other people. Most importantly, individuals develop a high or low sense of **self-efficacy** in a particular area of activity, the belief that one can ef-

fectively produce desired outcomes in that area. Whether you undertake an action such as going on a diet or studying for a test and whether you succeed depend greatly on whether you have a sense of self-efficacy with respect to that behavior.

Watson and Skinner may have believed that people are passively shaped by environment to become whatever those around them groom them to be, but Bandura does not. Because he views humans as active, cognitive beings, he holds that human development occurs through a continuous reciprocal interaction among the person (the individual's biological and psychological characteristics and cognitions), his or her behavior, and his or her environment—a perspective he calls **reciprocal determinism** (■ Figure 2.4). As Bandura sees it, environment does not rule, as it did in Skinner's thinking: people choose, build, and change their environments; they are not just shaped by them. Nor does biology rule; genetic influences on human behavior are evident, but cultural forces also change human environments (as when humans devised airplanes, indoor heating, and vaccines). The environments shaped by humans then influence biological evolution by influencing which traits increase the odds of survival (Bandura, 2000). And people's personal characteristics and behaviors affect the people around them, just as these people are influencing their personal characteristics and future behaviors.

Like Watson and Skinner, Bandura doubts that there are universal stages of human development. He maintains that development is context specific and can proceed along many paths. It is also continuous, occurring gradually through a lifetime of learning. Bandura acknowledges that children's cognitive capacities mature, so they can remember more about what they have seen and can imitate a greater variety of novel behaviors. Yet he also believes that children of the same age will be dissimilar if their learning experiences have differed considerably.

Obviously there is a fundamental disagreement between stage theorists such as Freud and Erikson and learning theorists such as Bandura. Learning theorists do not give a general description of the normal course of human development because they insist that there is no such description to give. Instead, they offer a rich account of the mechanisms through which behavior can change, using principles of learning that are universal in their applicability to understand how each individual changes

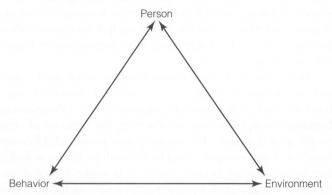

■ **FIGURE 2.4** Bandura's reciprocal determinism involves mutual influence of the person, the person's behavior, and the environment.

Learning Theorists: Notes on School Refusal

Anxiety disorders and phobias can be learned in a variety of ways. John Watson might hypothesize that Terrell had a traumatic experience at school—maybe a fire drill alarm scared him or he became sick and threw up in class. Through classical conditioning, the school building might become a conditioned stimulus for anxious responses.

B. F. Skinner would insist that we should analyze the consequences of going to school versus staying at home for Terrell to see whether those consequences can explain his behavior (C. A. Kearney, 2008). If Terrell's act of going to school results in punishing consequences (punches from a bully, harsh words from the teacher), the frequency of going to school will decline. And if acting sick is negatively reinforcing because it helps Terrell avoid the unpleasantness of going to school, "sick" behavior will become more frequent.

Terrell's mother could also be positively reinforcing stay-at-home behavior by allowing Terrell to spend quality time with her doing fun things and giving him extra attention and love when he is "sick."

Through observational learning, Albert Bandura would add, a child who merely witnesses another child's anxious behavior at school may learn to behave anxiously. It may also be important to understand what punishing consequences Terrell *believes* will occur if he attends school. And we should ask whether Terrell may have lost his sense of self-efficacy when faced with the new challenges of first grade.

Once it is clear how school refusal behavior is learned, behavioral therapies and more contemporary cognitive behavioral therapies based on learning principles can be applied to reduce Terrell's anxiety, reinforce going to school, and change any distorted thinking (Pina et al., 2009).

with age in unique ways (Goldhaber, 2000). We imagine what Watson, Skinner, and Bandura would say about school refusal in Exploration Box 2.3.

Strengths and Weaknesses

Pavlov's and Watson's demonstrations of classical conditioning, Skinner's work on operant conditioning, and Bandura's modern social cognitive theory with its highlighting of observational learning have contributed immensely to the understanding of development and continue to be influential. Learning theories are precise and testable. Carefully controlled experiments have shown how people might learn everything from altruism to alcoholism. Moreover, learning principles operate across the life span and can be used to understand behavior at any age. Finally, learning theories have incredibly important applications; they have been the basis for many highly effective behavioral and cognitive behavioral techniques for optimizing development and treating developmental problems.

Still, behavioral learning theories, and even Bandura's more recent social cognitive theory, leave something to be desired as explanations of human development. For instance, it has been demonstrated that reinforcing 3-month-old infants with smiles and gentle rubs on the chin whenever they happen to make babbling sounds, such as "bababa," causes them to babble more often than infants who receive the same social stimulation randomly, rather than only after each babbling sound they make (Weisberg, 1963). But does this mean that infants normally begin to babble *because* babbling is reinforced by their caregivers? Not necessarily. All normal infants, even deaf ones, babble around 4 months of age. Moreover, no matter what experiences are provided to newborns, they will not be maturationally ready to babble. We must suspect, then, that the maturation of the neural and muscular control required for babbling has more than a little to do with the onset of babbling during infancy.

This example highlights two criticisms of learning theories as theories of human development. First, learning theorists rarely demonstrate that learning is responsible for commonly observed developmental changes; they show through their experiments only that learning *might* have resulted in developmental change, as in the case of reinforcement increasing the frequency of babbling. Some critics wish that learning theorists would provide a fuller account of normal changes across the life span. Second, early learning theorists, and even Bandura, probably put too little emphasis on biological influences on development, such as genetic endowment and maturational processes, that affect how people respond to learning experiences. We may learn to fear snakes, for example. However, probably because snakes were a threat to our ancestors, we have evolved so that we are biologically prepared to be wary of these critters. Thus, 3- to 5-year-old children, whether they are already familiar with snakes or not, are quicker to find a target snake in the midst of several flowers than to find a target flower in the midst of several snakes (LoBue & DeLoache, 2008), and people learn to fear snakes more easily than they learn to fear bunnies or flowers (Ohman & Mineka, 2003). Today's learning theorists appreciate more than Watson and Skinner did that factors such as genetic endowment, previous learning, personality, and social context all affect how humans react to their learning experiences (Mineka & Zinbarg, 2006).

Checking Mastery

1. The Foxes try to control their teenage daughter's behavior by (a) giving her an allowance only if she does her weekly chores, (b) setting her weekend curfew earlier if she stays out later than she was supposed to the weekend before, and (c) allowing her to

get out of the distasteful task of cleaning the bathroom if she spends time with her grandmother. What specific consequences, using operant conditioning language, are illustrated by these three parenting strategies, and in each case, what effect do the parents hope to have on their daughter's behavior?

2. What are two main criticisms Albert Bandura might make of earlier behavioral learning theories?

Making Connections

1. Gert, age 78, fell and broke her hip a year ago and has become overly dependent on her daughter for help ever since, even though she can get around quite well now. How might (1) Freud or Erikson and (2) Watson, Skinner, or Bandura explain her old-age dependency?

2.5 Piaget: Cognitive Developmental Theory

After behavioral learning theories dominated the study of development in the 1950s and 1960s, many developmentalists began to look for a theory that was both more cognitive and more clearly developmental. They found what they wanted in the groundbreaking work of Jean Piaget. No theorist has contributed more to the understanding of children's minds than Piaget (1896–1980), a Swiss scholar who began to study children's intellectual development during the 1920s. This remarkable man developed quickly himself, publishing his first scientific work (a letter to the editor about an albino sparrow) at age 11. Eventually, Piaget blended his interest in zoology and the adaptation of animals to their environments with his interest in philosophy. He then devoted his career to the study of how humans acquire knowledge and use it to adapt to their world.

Piaget's lifelong interest in cognitive development emerged while he worked at the Alfred Binet laboratories in Paris on the first standardized IQ test. IQ tests estimate individuals' intelligence based on the number of questions they answer correctly. Piaget soon became interested in children's wrong answers and noticed that children of about the same age gave the same kinds of wrong answers. By questioning them to find out how they were thinking about the problems presented to them, he began to realize that young children do not simply know less than older children; instead, they think in a qualitatively different way. Eventually Piaget developed a theory to account for changes in thinking from infancy to adolescence, a theory we will explore more thoroughly in Chapter 7.

Constructivism

Influenced by his background in biology, Piaget (1950) viewed intelligence as a process that helps an organism adapt to its environment. The infant who grasps a cookie and brings it to her mouth is behaving adaptively, as is the adolescent who solves algebra problems or the mechanic who fixes cars. As humans ma-

Swiss psychologist Jean Piaget revolutionized the field of human development with his cognitive developmental theory of intellectual growth.

© Farrell Grehan/Corbis

ture, they acquire ever more complex cognitive structures, or organized patterns of thought or action, that aid them in adapting to their environments.

Piaget insisted that children are not born with innate ideas about reality, as some philosophers have claimed. Nor did he think children are simply filled with information by adults, as learning theorists believe. Piaget's position, called **constructivism**, was that children actively construct new understandings of the world based on their experiences. It is common for preschool children to invent their own ideas, saying that the sun is alive because it moves across the sky, that children get diseases if they tell lies or otherwise misbehave, or that babies are bought at the baby store and then put in their mommies' tummies.

How do children construct more accurate understandings of the world? By being curious and active explorers: watching what is going on around them, seeing what happens when they experiment on the objects they encounter, and recognizing instances in which their current understandings are inadequate to explain events. Children use their current understandings of the world to help them solve problems, but they also revise their understandings to make them better fit reality (Piaget, 1952). The *interaction* between biological maturation (most importantly, a developing brain) and experience (especially discrepancies between the child's understanding and reality) is responsible for the child's progress from one stage of cognitive development to a new, qualitatively different stage.

Stages of Cognitive Development

Piaget proposed four major periods of cognitive development: the sensorimotor stage (birth to age 2), the preoperational stage (ages 2 to 7), the concrete operations stage (ages 7 to 11), and the formal operations stage (ages 11 to 12 or older). These stages form what Piaget called an *invariant sequence*; that is, all children progress through the stages in the order they are listed without skipping stages or regressing to earlier stages. The ages given are only guidelines; different children progress at different rates.

The key features of each stage are summarized in ● **Table 2.3**. The core message is that humans of different ages think in qualitatively different ways (Inhelder & Piaget, 1958).

Infants in the **sensorimotor stage** deal with the world directly through their perceptions (senses) and actions (motor skills). They are unable to use symbols (gestures, images, or words representing real objects and events) to help them solve problems mentally. However, they learn a great deal about the world by exploring it, and they acquire tools for solving problems through their sensory and motor experiences.

The preschooler who has entered the **preoperational stage** of cognitive development has now developed the capacity for symbolic thought but is not yet capable of logical problem solving. The 4- or 5-year-old can use words as symbols to talk about a problem and can mentally imagine doing something before actually doing it. However, according to Piaget, preschool children are egocentric thinkers who have difficulty adopting perspectives other than their own and who may cling to incorrect ideas simply because they want them to be true. Lacking the tools of logical thought, preoperational children must also rely on their perceptions and as a result are easily fooled by appearances. Piaget demonstrated this by administering his famous conservation of liquid quantity task, in which a child is shown two short, wide glasses filled with equal amounts of water; sees the water poured from one of the squat glasses into a taller, thin-

Jean Piaget believed that children are naturally curious explorers who try to make sense of their environment and learn through their actions on it—a good thing for parents to remember when they encounter still another toddler-created disaster area!

© Marc Asnin 2005/Redux

ner glass; and is then asked which glass has more water, the squat glass or the taller glass. Preschool children fail to demonstrate **conservation**, the recognition that certain properties of an object or substance do not change when its appearance is altered in some superficial way. Tricked by the greater height of the water in the tall, thin glass, young children ignore the width of the glass

---

● TABLE 2.3 JEAN PIAGET'S FOUR STAGES OF COGNITIVE DEVELOPMENT

Stage (Age Range)	Description
Sensorimotor (birth to 2 years)	Infants use their senses and motor actions to explore and understand the world. At the start they have only innate reflexes, but they develop increasingly "intelligent" actions. By the end, they are capable of symbolic thought using images or words and can therefore plan solutions to problems mentally.
Preoperational (2 to 7 years)	Preschoolers use their capacity for symbolic thought to develop language, engage in pretend play, and solve problems. But their thinking is not yet logical; they are egocentric (unable to take others' perspectives) and are easily fooled by perceptions, failing conservation problems because they cannot rely on logical operations.
Concrete operations (7 to 11 years)	School-age children acquire concrete logical operations that allow them to mentally classify, add, and otherwise act on concrete objects in their heads. They can solve practical, real-world problems through a trial-and-error approach but have difficulty with hypothetical and abstract problems.
Formal operations (11 to 12 years and older)	Adolescents can think about abstract concepts and purely hypothetical possibilities and can trace the long-range consequences of possible actions. With age and experience, they can form hypotheses and systematically test them using the scientific method.

NOTE: Piaget's theory is elaborated upon in Chapter 7.

Cognition is an important influence on behavior; we need to understand how Terrell is thinking about both his home life and school.

We should assess his stage of cognitive development. Especially if he has not yet made the transition from the preoperational stage to the concrete-operational stage, his anxiety may be rooted in a faulty cause–effect analysis or a misunderstanding because he has not yet mastered logical operations. He may, for example, believe the serial murderer or terrorist he saw on TV will kill his mother next or that the school shooting that happened in another state will happen at his school. His egocentrism could make it even more likely that he would come to believe that these scary events will affect him.

and conclude that the amount of water had magically increased. Failing to appreciate that the process of pouring is reversible, they claim that the water would spill all over if it were poured back into its original glass.

School-age children who have advanced to the **concrete operations stage** are more logical than preschoolers. They use a trial-and-error approach to problem solving and do well on problems that involve thinking about concrete objects. These children can perform many important logical actions, or operations, in their heads on concrete objects (hence, the term *concrete operations*, and Piaget's description of the preschool child as *preoperational*). For example, they can mentally categorize or add and subtract objects, and they can mentally coordinate the height and width of glasses in order to solve conservation problems correctly. They can also draw sound, general conclusions based on their concrete or specific observations. However, they have difficulty dealing with abstract and hypothetical problems.

Adolescents who reach the **formal operations stage** are able to think more abstractly and hypothetically than school-age children. They can define *justice* abstractly, in terms of fairness, rather than concretely, in terms of the cop on the corner or the judge in the courtroom. They can formulate hypotheses or predictions in their heads, plan how to systematically test their ideas experimentally, and imagine the consequences of their tests. It often takes some years before adolescents can adopt a thoroughly systematic and scientific method of solving problems and can think logically about the implications of purely hypothetical ideas. Then they may be able to devise grand theories about what is wrong with their parents or the federal government or analyze the long-term consequences of legalizing drugs.

Obviously, children's cognitive capacities change dramatically between infancy and adolescence as they progress through Piaget's four stages of cognitive development. Infants, young children, school-age children, and adolescents and adults simply do not think the same way. What, then, do you suppose Piaget would have said about school refusal? Exploration Box 2.4 sketches his possible thoughts. Whereas Freud and Erikson might have looked to personality disorders or emotional conflicts for explanations, and Skinner and Bandura would have looked to specific learning experiences, Piaget probably would have hypothesized that cognitive immaturity, lack of knowledge, and faulty beliefs underlie many developmental problems.

Strengths and Weaknesses

Like Freud, Piaget was a true pioneer whose work has left a deep and lasting imprint on thinking about human development. You will see his influence throughout this text, for the mind that "constructs" understanding of the physical world also comes, with age, to understand sex differences, moral values, emotions, death, and a range of other important aspects of the human experience. Piaget's cognitive developmental perspective dominated the study of child development for about 3 decades, until the 1980s. Most developmentalists today continue to accept Piaget's basic beliefs that thinking changes in qualitative ways during childhood, that children are active in their own development, and that development occurs through an interaction of nature and nurture. Piaget's description of intellectual development has been tested and has been largely, although not wholly, supported. Finally, Piaget's ideas have influenced education and child rearing by encouraging teachers and parents to pitch their educational programs to children's levels of understanding and to stimulate children to discover new concepts through their own direct grappling with problems.

Still, Piaget has had his share of criticism (Lourenco & Machado, 1996; also see Chapter 7). For example, critics fault him for saying too little about the influences of motivation and emotion on thought processes. They also question whether Piaget's stages really hang together as coherent and general modes of thinking that can be applied to a variety of types of problems; research suggests that the thinking skills needed to solve different types of problems are acquired at different rates. Critics also conclude that Piaget underestimated the cognitive abilities of young children; recent studies suggest that children master some Piagetian concepts earlier than Piaget believed they did, although defenders of Piaget would question whether some of the simplified tasks used by later researchers really demonstrate that young children have fully mastered the concepts tested (Desrochers, 2008). Piaget is also charged with putting too little emphasis on the role of parents and other more knowledgeable people in nurturing cognitive development. And critics challenge the idea that all humans in every culture develop through the same stages toward the same endpoints. As a result, developmentalists began to seek theoretical perspectives that allowed more diversity in the pathways that cognitive development could take while retaining Piaget's theme that nature and nurture interact to produce developmental change.

Other Perspectives on Cognitive Development

Two important approaches to cognitive development that challenged some of Piaget's thinking are Vygotsky's *sociocultural perspective* (discussed in Chapter 7) and the *information-processing approach* (discussed in Chapter 8). We will briefly discuss them here to call attention to weaknesses in Piaget's cognitive developmental theory.

The **sociocultural perspective** on cognitive development offered by a contemporary of Piaget, Russian psychologist Lev Vygotsky, has become quite influential in recent years. Disagreeing with Piaget's notion of universal stages of cognitive development, Vygotsky maintained that cognitive development is shaped by the sociocultural context in which it occurs and grows out of children's interactions with members of their culture (Vygotsky, 1962, 1978). Each culture provides its members with certain tools of thought—most notably a language, but also tools such as pencils, art media, mathematical systems, and computers. The ways in which people in a particular culture approach and solve problems are passed from generation to generation through oral and written communication. Hence culture, especially as it is embodied in language, shapes thought. As a result, cognitive development is not the same universally; it varies across social and historical contexts. And whereas Piaget tended to see children as independent explorers, Vygotsky saw them as social beings who develop their minds through guided participation in culturally important activities in which parents, teachers, and other knowledgeable members of their culture provide "scaffolding" or support that facilitates learning.

Other challenges to Piaget came from scholars who saw a need to look more closely at the processes involved in thinking and factors affecting those processes. The **information-processing approach** to cognition, which became the dominant perspective starting in the 1980s, likens the human mind to a computer with hardware and software and examines the fundamental mental processes, such as attention, memory, decision making, and the like, involved in performing cognitive tasks. Development involves changes in the capacity and speed of the information-processing machine we call the brain, in the strategies used to process information, and in the information stored in memory. This approach is the focus of Chapter 8 and has guided research not only on attention, memory, and problem solving but also on gender-role development, social cognition, and many other topics addressed in this book.

Checking Mastery

1. Distinguish between concrete operational thinking and formal operational thinking in terms of what is operated upon mentally, using a specific example if you can.

2. What one major criticism would advocates of (a) the sociocultural perspective on cognitive development and (b) the

information-processing approach to cognition make of Piaget's cognitive developmental theory?

Making Connections

1. Although we will look at the implications of Piaget's theory for education more closely in Chapter 7, based on what you know so far, what recommendations would Piaget make to teachers of (a) 4-year-olds, (b) 9-year-olds, and (c) 14-year-olds to help them recognize the strengths and weaknesses of children at these ages?

2.6 Systems Theories

Systems theories of development (some are called contextual theories because they emphasize interactions between humans and the contexts in which they develop; some are called dynamic systems theories) generally claim that changes over the life span arise from ongoing transactions in which a changing organism and a changing environment affect one another (see, for example, Fogel, King, & Shanker, 2008; Gottlieb, Wahlsten, & Lickliter, 2006; Lerner, 2006). The individual and the physical and social contexts with which he interacts are inseparable parts of a larger system in which everything affects everything else. Development can take a variety of paths depending on the complex interplay of multiple influences.

Urie Bronfenbrenner's bioecological model, introduced in Chapter 1, illustrates a systems perspective on development: the individual, with her biologically based characteristics, is embedded in and interacts with four environmental systems over time. In Chapter 5, you will also encounter Esther Thelen's dynamic systems theory of motor development. Here, we highlight another theorist who emphasized that development grows out of a system of interacting influences, Gilbert Gottlieb (1929–2006), a developmental psychobiologist. Gottlieb believed that human development takes place in the context of our evolutionary history as a species and arises from ongoing interactions between biological and environmental influences. Although Bronfenbrenner started out interested in the environment and increasingly realized that biological influences on development were equally important, Gottlieb started out as a biologist and increasingly became convinced of the importance of environmental influences on what biologists had long believed were genetically influenced or innate phenomena.

Evolutionary Theory and Ethology

Gilbert Gottlieb's perspective grew out of earlier work looking at animal and human development in the context of evolutionary theory (Bjorklund & Pellegrini, 2002; Burgess & MacDonald, 2005; Gottlieb et al., 2006). In his tremendously influential theory of evolution, Charles Darwin (1859) maintained that genes that aid their bearers in adapting to their environment will be

Similarities between animals and humans suggest that many aspects of human development are the product of evolution.

passed on to future generations more frequently than genes that do not (see Chapter 3). Evolutionary theory therefore prompts us to ask how the characteristics and behaviors we commonly observe in humans today may have helped our ancestors adapt to their environments and consequently may have become part of the shared genetic endowment of our species.

Researchers inspired by Darwin's theory founded the field of **ethology**, the study of the evolved behavior of various species in their natural environments (J. Archer, 1992; Hinde, 1983). Noted ethologists Konrad Lorenz and Niko Tinbergen asked how many apparently innate, species-typical animal behaviors might serve adaptive functions in the sense that they contribute to survival. Ethologists maintain that behavior is adaptive only in relation to a particular environment; for example, nomadic wandering makes sense in an environment in which food is scarce but not in an environment in which food is abundant. As a result, they believed that it was essential to study behavior and development in its natural contexts using naturalistic observation. So, for example, they have recorded birdsongs in the wild, analyzed their features carefully, explored how male birds learn the songs characteristic of their species, and attempted to understand how songs aid birds in reproduction and survival. And they have studied in various species such phenomena as parent–infant attachment, play, dominance hierarchies, mating, and parenting. Sometimes ethologists just observe; other times they conduct experiments to determine how different environmental stimuli affect the development of species-typical patterns of behavior.

Ethologists suggest that humans, like other species, display species-specific behaviors that are the products of evolution and assist them in adapting to their environment. In Chapter 14, for example, we will encounter attachment theory, an influential perspective rooted in both psychoanalytic theory and ethological theory. Attachment theorists view the formation of close relationships between human infants and their caregivers, like the tendency of young ducks to follow their mothers, as evolved behavior that increases the odds that the young will survive. We will also discuss throughout this book contributions of modern **evolutionary psychology**, the application of evolutionary theory to understanding why humans think and behave as they do (Bjorklund & Pellegrini, 2002; Buss, 2008; Ellis & Bjorklund, 2005).

Gottlieb's Epigenetic Psychobiological Systems Perspective

While ethologists were examining the evolutionary roots of human behavior, developmental psychobiologist Gilbert Gottlieb was studying how products of evolution such as genes and hormones interact with environmental factors to guide the individual's development (1992, 2000, 2002; Gottlieb et al., 2006; Gottlieb & Halpern, 2008). According to Gottlieb's **epigenetic psychobiological systems perspective**, development is the product of interacting biological and environmental forces that form a larger system. It is possible to focus on the interplay of nature and nurture both at the level of the species interacting with its environment over the course of evolution and at the level of the individual, with his unique genetic makeup, interacting with his unique environment over the course of a lifetime (Li, 2003).

Gilbert Gottlieb sought to understand how biology and environment coact during the epigenetic process to produce development.

Species Change

The starting point in the epigenetic psychobiological systems perspective is recognition that evolution has endowed us with a human genetic makeup. We do not start out as *tabulae rasae*. Rather, we are predisposed to develop in certain directions rather than in others—for example, to develop so that we master language, use tools, display guilt, act aggressively, mate and bear children, and do the other things that humans do (Pinker, 2002). Each person's development takes place in the context of our evolutionary history as a species. We share many genes with our fellow humans because those genes enabled our ancestors to adapt to their environments.

However, genes and environment interact because humans actively and deliberately change their environments by farming, urbanizing, polluting, fighting infectious diseases, and so on. As we change our environments, through cultural evolution, we sometimes change the course of biological evolution. How? Because new environments may make different genes more critical to survival than earlier environments did. Consider that genes associated with a high tolerance for lactose in milk have become far more prevalent in human populations that have engaged in dairy farming than in other human populations—for example, more prevalent in Europe than in East Asia (Aoki, 1986; Voight et al., 2006). Over time, in the context of plenty of milk to drink, people with these gene variants were apparently more likely to survive than people without them. So, genes and environment interact at the species level, and both biological and cultural evolution contribute to change over time in the human species.

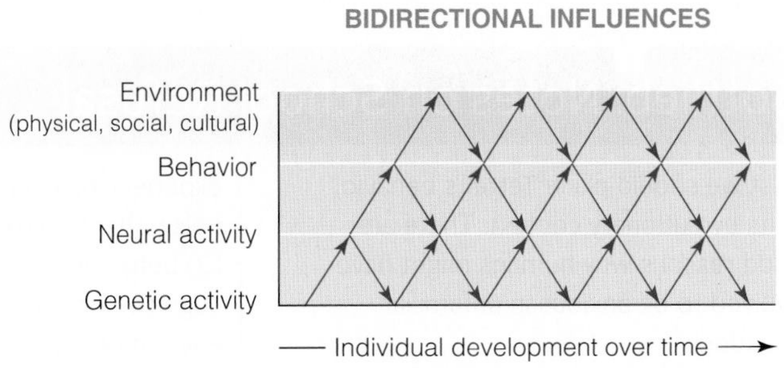

Epigenesis

Turning to change at the individual level, Gottlieb maintained that genes do not dictate how development will go; they only participate—along with environmental influences—in making certain developmental outcomes more probable than others. What happens in development depends on the all-important process of **epigenesis** (meaning "over and above" genes). Through epigenesis, nature and nurture (genes and environment) *co-act* to bring forth particular developmental outcomes—sometimes, surprising outcomes that are not easily predicted (see Spencer et al., 2009). In describing the epigenetic process, Gottlieb highlighted mutual influences over time involving (1) the activity of genes, which turn on and off at different points during development; (2) the activity of neurons; (3) the organism's behavior; and (4) environmental influences of all kinds—all part of a larger system, as shown in ■ **Figure 2.5**.

Gottlieb accused biologists of the past of wrongly claiming that genes dictate what happens in development in a one-directional and deterministic way and that genetic and physiological influences are therefore more causally important than environmental ones. We need to appreciate, he said, that each of his four levels is important and must be understood in its own right. Behavior cannot be explained, he argued, by reducing it to simpler components such as genes or neurons. In addition, we need to appreciate that behavior and environment

■ **FIGURE 2.5** Gottlieb's model of bidirectional influences. Moving from left to right, we see how the four levels of influence in Gottlieb's system mutually affect one another as the individual develops. Genes do not determine development; rather, through the epigenetic process, genetic influences interact with environmental influences, the individual's behavior, and activity at the neural level to make certain developmental outcomes more or less probable. Can you think of an example of each type of influence indicated by an arrow? SOURCE: Gottlieb, G. (1992). *Individual development and evolution: The genesis of novel behavior.* New York: Oxford University Press, p. 186. Copyright © 1991 by Oxford University Press, Inc. Reprinted by permission.

influence the activity of genes and the functioning of the brain, just as genes and the brain influence behavior and the environment. To illustrate this point using Gottlieb's terminology, consider that stimulation from the *environment*, gained partly through the infant's exploratory *behavior*, not only produces *neural activity* and changes the brain but also affects the *activity of genes*, which in turn influence the formation and functioning of the neural networks necessary for further development and behavior (Johnston & Edwards, 2002).

Gottlieb made his case for interacting levels of influence by demonstrating that behavior that most biologists assumed was innate or instinctive—etched in the genetic code of all members of a species in the course of evolution and automatically displayed—may or may not occur depending on the organism's early experience. He showed, for example, that the tendency of young ducks to prefer their mothers' vocal calls to those of other birds such as chickens is not as automatic as you might guess. Duckling embryos that were exposed to chicken calls before they hatched and then were prevented from vocalizing at birth, and therefore had no experience hearing ducklike calls, actually came to prefer the call of a chicken to that of a mallard duck (Gottlieb, 1991). This and other studies demonstrated that hearing duck vocalizations, whether generated by ducklings' mothers or by themselves, was necessary for ducklings to prefer the call of a mother duck.

Exciting new discoveries in genetic research, to be explored further in Chapter 3, are shedding further light on epigenesis

First we should place Terrell's behavior in its evolutionary context: There are good reasons why humans might have evolved to be anxious in unfamiliar situations.

We must consider the possible influences of each of the following factors on each of the others: (1) genes (Might he have a genetic predisposition to be anxious?), (2) neural activity (Has he been experiencing overarousal in response to a noisy, chaotic, stress-inducing classroom?), (3) behavior (Does he have immature cognitive or coping skills?), and (4) the environment (Could a gruff teacher, a bully, or an overprotective parent be contributing to his problem?) What about cultural influences? School refusal has been increasing in Japan as mothers and teachers increase pressure on children to succeed in school and as traditional family life in Japan breaks down (Kameguchi & Murphy-Shigematsu, 2001; Kameguchi, 2004). Characteristics of the school and the family environment should also be considered (C. A. Kearney, 2008).

In short, one must analyze the whole person–environment system over time, expecting reciprocal influences among multiple factors—not one simple cause.

---

and ways in which environment influences can alter the activity of genes. It has become clear that the biochemical environment of a cell, as influenced by factors such as nutrition and stress and even nurturing care early in life, can affect whether or not particular genes in that cell are expressed, or transcribed into RNA, so that they can guide the production of proteins and in turn influence the individual's emerging traits. As we will see in Chapter 3, this research is suggesting that what ultimately matters in development may not be what genes a person has but which of them are expressed or activated—and that environmental factors have a lot to do with this (Champagne & Mashoodh, 2009; also see Chapter 3).

The message is clear: genes do not determine anything (Gottlieb et al., 2006). Even seemingly instinctive, inborn patterns of behavior will not emerge unless the individual has both normal genes and normal early experiences. And it is rather silly, Gottlieb believed, to try to figure out how much of an individual's traits and behavior is caused by nature and how much is caused by nurture when genes and environment "coact" and are therefore inseparable and equally important. The nature–nurture issue simply vanishes from Gottlieb's perspective (Spencer et al., 2009).

In sum, the epigenetic psychobiological systems perspective holds that the development of the individual arises from complex interactions over time among genetic, neural, behavioral, and environmental influences operating as a system. Because genes have to be turned on with the help of environmental input in order to influence development, and even then only make particular developmental outcomes more or less probable, development is not genetically predetermined. Indeed, we cannot predict how the developmental story will end until we see what emerges from epigenesis, the long history of interactions among the multiple influences pictured in ■ **Figure 2.5**. Interestingly, then, Urie Bronfenbrenner, who initially emphasized cultural influences on development, and Gottlieb, who initially emphasized biological influences, ended up in close agreement that it is the interactions among biological and environmental forces that really count.

In Exploration Box 2.5, we imagine what Gottlieb might have thought about contributors to school refusal.

Strengths and Weaknesses

Systems theories of development are complex, but that is because life-span human development is complex. We can applaud Gottlieb, Bronfenbrenner, and like-minded theorists for conceptualizing development as the often unpredictable product of biological and environmental forces interacting within a complex system and challenging us to look closely at ongoing transactions between the individual and his or her environment.

Yet systems theories can be faulted for not yet providing a clear picture of the course of human development and for being only partially formulated and tested at this point. Indeed, an even more serious criticism can be made: systems perspectives may never provide any coherent developmental theory. Why? If we take seriously the idea that development can take a range of paths depending on a range of interacting influences both within and outside the person, how can we ever state generalizations about development that will hold up for most people? If change over a lifetime depends on the ongoing transactions between a unique person and a unique environment, is each life span unique? The problem is this: "For the contextual or systems theorist, often the only generalization that holds is, 'It depends.'" (Goldhaber, 2000, p. 33).

Human development may be more predictable than Gottlieb's theory implies when children with normal human biological endowments develop in normal human environments and, as a result, tend to change in similar directions at similar ages (MacDonald & Hershberger, 2005). Perhaps it is still possible to see humans as moving in orderly directions in many aspects of their development while also appreciating diversity and individuality in development. Perhaps it is possible to view developmental attainments such as formal-operational thinking not as inevitable, universal achievements but as attainments that are more or less *probable* depending on the coaction of the individual's genetic endowment and life experiences.

Checking Mastery

1. How might an ethologist go about studying influences on cooperation among preschool children?

2. Using one phrase or term each, describe (a) the relationship between nature and nurture in Gottlieb's epigenetic psychobiological systems perspective and (b) the way in which the two combine to influence development.

Making Connections

1. Speaking from the perspective of Gilbert Gottlieb, criticize two of the other theorists discussed in this chapter.

2.7 Theories in Perspective

That completes this survey of some grand and emerging theories of human development. Just as developmental scientists need theories to guide their work, every parent, teacher, human services professional, and observer of humans is guided by some set of basic assumptions about how humans develop and why they develop as they do. We hope that you will think about your own assumptions about human development by comparing the answers you gave to the questions in Engagement Box 2.1 at the start of the chapter with the summary information in ●**Table 2.4** and seeing which theorists' views are most compatible with your own.

Theories of human development can be grouped into even grander categories based on the broad assumptions they make (Goldhaber, 2000; P. H. Miller, 2010; Pepper, 1942; Reese & Overton, 1970). Stage theorists such as Freud, Erikson, and Piaget form one broad group and have much in common. They believe that development is guided in certain universal directions by biological–maturational forces within the individual. Humans unfold—much as a rose unfolds from its beginnings as a seed—according to a master plan carried in their genes, assuming that they grow up in a reasonably normal environment. They evolve through distinct or discontinuous stages that are universal and lead to the same final state of maturity. Parents who subscribe to the stage theory perspective on development, especially Piaget's, are likely to see themselves as *supporters* of development. They would tend to trust their children's biologically based tendencies to seek the learning opportunities they most need in order to develop their own minds. They would respond to their children's changing needs and interests, but they would not feel compelled to structure all their children's learning experiences. This position is like the philosophy of education incorporated in Montessori schools (Lillard, 2005).

By contrast, learning theorists such as Watson, Skinner, and Bandura emphasize the role of environment more than the role of biology in development. Parents who subscribe to a learning theory model of human development are not likely to trust genetically guided maturational forces to ensure that their children develop in healthy directions. Such parents are likely to act as *trainers*, assuming that their children will not develop properly (or at least will never be Harvard material) unless they are systematically exposed to particular learning experiences and shaped in positive directions.

Finally, systems and contextual theorists view biology and environment as inseparable components of a larger system. Humans contribute actively to the developmental process (as stage theorists such as Piaget maintain), but environment is also an active participant in the developmental drama (as learning theorists maintain). The potential exists for both qualitative (stagelike) change and quantitative change. Development can proceed along many paths depending on the intricate interplay of nature and nurture. Parents who adopt a systems theory of development are likely to appreciate that their children are influencing them just as much as they are influencing their children. They are likely to view themselves as *partners* with their children in the developmental process.

Our understanding of human development has changed, and will continue to change, as one prevailing view gives way to another. From the beginning of the study of human development at the turn of the 20th century through the heyday of Freud's psychoanalytic theory, a stage theory perspective prevailed, emphasizing biological forces in development (Parke et al., 1994). In the 1950s and 1960s, learning theories came to the fore, and attention shifted from biology toward environment and toward the view that children are blank tablets to be written on. Then, with the rising influence of cognitive psychology and Piaget's theory of cognitive development in the late 1960s and 1970s, a stage theory model emphasizing the interaction of nature and nurture gained prominence. Finally, in the 1980s and 1990s, we gained a fuller appreciation of both biological–genetic and cultural–historical influences on development.

Where are we today? The broad perspective on key developmental issues taken by systems theorists such as Bronfenbrenner and Gottlieb is the perspective that most 21st-century developmentalists have adopted. The field has moved beyond the extreme, black-or-white positions taken by many of its pioneers. We now appreciate that humans, although not tabulae rasae, have evolved so that they have the potential to develop in both good and bad directions; that human development is always the product of nature and nurture; that both humans and their environments are active in the developmental process; that development is both continuous and discontinuous in form; and that development has both universal aspects and aspects particular to certain cultures, times, and individuals. In short, the assumptions and theories that guide the study of human development have become increasingly complex as the incredible complexity of human development has become more apparent.

● TABLE 2.4 COMPARE YOURSELF WITH THE THEORISTS

In Engagement Box 2.1, you were asked to indicate your position on basic issues in human development by answering five questions. If you transcribe your answers (a, b, c, d, or e) in the appropriate boxes in the first column below, you can compare your stands with those of the theorists described in this chapter—and review the theories. With whom do you seem to agree the most?

	Your Answers (From ENGAGEMENT BOX 2.1)	Theory: Theorist					
		Psychoanalytic Theory: Freud's Psychosexual Theory	Psychoanalytic Theory: Erikson's Psychosocial Theory	Learning Theory: Skinner's Behavioral Theory	Learning Theory: Bandura's Social Cognitive Theory	Cognitive Developmental Theory: Piaget's Constructivism	Systems Theories: Gottlieb's Epigenetic Psychobiological Systems Perspective
MESSAGE		Biologically based sexual instincts motivate behavior and steer development through five psychosexual stages, oral to genital	Humans progress through eight psychosocial conflicts, from trust vs. mistrust to integrity vs. despair	Development is the product of learning from the consequences of one's behavior through operant conditioning	Development is the product of cognition, as illustrated by observational learning and human agency	Development proceeds through four stages of cognitive development, from sensorimotor to formal operations	Development takes many directions depending on transactions between a changing person and a changing environment
NATURE–NURTURE	Question 1	b. More nature (biology drives development; early experience in the family influences it, too)	c. Nature and nurture equally	e. Mostly nurture	d. More nurture	b. More nature (maturation interacting with experience guides all through the same stages)	c. Nature and nurture equally
GOODNESS–BADNESS OF HUMAN NATURE	Question 2	a. Bad (selfish, aggressive urges)	d. Good (capable of growth)	b. Neither good nor bad	b. Neither good nor bad	d. Good (curious)	c. Both good and bad (people have biologically based predispositions toward both)
ACTIVITY–PASSIVITY	Question 3	b. Passive (humans are influenced by forces beyond their control)	a. Active	b. Passive (humans are shaped by environment)	a. Active (humans influence their environments)	a. Active	a. Active
CONTINUITY–DISCONTINUITY	Question 4	a. Discontinuous (stagelike)	a. Discontinuous (stagelike)	c. Continuous (habits gradually increase or decrease in strength)	c. Continuous	a. Discontinuous (stagelike)	b. Both continuous and discontinuous
UNIVERSALITY–CONTEXT SPECIFICITY	Question 5	a. Universal	a. Universal (although stages may be expressed differently in different cultures)	b. Context specific (direction of development depends on experiences)	b. Context specific	a. Universal	b. Context specific

As we have emphasized, a main function of theories in any science is to guide research. Thus, Freud stimulated researchers to study inner personality conflicts, Skinner inspired them to analyze how behavior changes when its consequences change, and Piaget inspired them to explore children's modes of thinking. Different theories make different assumptions, stimulate different kinds of research, and yield different kinds of facts about development and explanations of them, as you will see throughout this book. Theorists who view the world through different lenses not only study different things in different ways but are likely to disagree even when the same "facts" are set before them, because they will interpret those facts differently (P. H. Miller, 2010). This is the nature of science.

Theories also guide practice. As you have seen, each theory of human development represents a particular way of defining developmental issues and problems. Often, how you define a problem determines how you attempt to solve it. To illustrate, consider unwanted teenage pregnancy. How do you think major developmental theorists would explain it, and how do you think each would go about trying to reduce the rate of teenage pregnancy in our society? Application Box 2.1 offers some ideas and will serve, too, as a review of the theories.

You need not choose one favored developmental theory and reject others. Because different theories often highlight different aspects of development, one may be more relevant to a particular issue or to a particular age group than another. Many developmentalists today are theoretical **eclectics** who rely on many theories, recognizing that no major theory of human development can explain everything but that each has something to contribute to our understanding.

Checking Mastery

1. How have stands on the nature–nurture issue changed during the 20th century from (a) Freud to (b) Skinner to (c) Gottlieb?

2. Of the theorists discussed in this chapter, who is the only one with something specific to say about development during adulthood?

Making Connections

1. You have decided to become an eclectic and to take from each of the four major perspectives in this chapter (psychoanalytic, learning, cognitive developmental, and systems theory) only one truly great insight into human development. What four ideas would you choose, and why?

2. Think about the development of cats and the development of humans. Which of the theories in this chapter are most and least applicable to both species—and why?

What approaches might you consider to reduce the rate of unwanted pregnancy at the high school you attended?

Although teenage pregnancy and birth rates have decreased since 1990, when more than 1 in 10 females aged 15 to 19 became pregnant each year and more than half gave birth (Guttmacher Institute, 2006), they have been creeping up again recently and are much higher in the United States than in other Western nations (Sullivan/Anderson, 2009). Valued in many traditional societies, pregnancy during the teen years is generally discouraged in modern societies like ours. Although pregnancy sometimes mobilizes a young woman's support network and helps her focus on school and work, too often it interrupts her education, limits her job prospects, and leaves her living in poverty and raising a child by herself (Furstenberg, 2005; Hoffman & Maynard, 2008).

Why are there so many unplanned teenage pregnancies, and what might we as a society do to prevent them? Think about it, and then compare your analyses to those of our main developmental theorists.

Psychoanalytic Theory

Teenagers get pregnant because they experience intense emotional conflicts during the genital stage of psychosexual development, Freud might say. Their new sexual urges are anxiety-provoking and may reawaken the sexual conflicts of the phallic stage. Teenagers who engage in risky sex may not have strong enough egos (to analyze the consequences) or superegos (to arouse guilt) to keep their selfish ids in check.

Erikson might also wonder about unresolved conflicts from earlier stages of development but might attribute unwanted teen pregnancy primarily to the adolescent psychosocial conflict of identity versus role confusion. In Erikson's view, adolescents seek a sense of identity by experimenting with different roles and behaviors to see what suits them; they try drugs, dye their hair orange, join radical groups, change majors every semester, and yes, have sex. Some adolescents may also try to find an easy resolution to their role confusion by prematurely latching onto an identity as the other's boyfriend or girlfriend rather than doing the hard work of experimenting to find out who they are (Erikson, 1968).

Psychoanalytic theorists tend to locate the causes of problems within the person. They would want to identify and target for intervention teenagers who are experiencing especially difficult psychic conflicts. High-risk teenagers might then be treated through psychoanalysis aimed at helping them resolve their conflicts. Although the psychoanalytic approach might work with teenagers who are psychologically disturbed, most teenagers who become pregnant are not (Farber, 2003).

Piaget's Cognitive Developmental Theory

Cognitive limitations, failure to anticipate consequences, and lack of knowledge may all influence sexual decision making, Piaget would say. Adolescents who are not yet solidly into the stage of formal operations may not be able to think through the long-range consequences of their sexual behavior. And misconceptions (pun intended!) about sex and contraception are rampant among adolescents (Aarons & Jenkins, 2002). In one study of 13- to 15-year-olds, more than 60% did not know that urinating after sex will not prevent pregnancy (Carrera et al., 2000).

According to Jean Piaget's cognitive developmental perspective, the solution to teenage pregnancy would be improved sex education programs—programs that correct misconceptions, provide teenagers with accurate information and strategies for avoiding unwanted and unprotected sex, and help even teens who have not yet reached the formal operations stage to think through the consequences of their sexual decisions. Carefully designed and comprehensive sex education programs can indeed delay initiation of sex, decrease number of sexual partners, and increase contraception use (Franklin & Corcoran, 2000; Kirby & Laris, 2009). However, education alone is often not enough, so perhaps we need to consider solutions that locate the causes of teenage pregnancy in the environment rather than in the individual's psychological weaknesses or cognitive deficiencies.

Learning Theorists

Through classical conditioning, John Watson might argue, teenagers may learn to associate the very presence of a partner with the pleasurable sensations associated with sexual activity. And, as B. F. Skinner might observe,

teenagers probably have unprotected sex because having sex is reinforcing, whereas using contraceptives is not. Finally, Albert Bandura might note that if a male *believes* that using a condom will decrease his sexual enjoyment, his belief may decrease the chances that he and his partner will use protection. Bandura would also emphasize observational learning, noting that teens who are exposed to a lot of sexually explicit material on television and in other media are more sexually active than other teens (Brown et al., 2006) and more prone to be involved in pregnancies (Chandra et al., 2008).

Learning theorists believe that changing the environment will change the person. In support of this belief, it appears that one effective approach to teenage pregnancy prevention is to make contraceptives readily available to teens through health clinics and to teach them how to use them (Franklin & Corcoran, 2000). This approach reflects a Skinnerian philosophy of encouraging desired behavior by making it more reinforcing and less punishing. Albert Bandura's social cognitive theory suggests that it might also help to provide teenagers with more role models of responsible sexual behavior and fewer examples of irresponsible sexual behavior to help them learn that the consequences of safe sex are likely to be more desirable than the consequences of early parenthood (Unger, Molina, & Teran, 2000).

Gottlieb's Epigenetic Psychobiological Systems Theory

Finally, Gilbert Gottlieb would first place behavior in its evolutionary context: sexual behavior is adaptive, after all; it has allowed humans to reproduce themselves for centuries. He would also look for multiple, interacting causes, analyzing the ongoing interactions between developing adolescents (the activity of their genes, their neural activity, and their behavior are all rapidly changing) and the changing world in which they are developing (their physical, social, and cultural environment). He would expect bidirectional influences throughout the developmental system; for

example, he would not be surprised to learn that just as poor parent and peer relations can increase the likelihood of risky sexual behavior, risky sexual behavior can negatively affect parent and peer relations (Henrich et al., 2006)

Gottlieb might also ask whether teenagers' cultural environment is one that considers teenage pregnancy a normal step in development or a social problem; in some cultures, including some lower-income subcultures in the United States, early motherhood is viewed as adaptive and teenage pregnancy is common (Davies et al., 2003; Farber, 2003). He might also consider whether the school environment engages or alienates students and whether a teenager's family environment is supportive or stressful. Mainly, he would recognize that there is not *one* cause of teenage pregnancy; there is a whole system of interacting causes.

Systems theorists such as Gilbert Gottlieb would recommend comprehensive programs that attempt to change *both* the person and the environment—or really, to change the whole system of interacting influences on development (Gottlieb & Halpern, 2008). Quick fixes are unlikely to work. The solution may require more than changing sexual behavior; it may need to address teenagers' broader socioemotional needs (Allen, Seitz, & Apfel, 2007). The solution may also require changing the social context— for example, changing how adolescents and their parents, peers, and partners interact and enabling youth in all segments of society to perceive opportunities to succeed in life if they postpone parenthood and pursue their educations (Farber, 2003).

You can see, then, that the theoretical position one takes has a profound effect on how one attempts to optimize development. In all likelihood, multiple approaches will be needed to address complex problems such as unwanted teenage pregnancy—and to achieve the larger goal of understanding human development.

Chapter Summary

2.1. Developmental Theories and the Issues They Raise

- Theories organize and explain the facts of human development and should be internally consistent, falsifiable, and supported by data.
- The five major issues in the study of human development are the goodness and badness of human nature, nature and nurture, activity and passivity, continuity and discontinuity, and universality and context specificity.

2.2. Freud: Psychoanalytic Theory

- In Freud's psychoanalytic theory, humans are irrational beings primarily driven by inborn biological instincts of which they are largely unconscious. The personality is partitioned into the id, ego, and superego (which emerge in that order).
- Libido is rechanneled across five psychosexual stages—oral, anal, phallic, latent, and genital. Each stage involves psychic conflicts that can result in fixation at a stage, create the need for defense mechanisms such as repression and regression, and can have lasting effects on personality.
- Biological needs drive development, but parents affect a child's success in dealing with conflicts and can contribute to emotional problems, especially if they are overly punitive.
- Although Freud called attention to the unconscious, to early experiences in the family, and to emotional development, his theory is not easily falsifiable and many of its specifics lack support.

2.3. Erikson: Neo-Freudian Psychoanalytic Theory

- Compared with Freud, neo-Freudian Erik Erikson emphasized biological urges less and social influences more; emphasized id less and ego more; held a more optimistic view of human nature and people's ability to overcome early problems; and theorized about the whole life span.
- According to Erikson, development proceeds through eight psychosocial stages involving issues of trust, autonomy, initiative, industry, identity, intimacy, generativity, and integrity. Parents, peers, and the larger culture influence how conflicts are resolved.
- The theories of both Freud and Erikson have been influential but are difficult to test and tend to describe development better than they explain it.

2.4. Learning Theories

- Learning theorists maintain that humans change gradually and can develop in many directions depending on environmental influences.
- Behaviorist Watson focused on the role of Pavlov's classical conditioning in the learning of emotional responses, and Skinner highlighted operant conditioning and the roles of reinforcement in strengthening behavior and punishment in weakening behavior.
- Bandura's social cognitive theory emphasizes the importance of cognitive processes in learning; observational learning, as well as human agency, including self-efficacy; and reciprocal determinism among person, behavior, and environment.
- Learning theories are well supported and applicable across the life span, but they do not necessarily explain normal developmental changes and underemphasize biological influences on development.

2.5. Piaget: Cognitive Developmental Theory

- Piaget's cognitive developmental perspective holds that intelligence is an adaptive process in which humans create new understandings of the world through their active interactions with it (constructivism).
- The interaction of biological maturation and experience causes children to progress through four universal, invariant, and qualitatively different stages of thinking: sensorimotor, preoperational, concrete operational, and formal operational.
- Despite Piaget's immense influence, developmentalists question whether development is as stagelike and universal as he claimed.

2.6. Systems Theories

- Systems theories view development as the product of ongoing transactions and mutual influence between the individual and his environment.
- Ethology asks how species-specific behaviors may have evolved, and Gottlieb's epigenetic psychobiological systems perspective highlights mutual influences among genes, neural activity, behavior, and environment—both over the course of evolution and during the epigenetic process.
- Systems theories are incomplete, however, and do not provide a coherent picture of human development.

2.7. Theories in Perspective

- During the 20th century, stage theories such as Freud's emphasizing biological forces gave way to learning theories emphasizing environmental influences and then to Piaget's cognitive developmental theory, which emphasizes the interaction of nature and nurture.
- Piaget's concept of universal stages has given way to more complex systems theories such as those of Bronfenbrenner and Gottlieb, who expect developmental outcomes to be more or less probable depending on multiple factors.
- Theories influence both research and practice, and many developmentalists are theoretical eclectics.

Checking Mastery Answers

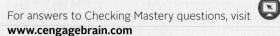

For answers to Checking Mastery questions, visit **www.cengagebrain.com**

Key Terms

Media Resources

Psychology CourseMate

Access an integrated eBook and chapter-specific learning
tools including flashcards, quizzes, videos, and more. Go to
www.cengagebrain.com

Jean Piaget Society

The Jean Piaget Society provides biographical information, links to other
Piaget resources on the web, and lists of suggested readings for those who
would like to learn more about Piaget's research and writings. To access,
see "web links" in Psychology CourseMate at www.cengagebrain.com

Sigmund Freud and the Freud Archives

A collection of links to resources related to Sigmund Freud and his
works. The list includes links to libraries, museums, and biographical
materials. To access, see "web links" in Psychology CourseMate at www
.cengagebrain.com

CengageNOW

www.cengagebrain.com
Go to www.cengagebrain.com to link to CengageNOW, your online
study tool. First take the Pre-Test for this chapter to get your Personalized
Study Plan, which will identify topics you need to review and direct you
to online resources. Then take the Post-Test to determine what concepts
you have mastered and what you still need work on.

Biological and Environmental Influences on Development

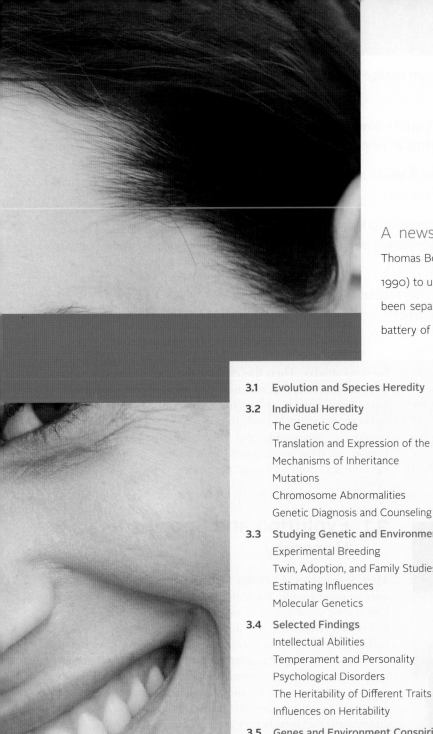
Odilon Dimier/PhotoAlto/Corbis

A newspaper story about Jim Lewis and Jim Springer inspired Thomas Bouchard Jr. and his associates (Bouchard, 1984; Bouchard et al., 1990) to undertake a study in which they reunited identical twins who had been separated soon after birth and asked them to complete a 50-hour battery of tests. Together after spending all but the first 4 weeks of their 39 years apart, Jim and Jim discovered that they had both married women named Linda—and then women named Betty. They named their first sons James Alan and James Allan, had dogs named Toy, and liked Miller Lite beer and Salem cigarettes.

Barbara Herbert and Daphne Goodship, also reunited after 39 years apart, both wore a beige dress and a brown velvet jacket when they met for the first time in London. They shared a habit of "squidging" (pushing up their noses), had fallen down the stairs at age 15, laughed more than anyone they knew, and never voted.

Identical twins Jessica and Rachel Wessell, despite their sharing the same genes, growing up together, and being close, are far from identical. One excels in math, the other in English. One has cerebral palsy and is in a wheelchair, possibly because of lack of oxygen to her brain at birth; her sister was in the marching band in high school (Helderman, 2003).

1. How do biological evolution and cultural evolution change the human species?

2. What do we inherit from our parents, what influences how genes are expressed, and what are the main mechanisms of inheritance?

3. How do researchers estimate the contributions of genes and environment to differences among us in development?

4. What are the contributions of genes and environment to individual differences in intellectual functioning, temperament and personality, and psychological disorders?

5. What is the significance of gene–environment interactions and gene–environment correlations in development?

Do we notice striking similarities between identical twins only because we are looking for them? Would we notice striking similarities between random pairs of people if we were looking for them? Do the similarities between twins we observe really occur because identical twins have identical genes, or is it because people treat individuals who look the same the same way? And how can we explain differences between individuals who have identical genes?

Identical twins share some remarkable similarities, even when separated early in life, but differ as well.

© Dennis Degnan/Corbis

Apparently the influence of genes on development must be taken seriously—but so must the influence of environment. How do nature and nurture, heredity and environment, contribute to the shaping of physical and psychological characteristics? That is the complex puzzle we grapple with in this chapter. Reading this chapter should increase your appreciation of genetic contributions to development, give you new insights into the importance of environmental influences, and most importantly reveal how nature and nurture work together to guide development. We invite you to take the short quiz in Engagement Box 3.1 to find out whether you come to this chapter with any misconceptions about genetic influence; the correct answers will become clear as you read and are provided in the box.

We begin with a brief look at ways in which genes make humans similar. Then the chapter turns to what each person inherits at conception and how this genetic endowment influences traits. Then it explores research findings on how genes and environment make individuals different from one another in intelligence, personality, and other important characteristics. Finally, we draw some general conclusions about heredity and environment from a life-span perspective.

3.1 Evolution and Species Heredity

Most descriptions of heredity focus on its role in creating differences among people. Some individuals inherit blue eyes, others brown eyes; some inherit blood type O, others blood type A or B. But isn't it remarkable that almost every one of us has two eyes and that we all have blood coursing through our veins? Virtually all of us also develop in similar ways at similar ages—walking and talking around 1 year, maturing sexually from 12 to 14, watching our skin wrinkle in our 40s and 50s. Such similarities in development and aging are a product of **species heredity**—the genetic endowment that members of a species have in common, including genes that influence maturation and aging processes. Humans can feel guilty but cannot fly; birds can fly but cannot feel guilty. Each species has a distinct heredity. Species heredity is one reason certain patterns of development and aging are universal.

To understand where we got our species heredity, we must turn to evolutionary theory. We introduced Gilbert Gottlieb's modern epigenetic psychobiological systems theory in Chapter 2. Here we go back to basics—to the path-blazing work of Charles Darwin (1809–1882; and see Dewsbury, 2009). Darwin's theory of evolution sought to explain how the characteristics of a species change over time and how new species evolve from earlier ones (Darwin, 1859). The theory has been and continues to be controversial, but it is well-supported; one evolutionary psychologist described it as

Genetic Influence: What Is Myth, What Is Reality?

Answer each of the following questions True or False to identify before reading this chapter any misconceptions about genetic influences you may have. Then watch for the correct answers and their explanations throughout the chapter and return to review the answers (printed upside down below).

__ 1. The most important reason that identical twins are similar psychologically is that they are treated similarly.

__ 2. The father, not the mother, determines the sex of a child.

__ 3. If a trait is highly influenced by genes, it is generally extremely hard for environmental forces to change it.

__ 4. Most important psychological traits like intelligence and extraversion are influenced by a single pair of genes.

__ 5. Environmental influences such as stress and diet can cause certain genes to become inactive.

__ 6. Homosexuality is genetically influenced, although environment plays an important role in its development too.

__ 7. Most childhood psychological disorders are caused by dysfunctional parenting rather than by genes.

__ 8. The contribution of genes to differences in intelligence typically decreases with age during childhood and adolescence as the effects of learning experiences become more evident.

__ 9. Biological siblings turn out about as similar in personality if they grow up apart as if they grow up in the same home.

__10. People's social attitudes and interests are influenced by environment rather than heredity.

Answers: 1. F (twins are treated similarly because they are so similar) 2. T (because sperm have either an X or a Y chromosome) 3. F (for example, genetically influenced IQ scores can be raised by enriched environments) 4. F (most are influenced by multiple genes) 5. T (environment influences gene expression) 6. T (genes and environment both contribute to homosexuality) 7. F (genes and unique or nonshared environment both play a role in psychological disorder; shared environment has little effect than their less intellectually inclined peers) 9. T (shared environment has little effect on personality) 10. T (attitudes and interests are modestly influenced by genetic makeup)

"as close to truth as any science is ever likely to get" (Barash, 2006, p. B10). Darwin's theory makes these main arguments:

1. *There is genetic variation in a species.* Some members of the species have different genes (and therefore different genetically influenced traits) than other members of the species do. If all members of the species were genetically identical, there would be no way for the genetic makeup of the species to change over time. Because novel genes arise through errors in cell division all the time (see later section on mutations), genetic variation is assured.

2. *Some genes aid adaptation more than others do.* Suppose that some members of a species have genes that make them strong and intelligent, whereas others have genes that make them weak and dull. Those with the genes for strength and intelligence would likely be better able to adapt to their environment—for example, to win fights for survival or to figure out how to obtain food.

3. *Genes that aid their bearers in adapting to their environment will be passed to future generations more frequently than genes that do not.* This is the principle of **natural selection**—the idea that nature "selects," or allows to survive and reproduce, those members of a species whose genes permit them to adapt to their environment. By contrast, genes that reduce the chances that an individual will survive and reproduce will become rarer over time because they will not be passed to many offspring. Through natural selection, then, the genetic makeup of a species slowly changes—and will continue to change as long as individuals with certain genetic makeups reproduce more frequently than individuals with other genetic makeups. Change can eventually

be sufficient to produce a new species. The result is what Darwin marveled at when he conducted observations in the Galapagos Islands: the incredible diversity of species on earth, each well adapted to its environment.

Now consider a classic example of evolution. H. B. D. Kettlewell (1959) carefully studied moths in England. There is genetic variation among moths that makes some dark and others light. By placing light and dark moths in several sites, Kettlewell found that in rural areas light-colored moths were most likely to survive but that in industrial areas dark moths were most likely to survive. The explanation? In rural areas, light-colored moths blend in well with light-colored trees and are therefore better protected from predators. Natural selection favors them. However, in sooty industrial areas, light-colored moths are easy pickings against the darkened trees, whereas dark moths are well disguised. When industry came to England, the proportion of dark moths increased; as pollution was brought under control in some highly industrialized areas, light-colored moths became more common again (Bishop & Cooke, 1975).

Notice, then, that evolution is not just about genes. It is about the *interaction between genes and environment*. A particular genetic makeup may enhance survival in one kind of environment but prove maladaptive in another. Which genes are advantageous, and therefore which become more common in future generations, depends on what environment a group experiences and what traits that environment demands. Genes that helped our ancestors hunt prey may not be as important in today's world as genes that help people master the Internet.

Checking Mastery

1. Biological evolution will not necessarily make humans better and better over time, but it *will* make them _____.
2. For natural selection to work and for a species to evolve, what must be true of the genetic makeup of a species?

Making Connections

1. Think of two human behaviors that you believe are so universal that they are probably built into our species heredity. Now, why might genes underlying these behaviors have been selected for in the course of evolution?
2. Think about people with a slow metabolism. Can you imagine an environment in which it would be beneficial to have a slow metabolism and another environment in which it could be harmful? What does this tell you about the "adaptiveness" of this human trait?

3.2 Individual Heredity

To understand how genes contribute to *differences* among humans, we must start at **conception**—the moment when an egg is fertilized by a sperm—look at the workings of genes, and then consider the mechanisms through which genes can influence traits.

The Genetic Code

A few hours after sperm penetrates ovum, the sperm cell begins to disintegrate, releasing its genetic material. The nucleus of the ovum releases its own genetic material, and a new cell nucleus is created from the genetic material provided by mother and father. This new cell, called a **zygote** and only the size of a pinhead, is the beginning of a human. Conception has occurred.

A sperm cell and an ovum each contribute 23 chromosomes to the zygote to give it 46 chromosomes total, organized into 23 pairs. **Chromosomes** are the threadlike bodies in the nucleus of each cell that are made up of genes, the basic units of heredity. Thus, of each chromosome pair—and of each pair of genes located on corresponding sites on a chromosome pair—one member came from the father and one member came from the mother.

Sperm and ova, unlike other cells, have only 23 chromosomes because they are produced through the specialized process of cell division called **meiosis**. At the start of this process, a reproductive cell in the ovaries of a female or the testes of a male that contains 46 chromosomes splits to form two 46-chromosome cells, and then these two cells each split again to form a total of four cells. In this last step, though, a special cell division process occurs in which each resulting cell receives only 23 chromosomes. The end product is one egg (and three nonfunctional cells that play no role in reproduction) in a female or four sperm in a male. Each resulting sperm cell or ovum thus has only one member of each of the parent's 23 pairs of chromosomes.

The single-celled zygote formed at conception becomes a multiple-celled organism through the more usual process

Each species has evolved through natural selection to be adapted to its environment.

© Stock Connection Distribution/Alamy

According to evolutionary theory, then, humans, like any other species, are as they are and develop as they do partly because they have a shared species heredity that evolved through natural selection. Solutions to problems faced by our ancestors thousands of years ago may have become built into the human genetic code. Not all human similarity is because of genes, however. Through the process of **cultural evolution**, we "inherit" from previous generations a characteristically human environment and tried and true ways of adapting to it, and we then learn to adjust to changing conditions and pass on what we learn to the next generation (Bjorklund & Pellegrini, 2002). This cultural evolution of the human species through learning and socialization of the young works much more quickly than biological evolution, especially in our age of globalization and instant messaging. In the end, the most significant legacy of biological evolution may be a powerful and very flexible brain that allows humans to learn from their experiences, to devise better ways of adapting to their environment and even changing it to suit them better, and, with the help of language, to share what they have learned (Bjorklund & Pellegrini, 2002; Ellis & Bjorklund, 2005).

TABLE 3.1 MITOSIS AND MEIOSIS COMPARED

	Mitosis	Meiosis in Males	Meiosis in Females
Begins	Conception	Puberty	Early in prenatal period when unripened ova form
Continues	Throughout life span	Throughout adolescence and adulthood	Through reproductive years; an ovum ripens each month of the menstrual cycle
Produces	Two identical daughter cells, each with 46 chromosomes like its parent	Four sperm, each with 23 chromosomes	One ovum and 3 nonfunctional polar bodies, each with 23 chromosomes
Accomplishes	Growth of human from fertilized egg, renewal of the body's cells	Formation of male reproductive cells	Formation of female reproductive cells

of cell division, **mitosis**. During mitosis, a cell (and each of its 46 chromosomes) divides to produce two identical cells, each containing the same 46 chromosomes. As the zygote moves through the fallopian tube toward its prenatal home in the uterus, it first divides into two cells; the two then become four, the four become eight, and so on, all through mitosis. Except for sperm and ova, all normal human cells contain copies of the 46 chromosomes provided at conception (● **Table 3.1**). Mitosis continues throughout life, creating new cells that enable us to grow and replacing old cells that are damaged.

Both members of a chromosome pair influence the same characteristics. Each chromosome consists of strands of deoxyribonucleic acid (**DNA**), the double helix molecule whose chemical code is our genetic endowment. DNA is made up of sequences of the chemicals A (adenine), C (cytosine), G (guanine), and T (thymine). Some of these sequences are functional units called genes (● **Figure 3.1**). Geneticists used to think humans had about 100,000 genes, but the actual number is more like 20,000–25,000 (International Human Genome Sequencing Consortium, 2004). Each gene, of which there can be several

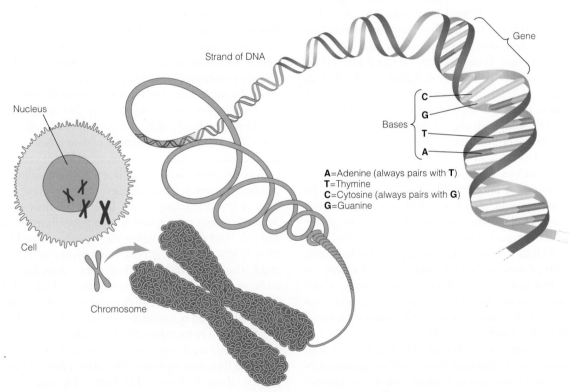

■ **FIGURE 3.1** The chromosomes in each cell consist of strands of DNA made up of sequences of the bases A, T, C, and G, some of which are functional units called genes. SOURCE: Adapted from *For DNA, a defining moment: With code revealed, challenge will be to find its meaning and uses. The Washington Post*, p. A16. Copyright © 2000 The Washington Post. All rights reserved. Reprinted by permission.

variants or **alleles**, provides instructions that lead to the production of particular proteins, the building blocks of all bodily tissues and of essential substances such as hormones, neurotransmitters, and enzymes (Rutter, Moffitt, & Caspi, 2006).

The Human Genome Project

Through the federally funded **Human Genome Project**, completed in 2003, researchers mapped the sequence of the chemical units or "letters" that make up the strands of DNA in a full set of human chromosomes (Weiss, 2003b). The raw material analyzed was DNA samples from a few humans of diverse racial backgrounds. The drudgery of this monstrous task was done by supercomputers and robots the size of small cars working alongside human technicians.

It is estimated that the human genome has 3.1 billion of the chemical constituents A, C, G, and T. However, it turns out that only about 2% of the human genome consists of what has traditionally been defined as genes: stretches of DNA that are transcribed into RNA, which then serves as a template for the production of particular proteins (Plomin & Davis, 2009). The remaining stretches of DNA were at first called "junk DNA," but it soon became clear that they are not junk at all—they play critical roles in regulating the activity of the protein-producing genes. It is now believed that genetic researchers got it wrong by focusing so much on the 2% of DNA (the protein-building genes) and should pay much more attention to the 98% and its regulatory functions (Plomin & Davis, 2009).

The Human Genome Project and the massive genome analysis projects that have followed it are yielding astounding new discoveries like this every year. The International HapMap Project, for example, described the genetic similarities and differences among 270 people from a variety of racial and ethnic groups around the world (Turnpenny & Ellard, 2005). It turns out that about 999 of 1000 base chemicals are identical in all humans; it is the remaining 1 of 1000 that makes us different.

Analysis of DNA samples is also shedding light on evolution. Analysis of the genome of the chimpanzee reveals that we share the large majority of our genes with other primates (Chimpanzee Sequencing and Analysis Consortium, 2005), and analysis of DNA from the bones of ancestors like the Neanderthals who lived 40,000 years ago is helping researchers piece together our family tree (Green et al., 2006). Analyses of DNA from groups around the world has revealed gene alleles or variants that have evolved in recent centuries, most likely in response to changes in the environments of modern human populations. A classic example is alleles that make people tolerate lactose in milk, which spread quite rapidly among Europeans as dairy farming became common, presumably because tolerating milk enhanced survival (McCabe & McCabe; Voight et al., 2006).

Through such studies, researchers are able to test in new ways some of the predictions of Darwin's theory and are gaining new insights into how the human species evolved, how it is unique as a species, and how humans are similar to and different from one another. As James Watson, codiscoverer of the double helix structure of DNA, said about the Human Genome Project, "We have the book, and now we've got to learn how to read it" (Weiss & Gillis, 2000, p. A12). There's no telling where it will all lead: In 2010, Craig Venter, one of the leaders of the effort to sequence the human genome, and his colleagues were able to apply their knowledge of gene sequencing to create artificial life (Gibson et al., 2010). They fabricated a computer-designed genome for a simple bacterium from the base chemicals A, C, G, and T and implanted it in the hollowed out cell of a different bacterium (yes, that was cheating a bit, but it proved necessary to make the human-designed genome kick into action). The result was a new, functioning bacterial cell that was able to multiply in the laboratory.

Genetic Uniqueness and Relatedness

To understand how people are both different from and like others genetically, consider that when a pair of parental chromosomes separates during meiosis, which of the two chromosomes will end up in a particular sperm or ovum is a matter of chance. And, because each chromosome pair separates independently of all other pairs, and because each reproductive cell contains 23 pairs of chromosomes, a single parent can produce 2^{23}—more than 8 million—different sperm or ova. Any couple could theoretically have at least 64 trillion babies without producing 2 children with identical genes.

The genetic uniqueness of children of the same parents is even greater than this because of a quirk of meiosis known as **crossing over**. When pairs of chromosomes line up before they separate, they cross each other and parts of them are exchanged, much as if you were to exchange a couple of fingers with a friend at the end of a handshake. Crossing over increases even more the number of distinct sperm or ova that an individual can produce. In short, it is incredibly unlikely that there ever was or ever will be another human exactly like you genetically. The one exception is **identical twins** (or identical triplets, and so on), also called monozygotic twins because they result when one fertilized ovum divides to form two or more genetically identical individuals. This happens in about 1 of every 250 births (Segal, 2005).

How genetically alike are parent and child or brother and sister? You and either your mother or your father have 50% of your genes in common because you received half of your chromosomes (and genes) from each parent. But if you have followed our mathematics, you will see that siblings may have many genes in common or few depending on the luck of the draw during meiosis. Because siblings receive half of their genes from the same mother and half from the same father, their genetic resemblance to each other is 50%, the same genetic resemblance as that of parent and child. The critical difference is that they share half of their genes *on the average*; some siblings share more and others fewer. Indeed, we have all known some siblings who are almost like twins and others who could not be more different if they tried.

Fraternal twins (also called dizygotic twins because two eggs are involved) result when two ova are released at approximately the same time and each is fertilized by a different sperm, as happens in about 1 of every 125 births (Plomin, 1990). Fraternal twins are no more alike genetically than brothers and sisters born at different times and can be of different sexes. Fraternal twins tend to run in families and have become more common in recent years because more couples are taking fertility drugs and undergoing in vitro fertilization (Segal, 2005).

Grandparent and grandchild, aunt or uncle and niece or nephew, and half brothers and half sisters have 25% of their genes in common on average. Thus, everyone except an identical twin is genetically unique, but each person also shares genes with kin that contribute to family resemblances.

Determination of Sex

Of the 23 pairs of chromosomes that each individual inherits, 22 (called *autosomes*) are similar in males and females. The chromosomes of the 23rd pair are the sex chromosomes. A male child has one long chromosome called an **X chromosome** and a short, stubby companion with far fewer genes called a **Y chromosome**. Females have two X chromosomes. The photos on this page show male and female chromosomes that have been photographed through a powerful microscope, then arranged in pairs and rephotographed in a pattern called a **karyotype** that allows their number and form to be studied.

Thanks to the Human Genome Project, we now know a good deal about the composition of X and Y chromosomes. Each X chromosome has almost 1100 genes, compared with only about 80 on a Y chromosome, many of which are involved in the production of sperm (Brown, 2005). It is now understood that most of the genes on one or the other of a female's two X chromosomes are normally inactivated early in the prenatal period and remain inactive in cells subsequently produced through mitosis (Ross et al., 2005).

Because a mother has only X chromosomes and a father's sperm cell has either an X chromosome or a Y chromosome (depending on which sex chromosome a sperm receives during meiosis), it is the father who determines a child's gender. If an ovum with its one X chromosome is fertilized by a sperm bearing a Y chromosome, the product is an XY zygote—a genetic male. A gene on the Y chromosome then sets in motion the biological events that result in male sexual development (Hawley & Mori,

1999; and see Chapter 12). If a sperm carrying an X chromosome reaches the ovum first, the result is an XX zygote—a genetic female. Perhaps if these facts had been known in earlier eras, women would not have been criticized, tortured, divorced, and even beheaded for failing to bear male heirs.

So a genetically unique boy or girl has roughly 20,000–25,000 protein-building genes and a lot of regulatory DNA on 46 chromosomes arranged in 23 pairs. How do these genes influence the individual's characteristics and development? It is still a mystery, but knowledge is increasing by leaps and bounds.

Translation and Expression of the Genetic Code

One does not have to understand cell biology to appreciate that environmental factors help determine which genetic potentials are translated into physical and psychological realities and which are not. Consider the genes that influence height. Some people inherit genes calling for exceptional height, and others inherit genes calling for a short stature. But **genotype**, the genetic makeup a person inherits, is different from **phenotype**, the characteristic or trait the person eventually has (for example, a height of 5 feet 8 inches). An individual whose genotype calls for exceptional height may or may not be tall. Indeed, a child who is severely malnourished from the prenatal period onward may have the genetic potential to be a basketball center but may end up too short to make the team. Environmental influences combine with genetic influences to determine how a particular genotype is translated into a particular phenotype—the way a person looks, thinks, feels, or behaves.

As you have seen, genes provide instructions for development by calling for the production of chemical substances. For example, genes set in motion a process that lays a pigment called *melanin* in the iris of the eye. Some people's genes call for much of this pigment, and the result is brown eyes; other people's genes

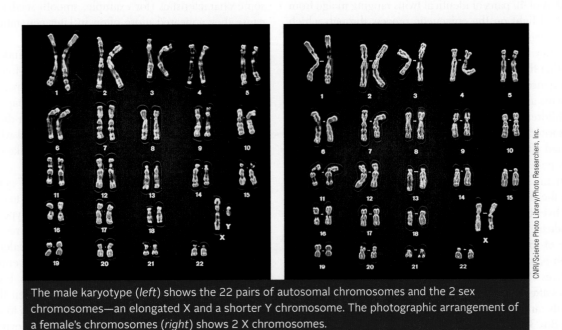

CNRI/Science Photo Library/Photo Researchers, Inc.

The male karyotype (*left*) shows the 22 pairs of autosomal chromosomes and the 2 sex chromosomes—an elongated X and a shorter Y chromosome. The photographic arrangement of a female's chromosomes (*right*) shows 2 X chromosomes.

call for less of it, and the result is blue eyes. Genetically coded proteins also guide the formation of cells that become neurons in the brain, influencing potential intelligence and personality.

But genes both influence and are influenced by the biochemical environment surrounding them during development, just as Gottlieb's epigenetic psychobiological systems theory emphasizes (Gottlieb, 2002). During embryonic development, a particular cell can become part of an eyeball or part of a kneecap depending on what cells are next to it and what they are doing. You should therefore think of the genetic "code" as written in erasable pencil rather than in indelible ink. Genes do not determine anything; rather, genes and environment coact to influence development and behavior throughout the life span (Johnston, 2008). A multitude of environmental factors—not only in the womb but throughout the life span—influence which genes are activated when (Gottesman & Hanson, 2005). Because all of a person's cells have the same genes on the same chromosomes, what makes brain, blood, and other cells different from each other is not what genes they contain but which of those genes are *expressed*.

Gene expression is the activation of particular genes in particular cells of the body at particular times; only if a gene is "turned on" is it influential. Gene expression, then, is what ultimately influences our traits. Gene expression is guided in part by genetic influences such as the action of regulatory DNA, but great interest is now being taken in the discovery that gene expression can also be affected by environmental factors such as diet, stress, toxins, and even early parenting (Champagne & Mashoodh, 2009; Zhang & Meaney, 2010).

How, despite having identical genes, can one identical twin develop schizophrenia, autism, or another significant disorder while the other does not? Environment has to be the answer, but it turns out that the story is more complicated and may involve genes too. Mario Fraga and his colleagues (2005) suspected that the answer might lie partly in gene expression—in which genes are turned on or off in each twin. They conducted analyses of the DNA and RNA of 40 pairs of identical twins ranging in age from 3 to 74 to shed light on the epigenetic process through which genetic and environmental influences translate genotype into phenotype. They found that older twin pairs were more different from each other than younger twin pairs in the patterns of activation of their genes. For example, a close analysis of the RNA of 3-year-old twins and 50-year-old twins showed that the genes of the young children had almost identical patterns of expression. If a gene was turned on in one twin, it was turned on in the other; if it was turned off in one twin, it was turned off in the other. By contrast, the genes of the 50-year-old twins were expressed very differently; many genes that were activated in one twin were deactivated in the other. What's more, those twins who had spent less of their lives together and had led different lifestyles (for example, as indicated by their eating habits, levels of physical activity, and use of tobacco, alcohol, drugs) showed greater differences in their patterns of gene activation than did twins who had led similar lives. This and other studies tell us that environmental influences affect gene expression, which in turn influences a person's traits and behavior (Zhang & Meaney, 2010). As Exploration Box 3.1 reveals, researchers have been making more amazing discoveries recently about what are now called epigenetic effects—ways in which environmental influences alter gene expression and, in turn, developmental outcomes.

In the end, no one completely understands the remarkable epigenetic process that transforms a single cell with its genetic endowment into millions of diverse cells—blood cells, nerve cells, skin cells, and so on—all organized into a living, behaving human. Nor do we fully understand how genes help bring about certain developments at certain points in the life span. Yet it is becoming clearer that genes are active players along with the environment in the developmental process throughout the life span and that having this gene or that gene may prove to be less important than which genes are expressed.

Mechanisms of Inheritance

Another way to approach the question of how genes influence human development is to consider the major mechanisms of inheritance—how parents' genes influence their children's traits. There are three main mechanisms of inheritance: single gene-pair inheritance, sex-linked inheritance, and polygenic (or multiple gene) inheritance.

Single Gene-Pair Inheritance

Through **single gene-pair inheritance**, each of thousands of human characteristics are influenced by only one pair of genes—one from the mother, one from the father (Turnpenny & Ellard, 2005). Although he knew nothing of genes, the 19th-century monk Gregor Mendel contributed greatly to our knowledge of single gene-pair inheritance and earned his place as the father of genetics by cross-breeding different strains of peas and carefully observing the outcomes (Henig, 2000). He noticed a predictable pattern to the way in which two alternative characteristics would appear in the offspring of cross-breedings—for example, smooth seeds or wrinkled seeds, green pods or yellow pods. He called some characteristics (for example, smooth seeds) *dominant* because they appeared more often in later generations than their opposite traits, which he called *recessive*.

As an illustration of the principles of Mendelian heredity, consider the remarkable fact that about three-fourths of us can curl our tongues upward into a tubelike shape, whereas one-fourth of us cannot. (We have no idea why.) It happens that there is a gene associated with tongue curling; it is a **dominant gene**, meaning that it will be expressed when paired with a **recessive gene**, a weaker gene that can be dominated (like one associated with the absence of tongue-curling ability).

The person who inherits one "tongue-curl" gene (label it U) and one "no-curl" gene (call it -) would be able to curl his tongue (that is, would have a tongue-curling phenotype) because the dominant tongue-curl gene overpowers the recessive no-curl gene. Using ■**Figure 3.2** as a guide, you can calculate the odds that parents with various genotypes for tongue curling will have children who can or cannot curl their tongues. Each cell of the figure shows the four possible types of children that can result when a father contributes one of his two genes to a sperm and a mother contributes one of her two genes to an ovum and a child is conceived.

Early Experience and Gene Expression

Until fairly recently, genetic scientists were far more focused on which genes people have than on which are turned on or off, but now there is great excitement about evidence that experience affects gene expression and, in turn, development. Michael Meaney, Francis Champagne, and their colleagues have shown through a series of elegant studies how the early experience of rat pups can affect the activity of their genes and, in turn, not only their development but that of their offspring (see Champagne & Mashoodh, 2009; Francis et al., 1999; Kaffman & Meaney, 2007).

If the mothers of rat pups are nurturant—if they regularly lick and groom their pups and nurse them with an arched back in the first week of life—the pups grow up able to handle stress well. If rat moms are neglectful and do not provide this tender tactile care, rat pups become timid and easily stressed adults. But why? The differences in pups' reactivity to stress were not due to heredity. Raising the pups of nurturant mothers with neglectful mothers and the pups of neglectful mothers with nurturant mothers demonstrated that it was rearing that mattered, not heredity. Rats turned out to be stress resistant if raised by nurturant mothers and stress reactive if raised by neglectful mothers, regardless of their biological parentage.

But these styles of responding to stress also were not acquired through learning. Rather, Meaney and his colleagues have found that early licking and grooming affect the development of the stress response system through their effects on gene expression. In properly licked and groomed pups, genes in the hippocampus of the brain that influence the regulation of stress hormones stay turned on, whereas in neglected pups these genes turn off, making the hippocampus less able to tone down stress hormone responses. Early care therefore has a lasting effect on development by altering gene expression in specific cells of the brain.

Too little licking and grooming in infancy also turns off genes that affect sensitivity to female hormones and later maternal behavior. As a result, daughters of neglectful mothers turn into neglectful mothers themselves. Here, then, we see epigenetic (rather than genetic) transmission of mothering styles across generations. The DNA sequence itself is not altered; rather, the early experience of neglected pups results in molecular codings attached to certain genes in their brains, codings that interfere with the transcription of DNA into RNA and the expression of these genes. These epigenetic codings on top of the DNA code are replicated in new cells produced through mitosis—and, remarkably, are passed on to offspring at conception.

What has been discovered, then, is no less than a whole new way in which parents influence their children besides genetic inheritance and social learning: *environmental influence on gene expression*. As a result, there is now keen interest in better understanding influences on and implications of gene expression. It appears, for example, that some diseases and disorders arise not because a normal gene is missing but because it is not expressed normally, possibly because of disruptions in epigenesis caused by a poor diet, toxins, or stressful experiences (Isles & Wilkinson, 2008). And there's now suggestive evidence that epigenetic effects on gene expression may help explain the transmission from mother to daughter of abusive parenting among both monkeys (Maestripieri, Lindell, & Higley, 2007) and humans (McGowan et al., 2009). But the cycle of neglect and abuse can be broken: Meaney and his colleagues find that negative epigenetic effects on stress response and parenting style can be reversed if young animals are raised by sensitive, nurturing mothers or if drugs that affect gene expression in critical parts of the brain are administered (McGowan, Meaney, & Szyf, 2008; Zhang & Meaney, 2010).

Human parents may not lick and groom their babies, but chances are that snuggling them sets in motion a different developmental process than abusing or neglecting them does. Meanwhile, understanding human development has become much more complicated now that we know more about gene expression. The challenge is to better understand which of a person's genes are turned on or off, and when, during development, and what genetic and environmental factors are shaping these patterns of gene expression.

If a father with the genotype UU (a tongue curler) and a mother with the genotype - - (a non–tongue curler) have children, each child they produce will have one dominant gene for tongue curling and one recessive gene for a lack of tongue curling (genotype U-) and each will be a tongue curler because the tongue-curl gene will rule. You can say that this couple has a 100% chance of having a tongue-curling child. Notice that two different genotypes, UU and U-, both produce the same phenotype: an acrobatic tongue.

A tongue-curling man and a tongue-curling woman can surprise everyone and have a child who lacks this amazing talent. These two parents both must have the U- genotype. If the father's recessive gene and the mother's recessive gene happen to unite in the zygote, they will have a non–tongue-curling child (with the genotype - -). The chances are 25%—one out of four—that this couple will have such a child. Of course, the laws of conception are much like the laws of cards. This couple could beat the odds and have a whole family of non–tongue-curling children, or they could have none. Because people who cannot curl their tongues must have the - - genotype, two non–tongue-curling parents will have only non–tongue-curling (- -) children.

● **Table 3.2** lists several other examples of dominant and recessive traits associated with single gene-pair inheritance. In some cases, a dominant gene incompletely dominates a recessive partner gene and the result is a new trait that blends the parents' traits—as when crossing red and white flowers produces pink

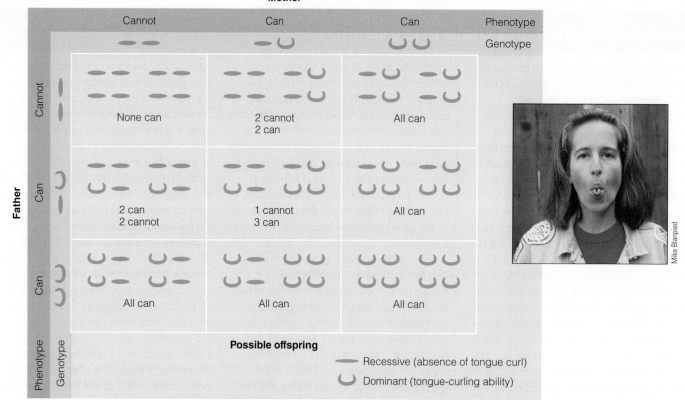

■ **FIGURE 3.2** Can you curl your tongue as shown? Tongue-curling ability is determined by a dominant gene; if you can curl your tongue, then either your mother or your father can, because one of them must have the dominant gene. All possibilities are shown in the figure; each of the nine boxes shows the gene combinations of the four possible children a particular mother and a particular father can have.

● **TABLE 3.2 EXAMPLES OF TRAITS INFLUENCED BY DOMINANT AND RECESSIVE GENES**

Dominant Trait	Recessive Trait	Dominant Trait	Recessive Trait
Brown eyes	Gray, green, hazel, or blue eyes	Pigmented skin	Albinism
Dark hair	Blond hair	Type A blood	Type O blood
Nonred hair	Red hair	Type B blood	Type O blood
Curly hair	Straight hair	Normal hearing	Congenital deafness
Normal vision	Nearsightedness	Normal blood cells	Sickle-cell disease*
Farsightedness	Normal vision	Huntington's disease*	Normal physiology
Roman nose	Straight nose	Normal physiology	Cystic fibrosis*
Broad lips	Thin lips	Normal physiology	Phenylketonuria (PKU)*
Extra digits	Five digits	Normal physiology	Tay-Sachs disease*
Double jointed	Normal joints		

*Condition described in this chapter.
SOURCES: Burns & Bottino, 1989; McKusick, 1990.

ones or when dark-skinned and light-skinned parents have a child with light brown skin. This phenomenon is called **incomplete dominance**. In other cases, two genes influence a trait but each is expressed in the product, as when crossing red and white flowers produces flowers with red and white streaks—a phenomenon called **codominance**. For example, an AB blood type is a mix of A and B blood types. Mendel got it mostly right, but single gene-pair inheritance is a bit more complex than he realized.

Sex-Linked Inheritance

Sex-linked characteristics are influenced by single genes located on the sex chromosomes rather than on the other 22 pairs of chromosomes. Indeed, you could say *X-linked* rather than *sex-linked* because most of these attributes are associated with genes located only on X chromosomes.

Why do far more males than females display red–green color blindness? The inability to distinguish red from green is caused by a recessive gene that appears only on X chromosomes. Recall that Y chromosomes are shorter than X chromosomes and have fewer genes. If a boy inherits the recessive color-blindness gene on the X chromosome his mother provides to him, there is no color-vision gene on his Y chromosome that could dominate the color-blindness gene. He will be color blind. By contrast, a girl who inherits the gene usually has a normal color-vision gene on her other X chromosome that can dominate the color-blindness gene (■ **Figure 3.3**). She would have to inherit two of the recessive color-blindness genes (one from each parent) to be color blind. **Hemophilia**, a deficiency in the blood's ability to clot, is also far more common among males than females because it is a sex-linked disorder associated with a recessive gene on X chromosomes.

Polygenic Inheritance

So far we have considered only the influence of single genes or gene pairs on human traits. Every week, it seems, we read in the newspaper that researchers have identified "the gene" for cancer, happiness, or some other human trait. However, most important human characteristics are **polygenic traits**; they are influenced by multiple pairs of genes, interacting with environmental factors, rather than by a single pair of genes. Examples of polygenic traits include height, weight, intelligence, personality, and susceptibility to cancer and depression.

When a trait like intelligence is influenced by multiple genes, many degrees of it are possible, depending on how many of the genes associated with the trait individuals inherit. The trait tends to be distributed in the population according to the familiar bell-shaped or normal curve. Many people are near the mean of the distribution; fewer are at the extremes. This is in fact the way intelligence and most other measurable human traits are distributed. At this point, we do not know how many gene pairs influence intelligence or other polygenic traits. What we can say is that unknown and probably large numbers of genes, interacting with environmental forces, create a range of individual differences in most important human traits (Plomin & Davis, 2009).

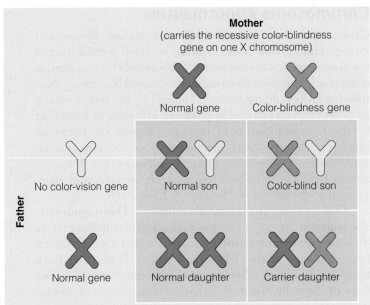

■ **FIGURE 3.3** The workings of sex-linked inheritance in red–green color blindness.

Mutations

We have described the three major mechanisms by which the genes inherited at conception influence traits: single gene-pair, sex-linked, and polygenic inheritance. Occasionally, however, a new gene appears as if out of nowhere; it is not passed on by a parent. A **mutation** is a change in the structure or arrangement of one or more genes that produces a new phenotype. For example, experts believe that the recessive gene for the sex-linked disorder hemophilia was a mutation first introduced into the royal families of Europe by Queen Victoria. New cases of hemophilia, then, can be caused by either sex-linked inheritance or spontaneous mutations. The odds that mutations will occur are increased by environmental hazards such as radiation and toxic industrial waste, but most mutations are just spontaneous errors in cell division (Turnpenny & Ellard, 2005).

Some mutations have beneficial effects and become more common in a population over time through natural selection. A good example is the gene associated with **sickle-cell disease**, a blood disease common among African Americans in which red blood cells take on a sickle shape (described in more detail later in the chapter). It probably arose as a mutation but became more prevalent in Africa, Central America, and other tropical areas over many generations because having one of the recessive sickle-cell genes protected people from malaria and allowed them to live longer and produce more children than people without the protective gene. Unfortunately, the sickle-cell gene does more harm than good where malaria is no longer a problem; carriers of the gene can be affected by some of the pain and difficulty breathing that affects individuals with sickle-cell disease. Thus, mutations can be either beneficial or harmful, depending on their nature and on the environment in which their bearers live.

Chromosome Abnormalities

Genetic endowment can also influence human development through **chromosome abnormalities**, in which a child receives too many or too few chromosomes (or abnormal chromosomes) at conception. Most such abnormalities are caused by errors in chromosome division during meiosis. Through an accident of nature, an ovum or sperm cell may be produced with more or fewer than the usual 23 chromosomes. In most cases, a zygote with the wrong number of chromosomes is spontaneously aborted; chromosome abnormalities are the main cause of pregnancy loss. However, around 1 child in 160 is born with more or, rarely, fewer chromosomes than the normal 46 (Simpson & Elias, 2003).

One familiar chromosome abnormality is **Down syndrome**, also known as *trisomy 21* because it is associated with three rather than two 21st chromosomes. Children with Down syndrome have distinctive eyelid folds, short stubby limbs, and thick tongues. Their levels of intellectual functioning vary widely, but they are typically classified as having some degree of mental retardation and therefore develop and learn at a slower pace than most children, although they can be helped along considerably through good special education and vocational programs (Roizen & Patterson, 2003). In some parts of the world, over half die in infancy, most often because of heart defects (Christianson, Howson, & Modell, 2006). However, in the United States and other wealthy nations, many people with Down syndrome are now living into middle age, when many of them develop signs of premature aging, including Alzheimer's disease, the degenerative brain disease that in some cases is associated with a gene on Chromosome 21 (Berney, 2009; and see Chapter 16).

What determines who has a child with Down syndrome and who does not? Chance, partly. The errors in meiosis responsible for Down syndrome can occur in any mother—or father. However, the chances of chromosome abnormalities and other birth defects increase as a parent's age increases (Cleary-Goldman et al., 2005). The chances of having a baby with Down syndrome are about 13 births in 10,000, or 1 birth in 733, in the United States (Centers for Disease Control and Prevention, 2006a). The odds increase with the mother's age, especially from about age 35 on (■ **Figure 3.4**). A father's age also affects the odds of having a child with Down syndrome, especially if his partner is at least 35 years old. Indeed, couples older than 40 have about 6 times the risk of having a child with Down syndrome as couples younger than 35 (Fisch et al., 2003).

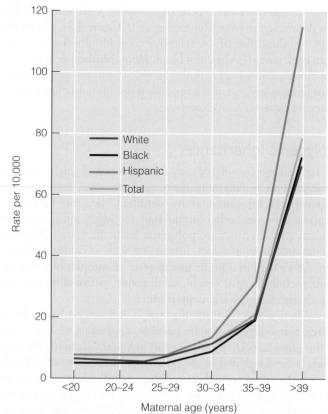

Children with Down syndrome have distinctive eyelid folds, short limbs, and thick tongues.

■ **FIGURE 3.4** The rate of Down syndrome births increases steeply as the mother's age increases. Source: "Down Syndrome Prevalence at Birth" (1994).

Why? As they age, ova and sperm are increasingly likely to be abnormal. Older mothers and fathers are also more likely than younger ones to have been exposed to environmental hazards that can damage ova or sperm—radiation, drugs, chemicals, viruses (Strigini et al., 1990). Finally, older mothers' bodies may be less likely than young mothers' bodies to spontaneously abort abnormal fetuses (Fisch et al., 2003). For a host of reasons, then, the fact that many adults today are delaying parenthood until their 30s or 40s is likely to translate into increased numbers of chromosome abnormalities.

Most other chromosome abnormalities involve a child's receiving either too many or too few sex chromosomes. Like Down syndrome, these sex chromosome abnormalities can be attributed mainly to errors in meiosis, errors that become increasingly likely in older parents and parents whose chromosomes have been damaged by environmental hazards (Wodrich, 2006). One example is **Turner syndrome**, in which a female (about 1 in 3000) is born with a single X chromosome (XO). These girls remain small and often have stubby fingers and toes, a "webbed" neck, and underdeveloped breasts. They are unable to reproduce, typically favor traditionally feminine activities, and often have lower-than-average spatial and mathematical reasoning abilities (Downey et al., 1991).

Another example is **Klinefelter syndrome**, in which a male (1 in 200) is born with one or more extra X chromosomes (XXY). Klinefelter males tend to be tall and generally masculine in appearance, but they are sterile and at puberty develop feminine sex characteristics such as enlarged breasts. Most have normal intelligence test scores, but many are below average in language skills and school achievement (Mandoki et al., 1991).

Finally, **fragile X syndrome** is worth noting because it is the most common hereditary cause of mental retardation (McConkie-Rosell et al., 2005; Wallis, 2008). In this condition, one arm of the X chromosome is only barely connected to the rest of the chromosome and looks as if it is about to break off— hence the term *fragile* (see photo below). Fragile X syndrome causes mental retardation or some degree of cognitive impair-

In fragile X syndrome, the X chromosome looks as though it might break apart, as illustrated by the purplish chromosome on the lower left.

ment in most affected persons and autism in some as well. The condition is usually not diagnosable until around age 3 unless parents know that fragile X runs in the family and ask for genetic testing so that their child can begin to receive early intervention services (Roberts et al., 2009).

The abnormal X chromosome is caused by sex-linked inheritance and therefore is more common among males than females. The affected individual has too many repeats or duplications of a sequence of three letters in the genetic code, and the result is lack of a protein important in keeping the proliferation of synapses, or connections between neurons of the brain, from spinning out of control (Wallis, 2008; O'Donnell & Warren, 2002). The number of repeats of the DNA segment responsible for fragile X syndrome increases from generation to generation in families with the sex-linked gene responsible for fragile X syndrome, causing more serious mental retardation in later generations of an affected family.

It has been discovered that family members who carry the gene but have less than the number of repeats of the gene sequence required for full-blown fragile X syndrome face risks of their own. Grandfathers and other male relatives of children with fragile X sometimes develop a syndrome involving tremors, balance problems, and intellectual decline in middle age, and mothers and other female relatives may experience problems with infertility and early menopause (Wallis, 2008; and see the website of the Fragile X Foundation at: www.fragilex.org).

Genetic Diagnosis and Counseling

Although you will be reassured to hear that 97% or more of babies will *not* be born with major birth defects, diseases and disorders associated with a single gene or pair of genes, polygene disorders, and chromosome abnormalities can profoundly affect human development (Brown, 2003; Simpson & Elias, 2003). **Genetic counseling** is a service that "helps people understand and adapt to the medical, psychological, and familial implications of genetic contributions to disease" (Resta et al., 2006, p. 77). Genetic counselors provide information on the nature, likelihood, effects, and treatment of genetically based diseases and disorders to people who suspect or learn that they or their unborn children are at risk. They provide the information their clients need to make decisions but are careful not to make the decisions for them (Turnpenny & Ellard, 2005).

Thanks to the Human Genome Project and related research, today's genetic counselors have access to more information than ever about genetic defects and can quickly and quite inexpensively collect and analyze DNA samples collected by swabbing the inside of people's cheeks. Although we advise caution, you can even order a test kit and mail in a sample of your DNA to be analyzed—for a price, of course—to determine whether you have any of a number of genes associated with diseases or other characteristics (Boodman, 2006; Weiss, 2008). To illustrate issues in genetic diagnosis and counseling and the workings of two important genetic disorders, we focus on sickle-cell disease and Huntington's disease. Several other genetic dis-

Disease	Description	Genetic Mechanism	Diagnosis and Treatment
Cystic fibrosis	Glandular problem results in mucus buildup in lungs that makes breathing difficult and shortens life; common among Caucasians	Recessive gene pair; carriers were protected from epidemics of diarrhea in Europe	DNA test can identify most carriers, but so many mutations are possible that the tests for all are not feasible. Hours of physical therapy and antibiotics delivered by aerosol spray to keep lungs clear can prolong life, and experimental gene therapy has had some success
Phenylketonuria (PKU)	Lack of enzyme needed to metabolize phenylalanine in milk and many other foods results in conversion of phenylalanine into an acid that attacks the nervous system and causes mental retardation	Recessive gene pair	Routinely screened for with a blood test at birth; special diet low in phenylalanine prevents brain damage
Hemophilia	Deficiency in blood's ability to clot; more common in males than in females	Sex-linked inheritance (gene on X chromosome)	DNA analysis of cells obtained through chorionic villus sampling (CVS) or amniocentesis can detect it; blood transfusions can improve clotting and reduce the negative effects of internal bleeding
Huntington's disease	Deterioration of the nervous system in middle age, associated with dementia, jerky movements, personality changes	Dominant gene; abnormal number of repetitions of DNA sequence	Test enables relatives to find out whether they have the gene; preimplantation genetic diagnosis of embryonic cells may be used to ensure a healthy child
Sickle-cell disease	Blood cells are sickle-shaped rather than round; stick together, make breathing difficult; and cause painful swelling of joints and blood clots; common in African Americans	Recessive gene pair; carriers were protected from malaria in Africa	Blood test can determine whether parents are carriers (newborns in the United States are screened with a blood test); antibiotics and blood transfusions prevent infections and relieve symptoms
Tay-Sachs disease	Metabolic defect results in accumulation of fat in a child's brain, degeneration of the nervous system, and early death; common in Jewish people from Eastern Europe	Recessive gene pair	Blood test can determine whether parents are carriers, and fetal DNA analysis can determine whether a child is affected; medication may help, but most victims die in childhood

Sources: Davidson, 2002; Kingston, 2002; Pritchard & Korf, 2008; Simpson & Elias, 2003; Turnpenny & Ellard, 2005.

eases, including cystic fibrosis, hemophilia, phenylketonuria (PKU), and Tay-Sachs disease, are described in ● Table 3.3.

Suppose an African American couple visits a genetic counselor, has a genetic test done, and learns that they both are carriers of the recessive gene for sickle-cell disease. Individuals with this disease have sickle-shaped blood cells that tend to cluster together and distribute less oxygen through the circulatory system than normal cells do (Davidson, 2002). They have great difficulty breathing and exerting themselves, experience painful swelling of their joints, and often die early as a result of blood clots and heart or kidney failure. The genetic counselor might tell the couple that about 9% of African Americans in the United States have the genotype we will call Ss; they carry one dominant gene (S) that calls for

round blood cells and one recessive gene (s) that calls for sickle-shaped blood cells (Thompson, 1975). Such people are called **carriers** because, although they do not have the disease, they can transmit the gene for it to their children. The child who inherits two recessive sickle-cell genes (ss) will have sickle-cell disease. The genetic counselor would therefore explain that an Ss father and an Ss mother (two carriers) have a one-in-four, or 25%, chance of having a child with sickle-cell disease (ss).

This couple also has a two-in-four, or 50%, chance of having a child who will be a carrier like themselves. This is significant, the counselor would say, because the dominant gene associated with round blood cells shows incomplete dominance. As a result, carriers of the sickle-cell gene have many round blood cells and

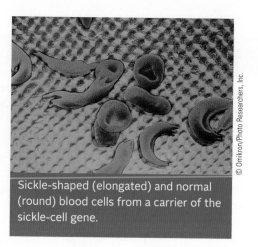

Sickle-shaped (elongated) and normal (round) blood cells from a carrier of the sickle-cell gene.

© Omikron/Photo Researchers, Inc.

some sickle-shaped cells (see the photo above). When they are at high altitudes, are given anesthesia, or are otherwise deprived of oxygen, carriers may experience symptoms of sickle-cell disease—difficulty breathing, painful swelling of the joints, and severe fatigue.

After providing the couple with this information, the genetic counselor might discuss prenatal screening procedures that can detect many genetic abnormalities prenatally. Three widely used techniques—amniocentesis, chorionic villus sampling, and ultrasound—as well as the newer methods of preimplantation genetic diagnosis and maternal blood sampling, are described in Exploration Box 3.2. For the parents whose tests reveal a normal embryo or fetus, there is relief. For parents who learn that their fetus has a serious defect, the choice between abortion and the challenges of raising a child with a serious disorder can be agonizing. In the case of sickle-cell disease, a blood test is used to screen newborns for the disease and affected children begin a life of treatment with blood transfusions and antibiotics to prevent infections (Davidson, 2002).

Now consider **Huntington's disease**, a famous (and terrifying) example of a genetic defect associated with a single dominant gene. This disease typically strikes in middle age and disrupts the normal transcription of RNA and the expression of genes in the brain and the peripheral nervous system (Anderson et al., 2008). Among the effects are motor disturbances such as slurred speech, an erratic and seemingly drunken walk, grimaces, and jerky movements; personality changes such as increased moodiness and irritability; and dementia or loss of cognitive abilities (Bishop & Waldholz, 1990; Sutton-Brown & Suchowersky, 2003). Any child of a parent with Huntington's disease is almost certain to develop the disease if she receives the dominant (but fortunately rare) Huntington's gene rather than its normal counterpart gene at conception; the risk for an individual who has a parent with Huntington's disease is therefore one out of two, or 50%. (You may wish to work the odds for yourself using the approach shown in Figure 3.2.)

In 1983, James Gusella and his colleagues studied a large family with many cases of Huntington's disease and traced the gene for it to Chromosome 4 (Bishop & Waldholz, 1990). This discovery led to the development of a test to enable the relatives of Huntington's victims to find out whether or not they inherited the gene. Interestingly, some want to know, but many do not, partly because they fear discrimination based on their genetic makeup, partly because they do not want to live with the knowledge that they will develop this awful disease (Bombard, 2009; Sutton-Brown & Suchowersky, 2003). If it turns out that a prospective parent has the gene and the couple wishes to have children, preimplantation genetic diagnosis (see Exploration Box 3.2) can be used to test fertilized eggs for the presence of the Huntington's gene, and the doctor can then implant only eggs without the gene in the mother's uterus.

Genetic counselors must keep up with breakthroughs in prevention, diagnosis, and treatment of genetically related diseases and disorders. For the many conditions that are polygenic in origin, it is usually not possible to do a definitive test or even give solid odds, but genetic counselors nonetheless can educate families and attempt to correct their misunderstandings.

Checking Mastery

1. Ted and Ned, fraternal twins, are not very alike at all. Give both a "nature" explanation and a "nurture" explanation of their differences.

2. Hairy forehead syndrome (we made it up) is caused by a single dominant gene, H. Using diagrams such as those in Figure 3.2 and Figure 3.3, figure out the odds that Herb (who has the genotype Hh) and Harriet (who also has the genotype Hh) will have a child with hairy forehead syndrome. Now repeat the exercise, but assume that hairy forehead syndrome is caused by a recessive gene, h, and that both parents again have an Hh genotype.

3. Juan has red–green color blindness. Knowing that he is color blind, what can you infer about his parents?

Making Connections

1. A DNA sample taken by swabbing a person's cheek can now reveal the person's entire genome. What do you think will be the positive and negative consequences of this scientific breakthrough for society? On balance, should we be pleased or concerned about this development?

2. As it becomes possible for parents to obtain genetic analyses of embryonic cells early in pregnancy and elect to continue or terminate the pregnancy based on the results, do you think parents should have the right to terminate any pregnancy they wish to terminate? Should they, for example, be able to terminate a female fetus if they want a boy, a fetus with a likely learning disability if they want a genius? Why or why not?

3. Are you aware of any genetically influenced diseases that run in your family? If so, what are they and what do you know (or what can you learn) about the mechanism involved?

Pregnant women, especially those over 35 or 40, turn to a variety of medical techniques to tell them in advance whether their babies are likely to be normal (Simpson & Elias, 2003; Turnpenny & Ellard, 2005; Wilfond & Ross, 2009).

Ultrasound

The easiest and most commonly used method is **ultrasound** (also called sonography), the use of sound waves to scan the womb and create a visual image of the fetus on a monitor screen. Ultrasound can indicate how many fetuses are in the womb and whether they are alive, and it can detect genetic defects that produce visible physical abnormalities. Prospective parents often enjoy "meeting" their child and can find out whether the child is going to be a girl or a boy. Ultrasound is widely used even when abnormalities are not suspected because it is considered very safe (Simpson & Elias, 2003).

Amniocentesis

To detect chromosome abnormalities such as Down syndrome and to determine, through DNA analysis, whether the genes for particular single gene-pair disorders are present, **amniocentesis** is used. A needle is inserted into the abdomen, a sample of amniotic fluid is withdrawn, and fetal cells that have been shed are analyzed. The risk of miscarriage associated with amniocentesis may not be the commonly cited 1 of 200 cases but as few as 1 in 1600 cases, making the procedure relatively safe and advisable for pregnant women over age 35 (Bornstein et al., 2009; Eddleman et al., 2006). Its main disadvantage is that it is not considered safe until the 15th week of pregnancy (Simpson & Elias, 2003).

Chorionic Villus Sampling

Chorionic villus sampling (CVS) involves inserting a catheter through the mother's vagina and cervix (or, less commonly, through her abdomen) into the membrane called the *chorion* that surrounds the fetus, and then extracting tiny hair cells from the chorion that contain genetic material from

the fetus. Sample cells are then analyzed for the same genetic defects that can be detected using amniocentesis. The difference is that chorionic villus sampling can be performed as early as the 10th week of pregnancy, allowing parents more time to consider the pros and cons of continuing the pregnancy if an abnormality is detected (Simpson & Elias, 2003). The risks of CVS are only slightly greater than those of amniocentesis.

Maternal Blood Sampling

Maternal blood sampling has been used for a number of years to test the mother's blood for various chemicals that can indicate an abnormality in the fetus, but now it can also be used to obtain embryonic DNA that has slipped through the placenta into the mother's blood—DNA that can then be analyzed with no risk at all to the fetus (Benn & Chapman, 2009; Chiu & Lo, 2006). This method of prenatal diagnosis has not been reliable until recently, but a technique for using this method to detect Down syndrome with high accuracy has just become available (Benn & Chapman, 2009; Skotko, 2009).

Maternal blood sampling of fetal DNA has the tremendous advantages of being noninvasive and usable early in the pregnancy. If it indeed becomes accurate enough, it may replace amniocentesis and CVS entirely. Meanwhile, the prospect that all pregnant women may soon have their blood analyzed for evidence of chromosome and other genetic abnormalities is raising ethical red flags, especially about the possibility that abortion rates will soar if more parents decide that they do not want babies with Down syndrome or other "undesirable" characteristics. Already data suggest that, due to high rates of termination of pregnancies that would produce a child with Down syndrome, the incidence of Down syndrome is lower than would be expected based on the growing number of older mothers (Skotko, 2009). There is a resulting need for better education of physicians and counseling of prospective parents about the nature of Down syndrome, as well

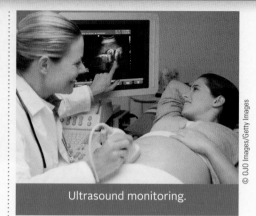

Ultrasound monitoring.

© OJO Images/Getty Images

as for more study of the implications of advances in maternal blood sampling (Benn & Chapman, 2009; Skotko, 2009).

Preimplantation Genetic Diagnosis

Finally, parents who know they are at high risk to have a baby with a serious condition can minimize their risk through **preimplantation genetic diagnosis**. This involves fertilizing a mother's eggs with a father's sperm in the laboratory using in vitro fertilization (IVF) techniques (see Chapter 4), conducting DNA tests on the first cells that result from mitosis of each fertilized egg, and implanting in the mother's uterus only eggs that do not have chromosome abnormalities or genes associated with disorders (Bick & Lau, 2006; Simpson & Elias, 2003). Although costly, this option may appeal to couples who would not consider abortion but do not want to have a child with a serious defect. Preimplantation genetic diagnosis, like maternal blood sampling, is controversial because parents could use it not only to prevent disorders and diseases but also to try to create "designer" children with the characteristics they prefer (Braude, 2006; Wilfond & Ross, 2009).

Prenatal diagnostic techniques such as ultrasound, amniocentesis, CVS, maternal blood sampling, and preimplantation genetic diagnosis can provide tremendously important information when there is reason to suspect a problem. Yet they clearly raise issues for society to grapple with as well.

3.3 Studying Genetic and Environmental Influences

How do researchers study the contributions of genes and environment to the normal range of variation among us in physical and psychological traits? **Behavioral genetics** is the scientific study of the extent to which genetic and environmental differences among people or animals are responsible for differences in their traits (Plomin et al., 2008; Rutter, 2006). It is impossible to say that a given person's intelligence test score is the result of, say, 80%, 50%, or 20% heredity and the rest environment. The individual would have no intelligence without both genetic makeup and experiences. It is, however, possible for behavioral geneticists to estimate the **heritability** of measured IQ and of other traits or behaviors. Heritability is the proportion of all the variability in the trait within a large sample of people that can be linked to genetic differences among those individuals. To say that measured intelligence is *heritable*, then, is to say that differences in tested IQ among the individuals studied are to some degree attributable to the different genetic endowments of these individuals. It is critical to understand that estimates of heritability differ from study to study depending on what sample is studied and how (Plomin et al., 2008).

It may seem from their title that *behavioral geneticists* tell us only about genetic contributions to development, but in fact their work tells us about the contributions of both genetic and environmental factors to differences among people. The variability in a trait that is not associated with genetic differences is associated with differences in experiences and other environmental influences. Behavioral geneticists gather evidence through experimental breeding; twin, adoption, and other family studies; and most recently molecular genetics techniques for studying specific genes (see Plomin et al., 2008).

Experimental Breeding

To study the relative influence of genes and environment on animal behavior, behavioral geneticists sometimes design breeding experiments, much like those Gregor Mendel conducted to discover the workings of heredity in plants. For example, **selective breeding** involves attempting to breed animals for a particular trait to determine whether the trait is heritable. In a classic study, R. C. Tryon (1940) tested numerous rats for the ability to run a complex maze. Rats that made few errors were labeled *maze bright*; those that made many errors were termed *maze dull*. Then, across several generations, Tryon mated bright rats with bright rats and dull rats with dull rats. If differences in experience rather than differences in genetic makeup had accounted for maze performance differences in the first generation of rats studied, selective breeding would have had no effect. Instead, across generations, the differences in learning performance between the maze-bright and maze-dull groups of rats became increasingly larger. Tryon demonstrated that maze-learning ability in rats is influenced by genetic makeup.

Selective breeding studies have also shown that genes contribute to such attributes as activity level, emotionality, aggressiveness, and sex drive in rats, mice, and chickens (Plomin et al., 2008). Because people do not take kindly to the idea of being selectively bred, such research cannot be done with humans. Instead, research on genetic influence in humans has relied primarily on determining whether the degree of genetic similarity between pairs of people is associated with the degree of physical or psychological similarity between them.

Twin, Adoption, and Family Studies

Twins have long been recognized as important sources of evidence about the effects of heredity. A simple type of **twin study** to untangle genetic and environmental influences involves determining whether identical twins reared together are more similar to each other in traits of interest than fraternal twins reared together. If genes matter, identical twins should be more similar because they have 100% of their genes in common, whereas fraternal twins share only 50% on average.

Today, most sophisticated twin studies include not only identical and fraternal twin pairs raised together but also identical and fraternal twins reared apart—four groups in all, differing in both the extent to which they share the same genes and the extent to which they share the same home environment (Bouchard & Pedersen, 1999). Identical twins separated near birth and raised in different environments—like the twins introduced at the beginning of the chapter—are particularly fascinating and informative because any similarities between them cannot be attributed to common family experiences.

Although it is widely used, the twin method has been criticized. Critics charge that identical twins could be more psychologically similar than fraternal twins, even if they are separated after birth, because they share a more similar prenatal environment than fraternal twins or other siblings do (Devlin, Daniels, & Roeder, 1997). Critics also charge that identical twins are treated more similarly than fraternal twins and that their more similar environment explains their greater similarity. Identical twins *are* treated more similarly. However, there appears to be little relationship between how similarly twins are treated and how similar they turn out to be psychologically (Loehlin, 1992; Plomin et al., 2008). The more similar treatment identical twins receive is most likely the effect rather than the cause of their psychological similarity (Reiss, 2005).

A second commonly used method is the **adoption study**. Are children adopted early in life psychologically similar to their biological parents, whose genes they share, or are they similar to their adoptive parents, whose environment they share? If adopted children resemble their biological parents in intelligence or personality, even though those parents did not raise them, genes must be influential. If they resemble their adoptive parents, even though they are genetically unrelated to them, a good case can be made for environmental influence. Like the twin method, the adoption method has proved useful but has been criticized. Researchers must appreciate that not only the genes of a biological mother but also the prenatal environment she provided could influence how an adopted child turns out (Gottlieb, Wahlsten, & Lickliter, 2006); to check for this possibility, it helps to determine whether biological father–child similarity is as great as biological mother–child similarity (Plomin et al., 2008). Researchers must also be careful to correct for the tendency of adoption agencies to place children in homes similar to those they were adopted from. Finally, researchers must recognize that because adoptive homes are generally above-average environments, adoption studies may underestimate the effects of the full range of environments children can experience (Stoolmiller, 1999; but see McGue et al., 2007).

Finally, researchers are conducting complex *family studies* that include pairs of siblings who have different degrees of genetic similarity—for example, identical twins, fraternal twins, full biological siblings, half siblings, and unrelated stepsiblings who live together in stepfamilies (Reiss et al., 2000). They are also measuring qualities of these family members' experiences to determine how similar or different the environments of siblings are. Researchers are even looking at twins and other pairs of relatives longitudinally so that they can assess the contributions of genes and environment to continuity and change in traits as individuals develop.

Estimating Influences

Having conducted a twin, adoption, or family study, behavioral geneticists use statistical calculations to estimate the degree to which heredity and environment account for individual differences in a trait of interest. When they study traits that a person either has or does not have (for example, a smoking habit or diabetes), researchers calculate and compare **concordance rates**—the percentage of pairs of people studied (for example, pairs of identical twins or adoptive parents and children) in which if one member of a pair displays the trait, the other does too. If concordance rates are higher for more genetically related than for less genetically related pairs of people, the trait is heritable.

Suppose researchers are interested in whether homosexuality is genetically influenced. They might locate men who are gay and who have twins, either identical or fraternal, locate their twin siblings, and find out whether they, too, are gay. In one study of this type (Bailey & Pillard, 1991), the concordance rate for identical twins was 52% (29 of the 56 twins of gay men were also gay), whereas the concordance rate for fraternal twins was 22% (12 of 54 twins of gay men were also gay). This finding and others suggest that genetic makeup contributes to both men's and women's sexual orientation (Bailey, Dunne, & Martin, 2000; Dawood, Bailey, & Martin, 2009). But notice that identical twins are *not* perfectly concordant. Environmental factors must also affect sexual orientation. After all, Bailey and Pillard found that in 48% of the identical twin pairs, one twin was gay but the other was not, despite their identical genes.

When a trait can be present in varying degrees, as is true of height or intelligence, correlation coefficients rather than concordance rates are calculated (see Chapter 1). In a behavioral genetics study of IQ scores, a correlation would indicate whether the IQ score of one twin is systematically related to the IQ score of the other, such that if one twin is bright, the other is bright, and if one is not so bright, the other is not so bright. The larger

Twins are concordant if they both display a trait of interest such as smoking.

the correlation for a group of twins, the closer the resemblance between members of twin pairs.

To better appreciate the logic of behavioral genetics studies, consider what Robert Plomin and his colleagues (1988) found when they assessed aspects of personality among twins in Sweden whose ages averaged 59. One of their measures assessed an aspect of emotionality—the tendency to be angry or quick tempered. The scale was given to many pairs of identical twins and fraternal twins—some pairs raised together, others separated near birth and raised apart. Correlations reflecting the degree of similarity between twins are presented in ● **Table 3.4**. From such data, behavioral geneticists can estimate the contributions of three factors to individual differences in emotionality: genes, shared environmental influences, and nonshared environmental influences.

1. *Genes.* In the example in Table 3.4, genetic influences are clearly evident, for identical twins are consistently more similar in emotionality than fraternal twins are. The correlation of 0.33 for identical twins reared apart also testifies to the importance of genetic makeup. These data suggest that emotionality is heritable and, more specifically, that about a third of the variation in emotionality in this sample can be linked to variations in genetic endowment.

2. *Shared environmental influences.* Individuals growing up in the same environment experience **shared environmental influences**, common experiences that work to make them similar—for example, a common parenting style or exposure to the same toys, peers, schools, and neighborhood. In Table 3.4, notice that both identical and fraternal twins are slightly more similar in

TABLE 3.4 CORRELATIONS FROM A TWIN STUDY OF THE HERITABILITY OF ANGRY EMOTIONALITY

	Raised Together	Raised Apart
Identical twin pairs	0.37	0.33
Fraternal twin pairs	0.17	0.09

By dissecting this table, you can assess the contributions of genes, shared environment, and nonshared environment to individual differences in angry emotionality.

Genes. Are identical twins more similar than fraternal twins? Yes: 0.37 is greater than 0.17, and 0.33 is greater than 0.09; therefore, greater genetic similarity is associated with greater emotional similarity.

Shared environment. Are twins who grow up together more similar than twins raised apart? Only a small effect of shared environment is evident: 0.37 is slightly greater than 0.33, and 0.17 is slightly greater than 0.09.

Nonshared environment. Are identical twins raised in the same home dissimilar, despite sharing 100% of their genes and the same environment? Yes: a correlation of 0.37 is far less than a perfect correlation of 1.00, suggesting a good deal of nonshared environmental influence.

SOURCE: From Plomin, R. et al. EAS temperaments during the last half of the life span: Twins reared apart and twins reared together. *Psychology and Aging, 3,* 1988. Copyright 1988 by The American Psychological Association. Reprinted by permission.

emotionality if they are raised together than if they are raised apart. These correlations tell us that shared environmental influences are evident but very weak: twins are almost as similar when they grew up in different homes as when they grew up in the same home.

3. *Nonshared environmental influences.* Experiences unique to the individual—those that are not shared by other members of the family and that work to make individuals different from each other—are referred to as **nonshared environmental influences**. Whether they involve being treated differently by parents, having different friends or teachers, undergoing different life crises, or even being affected differently by the same events, nonshared environmental influences make members of the same family different (Rowe, 1994). In Table 3.4, notice that identical twins raised together are not identical in emotionality, even though they share 100% of their genes *and* the same family environment; a correlation of 0.37 is much lower than a perfect correlation of 1.00. Any differences between identical twins raised together are attributable to differences in their unique, or nonshared, experiences plus any errors in measuring the trait of interest.

Anyone who has a brother or sister can attest that different children in the same family are not always treated identically by their parents. Moreover, studies of identical twins have revealed some systematic relationships in which differences in their prenatal environments, as indicated by different birth weights, and in their early family experiences can be linked to differences in such characteristics as their levels of anxiety, conduct problems, and academic achievement (Asbury, Dunn, & Plomin, 2006). Thus, failing to find strong shared environmental influences on a trait does not mean that family influences on development are unimportant. There could be strong nonshared environmental influences, both within and outside the home, working to make children in the same family different rather than similar.

Molecular Genetics

The Human Genome Project, by providing a map of the human genome, has opened the door to exciting new approaches to studying genetic and environmental influence. **Molecular genetics** is the analysis of particular genes and their effects. It involves identification of specific alleles or variants of genes that influence particular traits and comparisons of animals or humans who have these genes with those who do not. Thus, it opens doors to determining which specific genes may account for an overall contribution of genes to a trait in behavioral genetics research and to studying the effects of those genes in combination with the effects of specific environmental influences.

If researchers are not sure what genes contribute to a trait, they can now analyze research participants' entire genomes to

If you have brothers and sisters, do you think your parents treated you better or worse than they treated your siblings? If so, what might have been the effects of these nonshared environmental influences on your development?

© Getty Images/Tetra Images RF

identify which genes distinguish individuals who have a trait or do not or who score high or low on a measure of the trait (Butcher et al., 2008; Plomin & Davis, 2009). Molecular genetics is especially useful in identifying the multiple genes that contribute to polygenic traits—the genes that underlie evidence from twin and adoption studies that traits such as reading ability or depression are heritable (Plomin et al., 2008; Rende & Waldman, 2006). The goal is to be able to say, for instance, "This gene accounts for 20% of the variation, and these two other genes each account for 10% of the variation," in a phenotype or trait of interest.

So far, analyses based on molecular genetics have been disappointing in that they have failed to identify genes that account for large chunks of the variation in a trait. Rather, these analyses suggest that many genes contribute to each polygenic trait or disorder and that each gene's contribution is very small—usually less than 1% of the variation (Plomin & Davis, 2009).

If a specific gene's location and role are known, researchers may test DNA samples collected from study participants for the presence of the gene and determine how people who have a particular allele of a gene differ from those who have other variants of it. Consider Alzheimer's disease, the most common cause of dementia in later life (Williams, 2003; also see Chapter 16). Twin studies indicate that it is heritable (Gatz et al., 2006), but what genes are behind it? One allele of a gene called *apolipoprotein E (apoE4)* has been linked to a higher-than-normal risk of Alzheimer's. Although apoE4 is only one contributor to Alzheimer's disease and many Alzheimer's patients do not have the gene, researchers have been studying differences between individuals with the gene and individuals without it. In one such study (Hofer et al., 2002), elderly adults with the apoE4 gene showed greater memory deterioration over a 7-year period than did individuals without it, even though none of the participants had diagnosable Alzheimer's disease yet. Other researchers have found that having the apoE4 gene *and* experiencing an environmental risk factor such as head injury increases the odds of Alzheimer's disease still further, something college football players and boxers might want to note (Williams, 2003). Such research can help make possible early identification of people likely to develop Alzheimer's disease so that they can receive early treatment for it.

Despite its weaknesses, behavioral genetics research involving experimental breeding studies and twin, adoption, and family studies has taught us a great deal about the contributions of genes (heritability), shared environment, and nonshared environment to similarities and differences among humans. Molecular genetics research is now leading to exciting discoveries about which specific genes, interacting with which environmental factors, are responsible.

Checking Mastery

1. What does the following (hypothetical) table of correlations tell you about the contributions of genes, shared environment, and nonshared environment to use of marijuana?

	Raised together	Raised apart
Identical twins	+0.90	+0.40
Fraternal twins	+0.50	+0.10

2. What are two problems in adoption studies of genetic influence?
3. If twin studies show that genes strongly influence a psychological disorder, what good would it do to conduct molecular genetics studies of it?

Making Connections

1. Design both a twin study and an adoption study to examine the contributions of genes and environment to creativity. Explain what patterns of results would provide evidence of genetic or environmental influence.

2. Drawing on information about your family and friends, illustrate how genes, shared environmental influences, and nonshared environmental influences could each help explain why some teenagers are bigger risk takers behind the wheel of a car than others. Then design a study to find out which of these factors are most important.

3.4 Selected Findings

Findings from behavioral genetics studies have challenged and changed understandings of human development, as you will see throughout this book. We give a few examples here, drawn from studies of intellectual abilities, temperament and personality, and psychological disorders (see Kim, 2009; Plomin et al., 2008). Expect some surprises.

Intellectual Abilities

How do genes and environment contribute to individual differences in intellectual functioning, and how do their relative contributions change over the life span? Consider the average correlations between the IQ scores of different pairs of relatives presented in ●**Table 3.5**. These averages are primarily from a review by Thomas Bouchard Jr. and Matthew McGue (1981) of studies involving 526 correlations based on 113,942 pairs of children, adolescents, and adults. Clearly, correlations are higher when people are closely related genetically than when they are not and are highest when they are identical twins. Overall, the heritability of IQ scores is about 0.50, meaning that genetic differences account for about 50% of the variation in IQ scores and environmental differences account for the other half of the variation in the samples studied (Plomin, 1990; and see Segal & Johnson, 2009).

Can you detect the workings of environment in the table? Notice that (1) pairs of family members reared together are somewhat more similar in IQ than pairs reared apart; (2) fraternal twins, who should have especially similar family experiences because they grow up at the same time, tend to be more alike

TABLE 3.5 AVERAGE CORRELATIONS BETWEEN THE IQ SCORES OF PAIRS OF INDIVIDUALS

Family Pairs	Raised Together	Raised Apart
Identical twins	0.86	0.72
Fraternal twins	0.60	0.52
Biological siblings	0.47	0.24
Biological parent and child	0.42	0.22
Half siblings	0.31	—
Adopted siblings	0.34	—
Adoptive parent and adopted child	0.19	—
Unrelated siblings (same age, same home)	0.26	—

SOURCE: All but two of these averages were calculated by Bouchard and McGue (1981) from studies of both children and adults. The correlation for fraternal twins reared apart is based on data reported by Pedersen et al. (1985); that for unrelated children in the same home is based on data reported by Segal (2000).

than siblings born at different times; and (3) the IQs of adopted children are related to those of their adoptive parents. All these findings suggest that *shared* environmental influences tend to make individuals who live together more alike than if they lived separately. Notice, however, that genetically identical twins reared together are not perfectly similar. This is evidence that their unique or *nonshared* experiences have made them different.

Do the contributions of genes and environment to differences in intellectual ability change over the life span? You might guess that genetic influences would decrease as children accumulate learning experiences, but you would be wrong. Genetic endowment appears to *gain* rather than lose importance from infancy to adulthood as a source of individual differences in intellectual performance (McCartney, Harris, & Bernieri, 1990; Plomin & Spinath, 2004).

In a longitudinal study of identical and fraternal twins conducted by Ronald Wilson (1978, 1983), for example, identical twins scored no more similarly than fraternal twins on a measure of infant mental development during the first year of life; thus, evidence of heritability was lacking in infancy. This may be because powerful maturational forces keep redirecting infants back to the same species-wide developmental pathway, regardless of specific genetic makeup or experiences (McCall, 1981). The influence of individual heredity began to show by around 18 months of age, however. Identical twins even experienced more similar spurts in intellectual development than fraternal twins. Identical twins then stayed highly similar throughout childhood and into adolescence, the correlation between their IQ scores averaging about 0.85. Meanwhile, fraternal twins be-

came *less* similar over the years; the correlation between their IQ scores had dropped to 0.54 by adolescence. As a result, the heritability of IQ scores increased from infancy to adolescence.

Whereas the heritability of intelligence test performance increases with age, shared environmental influences become less significant with age, explaining about 30% of the variation in IQ in childhood and 20% in adolescence but close to 0% in adulthood (Kirkpatrick, McGue, & Iacono, 2009; McGue et al., 1993; Plomin & Spinath, 2004). Siblings are probably exposed to similar (shared) learning experiences when they are young and spend a good deal of time with their parents. As they age, they probably seek and have different (nonshared) life experiences. Partly because of their different genetic makeups, they may elicit different reactions from their parents, join different peer groups, encounter different teachers, develop different hobbies, go on to different colleges or universities and vocations, and so on.

Does evidence of the heritability of IQ scores mean that we cannot improve children's intellectual development by enriching their environment? Not at all. True, the IQs of adopted children are, by adolescence, correlated more strongly with the IQs of their biological parents than with the IQs of their adoptive parents. However, the *level* of intellectual performance that adopted children reach can increase dramatically (by 20 points on an IQ test) if they are adopted into more intellectually stimulating homes than those provided by their biological parents (Scarr & Weinberg, 1978, 1983; van IJzendoorn & Juffer, 2005). Most likely, then, stimulating environments help children realize more fully their genetically based potentials. It is critical for parents, teachers, and others concerned with optimizing development to understand that genetically influenced qualities can very often be altered.

How do genes and environment contribute to individual differences in intellectual functioning during adulthood? The influence of genes remains high. Genes also largely account for the considerable stability of intellectual ability from early adulthood to late middle age; a 55-year-old twin's score on a test of cognitive ability is likely to be as predictable from his co-twin's score at age 55 as from his own score at age 20 (Lyons et al., 2009). Changes in performance over the years have more to do with nonshared environmental influences. In old age, genetic influences on individual differences in intellectual functioning are still strong (Plomin et al., 2008). However, some studies suggest that heritability may diminish in very old age as diseases and other nonshared environmental influences make even identical twins more dissimilar than they were earlier in life (McGue & Johnson, 2008; Vogler, 2006).

Temperament and Personality

As parents know well, different babies have different personalities. In trying to describe infant personality, researchers have focused on aspects of **temperament**—tendencies to respond in predictable ways, such as sociability and emotional reactivity, that serve as the building blocks of later personality. (See Chapter 11 for more about temperament.) Genes contribute to individual differences in both early temperament and later personality

The temperament of infants is genetically influenced. These identical twins seem like easy babies, eager to socialize. (Notice that their arms are in the same positions as well.)

(Gagne, Vendlinski, & Goldsmith, 2009; Krueger & Johnson, 2008).

Arnold Buss and Robert Plomin (1984) reported average correlations from around 0.50 to 0.60 between the temperament scores of identical twins. The corresponding correlations for fraternal twins were not much greater than zero. Think about that: a zero correlation is what you would expect if fraternal twins were strangers living in different homes rather than siblings who, on average, share half their genes, the same home, and often the same bedroom! It does not seem to matter whether researchers look at fraternal twin pairs, ordinary siblings, or unrelated children adopted into the same family, *living in the same home generally does not make children more similar in personality* (Dunn & Plomin, 1990). This does not mean that the family is unimportant; it means that family influences do more to make children different from each other than to make them alike.

Similar conclusions have been reached about the contributions of genes and environment to adult personality (Krueger, Johnson, & Kling, 2006; Loehlin et al., 1998; see also Chapter 11). Of all the differences among adults on major dimensions of personality, about 40% of the variation is attributable to genetic differences (Loehlin, 1985). Only 5% of the variation reflects the effects of shared family environment. The remaining 55% of the variability in adult personalities is associated with nonshared environmental influences that make siblings different from each other.

Shared environmental influences can be important at times. For example, parents appear to influence their children to adopt attitudes and interests similar to their own, at least while the children are living at home (Eaves et al., 1997; Plomin et al., 2008). Shared environment also helps make adolescent siblings similar in the extent to which they engage in delinquent behavior and substance use, partly because siblings influence one another (Hopfer, Crowley, & Hewitt, 2003; Rowe, 1994). Shared environmental influences also show up in studies of child and adolescent psychological problems. Factors such as poor parent–child relationships and parent–child conflict sometimes cause multiple children in the same home to develop psychological problems (Burt, 2009).

Yet behavioral geneticists have discovered repeatedly that when it comes to many aspects of personality, unique, nonshared environmental influences rather than shared ones, along with genes, seem to be most significant (Reiss et al., 2000; Rowe, 1994). There is little evidence that parents mold all their children's personalities in similar directions. Increasingly, it seems more useful to ask how nonshared experiences inside and outside the home steer brothers and sisters along *different* developmental paths. There are plenty of possibilities (see Krueger & Johnson, 2008): for example, parents often develop unique relationships with each of their children, siblings grow up at different times and experience different family environments as a result, brothers and sisters may try to differentiate themselves from one another to establish their own identities, and, of course, different children may have different peer groups, teachers, and other experiences outside the home. But efforts to link differences in the personalities of brothers and sisters to specific differences in their experiences have been frustrating so far. Nonshared environmental influences appear to be idiosyncratic and hard to pin down (Burt, 2009; Dunn & Plomin, 1990; Reiss et al., 2000).

Psychological Disorders

As you will see in this book, both genes and environment contribute to psychological disorders across the life span—to alcohol and drug abuse, autism, depression, attention deficit hyperactivity disorder, eating disorders, aggressive and criminal behavior, Alzheimer's disease, and every other psychological disorder that has been studied (Plomin et al., 2008; Rende & Waldman, 2006; Rutter, 2006; and see Chapter 16). Usually it's a matter of multiple genes, along with multiple environmental factors, each making a small contribution to the development of a disorder.

Consider just one example. **Schizophrenia** is a serious mental illness that involves disturbances in logical thinking, emotional expression, and social behavior and that typically emerges in late adolescence or early adulthood. In the 1950s and 1960s, experts were convinced it was caused by mothers who were cold and inconsistent in their parenting style, but that has been proven wrong (Rowe & Jacobson, 1999). Now we know that genes contribute substantially to this disorder (Gottesman & Hanson, 2005). The average concordance rate for schizophrenia in identical twin pairs is 48%; if one twin has the disorder, in 48% of the pairs studied the other has it too (Gottesman, 1991; Owen & O'Donovan, 2003). By comparison, the concordance rate for fraternal twins is only 17%. In addition, children who have at least one biological parent who is schizophrenic have an increased risk of schizophrenia *even if they are adopted away early in life* (Heston, 1970). Thus, the increased risk these children face has more to do with their genes than with being brought up by a schizophrenic adult.

It is easy to conclude, mistakenly, that any child of a person with schizophrenia is doomed to become schizophrenic. But here are the facts: Whereas about 1% of people in the general population develop schizophrenia, about 10% of children who have a schizophrenic parent become schizophrenic (Gottesman, 1991; Plomin et al., 2008). So although children of parents with schizophrenia are at greater risk for schizophrenia than other children, approximately 90% of the children of one parent with schizophrenia do *not* develop the disorder. Even for the child of two parents with schizophrenia or for an identical twin whose twin develops the disorder, the odds of developing schizophrenia are only about one in two.

Clearly, then, environmental factors also contribute significantly to this mental illness. People do not inherit psychological disorders; they inherit *predispositions* to develop disorders. Genes and environment then interact so that a person who has inherited a genetic susceptibility to schizophrenia will likely not develop the disorder unless he also has stressful experiences that trigger the illness. For example, genetically at-risk children whose mothers come down with an infectious disease like the flu during pregnancy are at increased risk of schizophrenia, apparently due to damaging effects on the fetus's brain of the mother's immune system's response to infection (Patterson, 2007). Infants deprived of oxygen during delivery are also more likely to develop schizophrenia (Cannon et al., 2003). And adopted children who have a biological parent with schizophrenia are at greater risk of developing schizophrenia if they grow up in a dysfunctional adoptive home than if they grow up in a healthy family environment (Tienari et al., 2004).

In short, children may inherit predispositions to develop several problems and disorders; their experiences will interact with their genetic makeup to determine how well adjusted they turn out to be. Such research also shows that it is overly simple and often wrong to assume that any behavioral problem a child displays must be the result of bad parenting.

The Heritability of Different Traits

Although genes contribute to variation in virtually all human traits that have been studied, some traits are more heritable than others (Bouchard, 2004). ■ **Figure 3.5** presents, by way of summary, correlations obtained in the Minnesota Twin Study between the traits of identical twins raised apart and reunited later in life.

Observable physical characteristics, from eye color to height, are strongly associated with individual genetic endowment. Even weight is heritable; adopted children resemble their biological parents but not their adoptive parents in weight, even though their adoptive parents feed them (Grilo & Pogue-Geile, 1991). Certain aspects of physiology, such as measured brain activity and reactions to alcohol, are highly heritable, too (Lykken, Tellegen, & Iacono, 1982; Neale & Martin, 1989), as is level of physical activity (Eriksson, Rasmussen, & Tynelius, 2006). In addition, genetic differences among older adults contribute to differences in their functioning and changes in markers of aging such as lung capacity (Finkel et al., 2003a; Vogler, 2006). Genes also contribute to susceptibilities to many diseases associated

Characteristic

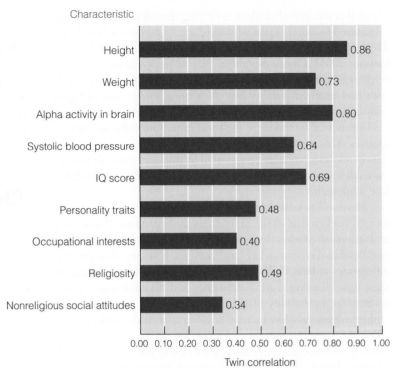

■**FIGURE 3.5** Correlations between the traits of identical twins raised apart in the Minnesota Twin Study. Source: From Bouchard, T. J., Jr., Lykken, D. T., McGue, M., Segal, N. L., & Tellegen, A. Sources of psychological differences: The Minnesota Study of Twins Reared Apart, *Science, 250*, pp. 223–228. Copyright © 1990, The American Association for the Advancement of Science. Reprinted with permission.

with aging, and genetic differences account for about one-third of the variation in longevity (Arking, 2006; see also Chapter 17).

If physical and physiological characteristics are strongly heritable, general intelligence is moderately heritable: 50% or more of the variation among people is attributable to genes. Somewhat less influenced by genes are aspects of temperament and personality, for which about 40% of the variation can be traced to genes, and susceptibility to many psychological disorders, for which heritability varies from condition to condition. Finally, genetic endowment even contributes, though only modestly, to differences in attitudes and interests—for example, political conservatism and vocational interests (Alford, Funk, & Hibbing, 2005; Olson et al., 2001; Rowe, 1994). It has proven difficult to find a human characteristic that is *not* to some degree heritable. For most psychological traits, genes often account for up to half the variation in a group; environmental factors (shared environmental factors to some extent in childhood, but more often nonshared environmental ones) account for the other half or more (Plomin et al., 2008).

Influences on Heritability

As mentioned, heritability is not a fixed quality; rather, it varies depending on the sample studied. First, it varies in relation to the age of the sample, as you have already seen. A fascinating example of this was revealed when an eating disorders survey was administered to female twins who were age 11 and prepubertal, age 11 and pubertal, and age 17 and pubertal (Klump, McGue, & Iacono, 2003). Genes explained 54% of the variation in survey responses indicative of high risk for eating disorders among girls who had reached puberty but 0% among the 11-year-old girls who had not yet reached puberty. For prepubertal girls, shared environmental factors were the most important influence on responses. This study hints that genes that help trigger eating disorders in adolescence may be activated by the biochemical changes associated with puberty and therefore may not be expressed before adolescence.

Heritability estimates also differ depending on the environmental background of the individuals studied. Many classic twin and adoption studies have involved children and adults from middle-class environments, and they have shown that genetic differences among children have a lot to do with differences in their IQs. However, Eric Turkheimer and his colleagues (2003) studied the heritability of IQ in a sample that included many children from very low income families as well as children from affluent homes. As shown in ■ **Figure 3.6**, among children from wealthy families, genes accounted for 72% of the variation in IQ, whereas shared environment was not very important—as in most previous studies. By contrast, genes explained only about 10% of the variation in IQ among children from poor families; instead, shared environmental influences accounted for almost 60% of the variation (see also Harden, Turkheimer, & Loehlin, 2007).

This finding could mean that a deprived and unstimulating environment drags most children down, regardless of whether their genetic potential is high or low, but that some families living in poverty are able to offer a home environment that helps their children thrive despite their economic disadvantage. In more affluent environments, children may have more freedom to build niches that suit their genetically based predispositions and that then make them more or less intellectually inclined depending on their unique genetic makeup (Kendler, 2003). It is clear that the heritability of a trait is not one fixed number. It is a range of numbers affected by the age, socioeconomic status, and other characteristics of the sample studied (Rutter et al., 2006).

Checking Mastery

1. Professor Gene Ohm is studying genetic influences on extraversion/introversion. Based on previous studies of genetic and environmental contributors to individual differences in personality, what should he expect?

2. Alan's biological parents both had schizophrenia, so he was placed in an adoptive home when he was only 1 year old. He grew up with his adoptive parents (neither of whom had psychological disorders) from then on. What would you tell Alan about his chances of becoming schizophrenic if you were a genetic counselor?

Making Connections

1. There's surely no gene that directly makes people politically liberal or politically conservative; yet political liberalism/conservatism is heritable. Develop an explanation of how genes could influence it. While you're at it, how might shared environment and nonshared environment influence it?

2. Sherrita believes that if intelligence is heritable, genes count for everything and nothing can be done to boost the intelligence of children who have low levels of it. Drawing on key evidence, convince Sherrita that she is wrong.

3.5 Genes and Environment Conspiring

What should we conclude about the influences of genes and environment and about the ways in which these two great forces in development conspire to make us what we are? Genes clearly do not orchestrate our growth before birth and then leave us alone. Instead, they are "turning on" and "turning off" in patterned ways throughout the life span, helping shape the attributes and behavioral patterns that we carry with us through our lives and changing their activity in response to environmental stimuli. No less important are environmental influences, from conception to death.

From infancy through childhood and adolescence, children's unique genetic potentials increasingly show themselves in their behavior. Identical twins start out similar and remain similar, but fraternal twins, like brothers and sisters generally, go their own ways and become increasingly dissimilar. Shared environ-

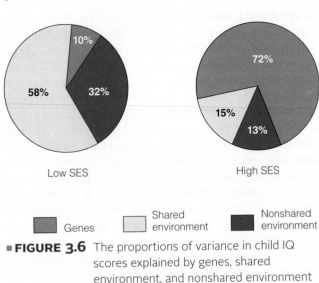

Low SES

High SES

■ Genes | ■ Shared environment | ■ Nonshared environment

■ **FIGURE 3.6** The proportions of variance in child IQ scores explained by genes, shared environment, and nonshared environment differ for children from low or high socioeconomic status (SES) environments.
Source: From Turkheimer, E., Haley, M., D'Onofrio, B., & Gottesman, I. I. Socioeconomic status modifies heritability of IQ in young children, *Psychological Science, 14(6),* 623–628. Reprinted by permission of Sage Publications.

mental influences—the forces that make children in the same family alike—are stronger early in life than they are later in life. Nonshared environmental influences—those unique experiences that make members of the family different—remain important throughout the life span. In short, as we move out of the home and into the larger world, we seem to become, increasingly, products of our unique genes and our unique experiences. But the two do not operate independently. Genes and environment are interrelated in interesting and important ways.

As you have seen throughout this chapter, behavioral geneticists try to establish how much of the variation observed in human traits such as intelligence can be attributed to individual differences in genetic makeup and how much can be attributed to individual differences in experience. Useful as that research is, it does not take us far in understanding the complex interplay between genes and environment over the life span (Turkheimer, 2000). As Ann Anastasi (1958) asserted many years ago, instead of asking *how much* is because of genes and how much is because of environment, researchers should be asking *how* heredity and environment work together to make us what we are. With that in mind, consider the workings of two tremendously important developmental mechanisms: gene–environment interactions and gene–environment correlations (Rowe, 2003; Rutter et al., 2006).

Gene–Environment Interactions

Genes provide us with potentials that are or are not realized depending on our experiences. Using the molecular genetics approach, Avshalom Caspi and his colleagues (2003) sought to understand why stressful life experiences cause some people but not others to become depressed. They performed DNA analysis on a large sample of New Zealanders to determine which alleles of a gene known to affect levels of the neurotransmitter serotonin in the brain each person in the sample had, knowing that a low serotonin level is linked to depression. They also administered surveys to measure the stressful events each person had experienced between ages 21 and 26, and whether at age 26 each person had experienced a diagnosable case of depression in the past year.

In ■ **Figure 3.7**, you can see that genes matter (having genes that predispose a person to depression results in a somewhat higher probability of depression overall than having genes that protect against depression). You also see that environment matters (overall, depression becomes more likely as the number of stressful events a person experiences increases). The real message in the figure, however, is embodied in the concept of **gene–environment interaction**: the effects of genes depend on what kind of environment we experience, and how we respond to the environment depends on what genes we have. In Figure 3.7, you see that individuals with two of the high-risk variants of the gene studied (called *5-HTTLPR*) are more vulnerable to depression than people with two of the protective variants of the gene *only* if they experience multiple stressful events. By comparison, even multiple stressful events will not easily cause people with the protective genes to become depressed. Thus, the genes people have make a difference only when their environment is stressful, and a stressful environment has an effect only on individuals with a genotype that predisposes them to depression. Genes and environment interact.

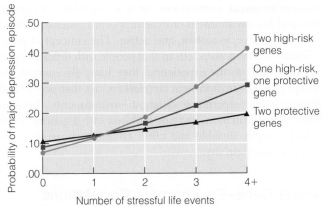

■ **FIGURE 3.7** The odds of a depressive episode at age 26 are highest for individuals who: (1) inherit two genes known to increase the risk of depression rather than two genes known to protect against depression, and (2) experience four or more stressful life events between ages 21 and 26. This is an example of gene–environment interaction: the effects of genetic makeup on depression depend on how stressful a person's environment is, and the effects of stressful life events depend on the person's genotype. SOURCE: From Caspi et al., Influences of Life Stress on Depression, *Science*, July 18, 2003, Fig. 1B. Copyright © 2003. Reprinted by permission of AAAS.

Although studies of particular gene–environment interactions like this do not always agree (Monroe & Reid, 2008), it often takes a combination of high-risk genes and a high-risk environment to trigger many psychological problems (Rutter, 2006). From an applied standpoint, it is also becoming clearer that psychological problems can be prevented by targeting individuals whose genes predispose them problems. In one recent study (Brody et al., 2009), for example, 11-year-olds with the high-risk variant of the same 5-HTTLPR gene studied by Caspi and his colleagues did not engage in risky behaviors such as substance use and sexual intercourse if their families participated in a prevention program that stressed good parenting skills and communication. They did engage in such behaviors if they were genetically predisposed to problem behavior and did not receive the prevention program—at much higher rates than peers who did not have high-risk genes. More and more evidence of gene–environment interactions is emerging as researchers look, as in Figure 3.7, at interactions between specific genes and specific experiences (Rutter et al., 2006).

Gene–Environment Correlations

Each person's genetic makeup also influences the kinds of experiences she seeks and has. Sandra Scarr and Kathleen McCartney (1983), drawing on the theorizing of Robert Plomin, John DeFries, and John Loehlin (1977), have proposed three kinds of gene–environment correlations, or ways in which a person's genes and his environment or experiences are systematically interrelated: passive, evocative, and active. The concept of gene–environment *interactions* tells us that people with different genes react differently to the experiences they have. By contrast, the concept of gene–environment *correlations* says that people with different genes experience different environments (Loehlin, 1992). As an illustration, imagine children with a genetic potential to be highly sociable and other children whose genes are likely to make them shy.

Passive Gene–Environment Correlations

The kind of home environment that parents provide for their children is influenced partly by the parents' genotypes. Because parents provide children not only with a home environment but also with their genes, the rearing environments to which children are exposed are correlated with (and are likely to suit) their genotypes.

For instance, sociable parents not only transmit their "sociable" genes to their children but also, because they have "sociable" genes, create a social home environment—inviting their friends over frequently, taking their children to many social events, and so on. The combination of genes for sociability and a social environment may make them more sociable than they would otherwise be. By contrast, the child with shy parents may receive genes for shyness *and* a correlated environment without much social stimulation.

Evocative Gene–Environment Correlations

A child's genotype also *evokes* certain kinds of reactions from other people. The smiley, sociable baby is likely to get more smiles, hugs, and social stimulation than the wary, shy baby—more opportunities to build social skills. Similarly, the sociable child may be chosen more often as a playmate by other children, the sociable adolescent may be invited to more parties, and the sociable adult may be given more job assignments involving public relations. In short, genetic makeup may affect the reactions of other people to a child and, hence, the kind of social environment that the child will experience.

Active Gene–Environment Correlations

Finally, children's genotypes influence the kinds of environments they *seek*. The individual with a genetic predisposition to be extraverted is likely to go to every party in sight, invite friends to the house, join organizations, and otherwise build a "niche" that is highly socially stimulating and that strengthens social skills. The child with genes for shyness may actively avoid large group activities and instead develop solitary interests.

Passive, evocative, and active genotype–environment correlations can all operate to influence a trait as parents and children choose and influence their environments (Rutter et al., 2006). However, Scarr and McCartney suggest that the balance of the three types of genotype–environment correlations shifts during

If the daughter of a runner turns out to be a good runner, is it because of genetic endowment or experience? We cannot say because genes and environment are correlated. Through passive gene–environment correlation, the children of athletes not only inherit their parent's genes but also grow up in sports-oriented family environments.

development. Because infants are at home a good deal, their environment is largely influenced by their parents through passive influences. Evocative influences operate throughout life; our characteristic, genetically influenced traits consistently prompt characteristic reactions in other people. Finally, as humans develop, they become increasingly able to build their own niches, so active gene–environment correlations become increasingly important.

Genetic Influences on Environment

Is there much evidence supporting Scarr and McCartney's claim that people's genes are correlated with, and possibly influence, their experiences in life? Indeed there is. Behavioral geneticists are discovering that measures of environment—especially the family environments of children—are themselves heritable (Butcher & Plomin, 2008)! What this means is that identical twins are more similar than fraternal twins, and biological siblings are more similar than adoptive siblings, in the environments they experience and in their perceptions of these environments. For example, there are genetically related similarities in:

- Both objective and perceived aspects of parenting style, such as warmth and the quality of the parent–child relationship (Plomin & Bergeman, 1991; Reiss, 2005)
- Time spent watching television (Plomin et al., 1990)
- Number of stressful life events experienced, especially events like divorcing one's spouse that the person could have helped to cause, as opposed to uncontrollable events like death of a parent (Kendler et al., 1993)

If our genetically influenced personality traits affect how others treat us and what experiences we seek and have, these findings make sense. For example, identical twins who are irritable and difficult could help create a conflict-ridden family environment, whereas calm and controlled children could help create a cohesive family environment (Krueger, Markon, & Bouchard, 2003).

Such findings challenge some of our most fundamental assumptions about human development. After all, they say that what we regard as purely environmental influences on development partly reflect the workings of heredity (Reiss et al., 2000; Rowe, 1994). As Robert Plomin (1990) suggests, we must constantly question our assumptions about nature and nurture. Suppose, he says, we find that parents who read to their children have brighter children than parents who do not read to their children. In the not-so-distant past, most developmentalists would have interpreted this finding rather uncritically as evidence that parents make important contributions to their children's intellectual development by reading to them. Without denying the importance of parents, suppose we offer this alternative interpretation: parents and children whose genes predispose them to be highly intelligent are more likely to seek opportunities to read than parents and children who are less intellectually inclined. If this is the case, can we be so sure that reading to children *causes* them to be brighter? Would we be able to show that reading to children is beneficial even when the parents and children involved are genetically unrelated?

Another example: If we observe that aggressive children tend to have parents who are negative and hostile toward them, can we be sure that the children's aggression was caused by negative parenting? Is it not also possible that they inherited genes that predisposed them to be irritable and aggressive themselves and made their parents hostile toward them? The evidence tell us that it works both ways: negative parents contribute to the development of antisocial behavior in children, but children genetically predisposed to be antisocial also bring out the worst in their parents (Larsson et al., 2008; O'Connor et al., 1998).

Perhaps the most convincing evidence of the importance of gene–environment correlations comes from an ambitious study by David Reiss, Jenae Neiderhiser, E. Mavis Hetherington, and Robert Plomin, summarized in their book *The Relationship Code* (2000). These researchers studied 720 pairs of same-sex adolescents who differed in their degree of biological relationship, from identical twins to biological siblings to unrelated stepsiblings. They measured environmental variables such as quality of parent–child interaction and adolescent adjustment variables such as self-esteem, sociability, depression, and antisocial behavior.

Repeatedly, genes shared by parents and adolescents partly or even largely accounted for relationships between children's experiences in the family and their developmental outcomes— for example, between negative parenting and antisocial behavior on the part of adolescents. In 44 of 52 instances in which significant relationships between measures of the family environment and adolescent adjustment were detected, genes influenced both family environment and adolescent adjustment and accounted for most of the relationship between the two (Reiss & Neiderhiser, 2000).

So genes and environment conspire to shape development. Genes influence how parents, peers, and others treat children. These environmental influences then contribute to the individual's development, often reinforcing genetically based predispositions.

Controversies Surrounding Genetic Research

As illustrated by debates over reproductive technologies, cloning, gene therapy, and stem cell research, our society is grappling with the complex and troubling public policy and ethical issues that have arisen as geneticists have gained the capacity to identify the carriers and potential victims of diseases and disorders, to give parents information that might prompt them to abort a fetus that does not meet their expectations, and to experiment with techniques for altering the genetic code through gene therapy (see McCabe & McCabe, 2008). As Application Box 3.1 illustrates, gene therapy with humans has not yet been very successful but is likely to be pursued more vigorously, along with stem cell therapies, as knowledge expands.

Likewise, behavioral genetics research is controversial among developmental scientists. On the one hand, it has provided important insights into human development: that genes are important, that the unique experiences of siblings are often more influential than those they share, that children influence parents just as parents influence children. Behavioral genetics research sometimes provides more convincing evidence of the effects of the environment on development than studies that do not take genes into account. As a result, more and more researchers are using twins and other biologically related pairs in their research so that they can better distinguish which apparent effects of experience are purely environmental and which at least partially reflect the workings of genes and gene–environment correlations (Johnson, Turkheimer, Gottesman, & Bouchard, 2009).

Nonetheless, some behavioral geneticists have overstated the importance of genes and underestimated the importance of

application 3.1

Prevention and Treatment of Genetic Conditions

Ultimately, genetic researchers want to know how the damaging effects of genes associated with diseases and disorders can be prevented, cured, or at least minimized. One of the greatest success stories in genetic research involves **phenylketonuria (PKU)**, a disorder caused by mutations in a single pair of recessive genes (Turnpenny & Ellard, 2005; Widaman, 2009). Affected children lack a critical enzyme needed to metabolize phenylalanine, a component of many foods (including milk). As phenylalanine accumulates in the body, it is converted to a harmful acid that attacks the nervous system and causes mental retardation and hyperactivity.

In the mid-1950s, scientists developed a special diet low in phenylalanine, and in 1961 they developed a simple blood test that could detect PKU soon after birth, before any damage had been done. Today, newborn infants are routinely screened for PKU, and affected children are immediately placed on the special (and, unfortunately, distasteful) diet (Miller, 1995). They must stay on it for their entire lives or risk deterioration in cognitive functioning (National Institutes of Health, 2000; Santos et al., 2006). It is especially important for a mother with PKU to stay on the special diet during pregnancy; otherwise, high levels of phenylalanine in her blood can harm her fetus, even if the fetus has only one of the PKU genes (Widaman, 2009).

Here, then, genetic research led to the prevention of one cause of mental retardation. And here is a clear-cut example of the interaction between genes and environment: a child will develop the condition and become mentally retarded if he inherits the PKU genes *and* eats a normal (high-phenylalanine) diet but not if he eats the special (low-phenylalanine) diet.

Guided by the Human Genome Project, medical researchers today are actively experimenting with **gene therapy**—interventions that involve substituting normal genes for the genes associated with a disease or disorder or otherwise altering a person's genetic makeup. In some experiments, viruses are used to carry normal replacement genes into an individual's cells (Turnpenny & Ellard, 2005). Gene therapy experiments to treat such genetic disorders as hemophilia (through infusions of normal genes into the blood) and the lung disease cystic fibrosis (using aerosol sprays to deliver normal genes to the lungs) have had some success (Griesenbach, Geddes, & Alton, 2006; Park & Gow, 2006; Walsh, 2003).

Yet progress in gene therapy has been slow because of a host of problems (Park & Gow, 2006; Weiss, 2003a). The death of Jesse Gelsinger, the first person to die in a gene therapy trial, was a sobering reminder of the risks. His immune system attacked the viruses that were to carry normal genes into his malfunctioning liver and destroyed not only the viruses but his own organs (Fischer, 2000). This 1999 tragedy resulted in stricter controls on gene therapy research and increased concern about ethical issues.

Although effective gene therapies undoubtedly will be developed, it is simpleminded to think that gene therapies will prevent or cure most diseases and disorders. Why? Because, as you now understand, most conditions are the product of multiple genes and environmental factors interacting. Researchers not only must deliver the right genes to the body in sufficient number to have the desired effect but also must get them to turn on and off when they should to produce normal functioning and control environmental factors as well. No "quick fix" such as the PKU diet will be possible.

Gene therapy experiments with mice promise to yield treatments that could benefit humans.

Some researchers see more promise in stem cell therapies in which undifferentiated **stem cells**—cells that have the potential to become many different types of specialized cells—are converted into the specialized cells needed by people with diseases and disorders and are transplanted into their bodies (McCabe & McCabe, 2008; Park, 2009). The use of embryonic stem cells for this purpose has been highly controversial, but researchers are now perfecting techniques that enable them to convert adult cells that have become specialized back into undifferentiated stem cells, as well as to reprogram adult cells to perform different functions (Park, 2009). Because the individual's own cells would be used to create therapeutic cells (for example, insulin-producing cells for people with diabetes), they would not be rejected by the person's immune system. Much remains to be learned, and there could turn out to be many bumps along the way, but the pace of progress is staggering, so stay tuned for more breakthroughs in both gene therapy and stem cell therapy.

family (Rutter, 2006), and that may have contributed to doubts among some developmentalists about the value of behavioral genetics research. The critics believe that techniques for calculating heritability attribute too much importance to genes and too little to environment by often giving genes credit for variation that is actually associated with gene–environment interactions or gene–environment correlations (McCartney, 2003; Rutter, 2006). Critics doubt that the influences of genes and environment on individual differences can ever be cleanly separated (Collins et al., 2000; Lerner, 2003). They even question whether it is worth trying to do so, insisting that behavioral genetics research will never tell us about what we should really want to understand: *epigenesis*, the long and complex process through which genes and environment, working together, steer development (Gottlieb, Wahlsten, & Lickliter, 2006).

Partly in response to criticism, behavioral geneticists are continually improving their methods of study and continue to offer new insights into genetic and environmental influences, as you will see throughout this book. Parents and helping professionals are likely to be in a better position to optimize development if they are sensitive to children's genetically based predispositions so that they can strengthen each child's adaptive tendencies and weaken or work around the maladaptive ones. Providing children with optimal experiences, of course, depends on knowing which environments stimulate healthy development and which do not. It is fitting, then, that the next chapter takes a closer look at early environmental influences on development.

Checking Mastery

Label each example below as an example of (a) gene–environment interaction, (b) passive gene–environment correlation, (c) evocative gene–environment correlation, or (d) active gene–environment correlation.

1. Roger inherited genes for artistic creativity from his parents and grew up watching them paint.

2. Kayla inherited genes for mathematical ability and has been taking extra math and science courses in college.

3. Sydney inherited a gene that can cause mental retardation but only in children who do not receive enough folic acid in their diet.

4. Andy got genes for anxiety, and his anxious behavior makes his parents overprotective of him.

Making Connections

1. Assume that genes predispose some people to be highly religious and some people to be unreligious and that some environments nurture religiosity and others do not. Explain how a gene–environment interaction and a gene–environment correlation could each help make Peter more religious than Paul.

2. What information in this chapter makes you think you will turn out very much like your parents—and what information suggests that this may not be the case at all?

Chapter Summary

3.1 Evolution and Species Heredity

- As humans, we develop similarly in part because we share a species heredity, the product of evolution.
- According to Darwin's theory of evolution, if there is genetic variation in a species—and if some genes aid members of the species in adapting to their environment and reproducing—those genes will become more common in the population over time through natural selection.
- Humans are also similar because they inherit a characteristically human environment, which they change through cultural evolution.

3.2 Individual Heredity

- Each human has an individual heredity provided at conception, when sperm and ovum, each with 23 chromosomes (thanks to meiosis), unite to form a single-cell zygote with 46 chromosomes. Parent and child share 50% of their genes in common; siblings share 50% on average.
- The chromosomes contain some 20,000–25,000 protein-building genes, along with regulatory DNA; the Human Genome Project and related studies have revealed similarities and differences between the genes of different human groups and different species.
- Environmental factors influence how a genotype (genetic makeup) is translated into a phenotype (actual traits); regulatory DNA and environmental factors influence the important process of gene expression throughout the life span.
- The three main mechanisms of inheritance are single gene-pair inheritance, sex-linked inheritance, and polygenic (multiple gene) inheritance. Some children are also affected by noninherited changes in gene structure (mutations); others, because of errors in meiosis, have chromosome abnormalities such as Down, Turner, Klinefelter, and fragile X syndromes.
- Genetic counseling offers information and guidance to people at risk for genetic conditions; abnormalities can be detected prenatally through amniocentesis, chorionic villus sampling, ultrasound, maternal blood sampling, and preimplantation genetic diagnosis.

3.3 Studying Genetic and Environmental Influences

- Behavioral geneticists conduct selective breeding and twin, adoption, and other family studies that describe resemblances between pairs of people using concordance rates and correlation coefficients. They then estimate the heritability of traits and the contributions of shared (with siblings) and nonshared (unique) environmental influences.
- Techniques of molecular genetics are used to identify and study particular gene variants and to compare people who do and do not have them.

3.4 Selected Findings

- Performance on measures of intelligence is a heritable trait. From infancy to adulthood, individual differences in mental ability more strongly reflect both individual genetic makeup and nonshared environmental influences, whereas shared environmental influences wane.
- Aspects of temperament and personality are also genetically influenced, and nonshared environmental influences are significant but shared environmental influences are not.

- Similarly, psychological disorders such as schizophrenia have a genetic basis but it often takes an interaction of genes and environmental stressors to produce disorder.
- Overall, physical and physiological characteristics are more strongly influenced by genetic endowment than are intellectual abilities and, in turn, temperament and personality traits, and finally attitudes and interests. Heritability differs depending on characteristics of the sample studied.

3.5 Genes and Environment Conspiring

- Both genes and nonshared environment are influential over the life span, but shared environmental influences generally become less important after childhood.
- Gene–environment interactions mean that environment influences how genes are expressed and that genes influence how people react to the environment. Passive, evocative, and active gene–environment correlations suggest that people experience and seek environments that often match and reinforce their genetic predispositions and that measures of environmental influence partly reflect genetic makeup.

Checking Mastery Answers

For answers to Checking Mastery questions, visit www.cengagebrain.com

Key Terms

species heredity **76**
natural selection **77**
cultural evolution **78**
conception **78**
zygote **78**
chromosome **78**
meiosis **78**
mitosis **79**
DNA **79**
allele **80**
Human Genome Project **80**
crossing over **80**
identical twins **80**
fraternal twins **80**
X chromosome **81**
Y chromosome **81**
karyotype **81**
genotype **81**
phenotype **81**
gene expression **82**
single gene-pair inheritance **82**

dominant gene **82**
recessive gene **82**
incomplete dominance **85**
codominance **85**
sex-linked characteristic **85**
hemophilia **85**
polygenic trait **85**
mutation **85**
sickle-cell disease **85**
chromosome abnormalities **86**
Down syndrome **86**
Turner syndrome **87**
Klinefelter syndrome **87**
fragile X syndrome **87**
genetic counseling **87**
carrier **88**
Huntington's disease **89**
ultrasound **90**
amniocentesis **90**
chorionic villus sampling (CVS) **90**

maternal blood sampling **90**
preimplantation genetic diagnosis **90**
behavioral genetics **91**
heritability **91**
selective breeding **91**
twin study **91**
adoption study **91**
concordance rate **92**
shared environmental influences **92**
nonshared environmental influences **93**

molecular genetics **93**
temperament **95**
schizophrenia **96**
gene–environment interaction **99**
gene–environment correlation **100**
phenylketonuria (PKU) **102**
gene therapy **102**
stem cell **102**

Media Resources

Psychology CourseMate

Access an integrated eBook and chapter-specific learning tools including flashcards, quizzes, videos, and more. Go to www.cengagebrain.com

Gene Therapy

Web presence for this journal features the most current research into genetic and cell-based technologies to treat disease. Host to a number of articles and reviews. To access, see "web links" in Psychology CourseMate at www.cengagebrain.com

Human Genome Project

The Human Genome Project is an international research effort aimed at characterizing the makeup of all 46 chromosomes by mapping sequences of their DNA. For a look at how this is done, as well as the latest in efforts to understand and prevent genetic defects and diseases, check out the website for the National Human Genome Research Institute. To access, see "web links" in Psychology CourseMate at www.cengagebrain.com

Understanding the DATA: Exercises on the Web (WWW)

www.cengagebrain.com
For additional insight on the data presented in this chapter, try out the exercises for these figures in Psychology CourseMate at

www.cengagebrain.com:

Table 3.5 Average Correlations between the IQ Scores of Pairs of Individuals

Figure 3.6 The proportions of variance in child IQ scores explained by genes, shared environment, and nonshared environment differ for children from low or high socioeconomic status (SES) environments.

Figure 3.7 The odds of a depressive episode at age 26 are highest for individuals who: (1) inherit two genes known to increase the risk of depression rather than two genes known to protect against depression, and (2) experience four or more stressful life events between ages 21 and 26. This is an example of gene–environment interaction: the effects of genetic makeup on depression depend on how stressful a person's environment is, and the effects of stressful life events depend on the person's genotype.

CengageNOW

www.cengagebrain.com

Go to www.cengagebrain.com to link to CengageNOW, your online study tool. First take the Pre-Test for this chapter to get your Personalized Study Plan, which will identify topics you need to review and direct you to online resources. Then take the Post-Test to determine what concepts you have mastered and what you still need work on.

The Prenatal Period and Birth

© Ryan McVay/Photodisc/Getty Images

At age 26, Serena was not thinking about getting pregnant. She and her boyfriend, Tony, were both getting adjusted to new jobs and working long hours. Serena tried to keep up with her regular exercise routine and struggled through a nasty sinus infection requiring treatment with antibiotics. She wasn't too concerned when she gained a few pounds but began to worry when she missed several menstrual periods. A visit to her doctor revealed that she was nearly 5 months pregnant, probably a result of the antibiotics decreasing the effectiveness of her birth control. Serena's mind raced as she considered all the things she had—or had not—done during recent months that might have influenced her unborn baby. Did she drink too much alcohol? Had she eaten a healthy diet? These thoughts were quickly followed by concerns about what the childbirth experience would be like and how she and Tony would adjust to this rather unexpected change in their lives.

We will answer these questions and more in this chapter on prenatal development, the birth experience, and the first hours and days of life. You will learn why the environment of the womb is so important and how it can set the stage for healthy development across the entire life span. The material in this chapter is a good illustration of how developmentalists seek to optimize development by using research to guide practices before, during, and after pregnancy.

1. How does development typically unfold during the prenatal period?

2. What factors can adversely affect prenatal development?

3. How can development during the prenatal and perinatal periods be optimized?

4. What risks face the newborn and how can these risks be minimized?

4.1 Prenatal Development

Perhaps at no time in the life span does development occur faster, or is environment more important, than between conception and birth. What maturational milestones normally occur during this period?

Conception

Midway through the menstrual cycle, every 28 days or so, females ovulate: an ovum (egg cell) ripens, leaves the ovary, and begins its journey through the fallopian tube to the uterus.

Usually the egg disintegrates and leaves the body as part of the menstrual flow. However, if the woman has intercourse with a fertile man around the time of ovulation, the 300 million or so sperm cells in his seminal fluid swim, tadpole style, in all directions. Of the approximately 300 sperm that survive the 6-hour journey into the fallopian tubes, one may meet and penetrate the ovum on its descent from the ovary (Sadler, 2010; see also ■ Figure 4.1). Once this one sperm penetrates the egg cell, a biochemical reaction occurs that repels other sperm and keeps them from entering the already fertilized egg. As explained in Chapter 3, conception, the beginning of life, occurs when the genetic material of the sperm and egg unite to form a single-celled zygote.

The process may sound simple, but as many as one in four couples experience difficulties conceiving despite their strong desires to have a child. **Infertility**—not being able to get pregnant after a year of trying—is equally likely to be traced to the man as the woman and stems from a variety of causes. For example, adolescents and adults who have contracted sexually transmitted infections may become infertile. Some couples are helped to conceive in relatively simple ways. A man may be ad-

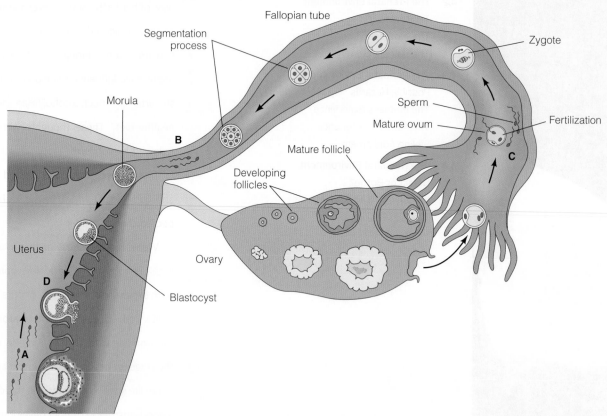

■ **FIGURE 4.1** Fertilization and implantation. (A) Millions of sperm cells have entered the vagina and are finding their way into the uterus. (B) Some spermatozoa are moving up the fallopian tube (there is a similar tube on the other side) toward the ovum. (C) Fertilization occurs. The fertilized ovum drifts down the tube, dividing and forming new cells as it goes, until it implants itself in the wall of the uterus (D) by the seventh or eighth day after fertilization.

vised to wear looser pants and underwear because an unusually high temperature in the testes interferes with sperm production. A woman may be asked to take her temperature to determine when she ovulates and is therefore most likely to become pregnant.

When simpler methods fail, some couples move on to more elaborate (and expensive) assisted reproductive technologies (ARTs), medical techniques used to increase fertility. ART techniques typically start with or include prescription drugs for the woman to stimulate her ovaries to ripen and release several eggs. If this is unsuccessful, couples and their doctors may proceed to **artificial insemination**, which involves injecting sperm, either from a woman's partner or from a donor, into her uterus. Or they may use **in vitro fertilization (IVF)**, in which several eggs are removed from a woman's ovary and manually combined with sperm in a laboratory dish before being returned to a woman's uterus in hopes that one egg will implant on the wall of the uterus. We should note that there are many variations of IVF, depending on who provides the eggs and the sperm. A couple wanting to have a child (the would-be biological mother and father) could donate both eggs and sperm and have the biological mother carry the baby to term. At the other end of the spectrum, an infant conceived through IVF could wind up with five "parents": a sperm donor, an egg donor, a surrogate mother in whom the fertilized egg is implanted, and a caregiving mother and father.

Infertility is costly, both economically and emotionally. In the United States, for example, the cost of IVF is about $12,400 for each attempt. The success rate for women who use their own fresh (rather than frozen) eggs is about 1 in 4 overall, but decreases as mothers get older (Centers for Disease Control, 2008). For women over the age of 42, the odds of a live birth following ART are about 1 in 10. Couples report that infertility is stressful, and unsuccessful treatment can have long-term psychosocial effects (Verhaak et al., 2005). Still, even couples who have not successfully conceived following infertility treatment are usually found to be well adjusted and stable, and looking back on the experience, they report positive growth in their lives as a result of this experience (Daniluk, 2001). Although their attempts to conceive were unsuccessful, they may feel satisfied that they actively pursued available options.

Prenatal Stages

The zygote contains the 46 chromosomes that are the genetic blueprint for the individual's development. It takes about 266 days (about 9 months) for the zygote to become a fetus of billions of cells that is ready to be born. This prenatal development is divided into three stages or periods: the germinal period, the embryonic period, and the fetal period.

The Germinal Period

The **germinal period** lasts approximately 2 weeks; the important events of this period are outlined in ● **Table 4.1**. For the first week or two, the zygote divides many times through mitosis, forming the **blastocyst**, a hollow ball of about 150 cells that is the

● TABLE 4.1 EVENTS OF THE GERMINAL PERIOD

Day	Event
1	Fertilization usually occurs within 24 hours of ovulation.
2	The single-celled zygote begins to divide 24–36 hours after fertilization.
3–4	The mass has 16 cells and is called a morula; it is traveling down the fallopian tube to the uterus.
5	An inner cell mass forms; the entire mass is called a blastocyst and is the size of a pinhead.
6–7	The blastocyst attaches to the wall of the uterus.
8–14	The blastocyst becomes fully embedded in the wall of the uterus. It now has about 250 cells.

size of the head of a pin. When the blastocyst reaches the uterus around day 6, it implants tendrils from its outer layer into the blood vessels of the uterine wall. This is quite an accomplishment; only about half of all fertilized ova are successfully implanted in the uterus. In addition, not all implanted embryos survive the early phases of prenatal development. Between 15 and 20% of recognized pregnancies are short-lived, ending in **miscarriage** before survival outside the womb is possible, and as many as 50% of *unrecognized* pregnancies are believed to terminate with miscarriage (Friebe & Arck, 2008; Sadler, 2010). Many of these early losses are because of genetic defects.

The Embryonic Period

The **embryonic period** occurs from the third to the eighth week after conception. During this short time, every major organ takes shape, in at least a primitive form, in a process called **organogenesis**. The layers of the blastocyst differentiate, forming structures that sustain development. The outer layer becomes both the **amnion**, a watertight membrane that fills with fluid that cushions and protects the embryo, and the **chorion**, a membrane that surrounds the amnion and attaches rootlike extensions called *villi* to the uterine lining to gather nourishment for the embryo. The chorion eventually becomes the lining of the **placenta**, a tissue fed by blood vessels from the mother and connected to the embryo by the umbilical cord. Through the placenta and umbilical cord, the embryo receives oxygen and nutrients from the mother and eliminates carbon dioxide and metabolic wastes into the mother's bloodstream. A membrane called the *placental barrier* allows these small molecules to pass through, but it prevents the large blood cells of embryo and mother from mingling. It also protects the developing child from many harmful substances, but as you will see shortly, it is not infallible; some dangerous substances slip through.

TABLE 4.2 EVENTS OF THE EMBRYONIC PERIOD

Week	Event
3	Now an embryo, the person-to-be is just 1/10 of an inch (2 mm) long. It has become elongated, and three layers emerge—the ectoderm, mesoderm, and endoderm.
4	The embryo is so curved that the two ends almost touch. The outer layer (ectoderm) folds into the neural tube. From the mesoderm, a tiny heart forms and begins to beat. The endoderm differentiates into a gastrointestinal tract and lungs. Between days 21 and 28, eyes develop.
5	Ears, mouth, and throat take shape. Arm and leg buds appear. The handplate from which fingers will emerge appears. The heart divides into two regions, and the brain differentiates into forebrain, midbrain, and hindbrain.
6–7	The embryo is almost 1 inch long. The heart divides into four chambers. Fingers emerge from the handplate, and primitive facial features are evident. The important process of sexual differentiation begins.
8	Most structures and organs are present. Ovaries and testes are evident. The embryo begins to straighten and assumes a more human appearance.

Meanwhile, the cells in the interior of the blastocyst give rise to the ectoderm, mesoderm, and endoderm. These will eventually evolve into specific tissues and organ systems, including the central nervous system (brain and spinal cord) from the ectoderm; muscle tissue, cartilage, bone, heart, arteries, kidneys, and gonads from the mesoderm; and gastrointestinal tract, lungs, and bladder from the endoderm (Sadler, 2010).

Development proceeds at a breathtaking pace (● Table 4.2). The beginnings of a brain are apparent after only 3–4 weeks, when the neural plate folds up to form the neural tube (■ Figure 4.2). The bottom of the tube becomes the spinal cord. "Lumps" emerge at the top of the tube and form the forebrain, midbrain, and hindbrain (■ Figure 4.3). The so-called primitive or lower portions of the brain develop earliest. They regulate such biological functions as digestion, respiration, and elimination; they also control sleep–wake states and permit simple motor reactions. These are the parts of the brain that make life possible.

In approximately 1 out of 1000 pregnancies, the neural tube fails to fully close (Sadler, 2010). When this happens at the bottom of the tube, it can lead to **spina bifida**, in which part of the spinal cord is not fully encased in the protective covering of the spinal column. Children with spina bifida typically have neurological problems ranging from very mild to severe depending on the location and size of the opening. Failure to close at the top

of the neural tube can lead to **anencephaly**, a lethal defect in which the main portion of the brain above the brain stem fails to develop (Sadler, 2010). Neural tube defects occur 25–29 days after conception and are more common when the mother is deficient in folic acid, a substance critical for normal gene function (Percy, 2007; Sadler, 2010). This illustrates the importance of good maternal nutrition for development, which we will have more to say about in a later section.

Other critical organs are also taking shape. Just 4 weeks after conception, a tiny heart not only has formed but also has begun to beat. The eyes, ears, nose, and mouth rapidly take shape in the second month, and buds appear that will become arms and legs. During the second month, a primitive nervous system also makes newly formed muscles contract. Only 60 days after conception, at the close of the embryonic period, the organism is a little over an inch long and has a distinctly human appearance.

The important process of sexual differentiation begins during the seventh and eighth prenatal weeks. First, undifferentiated tissue becomes either male testes or female ovaries: if the embryo inherited a Y chromosome at conception, a gene on it calls for the construction of testes; in a genetic female with two X chromosomes, ovaries form instead. The testes of a male embryo secrete **testosterone**, the primary male sex hormone that stimulates the development of a male internal reproductive system, and another hormone that inhibits the development of a female internal reproductive system. In the absence of these hormones, the embryo develops the internal reproductive system of a female.

Clearly the embryonic period is dramatic and highly important because it is when the structures that make us human evolve. Yet many pregnant women, either because they do not yet know they are pregnant—like Serena from the chapter opening story—or because they do not appreciate the value of early prenatal care, do not go to a doctor until *after* the eighth week of

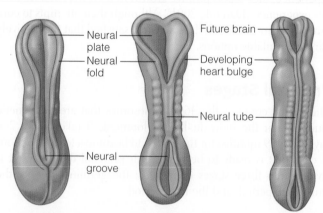

■ FIGURE 4.2 The nervous system emerges from the neural plate, which thickens and folds to form the neural groove. When the edges of the groove meet, the neural tube is formed. All this takes place between 18 and 26 days after conception.

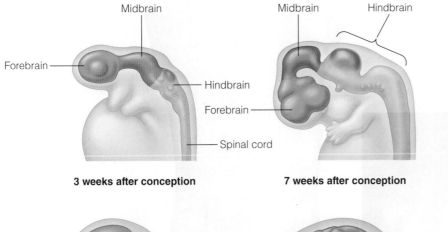

3 weeks after conception

7 weeks after conception

11 weeks after conception

At birth

■ **FIGURE 4.3** The brain at four stages of development, showing hindbrain, midbrain, and forebrain.

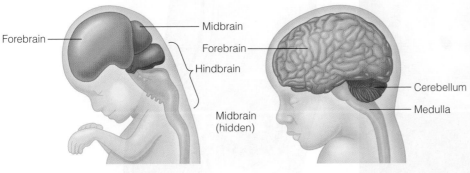

About a month after conception, this embryo is shown up against a cross-section of the placenta. The umbilical cord is shown at the bottom of the photo, connecting the embryo to its vital source of life in the womb. The eyes are clearly visible, as are the arms, legs, and ear buds. The fingers are just beginning to differentiate, and the mouth is formed.

prenatal development. By this time, it may be too late to prevent the damage that can be caused by an unhealthy lifestyle.

The Fetal Period

The **fetal period** lasts from the ninth week of pregnancy until birth (● Table 4.3). Neurons continue to proliferate (that is, multiply) at a staggering rate during this period; by one estimate, the number of neurons increases by hundreds of thousands every minute throughout all of pregnancy, with a concentrated period of proliferation occurring between 10 and 20 weeks after conception (Nelson, Thomas, & de Haan, 2006). As a result of this rapid proliferation, the young infant has around 100 billion neurons. Another period of proliferation takes place after birth, but this produces an increase in glial cells, not nerve cells. Glial cells function primarily as support cells for neurons. Once formed, neurons migrate from their place of origin to particular locations within the brain where they will become part of specialized functioning units. The impetus for migration is influenced by genetic instructions and by the biochemical environment in which brain cells find themselves. Neurons travel along the surface of glial cells and detach at programmed destinations in the developing brain. Neurons migrate to the closest or innermost parts of the brain first and to the farthest or outermost parts last, and much of this occurs between 8 and 15 weeks after conception.

In addition to multiplication and migration of cells, **differentiation** is occurring. Early in development, every neuron starts with the potential to become any specific type of neuron; what it becomes—how it differentiates—depends on where it migrates. Thus, if a neuron that would normally migrate to the visual cortex of an animal's brain is transplanted into the area of the cortex that controls hearing, it will differentiate as an auditory neuron instead of a visual neuron (Johnson, 2005). As noted in Chapter 3, some of these early cells that have not yet specialized have the capability of developing into any type of cell or tissue. Such stem cells are also present in adult tissue, but they are much more limited in number and ability to specialize. Adult stem cells may hold the key to new therapies involving tissue and organ transplants to replace damaged or diseased tissue. Scientists have much to learn, though, before any such therapies can become a reality (see Chapter 3).

Organ systems that formed during the embryonic period continue to grow and begin to function. Harmful agents will no longer cause major malformations because organs have already formed, but they can stunt the growth of the fetus and interfere with the wiring of its rapidly developing nervous system.

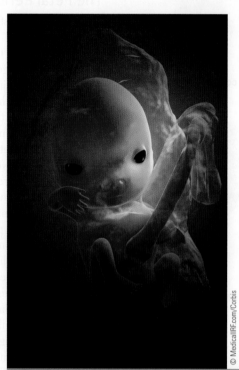

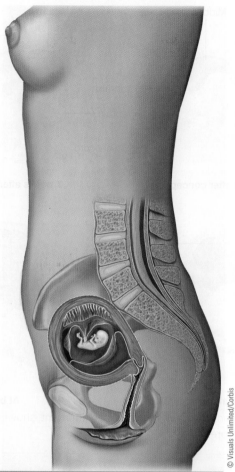

Here we see what the developing fetus looks like in the womb at 10 weeks after conception. Right, we see how things look at this same time on the outside: a "baby bump" is just barely visible on the mother, despite the amazing changes that have been taking place inside.

In the third month of pregnancy, distinguishable external sex organs appear, the bones and muscles develop, and the fetus becomes frisky: by the end of the third month (that is, by the end of the first third of pregnancy, or *trimester*), it moves its arms, kicks its legs, makes fists, and even turns somersaults. The mother probably does not yet feel all this activity because the fetus is still only about 3 inches long. Nonetheless, this tiny being can swallow, digest food, and urinate. All this "behaving" contributes to the proper development of the nervous system, digestive system, and other systems of the body, and it is consistent with the behaviors that we observe *after* birth (Kurjak et al., 2004).

During the *second trimester* (the fourth, fifth, and sixth months), more refined activities appear (including thumb sucking), and by the end of this period the sensory organs are functioning: premature infants as young as 25 weeks respond to loud noises and bright lights (Allen & Capute, 1986; Sadler, 2010). At about 23 weeks after conception, midway through the fifth month, the fetus reaches the **age of viability**, when survival outside the uterus is possible *if* the brain and respiratory system are sufficiently developed. The age of viability is earlier today than at any time in the past because medical techniques for keeping

fragile babies alive have improved considerably over the past few decades. In 2007 a baby girl believed to be the most premature baby to survive went home after 4 months of neonatal intensive care. She was born at 21 weeks and 6 days, weighing just 10 ounces. Despite this miracle, many infants born at 22–25 weeks do not survive, and of those who do, many experience chronic health or neurological problems. At one neonatal intensive care unit (NICU), for example, approximately 30% of infants born at 23 weeks' gestation do not survive, and of the survivors, approximately 30% have some sort of major impairment (Bell, 2009). Thus, the age of viability is an indicator of when survival *may be possible*, but it is by no means a guarantee of life or health.

During the *third trimester* (the seventh, eighth, and ninth months), the fetus gains weight rapidly. This time is also critical in the development of the brain, as is the entire prenatal period (see Chapter 5). Early in pregnancy, the basic architecture of the nervous system is developed. During the second half of pregnancy, neurons not only multiply at an astonishing rate (proliferation) but they also increase in size and develop an insulating cover, **myelin**, that improves their ability to transmit signals rapidly. Most importantly, guided by both a genetic blueprint and

● TABLE 4.3 EVENTS OF THE FETAL PERIOD

Week	Event
9	Bone tissue emerges, and the embryo becomes a fetus. The head of the fetus looks huge relative to the rest of the body—it takes up about half the total length of the fetus. The fetus can open and close its mouth and turn its head.
10–12	Fingers and toes are clearly formed. External genitalia have developed. Movements have increased substantially—arms and legs kick vigorously, but the fetus is still too small for the mother to feel all these movements. The fetus also shows "breathing" movements with its chest and some reflexes.
13–16	The heartbeat should be audible with a stethoscope. Fetal movements may become apparent to the mother. The fetus is about 4½ inches long, and the skeleton is becoming harder.
17–22	Fingernails and toenails, hair, teeth buds, and eyelashes grow. Brain development is phenomenal, and brainwaves are detectable.
23–25	These weeks mark the age of viability, when the fetus has a *chance* of survival outside the womb. It is about 12 inches long and weighs about 1 pound.
26–32	The fetus gains weight, and its brain grows. The nervous system becomes better organized.
33–38	The last 6 weeks of a full-term pregnancy bring further weight gain and brain activity. The lungs mature and begin to expand and contract.

early sensory experiences, neurons connect with one another and organize into working groups that control vision, memory, motor behavior, and other functions. For good reason, parents should be concerned about damage to the developing human during the first trimester, when the brain and other organs are forming. However, they should not overlook the significance of the second and third trimesters, which are critical to normal brain functioning and therefore to normal development.

As the brain develops, the behavior of the fetus becomes more like the organized and adaptive behavior seen in the newborn. For example, Janet DiPietro and her colleagues (2006, 2007) assessed heart rates and activity levels in fetuses at various prenatal intervals (between 20 and 38 weeks after conception), at 2 weeks of age, and again at 2 and 2½ years of age. Heart rate was relatively stable from the prenatal period into early childhood. By 36 weeks of gestation, heart rate activity and movement become increasingly organized into coherent patterns of waking and sleeping known as *infant states*. Fetuses whose heart rates and movements were concordant (that is, matched) at 36 weeks showed better regulation of their behavioral states at 2 weeks old. They were more alert, less irritable, better able to sustain their attention, and more likely to maintain control even during stressful parts of the postnatal examination. Beyond this, fetal heart rate variability was associated with mental development at age 2 and language development at age 2½. In particular, fetuses with slower and more variable heart rates had higher levels of mental and language development in early childhood compared with those who had faster and less variable heart rates. The researchers speculate that slow and variable heart rates may reflect optimal regulation of the nervous system.

DiPietro and her colleagues (1996b) also found that, with age, fetal heart rates become increasingly responsive to such stimuli as a vibrator placed on the mother's abdomen. Fetuses moved, on average, about once a minute and were active 20 to 30% of the time. At 20 weeks, fetuses spent only about 17% of

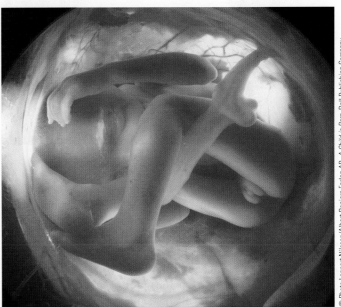

At 20 weeks, this male fetus is curled into the classic "fetal position" as his substantial growth begins to limit the space in the womb. In another 4 weeks, this little guy will reach the age of viability, when he might have a chance to survive outside the womb if born early.

their time in an organized infant state such as quiet sleep, active sleep, or active waking. By the end of the prenatal period, though, they were in one distinct state or another at least 85% of the time. They spent most of their time snoozing, especially in active sleep. Whereas in the 20th week of pregnancy they were almost never active and awake, by the 32nd week they spent 11 to 16% of their time in an active, waking state. The patterns de-

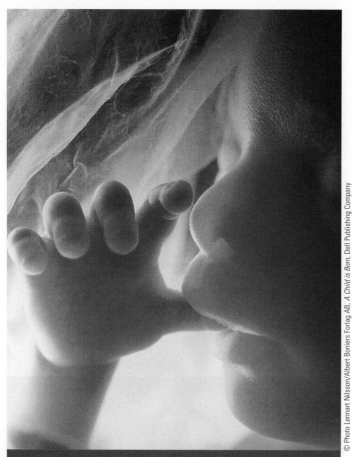

As it nears the end of the gestational period (38–40 weeks for a full-term infant), the fetus engages in many behaviors observed in newborns (here, it sucks its thumb).

© Photo Lennart Nilsson/Albert Bonniers Forlag AB, *A Child is Born*, Dell Publishing Company

Checking Mastery

1. What is conception, and what techniques can be used to assist conception?

2. What major developments occur during the third trimester of prenatal life?

3. When is survival outside the womb possible?

Making Connections

1. A close friend of yours believes she is about four weeks pregnant but is reluctant to schedule a visit with her doctor this early. What information would you give her about the importance of the first weeks of pregnancy? Would you advise her to seek prenatal care right away? If not, when would you advise her to seek care?

2. What ethical concerns should be considered with the use of artificial reproductive technologies? As technologies become more advanced in the future, what additional concerns may arise?

4.2 The Prenatal Environment

The mother's womb is the **prenatal environment** for the unborn child. Just as children are influenced by their physical and social environments, so too is the fetus affected by its surroundings. The physical environment includes everything from the molecules that reach the fetus's bloodstream before birth to the architecture of a home to the climate outside it. The social environment includes all the people who can influence and be influenced by the developing person and the broader culture. Although early theorists tended to view environment as a set of forces that shaped the individual, as though a person were just a lump of clay to be molded, we now know this is not the case. Recall the explanation from Chapter 1 of *reciprocal influences*: people shape their physical and social environments and are, in turn, affected by the environments they have helped create. For example, if a woman uses cocaine during pregnancy, her newborn may be extraordinarily fussy: environment has affected development. But a fussy baby is likely to affect his environment by irritating his mother, who then expresses her tenseness in her interactions with him; this makes him fussier, which aggravates his mother even more, and her aggravation, in turn, makes him even crankier. Such transactions between person and environment begin at the moment of conception.

The developing embryo-then-fetus is a vulnerable little creature. Research increasingly shows that events of the prenatal period can have lifelong effects on physical health and mental development (see, for example, Coe & Lubach, 2008; Hellemans et al., 2009). How then can development during this period be optimized? What hazards does the fetus face? "Experts" throughout history have offered several odd ideas about the effects of the prenatal physical environment on growth. For example, it was once believed that pregnant women could enhance their chances of bearing sons if they ate red meat and salty snacks, whereas eating vegetables and sweet snacks would supposedly increase the

tected in this and other studies suggest that important changes in the nervous system occur 28–32 weeks after conception, when premature infants are typically well equipped to survive. As the nervous system becomes more organized, so does behavior.

Interestingly, different fetuses display consistent differences in their patterns of heart rate and movement, and researchers have detected correlations between measures of fetal physiology and behavior and measures of infant temperament (DiPietro et al., 1996a, 2007; Werner et al., 2007). For example, active fetuses turned out to be active, difficult, and unpredictable babies, and fetuses whose states were better organized were also better regulated at 3 months old, as indicated by their waking fewer times during the night. The message is clear: Newborn behavior does not spring from nowhere; it emerges long before birth. There is a good deal of continuity between prenatal behavior and postnatal behavior.

By the middle of the ninth month, the fetus is so large that its most comfortable position in cramped quarters is head down with limbs curled in (the "fetal position"). The mother's uterus contracts at irregular intervals during the last month of pregnancy. When these contractions are strong, frequent, and regular, the mother is in the first stage of labor and the prenatal period is drawing to a close. Under normal circumstances, birth will occur within hours.

likelihood of having daughters (Springen, 2004). And until the early 1940s, it was widely—and wrongly—believed that the placenta was a marvelous screen that protected the embryo and fetus from nicotine, viruses, and all kinds of other hazards. In her book *Message in a Bottle: The Making of Fetal Alcohol Syndrome*, Janet Golden (2005) describes how experts and "regular folk" alike were reluctant to accept the findings that alcohol consumption during pregnancy could be harmful to the developing fetus because of the strongly held belief throughout much of history that the womb was a protective barrier. It wasn't until the early 1970s that we had the first official acknowledgment that this was not the case, when researchers identified a collection of symptoms in children whose mothers had consumed alcohol during pregnancy. (We will come back to this topic later in this section.)

Today we understand that transactions between the organism and its environment begin at conception. When all is right, the prenatal environment provides just the stimulation and support needed for the fetus to mature physically and to develop a repertoire of behaviors that allow it to seek more stimulation, which in turn contributes to the development of more sophisticated behavior. When the prenatal environment is abnormal, development can be steered far off track, as you will now see as we examine the influence of various substances. But just as exposure to some substances can place children at risk, other factors can enhance their developmental outcome, as you will see in later sections of this chapter.

Your main mission here is to discover the extent to which early environmental influences, interacting with genetic influences, make or break later development. The nature–nurture issue, then, is the central factor to consider when thinking about prenatal development and its influence on the developing person. Early environmental influences on development—bad and good—demand serious attention. Such influences interact with genetic makeup throughout the life span to make us who we are. If a common genetic heritage (species heredity) can make different human beings alike in some respects, so can similar environments. If unique genes make one person different from another, so do unique experiences.

Teratogens

A **teratogen** is any disease, drug, or other environmental agent that can harm a developing fetus (for example, by causing deformities, blindness, brain damage, or even death). The list of teratogens has grown frighteningly long, and the environment contains many potential teratogens whose effects on development have not yet been assessed. Before considering the effects of some major teratogens, however, let us emphasize that *only 15% of newborns have minor problems, and even fewer—perhaps 5%—have more significant anomalies due to teratogens* (Sadler, 2010). We will start with a few generalizations about the effects of teratogens, which we will then illustrate with examples:

- *Critical period.* The effects of a teratogenic agent are worst during the critical period when an organ system grows most rapidly.

- *Dosage and duration.* The greater the level of exposure and the longer the exposure to a teratogen, the more likely it is that serious damage will occur.
- *Genetic makeup.* Susceptibility to harm is influenced by the unborn child's and by the mother's genetic makeup. Some fetuses are more (or less) resistant to teratogens and some mothers are more (or less) able to detoxify teratogens (Percy, Lewkis, & Brown, 2007). Therefore, not all embryos and fetuses are affected, nor are they affected equally, by a teratogen.
- *Environment.* The effects of a teratogen depend on the quality of both the prenatal and the postnatal environments.

Look more closely at the first generalization, which is particularly important. A period of rapid growth is a **critical period** for an organ system—a time during which the developing organism is especially sensitive to environmental influences, positive or negative. As you will recall, organogenesis takes place during the embryonic period (weeks 3–8 of prenatal development). As ■ **Figure 4.4** shows, it is during this time—before many women even realize they are pregnant—that most organ systems are most vulnerable to damage. Moreover, each organ has a critical period that corresponds to its own time of most rapid development (for example, weeks 3–6 for the heart and weeks 4–7 for the arms and fingers). Once an organ or body part is fully formed, it is usually less susceptible to damage. However, because some organ systems—above all, the nervous system—can be damaged throughout pregnancy, *sensitive periods* might be a better term than *critical periods*.

Drugs

The principles of teratology can be illustrated by surveying just a few of the many drugs—prescription, over-the-counter, and social—that can disrupt prenatal development. More than half of pregnant women take at least one prescription or over-the-counter drug during pregnancy (Andrade et al., 2004). Under a doctor's close supervision, medications used to treat ailments and medical conditions are usually safe for mother and fetus. However, certain individuals exposed to certain drugs in certain doses at certain times during the prenatal period are damaged for life.

Thalidomide. In the late 1950s, the tranquilizer **thalidomide** was widely used in Europe to relieve morning sickness (the periodic nausea and vomiting many women experience during the first trimester of pregnancy). Presumably, the drug was safe; it had no ill effects in tests on pregnant rats. Tragically, however, the drug had adverse effects on humans. Indeed, more than any other drug, thalidomide alerted the world to the dangers of taking drugs during pregnancy.

Thousands of women who used thalidomide during the first 2 months of pregnancy gave birth to babies with all or parts of their limbs missing, with the feet or hands attached directly to the torso like flippers, or with deformed eyes, ears, noses, and hearts (Knightley et al., 1979). It soon became clear that there were critical periods for different deformities. If the mother had taken thalidomide 20–22 days after conception (34–36 days after

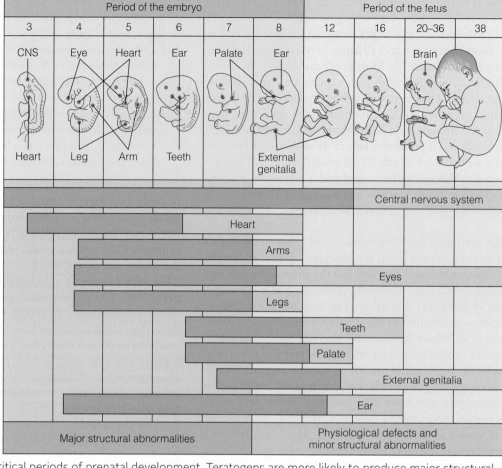

	Period of the embryo						Period of the fetus			
Prenatal week	3	4	5	6	7	8	12	16	20–36	38

Severity of defects (dark orange shading indicates the most highly sensitive period for teratogenic effects)

Central nervous system
Heart
Arms
Eyes
Legs
Teeth
Palate
External genitalia
Ear

Major structural abnormalities | Physiological defects and minor structural abnormalities

■ **FIGURE 4.4** The critical periods of prenatal development. Teratogens are more likely to produce major structural abnormalities during the third through the eighth prenatal week. Note, however, that many organs and body parts remain sensitive to teratogenic agents throughout the 9-month prenatal period.

SOURCE: Adapted from Moore, K. L. (1988). *The developing human.* Philadelphia: W. B. Saunders.

the first day of a woman's last menstrual period), her baby was likely to be born without ears. If she had taken it 22–27 days after conception, the baby often had missing or small thumbs; if thalidomide was taken between 27 and 33 days after conception, the child was likely to have stunted legs or no legs. And if the mother waited until 35 or 36 days after conception before using thalidomide, her baby was usually not affected. Thus, thalidomide had specific effects on development, depending on which structures were developing when the drug was taken.

Thalidomide, banned for years, is again being prescribed by physicians, this time for treatment of conditions associated with leprosy, acquired immunodeficiency syndrome (AIDS), tuberculosis, and some forms of cancer. Given its tragic past association with birth defects, the manufacturers of thalidomide have stamped each pill with a drawing of a pregnant woman inside a circle with a diagonal line through it (the universal "no" symbol) and have included a picture of a baby with the characteristic stunted limbs on the packaging accompanying the pills (Celgene Corporation, 2010). Critics, however, worry that these measures will not be enough to prevent future birth defects.

Tobacco. Warning labels on cigarette packages that smoking may damage fetuses have resulted in a decline, but not an absence, of smoking during pregnancy. The National Survey on Drug Use and Health (Substance Use, 2009) reports that 22% of women have smoked during their first trimester, when some may not yet know they are pregnant. The rate drops to 14% during the second and third trimesters, likely reflecting awareness of pregnancy and knowledge of the harmful effects of smoking on the developing fetus. Women who smoke experience higher rates of miscarriage than nonsmokers, and babies born to mothers who smoke grow more slowly in the womb and are at risk for prematurity, low birth weight, cleft lips (an opening in the top lip), and cleft palates (an opening in the roof of the mouth; Habek et al., 2002; Little, Cardy, & Munger, 2004). Smoking restricts blood flow to the fetus, which in turn reduces the levels of growth factors, oxygen, and nutrients that reach the fetus, leading to smaller size (Huijbregts et al., 2006; Meyer et al., 2009). More than half of infants born to women who smoke 20 or more cigarettes a day end up in neonatal intensive care and experience some degree of central nervous system impairment. Women do not even have

Classical singer Thomas Quasthoff was born in 1959 with the characteristic arm and leg defects associated with thalidomide, a drug prescribed in the late 1950s and early 1960s to relieve the nausea some women experience during pregnancy. From the nature of Quasthoff's condition—he stands about 4 feet tall and his arms are nearly missing, with hands attached close to his shoulders—we know that his mother took the drug 3–5 weeks after conception, a critical period for arm and leg formation.

The babies of smokers are also more susceptible than other babies to respiratory infections and breathing difficulties (Campos, Bravo, & Eugenin, 2009). The more a woman smokes during pregnancy, the more likely it is that her infant will experience growth retardation and neurological problems (Law et al., 2003; Romo, Carceller, & Tobajas, 2009). The risk of **sudden infant death syndrome (SIDS)**, in which a sleeping baby suddenly stops breathing and dies, also increases as the amount of smoking increases. And maternal smoking has been linked to mild cognitive difficulties and to conduct and behavior problems (NIDA, 2009b; Pickett et al., 2008; Stene-Larsen, Borge, & Vollrath, 2009). These effects appear to last at least into childhood. Finally, findings from longitudinal studies have led some researchers to conclude that chronic prenatal exposure to nicotine—a legal substance—may have more negative effects on central nervous system development than sporadic exposure to the illegal drug cocaine (Bada et al., 2005; Slotkin, 1998).

In sum, maternal smoking during pregnancy is unwise because it slows fetal growth and contributes to respiratory, cognitive, and conduct problems. These effects may be caused not only by nicotine and other chemicals in cigarettes but also by toxic by-products of smoking, such as carbon monoxide, which reduce the flow of blood and oxygen to the fetus. Further, we must consider that women who smoke during pregnancy are likely to be white, young, low-income, and less educated than women who do not smoke during pregnancy (Whalen et al., 2006). It may be that some of these other factors act independently or in conjunction with cigarette smoking to create the less than ideal outcomes seen among these exposed infants (Huijbregts et al., 2006). Exploration Box 4.1 describes a new research design that helps clarify the connection between maternal smoking and the outcomes observed in infants.

The good news is that even women who start their pregnancies as smokers can improve the outcome for their babies by quitting smoking during their pregnancy (Polakowski, Akinbami, & Mendola, 2009). The benefits are greatest for those women who quit during their first trimester but are also apparent for the babies of mothers who quit during their second trimester. Thus, women should be encouraged and supported to stop or reduce smoking during pregnancy.

to be heavy smokers during pregnancy for behavioral effects to be evident among their offspring. Newborns exposed to as few as 5 cigarettes a day in the womb are more irritable and score lower on standard assessments of behavioral functioning than other infants (Mansi et al., 2007). Often the small babies of smokers experience catch-up growth after they are born and reach normal size by the time they enter school, but the more their mothers smoked, the less likely it is that their growth will catch up completely (Kanellopoulos et al., 2007).

This pregnant woman poses with a cigarette held to her belly to make the point that maternal smoking has direct and measurable effects on the unborn baby. Smoking restricts the flow of blood and oxygen to the fetus, placing it at risk for low birth weight and premature delivery.

Alcohol. Alcohol consumed by the mother readily crosses the placenta, where it can directly affect fetal development and disrupt hormone functions of the placenta (Gabriel et al., 1998). Prenatal alcohol exposure disrupts the normal process of neuronal migration, leading to several outcomes depending on the severity of the effects. The most severe is a cluster of symptoms dubbed **fetal alcohol syndrome (FAS)**, with noticeable physical symptoms such as a small head and distinctive facial abnormalities (■ **Figure 4.5**). Children with

The Prenatal Effects of Smoking: Do They Result from Nature or Nurture?

As we have noted, smoking during pregnancy is associated with several negative consequences for the babies who were exposed in utero. But how do we know that the ill effects seen in these offspring are due to the prenatal exposure to smoke and not to other connections between mother and child, namely the genes that the mother has passed along? Until recently, we didn't know the answer to this. But thanks to a clever study by British researchers, we are now able to uncouple the influences of the prenatal environment from inherited influences. Frances Rice, Anita Thapar, and their colleagues (2007, 2009) realized that the key to untangling these influences would be to study two groups of children conceived through in vitro fertilization: Children who were the biological offspring of the mother (that is, the mother's own eggs were retrieved, fertilized, and then implanted in her womb) and children who were not biologically related to the mother (that is, a donor egg was fertilized and then implanted in her womb). The researchers looked at two dependent variables: birth weight and antisocial behavior at around age 6, and the rather striking findings are summarized in the table above.

	Low Birth Weight Due to Smoking	Elevated Antisocial Behaviors
Own Egg Used for IVF	Yes	Yes
Donor (Unrelated) Egg Used for IVF	Yes	No

Polluting the environment of the womb with the by-products of cigarette smoke results in lower birth weights. Lower birth weights were observed in the babies of mothers who smoked regardless of the genetic connection between mother and child. As for antisocial behaviors, these were observed in the offspring of smokers only when there was a genetic connection between mother and child. The children who were conceived with donor eggs and whose mothers smoked during pregnancy did not show elevated rates of antisocial behavior. Thus, a prenatal environment of smoke by-products does not increase antisocial behavior, but the mother's genetic contribution to her child does. There may be, for example, certain personality characteristics that make it more likely that a woman will smoke and that also contribute to antisocial behaviors that are passed along to offspring.

This research design, made possible by the advent of new reproductive technologies, is an innovative way to study the effects of nature versus early nurture. Moving forward, we can expect to see other issues studied with this design, allowing us to better understand which behaviors are influenced by the environment of the womb and which are products of inherited factors.

FAS are smaller and lighter than normal, and their physical growth lags behind that of their age-mates.

Children with FAS also show signs of central nervous system damage. As newborns, they are likely to display excessive irritability, hyperactivity, seizures, or tremors. Most children with FAS score well below average on IQ tests throughout childhood and adolescence, and many are mentally retarded (Howell et al., 2006; Nulman et al., 2007). Hyperactive behavior and attention deficits are also common among these children (Bhatara, Loudenberg, & Ellis, 2006). Longitudinal research indicates that more than 90% of children born with FAS have mental health problems later in life, including attention deficit hyperactivity disorder (ADHD) and conduct disorders (Fryer et al., 2007). They are also likely to get into trouble at school, break the law, and experience job-related problems (Autti-Rämö, 2000; Merrick et al., 2006). These problems may arise because children with FAS are less skilled at interpreting and processing social information in group situations, leading to interpersonal difficulties (McGee et al., 2009).

Although estimates vary widely, most surveys indicate that approximately 15% of pregnant women drink some alcohol during pregnancy; some of these admit to "risk drinking" (7 or more drinks per week or 5 drinks on one occasion; Centers for Disease Control, 2009). As a result, as many as 3 in 1000 babies in the United States are born with FAS and suffer its symptoms all their lives. This is by no means an insignificant number when you consider that each child with FAS costs an estimated $2 million over their lifetime, or approximately $4 billion a year in the United States alone (Centers for Disease Control, 2009). Children who were exposed prenatally to alcohol but do not have FAS experience milder alcohol-related effects labeled either *fetal alcohol effects* or *alcohol-related neurodevelopmental disorder* (Nulman et al., 2007). These individuals do not have all the features of FAS but have physical, behavioral, or cognitive problems or a combination of these. In Italy, where many people indulge in daily alcohol consumption with meals, the incidence of FAS and its milder forms is roughly 35 out of 1000 children (May et al., 2005).

How much drinking does it take to harm an unborn baby? In keeping with the dosage principle of teratology, mothers who consume larger quantities of alcohol are at greater risk for having children with alcohol-related complications (Roccella & Testa,

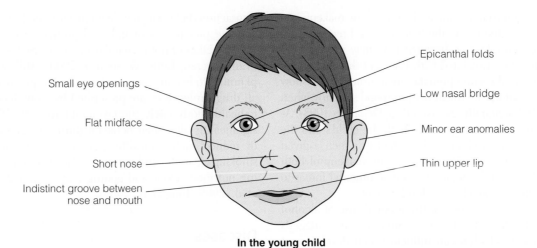

Small eye openings

Flat midface

Short nose

Indistinct groove between
nose and mouth

Epicanthal folds

Low nasal bridge

Minor ear anomalies

Thin upper lip

In the young child

■ **FIGURE 4.5** Characteristic features of a child with fetal alcohol syndrome (FAS). SOURCE:
From Sadler, T. W. (2004). Characteristic features of a child with fetal alcohol syndrome. In *Langman's
medical embryology* (9th ed.). Copyright © 2004, Lippincott, Williams, & Wilkins. Reprinted with
permission.

© George Steinmetz

Child with FAS, illustrating many features in the drawing. Such
children may also have cardiovascular and limb defects.

2003; Streissguth et al., 1999). The pattern of drinking is also important. Binge drinking (for women, consuming four or more drinks during a single session) has more negative effects on fetal development than consuming the same number of drinks across multiple sessions (Jacobson & Jacobson, 1999; Sayal et al., 2009). This makes sense when you consider that consuming four drinks in one evening results in higher blood alcohol levels for both mother and fetus than consuming one drink on each of four evenings. Finally, in keeping with the critical-period principle of teratogens, the effects of alcohol depend on which systems are developing at the time of exposure. The facial abnormalities associated with FAS result from consumption during the first trimester, when the face and skull bones are forming. During the second and third trimesters, there is much fetal growth as well as rapid brain development; thus, alcohol consumption during this latter part of pregnancy is likely to stunt growth and brain development.

No amount of drinking seems to be entirely safe. Even a mother who drinks less than an ounce a day is at risk to have a sluggish or placid newborn whose mental development is slightly below average (Jacobson et al., 1993). Other research shows that exposure to less than one drink per week during pregnancy is associated with mental health problems during childhood, at least among girls (Sayal et al., 2007). What is more, there is no well-defined critical period before or after which fetal alcohol effects cannot occur; drinking late in pregnancy can be as risky as drinking soon after conception.

Why do some babies of drinking mothers suffer ill effects but others do not? To answer this, you need to consider the nature–nurture issue again. First, the chances of damage depend partly on the mother's physiology—for example, on how efficiently she metabolizes alcohol and therefore how much is passed to the fetus (Shepard & Lemire, 2004). Complicating the situation, problem drinkers often have other issues that can aggravate the effects of alcohol on the fetus or cause independent damage that can be difficult to detangle from the effects of alcohol alone (Rodriguez et al., 2009). Women who consume unsafe levels of alcohol during pregnancy are also more likely to use drugs other than alcohol, smoke cigarettes, have inadequate prenatal care, and be young and single. Combining alcohol use with other risky behaviors increases the odds of pregnancy complications (Odendaal et al., 2009). In addition, consistent with the third principle of teratogenic effects, the embryo's genetic makeup and physical condition influence its ability to resist and recover from damage. So, for example, one fraternal twin may show all the physical abnormalities associated with FAS, but the other twin, although exposed to the same prenatal environment, may show almost none; by contrast, identical twins respond similarly when exposed to alcohol prenatally (Streissguth & Dehaene, 1993). As the third principle of teratology states, both the child's and the mother's characteristics influence the extent to which a given teratogen proves damaging. Thus, the genetic makeup of both the mother and the child interact with environmental forces to determine the effects of alcohol on development.

Finally, note that it is not just the mother's use of alcohol that can adversely affect development. Some research suggests that a father's use of alcohol can influence fetal development through transmission of the father's genetic makeup to his offspring (Knopik et al., 2009). Other research, however, shows that paternal drinking does not affect fetal development directly, but affects development indirectly through poor parenting (Knopik et al., 2009; Leonard & Das Eiden, 2002). Also, fathers who abuse alcohol or drugs are often with partners who abuse alcohol or drugs, making it difficult to separate the effects of the mother's use of these substances from the father's use (Frank et al., 2002a). Therefore, researchers still do not know whether a father's consumption of alcohol causes the problems or whether the problems arise from things often associated with a father's abuse of alcohol.

Cocaine. Although there is no "cocaine syndrome" with characteristic physical abnormalities such as those associated with FAS, cocaine use can damage the fetus. It can cause spontaneous abortion in the first trimester of pregnancy and premature detachment of the placenta or fetal strokes later in pregnancy (Diaz, 1997). Cocaine also contributes to fetal malnourishment, retarded growth, and low birth weight (Bada et al., 2005). At birth, a small proportion of babies born to cocaine users experience withdrawal-like symptoms such as tremors and extreme irritability and have respiratory difficulties (Diaz, 1997).

Cocaine-exposed infants show deficits on several measures of information processing (Singer et al., 1999) and sensory motor skills during their first year (Arendt et al., 1998). Fortunately, most problems caused by prenatal cocaine exposure do not persist into childhood (Frank et al., 2002b; Miller-Loncar et al., 2005). For problems that persist, it is unclear whether they are caused by the prenatal exposure to cocaine or by other prenatal or postnatal risk factors that affected infants may experience as the children of substance-abusing parents. For instance, many pregnant women who use cocaine also tend to smoke or drink alcohol during pregnancy (Nordstrom et al., 2005). In addition, cocaine-using mothers are less attentive to their babies and engage in fewer interactions with them during the first year than non–drug-using mothers or mothers who use drugs other than cocaine (Minnes et al., 2005).

● **Table 4.4** catalogs several substances and their known or suspected effects on the child. What should you make of these findings? You now understand that drugs do not damage all fetuses exposed to them in a simple, direct way. Instead, complex transactions between an individual with a certain genetic makeup and the prenatal, perinatal, and postnatal environments influence whether or not prenatal drug exposure does lasting damage (Van Beveren, Little, & Spence, 2000). Still, women who are planning to become pregnant or who are pregnant should avoid all drugs unless they are prescribed by a physician and essential to health. Fortunately, most women have gotten the message and significantly alter their behavior during pregnancy to eliminate or reduce such unhealthy practices as drinking alcohol and smoking cigarettes and to increase healthy behaviors such as eating nutritious foods and getting regular prenatal care (Crozier et al., 2009; Tong et al., 2009).

Diseases

Just as drugs can jeopardize the prenatal environment, so can diseases. Here we take a look at four diseases—rubella, diabetes, syphilis, and AIDS—that illustrate principles of teratogens. ● **Table 4.5** summarizes these and other maternal conditions that may affect prenatal development.

Rubella. In the early 1940s, a doctor discovered that many infants born to women affected by **rubella** (German measles) during pregnancy had one or more of a variety of defects, including blindness, deafness, heart defects, and mental retardation. Because rubella was fairly common, there were enough cases for doctors to see that the environment of the womb leaves the fetus vulnerable to outside influences. Rubella is most dangerous during the first trimester, a critical period in which the eyes, ears, heart, and brain are rapidly forming. Nearly 15% of pregnant women with rubella miscarry or experience a fetal death (Andrade et al., 2006). Yet not all babies whose mothers had rubella, even during the most critical period of prenatal development, will have problems. Birth defects occur in 60–85% of babies whose mothers had the disease in the first 2 months of pregnancy, in about 50% of those infected in the third month, and in only 16% of those infected in the fourth or fifth months (Kelley-Buchanan, 1988). Consistent with the critical-period principle, damage to the nervous system, eyes, and heart is most likely during that part of the first 8 weeks of pregnancy when each of these organs is forming, whereas deafness is more likely when the mother contracts rubella in weeks 6–13 of the pregnancy. Today, doctors stress that a woman should not try to become pregnant unless she has been immunized against rubella or has already had it. As a result of successful immunization programs, many women are now immune to this previously common infection. Nevertheless, recent outbreaks of rubella have been reported in several countries, including the Netherlands, Brazil, and Spain (de Mol et al., 2006; Torner et al., 2006).

Diabetes. Diabetes is a fairly common pregnancy complication, with most cases arising during pregnancy (gestational diabetes) rather than from pre-existing diabetes (Haffner, 2007). Diabetes results from elevated blood glucose levels. When glucose levels are well controlled with diet, there are few ill effects on the developing fetus. But in poorly controlled maternal diabe-

● TABLE 4.4 SOME DRUGS TAKEN BY THE MOTHER THAT AFFECT THE FETUS OR NEWBORN

Drug	Effects
Alcohol	Effects of prenatal exposure can include a small head, facial abnormalities, heart defects, low birth weight, and intellectual retardation (see main text).
Antiepileptic drugs	Drugs such as phenytoin (Dilantin), phenobarbital (Luminal), and carbamazepine (Tegretol), used to treat seizures, increase the incidence of cleft lip and palate, neural tube defects, kidney disease, and restricted growth (Kothare & Kaleyias, 2007). Approximately 1 in 12 infants exposed prenatally to antiepileptic drugs will develop a birth defect (Haffner, 2007).
Over-the-counter pain/fever reducers (acetaminophen, aspirin and ibuprofen)	An occasional low dose is okay, but used in large quantities, such drugs may cause neonatal bleeding and gastrointestinal discomfort. Large amounts of these over-the-counter pain relievers (e.g., Advil) have been associated with low birth weight, prematurity, and increased risk of miscarriage (Li, Liu, & Odouli, 2003; Rebordosa et al., 2009).
Chemotherapy drugs	Such drugs cross the placenta and attack rapidly dividing cells. They can increase malformations and lead to miscarriage, particularly when administered to the mother during the first trimester.
Marijuana	Heavy use of marijuana has been linked to premature birth, low birth weight, and mild behavioral abnormalities such as irritability at birth. It doesn't seem to influence general intelligence but may affect some of the skills that contribute to higher-level problem solving, including sustained attention and cognitive flexibility (Jacobsen et al., 2007).
Narcotics	Addiction to heroin, codeine, methadone, or morphine increases the risk of premature delivery and low birth weight. The newborn is often addicted and experiences potentially fatal withdrawal symptoms (e.g., vomiting and convulsions). Longer-term cognitive deficits are sometimes evident.
Sex hormones	Birth control pills containing female hormones have been known to produce heart defects and cardiovascular problems, but today's pill formulas are safer. Progesterone in drugs used to prevent miscarriage may masculinize the fetus. Diethylstilbestrol, once prescribed to prevent miscarriage, increased the risk of cervical cancer and created infertility and pregnancy problems in exposed daughters (DESAction, 2007; Kaufman et al., 2000).
Stimulants	Caffeine, found in coffees, teas, and many sodas, is a stimulant and diuretic. As such, it can increase blood pressure, heart rate, and urination. Heavy caffeine use has been linked to miscarriages, higher heart rates, growth restriction, and irritability at birth, but it does not seem to have long-lasting effects on development (CARE Study Group, 2008; Kaiser Permanente Division of Research, 2008). Cocaine is an illegal stimulate that can cause premature delivery, spontaneous abortion, and low birth weight, and it may result in later learning and behavioral problems (see main text). Prescription stimulants, such as amphetamines used to treat attention deficit disorder, have been linked to aggressive behavior and low school achievement in children whose mothers took them during pregnancy (Billing et al., 1994).
Tobacco	Babies of smokers tend to be small and premature, have respiratory problems, and sometimes show intellectual deficits or behavioral problems later in development (see main text). Sons whose mothers smoked during their pregnancy may later have fertility problems (Storgaard et al., 2003). Secondhand smoke in the pregnant woman's environment can increase her risk of miscarriage (George et al., 2006).

SOURCES: Modified from Creasy et al., 2009; Davidson & Myers, 2007; Friedman & Polifka, 2000; Haffner, 2007; Sadler, 2010; Shepard & Lemire, 2007.

tes, there is increased risk of premature delivery, stillbirth or miscarriage, immature lung development, and large fetal size (Brown & Satin, 2007; Haffner, 2007).

Syphilis. Now consider another teratogen, the sexually transmitted infection **syphilis**. Syphilis during pregnancy can cause mis-carriage or stillbirth (Genc & Ledger, 2000). Babies born alive to mothers who have syphilis, like those born to mothers who have rubella, often suffer blindness, deafness, heart problems, or brain damage. This shows that different teratogens—here, syphilis and rubella—can be responsible for the same problem. However, whereas rubella is most damaging in the early stage of pregnancy,

● TABLE 4.5 MATERNAL DISEASES AND CONDITIONS THAT MAY AFFECT AN EMBRYO, FETUS, OR NEWBORN

Disease or Condition	Effects
Sexually Transmitted Infections (STIs)	
Acquired immunodeficiency syndrome (AIDS)	If transmitted from mother to child, AIDS destroys defenses against disease and may lead to death. Mothers can acquire it through sexual contact or contact with contaminated blood (see main text).
Chlamydia	Chlamydia can lead to premature birth, low birth weight, eye inflammation, or pneumonia in newborns. This most common STI is easily treatable.
Gonorrhea	This STI attacks the eyes of the child during birth; blindness is prevented by administering silver nitrate eyedrops to newborns.
Herpes simplex (genital herpes)	This disease may cause eye and brain damage or death in the first trimester. Mothers with active herpes are advised to undergo cesarean deliveries to avoid infecting their babies during delivery, because 85% of infants born with herpes acquire the virus during birth through the birth canal.
Syphilis	Untreated, it can cause miscarriage or serious birth defects such as blindness and mental retardation (see main text).
Other Maternal Conditions or Diseases	
Chickenpox	Chickenpox can cause spontaneous abortion, premature delivery, and slow growth, although fewer than 2% of exposed fetuses develop limb, facial, or skeletal malformations.
Cytomegalovirus (CMV)	This common infection shows mild flulike symptoms in adults. About 25% of infected newborns develop hearing or vision loss, mental retardation, or other impairments, and 10% develop severe neurological problems or even die.
Diabetes	Well-controlled diabetes typically poses few, if any, prenatal complications. However, poorly controlled diabetes can lead to premature delivery or even fetal loss. In addition, maternal diabetes is associated with large-for-date fetuses, which can complicate delivery.
Influenza (flu)	The more powerful strains can cause spontaneous abortions or neural abnormalities early in pregnancy that may lead to decreased intelligence scores in adulthood (Eriksen, Sundet, & Tambs, 2009).
Rubella	Rubella may cause vision and hearing loss, mental retardation, heart defects, cerebral palsy, and microcephaly (see main text).
Toxemia	Affecting about 5% of mothers in the third trimester, its mildest form, preeclampsia, causes high blood pressure and rapid weight gain in the mother. Untreated, preeclampsia may become eclampsia and cause maternal convulsions, coma, and death of the mother, the unborn child, or both. Surviving infants may be brain damaged.
Toxoplasmosis	This illness, caused by a parasite in raw meat and cat feces, leads to blindness, deafness, and mental retardation in approximately 40% of infants born to infected mothers.

SOURCES: Modified from Bell, 2007; Ratcliffe, Byrd, & Sakornbut, 1996; Simpson & Creehan, 1996; Winn & Hobbins, 2000.

syphilis is most damaging in the middle and later stages of pregnancy. This is because syphilitic organisms cannot cross the placental barrier until the 18th prenatal week, providing a window of opportunity for treating the mother-to-be who finds out she has the disease. Even with appropriate treatment—penicillin—some infants are infected or die (Genc & Ledger, 2000).

AIDS. The sexually transmitted infection of greatest concern in recent decades is **acquired immunodeficiency syndrome**

(AIDS), the life-threatening illness caused by the human immunodeficiency virus (HIV). AIDS destroys the immune system and makes victims susceptible to "opportunistic" infections that eventually kill them unless they are treated with multiple drugs. HIV-infected mothers can transmit the virus to their babies (1) prenatally, if the virus passes through the placenta; (2) perinatally, when blood may be exchanged between mother and child as the umbilical cord separates from the placenta; or (3) postnatally, if the virus is transmitted during breast-feeding. Without treatment,

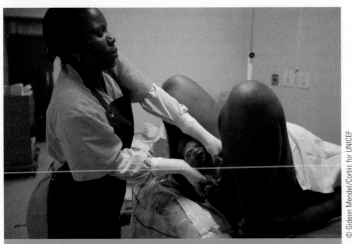

An HIV-positive mother gives birth in the small country of Lesotho, which borders South Africa. Knowledge of her HIV-positive status allowed this woman to enroll in a program to limit transmission of HIV to her unborn child. The baby will now receive a dose of AZT and other antiviral drugs, which will give her a chance for a healthy life.

somewhere between 15 and 35% of babies born to HIV-infected mothers will become infected (Newell, 2003). The rate is much lower if these mothers take azidothymidine (also called AZT) or zidovudine to treat the HIV, or if they and their newborns are given a drug called nevirapine, which helps block transmission of HIV at birth (Newell, 2003; Stringer et al., 2004). Bottle-feeding further reduces the rate of HIV transmission from affected mothers to their infants (Magoni et al., 2005). Infected infants now live longer than they did at the outset of the AIDS epidemic because of the development of appropriate treatments—75% are alive at age 5, and many survive into adolescence (King et al., 2002).

Although mother-to-child transmission of HIV in the United States has decreased significantly since peaking in 1992, it continues to be a tremendous problem in Africa and other parts of the world with AIDS epidemics. In 2007, for example, about 400,000 infants worldwide became infected with HIV from their mothers, most in sub-Saharan Africa (Avert, 2009).

Environmental Hazards

A mother can control what she ingests, but sometimes she cannot avoid a hazardous external environment. Next we discuss two environmental conditions—radiation and pollutants—that may endanger the unborn child.

Radiation. After atomic bombs were dropped on Hiroshima and Nagasaki in 1945, not one pregnant woman who was within one-half mile of the blasts gave birth to a live child, and 75% of those who were within a mile and a quarter of the blasts had stillborn infants or seriously handicapped children who died soon after birth (Apgar & Beck, 1974). Surviving children of

these mothers had a higher-than-normal rate of mental retardation and greater incidence of leukemia and cancers later in life (Centers for Disease Control, 2007a; Kodama, Mabuchi, & Shigematsu, 1996). The aftermath of these atomic bombs provides striking evidence of the devastating effects that can occur from prenatal exposure to radiation. But it doesn't take a Hiroshima-sized bomb to cause damage. Even clinical doses of radiation, such as those used in X-rays and cancer treatment, are capable of causing mutations, spontaneous abortions, and a variety of birth defects, especially if the mother is exposed between weeks 8 and 15 (Hill & Haffner, 2002). Therefore, expectant mothers are routinely advised to avoid X-rays unless they are essential to their own survival, as might be the case with women undergoing certain cancer treatments.

Pollutants. Following the 9/11 attacks and collapse of the World Trade Centers (WTC) in New York City, the air quality was extremely poor and those living in the vicinity were exposed to large amounts of potentially toxic pollutants. In the months after 9/11, researchers enrolled pregnant women in a longitudinal study to track potential effects of prenatal exposure to pollution on a variety of infant outcomes. They measured by-products of pollution evident in umbilical cord blood at birth. From this, they were able to conclude that the fetuses of women who were closer to the World Trade Centers did indeed have greater exposure to pollution. These infants were born lighter, shorter, and slightly earlier than a control group of babies whose mothers were not living near the WTC (Lederman et al., 2004). And three years later, some of the children showed decreased cognitive abilities (Perera et al., 2007). Was it the pollution alone or pollution in combination with the inevitable stress that was experienced by these women? Other research has found that 9/11 stress did not adversely affect birth outcomes, so pollution is the more probable explanation (Endara et al., 2009). But, importantly, there is another variable that the researchers considered: prenatal exposure to cigarette smoke (Lederman et al., 2004; Perera et al., 2007). It turns out that prenatal exposure to pollution *in combination with* cigarette smoke led to complications that were not present in the children who were exposed to just one of these prenatal risk factors. As we'll see later in this chapter, the more hazards that a child faces, the more likely it is that she will struggle to get back on track. Thus, with good postnatal care, children might overcome negative consequences of prenatal exposure to pollution or to cigarette smoke, but overcoming multiple risk factors is more of a challenge.

Exposure to heavy metals, such as lead in the air we breathe and the water we drink, is an ongoing concern. Children exposed prenatally to lead are smaller at birth and may be born preterm (Jelliffe-Pawlowski et al., 2006; Schell et al., 2006). They also show impaired intellectual functioning as infants in proportion to the amount of lead in their umbilical cords (Bellinger et al., 1987; Canfield et al., 2003). This finding holds true even after controlling for other differences among children, such as socioeconomic status. Postnatal lead exposure is also dangerous. It is estimated that one in four children under age 6 in the United States lives in a home with lead dust from old paint or old lead water pipes (Rogan & Ware, 2003). Exposure to even very low levels of lead—lower than previously thought to be safe—is associated with lowered mental function during childhood (Jedrychowski et al., 2009).

Mercury exposure typically results from eating fish or receiving a vaccination containing thimerosal as a preservative, although most vaccines today are thimerosal-free, particularly those recommended for children under the age of 6. Studies looking at prenatal exposure to mercury from maternal consumption of fish suggest adverse consequences, including delayed development and memory, attention, and language problems, with the effects commensurate to the amount of mercury exposure (Davidson & Myers, 2007). As for whether mercury from older vaccines had toxic effects on development, the vast majority of the research concludes that it did not (Davidson & Myers, 2007; Tozzi et al., 2009). However, some parents whose children developed autism following a vaccination continue to question whether there might be a link between the two events (see Chapter 16).

Finally, prenatal exposure to pesticides, dioxins, and polychlorinated biphenyls (PCBs) has also been associated with perinatal and postnatal problems (see Jedrychowski et al., 2006; Nakajima et al., 2006). For example, prenatal exposure to PCBs from maternal consumption of contaminated foods is associated with poor reflexes in infants and later learning difficulties, including lower IQ scores at age 9 (Davidson & Myers, 2007; Stewart et al., 2008).

Clearly there is a critical need for more research aimed at identifying a huge number of chemicals, wastes, and other environmental hazards that may affect unborn children. There are more than 85,000 chemicals "out there" to which children may be exposed, but fewer than 25% of these have been evaluated for toxicity (Davidson & Myers, 2007).

The message is unmistakable: The chemistry of the prenatal environment often determines whether an embryo or fetus survives and how it looks and functions after birth. A variety of teratogens can affect development, although as you have learned, the influence of teratogens varies. Effects are worst in critical periods when organ systems are growing most rapidly, and effects are more serious with greater exposure to teratogens. Not all embryos or fetuses are equally affected by the same teratogen; the genetic makeup of both the mother and her unborn child and the quality of the prenatal and postnatal environments all play a role in determining the effects. By becoming familiar with the information here and by keeping up with new knowledge, parents-to-be can do much to increase the already high odds that their unborn child will be normal as it approaches its next challenge: the birth process.

The Mother's State

What can parents, especially the mother-to-be, do to sustain a healthy pregnancy? Application Box 4.1 explores how parents can set the stage for a healthy pregnancy. Here we describe several characteristics of the mother—her age and race/ethnicity, emotional state, and nutritional status—that can affect the quality of the prenatal environment.

Age and Race/Ethnicity

At one end of the age spectrum, 11- and 12-year-old girls have given birth; at the other end of the spectrum, a 70-year-old woman from rural India made the record book by giving birth to twins after in vitro fertilization ("World's Oldest Mother," 2009). These are, however, unusual cases. The safest, and more typical, time to bear a child appears to be from about age 20 to age 40, as shown by the low birth weights and fetal mortality rates in ■ Figure 4.6.

Very young mothers have higher-than-normal rates of birth complications, including premature deliveries and **stillbirths**— fetal deaths late in pregnancy (20 or more weeks gestational age). The reproductive system of the teenager (19 years or younger) may not be physically mature enough to sustain a fetus to full term, making this group more vulnerable to having a low-birth-weight baby. However, the greater problem appears to be that teenagers often do not seek prenatal care and they are more likely to live in poverty and drink alcohol than mothers in their 20s and older (NSDUH, 2008). Unfortunately, these conditions are likely to persist after the birth, leading to increased death rates before their first birthday among infants born to mothers 15 years or younger (Phipps, Blume, & DeMonner, 2002).

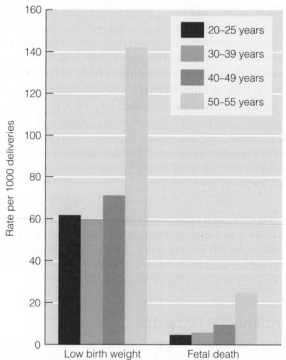

■ **FIGURE 4.6** Low birth weight and fetal death increase after maternal age 40, with marked increases after age 50.
SOURCE: Adapted from Salihu, H. M., Shumpert, M. N., Slay, M., Kirby, R. S., & Alexander, G. R. (2003). Childbearing beyond maternal age 50 and fetal outcomes in the United States. *Obstetrics and Gynecology, 102*, 1006–1014.

The more we learn about important environmental influences on human development, the better able we are to optimize environment and therefore to optimize development. Although the quality of an individual's environment matters throughout the life span, it seems sensible to do as much as possible to get a baby's life off to a good start because events of the prenatal period may set the stage for a lifetime of good (or poor) health. Ideally, pregnancies are planned rather than "discovered" after the fact, when it may be too late to make certain lifestyle changes. All women of childbearing age, for example, should eat a diet that contains the recommended amount of folic acid and should try to quit or reduce their smoking. Women who are thinking about getting pregnant should talk to their doctor about any prescription drugs they may be taking for ongoing medical conditions such as depression, high blood pressure, or diabetes. Doctors and mothers-to-be can develop a plan for how best to manage any preexisting conditions during a pregnancy. Having these discussions and making these lifestyle changes before pregnancy help ensure that the cards are stacked in favor of having a healthy baby.

Once a woman is pregnant, she should seek good prenatal care as quickly as possible so that she will learn how to optimize the well-being of both herself and her unborn child and so that any problems during the pregnancy can be managed appropriately. Although the recommendations for pregnant women are not complicated, they are not always followed. They boil down to such practices as eating a good diet, taking prenatal vitamins, protecting oneself against diseases, and avoiding drugs and alcohol. Women who become ill during pregnancy should always check with their doctor before taking even seemingly safe over-the-counter drugs. Women should avoid eating undercooked meat because of the risks of toxoplasmosis and *Escherichia coli (E. coli)* contamination, and they should be cautious of eating some fish, namely those larger fish that consume lots of little fish. These tend to have higher concentrations of mercury.

Most women can continue to engage in all their regular activities, including exercise, during pregnancy unless advised against it by their health-care provider. Exercise can help keep muscles toned for the rigors of childbirth and also provides a sense of positive well-being. Exercise and a healthy diet during pregnancy may also influence the baby's metabolism and could set the stage for adult weight. In addition, researchers are beginning to find that prenatal exposure to certain environmental toxins may "program" the endocrine system in ways that lead to obesity across all stages of the lifespan (see, for example, Newbold et al., 2009).

Women who want to do some home renovations in preparation for the baby's arrival should be careful of lead paint that may be present in older homes and avoid inhaling paint fumes in poorly ventilated rooms. They may also want to have someone else clean the cat's litter box, because cat feces is another source of the parasite that causes toxoplasmosis. For women who can't avoid litter box duty, having cats tested and treated before pregnancy can eliminate potential exposure to parasites.

Finally, many couples today also enroll in classes that prepare them for childbirth. These classes started in the 1940s to help reduce the fear and pain experienced by many women during labor and delivery. The **Lamaze method** of prepared childbirth teaches women to associate childbirth with pleasant feelings and to ready themselves for the process by learning exercises, breathing and pushing methods, and relaxation techniques that make childbirth easier (Lamaze, 1958). Couples who participate in childbirth preparation classes report a greater sense of control during labor and delivery, and this sense of control is associated with higher levels of satisfaction with the childbirth experience (Hart & Foster, 1997). Unfortunately, after delivery many women say that their prenatal classes did not go as far as they could have in providing practice with the coping strategies useful for a smooth delivery (Spiby et al., 1999).

As for older women, they are more likely to experience trouble getting pregnant. For those who do conceive, there is an increased risk of miscarriage, stillbirth, and low-birth-weight babies (Arck et al., 2008; Borders et al., 2007). In the past, many fetal deaths in older women were caused by genetic abnormalities or defects arising during the first weeks after conception, when the major organs are forming. With today's extensive prenatal testing of women older than 35, however, fewer babies are dying from genetic problems, partly because many such fetuses are identified early and aborted. Still, fetal death rates remain higher for older women, particularly for those over age 50 (Salihu et al., 2003). Compared with younger women, women over age 35 are more likely to release more than a single egg during ovulation, which increases their chances of conceiving fraternal twins (Beemsterboer et al., 2006). Though some women may be thrilled to learn that they are carrying twins, any multiple pregnancy and delivery carries additional health risks for the mother and the babies. Fetal mortality for higher-order pregnancies (three or more fetuses) is more than four times the rate for single pregnancies (MacDorman & Kirmeyer, 2009). Finally, keep in mind that despite the increased risks older women face in childbearing, most have normal pregnancies and healthy babies.

Does the mother's race/ethnicity impact pregnancy success? As ■ **Figure 4.7** shows, fetal mortality rates do vary with the race/ethnicity of the mother. Most notable is that non-Hispanic black women have fetal mortality rates that are more than twice the rates experienced by other women. The reasons for this disparity are not completely understood but include poorer preconception health of the mother and less prenatal care. In addition, non-Hispanic black mothers are more susceptible to premature

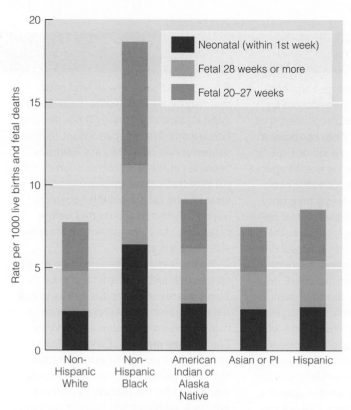

■ FIGURE 4.7 Fetal and neonatal mortality rates by race/ethnicity of mother. What factors might contribute to the markedly higher mortality rates for black infants (and fetuses)? SOURCE: Adapted from Figures 4 and 5 (p. 4) in MacDorman M. F., Hoyert D. L., Martin J. A., Munson M. L., & Hamilton B. E. (2007). Fetal and perinatal mortality, United States, 2003. *National Vital Statistics Reports, 55*(6). Available at: www.cdc.gov/nchs/data/nvsr/nvsr55/nvsr55_06.pdf. Accessed May, 2010.

labor, which creates numerous health concerns that we will discuss in a later section.

Emotional Condition

Is the prenatal environment affected by how the mother feels about being pregnant or how her life is going while she is pregnant? Life is filled with many stressors—both chronic (poverty, for example, or ongoing job stress) and acute (experiencing a serious car accident, for example, or the unexpected death of a loved one). Being pregnant does not make stress disappear; indeed, for some women with unintended or mistimed pregnancies, pregnancy may increase stress levels. How might the fetus be affected by the mother's experience of stress?

When a woman becomes emotionally aroused, her glands secrete powerful hormones such as adrenaline (also called epinephrine) that may cross the placental barrier and enter the fetus's bloodstream. At the least, these hormones temporarily in-

crease the fetus's motor activity. A temporarily stressful experience such as falling or receiving a scare will generally not damage mother or fetus. It is only when a mother experiences *prolonged and severe* emotional stress and anxiety during her pregnancy (as a result, for example, of the death of her husband, chronic illness of another child, or unemployment) that damage may be done (Borders et al., 2007; Hansen, Lou, & Olsen, 2001). The most likely effects on the fetus are a faster and more irregular heart rate and stunted prenatal growth, which can lower birth weight; premature birth; and birth complications (Berkowitz et al., 2003). Following birth, babies whose mothers had been highly stressed during pregnancy tend to be smaller, more active, more irritable, and more prone to crying than other babies (de Weerth, van Hees, & Buitelaar, 2003; Wurmser et al., 2006). They may experience delays in cognitive development and exhibit greater fearfulness as young children (Bergman et al., 2007; Laplante et al., 2008). Finally, acute maternal stress during the first trimester has been linked to the increased likelihood of developing schizophrenia, a serious mental disorder whose symptoms typically emerge in adolescence or early adulthood (Malaspina et al., 2008; St. Clair, 2005).

How might maternal stress stunt fetal growth and contribute to the offspring's irritability and anxiety? The mechanisms are not yet clear. The link between the mother's stressful experiences and small, premature babies may involve hormones, changes in the immune system, reduced blood flow through the arteries in the uterus, or even a poor diet (see DiPietro, Costigan, & Gurewitsch, 2003; Entringer et al., 2009; Huizink et al., 2008). Whatever the mechanism, it is clear that not all stressed mothers have babies who are small and arrive early. Indeed, Janet DiPietro and her colleagues (2006) found that mild to moderate stress experienced by otherwise healthy mothers during pregnancy may actually enhance fetal development. How can we reconcile these seemingly contradictory findings? What can we tell potential parents about the effects of stress—is it beneficial or harmful? It may depend on the effect that the stressful event has on the woman's daily life. If the event significantly disrupts daily life, child outcomes may be worse than if the mother's daily life is affected very little by the event (Laplante et al., 2004).

Stress and anxiety are not the only maternal emotional states to consider. Maternal depression during pregnancy may contribute to motor delays in newborns and influence their temperament (Davis et al., 2007; Lundy et al., 1999). Depression affects levels of neurotransmitters (brain chemicals) in both mothers and their newborns. Researchers have found a connection between these changes in neurotransmitter levels and certain immature motor responses of newborns. They do not yet know, however, whether these effects persist.

Nutritional Condition

At the turn of the last century, doctors advised mothers to gain a mere 10–15 pounds while pregnant. With better understanding of nutrition and pregnancy, doctors now recommend a well-balanced diet with about 300 additional calories per day, with a total weight gain of 25–35 pounds for normal-weight

What should women know about nutrition throughout pregnancy? What recommendations should this woman follow to ensure a healthy pregnancy?

women (Haffner, 2007). Healthy eating, including consuming lots of milk and leafy green vegetables, during pregnancy reduces the risk of having low-birth-weight babies (McCowan & Horgan, 2009). Doctors know that inadequate prenatal nutrition and lack of weight gain can be harmful. Severe maternal malnutrition, which occurs during famine, stunts prenatal growth and produces small, underweight babies (Stein et al., 1975; Susser & Stein, 1994). The effects of malnutrition depend on when it occurs. During the first trimester, malnutrition can disrupt the formation of the spinal cord, result in fewer brain cells, and even cause stillbirth (Susser & Stein, 1994). Restrictive dieting, use of diuretics, and disordered eating behaviors during the first trimester can also cause serious problems, such as neural tube defects (Carmichael et al., 2003). During the third trimester, malnutrition is most likely to result in smaller neurons, a smaller brain, and a smaller child overall.

The offspring of malnourished mothers sometimes show cognitive deficits as infants and children. Poor prenatal nutrition may also put some children at risk for certain diseases in adulthood, especially hypertension, coronary heart disease, and diabetes (Barker, 1998; Goldberg & Prentice, 1994). Some research challenges these conclusions, however. In many cases prenatal malnutrition does not have serious long-term effects on development, and among women who are adequately nourished, it is difficult to establish a connection between specific nutrients and birth outcome or later behaviors (Langley-Evans & Langley-Evans,

2003; Mathews, Youngman, & Neil, 2004). One exception to this is a deficiency of folic acid, which, as mentioned earlier, has been linked to neural tube defects. In 1998 the United States and Canada initiated mandatory folate enrichment of cereal products in an effort to increase folate levels of women of childbearing age. As ▪ **Figure 4.8** shows, these fortification programs have been associated with a decrease in the incidence of neural tube defects such as spina bifida and anencephaly (Hamilton, Martin, & Ventura, 2009). Although such fortification programs help, it may still be difficult to consume the "perfect" combination of foods to provide the full measure of recommended vitamins and minerals. Consequently, most health-care professionals prescribe prenatal vitamins for their pregnant patients.

Although prenatal nutrition is clearly important, much depends on whether a child receives an adequate diet and good care after birth. Dietary supplements, especially when combined with stimulating day care, can go a long way toward heading off the potentially damaging effects of prenatal malnutrition. Best, of course, is good nourishment before *and* after birth.

Now that we have had a chance to review the major teratogens that affect development during the prenatal period, go to Engagement Box 4.1 to check your understanding of this material.

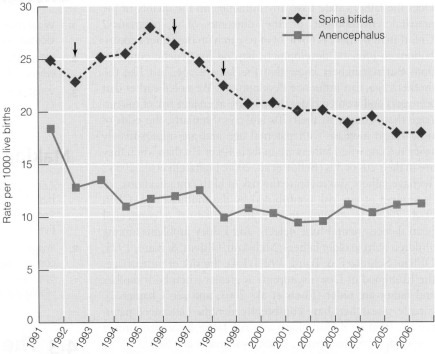

▪ **FIGURE 4.8** The incidence of neural tube defects such as spina bifida and anencephalus have decreased in the United States since the 1992 recommendation for all women of childbearing age to increase consumption of folic acid, the enrichment of cereal products with folic acid beginning in 1996, and the mandatory compliance with the folic acid fortification program in 1998. SOURCE: Adapted from Hamilton, B. E., Martin, J. A., & Ventura, S. J. (2009, March 18). Births: preliminary data for 2007. *National Vital Statistics Reports, 57* (12).

Check your understanding of how teratogens can influence the health and development of an unborn child by answering the following true–false questions.

_1. Most teratogens have their most devastating effects during the third trimester.

_2. Women should monitor their fish consumption during pregnancy.

_3. The fetus is protected from most environmental insults once it has fully implanted in the uterus and the umbilical cord has been completely established.

_4. Women who drink alcohol at any time during pregnancy will give birth to a baby with fetal alcohol syndrome.

_5. A woman's age and race/ethnicity affect the odds of a healthy pregnancy.

Answers: 1. F (The most serious problems occur during the first trimester when most major organs are forming.) 2. T (Some fish, such as swordfish, can contain high levels of the heavy metal mercury and should be avoided or eaten in small quantities.) 3. F (The umbilical cord is not a very good filter for many harmful substances. Carbon monoxide from cigarette smoke, for example, is actually "allowed" to cross the placenta before oxygen.) 4. F (Although FAS is a possibility, there are many variables that determine how an individual child will fare if exposed prenatally to alcohol. Certainly, the dosage generalization is important here: the more alcohol a woman drinks during pregnancy, the more likely it is that her child will have FAS or precursors to full-blown FAS.) 5. T (Women between the ages of 20 and 35 have the lowest rates of fetal mortality. Non-Hispanic black women have some of the highest rates of fetal mortality and premature labor.)

The Father's State

Does the father's state have any influence on the quality of the prenatal environment or the outcome of a pregnancy? Unfortunately, there is not a lot of research on the father's contributions to prenatal development beyond his genetic contribution. But researchers know that the father's age, just like the mother's age, can influence development. We noted earlier that teenagers and women older than 35 are at greater risk of miscarriage than women in their 20s and 30s. Similarly, the odds of miscarriage increase with paternal age and are approximately twice the rate when fathers are in their 40s or 50s than when they are in their 20s or 30s (Belloc et al., 2008; Frattarelli et al., 2008). Teenage fathers also increase the risk of birth complications, independent of any risk contributed by the mother's age (Chen et al., 2008). In addition, there is an elevated risk of congenital heart defects, neural tube defects, and kidney problems among children born to older fathers (McIntosh, Olshan, & Baird, 1995; Olshan, Schnitzer, & Baird, 1994). Like the risk of miscarriage, the likelihood of Down syndrome is greater when both mother and father are older (Fisch et al., 2003; and see Chapter 3). Finally, researchers have consistently identified advanced paternal age (that is, 50 and older) as a risk factor for schizophrenia (see Chapter 3; Rasmussen, 2006; Tsuchiya et al., 2005).

A father's exposure to environmental toxins can also affect a couple's children. A father's prolonged exposure to radiation, anesthetic gases used in operating rooms, pesticides, or other environmental toxins can damage the genetic material in his sperm and cause genetic defects in his children (Stone, 1992; Strigini et al., 1990). And the partners of men who have poor coping skills in response to stress are at increased risk of miscarriage (Zorn et al., 2008). In short, fathers, like mothers, should assess and, if need be, change their lifestyles and exposure to risk factors to optimize their chances of a healthy child.

Checking Mastery

1. What have researchers learned about the effects on the child of alcohol consumption during pregnancy?

2. What effects are likely to be seen among babies born to mothers who smoked throughout their pregnancies?

3. What principles can help us understand the effects of teratogens?

Making Connections

1. Consider Serena, whose story was summarized at the start of the chapter. What disadvantages might her child face, given Serena's lack of awareness of her pregnancy for the first four to five months?

2. Imagine you are asked to speak with a group of women who are considering a future pregnancy. The topic of your talk is how to optimize the development of their future child. What information would you want to convey to these women?

4.3 The Perinatal Environment

The **perinatal environment** is the environment surrounding birth; it includes influences such as drugs given to the mother during labor, delivery practices, and the social environment shortly after birth. Like the prenatal environment, the perinatal environment can greatly affect human development.

In most Western cultures, a dramatic shift in birthing practices occurred during the 20th century. In 1930, 80% of births took place at home; by 1990, this figure had plummeted to 1% (Zander & Chamberlain, 1999). This change in birth setting was accompanied by a shift from thinking about birth as a natural family event that occurred at home to thinking about it as a medical problem to be solved with high technology (Cassidy, 2006). In most cases, doctors assumed full authority for decisions regarding delivery.

Despite the continued medical setting of most births today, many couples want to give birth in a situation that combines the security of modern technology with a comfortable homelike feeling. Many hospitals have responded by restructuring their labor and delivery rooms and practices to give parents greater flexibility and control when it comes time to deliver. Today's parents are also pushing for greater voice in their delivery experiences (Carmichael, 2004). Mothers-to-be have several choices when it comes to who will assist with their delivery, including family physicians, obstetricians, specialists in maternal–fetal medicine, and midwives. For high-risk pregnancies associated with delivery complications, a maternal–fetal specialist, or **perinatologist**, is recommended. However, for the majority of women, personal preference can determine the best caregiver for pregnancy and delivery. In many countries, such as England and France, midwives have been the traditional pregnancy caregivers. For the past century, most (around 90%) women in the United States have relied on physicians or obstetricians for pregnancy care, but the use of midwives is slowly increasing, from 4% in 1990 to 8% more recently (Centers for Disease Control, 2006b). In general, midwives view pregnancy and delivery as natural life events rather than as medical events requiring medical intervention. They partner with the laboring mother-to-be to assist her with delivery but do not dictate the conditions of labor and delivery.

Another change in the delivery room is the presence of a spouse, partner, mother, sister, and/or friend to provide support and share in the miracle of birth. Most women find the support provided by this familiar person helpful and reassuring. Some women have the support of a *doula*—an individual trained to provide continuous physical and emotional support throughout the childbirth process. Such support tends to shorten labor by as much as half and to reduce the need for pain medication and assisted delivery such as use of forceps or vacuum (Hodnett et al., 2003; Scott, Klaus, & Klaus, 1999). The rate of cesarean sections is lower among women continuously supported by a doula or midwife (Dickinson et al., 2002). Mothers with continuous labor support also report more positive feelings about the birth experience, fewer symptoms of postnatal depression, and greater likelihood of breast-feeding than nonsupported mothers (Scott, Klaus, & Klaus, 1999). Clearly, then, the social context surrounding labor and delivery is important: women who receive more support during childbirth have more positive experiences.

Childbirth is a three-stage process (■ **Figure 4.9**). The first stage of labor begins as the mother experiences regular contractions of the uterus and ends when her cervix has fully dilated (widened) so that the fetus's head can pass through. This stage of labor lasts an average of 9 hours for firstborn children and 4–6 hours for later-born children, but it may last much longer (or shorter) depending on the individual and her circumstances

(Albers, 1999; Jones & Larson, 2003). It ends when the cervix has dilated to 10 centimeters. The second stage of labor is delivery, which begins as the fetus's head passes through the cervix into the vagina and ends when the baby emerges from the mother's body. This is when the mother is often told to "bear down" (push) with each contraction to assist her baby through the birth canal. For first deliveries, this stage takes about 1 hour; for later deliveries, it can be 15–20 minutes (Albers, 1999; Jones & Larson, 2003). Finally, the third stage of the birth process is the delivery of the placenta, which lasts only a few minutes.

When the birth process is completed, the mother (and often the father, if he is present) is typically physically exhausted, relieved to be through the ordeal of giving birth, and exhilarated all at once. Meanwhile, the fetus has been thrust from its carefree but cramped existence into a strange new world.

Possible Hazards

In most births the entire process goes smoothly, and parents and newborn quickly begin their relationship. Occasionally, however, problems arise.

Anoxia

One clear hazard during the birth process is **anoxia**, or oxygen shortage (also called *asphyxia*). Anoxia can occur for any number of reasons—for example, because the umbilical cord becomes pinched or tangled during birth, because sedatives given to the mother reach the fetus and interfere with the baby's breathing, because mucus lodged in the baby's throat prevents normal breathing, or because the baby is in a **breech presentation** (feet or buttocks first) during a vaginal delivery. If identified in advance, fetuses in breech position can be safely delivered by cesarean section to avoid possible anoxia that may occur with a vaginal delivery. Anoxia is dangerous primarily because brain cells die if they are starved of oxygen for more than a few minutes. Severe anoxia can initially cause poor reflexes, seizures, heart rate irregularities, and breathing difficulties. In the long run, severe anoxia can lead to memory impairment or **cerebral palsy**, a neurological disability primarily associated with difficulty controlling muscle movements; it also increases the risk of learning or intellectual disabilities and speech difficulties (Fehlings, Hunt, & Rosenbaum, 2007). Milder anoxia makes some infants irritable at birth or delays their motor and cognitive development but usually does not lead to permanent problems.

Fetal monitoring procedures during labor and delivery can alert caregivers to the possibility of anoxia and allow them to take preventive measures. For example, a vaginal delivery is nearly impossible for the 1 fetus in 100 that is found lying sideways in the uterus. The fetus must be turned to assume a head-down position or be delivered by **cesarean section**, a surgical procedure in which an incision is made in the mother's abdomen and uterus so that the baby can be removed. Now, consider the potential hazards associated with delivery procedures and technologies.

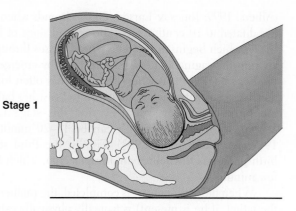

Stage 1

(A) Dilation of the cervix begins

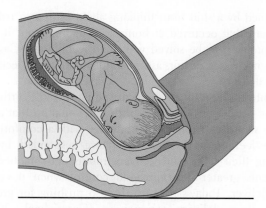

(B) Contractions are greatest and cervix opens completely

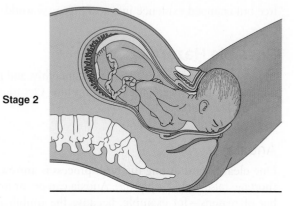

Stage 2

(C) Baby's head appears

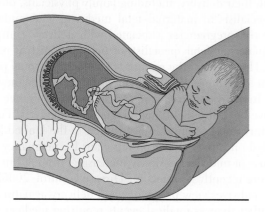

(D) Baby passes through the vagina

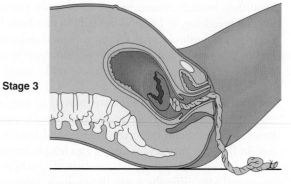

Stage 3

(E) Expulsion of the placenta

■ **FIGURE 4.9** The three stages of labor. Stage 1: (A) Contractions of the uterus cause dilation and effacement of the cervix. (B) Transition is reached when the frequency and strength of the contractions are at their peak and the cervix opens completely. Stage 2: (C) The mother pushes with each contraction, forcing the baby down the birth canal, and the head appears. (D) Near the end of stage 2, the shoulders emerge and are followed quickly by the rest of the baby's body. Stage 3: (E) With a few final pushes, the placenta is delivered.

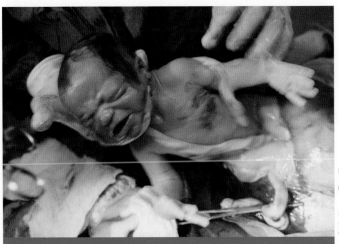

This woman is among the many thousands of women who undergo major abdominal surgery each year to deliver their babies. Why has the cesarean section rate risen to where it is today, and what are the concerns surrounding the high rate of C-section deliveries?

Complicated Delivery

In some cases, mothers may need assistance with delivery, possibly because labor has proceeded too long with too little to show for it or because of concern about the well-being of the baby or mother. For years, doctors frequently used forceps (an instrument resembling an oversized pair of salad tongs) to assist with a vaginal delivery. However, forceps on the soft skull of the newborn occasionally caused serious problems, including cranial bleeding and brain damage. Alternatively, doctors may use vacuum extraction ("suction") to assist difficult deliveries. This procedure has fewer risks associated with it, although it is not risk free. In a vacuum extraction, a cup is inserted through the opening of the birth canal and attached to the baby's head. Suction is applied to make the cup adhere to the baby's scalp; during each contraction and with the mother bearing down, the doctor uses the traction created by the suction to help deliver the baby. From the mother's point of view, vacuum extraction is less traumatic than forceps because the vacuum extractor takes up less space in the birth canal (and therefore is felt less) than forceps (Shihadeh & Al-Najdawi, 2001). For the baby, however, there is likely to be swelling of the scalp and some marking where the vacuum cup was attached. More serious injuries are possible if the vacuum is not properly used. Unfortunately, women who deliver with vacuum assistance report less satisfaction with the overall birth experience than mothers who deliver by other methods (Schindl et al., 2003).

Cesarean sections, too, have been controversial. Use of this alternative to normal vaginal delivery has prevented the death of many babies—for example, when the baby is too large or the mother is too small to permit normal delivery, when a fetus out of position cannot be repositioned, when the placenta prematurely separates from the uterus, or when fetal monitoring reveals that a birth complication is likely. Medical advances have made cesarean sections about as safe as vaginal deliveries, and few ill

effects on mothers and infants have been observed. But mothers who have "C-sections" do take longer to recover from the birth process and are sometimes less positive toward and involved with their babies, at least during the first month of life (DiMatteo et al., 1996; Swain et al., 2008). Nonetheless, the development of babies born by cesarean appears to be perfectly normal (Durik, Hyde, & Clark, 2000).

Many observers have questioned why cesarean deliveries have become so much more common—to the point that they accounted for nearly 32% of births in the United States in 2007 (Hamilton et al., 2009). By one estimate, 11% of first-time cesarean sections are unnecessary and 65% of second-time cesareans are unnecessary (Kabir et al., 2005). Some obstetricians readily opt for C-section deliveries because it protects them from the costly malpractice suits that might arise from complications in vaginal deliveries (Childbirth Connection, 2010). C-sections also generate more revenue for physicians and medical practices than vaginal deliveries (Grant, 2009). Contributing to the high rate of C-sections is the tendency for women who have had one C-section to deliver subsequent babies by C-section rather than attempting a vaginal delivery. Although there is a very small risk of complications with a vaginal delivery following a C-section, it is safe for the large majority of women (Landon et al., 2004). Finally, the high rate of C-section deliveries also reflects the fact that some mothers—and their doctors—prefer having a scheduled birth rather than contending with an unscheduled vaginal delivery. In one recent study, 55% of repeat C-sections were elective, not medically necessary (Tita et al., 2009). But mothers and their doctors need to be careful of the timing of elective C-sections. When nonemergency C-sections are performed at 38 weeks rather than 39 weeks, infants can experience greater respiratory complications (Tita et al., 2009). On the other side of this picture, C-sections performed at 41 or more weeks are also associated with complications, including risk of stillbirth. Thus, there is a fairly narrow window at 39–40 weeks when elective C-sections should be performed to optimize outcomes. Interestingly, mothers who undergo planned (as opposed to emergency) C-sections rate the birth experience more positively than any other group, including those who deliver vaginally (Schindl et al., 2003).

Medications

Some of us were delivered in an era when mothers were routinely drugged into unconsciousness during delivery so that they would not experience any pain, or if they did, they wouldn't remember it. Not surprisingly, concerns have been raised about medications given to mothers during the birth process—analgesics and anesthetics to reduce their pain, sedatives to relax them, and stimulants to induce or intensify uterine contractions. Sedative drugs that act on the entire body cross the placenta and can affect the baby. Babies whose mothers receive large doses of sedative medications during delivery are generally sluggish and irritable, are difficult to feed or cuddle during the first few days of life, and smile infrequently (Elbourne & Wiseman, 2000). In short, they act as though they are drugged. Think about it: Doses of medication large enough to affect mothers can have much greater effects on newborns who weigh only 7 pounds and have immature circulatory and excretory systems that cannot get rid of drugs for days.

Regional analgesics, such as epidurals and spinal blocks, reduce sensation in specific parts of the body. Because they do not cross the placenta, they have fewer ill effects on babies and are preferred by many physicians over sedative drugs that *do* cross the placenta. Epidurals are also rated by mothers as more effective for pain control than other forms of analgesics (Macario et al., 2000; Sheiner et al., 2000). But with these advantages mothers and physicians must weigh disadvantages, including longer labor times and increased need for forceps or vacuum assistance with epidurals (Cassidy, 2006; Halpern et al., 1998).

One of the most commonly used drugs is oxytocin (brand name Pitocin), which can initiate and speed up contractions—moving labor along more quickly. Oxytocin may be administered if a woman's labor seems to have stalled or if she is beyond her due date or the amniotic sac has broken without contractions. The body naturally produces low levels of oxytocin throughout pregnancy, and administering synthetic oxytocin to assist delivery is considered very safe.

In sum, taking obstetric medications is not as risky a business today as it once was, but it is still a decision that requires the pros and cons to be weighed carefully. The effects depend on which drug is used, how much is taken, when it is taken, and by which mother.

Possible hazards during birth, then, include anoxia; breech presentation; the need for assisted delivery through forceps, vacuum extraction, or cesarean section; and the use of medications for pain relief or to speed up labor. Fortunately, most deliveries, although unique from the parents' perspective, are routine from a clinical perspective. In the next section, we consider the birth experience from a family perspective.

The Mother's Experience

What is it really like to give birth to a child? For every woman who has given birth, you are likely to hear a unique birth story (Savage, 2001). Most mothers admit that they experienced severe pain and a good deal of anxiety, including feelings of outright panic (Waldenström et al., 1996). Yet most also emerged from the delivery room feeling good about their achievement and their ability to cope ("I did it!"). Overall, 77% felt the experience was positive and only 10% said it was negative. And, despite longer labors and more medication, first-time mothers did not perceive labor and delivery much differently than experienced mothers did.

What factors influence a mother's experience of birth? Psychological factors such as the mother's attitude toward her pregnancy, her knowledge and expectations about the birth process, her sense of control over childbirth, and the social support she receives from her partner or someone else are important determinants of her experience of delivery and of her new baby (Waldenström et al., 1996; Wilcock, Kobayashi, & Murray, 1997). Social support can be especially important. When the father, or another supportive person whose main role is to comfort the mother, is continuously present during labor and delivery, women experience less pain, use less medication, are less likely to have cesarean sections, and are more likely to feel good about the birth process (Hodnett & Osborn, 1989; Kennell et al., 1991).

Cultural Factors

The experience of childbearing is shaped by the cultural context in which it occurs. For example, different cultures have different views of the desirability of having children. In some, a large family is a status symbol, whereas in the People's Republic of China a "one-child policy" discourages multiple childbearing in hopes of slowing population growth and raising the standard of living. As a result of this policy, the average number of children a Chinese woman bears dropped from nearly five children in 1970 to fewer than two in recent years. The ratio of boys to girls has also changed; many parents want their one child to be a boy who can support them in old age and therefore abort female fetuses identified through ultrasound tests or abandon their female babies after they are born (Fitzpatrick, 2009).

Practices surrounding birth also differ widely. Consider three different birth scenarios that reflect different cultural beliefs about pregnancy and delivery. Among the Pokot people of Kenya, there is strong social support of the mother-to-be (O'Dempsey, 1988). The community celebrates the coming birth, and the father-to-be stops hunting lest he be killed by animals. As a result, he is available to support his wife. A midwife, aided by female relatives, delivers the baby. The placenta is buried in the goat enclosure, and the baby is washed in cold water and given a mixture of hot ash and boiled herbs so that it will vomit the amniotic fluid it has swallowed. Mothers are given plenty of time to recover. They go into seclusion for 1 month and devote themselves entirely to their babies for 3 months.

By contrast, in Uttar Pradesh in northern India, the blood associated with childbirth is viewed as polluting, and the whole event as shameful (Jeffery & Jeffery, 1993). A *dai*, a poorly paid attendant hired by the woman's mother-in-law, delivers the baby. The *dai* typically hates her menial, disgusting job, provides no pain relievers, discourages the mother from crying out in pain, and offers little emotional support. The mother is kept in the house for several days and in the family compound for weeks so that she will not pollute others. Because the baby is also believed to be polluted, its hair is shaved off.

Finally, among the !Kung San of Namibia, women typically labor by themselves (Cassidy, 2006). Giving birth alone is considered to be a strength. When labor begins, the !Kung woman goes off on her own and is expected to labor quietly. To do otherwise is considered a sign of weakness and possibly shows indifference toward the baby.

In contrast to these examples, childbirth in highly industrialized Western societies is highly "medicalized," with women hospitalized, hooked up to monitors, and separated from most friends and family members. Should we return to more traditional ways of birthing that view delivery less like a major medical event and more like a typical life event? As the Indian example illustrates, not all "traditional" practices would be viewed as in the best interests of parents and babies. Also, Western societies do a far better job than developing countries of preventing mother and infant mortality. In some areas of sub-Saharan

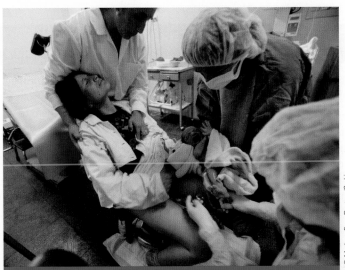

This Peruvian woman gives birth in an upright position, which reduces labor and delivery time by allowing gravity to assist with moving the baby down the birth canal. In societies that have medicalized childbirth, women are more likely to be lying horizontal on a bed, which may sound comfortable but is not the optimal laboring or birthing position.

Africa, for example, about 15% of babies die during childbirth or in the first year of life (CIA, 2009). In Western, industrial societies, infant mortality rates have dropped over the past 50 years from 3% (30 infants out of 1000) to nearly 0.5% (6 infants out of 1000) (CIA, 2009). Unfortunately, infant mortality is more than twice as high for black infants as for white infants (MacDorman & Mathews, 2008). The secret to a more optimal birth experience may be to blend beneficial traditional practices such as offering emotional support to new mothers with modern medical know-how.

Postpartum Depression

Some new mothers suffer from depression following the birth of their baby. As many as 60% of all new mothers report feeling tearful, irritable, moody, anxious, and depressed within the first few days after birth (Najman et al., 2000). This condition—the baby blues—is relatively mild, passes quickly, and is probably linked to the steep drops in levels of female hormones that normally occur after delivery and to the stresses associated with delivering a child and taking on the responsibilities of parenthood (not to mention coping with the lack of sleep experienced by many new mothers).

A second, and far more serious, condition is **postpartum depression**—an episode of clinical depression that lasts months rather than days in a woman who has just given birth. It affects approximately 1 in 10 new mothers (Cooper & Murray, 1998). Only rarely does a woman who has never had significant emotional problems become clinically depressed for the first time after giving birth. Most affected women have histories of depression, and many were depressed during pregnancy. Also, women

vulnerable to depression are more likely to become depressed if they are experiencing other life stresses on top of the stresses of becoming a mother (Honey, Bennett, & Morgan, 2003). Lack of social support—especially a poor relationship with a partner—also increases the odds (Boyce, 2003; Heh, 2003).

Postpartum depression has significant implications for the parent–infant relationship. One study compared the children of 58 mothers who experienced postpartum depression with the children of 42 nondepressed mothers over a 5-year period (Murray et al., 1999). The children of the depressed mothers were less securely attached to their mothers during infancy and were less responsive during interactions with their mothers at age 5. They also tended to respond negatively when another child approached them in a friendly manner.

Mothers who had been postnatally depressed report greater behavioral problems by their children. At age 11, children of postnatally depressed mothers show more violent behavior even when researchers control for family characteristics and later episodes of maternal depression (Hay et al., 2003). The violence exhibited by these children is associated with anger management problems, attention problems, and hyperactive behavior. Adolescents whose mothers had been postnatally depressed also show elevated levels of cortisol, which is associated with major depression (Halligan et al., 2004). The implication of these results is that early experiences with a depressed mother might predispose these children to later depression.

How exactly might maternal depression in the weeks and months following delivery affect children's behavior and increase their odds of developing depression? Mothers who are depressed tend to be relatively unresponsive to their babies and may even feel hostility toward them. They are tired, distracted, and often lack the energy needed to be fully engaged with their infants. Even though mothers typically recover from postnatal depression, research suggests that their early attitudes about their babies and the resulting pattern of early mother–child interactions set the stage for ongoing interaction problems that affect the child's behavior (Murray et al., 1999; Weinberg et al., 2006). The contribution of genes inherited from their depression-prone mothers and of stressful experiences before birth, after birth, or both can combine to precipitate depression in the child (Goodman, 2002). Thus, for their own sakes and for the sakes of their infants, mothers experiencing more than a mild case of the baby blues should seek professional help in overcoming their depression.

The Father's Experience

When birthing moved into hospitals, the medical establishment aggressively prohibited fathers from participating in their children's birth on the grounds that they would contaminate the sterile environment needed for a safe birth (Cassidy, 2006). It would take many decades, many lawsuits, and more progressive views about birth support before men were routinely accepted—and expected—in the delivery room. Today, many men prepare for fatherhood before delivery, attend prenatal classes with their partner, and are present for their child's birth. Fathers report that they want to be involved with their partner's pregnancy, although they don't always know how to make this happen (Draper, 2002).

Perhaps you have seen the TV show that tells story after story of women who did not realize they were pregnant until late in the pregnancy or even until the baby was being born. After viewers watch each woman's story, an announcer asks, "How could she not have known she was pregnant?" Good question. What are the symptoms or signs of pregnancy? How can women educate themselves to avoid a "surprise baby"? Here are some of the main reasons why women may not recognize a pregnancy:

1. Some women have a history of irregular periods and/or infertility. Some have even been told by their physicians that they are infertile or unlikely to conceive a child. With the mindset that they "can't get pregnant," these women often interpret signs of pregnancy in other ways. Fatigue from pregnancy may be attributed to poor sleep habits, and weight gain may be attributed to sluggish metabolism or less exercise.

2. Some women experience breakthrough bleeding during pregnancy. This may occur fairly regularly and women may assume it is their period. This may be especially likely if women with breakthrough bleeding also had irregular periods before their pregnancy.

3. Home pregnancy tests are not perfect. A woman may take one of these tests and get a false reading, suggesting that she is not pregnant when in fact she is. Women who suspect that a pregnancy is possible should schedule a visit with their health-care provider to have a more reliable test of pregnancy.

4. Birth control is not 100% effective. Some women will become pregnant while taking birth control, even when they take it reliably. But more often, women may not be as reliable as they should be—missing a dose, taking a dose late, or switching from one form of birth control to another. In addition, as with Serena in the chapter opener, the effectiveness of birth control can be diminished with certain illnesses or treatments for illnesses. Also, being a new mother and breastfeeding do *not* mean that a woman won't ovulate and potentially become pregnant again soon after childbirth.

5. Women who exercise strenuously may not menstruate regularly and may not be concerned if they go for months without menstruating. If they begin to put on a little weight from a pregnancy, this might lead them to exercise even more, keeping any pregnancy weight gain to a minimum.

6. Women who are obese may not notice any change in weight with a pregnancy. A tummy "bump" from a fetus may not be visible.

7. Some fetuses do not move around much and may not produce enough activity to be felt by the mother. In hindsight, some women do recall feeling activity in their bellies but attributed it, at the time, to indigestion or gas!

So if you are sexually active, be aware of even subtle changes in your body that could signal a pregnancy. These include breast tenderness, firmness, or tingling; fatigue; absence or changes in menstruation; lower backaches; headaches; nausea; increased urination; changes in sense of smell or taste or altered appetite; and skin changes. If there is any possibility that you are pregnant, visit a health-care provider to get checked out. If you are going to have a baby, you want to give it the best start in life by providing prenatal care as early as possible.

Like mothers, fathers experience the process of becoming a parent as a significant event in their lives that involves a mix of positive and negative emotions. Also like mothers, fathers tend to be anxious during pregnancy and birth and some even experience some of the same physiological symptoms as their pregnant partner. These symptoms, called **couvade** (from the French word meaning "to hatch"), include bloating, weight gain, fatigue, insomnia, and nausea (Cassidy, 2006). And before you conclude that these symptoms must be "all in their heads," consider that some research shows hormonal shifts among expectant fathers that are similar to the hormonal shifts experienced by pregnant women (Cassidy, 2006).

As for the labor period, new fathers report feeling scared, unprepared, helpless, and frustrated (Chandler & Field, 1997; Chapman, 2000; Hallgren et al., 1999). They find labor to be more work than they had expected and sometimes feel excluded as the nurses take over. For most men, attending prenatal classes with their partner improves their experience of childbirth, although for a few men the added knowledge that comes with these classes increases their anxiety (Greenhalgh, Slade, & Spiby, 2000). Stress levels among men tend to be highest during their partner's pregnancy and then decrease after the birth of the baby (Condon, Boyce, & Corkindale, 2004). Despite the stresses, negative emotions usually give way to relief, pride, and joy when the baby finally arrives (Chandler & Field, 1997). Indeed, most fathers find early contact with their babies special. As one father put it, "When my wife handed Anna to me, I was completely unprepared for the intense experience of fatherhood. I was overwhelmed by my feeling of belonging to and with this new child" (Reed, 1996, p. 52).

The thrill of having a new baby often intermingles with other emotions in the weeks and months after delivery as fathers struggle to become comfortable and confident in their new role as parent (Barclay & Lupton, 1999; St. John, Cameron, & McVeigh, 2005). Research reveals that nearly as many new fathers as new mothers experience symptoms of depression following the birth of their children (Paulson, Dauber, & Leiferman, 2006; Pinheiro et al., 2006; Wang & Chen, 2006). Fathers who

The birth of a baby affects more than the new mother and father; older siblings may have their worlds rocked until they have navigated their way through the changes that come with being a big sister or brother to a new sibling. It's unclear whether this older sister is thrilled or horrified at seeing her baby sister for the first time.

© Ariel Skelley/Corbis

Sibling Adjustment

In many families, it is not only mother and father who welcome and adjust to a new baby—there is often another child in the family who must adjust to the newest family member. There are many factors that influence how an older child deals with the arrival of a sibling. Brenda Volling (2005) applied an ecological systems approach to illustrate the multiple variables that influence a child's "transition to siblinghood." The quality of the child's immediate environment—the microsystem—in the weeks and months following the birth of a new baby affect the older sibling's behaviors and sense of well-being. A strong father–child relationship, for example, can help insulate an older sibling from effects of decreased maternal attention as mothers invest a great deal of time caring for the newborn.

The larger environment—the exosystem—also plays an important role. Mothers and fathers who receive strong social support from other family members or friends may be less stressed or tired, allowing them to provide better child care to the older sibling. And children who have good relationships with friends at the time their sibling is born develop more positive relationships with their sibling than children who lack good friendships (Kramer & Kowal, 2005).

Mothers with just one child tend to increase their work hours within a few years after childbirth. However, mothers who have a second child during this time tend to decrease their work hours (Baydar, Greek, & Brooks-Gunn, 1997). As a result, children without siblings may find themselves spending more time in group daycare settings outside the home, whereas children with new siblings, because their mothers are working less and home more, find themselves spending more of their time at home. One of these scenarios is not better or worse than the other, but they represent different environments for the older child, with the potential to shift their development along different paths.

Finally, it is also apparent that a child's age, gender, and personality affect how that child responds and adjusts to the arrival of a sibling. Very young children (younger than age 2 at the time of their sibling's birth) do not show the same disruption of mother–child attachment that often occurs with children who are between ages 2 and 5 when their sibling is born (Teti et al., 1996). It may be that very young children have not established the same expectations of the relationship or do not have the cognitive skills to process the change in the family situation brought on by the arrival of a sibling. In contrast, older children may have become accustomed to having all their parents' attention focused on them and are more disrupted in their routines and expectations when they have to share the family environment with a sibling.

are depressed interact less with their children. And like depressed mothers, depressed fathers report a lack of social support, suggesting that the postnatal period could be enhanced for both mothers and fathers with stronger support systems in place. In situations where mothers and fathers do not reside together, fathers tend to be only tangentially involved with their new babies. The involvement of nonresidential fathers depends on their relationship with the mother and their social support network (Fagan & Palkowitz, 2007).

One particular area that seems to trouble first-time fathers is their sexual relationship with their partners. Men expect their sex life to return to its prepregnancy state after the birth of their baby and are disappointed when it does not (Condon, Boyce, & Corkindale, 2004). They must forge a relationship with a new child as well as renegotiate their relationship with their partner.

Transitioning to parenthood can be challenging for both the mother-to-be and the father-to-be. Even couples who enjoy high levels of prepregnancy marital satisfaction experience postpartum declines in marital satisfaction (Doss et al., 2009; Lawrence et al., 2008). The decline in satisfaction is not short-lived, either; marital satisfaction remains depressed for at least 4 years following birth (Doss et al., 2009). Experiencing a planned pregnancy rather than an unexpected pregnancy helps to buffer the decline in marital satisfaction, at least for fathers (Lawrence et al., 2008). And both parents experience less depression and anxiety during the parenthood transition if they have a greater sense of control over events in their life (Keeton, Perry-Jenkins, & Sayer, 2008). Take a look at Exploration Box 4.2 to learn why some women may end up with a surprise package.

Checking Mastery

1. What steps occur during the process of childbirth?
2. What risks does the baby potentially face during the birth process?

Making Connections

1. Considering the research on birth and the perinatal environment, arrange the perfect birth experience for you and your baby and justify its features. Where would you be, who would be with you, and what would be done?
2. Some experts worry that cesarean sections are overused. What do you think? Should a woman be able to choose whether she delivers vaginally or by cesarean section? Should hospitals be permitted to force a woman to deliver by cesarean if they believe the fetus is in danger?

4.4 The Neonatal Environment

So now that parents have a baby, what do they do? Here we will look at the **neonatal** environment—the events of the first month and how parents might optimize the development of young infants.

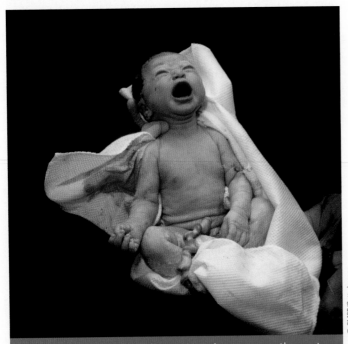

Welcome to the world, little one! Your journey over the past 9 months has been astonishing. At conception you received all the genetic material necessary to develop into the baby we now see. You have already taken your first breaths, and the umbilical cord that sustained you in the womb will soon be cut. After being cleaned and wrapped up, you will begin to interact with your family and explore the world around you.

© CMSP/Getty Images

There are marked differences in how parents interact with their newborns. As Meredith Small (1999) characterizes it, "Our ideas about parenting and infant care are as culturally constructed as what we wear, what we eat, or how we dance" (p. 41). For example, in societies where infant mortality is high, babies may not even be named or viewed as people until they seem likely to survive (Nsamenang, 1992). The Beng, who are concentrated in small farming towns along the Ivory Coast, believe that newborns are not entirely in this world but exist in the world the babies will eventually inhabit after death (Gottlieb, 2000). Once their umbilical cord stump falls off on the fourth or fifth day of life, they begin to inhabit this world but still vacillate between the two worlds for another 4–5 years. During this time, the Beng regard their children as vulnerable. Spiritual beliefs influence their child care practices, leading, for example, to twice-daily enemas for infants using a chili pepper solution.

Among the !Kung, a hunting and gathering society of the Kalahari Desert in southern Africa, babies are carried upright in slings during the day and they sleep in the same bed with their mothers at night. They are touched more than 70% of daytime hours, are breast-fed whenever they want (usually 20–40 times per day), and may not be weaned until the age of 4 (Hewlett, 1995). In general, infants in hunter–gatherer societies are indulged considerably, at least until their survival is assured.

Infant care practices are considerably different in modern, industrialized societies where infant mortality is lower. Infants in industrialized nations like the United States are touched only 12–20% of daytime hours, and they are often trained to breast-feed or bottle-feed on a schedule, usually 5–7 times a day (Hewlett, 1995). Babies may sleep in the same bed or room as their parents for just a few weeks before being settled into a crib in their own room, a practice that mothers in many other cultures, who sleep in the same bed with their babies until they are toddlers, find quite bizarre. Parents who do sleep with their babies should be mindful that babies are at increased risk of suffocation when they sleep in adult beds (Shapiro-Mendoza et al., 2009). Adults are obviously much larger and heavier, posing a hazard if they roll onto a baby while sleeping. But adult beds also have more bedding and pillows than an infant crib, and these can suffocate a tiny infant.

Regardless of where they live, new parents are often uncertain about how to relate to their babies and may find the period after birth stressful. T. Berry Brazelton (1979) devised a way to help parents appreciate their baby's competencies and feel competent themselves as parents. He developed a newborn assessment technique, the Brazelton Neonatal Behavioral Assessment Scale, which assesses the strength of infant reflexes and the infant's responses to 26 situations (for example, reactions to cuddling, general irritability, and orienting to the examiner's face and voice). Brazelton uses this test to teach parents to understand their babies as individuals and to appreciate many of the pleasing competencies that they possess. During "Brazelton training," parents observe the test being administered and learn how to administer it themselves to elicit smiles and other heartwarming responses from their babies.

Breast or Bottle?

Over time and across cultures, feeding practices vary considerably. Without question, breastfeeding is the most natural form of nutrition for newborns. And until modern times, it was the sole source of nourishment until solid foods were introduced. For a variety of reasons, breastfeeding in the United States reached an all-time low in the early 1970s, when only 1 in 4 mothers attempted to nurse their newborn infants. Bottle-feeding with formula had become the norm (Eiger and Olds, 1999). Since then, research has shown numerous advantages of breast milk over formula and all major health organizations (for example, the American Academy of Family Physicians, Canadian Paediatric Society, National Health Service of Great Britain, World Health Organization, and more) have advocated for exclusive breastfeeding for the first 6 months of life. As a result of public awareness campaigns regarding the advantages of breastfeeding, nearly 7 in 10 mothers now attempt to nurse their newborns (Ahluwalia, Morrow, & Hsia, 2006). But only 50% are still breastfeeding after a month, and less than one-third are still at it by 6 months (Wellbery, 2006).

The health benefits of breastfeeding are numerous and include fewer ear infections and respiratory tract problems for children and lower risk of ovarian cancer and early breast cancer for mothers (Ip et al., 2007). Children who breastfeed for at least 4 months have stronger lung function, almost certainly because breastfeeding requires infants to suck stronger and longer to obtain the same amount of milk as when bottle-feeding (Ogbuanu et al., 2008). In homes where a caregiver smokes cigarettes, breastfeeding offers some protection against the respiratory infections that frequently plague infants exposed to secondhand (passive) smoke (Yilmaz et al., 2009). Breast milk contains several substances that protect nursing infants from infections, and it has the perfect blend of nutrients for a quickly developing little person. For premature babies, breast milk has been referred to as "more of a medicine than a food" because of its positive effects on their immune systems and weight gain (Gross-Loh, 2006, p. 38). And mothers who breastfeed lose the weight gained during pregnancy more quickly than those who do not breastfeed following childbirth.

Given the health benefits of breastfeeding, why don't more women breast-feed? Women cite a number of reasons for not continuing with breastfeeding, including issues related to self (such as sore nipples) and issues related to the baby (for example, concerns that baby is not getting adequate nutrition) (Ahluwalia, Morrow, & Hsia, 2006; Thulier & Mercer, 2009). Young women, those from low socioeconomic backgrounds, and those with less education are less likely to breast-feed than other women (Ryan & Zhou, 2006). In one survey, 95% of the mothers with the highest education started breastfeeding compared with 73% of the mothers with the least education; by 6 months of age, 39% of the more educated mothers were still breastfeeding compared with just 15% of the less educated mothers (Van Rossem et al., 2009). Being employed outside the home is also associated with lower breastfeeding rates, presumably because of the logistical problems of breastfeeding while at work (Ryan & Zhou, 2006). Finally, fewer black mothers breastfeed than white mothers (Ip et al., 2007). Interestingly, Hispanic mothers have a fairly high rate of breastfeeding until they immigrate to the United States, and then the rate decreases with the amount of time in the United States (Gibson-Davis & Brooks-Gunn, 2006). This likely reflects U.S. cultural values toward breastfeeding, which are more ambivalent than those in many other countries. To improve breastfeeding rates, ambivalent (and in some cases, downright negative) views of breastfeeding need to be addressed so that women view breastfeeding as *the* option, not just *an* option.

Most hospitals promote breastfeeding and take time to teach new mothers successful breastfeeding techniques. However, one study found that hospitals may also inadvertently support bottle-feeding when they send new mothers home with gift packs containing formula samples (Rosenberg et al., 2008). The researchers found that mothers who went home with a gift pack containing formula were more likely to be using formula at 10 weeks postpartum than mothers who did not receive the formula in a gift pack. Despite the emphasis on breastfeeding while in the hospital, the formula in the gift pack may send the message that the hospital supports bottle-feeding and expects bottle-feeding at some point.

Breastmilk provides the perfect balance of nutrients for the developing infant.

© Ute Klaphake/Photofusion Picture Library

Identifying At-Risk Newborns

A few infants will be considered **at risk** for either short-term or long-term problems because of genetic defects, prenatal hazards, or perinatal damage. It is essential to these infants' survival and well-being that they be identified as early as possible. Newborns are routinely screened using the **Apgar test**, which provides a quick assessment of the newborn's heart rate, respiration, color, muscle tone, and reflexes (• **Table 4.6**). The test has been used for more than 50 years and, despite its low-tech nature, is still considered a valuable diagnostic tool (Casey, McIntire, & Leveno, 2001). The simple test is given immediately and 5 minutes after birth. It yields

Factors	Score		
	0	1	2
Heart Rate	Absent	Slow (<100 beats per minute)	Moderate (>100 beats per minute)
Respiratory Effort	Absent	Slow or irregular	Good; baby is crying
Muscle Tone	Flaccid; limp	Weak; some flexion	Strong; active motion
Color	Blue or pale	Body pink, extremities blue	Completely pink
Reflex Irritability	No response	Frown, grimace, or weak cry	Vigorous cry

scores of 0, 1, or 2 for each of the five factors, which are then added to yield a total score that can range from 0 to 10. Infants who score 7 or higher are in good shape. Infants scoring 4 or lower are at risk—their heartbeats are sluggish or nonexistent, their muscles are limp, and their breathing is shallow and irregular, if they are breathing at all. These babies will immediately experience a different postnatal environment than the normal baby experiences because they require medical intervention in intensive care units to survive, as you will see at the end of the chapter.

One particular group of at-risk babies that should be examined more closely are those with **low birth weight (LBW)**. As ● Table 4.7 illustrates, the younger (and smaller) babies are at birth, the lower their chances of survival. Approximately 8% of babies born in the United States have a low birth weight (less than 2500 grams, or 5½ pounds). Some of these babies are born at term and are called "small for gestational age," but many are born preterm (less than 37 weeks of gestation) and are more at risk as a result (■ **Figure 4.10**). The survival and health of these small infants is a concern, particularly for infants who are very small (less than 1500 grams or no more than 3.3 pounds). Prematurity is the leading cause of infant mortality. Although LBW infants account for about 8% of all births, they account for 65% of all infant deaths and nearly 60% of the money spent on pregnancies and deliveries (Callaghan et al., 2006; Schmitt, Sneed, & Phibbs, 2006). Very LBW infants are even more costly: they account for less than 1% of all births but 36% of the total hospital costs. Most fragile are the micropreemies—those weigh-ing less than 800 grams or 1.75 pounds at birth. The high emotional and economic costs of LBW have made this an important medical and societal issue.

We don't always know what causes LBW, but research has identified a number of factors regularly associated with it. For starters, LBW is strongly linked to low socioeconomic status, probably because poor women are more likely to have poor nutrition and inadequate prenatal care (Goldenberg & Culhane, 2007; Hughes & Simpson, 1995). African American mothers are twice as likely as non-Hispanic white mothers to experience premature delivery and LBW. In addition, many other risk factors that we have already described, such as smoking and stress, are linked to LBW. And not surprisingly, the more risk factors experienced during pregnancy, the greater the likelihood of delivering a small baby (Rosenberg, 2001).

Low birth weight is also associated with multiple births, which have increased substantially over the past several decades largely because of increased use of ovulation-stimulating drugs to treat infertility. In 1980 there were 37 higher-order multiple births (triplets or more) in every 100,000 births; by 1998 this figure had jumped to 194 higher-order multiples in every 100,000 births (Martin et al., 2005). Among single-birth infants, approximately 5% are LBW, but among twins, nearly half are LBW. Among higher-order multiples, 86% are low birth weight (Cohen et al., 1999). Higher-order multiples spend 8 times as long in the hospital as singleton infants and cost more than 6 times as much in hospital costs (Henderson et al., 2004).

● **TABLE 4.7 SURVIVAL AND HEALTH OF PREMATURE BABIES BY GESTATIONAL AGE**

Factor	Results (in Weeks and %)			
Number of completed weeks since last menstruation	<23 weeks	23 weeks	24 weeks	25 weeks
Percentage of babies who survive	0–15%	2–35%	17–58%	35–85%
Percentage of survivors with chronic lung disease	89%	57–70%	33–89%	16–71%
Percentage of survivors with a severe neurodevelopmental disability*	69%	30%	17–45%	12–35%

*Includes cerebral palsy, mental retardation, blindness or severe myopia, and deafness.
SOURCE: Based on data from Hack & Fanaroff, 1999.

The good news is that most LBW babies born since the advent of neonatal intensive care in the 1960s function within the normal range of development and experience significant catch-up growth during their first months and years of life (Chyi et al., 2008; Wilson-Costello et al., 2007). However, compared with normal-birth-weight children, LBW children, especially those with extremely LBW (less than 1000 grams, or 2 pounds 3 ounces) are at greater risk for numerous neurobehavioral problems, including blindness, deafness, cerebral palsy, poor academic achievement, autism, and health problems. Many of these problems persist into childhood and adulthood for the smallest and earliest preterm babies (Aarnoudse-Moens et al., 2009; Johnson et al., 2009). Respiratory difficulties are likely because premature babies have not yet produced enough **surfactant**, a substance that prevents the air sacs of the lungs from sticking together and therefore aids breathing. Surfactant therapy for LBW infants became common practice around 1990 and seems to improve the survival rate among the sickest infants. However, it has not entirely improved health or long-term achievement scores of LBW babies in general, perhaps because small, earlier-born babies, who have the most complications, are now surviving to be among the school-age population of LBW survivors (Hagen et al., 2006; Paul et al., 2006; see also Bode et al., 2009).

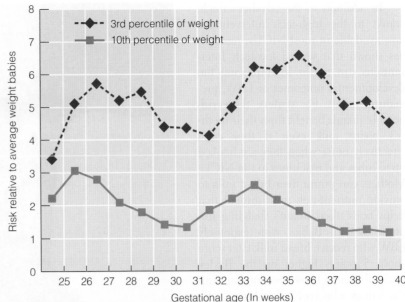

■ FIGURE 4.10 Mortality of low-birth-weight babies during the first month of life is affected by their gestational age (how long they were in the womb) as well as their weight, with smaller babies clearly at greater risk than heavier babies.

SOURCE: Adapted from Boulet, S. L., Alexander, G. R., Salihu, H. M., Kirby, R. S., & Carlo, W. A. (2006). Fetal growth risk curves: Defining levels of fetal growth restriction by neonatal death risk. *American Journal of Obstetrics and Gynecology, 195*, 1572–1577, Table 1. Copyright © 2006. Reprinted with permission from Elsevier.

Modern technology permits the survival of younger and smaller babies, but many experts believe we have reached the lowest limits of viability between 23 and 24 weeks of gestation. What is the long-term prognosis for premature babies?

In addition to the advances made thanks to the high-tech interventions now available in most NICUs, research has shown that several low-tech interventions can go far in improving the developmental outcomes of LBW, premature infants. For starters, these vulnerable infants benefit from their mother's breast milk even if they can't effectively nurse when they are hooked up to tubes and machines in the NICU. Mothers can pump their breast milk to provide nutrient-rich nourishment that helps boost their infant's fledgling immune system. Babies with extremely LBW who receive breast milk later score about 5 points higher on the Bayley Scale of Mental Development than similar babies who receive no breast milk (Vohr et al., 2006). And among babies receiving breast milk, there are measurable differences between those who consumed the largest quantities and those who consumed the least.

There is also evidence that skin-to-skin contact is therapeutic for these infants. Sometimes called **kangaroo care**, resting on a parent's chest helps maintain body temperature, heart rate, and oxygen levels in the blood (Feldman & Eidelman, 2003), and the rhythmic sound of the parent's heartbeat calms the infant and may help simulate the environment of the womb. Premature infants who experience kangaroo care settle into more mature patterns of quiet sleep and alert wakefulness than premature infants who do not receive this treatment. One of the nice things about kangaroo care is that both mothers and fathers can participate. Doing so improves parents' sensitivity to their infant and makes the dynamics among the trio more positive (Feldman et al., 2003).

In addition to skin-to-skin contact, Tiffany Field and her colleagues (Diego, Field, & Hernandez-Reif, 2005; Field et al., 2006) have shown that premature infants benefit from massage therapy. For example, in one study, premature babies received either light or moderate massage 3 times per day for 5 days (Field et al., 2006). Those who received moderate-pressure massage gained significantly more weight on each of the days of the therapy than the premature babies in the light-massage group. Babies receiving moderate massage seemed to be more relaxed and less aroused, which may have facilitated greater weight gain (Field et al., 2006). In addition, the massage increased the efficiency of the digestive system, which is also associated with greater weight gain (Diego, Field, & Hernandez-Reif, 2005).

Although the long-term health prognosis for LBW babies is now good, many children born with an extremely LBW continue to experience neurosensory impairments and academic problems throughout their childhood and teen years (Doyle & Anderson, 2005; Saigal et al., 2007). These cognitive deficits in childhood can be traced to deficits in attention, speed, and memory evident in preterm infants during their first year

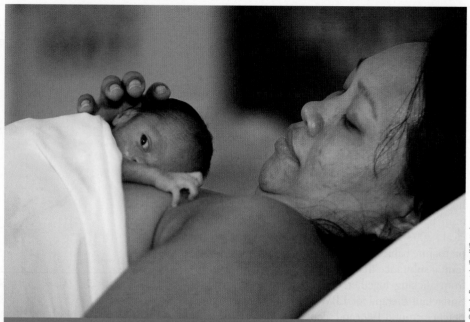

This 2 pound 10 ounce bundle is enjoying skin-to-skin contact with his mother. Such "kangaroo care" helps babies regulate body temperature and maintain a regular heart rate and oxygen levels in the blood.

© Paula Bronstein/Staff/Getty Images

(Rose et al., 2005). The fate of premature and LBW babies depends considerably on two factors. The first is their biological condition—their health and neurological status in particular. The second is the quality of the postnatal environment they experience. For instance, in a study of more than 8000 infants, Dennis Hogan and Jennifer Park (2000) found that the disadvantages of LBW were amplified for children of minority status growing up in poverty with a single parent. In contrast, LBW babies who live with two parents and whose mother is well educated, although they start out with delays, improve and may even catch up to the average child by age 8 (Ment et al., 2003). And children born with very LBW whose mothers are consistently responsive to them throughout infancy and toddlerhood attain higher levels of cognitive achievement than similar children with less responsive mothers (Smith, Landry, & Swank, 2006). In contrast, premature infants whose mothers are "out of synch" with them exhibit less mature outcomes at age 2 (Feldman & Eidelman, 2006).

Other research shows that at-risk infants can benefit from programs that teach their parents how to provide responsive care and appropriate intellectual stimulation to them once they are home. Home visits to advise parents, combined with a stimulating day care program for LBW toddlers, can teach mothers how to be better teachers of their young children and stimulate these children's cognitive development. In an ambitious project called the Infant Health and Development Program, premature and LBW infants at eight sites have benefited from such early intervention (McCormick et al., 2006). The program involves weekly home visits during the first year of life and then biweekly home visits and attendance by the infant at a special day care center for half a day every day from age 1 to age 3. Mothers are given child care education and support.

The program appears to help parents provide a more growth-enhancing home environment—for example, to give their babies appropriate toys and learning materials and to interact with them in stimulating ways. The intervention also helped these at-risk babies, especially the heavier ones, achieve more cognitive growth by age 3 than they would otherwise have achieved. An impressive 14-point boost in IQ scores at age 3 for heavier LBW children who received the intervention had dropped to a 4-point advantage over control group children at age 8, but this small advantage was still evident at age 18 (McCarton et al., 1997; McCormick et al., 2006). Children who weighed 2000 grams (4 pounds 6 ounces) or less at birth did not get much benefit from the program. Other research similarly shows that early intervention effects on premature infants fade over time (Johnson et al., 2005). Researchers have more to learn, then, about what it takes to keep the development of at-risk children on a positive track after the perinatal period comes to a close. However, everything we know about life-span environmental forces suggests that supportive parents and programs can do a great deal to optimize every child's development. It seems that premature, LBW babies can achieve normal levels of intellectual functioning during childhood when they live in middle-class homes, when their mothers are relatively educated, and most importantly, when their mothers, rich or poor, are consistently attentive and responsive when interacting with them (Smith, Landry, & Swank, 2006).

Studies such as these raise a larger issue about the importance of early experience. Some developmentalists take seriously the concept of critical (or sensitive) periods in early development. Others stress the resilience of human beings, their ability to rebound from early disadvantages and to respond to environmental influences throughout their lives rather than only during so-called critical periods. Which is it?

Risk and Resilience

To what extent does harm done in the prenatal or perinatal period last, and to what extent can postnatal experiences make up for it? You have encountered many examples in this chapter of what can go wrong before or during birth. Some damaging effects are clearly irreversible: the thalidomide baby will never grow normal arms or legs, and the child with FAS will always be mentally retarded. Yet throughout history, many children turned out fine even though their mothers—unaware of many risk factors—smoked and drank during their pregnancies, received heavy doses of medication during delivery, or experienced serious illness. So, although many factors place a fetus at risk and increase the likelihood of problems after birth, not all at-risk infants end up with problems (Fraser, 2004). Is it also possible that some babies exposed to and clearly affected by risks recover from their deficiencies later in life?

Indeed it is, and researchers now have the results of major longitudinal studies that say so. For 40 years, Emmy Werner and her colleague Ruth Smith studied a group of babies born in 1955 on the island of Kauai in Hawaii (Werner, 1989a, 1989b; Werner & Smith, 1982, 1992, 2001). This was a monumental undertaking. All women of Kauai who were to give birth in 1955 were interviewed in each trimester of pregnancy, and physicians noted any prenatal, perinatal, or postnatal complications. On the basis of this information, each baby was categorized as having been exposed to severe, moderate, mild, or no prenatal or perinatal stress. At ages 1, 2, 10, 18, 32, and 40 years, researchers diligently tracked down their participants and conducted interviews (initially with the mothers and later with the children), administered psychological and cognitive tests, rated the quality of the family environment, and conducted medical examinations. Remarkably, at the 40-year follow-up, 70% (489 of 698) of the original group of babies born in 1955 still participated in the study.

One-third of the children classified as at risk showed considerable resilience, getting themselves back on a normal course of development. Through this self-righting capacity, they were able to mature into competent, successful adults with no evident learning, social, or vocational problems despite being at risk for poor outcomes. Two major findings emerge from this research:

- The effects of prenatal and perinatal complications decrease over time.
- The outcomes of early risk depend on the quality of the postnatal environment.

The postnatal environments of these successful at-risk children included two types of protective factors, influences that prevent the damaging effects of risk factors or help children overcome disadvantages. These are:

- *Personal resources.* Possibly because of their genetic makeup, some children have qualities such as intelligence, sociability, and communication skills that help them choose or create more nurturing and stimulating environments and cope with challenges. For example, parents and other observers noted that these children were agreeable, cheerful, and self-confident as infants, which elicited positive caregiving responses. They also believed that they were in control of their own fates—that through their actions, they could bring about positive outcomes.
- *Supportive postnatal environment.* Some at-risk children receive the social support they need within or outside the family. Most importantly, they are able to find at least one person who loves them unconditionally and with whom they feel secure.

Clearly, hazards during the important prenatal and perinatal periods can leave lasting scars, and yet many children show remarkable resilience. There seem to be some points in the life span, especially early on, in which both positive and negative environmental forces have especially strong effects. Yet *environment matters throughout life*. It would be a mistake to assume that all children who have problems at birth are doomed. In short, early experience by itself can, but rarely does, make or break development; later experience counts, too, sometimes enough to turn around a negative course of development.

Checking Mastery

1. What are two things you can do during your baby's first weeks and months of life to ensure a healthy start to life?

2. What are two factors that allow some babies to show resilience to negative events of the prenatal or perinatal periods?

Making Connections

1. Find out if your mother and grandmothers breastfed their children, including you, and for how long. What are your thoughts on the breast-versus-bottle choice? What factors might make it more or less likely that you will breastfeed (or have breastfed if you are already a parent)?

2. Given the high costs of low birth weight, what programs would you make part of a national effort to reduce the number of LBW babies born each year?

Chapter Summary

4.1 Prenatal Development

- Prenatal development begins with conception and proceeds through the germinal, embryonic, and fetal periods.

- Some couples experience difficulties conceiving and turn to assisted reproduction technologies to assist them with having a baby. These include drugs to stimulate the ovaries to release eggs, artificial insemination to inject sperm into a woman's uterus, and in vitro fertilization to fertilize an egg outside the womb and then insert it into a woman's uterus or fallopian tube.

- The germinal period lasts about 2 weeks. During this time, the single-celled zygote created when a sperm penetrates an egg repeatedly multiplies and travels to the uterus where it implants itself.

- The embryonic period lasts through the eighth week after conception. Every major organ takes shape during this time in a process called organogenesis. The placenta forms and connects the embryo to its mother through the umbilical cord. Major developments occur during this time, including formation and beating of the heart and the start of sexual differentiation.

- The fetal period lasts from the ninth week after conception until the end of pregnancy. The body and brain undergo much growth during this time. Neurons multiply, migrate, and differentiate into what they will finally become. The age of viability is reached at around 23–24 weeks' gestation.

- Growth during the prenatal period is faster than during any other period of the life span.

4.2 The Prenatal Environment

- The womb is an environment and can affect the embryo/fetus in positive as well as negative ways.

- Teratogens include diseases, drugs, or other environmental agents that can harm the developing fetus. Teratogens are most damaging to an organ during the time when the organ is developing most rapidly. In addition, the longer and stronger the exposure to a teratogen, the more likely that damage will occur to the developing child. The genetic makeup of both mother and unborn baby influence the effect of a teratogen, as does the quality of the prenatal and postnatal environments.

- Numerous drugs—prescription, over-the-counter, and recreational—have been found to have teratogenic effects. One of the most widely used drugs—alcohol—results in a cluster of symptoms that have lifelong effects on the children who are exposed prenatally.

- Diseases such as rubella (German measles), syphilis, and AIDS can adversely affect the developing baby, as can environmental hazards such as radiation and pollution.

- Some aspects of the mother can influence the quality of the prenatal environment, including her age, emotional state, and nutritional status. Women in their 20s have the lowest rates of pregnancy and birth complications. Women who experience prolonged and severe emotional stress during pregnancy may give birth to smaller babies. Good nutrition is important throughout pregnancy and is often supplemented with vitamins and fortified foods.

- Characteristics of the father, such as his age, may also affect the baby.

4.3 The Perinatal Environment

- The perinatal environment includes delivery practices and drugs used to assist with delivery. Many births today take place in the medical setting of a hospital or birthing center.

- Childbirth is a three-stage process that begins with regular contractions of the uterus and dilation of the cervix. The second stage of labor is the actual delivery of the baby out of the woman's body. The third stage is the delivery of the placenta.

- Among the possible birth complications is anoxia, or an oxygen shortage, which may occur for a variety of reasons. Anoxia can lead to brain damage or cerebral palsy if the brain is deprived of oxygen for more than a few minutes.

- Some babies must be assisted through the birth canal with vacuum extraction or forceps. Some women undergo a cesarean section, or surgical removal of the baby. Many women in Western cultures are given medications to assist with delivery. Most common are epidural or spinal blocks to reduce pain and oxytocin to promote contractions.

- The experience of pregnancy and childbirth vary widely, across cultures as well as across women within a culture. Some women experience mild to moderate depression following childbirth. Fathers, too, often need time to adjust to the life changes that accompany becoming a parent, as do older siblings.

4.4 The Neonatal Environment

- The neonatal environment refers to the events of the first month or so after delivery. Caring for a newborn varies across cultures. Nearly all cultures promote breastfeeding as the ideal way to nourish the young infant. For a variety of reasons, some mothers bottle-feed their newborns or switch to bottle-feeding after a trial run with breastfeeding.

- Some infants are considered to be at risk for short-term or long-term problems and must receive extra care during the neonatal period. Babies born prematurely and who have low birth weight are at risk for a number of complications.

- Many at-risk babies show remarkable resilience and outgrow their problems, especially if they have personal resources, such as sociability and intelligence, and grow up in stimulating and supportive postnatal environments where someone loves them.

Checking Mastery Answers

For answers to Checking Mastery questions, visit **www.cengagebrain.com**

Key Terms

Media Resources

Psychology CourseMate

Access an integrated eBook and chapter-specific learning tools including flashcards, quizzes, videos, and more. Go to **www.cengagebrain.com**

Birth Defects: Center for Disease Control

The website for the National Center on Birth Defects and Developmental Disabilities includes links to information on birth defects and disabilities, press releases, and current health news. To access, see "web links" in Psychology CourseMate at www.cengagebrain.com

The Visible Embryo

The Visible Embryo is a multiple award-winning website that offers an amazing amount of text and graphic information on the human organism as it develops from ovulation through the fetal stage. One nice element is the visible "spiral" depicting 23 distinct stages of prenatal change. The website also features links to information on key pregnancy issues. To access, see "web links" in Psychology CourseMate at www .cengagebrain.com

Understanding the DATA: Exercises on the Web

www.cengagebrain.com
For additional insight on the data presented in this chapter, try out the exercises for these figures in Psychology CourseMate at
www.cengagebrain.com:

Figure 4.6 Low birth weight and fetal death increase after maternal age 40, with marked increases after age 50.

Table 4.7 Survival and Health of Premature Babies by Gestational Age

Figure 4.10 Mortality of low-birth-weight babies during the first month of life is affected by their gestational age (how long they were in the womb), as well as their weight, with smaller babies clearly at greater risk than heavier babies.

CengageNOW

www.cengagebrain.com
Go to www.cengagebrain.com to link to CengageNOW, your online study tool. First take the Pre-Test for this chapter to get your Personalized Study Plan, which will identify topics you need to review and direct you to online resources. Then take the Post-Test to determine what concepts you have mastered and what you still need work on.

Physical Development and Health

"Josh is a 12-year-old boy with constitutional growth delay. Although he has grown at a normal rate throughout childhood, his height is below the 5th percentile line on the growth chart. His bone age is delayed by 2 to 3 years, so he is unlikely to reach a normal adult height. He has always been the smallest child in his class, and the size difference is getting more noticeable as some of his classmates begin their growth spurts: Josh looks more like a 4th grader than a 7th grader. He is having school problems this year, after moving into a new school. His teachers report that 'he's either a clown or a bully in class, and he just does not pay attention.' He likes sports and is good at soccer, but the coach does not want to let him try out for the team—he is afraid Josh will get hurt. The older boys at school sometimes pick him up and carry him around, calling him 'Peewee' and 'Squirt.' He has started spending a lot of time alone in his room and does not seem interested in anything. After his last visit to the doctor, he said, 'I'm sick of hearing how tall I'll be in 10 years. I'm a shrimp now, and that is all that matters'" (Rieser & Underwood, 2002, p. 43).

Ask Yourself This

1. What are the most important postnatal changes in the brain?

2. What physical challenges face the infant, and what accomplishments do they typically achieve during the first year or so of life?

3. How do nutrition and physical activity affect development, and what can be done to foster a healthy lifestyle at all ages?

4. How does puberty unfold for males and females, and how does its timing influence them?

5. What are the most typical physical changes experienced by older adults?

Josh's case illustrates the complexity as well as the significance of growth and development. Although he is growing at the normal *rate* of development, he is still markedly shorter than other boys his age. What are the processes underlying Josh's growth? And what are the psychological implications for Josh and other children, adolescents, and adults of the physical and health changes that occur throughout the life span?

These are the sorts of questions that we address in this chapter on health and physical development. We start with an overview of the major physical systems, most notably the nervous system, that underlie human functioning. We also look at the reproductive system as it matures during adolescence and then changes during adulthood. And we watch the physical self in action, as motor skills develop during childhood and as physical fitness and motor behaviors change during adulthood. We identify influences on health, physical development, and aging so that you can better understand why some children develop—and some older adults age—more rapidly than others.

5.1 Building Blocks of Growth and Development

Physical capabilities are fundamental to what people are able to do in life. A 5-year-old child is physically able to experience the world in ways markedly different from those available to a 5-month-old infant. 5-year-old Mariah, for example, can throw a ball with her mom, run with her dog, play hopscotch with her friends, feed and dress herself, and enjoy many of the rides at the amusement park. Changes in her brain have increased her memory abilities and capacity to think, and her language skills are astounding compared with those of the 5-month-old. Yet Mariah and other 5-year-olds are limited by their physical selves. It will be years before their brains are fully developed, allowing greater concentration and more sophisticated thought processes. Their strength and coordination on motor tasks will continue to improve, and their bodies will grow taller and heavier and will mature sexually.

Human growth and development is an incredibly complex process, influenced by both genetic and environmental factors. At certain times and for certain developments, genetic influences dominate, whereas at other times, environmental influences are more powerful. But as we have explained in previous chapters, genetic and environmental forces are always working together. Consider height. The average female in the United States is just over 5 feet 4 inches (164 cm) and the average male is about 5 feet 10 inches (178 cm), but there is considerable variability. Until her death in 2008, Sandy Allen was the tallest woman in the United States at just over 7 feet 7 inches. In contrast, most women with Turner syndrome (see Chapter 3) are nearly 3 feet shorter than this—4 feet 8 inches on average. Even among those considered within the average range of height, there is variability. Genes account for some of this: tall

What are the genetic and environmental influences on height? Will the son of NBA star LeBron James be as tall as his father?

people tend to have tall parents, whereas short people often have "short genes" hanging on their family tree. Heritability studies confirm a strong genetic influence in height (Lettre, 2009).

But as noted in Chapter 3, even if you inherit the genetic propensity to be tall (or short), environment can influence the expression of those genes. If you lack adequate nutrition, for example, you may not realize your full growth potential. And consider the case of children with **celiac disease**, an inherited digestive problem in which gluten (the proteins found in all wheat products) triggers an immune response that damages the small intestine. This leaves affected children unable to absorb nutrients from food despite adequate consumption. Their disease leads to malnutrition, which stunts growth and delays puberty. Early diagnosis for the estimated 3 million Americans with celiac disease is key to long-term health. As ■ Figure 5.1 shows, treatment in the form of a gluten-free diet restores absorption of nutrients and leads to dramatic **catch-up growth**. This catch-up growth after a period of malnutrition or illness reflects the body's struggle to get back on the growth course it is genetically programmed to follow.

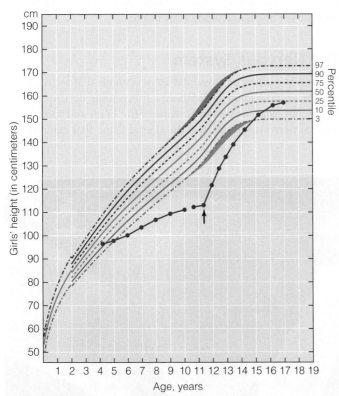

■ **FIGURE 5.1** This shows the rather dramatic catch-up growth that has occurred in a girl following treatment at around age 11 for her celiac disease. Source: From Cameron N. (Ed.). (2002). *Human growth and development.* New York: Academic Press. Copyright © 2002. Reprinted with permission of Elsevier.

To understand more fully how growth can be influenced by genes and environments, we need to consider the workings of the endocrine and nervous systems.

The Endocrine System

The endocrine, or hormonal, system consists of a group of **endocrine glands** that secrete chemicals called *hormones* directly into the bloodstream. Perhaps the most critical of the endocrine glands is the **pituitary gland**, the so-called master gland located at the base of the brain. Directly controlled by the hypothalamus of the brain, it triggers the release of hormones from all other endocrine glands by sending hormonal messages to those glands. Moreover, the pituitary produces **growth hormone**, which triggers the production of specialized hormones that directly regulate growth. Children who lack adequate growth hormone are unlikely to exceed 4 feet (or 130 cm) in height as adults if left untreated. Treatment with synthetic growth hormones can lead to near-expected adult height if administered early—well before the start of puberty (Bajpai et al., 2006; Reiter et al., 2006).

Children born small for their gestational age are often shorter as adults. Some of these children may also benefit from growth hormone therapy, but results with this group have been variable and additional research is needed to determine why some children benefit and others do not (Maiorana & Cianfarani, 2009). Adults who use human growth hormone in an attempt to enhance their athletic performance are at risk for a variety of health conditions, including cardiac problems and insulin resistance (Holt & Sönksen, 2008). Despite widespread beliefs about its potential performance-enhancing benefits, there are no clinically documented benefits to athletes who inject human growth hormone (O'Mathúna, 2006).

The thyroid gland also plays a key role in physical growth and development and in the development of the nervous system. Children whose mothers had a thyroid deficiency during pregnancy can experience intellectual problems (LaFranchi, Haddow, & Hollowell, 2005). Thyroid deficiency during infancy can also lead to mental retardation and slow growth if unnoticed and untreated (see Zimmerman, 2007). Children who develop a thyroid deficiency later in life will not suffer brain damage, because most of their brain growth will have already occurred, but their physical growth will slow drastically.

In Chapter 4 you learned about another critical role of the endocrine system. A male fetus will not develop male reproductive organs unless (1) a gene on his Y chromosome triggers the development of the testes (which are endocrine glands), and (2) the testes secrete the most important of the male hormones, testosterone. Male sex hormones become highly important again during adolescence. When people speak of adolescence as a time of "raging hormones," they are quite right. The testes of a male secrete large quantities of testosterone and other male hormones (called **androgens**). These hormones stimulate the production of growth hormone, which in turn triggers the adolescent growth spurt. Androgens are also responsible for the development of the male sex organs and contribute to sexual motivation during adulthood.

● TABLE 5.1 HORMONAL INFLUENCES ON GROWTH AND DEVELOPMENT

Endocrine Gland	Hormones Produced	Effects on Growth and Development
Pituitary	Growth hormone	Regulates growth from birth through adolescence; triggers adolescent growth spurt
	Activating hormones	Signal other endocrine glands (such as ovaries and testes) to secrete their hormones
Thyroid	Thyroxine	Affects growth and development of the brain and helps regulate growth of the body during childhood
Testes	Testosterone	Are responsible for development of the male reproductive system during the prenatal period; directs male sexual development during adolescence
Ovaries	Estrogen and progesterone	Are responsible for regulating the menstrual cycle; estrogen directs female sexual development during adolescence
Adrenal glands	Adrenal androgens	Play a supportive role in the development of muscle and bones; contribute to sexual motivation

Meanwhile, in adolescent girls, the ovaries (also endocrine glands) produce larger quantities of the primary female hormone, **estrogen**, and of progesterone. Estrogen increases dramatically at puberty, stimulating the production of growth hormone and the adolescent growth spurt, much as testosterone does in males. It is also responsible for the development of the breasts, pubic hair, and female sex organs and for the control of menstrual cycles throughout a woman's reproductive years. Progesterone is sometimes called the "pregnancy hormone" because it orchestrates bodily changes that allow conception and then support a pregnancy. Finally, the adrenal glands secrete androgen-like hormones that contribute to the maturation of the bones and muscles in both sexes. The maturation of the adrenal glands during middle childhood results in sexual attraction well before puberty in both boys and girls and relates to sexual orientation in adulthood (Del Giudice, 2009; McClintock & Herdt, 1996). The roles of different endocrine glands in physical growth and development are summarized in ● Table 5.1.

In adulthood, endocrine glands continue to secrete hormones, under the direction of the hypothalamus and the pituitary gland, to regulate bodily processes. For example, thyroid hormones help the body's cells metabolize (break down) foods into usable nutrients, and the adrenal glands help the body cope with stress. Throughout the life span, then, the endocrine system works with the nervous system to keep the body on an even keel. Yet changes occur; for example, declines in levels of sex hormones are associated with menopause. And, as you will see in Chapter 17, some theorists believe that changes in the functioning of the endocrine glands late in life help bring about aging and death.

In short, the endocrine system, in collaboration with the nervous system, is centrally involved in growth during childhood,

physical and sexual maturation during adolescence, functioning over the life span, and aging later in life.

The Nervous System

None of the physical or mental achievements that we regard as human would be possible without a functioning nervous system. Briefly, the nervous system consists of the brain and spinal cord (central nervous system) and the neural tissue that extends into

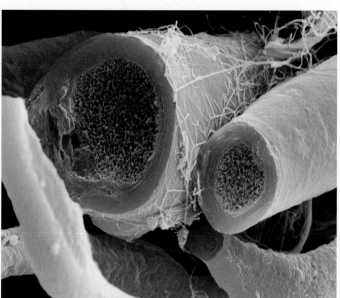

These nerve fibers are covered with myelin, shown here in pink. What role does myelin play in neural activity?

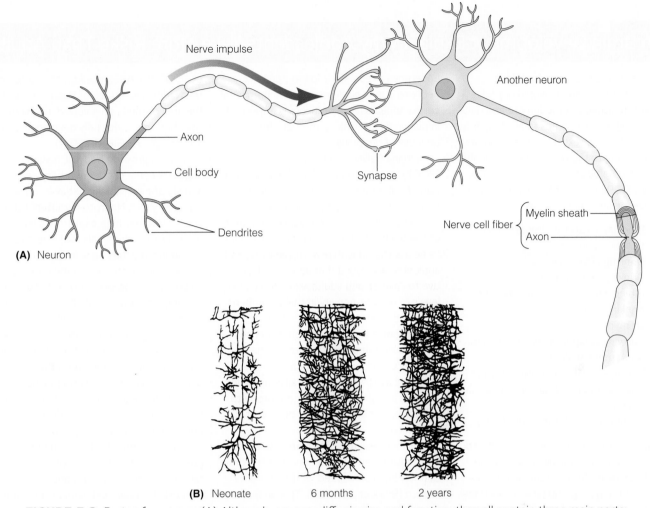

■ FIGURE 5.2 Parts of a neuron. (A) Although neurons differ in size and function, they all contain three main parts: the dendrites, which receive messages from adjacent neurons; the cell body; and the axon, which sends messages across the synapse to other neurons. (B) The formation of dendrites leading to new connections among existing neurons, as well as the myelination of neural pathways, accounts for much of the increase in brain weight during a baby's first 2 years.

all parts of the body (peripheral nervous system). Its basic unit is a **neuron** (■ Figure 5.2). Although neurons come in many shapes and sizes, they have some common features. Branching, bushy dendrites receive signals from other neurons, and the long axon of a neuron transmits electrical signals to other neurons or, in some cases, directly to a muscle cell. The axon of one neuron makes a connection with another neuron at a tiny gap called a **synapse**. By releasing neurotransmitters stored at the ends of its axons, one neuron can either stimulate or inhibit the action of another neuron.

The axons of many neurons become covered by a fatty sheath called *myelin*, which acts like insulation to speed the transmission of neural impulses. The process of **myelination**—neurons becoming encased in this protective substance that speeds transmission—begins prenatally but continues for many years after birth, proceeding from the spinal cord to the hindbrain, midbrain, and forebrain. Myelination has numerous im-

plications for developmental changes observed across the lifespan. For instance, toddlers experience a vocabulary spurt following a period of rapid myelination of those parts of the brain involved in language development (Pujol et al., 2006). And teenagers are more likely than children to ask hypothetical "what if" questions and to reason about weighty abstractions such as truth and justice, which corresponds to myelination within the prefrontal lobes during adolescence. Progressive myelination of the pathways involved in attention and concentration helps explain why infants, toddlers, school-age children, and even young adolescents have shorter attention spans than do older adolescents and adults (Tanner, 1990). Changes in the brain during adolescence may also account for some of the risky behaviors associated with this period (see Exploration Box 5.1). Finally, continued myelination into adulthood may account for adults being more able than teenagers to integrate thoughts and emotions (Benes, 1998; Nelson, Thomas, & de Haan, 2006).

Can Brain Development Explain Why Adolescents Take More Risks Than Adults?

Adolescents are notorious for taking chances that most adults would not take. They often display poor judgment and decision making when it comes to alcohol, drug, and cigarette use; sexual activities; and driving. According to the Department of Health and Human Services (Youth Risk Behavior Survey, 2009), risky behaviors during adolescence include the following:

- Smoking cigarettes (reported by 20% of adolescents)
- Drinking alcohol (45%)
- Drinking and driving (10%)
- Riding with a driver who has been drinking (29%)
- Using marijuana (20%)
- Carrying weapons (18% overall but 30% among males)
- Having sex without a condom (39%)
- Using alcohol or drugs before sexual intercourse (23%)
- Getting into a physical fight (35%)

Various explanations have been offered for adolescents' risk taking, including the need to separate from parents and the influence of the peer group (see, for example, Arnett, 2000). However, several researchers are also beginning to find connections between brain development and risky behavior during adolescence. Linda Spear (2000b) found that the prefrontal cortex—that part of the brain involved in control of emotions and decision making—decreases in size and undergoes a reorganization of neural connections during adolescence. The prefrontal cortex appears to be particularly important in planning and thinking through the consequences of decisions.

Adriana Galvan and her colleagues (2007) found a connection among anticipation of outcomes as positive or negative, brain activity, and engaging in risky behavior. The researchers measured activity in a part of the brain called the accumbens (thought to be associated with reward, pleasure, and addiction) and found that adolescents, relative to children and adults, exhibited higher levels of activity. Activity in the accumbens increased when adolescents anticipated both negative and positive consequences of risk taking. Importantly, though, the researchers found individual differences across all ages, showing that although adolescents as a group may be more prone to risk-taking behaviors, this is not true of all adolescents.

In other research, teenagers displayed less activity than adults in a part of the brain that has been associated with a desire for reward (Bjork et al., 2004). This underactivity may mean that teens need more stimulation to achieve the same level of reward that others achieve with less stimulation, leading them to engage in more risky behaviors. Consistent with this, sensation seeking increases between ages 10 and 15 before leveling off and then declining (Steinberg, et al., 2008). Also, research conducted by the National Institutes of Health shows that the area of the brain involved in inhibiting risky behavior is not fully developed until around age 25 (Giedd, 2004).

Thus, a growing body of research suggests some connection between brain activity and risk-taking behavior during the teen years. Neurotransmitters (brain chemicals) may help explain this link. Animal research reveals that one chemical, dopamine, reaches peak levels during adolescence in the prefrontal cortex and limbic system before dropping and then leveling off (Lewis et al., 1998). This chemical is involved in novelty seeking and in determining the motivational value of activities (Spear, 2000a). If this holds true for human adolescents, then their risky behaviors may reflect a combination of seeking new experiences and finding certain stimuli more attractive or motivating—both influenced by changes in brain chemistry and incomplete development of the prefrontal cortex during adolescence. So far, the research with humans seems to support this brain–behavior connection. The adolescent brain, then, is still a work in progress, and some risk taking by teenagers may be par for the course until further brain developments, such as maturation of the prefrontal cortex, refine their good judgment and decision making (Steinberg, 2007).

Now imagine a brain with as many as 100 billion neurons and each neuron communicating through synapses to thousands of others. How does this brain develop to make adults more physically and mentally capable than infants? Is it that adults have more neurons than infants do? Do they have more synapses connecting neurons or a more organized pattern of connections? And what happens to the brain in later life?

Brain Development

In Chapter 4 we traced the amazing evolution of the brain during the prenatal period. Here we pick up the story by looking at what goes on in the brain from birth onward. Although the brain is proportionately the largest and most developed part of the body at birth, much of its development takes place after birth. At birth, the brain weighs about 25% of its adult weight; by age 2, it reaches 75% of its adult weight; and by age 5, the brain has achieved 90% of its adult weight.

The development of the brain early in life is heavily influenced by the unfolding of a genetic program that has evolved over many generations. But genes are not the only influence—an individual's experiences are also crucial to brain development. As Charles Nelson and colleagues (2006) describe it, "the brain's circuitry must rely on experience to customize connections to serve the needs of the individual" (p. 3). Assuming that the infant has normal opportunities to explore and experience the world, the result will be a normal brain and normal development.

Thus, the brain, especially early in its formation, has great **plasticity**; that is, it is responsive to the individual's experiences and can develop in a variety of ways (Kolb & Whishaw, 2008). On the negative side, the developing brain is highly vulnerable to damage if it is exposed to drugs or diseases (recall the description of teratogens in Chapter 4) or if it is deprived of sensory and motor experiences. On the positive side, this highly adaptable brain can often recover successfully from injuries. Neurons that are not yet fully committed to their specialized functions can often take over the functions of damaged neurons. Moreover, the immature brain is especially able to benefit from stimulating experiences. Rats that grow up in enriched environments with plenty of sensory stimulation develop larger, better-functioning brains with more synapses than rats that grow up in barren cages (Greenough, Black, & Wallace, 1987; Nilsson et al., 1999). Brain plasticity is greatest early in development. However, the organization of synapses within the nervous system continues to change in response to experience throughout the life span. Animals put through their paces in mazes grow bushier dendrites, whereas their brains lose some of their complexity if the animals are then moved to less stimulating quarters (Thompson, 2000).

In short, the *critical*, or *sensitive*, *period* for brain development—the time when it proceeds most rapidly—is during the late prenatal period and early infancy. The developing brain is characterized by a good deal of plasticity: normal genes may provide rough guidelines about how the brain should be configured, but early experience determines the architecture of the brain.

One important feature of the developing organization of the brain is the **lateralization**, or asymmetry and specialization of functions, of the two hemispheres of the cerebral cortex. Instead of developing identically, the functions controlled by the two hemispheres diverge. In most people, the left cerebral hemisphere controls the right side of the body and is adept at the *sequential* (that is, step-by-step) processing needed for analytic reasoning and language processing. The right hemisphere generally controls the left side of the body and is skilled at the *simultaneous* processing of information needed for understanding spatial information and processing visual–motor information as well as the emotional content of information (Kensinger & Choi, 2009). Although it is an oversimplification, the left hemisphere is often called the *thinking* side of the brain, whereas the right hemisphere is called the *emotional* brain.

Having two hemispheres of the brain is not the same as having two brains. The hemispheres "communicate" and work together through the corpus callosum, "the super-highway of neurons connecting the halves of the brain" (Gazzaniga, 1998, p. 50). Even though one hemisphere might be more active than the other during certain tasks, they both play a role in all activities. For example, the left hemisphere is considered the seat of language because it controls word content, grammar, and syntax, but the right hemisphere processes melody, pitch, sound intensity, and the affective content of language.

If one hemisphere is damaged, it may be possible for the other hemisphere to "take over" the functions lost. For example, most children who have one hemisphere removed to try to reduce or eliminate severe seizures regain normal language function (Liégeois et al., 2008; Vining et al., 1997). It does not matter whether the remaining hemisphere is the left or the right. Thus, although the left hemisphere processes language in most people (perhaps 92%), the right hemisphere may also be able to fill this function, although it is not yet known how this possibility might be limited—or enhanced—by age or other characteristics of the individual (Gazzaniga, 1998; Knecht et al., 2000).

When does the brain become lateralized? Signs of brain lateralization are clearly evident at birth. Newborns are more likely to turn their heads to the right than to the left (Thompson & Smart, 1993), and one-quarter clearly prefer the right hand in their grasp reflex (Tan & Tan, 1999). Newborns may also show more left hemispheric response to speech sounds (Kotilahti et al., 2009), although this response becomes stronger and more reliable in the second half of the first year (Holowka & Petitto, 2002).

Signs of lateralization so early in life suggest that it has a genetic basis. Further support for the role of genes comes from family studies of handedness. Overall, about 9 in 10 people rely on their right hands (or left hemispheres) to write and perform other motor activities. Males are somewhat more likely to be left-handed than females (Vuoksimaa et al., 2009). In families where both parents are right-handed, the odds of having a left-handed child are only 2 in 100. These odds increase to 17 in 100 when one parent is left-handed and to 46 in 100 when both parents are left-handed (Springer & Deutsch, 1997). Although this suggests a genetic basis to handedness, it could also indicate that children become left-handed because of experiences provided by left-handed parents. However, experience would not account for head-turning preferences in young infants or for the differential activation of the left and right hemispheres observed in newborns when listening to speech sounds.

Overall, then, the brain appears to be structured very early so that the two hemispheres of the cortex will be capable of specialized functioning. As we develop, most of us come to rely more on the left hemisphere to carry out language processing and more on the right hemisphere to do such things as perceive spatial relationships and emotions. We also come to rely more consistently on one hemisphere, usually the left, to control many of our physical activities.

When does the brain complete its development? In the past, we might have answered that the brain was fully developed by the end of infancy, or even by the end of pregnancy. Today, however, the answer is that *brain development is never truly complete*. The brain is responsive to experience and is capable of **neurogenesis**, the process of generating new neurons, across the life span. Consider first some research with mice. Mice that regularly workout on their treadmills (that is, running wheels) learn more quickly to navigate through a maze than their couch potato counterparts (mice without running wheels) (Pereira

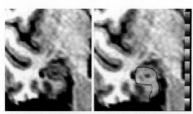

Pre-exercise   Post-exercise

© Copyright 2010 National Academy of Sciences, U.S.A.

Your brain on exercise. Using magnetic resonance imaging (MRI) technology that maps cerebral blood volume, researchers have found evidence of increased blood volume in a region of the hippocampus after exercise. This suggests the brain is capable of neurogenesis and could pave the way for developing new treatments for various conditions.

et al., 2007). By examining the brain tissue of the active mice, researchers found evidence of neurogenesis—new neurons were being created in response to the mouse's activity. And it turns out that adult songbirds can learn new songs with the help of new neurons (Goldman, 2008).

Neurogenesis in adult humans was once considered an impossibility, but recent evidence shows that it is indeed possible (see Gage, Song, & Kempermann, 2008a). Injured at age 19 in a serious car accident, Terry Wallis suffered severe brain damage and existed in a minimally conscious state for nearly 20 years (Hopkins, 2006). Doctors had assumed that recovery was not possible, but one day Terry "woke up" and began to talk. Although he remains disabled from injuries sustained during the accident, he has regained some functions and can communicate. Doctors attribute his miracle awakening to generation of new neurons and connections in the brain.

Fred Gage and his colleagues studied the effects of exercise on brain activity in a small group of adults (Pereira et al., 2007; and see Gage, Song, & Kempermann, 2008b). The adults were given a learning task, completed a 3-month aerobic exercise program, and were then given another learning task. Learning was improved following the exercise program. The researchers could not examine actual brain tissue after exercise as they do with mice. However, they did study blood volume in the brain and found that it was almost twice as high in the hippocampus, a part of the brain involved in learning and memory. This increased blood volume seems to be associated with production of new neurons.

Thus, the brain displays plasticity early in life and signs of neurogenesis throughout life. It can change in response to physical and mental exercise. It may be able to regenerate some functions following injury, which holds great promise for future therapies for patients with a wide range of conditions such as

stroke (Lindvall & Kokaia, 2008), epilepsy (Jessberger & Parent, 2008), and degenerative diseases such as Parkinson's and Alzheimer's (Brundin, Winkler, & Masliah, 2008). But what about the average person? What happens to the typical brain as it ages?

The Aging Brain

Many people fear that aging means losing brain cells and ultimately becoming "senile." As you will see in Chapter 16, Alzheimer's disease and other conditions that cause serious brain damage and dementia are *not* part of normal aging; they do not affect most older people. Normal aging is associated with gradual and relatively mild degeneration within the nervous system—some loss of neurons, diminished functioning of many remaining neurons, and potentially harmful changes in the tissues surrounding and supporting the neurons, such as the protective myelin covering (Hof & Mobbs, 2001; Peters, 2002). Just as brain weight and volume increase over the childhood years, they decrease over the adult years, especially after age 50 (Courchesne et al., 2000; Resnick, 2000). As people age, more of their neurons atrophy or shrivel, transmit signals less effectively, and ultimately die (Hof & Mobbs, 2001). Elderly adults may end up with 5–30% fewer neurons, depending on the brain site studied, than they had in early adulthood. Neuron loss is greater in the areas of the brain that control sensory and motor activities than in either the association areas of the cortex (involved in thought) or the brain stem and lower brain (involved in basic life functions such as breathing) (Whitbourne, 2008).

Other signs of brain degeneration besides neuron loss include declines in the levels of important neurotransmitters; the formation of "senile plaques," hard areas in the tissue surrounding neurons that may interfere with neuronal functioning and are seen in abundance in people with Alzheimer's disease; and reduced blood flow to the brain, which may starve neurons of the oxygen and nutrients they need to function (Hof & Mobbs, 2001). One of the main implications of such degeneration, as you will see later, is that older brains typically process information more slowly than younger brains do.

On the positive side, research shows that middle age brings greater integration of the left and right hemispheres, which may help increase creativity and cognitive functioning (Cohen, 2005). And the brain can remain healthy with exercise—both mental puzzles and physical aerobic workouts. Older adults who engage in high levels of aerobic activity show enhanced mental performance and corresponding increases in activity in certain regions of the brain (Colcombe et al., 2004).

What does it mean for older adults that both degeneration and plasticity—both losses and gains—characterize the aging brain? In some people, degeneration may win and declines in intellectual performance will occur. In other people, plasticity may prevail; their brains may form new and adaptive neural connections faster than they are lost so that performance on some tasks may actually improve with age (at least until very old age). For example, in his book *The Mature Mind: The Positive Power of the Aging Brain*, Gene Cohen (2005) argues that several forms of sophisticated thinking emerge only during middle and older adulthood. As you will see in Chapters 7, 8, and 9, older adults vary widely in how effectively they learn, remember, and think, and in how well their intellectual abilities hold up as they age. On average, however, plasticity and growth may make up for degeneration until people are in their 70s and 80s. One key to maintaining or even improving performance in old age is to avoid the many diseases that can interfere with nervous system functioning. Another key is to remain intellectually active—to create an "enriched environment" for the brain. You can reject the view that aging involves nothing but a slow death of neural tissue. Old brains *can* learn new tricks.

Principles of Growth

Now that you know something about the endocrine and nervous systems, and how they contribute to growth early in life, is it possible to make general predictions about growth patterns? To do so, researchers often apply three general principles that underlie growth. It is easiest to see these principles in action during infancy when growth is fast. For instance, you have probably noticed that young infants seem to be all head compared with older children and adults. That is because growth follows the **cephalocaudal principle**, accord-

ing to which growth occurs in a head-to-tail direction. This pattern is clear in ■**Figure 5.3**: The head is far ahead of the rest of the body during the prenatal period and accounts for about 25% of the newborn's length and 13% of total body weight. But the head accounts for only 12% of an adult's height and 2% of an adult's weight (Zemel, 2002). During the first year after birth, the trunk grows the fastest; in the second year, the legs are the fastest growing part of the body.

While infants are growing from the head downward, they are also growing and developing muscles from the center outward to the extremities. This **proximodistal principle** of growth can be seen during the prenatal period, when the chest and internal organs form before the arms, hands, and fingers. During the first year of life, the trunk is rapidly filling out but the arms remain short and stubby until they undergo their own period of rapid development.

A third important principle of growth and development is the **orthogenetic principle**. This means that development starts globally and undifferentiated and moves toward increasing differentiation and hierarchical integration (Werner, 1957). Consider a human who starts as a single, undifferentiated cell at conception. As growth proceeds, that single cell becomes billions of highly specialized cells (neurons, blood cells, liver cells, and so on). These differentiated cells become organized, or integrated, into functioning systems such as the brain or the digestive system.

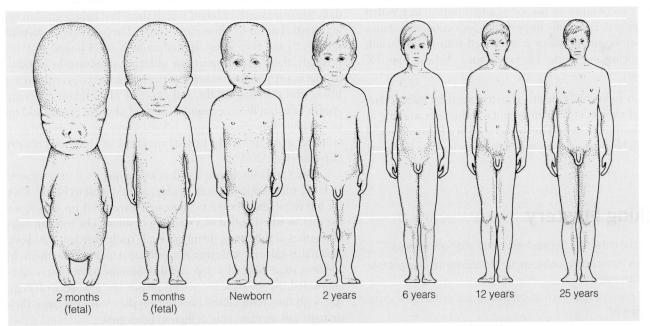

| 2 months (fetal) | 5 months (fetal) | Newborn | 2 years | 6 years | 12 years | 25 years |

■**FIGURE 5.3** The cephalocaudal ("head-to-tail") principle of growth is illustrated in our body proportions from the fetal period through adulthood. At 2 months after conception, your head made up *half* of your total body length, but now, as an adult, your head is a mere 12–13% of your adult height. By contrast, during this same time frame, your legs have gone from being only about 12–13% of your early prenatal length to about half of your adult height.

Having looked at the building blocks of growth and development, you are ready to examine the development, aging, and health of the physical self. We concentrate on the body (its size, composition, and functioning) and the use of body and brain in physical activities such as locomotion and finely controlled movements. We also consider factors that are important to health at different ages. In doing so, we turn once again to a life-span model.

A Life-Span Developmental Model of Health

The life-span developmental perspective introduced in Chapter 1 can be applied to a consideration of health and physical change as we age. We can summarize a life-span model of health as follows:

- Health is a lifelong process. It is influenced by personal choices over the life span and is constantly changing in response to these choices.
- Health is determined by both genetic and environmental influences. "It has genetic origins; it develops during infancy, childhood, and adulthood as a result of gene-environment interactions" (Aldwin, Spiro, & Park, 2006; p. 85).
- Health—and its study—is multidimensional. Health is a constellation of "physical, mental, and social well-being and not merely the absence of disease or infirmity" (Aldwin, Spiro, & Park, 2006; p. 86).
- Changes in health involve both gains and losses; health both improves and declines over the life span in response to many factors.
- Health occurs in a sociohistorical context and can be enhanced or constrained by the social and historical factors that contribute to it. Especially important is socioeconomic status. Lower socioeconomic status is associated with poorer health and well-being and shorter life expectancy (Aldwin, Spiro, & Park, 2006).

Thus, an individual's health is determined by genetic factors, personal choice, and environmental influences working in concert across the life span. The importance of a life-span model of health will be clear as we view health in each of the following sections.

Checking Mastery

1. What is the difference between plasticity and neurogenesis?
2. How does myelination contribute to developmental changes that we can observe?
3. What is one example each of cephalocaudal and proximodistal development?

Making Connections

1. In what ways is brain plasticity an advantage and in what ways might it be a disadvantage to the developing human?

2. Why is it important to view health from a life-span developmental perspective? Can you illustrate three aspects or components of this perspective as they apply to you or members of your family?

5.2 The Infant

Infancy is characterized by rapid growth, continued brain development, emergence of locomotor skills, and impressive sensory and reflexive capabilities. Understanding the newborn's capacities and limitations brings a fuller appreciation of the dramatic changes that take place between birth and adulthood.

Rapid Growth

Newborns are typically about 20 inches long and weigh 7–7½ pounds. However, weight and length at birth can mislead about eventual weight and height because the growth of some fetuses is stunted by a poor prenatal environment (Lejarraga, 2002). Size during the first few months of life is related more to prenatal experiences (environment) than to size of parent (genes). This is easy to see in twins and other multiple births, because their prenatal growth is significantly restricted by siblings competing for the limited space in the mother's womb.

In the first few months of life, infants grow rapidly, gaining nearly an ounce of weight a day and an inch in length each month. By age 2, they have already attained about half of their eventual adult height and weigh 27–30 pounds on average. Although we usually think of growth as a slow and steady process, daily measurements of infant length show that babies grow in fits and starts (Lampl & Thompson, 2008). They may go weeks with no growth and then shoot up half an inch in 24 hours! Not surprisingly, these growth spurts are often accompanied by irritability that many parents, unaware of the phenomenal growth taking place, find puzzling. In the end, 90–95% of an infant's days are growth free, but their occasional bursts of physical growth add up to substantial increases in size. Infants whose overall weight gain outpaces gains in length (height) are at risk of childhood obesity (Taveras et al., 2009).

Bones and muscles are also developing quickly during infancy. At birth, most bones are soft, pliable, and difficult to break. They are too small and flexible to allow newborns to sit up or balance themselves when pulled to a standing position. The soft cartilage-like tissues of the young infant gradually ossify (harden) into bony material as calcium and other minerals are deposited into them. In addition, more bones develop, and they become more closely interconnected. As for muscles, young infants are relative weaklings. Although they have all the muscle cells they will ever have, their strength will increase only as their muscles grow.

Newborn Capabilities

Newborns used to be viewed as helpless little organisms ill prepared to cope with the world outside the womb. We now know that they are quite well equipped to begin life. Just what can a newborn do? Among the most important capabilities are reflexes, functioning senses, a capacity to learn, and organized, individualized patterns of waking and sleeping. In this chapter, we'll examine their reflexes and behavioral patterns; in subsequent chapters, we address their sensory abilities and their potential to learn from experience.

Reflexes

One of the newborn's greatest strengths is a set of useful reflexes. A **reflex** is an unlearned and involuntary response to a stimulus, such as when the eye automatically blinks in response to a puff of air. ● **Table 5.2** lists some reflexes that can be readily observed in all normal newborns. These seemingly simple reactions are actually quite varied and complex patterns of behavior that provide infants with a way to begin interacting with their world (von Hofsten, 2007).

Some reflexes are called *survival reflexes* because they have clear adaptive value. Examples include the breathing reflex (useful for obvious reasons), the eye-blink reflex (which protects against bright lights or foreign particles), and the sucking reflex (needed to obtain food). Those called *primitive reflexes* are not clearly useful; many are believed to be remnants of evolutionary history that have outlived their purpose (but see Schott & Rossor, 2003, for another perspective). The Babinski reflex is a good example. Why would it be adaptive for infants to fan their toes when the bottoms of their feet are stroked? Frankly, we don't know. Other primitive reflexes may have some adaptive value, at least in some cultures. For example, the grasping reflex may help infants carried in slings or on their mothers' hips to hang on. Finally, some primitive reflexes—for example, the stepping reflex—are forerunners of useful voluntary behaviors that develop later in infancy. The expression of primitive reflexes at age 6 weeks, however, is not related to the expression of later motor behaviors (Bartlett, 1997). Thus, infants who demonstrate a strong primitive grasping reflex at 6 weeks are not necessarily the infants who demonstrate a strong voluntary grasp later in infancy.

Primitive reflexes typically disappear during the early months of infancy. For instance, the grasping reflex becomes weak by 4 months and is replaced by voluntary grasping. These primitive reflexes are controlled by the lower, subcortical areas of the brain and are lost as the higher centers of the cerebral cortex develop and make voluntary motor behaviors possible. Even though many primitive reflexes are not very useful to infants, they have proven to be useful in diagnosing infants' neurological problems. If such reflexes are not present at birth—or if they last too long in infancy—physicians know that something is wrong with a baby's nervous system. The existence of reflexes at birth tells them that infants are ready to respond to stimulation in adaptive ways. The disappearance of certain reflexes tells them that the nervous system is developing normally and that experience is affecting both brain and behavior. Thus, we see that the presence and then the absence of reflexes can serve as a general indicator of neurological health.

Behavioral States

Another sign that newborns are healthy and equipped for life is their ability to establish organized and individualized patterns of daily activity. Settling into an organized sleep–wake pattern is an indication that the baby is integrating biological, physiological, and psychosocial information (Sadeh, 1994, 1996). Infants must move from short sleep–wake cycles distributed throughout the day and night to a pattern that includes longer sleep periods at night with longer wake periods during the day. Much to their tired parents' dismay, newborns have no clear sense of night or day and may wake every 1–4 hours. By 3 months, infants begin to establish a predictable sleep–wake cycle, which becomes fairly stable by 6 months of age. Infants who get more sleep at night tend to be more easygoing during the day (Spruyt et al., 2008). Are they more easygoing because they are well rested from a good night's sleep, or do they sleep well at night because they are easygoing? We don't know the answer to this in infants, but we do know that adults who are normally easygoing can be irritable when deprived of sleep, so perhaps this is true for infants as well. Newborns spend half of their sleeping hours in active sleep, also called **REM sleep** (for the rapid eye movements that occur during it). Infants older than 6 months spend only 25–30% of their total sleep in REM sleep, which more closely resembles the 20% that adults spend in REM sleep.

Why do young infants sleep so much and spend so much more time in REM sleep than adults? Some research suggests that sleep patterns in infancy are associated with brain maturation and plasticity (see, for example, Dang-Vu et al., 2006; Peirano & Algarín, 2007). REM sleep in particular may be important for learning and memory processes (Diekelmann, Wilhelm, & Born, 2009). This may help explain why infants, who have so much to learn, spend more time in this sleep. Daphne and Charles Maurer (1988) suggest that infants use sleep to regulate sensory stimulation. Being bombarded by too much stimulation can "overload" the immature nervous system. To reduce the stimulation, infants tend to become less active, grow quieter, and shift into sleep. This may explain why infants are notoriously fussy at the end of a busy day—often at dinnertime when parents are tired and hoping for some peace. The infant's nervous system can be overstimulated by the flood of stimulation received during the day. Somehow, the arousal needs to be reduced—perhaps by crying and then sleeping. Adults sometimes marvel at how infants can sleep through the loudest noises and the brightest lights, but being able to do so may serve a valuable function. As Application Box 5.1 shows, sleep is important across the life span and inadequate sleep can take its toll in a variety of ways.

Physical Behavior

The motor behaviors of newborns are far more organized and sophisticated than they appear at first glance, but newborns are not ready to dance or thread needles. By age 2,

● TABLE 5.2 MAJOR REFLEXES OF FULL-TERM NEWBORNS

Reflexes	Developmental Course	Significance
Survival Reflexes		
Breathing reflex	Permanent	Provides oxygen; expels carbon dioxide
Eye-blink reflex	Permanent	Protects eyes from bright light or foreign objects
Pupillary reflex: Constriction of pupils to bright light; dilation to dark or dimly lit surroundings	Permanent	Protects against bright light; adapts visual system to low illumination
Rooting reflex: Turning a cheek toward a tactile (touch) stimulus	Weakens by 2 months; disappears by 5 months	Orients child to breast or bottle
Sucking reflex: Sucking on objects placed (or taken) into mouth	Is gradually modified by experience over the first few months after birth; disappears by 7 months	Allows child to take in nutrients
Swallowing reflex	Is permanent but modified by experience	Allows child to take in nutrients; protects against choking
Primitive Reflexes		
Babinski reflex: Fanning then curling toes when bottom of foot is stroked	Disappears by 12–18 months of age	Presence at birth and disappearance in first year indicate normal neurological development
Grasping reflex: Curling fingers around objects (such as a finger) that touch the baby's palm	Disappears in first 3–4 months; is replaced by a voluntary grasp	Presence at birth and later disappearance indicate normal neurological development
Moro reflex: Loud noise or sudden change in position of baby's head will cause baby to throw arms outward, arch back, then bring arms toward each other	Disappears by 4 months; however, child continues to react to unexpected noises or a loss of bodily support by showing startle reflex	Presence at birth and later disappearance (or evolution into startle reflex) indicate normal neurological development (which does not disappear)
Swimming reflex: Infant immersed in water will display active movements of arms and legs and will involuntarily hold breath (thus staying afloat for some time)	Disappears in first 4–6 months	Presence at birth and later disappearance indicate normal neurological development
Stepping reflex: Infants held upright so that their feet touch a flat surface will step as if to walk	Disappears in first 8 weeks unless infant has regular opportunities to practice it	Presence at birth and later disappearance indicate normal neurological development

Preterm infants may show little to no evidence of primitive reflexes at birth, and their survival reflexes are likely to be irregular or immature. However, the missing reflexes will typically appear soon after birth and will disappear a little later than they do among full-term infants.

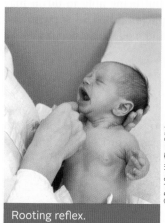

Rooting reflex.

© Paul Conklin/PhotoEdit Inc.

Grasping reflex.

© Ocean/Corbis

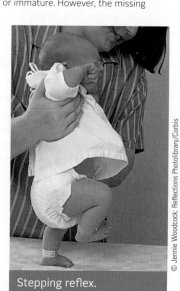

Stepping reflex.

© Jennie Woodcock; Reflections Photolibrary/Corbis

however, immobile infants have become toddlers, walking up and down stairs by themselves and using their hands to accomplish simple self-care tasks and to operate toys. How do the motor skills involved in walking and manipulating objects develop?

Locomotor Development

●**Table 5.3** shows the age at which half of U.S. infants master particular motor milestones. This average age of mastery is called the **developmental norm** for a skill. Developmental norms such as these must be interpreted carefully. They depend on the group studied (children walk earlier today than they used to and walk earlier in some cultures than in others), and they hide a good deal of variation among children, even in the sequence in which skills are mastered (von Hofsten, 1993). Finally, most children who master a skill earlier or later than the developmental norm are still within the normal range of development. Parents should not be alarmed if their child is 1 or 2 months "behind" the norm; only significantly delayed achievement of key skills such as sitting up or walking is cause for concern.

● TABLE 5.3 AGE NORMS FOR IMPORTANT MOTOR MILESTONES DURING THE FIRST YEAR

Age (in Months)	Milestone
2	Lifts head up when lying on stomach
3	Rolls over from stomach to back; holds head steady when being carried
4	Grasps a cube or other small object
5	Sits without support toward end of month
6	Stands holding on to something
7	Rolls over from back to stomach and may begin to crawl or creep; shows thumb opposition
8	Pulls self up to standing position
9	Walks holding on to furniture; bangs two objects together
10	Plays clapping games (e.g., pat-a-cake)
11	Stands alone
12	Walks well alone; drinks from a cup

Based on European American, Hispanic, and African American children in the United States. Indicates the age at which 50% of infants have demonstrated the skill. Keep in mind that there are large individual differences in when infants display various developmental milestones.
SOURCES: Bayley, 1993; Frankenburg et al., 1992; WHO Multicentre Growth Reference Study Group, 2006.

Can you recognize the workings of the cephalocaudal and proximodistal principles of development in the milestones in Table 5.3? Early motor development follows the cephalocaudal principle because the neurons between the brain and the muscles acquire myelin sheaths in a head-to-tail manner. Thus, infants can lift their heads before they can control their trunks enough to sit, and they can sit before they can control their legs to walk. The proximodistal principle of development is also evident in early motor development. Activities involving the trunk are mastered before activities involving the arms and legs, and activities involving the arms and legs are mastered before activities involving the hands and fingers or feet and toes. Therefore, infants can roll over before they can walk or bring their arms together to grasp a bottle, and children generally master **gross motor skills** (skills such as kicking the legs or drawing large circles that involve large muscles and whole-body or limb movements) before mastering **fine motor skills** (skills such as picking Cheerios off the breakfast table or writing letters of the alphabet that involve precise movements of the hands and fingers or feet and toes). As the nerves and muscles mature downward and outward, infants gradually gain control over the lower and the peripheral parts of their bodies.

The orthogenetic principle is also evident in early motor development. A young infant is likely to hurl his body as a unit at a bottle of milk held out to him (a global response). An older infant gains the ability to move specific parts of her body separately (a differentiated response); she may be able to extend one arm toward the bottle without extending the other arm, move the hand but not the arm to grasp it, and so on, making distinct, differentiated movements. Finally, the still older infant is able to coordinate separate movements in a functional sequence—reaching for, grasping, and pulling in the bottle while opening his mouth to receive it and closing his mouth when the prize is captured (an integrated response).

Crawling. Life changes dramatically for infants and their parents when the infants become mobile. As Karen Adolph (2008) describes it, "locomotion is one of infants' greatest accomplishments" (p. 213). Their **locomotion**, or movement from one place to another, is accomplished in a variety of interesting ways, including "rolling, bum shuffling, belly crawling, hands-and-knees crawling, cruising sideways along furniture, supported stepping, independent walking, and so on" (Adolph, 2008, p. 213). However they start, most infants around 10 months old end up crawling on their hands and knees, and they all seem to figure out that the best way to keep their balance is to move the diagonal arm and leg at the same time (Adolph & Berger, 2006).

With their new mobility, infants are better able to explore the objects around them and to interact with other people. Experience moving through the spatial world contributes to cognitive, social, and emotional development (Adolph & Berger, 2006). For example, crawling contributes to more frequent social interactions with parents and to the emergence of a healthy fear of heights.

It is interesting to note that fewer infants crawl today than in the past, moving directly to cruising on their legs instead of crawl-

"Impaired by sleep loss, individuals start a task feeling fine. Minutes later, however, heads begin to nod, and the rate of deterioration accelerates. Instead of being able to sustain attention for a 45-minute lecture in a classroom, for example, a student might be able to manage only 3 to 5 minutes" (National Academy of Sciences, 2000, p. 15).

How much sleep do you need, and what happens when you do not get enough? As the graph in this box illustrates, sleep needs change with age, with infants needing the most and adults the least number of hours per night. Experts recommend that 2- to 5-year-olds should get about 12 hours of sleep every night, school-age children should get about 10 hours, teens should get about 9 hours of sleep, and adults should get roughly 8 hours (National Sleep Foundation, 2009). Reports from children and their parents suggest that sleeping problems are common, and sleep experts believe school officials need training to identify and respond to sleep issues among their students (Buckhalt, Wolfson, & El-Sheikh, 2009; Gregory, Fijsdijk, & Eley, 2006).

Infants who get less sleep at night are more irritable during the day, and those who go to bed later, and perhaps get less sleep as a result of being up later, gain less weight than their early-to-bed counterparts (Adachi et al., 2008). Among preschoolers, lack of a good night's sleep is associated with behavioral problems such as acting out and not complying with requests (Lavigne et al., 1999). Teachers report that at least 10% of their elementary school–age students have trouble staying awake in the classroom (Owens et al., 2000). School-age children who do not get adequate sleep at night perform poorly on a variety of memory tasks and experience problems at school (Smaldone, Honig, & Byrne, 2007; Steenari et al., 2003).

Getting a good night's sleep only seems to get more difficult as children move into middle school. Katia Fredriksen and her colleagues (2004) found that sixth-graders who got too little sleep had lower self-esteem, poorer grades, and more depression symptoms than their well-rested peers. In contrast, 9- to 12-year-olds who extend their sleep just 40–60 minutes can increase their performance significantly (Sadeh, Gruber, & Raviv, 2003).

© moodboard/Corbis

Teenagers are especially likely to be at risk for daytime sleepiness and the consequences associated with fatigue. Changes in the sleep–wake cycle, melatonin production, and circadian rhythms during adolescence mean that the "natural" time for falling asleep shifts later. Research shows that the level of melatonin (a sleep-promoting hormone) rises later at night for teens than for children or adults (National Sleep Foundation, 2009). Teens report later bedtimes from age 12 to age 18, and only 20% of them get the optimal amount of sleep on school nights. Although psychosocial factors may also contribute to later bedtimes than in childhood (for example, doing homework or text messaging with friends late into the night), biological factors—puberty in particular—seem primarily responsible. Teens who go to bed at 11 p.m. should not wake up until around 8 a.m. if they are to get the recommended amount of sleep. However, most teens find themselves getting out of bed around 6:30 a.m. to get to school on time (see the graph in this box). High schools typically start earlier than elementary schools, often by 7:30 a.m. to accommodate bus schedules. Thus, just when their biological clocks are pushing back sleep times at night, schools are getting teens up earlier in the morning.

What are the consequences for teens who do not get enough sleep? Teens report greater sleepiness during the day, which is associated with decreased motivation, especially for "boring" tasks (Dahl, 1999). Tired teens may be able to successfully navigate a favorite class or read a particularly good book, but these same teens may have trouble completing an assignment in their least favorite subject or studying for an exam. Teens who have had their sleep restricted display increased sleepiness in proportion to the number of nights that their sleep is reduced. But surprisingly—at least to many adults—these same teens "perk up" in the evenings and show high levels of energy that discourage them from going to bed early (National Academy of Sciences, 2000).

Teens who sleep less at night or who stay up later on the weekends than their peers report higher levels of depression, irritability, and lack of tolerance for frustration (Dahl, 1999; Wolfson & Carskadon, 1998). They may also have difficulty controlling their emotional responses, which leads to greater expression of aggression or anger (Dahl, 1999). As with younger children, teens who do not get enough sleep have trouble concentrating in school, experience short-term memory problems, and may doze off in class (National Sleep Foundation, 2009).

Finally, what happens when adults are sleep deprived? Young adults sleep 7–8 hours per night; this decreases to 6½–7½ hours during middle age and drops even further during old age. When they are raising children, which corresponds to the time career demands are likely to be high,

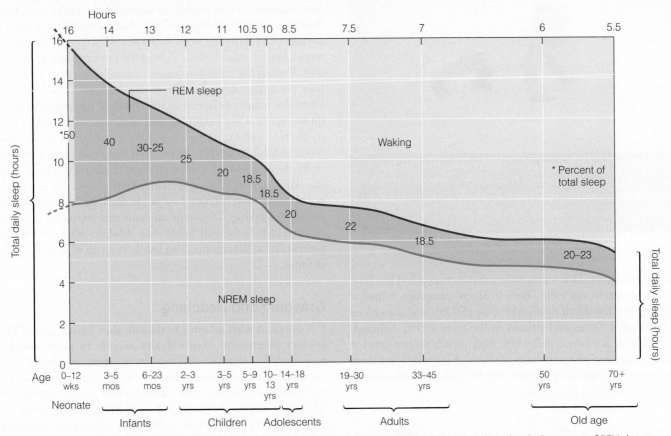

Graph showing changes with age in the total amount of daily sleep and the percentage of REM sleep. There is a sharp drop in the amount of REM sleep after the early years, falling from 8 hours at birth to less than 1 hour in old age. The change in the amount of non-REM (NREM) sleep is much less marked, falling from 8 hours to about 5 hours over the life span. SOURCE: www.sleephomepages.org.

many adults (about two-thirds) report that they do not get enough sleep (National Sleep Foundation, 2009). And 1 out of every 5 parents reports that daily functioning is impaired at least several days a week because the parent feels so tired. The implications of this for worker productivity and safety are tremendous.

Older adults, although they sleep less at night, often compensate by taking a nap during the day. They are also more likely to report sleep problems such as difficulty staying asleep and repeated awakenings during the night. Changes in physiology, such as decreased production of melatonin and growth hormone, both of which help regulate sleep, contribute to the sleep problems experienced by older adults. In addition, older adults are more likely to experience health problems such as arthritis and congestive heart failure that disrupt sleep and to take medications that decrease sleep (National Sleep Foundation, 2009).

For all ages, learning more about sleep needs and the effects of sleep deprivation can lead to healthy lifestyle changes.

Adhering to a regular bedtime and wake time on the weekends and on school and work days can help maintain healthy sleep habits. Unfortunately, "sleeping in" on the weekends alters the sleep–wake cycle and makes it more difficult to get up early for work or school Monday morning. So, next time you find yourself dozing off in class or at work, do not jump to the conclusion that the work you are doing is boring. It may be that your sleep–wake cycle is out of sync with the schedule imposed on you by school or work.

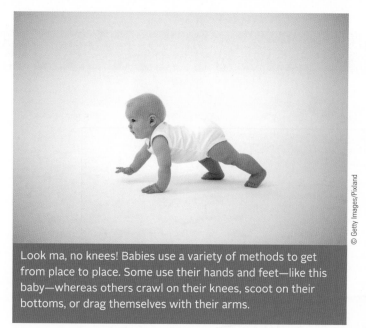

Look ma, no knees! Babies use a variety of methods to get from place to place. Some use their hands and feet—like this baby—whereas others crawl on their knees, scoot on their bottoms, or drag themselves with their arms.

and unstable" (Thelen, 1984, p. 246; see also Spencer et al., 2006).

In many cases, the infant who has recently impressed her parents by staggering across the room in an upright position seems to regress by reverting to crawling. By collecting an enormous number of observations of infants' daily movements, Karen Adolph and her colleagues (2008) have found that it takes an average of 13 starts and stops over a period of days and sometimes weeks before infants show consistent performance of a motor skill. During the transition period of acquiring a new motor skill, they are truly taking "one step forward, two steps backward." From the infant's perspective, the apparent regression in skills is quite logical. They have mastered crawling and are quite fast at it, whereas walking on two legs is hard work and can slow them down (Adolph & Berger, 2006). So if they have important things to do, they might find it more efficient to use their reliable crawling skills than to labor at walking. With a little bit of practice, walking will soon become routine. Indeed, by 14 months of age, infants are taking 2000 steps an hour and travelling a distance equivalent to 7 football fields! (see Adolph, 2008). No wonder parents feel as though they can barely keep up with their toddlers at times.

Grasping and Reaching

If you look at what infants can do with their hands, you will find another progression from reflexive activity to more voluntary, coordinated behavior. As you have seen, newborns come equipped with a grasping reflex. It weakens from age 2 months to age 4 months, and for a time infants cannot aim their grasps well. They take swipes at objects and even make contact more than you would expect by chance, but they often miss. And rather than opening their hands to grasp what they are reaching for, they make a fist (Wallace & Whishaw, 2003).

By the middle of the first year, infants grasp objects well, although they use a rather clumsy, clamplike grasp in which they press the palm and outer fingers together—the **ulnar grasp**. Initially, they reach for objects using jerky movements and a locked elbow (Berthier & Keen, 2006). By 6 months of age, they are able to bend their elbow, and their reaching movements become increasingly smooth and responsive to characteristics of an object over the next 6–12 months (Barrett & Needham, 2008). They anticipate how they need to adjust their hand so that it can effectively grasp an approaching object (von Hofsten, 2007). We can again see the workings of the proximodistal principle of development as we watch infants progress from controlling their arms, then their hands, and finally their individual fingers enough to use a **pincer grasp**, involving only the thumb and the forefinger (or another finger). The pincer grasp appears as early as 5 months and is reliable by the infant's first birthday (Wallace & Whishaw, 2003).

By 16 months, infants can scribble with a crayon, and by the end of the second year they can copy a simple horizontal or vertical line and even build towers of five or more blocks. They are rapidly gaining control of specific, *differentiated* movements, then *integrating* those movements into whole, coordinated actions. They use their new locomotor and manipulation skills to

ing on their knees. This seems to be a result of spending less time on their stomachs since the "Back to Sleep" campaign, aimed at reducing sudden infant death syndrome (SIDS), was introduced in the United States and Britain in the early 1990s. Although some parents are concerned when their infants do not crawl at the age suggested by many baby manuals, it turns out that there is no great developmental significance to crawling. Babies can go directly from sitting to walking.

Walking. Although parents must be on their toes when their infants first begin walking, they take great delight in witnessing this new milestone in motor development, which occurs around infants' first birthday. According to Esther Thelen (1984, 1995), the basic motor patterns required for walking are present at birth. They are evident in the newborn's stepping reflex and in the spontaneous kicking of infants lying down. Indeed, Thelen noticed that the stepping reflex and early kicking motions were identical. She began to question the traditional understanding that early reflexes, controlled by subcortical areas of the brain, are inhibited once the cortex takes control of movements. Thelen showed that it simply requires more strength to make the walking motion standing up (as in the stepping reflex) than to make it lying down (as in kicking). She demonstrated that babies who no longer showed the stepping motion when placed standing up on a table did show it when suspended in water because less muscle power was needed to move their chunky legs. The upshot? Infants need more than a more mature nervous system to walk; they must also develop more muscle and become less top-heavy. Even when they begin to walk, they lack good balance partly because of their big heads and short legs. Steps are short; legs are wide apart; and hips, knees, and ankles are flexed. There is much teetering and falling, and a smooth gait and good balance will not be achieved for some time. Thelen's point is that adults would walk funny, too, if they, like infants, were "fat, weak,

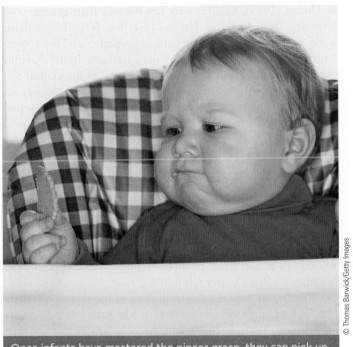

Once infants have mastered the pincer grasp, they can pick up all sorts of objects.

© Thomas Barwick/Getty Images

learn about and adapt to the world around them. By cornering bugs and stacking Cheerios, they develop their minds.

Motor Skills as Dynamic Action Systems

How do motor skills emerge? Thelen (1995, 1996) observed infants throughout their first year and discovered that they spent a great deal of time engaged in **rhythmic stereotypies**. That is, the infants moved their bodies in repetitive ways—rocking, swaying, bouncing, mouthing objects, and banging their arms up and down. Thelen found that infants performed these rhythmic stereotypies shortly before a new skill emerged but not after the skill had become established. Thus, infants might rock back and forth while on their hands and knees, but once they were crawling, they no longer rocked.

Esther Thelen's work has culminated in the development of the **dynamic systems theory** to explain such motor developments (Thelen & Smith, 1994; see also Spencer et al., 2006). According to dynamic systems theory, developments take place over time through a "self-organizing" process in which children use the sensory feedback they receive when they try different movements to modify their motor behavior in adaptive ways (Smith & Thelen, 1993; von Hofsten, 2007). Behaviors that seem to emerge in a moment of time are actually the cumulative effects of motor decisions that the infant makes over a longer time (Spencer et al., 2006). In this view, motor milestones such as crawling and walking are the learned outcomes of a process of interaction with the environment in which infants do the best they can with what they have in order to achieve their goals (Thelen, 1995). Thus, development is highly individualistic: "infants must explore a wide range of behaviors to discover and

select their own unique solutions in the context of their intrinsic dynamics and movement history" (Spencer et al., 2006; p. 1528). Neural maturation, physical growth, muscle strength, balance, and other characteristics of the child interact with gravity, floor surfaces, and characteristics of the specific task to influence what children can and cannot learn to do with their bodies.

Consistent with the dynamic systems approach, Karen Adolph and Anthony Avolio (2000) found that young toddlers could adjust their walking to changes in both their body dimensions and the slope of a walkway. The researchers had young toddlers walk on slopes of different degrees while wearing a vest with removable "saddlebags" that could be weighted to simulate changes in their body dimensions (■ **Figure 5.4**). The weights added mass and shifted the toddlers' center of gravity, akin to what happens when toddlers grow. Would toddlers be able to compensate for the changes in their body and their environment? Yes—they adjusted their motor skills to adapt to rapid

■ **FIGURE 5.4** Adolph and Avolio's walkway with adjustable slope. Infants are outfitted with weighted saddlebags to alter their body mass and center of gravity. While an experimenter stays beside infants to ensure safety, parents stand at the end of the walkway and encourage their child to walk toward them. Source: From Adolph K. E. & Avolio, A. M. Walking infants adapt locomotion to changing body dimensions. *Journal of Experimental Psychology: Human Perception and Performance, 26,* 1148–1166. Copyright © 2000 by The American Psychological Association. Reprinted with permission of the American Psychological Association.

"growth" of their bodies and to changes in their environment (Adolph & Berger, 2006). Like adults carrying a heavy load on their shoulders, toddlers bent their knees and kept their upper bodies stiffly upright to maintain their balance with heavier loads. Toddlers with greater walking experience did better than those with less experience (Garciaguirre, Adolph, & Shrout, 2007). Toddlers also seemed to recognize when the walkway was too steep for safe travel—they either avoided it or scooted down on their bottoms or on their hands and knees. Young walkers (16 months) are also clever enough to figure out that they can use handrails to help maintain their balance while walking across bridges (Berger & Adolph, 2003). Further, they quickly discover that a sturdy handrail offers more support than a "wobbly" handrail and they are more adventuresome when they can use a sturdy handrail for support (Berger, Adolph, & Lobo, 2005). If they are not sure how to proceed across a potentially unstable surface, they look to their mothers for advice. With mother's encouragement, 75% of infants will try to navigate a questionable slope; only 25% of infants are brave enough to give it a shot when mothers express discouragement (Karasik et al., 2008; Tamis-Lemonda et al., 2008).

As every parent knows, toddlers do not become proficient walkers without experiencing more than a few falls—as many as 15 per hour by one estimate (see Adolph, 2008). As it turns out, these tumbles may help walkers learn which surfaces are safe and which ones may be problematic (Joh & Adolph, 2006). With age, toddlers become increasingly adept at figuring out how to avoid falls. Finally, changes in one area of the dynamic system influence other areas. When toddlers start to walk, it temporarily disrupts their previously established ability to balance themselves while sitting (Chen et al., 2007). It's as if toddlers experience a "recalibration of an internal model for the sensorimotor control" of their bodies (Chen et al., 2007, p. 16).

What does this dynamic systems perspective say about the contribution of nature and nurture to development? According to Thelen (1995), toddlers walk not because their genetic code programs them to do so but because they learn that walking works well given their biomechanical properties and the characteristics of the environments they must navigate. In the dynamic systems approach, nature (that is, maturation of the central nervous system) and nurture (sensory and motor experience) are both essential and largely inseparable. Feedback from the senses and from motor actions is integrated with the ever-changing abilities of the infant. Having learned how to adjust one motor skill (such as crawling) to successfully navigate environmental conditions, however, does not mean that infants will generalize this knowledge to other motor skills (such as walking; see Adolph & Berger, 2006). Different motor skills present different challenges. Crawling infants, for instance, must learn to avoid such dangers as bumping their head on table legs. Walking infants face other challenges, such as not toppling over when turning around. To master these challenges, infants need opportunities to gather feedback from each motor activity.

Finally, an important contribution of the dynamic systems approach to motor development is its integration of action with thought (von Hofsten, 2007). The motor behaviors we have been describing are not separate and distinct from the child's knowledge. Children have to think about how to organize their movements to optimize what they are able to get from their ever-changing environment. Thus, there is far more to motor development than implied by norms indicating when we might expect infants to sit up, stand alone, or walk independently. The emergence of motor skills is complex and is closely connected to perceptual–cognitive developments.

Health and Wellness

What typical health issues must infants—and their parents—navigate? As noted in the previous chapter, modern medicine has made it possible for smaller and smaller babies to survive premature delivery, but sadly, most babies born weighing less than 750 grams (1 pound 10½ ounces) die within the first year (MacDorman & Matthews, 2008). The health problems associated with premature delivery and low birth weight often continue to challenge infants throughout their first year and beyond, illustrating one of the principles of the life-span model of health: Some events can have lifelong effects on health. Only about 12% of babies in the United States are premature, but as many as one-third of infant deaths are caused by complications of premature birth, making this the second leading cause of infant death (MacDorman & Mattews, 2008). **Congenital malformations**—defects that are present at birth, either from genetic factors or prenatal events—are the leading cause of death during the first year. Such malformations include heart defects, spina bifida, Down syndrome, cleft palates, and more.

Infant health has been dramatically improved in recent decades by administering vaccinations aimed at protecting infants from a variety of diseases (such as diphtheria, pertussis, polio, and measles). The approximately 20% of infants who do *not* receive the recommended immunizations are more likely to contract illnesses that can compromise their health. Unfortunately, socio-

What might this toddler learn from his experience of falling? Should parents be concerned about such tumbles in early childhood?

© Laurence Mouton/ZenShui/Corbis

economic status in the United States often determines who has access to health-care services that cover immunizations. As the life-span model maintains, one's sociohistorical context influences health.

Thus, health during infancy starts well before birth with prenatal care that helps prevent and/or treat potential congenital anomalies and preterm birth. Health after birth is enhanced by well-baby visits to the doctor to ensure that development is proceeding normally and by following recommendations for prevention of illness.

Checking Mastery

1. What are two infant reflexes that may help ensure survival in the early months of life?

2. How do infants learn to get around in the world once their muscles are strong enough to support their body weight?

Making Connections

1. Why has Esther Thelen characterized the emergence of motor skills as a dynamic system? What does this mean with respect to acquiring motor skills?

2. Recall a time when you learned a new motor skill—for example, how to inline skate or hit a golf ball. Can you apply the dynamic systems approach to understand how your skill developed over time and what influenced its development?

5.3 The Child

Development of the body and of motor behavior during childhood is slower than it was during infancy, but it is steady. You need only compare the bodies and the physical feats of the 2-year-old and the 10-year-old to be impressed by how much change occurs over childhood.

Steady Growth

Slow and steady is probably the best way to describe the growth that occurs throughout much of childhood. From age 2 until puberty, children gain about 2–3 inches and 5–6 pounds every year. This growth is often tracked on a growth chart like the one shown in ■ **Figure 5.5**. This allows physicians and families to see how a particular child is progressing relative to other children of the same age and gender and to graph the pattern of growth over time. Children who are markedly different—higher, lower, or more erratic in their growth rate—may warrant additional investigation.

During middle childhood (ages 6–11), children may seem to grow little, probably because the gains are small in proportion to the child's size (4–4½ feet and 60–80 pounds on average) and therefore harder to detect. The cephalocaudal and proximodistal principles of growth continue to operate. As the lower parts of the

body and the extremities fill out, the child takes on more adult-like body proportions. The bones continue to grow and harden, and the muscles strengthen.

Physical Behavior

Infants and toddlers are capable of controlling their movements in relation to a *stationary* world, but children master the ability to move capably in a *changing* environment (Sayre & Gallagher, 2001). They must learn to modify their movements to adapt to changes in environment. This allows them to bring their hands together at just the right time to catch a ball and to avoid bumping into moving people when walking through a crowded mall. They also refine many motor skills. For example, young children throw a ball only with the arm, but older children learn to step forward as they throw. Their accuracy throwing a ball increases around age 7, as does their speed of throwing (Favilla, 2006). Thus, older children can throw a ball farther than younger ones can, not just because they are bigger and stronger but also because they can integrate multiple body movements—raising their arm, turning their body, stepping forward with one foot, and pushing their body forward with the other foot (Sayre & Gallagher, 2001).

The toddler in motion appears awkward compared with the older child, who takes steps in more fluid and rhythmic strides and is better able to avoid obstacles. And children quickly become able to do more than just walk. By age 3, they can walk or run in a straight line, although they cannot easily turn or stop while running. By age 4, children are getting so talented with their motor skills that they can trace a figure with one hand while tapping a pen with their other hand (Otte & van Mier, 2006). Kindergarten children can integrate two motor skills—hopping on one foot with walking or running—into mature skipping (Loovis & Butterfield, 2000). With each passing year, school-age children can run a little faster, jump a little higher, and throw a ball a little farther. Their motor skills are also responsive to practice. In one study, children improved their arm movements 25–30% with practice—an impressive accomplishment compared with the 10% improvement shown by adults who practiced (Thomas, Yan, & Stelmach, 2000). There are some gender differences in motor skills, with boys slightly ahead in throwing and kicking and girls somewhat ahead in hopping and tasks that require manual dexterity (Junaid & Fellowes, 2006; Van Beurden et al., 2002). These differences seem to arise primarily from practice and different expectations for males and females rather than from inherent differences between the sexes.

From age 3 to age 5, eye–hand coordination and control of the small muscles are improving rapidly, giving children more sophisticated use of their hands. At age 3, children find it difficult to button their shirts, tie their shoes, or copy simple designs. Their drawings often look more like scribbles than pictures. By age 5, children can accomplish all of these feats and can cut a straight line with scissors or copy letters and numbers with a crayon. Their drawings become recognizable and are increasingly realistic and detailed. The typical 5- to 6-year-old can also tie her shoes and even use a knife to cut soft foods. By age 8 or age 9, children can use household tools such as screwdrivers and

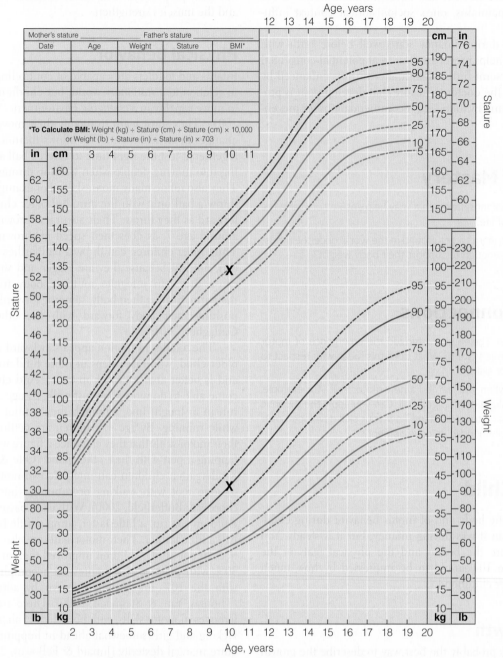

2 to 20 years: boys
Stature-for-age and weight-for-age percentiles

NAME _____

RECORD # _____

■ FIGURE 5.5 Growth patterns throughout infancy and childhood are typically tracked with a chart that shows weight and height of an individual child over time relative to normative data. In this example, the lower X indicates that this 10-year-old boy weighs about 95 pounds, which is at the 90th percentile for weight: he is heavier than 90% of other boys at this age. The higher X shows that his height is about 53 inches (135 centimeters), which is at the 25th percentile: he is taller than 25% of other boys at this age. Together, these data may suggest that the boy is gaining weight at a faster pace than he is gaining height. Figure 5.1 illustrates height percentiles for girls.

have become skilled performers at games that require eye–hand coordination. Handwriting quality and speed also improve steadily from age 6 to age 15 (van Galen, 1993).

Finally, older children have quicker reactions than young children do. When dogs suddenly run in front of their bikes, they can do something about it. In studies of **reaction time**, a stimulus, such as a light, suddenly appears and the subject's task is to respond to it as quickly as possible—for example, by pushing a button. These studies reveal that reaction time improves steadily throughout childhood (Eaton & Ritchot, 1995; Yan et al., 2000). As children age, they can carry out any number of cognitive processes more quickly. This speeding up of neural responses with age contributes in important ways to steady improvements in memory and other cognitive skills from infancy to adolescence (see Chapter 8).

Health and Wellness

Children's health is influenced by a multitude of factors, some of which are beyond their control. For instance, parents' education and socioeconomic status affect their children's health (Chen, Martin, & Matthews, 2006). Children whose parents are less educated are more likely to experience poor or fair health than children with more educated parents. This is particularly true for black children and white children, but less true for Hispanic children and Asian children, whose health outcomes may be buffered by strong social networks that cut across educational and socioeconomic levels (■ **Figure 5.6**). Clearly, then, the sociohistorical context of development plays a role in children's health and well-being.

Accidents constitute a major category of negative influences on children's health and well-being. Childhood is unfortunately marked by numerous unintentional injuries, making accidents the leading cause of death throughout the childhood years (CDC, 2009a). Crashes involving motor vehicles cause the largest number of fatal injuries during childhood. Parents can reduce the possibility of motor vehicle injuries by properly strapping their infants and young children into car seats, or as they get older, insisting that they sit in the backseat with a shoulder-strap seat belt. Nutrition continues to be an important contributor to health throughout childhood, as it was during infancy. Much to parents' dismay, though, the toddler who sampled all sorts of new foods may turn into a picky eater during childhood. One reason for this is that the rate of growth has slowed down, diminishing children's appetites. Still, they need to have a well-balanced diet that addresses their nutritional needs. Unfortunately, societal influences often inadvertently encourage poor eating habits rather than good ones. Many children eat fast foods, which are often fried, and snack on foods high in carbohydrates and low on nutritional value. A determined group of researchers staked out local convenience stores that were located near urban schools (Borradaile et al., 2009). These were small stores within 4 blocks of the schools that were frequented by children on their way to and from school. For months, the researchers tracked everything

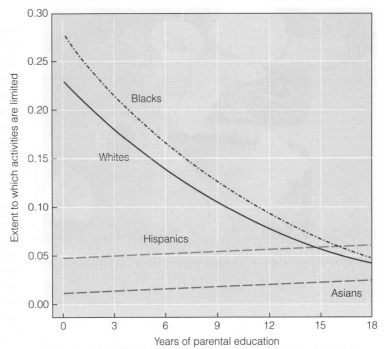

■ **FIGURE 5.6** Among white families and black families, parents' education levels influence the extent to which children's activities are limited by poor or fair health: children have more limitations when their parents are less educated. This is not true among Hispanic families and Asian families. SOURCE: From Chen, E., Martin, A. D., & Matthews, K. A. (2006). Understanding health disparities: The role of race and socioeconomic status in children's health. *American Journal of Public Health, 96,* 702–705. Reprinted by permission of the American Public Health Association.

the children purchased, briefly surveyed them regarding their purchases, and later analyzed the nutritional content of the food and beverages purchased. The most frequently purchased item was chips, followed by candy, and then sugar-sweetened artificially flavored drinks. In other words, the children were buying fatty, sugary foods and beverages with little nutritional value but high caloric value. Amazingly, these children spent an average of just $1 dollar to ingest an average of 356 empty calories. What a bargain!

Parents can help children to become healthy eaters by regularly offering a variety of healthy foods and modeling healthy eating habits. Parents can also steer children away from the sugary sodas and other sugar-sweetened beverages that have become so very popular. A survey of fluid intake across childhood indicates that sodas and artificially flavored drinks make up a large portion of the fluids that children consume (Borradaile et al., 2009; He, Marrero, & MacGregor, 2008). Sodas not only contribute to weight gain and obesity, they are also associated with lower consumption of milk and intake of calcium, an important nutrient for bone health (Keller et al., 2009; Lim et al., 2009). Preschoolers who consume sugary sodas between meals are more than twice as likely to be overweight by the time they start school than pre-

A steady diet of cheeseburgers, fries, and sodas is one of the reasons why many Americans are overweight and rates of obesity have increased, even among children.

Health during childhood can be fostered not only by a good diet but also by regular physical activity. Children should do at least 60 minutes of moderate or vigorous physical activity everyday (CDC, 2009c). Many children don't achieve this goal, but those who do are more physically fit than children who lead a more sedentary lifestyle (see Tuckman, 1999, for a review). The benefits of exercise go beyond physical fitness; physical activity may enhance cognitive and psychological functioning. One researcher has referred to exercise as "brain food" (Ploughman, 2008). In a review of studies on children's participation in physical activity and their academic performance, Roy Shepard (1997) concluded that increased physical activity was associated with improved academic skills. But these data are largely correlational, and many factors may explain the connection between physical activity and academic performance. For instance, Mark Tremblay and colleagues (Tremblay, Inman, & Willms, 2000) found that although regular participation in physical activity did not strongly influence 12-year-olds' academic performance, it did positively affect their self-esteem. Students who are healthier and feel better about themselves may perform better in the classroom. Other research suggests that children's physical activity must be sustained and vigorous before academic benefits will be realized (Tomporowski et al., 2008).

Unfortunately, our contemporary lifestyles may inadvertently promote physical inactivity, which may explain why the fitness levels of children have shown a measurable decline in recent years (see, for example, Powell et al., 2009). The average child spends 5–6 hours every day watching television or videos, playing video games, and working or playing on the computer (Roberts & Foehr, 2004). Children who watch more than 5 hours of television a day are about 5 times more likely to be overweight than children who watch 2 hours a day or less, perhaps because they get little exercise and eat the junk foods they see advertised on TV. At the same time, some schools have reduced recess time and physical education requirements. Most kids get chauffeured everywhere they need to go in the family car, further decreasing their opportunities for walking and physical activity. As a result, an increasing number of American children are overweight and meet the criterion for **obesity**—being 20% or more above the "ideal" weight for your height, age, and sex. As ■ **Figure 5.7** shows, obesity rates among

schoolers who do not (Dubois et al., 2007). Finally, there is also evidence that children may eat more at home and gain more weight if they are living in a stressful home situation. Craig Gunderson and his colleagues (2008) found that young children eat more "comfort foods" when their mothers are stressed, but only if these foods are available to them. This illustrates Bronfenbrenner's exosystem: a child is influenced by things going on in the mother's life that may relate to her work, finances, and other factors that do not directly involve the child but still affect the child.

Schools are also in a position to influence children's eating habits and health. Students who attend schools with breakfast programs have healthier weights than students in schools without breakfast programs, as indicated by **body mass index (BMI)**, a marker of body fat calculated from a person's height and weight (Gleason & Dodd, 2009). Children who participate in their school's meal programs consume more milk, vegetables, and 100% fruit juice than children not participating (Condon, Crepinsek, & Fox, 2009). Further, children who eat a regular breakfast, either at home or at school, are less likely to snack or lunch on high-fat foods.

School lunches may pose special risks to health. A survey of school meals shows that lunches offered to students contain more fat than the breakfasts (Crepinsek et al., 2009). Elementary school children who have French fries as a school lunch option are heavier than children whose schools do not offer French fries (Fox et al., 2009). In addition to being above recommended levels of fat, school lunches tend to have higher than recommended levels of sodium and lower amounts of fiber (Clark & Fox, 2009; Crepinsek et al., 2009). Schools are taking action to improve the nutrition of the foods offered to students for lunch and are reducing the availability of unhealthy snack items, such as French fries as a regular a la carte item and vending machines that offer fatty snacks and sugary sodas (Briefel et al., 2009). Perhaps because they have a more vocal student body, secondary schools lag behind elementary schools in eliminating the unhealthy options that contribute to higher BMIs (Story, Nanney, & Schwartz, 2009).

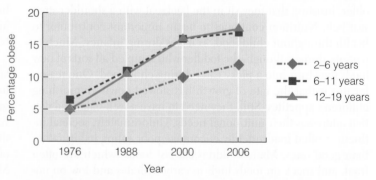

■ **FIGURE 5.7** Obesity rates have increased over the past 30 years among all age groups of children. Source: CDC, 2009. NHANES surveys (1976–1980 and 2003–2006) available at: www.cdc.gov/obesity/childhood/prevalence.html.

children have nearly tripled over the past 30 years and are especially high among ethnic minority children (Skelton et al., 2009).

Children who live in neighborhoods that provide opportunities for safe outdoor activities are less likely to be overweight than their peers who live in settings that offer few such opportunities (Committee on Environmental Health, 2009). Particularly for families in urban neighborhoods, if parents do not believe that it is safe for their children to play outdoors, children tend to replace outdoor activity with sedentary indoor activity such as watching television (Cecil-Karb & Grogan-Kaylor, 2009). But indoor activity does not have to be completely sedentary. Children who play *active* sports or fitness video games—those that require fairly rigorous movement—benefit in comparison to children who play only the traditional, inactive video games, although they do not benefit as much as they would from physically participating in the actual sport (Daley, 2009; Graf et al., 2009; Graves et al., 2008). Further, children who attend preschools with more portable equipment (for example, balls and bikes) engage in more physical activity over the course of the day compared with children who attend preschools with more fixed equipment (such as swing sets) (Dowda et al., 2009). But even the environments that encourage the most activity cannot turn every couch potato into an athletic powerhouse. Some children are predisposed by temperament to lead more sedentary lifestyles and resist even the most engaging playground equipment and incentives to be physically engaged (Saudino & Zapfe, 2008). Thus, characteristics of the environment in combination with characteristics of the child affect activity levels.

Checking Mastery

1. What are the major factors that contribute to health during childhood?

2. What are two things that schools or parents can do to influence children's eating behaviors in order to help them maintain or achieve a healthy weight?

Making Connections

1. Develop a model plan for reducing childhood injuries. Based on children's burgeoning physical and motor skills, what would be your focus for helping parents, schools, and neighborhoods keep their children as safe as possible?

2. Design an intervention to reduce childhood obesity and indicate how you will assess the effectiveness of your intervention.

5.4 The Adolescent

Adolescents are intensely focused on their physical self, and rightly so—dramatic physical changes are taking place during this period. Consider your own transformation from child to adult. You rapidly grew taller and took on the body size and proportions of an adult during your growth spurt. Moreover, you experienced **puberty**—the processes of biological change that result in an individual's attaining sexual maturity and becoming capable of producing a child. We look at both these processes.

The Growth Spurt

As noted earlier in the chapter, the **adolescent growth spurt** is triggered by an increase in the level of growth hormones circulating through the body during adolescence. Boys and girls grow at different rates, as do different body parts. Girls' peak rate of growth for height is just under 12 years; for boys it is 13.4 years (Geithner et al., 1999). The peak rate of growth for weight is 12.5 years for girls and 13.9 years for boys. Thus, boys lag behind girls by 1 to 2 years. Both sexes return to a slower rate of growth after the peak of their growth spurts. Like infants, adolescents may grow in spurts rather than continuously. Girls achieve their adult height by around 16 years; boys are still growing at 18, 19, or even 20 years (National Center for Health Statistics, 2007a).

Muscles also develop rapidly in both sexes, with boys normally gaining a greater proportion of muscle mass than girls do. Total body weight increases in both sexes, but it is distributed differently: girls gain extra fat, primarily in the breasts, hips, and buttocks; boys develop broader shoulders.

Sexual Maturation

Long before the physical signs of puberty are evident, the body is changing to prepare for sexual maturity. The adrenal glands increase production of adrenal androgens sometime between the ages of 6 and 8 in both boys and girls. Known as **adrenarche**, this circulation of adrenal hormones contributes partly to such secondary sex characteristics as pubic and axillary (underarm) hair. But the more obvious signs of sexual maturity emerge with increased production of gonadal hormones (those produced by the testes or ovaries): androgens in males and estrogen and progesterone in females. The gonadal hormones are primarily responsible for the development of secondary sexual characteristics and sexual maturity.

Progression through puberty and attainment of sexual maturity is often measured using the "Tanner Scale," named for the British pediatrician who developed it (see Marshall & Tanner, 1969; 1970). The Tanner Scale includes five stages ranging from prepubertal—no evidence of secondary sexual characteristics—to adult secondary sexual characteristics (• **Table 5.4**). For girls, the most dramatic event in the sexual maturation process is **menarche**—the first menstruation—normally between ages 11 and 14, with an average of about 12 years. Menstruation is the process of shedding the lining of a uterus prepared to support a fertilized egg. However, young girls often begin to menstruate before they have begun to ovulate, so they may not be capable of reproducing for a year or more after menarche (Spear, 2000a).

There is a great deal of variability in when secondary sex characteristics (such as breast buds and pubic hair) appear. Sexual maturation also proceeds at different rates in different ethnic groups. Several studies have found that African American and Mexican American girls begin to experience pubertal

● TABLE 5.4 TANNER'S STAGES OF SECONDARY SEXUAL CHARACTERISTICS AND ANNUAL GROWTH (IN INCHES) FOR BOYS AND GIRLS

Stage	Boys	Girls: Breasts	Boys and Girls: Pubic Hair
I	Prepubertal AG: 2–2.5 inches	Prepubertal AG: 2–2.5 inches	Prepubertal: no hair
II Boys: ages 12.5–14.5 Girls: ages 10–12	Testes: a bit larger (first sign in boys) Scrotum: red Penis: still childlike but erections common AG: 2.75–3.25 inches	Breast: small bud, widened areola AG: 2.8–3.2 inches	Boys: scant at base of scrotum Girls: scant on labia majora
III Boys: ages 13–15 Girls: ages 11–13	Testes: larger Scrotum: darker Penis: increases in length AG: 3.25 inches	Breasts: larger and more elevated AG: 3.2 inches	Hair more curly and coarser moving towards thighs
IV Boys: ages 13.5–15.5 Girls: ages 12–14	Testes: more enlargement Scrotum: more darkening Penis: becomes thicker AG: 4 inches	Breasts: secondary mound of areola from body AG: 2.8 inches	Adult-type hair covering genitalia but not on thighs
V Boys: ages 14–18 Girls: ages 14–18	Testes, scrotum, and penis all adult Final height by 18–19 years	Breasts: adult shape and size Final height by 16 years	Adult-type hair that extends to inner thighs

AG = annual growth.

Adapted from Pediatrics Now. (2009) *Puberty resource page.* Available at: www.pediatricsnow.com/PubertyResourcePage.html#tannerstages. Accessed March, 2010. Information originally presented in Marshall & Tanner, 1969; Marshall & Tanner, 1970.

changes earlier than European American girls (Chumlea et al., 2003; Wu, Mendola, & Buck, 2002). At age 9, for example, 49% of African American girls have begun to develop breasts compared with only 16% of European American girls and 25% of Mexican American girls (Wu, Mendola, & Buck, 2002). A few girls (1% of European Americans and 3% of African Americans) show signs of breast or pubic hair development at age 3, and a few have not begun to mature even at age 12 (Herman-Giddens et al., 1997). In addition, a girl's weight at birth as well as the amount of weight she gains during childhood both influence the timing of menarche: the lighter she is at birth and the more weight she gains during childhood, the earlier she tends to begin menstruating (Sloboda et al., 2007; Tam et al., 2006).

For the average boy, the sexual maturation process begins around age 11 to age 11½ with an initial enlargement of the testes and scrotum (the saclike structure that encloses the testes). Unpigmented, straight pubic hair appears soon thereafter, and about 6 months later, the penis grows rapidly about the same time that the adolescent growth spurt begins (see Table 5.4). The marker of sexual maturation most like menarche in girls is **semenarche**, or a boy's first ejaculation—the emission of seminal fluid in a "wet dream" or while masturbating. It typically occurs around age 13. Just as girls often do not ovulate until sometime

after menarche, boys often do not produce viable sperm until sometime after their first ejaculation.

Somewhat later, boys begin to sprout facial hair, first at the corners of the upper lip and finally on the chin and jawline. As the voice lowers, many boys have the embarrassing experience of hearing their voices "crack" uncontrollably up and down between a squeaky soprano and a deep baritone, sometimes within a single sentence. Boys may not see the first signs of a hairy chest until their late teens or early 20s, if at all.

What determines an adolescent's rate of development? Genes are part of the answer: identical twins typically begin and end their growth spurts at very similar times, and early or late maturation tends to run in families (Silventoinen et al., 2008). In both sexes, the changes involved in physical and sexual maturation are triggered when the hypothalamus of the brain stimulates activity in the endocrine system (see the description at the beginning of this chapter). Boys and girls have similar levels of both male and female sex hormones during childhood. By the time sexual maturation is complete, however, males have larger quantities of male hormones (androgens, including testosterone) circulating in their blood than females do, whereas females have larger quantities of female hormones (estrogen, progesterone, and others).

Physical and sexual maturation, then, are processes set in motion by the genes and executed by hormones. But environment also plays its part in the timing of maturation. This is dramatically illustrated by the **secular trend**—the historical trend in industrialized societies toward earlier maturation and greater body size. In 1840, for example, the average age of menarche was 16½ years, a full 4 years later than it is today (Rees, 1993). And over a recent 15-year period (1991 to 2006), emergence of breast tissue began a full year earlier (Aksglaede et al., 2009).

What explains the secular trend? Better nutrition and advances in medical care seem to be the major factors (Gluckman & Hanson, 2006). As ●**Table 5.5** shows, the age of menarche

● **TABLE 5.5 MEDIAN AGE OF MENARCHE & EMERGENCE OF SECONDARY SEXUAL CHARACTERISTICS (IF AVAILABLE) IN SELECT COUNTRIES**

	Stage 2 Breast	Stage 2 Pubic Hair	Menarche
Mexico			12
Greece			12.29
Brazil			12.3
China	9.2	10.4	12.3
U.S.	10.0	10.5	12.4
Turkey	10.16	10.57	12.41
Egypt	10.71	10.46	12.44
Ireland			12.53
Iran	10.15	10.78	12.65
Germany			12.8
Canada			12.9
U.K.	10.14	10.92	12.9
Taiwan			13
Denmark	9.86		13.13
Tanzania			14.3
Bangladesh			15.1
North Korea (refugees)			16

Sources: Aksglaede et al. (2009); Bau et al (2009); Bosch et al. (2008); Chang & Chen (2008); Gohlke & Woelfle (2009); Harris, Prior, & Koehoorn (2008); Hosny et al. (2005); Juul et al. (2006); Kashani et al. (2009); Ku et al. (2006); Ma et al. (2009); McDowell, Brody, & Hughes (2007); O'Connell et al. (2009); Papadimitriou et al. (2008); Rabbani et al. (2008); Rebacz (2009); Rubin et al. (2009); Semiz et al. (2008); Silva & Padez (2006); Torres-Mejia et al. (2005).

varies across countries and tends to be earlier in countries with good nutrition, long life expectancies, and high literacy rates, reflecting the effect of both biological and environmental factors (Thomas et al., 2001). In industrialized nations, today's children are more likely than their parents or grandparents to reach their genetic potential for maturation and growth because they are better fed and less likely to experience growth-retarding illnesses. Even within the relatively affluent U.S. society, poorly nourished adolescents—both boys and girls—mature later than well-nourished ones do. Girls who are taller and heavier as children tend to mature earlier than other girls (Lee et al., 2007). By contrast, girls who engage regularly in strenuous physical activity and girls who suffer from anorexia nervosa (the life-threatening eating disorder that involves dieting to the point of starvation) may begin menstruating late or stop menstruating after they have begun. These variations seem to be tied not to overall weight but to skeletal development, particularly maturation of the pelvic bones necessary for delivering a baby (Ellison, 2002).

Family situations can also affect the timing of puberty in girls. For instance, Bruce Ellis and Judy Garber (2000) found that girls whose mothers were depressed were likely to experience early puberty, as were girls who had a stepfather or mother's boyfriend present in the home. In particular, girls who were relatively young when an unrelated male moved into the house and whose mothers and stepfathers or boyfriends had a more conflicted, stressful relationship were likely to experience early sexual maturity. Even without a stepfather or boyfriend present in the home, girls experience earlier puberty when their family is disrupted by a separation or divorce that removes their biological father from the home at an early age (Tither & Ellis, 2008). This is especially true if the father, prior to leaving, displayed dysfunctional behaviors, at least in the eyes of his daughters. And harsh mothering at a young age also seems to precipitate earlier puberty and menarche (Belsky et al., 2007). The common thread in all this research is stress in the girls' lives, starting at a relatively young age (see also Chisholm et al., 2005). Over time, stress can affect many bodily systems and functions and early menarche may be one by-product of these changes. Truly, then, physical and sexual maturation are the products of an interaction between heredity and environment, with some environments delaying maturation and others hastening it.

Psychological Implications

As noted previously, there are large individual differences in the timing of physical and sexual maturation. An early-maturing girl may develop breast buds at age 8 and reach menarche at age 10, whereas a late-developing boy may not begin to experience a growth of his penis until age 14½ or a height spurt until age 16. Within a middle school, then, there is a wide assortment of bodies, ranging from entirely childlike to fully adultlike. It is no wonder adolescents are self-conscious about their appearance!

What psychological effects do the many changes associated with puberty have on adolescents? In many cultures, girls approaching or experiencing puberty tend to become concerned about their appearance and worry about how others will respond to them. One adolescent girl may think she is too tall, another that she is too short. One may try to pad her breasts; another may hunch her shoulders to hide hers. Not surprisingly, research confirms that individual reactions to menarche vary widely, with many girls reporting a mixture of positive and negative feelings and some confusion about the process (Koff & Rierdan, 1995; Moore, 1995). Unfortunately, cultural views about menstruation are often negative, and girls internalize these negative myths about what to expect. Many also develop poor body images, possibly because they are bothered by the weight gains that typically accompany menarche (McCabe & Ricciardelli, 2004).

What about boys? Their body images are more positive than those of girls, and they are more likely to welcome their weight gain and voice changes. But they hope to be tall, hairy, and handsome, and they may become preoccupied with their physical and athletic prowess. For boys like Josh, who was introduced at the beginning of this chapter, slow growth and/or short stature can be the source of significant grief. Josh experiences **constitutional growth delay**, which is characterized by being small for age (at or below the fifth percentile on a growth chart) and late entering puberty, but growing at a normal or near-normal pace. Eventually, these children tend to catch-up with their peers, but they may experience a rocky emotional road during adolescence as the smallest kid in the class, the last picked for sports, and the one least likely to be noticed in a romantic way by peers who are more developed. Their smaller size often means that others perceive them as younger and less mature.

Whereas menarche is a memorable event for girls, boys are often unaware of some of the physical changes they are

Why are boys generally more positive than girls about the physical changes in their bodies during adolescence?

experiencing. They notice their first ejaculation, but they rarely tell anyone about it and often were not prepared for it (Stein & Reiser, 1994). Although males express a mix of positive and negative reactions to becoming sexually mature, they generally react more positively to semenarche than girls do to menarche; 62% of boys regard semenarche positively, whereas only 23% of girls view menarche positively (Seiffge-Krenke, 1998).

Pubertal changes may prompt changes in family relations. Adolescents physically distance themselves from their parents by engaging in less body contact, especially with fathers, and they go to great lengths to avoid being seen naked by their parents (Schulz, 1991, in Seiffge-Krenke, 1998). Likewise, parents seem to restructure the parent–child relationship, placing greater distance between themselves and their children. Perhaps as a result of the barriers erected between adolescents and their parents, teens become more independent and less close to their parents (Steinberg, 1989). They are also more likely to experience conflicts with their parents, especially with their mothers—more often about minor issues such as unmade beds, late hours, and loud music than about core values. Hormone changes in early adolescence may contribute to this increased conflict with parents and to moodiness, bouts of depression, lower or more variable energy levels, and restlessness (Buchanan, Eccles, & Becker, 1992). However, cultural beliefs about family relations and about the significance of becoming an adult also influence parent–child interactions during adolescence. For example, many Mexican American boys and their parents appear to become closer rather than more distant during the peak of pubertal changes (Molina & Chassin, 1996).

Even when parent–child relationships are disrupted during early adolescence, they become warmer once the pubertal transition is completed. Parents—mothers and fathers alike—can help adolescents adjust successfully to puberty by maintaining close relationships and helping adolescents accept themselves (Swarr & Richards, 1996). Overall, you should not imagine that the physical and hormonal changes of puberty cause direct and straightforward psychological changes in the individual. Instead, biological changes interact with psychological characteristics of the person and with changes in the social environment to influence how adolescence is experienced (Magnusson, 1995; Paikoff & Brooks-Gunn, 1991).

Early versus Late Development

If "timely" maturation has psychological implications, what is it like to be "off time"—to be an early or late developer? The answer depends on whether we are talking about males or females and also on whether we examine their adjustment during adolescence or later on.

Consider the short-term effect of being an early-developing or late-developing boy. Early-developing boys are judged to be socially competent, attractive, and self-assured, and they enjoy greater social acceptance by their peers (Bulcroft, 1991). There are some negative aspects of being an early-maturing boy, namely increased risk of earlier involvement in substance use and other problem behaviors such as bullying, aggression, and delinquency (Kaltiala-Heino et al., 2003; Lynne et al., 2007). By comparison, late maturation in boys has more negative effects. Late-maturing boys like Josh tend to be more anxious and less sure of themselves, and they experience more behavior and adjustment problems (Dorn, Susman, & Ponirakis, 2003). As a group, they even score lower than other students do, at least in early adolescence, on school achievement tests (Dubas, Graber, & Petersen, 1991). However, on the positive side, late-maturing boys are less likely to drink alcohol during adolescence (Bratberg et al., 2005).

Now consider early-maturing and late-maturing girls. Traditionally, physical prowess has not been as important in girls' peer groups as in boys', so an early-developing girl may not gain much status from being larger and more muscled. In addition, because girls develop about 2 years earlier than boys do, a girl may be subjected to ridicule for a time—the only one in her grade who is developed and thus the target of some teasing. Perhaps for some of these reasons, early maturation appears to be more of a disadvantage than an advantage for girls. The early-maturing girl expresses higher levels of body dissatisfaction than her prepubertal classmates and may engage in unsafe dieting and exercising as a result of this discomfort (McCabe & Ricciardelli, 2004). In addition, early-maturing girls tend to be popular with boys and often end up socializing with an older peer group; consequently, they are likely to become involved in dating, smoking, drinking, having sex, and engaging in minor troublemaking at an early age (Bratberg et al., 2005; Burt et al., 2006; Carter et al., 2009; Ge et al., 2006). Girls who experience early puberty and early sex report higher levels of depression, but it's not yet clear which comes first: Does being depressed ignite biochemical changes in the body, triggering early puberty and sexual activity? Or does experiencing early puberty and sexual activity lead to being depressed? Additional research is needed to untangle these issues (see Kaltiala-Heino, Kosunen, & Rimpelä, 2003).

Late-maturing girls (like late-maturing boys) may experience some anxiety as they wait to mature, but they do not seem to be as disadvantaged as late-maturing boys. Indeed, whereas later-developing boys tend to perform poorly on school achievement tests, later-developing girls outperform other students (Dubas, Graber, & Petersen, 1991). Perhaps late-developing girls focus on academic skills when other girls have shifted some of their focus to extracurricular activities.

Do differences between early and late developers persist into later adolescence and adulthood? Typically, they fade with time. By late high school, for example, differences in academic performance between early and late maturers have largely disappeared (Dubas, Graber, & Petersen, 1991). When tracked into adulthood, though, early maturing girls have not attained as much education as those who were not early maturing (Johansson & Ritzén, 2005). And there may be lasting effects of some of the risky behaviors engaged in by early-maturing girls (such as sex and drinking). Early-maturing girls have a greater likelihood than all other groups of experiencing long-term adjustment problems, including anxiety and depression (Graber et al., 1997). Some of the advantages of being an early-maturing boy may carry over into adulthood, but early-maturing boys also seem to be more rigid and conforming than late-maturing ones, who may learn some lessons about coping in creative ways from their struggles as adolescents.

Overall, then, late-maturing boys and early-maturing girls are especially likely to find the adolescent period disruptive. However, psychological differences between early-maturing and late-maturing adolescents become smaller and more mixed in quality by adulthood. It is also important to note that differences between early and late maturers are relatively small and that many factors besides the timing of maturation influence whether this period goes smoothly or not. For example, girls who make the transition from elementary to middle school at the same time they experience puberty exhibit greater adjustment problems than girls who do not experience a school transition and pubertal changes simultaneously (Simmons & Blyth, 1987).

Finally, and perhaps most important, the effects of the timing of puberty depend on the adolescent's perception of whether pubertal events are experienced early, on time, or late (Seiffge-Krenke, 1998). Thus, one girl may believe she is a "late bloomer" when she does not menstruate until age 14. But another girl who exercises strenuously may believe that menarche at age 14 is normal because delayed menarche is typical of serious athletes. Peer and family-member reactions to an adolescent's pubertal changes are also instrumental in determining the adolescent's adjustment. This may help explain the difference in adjustment between early-maturing boys and early-maturing girls. Parents may be more concerned and negative about their daughter's emerging sexuality than they are about their son's. These attitudes may be inadvertently conveyed to teens, affecting their experience of puberty and their self-concept.

Physical Behavior

The dramatic physical growth that occurs during adolescence makes teenagers more physically competent than children. Rapid muscle development over the adolescent years makes both boys and girls noticeably stronger than they were as children (Seger & Thorstensson, 2000). Their performance of large-muscle activities continues to improve: An adolescent can throw a ball farther, cover more ground in the standing long jump, and run much faster than a child can (Keough & Sugden, 1985). Unfortunately, many adolescents are not as active as they should be, and girls are more sedentary than boys. By age 10–11, girls engage in less rigorous outdoor activities and report more environmental obstacles to physical activity than boys (University of Exeter, 2009; Yan et al., 2009). Boys' larger musculature may give them an advantage over girls in activities that require strength. But larger muscles cannot explain why girls are less active. Gender-role socialization may be partly responsible. As girls mature sexually and physically, they are often encouraged to be less "tomboyish" and to become more involved in traditionally "feminine" (often more sedentary) activities. Studies of world records in track, swimming, and cycling suggest that as gender roles have changed in the past few decades, women have been improving their performances, and the male–female gap in physical performance among top athletes has narrowed dramatically (Sparling, O'Donnell, & Snow, 1998; Whipp & Ward, 1992). This shows that, although fewer young women are as physically active as we might like, they are indeed capable of achieving the highest levels of physical activity and fitness.

Health and Wellness

Adolescents should be reaching their peak of physical fitness and health and, indeed, many adolescents are strong, fit, and energetic. Unfortunately, the sedentary lifestyle of modern society may be undermining the health and fitness of an increasing number of teens. Fitness tests of American teenagers show that an alarming one-third of them have poor physical fitness (Carnethon, Gulati, & Greenland, 2005). Teens may be doing well in school, but they are flunking treadmill tests that measure heart and lung function. Today's teens are showing up with high blood pressure, high cholesterol, and high blood sugar, putting them at risk for heart disease at earlier ages than previous generations of teens.

As with children, the number of teens who meet the criteria for obesity has also increased in recent decades. Some of the same issues that we discussed earlier regarding children's weight also apply to adolescents. Adolescents have more sedentary lifestyles and consume more empty calories than they need, often in

the form of beverages. Adolescents who drink more calorie-dense, nutrient-poor beverages not only gain weight, they have higher systolic blood pressure (Nguyen et al., 2009). The weight and the blood pressure put them at risk for later health problems including heart and kidney disease, diabetes, liver problems, and arthritis. Rates of **diabetes**—high levels of sugar in the blood—have significantly increased in recent years among adolescents, with more and more teens now taking antidiabetic drugs (Hsia et al., 2009).

Obesity is usually the product of both nature and nurture: heredity is perhaps the most important factor, but poor eating habits, inactivity, and parent behaviors contribute (Gable & Lutz, 2000; Steffen et al., 2009). Children and adolescents whose parents are overweight have twin risk factors for becoming overweight themselves: the genes that their parents have passed along to them that may predispose them to be overweight and the environment that is created for them by overweight parents (Steffen et al., 2009; Thibault et al., 2009). For instance, overweight parents are less likely to engage their children in vigorous physical activity and they are more likely to model sedentary behaviors such as watching television. Overweight parents are also more likely to be economically disadvantaged, so they purchase less expensive foods that are often high in calories and low in nutritional value. Adolescents who are overweight tend to gravitate toward other overweight teens (Valente et al., 2009). Being friends with other teens who are overweight may be comfortable in that it reduces the stigma of being overweight. Unfortunately, individuals who are overweight as adolescents—even those who slim down as adults—run a greater-than-average risk of coronary heart disease and a host of other health problems decades later (Kvaavik et al., 2009; Must et al., 1992).

The leading causes of death among teens are unintentional injuries (mostly from motor vehicles) and violence, including homicides and suicides (Centers for Disease Control, 2009e). Other health risks that may originate during adolescence include alcohol and drug use and cigarette smoking. Lifestyle choices made by adolescents have important implications for their health, both in the short term and in the long term. Consider the one out of four high school students who report occasional heavy or binge drinking (Centers for Disease Control, 2009e). Teens under the influence of alcohol are more likely to make additional risky choices: (1) They are more likely to smoke cigarettes and the more they smoke, the more likely they are to become addicted to nicotine. (2) They are more likely to engage in risky sexual behaviors including sex with multiple partners and unprotected sex. In turn, these behaviors are associated with unintended pregnancies and sexually transmitted diseases. (3) They are more likely to get into a car where the driver has been drinking, which greatly increases the risk of an accident. (4) They are more likely to get into physical fights, experience academic problems, and engage in illegal behaviors. These behaviors, or the predisposition to these behaviors, may have been present before the alcohol use, but alcohol use can still exacerbate the problems. By some analyses, making the decision not to drink during adolescence may be one of the teen's most important health decisions.

A mother and her daughter attend a local fair. What factors have contributed to this girl's weight, and what health issues might she face?

© Frank Siteman/Science Faction/Corbis

1. What are the major physical milestones of adolescence for boys and girls?

2. Which group of kids is likely to have the "best" experience of puberty and which group is likely to experience more problems with the process of puberty?

3. What factors affect timing of menarche in girls?

4. What is the most frequent cause of death during adolescence?

Making Connections

1. What are the most significant health concerns during adolescence? If you could get adolescents to change one or two behaviors to improve their health, what would they be and why?

2. How would you counsel the parents of an early-maturing girl so that they understand the risks she may face and what they can do to help her adjust successfully?

5.5 The Adult

The body of the mature adolescent or young adult is at its prime in many ways. It is strong and fit; its organs are functioning efficiently; it is considered to be in peak health. But it is aging, as it has been all along. Physical aging occurs slowly and steadily over the life span. Physical and health changes begin to have noticeable effects on appearance and functioning in middle age and have an even more significant effect by the time old age is reached, although more so in some people than in others.

In the next sections, we discuss typical changes that occur as we progress through middle adulthood and old age. We also look at health issues that can challenge us and consider what it takes to age successfully. You will learn that lifestyle choices play a key role in your overall health and longevity, which you can estimate by answering the questions in the Engagement Box 5.1.

Typical Changes

What changes can we expect across adulthood and old age? There are usually some changes in appearance, physical functioning, and the reproductive system, as well as a slowing of motor responses. Let's look at each of these areas in more detail.

Appearance and Physical Functioning

Only minor changes in physical appearance occur in the 20s and 30s, but many people notice signs that they are aging as they reach their 40s. Skin becomes wrinkled, dry, and loose, especially among people who have spent more time in the sun.

Hair thins and often turns gray from loss of pigment-producing cells. And to most people's dismay, they put on extra weight throughout much of adulthood as their metabolism rate slows but their eating and exercise habits do not adjust accordingly. This "middle-aged spread" could be controlled by regular exercise but it occurs when many adults feel they have little time to exercise because family and work responsibilities demand a great deal of their time. Just 30% of adults engage in any physical activity during their leisure time, less than 20% do strength training, and few engage in the level of aerobic exercise needed to maintain, let alone improve, their fitness (CDC/NCHS, 2008). Consequently, many middle-aged adults are overweight or even obese. As ■ **Figure 5.8** shows, nearly 25% of non-Hispanic white, 30% of Hispanic, and 35% of non-Hispanic black adults are obese (CDC, 2009b).

Obesity is a multifaceted problem that carries health burdens (heart disease, type 2 diabetes, certain cancers, and stroke), social stigma, and financial costs to the individual as well as to society. The annual health care cost of obesity in the United States is estimated at $147 billion dollars, with each individual obese person spending 42% more per year on health care than their normal-weight counterpart (CDC, 2009d). The U.S. Department of Health and Human Services has identified obesity as one of the most significant health-care concerns facing Americans and has issued a number of recommended strategies for combating obesity. These include promoting healthy foods and beverages, discouraging consumption of those foods and beverages that add calories but not nutrition, and increasing physical activity through a variety of community programs. The upward trend in obesity rates must be curbed or future generations will face the prospect of shorter life spans than their parents or grandparents.

As people move into their 60s and beyond, they typically begin to lose some weight (Whitbourne, 2008). Unfortunately, this loss of weight in old age is not from losing the fat gained in middle age but from losing valuable muscle and bone. Importantly, it is not age per se that reduces muscle mass but rather the sedentary lifestyle adopted by many older adults. When Abby King and colleagues (2000) surveyed nearly 3000 women in middle and later adulthood, they found that only 9% met the criteria for being regularly active. And as age increased, level of activity decreased. Age is not the only culprit, however, in making adults less active; low level of education, poor neighborhood characteristics, and personal factors (such as caregiving responsibilities and lack of energy) also influence whether or not adults exercise (King et al., 2000).

Aging also involves a gradual decline in the efficiency of most bodily systems from the 20s on. Most systems increase to a peak sometime between childhood and early adulthood and decline slowly thereafter. No matter what physical function you look at—the capacity of the heart or lungs to meet the demands of exercise, the ability of the body to control its temperature, the ability of the immune system to fight disease, or strength—the gradual effects of aging are evident. For example, Monique Samson and her colleagues (2000) assessed handgrip strength in

By the end of this decade, experts believe that there will be more than 300,000 people over the age of 100 in the United States (Schoemaker & Schoemaker, 2010). Is there a 100th birthday in your future? Take the following longevity quiz and get an estimate of your personal life expectancy. Start with the average life expectancy of 80 years if you are female and 75 years if you are male. Then add and subtract years as you answer each question below to arrive at an idea of your life expectancy. If you notice you are subtracting years as a result of certain poor lifestyle choices, you can take actions to alter these choices as you move forward in life.

___ 1. Add 5 years if two or more of your grandparents lived to 80 or beyond.

___ 2. Subtract 4 years if any parent, grandparent, or sibling died of heart attack or stroke before 50.

___ 3. Subtract 2 years if anyone died from these diseases after age 50 but before 60.

___ 4. Subtract 3 years for each case of diabetes, thyroid disorder, breast cancer, cancer of the digestive system, asthma, or chronic bronchitis among parents or grandparents.

___ 5. If you are married, add 4 years. If you are over age 25 and not married, subtract 1 year for every decade not married.

___ 6. Add 2 years if your family income places you in the middle-class or higher socioeconomic category.

___ 7. Subtract 3 years if you have been poor for most of your life.

___ 8. Subtract 1 year for every ten pounds you are overweight.

___ 9. If your belly measurement is bigger than your chest measurement, subtract 2 years.

___ 10. Add 3 years if you are over 40 and not overweight.

___ 11. Add 3 years if you exercise regularly and moderately (e.g., jogging 3 times a week). Add another 2 years if your regular exercise is *vigorous* (e.g., long-distance running).

___ 12. Subtract 3 years if your job is sedentary or add 3 years if your job is active.

___ 13. Add 2 years if you are a light drinker (1–3 drinks per day) but subtract 5–10 years if you are a heavy drinker (more than 4 drinks per day).

___ 14. Subtract 8 years if you smoke 2 or more packs of cigarettes per day. If you smoke anything less than this, subtract 2 years.

___ 15. Add 2 years if you are a reasoned, practical person, but subtract 2 years if you are aggressive, intense, and competitive.

___ 16. Add 1–3 years if you are basically happy and content with life, but subtract 1–5 years if you are often unhappy, worried, and often feel guilty. (Use your best judgment on how happy/unhappy you are to determine how many years to add or subtract.)

___ 17. Add 1 year if you attended 4 years of school beyond high school. Add an additional 3 years if you attended 5 or more years beyond high school.

___ 18. Add 4 years if you have lived most of your life in a rural environment, but subtract 2 years if you have lived most of your life in an urban environment.

___ 19. Subtract 5 years if you sleep more than nine hours a day.

___ 20. Add 3 years if you have regular medical checkups and regular dental care. Add another year if you floss your teeth every day.

___ 21. Subtract 2 years if you are frequently ill.

Source: Adapted from Woodruff-Pak, D. (1988). *Psychology and aging.* Englewood Cliff, NJ: Prentice-Hall.

---

healthy men and women between ages 20 and 80. Women showed only small decreases in muscle strength before age 55 but much larger decreases after age 55. Men showed steady loss of muscle strength across all ages studied. It turns out that hand-grip strength in middle age is a good predictor of disability and ability to function in later life: those with weaker handgrip in middle age are more likely to have greater functional limitations and disabilities 25 years later (Rantanen et al., 1999). Researchers also find that arm movements are slower and more variable among older adults, which has implications for functioning (Yan, Thomas, Stelmach, 1998). Everyday activities such as bathing and dressing will take more time with slower arm movements.

It should be noted, however, that individual differences in physiological functioning increase with age (Harris et al., 1992).

That is, aerobic capacity and other physiological measurements vary more widely among 70-year-olds than among 20-year-olds. Even though the *average* old person is less physiologically fit than the *average* young person, *not all older people have poor physiological functioning*. Older adults who remain physically active retain greater strength and faster reaction times (Amara et al., 2003; Hatta et al., 2005).

Another fact of physical aging is a decline in the **reserve capacity** of many organ systems—that is, their ability to respond to demands for extraordinary output, such as in emergencies (Goldberg & Hagberg, 1990). For example, old and young people do not differ much in resting heart rates, but older adults, even if they are disease-free, will have lower maximal heart rates (Lakatta, 1990). This means that older adults who do not feel

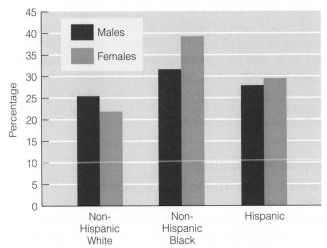

■ FIGURE 5.8 Prevalence of obesity among adults varies across race/ethnicity: non-Hispanic black women have the highest rates and non-Hispanic white women have the lowest. Overall, though, 1 in 4 adults meets the criteria for obesity.

very old as they go about their normal routines may feel very old indeed if they try to run up mountains.

Older adults are often less fit than younger ones because they decrease their involvement in vigorous physical activity as they get older—females earlier than males (Ruchlin & Lachs, 1999). Older adults who are socially isolated and lonely reduce their physical activity even more than those who maintain strong social connections (Hawkley, Thisted, & Caciappo, 2009). By

Older adults, like adolescents, often struggle to come to terms with the physical changes they experience as they age.

late adulthood, older adults may find that they get tired just climbing stairs or carrying groceries; running a marathon is out of the question. The average older person tires more quickly and needs more time to recover after vigorous activity than the average younger person.

Psychological Implications

Some people, influenced by societal stereotypes to equate "old" with "unattractive," find the physical changes in their appearance and functioning that occur with age difficult to accept. American society values youth and devalues old age and the physical changes that often accompany it. What are the psychological implications of growing older under these conditions? Negative stereotypes about older adults abound—they are sickly, frail, forgetful, unattractive, dependent, or otherwise incompetent. Such stereotypes can lead to **ageism**, or prejudice against elderly people. Most elderly adults have internalized these negative views but believe they apply to other older adults and not to themselves.

How do older adults feel about themselves and the changes in their physical appearance and functioning? Some adults are bothered by their physical appearance, women more so than men and white women somewhat more so than women of color (Frederick, Peplau, & Lever, 2006; Grabe & Hyde, 2006). Women often focus their clothes' shopping on finding the best camouflage for their perceived body flaws (Tiggemann & Lacey, 2009). But the larger concern seems to be the ability to continue functioning at a desirable level. Laura Hurd (1999) interviewed women between ages 50 and 90 who attended programs at a "senior center." She found that the women actively worked to distance themselves from the "old" category and to remain in the "not old" category. These categories were defined not by age but by what individuals can and cannot do. Generally, the women believed that they were not old because they had the physical and mental abilities to avoid nursing home care. In particular, they believed that remaining active—both physically and socially—was the key to avoiding becoming old. Women who considered themselves "not old" believed that men and women who were old had given in to the stereotypes of aging by being inactive and solitary.

As you have seen, many older adults, even those who consider themselves "not old," have chronic diseases and impairments. Still, the majority of people 65 and older say they are in excellent, very good, or good health (Federal Interagency Forum, 2008). Whites are more likely to report they are in good health than Blacks or Hispanics (76% compared to 60% and 62%). Relatively few older adults say they need assistance with daily activities, although the figure climbs with age—from 9% of those age 65 to age 69 to 50% of those age 85 and older (Hobbs, 1996). Although having a chronic disease or disability tends to lower an older person's sense of well-being, many people with arthritis, diabetes, and other difficulties are no less content with their lives than anyone else (Kempen et al., 1997). Clearly, most older people are able to retain their sense of well-being and their ability to function independently despite an increased likelihood of impairments.

The Reproductive System

During most of adulthood, the sex hormones that start to be secreted during adolescence help ensure interest in sexual behavior and the ability to have children, but they also have psychological implications and affect the experience of aging. In men, testosterone levels fluctuate annually, with the highest levels detected in June and July (Andersson et al., 2003), and daily (Harman & Talbert, 1985). Men with high levels of testosterone tend to be more sexually active and aggressive than other men (Archer, 1991; Schiavi et al., 1991). Otherwise, it is not clear that changes in men's hormone levels are tied to changes in their moods and behavior.

By contrast, hormone levels in women shift drastically each month as they progress through their menstrual cycles. These shifts have psychological implications for some women. Estrogen and progesterone levels rise to a peak at midcycle, when a woman is ovulating, and decline as she approaches her menstrual period. The cyclic changes in hormones may lead to such symptoms as bloating, moodiness, breast tenderness, and headaches during the days just before the menstrual flow, symptoms collectively referred to as **premenstrual syndrome (PMS)**. Estimates of how many women experience PMS vary substantially. Among women age 21 to age 64, 41% report that they experience PMS and another 17% report at least some symptoms before menstruation (Singh et al., 1998). A majority of adolescent women report noticeable symptoms related to their menstrual cycle (Cleckner-Smith, Doughty, & Grossman, 1998). It's likely that close to 10% of women experience symptoms severe enough to interfere with their ability to perform daily activities (e.g., Potter et al., 2009; Yonkers, O'Brien, & Eriksson, 2008).

However, there is some debate about the validity of PMS. In research where women are simply asked to complete mood surveys every day and do not know that their menstrual cycles are being studied, most report little premenstrual mood change (Englander-Golden et al., 1986). This suggests that expectations and not hormones play a role in many cases of PMS. Only a few women—probably fewer than 5%—experience significant PMS. Changes in estrogen and progesterone levels may be responsible (Schmidt et al., 1998). Women with severe PMS may find relief when treated with antidepressant drugs such as Prozac (Dimmock et al., 2000). For women with milder forms of PMS, treatment with calcium and vitamin D may alleviate symptoms because the low estrogen levels experienced prior to menstruation can interfere with the absorption of these substances by the body (Thys-Jacobs, 2000). Clearly, individuals vary in how they experience menstrual cycles.

Genetic endowment influences the extent to which a woman experiences both premenstrual and menstrual distress (Condon, 1993; Kendler et al., 1992). Social factors also play a role. Learned societal stereotypes of what women "should" experience at different phases of the menstrual cycle appear to influence what women experience and report (Ainscough, 1990; Englander-Golden et al., 1986). Most likely, then, biological, psychological, social, and cultural factors all contribute to a woman's experience of the menstrual cycle during her adult life (McFarlane & Williams, 1990).

Female Menopause

Like other systems of the body, the reproductive system ages. The ending of a woman's menstrual periods in midlife is called **menopause**. The average woman experiences menopause at age 51, and the usual age range is from 45 to 54. The process takes place gradually over 5–10 years as periods become either more or less frequent and less regular. Levels of estrogen and other female hormones decline so that the woman who has been through menopause has a hormone mix that is less "feminine" and more "masculine" than that of the premenopausal woman. When menopause is completed, a woman is no longer ovulating, no longer menstruating, and no longer capable of conceiving a child.

The age at which a woman reaches menopause is somewhat related to both the age at which she reached menarche and the age at which her mother reached menopause (Varea et al., 2000). Although life expectancy has increased and the age of menarche has decreased over history as part of the secular trend, the age of menopause does not appear to have changed much and is similar from culture to culture (Brody et al., 2000). What has changed is that women are now living long enough to experience a considerable period of postmenopausal life.

Society holds rather stereotypic views of menopausal women. They are regarded as irritable, emotional, depressed, and unstable. How much truth is there to this stereotype? Not much. About two-thirds of women in U.S. society experience **hot flashes**—sudden experiences of warmth and sweating, usually centered around the face and upper body, that occur at unpredictable times, last for a few seconds or minutes, and are often followed by a cold shiver (Whitbourne, 2008). Many also experience vaginal dryness and irritation or pain during intercourse. Still other women experience no symptoms.

What about the psychological symptoms—irritability and depression? Again, researchers have discovered wide variation among menopausal women—and not much truth to the negative stereotypes. In a particularly well-designed study, Karen Matthews and her associates (Matthews, 1992; Matthews et al., 1990) studied 541 initially premenopausal women over a 3-year period, comparing those who subsequently experienced menopause with women of similar ages who did not become menopausal. The typical woman entering menopause initially experienced some physical symptoms such as hot flashes. Some women also reported mild depression and temporary emotional distress, probably in reaction to their physical symptoms, but only about 10% could be said to have become seriously depressed in response to menopause. Typically, menopause had no effect on the women's levels of anxiety, anger, perceived stress, or job dissatisfaction. When women do experience severe psychological problems during the menopausal transition, they often had those problems well before the age of menopause (Greene, 1984).

Women who have been through menopause generally say it had little effect on them or that it even improved their lives; they are usually more positive about it than women who have not been through it yet (Gannon & Ekstrom, 1993; Wilbur, Miller, & Montgomery, 1995). For most women, menopause brings no changes in sexual interest and activity, although sexual activity gradually declines in both women and men over the adult years (Laumann, Paik, & Rosen, 1999). In short, despite all the negative stereotypes, menopause seems to be "no big deal" for most women. Indeed, many women find the end of monthly periods to be quite liberating.

Why do some women experience more severe menopausal symptoms than others do? Again, part of the answer may lie with biology. Women who have a history of menstrual problems (such as PMS) report more menopausal symptoms, both physical and psychological (Morse et al., 1998). Thus, some women may experience greater biological changes. But psychological and social factors of the sort that influence women's reactions to sexual maturation and to their menstrual cycles also influence the severity of menopausal symptoms. For example, women who expect menopause to be a negative experience are likely to get what they expect (Matthews, 1992). There is also a good deal of variation across cultures in how menopause is experienced. It appears that the effect of menopause is colored by the meaning it has for the woman, as influenced by her society's prevailing views of menopause and by her own personal characteristics.

For years, **hormone replacement therapy**, or **HRT** (taking estrogen and progestin to compensate for hormone loss at menopause), was considered an effective cure for the symptoms that many women experience with menopause. HRT relieves physical symptoms of menopause, such as hot flashes and vaginal dryness, and prevents or slows osteoporosis. Unfortunately, this trust in HRT was shattered in 2002 by a large government study that found that HRT increases women's chances of developing breast cancer and experiencing heart attacks and strokes (Women's Health Initiative, 2004). For most women, these risks outweigh the benefits of HRT, particularly if the hormones estrogen and progestin are taken over a long period. For women with severe menopausal symptoms associated with decreasing production of hormones, short-term HRT (for example, up to 2 years) may be warranted. In the year following publication of the research, sales of hormones dropped by 40% (Grady, 2006) and women and their physicians have been scrambling for alternative treatments. To date, however, the benefits and pitfalls of these alternatives, such as soy, have not been documented. Lifestyle changes such as exercising and getting adequate sleep may be the best options for menopausal women because they alleviate some complaints and are safe.

Male Andropause

Obviously, men cannot experience menopause because they do not menstruate. They also do not experience the sharp drop in hormones that accompanies menopause in women. But over the past decade, some research has pointed to the possibility that men experience andropause as they age. **Andropause**, slower and not as dramatic as menopause in women, is characterized by decreasing levels of testosterone and a variety of symptoms including low libido, fatigue and lack of energy, erection problems, memory problems, and loss of pubic hair (Tan & Pu, 2004; Vermeulen, 2000; Wu, Yu, & Chen, 2000). By age 80, men have between 20 and 50% of the testosterone that they had at age 20. The sperm produced by older men may not be as active as those produced by younger men. Still, men can father children long after women become incapable of bearing children.

Some research reports that testosterone levels are markedly lower among men over age 50 with symptoms of andropause than among men without symptoms (Wu, Yu, & Chen, 2000). But other research does not show a clear connection between andropause symptoms and testosterone levels (see, for example, Vermeulen, 2000). In one study, for example, half of 50- to 70-year-old men complained of erectile dysfunction despite having sufficient levels of testosterone; most of these cases of erectile dysfunction are caused by medical conditions such as diabetes and not by lower hormone production (Gould, Petty, & Jacobs, 2000).

In sum, the changes associated with andropause in men are more gradual, more variable, and less complete than those associated with menopause in women. As a result, men experience fewer psychological effects. Frequency of sexual activity does decline as men age. However, this trend cannot be blamed entirely on decreased hormone levels, because sexual activity often declines even when testosterone levels remain high (Gould, Petty, & Jacobs, 2000; see also Chapter 12 on sexuality).

Slowing Down

You may have noticed, as you breeze by them on the sidewalk, that older adults often walk more slowly than young people do. Indeed, research suggests that the amount of time stoplights provide for pedestrians to cross the street is not enough for the 99% of people age 72 or older who walk at a pace slower than 4 feet per second (Langlois et al., 1997). Some older adults also walk as if they were treading on a slippery surface—with short, shuffling steps and not much arm movement—an adaptive strategy, perhaps, since falls in old age can be deadly.

It's not just walking that slows with age. On average, older adults perform many motor actions more slowly and with less coordination than younger adults do (Whitbourne, 2008). In a study comparing younger adults (18–24 years) with older adults (62–72 years) on five motor tasks, the older adults performed more slowly on all five (Francis & Spirduso, 2000). The older adults were especially slow on fine motor tasks requiring object manipulation, such as inserting pegs in holes. They also have more trouble when tasks are novel and when they are complex—for example, when any one of several stimuli might appear on a screen and each requires a different response (Sliwinski et al., 1994; Spirduso & MacRae, 1990). On average, older adults take 1½ to 2 times longer than young adults to respond on a range of cognitive tasks that require speedy answers (Lima, Hale, & Myerson, 1991).

What accounts for the slowing of motor performance in old age? One hypothesis is that the ability to produce complex behavior declines with age (Newell, Vaillancourt, & Sosnoff, 2006). Putting together the multiple components that comprise complex tasks becomes increasingly difficult as we age (Kolev, Falkenstein, & Yordanova, 2006; Shea, Park, & Braden, 2006). Motor responses also likely slow because the brain itself slows. Gerontologist James Birren has argued that *the* central change that comes about as people age is a slowing of the nervous system (Birren & Fisher, 1995). It affects not only motor behavior but also mental functioning, and it affects most elderly people to at least some degree.

At age 81, Marie Pastor earned her GED, or high school equivalency test. Such mental "exercise" later in life is likely to contribute to neural growth in the aging brain and compensate for neural degeneration.

You should not expect all old people to be slow in all situations, however. The reaction times of older adults vary greatly (Yan, Thomas, & Stelmach, 1998; Yan et al., 2000). Physically fit older people and those free from cardiovascular diseases have quicker reactions than peers who lead sedentary lives or have diseases, although they are still likely to be slower than they were when they were younger (Earles & Salthouse, 1995; Spirduso & MacRae, 1990). Aerobic exercise or experience playing video games can also speed the reactions of older adults (Dustman et al., 1989, 1992). In addition, experience can help elderly people compensate for a slower nervous system so that they can continue to perform well on familiar motor tasks.

Disease, Disuse, or Abuse?

Many aspects of physical functioning seem to decline over the adult years in many individuals. But an important question arises: when researchers look at the performance of older people, are they seeing the effects of aging alone or the effects of something else? The "something else" could be disease, disuse of the body, abuse of the body—or all three.

Most older people have at least some chronic *disease* or impairment, such as arthritis or heart disease. How would an elderly person function if she could manage to stay disease-free? Birren

and his colleagues (1963) addressed this question in a classic study of men aged 65–91. Extensive medical examinations were conducted to identify two groups of elderly men: (1) those who were almost perfectly healthy and had no signs of disease and (2) those who had slight traces of some disease in the making but no clinically diagnosable diseases. Several aspects of physical and intellectual functioning were assessed in these men, and the participants were compared with young men.

The most remarkable finding was that the healthier group of older men hardly differed from the younger men. They were equal in their capacity for physical exercise, and they beat the younger men on measures of intelligence requiring general information or knowledge of vocabulary words. Their main limitations were the slower brain activity and reaction times that seem to be so basic to the aging process. Overall, aging in the absence of disease had little effect on physical and psychological functioning. However, the men with slight traces of impending disease were deficient on several measures. Diseases that have progressed to the point of symptoms have even more serious consequences for performance.

So it is possible that disease, rather than aging, accounts for many declines in functioning in later life. We must note, however, that Birren and his colleagues had a tough time finding the perfectly healthy older people they studied. Most older people experience both aging and disease, and it is difficult to separate the effects of the two. Although aging and disease are distinct, increased vulnerability to disease is one part—and an important part—of normal aging.

Disuse of the body also contributes to steeper declines in physical functioning in some adults than in others. John Masters and Virginia Johnson (1966) proposed a "use it or lose it" maxim to describe how sexual functioning deteriorates if a person engages in little or no sexual activity. The same maxim can be applied to other systems of the body. Muscles atrophy if they are not used, and the heart functions less well if a person leads a sedentary life (Rosenbloom & Bahns, 2006). Changes such as these in some aging adults are much like the changes observed in people of any age confined to bed for a long time (Goldberg & Hagberg, 1990). The brain also needs "mental exercise" to display plasticity and to continue to function effectively in old age (Black, Isaacs, & Greenough, 1991). In short, most systems of the body seem to thrive on use, but too many people become inactive as they age (Rosenbloom & Bahns, 2006).

Finally, *abuse* of the body contributes to declines in functioning in some people. Excessive alcohol consumption, a high-fat diet, and smoking are all clear examples. In addition, some older adults abuse drugs, either illicit or prescription, intentionally or unintentionally (Dowling, Weiss, & Condon, 2008; Martin, 2008). Experts believe that we may see an increase in recreational use of drugs among the elderly as the baby boomers who came of age during the drug culture of the 1960s retire (Gfroerer, 2003; Han, 2009). Drugs typically affect older adults more powerfully than they do younger adults; they can also interact with one another and with the aging body's chemistry to impair functioning (Cherry & Morton, 1989; Lamy, 1986).

Overall, then, poor functioning in old age may represent any combination of the effects of aging, disease, disuse, and abuse. We may not be able to do much to change basic aging processes but as you will see in the next section, we can change our lifestyles to optimize the odds of a long and healthy old age.

Health and Wellness

By the time people are 65 or older, it is hard to find many who do not have something wrong with their bodies. Acute illnesses such as colds and infections become less frequent from childhood on, but chronic diseases and disorders become more common. National health surveys indicate that many of the 70-and-older age group have at least one chronic impairment—whether a sensory loss, arthritis, hypertension, or a degenerative disease (Federal Interagency Forum, 2008). Arthritis alone affects 43% of elderly men and 54% of elderly women; in addition, about half have hypertension (high blood pressure), and about one-third have heart disease (Federal Interagency Forum, 2008). Among older adults who live in poverty, many of whom are members of a minority group, health problems and difficulties in day-to-day functioning are even more common and more severe (Clark & Maddox, 1992; Hobbs, 1996). Still, as ■ **Figure 5.9** suggests, only a minority of adults report physical limita-

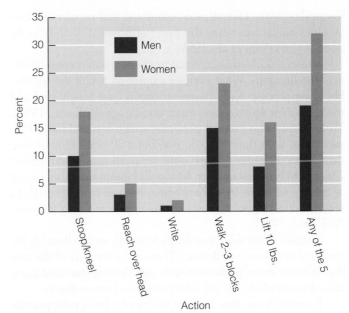

■ **FIGURE 5.9** Percentage of older adults (65+ years) who report limitations in some basic physical functions. More women than men report functional limitations.

tions; most adults maintain the physical capabilities that allow them to function successfully.

Again, though, it is important to note that there is tremendous variability in the health, wellness, and functioning of older adults. Some are limited by health problems, but others enjoy active, healthy lives. Indeed, some older adults are far more active than younger ones! For instance, Michael Stones and Albert Kozma (1985) cite the example of a 98-year-old man who could run a marathon (26.2 miles) in 7½ hours! And former president George Bush marked the occasion of his 85th birthday by skydiving, commenting to the press that it was "better than just drooling in a corner."

What factors might account for such differences and what do we know about staying healthy in older adulthood? For one, older adults who exercise reap many benefits. Exercise can improve cardiovascular and respiratory functioning, slow bone loss, and strengthen muscles. In one study, older athletes (average age 69 years) were compared with older nonathletes on several physiological measures following exercise. The athletes showed better oxygen uptake capacity and greater cardiovascular stamina than the nonathletes (Jungblut et al., 2000). In another study, elderly adults who did low-intensity exercise and weight lifting for 1 year became stronger and more flexible and experienced less pain as a result (Sharpe et al., 1997). Exercise can make aging adults feel less stressed and happier, and it can enhance their cognitive functioning (Barnes et al., 2003; Rowe & Kahn, 1998; Yaffe et al., 2001). Physical activity is also associated with a lower incidence of depression among older adults (Lampinen, Heikkinen, &

Ruoppila, 2000). Overall, it is estimated that regular exercise by older adults can delay the onset of physical disabilities by up to 7 years (Vita et al., 1998).

Exercise is clearly beneficial to physical and mental health over the life span. What exercise cannot do is halt the inevitable aging process. Even frequent joggers gain weight and add inches to their waists as they enter middle age (Williams, 1997). True, people who exercise generally weigh less and have slimmer waists than those who do not, but a 30-year-old man who runs 20 to 30 miles a week until he is 50 would add almost 2 inches to his waist anyway; he would have to run farther each year to avoid it. To try to beat aging, then, it is not enough to remain active; a person must become *more* active over the years (Williams, 1997).

Another factor that contributes to health and wellness is the presence or absence of disease. There are a number of diseases that become more prominent with age. Among the most common diseases of old age are osteoporosis and osteoarthritis.

Extreme bone loss in later life results from **osteoporosis** (meaning "porous bone"), a disease in which a serious loss of minerals leaves the bones fragile and easily fractured. It involves pain and can result in death if the victim falls and fractures a hip. Nearly one-third of elderly adults who fracture a hip die within 1 year; hip fractures are also a leading cause of nursing home admissions (Whitbourne, 2008). One fall can change an older person's entire lifestyle, requiring a shift from independent living to assisted living. Not surprisingly, adults who have experienced a fall often begin to restrict their activities out of fear of falling again. Unfortunately, less activity can make them more vulnerable because it can lead to further decreases of muscle and bone mass (Whitbourne, 2008). Osteoporosis is a special problem for older women, who never had as much bone mass as men and whose bones tend to thin rapidly after menopause. European and Asian women with light frames, those who smoke, and those with a family history of osteoporosis are especially at risk.

What can be done to prevent osteoporosis? For starters, dietary habits can influence a person's risk for osteoporosis. Many individuals do not get enough calcium to develop strong bones when they are young or to maintain bone health as they age (Kart, Metress, & Metress, 1992). Weight-bearing exercises such as walking or jogging can help prevent osteoporosis, as can the hormone replacement therapy (HRT) that some women take following menopause (but see this chapter's earlier section, "Female Menopause," for a discussion of concerns about HRT). It is increasingly evident that good bone health starts in childhood and adolescence (Krucoff, 2000). Girls and young women who are physically active and eat a healthy diet develop higher bone density that protects them from bone loss in later life.

The joints also age over the adult years. The cushioning between bones wears out, and the joints stiffen. Many older adults experience pain or discomfort from arthritis, or joint inflammation. The most common joint problem among older adults is **osteoarthritis**, which results from gradual deterioration

Four sisters from David Snowden's "nun study." What factors have contributed to the unusual longevity of some of the sisters?

© Ruth Ann Shanklin Jackson

of the cartilage that cushions the bones from rubbing against one another. For some older adults, joint disease is deforming and painful and limits their activities. The older person who can no longer fasten buttons, stoop to pick up dropped items, or even get into and out of the bathtub may easily feel incompetent and dependent (Whitbourne, 2008).

Successful Aging

Everyone wants to age "successfully"; that is, maintain good health and be free of diseases that might limit physical and mental skills and the ability to actively participate in desired daily activities (Rowe & Kahn, 1998). Older adults want to be as independent as possible and pursue a lifestyle that makes them feel satisfied. Researchers are beginning to learn some of the secrets to successful aging.

In 1986, David Snowdon (2002) began the Nun Study with 678 nuns ranging in age from 75 to 106 years. Snowdon, an epidemiologist, chose to study the nuns because they were very similar with respect to socioeconomic status, housing, health care, and diet. In this remarkable longitudinal study, participants underwent annual mental and physical testing, provided complete access to a lifetime of health records, and agreed to donate their brains for examination following their deaths.

The first finding to emerge from the Nun Study was that level of education affected longevity and health. Those with a college degree lived longer and were more likely to remain independent. The risk of death among the college-educated nuns was lower at every age. Another major finding was that the nuns who were active, both physically and mentally, lived longer and healthier than nuns who were not as active.

A unique aspect of the Nun Study was that each nun had written an autobiography prior to taking her vows (average age of 22 years) and, decades later, these autobiographies became part of the data analyzed for the study. This analysis revealed that older nuns who were healthy had used more complex vocabulary in their autobiographies decades earlier (on average, 60 years earlier). They used words such as "particularly, privileged, and quarantined" as opposed to simple words such as "girls, boys, and sick" that were used by nuns who later developed symptoms of Alzheimer's disease (Snowdon, 2002, p. 107). In particular, idea density, a measure of language-processing ability, measured in early adulthood predicts mental functioning in later adulthood. In addition, nuns whose autobiographies expressed more positive emotions lived longer than nuns whose autobiographies expressed fewer positive emotions.

The message to take away from such research is that both physical and mental activity, along with a positive attitude, can help slow the effects of aging on both the body and brain. As noted earlier, we can't avoid the biological reality of aging, but we can make choices across the life span that will increase the odds of aging successfully. Clearly, then, our health and well-being are influenced by an interaction of environmental and genetic factors.

Checking Mastery

1. Name several lifestyle factors that affect longevity.

2. What have we learned about successful aging from the "Nun Study"?

Making Connections

1. Many (indeed, most) stereotypes of the physical aging process are negative and depressing. What in this chapter gives you reason to be more optimistic about aging, and why? Cite specific concepts and research findings.

2. Suppose you set as your goal reaching age 100 in superb physical condition. Describe and justify a plan for achieving your goal, then indicate why you might not make it despite your best efforts.

Chapter Summary

5.1 Building Blocks of Growth and Development

- Growth is influenced by genes and environments, through the working of the endocrine and nervous systems. The nervous system consists of the brain, the spinal cord, and peripheral neurons. Endocrine glands such as the pituitary, thyroid, testes, and ovaries regulate behavior by secreting hormones directly into the bloodstream. The workings of the endocrine and nervous systems can be hindered or enhanced by environmental forces. During childhood, neural transmission speeds up and lateralization of various brain functions, although present at birth, becomes more evident in behavior.
- During adolescence, the brain (especially the prefrontal cortex) continues to develop, permitting sustained attention and strategic planning.
- The adult brain is capable of some degree of neurogenesis.
- The aging brain exhibits both degeneration and plasticity. Neurons atrophy and die, and blood flow to the brain decreases; but the aging brain forms new synapses to compensate for neural loss and reorganizes itself in response to learning experiences.
- Physical growth proceeds according to the cephalocaudal (head-to-tail), proximodistal (center outward), and orthogenetic (global and undifferentiated to differentiated and integrated) principles.
- Health is best viewed from a life-span developmental perspective emphasizing genes, personal choice, and environmental factors in interaction.

5.2 The Infant

- The physical changes that occur during the short period of infancy are awe-inspiring. Infants gain significant height and weight, their bones harden, and their muscles become strong enough to support locomotion and grasping.
- Infants come into the world equipped with reflexes and organized states that allow them to adapt to their environments.
- Major motor milestones are achieved during infancy, including crawling, walking, reaching, and grasping. These accomplishments are best understood within a dynamic systems model. This model suggests that infants "self-organize" their motor development by using sensory feedback they receive from their movements to modify their motor behavior in adaptive ways.
- Congenital malformations and complications of preterm birth are the leading causes of infant mortality. Preventative medicine such as well-baby visits to the doctor and vaccinations can improve infant health.

5.3 The Child

- There is steady and marked improvement in all aspects of physical growth and motor behavior over the childhood years.
- Physical activity is an important component of health during childhood. Children's health is also influenced by their parents' socioeconomic status and lifestyle choices.
- Accidental injuries are the leading cause of death during childhood, with motor vehicle accidents topping the list of injury causes.

- Health is enhanced with proper nutrition and regular physical activity. Current lifestyles have decreased physical activity and increased sedentary media time, resulting in increased weight among today's children.

5.4   The Adolescent

- The adolescent period is marked by physical growth—the adolescent growth spurt—and attainment of puberty or sexual maturity. Girls experience their growth spurt at a younger age than do boys. The major milestone of sexual maturity for girls is menarche—their first menstruation. For boys, it is the less noted experience of semenarche, or first ejaculation. A combination of genes, hormones, and environmental factors determine the timing and rate of growth and puberty.

- The physical changes of adolescence are significant and have psychological implications. Girls' experience is often on the negative side, whereas boys tend to report a more positive reaction to growth and puberty. Boys who mature early experience largely positive benefits whereas late-maturing boys have a more negative experience. In contrast, girls who mature early are sometimes disadvantaged by teasing from their peers and the influence of the older peers with whom they often socialize. Late-maturing girls seem to benefit academically, possibly because they continue to spend more time on schoolwork than their early-maturing peers.

- Adolescents are a relatively healthy bunch, but the fitness level of some teens is poor because of a lack of physical activity. Accidental injuries and violence are the leading causes of death during adolescence and include motor vehicle accidents, suicides, and homicides.

5.5   The Adult

- Changes in appearance and functioning start to become evident during middle adulthood, and declines are noticeable in most older adults. There are large individual differences in physical functioning of older adults. Negative stereotypes about aging may lead many older adults to negatively interpret the natural changes that accompany aging.

- For both sexes, changes in the reproductive system are a normal part of aging. Women experience menopause, a cessation of menstruation and an end of child-bearing years. Men experience andropause, a more gradual change in their reproductive system. The experience of menopause is variable and a variety of treatments are available to treat the symptoms.

- Aging, disease, disuse, and abuse of the body all affect performance in later life. Healthy older people function much like younger people except for their slower reactions, but the development of chronic diseases is a fact of aging for most people.

- Health and well-being during adulthood are influenced by genetic predispositions acting in concert with the environment and lifestyle choices. Exercise can enhance both physical and mental functioning. Common diseases among older adults include osteoporosis, which leads to fragile bones, and osteoarthritis, or joint inflammation.

- Physical and mental activity, as well as a positive attitude, improve the odds of successful aging.

Checking Mastery Answers

For answers to Checking Mastery questions, visit
www.cengagebrain.com

Key Terms

celiac disease **147**
catch-up growth **147**
endocrine gland **147**
pituitary gland **147**
growth hormone **147**
androgens **147**
estrogen **148**
neuron **149**
synapse **149**
myelination **149**
plasticity **151**
lateralization **151**
neurogenesis **151**
cephalocaudal principle **153**
proximodistal principle **153**
orthogenetic principle **153**
reflex **155**
REM sleep **155**
developmental norm **157**
gross motor skills **157**
fine motor skills **157**
locomotion **157**
ulnar grasp **160**
pincer grasp **160**
rhythmic stereotypies **161**

dynamic systems theory **161**
congenital malformations **162**
reaction time **165**
body mass index (BMI) **166**
obesity **166**
puberty **167**
adolescent growth spurt **167**
adrenarche **167**
menarche **167**
semenarche **168**
secular trend **169**
constitutional growth delay **170**
diabetes **172**
reserve capacity **174**
ageism **175**
premenstrual syndrome (PMS) **176**
menopause **176**
hot flashes **176**
hormone replacement therapy (HRT) **177**
andropause **177**
osteoporosis **180**
osteoarthritis **180**

Media Resources

Psychology CourseMate

Access an integrated eBook and chapter-specific learning tools including flashcards, quizzes, videos, and more. Go to **www.cengagebrain.com**

Early Physical Development Tracker

The Early Childhood Physical Development section of Wholefamily.com summarizes key milestones in physical development during the first six years of life. This section also features definitions of key terms and development checklists. To access, see "web links" in Psychology CourseMate at www.cengagebrain.com

PBS Whole Child: ABCs of Physical Development

The ABC's of Child Development presents a number of physical development stages through which a child will pass in his or her first 5 years of life. These milestones are presented in a colorful and easy-to-follow timeline. To access, see "web links" in Psychology CourseMate at www.cengagebrain.com

Understanding the DATA:
Exercises on the Web

www.cengagebrain.com
For additional insight on the data presented in this chapter, try out the exercises for these figures in Psychology CourseMate at
www.cengagebrain.com:

Figure 5.1 This shows the rather dramatic catch-up growth that has occurred in a girl following treatment at around age 11 for her celiac disease.

Table 5.5 Median age of menarche and emergence of secondary sexual characteristics (if available) in select countries.

CengageNOW

www.cengagebrain.com
Go to www.cengagebrain.com to link to CengageNOW, your online study tool. First take the Pre-Test for this chapter to get your Personalized Study Plan, which will identify topics you need to review and direct you to online resources: . Then take the Post-Test to determine what concepts you have mastered and what you still need work on.

Perceptual Development

As a young child, Elizabeth M. bumped into objects and was considered to be clumsy and a bit "slow." When her first-grade teacher reported that she could not see the board even from the first row of desks, a visit to the eye doctor revealed that Elizabeth's visual acuity was, at best, 20/200. She could see the big E at the top of the vision chart, but nothing else. After being outfitted with thick-lensed glasses, Elizabeth demonstrated that she was far from clumsy and slow. She excelled in academics and graduated in the top of her class. Still, eye problems continued to plague her. Twice, she experienced a tear in her retina. The first one was repaired successfully, but the second one led to retinal detachment and further loss of vision in this eye. To make matters worse, Elizabeth was diagnosed in early adulthood with retinitis pigmentosa, which initially affected her night vision and peripheral vision and eventually claimed what remained of her vision.

1. How well do the sensory systems function during infancy? What changes occur in sensory capabilities over the period of infancy?

2. How do researchers know what infants understand about their worlds?

3. What can we conclude about the perceptual abilities and preferences of a typical infant?

4. How does attention change across the life span, and what characterizes a problem with attention?

5. What typical changes in sensory abilities occur with age?

Possibly one reason that sensation and perception may not seem important is that they occur so effortlessly for most people. And as long as the sensory–perceptual systems are in good working order, we tend to take them for granted. But as soon as there is a "glitch" in the system, we become painfully aware of the limitations imposed when, for example, we lose our vision or sense of smell.

There is another reason to be interested in sensation and perception. They have long been at the center of a debate among philosophers and, more recently, developmental scientists about how we gain knowledge of reality.

In what ways might our lives be changed if, like Elizabeth, we had compromised vision or no vision? Would our perception of the world be altered because this one sense was not providing normal input? Would other senses become more finely tuned to compensate for vision loss? In this chapter, we answer these questions and more as we examine how our senses provide us with the building blocks for understanding the world around us. We discuss the tremendous flood of sensations bombarding the infant and how infants come to "make sense" of this information. We trace the changes in sensation and perception through childhood, adolescence, and early adulthood, and then look at some of the inevitable declines that occur in middle and later adulthood. We also look at the important role that attention plays in our awareness of the world around us and why some information is noticed and other information seems to drop off our "radar screens."

Psychologists have long distinguished between sensation and perception. **Sensation** is the process by which sensory receptor neurons detect information and transmit it to the brain. From birth, infants sense their environment. They detect light, sound, odor-bearing molecules in the air, and other stimuli. But do they *understand* the patterns of stimulation coming in from the various sense organs? This is where **perception,** or the interpretation of sensory input, comes into play: recognizing what you see, understanding what is said to you, knowing that the odor you have detected is a sizzling steak, and so on. But let's be clear about something: The sense organs are not passive receptacles that detect and merely pass along information to the brain. Your eyes, nose, tongue, ears, and skin actually help shape the brain (Brynie, 2009). Before we look at how this occurs, we will start with a more basic question: Why should you care about the development of sensation and perception?

Sensation and perception are at the heart of human functioning. *Everything you do depends on your ability to sense and perceive the world around you.* You would have a tough time as a student if you could neither read printed words nor understand speech. Indeed, you would not be able to walk to class without the aid of the body senses that control movement.

6.1 Issues of Nature and Nurture

Does the ability to perceive the world around us depend solely on innate biological factors, or is this ability acquired through experience and learning? **Constructivists** come down on the side of nurture (Kellman & Arterberry, 2006). They argue that perceptions of the world are constructed over time through learning. Yes, we come equipped at birth with functioning sensory systems, but understanding the input coming in through our senses requires interacting with the environment and "learning to infer the meanings of our sensations" (Kellman & Arterberry, 2006, p. 112). For instance, the retinal image of an object located 50 feet from an observer is different from the retinal image of the same object located just 10 feet from the observer. According to the constructivists, we need experience with viewing objects at various distances to learn how to interpret the different retinal images that they project. With experience, we create an association between the retinal image (for example, small) and its meaning (for example, distant object).

On the nature side of the issue are the **nativists,** who argue that perception is *not* created by interpreting external input—that instead innate capabilities and maturational programs are the driving forces in perceptual development (Kellman & Arterberry, 2006). Infants come equipped with basic sensory capabilities, which are further refined according to an innate plan. Nativists would argue that the infant does not need experience to learn how to interpret different retinal images cast by the same object at different distances. The brain automatically understands the meaning of different retinal images created as we move about our world (for example, a small image is automatically "read" by the brain as distant object). Thus, from the nativist perspective, perception is direct—it does not require interpretation based on previous experience (Kellman & Arterberry, 2006).

Although the constructivist view of perception has long been popular, more sophisticated methods of assessing infants' capabilities are yielding new findings about their perceptual abilities. As a result, some researchers have shifted toward a more nativist perspective to understand the origins of some aspects of perception.

In what ways are the perceptual experiences of infants and adults similar, and in what ways are they different because of the adult's greater experience with the world?

Nature–nurture issues also arise in the study of declines in sensory and perceptual abilities in later life. Are these declines universal, suggesting that they are the product of fundamental aging processes? Or do they differ greatly from person to person and result from factors other than aging, such as disease or exposure to ultraviolet rays, loud noise, and other environmental influences known to damage the senses? Just as researchers must pin down the contributions of nature and nurture to early perceptual development, so they must clarify the roles of nature and nurture in perceptual aging.

In the next section, we look closely at sensation and perception in infancy because this is when most fundamental perceptual capacities emerge. Later, you will see how much more "intelligent" the senses become during childhood and adolescence and will question the image of old age as a time of little more than sensory decline.

Checking Mastery

1. How is perception different from sensation?
2. What is the difference in how constructivists and nativists view sensation and perception?

Making Connections

1. How could you demonstrate that perception of an object's distance is innate rather than constructed through experience?

6.2 The Infant

The pioneering American psychologist William James (1890) claimed that sights, sounds, and other sensory inputs formed a "blooming, buzzing confusion" to the young infant. James was actually noting that impressions from the several senses are fused rather than separable, but his statement has since been quoted to represent the view that the world of the young infant is hopelessly confusing.

Today the accepted view is that young infants have far greater perceptual abilities than anyone suspected. Their senses are functioning even before birth, and in the first few months of life they show many signs that they are perceiving a coherent rather than a chaotic world. Why the change in views? It is not that babies have become smarter. It is that researchers have become smarter. They have developed more sophisticated methods of studying what infants can and cannot do. Infants, after all, cannot tell researchers directly what they perceive, so the trick has been to develop ways to let their behavior speak for them.

Assessing Sensory and Perceptual Abilities

As researchers have devised more ingenious ways of testing the perceptual capacities of young infants, they have uncovered more sophisticated capacities at younger ages. The main methods used to study infant perception are the habituation, preferential looking, evoked potentials, and operant conditioning techniques (Cohen & Cashon, 2006; Gibson & Pick, 2000).

Habituation

Humans of all ages lose interest in a stimulus if it is presented repeatedly. This process of learning to be bored with a stimulus is called **habituation.** Suppose researchers repeatedly present the same visual stimulus (such as a blue circle) to an infant; eventually the infant becomes bored and looks away—the infant habituates. If the researchers then present a different stimulus (such as a red circle) and the infant regains interest, researchers know that the infant has discriminated between the two stimuli—has noticed a difference between the blue and red circles (Cohen & Cashon, 2006). This procedure can be used to test for discrimination of stimuli by all the senses—vision, hearing, touch, and even taste and smell.

Preferential Looking

Alternatively, researchers can present an infant with two stimuli at the same time and measure the length of time the infant spends looking at each. A preference for one over the other, like responding to a novel stimulus in the habituation paradigm, indicates that the infant discriminates between the two stimuli. What if the infant looks equally long at the two stimuli? Then it is unclear what researchers can conclude; the infant may discriminate between the stimuli but may simply not like one better

This youngster does not seem at all bothered by wearing an "electrode cap" that allows researchers to measure electrical activity of different regions of the brain while the infant is exposed to various visual or auditory stimuli.

© Infant Auditory Lab, McMaster University

than the other. It is also possible that infants have a preference but do not display it with preferential looking (Rovee-Collier, 2001). They may reveal this preference when tested with an alternative method, such as an opportunity to interact with the preferred object.

Evoked Potentials

Researchers can get an idea of how the brain responds to stimulation by measuring its electrical activity with small metal disks (electrodes) attached to the skin's surface. The infant simply sits in a comfortable seat and watches or listens to various stimuli. The electrodes and computer record the brain's response to these stimuli so that researchers can "see" what is going on inside the brain.

Operant Conditioning

As you learned in Chapter 2, humans will repeat a response that has a pleasant consequence; that is, they are capable of learning through operant conditioning. Young infants are not easily conditioned, but they can learn to suck faster or slower or to turn their head to the side when a certain stimulus is presented if they are reinforced for that response. Suppose that you want to determine whether infants can distinguish between two speech sounds. First, an infant might be conditioned over several trials to turn his head every time he hears a sound—perhaps by being shown an interesting toy or being given a taste of milk. Then a second sound would be presented; if the infant turns his head, it suggests that the two sounds are perceived as equivalent; if the

infant does *not* turn his head, you can conclude that the two sounds have been discriminated.

Methods for studying infant perception have their limitations. For example, infants may not respond to a difference between stimuli for reasons unrelated to an inability to discriminate between them. Still, these techniques, with others, have revealed a good deal about what infants perceive and what they do not, as you will now see.

Vision

Most of us tend to think of vision as our most indispensable sense. Because vision is indeed important, we examine its early development in some detail before turning to the other major senses.

Basic Capacities

The eye functions by taking in stimulation in the form of light and converting it to electrochemical signals to the brain. How well does the newborn's visual system work? From the first minutes of life, the infant can detect changes in brightness and can visually track a slow-moving picture or object (Slater, 2004). Failure to follow an object when the object is presented within normal viewing range is often an early indicator of a visual problem. Even among sighted newborns, visual capabilities are lacking when compared with those of a child or an adult. At birth, newborns' **visual acuity,** or the ability to perceive detail, is 40 times worse than an adult's, but improves across the first month of life to roughly the equivalent of 20/120 vision on the standard eye chart—being able to see only the big E at the top of the chart (Hamer, 2009; ■ **Figure 6.1**). Objects are blurry to young infants unless they are about 8 inches from the face or are bold patterns with sharp light–dark contrasts—the face of a parent, for example. The young infant's world is also blurred because of limitations in **visual accommodation**—the ability of the lens of the eye to change shape to bring objects at different distances into focus. It is likely to take 6 months to 1 year before the infant can see as well as an adult (Slater, 2004).

Very young infants also see the world in color, not in black and white as some early observers thought (Zemach, Chang, & Teller, 2006). How do researchers know this? Suppose they accustom an infant to a blue disk using the habituation technique. What will happen if they then present either a blue disk of a different shade or a green disk? Infants 4 months old will show little interest in a disk of a different blue but will be attentive to a green disk—even when the light reflected from these two stimuli differs in wavelength from the original blue stimulus by the same amount (Schiffman, 2000). Thus, 4-month-olds appear to discriminate colors and categorize portions of the continuum of wavelengths of light into the same basic color categories (red, blue, green, and yellow) that adults do. Color vision is present at birth, but newborns cannot discriminate some color differences well because their receptors are not yet mature. By 2–3 months, however, color vision is mature (Goldstein, 2007). Like adults, 4-month-old infants can detect a colored stimulus on a back-

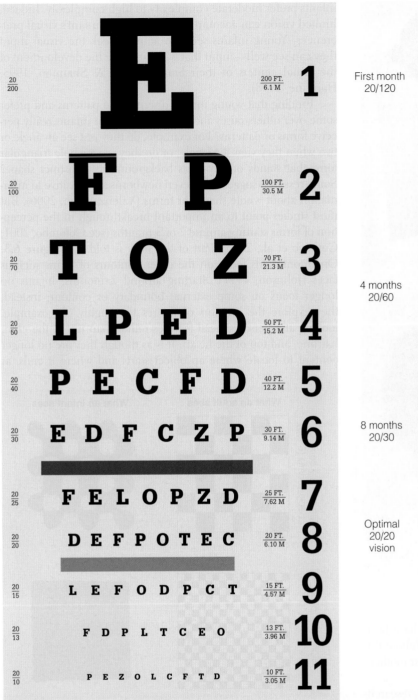

20/200	E	200 FT. / 6.1 M	**1** First month 20/120
20/100	F P	100 FT. / 30.5 M	**2**
20/70	T O Z	70 FT. / 21.3 M	**3**
20/50	L P E D	50 FT. / 15.2 M	**4** 4 months 20/60
20/40	P E C F D	40 FT. / 12.2 M	**5**
20/30	E D F C Z P	30 FT. / 9.14 M	**6** 8 months 20/30
20/25	F E L O P Z D	25 FT. / 7.62 M	**7**
20/20	D E F P O T E C	20 FT. / 6.10 M	**8** Optimal 20/20 vision
20/15	L E F O D P C T	15 FT. / 4.57 M	**9**
20/13	F D P L T C E O	13 FT. / 3.96 M	**10**
20/10	P E Z O L C F T D	10 FT. / 3.05 M	**11**

■ **FIGURE 6.1** The Snellen chart is often used to estimate a person's visual acuity. Although 20/20 vision is frequently assumed to be the "best" vision, 20/10 on the Snellen chart would actually be optimal vision. At birth, visual acuity may be as poor as 20/400, improving to 20/120 over the first month and to 20/30 by 8 months.

Infants are able to see what they need to see (Hainline, 1998). Even newborns can perceive light and dark, focus on nearby objects, distinguish colors, and see simple patterns. But does all this visual stimulation make any sense?

Pattern Perception

Over years of testing, researchers have found that even young infants prefer to look at certain patterns more than others. What are the properties of patterns that "turn infants on"? For one thing, young infants are attracted to patterns that have a large amount of light–dark transition, or **contour**; they are responsive to sharp boundaries between light and dark areas (Banks & Shannon, 1993; Farroni et al., 2005). This is perhaps why it was once mistakenly thought that infants could only see in black and white. They can detect color, but often the pastel colors presented to young infants do not have enough contrast to be detected (Brown & Lindsey, 2009). Black and white objects, however, offer this contrast, as do bold colors.

Second, young infants are attracted to displays that are dynamic (as opposed to static) or contain *movement* (Courage, Reynolds, & Richards, 2006; Kavsek & Yonas, 2006). Newborns can and do track a moving target with their eyes, although their tracking at first is imprecise and likely to falter unless the target is moving slowly (Easterbrook et al., 1999; Slater, 2004). Infants also look longer at moving objects and perceive their forms better than those of stationary ones (Johnson & Aslin, 1995; Slater 2004).

Finally, young infants seem to be attracted to *moderately complex* patterns. They prefer a clear pattern (for example, a bold checkerboard pattern) to either a blank stimulus or an elaborate one such as a page from the *New York Times* (Fantz & Fagan, 1975). As infants mature, they prefer more complex stimuli.

One special pattern that has garnered much attention from researchers is the human face. Early research showed that young infants preferred to look at schematic drawings of faces rather than other patterned stimuli and that faces elicited more visual tracking by young infants than other targets (Gamé, Carchon, & Vital-Durand, 2003). Other research shows that within hours of birth, infants prefer their mother's face to a strange woman's face (see Sai, 2005). These findings seem to suggest an inborn tendency to orient to faces and even to recognize a particular face. But as you have just learned, infants prefer contour, movement, and moderate complexity. Human faces have all of these physical properties. In addition, research shows that newborns have a preference for patterns that have more information in their upper visual field—that is, patterns that are "top heavy" (Cassia et al., 2006; Cassia, Turati, & Simion, 2004; Turati, 2004). Again, faces are top heavy. As for being able to visually pick out their mother's face from a lineup, it

ground that is a different shade of the same color (Franklin, Pilling, & Davies, 2005). However, like adults, they are *faster* at detecting the stimulus on a background of a different color.

In short, the eyes of the young infant are not working at peak levels, but they are working. As one researcher summarizes it:

At 2 months, Jordan is attracted to the mobile's well-defined contours (or light–dark contrasts) and bold patterns (which are neither too simple nor too complex).

© Laura Dwight/Corbis

infants prefer moderate complexity to high complexity. Indeed, limited vision can account for several of the infant's visual preferences. Young infants seem to actively seek the visual input they can see well—input that will stimulate the development of the visual centers of their brains (Banks & Shannon, 1993; Hainline, 1998).

Finding that young infants discriminate patterns and prefer some over others raises another question. Can infants really perceive forms or patterns? For example, do they just see an angle or two when they view a triangle, or do they see a whole triangular form that stands out from its background as a distinct shape? Some research suggests that even newborns are sensitive to information about whole shapes or forms (Valenza et al., 2006). But most studies point to an important breakthrough in the perception of forms starting around 2 or 3 months (see Colombo, 2001; Courage et al., 2006). Part of the story is told in ■ Figure 6.3. One-month-olds focus on the outer contours of forms such as faces (Johnson, 1997). Starting around 2 months, infants no longer focus on some external boundary or contour; instead, they explore the interiors of figures thoroughly (for example, looking at a person's facial features rather than just at the chin, hairline, and top of the head). It is as though they are no longer content to locate where an object starts and where it ends, as

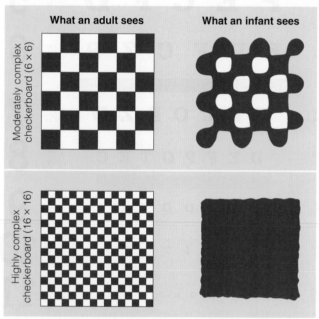

■ **FIGURE 6.2** What the young eye sees. By the time these two checkerboards are processed by eyes with undeveloped vision, only the checkerboard at top left may have a pattern remaining. Blurry vision in early infancy helps explain a preference for moderately complex rather than highly complex stimuli. Source: From Haith M. M. & Campos J. J. (Eds.) & Mussen P. H. (Gen Ed.), *Handbook of Child Psychology: Vol. 2, Infancy and Developmental Psychology* (4th ed.) Copyright © 1983. Reprinted with permission of John Wiley & Sons, Inc.

turns out that newborns can only do this when they have been exposed to their mother's face *along with her voice*. Without this auditory–visual coupling, neonates fail to recognize their mother's face (Sai, 2005).

To recap what has been covered up to this point, researchers know that infants younger than 2 months have visual preferences, and they also know something about the physical properties of stimuli that attract infants' attention. Martin Banks and his colleagues have offered a simple explanation for these early visual preferences: *Young infants prefer to look at whatever they can see well* (Banks & Ginsburg, 1985). Based on a complex mathematical model, Banks has been able to predict how different patterns might look to a young infant. ■ Figure 6.2 gives an example. Because the young infant's eye is small and its neural receptors are immature, it has poor visual acuity and sees a highly complex checkerboard as a big, dark blob. The pattern in a moderately complex checkerboard can be seen. Less-than-perfect vision would therefore explain why young

1-month-old   2-month-old

Visual scanning of a geometric figure by 1- and 2-month-old infants

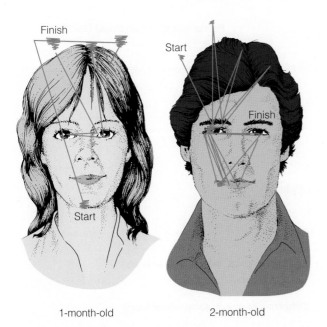

1-month-old   2-month-old

Visual scanning of the human face by 1- and 2-month-old infants

■ FIGURE 6.3 Visual scanning in early infancy. The 1-month-old seems to be trying to locate where an object begins and ends, whereas the 2-month-old seems to be on the way to figuring out what an object is by exploring it inside and out. Source: Adapted from Salapatek, 1975.

1-month-olds tend to do; they seem to want to know what it is. During this time, infants also become better at shifting their attention or disengaging from a stimulus (Colombo, 2001; Courage et al., 2006). Initially, their gaze seems to become "stuck" on the fixated object, and they have difficulty shifting it to another object. As you might imagine, this difficulty with shifting gaze limits what young infants can take in from their environment.

Much remains to be learned about early perception of faces. An intense nature–nurture debate still rages about whether infants have an innate ability to perceive faces or can do so only after they have had some experience looking at faces (Cassia et al., 2006; Johnson & de Haan, 2001; Slater, 2004). Still, we can conclude that infants truly perceive a meaningful face, not merely an appealing pattern, by 2–3 months of age. By then, infants smile when they see faces as though they recognize them as familiar and appreciate their significance. So it goes with pattern perception more generally: as infants gain experience with different objects, their attention is drawn to certain objects not only because they have certain physical properties, but also because their forms are recognized as familiar.

Depth Perception

Another important aspect of visual perception involves perceiving depth and knowing when objects are near or far. Although it can take years to learn to judge the size of objects in the distance, very young infants have some intriguing abilities to interpret spatial cues involving nearby objects. For example, they react defensively when objects move toward their faces; blinking in response to looming objects first appears around 1 month and becomes more consistent over the next few months (Kayed & van der Meer, 2007; Nanez & Yonas, 1994). As Exploration Box 6.1 describes, young infants also seem to operate according to the principle of **size constancy**: they recognize that an object is the same size despite changes in its distance from the eyes.

Does this evidence of early spatial perception mean that infants who have begun to crawl know enough about space to avoid crawling off the edges of beds or staircases? The first attempt to examine depth perception in infants was carried out in classic research by Eleanor Gibson and Richard Walk (1960) using an apparatus called the **visual cliff**. This cliff consists of an elevated glass platform divided into two sections by a center board. On the "shallow" side a checkerboard pattern is placed directly under the glass. On the "deep" side the pattern is several feet below the glass, creating the illusion of a drop-off or "cliff." Infants are placed on the center board and coaxed by their mothers to cross both the shallow and the deep sides. Testing infants 6½ months of age and older, Gibson and Walk found that 27 of 36 infants would cross the shallow side to reach Mom, but only 3 of

An infant on the edge of a visual cliff, being lured to cross the "deep" side.

© Mark Richards/PhotoEdit Inc.

Do Infants Understand Size Constancy?

Carl Granrud (2006) assessed whether young infants understand size constancy, the fact that objects are perceived as the same size even when they project different images on the retina because of their distance from us. To start, 4-month-olds were habituated to either a 6-cm disk or a 10-cm disk presented at different distances (see the figure in this box). They were then tested to see whether they would prefer to look at a disk that was the same size but cast a different retinal image or one that was a different size but cast the same retinal image. The infants responded on the basis of actual object size, not size of the retinal image cast by the object.

They preferred to look at the disk that was a novel size rather than the one that cast the same retinal image as during the habituation phase. This indicates that infants recognize the size of an object even when the object is presented at different distances and thus produces different images on the retina.

Habituation Phase:

A — 18-cm distance 6-cm disk

OR

B — 50-cm distance 10-cm distance

Retinal Image of Habituated Disk

Test Phase:

A — 30-cm distance
- Same-size object; different retinal image
- Different-size object; same retinal image

OR

B — 30-cm distance
- Different-size object; same retinal image
- Same-size object; different retinal image

Which disk will infants prefer? The one that is the same size as what they were habituated to in the previous phase, or the one that projects the same retinal image as in the habituation phase? Whether they were in condition A or B, they preferred the different-sized object in the test phase. SOURCE: From Granrud C. E. (2006). Size constancy in infants: 4-month-olds' responses to physical versus retinal image size. *Journal of Experimental Psychology: Human Perception and Performance, 32,* 1398–1404. Copyright © 2006 American Psychological Association. Reprinted with permission.

36 would cross the deep side. Most infants of crawling age (typically 7 months or older) clearly perceive depth and are afraid of drop-offs.

But the testing procedure used by Gibson and Walk depended on the ability of infants to crawl. Would younger infants who cannot yet crawl be able to perceive a drop-off? Joseph Campos and his colleagues (Campos, Langer, & Krowitz, 1970) found that when they slowly lowered babies over the shallow and deep sides of the visual cliff, babies as young as 2 months had a slower heart rate on the deep side than on the shallow side. Why slower? When we are afraid, our hearts beat faster, not slower. A slow heart rate is a sign of interest. So, 2-month-old infants *perceive a difference* between the deep and the shallow sides of the visual cliff, but they have not yet learned to *fear* drop-offs.

Fear of drop-offs appears to be learned through crawling—and perhaps falling now and then, or at least coming close to it (Campos, Bertenthal, & Kermoian, 1992). Some beginning crawlers will shuffle right off the ends of beds or the tops of stairwells if they are not watched carefully. However, fear of drop-offs is stronger in infants who have logged a few weeks of crawling than in infants of the same age who do not yet crawl. Both maturation and normal experiences moving about contribute to the perception and interpretation of depth, it seems.

Organizing a World of Objects

Another challenge in perceptual development is to separate the visual field into distinct objects, even when parts of objects are hidden behind other objects. From an early age, infants show remarkable abilities to organize and impose order on visual scenes in much the same way that adults do. For example, Katherine Van Giffen and Marshall Haith (1984) reported that 3-month-olds, but not 1-month-olds, will focus their attention on a small irregularity in an otherwise well-formed circle or square pattern, as if they appreciated that it is a deviation from an otherwise well-formed and symmetrical pattern.

Infants must also determine where one object ends and another begins. Elizabeth Spelke and her colleagues (Kellman & Spelke, 1983; Spelke, 1990) have concluded that young infants are sensitive to several cues about the wholeness of objects, especially cues available when an object moves. For example, 4-month-olds seem to expect all parts of an object to move in the same direction at the same time, and they therefore use common motion as an important cue in determining what is or is not part of the same object (Kellman & Spelke, 1983). It takes infants longer, until about 6 months of age, to determine the boundaries or edges of stationary objects (Gibson & Pick, 2000). Amy Needham (1999) has found that 4-month-old babies, like adults, use object shape to figure out that two objects side by side are separate. They also use *good form* (for example, logical continuation of a line) to perceive an object's unity or wholeness (Johnson et al., 2000). Thus, babies appear to have an innate ability to organize a visual scene into distinct objects, and they are better able to make sense of a world in motion—a world like the one they live in—than to make sense of a stationary world.

The Infant as an Intuitive Theorist

That is not all. Researchers have been exploring infants' understandings of the physical laws that govern objects. For example, Elizabeth Spelke and her colleagues have been testing infants to determine what they know of Newtonian physics and the basic laws of object motion (Spelke & Hermer, 1996). Do babies know that a falling object will move downward along a continuous path until it encounters an obstruction? Spelke's studies suggest that infants only 4 months of age seem surprised when a ball dropped behind a screen is later revealed below a shelf rather than resting on it. They look longer at this "impossible" event than at the comparison event in which the ball's motion stops when it reaches a barrier. By 6 months, infants seem surprised when a ball drops behind a screen and then, when the screen is lifted, appears to be suspended in midair rather than lying at the bottom of the display unit (Kim & Spelke, 1992; Spelke et al., 1992). This hints that they know something about the laws of gravity. Do infants understand any other simple principles of physics? Yes; 4-month-olds watching a moving object disappear behind the left side of a screen seem to expect to see the object reappear from the right side of the screen (Bremner et al., 2005). And 4-month-olds are also surprised when a wide object disappears into a narrow container (Wang, Baillargeon, & Brueckner, 2004). By 6 months of age, infants understand that someone else must be able to perceive an object before that person can show a preference for that object or act upon that object (Luo & Johnson, 2009).

Such findings have led some developmentalists to conclude that young infants do more than just sense the world—they come equipped with organized systems of knowledge, called **intuitive theories**, which allow them to make sense of the world (Gelman, 1996; Wellman & Gelman, 1992). From an early age, children distinguish between the domains of knowledge adults know as physics, biology, and psychology. They organize their knowledge in each domain around causal principles and seem to understand that different causal forces operate in different domains (for example, that desires influence the behavior of humans but not of rocks). According to this intuitive theories perspective, young infants have innate knowledge of the world, and they perceive and even reason about it much as adults do. Coming to know the physical world is then a matter of fleshing out understandings they have had all along rather than constructing entirely new ones as they age (Spelke, 1994). All in all, it is clear that young infants know a good deal more about the world around them than anyone imagined, although they learn more as they get older.

Hearing

Hearing is at least as important to us as vision, especially because we depend on it to communicate with others through spoken language. As Anne Fernald (2004) notes, "while vision may be primary in enabling infants to learn about the physical world, audition plays a powerful role in initiating infants into a social world" (p. 37).

The process of hearing begins when moving air molecules enter the ear and vibrate the eardrum. These vibrations are transmitted to the cochlea in the inner ear and are converted to signals that the brain interprets as sounds.

Basic Capacities

Newborns can hear well—better than they can see. They can also localize sounds: they are startled by loud noises and will turn from them, but they will turn toward softer sounds (Field et al., 1980; Morrongiello et al., 1994). Even fetuses can hear some of what is going on in the world outside the womb as much as 3 months before birth (Saffran, Werker, & Werner, 2006). Researchers have detected changes in fetal heart rates that correspond to changes in sounds they are exposed to while in their mother's womb (Fifer, Monk, & Grose-Fifer, 2004; Saffran et al., 2006). Infants seem to prefer listening to auditory stimuli that are relatively complex, a finding that is consistent with the preference for moderate complexity that we saw with visual stimuli (Richard et al., 2004).

Although sensory impairments can change the course of normal life-span development, much can be done to help even those individuals born totally deaf or blind develop in positive directions and function effectively in everyday life. Let's briefly examine interventions for infants and children who have hearing impairments. Why tackle hearing impairments and not another sensory system? Because several estimates suggest that hearing impairments take a heavy toll on the individual and on society. Researchers at Johns Hopkins University, for example, estimate that more than $1 million will be spent over the lifetime of each infant or child who becomes deaf before acquiring language (Mohr et al., 2000).

For the 2 to 3 in 1000 infants born deaf or hearing impaired, early identification and treatment are essential if they are to master spoken language. Until recently, the average hearing-impaired child was not identified until age 2½ or older, usually when it became clear that his language skills had not developed normally (National Institutes of Health, 2006; Saffran, Werker, & Werner, 2006). Because children who receive no special intervention before age 3 usually have lasting difficulties with speech and language, most states have now mandated that all newborns be screened for hearing loss before they leave the hospital. How do you test the hearing of newborns? By using the auditory evoked potentials described at the beginning

of the chapter and determining whether sounds trigger normal activity in the brain. Infants' behaviors also give physicians clues about their hearing. Does she turn her head when spoken to? Does he react to loud noises? Is she soothed by your voice? If the answers to these questions are no, a more thorough examination is warranted.

Once hearing-impaired infants are identified, interventions can be planned. Many programs attempt to capitalize on whatever residual hearing these children have by equipping them with hearing aids. Today, even profoundly deaf children can be helped to hear through an advanced amplification device called the **cochlear implant** (see the photo in this box). The device is implanted in the inner ear through surgery and connected to a microphone worn outside the ear. It works by bypassing damaged hair cells (sensory receptors located in the inner ear) and directly stimulating the auditory nerve with electrical impulses.

Deaf children provided with cochlear implants by age 4 recognize more spoken words and speak more intelligibly than do children who receive them later in childhood, though even children given implants later in life can benefit (Harrison, Gordon, & Mount, 2005). Indeed, research shows that the rate of language development among children with cochlear implants is similar to that of children with normal hearing (Miyamoto,

Houston, & Bergeson, 2005; Schery & Peters, 2003). In addition, speech production and speech perception are improved in deaf children who have cochlear implants compared with deaf children who have traditional hearing aids, although performance still falls short of that of children with normal hearing (Houston et al., 2005; Schery & Peters, 2003). Performance is especially enhanced if there is earlier implantation and more auditory training following placement of the implant. Children with two cochlear implants—one in each ear—show additional benefits, particularly for localizing sounds (Godar, Grieco, & Litovsky, 2007). For some, cochlear implants have truly opened up new horizons that they thought were not possible before the implant (see, for example, Denworth, 2006; Mishori, 2006).

Why, then, are not all hearing-impaired children provided with cochlear implants? First, they require surgery and are expensive—although the expense of cochlear implants may be offset by educational savings down the road (Cheng et al., 2000). Also, despite their benefits, cochlear implants do not have the full support of the deaf community (Bollag, 2006; Tucker, 1998). Deaf children who use them, some say, will be given the message that they should be ashamed of being deaf. They will be deprived of participation in the unique culture that has developed in communities of deaf people who share a

Although the auditory sense is working before birth, infants appear to be a little less sensitive to very soft sounds than adults are (Saffran et al., 2006). As a result, a soft whisper may not be heard. Still, newborns can discriminate among sounds within their range of hearing that differ in loudness, duration, direction, and frequency or pitch, and these basic capacities improve rapidly during the first months of life (Fernald, 2004). In general, the sounds that penetrate the womb before birth are the ones that are the easiest for the infant to hear after birth (Elliot, 1999).

Speech Perception

Young infants seem to be well equipped to respond to human speech and, indeed, show a preference for speech over non-speech sounds (Vouloumanos & Werker, 2007). In many ways,

it seems as though the human brain was designed to produce and understand language (Byrnie, 2009). We can discriminate basic speech sounds—called **phonemes**—very early in life. Peter Eimas (1975b, 1985) pioneered research in this area by demonstrating that infants 2–3 months old could distinguish similar consonant sounds (for example, *ba* and *pa*). In fact, infants seem to detect the difference between the vowels *a* and *i* from the second day of life (Clarkson & Berg, 1983). They can even distinguish between standard sounds (those that occur regularly in a language) and deviant sounds (those that occur rarely) in the first few days of life (Ruusuvirta et al., 2003). By 3 months, they have developed a sound category system that allows them to recognize a phoneme even when it is spoken by different people (Marean, Werner, & Kuhl, 1992; Winkler et al., 2003). These are impressive accomplishments.

common language and identity. Because their hearing will still be far from normal, they may feel they do not belong to either the deaf or the hearing world (Arana-Ward, 1997; Fryauf-Bertschy et al., 1997).

The correct amplification device and auditory training has proven effective in improving the ability of hearing-impaired infants and preschoolers to hear speech and learn to speak. Yet for other deaf and severely hearing-impaired children, the most important thing may be early exposure to sign language. Early intervention programs for parents of deaf infants can teach them strategies for getting their infants' attention and involving them in conversations using sign (Chen, 1996). The earlier in life deaf children acquire some language system, whether spoken or signed, the better their command of language is likely to be later in life (Mayberry & Eichen, 1991). Deaf children whose parents are deaf and use sign language with them, as well as deaf children of hearing parents who participate in early intervention programs, generally show normal patterns of development, whereas children who are not exposed to any language system early in life suffer for it (Marschark, 1993).

Three-year-old Mustafa Ghazwan has just had his cochlear implant activated and will begin auditory training to learn how to interpret the impulses that it transmits to his auditory nerve.

© Kim Komenich/*San Francisco Chronicle/Corbis*

Infants can actually make some speech sound discriminations better than adults (Werker & Desjardins, 1995). They begin life biologically prepared to learn any language humans anywhere speak. As they mature, they become especially sensitive to the sound differences significant in their own language and less sensitive to sound differences irrelevant to that language. For example, young infants can easily discriminate the consonants *r* and *l* (Eimas, 1975a). So can adults who speak English, French, Spanish, or German. However, the Chinese and Japanese languages make no distinction between *r* and *l*, and adult native speakers of those languages cannot make this particular auditory discrimination as well as young infants can (Miyawaki et al., 1975). Similarly, infants raised in English-speaking homes can make discriminations important in Hindi but nonexistent in English, but English-speaking adults have trouble doing so (Werker et al., 1981).

By 1 year of age, when infants are just beginning to utter their first words, they have already become insensitive to contrasts of sounds that are not made in their native language (Rivera-Gaxiola, Silva-Pereyra, & Kuhl, 2005; Werker & Desjardins, 1995). Further, they show *increased* sensitivity to native language sounds (Kuhl et al., 2006). Their early auditory experiences have shaped the formation of neural connections, or synapses, in the auditory areas of their brains so that they are optimally sensitive to the sound contrasts that they have been listening to and that are important in the language they are acquiring (see Chapter 10).

Newborns are especially attentive to female voices (Ecklund-Flores & Turkewitz, 1996), but can they recognize their mother's voice? Indeed they can. Even unborn fetuses can distinguish their mother's voice from a stranger's voice. How do we know this? Canadian researchers measured fetal heart rate in response to a tape recording (played over the mother's stomach) of either their mother's voice or a stranger's voice (Kisilevsky et al., 2003). Heart rates increased in response to their mother's voice and decreased in response to the stranger's voice, indicating that fetuses detected a difference between the two. Newborns will learn to suck faster on a special pacifier when it activates a recording of the mother's voice (DeCasper & Fifer, 1980).

Does this early recognition extend to fathers' voices? Sorry, men, apparently not. Even by 4 months, infants show no preference for their father's voice over the voice of a strange man (Ward & Cooper, 1999). They can detect differences between various male voices, however, indicating that the lack of preference for the father's voice is not because of a failure to distinguish it.

Why would infants prefer their mother's but not their father's voice? We need to look at what is happening before birth to answer this. Anthony DeCasper and Melanie Spence (1986) had mothers recite a passage (for example, portions of Dr. Seuss's *The Cat in the Hat*) many times during the last 6 weeks of their pregnancies. At birth, the infants were tested to see if they would suck more to hear the story they had heard before birth or to hear a different story. Remarkably, they preferred the familiar story. Somehow these infants were able to recognize the distinctive sound pattern of the story they had heard in the womb. Auditory learning before birth could also explain why newborns prefer to hear their mother's voice to those of unfamiliar women but do not show a preference for their father's voice. They are literally bombarded with their mother's voice for months before birth, giving them ample opportunity to learn its auditory qualities.

So hearing is more developed than vision at birth. Infants can distinguish among speech sounds and recognize familiar sound patterns such as their mother's voice soon after birth. Within the first year, they lose sensitivity to sound contrasts insignificant in the language they are starting to learn, and they further refine their auditory perception skills. Unfortunately, some infants experience hearing problems, placing them at risk for language and communication problems. Application Box 6.1 examines the importance of early identification and treatment of hearing problems.

The Chemical Senses: Taste and Smell

Can newborns detect different tastes and smells? Both of these senses rely on the detection of chemical molecules; thus, the characterization of them as the "chemical senses." The sensory receptors for taste—taste buds—are located mainly on the tongue. In ways not fully understood, taste buds respond to chemical molecules and produce perceptions of sweet, salty, bitter, or sour tastes. At birth, babies can clearly distinguish sweet, bitter, and sour tastes and show a preference for sweets. Indeed, sugar water—but not plain water—may help calm babies who are experiencing mildly stressful events. Some research had even suggested that sugar water may help alleviate pain experienced by infants during routine tests, but more recent research disputes this (Marceau, Murray, & Nanan, 2009).

Different taste sensations also produce distinct facial expressions in the newborn. Newborns lick their lips and sometimes

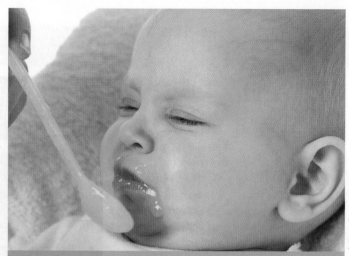

From birth, infants respond to tastes. In response to a sugar solution, newborns part their lips, lick their upper lips, make sucking movements, and sometimes smile. In response to bitter tastes, they purse their lips or open their mouths with the corners down and drool.

smile when they are tasting a sugar solution but purse their lips and even drool to get rid of the foul taste when they are given a bitter solution (Mennella et al., 2009; Steiner, 1979). Their facial expressions become increasingly pronounced as a solution becomes sweeter or more bitter, suggesting that newborns can discriminate different concentrations of a substance. Even before birth, babies show a preference for sweets when they swallow more amniotic fluid that contains higher concentrations of sugar than amniotic fluid with lower concentrations of sugar (Fifer, Monk, & Grose-Fifer, 2004).

Although we may have a general—and innate—preference for sweets and avoidance of bitters, flavor preferences are highly responsive to learning (Myers & Sclafani, 2006). Research by Julie Mennella and her colleagues (2004, 2006, 2009) suggests that food preferences may be influenced by early tastes that we are exposed to during infancy. Starting at 2 weeks of age, infants were fed one of two formulas for 7 months. One formula was bland, and the other was bitter and tasted sour, at least to most adults. After this period, the babies who had been fed the sour formula continued to consume it, but the other infants refused when it was offered to them. By 4–5 years, children fed the unpleasant-tasting formula were more likely to consume other sour-tasting foods (for example, a sour-flavored apple juice) than children exposed to only bland-tasting formula (Beauchamp & Mennella, 2009; Mennella & Beauchamp, 2002; Mennella et al., 2009).

Such research may be key to helping researchers understand why some people are picky eaters, whereas others are open to a wide variety of tastes. Greater exposure to a variety of flavors during infancy—what a breast-fed baby with a mother who eats many different foods might experience—may lead to a more adventuresome eater later on. These early experiences with different flavors may also extend to the prenatal period and

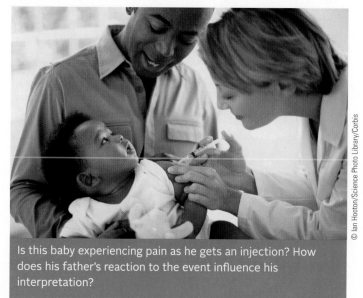

Is this baby experiencing pain as he gets an injection? How does his father's reaction to the event influence his interpretation?

Touch, Temperature, and Pain

Receptors in the skin detect touch or pressure, heat or cold, and painful stimuli. The sense of touch seems to be operating nicely before birth and, with the body senses that detect motion, may be among the first senses to develop (Elliot, 1999; Field, 1990). You saw in Chapter 5 that newborns respond with reflexes if they are touched in appropriate areas. For example, when touched on the check, a newborn will turn her head and open her mouth. Even in their sleep, newborns will habituate to strokes of the same spot on the skin but respond again if the tactile stimulation is shifted to a new spot—from the ear to the lips, for example (Kisilevsky & Muir, 1984). And like the motor responses described in Chapter 5, sensitivity to tactile stimulation develops in a cephalocaudal (head-to-toe) direction, so the face and mouth are more sensitive than lower parts of the body. No wonder babies like to put everything in their mouths—the tactile sensors in and around the mouth allow babies to collect a great deal of information about the world. Most parents quickly recognize the power of touch for soothing a fussy baby. Touch has even greater benefits: Premature babies who are systematically stroked over their entire body gain more weight and exhibit more relaxed behavior and more regular sleep patterns than premature babies who are not massaged (Field et al., 2006; Scafidi, Field, & Schanberg, 1993).

Newborns are also sensitive to warmth and cold; they can tell the difference between something cold and something warm placed on their cheeks (Elliot, 1999). Finally, young babies clearly respond to painful stimuli such as needle pricks. For obvious ethical reasons, researchers have not exposed infants to severely painful stimuli. However, analyses of babies' cries and facial movements as they receive injections and have blood drawn leave no doubt that these procedures are painful. Even premature babies show cortical responses to pain (Slater et al., 2006). And pain is responsive to learning. For example, researchers have compared infants born to diabetic mothers, who have their heels pricked every few hours after birth to test their blood sugar levels, with infants born to nondiabetic mothers (Taddio, 2002). Both groups of infants have blood drawn from the back of their hands before they leave the hospital so several routine tests can be conducted. The infants who have already had their heels pricked show a larger response to having blood drawn than the infants who have never experienced presumably painful needle pricks in their feet. Indeed, some infants who had already experienced the heel pricks began to grimace when the nurse prepared their skin for the needle prick, indicating that they had learned from their prior experiences that a painful moment was coming.

Such research challenges the medical wisdom of giving babies who must undergo major surgery little or no anesthesia. It turns out that infants are more likely to survive heart surgery if they receive deep anesthesia that keeps them unconscious during the operation and for a day afterward than if they receive light anesthesia that does not entirely protect them from the stressful experience of pain (Anand & Hickey, 1992). And the American Academy of Pediatrics (2000) recommends that local anesthesia be given to newborn males undergoing circumcision. Finally, breastfeeding during painful events such as getting a vaccination

exposure to different chemicals in the amniotic fluid (Fifer et al., 2004; see also Beauchamp & Mennella, 2009). Although learning plays a role in taste preferences, we cannot discount genetic predispositions. Discovery of a "taste gene" has shown that genetic variation can account for a lot of the variation in children and adults' perception of bitterness and some of the variation in children's perception of sweetness (Mennella, Pepino, & Reed, 2005).

The sensory receptors for smell, or **olfaction**, are located in the nasal passage. Like taste, the sense of smell is working well at birth. Newborns react vigorously to unpleasant smells such as vinegar or ammonia and turn their heads away (Rieser, Yonas, & Wilkner, 1976). Even premature babies (born at 28 weeks of gestation) are capable of detecting various odors. Newborns also reliably prefer the scent of their own amniotic fluid over that of other amniotic fluid, suggesting that olfactory cues are detectable prenatally (Schaal, Barlier, & Soussignan, 1998). Exposure to a familiar odor—their own amniotic fluid or their mother's breast milk—can also calm newborns, resulting in less crying when their mothers are absent or when they undergo a painful procedure (Nishitani et al., 2009; Rattaz, Goubet, & Bullinger, 2005). All babies also show a preference for the smell of human milk over formula, even if they have consumed only formula (Delaunay-El Allam, Marlier, & Schaal, 2006; Marlier & Schaal, 2005). Furthermore, babies who are breast-fed can recognize their mothers solely by the smell of their breasts or underarms within 1 or 2 weeks of birth (Cernoch & Porter, 1985; Porter et al., 1992; Vaglio, 2009). Babies who are bottle-fed cannot, probably because they have less contact with their mothers' skin. On the flip side, mothers can identify their newborns by smell, and they are less repulsed by the odor of their own infant's dirty diaper than by one from an unfamiliar infant (Case, Repacholi, & Stevenson, 2006; Porter, 1999). Thus, the sense of smell we often take for granted may help babies and their parents get to know each other.

or having blood drawn has been shown to reduce the behavioral signs that infants are experiencing pain with these events (Codipietro, Ceccarelli, & Ponzone, 2008).

You have now seen that each of the major senses is operating in some form at birth and that perceptual abilities improve dramatically during infancy. Let us ask one final question about infant perception: Can infants meaningfully integrate information from the different senses?

Integrating Sensory Information

It would obviously be useful for an infant attempting to understand the world to be able to put together information gained from viewing, fingering, sniffing, and otherwise exploring objects. It now seems clear that the senses function in an integrated way at birth. For instance, newborns will look in the direction of a sound they hear, suggesting that vision and hearing are linked. Moreover, infants 8–31 days old expect to feel objects that they can see and are frustrated by a visual illusion that looks like a graspable object but proves to be nothing but air when they reach for it (Bower, Broughton, & Moore, 1970). Thus, vision and touch, as well as vision and hearing, seem to be interrelated early in life. This integration of the senses helps babies perceive and respond appropriately to the objects and people they encounter (Hainline & Abramov, 1992; Walker-Andrews, 1997).

A more difficult task is to recognize through one sense an object familiar through another, a process called **cross-modal perception**. This capacity is required in children's games that involve feeling objects hidden in a bag and identifying what they are by touch alone. Some researchers (for example, Streri, 2003; Streri & Gentaz, 2004) report that newborns can recognize an object by sight that they had previously touched with their hand. But other researchers have had trouble demonstrating cross-modal perception in such young infants (for example, Maurer, Stager, & Mondloch, 1999). Apparently, early cross-modal perception is a fragile ability dependent on various task variables such as which hand is used to manipulate the object (Streri & Gentaz, 2004). Consistent oral-to-visual cross-modal transfer is shown by 3 months of age (illustrated by infants' ability to visually discriminate an object previously experienced by mouthing or sucking it), and other forms of cross-modal perception are reliably displayed at 4–7 months (Streri & Pecheux, 1986; Walker-Andrews, 1997). By that age, for example, infants integrate vision and hearing to judge distance; they prefer to look at an approaching train that gets louder and a departing one that gets quieter rather than at videos in which sound and sight are mismatched (Pickens, 1994). Nevertheless, performance on more complex cross-modal perception tasks that require matching patterns of sounds with patterns of visual stimuli continues to improve throughout childhood and even adolescence (Bushnell & Baxt, 1999).

Researchers now conclude that impressions from the different senses are "fused" early in life, much as William James believed, but they do not create the "blooming, buzzing confusion" he described. Rather, this early sensory integration may make it easier for babies to perceive and use information that comes to

Intersensory perception. The ability to recognize through one sense (here, touch) what has been learned through another (vision) increases with age during infancy and childhood. Here, the birthday girl must identify prizes in the bag by touch alone.

them through multiple channels simultaneously (Walker-Andrews, 1997). Then, as the separate senses continue to develop and each becomes a more effective means of exploring objects, babies become more skilled at cross-modal perception and are able to coordinate information gained through one sense with information gained through another.

Influences on Early Perceptual Development

The perceptual competencies of even very young infants are remarkable, as is the progress made within the first few months of life. All major senses begin working before birth and are clearly functioning at birth; parents would be making a huge mistake to assume that their newborn is not taking in the sensory world. Many perceptual abilities—for example, the ability to perceive depth or to distinguish melodies—emerge within just a few months of birth. Gradually, basic perceptual capacities are fine-tuned, and infants become more able to interpret their sensory experiences—to recognize a pattern of light as a face, for example. By the end of the second year, the most important aspects of perceptual development are complete. The senses and the mind are working to create a meaningful world of recognized objects, sounds, tastes, smells, and bodily sensations.

The fact that perceptual development takes place so quickly can be viewed as support for the "nature" side of the nature–nurture debate. Many basic perceptual capacities appear to be innate or to develop rapidly in all normal infants. What, then, is the role of early sensory experience in perceptual development?

Early Experience and the Brain

Classic studies that would ultimately lead to a Nobel Prize for David Hubel and Torsten Wiesel showed that depriving newborn kittens of normal visual experience by suturing one eye closed for 8 weeks resulted in a lack of normal connections between that eye and the visual cortex—and blindness even after the eye had been reopened (Hubel & Wiesel, 1970). Even as little as 1 week of deprivation during the critical period of the first 8 weeks of life can lead to permanent vision loss in the kitten (Kandel & Jessell, 1991). By contrast, depriving an adult cat's eye of light does not lead to permanent damage.

In humans, it is probably more accurate to characterize the effects of early experience on vision in terms of **sensitive periods** rather than critical periods (Armstrong et al., 2006). A sensitive period is "a window of time during which an individual is *more* affected by experience, and thus has a higher level of plasticity than at other times throughout life" (p. 326). Terri Lewis and Daphne Maurer (2005, 2009) provide evidence for multiple sensitive periods during which vision can be influenced by experience. First, there is the period they call visually driven normal development. This is when expected developmental changes in vision will occur with exposure to "normal" visual input; these changes will not occur if visual input is absent. Second, there is a sensitive period for damage; that is, there is a period when abnormal or absent visual input is likely to lead to permanent deficits in some aspect of vision. Third, there is a sensitive period for recovery when the visual system has the potential to recover from damage (Lewis & Maurer, 2005, p. 164).

Sensory experience is vital in determining the organization of the developing brain. Imagine what visual perception would be like in an infant who was blind at birth but later had surgery to permit vision. This is the scenario for perhaps 3 of every 5000 infants with congenital **cataracts**, a clouding of the lens that leaves these infants nearly blind from birth if it is not corrected. In the past, surgery to remove cataracts was often delayed until infants were older. But such delays meant that infants had weeks, months, or even years with little or no visual input. Consequently, some never developed normal vision even after the lens defect was removed.

It turns out that the visual system requires stimulation early in life, including patterned stimulation, to develop normally. Although the visual system has some plasticity throughout childhood, the first 3 months of life are considered critical (Lambert & Drack, 1996). During this time, the brain must receive clear visual information from both eyes. Unfortunately, not all infants with cataracts are identified early enough to benefit from surgery. One recent study found that even with visual screening programs for newborns before they leave the hospital, the vast majority of congenital cataracts are still not identified during the neonatal (first month) period (Sotomi et al., 2007). Early identification is essential. Identification and removal of cataracts by 10 weeks of age is associated with better long-term outcomes than identification and removal after this age (Lambert et al., 2006). Even after surgery restores their sight, these infants have difficulty, at least initially, perceiving their visual world clearly (Maurer, Mondloch, & Lewis, 2007). Acuity after surgery is what you might find in a newborn without cataracts—in other words, rather poor (Maurer et al., 1999). But it improves significantly during the month following surgery.

Years after corrective surgery, individuals who missed out on early visual experience because of congenital cataracts show normal visual abilities in some areas, such as sensitivity to low spatial frequencies (for example, wide stripes) and recognition of faces based on the *shape* of facial features. However, they struggle with certain other visual tasks, including the ability to distinguish between mid- and high spatial frequencies (for example, medium and narrow strips) as well as holistic face processing and recognizing faces based on *spacing* of facial features. What might account for this pattern?

Daphne Maurer and her colleagues (2007) argue that the lingering deficits reflect sleeper effects of early visual deficits. Thus, patterned visual input early in life is critical to developing later sensitivity to detail and holistic face processing. Even though these abilities do not normally develop until after early infancy—and after corrective surgery has been done—early visual deprivation likely affects the brain in a way that prevents infants from developing these abilities even when normal visual input is restored (Maurer et al., 2007). Clearly, then, early visual experiences influence later visual perception.

The same message about the importance of early experience applies to the sense of hearing: exposure to auditory stimulation early in life affects the architecture of the developing brain, which in turn influences auditory perception skills (Finitzo, Gunnarson, & Clark, 1990). Children with hearing impairments who undergo a cochlear implant, which bypasses damaged nerve cells in their inner ear, may struggle for months to understand the meaning of signals reaching their brain through the implant before they derive benefits (Allum et al., 2000; see also Application Box 6.1). Although the brain is being fed information, it must learn how to interpret these signals. Otherwise, the signals are a crashing jumble of nonsense that can be worse than not hearing (Colburn, 2000). The conclusion is clear: Maturation alone is not enough; normal perceptual development also requires normal perceptual experience. The practical implication is also clear: Visual and hearing problems in children should be detected and corrected as early in life as possible (Joint Committee on Infant Hearing, 2000).

The Infant's Active Role

Parents need not worry about arranging the right sensory environment for their children because young humans actively seek the stimulation they need to develop properly. Infants are active explorers and stimulus seekers; they orchestrate their own perceptual, motor, and cognitive development by exploring their environment and learning what it will allow them to do (Gibson, 1988; Gibson & Pick, 2000).

According to Eleanor Gibson (1988), infants proceed through three phases of exploratory behavior:

1. From birth to 4 months, infants explore their immediate surroundings, especially their caregivers, by looking and listening, and they learn a bit about objects by mouthing them and watching them move.
2. From 5 to 7 months, once the ability to voluntarily grasp objects has developed, babies pay far closer attention to objects, exploring objects with their eyes as well as with their hands.
3. By 8 or 9 months, after most have begun to crawl, infants extend their explorations into the larger environment and carefully examine the objects they encounter on their journeys, learning all about their properties. Whereas a 4-month-old infant may merely mouth a new toy and look at it now and then, a 12-month-old will give it a thorough examination—turning it, fingering it, poking it, and watching it intently (Ruff et al., 1992).

By combining perception and action in their exploratory behavior, infants actively create sensory environments that meet their needs and contribute to their own development (Eppler, 1995). As children become more able to attend selectively to the world around them, they become even more able to choose the forms and levels of stimulation that suit them best.

Cultural Variation

Do infants who grow up in different cultural environments encounter different sensory stimulation and perceive the world in different ways? Perceptual preferences obviously differ from culture to culture. In some cultures, people think heavier women are more beautiful than slim ones or relish eating sheep's eyeballs or chicken heads. Are more basic perceptual competencies also affected by socialization?

People from different cultures differ little in basic sensory capacities, such as the ability to discriminate degrees of brightness or loudness (Berry et al., 1992). However, their perceptions and interpretations of sensory input can vary considerably. For example, you have already seen that children become insensitive, starting at the end of the first year of life, to speech sound contrasts that they do not hear regularly because they are not important in their primary language. Michael Lynch and his associates (1990) have shown that the same is true for perceptions of music. Infants from the United States, they found, noticed equally notes that violated either Western musical scales or the Javanese

pelog scale. This suggests that humans are born with the potential to perceive music from a variety of cultures. However, American adults were less sensitive to bad notes in the unfamiliar Javanese musical system than to mistuned notes in their native Western scale, suggesting that their years of experience with Western music had shaped their perceptual skills.

Another example of cultural influence concerns the ability to translate perceptions of the human form into a drawing. In Papua New Guinea, where there is no cultural tradition of drawing and painting, children aged 10–15 who have had no schooling do not have much luck drawing the human body; they draw scribbles or tadpolelike forms far more often than children in the same society who have attended school and have been exposed many times to drawings of people (Martlew & Connolly, 1996; ■ Figure 6.4). We all have the capacity to create two-dimensional representations, but we apparently develop that capacity more rapidly if our culture provides us with relevant experiences. Many other examples of the effects of cultural learning experiences on visual and auditory perception can be cited (Berry et al., 1992).

■ **FIGURE 6.4** These human figures were drawn by children between the ages of 10 and 15. On the left, the drawings were made by children in Papua New Guinea, who often lack experience with drawing the human form and produce figures much like those done by far younger children (such as 4-year-olds) in the United States. The drawing on the right was made by a 12-year-old child in the United States. The contrast between the drawings on the left and the one on the right illustrates how cultural experience influences the ability to translate visual perceptions into representations on the page. SOURCE: From Human figure drawings by schooled and unschooled children in Papua New Guinea by M. Matthew and K. J. Connolly from *Child Development, 67*, p. 2743–2762. Reprinted by permission of John Wiley & Sons, Inc.

Checking Mastery

1. Describe two procedures used by researchers to assess perceptual abilities of infants.

2. During their first few months of life, what can infants see best?

3. What have we learned from DeCasper and Spence's "Cat in the Hat" study?

Making Connections

1. Drawing on your knowledge of the sensory and perceptual capacities of newborns, put yourself in the place of a newborn just emerging from the womb and describe your perceptual experiences.

2. How would you design a nursery for an infant to make the best use of his sensory and perceptual abilities?

6.3 The Child

There are some refinements of the sensory systems during childhood. For example, visual acuity improves to adult levels sometime between 4 and 6 years, and sensitivity to contrasts develops completely by about 7 years of age (Maurer et al., 2007). Recognition of odors improves between ages 6 and 11, at which point it reaches adult levels (Stevenson, Mahmut, & Sundqvist, 2007). For the most part, though, sensory and perceptual development is largely complete by the end of infancy. Is there anything left to accomplish during childhood? Mostly, sensory and perceptual development during this time is a matter of children learning to use their senses more intelligently. For example, children rapidly build knowledge of the world so that they can recognize and label what they sense, giving it greater meaning. As a result, it becomes even harder to separate perceptual development from cognitive development.

The Development of Attention

Much of perceptual development in childhood is really the development of **attention**—the focusing of perception and cognition on something in particular. Youngsters become better able to use their senses deliberately and strategically to gather the information most relevant to a task at hand.

Infants actively use their senses to explore their environment, and they prefer some sensory stimuli to others. Selective as they are, though, young infants do not deliberately choose to attend to faces and other engaging stimuli. Instead, a novel stimulus attracts their attention and, once their attention is "caught," they sometimes seem unable to turn away (Butcher, Kalverboer, & Geuze, 2000; Ruff & Rothbart, 1996). Thus, there is some truth to the idea that the attention of the infant or very young child is "captured by" something and that of the older child is "directed toward" something. This difference has been described as the difference between having an **orienting** system that reacts to events in the environment versus having a focusing system that deliberately seeks out and maintains attention to events (Ruff & Rothbart, 1996). As children get older, three things change: their attention spans become longer, they become more selective in what they attend to, and they are better able to plan and carry out systematic strategies for using their senses to achieve goals.

Longer Attention Span

If you have spent any time in the company of young children, then you are probably aware that they have short attention spans. Researchers know that they should limit their experimental sessions with young children to a few minutes, and nursery-school teachers often switch classroom activities every 15–20 minutes. Even when they are doing things they like, such as watching a television program or playing with a toy, 2- and 3-year-olds spend far less time concentrating on the program or the toy than older children do (Ruff & Capozzoli, 2003; Ruff & Lawson, 1990). In one study of sustained attention, children were asked to put strips of colored paper in appropriately colored boxes (Yendovitskaya, 1971). Children aged 2–3 worked for an average of 18 minutes and were easily distracted, whereas children aged 5–6 often persisted for 1 hour or more. Further improvements in sustained attention occur from ages 5–6 to ages 8–9 as those parts of the brain involved with attention become further myelinated (Betts et al., 2006). Beyond ages 8–9 there is not much increase in length of sustained attention, but children do become more accurate on tasks requiring sustained attention over the next few years (Betts et al., 2006).

More Selective Attention

Although infants clearly deploy their senses in a selective manner, they are not good at controlling their attention—deliberately concentrating on one thing while ignoring something else, or what is known as **selective attention**. With age, attention becomes more selective and less susceptible to distraction. As infants approach 2 years, they become able to form plans of action, which then guide what they focus on and what they ignore (Ruff & Rothbart, 1996).

Research suggests that preschool children have an adultlike orienting system but an immature focusing system of attention (Ristic & Kingstone, 2009). Between approximately 3½ and 4 years, there is a significant increase in focused attention. Kathleen Kannass and John Colombo (2007) tested 3½- and 4-years-olds while they worked on a task under one of three conditions: no distraction, constant distraction (a TV program in an unfamiliar language played continuously in the background), or intermittent distraction (the same TV program played in the background but was frequently turned on and off as the children worked). Among the 3½-year-olds, the two groups working with any distraction had more trouble completing their task than the group working without distraction. Among the 4-year-olds, only the group working with constant distraction had trouble finishing the task. Those working with intermittent distraction were able to stay as focused on the task as children working without distraction. Finally, the researchers found that when a distracter was present, looking away from their task led to worse performance, whereas looking away when there was no distraction did not impair performance. These findings should suggest to parents and teachers of young children that performance will be better if distractions in task materials and in the room are kept to a minimum. In particular, the presence of a continuous distracter will lead to trouble completing tasks (Kannass & Colombo, 2007).

More Systematic Attention

Finally, as they age, children become more able to plan and carry out systematic perceptual searches. You have already seen that older infants are more likely than younger ones to thoroughly explore a pattern. Research with children in the former Soviet Union reveals that visual scanning becomes considerably more detailed and exhaustive over the first 6 years of life (Zaporozhets, 1965). But the most revealing findings come from studies of how children go about a visual search. In general, children search more slowly than adults (Donnelly et al., 2007) but they are also less efficient. Elaine Vurpillot (1968) recorded the eye movements of 4- to 10-year-olds trying to decide whether two houses, each with several windows containing various objects, were identical or different. As ■ **Figure 6.5** illustrates, children ages 4 and 5 were not systematic. They often looked at only a few windows and, as a result, came to wrong conclusions. In contrast, most children older than 6 were very systematic; they typically checked each window in one house with the corresponding window in the other house, pair by pair. For most, improvements in visual search continue to be made throughout childhood and into early adulthood (Burack et al., 2000). For some, performance will be affected by attention problems, as we'll see in the next section.

Problems of Attention

Upon entering high school I was determined to make high honor roll every quarter. It didn't quite work out that way though. . . . I was completely lost. I couldn't focus on work, I couldn't pay attention in class, and I couldn't concentrate on homework, rarely completing it as a result. Emotionally, I didn't really know how to handle it. I was completely frustrated because I didn't understand why I was having such trouble. . . . My teachers knew I had the potential to do well, but they just figured I was lazy and not motivated. My parents were angry with me because my teachers told them I never did my homework. Nobody understood that it wasn't because I was lazy or not motivated; I really did care about my grades.

I would try to sit down and write a paper, but there were too many thoughts in my head and too many things going on around me to even get a paragraph down. I would sit in the front row of my math class, with my notebook open and ready to take notes, but then something would catch my eye out the window and I'd miss the whole lesson. (Stone, 2009)

In this story, Rachel Stone describes her struggles with sustaining and focusing her attention, illustrating a key feature of one of the most commonly diagnosed developmental disorders. Someone has **attention deficit hyperactivity disorder (ADHD)** if some combination of the following three symptoms is present (DSM-IV TR; see also Selikowitz, 2009; Weyandt, 2007):

1. *Inattention.* The child does not seem to listen, is easily distracted, has trouble following instructions, does not stick to activities or finish tasks, and tends to be forgetful and unorganized.
2. *Impulsivity.* The child acts before thinking and cannot inhibit urges to blurt something out in class or conversations or have a turn in a group activity.
3. *Hyperactivity.* The child is restless, perpetually fidgeting, finger tapping, or chattering, and has trouble remaining seated at desk.

5-year-old: "The same"

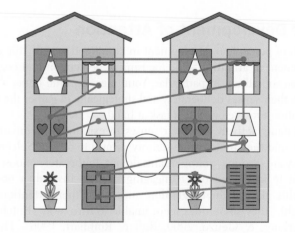

8-year-old: "Not the same"

■ **FIGURE 6.5** Are the houses in each pair identical or different? As indicated by the lines, 8-year-olds are more likely than 5-year-olds to answer correctly because they systematically scan the visual features of the two pictures. SOURCE: Adapted from Vurpillot, 1968.

Many children with attention problems appear to be daydreaming or "spaced out" in settings that require selective or sustained attention.

© Wolfgang Flamisch/Corbis

Somewhere between 5 and 9% of school-age children meet the diagnostic criteria for ADHD (Froehlich et al., 2007; Polancyzk et al., 2007) and at least two boys for every girl have the disorder, although girls may be underdiagnosed because they often do not show as much of the hyperactivity and acting out associated with ADHD as boys do (Weyandt, 2007). Because behaviors of hyperactivity are more easily observable, children with predominantly hyperactivity-impulsivity symptoms are diagnosed around age 8, 2 years earlier than those children with predominantly inattention symptoms (Mayo Clinic, 2009; Weyandt, 2007). The inattentive subtype of ADHD is roughly twice as common as the hyperactive-impulsive subtype (Froehlich et al., 2007).

Developmental Course

ADHD expresses itself differently at different ages. When the predominant symptom is hyperactivity-impulsivity, the condition often reveals itself in infancy. As infants, children with ADHD are typically very active, have difficult temperaments, and show irregular feeding and sleeping patterns (Teeter, 1998). As preschool children, they are in perpetual motion, quickly moving from one activity to another. Because most young children are energetic and have short attention spans, behavior must be evaluated in relation to developmental norms; otherwise, we might mistake most average 3- and 4-year-olds for hyperactive children. Finally, by the grade-school years, overactive behavior is less of a problem, but children with ADHD are fidgety, restless, and inattentive to schoolwork (American Psychiatric Association, 2000).

What becomes of hyperactive children later in life? It used to be thought that they outgrew their problems, so parents sometimes delayed getting help, expecting their children's difficulties to go away by adolescence. Most children with ADHD do outgrow their overactive behavior (DuPaul & Stoner, 2003). However, as illustrated by Rachel's story, adolescents with ADHD continue to be restless, to have difficulty concentrating on their academic work, and to behave impulsively; they often perform poorly in school or drop out, and they are prone to committing reckless delinquent acts without thinking about the consequences (Brassett-Harknett & Butler, 2007).

The picture is somewhat more positive by early adulthood; yet many individuals with ADHD get in trouble because they have lapses of concentration, make impulsive decisions, and procrastinate (Brassett-Harknett & Butler, 2007; Schmidt & Petermann, 2009). In one study following hyperactive and control children from about age 7 to age 21, the hyperactive adults had lower educational attainment and achievement, had been fired more and received lower performance ratings from their employers, had fewer close friends and more problems in social relations, and had become involved in sexual activity and parenthood earlier (Barkley et al., 2006). Outcomes were especially poor for those who had conduct disorders (see Chapter 13) along with their ADHD as children; this subgroup is also likely to have more than its share of car accidents and law breaking, to abuse alcohol and drugs, and to have emotional problems as adults (Schmidt & Petermann, 2009; Selikowitz, 2009). The more severe the ADHD symptoms and associated problems such as aggression in childhood, the more likely it is that later life outcomes will be poor (Pelham et al., 2004). Overall, an estimated 20% of ADHD children outgrow their problems, 20% continue to have severe problems as adults, and 60% continue to have at least mild problems throughout their lives (Selikowitz, 2009). More than 4% of adults in the United States appear to have diagnosable ADHD, and many could benefit from treatment (Kessler et al., 2006). Complete the short assessment in Engagement Box 6.1 to determine whether you have behaviors characteristic of adult ADHD.

Suspected Causes

What causes this disorder? Researchers have long agreed that ADHD has a neurological basis, but they have had difficulty pinpointing it until recently. No consistent evidence of brain damage or of structural defects in the brain is found in most children with ADHD. It is widely agreed, though, that the brains of children with ADHD work differently than the brains of other children and that the cause is most likely differences in brain chemistry rather than physical brain damage. Russell Barkley (1997, 2000) put forth the view that the frontal lobes of individuals with ADHD do not function properly, resulting in deficien-

Check the box that best describes how you have felt and conducted yourself over the past 6 months.

	Never	Rarely	Sometimes	Often	Very Often
1. How often do you have trouble wrapping up the final details of a project once the challenging parts have been done?					
2. How often do you have difficulty getting things in order when you have to do a task that requires organization?					
3. How often do you have problems remembering appointments or obligations?					
4. When you have a task that requires a lot of thought, how often do you avoid or delay getting started?					
5. How often do you fidget or squirm with your hands or feet when you have to sit down for a long time?					
6. How often do you feel overly active and compelled to do things, like you were driven by a motor?					

Add up the number of check marks in the shaded boxes. If you have four or more checks in the shaded boxes, then you may want to talk to a professional about your behaviors and feelings to determine if you might have adult ADHD. Remember that this self-assessment is not a definitive diagnosis and needs follow-up if your answers are suggestive of ADHD.

SOURCE: Adapted from the World Health Organization's 18-question Adult ADHD Self-Report Scale, Version 1.1 (Adult ASRS-V1.1), Symptom Checklist. ASRS-V1.1 Screener Copyright © 2003 World Health Organization (WHO). Reprinted by permission.

cies in executive functions, most importantly difficulty inhibiting and otherwise regulating one's behavior. This view has received a good deal of support, although not all individuals with ADHD show executive function impairments and not all executive functions are impaired (Seidman, 2006). Low levels of the neurotransmitters dopamine and norepinephrine, which are involved in communication among neurons in the frontal lobes, may be at the root of executive function impairments (Selikowitz, 2009; Weyandt, 2007).

Genes predispose some individuals to develop ADHD and probably underlie the physiological problems that give rise to it. One identical twin is highly likely to have it if the other does, and first-degree relatives of someone with ADHD (including parents)

have 4 to 5 times the usual risk (Thapar, 2003). Genes account for 60–90% of the variation in ADHD among individuals, non-shared environmental factors for the rest (Franke, Neale, & Faraone, 2009; Waldman & Gizer, 2006). There is not one ADHD gene, however. Instead, researchers have identified several gene variants common in individuals with ADHD that influence levels of dopamine, serotonin, and other relevant neurotransmitters in their brains (Smith, Mick & Faraone, 2009; Waldman & Gizer, 2006).

Environmental influences are also important, not so much as the main cause of ADHD but as forces that help determine whether a genetic potential turns into a reality and whether the individual adapts well or poorly as she develops (Brassett-Harknett

& Butler, 2007). Misconceptions that ADHD is due to consuming sugar or food additives such as red food coloring have long been put to rest, although allergies are an issue for a small number of children with ADHD (Weyandt, 2007). Carefully controlled studies comparing diets with and without the suspected culprit foods typically offer no support for diet theories. Low birth weight and maternal smoking and alcohol use during pregnancy, both associated with a shortage of oxygen prenatally, do appear to contribute to some cases of ADHD (Banerjee, Middleton, & Faraone, 2007; Lehn et al., 2007). And genes and environment may interact: individuals who inherit genes that adversely affect dopamine levels and who also experience family adversity show more ADHD symptoms than children who do not have both genes and environment working against them (Laucht et al., 2007).

Treatment

Many children with ADHD are given stimulant drugs such as methylphenidate (Ritalin), and most are helped by these drugs. Although it may seem odd to give overactive children stimulants, the brains of individuals with ADHD are actually under-aroused. These drugs increase levels of dopamine and other neurotransmitters in the frontal lobes of the brain to normal levels and, by doing so, allow these children to concentrate (Selikowitz, 2009). Listen to Rachel, who described her struggles with attention at the beginning of this section, on her transformation with stimulant medication:

> After hitting rock bottom the middle of sophomore year, I was finally retested for ADD. I was put on the medication Adderall one month before sophomore year concluded. I was able to pull up all my grades and end up with an eighty-five for my fourth quarter average, making the honor roll for the first time in my high school career.
>
> Things only got better with junior year. My second quarter average was twenty points higher than it was second quarter of sophomore year. I feel that my best achievement was in math. I almost didn't pass math sophomore year, and almost didn't take it junior year because I didn't think it would be worth it. With the Adderall, I was able to focus in class and remember how much I liked math! I ended up with the highest average in the pre-calculus classes, a 100% homework average for the year; I also received the 11th grade math award for achievement and effort (Stone, 2009).

Why, then, does controversy surround the use of stimulants with ADHD children? Some critics feel that these drugs are prescribed to too many children, including some who do not have ADHD (Mayes, Bagwell, & Erkulwater, 2009). Although it is probably true that Ritalin and other stimulants are overprescribed in some communities, it is also true that many children with ADHD who could benefit from drug treatment go untreated. Others are concerned that stimulant drugs have undesirable side effects such as loss of appetite and headaches (see Mayes et al., 2009). Moreover, they do not cure ADHD; they improve functioning only until their effects wear off. And so far, there is not much evidence that individuals with ADHD who took stimulants as children function better as adolescents or adults than those who did not, although some studies are beginning to show beneficial longer-term effects on attention and behavior (Mayes et al., 2009).

Many experts have concluded that stimulant drugs cannot resolve all the difficulties faced by individuals with ADHD and their families but that they are part of the answer, not only in childhood but continuing into adulthood.

Might behavioral treatment work better than drug treatment? The Multimodal Treatment of Attention Deficit Hyperactivity Disorder Study (MTA), a national study of 579 children with ADHD ranging in age from 7 to 9, is the best source of information about the pros and cons of medication and behavioral treatment for ADHD (Jensen et al., 2001). This study compared children who received optimally delivered medication, state-of-the-art behavioral treatment (a combination of parent training, child training through a summer program, and school intervention), a combination of the two approaches, or routine care in the community. The findings were clear: Medication alone was more effective than behavioral treatment alone or routine care in reducing ADHD symptoms (see also Scheffler et al., 2009). However, a combination of medication and behavioral treatment was superior to medication alone when the goal was defined as not only reducing ADHD symptoms but also improving academic performance, social adjustment, and parent–child relations. Continued follow-up of children who had been in the MTA study has raised questions about the long-term effectiveness of medication treatment versus other treatments, leading one of the authors to conclude that medication must be carefully monitored so that it is prescribed at optimal levels and at optimal times during the course of the disorder (Jensen et al., 2007). Most experts agree that a coordinated effort is needed for the best outcomes. This includes behavioral programs designed to teach children with ADHD to stay focused on tasks, control their impulsiveness, and interact socially; parent training designed to help parents understand and manage the behavior of these often-difficult youngsters; and interventions at school to structure the learning environment (Chronis, Jones, & Raggi, 2006; Weyandt, 2007).

Checking Mastery

1. What are three ways that attention improves during childhood?
2. What three behavioral symptoms characterize ADHD?

Making Connections

1. You have an unlimited budget for redesigning a local child care center that serves children 6 weeks to 6 years old. Given what you know about sensory and perceptual capabilities of infants and young children, what equipment and toys will you purchase, and how will you remodel and redecorate the rooms?

2. Some experts believe that ADHD is overdiagnosed and overtreated with medications. There are others, however, who believe that not enough cases of ADHD are being identified and treated. What is your position on diagnosis and treatment of ADHD? Can you support your position with facts?

6.4 The Adolescent

There is little news to report about sensation, attention, and perception during adolescence, except that some developments of childhood are not completed until then. Several issues during this time, though, warrant discussion: refinements in attention, potential insults to hearing from exposure to loud noise, and expanding taste horizons.

Attention

It is fairly clear that adolescents have longer attention spans than children. They can, for example, sit through longer classes, work on papers or study for lengthier periods of time, and take tests that last as long as 3–4 hours (for example, the SAT). The ability to sustain attention improves considerably between childhood and adulthood (McKay et al., 1994). This seems to be tied to increased myelination of those portions of the brain that help regulate attention (Tanner, 1990). As we noted in Chapter 5, a myelin coating on neurons helps insulate them to speed up transmission of neural impulses.

In addition, adolescents become still more efficient at ignoring irrelevant information so that they can concentrate on the task at hand. Not only do they learn more than children do about material they are supposed to master, but they also learn *less* about distracting information that could potentially interfere with their performance (Miller & Weiss, 1981). Children have the rudimentary skills to adapt to distractions, but compared with adolescents and adults, they are slowed down and more likely to be thrown off track by distracters.

Similarly, adolescents can divide their attention more systematically between two tasks. For instance, Andrew Schiff and Irwin Knopf (1985) watched the eye movements of 9-year-olds and 13-year-olds during a two-part visual search task. Children were to push a response key when particular symbols appeared at the center of a screen and to remember letters flashed at the corners of the screen. The adolescents developed efficient strategies for switching their eyes from the center to the corners and back at the right times. The 9-year-olds had an unfortunate tendency to look at blank areas of the screen or to focus too much attention on the letters in the corners of the screen, thereby failing to detect the symbols in the center.

Hearing

Adolescence should be a period of optimal acuity of all the senses, but in today's world of rock concerts, MP3 players, power equipment, and so on, auditory acuity can become compromised in some adolescents. As ●Table 6.1 shows, loud sounds—those above 75 decibels—may leave the listener with a loss of hearing. Fans of loud music, beware: The noise at rock concerts and nightclubs is often in the 120-decibel to 130-decibel range, well above the level where damage may occur. And if you can hear the music coming from the headset of your friend's iPod or other MP3 player, your friend may be damaging her hearing.

Adolescents are skilled at dividing their attention among several tasks. What are the pros and cons of such multitasking?

The most common outcome of noise exposure is **tinnitus**, or ringing sounds in one or both ears that can last for days, weeks, or indefinitely. A majority—as many as 85%—of concert attendees report experiencing tinnitus (Bogoch, House, & Kudla, 2005; Chung et al., 2005). Hearing problems associated with short periods of exposure to loud sounds may be temporary, but damage

● TABLE 6.1 NOISE LEVELS

Noise	Number of Decibels
Whisper	30
Quiet room	40
Normal speech	60
City traffic	80
Lawnmower	90
Rock concerts	110–140
Jet plane takeoff	120
Jackhammer	130
Firearm discharge	140

The healthy ear can detect sounds starting at 0 decibels. Damage to hearing can start between 75 and 80 decibels and is more likely with long-term exposure to loud sounds.

from regular exposure to these same sounds can accumulate over time, leading to moderate or even severe hearing loss by adulthood.

Many teens report that they are aware of the potential for hearing loss from exposure to loud sounds, but they do not believe that hearing loss is a serious health concern for them (Chung et al., 2005). Thus, despite their awareness that noise exposure can lead to hearing loss and warnings from parents and health officials that noise can be hazardous, teens do little to protect their hearing because hearing loss is not perceived as an important issue. Few wear earplugs at concerts or ear protectors when operating power equipment (Bogoch et al., 2005; Chung et al., 2005). Part of the problem is the perception that ear protection is not "cool." Teens who are more open to behavioral change and those who are less concerned about appearance are more willing to use ear protection (Bogoch et al., 2005). In addition, teens from higher socioeconomic backgrounds tend to rate noise exposure as more negative, and therefore are more open to ear protection, than teens from lower socioeconomic backgrounds (Widén & Erlandsson, 2004; Widén et al., 2009).

Educational programs to improve hearing protection among teens need to focus on several issues to be effective. They need to help teens recognize that there may be long-term consequences of noise exposure; damage to the auditory system can accumulate over time. Second, they need to address teens' perception that hearing loss is not an important health issue. Until hearing is perceived as a priority, teens and others will have little motivation to protect this sensory system. And finally, education programs need to reduce the stigma associated with wearing hearing protection so teens feel comfortable making the decision to protect their hearing when they are in settings with loud noise.

Another Look at the Chemical Senses

Taste

Earlier, we introduced four basic tastes (sweet, sour, bitter, and salty) and discussed how smell contributes to the taste of foods. Now we take our discussion of the chemical senses a few steps further and consider whether there are any noticeable changes in taste during adolescence.

Many researchers believe that there is a fifth taste, called **umami** from a Japanese word that roughly translates to "savory" or "brothy." Umami is associated with the amino acid glutamate, which is often found in proteins and can be purchased in concentrated form in little containers of MSG found in the spice aisle of your local grocery store. By itself, glutamate is not very tasty, but when combined with certain odors, it is perceived as a delicious flavor (Rolls, 2009). People have varying degrees of sensitivity to the umami flavor, which seems to be determined by genes (Beauchamp, 2009; Stein, 2009). This may help explain why some people enjoy protein-rich foods more than other people.

In addition, it turns out that your sense of taste is mediated by more than smell and taste receptors on the tongue. It is also determined by something called "chemosensory irritation," which is the reaction of your skin—in your mouth and nose—to certain chemical compounds of foods (Beauchamp & Mennella, 2009). When you feel the burn from hot peppers, the cooling sensation from menthol, or the tingle from a carbonated beverage, you are experiencing chemosensory irritation. This irritation of your skin contributes to your experience of a food, with, for example, some people reporting that they love to "feel the burn" of hot peppers and others completely turned off by it.

Taste is also influenced by cognition: You taste what you expect to taste. From past experience, we learn to associate certain features of food with certain tastes. For instance, brightly colored juices are thought to be tastier than their pale counterparts, even when the juices are identical other than the addition of a few drops of artificial coloring to some (Hoegg & Alba, 2007). Thus, we see a bright orange liquid in a cup and we believe that this will be more flavorful than a pale orange liquid.

Research suggests that taste undergoes several changes during adolescence. First, there is a slight decline in preference for sweets and an increased sensitivity to—and liking of—sour tastes (University of Copenhagen, 2008). A preference for sour tastes, or at least a tolerance for sour tastes, is associated with willingness to try new foods and expand food horizons. This slight shift in an adolescent's taste palette leads to another difference between the child and adolescent: Adolescents are more likely to have an *acquired taste* for previously disliked or avoided foods. Most children may not enjoy, for example, eating snails (escargot) or fried squid (calamari), but many adolescents and adults have learned that these items can be quite tasty! Teenagers are more likely to enjoy foods with strong or strange tastes because they have had more opportunity to "acquire" these tastes through multiple exposures. Teenagers loosen up on the childhood tendency to reject new foods, and they are more open to experimenting with foods that may have odd textures or odors (Segovia et al., 2002). Of course, there are large individual differences in taste, with some teenagers enjoying very hot, spicy foods and others rejecting anything that has just a tiny amount of spice. Take the test in Engagement Box 6.2 to see if you might be a supertaster who is more sensitive to low levels of chemicals hitting your taste receptors.

Smell

Interestingly, gender differences play a role in the sense of smell during adolescence and adulthood, with women generally demonstrating greater sensitivity than men to a variety of odors (Doty & Cameron, 2009; Hummel et al., 2007). This may reflect hormonal differences between men and women and the effect of different hormonal patterns on detection and interpretation of the chemicals that comprise odors. Moreover, among women, hormonal changes seem to influence sensitivity to different smells (Lundström, McClintock, & Olsson, 2006). Women who are fertile may use odor as part of their criteria for selecting a desirable mate, judging the body odor of some men—those who have symmetrical or balanced physical features—as more desirable than the body odor of other men during the time they are ovulating (Foster, 2008; Yamazaki & Beauchamp, 2007). Symmetry (having balanced features) may be a biological marker of better health.

Approximately 25% of the adult population has substantially more taste receptors than the other 75%, making them super sensitive to tastes (see Taste Science, 2010). The definitive supertaster test consists of a small paper filter that is infused with a special chemical. When placed on the tongue of a supertaster, it is perceived as incredibly bitter, but tastes bland or mildly bitter to those without the supertaster gene. Your answers to the following questions will give you an estimate of whether you might be a supertaster.

1. Do you enjoy or despise grapefruit juice?
2. Do you like milk chocolate or dark chocolate?
3. Do you hate raw broccoli or Brussels sprouts or think these veggies are okay or even good?
4. As a child, did you eat lots of vegetables?
5. Do you often think that desserts or cookies are too sweet while others report that the same foods taste just right?

Supertasters are likely to have a strong dislike for the bitter tastes of grapefruit juice, dark chocolate, or raw broccoli/Brussels sprouts. As children, supertasters avoided vegetables because they tasted "too strong." Supertasters are likely to think that too much sweetener has been used in foods and would prefer less sugar. To follow up, you can perform this relatively simple test using a drop of blue food coloring and a small piece of wax paper that you have punched with a single hole–puncher. Place a few drops of the blue food coloring on your tongue. Place the wax paper that has the hole punched in it over the blue patch on your tongue. Now carefully count the little pink circles that are within the circle. If you have a lot (25 or more) of little pink circles, then you have more than the average number of papillae and are a supertaster (each papillae contains 6–15 taste buds). If you have very few pink circles (less than 6), then you are a nontaster and are probably insensitive to bitter and other strong tastes. Anything between these two extremes is where most of us (50%) fall. With our average number of papillae, we enjoy most foods and don't find them too bitter or too sweet, but also don't find them bland.

© Koval Image Creation/Getty Images

This tongue has an average number of papillae, or bumps containing taste buds. The tongue of a "supertaster" would have as many as twice the papillae seen here.

Men, too, may use differences in women's body odors as a component of mate selection, rating odor during ovulation as more pleasant than odor at other times of women's menstrual cycles (Singh & Bronstad, 2001). Evolutionary theory would predict that men and women want to select a mate who is healthy and capable of reproduction, and odor may provide some clues in this regard. Both men and women report that odor is an important consideration in choosing romantic partners, even though most cannot clearly articulate what constitutes a "good" or a "bad" smelling person (Sergeant et al., 2005). But if you are out with a woman, be forewarned: Women are more sensitive to body odor than men, and it is more difficult to cover up body odor so that women do not detect it, whereas perfumes and other cover-ups often fool men (Wysocki et al., 2009). We learned earlier that babies and their mothers can recognize one another through smell. Now we see that odor is also important in later relationships, perhaps serving as a filter to allow some people to get close and discourage others.

Checking Mastery

1. What concerns might we have regarding hearing during the adolescent years?
2. What are two observations regarding the chemical senses during adolescence?

Making Connections

1. You are a tutor and want a 5-year-old and a 13-year-old to systematically compare pairs of maps to determine whether they are similar or different. What can you expect of each child, and what can you do to optimize the performance of the younger child?

2. Design an educational unit for a high school health class that is aimed at reducing the incidence of noise-induced hearing loss.

6.5 The Adult

What becomes of sensory and perceptual capacities during adulthood? There is good news and bad news, and we might as well dispense with the bad news first: Sensory and perceptual capacities decline gradually with age in the normal person. Whispers become harder to hear, seeing in the dark becomes difficult, food may not taste as good, and so on. Often these declines begin in early adulthood and become noticeable in the 40s, sometimes giving middle-aged people a feeling that they are getting old. Further declines take place in later life, to the point that you would have a hard time finding a person age 65 or older who does not have at least a mild sensory or perceptual impairment. The good news is that these changes are gradual and usually minor. As a result, we can usually compensate for them, making small adjustments such as turning up the volume on the TV set or adding a little extra seasoning to food. Because the losses are usually not severe, and because of the process of compensation, only a minority of old people develop serious problems such as blindness and deafness.

The losses we are describing take two general forms. First, sensation is affected, as indicated by raised **sensory thresholds**. The threshold for a sense is the point at which low levels of stimulation can be detected—a dim light can be seen, a faint tone can be heard, a slight odor can be detected, and so on. Stimulation below the threshold cannot be detected, so the rise of the threshold with age means that sensitivity to very low levels of stimulation is lost. (You saw that the very young infant is also insensitive to some very low levels of stimulation.)

Second, perceptual abilities decline in some aging adults. Even when stimulation is intense enough to be well above the detection threshold, older people sometimes have difficulty processing or interpreting sensory information. As you will see, they may have trouble searching a visual scene, understanding rapid speech in a noisy room, or recognizing the foods they are tasting.

So sensory and perceptual declines are typical during adulthood, although they are far steeper in some individuals than in others and can often be compensated for. These declines involve both a rise of thresholds for detecting stimulation and a weakening of some perceptual abilities.

Vision

We begin with a question that concerns many people as they get older: Will I lose my eyesight? For most people, the answer is no. Fewer than 2% of adults older than 70 are blind

TABLE 6.2 PERCENTAGE OF ADULTS 70 YEARS AND OLDER WHO EXPERIENCE VISION PROBLEMS

Vision Condition	Percentage of Adults 70 and Older
Cataract(s)	57%
Visual Impairment	20%
Glaucoma	9%
Macular Degeneration	6%
Retinopathy from Diabetes	4%
Workplace Eye Injury	4%

Source: Adapted from *MMWR Weekly*, 2006b.

in both eyes, and only 4.4% are blind in one eye, but these numbers increase as we go through our 80s and 90s (Campbell et al., 1999). Although most adults will not be blind, many experience some vision problems as shown in ●Table 6.2. In particular, more than half of older adults develop cataracts, or cloudiness of the normally clear lens. Why do these changes in the visual system occur, and is there anything you can do to prevent losses? Before we answer these questions, we need to briefly review the basic workings of the visual system.

As ■Figure 6.6 shows, light enters the eye through the cornea and passes through the pupil and lens before being projected (upside down) on the retina. From here, images are relayed to the brain by the optic nerve at the back of each eye. The pupil of the eye automatically becomes larger or smaller depending on the lighting conditions, and the lens changes shape, or accommodates, to keep images focused on the retina. In adolescents and young adults, the visual system is normally at peak performance. Aging brings changes to all components of the visual system.

Changes in the Pupil

As we age, our pupils become somewhat smaller and do not change as much when lighting conditions change. As a result, older adults experience greater difficulty when lighting is dim, when it is bright, and when it suddenly changes. Approximately one-third of adults older than 85 exhibit a tenfold loss of the ability to read low-contrast words in dim lighting (Brabyn, 2000). ■Figure 6.7 shows how visual acuity decreases only slightly with age under ideal conditions—strong contrast and bright light. But when contrast is poor, and especially when poor contrast is combined with low light levels, the drop in visual acuity is sharper (Haegerstrom-Portnoy, Schneck, & Brabyn, 2000). Findings such as these

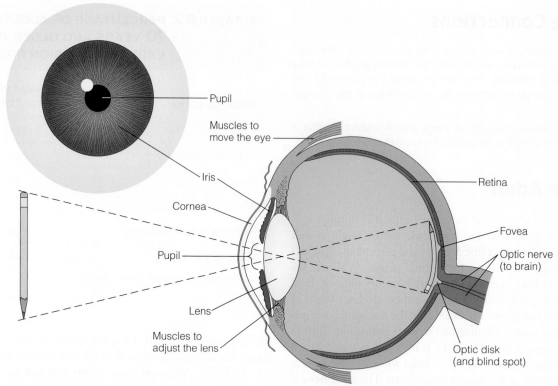

■ **FIGURE 6.6** The human eye and retina. Light passes through the cornea, pupil, and lens and falls on the light-sensitive surface of the retina, where images of objects are projected upside down. The information is relayed to the brain by the optic nerve.

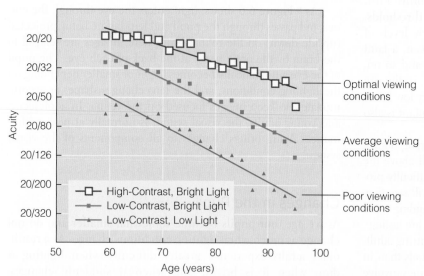

■ **FIGURE 6.7** Visual acuity of older adults under optimal (high contrast and bright light), average (low contrast and bright light), and poor (low contrast and low light) stimulus conditions. SOURCE: Adapted from Haegerstrom-Portnoy, G., Schneck, M. E., & Brabyn, J. A. (1999). Seeing into old age: Vision function beyond acuity. *Optometry and Vision Science, 76,* 141–158. Reprinted by permission of Lippincott, Williams, and Wilkins.

explain why older adults often have difficulty reading menus in restaurants with dim lighting. To compensate, they might use a small flashlight. And restaurants could help by providing menus printed with sharp contrast (black print on a pure white background).

When walking into the sunlight after watching a movie in a darkened theater, older adults' pupils are slower than younger adults' to change from large to small, a process that helps reduce the glare of bright lights. In one study, adults older than 85 years took more than 2 minutes to recover from glare, whereas adults younger than 65 needed less than 15 seconds (Brabyn, 2000).

Similarly, **dark adaptation**—the process in which the eyes adapt to darkness and become more sensitive to the low level of light available—occurs more slowly in older individuals than in younger ones (Fozard & Gordon-Salant, 2001). As a result, the older person driving at night may have special problems when turning onto a dark road from a lighted highway.

As adults age, they typically find they are more bothered by glare and need corrective lenses.

Changes in the Lens

The lens of the eye also undergoes change with age. It has been gaining new cells since childhood, making it denser and less flexible later in life. It cannot change shape, or accommodate, as well to bring objects at different distances into focus. The lens is also yellowing, and both it and the gelatinous liquid behind it are becoming less transparent. The thickening of the lens with age leads to **presbyopia**, or the decreased ability of the lens to accommodate objects close to the eye. Over the years, an adult may, without even being aware of it, gradually move newspapers and books farther from the eye to make them clearer—a form of compensation for decline. Eventually, however, the arms may simply be too short to do the trick any longer. Middle-aged adults cope with problems of near vision by getting reading glasses (or, if they also have problems with distance vision, bifocals); reading fine print may still be a problem, however.

As for distance vision, visual acuity as measured by standard eye charts increases in childhood, peaks in the 20s, remains steady through middle age, and steadily declines in old age (Evans et al., 2002; Klein et al., 2001). The implications for the average adult are fairly minor. For example, in one major study, 3 out of 4 older adults (75 years and older) had good corrected vision (Evans et al., 2002). At worst, most of them could see at 20 feet what a person with standard acuity can see at 25 feet—not a big problem. Among the oldest adults—those in their 90s—37% are visually impaired, but only 7% have lost all functional vision. Several studies show that women experience greater declines in visual acuity than men (see, for example, Bailey et al., 2006). Older women with declining vision are more susceptible to falling and fracturing a bone, which is a serious threat to their independence (Pedula et al., 2006). Fracturing a hip often triggers a shift from independent to assisted living and can even be fatal. And poor vision that is not correctable can seriously decrease older adults' quality of life. According to one estimate, older adults with poor visual acuity (20/40 or worse) were as impaired as those with a major medical problem such as stroke (Chia et al., 2004).

Thus, even though most of us will not be blind, we may need to wear corrective lenses and should regularly monitor our vision. The minority of elderly people who experience serious declines in visual acuity typically suffer from pathological conditions of the eye. These conditions become more prevalent in old age but are not part of aging itself. For example, cataracts are the leading cause of visual impairment in old age. Most older adults have some degree of lens clouding, and significant clouding is present in more than half of adults older than 70 years, often from lifelong heavy exposure to sunlight and its damaging ultraviolet rays (Fozard & Gordon-Salant, 2001). Fortunately, cataracts can be removed through surgery, which can improve vision and prevent blindness.

Retinal Changes

Researchers also know that the sensory receptor cells in the retina may die or not function in later life as efficiently as they once did. The serious retinal problem **age-related macular degeneration (AMD)** results from damage to cells in the retina responsible for central vision. Vision becomes blurry and begins to fade from the center of the visual field, leading to blank or dark space in the center of the image. Because cataracts are now often successfully corrected with surgery, age-related macular degeneration has become the leading cause of blindness in older adults. The causes of macular degeneration are largely unknown, but some research points to a genetic contribution; other research shows a connection with cigarette smoking (Evans, 2001). Currently, there is no cure for macular degeneration, but several researchers are working to develop retinal implants that would stimulate the remaining cells of the retina and restore some useful vision (Boston Retinal Implant Project, 2009). In addition, some doctors prescribe vitamin and mineral supplements that have had some success in slowing the progression of AMD, preserving useful vision for as long as possible.

Changes in the retina also lead to decreased visual field, or a loss of peripheral (side) vision. Looking straight ahead, an older adult may see only half of what a young adult sees to the left and the right of center. Can you think of activities that might be hindered by a decreased visual field? Driving a car comes to mind. For example, when approaching an intersection, you need to be able to see what is coming toward you as well as what is coming from the side roads. Exploration Box 6.2 describes some other sensory changes that might make driving more hazardous for older people.

Significant loss of peripheral vision can lead to tunnel vision, a condition often caused by retinitis pigmentosa or by glaucoma. **Retinitis pigmentosa (RP)** is a group of hereditary disorders that all involve gradual deterioration of the light-sensitive cells of the retina. Symptoms of RP can appear as early as childhood, but they are more likely to be diagnosed in adulthood,

Aging Drivers

Older drivers are perceived by many as more accident prone and slower than other drivers. Perhaps you have had the experience of zipping down the interstate when a slow-moving car driven by an elderly adult pulls into your path, forcing you to brake quickly. Is this experience representative, and is the stereotype of older drivers accurate? This is an important question, because 20% of all drivers will be older than 65 years by 2030 (Braver & Trempel, 2004; Lyman et al., 2002).

It is true that older adults (70 years and older) are involved in more automobile fatalities than middle-aged adults (see the graph in this box). But the most accident-prone group is young drivers between ages 16 and 24 (Insurance Institute for Highway Safety, 2009). When you take into account that young people drive more than elderly people, it turns out that both elderly drivers and young drivers have more accidents *per mile driven* than middle-aged drivers (Insurance Institute for Highway Safety, 2009).

Why is driving hazardous for elderly adults? Clearly, vision is essential to driving; vision accounts for approximately 90% of the information necessary to operate and navigate a car (Messinger-Rapport, 2003). Limited visual acuity or clarity is one component of problematic driving, but as noted in the main text, poor acuity is fairly easy to correct. Therefore, although older adults cite concerns about eyesight as one reason to limit or avoid driving, it cannot account for all the problems older drivers have (Ragland, Satariano, & MacLeod, 2004).

Diminished peripheral vision also makes driving hazardous because good drivers must be able to see vehicles and pedestrians approaching from the side. Half the fatal automobile accidents involving older drivers occur at intersections, and older drivers are more than twice as likely as young drivers to have problems making left turns (Uchida, Fujita, & Katayama, 1999). Older drivers who realize that they have diminished peripheral vision begin to restrict their driving, but not enough do so to improve the fatal crash rates among older adults (Ross et al., 2009).

Not only must drivers see obstacles moving toward them, they must evaluate the speed and trajectory of these objects and in-tegrate this information with their own speed and trajectory to determine a course of action. For example, is the car approaching from the left going to hit my car, or will I be through the intersection before it reaches me? Unfortunately, perceiving moving objects is a problem for older adults, even those who have good visual acuity (Erber, 2005). Simultaneously processing multiple pieces of information is also difficult for older adults. Thus, older drivers have trouble reading street signs while driving (Dewar, Kline, & Swanson, 1995), and they are less able than younger adults to quickly change their focus from the dashboard to the rearview mirror to the road ahead.

After understanding the dynamics of a potentially dangerous situation, the driver must be able to react quickly to threats (for example, a child chasing a ball into the street). As you learned in Chapter 5, older adults typically have slower response times than younger adults; thus, they need more time to react to the same stimulus (Horswill et al., 2008). Finally, older adults are slower to recover from glare and to adapt to the dark, which makes night driving problematic. But the driving records of older adults are not as bad as might be expected, because many of them compensate for visual and other perceptual difficulties and slower reactions by

driving less frequently, especially in conditions believed to be more hazardous—at night, during rush hour, and when the weather is poor (Messinger-Rapport, 2003). Older adults with visual problems such as cataracts and those with cognitive problems are more likely to limit their driving than older adults without these problems (Messinger-Rapport, 2003). Some states have responded to concerns about elderly drivers with mandatory road retesting for license renewal, but most states have no distinct policies about license renewal for older adults. It is not that states do not care; rather, they face strong opposition from groups such as the American Association of Retired Persons and individual older adults (Cobb & Coughlin, 1998). To give up driving is to give up a big chunk of independence, something anyone would be loath to do. Most people want to find ways to drive safely as long as possible.

There is good news: Older drivers who return to the classroom for a refresher course on safe driving and get behind-the-wheel training can improve their driving (Marottoli, 2007). By understanding the strengths and limitations of their sensory–perceptual abilities, older adults will be in a good position to keep driving safely. Remember that the next time you are stuck behind a slow driver.

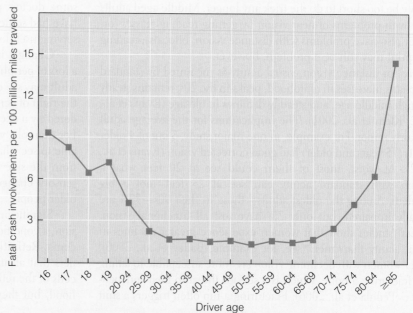

Fatal crash involvement by age. SOURCE: Insurance Institute, 2009.

when the symptoms have become more apparent. Individuals with RP often have a history of visual problems at night and a gradual loss of peripheral vision. Like AMD, retinal deterioration cannot be cured, but some promising research suggests that treatment with vitamin A can slow (not eliminate) the progress of the disease (Berson, 2000; Sibulesky et al., 1999).

In **glaucoma**, increased fluid pressure in the eye can damage the optic nerve and can cause a progressive loss of peripheral vision and, ultimately, blindness. Glaucoma becomes more common over age 50. The key is to prevent the damage before it occurs, using eyedrops or surgery to lower eye fluid pressure. In many cases, however, the damage is done before people experience visual problems; only regular eye tests can reveal the buildup of eye pressure that spells trouble.

To recap, you can expect some changes in vision as you age. (See ■ **Figure 6.8** for a view of how the world looks through aging eyes affected by the conditions discussed here.) Sensory thresholds increase with age so that you need higher levels of stimulation than when you were young. Acuity, or sharpness of vision, decreases, and it takes longer for eyes to adapt to changes. Fortunately, it is possible to correct or compensate for most of these "normal" changes. And older adults who have good family support systems and personal coping mechanisms that focus on acceptance rather than wishful thinking adapt more successfully to visual impairment (Reinhardt, Boerner, & Horowitz, 2009). Some older adults will experience serious visual problems, such as those caused by changes in the retina, but early detection and treatment can preserve vision in most adults.

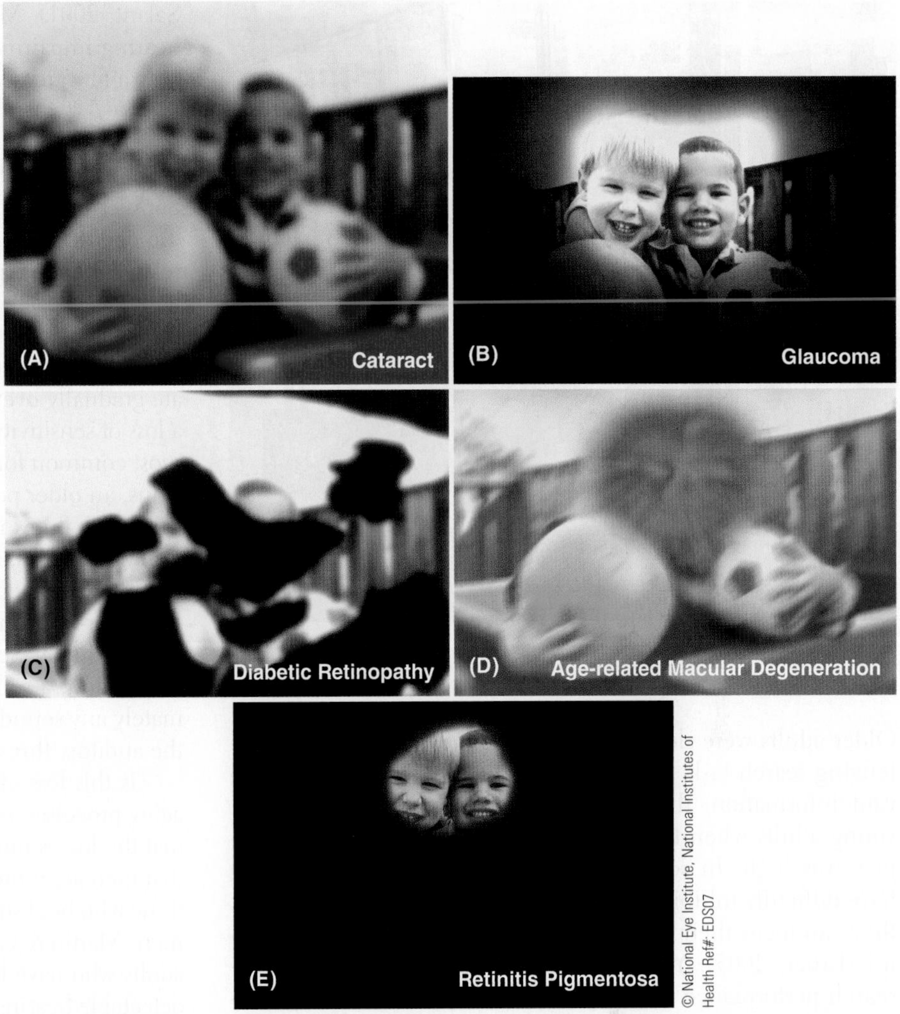

■**FIGURE 6.8** These photos illustrate how a scene might be viewed by someone with various eye conditions: A, cataracts; B, glaucoma; C, diabetic retinopathy; D, age-related macular degeneration; E, retinitis pigmentosa. © National Eye Institute, National Institutes of Health Ref#: EDS05

Attention and Visual Search

As you learned earlier in this chapter, perception is more than just seeing. It is using the senses intelligently and allocating attention efficiently. Some stimuli are more likely to capture attention than others. In a carefully designed series of studies, Greg West and his colleagues (West, Anderson, & Pratt, 2009) demonstrated that adults give prior attention to visual displays that signal a threat; for example, an angry face is attended to before a neutral face. Even among images that are not threatening, some are more likely to capture attention than others. Adults are typically able to control their attention to a greater extent than are children, deliberately focusing on the most relevant information and ignoring irrelevant

information. What happens as we get older? Do we retain this ability to focus and sustain our attention on relevant information?

Several studies show that older adults do worse than younger ones on tests that require dividing attention between two tasks (divided attention) or selectively attending to certain stimuli while ignoring others (selective attention; see Juola et al., 2000; Madden & Langley, 2003). The more distracters a task involves, the more the performance of elderly adults falls short of the performance of young adults. In everyday life, this may translate into difficulty carrying on a conversation while driving or problems locating the asparagus amid all the frozen vegetables at the supermarket.

In one test of visual search skills, Charles Scialfa and his colleagues (Scialfa, Esau, & Joffe, 1998) asked young adults and elderly adults to locate a target (for example, a blue horizontal line) in a display where the distracter items were clearly different (for example, red vertical lines) or in a more difficult display where the distracters shared a common feature with the target (for example, blue vertical and red horizontal lines).

An older adult is likely to find the ice cream as efficiently as a younger adult in a familiar supermarket but may have difficulty with this visual search task if the supermarket is unfamiliar.

Older adults were slower and less accurate on the more challenging search task. They were also more distracted by irrelevant information; they were especially slow compared with young adults when the number of distracter items in the display was high. In some situations, elderly people appear to have difficulty inhibiting responses to irrelevant stimuli so that they can focus their attention more squarely on relevant stimuli (Erber, 2005). Yet older adults can improve their visual search performance with practice, and they are more successful when they strategically use a feature of the display (for example, color) to help guide their search (Madden, Gottlob, & Allen, 1999).

In short, older adults have their greatest difficulties in processing visual information when the situation is *novel* (when they are not sure exactly what to look for or where to look) and when it is *complex* (when there is a great deal of distracting information to search through or when two tasks must be performed at once). By contrast, they have fewer problems when they have clear expectations about what they are to do and when the task is not overly complicated (Madden, 2007). Thus, an older factory worker who has inspected radios for years may be just as speedy and accurate as a younger worker at this well-practiced, familiar task, but he might perform relatively poorly if suddenly asked to inspect pocket calculators and look for a much larger number of possible defects—a novel and complex task.

Hearing

There is some truth to the stereotype of the hard-of-hearing older person. Hearing impairment is approximately three times as prevalent as visual impairment among older adults (Davila et al., 2009). As many as 90% of individuals older than 65 have at least mildly impaired hearing, and hearing becomes progressively worse with age (Cruickshanks et al., 2010; Fozard & Gordon-

Salant, 2001). Most older people experience mild to moderate hearing impairments, some experience severe hearing loss, and only a few are deaf (Dalton et al., 2004).

Basic Capacities

Sources of hearing problems range from excess wax buildup in the ears to infections to a sluggish nervous system. Most age-related hearing problems seem to originate in the inner ear, however (Fozard & Gordon-Salant, 2001). The cochlear hair cells that serve as auditory receptors, their surrounding structures, and the neurons leading from them to the brain degenerate gradually over the adult years. The most noticeable result is a loss of sensitivity to high-frequency or high-pitched sounds, the most common form of **presbycusis**, or problems of the aging ear. Thus, an older person may have difficulty hearing a child's high voice, the flutes in an orchestra, and high-frequency consonant sounds such as *s*, *z*, and *ch* (Whitbourne, 2008) but may have less trouble with deep voices, tubas, and sounds such as *b*. After age 50, lower-frequency sounds also become increasingly difficult to hear (Kline & Scialfa, 1996). Thus, to be heard by the average older adult, a sound—especially a high-pitched sound but ultimately any sound—must be louder than it needs to be to exceed the auditory threshold of a younger adult.

Is this loss of hearing with age the inevitable result of basic aging processes, or is it caused by other factors? Researchers know that the loss is more noticeable among men than among women, that men are more likely to work in noisy industrial jobs, and that those who hold such jobs experience more hearing loss than other men (Martin & Clark, 2002; Reuben et al., 1998). But even when adults who have held relatively quiet jobs are studied, men show detectable hearing losses earlier in life (in their 30s) and lose hearing sensitivity at a faster rate than women do (Pearson et al., 1995). It seems, then, that most people, men more than women, will experience some loss of sensitivity to high-frequency sounds as part of the basic aging process, but that certain people will experience more severe losses because of their experiences.

Speech Perception

Perhaps the most important thing we do with our ears in everyday life is listen to other people during conversations. The ability to hear is one requisite for understanding speech, but this complex auditory perception task also depends on cognitive processes such as attention and memory. How well do aging adults do?

Older adults typically have more difficulty understanding conversation than younger adults do, even under ideal listening conditions. This age difference becomes smaller when differences in hearing are controlled but it does not entirely disappear. Under poor listening conditions—for example, loud background noise—group differences between older and young adults are larger, even when individual differences in hearing are accounted for (Schneider et al., 2000). Thus, older adults may recall fewer details of a conversation that takes place in a crowded, noisy restaurant.

Age-related declines in auditory sensitivity (that is, acuity) are partly responsible, but cognitive declines also seem to contribute to the observed declines in speech perception among older adults

Aiding Adults with Hearing Impairments

In Application Box 6.1, we examined ways to help infants and children who have hearing impairments, often from birth. Here we consider the other end of the life span. What can be done to assist hearing-impaired adults, most of whom were born with normal hearing? Unfortunately, many older adults are reluctant to admit that they have a hearing problem and do not seek assistance. And among those who admit to having a hearing problem, many refuse to wear a hearing aid because they feel it stigmatizes them as old, or they report that hearing aids do not work or do not help them to hear better (Lupsakko, Kautiainen, & Sulkava, 2005).

Those who do not have their hearing corrected may suffer depression, decreased independence, and strained relationships (Appollonio et al., 1996). Imagine how hard social interaction can become if you cannot understand what is being said, misinterpret what is said, or have to keep asking people to repeat what they said. One 89-year-old woman became extremely depressed and isolated: "There is an *awfulness* about silence....I am days without speaking a word. It is affecting my voice. I fear for my mind. I cannot hear the alarm clock, telephone ring, door bell, radio, television—or the human voice" (Meadows-Orlans & Orlans, 1990, pp. 424–425). In contrast, among those older adults who do use hearing aids, quality of life improves (Vuorialho, Karinen, & Sorri, 2006). We tend to think of vision as our most important sense, but hearing impairments may be more disruptive than visual impairments to cognitive and social functioning. Still, many individuals cope well with their hearing impairments and maintain active, satisfying lifestyles.

Hearing aids, although beneficial, cannot restore normal hearing; they tend to distort sounds and to magnify background noise as well as what the wearer is trying to hear. In addition, many older people are ill served by hearing aids that are of poor quality or that are poorly matched to their specific hearing problems. Because cochlear implants work best for individuals exposed to spoken language before they lost their hearing, elderly people are ideal candidates for them. They tolerate the surgical procedure required for implantation well, and their hearing-test scores increase significantly (Kelsall, Shallop, & Burnelli, 1995). In addition, adults who receive cochlear implants report that their quality of life improves significantly (Faber & Grontved, 2000). Cochlear implants, however, cannot work overnight miracles; it can take months, even years, to learn how to interpret the messages relayed by the implant to the brain (Colburn, 2000).

Finally, the physical and social environment can be modified to help people of all ages with hearing losses. For example, furniture can be arranged to permit face-to-face contact; lights can be turned on to permit use of visual cues such as gestures and lip movements. Then there are the simple guidelines we can follow to make ourselves understood by hearing-impaired people. One of the most important is to avoid shouting. Shouting not only distorts speech but also raises the pitch of the voice (therefore making it more difficult for elderly people to hear); it also makes it harder for the individual to read lips. It is best to speak at a normal rate, clearly but without overarticulating, with your face fully visible at a distance of about 3–6 feet.

With modern technology, appropriate education, effective coping strategies, and help from those who hear, hearing-impaired and deaf individuals of all ages can thrive.

(Cervera et al., 2009; Murphy, Daneman, & Schneider, 2006). Patricia Tun and her colleagues (Tun, McCoy, & Wingfield, 2009) compared two groups of older and younger adults: those with good and poor hearing. Participants listened to words and then recalled as many of these words as possible. On half the trials, they did this while also performing a simple visual tracking task. Older adults with good hearing performed significantly worse than young adults with good hearing, so there is more to the recall of spoken words than having good auditory acuity. Moreover, the additional attentional demands of the second task had no significant effect on the younger adults, regardless of whether they had good or poor hearing, but older adults were disadvantaged by increased attentional demands and recalled few spoken words when they had to divide their attention.

In addition, auditory perception tasks, like visual perception tasks, are more difficult for older people when they are novel and complex. In familiar, everyday situations, older adults are able to use contextual cues to interpret what they hear (Fozard & Gordon-Salant, 2001). In one study, for example, elderly adults were about as able as young adults to recall meaningful sentences they had just heard (Wingfield et al., 1985). However, they had serious difficulty repeating back grammatical sentences that made no sense or random strings of words, especially when these meaningless stimuli were spoken rapidly. So an older person may be able to follow an ordinary conversation but not a technical presentation on an unfamiliar topic—especially if the speaker makes the task harder by talking too fast.

Overall, then, most older adults have only mild hearing losses, especially for high-frequency sounds, and only minor problems understanding everyday speech, at least under good listening conditions. In addition, they can compensate for their difficulties successfully—for example, by reading lips and relying on contextual cues. Novel and complex speech heard under poor listening conditions is likely to cause more trouble. Fortunately, there are ways older people can improve their hearing or compensate for its loss, as Application Box 6.2 describes.

Aging of the Chemical Senses

Does the aging of sensory systems also mean that older people become less able to appreciate tastes and aromas? On average, yes: there is a general decline in sensitivity to taste, with older men showing somewhat greater decline than older women (Mojet, Christ-Hazelhof, & Heidema, 2001). But keep in mind that there is great variability: some older adults will continue to have keen senses of smell and taste while others experience sharp declines in these chemical senses. Thus, some older adults may report that food tastes bland and use larger amounts of salt and seasonings than they used when they were younger. In addition, both middle-aged and older adults sometimes have difficulty discriminating among tastes that differ in intensity (Nordin et al., 2003). In one study, adults over 70 were less able than young adults to reliably judge one solution to be saltier, more bitter, or more acidic than another (Weiffenbach, Cowart, & Baum, 1986). In part, this may occur because older adults are more likely than younger adults to take medications that interfere with the taste receptors (Schiffman, 2009). In addition, older adults tend to produce less saliva than younger adults, and saliva facilitates distribution of the chemical molecules carrying information about taste around the mouth (Byrnie, 2009). Interestingly, though, older adults do not have difficulty distinguishing degrees of sweetness; people apparently do not lose the sweet tooth they are born with!

The ability to perceive odors also typically declines with age. Sensitivity to odors increases from childhood to early adulthood then declines during adulthood, more so with increasing age (Finkelstein & Schiffman, 1999; Ship et al., 1996). However, differences among age groups are usually small, and many older people retain their sensitivity to odors. The age decline depends on the type of odor: older adults can identify and remember unpleasant odors just as well as younger adults, although they show some decline in their ability to detect and remember pleasant odors (Larsson, Öberg-Blåvarg, & Jönsson, 2009). Women are more likely than men to maintain their ability to label odors in scratch-and-sniff tests, partly because they are less likely than men to have worked in factories and been exposed to chemicals that could damage the chemical receptors involved in odor perception (Corwin, Loury, & Gilbert, 1995; Ship & Weiffenbach, 1993). Also, healthy adults of both sexes retain their sense of smell better than do those who have diseases, smoke, or take medications (Wilson et al., 2006). Again, then, perceptual losses in later life are part of the basic aging process but vary from person to person depending on environmental factors.

How do declines in the senses of taste and smell affect the older person's experience of the foods they eat? Susan Schiffman (1977) blindfolded young adults and elderly adults and asked them to identify blended foods by taste and smell alone. As ● **Table 6.3** reveals, the older people were correct less often than the college students were. But was this because of a loss of taste sensitivity or smell sensitivity? Or was it a cognitive problem—difficulty coming up with the name of a food that was sensed?

Claire Murphy (1985) attempted to shed light on these questions by presenting young and elderly adults with 12 of the blended foods used by Schiffman. She observed that older people often came up with the wrong specific label but the right idea (identifying sugar as fruit or salt as peanuts, for example). Thus, at least some of their difficulty may have been cognitive. Murphy also tested women whose nostrils were blocked and found that both young and elderly women did miserably when they could

● **TABLE 6.3 AGE DIFFERENCES IN RECOGNITION OF FOODS**

Percentage Recognizing Food

Pureed Food Substance	College Students (ages 18–22)	Elderly People (ages 67–93)
Fruits		
Apple	93%	79%
Banana	93%	59%
Pineapple	93%	86%
Strawberry	100%	79%
Tomato	93%	93%
Vegetables		
Broccoli	81%	62%
Carrot	79%	55%
Corn	96%	76%
Cucumber	44%	28%
Green pepper	78%	59%
Meat/Fish		
Beef	100%	79%
Fish	89%	90%
Pork	93%	72%

Elderly adults have more difficulty than young college students in identifying most blended foods by taste and smell alone. Percentages of those recognizing food include reasonable guesses such as "orange" in response to "apple." Notice that some foods (for example, cucumber) are difficult for people of any age to identify by taste and smell alone. Appearance and texture are important to the recognition of such foods. SOURCE: Schiffman, S. (1977). Food recognition by the elderly. *Journal of Gerontology, 32.* Reprinted by permission of Oxford University Press.

not smell and had to rely on taste alone. These findings suggest that a reduced ability to identify foods in old age is less because of losses in the sense of taste than because of the small losses in the sense of smell as well as declines in the cognitive skills required to remember and name what has been tasted (Murphy, Nordin, & Acosta, 1997).

If foods do not have much taste, an older person may lose interest in eating and may not get proper nourishment (Rolls, 1999). Alternatively, an older person may overuse seasonings such as salt or may eat spoiled food, which can threaten health in other ways. Yet these problems can be remedied. For example, when flavor enhancers were added to the food in one nursing home, elders ate more, gained muscle strength, and had healthier immune system functioning than they did when they ate the usual institutional fare (Schiffman & Warwick, 1993).

● TABLE 6.4 PERCENTAGE OF OLDER ADULTS WITH VARIOUS IMPAIRMENTS WHO REPORT LIMITS ON ACTIVITIES

Activity	With Visual Impairments	With Hearing Impairments	With Both Visual and Hearing Impairments	Without Visual or Hearing Impairments
Difficulty walking	43.3%	30.7%	48.3%	22.2%
Difficulty getting outside	28.6%	17.3%	32.8%	11.9%
Difficulty getting in or out of a bed or chair	22.1%	15.1%	25.0%	10.4%
Difficulty taking medicines	11.8%	7.7%	13.4%	5.0%
Difficulty preparing meals	18.7%	11.6%	20.7%	7.8%

SOURCE: Adapted from Campbell et al., 1999.

Conclusions about changes in taste and smell must be considered in perspective. These sensory and perceptual abilities are highly variable across the entire life span, not just in older adulthood. Taste and smell receptors are replaced throughout the life span and are influenced by such environmental factors as smoke, medications, and extreme temperatures. This means that, under optimal environmental conditions, many older adults will not experience deficits: They can continue to smell the roses and enjoy their food.

Touch, Temperature, and Pain

By now you have seen numerous indications that older adults are often less able than younger adults to detect weak sensory stimulation. This holds true for the sense of touch. The detection threshold for touch increases and sensitivity is gradually lost from middle childhood on (Erber, 2005). It is not clear that minor losses in touch sensitivity have many implications for daily life, however.

Similarly, older people may be less sensitive to changes in temperature than younger adults are (Frank et al., 2000). Some keep their homes too cool because they are unaware of being cold; others may fail to notice that it is too hot. Because older bodies are less able than younger ones to maintain an even temperature, elderly people face an increased risk of death in heat waves or cold snaps (Worfolk, 2000).

It seems only fair that older people should also be less sensitive to painful stimulation, but are they? They are indeed less likely than younger adults to report *weak* levels of stimulation as painful, although the age differences in pain thresholds are not large or consistent (Verrillo & Verrillo, 1985). Yet older people seem to be no less sensitive to stronger pain stimuli. Unfortunately, older adults are more likely to experience chronic pain than younger adults but are less likely to obtain adequate pain relief (Gloth, 2000). Adults with arthritis, osteoporosis, cancer, and other diseases who also experience depression and anxiety are especially likely to perceive pain. Treating these secondary conditions and administering effective pain relief can improve the daily functioning and psychological well-being of older adults.

The Adult in Perspective

Of all the changes in sensation and perception during adulthood that we have considered, those involving vision and hearing appear to be the most important and the most universal. Not only do these senses become less keen, but older people also use them less effectively in such complex perceptual tasks as searching a cluttered room for a missing book or following rapid conversation in a noisy room. Declines in the other senses are less serious and do not affect as many people.

Although people compensate for many sensory declines, their effects cannot be entirely eliminated. At some point, aging adults find that changes in sensory abilities affect their activities. As ● **Table 6.4** shows, older adults with one or two sensory impairments are more likely to experience difficulty with basic tasks of living—walking, getting outside, getting in or out of bed or a chair, taking medicines, or preparing meals. Notice, however, that even older adults without sensory impairments report some difficulty with these tasks. People who are limited by sensory impairments usually have physical or intellectual impairments as well, most likely because of general declines in neural functioning that affect both perception and cognition (Baltes & Lindenberger, 1997; Salthouse et al., 1996). Most older adults, even those with sensory impairments, are engaged in a range of activities and are living full lives. Thus, although most adults will experience some declines in sensory abilities with age, these changes do not need to detract from their quality of life.

Checking Mastery

1. What are the most common eye problems experienced by older adults?

2. What is the greatest functional difficulty with hearing loss among older adults?

3. Which taste is best perceived across the life span (that is, there is little loss of acuity)?

Making Connections

1. You have been hired to teach a cooking course to elderly adults. First, analyze the perceptual strengths and weaknesses of your students: What perceptual tasks might be easy for them, and what tasks might be difficult? Second, considering at least three senses, think of five strategies you can use to help your students compensate for the declines in perceptual capacities that some of them may be experiencing.

2. You are the coordinator for social and educational activities at your community center, which means you work with people of all ages, ranging from the youngest infants to the oldest adults. In planning activities, what should you consider in trying to capture and hold the attention of different age groups?

Chapter Summary

6.1 Issues of Nature and Nurture

- Sensation is the detection of sensory stimulation, and perception is the interpretation of what is sensed.
- Constructivists argue that the newborn is a "blank slate" and must acquire an understanding of the world through experience with sensory inputs. Thus, according to the constructivist perspective, nurture drives the development of perception.
- Nativists believe that each person is born with some innate understanding of how to interpret sensory information. Thus, according to the nativists, the origin of perception is largely nature.

6.2 The Infant

- Methods of studying infant perception include habituation, evoked potentials, preferential looking, and operant conditioning techniques.
- The visual system is fairly well developed at birth. Infants younger than 2 months old discriminate brightness and colors and are attracted to contour, moderate complexity, and movement. Starting at 2 or 3 months, infants more clearly perceive whole patterns such as faces and seem to understand a good deal about objects and their properties, guided by intuitive theories of the physical world.
- Spatial perception develops rapidly, and by about 7 months infants not only perceive drop-offs but also fear them.
- The auditory sense is well developed at birth. Young infants can recognize their mother's voice and distinguish speech sounds that adults cannot discriminate.
- The senses of taste and smell are also well developed at birth. In addition, newborns are sensitive to touch, temperature, and pain.
- Infants develop cross-modal perception around 3–6 months of age, although this ability to recognize through one sense what was learned by a different sense continues to develop through later infancy and childhood.
- The early presence of sensory and perceptual abilities suggests that they are innate, but they are also clearly influenced by early experiences. Certain experiences may be necessary for normal visual perception to develop, suggesting a sensitive period for the visual system.
- Infants actively seek out stimulation by exploring their environments, which typically provides them with the stimulation they need to develop normal sensory and perceptual skills.

6.3 The Child

- Sensory skills undergo little change during childhood, although children learn better how to use the information coming in through their senses.
- Learning to control attention is an important part of perceptual development during childhood. Infants and young children are selectively attentive to the world around them, but they have not fully taken charge of their attentional processes.
- With age, children become more able to concentrate on a task for a long period, to focus on relevant information and ignore distractions, and to use their senses in purposeful and systematic ways to achieve goals.
- Infants and children who can control and sustain their attention are more successful at problem solving.
- Some children experience significant problems with attention and may be diagnosed with attention deficit hyperactivity disorder if they exhibit some combination of inattention, hyperactivity, and impulsivity. Rates of ADHD have escalated over the past two decades, as has the use of stimulant medications to treat the symptoms.

6.4 The Adolescent

- Basic perceptual and attentional skills are perfected during adolescence. Adolescents are better than children at sustaining their attention and using it selectively and strategically to solve the problem at hand.
- Exposure to loud noise can cause tinnitus or ringing sounds in the ear that can be temporary or permanent. Damage to the auditory system from exposure to loud noise can accumulate over time, leading eventually to hearing impairment. Teens are aware that loud noise can cause hearing loss, but most do not rate this as a serious health concern and do not take measures to protect their hearing.
- The chemical senses operate at adult levels, as illustrated by detection of the taste umami and sensitivity to body odor, which may contribute to mate selection.

6.5 The Adult

- During adulthood, sensory and perceptual capacities gradually decline in most individuals, although many changes are minor and can be compensated for. Sensory thresholds—the amount of stimulation required for detection—rise, and perceptual processing of sensory information often declines. Moderate to severe declines that are not corrected can lead to declines in activities and quality of life among older adults.
- Visual changes include cataracts (clouding of the lens), reduced ability of the pupil to change in response to changes in light, thickening of the lens leading to decreased acuity (presbyopia), and retinal changes such as age-related macular degeneration and retinitis pigmentosa. Glaucoma, increased fluid pressure in the eye, becomes more common with age and can lead to blindness if untreated.
- Presbycusis—changes in hearing associated with aging—affects many older adults and most commonly leads to trouble detecting high-pitched sounds. Older adults have more difficulty with speech perception, especially under noisy conditions, than younger adults. Hearing aids can significantly improve older adults' abilities to detect sounds.
- Many older people have difficulty recognizing or enjoying foods, largely because of declines in the sense of smell and memory; touch, temperature, and pain sensitivity also decrease slightly, but intense pain stimuli still hurt.

Checking Mastery Answers

For answers to Checking Mastery questions, visit **www.cengagebrain.com**

Key Terms

sensation **186**
perception **186**
constructivists **186**
nativists **186**
habituation **187**
visual acuity **188**
visual accommodation **188**
contour **189**
size constancy **191**
visual cliff **191**
intuitive theories **193**
cochlear implant **194**
phonemes **194**
olfaction **197**
cross-modal perception **198**
sensitive periods **199**
cataracts **199**
attention **201**
orienting system **201**
selective attention **201**
attention deficit hyperactivity disorder (ADHD) **202**
tinnitus **206**
umami **207**
sensory threshold **209**
dark adaptation **210**
presbyopia **211**
age-related macular degeneration (AMD) **211**
retinitis pigmentosa (RP) **211**
glaucoma **213**
presbycusis **214**

Media Resources

Psychology CourseMate

Access an integrated eBook and chapter-specific learning tools including flashcards, quizzes, videos, and more. Go to **www.cengagebrain.com**

NIMH: Attention Deficit Hyperactivity Disorder

A list of frequently asked questions concerning Attention Deficit Hyperactivity Disorder. Topics covered include causes, symptoms, diagnosis, and treatment. To access, see "web links" in Psychology CourseMate at www.cengagebrain.com

Seeing, Hearing, and Smelling Your World

This website contains a number of articles presenting the latest research findings concerning the senses. To access, see "web links" in Psychology CourseMate at www.cengagebrain.com

Understanding the DATA: Exercises on the Web

www.cengagebrain.com
For additional insight on the data presented in this chapter, try out the exercises for these figures in Psychology CourseMate at
www.cengagebrain.com:

Figure 6.1 The Snellen chart is often used to estimate a person's visual acuity. Although 20/20 vision is frequently assumed to be the "best" vision, 20/10 on the Snellen chart would actually be optimal vision. At birth, visual acuity may be as poor as 20/400, improving to 20/120 over the first month and to 20/30 by 8 months.

Table 6.4 Percentages of older adults with various impairments who report limits on activities

CengageNOW

www.cengagebrain.com
Go to www.cengagebrain.com to link to CengageNOW, your online study tool. First take the Pre-Test for this chapter to get your Personalized Study Plan, which will identify topics you need to review and direct you to online resources: . Then take the Post-Test to determine what concepts you have mastered and what you still need work on.

Cognitive Development

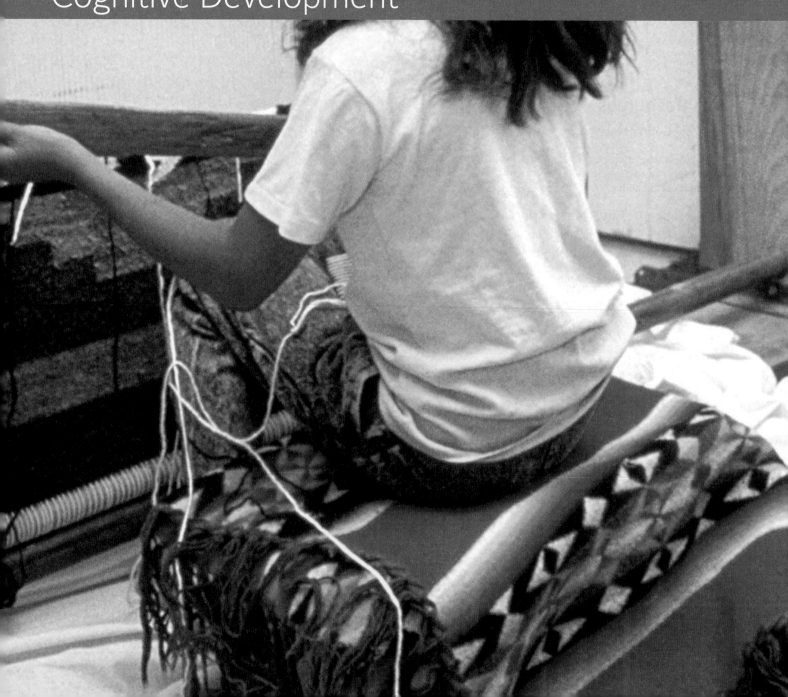

"Consider what would happen if children of various ages were given a metal magnet for the first time. Six-month-olds might accommodate to the unfamiliar metallic taste, the peculiar (horseshoe) shape, and the sound of the magnet being dropped....Three-year-olds, if given an assortment of objects, might accommodate to the fact that some of the objects cling to the magnet and might entertain explanations such as "stickiness" and "wanting to stay together." Nine-year-old children might hypothesize that only objects with certain characteristics are attracted to the magnet and might test out the conditions in which magnetism occurs—through glass, water, and certain distances. Only in adolescence could children accommodate by formulating an abstract theory of magnetism and simultaneously consider all of the variables involved, such as the size and shape of the magnet and the distance from the object." (Miller, 2002, pp. 65–66)

© Paul Conklin/PhotoEdit Inc.

221

1. What are the essential features of children's thought in each of Piaget's stages?

2. How—by what processes—does thought change according to Piaget's theory?

3. What are the primary strengths and weaknesses of Piaget's theory?

4. What has Vygotsky's theory contributed to our understanding of cognition?

5. How do the approaches of Piaget and Vygotsky compare to one another—in what ways are they similar and how do they differ?

In this example, four children—an infant, a 3-year-old, a 9-year-old, and an adolescent—interact with the same object, a magnet, but their interactions are influenced by their current level of development and lead to very different understandings. The infant is competent at getting objects into her mouth and so goes the magnet. The 3-year-old is probably amused by how some objects stick to the magnet without having any clue why this occurs. The 9-year-old may do some trial-and-error testing to see which objects stick to the magnet, and from this develops a fairly logical understanding of magnetism. The adolescent can generate hypotheses about magnetism, systematically test these hypotheses, and create an abstract understanding of the properties of magnetism. At least this is what Jean Piaget proposed after painstakingly observing and testing children of different ages. Others of us might have simply concluded that these children were manipulating a magnet. But psychology was significantly altered by Piaget's curiosity and desire to figure out precisely what children were thinking and why their responses changed with age.

In this chapter, we begin to examine the development of **cognition**—the activity of knowing and the processes through which knowledge is acquired and problems are solved. Humans are cognitive beings throughout the life span, but as the magnet example suggests, our minds change in important ways. We concentrate on the influential theory of cognitive development proposed by Jean Piaget, who traced growth in cognitive capacities during infancy, childhood, and adolescence, and then ask what becomes of these capacities during adulthood. We also consider an alternative view: Lev Vygotsky's sociocultural perspective on cognitive development. Both theorists have changed how we think about cognitive functioning and education. We explore Piaget and Vygotsky's ideas for improving cognitive skills at the end of this chapter; we will revisit these ideas in Chapter 10 when we cover language and education.

7.1 Piaget's Constructivist Approach

Piaget was an exceptional person. As you learned in Chapter 2, he became intrigued by children's mistakes because he noticed that children of the same age often made similar kinds of mental

mistakes—errors typically different than those made by younger or older children. Could these age-related differences in error patterns reflect developmental steps, or stages, in intellectual growth? Piaget thought so, and he devoted his life to studying *how* children think, not just *what* they know (Flavell, 1963). Although many of Piaget's ideas were initially formulated in the 1920s, there was little knowledge of his work in North America until the 1960s, when John Flavell's (1963) summary of Piaget's theory appeared in English.

Piaget began his studies with close observation of his own three children as infants: how they explored new toys, solved simple problems that he arranged for them, and generally came to understand themselves and their world. Later, Piaget studied larger samples of children through what has become known as his **clinical method**, a flexible question-and-answer technique

Piaget spent a lifetime carefully observing children and presenting them with problem solving opportunities.

Yves de Braine/Black Star

used to discover how children think about problems. Consider the following exchange between Piaget and 6-year-old Van (Piaget, 1926, p. 293):

> Piaget: Why is it dark at night?
> Van: Because we sleep better, and so that it shall be dark in the rooms.
> Piaget: Where does the darkness come from?
> Van: Because the sky becomes grey.
> Piaget: What makes the sky become grey?
> Van: The clouds become dark.
> Piaget: How is that?
> Van: God makes the clouds become dark.

Many contemporary researchers consider this method imprecise because it does not involve asking standardized questions of all children tested, but Piaget (1926) believed that the investigator should have the flexibility to pursue an individual child's line of reasoning to fully understand that child's mind. Using his naturalistic observations of his own children and the clinical method to explore how children understand everything from the rules of games to the concepts of space and time, Piaget formulated his view of the development of intelligence.

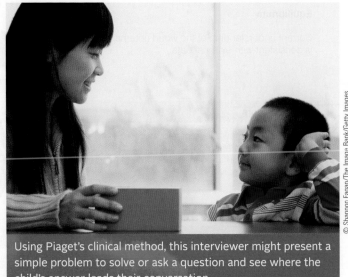

Using Piaget's clinical method, this interviewer might present a simple problem to solve or ask a question and see where the child's answer leads their conversation.

What Is Intelligence?

Piaget's definition of intelligence reflects his background in biology: *intelligence is a basic life function that helps an organism adapt to its environment.* You can see adaptation when you watch a toddler figuring out how to work a jack-in-the-box, a school-age child figuring out how to divide treats among friends, or an adult figuring out how to operate a new digital camera. The newborn enters an unfamiliar world with few means of adapting to it other than working senses and reflexes. But Piaget viewed infants as active agents in their own development, learning about the world of people and things by observing, investigating, and experimenting.

As infants and children explore their world, their brains respond by creating schemes (sometimes called *schema* in the singular and *schemata* in the plural). **Schemes** are cognitive structures—organized patterns of action or thought that people construct to interpret their experiences (Piaget, 1952, 1977). Schemes are like having a set of rules or procedures that structure our cognition (Meadows, 2006). For example, the infant's grasping actions and sucking responses are early behavioral schemes, patterns of action used to adapt to different objects. During their second year, children develop symbolic schemes, or concepts. They use internal mental symbols such as images and words to represent or stand for aspects of experience, such as when a young child sees a funny dance and carries away a mental model of how it was done. Older children become able to manipulate symbols in their heads to help them solve problems, such as when they add two numbers together mentally rather than on paper or with the aid of their fingers.

As children develop more sophisticated schemes, or cognitive structures, they become increasingly able to adapt to their environments. Because they gain new schemes as they develop, children of different ages will respond to the same stimuli differ-

ently. The infant may get to know a shoe mainly as something to chew, the preschooler may decide to let the shoe symbolize or represent a telephone and put it to her ear, and the school-age child may mentally count its shoelace eyelets.

How Does Intelligence Develop?

Piaget took an interactionist position on the nature–nurture issue: children actively create knowledge by building schemes from their experiences (nurture), using two inborn (nature) intellectual functions, which he called organization and adaptation. These processes operate throughout the life span. Through **organization**, children systematically combine existing schemes into new and more complex ones. Thus, their minds are not cluttered with an endless number of independent facts; they contain instead logically ordered and interrelated actions and ideas. For example, the infant who gazes, reaches, and grasps will organize these simple schemes into the complex structure of visually directed reaching. Complex cognitive structures in older children grow out of reorganizations of simpler structures.

Adaptation is the process of adjusting to the demands of environment (Piaget, 1971). It occurs through two complementary processes, assimilation and accommodation. Imagine that you are a 2-year-old, that the world is still new, and that you see your first horse. What will you make of it? You likely will try to relate it to something familiar. **Assimilation** is the process by which we interpret new experiences in terms of existing schemes or cognitive structures. Thus, if you already have a scheme that mentally represents your knowledge of dogs, you may label this new beast "doggie." Through assimilation, we deal with our environment in our own terms, sometimes bending the world to squeeze it into our existing categories. Throughout the life span, we rely on our existing cognitive structures to understand new events.

But if you notice that this "doggie" is bigger than most dogs and that it has a mane and an awfully strange "bark," you may be

Equilibrium		
Current understanding of the world (internal data) is consistent with external data.		Small furry animals with fluffy tails are called cats. They meow and smell nice.
Disequilibrium		
Along comes a new piece of information that does not fit with current understanding of the world, leading to disequilibrium—an uncomfortable state of mind that the child seeks to resolve.		That's strange—this small furry creature has a fluffy tail but it doesn't meow and it certainly doesn't smell nice!
Assimilation and accommodation		
This unbalanced (confused) state can be resolved through the processes of organization and adaptation (assimilation and accommodation).		This can't be a cat. Mommy called it a skunk, which must be a different kind of animal.
Equilibrium		
These lead to a new way of understanding the world—a new state of equilibrium.		I'll have to remember that skunks and cats are different types of animals.

■ **FIGURE 7.1** Process of change in Piaget's theory.

prompted to change your understanding of the world of four-legged animals. **Accommodation** is the process of modifying existing schemes to better fit new experiences. Perhaps you will need to invent a new name for this animal or ask what it is and revise your concept of four-legged animals accordingly.

If we always assimilated new experiences, our understandings would never advance. Piaget believed that all new experiences are greeted with a mix of assimilation and accommodation. Once we have schemes, we apply them to make sense of the world, but we also encounter puzzles that force us to modify our understandings through accommodation. According to Piaget, when new events seriously challenge old schemes, or prove our existing understandings to be inadequate, we experience cognitive conflict. This cognitive conflict, or disequilibrium, then stimulates cognitive growth and the formation of more adequate understandings (Piaget, 1985; ■ **Figure 7.1**). This occurs because mental conflict is not pleasant; we are motivated to reduce conflict through what Piaget called **equilibration**, the process of achieving mental stability where our internal thoughts are con-

sistent with the evidence we are receiving from the external world (Piaget, 1978).

Intelligence, then, in Piaget's view, develops through the interaction of the individual with the environment. Nature provides the complementary processes of assimilation and accommodation that make adaptation to environments possible. The processes of adaptation and organization are driven by an innate tendency to maintain equilibrium. As a result of the interaction of biological maturation and experience, humans progress through four distinct stages of cognitive development:

1. The sensorimotor stage (birth to roughly 2 years)
2. The preoperational stage (roughly 2–7 years)
3. The concrete operations stage (roughly 7–11 years)
4. The formal operations stage (roughly 11 years and beyond)

These stages represent qualitatively different ways of thinking and occur in an invariant sequence—that is, in the same order in all children. However, depending on their experiences, children may progress through the stages at different rates, with some moving more rapidly or more slowly than others. Thus, the age ranges associated with the stages are only averages. A child's stage of development is determined by his reasoning processes, not his age.

Checking Mastery

1. What is a schema in Piaget's theory?
2. Define and give an example of assimilation and accommodation.

Making Connections

1. In our electronic global world, children are exposed to a great deal of information, but their understanding of this information is far from adultlike. Using Piaget's model, how would you move children toward a better understanding of natural disasters such as the 2010 earthquake in Chile and the subsequent tsunamis that this triggered?
2. Using your own experiences, provide a unique example of how the inborn processes of organization and adaptation operate.

7.2 The Infant

Piaget's sensorimotor stage, spanning the 2 years of infancy, involves coming to know the world through senses and actions. The dominant cognitive structures are behavioral schemes—patterns of action that evolve as infants begin to coordinate sensory input (seeing and mouthing an object) and motor responses (grasping it). Because infants solve problems through their actions rather than with their minds, their mode of thought is qualitatively different from that of older children.

Substages of the Sensorimotor Stage

The six substages of the sensorimotor stage are outlined in ● Table 7.1. At the start of the sensorimotor period, infants may not seem highly intelligent, but they are already active explorers of the world around them. Researchers see increasing signs of intelligent behavior as infants pass through the substages, because they are gradually learning about the world and about cause and effect by observing the effects of their actions. They are transformed from reflexive creatures who adapt to their environment using their innate reflexes to reflective ones who can solve simple problems in their heads.

The advances in problem-solving ability captured in the six substages of the sensorimotor period bring many important changes. Consider changes in the quality of infants' play activities. During the first month, young infants react reflexively to internal and external stimulation. In the primary circular reactions substage (1–4 months), they are more interested in their own bodies than in manipulating toys. Moving their tongues or fingers around is entertainment enough at this age. Piaget named this substage **primary circular reactions** because he observed infants repeating (hence, the term *circular*) actions relating to their own bodies (that is, primary to themselves) that had initially happened by chance. Piaget reports the example of his son, Laurent, at just over 1 month accidentally getting his thumb in his mouth. It falls out. This happens again on another day. Indeed, since the first accidental occurrence, Piaget observes it happening over and over again.

● TABLE 7.1 THE SUBSTAGES AND INTELLECTUAL ACCOMPLISHMENTS OF THE SENSORIMOTOR PERIOD

Substage	Description
1. Reflex activity (birth–1 month)	Active exercise and refinement of inborn reflexes (e.g., accommodate sucking to fit the shapes of different objects)
2. Primary circular reactions (1–4 months)	Repetition of interesting acts centered on the child's own body (e.g., repeatedly suck a thumb, kick legs, or blow bubbles)
3. Secondary circular reactions (4–8 months)	Repetition of interesting acts on objects (e.g., repeatedly shake a rattle to make an interesting noise or bat a mobile to make it wiggle)
4. Coordination of secondary schemes (8–12 months)	Combination of actions to solve simple problems (e.g., bat aside a barrier to grasp an object, using the scheme as a means to an end); first evidence of intentionality
5. Tertiary circular reactions (12–18 months)	Experimentation to find new ways to solve problems or produce interesting outcomes (e.g., explore bathwater by gently patting it, then hitting it vigorously and watching the results; or stroke, pinch, squeeze, and pat a cat to see how it responds to varied actions)
6. Beginning of thought (18–24 months)	First evidence of insight; solve problems mentally, using symbols to stand for objects and actions; visualize how a stick could be used (e.g., move an out-of-reach toy closer); no longer limited to thinking by doing

Increasingly, a finger or thumb successfully makes it into the mouth, which pleases Laurent. He seeks opportunities to repeat this pleasant action involving his body (alas, Laurent was not to be a thumb-sucker for very long—by 2 or 3 months of age, Piaget had bandaged his son's hands to bring this habit to an end).

By the third substage of secondary circular reactions (4–8 months), infants derive pleasure from repeatedly performing an action, such as sucking or banging a toy. Now the repetitive actions are called **secondary circular reactions** because they involve something in the infant's external environment (that is, secondary to the self). In the fourth substage (8–12 months), called **coordination of secondary schemes**, infants combine (that is, coordinate) secondary actions to achieve simple goals such as when they *push* an obstacle out of the way in order to *grasp* a desired object.

Later, when they reach the substage of tertiary circular reactions (12–18 months), infants experiment in varied ways with toys, exploring them thoroughly and learning all about their properties. In this stage, a true sense of curiosity and interest in novel actions appears. Piaget defined a **tertiary circular reaction** as "interest in novelty for its own sake" (Ginsburg & Opper, 1988, p. 57). Now it is interesting to the baby to repeat an action with variations, such as the infant who experiments with all the many ways that oatmeal can land on the floor and walls when launched from a highchair in different directions and at different velocities.

With the final substage, the beginning of thought (about 18 months), comes the possibility of letting one object represent another so that a cooking pot becomes a hat or a shoe becomes a telephone—a simple form of pretend play made possible by the

capacity for symbolic thought. It is also in this stage, according to Piaget, that infants can imitate models no longer present, because they can now create and later recall mental representations of what they have seen.

The Development of Object Permanence

Another important change during the sensorimotor period concerns the infant's understanding of the existence of objects. According to Piaget, newborns lack an understanding of **object permanence** (also called *object concept*). This is the fundamental understanding that objects continue to exist—they are permanent—when they are no longer visible or otherwise detectable to the senses. It probably does not occur to you to wonder whether your coat is still in the closet after you shut the closet door (unless perhaps you have taken a philosophy course). But very young infants, because they rely so heavily on their senses, seem to operate as though objects exist only when they are perceived or acted on. According to Piaget, infants must construct the notion that reality exists apart from their experience of it.

Piaget believed that the concept of object permanence develops gradually over the sensorimotor period. Up through roughly 4–8 months, it is "out of sight, out of mind"; infants will not search for a toy if it is covered with a cloth or screen. By substage 4 (8–12 months), they master that trick but still rely on their perceptions and actions to "know" an object (Piaget, 1952). After his 10-month-old daughter, Jacqueline, had repeatedly retrieved a toy parrot from one hiding place, Piaget put it in a new spot while she watched him. Amazingly, she looked in the original hiding place. She seemed to assume that her behavior determined where the object would appear; she did not treat the object as if it existed apart from her actions or from its initial location. The surprising tendency of 8- to 12-month-olds to search for an object in the place where they last found it (A) rather than in its new hiding place (B) is called the **A-not-B error**. The likelihood of infants making the A-not-B error increases with lengthier delays between hiding and searching and with the number of trials in which the object is found in spot A (Marcovitch & Zelazo, 1999).

Some research suggests that task demands and physical limitations of infants influence performance on the A-not-B task (Lew et al., 2007). To evaluate this, Ted Ruffman and his colleagues (2005) conducted a series of studies and concluded that multiple factors do influence performance, but infants do indeed have a conceptual problem when it comes to understanding that the object is located at B and not at A.

In substage 5, the 1-year-old overcomes the A-not-B error but continues to have trouble with invisible displacements—as when you hide a toy in your hand, move your hand under a pillow, and then remove your hand, leaving the toy under the pillow. The infant will search where the object was last seen, seeming confused when it is not in your hand and failing to look under the pillow, where it was deposited. Finally, by 18 months or so, the infant is capable of mentally representing such invisible moves and conceiving of the object in its final location. According to Piaget, the concept of object permanence is fully mastered at this point.

Does research support Piaget? Recent studies suggest that infants may develop at least some understanding of object perma-

Infants have a range of behavioral schemes, such as grasping, that allow them to explore new objects. Each scheme is a general pattern of behavior that can be adjusted to fit specific objects such as the spoon held tightly by this hungry guy.

© Bubbles Photolibrary/Alamy

nence far earlier than Piaget claimed (Baillargeon, 2002; Ruffman, Slade, & Redman, 2005). For example, Renee Baillargeon and her colleagues have used a method of testing for object concept that does not require reaching for a hidden object, only looking toward where it should be. In one study, infants as young as 2½ months seemed surprised (as demonstrated by looking longer) when a toy that had disappeared behind one screen (left side of ■ Figure 7.2) reappeared from behind a second screen (right side of Figure 7.2) *without* appearing in the open space between the two screens (Aguiar & Baillargeon, 1999).

At this young age, however, understanding of hidden objects is still limited. Consider the scenario shown in ■ Figure 7.3. In the high-window condition, a toy is hidden as it moves along a track behind a block that has a window located at its top. There is nothing odd about this condition. In the low-window condition, a toy *should* be visible as it moves along a track behind a block that has a window located at its bottom, but it is not. To someone who understands the properties of object permanence, this should strike them as odd. At 2½ months, infants do not show signs that they detect a difference between an object moving along a track under the high-window and low-window conditions. But just 2 weeks later, 3-month-olds look longer at the low-window event compared with the high-window event, as if surprised (Aguiar & Baillargeon, 2002). Thus, by 3 months, infants have gained an understanding that objects have qualities that should permit them to be visible when nothing is obstructing them.

In an unusual study of toddlers' advanced understanding of object permanence, researchers compared healthy 2-year-olds with 2-year-olds with spinal muscular atrophy (SMA), which is characterized by normal IQ but severe muscle problems limiting children's movement (Riviere & Lecuyer, 2003). Based on Piaget's original reaching task, infants watch as a hand picks up a toy and then "visits" three separate cloths, depositing the toy under the second location before moving to the last cloth. Healthy toddlers incorrectly searched under the third cloth for the toy, whereas the SMA toddlers correctly searched under the

■ **FIGURE 7.2** Test stimuli used by Aguiar and Baillargeon (1999, 2002). The doll moves behind the screen on the left and reappears on the right side of the second screen without appearing in the space between screens. SOURCE: From Aguiar & Baillargeon, Developments of young infants' reasoning about occluded objects, *Cognitive Psychology, 45,* p. 267–336, Figure 1. Reprinted by permission of Elsevier.

second cloth. In a second study, researchers made healthy toddlers wait before they were allowed to search, and with this delay, they too responded correctly by searching under the second cloth. What explains this? Healthy toddlers may quickly and impulsively search at the location where an object is likely to be hidden (where the hand was last seen), but when given more time to think about it, they can go beyond their first impulsive response to search successfully. SMA toddlers have this extra

High-window event

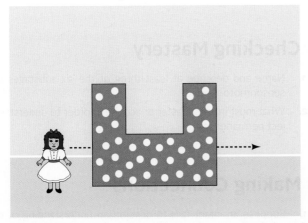

Low-window event

■ **FIGURE 7.3** There is nothing to be surprised about in the high-window event, but in the low-window event, the doll should (but does not) appear in the middle space as it moves along the track. SOURCE: From Aguiar & Baillargeon, Developments of young infants' reasoning about occluded objects, *Cognitive Psychology, (2002) 45,* p. 267–336, Figure 2. Reprinted by permission of Elsevier.

At 5 months, almost everything ends up in Eleanor's mouth. According to Jean Piaget, infants in the sensorimotor stage of development learn a great deal about their world by investigating it with their senses and acting motorically on this information.

time "built in." Because of their muscle problems, SMA toddlers are slower at searching and have less experience with manual searches than other children. They are less likely to make an impulsive reach in the wrong direction because of the time and effort required to reach. This research suggests that success at object permanence tasks may depend on more than a cognitive awareness of the properties of objects: success also could be influenced by task conditions such as the time interval between seeing something hidden and being able to search for it.

In general, then, it seems that babies sometimes know a good deal more about object permanence than they reveal through their actions when they are given the kinds of search tasks originally devised by Piaget (Baillargeon, 2002). Such findings, however, are not necessarily inconsistent with Piaget's findings (Haith & Benson, 1998). Indeed, Piaget contended that looking behaviors were developmental precursors to the reaching behaviors that he assessed. He did not believe, however, that looking represented complete understanding of object permanence (Fischer & Bidell, 1991; Haith & Benson, 1998). An analysis of infants' looking behaviors by Carolyn Rovee-Collier (2001) suggests that Piaget was wise to distinguish between infants' looking and reaching. In some situations, looking may developmentally precede reaching for an object, as Piaget suggested. In other situations, however, infants' actions may reveal a more sophisticated understanding of the world than looking would indicate. Regardless of the specific measure researchers use, infants gradually become more skilled at acting on their knowledge by searching in the right spot. They improve their looking and reaching skills between 8 and 12 months, and by the end of the sensorimotor period, they are masters of even very complex hide-and-seek games (Moore & Meltzoff, 1999; Newman, Atkinson, & Braddick, 2001).

The Emergence of Symbols

The crowning achievement of the sensorimotor stage is internalizing behavioral schemes to construct mental symbols that can guide future behavior. Now the toddler can experiment mentally and can therefore show a kind of insight into how to solve a problem. This new **symbolic capacity**—the ability to use images, words, or gestures to represent or stand for objects and experiences—enables more sophisticated problem solving. To illustrate, consider young Lucienne's actions after she watches her father—Piaget—place an interesting chain inside a matchbox (Piaget, 1952, pp. 337–338):

> [To open the box], she only possesses two preceding schemes: turning the box over in order to empty it of its contents, and sliding her fingers into the slit to make the chain come out. It is of course this last procedure that she tries first: she puts her finger inside and gropes to reach the chain, but fails completely. A pause follows during which Lucienne manifests a very curious reaction. . . . She looks at the slit with great attention; then several times in succession, she opens and shuts her mouth, at first slightly, then wider and wider! [Then]. . . . Lucienne unhesitatingly puts her finger in the slit, and instead of trying as before to reach the chain, she pulls so as to enlarge the opening. She succeeds and grasps the chain.

Lucienne uses the symbol of opening and closing her mouth to "think" through the problem. In addition to permitting mental problem solving, the symbolic capacity will appear in the language explosion and pretend play so evident in the preschool years.

In all, children's intellectual achievements during the six substages of the sensorimotor period are remarkable. By its end, they have become deliberate thinkers with a symbolic capacity that allows them to solve some problems in their heads, and they have a grasp of object permanence and many other concepts.

Checking Mastery

1. Name and describe at least three of the six substages of the sensorimotor period.

2. What must infants master or acquire in order to understand object permanence?

Making Connections

1. Suppose an infant fails to develop an understanding of object permanence. How would this deficit influence his behavior and knowledge of the world?

2. Trace the emergence of a goal-directed behavior, such as opening a cabinet door to get to a box of animal crackers, through the six sensorimotor substages.

7.3 The Child

No one has done more to make us aware of the surprising turns that children's minds can take than Piaget, who described how children enter the preoperational stage of cognitive development in their preschool years and progress to the stage of concrete operations as they enter their elementary school years.

The Preoperational Stage

The preoperational stage of cognitive development extends from roughly 2 to 7 years of age. The *symbolic capacity* that emerged at the end of the sensorimotor stage runs wild in the preschool years and is the greatest cognitive strength of the preschooler. Imagine the possibilities: The child can now use words to refer to things, people, and events that are not physically present. Instead of being trapped in the immediate present, the child can refer to past and future. Pretend or fantasy play flourishes at this age: blocks can stand for telephones, cardboard boxes for trains. Some children—especially first-borns and only children who do not have ready access to play companions—even invent **imaginary companions** (Hoff, 2005a). Some of these imaginary companions are humans, and some are animals; they come with names like Zippy, Simply, Fake Rachel, and Sargeant Savage (Taylor et al., 2004). Their inventors know their companions are not real. Although parents may worry about such flights of fancy, they are normal. In fact, imaginative uses of the symbolic capacity are associated with advanced cognitive and social development, as well as higher levels of creativity and imagery (Bouldin, 2006; Hoff, 2005b).

Yet the young child's mind is limited compared with that of an older child, and it was the limitations of preoperational thinking that Piaget explored most thoroughly. Although less so than infants, preschoolers are highly influenced by their immediate perceptions. They often respond as if they have been captured by, or cannot go beyond, the most perceptually salient aspects of a situation. This focus on **perceptual salience**, or the most obvious features of an object or situation, means that preschoolers can be fooled by appearances. They have difficulty with tasks that require them to use logic to arrive at the right answer. Their "logic," if we can indeed refer to it as logic at all, is based on their intuitions. We can best illustrate this reliance on perceptions and lack of logical thought by considering Piaget's classic tests of conservation (also see Exploration Box 7.1).

Lack of Conservation

One of the many lessons about the physical world that children must master is the concept of **conservation**—the idea that certain properties of an object or substance do not change when its appearance is altered in some superficial way (■**Figure** 7.4). So find a 4- or 5-year-old and try Piaget's conservation-of-liquid-quantity task. Pour equal amounts of water into two identical glasses, and get the child to agree that she has the same amount of water. Then, as the child watches, pour the water from one glass into a shorter, wider glass. Now ask whether the two containers—the tall, narrow glass and the shorter, broader one—have the same amount of water to drink or whether one has more water. Children younger than 6 or 7 will usually say that the taller glass has more water than the shorter one. They lack the understanding that the volume of liquid is conserved despite the change in the shape it takes in different containers.

How can young children be so easily fooled by their perceptions? According to Piaget, the preschooler is unable to engage in **decentration**—the ability to focus on two or more dimensions of a problem at once. Consider the conservation task: the child must focus on height and width simultaneously and recognize that the increased width of the short, broad container compensates for its lesser height. Preoperational thinkers engage in **centration**—the tendency to center attention on a single aspect of the problem. They focus on height alone and conclude that the taller glass has more liquid; or, alternatively, they focus on width and conclude that the short, wide glass has more. In this and other ways, preschoolers seem to have one-track minds.

A second contributor to success on conservation tasks is **reversibility**—the process of mentally undoing or reversing an action. Older children often display mastery of reversibility by suggesting that the water be poured back into its original container to prove that it is still the same amount. The young child shows irreversibility of thinking and may insist that the water would overflow the glass if it were poured back. Indeed, one young child tested by a college student shrieked, "Do it again!" as though pouring the water back without causing the glass to overflow were some unparalleled feat of magic.

Finally, preoperational thinkers fail to demonstrate conservation because of limitations in **transformational thought**—the ability to conceptualize transformations, or processes of change from one state to another, as when water is poured from one glass to another (see Figure 7.4). Preoperational thinkers engage in **static thought**, or thought that is fixed on end states rather

Until an infant masters the concept of object permanence, objects that are outside of his visual sight are "out of mind."

Can There Really Be a Santa Claus?

Many young children around the world believe in Santa Claus, St. Nicholas, the Tooth Fairy, or a similar magical being. Children whose parents endorse and promote Santa or another mythical being are more likely to believe than children whose parents do not (Harris et al., 2006; Woolley et al., 2004). After all, children normally trust their parents and accept their statements about Santa at face value. Children also tend to accept supporting evidence of Santa (for example, there are presents under the tree) without questioning whether this evidence is conclusive proof of Santa's existence (Tullos & Wooley, 2009).

At what point, and why, do their beliefs in these figures begin to waiver? Research with 5- and 6-year-old children shows that they are already somewhat less confident about the existence of Santa and the Tooth Fairy than they are about two invisible but scientifically proven entities—germs and oxygen (Harris et al., 2006). According to Piaget's theory, children would begin to seriously question the existence of Santa Claus when they acquire concrete-operational thought. With their ability to reason logically, they may begin to ask questions such as, "How can Santa Claus get around to all those houses in one night?" "How can one sleigh hold all those gifts?" "Why haven't I ever seen a reindeer fly?" and "How does Santa get into houses without chimneys?"

What made sense to the preoperational child no longer adds up to the logical, concrete-operational thinker. With their focus on static endpoints, preschool-age children may not have a problem imagining presents for all the children in the world (or at least those on the "nice" list) sitting at the North Pole waiting to be delivered and then sitting under decorated trees Christmas morning. But once children understand transformations, they are confronted with the problem of how all those presents get from the North Pole to the individual houses in record time. The logical thinker notes that the gifts under the tree are wrapped in the same paper that Mom has in her closet. Some children question why gifts sport certain brand labels if Santa and his elves spent the year making gifts in their workshop. Thus, children begin using evidence to build a case against Santa (Tullos & Woolley, 2009).

As adults, we can resolve some of these inconsistencies for children to help maintain children's beliefs in Santa Claus. We can, for example, point out that Santa has many helpers and that reindeer native to the North Pole are unlike those ever seen in the wild or in a zoo. Some parents who want to perpetuate the Santa myth get tough and simply tell their children that nonbelievers will not get any presents. So the level of cognitive development and the surrounding culture play roles in whether or not children believe in Santa Claus and for how long.

than the changes that transform one state into another, as when the water is sitting in the two glasses, not being poured or manipulated.

Preoperational children do not understand the concept of conservation, then, because they engage in centration, irreversible thought, and static thought. The older child, in the stage of concrete operations, has mastered decentration, reversibility, and transformational thought. The correct answer to the conservation task is a matter of logic to the older child; there is no longer a need to rely on perception as a guide. Indeed, a 9-year-old tested by another of our students grasped the logic so well and thought the question of which glass had more water so stupid that she asked, "Is this what you do in college?"

Egocentrism

Piaget believed that preoperational thought also involves **egocentrism**—a tendency to view the world solely from one's own perspective and to have difficulty recognizing other points of view. For example, he asked children to choose the drawing that shows what a display of three mountains would look like from a particular vantage point. Young children often chose the view that corresponded to their own position (Piaget & Inhelder, 1956). Similarly, young children often assume that if they know something, other people do, too (Ruffman & Olson, 1989). The same holds for desires: the 4-year-old who wants to go to McDonald's for dinner may say that Mom and Dad want to go to McDonald's, too, even if Mom does not like burgers or chicken nuggets and Dad would rather order Chinese takeout.

Difficulty with Classification

The limitations of relying on perceptions and intuitions are also apparent when preoperational children are asked to classify objects and think about classification systems. When 2- or 3-year-old children are asked to sort objects on the basis of similarities, they make interesting designs or change their sorting criteria

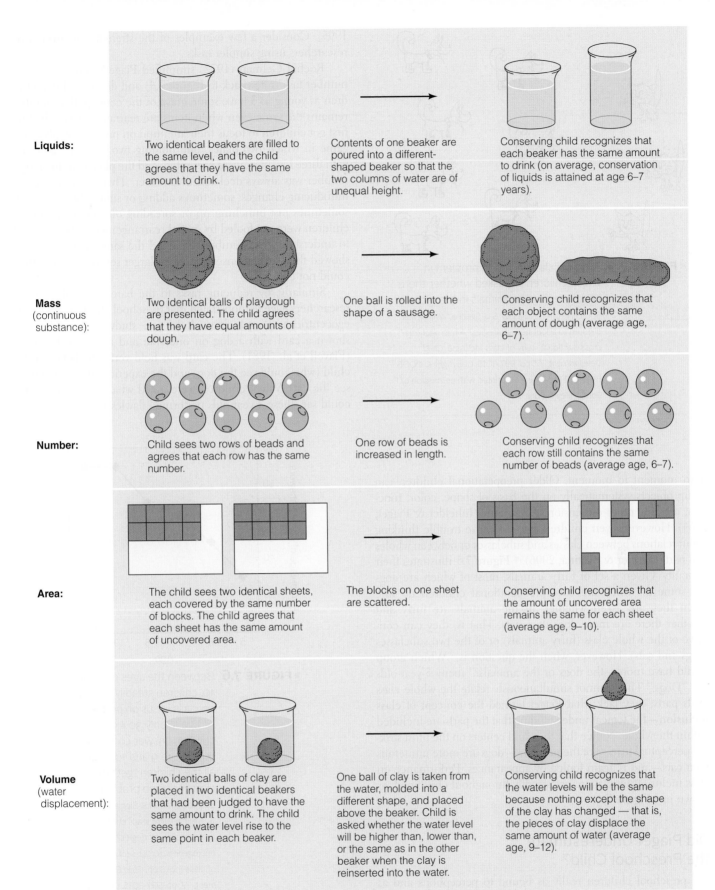

Liquids:

Two identical beakers are filled to the same level, and the child agrees that they have the same amount to drink.

Contents of one beaker are poured into a different-shaped beaker so that the two columns of water are of unequal height.

Conserving child recognizes that each beaker has the same amount to drink (on average, conservation of liquids is attained at age 6–7 years).

Mass (continuous substance):

Two identical balls of playdough are presented. The child agrees that they have equal amounts of dough.

One ball is rolled into the shape of a sausage.

Conserving child recognizes that each object contains the same amount of dough (average age, 6–7).

Number:

Child sees two rows of beads and agrees that each row has the same number.

One row of beads is increased in length.

Conserving child recognizes that each row still contains the same number of beads (average age, 6–7).

Area:

The child sees two identical sheets, each covered by the same number of blocks. The child agrees that each sheet has the same amount of uncovered area.

The blocks on one sheet are scattered.

Conserving child recognizes that the amount of uncovered area remains the same for each sheet (average age, 9–10).

Volume (water displacement):

Two identical balls of clay are placed in two identical beakers that had been judged to have the same amount to drink. The child sees the water level rise to the same point in each beaker.

One ball of clay is taken from the water, molded into a different shape, and placed above the beaker. Child is asked whether the water level will be higher than, lower than, or the same as in the other beaker when the clay is reinserted into the water.

Conserving child recognizes that the water levels will be the same because nothing except the shape of the clay has changed — that is, the pieces of clay displace the same amount of water (average age, 9–12).

■ **FIGURE 7.4** Some common tests of the child's ability to conserve. Source: From R. Gelman, the nature and development of early number concepts, H.W. Reese (ED.), *Advances in Child Development and Behavior, 7.* Copyright © 1972 by Academic Press. Reprinted with permission of Elsevier.

■ FIGURE 7.5 A typical class inclusion problem in which children are asked whether there are more dogs or animals in the picture.

Source: From R.S. Siegler & J. Svetina, What leads children to adopt new strategies? A microgenetic/cross-sectional study of class-inclusion, *Child Development*, 77, pp. 997–1015. Copyright © 2006, Blackwell Publishing. Reprinted with permission of John Wiley & Sons, Inc.

from moment to moment. Older preoperational children can group objects systematically on the basis of shape, color, function, or some other dimension of similarity (Inhelder & Piaget, 1964). However, even children ages 4–7 have trouble thinking about relations between classes and subclasses or between wholes and parts (Siegler & Svetina, 2006). **■ Figure 7.5** illustrates their difficulty. Given a set of furry animals, most of which are dogs but some of which are cats, preoperational children do fine when they are asked whether all the animals are furry and whether there are more dogs than cats. That is, they can conceive of the whole class (furry animals) or of the two subclasses (dogs and cats). However, when the question is, "Which group would have more—the dogs or the animals?" many 5-year-olds say, "Dogs." They cannot simultaneously relate the whole class to its parts; they lack what Piaget termed the concept of **class inclusion**—the logical understanding that the parts are included within the whole. Notice that the child centers on the most striking perceptual feature of the problem—dogs are more numerous than cats—and is again fooled by appearances. Performance on class inclusion tasks increases steadily throughout childhood, as shown in **■ Figure 7.6**.

Did Piaget Underestimate the Preschool Child?

Are preschool children really as bound to perceptions and as egocentric as Piaget believed? Many developmentalists believe that Piaget underestimated the competencies of preschool children by giving them very complex tasks to perform (Bjorklund,

1995). Consider a few examples of the strengths uncovered by researchers using simpler tasks.

Rochel Gelman (1972) simplified Piaget's conservation-of-number task (refer back to Figure 7.4) and discovered that children as young as 3 have some grasp of the concept that number remains the same even when items are rearranged spatially. She first got children to focus their attention on number by playing a game in which two plates, one holding two toy mice and one with three toy mice, were presented; and the plate with the larger number was always declared the winner. Then Gelman started introducing changes, sometimes adding or subtracting mice but sometimes just bunching up or spreading out the mice. Young children were not fooled by spatial rearrangements; they seemed to understand that number remained the same. However, they showed their limitations when given larger sets of numbers they could not count.

Similarly, by reducing tasks to the bare essentials, several researchers have demonstrated that preschool children are not as egocentric as Piaget claimed. In one study, 3-year-olds were shown a card with a dog on one side and a cat on the other (Flavell et al., 1981). The card was held vertically between the child (who could see the dog) and the experimenter (who could see the cat). When children were asked what the experimenter could see, these 3-year-olds performed flawlessly.

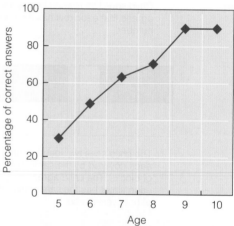

■ FIGURE 7.6 Between the ages of 5 and 10, children steadily improve on class inclusion problems. At age 5, only 30% of children answer correctly, but by age 9 and 10, nearly all the children "get" the class inclusion problem.

SOURCE: From R.S. Siegler & J. Svetina, What leads children to adopt new strategies? A microgenetic/cross-sectional study of class-inclusion, *Child Development*, 77, pp. 997–1015. Copyright © 2006. Reprinted with permission of John Wiley & Sons, Inc.

Finally, preschool children seem to have a good deal more understanding of classification systems than Piaget believed. Sandra Waxman and Thomas Hatch (1992) asked 3- and 4-year-olds to teach a puppet all the different names they could think of for certain animals, plants, articles of clothing, and pieces of furniture. The goal was to see whether children knew terms associated with familiar classification hierarchies—for example, if they knew that a rose is a type of flower and is a member of the larger category of plants. Children performed well, largely because a clever method of prompting responses was used. Depending on which term or terms the children forgot to mention (rose, flower, or plant), they were asked about the rose: "Is this a dandelion?" "Is this a tree?" "Is this an animal?" Often, children came up with the correct terms in response (for example, "No, silly, [it's not an animal] it's a plant!"). Even though young children typically fail the tests of class inclusion that Piaget devised, then, they appear to have a fairly good grasp of familiar classification hierarchies.

Studies such as these have raised important questions about the adequacy of Piaget's theory and have led to a more careful consideration of the demands placed on children by cognitive assessment tasks. Simplified tasks that focus children's attention on relevant aspects of the task and do not place heavy demands on their memories or verbal skills tend to reveal that young children develop sound understandings of the physical world earlier than Piaget thought. Yet Piaget was right in arguing that preschool children, although they have several sound intuitions about the world, are more perception-bound and egocentric thinkers than elementary school children are. Preschool children still depend on their perceptions to guide their thinking,

and they fail to grasp the logic behind concepts such as conservation. They also have difficulty applying their emerging understanding to complex tasks that involve coordinating two or more dimensions.

The Concrete Operations Stage

About the time children start elementary school, their minds undergo another transformation. Piaget's third stage of cognitive development extends from roughly 7 to 11 years of age. The concrete operations stage involves mastering the logical operations missing in the preoperational stage—becoming able to perform mental actions on objects, such as adding and subtracting Halloween candies, classifying dinosaurs, or arranging objects from largest to smallest. This allows school-age children to think effectively about the objects and events they experience in everyday life. For every limitation of the preoperational child, there is a corresponding strength of the concrete-operational child. These contrasts are summarized in ● Table 7.2.

Conservation

Given the conservation-of-liquid task (refer again to Figure 7.4), the preoperational child centers on either the height or the width of the glasses, ignoring the other dimension. The concrete-operational child can decenter and juggle two dimensions at once. Reversibility allows the child to mentally reverse the pouring process and imagine the water in its original container. Transformational thought allows the child to better understand the process of change involved in pouring the water. Overall, armed

● TABLE 7.2 COMPARISON OF PREOPERATIONAL AND CONCRETE-OPERATIONAL THINKING

Preoperational Thinkers	Concrete-Operational Thinkers
Fail conservation tasks because they have:	Solve conservation tasks because they have:
• *Irreversible thought*—Cannot mentally undo an action.	• *Reversibility of thought*—Can mentally reverse or undo an action.
• *Centration*—Center on a single aspect of a problem rather than two or more dimensions at once.	• *Decentration*—Can focus on two or more dimensions of a problem at once.
• *Static thought*—Fail to understand transformations or processes of change from one state to another.	• *Transformational thought*—Can understand the process of change from one state to another.
Perceptual salience. Understanding is driven by how things look rather than derived from logical reasoning.	*Logical reasoning.* Children acquire a set of internal operations that can be applied to a variety of problems.
Transductive reasoning. Children combine unrelated facts, often leading them to draw faulty cause–effect conclusions simply because two events occur close together in time or space.	*Inductive reasoning.* Children draw cause–effect conclusions logically, based on factual information presented to them.
Egocentrism. Children have difficulty seeing things from other perspectives and assume that what is in their mind is also what others are thinking.	*Less egocentrism.* Children understand that other people may have thoughts different from their own.
Single classification. Children classify objects by a single dimension at one time.	*Multiple classification.* Children can classify objects by multiple dimensions and can grasp class inclusion.

with logical operations, the child now knows that there must be the same amount of water after it is poured into a different container; the child has logic, not just appearance, as a guide.

Looking back at the conservation tasks in Figure 7.4, you will notice that some forms of conservation (for example, mass and number) are understood years earlier than others (area or volume). Piaget maintained that operational abilities evolve in a predictable order as simple skills that appear early are reorganized into increasingly complex skills. He used the term **horizontal décalage** for the idea that different cognitive skills related to the same stage of cognitive development emerge at different times.

Seriation and Transitivity

To appreciate the nature and power of logical operations, consider the child's ability to think about relative size. A preoperational child given a set of sticks of different lengths and asked to arrange them from biggest to smallest is likely to struggle, awkwardly comparing one pair of sticks at a time. Concrete-operational children are capable of the logical operation of **seriation**, which enables them to arrange items mentally along a quantifiable dimension such as length or weight. Thus, they perform this seriating task quickly and correctly.

Concrete-operational thinkers also master the related concept of **transitivity**, which describes the necessary relations among elements in a series. If, for example, John is taller than Mark, and Mark is taller than Sam, who is taller—John or Sam? It follows logically that John must be taller than Sam, and the concrete operator grasps the transitivity of these size relationships. Lacking the concept of transitivity, the preoperational child will need to rely on perceptions to answer the question; she may insist that John and Sam stand next to each other to determine who is taller. Preoperational children probably have a better understanding of such transitive relations than Piaget gave them credit for (Gelman, 1978; Trabasso, 1975), but they still have difficulty grasping the logical necessity of transitivity (Chapman & Lindenberger, 1988).

Other Advances

The school-age child overcomes much of the egocentrism of the preoperational period, becoming increasingly better at recognizing other people's perspectives. Classification abilities improve as the child comes to grasp the concept of class inclusion and can bear in mind that subclasses (brown beads and white beads) are included in a whole class (wooden beads). Mastery of mathematical operations improves the child's ability to solve arithmetic problems and results in an interest in measuring and counting things precisely (and sometimes in fury if companions do not keep accurate score in games). Overall, school-age children appear more logical than preschoolers because they possess a powerful arsenal of "actions in the head."

But surely, if Piaget proposed a fourth stage of cognitive development, there must be some limitations to concrete operations. Indeed, there are. This mode of thought is applied to objects, situations, and events that are real or readily imaginable (thus the term *concrete operations*). As you will see in the next section, concrete operators have difficulty thinking about abstract ideas and unrealistic hypothetical propositions.

Checking Mastery

1. Name three ways that preoperational thought is limited relative to concrete-operational thought.

2. What is the defining feature of concrete-operational thought?

Making Connections

1. As a substitute teacher, you sometimes find yourself teaching young children who are mostly preoperational thinkers, while at other times you are teaching children who are concrete-operational thinkers. How would you adjust your lesson plan on stream ecology or global warming to best address these different levels of thought?

7.4 The Adolescent

Although tremendous advances in cognition occur from infancy to the end of childhood, other transformations of the mind are in store for the adolescent. If teenagers become introspective, question their parents' authority, dream of perfect worlds, and contemplate their futures, cognitive development may help explain why.

The Formal Operations Stage

Piaget set the beginning of the formal operations stage of cognitive development around age 11 or 12 and possibly later. If concrete operations are mental actions on objects (tangible things and events), formal operations are mental actions on ideas. Thus, the adolescent who acquires formal operations can mentally juggle and think logically about ideas, which cannot be seen, heard, tasted, smelled, or touched. In other words, formal-operational thought is more hypothetical and abstract than concrete-operational thought; it also involves adopting a more systematic and scientific approach to problem solving (Inhelder & Piaget, 1964).

Hypothetical and Abstract Thinking

If you could have a third eye and put it anywhere on your body, where would you put it, and why? That question was posed to 9-year-old fourth-graders (concrete operators) and to 11- to 12-year-old sixth-graders (the age when the first signs of formal operations often appear). In their drawings, all the 9-year-olds placed the third eye on their foreheads between their existing eyes; many thought the exercise was stupid. The 11- and 12-year-olds were not as bound by the realities of eye location. They could invent ideas contrary to fact (for example, the idea of an eye in a palm) and think logically about the implications of such ideas (■ Figure 7.7). Thus, concrete operators deal with realities, whereas formal operators can deal with possibilities, including those that contradict known reality.

Formal-operational thought is also more abstract than concrete-operational thought. The school-age child may define the justice system in terms of police and judges; the adolescent may define it more abstractly as a branch of government con-

Tanya's response   Ken's response   John's response

■ **FIGURE 7.7** Where would you put a third eye? Tanya (age 9) did not show much inventiveness in drawing her "third eye." But Ken (age 11) said of his eye on top of a tuft of hair, "I could revolve the eye to look in all directions." John (also 11) wanted a third eye in his palm: "I could see around corners and see what kind of cookie I'd get out of the cookie jar." Ken and John show early signs of formal-operational thought.

cerned with balancing the rights of different interests in society. Also, the school-age child may be able to think logically about concrete and factually true statements, as in this syllogism: If you drink poison, you will die. Fred drank poison. Therefore, Fred will die. The adolescent can do this but also engage in such if–then thinking about contrary-to-fact statements ("If you drink milk, you will die") or symbols (If P, then Q. P, therefore Q).

Scientific Reasoning

Formal operations also permit systematic and scientific thinking about problems. One of Piaget's famous tests for formal-operational thinking is the pendulum task (■ **Figure 7.8**). The

child is given several weights that can be tied to a string to make a pendulum and is told that he may vary the length of the string, the amount of weight attached to it, and the height from which the weight is released to find out which of these factors, alone or in combination, determines how quickly the pendulum makes its arc. How would you go about solving this problem?

The concrete operator is likely to jump right in without much advanced planning, using a trial-and-error approach. That is, the child may try a variety of things but fail to test different hypotheses systematically—for example, the hypothesis that the shorter the string is, the faster the pendulum swings, all other factors remaining constant. Concrete operators are therefore unlikely to solve the problem. They can draw proper conclusions

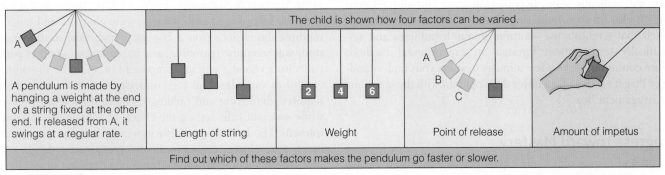

A pendulum is made by hanging a weight at the end of a string fixed at the other end. If released from A, it swings at a regular rate.	The child is shown how four factors can be varied.			
	Length of string	Weight	Point of release	Amount of impetus
Find out which of these factors makes the pendulum go faster or slower.				

■ **FIGURE 7.8** The pendulum problem. SOURCE: From E. Labinowicz, The pendulum problem, *The Piaget primer*, p. 83. Copyright © 1980 Pearson Education. Reprinted with permission.

In this conservation-of-area task, Rachel first determines that the yellow boards have the same amount of space covered by blocks. But after the blocks are rearranged on one of the boards, she fails to conserve area, indicating that one board now has more open space.

from their observations—for example, from watching as someone else demonstrates what happens if a pendulum with a short string is compared with a pendulum with a long string.

What will the formal-operational individual do? In all likelihood, the child will first sit and think, planning an overall strategy for solving the problem. All the possible hypotheses should be generated; after all, the one overlooked may be the right one. Then it must be determined how each hypothesis can be tested. This is a matter of **hypothetical-deductive reasoning**, or reasoning from general ideas or rules to their specific implications. In the pendulum problem, it means starting with a hypothesis and tracing the specific implications of this idea in an if–then fashion: "If the length of the string matters, then I should see a difference when I compare a long string with a short string while holding other factors constant." The trick in hypothesis testing is to vary each factor (for example, the length of the string) while holding all others constant (the weight, the height from which the weight is dropped, and so on). (It is, by the way, the length of the string that matters; the shorter the string, the faster the swing.)

In sum, formal-operational thought involves being able to think systematically about hypothetical ideas and abstract concepts. It also involves mastering the hypothetical-deductive approach that scientists use—forming many hypotheses and systematically testing them through an experimental method. Before continuing, take a few minutes to assess your understanding of Piaget's stages of cognitive development with the questions in Engagement Box 7.1.

Progress toward Mastery

Are 11- and 12-year-olds really capable of all these sophisticated mental activities? Anyone who has had dealings with this age group will know that the answer to this question is usually not. Piaget (1970) described the transition from concrete operations

to formal operations as taking place gradually over years. Many researchers have found it useful to distinguish between early and late formal operations. For example, 11- to 13-year-olds just entering the formal operations stage are able to consider simple hypothetical propositions such as the three-eye problem. But most are not yet able to devise an overall game plan for solving a problem or to systematically generate and test hypotheses. On a battery of Piagetian tasks designed to evaluate scientific reasoning, 11- to 14-year-old girls correctly solved only 20–30% of the problems (Martorano, 1977). By ages 16–17 this had improved, but only to 50–60% correct. Even with training, 11- to 12-year-olds continue to struggle to systematically coordinate multiple variables, although they may do fine on single-variable tasks (Kuhn, Pease, & Wirkala, 2009). Throughout adolescence, responses to scientific reasoning tasks reflect biases indicating that students more readily accept evidence consistent with their preexisting beliefs than evidence inconsistent with these beliefs (Klaczynski & Gordon, 1996a, 1996b; Kuhn, 1993).

Consider the findings from the Munich Longitudinal Study on the Ontogenesis of Individual Competencies (LOGIC) study (see Bullock, Sodian, & Koerber, 2009; Schneider & Bullock, 2009; Weinert & Schneider, 1999). LOGIC began in the 1980s with 200 school-aged children who were observed and tested on multiple dimensions over a 20-year period. One of the areas of study was scientific reasoning, and in particular, whether participants understood a crucial component of scientific reasoning—control of variables. Did they understand that scientific testing requires identifying and holding constant all relevant variables while systematically testing the effects of varying the variable of interest? The LOGIC participants were given a group of experiments to evaluate; each experiment contained a design error, such as not keeping all variables but one constant or not having a comparison group for an intervention study. In addition to evaluating experimental designs, participants were also tested to determine if they could produce their own experiments.

1. Baby Joel seems to be fascinated with the dog's tail: He repeatedly kicks at it with his foot, which makes the dog wag his big tail. Joel finds this highly amusing. This suggests that Joel is in which substage of the sensorimotor period?
   a. Primary circular reactions
   b. Secondary circular reactions
   c. Coordination of secondary schemes
   d. Tertiary circular reactions

2. Bill is playing with his infant daughter, Skylar, showing her a stuffed bear and then dropping it behind the sofa. Skylar seems interested in the toy when it is in front of her, but as soon as Bill drops it behind the sofa, she stops "playing" the game and looks at other things. This illustrates that Sklyar:
   a. Has not yet developed object permanence
   b. Is not really interested in the toy
   c. Is mentally trying to figure out where the toy has gone after it is dropped
   d. Is still operating with secondary circular reactions but has not yet learned to combine them to solve the problem

3. Which of the following statements is TRUE regarding Piaget's first stage of cognitive development?
   a. Piaget may have overestimated infants' abilities by allowing them multiple attempts to solve problems.
   b. Infants progress through the substages in an individualized order that does not permit researchers to make any generalizations about developments of this stage.
   c. Piaget underestimated infants' abilities because he placed many task demands on them in assessing their knowledge.
   d. Piaget was right on the mark with his description of the ages when infants typically acquire symbolic logic.

4. Jeremy used to just bang his shoe on the coffee table, but now he has started holding it up to his ear and "talking" to it as if he is using a telephone. Jeremy has acquired:
   a. Decentration
   b. Transformational thought
   c. Symbolic capacity
   d. Object permanence

5. Mira emphatically tells her older brother that "there *is* a Santa Claus because I see lots of presents under the tree!" Mira's thinking reflects:
   a. The "A-not-B error"
   b. Conservation

   c. Transformational thought
   d. The influence of perceptual salience

6. When Mom presents the kids with some cookies, big sister Kim immediately grabs for the unbroken cookie, saying she doesn't want the broken one. Little sister Sal happily takes the cookie broken in half, saying, "Ha-ha! I got more than you!" Sal seems to lack an understanding of:
   a. Egocentrism
   b. Conservation
   c. Class inclusion
   d. Object permanence

7. Ramon understands that if A is bigger than B, and B is bigger than C, then A must also be bigger than C. This shows that he has mastered:
   a. Transitivity
   b. Horizontal decalage
   c. Seriation tasks
   d. Reversibility of thought

8. Kira is furious that her father won't let her go out with a friend on a school night. She screams, "You have no idea what I'm feeling! You just want me to be miserable." Kira's response indicates that she:
   a. Has not yet acquired conservation of thought
   b. Is spoiled or has unreasonable parents
   c. Shows centration of thought
   d. Shows adolescent egocentrism

9. An important distinction between concrete operational thought and preoperational thought is:
   a. The acquisition of logical reasoning skills in the concrete stage
   b. The acquisition of symbolic logic in the concrete stage
   c. The acquisition of hypothetical thinking in the concrete stage
   d. The use of deductive reasoning in the concrete stage

10. The defining difference between concrete operational thought and formal operational thought is:
    a. The use of logical reasoning
    b. The ability to reason about abstract and hypothetical problems
    c. The ability to imagine performing before an audience
    d. The ability to use relativistic thinking

Answers: 1. B 2. A 3. C 4. C 5. D 6. B 7. A 8. D 9. A 10. B

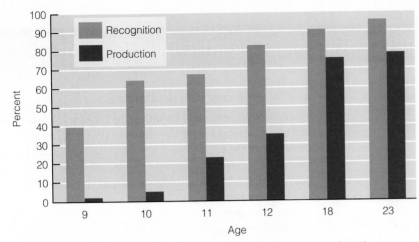

As ■ **Figure 7.9** shows, most participants, even those as young as 10, showed an understanding of this important principle of scientific thinking. However, there was a marked difference between their ability to recognize good scientific reasoning and their ability to produce it. For example, among 12-year-olds, more than 80% could recognize good and bad examples of experiments, but only 35% could create a good experiment themselves. By age 18, though, the ability to create a good experiment was catching up to the ability to recognize a good experiment (91% versus 85%). Thus, adolescents show an awareness of scientific reasoning ("I know it when I see it"), but they may not be able to produce logical scientific reasoning skills until they are older.

Piaget claimed that intuitive reasoning is *replaced* by scientific reasoning as children age, but it turns out that the two forms of reasoning—intuitive and scientific—*coexist* in older thinkers (Klaczynski, 2000, 2001, 2009). Being able to shift between intuitive and scientific reasoning provides flexibility in problem-solving situations as long as the thinker can effectively select the appropriate strategy. However, like children (and adults), adolescents often seem to adopt an intuitive or experiential strategy, leading them to conclusions inconsistent with scientific judgment (Amsel et al., 2008; Klaczynski, 2001). With age, however, adolescents are increasingly able to **decontextualize**, or separate prior knowledge and beliefs from the demands of the task at hand (Kuhn & Franklin, 2006; Stanovich & West, 1997). For example, someone who believes that males are better at math than females may find it difficult to accept new evidence that girls attain higher classroom math grades than boys if intuitions based on their prior experiences do not allow them to scientifically process the new information. Decontextualizing increases the likelihood of using reasoning to analyze a problem logically rather than relying on intuition or faulty existing knowledge.

There is some evidence that recent cohorts of teens (ages 13–15) are better able than earlier cohorts to solve formal-operational tasks. For example, 66% of teens tested in 1996 showed formal-operational thought on a probability test, whereas 49% of teens tested in 1967 showed such skills (Flieller, 1999). Why might formal-operational skills improve over time? Changes in school curricula are the likely explanation. Notably, science curricula were revised in the 1960s and have increasingly incorporated more hands-on discovery learning activities (Bybee, 1995). The achievement of formal-operational thinking depends on opportunities to learn scientific reasoning, as through exposure to math and science education (Babai & Levit-Dori, 2009; Karpov, 2005). The more hands-on the learning, the greater the benefit to performance on hands-on formal-operational tasks.

Several cross-cultural studies have tried to clarify the role of educational experience in cognitive development by studying naturally occurring groups that differ in whether or not adults have had structured schooling. The results of such research show that both age and education level influence performance on formal-operational tasks. For instance, adults with some formal education are able to solve logic problems, whereas adults in the same culture with no formal education are not able to do so (Luria, 1974/1976). Similarly, college and university students outperform adults with no advanced education in solving certain types of formal logic problems, and adults without advanced education in turn outperform adolescents who have not yet acquired as much education (Mwamwenda, 1999; Mwamwenda & Mwamwenda, 1989).

Progress toward the mastery of formal operations is slow, at least as measured by Piaget's scientific tasks. These findings have

Adolescents are more likely than children to benefit from some types of science instruction because formal-operational thought opens the door for reasoning about abstract and hypothetical material.

Humor and Cognitive Development

At age 5, John repeatedly tells his mother the following joke: Why did the football coach go to the bank? Answer: To get his quarter back. When his mom asks him why this is funny, he replies that the coach lost his quarter and needed to get it back. He misses the whole idea that the humor of the joke depends on the double meaning of "quarter back." He repeats it only because of the chuckles it elicits from his listeners, who are amused not by the joke itself but because he is so earnest in his attempt to tell a joke. What really tickles John's funny bone is anything that looks or sounds silly—calling a "shoe" a "floo" or a "poo," for example. At 5 years old, John is likely to laugh at a variety of verbal behaviors such as silly songs, comments, or words. In comparison, his 3-year-old sister is likely to dissolve into laughter at the sight of a silly face or the repetition of "potty words" (Martin, 2007).

With the onset of concrete-operational thought and advances in awareness of the nature of language, children come to appreciate jokes and riddles that involve linguistic ambiguities. The "quarter back" joke boils

© Photo and Co/Lifesize/Getty Images

down to a classification task. School-age children who have mastered the concept of class inclusion can keep the class and subclasses in mind at once and move mentally between the two meanings of "quarter back." Appreciation of such puns is high among second-graders (7- to 8-year-olds) and continues to grow until fourth or fifth grade (Martin, 2007; McGhee, 1979). With their newfound appreciation of linguistic double meanings, 7- to 8-year-olds are likely to find the following riddle fairly amusing (McGhee, 1979, p. 77):

"Why did the old man tiptoe past the medicine cabinet?

Because he did not want to wake up the sleeping pills."

The ability to appreciate such riddles may also signal greater cognitive competence. Children who are better at solving riddles are also better at reading and other language tasks (Ely, 1997).

As their language and social skills expand, children also become more able to understand sarcasm, irony, and other discrepancies between what is said and what is meant, such as when a teacher says to a noisy 8-year-old, "My, but you're quiet today" (Martin, 2007). To appreciate irony, children need the cognitive ability to infer the speaker's intentions, using what is called their "theory of mind," which we will discuss further in Chapter 13. Children first develop an understanding that irony can be used to "soften" a criticism, but appreciating the humor in ironic criticism is slower to develop

(Creusere, 1999; Martin, 2007). Further, understanding ironic criticisms (such as saying "Well, aren't you in a pleasant mood today" to a grumpy sibling) emerges earlier than understanding ironic compliments (such as "What a bad play," following a great soccer kick).

Children's tastes in humor change again when they enter the stage of formal operations around age 11 or 12. Simple riddles and puns are no longer cognitively challenging enough, it seems, and are likely to elicit loud groans (McGhee, 1979). Adolescents and adults are more amused by subtle forms of irony than by the obvious irony that is understood by the child (Dews et al., 1996). Adolescents also appreciate jokes that involve an absurd or contrary-to-fact premise and a punch line that is logical if the absurd premise is accepted. The humor in "How do you fit six elephants into a Volkswagen?" depends on appreciating that "three in the front and three in the back" is a perfectly logical answer only if you accept the hypothetical premise that multiple elephants could fit into a small car. Reality-oriented school-age children may simply consider this joke stupid; after all, elephants cannot fit into cars. Clearly, then, children cannot appreciate certain forms of humor until they have the required cognitive abilities. Research on children's humor suggests that children and adolescents are most attracted to jokes that challenge them intellectually and that contain content relevant to their developmental stage (Martin, 2007; McGhee, 1979).

major implications for secondary-school teachers, who are often trying to teach abstract material to students with a range of thinking patterns. Teachers may need to give concrete thinkers extra assistance by using specific examples and demonstrations to help clarify general principles.

Implications of Formal Thought

Formal-operational thought contributes to other changes in adolescence—some good, some not so good. First, the good news: As you will see in upcoming chapters, formal-operational thought may prepare the individual to gain a sense of identity,

think in more complex ways about moral issues, and understand other people better. Advances in cognitive development help lay the groundwork for advances in many other areas of development, including the appreciation of humor, as shown in Exploration Box 7.2.

Now, the bad news: Formal operations may also be related to some of the more painful aspects of the adolescent experience. Children tend to accept the world as it is and to heed the words of authority figures. The adolescent armed with formal operations can think more independently, imagine alternatives to present realities, and raise questions about everything from why parents set certain rules to why there is injustice in the

A teenage boy may feel that everyone is as preoccupied with his appearance as he is, a form of adolescent egocentrism known as the imaginary audience phenomenon.

world. Questioning can lead to confusion and sometimes to rebellion against ideas that do not seem logical enough. Some adolescents become idealists, inventing perfect worlds and envisioning logical solutions to problems they detect in the imperfect world around them, sometimes losing sight of practical considerations and real barriers to social change. Just as infants flaunt the new schemes they develop, adolescents may go overboard with their new cognitive skills, irritate their parents, and become frustrated when the world does not respond to their flawless logic.

Some years ago, David Elkind (1967) proposed that formal-operational thought also leads to **adolescent egocentrism**—difficulty differentiating one's own thoughts and feelings from those of other people. The young child's egocentrism is rooted in ignorance that different people have different perspectives, but the adolescent's reflects an enhanced ability to reflect about one's own and others' thoughts. Elkind identified two types of adolescent egocentrism: the imaginary audience and the personal fable.

The **imaginary audience** phenomenon involves confusing your own thoughts with those of a hypothesized audience for your behavior. Thus, the teenage girl who ends up with pizza sauce on the front of her shirt at a party may feel extremely self-conscious: "They're all thinking what a slob I am! I wish I could crawl into a hole." She assumes that everyone in the room is as preoccupied with the blunder as she is. Or a teenage boy may spend hours in front of the mirror getting ready for a date, then may be so concerned with how he imagines his date is reacting to him that he hardly notices her: "Why did I say that? She looks bored. Did she notice my pimple?" (She, of course, is equally preoccupied with how she is playing to her audience. No wonder teenagers are often awkward and painfully aware of their every slip on first dates.)

The second form of adolescent egocentrism is the **personal fable**—a tendency to think that you and your thoughts and feelings are unique (Elkind, 1967). If the imaginary audience is a product of the inability to differentiate between self and other, the personal fable is a product of differentiating too much. Thus, the adolescent in love for the first time imagines that no one in the history of the human race has ever felt such heights of emotion. When the relationship breaks up, no one—least of all a parent—could possibly understand the crushing agony. The personal fable may also lead adolescents to feel that rules that apply to others do not apply to them. Thus, they will not be hurt if they speed down the highway without wearing a seat belt or drive under the influence of alcohol. And they will not become pregnant if they engage in sex without contraception, so they do not need to bother with contraception. As it turns out, high scores on measures of adolescent egocentrism are associated with behaving in risky ways (Greene et al., 1996; Holmbeck et al., 1994).

Elkind hypothesized that the imaginary audience and personal fable phenomena should increase when formal operations are first being acquired and then decrease as adolescents get older, gain fuller control of formal operations, and assume adult roles that require fuller consideration of others' perspectives. Indeed, both the self-consciousness associated with the imaginary audience and the sense of specialness associated with the personal fable are most evident in early adolescence and decline by late high school (Elkind & Bowen, 1979; Enright, Lapsley, & Shukla, 1979). Adolescent egocentrism may persist, however, when adolescents have insecure relationships with their parents—when they do not feel that their parents are supportive of them or reliable sources of security (see Chapter 14). Such parent–adolescent relationships may make teens self-conscious and may make them appear to lack self-confidence even as older adolescents (Ryan & Kuczkowski, 1994).

Contrary to what Piaget and Elkind hypothesized, however, researchers have been unable to link the onset of the formal operations stage to the rise of adolescent egocentrism (Gray & Hudson, 1984; O'Connor & Nikolic, 1990). It seems that adolescent egocentrism may arise when adolescents acquire advanced social perspective–taking abilities and contemplate how other people might perceive them and react to their behavior (Lapsley et al., 1986; Vartanian & Powlishta, 1996).

Furthermore, research by Joanna Bell and Rachel Bromnick (2003) suggests that adolescents are preoccupied with how they present themselves in public not because of an imaginary audience but because of a *real audience*. That is, research indicates that adolescents are aware that there are real consequences to how they present themselves. Their popularity and peer approval, as well as their self-confidence and self-esteem, are often influenced by how others (the real audience) perceive them. Adults, too, are aware that their actions and appearance are often judged by others, but although these adult concerns are usually assumed to be realistic, similar concerns by adolescents are sometimes viewed, perhaps unfairly, as trivial (Bell & Bromnick, 2003).

Checking Mastery

1. What change in thinking marks the shift from concrete to formal-operational thinking?

2. What is the hypothetical-deductive approach to thinking?

Making Connections

1. Consider one or more assignments or tests that you recently completed for one (or more) of your courses. Conduct an analysis to determine whether your responses reflect primarily a concrete or a formal level of thinking. If they were primarily concrete, was this appropriate to the task demands? What distinguished the assignments that elicited concrete-operational answers from those that elicited formal-operational answers?

2. Design an educational plan or program that you think would help foster formal-operational thought in students who have not yet mastered it.

7.5 The Adult

Do adults think differently than adolescents do? Does cognition change over the adult years? Until fairly recently, developmentalists have not asked such questions. Piaget indicated that the highest stage of cognitive development, formal operations, was fully mastered by most people between age 15 and age 18. Why bother studying cognitive development in adulthood? As it turns out, it has been worth the effort. Research has revealed limitations in adult performance that must be explained, and it suggests that at least some adults progress beyond formal operations to more advanced forms of thought (Jacobs & Klaczynski, 2002).

Limitations in Adult Cognitive Performance

If many high school students are shaky in their command of formal operations, do most of them gain fuller mastery after the high school years? Gains are indeed made between adolescence and adulthood (Blackburn & Papalia, 1992). However, only about half of all college students show firm and consistent mastery of formal operations on Piaget's scientific reasoning tasks (Neimark, 1975). Similarly, sizable percentages of American adults do not solve scientific problems at the formal level, and there are some societies in which no adults solve formal-operational problems (Neimark, 1975).

Why do more adults not do well on Piagetian tasks? An average level of performance on standardized intelligence tests seems to be necessary for a person to achieve formal-operational thought (Inhelder, 1966). What seems more important than basic intelligence, however, is formal education (Neimark, 1979). In cultures in which virtually no one solves Piaget's problems, people do not receive advanced schooling. If achieving formal-operational thought requires education or specific experiences, Piaget's theory may be culturally biased, and his stages may not be as universal as he believed.

But neither lack of intelligence nor lack of formal education is a problem for most college students. Instead, they have difficulty with tests of formal operations when they lack expertise in a domain of knowledge. Piaget (1972) suggested that adults are likely to use formal operations in a field of expertise but to use concrete operations in less familiar areas. This is precisely what seems to happen. For example, Richard De Lisi and Joanne Staudt (1980) gave three kinds of formal-operational tasks—the pendulum problem, a political problem, and a literary criticism problem—to college students majoring in physics, political science, and English. As ■ Figure 7.10 illustrates, each group of students did well on the problem relevant to that group's field of expertise. On problems outside their fields, however, about half the students failed. Consistent with this, other research shows that task relevancy affects performance on reasoning tasks (Sebby & Papini, 1994). Possibly, then, many adolescents and adults fail to use formal reasoning on Piaget's scientific problems simply because these problems are unfamiliar to them and they lack relevant expertise.

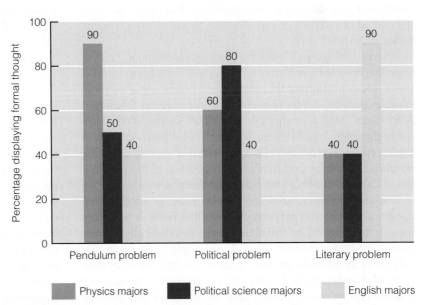

■ **FIGURE 7.10** Expertise and formal operations. College students show the greatest command of formal-operational thought in the subject area most related to their major. SOURCE: From R. Di Lisi & J. Staudt, Individual differences in college students' performance on formal operations task, *Journal of Applied Developmental Psychology*, 1, pp. 206–208. Copyright © 1980 by permission of Elsevier.

As Kurt Fischer (Fischer, 1980; Fischer, Kenny, & Pipp, 1990) maintains, each person may have an optimal level of cognitive performance that will show itself in familiar and well-trained content domains. However, performance is likely to be highly inconsistent across content areas unless the person has had a chance to build knowledge and skills in all these domains. More often, adults may use and strengthen formal modes of thinking only in their areas of expertise. By adopting a contextual perspective on cognitive development, you can appreciate that the individual's experience and the nature of the tasks she is asked to perform influence cognitive performance across the life span (Salthouse, 1990).

Growth beyond Formal Operations?

While some researchers have been asking why adults sometimes perform so poorly on cognitive tasks, others have been asking why they sometimes perform so well. Take Piaget. Was his ability to generate a complex theory of development no more than the application of formal-operational thought? This seems unlikely and, indeed, Fernando Vidal (1984) uses Piaget's own writings as a teen and young man to show how his thinking shifted over time from largely formal operational to something beyond formal operations. Others have argued that formal operations involves applying logic to a *closed* set of ideas and not to *open* sets of ideas that characterize most adult issues (Broughton, 1984; Ricco, 1990). To illustrate this, consider again the pendulum problem. A defined or closed set of variables is associated with this problem; solving the problem is possible by systematically applying logic to this closed set of variables. You do not need to go beyond the problem set. But how do adults make decisions about complex dilemmas and problems that have no well-defined set of variables or variables that are constantly changing rather than static?

Several intriguing ideas have been proposed about stages of cognitive development that may lie beyond formal operations—that is, about **postformal thought**, ways of thinking that are more complex than those of the formal operational stage (see Commons & Richards, 2003; Commons & Ross, 2008; Gurba, 2005). How might thought be qualitatively different in adulthood than it is in adolescence? Several theorists have taken a shot at exploring postformal thinking, and here we consider two of the possibilities: relativistic thinking and dialectical thinking.

As noted earlier, adolescents who have attained formal operations sometimes get carried away with their new powers of logical thinking. They insist that there is a logically correct answer for every question—that if you simply apply logic, you will arrive at the right answer, at some absolute truth. In contrast, adults often think flexibly and recognize that there is not a single right or wrong answer; there are shades of gray to many problems and flexible or creative thinking may be required to successfully navigate many of the complex issues of the adult world. Thus, adults are more likely to engage in **relativistic thinking**, or understanding that knowledge depends on its context and the subjective perspective of the knower (Marchand, 2002; Sinnott, 1984, 1996). Whereas an absolutist assumes that

truth lies in the nature of reality and that there is only one truth, a relativist assumes that his starting assumptions influence the "truth" discovered and that a problem can be viewed in multiple ways.

Consider this logic problem: "A grows 1 cm per month. B grows 2 cm per month. Who is taller?" (Yan & Arlin, 1995, p. 230). The absolutist might say, "B," based on the information given, but the relativist would be more likely to say, "It depends." It depends on how tall A and B were to begin with and on how much time passes before their heights are measured. The relativistic thinker will recognize that the problem is ill defined and that further information is needed, and he will be able to think flexibly about what the answer would be if he made certain assumptions rather than others.

Or consider this problem, given to preadolescents, adolescents, and adults by Gisela Labouvie-Vief and her colleagues (1983, p. 5):

John is known to be a heavy drinker, especially when he goes to parties. Mary, John's wife, warns him that if he gets drunk one more time she will leave him and take the children. Tonight John is out late at an office party. John comes home drunk.

Does Mary leave John? Most preadolescents and many adolescents quickly and confidently said, "Yes." They did not question the assumption that Mary would stand by her word; they simply applied logic to the information they were given. Adults were more likely to realize that different starting assumptions were possible and that the answer depended on which assumptions were chosen. One woman, for example, noted that if Mary had stayed with John for years, she would be unlikely to leave him now. This same woman said, "There was no right or wrong answer. You could get logically to both answers" (p. 12). Postformal thinkers seem able to devise more than one logical solution to a problem (Sinnott, 1996).

In a fascinating study of cognitive growth over the college years, William Perry (1970) found that beginning college students often assumed that there were absolute, objective truths to be found by consulting their textbooks or their professors. They looked to what they believed were authoritative sources for *the* answer to a question, as if all problems have a single, correct answer. As their college careers progressed, they often became frustrated in their search for absolute truths. They saw that many questions seemed to have several answers, depending on the perspective of the respondent. Taking the extremely relativistic view that any opinion was as good as any other, several of these students said they were not sure how they could ever decide what to believe. Eventually, many understood that some opinions can be better supported than others; they were then able to commit themselves to specific positions, fully aware that they were choosing among relative perspectives.

Between adolescence and adulthood, then, many people start as absolutists, become relativists, and finally make commitments to positions despite their more sophisticated awareness of the nature and limits of knowledge (Sinnott, 1996). Not surprisingly, students at the absolute level of thinking use fewer thinking styles; they stick mainly with traditional or conventional

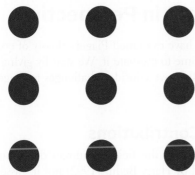

FIGURE 7.11 Your task is to connect all 9 dots using four straight lines or less, without lifting your pen or pencil from the paper. Hint: To be successful, you need to think outside the box! To see a solution to this problem, go to Psychology CourseMate at www.cengagebrain.com

modes of thinking (Zhang, 2002). Students who are relativistic thinkers use a greater variety of thinking styles, including ones that promote creativity and greater cognitive complexity (see Wu & Chiou, 2008). Some refer to this as "thinking outside the box," or thinking unconventionally. Try the 9-dot problem in ■ **Figure 7.11** to see if you can think outside the box. (You can find the answer online.)

Another possibility for advanced thought beyond formal operations is **dialectical thinking**, or detecting paradoxes and inconsistencies among ideas and trying to reconcile them (Basseches, 1984, 2005; Kramer, 1989; Riegel, 1973). For example, you engage in dialectical thinking when you recognize that the problem facing you is multifaceted and will be difficult to solve; you "wrestle" with it mentally, considering the various possibilities and trying to reconcile the pieces that do not immediately make sense to you. You may solicit input from several trusted friends and then consider the pros and cons of each possible solution. Finally, you make a decision on the best way to address the problem, knowing that it is not necessarily a perfect solution, but it is the best option under the current conditions. By engaging in dialectical thinking, advanced thinkers repeatedly challenge and change their understanding of what constitutes "truth." For example, they may arrive at one conclusion, then think of an idea that contradicts their conclusion, and then synthesize the two ideas into a more complete understanding. They realize that the search for truth is an ongoing process and can take them down many different paths.

In an attempt to integrate various postformal ideas, Helena Marchand (2002) suggests these common features:

1. Understanding that knowledge is relative, not absolute; there are far more shades of gray than there are clear dichotomies of knowledge.
2. Accepting that the world (physical and mental) is filled with contradictions: inconsistent information can exist side by side.
3. Attempting to integrate the contradictions into some larger understanding.

Environments that expose us to a wider range of ideas, roles, and experiences seem to foster this higher level of thinking. College students who have greater diversity among their friends tend to exhibit more of these postformal characteristics than those whose friends are very similar (Galupo, Cartwright, & Savage, 2009). Among high school and college students, females report more gender role diversity than males and also a more relativistic perspective on relationships (Kramer & Melchior, 1990).

It is not yet clear whether relativistic, dialectical, or other forms of advanced thinking might qualify as a new, postformal stage of cognitive development. Marchand (2002) concludes that a fifth stage of postformal thought may not be warranted. Adult thought may indeed be different or more advanced than the formal-operational thought of adolescence. Much research confirms that cognitive growth does not end in adolescence. Yet the characteristics of adult thought may not follow the same Piagetian principles that organize the four recognized stages of his theory. That is, adult thought may not reflect a qualitatively different, structural change in thinking that is universal and irreversible (Lerner, 2006).

Aging and Cognitive Skills

What becomes of cognitive capacities in later adulthood? Some mental abilities decline as the average person ages, and it appears that older adults often have trouble solving Piagetian tests of formal-operational thinking (Blackburn & Papalia, 1992). Indeed, elderly adults sometimes perform poorly relative to young and middle-aged adults even on concrete-operational tasks assessing conservation and classification skills.

This does not mean that elderly adults regress to immature modes of thought. For one thing, these studies have involved cross-sectional comparisons of different age groups. The poorer performance of older groups does not necessarily mean that cognitive abilities are lost as people age. It could be caused by a cohort effect, because the average older adult today has had less formal schooling than the average younger adult has had. Older adults attending college tend to perform as well as younger college students on tests of formal operations (Blackburn, 1984; Hooper, Hooper, & Colbert, 1985). Moreover, brief training can quickly improve the performance of older adults long out of school, which suggests that the necessary cognitive abilities are there but merely need to be reactivated (Blackburn & Papalia, 1992).

Questions have also been raised about the relevance of the skills assessed in Piagetian tasks to the lives of older adults (Labouvie-Vief, 1985). Not only are these problems unfamiliar to many older adults, but they also resemble the intellectual challenges that children confront in school, not those that most adults encounter in everyday contexts. Thus, older people may not be motivated to solve them. Also, older adults may rely on modes of cognition that have proved useful to them in daily life but that make them look cognitively deficient in the laboratory (Salthouse, 1990).

Consider this example: Kathy Pearce and Nancy Denney (1984) found that elderly adults, like young children but unlike other age groups, often group two objects on the basis of some functional relationship between them (for example, putting a pipe and matches together because matches are used to light pipes) rather than on the basis of similarity (for example, putting a pipe and a cigar together because they are both ways of smoking tobacco). In school and in some job situations, Pearce and Denney suggest, people are asked to group objects on the basis of similarity, but in everyday life it may make more sense to associate objects commonly used together.

Such findings suggest that what appear to be deficits in older people may merely be differences in style. Similar stylistic differences in classification skills have been observed cross-culturally and can, if researchers are not careful, lead to the incorrect conclusion that uneducated adults from non-Western cultures lack basic cognitive skills. A case in point: Kpelle adults in Africa, when asked to sort foods, clothing, tools, and cooking utensils into groups, sorted them into pairs based on functional relationships. "When an exasperated experimenter finally asked, 'How would a fool do it?' he was given sorts of the type that were initially expected—four neat piles with foods in one, tools in another, and so on" (Glick, 1975, p. 636).

So today's older adults appear not to perform concrete-operational and formal-operational tasks as well as their younger contemporaries do. Planners of adult education for senior citizens might bear in mind that some (although by no means all) of their students may benefit from more concrete forms of instruction. However, these differences may be related to factors other than age, such as education and motivation; an age-related decline in operational abilities has not been firmly established. Most importantly, older adults who perform poorly on unfamiliar problems in laboratory situations often perform far more capably on the sorts of problems that they encounter in everyday contexts (Cornelius & Caspi, 1987; Salthouse, 1990).

Checking Mastery

1. When, or under what conditions, is an adult most likely to use formal-operational thinking?

2. What is relativistic thinking?

Making Connections

1. How important is it to achieve formal-operational thought? What limitations would you experience at work and school if you operated at a concrete-operational level all the time and never progressed to formal-operational thought?

2. What sorts of questions or answers do you contribute to class discussions? Do they reflect primarily concrete operational, formal operational, or something beyond formal operational thinking such as relativistic or dialectical thinking?

7.6 Piaget in Perspective

Now that you have examined Piaget's theory of cognitive development, it is time to evaluate it. We start by giving credit where credit is due, then we consider challenges to Piaget's version of things.

Piaget's Contributions

Piaget is a giant in the field of human development. As one scholar quoted by Harry Beilin (1992) put it, "assessing the impact of Piaget on developmental psychology is like assessing the impact of Shakespeare on English literature or Aristotle on philosophy—impossible" (p. 191). It is hard to imagine that researchers would know even a fraction of what they know about intellectual development without Piaget's groundbreaking work.

One sign of a good theory is that it stimulates research. Piaget asked fundamentally important questions about how humans come to know the world and showed that we can answer them "by paying attention to the small details of the daily lives of our children" (Gopnik, 1996, p. 225). His cognitive developmental perspective has been applied to almost every aspect of human development, and the important questions he raised continue to guide the study of cognitive development. Thus, his theory has undoubtedly stimulated much research in the decades following its creation.

We can credit Piaget with some lasting insights (Flavell, 1996). He showed us that infants are active in their own development—that from the start they seek to master problems and to understand the incomprehensible by using the processes of assimilation and accommodation to resolve their cognitive disequilibrium. He taught us that young people think differently than older people do—and often in ways we never would have suspected. The reasoning of preschoolers, for example, often defies adult logic, but it makes sense in light of Piaget's insights about their egocentrism and reliance on the perceptual salience of certain aspects of a situation. School-age children have the logical thought processes that allow them to excel at many tasks, but they draw a blank when presented with hypothetical or abstract problems. And adolescents are impressive with their scientific reasoning skills and their ability to wrestle with abstract problems, but they may think so much about events that they get tangled with new forms of egocentrism.

Finally, Piaget was largely right in his basic description of cognitive development. The sequence he proposed—sensorimotor to preoperational to concrete operations to formal operations—seems to describe the course and content of intellectual development for children and adolescents from the hundreds of cultures and subcultures that have been studied (Flavell, Miller, & Miller, 1993). Although cultural factors influence the rate of cognitive growth, the direction of development is always from sensorimotor thinking to preoperational thinking to concrete operations to, for many, formal operations (or even postformal operations). Piaget's account of development remains relevant to our understanding of current issues in the field of cognition (Kuhn, 2008).

Challenges to Piaget

Partly because Piaget's theory has been so enormously influential, it has had more than its share of criticism: some of this has been mild—suggesting the need for minor tweaking of the theory—whereas other criticism has been more severe. John Broughton (1984), for example, concluded that Piaget's theory is fundamentally flawed and should be thrown out. Despite Broughton's self-proclaimed revolutionary position on Piaget, most challenges have used the decades of accumulated research on Piaget's theory to offer targeted refinements to specific areas of the theory. Here, we focus on five common criticisms (see Lourenco & Machado, 1996):

1. *Underestimating young minds.* Piaget seems to have underestimated the cognitive abilities of infants and young children, although he emphasized that he was more interested in understanding the sequences of changes than the specific ages at which they occur (Lourenco & Machado, 1996). When researchers use more familiar problems than Piaget's and reduce tasks to their essentials, hidden competencies of young children—and of adolescents and adults—are sometimes revealed.

2. *Failing to distinguish between competence and performance.* Piaget sought to identify underlying cognitive competencies that guide performance on cognitive tasks. But there is an important difference between understanding a concept and passing a test designed to measure it. The age ranges Piaget proposed for some stages may have been off target partly because he tended to ignore the many factors besides competence that can influence task performance—everything from the individual's motivation, verbal abilities, and memory capacity to the nature, complexity, and familiarity of the task used to assess mastery. Piaget may have been too quick to assume that children who failed one of his tests lacked competence; they may only have failed to demonstrate their competence in a particular situation.

    Perhaps more importantly, Piaget may have overemphasized the idea that knowledge is an all-or-nothing concept (Schwitzgebel, 1999). Instead of having or not having a particular competence, children probably gain competence gradually and experience long periods between not understanding and understanding. Many of the seemingly contradictory results of studies using Piagetian tasks can be accounted for with this idea of gradual change in understanding. For instance, Piaget argued that infants do not show understanding of object permanence until 9 months, but other research indicates that at least some understanding of object permanence is present at 4 months (Ruffman et al., 2005). If researchers accept that conceptual change is gradual, then they can stop debating whether competence is present or not present at a particular age.

3. *Wrongly claiming that broad stages of development exist.* According to Piaget, each new stage of cognitive development is a coherent mode of thinking applied across a range of problems. Piaget emphasized the consistency of thinking *within a*

stage and the difference *between* stages (Meadows, 2006). Yet individuals are often inconsistent in their performance on different tasks that presumably measure the abilities defining a given stage. For example, conservation of liquid is acquired earlier than conservation of volume. Researchers increasingly argue that cognitive development is domain specific—that is, it is a matter of building skills in particular content areas—and that growth in one domain may proceed much faster than growth in another (Fischer, Kenny, & Pipp, 1990). In addition, the transitions between stages are not swift and abrupt, as most of Piaget's writings suggest, but are often lengthy (over several years) and subtle (see Meadows, 2006). It is not always clear when a child has made the shift from one set of structures to a more advanced set of structures, particularly when we consider the two stages based on logical structures—concrete and formal operations.

4. *Failing to adequately explain development.* Several critics suggest that Piaget did a better job of describing development than of explaining how it comes about (Bruner, 1997; Meadows, 2006). To be sure, Piaget wrote extensively about his interactionist position on the nature–nurture issue and did as much as any developmental theorist to tackle the question of how development comes about. Presumably, humans are always assimilating new experiences in ways that their level of maturation allows, accommodating their thinking to those experiences, and reorganizing their cognitive structures into increasingly complex modes of thought. Yet this explanation is vague. Researchers need to know far more about how specific maturational changes in the brain and specific kinds of experiences contribute to important cognitive advances.

5. *Giving limited attention to social influences on cognitive development.* Some critics say Piaget paid too little attention to how children's minds develop through their social interactions with more competent individuals and how they develop differently in different cultures (Karpov, 2005). Piaget's child often resembles an isolated scientist exploring the world alone, but children develop their minds through interactions with parents, teachers, peers, and siblings. True, Piaget had interesting ideas about the role of *peers* in helping children adopt other perspectives and reach new conclusions (see Chapter 13 on moral development). But he did not believe that children learned much from their interactions with *adults*. This may seem counterintuitive, but Piaget believed that children see other children, but not adults, as "like themselves." Hearing a different perspective from someone like oneself can trigger internal conflict, but hearing a perspective from someone different from oneself may not be viewed as a challenge to one's current way of thinking because the person—and their views—are simply too different. Thus, in Piaget's model, no notable cognitive conflict, and therefore little cognitive growth, occurs from children interacting with adults. As you will see shortly, the significance of social interaction and culture for cognitive development is the basis of the perspective on cognitive development offered by one of Piaget's early critics, Lev Vygotsky.

Checking Mastery

1. What are two of Piaget's major contributions to our understanding of cognitive development?

2. What are three problems with, or challenges to, Piaget's theory of cognitive development?

Making Connections

1. How might Piaget's theory be updated to accommodate the research findings that have emerged since he constructed his theory?

2. Considering the differences among preoperational thought, concrete-operational thought, and formal-operational thought, what should parents keep in mind as they interact with their 4-year-old, 8-year-old, and 17-year-old children?

7.7 Vygotsky's Sociocultural Perspective

You can gain additional insight into Piaget's view of cognitive development by considering the quite different sociocultural perspective of Lev Vygotsky (1962, 1978; see also Karpov, 2005). This Russian psychologist was born in 1896, the same year as Piaget, and was an active scholar in the 1920s and 1930s when Piaget was formulating his theory. For many years, Vygotsky's work was banned for political reasons in the former Soviet Union, and North American scholars lacked English translations of his work, which limited consideration of Vygotsky's ideas until recent decades. In addition, Vygotsky died of tuberculosis at age 38, before his theory was fully developed. However, his main theme is clear: cognitive growth occurs in a sociocultural context and evolves out of the child's social interactions.

Culture and Thought

Culture and society play a pivotal role in Vygotsky's theory. Indeed, intelligence in the Vygotskian model is held by the group, not the individual, and is closely tied to the language system and other tools of thinking the group has developed over time (Case, 1998). Culture and social experiences affect how we think, not just what we think.

Consider some research by Vygotsky's colleague, Alexander Luria, who tested groups of 9- to 12-year-old children growing up in different social environments. Children were given target words and asked to name the first thing that came to mind when they heard each word. Luria found that children growing up in a remote rural village with limited social experiences gave remarkably similar responses, whereas children growing up in a large city gave more distinctly individual answers. Vygotsky and Luria believed that this difference reflected the city children's broader exposure to various aspects of culture. On their own, the rural children were unable to develop cer-

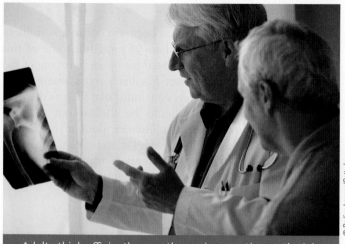

Adults think efficiently once they gain expertise on the job.

© Radius Images/Getty Images

tain types of knowledge. Knowledge, then, depends on social experiences.

Vygotsky would not be surprised to learn that formal-operational thought is rarely used in some cultures; he expected cognitive development to vary from society to society depending on the mental tools such as the language that the culture values and makes available. How do children acquire their society's mental tools? They acquire them by interacting with parents and other more experienced members of the culture and by adopting their language and knowledge (Frawley, 1997).

Social Interaction and Thought

Consider this scenario: Annie, a 4-year-old, receives a jigsaw puzzle, her first, for her birthday. She attempts to work the puzzle but gets nowhere until her father sits down beside her and gives her some tips. He suggests that it would be a good idea to put the corners together first. He points to the pink area at the edge of one corner piece and says, "Let's look for another pink piece." When Annie seems frustrated, he places two interlocking pieces near each other so that she will notice them. And when she succeeds, he offers words of encouragement. As Annie gets the hang of it, he steps back and lets her work more independently. This kind of social interaction, said Vygotsky, fosters cognitive growth.

How? First, Annie and her father are operating in what Vygotsky called the **zone of proximal development**—the gap between what a learner can accomplish independently and what she can accomplish with the guidance and encouragement of a more skilled partner. Skills within the zone are ripe for development and are the skills at which instruction should be aimed. Skills outside the zone are either well mastered already or still too difficult. In this example, Annie obviously becomes a more competent puzzle-solver with her father's help than without it. More importantly, she will internalize the problem-solving techniques that she discovered in collaboration with her father, working together in her zone of proximal development, and will use them on her own, rising to a new level of independent mastery.

What began as a social process involving two people becomes a cognitive process within one.

An important implication of the zone of proximal development is that knowledge is not a fixed state and no single test or score can adequately reflect the range of a person's knowledge. The mind has potential for unlimited growth. Development consists of moving toward the upper range of the zone using the tools of society such as the language and the inventions it has created. The upper limit continues to move upward in response to cultural changes (Smagorinsky, 1995). Support for Vygotsky's idea of the zone of proximal development comes from various sources, including research showing that children's performance on assisted learning tasks is a good predictor of their future achievement (Meijer & Elshout, 2001). And research on pairing less-skilled readers with more-skilled ones shows that reading fluency increases substantially when the less-skilled readers are provided with a model of good reading and encouragement (Nes, 2003).

In many cultures, children do not go to school with other children to learn, nor do their parents explicitly teach them tasks such as weaving and hunting. Instead, they learn through **guided participation**—by actively participating in culturally relevant activities with the aid and support of their parents and other knowledgeable guides (Rogoff, 1998). Jerome Bruner (1983) had a similar concept in mind when he wrote of the many ways in which parents provide **scaffolding** for their children's development; that is, the more skilled person gives structured help to a less skilled learner but gradually reduces the help as the less skilled learner becomes more competent. By calling attention to guided participation processes, in the zone of proximal development, Vygotsky was rejecting Piaget's view of children as independent explorers in favor of the view that they learn more sophisticated cognitive strategies through their interactions with more mature thinkers. To Piaget, the child's level of cognitive development determines what he can learn; to Vygotsky, learning in collaboration with more knowledgeable companions drives cognitive development.

According to Lev Vygotsky's theory, cognitive development is shaped by the culture in which children live and the kinds of problem-solving strategies that adults and other knowledgeable guides pass on to them.

By working with a more knowledgeable partner, this child is able to accomplish more than would be possible on his own. According to Lev Vygotsky, the difference between what a child can accomplish alone and with a partner is the zone of proximal development.

Tools of Thought

Vygotsky believed that mental activity, like physical activity, is mediated by tools (Karpov, 2005). If a child wants to start a garden, we wouldn't send her outside empty handed and say, "Go ahead and make a garden." We would, instead, equip her with an array of tools—shovel, rake, gloves, fertilizer, seeds, and so on—that have already been proven useful for accomplishing this task. Further, we would probably show her how to best use these tools to accomplish the desired task. We might show the child how to poke holes in the soil and drop seeds inside, watch while the child attempted this, and perhaps correct her if she pushed the seeds in too deep. As the child practices and masters the use of the tools presented by the adult, the child adopts the tools as her own. The same process is involved in passing along culturally derived tools for mental activity.

In Vygotsky's view, adults use a variety of tools to pass culturally valued modes of thinking and problem solving to their children. Spoken language is the most important tool, but writing, using numbers, and applying problem-solving and memory strategies also convey information and enable thinking (Vygotsky, 1978). The type of tool used to perform a task influences performance on the task. Consider a study by Dorothy Faulkner and her colleagues (2000) with 9- and 10-year-old children. Children worked in pairs on a science project (a task developed by Inhelder and Piaget that involves figuring out which chemicals to combine to make a colored liquid), using either a computer simulation of the task or the actual physical materials. The children who worked with the computerized version talked more, tested more possible chemical combinations, and completed the task more quickly than children who worked with the physical materials. The computer, then, was a tool that changed the nature of the problem-solving activity and influenced performance, as Vygotsky would have predicted.

Look more closely at Vygotsky's notion of how tools—especially language—influence thought. Whereas Piaget maintained that cognitive development influences language development, Vygotsky argued that language shapes thought in important ways and that thought changes fundamentally once we begin to think in words (Bodrova & Leong, 1996). Piaget and Vygotsky both noticed that preschool children often talk to themselves as they go about their daily activities, almost as if they were play-by-play sports announcers. ("I'm putting the big piece in the corner. I need a pink one. Not that one—this one.") Two preschool children playing next to each other sometimes carry on separate monologues rather than conversing. Piaget (1926) regarded such speech as egocentric—further evidence that preoperational thinkers cannot yet take the perspectives of other people (in this case, their conversation partners) and therefore have not mastered the art of social speech. He did not believe that egocentric speech played a useful role in cognitive development.

In contrast, Vygotsky called children's recitations **private speech**—speech to oneself that guides one's thought and behavior. Rather than viewing it as a sign of cognitive immaturity, he saw it as a critical step in the development of mature thought and as the forerunner of the silent thinking-in-words that adults engage in every day. Adults guide children's behavior with speech, a tool that children adopt and initially use externally, just as adults did with them. Gradually, this regulatory speech is internalized.

Studies conducted by Vygotsky and other researchers support his claim. For example, in one set of studies, Vygotsky (1934/1962) measured children's private speech first as they worked unimpeded on a task, then as they worked to overcome an obstacle placed in their path. Their use of private speech increased dramatically when they confronted an interruption of their work—a problem to solve. Thus, young children rely most heavily on private speech when they are struggling to solve difficult problems (Berk, 1992). Even adults sometimes revert to thinking aloud when they are stumped by a problem (John-Steiner, 1992).

The incidence of private speech varies with age and task demands. Both 3- and 4-year-olds use private speech, but 4-year-olds are more likely to use it systematically when engaged in a sustained activity. Four-year-olds are presumably more goal oriented than 3-year-olds and use private speech to regulate their behavior and achieve their goals (Winsler, Carlton, & Barry, 2000). As the task becomes familiar and children gain competence, the use of private speech decreases (Duncan & Pratt, 1997). Private speech is also more frequent during open-ended activities (such as pretend play) that have several possible outcomes than during closed-ended tasks that have a single outcome (Krafft & Berk, 1998). Open-ended activities tend to be directed more by the child than by an adult; they allow children to alter the difficulty level of the task so that it is appropriately challenging. In contrast, adult-directed activities provide fewer opportunities for children to regulate their own behavior.

Intellectually capable children rely more heavily on private speech in the preschool years and make the transition to inner speech earlier in the elementary school years than their less academically capable peers do (Berk & Landau, 1993). This sug-gests that the preschool child's self-talk is indeed a sign of cognitive maturity, as Vygotsky claimed, rather than a sign of immature egocentrism, as Piaget claimed.

In addition, heavy use of private speech contributes to effective problem-solving performance—if not immediately, then when children encounter similar problems in the future (Behrend, Rosengren, & Perlmutter, 1989; Bivens & Berk, 1990). The amount of private speech and the nature of what the child says are both related to performance (Chiu & Alexander, 2000). In particular, children who use private speech to talk themselves through a problem ("No, I need to change this. Try it over here. Yes, that's good.") show greater motivation toward mastery; that is, they are more likely to persist on a task even without adult prodding (Chiu & Alexander, 2000). Thus, private speech not only helps children think their way through challenging problems but also allows them to incorporate into their own thinking the problem-solving strategies they learned during their collaborations with adults. Notice that, as in guided participation, what is at first a social process becomes an individual psychological process. In other words, social speech (for example, the conversation between Annie and her father as they jointly worked a puzzle) gives rise to private speech (Annie talking aloud, much as her father talked to her, as she then tries to work the puzzle on her own), which in turn goes "underground" to become first mutterings and lip movements and then inner speech (Annie's silent verbal thought).

Evaluation of Vygotsky

Although many scholars find Vygotsky's ideas a refreshing addition to Piaget's, some concerns should be noted. Piaget has been criticized for placing too much emphasis on the individual and not enough on the social environment; Vygotsky has been criticized for placing too much emphasis on social interaction (Feldman & Fowler, 1997). Vygotsky seemed to assume that all knowledge and understanding of the world is transmitted through social interaction. But at least some understanding is individually constructed, as Piaget proposed. Vygotsky and Piaget are often presented as opposites on a continuum representing the extent to which cognitive development derives from social experience. However, a careful reading of the two theorists reveals that they are not as dissimilar as they are often presented to be (DeVries, 2000; Matusov & Hayes, 2000). Both Piaget and Vygotsky acknowledge the importance of the social context of development. Still, there are differences in their emphasis. ● Table 7.3 summarizes some of the differences between Vygotsky's sociocultural perspective and Piaget's cognitive developmental view. Application Box 7.1 explains their views on improving cognitive functioning.

Pause for a moment and consider the remarkable developmental accomplishments we described in this chapter. The human mind's capacity for thought is awesome. Because the human mind is so complex, you should not be surprised that it is not yet understood. Piaget attacked only part of the puzzle, and he only partially succeeded. Vygotsky alerted us to sociocultural influences on cognitive development but died before he could formalize his theory. As you will see in Chapters 8 and 9, other ways to think about mental development are needed.

TABLE 7.3 A COMPARISON OF VYGOTSKY AND PIAGET

Vygotsky's Sociocultural View	Piaget's Cognitive Developmental View
Processes of animal and human development are fundamentally different.	Processes of animal and human development are fundamentally the same.
Cognitive development is different in different social and historical contexts.	Cognitive development is mostly the same universally.
Appropriate unit of analysis is the social, cultural, and historical context in which the individual develops.	Appropriate unit of analysis is the individual.
Cognitive growth results from social interactions (guided participation in the zone of proximal development).	Cognitive growth results from the child's independent explorations of the world.
Children and their partners co-construct knowledge.	Children construct knowledge on their own.
Social processes become individual psychological ones (e.g., social speech becomes inner speech).	Individual, egocentric processes become more social (e.g., egocentric speech becomes social speech).
Adults are especially important because they know the culture's tools of thinking.	Peers are especially important because the cognitive conflict triggered by different perspectives of other children is not so overwhelming that it cannot be resolved.
Learning precedes development (tools learned with adult help become internalized).	Development precedes learning (children cannot master certain things until they have the requisite cognitive structures).
Training can help mediate development.	Training is largely ineffective in "speeding up" development.

Checking Mastery

1. What theme is stressed in Vygotsky's theory that is largely missing in Piaget's theory?
2. What is the zone of proximal development?

Making Connections

1. Create descriptions of a Piagetian preschool and a Vygotskian preschool. What are the main differences in how children will be assessed, what they will be taught, and how they will be taught?
2. Piaget and Vygotsky differed in their views of the importance of the individual versus society. Compare their positions on individual versus society in terms of cognitive development.

What do the theories of Piaget and Vygotsky have to contribute to the goal of optimizing cognition? Studies suggest that many Piagetian concepts can be taught to children who are slightly younger than the age at which the concepts would naturally emerge. Training is sometimes difficult, and it does not always generalize well to new problems, but progress can be achieved. Dorothy Field (1981), for example, demonstrated that 4-year-olds could be trained to recognize the identity of a substance such as a ball of clay before and after its appearance is altered—that is, to understand that although the clay looks different, it is still the same clay and has to be the same amount of clay. Field found that nearly 75% of the children given this identity training could solve at least three of five conservation problems 2–5 months after training.

Similar training studies have demonstrated that children who function at the late concrete operations stage can be taught formal operations (Adey & Shayer, 1992). Researchers have had even more luck improving the cognitive performance of older adults, sometimes with simple interventions (Blackburn & Papalia, 1992). Make no mistake: No one has demonstrated that 2-year-olds can be taught formal operations. But at least these studies establish that specific training experiences can somewhat speed a child's progress through Piaget's stages or bring out more advanced capacities in an adult performing at a less advanced level.

In truth, Piaget disapproved of attempts by Americans to speed children's progress through his stages (Piaget, 1970). He believed parents should provide young children with opportunities to explore their world and teachers should use a discovery approach in the classroom that allows children to learn by doing. Given their natural curiosity and normal opportunities to try their hand at solving problems, children would construct ever more complex understandings on their own. Many educators have incorporated Piaget's ideas about discovery-based education into their lesson plans, especially in science classes. Teachers have also taken seriously Piaget's notion that children understand material best if they can assimilate it into their existing understandings. Finding out what the learner already knows or can do and providing instruction matched to the child's level of development are in the spirit of Piaget.

What would Vygotsky recommend to teachers who want to stimulate cognitive growth? As you might guess, Vygotsky's theoretical orientation leads to a different approach to education than Piaget's does—a more social one. Whereas students in Piaget's classroom would most likely be engaged in independent exploration, students in Vygotsky's classroom would be involved in guided participation, "co-constructing" knowledge during interactions with teachers and more knowledgeable peers. The roles of teachers and other more skillful collaborators would be to organize the learning activity, break it into steps, provide hints and suggestions carefully tailored to the student's abilities, and gradually turn over more of the mental work to the student. According to Vygotsky's sociocultural perspective, the guidance provided by a skilled partner will then be internalized by the learner, first as private speech and eventually as silent inner speech. Education ends up being a matter of providing children with tools of the mind important in their culture, whether hunting strategies or computer skills (Berk & Winsler, 1995; Bodrova & Leong, 1996).

Is there evidence that one of these theoretical approaches might be superior to the other? Consider what Lisa Freund (1990) found when she had 3- to 5-year-old children help a puppet with a sorting task: deciding which furnishings (sofas, beds, bathtubs, stoves, and so on) should be placed in each of six rooms of a dollhouse that the puppet was moving into. First the children were tested to determine what they already knew about proper furniture placement. Then each child worked at a similar task, either alone (as might be the case in Piaget's discovery-based education, although here children were provided with corrective feedback by the experimenter) or with his or her mother (Vygotsky's guided learning). Finally, to assess what they had learned, Freund asked the children to perform a final, rather complex furniture-sorting task. The results were clear: Children who had sorted furniture with help from their mothers showed dramatic improvements in sorting ability, whereas those who had practiced on their own showed little improvement. Moreover, the children who gained the most from guided participation with their mothers were those whose mothers talked the most about how to tackle the task. Collaborating with a competent peer can also produce cognitive gains that a child might not achieve working alone (Azmitia, 1992; Gauvain & Rogoff, 1989).

So children do not always learn the most when they function as solitary scientists, seeking discoveries on their own; often, conceptual growth springs more readily from children's interactions with other people—particularly with competent people who provide an optimal amount of guidance. Yet it would seem that many children might benefit most from the best of both worlds: opportunities to explore on their own and supportive companions to offer help when needed.

Chapter Summary

7.1 Piaget's Constructivist Approach

- Jean Piaget developed a theory of how children come to know their world by constructing their own schemes or cognitive structures through active exploration.
- Studying children using the clinical method, a flexible question-and-answer technique, Piaget formulated four stages of cognitive development in which children construct increasingly complex schemes through an interaction of maturation and experience.
- Intelligence is a basic life function that allows organisms (including humans) to adapt to the demands of their environment.
- Children adapt to the world through the processes of organization and adaptation (assimilating new experiences to existing understandings and accommodating existing understandings to new experiences).

7.2 The Infant

- Infants progress through six substages of the sensorimotor period by perceiving and acting on the world; they progress from using their reflexes to adapt to their environment to using symbolic or representational thought to solve problems in their heads.
- Major accomplishments of the sensorimotor stage include the development of object permanence, or the realization that objects continue to exist even when they are not directly experienced, and the symbolic capacity, or the ability to allow one thing to represent something else. The emergence of the symbolic capacity paves the way for language and pretend play.

7.3 The Child

- In the preoperational stage, preschool-age children do not yet reason logically; instead they rely on perceptually salient features of a task or object. Their pre-logical set of cognitive structures leads them to have trouble with conservation and classification tasks. In particular, preoperational children lack the abilities to decenter, reverse thought, and understand transformations. In addition, they tend to be egocentric—viewing the world from their own perspective and not recognizing others' points of views.
- Concrete-operational thinkers can reason logically about concrete information, which allows them to solve conservation and classification tasks. Concrete-operational children have acquired the abilities of decentration, reversibility of thought, and transformational thought. They can think about relations, grasping seriation and transitivity, and they understand the concept of class inclusion.

7.4 The Adolescent

- Adolescents may advance to Piaget's last stage of cognitive development—formal-operational thought, in which they can think about abstract concepts and apply their logical reasoning to hypothetical problems. Formal-operational thinkers can simultaneously consider multiple task components.

- Formal-operational thought may give rise to special forms of egocentrism, namely, the imaginary audience and personal fable.

7.5 The Adult

- Many adults seem to function at the concrete-operational level, rather than at Piaget's highest level of formal-operational thought. Formal-operational thought appears to be highly dependent on formal education. It is also influenced by culture and area of expertise.
- Some adults may acquire advanced levels of thought not considered by Piaget, such as relativistic thinking, or understanding that knowledge is dependent on the knower's subjective perspective, and dialectical thinking, or detecting and reconciling contradictory ideas.

7.6 Piaget in Perspective

- Piaget's theory has stimulated much research over the years, which has added considerably to our understanding of cognitive development. Piaget showed us that infants are active, not passive, in their own development. He argued that children think differently during different phases of their development, as reflected in his four qualitatively different stages.
- Piaget has been criticized for underestimating the capacities of infants and young children, not considering factors besides competence that influence performance, failing to demonstrate that his stages have coherence, offering vague explanations of development, and underestimating the role of language and social interaction in cognitive development.

7.7 Vygotsky's Sociocultural Perspective

- Lev Vygotsky's sociocultural perspective emphasizes cultural and social influences on cognitive development more than Piaget's theory does.
- Through guided participation in culturally important activities, children learn problem-solving techniques from knowledgeable partners sensitive to their zone of proximal development.
- Language is the most important tool that adults use to pass culturally valued thinking and problem solving to their children. Language shapes their thought and moves from social speech to private speech and later to inner speech.

Checking Mastery Answers

For answers to Checking Mastery questions, visit **www.cengagebrain.com**

Key Terms

Media Resources

Psychology CourseMate

Access an integrated eBook and chapter-specific learning tools including flashcards, quizzes, videos, and more. Go to **www.cengagebrain.com**

Jean Piaget's Genetic Epistemology: Appreciation and Critique

This website, maintained by Robert Campbell of Clemson University, offers the visitor a highly detailed biography of Piaget's life and works, as well as a detailed critique of Piaget's theory. To access, see "web links" in Psychology CourseMate at www.cengagebrain.com

Vygotsky Archives

The Lev Vygotsky Archives is a tremendous resource for anyone seeking information on the life and work of this famous Soviet theorist. Highlights include direct access to several important written works and an image gallery. To access, see "web links" in Psychology CourseMate at www.cengagebrain.com

Understanding the DATA: Exercises on the Web

www.cengagebrain.com
For additional insight on the data presented in this chapter, try out the exercises for these figures in Psychology CourseMate at

www.cengagebrain.com:

Figure 7.6 Between the ages of 5 and 10, children steadily improve on class inclusion problems. At age 5, only 30% of children answer correctly, but by age 9 and 10, nearly all the children "get" the class inclusion problem.

Figure 7.10 Expertise and formal operations. College students show the greatest command of formal–operational thought in the subject area most related to their major.

CengageNOW

www.cengagebrain.com
Go to www.cengagebrain.com to link to CengageNOW, your online study tool. First take the Pre-Test for this chapter to get your Personalized Study Plan, which will identify topics you need to review and direct you to online resources. Then take the Post-Test to determine what concepts you have mastered and what you still need work on.

8

Information Processing and Memory

© Radius Images/Corbis

What would it be like to remember nearly every day of your life? Elizabeth Parker, Larry Cahill, and James McGaugh (2006) describe the case of "AJ," a woman of average intelligence born in 1965, who has extraordinary recall for most days of her life since childhood. When given a date, such as October 4, 1989, she reports that she "sees" the day...sees the events of that day unfold in her head...experiences the events as if they were current...and effortlessly recalls information from the day. Her memories are highly personal, revolving around her daily activities. Interestingly, she was an average student with no special ability to memorize facts and figures unconnected to her personally. She went on to write her memoir, using her real name of Jill Price, describing her memory as a movie constantly playing in her head as if on a split screen, with the present running on one half of the screen and her past running on the other half (Price, 2008). Obviously, AJ, or Jill Price as we now know her, has a highly unusual memory. Most of us have more ordinary skills with a host of strengths and weaknesses. Even so, our memory is a vital aspect of who we are and what we do; it allows us to learn from the past, function in the present, and plan for the future.

Ask Yourself This

1. How do information processing theorists propose that our memory is organized?

2. How can we assess infants' memory capabilities and what have we learned about memory during infancy?

3. What are the four major hypotheses about why learning and memory improve throughout childhood?

4. How and why is the memory of an adolescent stronger than a child's?

5. What are the strengths and weaknesses of the adult's memory?

Jill Price has extraordinary autobiographical memory for the events of her past. When given a specific date, she can tell you what she was doing on that date and other events that happened to the extent that she experienced them in the past. If someone gave you a date from 5, 10, or 15 years ago, would you be able to recall what you were doing on that day?

In this chapter, we consider how **memory**, our ability to store and later retrieve information about past events, develops and changes over the life span. We also continue examining cognitive development by looking at a view different from Jean Piaget's and Lev Vygotsky's approaches, described in the last chapter. Cognitive psychologists, influenced by the rise of computer technology, began to think of the brain as a computer that processes input and converts it to output (correct answers on tests, for example). This information-processing perspective has revealed much about how the capacities to acquire, remember, and use information change over the life span.

8.1 The Information-Processing Approach

The information-processing approach to cognition emerged amid growing evidence that the behaviorist approach could not easily or fully account for performance on all learning and memory tasks, particularly those of higher complexity. Consider learning from this textbook. Obviously, some complex processes occur between when you register the pattern of print on this page and when you write an essay about it. To account for these processes, behaviorists such as John B. Watson and B. F. Skinner (see Chapter 2) would have to describe chains of mental stimuli and responses between an external stimulus (for instance, the printed page) and an overt response (for example, writing an essay). This approach proved cumbersome at best, as more cognitively oriented learning theorists, such as Albert Bandura, recognized.

Into this picture came computers, with their capacity to systematically convert input to output. The computer seemed to provide a good analogy to the human mind, and indeed, efforts to program computers to play chess and solve other problems as well as human experts helped scientists understand a great deal about the strengths and limitations of human cognition (Newell & Simon, 1961; Simon, 1995). The computer, then, was the model for the **information-processing approach** to human cognition, which emphasizes the basic mental processes involved in attention, perception, memory, and decision making. And just as today's more highly developed computers have greater capacity than those of the past, maturation of the nervous system plus experience presumably enables adults to remember more than young children can and to perform more complex cognitive feats with greater accuracy (Kail & Bisanz, 1992). Let's look at a very popular model of how the computer analogy has been applied to understanding human memory processes.

Memory Systems

Any computer has a limited capacity, associated with its hardware and software, for processing information. The computer's hardware is the machine itself—its keyboard (or input system), its storage capacity, and so on. The mind's "hardware" is the nervous system, including the brain, the sensory receptors, and their neural connections. The computer's software consists of the programs used to manipulate stored and received information: word processing, statistics programs, and the like. The mind, too, has its "software"—rules, strategies, and other mental "programs" that specify how information is to be registered, interpreted, stored, retrieved, and analyzed.

■ **Figure 8.1** presents an early and influential conception of the human information-processing system offered by

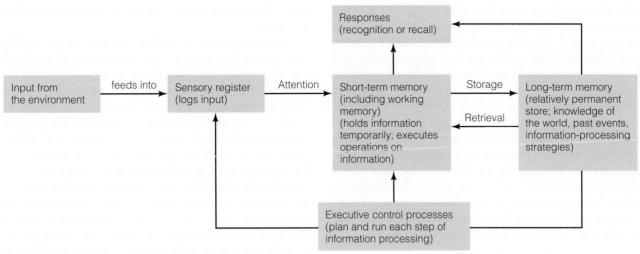

■ **FIGURE 8.1** A model of information processing. Source: Adapted from Atkinson & Shiffrin (1968).

Richard Atkinson and Richard Shiffrin (1968). If your history professor says that the U.S. Constitution was ratified in 1789, this statement is an environmental stimulus. Assuming that you are not lost in a daydream, your **sensory register** will log it, holding it for a fraction of a second as a kind of afterimage (or, in this example, a kind of echo). Much that strikes the sensory register quickly disappears without further processing. Attentional processes (see Chapter 6) have a good deal to do with what information enters the sensory register and may be processed further. If you think you may need to remember 1789, it will be moved into **short-term memory**, which can hold a limited amount of information (about seven items or chunks of information) for several seconds. For example, short-term memory can hold onto a telephone number while you dial it. Most cognitive researchers distinguish between passive and active forms of short-term memory and use the term **working memory** to refer to a mental "scratch pad" that temporarily stores information while actively operating on it (Baddeley, 1986, 1992). It is what is "on one's mind," or in one's consciousness, at any moment. As you know, people can juggle only so much information at once without some of it slipping away or "falling out" of working memory.

To illustrate working memory, look at the following seven numbers. Then look away and add the numbers in your head while trying to remember them:

7 2 5 6 1 4 7

Most likely, having to actively manipulate the numbers in working memory to add them disrupted your ability to rehearse them to remember them. People who are fast at adding numbers would have better luck than most people, because they would have more working-memory space left for remembering the items (Byrnes, 1996).

To be remembered for any length of time, information must be moved from short-term memory into **long-term memory**, a relatively permanent store of information that represents what most people mean by memory. More than likely, you will hold the professor's statement in short-term memory just long enough to record it in your notes. Later, as you study your notes, you will rehearse the information in working memory to move it into long-term memory so that you can retrieve it the next day or week when you are taking the test. For Jill Price, this transfer of information from short-term to long-term memory seems to occur effortlessly and automatically, at least for events that are personally connected to her.

This simplified model shows what you must do to learn and remember something. The first step is **encoding** the information: getting it into the system. If it never gets in, it cannot be remembered. Second, information undergoes **consolidation**, during which it is processed and organized in a form suitable for long-term storage. Consolidation transforms the immediate sensory-perceptual experience of an event into a long-lasting memory trace, a process that is facilitated by sleep (Diekelman & Born, 2010; Kopasz et al., 2010). In the absence of consolidation, the information would not make the leap from the first step of encoding to the third step of storage (Banai et al., 2010). **Storage**, of course, refers to holding information in a long-term memory store. Memories fade over time unless they are appropriately stored in long-term memory. It is clear that storing memories is a *constructive process* and not a static recording of what was encoded. As Mary Courage and Nelson Cowan (2009) describe it, "human memory does not record experience as a video camera would, but rather as an historian would: as a dynamic and inferential process with reconstructions that depend on a variety of sources of information" (p. 2).

Finally, for the memory process to be complete, there must be **retrieval**—the process of getting information out when it is needed. People say they have successfully remembered something when they can retrieve it from long-term memory. Retrieval can be accomplished in several ways. If you are asked a multiple-choice question about when the Constitution was ratified, you need not actively retrieve the correct date; you merely need to recognize it among the options. This is an example of **recognition memory**. If, instead, you are asked, "When was the Constitution ratified?" this is a test of **recall memory**; it requires active retrieval without the aid of cues. Between recognition and recall memory is **cued recall memory**, in which you would be given a hint or cue to facilitate retrieval (for example, "When was the Constitution ratified? It is the year the French Revolution began and rhymes with *wine*."). Most people find questions requiring recognition memory easier to answer than those requiring cued recall, and those requiring cued recall easier than those requiring pure recall. This holds true across the life span, which suggests that many things people have apparently encoded or learned are "in there someplace" even though they may be difficult to retrieve without cues. Breakdowns in remembering may involve difficulties in initial encoding, storage, or retrieval.

Implicit and Explicit Memory

Memory researchers have concluded that the long-term memory store responds differently depending on the nature of the task. They distinguish between **implicit memory** (including what is called procedural memory), which occurs unintentionally, automatically, and without awareness, and **explicit memory** (also called declarative memory), which involves deliberate, effortful recollection of events (■ Figure 8.2). Explicit memory is tested through traditional recognition and recall tests (such as a course's final exam with multiple choice and essay questions) and can be further divided into **semantic memory** for general facts and **episodic memory** for specific experiences. Most memory experts agree that explicit memories, whether they are semantic general knowledge or the specific personal memories that make up episodic memories, are deeply entwined with language. To further clarify the two types of explicit memory, an example of semantic memory would involve *knowing* that the Twin Towers in New York City collapsed on 9-11-2001. Episodic memory would involve *remembering* where you were and what you were doing when you learned that airplanes had crashed into the Twin Towers. The first example illustrates general knowledge of the event, whereas the second example is a personal recollection of the event.

Implicit memory is a different beast. Learners are typically unaware that their memory is being assessed with implicit "tests." Consider an example: individuals are exposed to a list of words (*orange, tablet, forest*, and so on) to be rated for likeability, not to be memorized. In a second task, they are given word stems such as *tab*___ and asked to complete them with the first word that comes to mind. People who are exposed to the word *tablet* in the initial task are more likely than people who are not exposed to the word to come up with *tablet* rather than *table* or *tabby* to complete the word stem, demonstrating that they learned something from their earlier exposure to the words even though they were not trying to learn. Adults with amnesia do poorly on tests of explicit memory in which they study words and then are asked to finish word stems such as *tab*___ with a word they studied earlier. Amazingly, however, if they are merely exposed to a list of words and then given an implicit memory test that asks them to write the first word that comes to mind, they do fine (Graf, Squire, & Mandler, 1984). Many forms of amnesia destroy explicit memory but leave implicit memory undamaged (Schacter, 1996). As Patricia Bauer (2007) describes it, explicit memory is fallible—subject to forgetting—whereas implicit memory is largely infallible—it remains intact.

Research makes it clear that implicit and explicit memories are two distinct components of long-term memory that operate independently. It is not surprising, then, that research on the neural basis of memory shows that different parts of the brain are involved in the different forms of memory. Procedural memory (such as memory of how to ride a bike), which is a type of implicit memory, is mediated by an area of the forebrain called the striatum. Explicit memory is largely localized in the medial temporal lobe of the brain (*medial* refers to the middle of the brain and the temporal lobe is located at the base of the brain). In particular, the medial temporal structures are thought to be crucial to consolidating information into a memory trace for long-term storage (Bauer, 2009). Damage to a specific region of the medial temporal lobe—the hippocampus—leads to significant impairments in creating new episodic memories, such as recalling that you went to the dentist on Monday morning (Vargha-Khadem et al., 1997).

The actual storage and retrieval of the information take place in whichever cortex originally encoded or was activated by the information. For example, vocabulary seems to be stored in the limbic-temporal cortex, as evidenced by the vocabulary impairment experienced by individuals with damage to this part of the brain (Bauer, 2009). Thus, sensory information initially activates one of the cortical association areas distributed throughout the brain. This information then passes to the medial temporal lobe for consolidation. If and when this consolidation occurs, the resulting memory trace is stored in the cortical association area of the brain that first registered the information, and it is from this area that the information must be retrieved.

```
                          Memory
                            |
          +-----------------+-----------------+
          |                                   |
       Explicit                            Implicit
     (Declarative)                      (Nondeclarative)
          |                                   |
     +----+----+              +---------------+---------------+
     |         |              |               |               |
  Episodic  Semantic       Skills,         Priming          Other
  (Events)  (Facts,        procedures,                    (e.g., classical
            general        habits                          conditionings,
            knowledge)                                     habituation)
     |
Autobiographical
```

■ FIGURE 8.2 Types of memory. Based on Squire (2004).

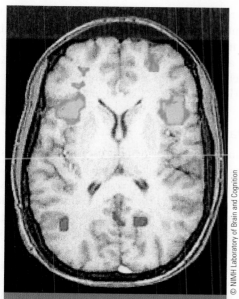

Advances in brain imaging have allowed researchers to "see" memory and problem solving by looking at patterns of blood flow in different regions of the brain. The yellow portions in this image show increased areas of blood flow as the person was remembering the image of a face.

© NIMH Laboratory of Brain and Cognition

Research suggests that implicit memory develops earlier in infancy than explicit memory (Bauer, 2008; Schneider, 2004). Explicit memory improves as the hippocampus becomes more mature during the second half of the first year (Nelson, Thomas, & de Haan, 2006). Further, the two types of memory follow different developmental paths. Explicit memory capacity increases from infancy to adulthood, then declines in later adulthood. By contrast, implicit memory capacity changes little; young children often do no worse than older children and elderly adults often do no worse than younger adults on tests of implicit memory (Schneider, 2004; Schneider & Bjorklund, 1998). Research on implicit memory shows that young and old alike learn and retain a tremendous amount of information from their everyday experiences without any effort.

Problem Solving

Now imagine that you are asked how many years passed between the signing of the Declaration of Independence (1776, remember?) and the ratification of the Constitution. This is a simple example of **problem solving**, or use of the information-processing system to achieve a goal or arrive at a decision (in this case, to answer the question). Here, too, the information-processing model describes what happens between stimulus and response. The question will move through the memory system. You will need to draw on your long-term memory to

understand the question, then you will have to search long-term memory for the two relevant dates. Moreover, you will need to locate your stored knowledge of the mathematical operation of subtraction. You will then transfer this stored information to working memory so that you can use your subtraction "program" (1789 minus 1776) to derive the correct answer.

Notice that processing information successfully requires both knowing what you are doing and making decisions. This is why the information-processing model (see Figure 8.1) includes **executive control processes** involved in planning and monitoring what is done. These control processes run the show, guiding the selection, organization, manipulation, and interpretation of information throughout. Stored knowledge about the world and about information processing guides what is done with new information.

Cognitive psychologists now recognize that information processing is more complex than this model or similar models suggest (Bjorklund, 1997). For example, they appreciate that people, like computers, engage in "parallel processing," carrying out many cognitive activities simultaneously (for example, listening to a lecture and taking notes at the same time) rather than performing operations in a sequence (such as solving a math problem by carrying out a series of ordered steps). They also appreciate that different processing approaches are used in different domains of knowledge. Still, the information-processing approach to cognition has the advantage of focusing attention on how people remember things or solve problems, not just on what they recall or what answer they give. A young child's performance on a problem could break down in any number of ways: The child might not be paying attention to the relevant aspects of the problem, might be unable to hold all the relevant pieces of information in working memory long enough to do anything with them, might lack the strategies for transferring new information into long-term memory or retrieving information from long-term memory as needed, might simply not have enough stored knowledge to understand the problem, or might not have the executive control processes needed to manage the steps for solving problems. If researchers can identify how information processes in the younger individual differ from those in the older person, they will gain much insight into cognitive development.

Many processes involved in memory and problem solving improve between infancy and adulthood and then decline somewhat in old age, although this pattern is not uniform for all processes or all people. Our task in this chapter is to describe these age trends and, of greater interest, to try to determine why they occur.

Checking Mastery

1. What steps are required in order to learn, remember, and recall material?

2. What is the difference between implicit and explicit memory?

3. Why are recognition tasks generally easier than recall tasks?

Making Connections

1. Consider your own memory profile. On what types of memory tasks and under what conditions is your memory good, and conversely, which types of tasks and conditions challenge your memory?

2. In creating a memory assessment, how would you tap into someone's implicit memories as opposed to their explicit memories?

8.2 The Infant

You have already seen that infants explore the world thoroughly through their senses. But are they remembering anything of their experiences? First, look at what research on information processing has taught developmentalists about early memory; then, consider whether infants demonstrate problem-solving skills.

Memory

Assessing infant memory requires some ingenuity because infants cannot tell researchers what they remember (Bauer, 2007; Courage & Cowan, 2009). Several methods have been used to uncover infants' memory capabilities. Here we consider imitation, habituation, and operant conditioning techniques before examining infants' abilities to recall previously presented information.

Imitation

Researchers can learn something about memory by noting whether or not infants can imitate an action performed by a model. Some studies suggest that young infants, even newborns, can imitate certain actions, such as sticking out the tongue or opening the mouth (see Meltzoff, 2004). These findings are exciting because they challenge Piaget's claim that infants cannot imitate actions until about 1 year, when they have some ability to represent mentally what they have seen.

At first, such findings were viewed with skepticism by some, who believed that early tongue protrusions did not demonstrate true imitation but instead reflected reflexive responses to specific stimuli or attempts to "explore" interesting sights (see, for example, Bjorklund, 1995; Jones, 1996). However, observations of infants sticking out their tongues and moving their mouths in ways consistent with a model have now been replicated

with different populations (Meltzoff & Moore, 1997). In addition, infants as young as 6 months display **deferred imitation**, the ability to imitate a novel act after a delay, which clearly requires memory ability (see Bauer, 2007; Rovee-Collier & Cuevas, 2009). Deferred imitation may represent an early form of explicit memory (Rovee-Collier & Cuevas, 2009).

Habituation

Another method to assess memory uses habituation, a simple and often overlooked form of learning introduced in Chapter 6. Habituation—learning *not* to respond to a repeated stimulus—might be thought of as learning to be bored by the familiar (for example, eventually not hearing the continual ticking of a clock or the drip of a leaky faucet) and is evidence that a stimulus is recognized as familiar. From birth, humans habituate to repeatedly presented lights, sounds, and smells; such stimuli are recognized as "old hat" (Rovee-Collier & Cuevas, 2009). Indeed, as we noted in Chapter 5, even fetuses demonstrate through habituation that they can learn and remember (Dirix et al., 2009). It is clear that newborns are capable of recognition memory and prefer a new sight to something they have seen many times. As they age, infants need less "study time" before a stimulus becomes old

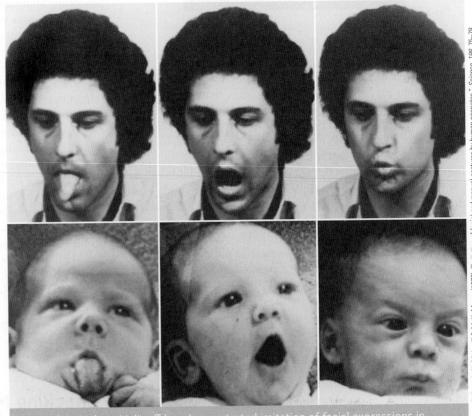

Researcher Andrew Meltzoff has demonstrated imitation of facial expressions in newborns. These sample photographs are from videotaped recordings of 2- to 3-week-old infants imitating tongue protrusion, mouth opening, and lip protrusion. Of the three responses shown here, tongue protrusion is the most reliably observed.

© From A. N. Meltzoff & M. K. Moore (1977). "Imitation of facial and manual gestures by human neonates." *Science, 198, 75–78.*

hat, and they can retain what they have learned for days or even weeks (Rovee-Collier & Cuevas, 2009).

Operant Conditioning

To test long-term memory of young infants, Carolyn Rovee-Collier and her colleagues devised a clever task that relies on the operant conditioning techniques introduced in Chapter 2 (see Rovee-Collier & Cuevas, 2009). When a ribbon is tied to a baby's ankle and connected to an attractive mobile, the infant will shake a leg now and then and learn in minutes that leg kicking brings about a positively reinforcing consequence: the jiggling of the mobile.

To test infant memory, the mobile is presented at a later time to see whether the infant will kick again. To succeed at this task, the infant must not only recognize the mobile but also recall that the thing to do is to kick. Before we review the re-

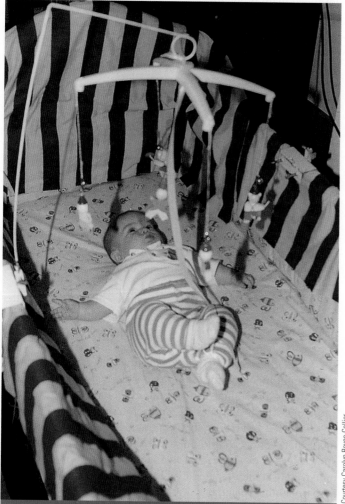

Courtesy Carolyn Rovee-Collier

When ribbons are tied to their ankles, young infants soon learn to make a mobile move by kicking their legs. Carolyn Rovee-Collier has made use of this operant conditioning paradigm to find out how long infants will remember the trick for making the mobile move.

search findings, what type of memory do you believe this task assesses? Consider whether infants are deliberately and effortfully remembering something or are unintentionally and automatically learning and remembering a connection between their kicking and the movement of the mobile. This task is tapping into implicit or procedural memory (Rovee-Collier & Cuevas, 2009). When given two 9-minute training sessions, 2-month-olds remember how to make the mobile move for up to 2 days, 3-month-olds for about 1 week, and 6-month-olds for about 2 weeks (Rovee-Collier & Cuevas, 2009). Using a modification of this task for older infants, Carolyn Rovee-Collier and her colleagues (2009) have shown that by 18 months, infants can remember for at least 3 months—rather impressive! Further, the researchers could enhance young infants' memory by giving them three 6-minute learning sessions rather than two 9-minute sessions. Although the total training time is the same in the two conditions, the distributed, or spread out, training is more effective. As it turns out, distributed practice is beneficial across the life span (Son, 2004).

What if stronger cues to aid recall are provided? Three-month-old infants who were reminded of their previous learning, by seeing the mobile move 2–4 weeks after their original learning experience, kicked up a storm as soon as the ribbon was attached to their ankles, whereas infants who were not reminded showed no sign of remembering to kick (Rovee-Collier & Barr, 2004). It seems, then, that cued recall (in this case, memory cued by the presence of the mobile or, better yet, its rotation by the experimenter) emerges during the first couple of months of life and that infants remember best when they are reminded of what they have learned. Other research shows that verbal reminders are also effective with 15-month-olds and can help them remember an event after a month as well as they did after a week (Hayne & Simcock, 2009).

However, this research also suggests that young infants have difficulty recalling what they have learned if cues are insufficient or different. They have trouble remembering when the mobile (for example, the specific animals hanging from it) or the context in which they encountered it (for example, the design on the playpen liner) is even slightly different from the context in which they learned. In short, early memories are *cue-dependent* and *context-specific*.

Recall

When are infants capable of pure recall—of actively retrieving information from memory when no cues are available? As noted earlier, infants as young as 6 months, given repeated exposure to a model's actions, can imitate novel behaviors (for example, pushing a button on a box to produce a beep) after a 24-hour delay (Barr, Dowden, & Hayne, 1996). As infants age, they demonstrate recall or deferred imitation over longer periods. By 6 months, infants can defer their imitation of an action over a longer delay and can recall the order of a simple sequence of events (Bauer, 2007). By age 2, events can be recalled for months, and recall is more flexible—less bound by the specific cues present at the time of learning (Hayne & Simcock, 2009; Klein & Meltzoff, 1999).

Patricia Bauer (1996, 2000) and her colleagues have shown sequences of actions to infants of different ages and then asked them to imitate what they saw—for example, putting a teddy bear in bed, covering him with a blanket, and reading him a story. Infants as young as 13 months can reconstruct a sequence of actions for as long as 3 months afterward. Older infants (16 months and 20 months) can store and retrieve events for 12 months after exposure (Bauer et al., 2000). Much like children and adults, infants remember best when they have repeated exposures to what they are to remember, when they are given plenty of cues to help them remember, and when the events they must remember occur in a meaningful or logical order.

By age 2, infants have become verbal and can use words to reconstruct events that happened months earlier. In one study, for example, researchers interviewed young children about emergency room visits for accidents the children had between about 1 and 3 years of age (Peterson & Rideout, 1998). Interviews were conducted soon after the ER visits and 6, 12, 18, or 24 months later. Children who were 18 months or younger at the time of their ER visit were unable to verbally recall aspects of their visits after a 6-month delay, but children 20 months or older were able to do so. Children who were at least 26 months old at the time of their ER visit could retain information and answer verbal questions about their experiences for at least 2 years following the event. It's clear that language helps memory performance (Hayne & Simcock, 2009).

Problem Solving

Infants, like children and adults, face problem-solving tasks every day. For example, they may want to obtain an object beyond their reach or to make a toy repeat the interesting sound it produced earlier. Can infants overcome obstacles to achieve desired goals? It appears they can. In one study, infants were presented with an object out of their reach; however, by pulling on a cloth, they could drag the object to within reach (Willats, 1990). Although 6-month-olds did not retrieve the object, 9-month-olds solved this problem. Even the younger infants were successful when given hints about how they might retrieve the object (Kolstad & Aguiar, 1995). By 14 months of age, infants have figured out that adults are often useful sources of information in problem-solving situations (Goubert et al., 2006). As they get older, infants increasingly pay attention to the cues provided by adults and they increasingly solicit help by pointing, reaching, or otherwise letting the adult know that assistance is needed. Simple problem-solving behaviors improve considerably over the first 2 years of life and then, as you will see shortly, flourish during childhood.

Checking Mastery

1. How does the habituation task allow researchers to assess an infant's memory abilities?

2. At what age do infants begin to show reliable memory for events?

Making Connections

1. Uncle Jed says there is no way a baby can learn or remember anything. His position is that babies just eat, sleep, cry, and poop. What three key pieces of evidence might you use to convince Uncle Jed that there is something going on inside the infant's head in terms of learning and memory?

2. Would you characterize infants' memory as robust or fragile? What factors influence the robustness of infants' memory?

8.3 The Child

The 2-year-old is already a highly capable information processor, as evidenced by the rapid language learning that takes place at this age. But dramatic improvements in learning, memory, and problem solving occur throughout the childhood years as children learn everything from how to flush toilets to how to work advanced math problems.

Explaining Memory Development

In countless situations, older children learn faster and remember more than younger children do. For example, 2-year-olds can repeat back about two digits immediately after hearing them, 5-year-olds about four digits, and 10-year-olds about six digits. And second-graders not only are faster learners than kindergartners but also retain information longer (Howe, 2000). Why is this? Here are four major hypotheses about why learning and memory improve, patterned after those formulated by John Flavell and Henry Wellman (1977):

1. *Changes in basic capacities.* Older children have higher-powered "hardware" than younger children do; neural advances in their brains have contributed to more working-memory space for manipulating information and an ability to process information faster.

2. *Changes in memory strategies.* Older children have better "software"; they have learned and consistently use effective methods for putting information into long-term memory and retrieving it when they need it.

3. *Increased knowledge about memory.* Older children know more about memory (for example, how long they must study to learn things thoroughly, which kinds of memory tasks take more effort, and which strategies best fit each task).

4. *Increased knowledge about the world.* Older children know more than younger children about the world in general. This knowledge, or expertise, makes material to be learned more familiar, and familiar material is easier to learn and remember than unfamiliar material.

Do Basic Capacities Change?

Because the nervous system continues to develop in the years after birth, it seems plausible that older children remember more than younger children do because they have a better "computer"—a larger or more efficient information-processing system. We can quickly rule out the idea that the storage capacity of long-term memory impairs memory performance. There is no consistent evidence that the capacity changes after the first month of life (Perlmutter, 1986). In fact, young and old alike have more room for storage than they could ever use. If long-term storage capacity does not contribute to developmental differences in memory, then what about the encoding and consolidation processes needed to move information into long-term storage? Encoding begins with the sensory registration of stimuli from the environment. As we learned in Chapter 6, the sensory systems are working fairly well from a very early age and undergo only slight improvements during the first year. Thus, the sensory register itself is an unlikely source of much developmental variation in memory. What *does* seem to matter is how information is handled once it has reached the sensory register. This is the job of working memory and leads to the consolidation of memories so that a lasting record is placed into long-term storage.

To test short-term memory, researchers quickly present a list of items (such as numbers) then count the number of items that a person can recall in order. Measured this way, the basic features of working memory are in place by age 4 but improvements on a variety of working-memory tasks are evident across childhood and into adolescence (Alloway, Gathercole, & Pickering, 2006). In particular, there is significant improvement in *capacity* of short-term memory between ages 6–7 and ages 12–13, at which point, capacity shows little additional change (Cowan et al., 2010). These improvements correspond to maturation of the hippocampus and other parts of the brain believed to be centrally involved in consolidation of memories. We also know that the *speed* of mental processes improves with age, and this allows older children and adults to simultaneously perform more mental operations in working memory than young children can (Cowan et al., 2010). As basic mental processes become automatic, they can also be performed with little mental effort. This, in turn, frees space in working memory for other purposes, such as storing the information needed to solve a problem.

This focus on changes in working memory has been featured in revisions of Piaget's theory of cognitive development proposed by neo-Piagetian theorists who retain Piaget's original emphasis on stages and qualitative change, but try to articulate the processes of change more concretely. For example, Robbie Case (Case, 1985; Marini & Case, 1994) proposed that more advanced stages of cognitive development are made possible because children make better use of the available space in their working memory. Recall from Chapter 7 Piaget's finding that preschoolers tend to *center* on one aspect of a problem and lose sight of another (for example, to attend to the height of a glass but ignore its width, or vice versa). Perhaps, say the neo-Piagetians, this is not a matter of lacking certain cognitive structures; perhaps young children simply do not have enough working-memory capacity to keep both pieces of information in mind at once and to coordinate them. Similarly, young children may do poorly on memory tasks because they cannot keep the first items on a list in mind while processing later ones. And they may fail to solve mathematical problems correctly because they cannot keep the facts of the problem in mind while they are performing the calculations.

Some research suggests that the degree of improvement in short-term memory capacity that is evident as children age depends on what is tested or how it is tested. That is, short-term memory capacity is domain-specific—it varies with background knowledge and type of task (Conklin et al., 2007; Schneider, 2004). Greater knowledge in a domain or area of study increases the speed with which new, related information can be processed. In other words, the more you know about a subject, the faster you can process information related to this subject. In addition, more complex tasks consume more working-memory resources than less complex tasks (Luciana et al., 2005).

In sum, the basic capacities of the sensory register and long-term memory do not change much with age. There are, however, improvements with age in operating speed and efficiency of working memory, which includes improvements in the consolidation process through which memories are processed for long-term storage. These changes correspond to maturational changes in the brain. During infancy, brain activity during working-memory tasks is scattered and general (Bell & Wolfe, 2007). By age 4 or 5, working memory has found its "home" in the frontal lobes of the brain. Maturation of the frontal lobes continues throughout childhood and adolescence, bringing further improvements in working memory and consolidation of memories (Bauer, 2009).

Do Memory Strategies Change?

If shown the 12 items in ■ **Figure 8.3**, 4-year-olds might recall only 2–4 of them, 8-year-olds would recall 7–9 items, and adults might recall 10–11 of the items after a delay of several minutes. Are there specific memory strategies that evolve during childhood to permit this dramatic improvement in performance?

Children as young as 2 years can deliberately remember to do "important" things, such as reminding Mom to buy candy at

■ **FIGURE 8.3** A memory task. Imagine that you have 120 seconds to learn the 12 objects pictured here. What tricks or strategies might you devise to make your task easier?

the grocery store. They are more likely to use external memory aids (for example, pointing at or holding a toy pig when asked to remember where it was hidden) if they are instructed to remember than if they are not (Fletcher & Bray, 1996). However, children younger than 4 show little flexibility in switching from an ineffective strategy to an effective one, and they typically do not generate new strategies even as they gain experience with a task (Chen, 2007). In contrast, many 4- and 5-year-olds will flexibly switch strategies and generate new strategies, making them more effective on memory tasks than younger children. Four-year-olds can also selectively focus on relevant information and ignore irrelevant information, although this ability will become more robust with age and experience (Schwenck, Bjorklund, & Schneider, 2009). Younger children have a tendency to make **perseveration errors**: they continue to use the same strategy that was successful in the *past* despite the strategy's *current* lack of success. Thus, if they previously found their favorite toy under the sofa, they search this location on future occasions when the toy is lost (Chen, 2007). They seem to be unable to get the old strategy—ineffective in the new situation—out of their mind and move on to a different strategy that could potentially be successful. By age 4, we see a decline in these perseveration errors.

Yet even 4-year-olds have not mastered many of the effective strategies for moving information into long-term memory. For example, when instructed to remember toys they have been shown, 3- and 4-year-olds will look carefully at the objects and will often label them once, but they only rarely use the memory strategy called **rehearsal**—the repeating of items they are trying to learn and remember (Baker-Ward, Ornstein, & Holden, 1984). To rehearse the objects in Figure 8.3, you might simply say, "apple, truck, grapes. . . ." repeatedly. John Flavell and his associates found that only 10% of 5-year-olds repeated the names of pictures they were asked to recall, but more than half of 7-year-olds and 85% of 10-year-olds used this strategy (Flavell, Beach, & Chinsky, 1966).

Another important memory strategy is **organization**, or classifying items into meaningful groups. You might lump the apple, the grapes, and the hamburger in Figure 8.3 into a category of foods and form other categories for animals, vehicles, and baseball equipment. You would then rehearse each category and recall it as a cluster. Another organizational strategy, *chunking*, is used to break a long number (6065551843) into manageable subunits (606-555-1843, a phone number). Organization is mastered later in childhood than rehearsal. Until about age 9 or 10, children are not much better at recalling lists of items that lend themselves readily to grouping than they are at recalling lists of unrelated words (Bjorklund, Dukes, & Brown, 2009).

Finally, the strategy of **elaboration** involves actively creating meaningful links between items to be remembered. Elaboration is achieved by adding something to the items, in the form of either words or images. Creating and using a sentence such as "the apple fell on the horse's nose" could help you remember two of the items in Figure 8.3. Elaboration is especially helpful in learning foreign languages. For example, you might link the Spanish word *pato* (pronounced pot-o) to the English equivalent *duck* by imagining a duck with a pot on its head. Children who can elaborate on the relationship between two items (for example,

generating similar and different features of the items) have improved retention of these items (Howe, 2006).

Memory or encoding strategies develop in a fairly predictable order, with rehearsal emerging first, followed by organization, and then by elaboration. Children do not suddenly start using strategies, however. According to Patricia Miller (Miller, 1990, 1994; Miller & Seier, 1994), they typically progress through four phases on their way to successful strategy use. Initially, children have a **mediation deficiency**, which means they cannot spontaneously use or benefit from strategies, even if they are taught how to use them. Children with mediation deficiencies seem qualitatively unable to grasp the concept of the strategy. This gives way to a different kind of problem, a **production deficiency**, in which children can use strategies they are taught but do not produce them on their own. The third phase is a **utilization deficiency**, in which children spontaneously produce a strategy but their task performance does not yet benefit from using the strategy. This seems to be a precursor to the final stage in which children exhibit effective strategy use by both producing and benefiting from a memory strategy.

There is ample evidence of utilization deficiencies across various age groups and for different types of strategies (see Pressley & Hilden, 2006; Schwenck, Bjorklund, & Schneider, 2007). Why would children who use a strategy fail to benefit from it? One possibility is that using a new strategy is mentally taxing and leaves no free cognitive resources for other aspects of the task (Pressley & Hilden, 2006). Once using the strategy becomes routine, then other components of the task can be addressed simultaneously. Whatever the reason for utilization defi-

What memory strategies could this girl use to help her remember where she hid her birthday treasures?

Have you noticed that the material in this chapter has great potential value to teachers? The information-processing perspective has yielded improved methods for diagnosing learning problems and improving instruction. Here we focus on interventions aimed at boosting the memory skills of young children. Just how much can be achieved through training?

Garrett Lange and Sarah Pierce (1992) took on the challenge of teaching the memory strategy of organization (grouping) to 4- and 5-year-olds. Using pictures of objects and animals as the stimuli, they taught these preschoolers a "group-and-name trick" that involved sorting items to be learned into groups based on similarity, naming the group, naming the items within the group, and, at recall, naming the group before calling out the items within that group. Because such memory-training programs have not always been successful, these researchers attempted to increase motivation through encouragement and praise. They even included training in metamemory: They made sure children understood the rationale for the sorting strategy, knew when it could be used, and could see firsthand that it could improve their performance.

How successful was the training? These children did virtually no sorting of items to be learned before they were trained, but they did a good deal of it after training, even 7 days later. They clearly learned to use the organization strategy they were taught. They also outperformed untrained control children on measures of recall, but the gains in recall were fairly small compared with the much larger gains in strategy use. This discrepancy between gains in strategy use and gains in recall performance shows that these young children experienced utilization deficiencies: They could not derive full benefit from the memory strategy they were taught, possibly because they did not have the working-memory capacity to carry out the strategy.

Other programs that teach memory strategies and metacognitive skills to elementary-school children often work much better, especially with children who are underachievers and who may be capable of executing strategies but fail to do so on their own (Hattie, Biggs, & Purdie, 1996). Still, the benefits of training are often domain specific: they do not generalize to learning tasks different from those that were the focus of training. Perhaps this makes sense if you realize that the strategies that work best in learning math skills may be different from the strategies that work best in learning historical facts or basketball skills.

---

ciencies, they reflect a child–task interaction; that is, it is not task difficulty per se, but how difficult a task is for a particular child, that matters (Bjorklund et al., 2009).

Using effective storage strategies to learn material is only half the battle; retrieval strategies can also influence how much is recalled. Indeed, retrieving something from memory can often be a complex adventure when solving problems, such as when you try to remember when you went on a trip by searching for cues that might trigger your memory ("Well, I still had long hair then, but it was after Muffy's wedding, and. . . ."). In general, young children rely more on external cues for both encoding and retrieving information than do older children (Schneider & Pressley, 1997). Thus, young children may need to put their toothbrushes next to their pajamas so that they have a physical reminder to brush their teeth before they go to bed. Older children are less likely to need such external cues but may continue to use them throughout elementary school (Eskritt & Lee, 2002). In many ways, then, command of memory strategies increases over the childhood years, but the path to effective strategy use is characterized more by noticeable jumps than by steady increases (Bjorklund et al., 2009; Schneider, Kron-Sperl, & Hünnerkopf, 2009). Application Box 8.1 looks at whether children can be taught strategies to improve their memory.

Does Knowledge about Memory Change?

The term **metamemory** refers to knowledge of memory and to monitoring and regulating memory processes. It is knowing, for example, what your memory limits are, which memory strategies are more or less effective, and which memory tasks are more or less difficult. It is also noting that your efforts to remember something are not working and that you need to try something different. Metamemory is one aspect of **metacognition**, or knowledge of the human mind and of the range of cognitive processes. Your store of metacognitive knowledge might include an understanding that you are better at learning a new language than at learning algebra, that it is harder to pay attention to a task when there is distracting noise in the background than when it is quiet, and that it is wise to check a proposed solution to a problem before concluding that it is correct.

When do children first show evidence of metacognition? If instructed to remember where the *Sesame Street* character Big Bird has been hidden so that they can later wake him up, even 2- and 3-year-olds will go stand near the hiding spot, or at least look or point at that spot; they do not do these things as often if Big Bird is visible and they do not need to remember where he is (DeLoache, Cassidy, & Brown, 1985). By age 2, then, children understand that to remember something, you have to work at it. Researchers have found that 3-year-olds understand the difference between thinking about an object in their heads and experiencing it in reality and that 4-year-olds realize behavior is guided by beliefs (Flavell, 1999). These findings indicate that metacognitive awareness is present at least in a rudimentary form at a young age but there continue to be significant improvements throughout childhood (Ghetti, Lyons, & Cornoldi, 2008; MacKinlay et al., 2009).

Are increases in metamemory a major contributor to improved memory performance over the childhood years? Children with greater metamemory awareness demonstrate better memory ability, but several factors influence the strength of this relationship (Bjork & Bjork, 1998; Schneider, 2004). Researchers are most likely to see a connection between metamemory and memory performance among older children and among children who have been in situations in which they must remember something (DeMarie & Ferron, 2003; Schneider & Bjorklund, 1998). Not only is task experience important, but the nature of the task is also relevant. Awareness of memory processes benefits even young children on tasks that are simple and familiar and where connections between metamemory knowledge and memory performance are fairly obvious (Schneider & Sodian, 1988). Yet children who know what to do may not always do it, so good metamemory is no guarantee of good recall (Schneider & Pressley, 1997). It seems that children not only must know that a strategy is useful but also must know why it is useful in order to be motivated to use it and to benefit from its use (Justice et al., 1997). Metamemory is also influenced by children's language skills and by their general knowledge about mental states and their roles in behavior—what is known as theory of mind (Lockl & Schneider, 2007; see Chapter 13 for definition and discussion). The links between metamemory and memory performance, although not perfect, are strong enough to suggest the merits of teaching children more about how memory works and how they can make it work more effectively for them.

Does Knowledge of the World Change?

Ten-year-olds have greater semantic memory than two-year-olds do. That is, they know considerably more about the world in general. The individual's knowledge of a content area to be learned, or **knowledge base**, as it has come to be called, clearly affects learning and memory performance. Think about the difference between reading about a topic that you already know well and reading about a new topic. In the first case, you can read quickly because you are able to link the information to the knowledge you have already stored. All you really need to do is check for any new information or information that contradicts what you already know. Learning about a highly unfamiliar topic is more difficult ("It's Greek to me").

Perhaps the most dramatic illustration of the powerful influence of knowledge base on memory was provided by Michelene Chi (1978). She demonstrated that even though adults typically outperform children on tests of memory, this age difference could be reversed if children have more expertise than adults. Chi recruited children who were expert chess players and compared their memory skills with those of adults who were familiar with the game but lacked expertise. On a test of memory for sequences of digits, the children recalled fewer than the adults did, demonstrating their usual deficiencies. But on a test of memory for the locations of chess pieces, the chil-

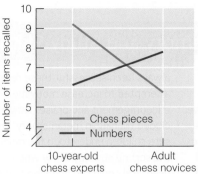

■ **FIGURE 8.4** Effects of expertise on memory. Michelene Chi found that child chess experts outperformed adult chess novices on a test of recall for the location of chess pieces (although, in keeping with the usual developmental trend, these children could not recall strings of numbers as well as adults could).

dren clearly beat the adults (■ **Figure** 8.4). Because they were experts, these children were able to form more and larger mental chunks, or meaningful groups, of chess pieces, which allowed them to remember more. When child experts were compared with adult experts, there were no differences in performance (Schneider et al., 1993).

Pause to consider the implications: On most tasks, young children are the novices and older children or adults are the experts. Perhaps older children and adults recall longer strings of digits because they are more familiar with numbers than young children are, not because they have better basic learning capacities. Perhaps they recall more words in word lists simply because they have more familiarity with language. Perhaps memory improves over childhood simply because older children know more about all kinds of things than younger children do (Bjorklund, 1995).

In their areas of expertise—whether baseball, dinosaurs, Pokémon cards, or *Harry Potter* trivia—children appear to develop highly specialized and effective strategies of information processing, just as the young chess players studied by Chi apparently had. Indeed, children with low general intellectual ability but high expertise sometimes understand and remember more about stories in their area of expertise than do children with higher intellectual ability but less expertise (Schneider, Bjorklund, & Maier-Bruckner, 1996). Knowledge in a content area probably allows you to make better use of the limited capacity of working memory. It seems that the more you know, the more you *can* know.

Revisiting the Explanations

We can now draw four conclusions about the development of learning and memory:

1. Older children are faster information processors and can juggle more information in working memory. Maturation of the nervous system leads to improvements in consolidation of

memories. Older and younger children, however, do not differ in terms of sensory register or long-term memory capacity.

2. Older children use more effective *memory strategies* in encoding and retrieving information. Acquisition of memory strategies reflects qualitative rather than quantitative changes.

3. Older children know more about memory, and good *metamemory* may help children choose more appropriate strategies and control and monitor their learning more effectively.

4. Older children know more in general, and their larger *knowledge base* improves their ability to learn and remember. A richer knowledge base allows faster and more efficient processing of information related to the domain of knowledge.

Is one of these explanations of memory development better than the others? Darlene DeMarie and John Ferron (2003) tested whether a model that includes three of these factors—basic capacities, strategies, and metamemory—could explain recall memory better than a single factor. For both younger (5–8 years) and older (8–11 years) children, the three-factor model predicted memory performance better than a single-factor model. Use of memory strategies was an especially strong direct predictor of recall. Importantly, there were also correlations among factors. Having good basic capacities, for example, was related to advanced metamemory and to command of strategies and had both direct and indirect influences on recall. So all these phenomena may contribute something to the dramatic improvements in learning and memory that occur over the childhood years. We return to these four hypotheses when we consider changes in learning and memory in adulthood.

Autobiographical Memory

Children effortlessly remember all sorts of things: a birthday party last week, where they left their favorite toy, what to do when they go to a fast-food restaurant. Much of what children remember and talk about consists of personal experiences or events that have happened to them at a particular time and place. These **autobiographical memories**, episodic memories of personal events, are essential ingredients of present and future experiences as well as our understanding of who we are (see Dere et al., 2008). The extraordinary memory ability of Jill Price, the woman described in this chapter's opener, involves autobiographical memory of the personal events of her life. Here we look at how autobiographical memories are stored and organized and at factors that influence their accuracy.

When Do Autobiographical Memories Begin?

You learned earlier in this chapter that infants and toddlers are able to store memories. You also know that children and adults have many specific autobiographical events stored in long-term memory. Yet research shows that older children and adults exhibit **childhood** (or infantile) **amnesia**; that is, they have few autobiographical memories of events that occurred during the first few years of life (Hayne & Simcock, 2009). As Patricia Bauer (2007) notes, memories for the first few years of life seem to fall into a large black hole from which there is no return.

To determine how old we have to be when we experience significant life events to remember them, researchers typically ask adults to answer questions about early life experiences such as the birth of a younger sibling, a hospitalization, the death of a family member, or a family move early in life. In one study using this method, college students were able to recall some information from events that happened as early as age 2 (Usher & Neisser, 1993). But age 2 seems to be the lowest age limit for recall of early life events as an adult. Other research shows that most adults do not remember much until they were 4 or 5 years old (Davis, Gross, & Hayne, 2008; Jack & Hayne, 2007). For example, Nicola Davis and her colleagues (2008) asked college students who had experienced the birth of a younger sibling by the age of 5 to recall as much as they could about this early event. As ■ Figure 8.5 shows, college students who had been 1, 2, or 3 years old at the time recalled very little of the event, but those who were 4 or 5 when their sibling was born recalled significantly more. Even Jill Price, with her unusual autobiographical memory, does not recall events from before she was about 2 years old (Parker et al., 2006).

Why do we remember little about our early years? As you have seen, infants and toddlers are certainly capable of encoding their experiences (Cleveland & Reese, 2008). Also, young preschool children seem able to remember a good deal about events that occurred when they were infants even though older children and adults cannot (Bauer, 1996; Fivush, Gray, & Fromhoff, 1987). One explanation of childhood amnesia is that infants and toddlers may not have enough space in working memory to hold the multiple pieces of information about actor, action, and set-

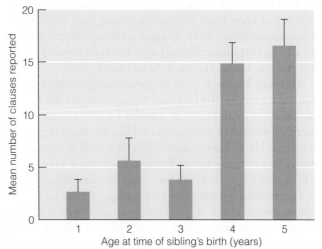

■ **FIGURE 8.5** College students' recall of the birth of a younger sibling increases as a function of how old they were at the time of the event. Those who were at least 4 years of age when their sibling was born recall much more than those who were younger than 4. Source: From Davis, N., Gross, J., & Hayne, H. (2008). Defining the boundary of childhood amnesia. *Memory, 16*(5), 465–474, Figure 2. Reprinted by permission of Taylor & Francis Group.

ting needed to encode and consolidate a coherent memory of an event. As you learned earlier in this chapter, functional working-memory capacity increases with age as the brain, particularly the frontal lobe, matures. But this explanation is unsatisfactory because, as we have just noted, toddlers can remember these events, indicating that they were encoded to some degree.

Perhaps infants' lack of language is the answer. Because autobiographical memory seems to rely heavily on language skills, we would expect such memories to increase with increased language skills. Gabrielle Simcock and Harlene Hayne (Simcock & Hayne, 2002, 2003, Hayne & Simcock, 2009) assessed the verbal skills of young children (27, 33, and 39 months old) who participated in a unique event involving a "magic shrinking machine" that seemingly made items smaller in a matter of seconds. After a 6- or 12-month delay, children were tested for both verbal recall (answers to open-ended questions) and nonverbal recall (identification of photos of the items used in the activity) of the unique event. Their nonverbal recall improved across the age groups but was good at all ages. Verbal recall was poor and depended on the simpler verbal skills present at the time of encoding rather than the more developed verbal skills present at the time of recall. In other words, "children's verbal reports of the event were frozen in time" (p. 229). So a relative lack of verbal skills during the first few years of life may limit what we are able to recall from this period.

Although toddlers may have limited verbal skills, their parents presumably do not. There are large individual differences in toddler–parent "conversations" about past events (Fivush, 2009). An examination of mother–toddler conversations about past events shows that some mothers provide rich elaborations of these events, whereas others do not, in the course of conversing with their toddlers (Fivush, 2009). Years later, adolescents whose mothers had been more elaborative during their early mother–toddler conversations have stronger autobiographical memories than adolescents whose mothers were less elaborative (Jack et al., 2009; see also Reese, Hayne, & MacDonald, 2008).

Although language is an important component of autobiographical memories, the language explanation, like the encoding explanation, does not entirely account for why children cannot remember nonverbal information such as the faces of preschool classmates (Lie & Newcombe, 1999). We need to consider that toddlers lack a strong sense of self and as a result may not have the necessary pages on which they can write memories of personally experienced events (Howe, Courage, & Rooksby, 2009). Without a sense of self, it is difficult to organize events as "things that happened to *me*." Indeed, young children's ability to recognize themselves in a mirror is a good predictor of children's ability to talk about their past (see Howe et al., 2009).

Finally, some researchers have also tried to explain childhood amnesia in terms of **fuzzy-trace theory** (Reyna & Brainerd, 1995). According to this explanation, children store verbatim and general accounts of an event separately. Verbatim information (such as word-for-word recall of a biology class lecture) is unstable and likely to be lost over long periods (Leichtman & Ceci, 1993); it is easier to remember the gist of an event (for example, recall of the general points covered in a biology lecture) than the details (Brainerd & Reyna, 1993; Koriat, Goldsmith, & Pansky, 2000). With age, we are increasingly likely to rely on gist mem-

ory traces, which are less likely to be forgotten and are more efficient than verbatim memory traces in the sense that they take less space in memory (Brainerd & Gordon, 1994; Klaczynski, 2001). Children pass through a transition period from storing largely verbatim memories to storing more gist memories, and the earlier verbatim memories are unlikely to be retained over time (Howe, 2000).

As you can see, there are plenty of ideas about the causes of childhood amnesia but still no firm explanation of why a period of life that is highly important to later development is a blank for most of us. Young children certainly encode many experiences and demonstrate recall during early childhood for these events. But due to a lack of sufficient working memory to encode events, language skills, a sense of self, or encoding only a "fuzzy trace" of what happened, the events of our early childhood do not seem to undergo the *consolidation* needed to store robust memories of this time (Bauer et al., 2007).

Scripts

As children engage in routine daily activities such as getting ready for bed or eating at a fast-food restaurant, they construct **scripts** or **general event representations** (GERs) of these activities (Nelson, 1986; Schank & Abelson, 1977). Scripts or GERs represent the typical sequence of actions related to an event and guide future behaviors in similar settings (Hudson & Mayhew, 2009). For instance, children who have been to a fast-food restaurant might have a script like this: You wait in line, tell the person behind the counter what you want, pay for the food, carry the tray of food to a table, open the packages and eat the food, gather the trash, and throw it away before leaving. With this script in mind, children can act effectively in similar settings. Children as young as 3 years use scripts when reporting familiar events (Hudson & Mayhew, 2009; Nelson, 1997). When asked about their visit to a fast-food restaurant the day before, children usually report what happens *in general* when they go to the res-

Children develop scripts in memory for routine activities, such as visiting a fast-food restaurant, that guide their behavior in these situations.

taurant rather than what specifically happened during yesterday's visit (Kuebli & Fivush, 1994). As children age, their scripts become more detailed. Perhaps more important than age, however, is experience: Children with greater experience of an event develop richer scripts than children with less experience (DeMarie, Norman, & Abshier, 2000).

Eyewitness Memory

Children's scripts affect their memory for future events as well as their recollection of past events. For example, when presented with information inconsistent with their scripts, preschoolers may misremember the information so that it better fits their script (Nelson & Hudson, 1988). Four-year-old Damian may have a script for birthdays that includes blowing out candles, eating cake, and opening presents. Although his brother is sick on his birthday and eats applesauce instead of cake, Damian later recalls that they all ate cake before opening presents. This demonstrates that memory is a reconstruction, not an exact replication (Hudson & Mayhew, 2009). This, in turn, has significant implications for **eyewitness memory** (or testimony), or the reporting of events witnessed or experienced—for example, a child's reporting that she saw her little brother snitch some candy before dinner. Children are increasingly asked to report events that have happened in the context of abuse cases or custody hearings. To what extent can you "trust" a child's memory in these situations? What factors influence the accuracy of children's episodic memory when providing testimony?

When asked generally about events ("Tell me what happened at Uncle Joe's house"), preschoolers recall less information than older children, but the recall of both groups is accurate (Pipe & Salmon, 2009; Pipe, Thierry, & Lamb, 2007). General prompts (such as "What happened next?" or "Tell me more about that…") can elicit additional recall of information (Pipe & Salmon, 2009). Specific questions ("Was Uncle Joe wearing a red shirt?") can also elicit more information, but accuracy of recall begins to slip (Hilgard & Loftus, 1979). This is especially true as the questions become more directed or leading ("Uncle Joe touched you here, didn't he?"). Preschool-age children, more so than older children and adults, are suggestible; they can be influenced by information implied in direct questioning and by relevant information introduced after the event (Bjorklund, Brown, & Bjorklund, 2002).

Perhaps it is unfortunate, then, that preschoolers, because they initially offer less information in response to open-ended questions, are asked a larger number of directed questions than older children (Baker-Ward et al., 1993; Price & Goodman, 1990). They are also frequently subjected to repeated questioning, which increases errors in reporting among children (Bjorklund, Brown, & Bjorklund, 2002). Although repeated questioning with general, open-ended questions can increase accuracy, repeated questioning with directed or closed questions can decrease accuracy (Memon & Vartoukian, 1996). For example, in a study with 5- and 6-year-olds, researchers "cross-examined" children about events that occurred on a field trip to a police station during which the children saw a jail cell and police car and were fingerprinted and photographed (Zajac &

Hayne, 2003). After a delay of 8 months, children's memories were probed using irrelevant, leading, and ambiguous questions like those you might hear in a courtroom. Many children "cracked" under the pressure as evidenced by backing down and changing their answers in response to the questioning. Fully 1 out of 3 children changed *all* their answers, and most changed at least one answer. So although children can demonstrate accurate recall when asked clear and unbiased questions, this study shows that young children's memory for past events can quickly become muddied when the questioning becomes tough.

Problem Solving

Memories are vital to problem-solving skills. To solve any problem, a person must process information about the task, as well as use stored information, to achieve a goal. Thus, working memory in particular is a critical component of problem solving (Lee, Ng, & Ng, 2009). How do problem-solving capacities change during childhood? Piaget provided one answer to this question by proposing that children progress through broad stages of cognitive growth, but information-processing theorists were not satisfied with this explanation. They sought to pinpoint more specific reasons why problem-solving prowess improves so dramatically as children age.

Consider the problem of predicting what will happen to the balance beam in ■ **Figure 8.6** when weights are put on each side of the fulcrum, or balancing point. The goal is to decide which way the balance beam will tip when it is released. To judge correctly, you must take into account both the number of weights and their distances from the fulcrum. Piaget believed that concrete operational thinkers can appreciate the significance of either the amount of weight or its distance from the center but will not grasp the inverse relationship between the two factors. Only when they reach the stage of formal operations will new cognitive structures allow them to understand that balance can be maintained by decreasing a weight *and* moving it farther from the fulcrum or by increasing a weight *and* moving it closer to the fulcrum (Piaget & Inhelder, 1969).

Robert Siegler (1981, 2000) proposed that the information-processing perspective could provide a fuller analysis. His **rule assessment approach** determines what information about a

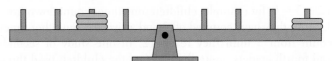

■ **FIGURE 8.6** The balance beam apparatus used by Robert Siegler to study children's problem-solving abilities. Which way will the balance beam tip? Source: From R. S. Siegler, Developmental sequences within and between concepts, *Monographs of the Society for Research in Child Development, 46*, (2, Serial No. 189). Copyright © 1981. Reprinted with permission of John Wiley & Sons, Inc.

problem children take in and what rules they then formulate to account for this information. This approach assumes that children's problem-solving attempts are not hit or miss but are governed by rules; it also assumes that children fail to solve problems because they fail to encode all the critical aspects of the problem and are guided by faulty rules.

Siegler (1981) administered balance beam problems to individuals ages 3–20. He detected clear age differences in the extent to which both weight and distance from the fulcrum were taken into account in the rules that guided decisions about which end of the balance beam would drop. Few 3-year-olds used a rule; they guessed. By contrast, 4- and 5-year-olds were governed by rules. More than 80% of these children used a simple rule that said the side of the balance beam with greater weight would drop; they ignored distance from the fulcrum. By age 8, most children had begun to consider distance from the fulcrum and weight under some conditions: when the weight on the two sides was equal, they appreciated that the side of the balance beam with the weights farthest from the fulcrum would drop. By age 12, most children considered both weight and distance on a range of problems, although they still became confused on complex problems in which one side had more weights but the other had its weights farther from the fulcrum. Finally, 30% of 20-year-olds discovered the correct rule—that the pull on each arm is a function of weight times distance. For example, if there are three weights on the second peg to the left and two weights on the fourth peg to the right, the left torque is $3 \times 2 = 6$ and the right torque is $2 \times 4 = 8$, so the right arm will drop.

The increased accuracy of young adults comes with a price—increased time to solve the problem (van der Maas & Jansen, 2003). Although, in general, information-processing time gets faster with age, the complex rules needed to successfully solve all the variations of the balance beam problem demand more time. So on some problems, adults are slower than children because they are using a more sophisticated strategy.

In most important areas of problem solving, Siegler (1996) concluded, children do not simply progress from one way of thinking to another as they age, as his balance beam research suggested. Instead, in working problems in arithmetic, spelling, science, and other school subjects, most children in any age group use multiple rules or problem-solving strategies rather than just one. In working a subtraction problem such as $12 - 3 = 9$, for example, children sometimes count down from 12 until they have counted off 3 and arrive at 9 but other times count from 3 until they reach 12. In one study of second- and fourth-graders, more than 90% of the children used three or more strategies in working subtraction problems (Siegler, 1989).

Similarly, Michael Cohen (1996) found that most preschoolers used all possible strategies when attempting to solve a practical mathematical problem in the context of playing store. He also found that children's selection and use of strategies became more efficient over multiple task trials; that is, they increasingly selected strategies that would allow them to solve the task in fewer steps.

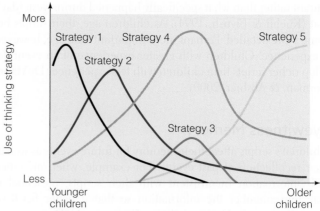

■ **FIGURE 8.7** Cognitive development may resemble overlapping waves more than a staircase leading from one stage to another. Children of a particular age typically use multiple thinking strategies rather than just one.

Source: From *Emerging minds: The process of change in children's thinking* by Siegler. Copyright © 1996 by Oxford University Press, Inc. Used by permission of Oxford University Press, Inc.

Such results suggest that cognitive development works much as evolution does, through a process of natural selection in which many ways of thinking are available and the most adaptive survive (DeLoache, Miller, & Pierroutsakos, 1998; Siegler, 1996, 2000). Rather than picturing development as a series of stages resembling stairsteps, Siegler argues, we should picture it as overlapping waves, as shown in ■ **Figure** 8.7. Siegler (2006) summarizes the **overlapping waves theory** as a "process of variability, choice, and change" (p. 478). Thus, the development of problem-solving skills is a matter of knowing and using a variety of strategies, becoming increasingly selective with experience about which strategy to use, and changing or adding strategies as needed. At each age, children have multiple problem-solving strategies available to them. As children gain more experience, which typically occurs as they age, they decrease their use of less-adaptive strategies and increase their use of more-adaptive strategies; occasionally, new strategies may appear. Strategies evolve from their initial acquisition in a particular context to their generalization to other contexts, which helps strengthen the fledgling strategies (Siegler, 2006). Gradually, children not only learn to choose the most useful strategy for a problem but also become increasingly effective at executing new strategies. Familiarity with a task and with strategies frees processing space, allowing children to engage in more metacognitive analysis of the strategies at their disposal (Whitebread, 1999). Throughout, there is significant variability—both between children and within the same child across time and tasks.

Notice the difference between this information-processing explanation and Piaget's explanation of cognitive change. Piaget argued that change is qualitative, with new, more effective strategies replacing older, less effective strategies all at once as children move from one stage to another. Siegler argues that strategies emerge gradually and become more effective over time, with multiple strategies available any time.

Imagine how effective teachers might be if they, like Siegler, could accurately diagnose the information-processing strategies of their learners to know what each child is noticing (or failing to notice) about a problem and what rules or strategies each child is using when. Like a good car mechanic, the teacher would be able to pinpoint the problem and encourage less use of faulty strategies and rules and more use of adaptive ones. Much remains to be learned about how problem-solving strategies evolve as children age, and why. However, the rule assessment approach and overlapping waves theory give a fairly specific idea of what children are doing (or doing wrong) as they attack problems and illustrate how the information-processing approach to cognitive development provides a different view of development than Piaget's account does.

Checking Mastery

1. What are two reasons why older children have improved memories relative to younger children?

2. How do scripts or GERs relate to memory?

3. What is the "take-home" message of the overlapping waves theory of problem solving?

Making Connections

1. You are a first-grade teacher, and one of the first things you notice is that some of your students remember a good deal more than others about the stories you read to them. Based on what you have read in this chapter, what are your main hypotheses about why some children have better memories than other children the same age?

2. You have been called in to interview a young child who may have witnessed a shooting. Given the research on children's memory, how will you gather information from your young witness?

3. If you are typical, then you probably have few, if any, memories from the period of your infancy and even toddlerhood. Why can't we remember the early events of our lives?

8.4 The Adolescent

Although parents in the midst of reminding their adolescent sons and daughters to do household chores or homework may wonder whether teenagers process any information at all, learning, memory, and problem solving continue to improve considerably during the adolescent years. Research on episodic memory shows that the performance of young teens (11–12 years) is quite similar to that of children, and both groups do markedly worse than young adults (Brehmer et al., 2007). Clearly, then, there is room for improvement during adolescence. How does this improvement occur?

Strategies

First, new learning and memory strategies emerge. It is during adolescence that the memory strategy of elaboration is mastered (Schneider & Pressley, 1997). Adolescents also develop and refine advanced learning and memory strategies highly relevant to school learning—for example, note-taking and underlining skills. Ann Brown and Sandra Smiley (1978) asked students from 5th to 12th grade (approximately 11–18 years) to read and recall a story. Some learners were asked to recall the story immediately; others were given an additional 5 minutes to study it before they were tested. Amazingly, fifth-graders gained almost nothing from the extra study period except for those few who used the time to underline or take notes. The older middle school students benefited to an extent, but only senior high school students used underlining and note-taking methods effectively to improve their recall. When some groups of students were told specifically that they could underline or take notes if they wished, fifth-graders still did not improve, largely because they tended to underline everything rather than to highlight the most important points.

Adolescents also make more deliberate use of strategies that younger children use unconsciously (Bjorklund, 1985). For example, they may deliberately organize a list of words instead of simply using the organization or grouping that happens to be there already. And they use existing strategies more selectively. For example, they are adept at using their strategies to memorize the material on which they know they will be tested and at letting go of irrelevant information (Bray, Hersh, & Turner, 1985; Lorsbach & Reimer, 1997). To illustrate, Patricia Miller and Michael Weiss (1981) asked children to remember the locations of animals that had been hidden behind small doors and to ignore the household objects hidden behind other doors. As ▪Figure 8.8 shows, 13-year-olds recalled more than 7- and

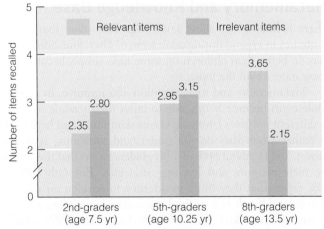

▪**FIGURE 8.8** Adolescents are better able than children to concentrate on learning relevant material and to ignore irrelevant material.

Source: From P. H. Miller & M. G. Weiss, Children's attention allocation, understanding of attention and performance on the incidental learning task, *Child Development, 52*, pp. 1183–1190. Reprinted with permission of John Wiley & Sons, Inc.

10-year-olds about where the animals had been hidden, but they remembered less about task-irrelevant information (the locations of the household objects). Apparently, they are better able to push irrelevant information out of working memory so that it does not interfere with task performance (Lorsbach & Reimer, 1997). So, during elementary school, children get better at distinguishing between what is relevant and what is irrelevant, but during adolescence they advance further by selectively using their memory strategies only on the relevant material. If it is not going to be on the test, forget it!

Basic Capacities

Adolescents make other strides besides these changes in memory strategies. Basic capacities continue to increase; for example, adolescents perform any number of cognitive operations faster than children do (Kail, 1991). As discussed earlier in this chapter, adolescents have greater functional use of their working memory because maturational changes in the brain allow them to process information more quickly and to simultaneously process more chunks of information. Older teens (16–20 years) perform better than younger ones (less than 15 years) on highly complex cognitive tasks that require them to use recalled information to strategically direct their search behavior (Luciana et al., 2005). There is no difference, though, on tasks of low complexity such as face recognition. Some research suggests that face recognition has a different neural basis than other forms of memory (MacKenzie & Donaldson, 2009). This may explain why face recognition appears early in life and is relatively robust throughout the life span.

Metamemory and Knowledge Base

There is little to say about knowledge base other than that it continues to expand during adolescence. Therefore, adolescents may do better than children on some tasks simply because they know more about the topic.

Metamemory and metacognition also improve. In general, adolescents become better able to tailor their reading strategies to different purposes (studying versus skimming) and better able to realize when they do not understand something (Baker & Brown, 1984). About 80% of 12th graders report that they monitor their memory and learning strategies. But only 50% to 60% report that they think in advance to develop an effective plan for a difficult task or think back after completing a task to evaluate what worked or did not work (Leutwyler, 2009). Clearly, this leaves room for improvements beyond adolescence.

Successful metacognition can be seen in adolescents choosing the strategy of elaboration over rote repetition when they realize that the former is more effective (Pressley, Levin, & Ghatala, 1984). Adolescents are also fairly accurate at monitoring whether or not they have allocated adequate study time to learn new material (Kelemen, 2000). Teens typically allo-

cate more study time to information judged to be difficult, indicating that they understand this material needs additional processing to be retained (Thiede & Dunlosky, 1999). Interestingly, when pressed for time, college students devote more study time to easy items (Son & Metcalfe, 2000). Apparently, they decide it is futile to work on the difficult material when they do not have adequate time, so they spend their time on what seems most likely to pay off. Hopefully, you can see the implication of this for your own studying: Set aside enough time to study all the material; otherwise, you may end up in a time crunch reviewing only the easy material. And take comfort in knowing that the better you learn something now, the more likely you will remember this material 20, 30, even 50 years from now (Bahrick 1984; Conway, Cohen, & Stanhope, 2006). For more tips on how to improve your memory, visit Engagement Box 8.1.

It is interesting to note that that the extent to which metacognition is employed varies by gender and socioeconomic background (Leutwyler, 2009). Adolescent girls consistently report using more metacognitive strategies than adolescent boys. This may help explain why girls earn higher grades in school than boys, a finding that we will explore in greater detail in Chapter 10. And students from higher socioeconomic backgrounds report more use of metacognitive strategies than their lower socioeconomic peers. Families with higher socioeconomic status may have more resources such as books in the home and may talk more explicitly about effective learning strategies.

Growth in strategies, basic capacities, knowledge base, and metacognition probably also helps explain the growth in everyday problem-solving ability that occurs during the adolescent years. Teenagers perfect several information-processing skills and become able to apply them deliberately and spontaneously across a variety of tasks.

Checking Mastery

1. What are the differences in basic memory capacities of children and adolescents?

2. What memory improvements are we likely to notice when a child becomes an adolescent?

Making Connections

1. Using the information-processing model presented earlier in the chapter (see Figure 8.1), explain why 17-year-old Nathaniel outperforms his 7-year-old sibling when asked to recall a TV program on the Civil War both watched last week.

2. Abigail has a big exam coming up—the results could determine whether or not she earns a scholarship for college. How should she prepare for the exam and what characteristics of the test itself or the testing conditions might affect her performance?

engagement 8.1

Improve Your Memory!

What are some practical steps you can use to improve your memory? First, keep in mind that your brain, which is absolutely essential for memory, does not operate in isolation from the rest of you. Your brain, and therefore your memory, is affected by such factors as the amount of sleep you get, your nutrition, and your physical activity.

Consider sleep. The process of consolidation of memories is critical to moving them into long-term storage and is improved with sleep. Try reviewing to-be-remembered information right before you go to sleep at night and then get the recommended hours of sleep for your age (see Chapter 5). Studying in the afternoon and then taking a nap has also been shown to help consolidate memories. And before you start to study, plan to do some aerobic exercise. This increases oxygen to your brain and also helps you stay alert and focused once you settle down to study. As for nutrition, a growing body of research suggests that omega-3 fatty acids contribute to brain function, as do B vitamins and antioxidants. A good meal for your brain might be salmon, spinach salad, and a strawberry-blueberry smoothie.

So you have adopted healthy eating, exercise, and sleep habits. What can you do to improve your memory when actually studying course material for that upcoming test? We'll focus on a few things that will assist with encoding and consolidation of memories, as well as some helpful hints for retrieval.

1. PAY ATTENTION! If you are daydreaming in class or thinking of something else while reading, you will not encode the information to be learned. If you don't encode it, you will be out of luck when it comes time to retrieve the memory—it simply won't be there. To increase your attention, reduce the distractions that may be present in your environment.

2. ORGANIZE AND MAKE CONNECTIONS to existing knowledge. Organizing to-be-learned material into logical groups can aid in consolidation and storage of the information. What is logical depends on each individual and each task. The organizational scheme must make sense to the learner in the context that it needs to be learned. Consolidation is also more likely to occur when the new material can be related to existing knowledge. Think of how you might use familiar ideas to help you remember new ideas.

3. USE STRATEGIES that enrich and elaborate the new material. Repeating items over and over is a simplistic strategy that helps store fairly simple facts. You need to dig deeper into your toolbox of strategies and choose those that will create richer connections to existing material or will allow you to elaborate the new material. Examples of these strategies might be to associate each new word to an existing concept; this could be taken a step further—elaborated—by thinking of the similarities and differences between the new and old material. Or think of an acronym using the first letter of each to-be-learned word. You could create a story that ties together a new set of concepts that you want to recall later; by retelling the story, you recall the concepts.

4. CUSTOMIZE YOUR LEARNING STRATEGIES to optimize your learning style. Some research suggests that students who use the strategy of verbal elaboration (that is, creating sentences about the material) have better recall than students who use mental imagery or another visual strategy (Kirchhoff & Buckner, 2006). But this same research also showed that individuals choose different strategies to learn the same material. Some learners tend to be more visual, whereas others excel with more verbal material and strategies.

5. OVERLEARN new material. If you study new material just enough to recognize or recall it for a short period, chances are good you will forget a considerable amount of this material. To prevent this from happening, you need to overlearn the material. Don't stop studying when you reach that point where you think you might be able to remember the material if you take the test very soon. Keep studying until retrieval of the information becomes quick and effortless. There is evidence that overlearning strengthens the neural connections involved in storing information and makes it more likely that you will be able to retrace these neural paths when it comes time to retrieve it.

8.5 The Adult

If you are about age 20, you will be pleased to know that the young adult college student has served as the standard of effective information processing against which all other age groups are compared. In other words, information processing is thought to be most efficient—at its peak—in young adults. Still, improvements in cognitive performance continue during the adult years before aging begins to take its toll on some memory and problem-solving capacities.

Developing Expertise

Comparing people new to their chosen fields of study with those more experienced tells researchers that experience pays off in more effective memory and problem-solving skills. In Chapter 7, you saw that people in Piaget's highest stage of cognitive development, formal operations, often perform better in their areas of specialization than in unfamiliar areas. Similarly, information-processing research shows that adults often function best cognitively in domains in which they have achieved expertise (Byrnes, 1996; Ericsson, 1996; Glaser & Chi, 1988). It seems to take about 10 years of training and experience to become a true expert in a field and to build a rich and well-organized knowledge base (Ericsson, 1996). But once this base is achieved, the expert not only knows and remembers more but thinks also more effectively than individuals who lack expertise.

Consider first the effects of semantic memory, or knowledge base, on performance. How might adults who are baseball experts and adults who care little for baseball perceive and remember the same game? George Spilich and his associates (1979) had baseball experts and novices listen to a tape of a half inning of play. Experts recalled more of the information central to the game—the important plays and the fate of each batter, in proper order—whereas novices were thrown off by irrelevant facts such as the threatening weather conditions and the number of people attending the game. Experts also recalled more details—for example, noting that a double was a line drive down the left-field line rather than just a double. At any age, experts in a field are likely to remember new information in that content domain more fully than novices do (Morrow et al., 1994).

In addition, experts are able to use their elaborately organized and complete knowledge bases to solve problems effectively and efficiently (Proffitt, Coley, & Medin, 2000). They are able to size up a situation quickly, see what the problem really is, and recognize how the new problem is similar to and different from problems encountered in the past (Glaser & Chi, 1988). They can quickly, surely, and almost automatically call up the right information from their extensive knowledge base to devise effective solutions to problems and to carry them out efficiently.

Are the benefits of expertise content-specific, or does gaining expertise in one domain carry over into other domains and make a person a more generally effective learner or problem solver? This is an interesting and important question. One research team (Ericsson, Chase, & Faloon, 1980) put an average college

Adults who have gained proficiency in their chosen fields can draw from their well-organized knowledge bases to find just the right information to fit the problem at hand. Solving problems is automatic and effortless for experts.

student to work improving the number of digits he could recall. He practiced for about 1 hour a day, 3–5 days a week, for more than 1½ years—more than 200 hours in all. His improvement? He went from a memory span of 7 digits to one of 79 digits! His method involved forming meaningful associations between strings of digits and running times—for example, seeing 3492 as "3 minutes and 49 point 2 seconds, near world-record mile time" (p. 1181). It also involved chunking numbers into groups of three or four, then organizing the chunks into large units.

Did all this work pay off in a better memory for information other than numbers? Not really. When he was given letters of the alphabet to recall, this young man's memory span was unexceptional (about six letters). Clearly the memory ability he developed was based on strategies of use only in the subject matter he was trying to remember. Similarly, Bob Petrella, a man with an exceptional memory for anything and everything related to sports, turns out to have ordinary prospective memory, or remembering things that need to be done in the future (ABCNews, 2010). And Jill Price, who we introduced at the beginning of this chapter, has no special ability to memorize numbers or facts despite her near perfect episodic memory of events from every day of her life since age 14 (Parker et al., 2006). Each expert apparently relies on domain-specific knowledge and domain-specific information-processing strategies to achieve cognitive feats (Ericsson & Kintsch, 1995; Schunn & Anderson, 1999).

Overall, experts know more than novices do, their knowledge base is more organized, and they are able to use their knowledge and the specialized strategies they have devised to learn, remember, and solve problems efficiently in their areas of expertise—but not in other domains. In effect, experts do not need to think much; they are like experienced drivers who can put themselves on "autopilot" and carry out well-learned routines quickly and accurately. By gaining expertise over the years, adults can often compensate to some extent for age-related losses in information-processing capacities (Jastrzembski, Charness, & Vasyukova, 2006).

Autobiographical Memory

Earlier in this chapter, we examined the emergence of autobiographical memories and you learned that most adults do not remember much about their first few years of life. Yet we also noted that the long-term memory store seems limitless in terms of space and longevity. Is everything we have ever experienced "in there" somewhere? Unless you are like Jill Price with near perfect recall of life events, this seems unlikely. Most adults report difficulties recalling past events. So what determines whether an event is likely to be recalled at a later point in time? We will consider four factors identified by Patricia Bauer (2007) that may influence autobiographical memories: personal significance, distinctiveness, emotional intensity, and life phase of the event.

To begin, most people believe that the personal significance of an event affects our memory for the event—that events of great importance to the self will be remembered better than less important events. As it turns out, the personal significance of an event, as rated at the time the event occurs, has almost no effect on one's ability to later recall the event. It may be that what was once considered important becomes less so with the passage of time and with the broader perspective gained over the years. For example, imagine that at age 19, you break up with your boyfriend of 2 years. This is traumatic and of great importance to you as a 19-year-old. You expect you'll never get over it and that the details of the event will be forever etched into your memory. But over the next 10, 20, 30 years, or more, so many other events occur that the importance of this youthful breakup fades as you date others, marry, work, raise children, and so on.

In contrast, the distinctiveness or uniqueness of an event has been consistently associated with better recall (Bauer, 2007). The more unique an event is, the more likely it is to be recalled later on, and to be recalled as a distinct event with relevant details. Common events and experiences are often recalled, if at all, as multiple events lumped together as one (Burt, Kemp, & Conway, 2003). Thus, if you attended the same camp every summer throughout your childhood, you may retain fond memories of your experiences at the camp. But the chances are good that you have integrated in your memory many of the common and similar camp experiences: you remember singing songs around the campfire, but because you did this every year of the camp, you don't recall the experience of this one year as separate from your experience of this other years. On the other hand, if one year a camper did something highly unusual during one of these campfire sing-a-longs (for example, streaked through the fire), you may indeed remember this particular event for many years to come because of its uniqueness.

Bauer (2007) notes that the affective or emotional intensity of an event also influences later recall. Events associated with either highly negative or highly positive emotions are recalled better than events that were experienced in the context of more neutral emotions. This enhanced memory for emotion-arousing events occurs even though the emotion associated with the event tends to dissipate with time, especially if it is a negative emotion (Paz-Alonso et al., 2009). It is likely that strong emotions activate the body's arousal system and the neural components associated with arousal enhance encoding and consolidation of events.

Finally, research on autobiographical memory has revealed that people recall more information from their teens and 20s than from any other time except the near present (Fitzgerald, 1999; Rubin, 2002; Rybash, 1999). ■ **Figure 8.9** shows the number of memories recalled by 70-year-old adults. Not surprisingly, they recalled a lot from their recent past (for example, age 65). But the number of memories recalled from about ages 15–25 was higher than the number recalled from other points of the life span. Why? Possibly, this phase of life is more memorable because it is instrumental in shaping who people are as adults—their identity—and is often full of significant life changes (Fitzgerald, 1999). David Rubin (2002) suggests that the *bump*, as he calls it, occurs because memories from adolescence and early adulthood are more easily accessible than memories from other periods of the life span. They are more accessible because of their distinctiveness and the effort applied by adolescents and young adults to understanding the meaning of the events (Rubin, Rahhal, & Poon, 1998).

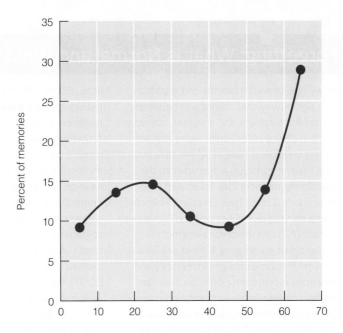

■ **FIGURE 8.9** Seventy-year-olds recall the times of their lives: What does this graph illustrate about the recall of autobiographical memories by older adults? Source: From D. C. Rubin, S. E. Wetzler, & R. D. Nebes, Autobiographical memory across the adult lifespan. In D. C. Rubin (ed.), *Autobiographical memory.* Copyright © 1986 Cambridge University Press. Reprinted with permission.

Memory and Aging

No less an expert on learning than B. F. Skinner complained about memory problems: "One of the more disheartening experiences of old age is discovering that a point you have just made—so significant, so beautifully expressed—was made by you in something you published a long time ago" (Skinner, 1983, p. 242). Most elderly adults report that they have at least minor difficulties remembering things (Smith et al., 1996). They are especially likely to have trouble recalling names and items they will need later; they are also more upset than young adults by memory lapses, perhaps because they view them as signs of aging (Cavanaugh, Grady, & Perlmutter, 1983). Exploration Box 8.1 describes when forgetfulness is normal and when it is indicative of a more serious problem.

Areas of Strength and Weakness

Much research indicates that, on average, older adults learn new material more slowly and sometimes learn it less well than young and middle-aged adults do and that they remember what they have learned less well. However, the following qualifications are important and will be expanded on in the following sections:

- Most of the research is based on cross-sectional studies that compare age groups, which suggests that the age differences detected could be related to factors other than age. (If needed, you can refresh your memory of the strengths and weaknesses of cross-sectional designs by referring back to Chapter 1.)

As we age, or watch parents and grandparents age, how can we distinguish between normal forgetfulness and abnormal memory changes? Many older adults worry that forgetting an appointment or where they put their reading glasses is a precursor to the devastating memory loss associated with Alzheimer's disease (see Chapter 16). Fortunately, most of us will not develop Alzheimer's disease (AD) and the atypical memory changes that accompany it. Most will, however, exhibit some changes in memory and information-processing skills. So how can we discriminate between normal memory changes and those associated with disease?

Cynthia Green (2001) suggests three criteria that can be used to alert us to atypical memory problems:

- Has memory gotten noticeably worse over the past 6 months?
- Do memory problems interfere with everyday activities at home or work?
- Are family and friends concerned about an individual's memory problems?

Answering "yes" to these questions may indicate unusual memory loss that should be evaluated by a professional.

In practical terms, it is normal to forget where you put something but abnormal to forget how to use it (Cherry & Smith, 1998). Thus, do not worry when Grandpa cannot find his car keys, but be alert if he cannot remember how to use them when they are in his hand. Similarly, it is normal to forget a new phone number you recently looked up in the phone book but abnormal to forget phone numbers you have known and used for years.

Researchers who study memory now believe there is a third type of memory loss that distinguishes normal loss with age from unhealthy disease-related loss (Brandt et al., 2009; Petersen et al., 1997, 2001). Individuals with **mild cognitive impairment** experience significant memory problems—forgetting important appointments, having trouble learning new names, and repeating themselves to the same person—but otherwise do not appear to be suffering from dementia. At least not yet. Some research suggests that a majority of those with mild cognitive impairment will eventually develop forms of dementia such as Alzheimer's disease (Fischer et al., 2007; Maioli et al., 2007). Research also suggests that patients with mild cognitive impairment display deficits on other cognitive tasks as well, which could mean their problem is more general than memory impairment (Ribeiro, de Mendonca, & Guerreiro, 2006). This is a serious concern because 22% of older adults may have mild cognitive impairment and will require increased assistance as they continue to age (Plassman et al., 2008).

The good news is that age-related memory loss may be preventable, and some losses may be reversible. Reducing stress, for example, is one way to improve memory performance (Bremner & Narayan, 1998). Chronic stress elevates levels of cortisol in the brain, which impedes memory. A study by the MacArthur Foundation found that three things predicted good memory over time: physical fitness and activity, mental activity, and a sense of control over life events (Rowe & Kahn, 1998). Mental activity—working crossword puzzles, reading, playing musical instruments—increases connections among neurons. Physical activity seems to release chemicals that protect neurons involved in cognitive function. Older adults who engage in moderate to high levels of physical activity are less likely to develop cognitive impairment than those who are not active (Etgen et al., 2010). Thus, remaining physically and mentally active can help protect against memory loss associated with aging. Having a sense of control over memory can boost both confidence and memory performance.

In sum, significant memory loss is not likely among healthy older adults. It is true that, relative to young adults, older adults exhibit poorer memory performance in some situations. But these changes are minor and can often be avoided or minimized by remaining physically and mentally active. Families and professionals should be on the lookout for older adults who show marked declines in their memory performance. They may be experiencing mild cognitive impairment and may eventually develop Alzheimer's disease and impaired memory. The earlier they are identified and receive treatment, the better (see Chapter 16).

© Hans Neleman/Corbis

- Declines, when observed, typically do not become noticeable until we hit our 70s.
- Difficulties in remembering affect elderly people more noticeably as they continue to age and are most severe among the oldest elderly people.
- Not all older people experience these difficulties.
- Not all kinds of memory tasks cause older people difficulty.

Studies of memory skills in adulthood suggest that the aspects of learning and memory in which older adults look most deficient in comparison with young and middle-aged adults are some of the same areas in which young children compare unfavorably with older children (see Bauer, 2007). The following sections describe some of the major weaknesses—and, by implication, strengths—of older adults' memory skills.

Timed Tasks. On average, older adults are slower than younger adults to learn and retrieve information; they may need to go through the material more times to learn it equally well and may need more time to respond when their memory is tested. Thus, they are hurt by time limits (Finkel et al., 2003).

Unfamiliar or Artificial Content. Older adults fare especially poorly compared with younger adults when the material to be learned is unfamiliar or meaningless—when they cannot tie it to their existing knowledge. In a convincing demonstration of how familiarity influences memory, researchers had young and elderly adults examine words likely to be more familiar to the young adults at the time of the testing (for example, *dude, disco,* and *bummer*) and words from the past likely to be more familiar to the older adults (for example, *pompadour, gramophone,* and *vamp*). Young adults outperformed older adults on the "new" words, but older adults outperformed young adults on the "old" words (Barrett & Wright, 1981). Many memory tasks involve learning unfamiliar material and thus do not allow older adults to use their knowledge base.

Similarly, older adults perform significantly worse in laboratory contexts but can often outperform younger adults in naturalistic contexts (Henry et al., 2004). So when the task is meaningful—such as remembering to take your medicine every morning—older adults may be able to draw on their greater experience or knowledge bases to enhance their memory performance.

Unexercised Skills. Older adults are also likely to be at a disadvantage when they are required to use learning and memory skills that they rarely use in daily life; they hold their own when they can rely on well-practiced skills that have become effortless and automatic with practice. For example, Lynne Reder, Cynthia Wible, and John Martin (1986) found that elderly adults were just as good as young adults at judging whether sentences presented to them were plausible based on a story they had read. Judging whether something makes sense in the context of what has been read is a well-exercised ability. However, older adults

were deficient when it came to judging whether specific sentences had or had not appeared in the story—a skill seldom used outside school. It seems that older adults read to get the gist or significance of a story and do not bother with the details, a strategy that may be adaptive if they have no need to memorize details and if their ability to do so has fallen off with age (Adams, 1991; Stine-Morrow, Loveless, & Soederberg, 1996). In other ways, age differences are smaller when well-practiced skills are assessed than when less-practiced skills are assessed (Denney, 1982).

Recall versus Recognition. Older adults are likely to be more deficient on tasks requiring recall memory than on tasks requiring only recognition of what was learned (Charles, Mather, & Carstensen, 2003). In one study of memory for high school classmates (Bahrick, Bahrick, & Wittlinger, 1975), even adults who were almost 35 years past graduation could recognize which of five names matched a picture in their yearbook about 90% of the time. However, the ability to actively recall names of classmates when given only their photos as cues dropped considerably as the age of the rememberer increased. A large gap between recognition and recall shows that older people have encoded and stored the information but cannot retrieve it without the help of cues. Sometimes older adults fail to retrieve information because they never thoroughly encoded or learned it, but at other times they simply cannot retrieve information that is "in there."

Explicit Memory Tasks. Finally, older adults seem to have more trouble with explicit memory tasks that require mental effort than with implicit memory tasks that involve more automatic mental processes (Hoyer & Verhaeghen, 2006). Older adults, then, have little trouble with skills and procedures that have been routinized over the years—established as habits. But even though explicit memory declines, the magnitude of the decline varies with the type of explicit memory. Older adults retain fairly good semantic memory (general factual knowledge accumulated over time) but show steady declines in episodic memory (recall of specific events that are tied to a specific time and place) (see, for example, Spaniol, Madden, & Voss, 2006).

Overall, these findings suggest that older adults, like young children, have difficulty with tasks that are cognitively demanding—that require speed, the learning of unfamiliar material, the use of unexercised abilities, recall rather than recognition, or explicit and effortful rather than implicit and automatic memory. Yet older adults and young children have difficulty for different reasons, as you will now see.

Explaining Declines in Old Age

In asking why some older adults struggle with some learning and memory tasks, we will first return to the hypotheses used to explain childhood improvements in performance: knowledge base, metamemory, strategy use, and basic processing capacities. Then we will consider some additional possibilities.

Knowledge Base. If you start with the hypothesis that differences in knowledge base explain memory differences between older and younger adults, you immediately encounter a problem: Young children may lack knowledge, but elderly adults do not. Indeed, older adults are generally at least as knowledgeable as young adults: semantic memory *increases* until about age 65 (Rönnlund et al., 2005). Verbal knowledge shows no decrease throughout mid- and older adulthood and may not decline until we are pushing 90 (Park et al., 2002; Rönnlund et al., 2005; Singer et al., 2003)! Older adults know more than younger adults about real-world categories of information such as U.S. presidents, countries, international cities, and bodies of water (Foos & Sarno, 1998). In an important study, Harry Bahrick (1984) tested adults of various ages on their retention of Spanish vocabulary from high school or college classes. Amazingly, as much as 50% of the vocabulary learned was retained nearly *50 years* later! And it may be worth your time and effort to learn as much as you can in your classes now: Bahrick also found that the more classes taken in a subject and the higher the grades in those courses, the better the retention of this material in the years to come. Adults who took several Spanish classes and earned As remembered more Spanish vocabulary 50 years later compared to adults who took one Spanish class and earned Cs after a delay of just 1 year. Information that undergoes meaningful consolidation can clearly be retained in long-term memory for many years to come. So deficiencies in knowledge base are probably not the source of most memory problems that many older adults display. On the contrary, gains in knowledge probably help older adults compensate for losses in information-processing efficiency (Salthouse, 1993). Thus, older pilots are as adept as younger pilots and better than nonpilots at repeating back flight commands, but they show the usual effects of aging if they are given tasks less relevant to their work (Morrow et al., 1994). Older adults also perform better than younger adults on memory tasks in which they can spontaneously use analogies, another indication that a rich knowledge base can aid memory (Caplan & Schooler, 2001). Knowledge enhances learning. Indeed, as Paul Baltes has put it, "Knowledge is power!" (Baltes, Smith, & Staudinger, 1992, p. 143).

Metamemory. Could elderly adults, like young children, be deficient in the specific knowledge called metamemory? Is their knowledge of some of the strategies that prove useful in school learning—and in laboratory memory tasks—rusty? This theory sounds plausible, but research shows that older adults seem to know as much as younger adults about such things as which memory strategies are best and which memory tasks are hardest (Light, 1991). They can monitor their memory to assist their learning (Hines, Touron, & Herzog, 2009). Still, older adults are more likely than younger ones to misjudge the accuracy of some aspects of their memory, such as the source of the memories (Dodson, Bawa, & Krueger, 2007).

So whereas metamemory seems largely intact across the life span, there may be some isolated areas of weakness. Moreover, although older adults know a lot about memory, they express

At age 76, Yvette Kelly uses a memory program to exercise her information processing skills. Research suggests that both physical and mental workouts can aid memory across the lifespan.

more negative beliefs about their memory skills than do younger adults (Cavanaugh, 1996). Memory loss may contribute to a drop in confidence in memory skills, but negative beliefs about memory skills also appear to hurt memory performance (Hess, 2006). Therefore, it's not clear whether declines in actual memory performance lead to the development of negative beliefs about memory or whether negative beliefs—either your own or those of the surrounding culture—undermine memory performance (Hess, 2006; Hess et al., 2009).

To understand the connection between memory performance and stereotypes, Becca Levy and Ellen Langer (1994) tested the memory of young and elderly adults (ages 59–91) in three groups: hearing Americans, deaf Americans, and hearing Chinese. In both the American deaf and Chinese cultures, elders are respected and negative stereotypes of intellectual aging are not as prevalent as they are among hearing Americans. As ■ **Figure 8.10** shows, young adults in the three groups performed about equally well on a set of recall tasks, but Chinese elders clearly outperformed both deaf American elders (who were second best) and hearing American elders. Elderly Chinese adults scored only a little lower than young Chinese adults despite having less education. In addition, those older people in the study who believed that aging brings about memory loss performed more poorly than those who did not hold this belief. Levy (1996) has also shown that activating negative stereotypes in the minds of elderly adults (through rapid, subliminal presentation of words such as *Alzheimer's* and *senile* on a computer screen) causes them to perform worse on memory tests and to express less confidence in their memory skills than when positive stereotypes of old age are planted in their minds (through words such as *wise* and *sage*). Findings such as these clearly call into question the idea of a universal decline in memory skills in later life and point to the influence of culture and its views of aging on performance.

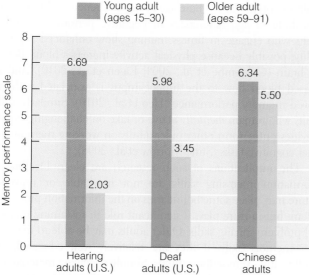

Young adult
(ages 15–30)

Older adult
(ages 59–91)

■ **FIGURE 8.10** Declines in memory skills in old age are not universal. In deaf culture and in Chinese culture, elderly people are not stereotyped as forgetful or senile. Perhaps as a result, Chinese elders perform almost as well as young Chinese adults on memory tasks, whereas in the United States, elders, especially in the hearing population, perform poorly. SOURCE: Adapted from B. Levy & B. Langer, Aging free from negative stereotypes: Successful memory in China and among the American deaf, *Journal of personality and social psychology*, 66, pp. 989–997. Copyright © 1994 by the American Psychological Association. Reprinted with permission.

Memory Strategies. What about the hypothesis that failure to use effective memory strategies accounts for deficits in old age? Many older adults do not spontaneously use strategies such as organization and elaboration even though they know them and are capable of using them (Light, 1991; Smith & Earles, 1996). This may be an important part of the problem when older adults are asked to deliberately memorize something. Older adults' biggest problem, though, seems to be with effective *retrieval* of details of an event and not with the original *encoding* of the event (Thomas & Bulevich, 2006). This can be seen in the increased incidence of *tip-of-the-tongue* episodes, where individuals have the feeling that they know something such as a person's name but cannot retrieve it (Bucur et al., 2008). Although most of us experience at least an occasional episode of the tip-of-the-tongue phenomenon, older adults have more frequent episodes as they attempt to retrieve stored information. Thus, retrieval strategies may be more susceptible to aging than encoding strategies. But why do many older adults fail to use effective memory and retrieval strategies?

Basic Processing Capacities. The answer may lie in the fourth hypothesis—the notion that basic processing capacities change with age. Which capacities? Much attention has focused on declines in the capacity to use working memory to operate actively on a lot of information simultaneously. Working-memory capacity increases during childhood and adolescence, peaks around age 45, then begins to decline (Swanson, 1999). Moreover, working-memory capacity predicts how well adults will perform on a range of cognitive tasks (Hoyer & Verhaeghen, 2006). Older adults do fine on short-term memory tasks that require them to juggle just a few pieces of information in working memory. However, when the amount of information that they are to "operate on" increases, they begin to show deficits. Older adults may have more trouble than younger ones ignoring irrelevant task information. For instance, trying to memorize a list of words while walking is more problematic for older adults than for middle-aged or younger adults (Li et al., 2001; Lindenberger, Marsiske, & Baltes, 2000). Brain research confirms that older adults show increased activity in parts of the brain associated with inhibition of task-irrelevant information (Stevens et al., 2008). Thus, their working-memory space may become cluttered with unnecessary information, limiting the space available for the task at hand (Hoyer & Verhaeghen, 2006).

Limitations in working-memory capacity are most likely rooted in slower functioning of the nervous system both early and late in life (see Hartley, 2006; also see Chapter 5). Much research shows that speed of processing increases during childhood and adolescence, peaks in early adulthood, then declines slowly over the adult years (Baudoin et al., 2009). The age differences in performance on cognitive tasks often shrink when age differences in speed of information processing are taken into account and controlled. Experience in a domain of learning can certainly enhance performance, but if children and older adults generally have sluggish "computers," they simply may not be able to keep up with the processing demands of complex learning and memory tasks (Hartley, 2006).

Using brain imaging techniques, researchers have also begun to identify different patterns of activity during memory tasks in the prefrontal cortex of younger and older adults (see, for example, Galdo-Alvarez, Lindin, & Diaz, 2009; Rypma et al., 2001). Although some studies show underactivity in older adults' brains, others show overactivity. Underactivity in the older brain is assumed to result from a deficiency of either the hardware of the brain or of the software it uses, such as the strategies that could be employed on a task (Reuter-Lorenz & Cappell, 2008). Overactivity, on the other hand, may indicate that the older brain is trying to compensate for age-related losses. By compensating, or working harder, the older brain may be able to perform as well as its younger counterpart, at least until this overactivity can no longer overcome steeper age-related declines (Meulenbroek et al., 2010).

Slow neural transmission, then, may be behind limitations in working memory in both childhood and old age (Bailey, Dunlosky, & Hertzog, 2009). Limitations in working memory, in turn, may contribute not only to limitations in long-term memory but also to difficulties performing a range of cognitive tasks, including problem-solving tasks and tests of intelligence, even those that have no time limits (Hartley, 2006; Salthouse, 2000).

To this point, then, you might conclude that many older adults, although they have a vast knowledge base and a good deal of knowledge about learning and memory, experience declines in basic processing capacity that make it difficult for them to carry out memory strategies that will drain their limited working-memory capacity. But the basic processing capacity hypothesis cannot explain everything about age differences in memory. You must consider some additional hypotheses, including sensory changes and a variety of contextual factors.

Sensory Changes. As you learned in Chapter 6, older adults experience declines in sensory abilities. Might these affect memory performance? Yes indeed. Research shows that visual and auditory skills are often better predictors than processing speed of cognitive performance among older adults (Anstey, Hofer, & Luszcz, 2003; Baltes &Lindenberger, 1997). As noted in Chapter 6, many older adults experience some hearing loss. Even young adults, when tested under moderately noisy conditions, show short-term memory performance decreases (Murphy et al., 2000). Sensory loss at any age may tax available processing resources, leading to memory deficits.

Contextual Contributors. Many researchers have adopted a contextual perspective on learning and memory, emphasizing both biological and genetic factors along with environmental and situational factors (Blanchard-Fields, Chen, & Norris, 1997; Dixon, 1992). They emphasize that performance on learning and memory tasks is the product of an interaction among (1) characteristics of the learner, such as goals, motivations, abilities, and health; (2) characteristics of the task or situation; and (3) characteristics of the broader environment, including the cultural context, in which a task is performed. They are not convinced that there is a universal biological decline in basic learning and memory capacities because older individuals often perform capably in certain contexts.

First, cohort differences in education and IQ can explain age differences in some learning and memory skills. Elderly people today are less educated, on average, than younger adults are, and they are further removed from their school days. When education level is controlled for, age differences shrink, although they do not disappear (Nilsson et al., 2002; Rönnlund et al., 2005). Thus, to some extent, education can compensate for aging. Older adults who are highly educated or who have high levels of intellectual ability often perform as well as younger adults (Cherry & LeCompte, 1999; Haught et al., 2000).

Similarly, health and lifestyle differences between cohorts may contribute to age differences in learning and memory. Older adults are more likely than younger adults to have chronic or degenerative diseases, and even mild diseases can impair memory performance (Houx, Vreeling, & Jolles, 1991; Hultsch, Hammer, & Small, 1993). Older adults also lead less active lifestyles and perform fewer cognitively demanding activities than younger

adults do, on average. These age group differences in lifestyle also contribute to age differences in cognitive performance. Older adults who engage in fitness training show enhanced cognitive ability, possibly because physical activity increases blood flow to the brain (Colcombe et al., 2004; Etgen et al., 2010). And increased blood flow to the hippocampus is associated with improved memory performance (Heo et al., 2010). Similarly, older adults who remain *mentally* active or take on challenging mental activities outperform other older adults on working memory and other cognitive tasks (Stine-Morrow et al., 2008).

The implications of such research are clear: Declines in information-processing skills are not inevitable or universal. Nature may place some boundaries on the information-processing system, but nurture plays a significant role in sustaining memory and problem-solving skills. Older adults may be able to maintain their memory skills if they are relatively well educated, stay healthy, and exercise their minds. Simply reviewing material after its presentation can help them improve their memory performance (Koutstaal et al., 1998; see Exploration Box 8.2 for more ways to improve memory of older adults). Still, factors such as education and health cannot account completely for age differences in cognitive performance.

Perhaps the truth lies somewhere between the basic processing capacity view, which emphasizes nature by pointing to a universal decline in cognitive resources such as speed and working memory that affect performance on many cognitive tasks, and the contextual view, which emphasizes nurture. Contextual theorists stress variability from person to person and situation to situation based on cohort differences, motivational factors, and task demands. Most adults, at least if they live to an advanced old age, may experience some loss of basic processing resources. However, they may also have developed specialized knowledge and strategies that allow them to compensate for these losses as they carry out the everyday cognitive activities most important to them (Baltes, Smith, & Staudinger, 1992).

Problem Solving and Aging

You know that problem-solving skills improve steadily from early childhood through adolescence, but what becomes of them in adulthood? On the one hand, you might expect to see a decline in problem-solving prowess paralleling declines in learning and memory performance. On the other hand, if adults increase their knowledge bases and develop expertise as they age, might not older adults outwit younger novices on many problem-solving tasks?

Familiar versus Unfamiliar Tasks

When given traditional problem-solving tasks to perform in the laboratory, young adults typically perform better than middle-aged adults, who in turn outperform older adults (Denney, 1989). However, consider research using the Twenty Questions task. Subjects are given an array of items and asked to find out, using as few questions as possible, which item the experimenter has in mind (■ **Figure 8.11**). The soundest problem-solving

Can You Teach an "Old Dog" New Tricks?

In an important study of cognitive training effects, Sherry Willis and her colleagues for the ACTIVE Study Group (2006) followed four groups of older adults (average age of 74 years) over a period of 5 years. The groups differed in the type of cognitive training they received at the beginning of the study:

- Memory training—participants were taught strategies of organization, visualization, and association to remember verbal material.
- Reasoning training—participants were taught strategies for detecting a pattern in a series of letters or words.
- Speed training—participants learned to complete visual search tasks in increasingly less time, and they were trained to divide their attention between two tasks.
- No training—these participants served as a control group.

How did the groups fare after 5 years? Compared with the control group, the adults who received memory training still did better on memory tasks; those who received reasoning training performed better on reasoning tasks; and those who received speed training were much faster. Importantly, the benefits of training were evident not just on laboratory tasks but on activities important to daily living such as driving or understanding the interactions and side effects of prescription drugs.

This study and others (see Hertzog et al., 2009) show that older adults can profit from mental exercise that increasingly challenges them. Just as physical exercise contributes to overall physical well-being, mental exercise contributes to overall mental well-being. And just as your physical workouts need to increasingly challenge you (if you start out walking a half-mile at a slow pace, you need to increase your distance and/or your pace to reap the most benefits), your mental workouts must become more rigorous. If you start out solving easy Sudoku puzzles, you need to push yourself to move on to more difficult ones.

Consider the real-world memory problem of understanding and remembering information about drug prescriptions, which older adults often struggle more with compared with younger adults. By writing clear, organized instructions and spending time explaining to older patients what they are to do, health-care professionals can simplify the learning task (Morrell, Park, & Poon, 1989). Alternatively, older adults can be given external memory aids. Denise Park and her colleagues (1992) explored the benefits of two such aids: an organization chart (a poster or pocket-sized table giving an hour-by-hour account of when drugs should be taken) and a medication organizer (a dispenser with columns for different days of the week and pill compartments for times of the day). Adults older than 70 more often took their pills correctly when they were given both the chart and the organizer than when they were given one or neither. Because researchers know that poor health is one contributor to poor memory functioning, it makes especially good sense to reduce the cognitive demands on old and ailing patients by letting external memory aids do the mental work for them. Surely the best of all possible worlds for the aging learner would be one in which materials and teaching techniques are tailored to the learner's information-processing capacities and in which training is offered in how to stretch those capacities.

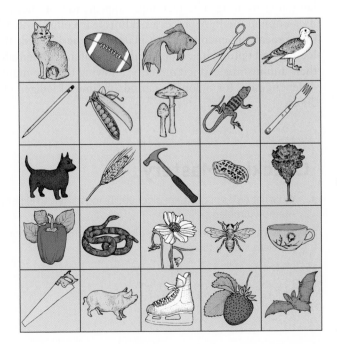

■ FIGURE 8.11 A Twenty Questions game. You can try it on a young child or a friend by thinking of one item in the group and asking your testee to find out which it is by asking you yes–no questions. Look for the constraint-seeking questions (for example, "Is it animate?"), and note the total number of questions required to identify the correct item.

strategy is to ask **constraint-seeking questions**—ones that rule out more than one item (for example, "Is it an animal?"). Young children and older adults tend to pursue specific hypotheses instead ("Is it a pig?" "Is it a pencil?"). Consequently, they must ask more questions to identify the right object. However, if the task is altered to make it more familiar (for example, through the use of playing cards as stimuli), then older adults do far better. The familiarity of the material allows them to draw on their knowledge base to solve the problem. Thus, older adults are capable of using effective problem-solving strategies but do not use them in some contexts, especially when given unfamiliar tasks in a laboratory.

What if adults are asked to deal with real-life problems such as grease fires in the kitchen, family squabbles, or refrigerators that break down in the middle of the night? Nancy Denney and Kathy Pearce (1989) asked elderly adults to help them devise everyday problems that would be meaningful and familiar to older individuals. One problem was to generate ideas about how a 65-year-old recently widowed woman could improve her social life; another was to advise an elderly couple living on Social Security what to do when they were unable to pay their heating bill one winter. On these everyday problems, performance increased from early adulthood to middle age and declined in old age.

Other findings echo this one: When given everyday problems to which they can apply the expertise they have gained through experience, middle-aged adults often outperform young adults. Elderly adults sometimes equal and sometimes do worse than young and middle-aged adults; either way, they show smaller deficits on the everyday problems than they do on unfamiliar problems in the laboratory (Berg & Klaczynski, 1996; Marsiske & Willis, 1995). Ultimately, declines in basic capacities may limit the problem-solving skills of many elderly adults, not only in the laboratory but also in real life (Denney, 1989; Kasworm & Medina, 1990). You should bear in mind, however, that cognitive competence among older adults varies widely because of differences in health, education, experience, and so on.

Selection, Optimization, and Compensation

Some cognitive researchers believe that older adults may approach problem solving differently than younger adults. It's true that younger adults generate more possible solutions to a problem than do older adults. But the solutions generated by older adults tend to be more goal-focused and selective, emphasizing quality over quantity (Marsiske & Margrett, 2006). When faced with a broken water pipe in the middle of the night, an older couple may generate one solution—call their grown son who lives down the street. Although this may not seem like an ideal solution to the son, the older adults may realize that this is the easiest and fastest solution.

In addition, researchers have proposed a selection, optimization, and compensation (SOC) framework to understand how older adults may cope with and compensate for their diminishing cognitive resources (Riediger, Li, & Lindenberger, 2006; and see Chapter 11). Older adults may adapt to changes in their problem-solving skills by finding ways to make up for cognitive skills that have grown rusty (compensation—for example, writing down items to remember if your memory skills are failing) so that they can maintain and strengthen those skills most useful to them in everyday life (selection and optimization). If your resources are limited or unstable, then you can't take on everything; you need to be selective. Choose those tasks that are most important or have to be done. For example, prepare dinner (after all, you have to eat), but don't worry about getting every surface of the house dusted. Focus on what you do well—optimize your strengths and minimize weaknesses. If you still have the skills to balance a checkbook and this is something your partner struggles with, then you should take over managing the checkbook. If your vision is so bad that you cannot tell that your "clean" dishes have chunks of food remaining on them, then offload this task to a dishwasher or partner.

Researchers have investigated whether this selection, optimization, and compensation model can be applied to help older adults overcome weaknesses in explicit memory by taking advantage of their relative strength of implicit memory. For instance, Cameron Camp and his colleagues (Camp et al., 1996; Camp & McKitrick, 1992) have tried to help patients with dementia caused by Alzheimer's disease use the implicit memory capacities that they, like people with amnesia, retain even though they have serious deficits in explicit memory. For example, they have taught patients with Alzheimer's disease to remember the names of staff members by having the patients name photos of staff members repeatedly and at ever longer intervals between trials. People who could not retain names for more than a minute were able to recall the names weeks later after training. The technique appears to work because it uses implicit memory processes; adults learn effortlessly when they repeatedly encounter the material to be learned. By selecting and optimizing, older adults can often compensate for their diminishing explicit memory, allowing them to maintain independence for a longer period of time (Riediger et al., 2006).

Checking Mastery

1. On what types of tasks are older adults most likely to experience memory problems?

2. How can adults minimize the effects of aging on memory and problem-solving tasks?

Making Connections

1. As a teacher in an Elderhostel program for older adults, you want to base your teaching methods on knowledge of the information-processing capacities of elderly adults. What practical recommendations would you derive from (a) the view that there is a universal decline with age in basic processing capacities and (b) the contextual perspective on cognitive aging?

2. Revisit Figure 8.9 showing the distribution of autobiographical memories over the life span. What factors might account for the rise and fall of autobiographical memories at different phases of the life span?

3. Every time your mother and grandmother forget something, they express concerns about "losing it" and "getting senile." Knowing that you have taken a course in life-span human development, they seek you out for reassurance. What can you tell them about memory and aging that might alleviate their concerns?

Chapter Summary

8.1 The Information-Processing Approach

- The information-processing approach uses a computer analogy to illustrate how the mind processes information. The human "computer" takes in information through the sensory registers, which hold the information for a very brief period.
- If the person pays attention to the information that "hits" the sensory register, then it is further processed in short-term, or working, memory.
- Eventually, information may be stored in long-term memory, which seems to be unlimited in terms of size and permanency. In order for something to move into the long-term memory store, it must undergo a process of consolidation in which a memory trace of the event is created.
- Encoding and retrieval strategies influence memory performance. Types of retrieval include recognition, recall, and cued recall.
- Explicit memory is deliberate and effortful and changes over the life span, whereas implicit memory is automatic and relatively stable over the life span. Explicit and implicit memories are separate components of long-term memory and are localized in different parts of the brain.
- Stored memories are instrumental to success at problem solving, or using stored information to achieve a goal. Executive control processes select, organize, manipulate, and interpret what is going on in the context of problem solving.

8.2 The Infant

- Using imitation, habituation, and operant-conditioning techniques, researchers have gone from believing that infants have no memory beyond a few seconds to appreciating that even young 1-year-olds can recall experiences for weeks and even months under certain conditions.

- Infants clearly show recognition memory for familiar stimuli at birth and cued recall memory by about 2 months. More explicit memory, which requires actively retrieving an image of an object or event no longer present, appears to emerge toward the end of the first year. By age 2, it is even clearer that infants can recall events that happened long ago, for they, like adults, use language to represent and describe what happened.
- Simple problem solving improves throughout infancy, and infants realize that they can get adults to help them solve problems.

8.3 The Child

- Basic information-processing capacity increases as the brain matures and fundamental processes are automated to free working-memory space.
- Memory strategies such as rehearsal, organization, and elaboration improve. Metamemory improves and the general knowledge base grows. All these changes improve the processing of new information in areas of expertise.
- According to Robert Siegler, even young children use systematic rules to solve problems, but their problem-solving skills improve as they replace faulty rules with ones that incorporate all the relevant aspects of the problem. Multiple strategies are used at any age so that development proceeds through a natural selection process and resembles overlapping waves more than a set of stair-steps leading from one way of thinking to the next.
- Memory improves during childhood with increased efficiency of basic information-processing capacities, greater use of memory strategies, improvement in metamemory, and growth of general knowledge base.
- By age 3, children store routine daily events as scripts that they can draw on in similar situations. Our scripts influence what we remember about an event, which is also influenced by information related to but coming after the event.
- Much of what we remember is autobiographical. Even though infants and toddlers show evidence of memory, older children and adults often experience childhood amnesia, or lack of memory for events that happened during infancy and early childhood.

8.4 The Adolescent

- Adolescents master advanced learning strategies such as elaboration, note taking, and underlining, and they use their strategies more deliberately and selectively.
- Adolescents have larger knowledge bases, and their metamemory skills also improve and contribute to increased memory performance and problem-solving ability.

8.5 The Adult

- As adults gain expertise in a domain, they develop large and organized knowledge bases and highly effective, specialized, and automated ways of retrieving and using their knowledge.
- Many older adults perform less well than young adults on memory tasks that require speed, the learning of unfamiliar or meaningless material, the use of unexercised abilities, recall rather

than recognition memory, and explicit rather than implicit memory.

- Declines in basic processing capacity and difficulty using strategies, plus contextual factors such as cohort differences and the irrelevance of many laboratory tasks to everyday life, contribute to age differences in memory.
- On average, older adults also perform less well than younger adults on laboratory problem-solving tasks, but everyday problem-solving skills are likely to improve from early adulthood to middle adulthood and to be maintained in old age.

Checking Mastery Answers

For answers to Checking Mastery questions, visit
www.cengagebrain.com

Key Terms

memory **256**
information-processing
  approach **256**
sensory register **257**
short-term memory **257**
working memory **257**
long-term memory **257**
encoding **257**
consolidation **257**
storage **257**
retrieval **257**
recognition memory **258**
recall memory **258**
cued recall memory **258**
implicit memory **258**
explicit memory **258**
semantic memory **258**
episodic memory **258**
problem solving **259**
executive control processes **259**
deferred imitation **260**

perseveration errors **264**
rehearsal **264**
organization (as memory
  strategy) **264**
elaboration **264**
mediation deficiency **264**
production deficiency **264**
utilization deficiency **264**
metamemory **265**
metacognition **265**
knowledge base **266**
autobiographical memories **267**
childhood amnesia **267**
fuzzy-trace theory **268**
script **268**
general event representation **268**
eyewitness memory **269**
rule assessment approach **269**
overlapping waves theory **270**
mild cognitive impairment **276**
constraint-seeking questions **282**

Media Resources

Psychology CourseMate

Access an integrated eBook and chapter-specific learning tools including flashcards, quizzes, videos, and more. Go to **www.cengagebrain.com**

Improving Memory: Understanding Age-Related Memory Loss

A series of articles contributed by Harvard Medical School on the topics of Memory and Age-Related Memory Loss. Some articles delve into topics like forgetting, cognitive impairment, and improving everyday memory. To access, see "web links" in Psychology CourseMate at www.cengagebrain.com

Memory Improvement Techniques

This Mind Tools-sponsored site offers an extensive list of articles on methods of improving memory. It also contains links to several articles that explain how specific memory strategies work. To access, see "web links" in Psychology CourseMate at www.cengagebrain.com

Understanding the DATA: Exercises on the Web

www.cengagebrain.com

For additional insight on the data presented in this chapter, try out the exercises for these figures in Psychology CourseMate at

www.cengagebrain.com:

Figure 8.4 Effects of expertise on memory. Michelene Chi found that child chess experts outperformed adult chess novices on a test of recall for the location of chess pieces (although, in keeping with the usual developmental trend, these children could not recall strings of numbers as well as adults could).

Figure 8.8 Adolescents are better able than children to concentrate on learning-relevant material and to ignore irrelevant material.

Figure 8.10 Declines in memory skills in old age are not universal. In deaf culture and Chinese culture, elderly people are not stereotyped as forgetful or senile. Perhaps as a result, Chinese elders perform almost as well as young Chinese adults on memory tasks, whereas in the United States, elders, especially in the hearing population, perform poorly.

CengageNOW

www.cengagebrain.com

Go to www.cengagebrain.com to link to CengageNOW, your online study tool. First take the Pre-Test for this chapter to get your Personalized Study Plan, which will identify topics you need to review and direct you to online resources. Then take the Post-Test to determine what concepts you have mastered and what you still need work on.

Intelligence

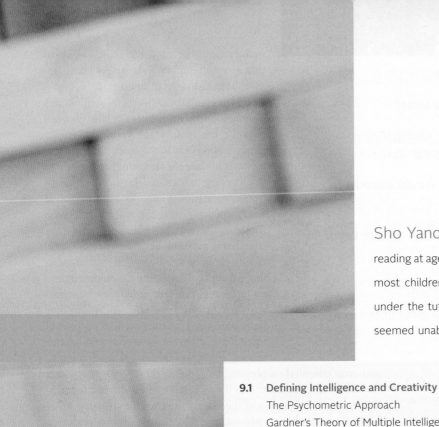
© Indeed/Photodisc/Getty Images

Sho Yano was born in Oregon, USA, and started writing at age 2, reading at age 3, and playing and composing music at age 4. By age 7, when most children are starting first grade, Sho was doing high school work under the tutelage of his mother because the gifted school he attended seemed unable to keep pace with his learning needs. He started college at age 9, and at age 12 he became the youngest person to enter the University of Chicago's joint MD/PhD program. He purportedly has an IQ of over 200 (*60 Minutes*, December 27, 2006).

At age 35, Michael lives in an institution for the mentally retarded. He has been labeled profoundly retarded and has an IQ score of 17, as nearly as it can be estimated. Michael responds to people with grins and is able to walk haltingly, but he cannot feed or dress himself and does not use language.

1. What are the most prominent views of intelligence?

2. How accurate and useful are the standard IQ tests?

3. What evidence supports the conclusion that intelligence is influenced by genetic factors? By environmental factors?

4. Are there any available infant measures that would allow us to predict later intelligence?

5. What is creativity, and how does it change across the life span? How does creativity relate to intelligence?

6. Why are there racial/ethnic differences in test scores?

7. What are the characteristics of individuals who fall at the extreme ends of the intelligence scale?

As these examples indicate, the range of human intellectual abilities is immense. So far, much of the material on cognitive development in this book has focused on what human minds have in common, not on how they differ. Piaget, after all, was interested in identifying universal stages of cognitive development. And the information-processing approach has been used

Some gifted children thrive as college students, such as Sho Yano, shown here, who entered college at age 9.

© Associated Press

mainly to understand the basic cognitive processes all people rely on to learn, remember, and solve problems.

This chapter continues the exploration of how the human mind normally changes over the life span. Here we introduce still another approach to the study of the mind: the psychometric, or testing, approach to intelligence, which led to the creation of intelligence tests. Many people find it hard to say anything nice about IQ tests. These measures have their limitations, and they have been misused. Yet they have also provided researchers with a good deal of information about intellectual development and about variations in intellectual performance. Further, since their inception they have been used for the practical purpose of identifying different levels of intelligence among school children, military recruits, and even potential employees.

This chapter examines how performance on intelligence tests typically changes and stays the same over the life span, what IQ tests reveal about a person, and why people's IQ scores differ. It also looks at both gifted and intellectually disabled individuals from a life-span perspective. We will also discuss creativity, a type of intellectual ability not measured by traditional intelligence tests. Before going further, take the quiz in Engagement Box 9.1 to see if you have any misconceptions about intelligence and intelligence tests; this chapter will clarify why the correct answers are correct.

9.1 Defining Intelligence and Creativity

Let's begin by trying to understand intelligence, as defined by some of the most prominent scholars in this field. As noted in Chapter 7, Piaget defined intelligence as thinking or behavior that is adaptive. Other experts have offered different definitions, many of them centering on the ability to think abstractly or to solve problems effectively (e.g., Sternberg, 2010a, 2010b). Early definitions of intelligence tended to reflect the assumption that intelligence reflects innate ability—that it is genetically determined and fixed at conception. But it has become clear that intelligence is not fixed, that it is changeable and subject to environmental influence (Nisbett, 2009). As a result, an individual's intelligence test scores sometimes vary considerably over a lifetime. Bear in mind that understanding of this complex human quality has changed since the first intelligence tests were created at the turn of the last century—and that there is still no single, universally accepted definition of intelligence. Linda Gottfredson and Donald Saklofske (2009) recently concluded that the field has shifted away from trying to answer the question of what intelligence is to discussing the research findings that have emerged from using intelligence tests, whatever it is these might be measuring.

Answer each question true or false:

__ 1. On the leading tests of intelligence, a score of 100 is average.

__ 2. Most scholars now conclude that there is no such thing as general intelligence; there are only separate mental abilities.

__ 3. Individuals who are intellectually gifted are typically gifted in all mental abilities.

__ 4. Intellectually gifted children do well in school but are more likely than most children to have social and emotional problems.

__ 5. IQ predicts both a person's occupational status and his success compared with others in the same occupation.

__ 6. On average, performance on IQ tests declines for people in their 70s and 80s.

__ 7. Qualities associated with wisdom are as common among young and middle-aged adults as among elderly adults.

__ 8. It has been established that children's IQs are far more influenced by their environments than by their genes.

__ 9. How well a child does on a test of creativity cannot be predicted well from her IQ score.

__ 10. Creative achievers (great musicians, mathematicians, writers, and so on) typically do all their great works before about age 40 or 45 and produce only lesser works from then on.

Answers: 1-T, 2-F, 3-F, 4-F, 5-T, 6-T, 7-T, 8-F, 9-T, 10-F

The Psychometric Approach

The research tradition that spawned the development of standardized tests of intelligence is the **psychometric approach**. According to psychometric theorists, intelligence is a trait or a set of traits that characterizes some people to a greater extent than others. The goals, then, are to identify these traits precisely and to measure them so that differences among individuals can be described. But from the start, experts could not agree on whether intelligence is one general cognitive ability or many specific abilities.

Early on, Charles Spearman (1927) proposed a two-factor theory of intelligence consisting of a general mental ability (called *g*) that contributes to performance on many different kinds of tasks. This *g* factor is what accounts for Spearman's observation that people were often consistent across a range of tasks. For example, general intelligence has been found to correlate with performance on exams in 25 different academic subjects (Deary et al., 2007). However, Spearman also noticed that a student who excelled at most tasks might score low on a particular measure (for example, memory for words). So he proposed a second aspect of intelligence: *s*, or special abilities, each of which is specific to a particular kind of task. Some research suggests that *g* may play a greater role in IQ test performance during childhood than adolescence (Kane & Brand, 2006). By adolescence, many effortful processes that underlie expression of *g* have become automated, freeing up cognitive resources to hone certain specific abilities.

Raymond Cattell and John Horn have greatly influenced current thinking concerning intelligence by distinguishing between two broad dimensions of intellect: fluid intelligence and crystallized intelligence (Cattell, 1963; Horn & Cattell, 1967; Horn & Noll, 1997). **Fluid intelligence** is the ability to use your mind actively to solve novel problems—for example, to solve verbal analogies, remember unrelated pairs of words, or recognize relationships among geometric figures (■**Figure 9.1**). The skills involved— reasoning, seeing relationships among stimuli, and drawing

inferences—are usually not taught and are believed to represent a person's "raw information processing power" (Gottfred & Saklofske, 2009). **Crystallized intelligence**, in contrast, is the use of knowledge acquired through schooling and other life experiences. Tests of general information (At what temperature does water boil?), word comprehension (What is the meaning of *duplicate*?), and

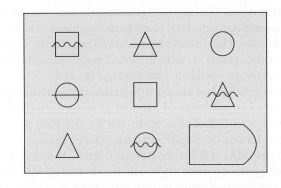

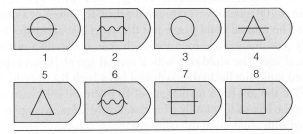

Answer: 7

■**FIGURE 9.1** An item assessing fluid intelligence (similar to those in a test called the Raven Progressive Matrices Test). Which of the numbered pieces completes the design?

numerical abilities (What is 23 × 3?) are all measures of crystallized intelligence. Thus, fluid intelligence involves using your mind in new and flexible ways, whereas crystallized intelligence involves using what you have already learned through experience.

Obviously, there is no single answer to the question *What is intelligence?* Nonetheless, some consensus has emerged from the vast amount of research conducted over the years on this construct. Intelligence is most often viewed as a hierarchy that includes (1) a general ability factor at the top that influences how well people do on a range of cognitive tasks; (2) a few broad dimensions of ability that are distinguishable in factor analyses (for example, fluid intelligence, crystallized intelligence, memory capacity, and processing speed); and (3) at the bottom, many specific abilities such as numerical reasoning, spatial discrimination, and word comprehension that also influence how well a person performs cognitive tasks that tap these specific abilities (Carroll, 1993; Horn & Noll, 1997).

One of the most significant contributions to the psychometric approach to intelligence occurred in 1904 when Alfred Binet and Theodore Simon were commissioned by the French government to devise a test that would identify "dull" children who might need special instruction. Binet and Simon devised a large battery of tasks measuring the skills believed to be necessary for classroom learning: attention, perception, memory, reasoning, verbal comprehension, and so on. Items that discriminated between normal children and those described by their teachers as slow were kept in the final test.

This forerunner of the modern IQ test was soon revised so that the items were age-graded. For example, a set of "6-year-old" items could be passed by most 6-year-olds but by few 5-year-olds; "12-year-old" items could be handled by most 12-year-olds but not by younger children. This approach permitted the testers to describe a child's **mental age**—the level of age-graded problems that the child is able to solve. Thus, a child who passes all items at the 5-year-old level but does poorly on more advanced items—regardless of the child's actual age—is said to have a mental age of 5.

Binet's test became known as the **Stanford-Binet Intelligence Scale** after Lewis Terman of Stanford University translated and published a revised version of the test for use with American children. Terman developed a procedure for comparing a child's mental age (MA) with his chronological age (CA) by calculating an **intelligence quotient (IQ)**, which consisted of MA divided by CA and then multiplied by 100 ($IQ = MA/CA \times 100$). An IQ score of 100 indicates average intelligence, regardless of a child's age: The normal child passes just the items that age-mates typically pass; mental age increases each year, but so does chronological age. The child of 8 with a mental age of 10 has experienced rapid intellectual growth and has a high IQ (specifically, 125); if she still has a mental age of 10 when she is 15 years old, then she has an IQ of only 67 and is clearly below average compared with children of the same age.

The Stanford-Binet, now in its fifth edition, is still in use (Roid, 2003). Its **test norms**—standards of normal performance expressed as average scores and the range of scores around the average—are based on the performance of a large, representative sample of people (2-year-olds through adults) from many socioeconomic and racial backgrounds. The concept of mental age is no longer used to calculate IQ; instead, individuals receive scores

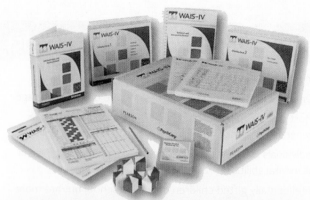

The Wechsler Adult Intelligence Scale (WAIS), revised in 2008, assesses cognitive ability in adults ages 16 through 90. A qualified administrator uses the colored blocks and other materials shown here to evaluate an individual's verbal comprehension, perceptual reasoning, working memory, and processing speed, all of which contribute to intelligence.

that reflect how well or how poorly they do compared with others of the same age. An IQ of 100 is still average, and the higher the IQ score an individual attains, the better the performance is in comparison with that of age-mates.

David Wechsler constructed a set of intelligence tests, collectively referred to as the **Wechsler Scales**, also in wide use. The Wechsler Preschool and Primary Scale of Intelligence (WPPSI) is for children between ages 3 and 8 (Wechsler, 2002). The Wechsler Intelligence Scale for Children (WISC-IV) is appropriate for schoolchildren ages 6 to 16 (Wechsler, 2003), and the Wechsler Adult Intelligence Scale (WAIS-IV) is used with adults (Wechsler, 2008). The Wechsler tests yield a verbal IQ score based on items measuring vocabulary, general knowledge, arithmetic reasoning, and the like and a performance IQ based on such nonverbal skills as the ability to assemble puzzles, solve mazes, reproduce geometric designs with colored blocks, and rearrange pictures to tell a meaningful story. As with the Stanford-Binet, a score of 100 is defined as average performance for the person's age. A person's full-scale IQ is a combination of the verbal and performance scores.

Scores on both the Stanford-Binet and Wechsler Scales form a **normal distribution**, or a symmetrical, bell-shaped spread around the average score of 100 (■ **Figure 9.2**). Scores around the average are common; very high and very low scores are rare. About two-thirds of people taking one of these IQ tests have scores between 85 and 115, which corresponds to the spread or range of scores within one **standard deviation** above and below the average score. Fewer than 3% have scores of 130 or above, a score often used as one criterion of giftedness. Similarly, fewer than 3% have IQs below 70, a cutoff commonly used to define intellectual disability.

In the end, the intelligence tests guided by psychometric theories have emphasized general intellectual ability by summarizing performance in a single IQ score, and they have assessed only some of the specialized abilities humans possess. Critics believe traditional psychometric tests have not fully described what it means to be an intelligent person, and some have offered

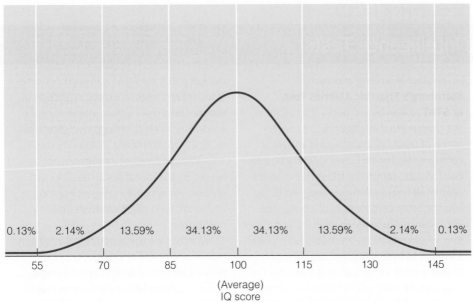

■ **FIGURE 9.2** A normal distribution curve showing traditional intelligence testing scores in the classic bell shape around the average score of 100.

moods; demonstrated by salespeople and psychologists.

7. *Intrapersonal intelligence*. Understanding of one's own feelings and inner life.
8. *Naturalist intelligence*. Expertise in the natural world of plants and animals.

Traditional IQ tests emphasize linguistic and logical–mathematical intelligence, and to some extent they test spatial intelligence, perhaps because those are the forms of intelligence Western societies value most highly and work the hardest to nurture in school. But IQ tests can be faulted for ignoring most of the other forms of intelligence. Although Gardner does not claim that his is the definitive list of intelligences, he presents evidence suggesting that each of these eight abilities is distinct. For example, it is clear that a person can be exceptional in one ability but poor in others—witness **savant syndrome**, the phenomenon in which extraordinary talent in a particular area is displayed by a person otherwise mentally retarded (Treffert, 2000). Leslie Lemke, one such individual, is affected by cerebral palsy, blindness, and intellectual disability, and could not talk until he was an adult (Treffert, 2000). Yet he can hear a musical piece once and play it flawlessly on the piano or imitate songs in perfect German or Italian even though his own speech is still primitive. He apparently has a high level of musical intelligence. Other savants, despite IQs below 70, can draw well enough to gain admittance to art school or can calculate on the spot what day of the week it was January 16, 1909 (Hermelin & Rutter, 2001). Some scholars think that the skills shown by savants are so specific and depend so much on memory that they do not qualify as separate "intelligences" (Nettelbeck & Young, 1996). However, Gardner insists that savant syndrome simply cannot be explained by theories that emphasize a general intelligence factor, *g*.

Gardner also marshals evidence to show that each intelligence has its own distinctive developmental course. Many great musical composers and athletes, for example, revealed their genius in childhood, whereas exceptional logical–mathematical intelligence typically shows up later, after the individual has gained the capacity for abstract thought and has mastered an area of science. Finally, Gardner links his distinct intelligences to distinct structures in the brain, arguing that the eight intelligences are neurologically distinct.

alternative ways of thinking about intelligence that represent challenges to the traditional view. Reading about these approaches in the following sections will help you capture the nature of intelligence and appreciate the limitations of the tests used to measure it. In addition, Exploration Box 9.1 examines two modern alternatives to assessment of intelligence.

Gardner's Theory of Multiple Intelligences

Howard Gardner (1993, 1999/2000; Chen & Gardner, 1997) rejects the idea that a single IQ score is a meaningful measure of human intelligence. He argues that there are many intelligences, most of which have been ignored by the developers of standardized intelligence tests. Instead of asking, "How smart are you?" researchers should be asking, "How are you smart?" and identifying people's strengths and weaknesses across the full range of human mental faculties (Chen & Gardner, 1997). Gardner (1993, 2000) argues that there are at least eight distinct intellectual abilities:

1. *Linguistic intelligence*. Language skills, such as those seen in the poet's facility with words.
2. *Logical–mathematical intelligence*. The abstract thinking and problem solving shown by mathematicians and computer scientists and emphasized by Piaget.
3. *Musical intelligence*. Based on an acute sensitivity to sound patterns.
4. *Spatial intelligence*. Most obvious in great artists who can perceive things accurately and transform what they see.
5. *Bodily-kinesthetic intelligence*. The skillful use of the body to create crafts, perform, or fix things; shown, for example, by dancers, athletes, and surgeons.
6. *Interpersonal intelligence*. Social intelligence, social skill, exceptional sensitivity to other people's motivations and

Sternberg's Triarchic Theory

Agreeing with Gardner that traditional IQ tests do not capture all that it means to be an intelligent person, Robert Sternberg (1985, 1988, 2003, 2009) has proposed a **triarchic theory of intelligence**

Alternatives to Traditional Intelligence Tests

Although the Stanford-Binet Intelligence Scale and the Wechsler Scales continue to dominate the assessment field, concerns about what these scales truly measure has led to the creation of several alternatives. Alan Kaufman and Nadeen Kaufman, for example, designed the Kaufman Assessment Battery for Children (K-ABC-II; Kaufman & Kaufman, 2003). This test, based on information-processing theory, focuses on *how* children solve problems rather than on *what* problems they solve (Kaufman, 2001; Sparrow & Davis, 2000). The K-ABC-II, which is appropriate for children ages 3–18, has two subscales. One measures a child's ability to process information sequentially; the other measures the ability to integrate several pieces of information. The test also has a separate section of questions to assess children's achievement or acquired knowledge.

Another promising approach is **Sternberg's Triarchic Abilities Test, or STAT**, driven by his theory (discussed in the chapter) that intelligence is a convergence of practical, creative, and analytical components. The test uses a variety of question formats, combining those found on traditional IQ tests with those designed to tap into the other components of intelligence. For instance, students write an essay on how they would reform their school system, offer solutions to everyday dilemmas such as how to plan a route around an obstacle, infer the meanings of "fake words" from the sentence context, and figure out analogies based on counterfactual information. Some studies suggest that the STAT is a valid measure of the three components of intelligence that it is intended to assess (see, for example, Sternberg et al., 2001). In addition, there is

evidence that the STAT can augment other standardized tests to extend prediction of school performance from elementary and secondary levels to college level (Stemler et al., 2006; Sternberg, 2009). By tapping into different types of intelligence not assessed by traditional tests, the STAT can uncover exceptional intelligence among individuals who might otherwise be overlooked.

Whether we use a traditional intelligence test or one of the alternatives, trying to boil down a person's intelligence to a single score is a formidable task. Human mental functioning is truly complex. Intelligence tests can provide us with only a snapshot in time—an estimate that is not always a good indicator of the person's underlying intellectual competence.

that emphasizes three components that jointly contribute to intelligent behavior: practical or contextual, creative or experiential, and analytic components (■ **Figure 9.3**).

First, according to the **practical component**, what is defined as intelligent behavior varies from one sociocultural context to another. What might be intelligent in one context may be quite illogical in another. People who are high in this practical component of intelligence can adapt to the environment that they find themselves in, and they can shape the environment to optimize their strengths and minimize their weaknesses. These people have "street smarts," or common sense.

Just as intelligent behavior varies from one context to another, it also changes over time. Numerical abilities may not play as important a role in intelligent behavior now that calculators and computers are widely used, for example, whereas analytical skills may be more important than ever in a complex, urban world. And certainly the infant learning how to master new toys shows a different kind of intelligence than the adult mastering a college curriculum. Thus, the definition of the intelligent infant must differ from the definition of the intelligent adult.

The practical component of Sternberg's triarchic theory, then, defines intelligent behavior differently depending on the sociocultural context in which it is displayed. Intelligent people adapt to the environment they are in (for example, a job setting), shape that environment to make it suit them better, or find a better environment. They can walk into a new situation, quickly evaluate it, and adapt their behavior to be successful in this new context. Although recognized by many people as an important

form of intelligence, this real-world adaptability is not assessed by traditional intelligence tests.

According to the **creative component** of the triarchic theory, what is intelligent when a person first encounters a new task is not the same as what is intelligent after extensive experience with that task. The first kind of intelligence, *response to novelty*, requires active and conscious information processing. Sternberg believes that relatively novel tasks provide the best measures of intelligence because they tap the individual's ability to come up with creative ideas or fresh insights.

In daily life, however, people also perform more or less intelligently on familiar and repetitive tasks (driving a car, for example). This second kind of intelligence reflects **automatization**, or an increased efficiency of information processing with practice. It is intelligent to develop little "programs in the mind" for performing common, everyday activities efficiently and unthinkingly. Thus, according to Sternberg, it is crucial to know how familiar a task is to a person before assessing that person's behavior. For example, giving people of two different cultural groups an intelligence test whose items are familiar to one group and novel to the other introduces **culture bias** into the testing process, making it difficult to obtain a fair assessment of the groups' relative abilities.

The third aspect of the triarchic theory, the **analytic component**, focuses on information-processing skills that are assessed by traditional intelligence tests. These include thinking critically and analytically. Specifically, people who are high on this component can plan what to do, monitor progress, filter out irrelevant information and focus on the relevant, compare new information to existing knowledge, and evaluate outcomes.

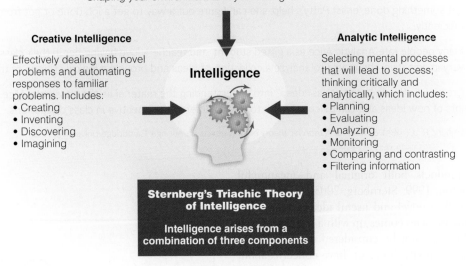

Practical Intelligence

Practical intelligence, or "street smarts," means successfully solving problems that arise in your everyday life. This includes:
- Adapting to the environment you are in
- Selecting environments in which you can succeed
- Shaping your environment to fit your strengths

Creative Intelligence

Effectively dealing with novel problems and automating responses to familiar problems. Includes:
- Creating
- Inventing
- Discovering
- Imagining

Intelligence

Analytic Intelligence

Selecting mental processes that will lead to success; thinking critically and analytically, which includes:
- Planning
- Evaluating
- Analyzing
- Monitoring
- Comparing and contrasting
- Filtering information

Sternberg's Triachic Theory of Intelligence

Intelligence arises from a combination of three components

■ **FIGURE 9.3** Sternberg's triarchic theory of intelligence includes three components: analytic, practical, and creative intelligences.

As an information-processing theorist, Sternberg believes that the theories of intelligence underlying the development of traditional IQ tests ignore *how* people produce intelligent answers. He argues that a full picture of intelligence includes not only the number of answers people get right but also the processes they use to arrive at their answers and the efficiency with which they use those processes. So, to fully assess how intelligent people are, researchers must consider the practical *context* in which they perform (their age, culture, and historical period), their ability to respond

creatively to new tasks, and their *analytic* strategies. Individuals who are intelligent, according to this triarchic model, are able to carry out logical thought processes efficiently and effectively to solve both novel and familiar problems and to adapt to their environment. Before moving on, review Sternberg's three components of intelligence with the examples provided in ● **Table 9.1.**

Sternberg (1999b; 2003) expanded his triarchic theory of intelligence to include what he calls the theory of **successful intelligence.** According to this view, people are intelligent "to the extent that they have the abilities needed to succeed in life, according to their own definition of success within their sociocultural context" (2003, p. xvi). These individuals are strong in all three areas—practical, creative, and analytic. Thus, intelligence is not just the ability to do well in school, something measured by traditional intelligence tests, but also the ability to do well in life (Sternberg, 2004). Smart people find ways to optimize their strengths and minimize their weaknesses so that they can succeed. They select environments (including occupations) that suit their profile of abilities, or, to the extent possible, they modify their abilities or environments. Unfortunately, today's widely used tests of intelligence do not reflect this multifaceted view of intelligence; they instead focus on analytic intelligence.

© AP Photo/Michelle McLoughlin

What has Robert Sternberg contributed to our understanding of intelligence?

Creativity

According to Sternberg, creativity is one of the three main components of intelligence. Most scholars define **creativity** as the ability to produce novel responses appropriate in context and

STERNBERG'S TRIARCHIC THEORY OF INTELLIGENCE: EXAMPLES OF THREE HYPOTHETICAL STUDENTS, EACH EXCELLING AT ONE OF THE THREE COMPONENTS

Component	Description of Hypothetical Student
Practical	Practical Patty is not terribly creative, nor does she get the best grades in the classroom. However, if you want to get something done, enlist Patty's help; she can figure out a way to get a job done or get from point A to point B efficiently.
Analytic	Many people rate Analytic Alice as a gifted student, and teachers love having her in their classrooms. Although not very imaginative, she is able to analyze a collection of ideas and provide a logical critique of them.
Creative	Creative Cathy does not get as "deep" into understanding the material as her classmate Alice. But she generates lots of new ideas and can be counted on to offer a different perspective in class discussions.

SOURCE: Adapted from Sternberg, R. J. (1985). *Beyond IQ: A triarchic theory of intelligence.* Cambridge: Cambridge University Press.

valued by others—products both original and meaningful (Simon, 2001; Simonton, 1999; Sternberg, 2003). Thus, someone who comes up with a novel and useful idea is considered creative, whereas someone who comes up with a novel idea that has no apparent value may not be considered creative. Some researchers who study creativity, however, have concerns about defining as creative only those ideas that are deemed useful (see Smith, 2005). After all, who decides what is useful, and who is to say whether something will be valued by someone at some time? Consequently, some researchers examine all novel outputs and not just those that are deemed useful or valuable. Before reading further, you may want to test your creativity with the problems in ■ Figure 9.4.

An early study of creativity found that highly creative students were not necessarily the ones who earned high grades in the classroom (Wallach & Kogan, 1965). It turns out that IQ scores and creativity scores do not correlate very well because they measure two different types of thinking. IQ tests measure **convergent thinking**, which involves "converging" on the best answer to a problem. In contrast, creativity involves **divergent thinking**, or coming up with a variety of ideas or solutions to a problem when there is no single correct answer. Responses on divergent thinking tasks can be analyzed along three dimensions: the originality or uniqueness of the generated ideas, the flexibility of or number of different categories expressed by the ideas, and the fluency of the ideas (Runco, 2007). This last one—ideational fluency, or the sheer number of different (including novel) ideas that a person can generate—is most often used to assess creativity because it is easy to score. Quick—list all the uses you can think of for a pencil. An uncreative person might say you could write letters, notes, postcards, and so forth; by contrast, one creative person envisioned a pencil as "a backscratcher, a potting stake, kindling for a fire, a rolling pin for baking, a toy for a woodpecker, or a small boat for a cricket" (Richards, 1996, p. 73).

This use of divergent thinking tasks to assess creativity reflects a psychometric, or testing, approach. That is, it assumes that creativity is a trait that is held to a greater or lesser degree by individuals and can be measured. While the psychometric approach can be useful, it may not consider the complexity or multitude of fac-

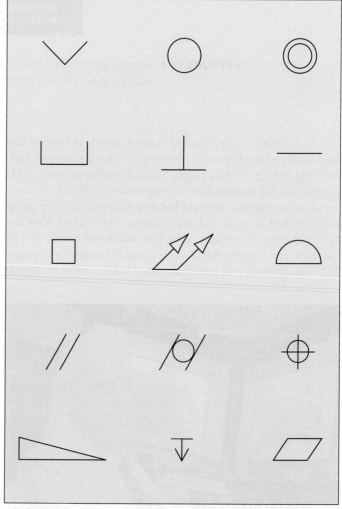

■**FIGURE 9.4** Are you creative? Make something out of each shape here. SOURCE: From www.zenstorming.com/mindopeningexercise.pdf. Reprinted by permission of Michael Plishka.

tors that constitute creativity. This is where Sternberg's *confluence approach* is valuable (Sternberg, 2006). Confluence is the convergence or coming together of several factors to form a new product. Sternberg argues that creativity is a confluence of many factors, each added in appropriate concentrations at the proper time. Thus, we might think of creativity as analogous to making a good soufflé: It requires certain ingredients in specific amounts combined in a particular order, baked at the proper temperature for the right amount of time. All these things must come together or your soufflé will be a flop. And so it is with creativity.

The "ingredients" for creativity include the intellectual skills that make up intelligence, knowledge of the field in which the creativity might emerge, a mind that is open to new ways of thinking, personality characteristics that include calculated risk taking and willingness to pursue and overcome obstacles, motivation, and an environment that is supportive of creative ideas (Sternberg, 2006). Then all these components must converge. As Sternberg (2009) puts it, this involves "more than a simple sum of a person's level on each component" (p. 107). For example, some components might need to be present in certain amounts, as would be the case with knowledge of a field: it is unlikely that anyone without knowledge in a field will come up with a creative idea in this unknown field. Sometimes, though, having more of one component might compensate for having less of another component. Sternberg (2009) gives the example of someone who is highly motivated to generate new ideas despite being in an environment that does not reward this kind of thinking; this person's high motivation may compensate for the lack of support from the environment.

A minimum of intelligence is probably required for creativity (Runco, 2007; Simonton, 1999). Highly creative people rarely have below-average IQs. However, among people who have average or above-average IQs, an individual's IQ score is essentially unrelated to her level of creativity. Finally, we might have someone who has the intelligence and the knowledge of a field to suggest that she could generate some great new ideas, but if this person has a personality that is not open to new experiences and seeks to minimize risk taking, then this person is unlikely to demonstrate high levels of creativity (Lynn, 2008a).

As you can see, although the two constructs are related, intelligence, with its focus on convergent thinking, and creativity, with its focus on divergent thinking, are distinct. In subsequent sections, as we discuss the intellectual profiles of children, adolescents, and adults, we will also consider the development of their creative selves. Note, however, that the infant is not included in our discussion of creativity because, to date, researchers have not developed a method for uncovering signs of creativity at this young age.

Checking Mastery

1. What is the difference between fluid and crystallized intelligence?

2. What is the main point of Gardner's theory of intelligence?

3. What three factors contribute to intelligence according to Sternberg?

Making Connections

1. Imagine that you are chosen to head a presidential commission on intelligence testing whose task it is to devise an IQ test for use in the schools that is better than any that currently exists. Sketch out the features of your model IQ test. What would be included and excluded from your definition of intelligence? How would you measure intelligence? In what ways would your test improve upon the tests that are currently used?

2. Traditional IQ tests assess convergent thinking. Should they also assess divergent thinking? Why or why not?

9.2 The Infant

As you saw in Chapters 7 and 8, the mind develops rapidly in infancy. But how can an infant's intellectual growth be measured? Is it possible to identify infants who are more or less intelligent than their age-mates? And how well does high (or low) intelligence in infancy predict high (or low) intelligence in childhood and adulthood?

Developmental Quotients

None of the standard intelligence tests can be used with children much younger than 3, because the test items require verbal skills and attention spans that infants and toddlers do not have. Some developmentalists have tried to measure infant intelligence by assessing the rate at which infants achieve important developmental milestones. Perhaps the best known and most widely used infant test is the **Bayley Scales of Infant Development** (Bayley, 1993). This test, designed for infants and toddlers ages 1 month to 42 months, has three parts:

- The *motor scale*, which measures the infant's ability to do such things as grasp a cube and throw a ball

The Bayley Scales of Infant Development are used to assess infants and toddlers. How would you evaluate the usefulness of the Bayley?

- The *mental scale*, which includes adaptive behaviors such as reaching for a desirable object, searching for a hidden toy, and following directions
- The *behavior rating scale*, a rating of the child's behavior on dimensions such as goal-directedness, emotional regulation, and social responsivity

On the basis of the first two scores, the infant is given a **developmental quotient (DQ)** rather than an IQ. The DQ summarizes how well or how poorly the infant performs in comparison with a large norm group of infants and toddlers the same age.

Infant Intelligence and Later Intelligence

As they age, infants progress through many developmental milestones of the kind assessed by the Bayley scales, so such scales are useful in charting infants' developmental progress. They are also useful in diagnosing neurological problems and mental retardation—even when these conditions are mild and difficult to detect through standard pediatric or neurological examinations (Escalona, 1968; Honzik, 1983). But developmentalists have also been interested in the larger issue of continuity versus discontinuity in intellectual development: Is it possible to predict which infants are likely to be gifted, average, or intellectually disabled during the school years?

Not from their DQ Scores. Correlations between infant DQ and child IQ are low, sometimes close to zero. The infant who does well on the Bayley scales or other infant tests may or may not obtain a high IQ score later in life (Honzik, 1983; Rose et al., 1989). True, the infant who scores low on an infant test often turns out to be intellectually disabled, but otherwise there seems to be a good deal of discontinuity between early and later scores—at least until a child is 4 or older.

What might explain the poor connection between scores on infant development scales and children's later IQs? Perhaps the main reason is that infant tests and IQ tests tap qualitatively different kinds of abilities (Columbo, 1993). Piaget would undoubtedly approve of this argument. Infant scales focus heavily on the sensory and motor skills that Piaget believed are so important in infancy; IQ tests such as the Stanford-Binet and WISC-IV emphasize more abstract abilities, such as verbal reasoning, concept formation, and problem solving.

Robert McCall (1981, 1983) offers a second explanation, arguing that the growth of intelligence during infancy is highly influenced by powerful and universal maturational processes. Maturational forces (such as the unfolding of the genetic blueprint for intelligence) pull infants back on course if environmental influences (such as growing up in an impoverished home and neighborhood) cause them to stray. For this reason, higher or lower infant test scores are likely to be nothing more than temporary deviations from a universal developmental path. As the child nears age 2, McCall argues, maturational forces become less strong, so individual differences become larger and more stable over time. Consistent differences related to both individual genetic makeup and environment begin to emerge.

Should researchers give up on trying to predict later IQ on the basis of development in infancy? Perhaps not yet. The information-processing approach has given new life to the idea that there is continuity in intelligence from infancy to childhood. Several researchers have found that certain measures of infant attention predict later IQ better than infant intelligence tests do. For example, speed of habituation (how fast the infant loses interest in a repeatedly presented stimulus) and preference for novelty (the degree to which an infant prefers a novel stimulus to a familiar one), assessed in the first year of life, have an average correlation of about 0.45 with IQ in childhood, particularly with verbal IQ and memory skills (McCall & Carriger, 1993; Rose & Feldman, 1997; Rose, Feldman, & Jankowski, 2003). Thus, the infant who quickly becomes bored and likes novelty over familiarity is likely to be brighter in childhood than the infant who is slow to habituate and does not like novelty. In addition, fast reaction time in infancy (time taken to look in the direction of a visual stimulus as soon as it appears) predicts later IQ about as well as speed of habituation and novelty preferences scores (Dougherty & Haith, 1997).

From this, we can characterize the "smart" infant as the speedy information processor—the infant who quickly becomes bored by the same old thing, seeks novel experiences, and soaks up information rapidly. There seems to be some continuity between infant intelligence and childhood intelligence after all. Such Bayley scale accomplishments as throwing a ball are unlikely to carry over into vocabulary-learning or problem-solving skills in childhood. However, the extent to which the young infant processes information quickly can predict the extent to which he will learn quickly and solve problems efficiently later in childhood.

Checking Mastery

1. What does a developmental quotient (DQ) assess?
2. What characteristics or behaviors of infants are associated with later intelligence?

Making Connections

1. Are there specific activities that parents should be doing with their infants to ensure that they develop to their intellectual potential? What might some of these activities be?

9.3 The Child

Over the childhood years, children generally become able to answer more questions, and more difficult questions, on IQ tests. That is, their mental ages increase. But what happens to the IQ scores of individual children, which reflect how they compare with peers?

How Stable Are IQ Scores during Childhood?

It was once assumed that a person's IQ reflected her genetically determined intellectual capacity and therefore would remain stable over time. In other words, a child with an IQ of 120 at age 5 was expected to obtain a similar IQ at age 10, 15, or 20. Is this idea supported by research? As you have seen, infant DQs do not predict later IQs well. However, starting around age 4 there is a fairly strong relationship between early and later IQ, and the relationship grows even stronger by middle childhood. ● Table 9.2 summarizes the results of a longitudinal study of 220 children ages 4 to 12 (Weinert & Hany, 2003; Weinert & Schneider, 1999). The shorter the interval between two testings, the higher the correlation between children's IQ scores on the two occasions. Even when several years have passed, however, IQ seems to be a stable attribute: the scores that children obtain at age 7 are clearly related to those they obtain 5 years later, at age 12.

These correlations do not reveal everything, however. They are based on a large group of children, and they do not necessarily mean that the IQs of individual children will remain stable over the years. As it turns out, many children show sizable ups and downs in their IQ scores over the course of childhood. Patterns of change differ considerably from child to child, as though each were on a private developmental trajectory (Gottfried et al., 1994). One team of researchers looked at the IQ scores of 140 children who had taken intelligence tests at regular intervals from age 2 to age 17 (McCall, Applebaum, & Hogarty, 1973). The average difference between a child's highest and lowest scores was a whopping 28.5 points. About one-third showed changes of more than 30 points, and one child changed by 74 IQ points.

How do researchers reconcile the conclusion that IQ is relatively stable with this clear evidence of instability? They can still conclude that, within a group, children's standings (high or low) in comparison with peers stay stable from one point to another during the childhood years (Sternberg, Grigorenko, & Bundy, 2001). But many individual children experience drops or gains in IQ scores over the years. Remember, however, that this relates to performance on IQ tests rather than underlying intellectual competence. IQ scores are influenced not only by people's intelligence but also by their motivation, testing procedures and conditions, and many other factors that we will discuss in this chapter. As a result, IQ may be more changeable over the years than intellectual ability.

Causes of Gain and Loss

Some wandering of IQ scores upward or downward over time is just random fluctuation—a good day at one testing, a bad day at the next. Yet there are patterns. Children whose scores fluctuate the most tend to live in unstable home environments; their life experiences fluctuate between periods of happiness and turmoil.

In addition, some children gain IQ points over childhood and others lose them. Who are the gainers, and who are the losers? Gainers seem to have parents who foster achievement and who are neither too strict nor too lax in child rearing (McCall et al., 1973). Noticeable drops in IQ with age often occur among children who live in poverty. Otto Klineberg (1963) proposed a **cumulative-deficit hypothesis** to explain this: impoverished environments inhibit intellectual growth, and these negative effects accumulate over time. There is some support for the cumulative-deficit hypothesis, especially when a child's parents are not only poor but also low in intellectual functioning themselves (Jensen, 1977; Ramey & Ramey, 1992). Exploration Box 9.2 examines research on the effectiveness of various early intervention programs designed to raise the IQ scores and academic success of children living in poverty.

The Emergence of Creativity

We often hear young children's play activities and artwork described as "creative." When does creativity emerge, and what is the child who scores high on tests of creativity like? To answer the first question, researchers have measured divergent thinking at different ages throughout childhood. Early on, it became apparent that preschool-aged children display fairly high levels of divergent thought—generating many original ideas. But creative output begins to decline somewhat as children enter kindergarten and first grade, and drops even further by fourth grade (see Gardner, 1982; Torrance, 1988). Following this fourth-grade slump, as it is called among creativity researchers, levels of divergent thinking rise again after the age of 12 (Runco, 2007; Smith & Carlsson, 1990).

More recent research suggests that the peaks and valleys of creative thought during childhood are not as large as originally reported, although there is some drop-off during elementary school (Claxton, Pannells, & Rhoads, 2005). This may reflect the demands of school and peers to conform to the group rather than to be a "free spirit" (Gardner, 1982).

To address the second question, what the creative child is like, one group of researchers compared children who had high creativ-

---

● **TABLE 9.2 CORRELATIONS OF IQS MEASURED AT VARIOUS AGES**

Age of Child at Initial IQ Test	Correlation of IQ Scores When Retested at Age 9	Correlation of IQ Scores When Retested at Age 12
4	0.46	0.42
5	0.47	0.49
7	0.81	0.69
9	—	0.80

SOURCE: From Weinert, F. E. & Haney, E. A., The stability of individual differences in intellectual development: Empirical evidence, theoretical problems, and new research questions, in Sternberg R. J., Lautrey J., & Lubart T. I. (eds.), Models of intelligence: International perspectives. Copyright © 2003 by the American Psychological Association. Reprinted with permission.

Early Intervention

During the 1960s, several programs were launched to enrich the early learning experiences of disadvantaged preschoolers. Project Head Start is perhaps the best known of these interventions. The idea was to provide a variety of social and intellectual experiences that might better prepare these children for school. High-quality Head Start programs provide the nutrition, health care, parent training, and intellectual stimulation that can get disadvantaged children off to a good start. At first, Head Start and similar programs seemed to be a smashing success; children in the programs were posting average gains of about 10 points on IQ tests. But then discouragement set in: By the time children reached the middle years of grade school, their IQs were no higher than those of control-group children (Gray, Ramsey, & Klaus, 1982). Such findings led Arthur Jensen (1969) to conclude that "compensatory education has been tried and it apparently has failed" (p. 2).

But that was not the end of the story. Children in some of these programs have been followed into their teens, 20s, and beyond. It turns out that Project Head Start and other early intervention programs do in fact offer some long-term benefits (e.g., Ludwig & Phillips, 2008). This is what we have learned:

- Children who participate in early intervention programs show immediate gains on IQ and school achievement tests, whereas nonparticipants do not. Although these gains rarely last more than 3 or 4 years after the program has ended, effects on measures other than IQ are more encouraging. In one first-grade classroom-based intervention program, students attained higher scores on standardized achievement tests when they reached 12th grade (Bradshaw et al., 2009).

High-quality Head Start programs provide the nutrition, health care, parent training, and intellectual stimulation that can get disadvantaged children off to a good start.

ity scores but normal-range IQ scores with children who scored high in IQ but not in creativity (Getzels & Jackson, 1962). Personality measures suggested that the creative children showed more freedom, originality, humor, aggression, and playfulness than the high-IQ children. Perhaps as a result, the high-IQ children were more success oriented and received more approval from teachers. The unconventional responses of highly creative children are not always appreciated in the conventional classroom (Runco, 2007). Compared with their less creative peers, creative children also engage in more fantasy or pretend play, often inventing new uses for familiar objects and new roles for themselves (Kogan, 1983). They have active imaginations, and their parents are often tolerant of their sometimes unconventional ideas (Runco, 2007). Finally, creative children are more likely to be open to new experiences and ideas, as are their parents (Simonton, 1999).

As you will see later in this chapter, average IQ scores differ across racial and socioeconomic groups, but scores on creativity tests usually do not, nor do self-perceptions of one's creativity (Kaufman, 2006; Kogan, 1983). Moreover, genetic influences (a source of individual differences in IQ) have little to do with performance on tests of creativity; twins are similar in the degree of creativity they display, but identical twins are typically no more similar than fraternal twins (Plomin, 1990; Reznikoff et al., 1973). This suggests that certain qualities of the home environment tend to make brothers and sisters alike in their degree of creativity. What qualities? Although there is little research to go on, parents of creative children and adolescents tend to value nonconformity and independence, accept their children as they are, encourage their curiosity and playfulness, and grant them a good deal of freedom to explore new

- Compensatory education improves both children's and mothers' attitudes about achievement. When asked to describe something that has made them feel proud of themselves, program participants are more likely than nonparticipants to mention scholastic achievements or (in the case of 15- to 18-year-olds) job-related successes. Mothers of program participants tend to be more satisfied with their children's school performance and to hold higher occupational aspirations for their children.

- Program participants are more likely than nonparticipants to complete high school and to attend some college (Garces, Thomas, & Currie, 2002; Schweinhart et al., 2005). They are less likely to be assigned to special education classes, to be retained in a grade, or to drop out of high school (Bradshaw et al., 2009).

- There is even some evidence that teenagers who have participated in early compensatory education are less likely to experience such negative life events as teen pregnancy and delinquency than nonparticipants. By age 40, they are less likely to have had multiple arrests (Schweinhart et al., 2005).

In sum, longitudinal evaluations suggest that compensatory education does work. Programs seem most effective if they start early, last long, and involve several components. For example, Craig Ramey and his colleagues (Campbell et al., 2001; Campbell & Ramey, 1995; Campbell, Shirley, & Caygill, 2002) have reported outstanding success with the Abecedarian Project, an early intervention for extremely disadvantaged, primarily African American children that involved an intellectually stimulating day care program, home visits and efforts to involve parents in their children's development, and medical and nutritional care from early infancy to kindergarten entry. Program participants outperformed nonparticipants throughout childhood and into adolescence. By age 15, the impressive IQ advantage they had shown as young children had narrowed to less than 5 points, but they continued to perform better on math and reading achievement tests, were less likely to have been held back a grade, and were less in need of special education services. Some children in the study were randomly assigned to a group whose intervention did not begin until school age, when a teacher worked with their regular teachers and their parents over a 3-year period. These

children did not show as many gains as those who received the preschool intervention, suggesting that it is best to intervene early in children's lives (Campbell & Ramey, 1995). An early start is the premise behind the Born to Learn curriculum, which starts during the first year of life and shows benefits by age 3 (Drotar et al., 2008).

The success of early compensatory education for at-risk preschoolers has led some experts in the field to call for mandatory preschool education for all children (Barnett et al., 2007). Although many young children do attend some sort of program prior to entering kindergarten, the programs are quite varied in their quality and focus. A universal preschool system would aim to reduce these inequalities. Not all experts, though, agree that universal preschool should be the goal (Stipek & Hakuta, 2007). Instead, they believe that improving the existing preschool programs that target at-risk children, such as Head Start, Abecedarian Project, and Born to Learn, will help ensure that "no child starts from behind," struggling to catch up to peers on cognitive and social skills that they did not have the opportunity to develop at home (Stipek & Kahuta, 2007, p. 129).

possibilities on their own (Harrington, Block, & Block, 1987; Runco, 1992). In some cases, the parent–child relationship is even distant; a surprising number of eminent creators seem to have experienced rather lonely, insecure, and unhappy childhoods (Ochse, 1990; Simonton, 1999). Out of their adversity may have come an active imagination and a strong desire to develop their talents. Indeed, several early studies suggested that childhood adversity was a common theme among highly creative individuals—that adversity was the driving force behind their creativity (see, for example, Goertzel & Goertzel, 1962).

Although this may be true for some creative individuals, it is certainly not true for all of them. Overall, then, creative abilities are influenced by factors distinct from those that influence the cognitive abilities measured on IQ tests.

Checking Mastery

1. Once children reach elementary school, how stable are their IQ scores as a group?

2. What is one reason for an individual's IQ score to increase and what is one reason for an individual's IQ score to decrease during childhood?

Making Connections

1. Would you want to know your IQ or your child's IQ? How might this knowledge affect you? Would you think or act any differently if you learned that you (or your child) had an IQ of 105 versus an IQ of 135? You might also consider whether teachers should

know their students' IQ scores. What are some potential pros and cons of teachers having access to this information?

2. Would you rather have a child who has average intelligence but is highly creative or one who has high intelligence but average creativity? What are the pros and cons of each?

9.4 The Adolescent

Intellectual growth is rapid during infancy and childhood. What happens during adolescence, and how well does IQ predict school performance?

Continuity between Childhood and Adulthood

Intellectual growth continues its rapid pace in early adolescence, then slows and levels off in later adolescence (Thorndike, 1997). As noted in Chapter 5, a spurt in brain development occurs around age 11 or age 12, when children are believed to enter Piaget's formal operational stage. Brain development may give children the information-processing speed and working-memory capacity they need to perform at adultlike levels on IQ tests (Kail & Salthouse, 1994). Thus, basic changes in the brain in early adolescence may underlie a variety of cognitive advances—the achievement of formal operations, improved memory and information-processing skills, and better performance on tests of intelligence.

Although adolescence is a time of impressive mental growth, it is also a time of increased stability of individual differences in intellectual performance. During the teen years, IQ scores become even more stable than they were in childhood and strongly predict IQ in middle age (Deary et al., 2004). Even while adolescents as a group are experiencing cognitive growth, then, each adolescent is establishing a characteristic level of intellectual performance that will most likely be carried into adult life unless the individual's environment changes dramatically.

IQ and School Achievement

The original purpose of IQ tests was to estimate how well children would do in school, and they do this fairly well. Correlations between children's and adolescents' IQ scores and their grades range from 0.50 to 0.86, making general intellectual ability one of the best predictors of school achievement available (Deary et al., 2007; Neisser et al., 1996). Adolescents with high IQs are also less likely to drop out of high school and more likely to go on to college than their peers with lower IQs; the correlation between IQ and years of education obtained averages 0.55 (Neisser et al., 1996). However, IQ scores do not predict college grades as well as they predict high school grades (Brody & Brody, 1976). Most college students probably have at least the average intellectual ability needed to succeed in college; success is therefore more influenced by personal qualities such as motivation. Overall, an IQ score is a good predictor of academic achievement, but it does not reveal everything about a student. Factors such as work habits, interests, and motivation to succeed also affect academic achievement.

Fostering Creativity

We noted earlier that there is some dip in creativity during elementary school. What happens during adolescence? According to Howard Gardner (1993), adolescents often regain the innovativeness and freedom of expression they had as preschoolers and put it to use, with the technical skills they gained as children, to produce highly creative works. The ages at which creativity flourishes or is stifled seem to vary from culture to culture depending on when children are pressured to conform (Torrance, 1975). Overall, the developmental course of creativity is not so predictable or steady as the increase in mental age seen on measures of IQ. Instead, creativity seems to wax and wane with age in response to developmental needs and task demands. For example, in one study, researchers found that sixth-graders demonstrated greater creativity than college students on one type of task, but the college students outperformed the sixth-graders on a different task of creativity (Wu et al., 2005; see also Runco, 2006). In other research (Claxton et al., 2005), creative thinking remained fairly stable from fourth to ninth grade, but creative *feelings* increased significantly throughout adolescence. Creative feelings include curiosity, imagination, and willingness to take calculated risks. So teens may be feeling more creative than children even if they are not expressing creativity in their actions. What about your creativity? If you tried the exercise in Figure 9.4, compare your responses to the sample responses in ■ **Figure 9.5**.

Is it possible to foster creativity? Training studies indicate that people can learn techniques to improve their creativeness (Ma, 2006; Scott et al., 2004). But training may only be effective if the person's environment supports and rewards creativity. Researchers have looked at individuals who demonstrate creativity in a particular field to try to identify the factors that contribute to their accomplishments. David Feldman (1982, 1986), for example, has studied children and adolescents who are prodigies in such areas as chess, music, and mathematics. These individuals were generally similar to their peers in areas outside their fields of expertise. What contributed to their special achievements? On the nature side, they had *talent* as well as a powerful *motivation* to develop their special talents—a real passion for what they were doing. Olympic gymnast Olga Korbut put it well: "If gymnastics did not exist, I would have invented it" (Feldman, 1982, p. 35). Other research confirms that internal motivation and a thirst for challenge are crucial elements of creative productivity (Sternberg, 2006; Yeh & Wu, 2006). Individuals with a positive outlook also seem more likely to display creativity, perhaps because they are more open to challenges and derive more pleasure from challenges (see Yeh & Wu, 2006). Creative thinkers have other personal qualities as well—they display a willingness to take risks and are able to put up with some ambiguity without becoming frustrated (Proctor & Burnett, 2004; Sternberg, 2006).

On the nurture side, creative individuals seem to be blessed with *environments* that recognize, value, and nurture their creative endeavors (Sternberg, 2006). Their environments

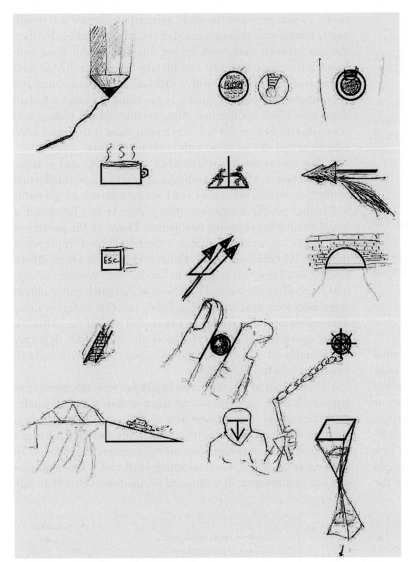

■ **FIGURE 9.5** How creative were you with the shapes in Figure 9.4? Compare your responses to those shown here. SOURCE: www.zenstorming.com/mindopeningexercise.pdf.

Creativity often increases during adolescence as talents emerge and are fostered by a supportive environment.

allow them a certain degree of independence to explore different fields and acquire knowledge of their chosen field. According to Feldman (1982), the child with creative potential in a specific field must become intimately familiar with the state of the field if he is to advance or transform it, as the groundbreaking artist or musician does. Thus, building a knowledge base is a necessary, although not sufficient, component of creativity (Sternberg, 2006). So parents can help foster creativity by giving their children freedom to explore and opportunities to experiment with ideas and activities. But talent and creativity can be squashed if parents and trainers are too pushy. For example, David Helfgott, the Australian pianist who was the subject of the movie *Shine*, was nearly destroyed by an abusive father who pushed him unmercifully to master difficult pieces (Page, 1996). Cellist Yo-Yo Ma, a prodigy himself, says this about nurturing young musicians:

If you lead them toward music, teach them that it is beautiful, and help them learn—say, "Oh, you love music, well, let's work on this piece together, and I'll show you something. . . ." That's a *creative* nurturing. But if you just push them to be stars, and tell them they'll become rich and famous—or, worse, if you try to live through them—that is damaging. (Page, 1996, p. G10)

Finally, we should ask whether performance on the tests of creativity used in studies of creative development predict actual creative accomplishments, such as original artwork or outstanding science projects. Some researchers have found that scores on creativity tests administered in either elementary or secondary school predict creative achievements, such as inventions and writing novels, in adulthood (Howieson, 1981; Runco, 1992; Torrance, 1988). However, just as it is a mistake to expect IQ to predict accomplishments, it may also be a mistake to expect tests of creativity to do so with any great accuracy (Albert, 1996). Why? First, creativity is expressed in different ways at different points in the life span; engaging in imaginative play as a child is correlated with high scores on tests of creativity (Russ, 1996) but may have little to do with being a creative scientist or musician as an adult. Also, creativity tests, like IQ tests, attempt to measure a general cognitive ability when many specific talents exist, and each (artistic, mathematical, musical, and so on) requires distinct skills and experiences, as suggested by Gardner's theory of multiple intelligences.

Checking Mastery

1. Is creativity or intelligence more stable during adolescence?
2. What is one environmental factor that could help enhance creativity?

Making Connections

1. To what extent have your schools fostered creativity? Is this something that *can* be fostered in schools and *should* it be fostered in schools?

2. IQ scores stabilize in adolescence and are highly correlated with adult IQ scores. Given this stability, should greater use be made of IQ scores? If so, what would be one or two meaningful uses of IQ scores during adolescence?

9.5 The Adult

We turn our attention now to intelligence during adulthood. Do IQ scores predict achievement and success after people have left school? Does performance on IQ tests change during the adult years? And do IQ scores decline in old age, as performance on Piagetian cognitive tasks and some memory tasks does?

IQ and Occupational Success

What is the relationship between IQ and occupational status? Professional and technical workers (such as scientists and engineers) score higher on IQ tests than white-collar workers (such as bank managers), who in turn score higher than blue-collar, or manual, workers (such as construction workers) (Nyborg & Jensen, 2001; Schmidt & Hunter, 2004). The connection among intelligence, income, and occupational prestige is striking when we look at findings from a longitudinal study using a large U.S. sample (Judge, Klinger, & Simon, 2010). ▪ **Figure 9.6** shows that over the

nearly 30-year period of the study, general intelligence was significantly related to both income and occupational prestige. Further, the gap between those with higher intelligence and those with lower intelligence widened considerably over time. Those with higher intelligence started with a slight advantage for income and occupational prestige but quickly began rising at a faster rate than those with lower intelligence. Also, income did not plateau and occupational prestige did not drop among those with higher intelligence as they did for those with lower intelligence.

The reason for the relationship between IQ and occupational success is clear: It undoubtedly takes more intellectual ability to complete law school and become a lawyer, a high-status and higher paying occupation, than it does to be a farmhand, a low-status and lower-paying occupation. However, the prestige or status of the occupation is not as important as the complexity of the work (Gottfredson, 1997; Kuncel, Hezlett, & Ones, 2004). Greater intelligence is required to handle more complex or cognitively challenging work. Those with higher intelligence obtain more education and training and they use this to tackle more demanding jobs, which leads to a faster and steeper rise to the top of the occupational ladder (Judge et al., 2010). Still, IQs vary considerably in every occupational group, so many people in low-status jobs have high IQs.

Now a second question: Are bright lawyers, electricians, or farmhands more successful or productive than their less intelligent colleagues? The answer here is also yes. The correlation between scores on tests of intellectual ability and such measures of job performance as supervisor ratings averages +0.30 to +0.50 (Neisser et al., 1996). General intellectual ability seems to predict job performance in a range of occupations better than any

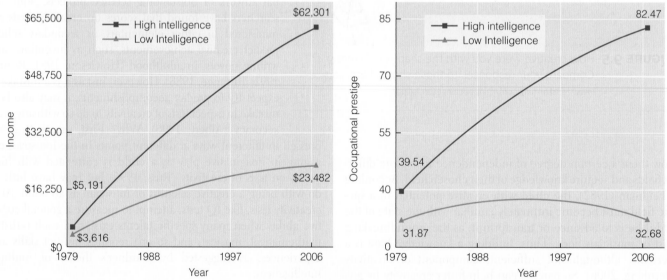

▪ **FIGURE 9.6** The two graphs show income *(left)* and occupational prestige *(right)* of participants over nearly 30 years in relation to their intelligence test performance: Those with high intelligence start with a slight advantage over their less intelligent peers but quickly leave them behind. Why don't those with lower intelligence keep rising at the same rate over the years? SOURCE: From Judge, T. A., Klinger, R. L., & Simon, L. S. (2010). Time is on my side: Time, general mental ability, human capital, and extrinsic career success. *Journal of Applied Psychology, 95,* 1, 92–107. Figure 2. Copyright © 2010 American Psychological Association. Reprinted by permission.

other indicator, and it predicts likelihood of success as accurately for members of racial and ethnic minority groups as for whites (Gottfredson, 2002; Schmidt & Hunter, 1998, 2004). More intellectually capable adults are better able to learn what they need to know about their occupations and to solve the problems that arise. This literally pays off, as shown in Figure 9.6: Individuals with greater cognitive ability earn more money than those with lower cognitive ability (Judge et al., 2010).

IQ and Health

People who score higher on measures of intelligence tend to be healthier and live longer than those who score lower on these tests (see, for example, Gottfredson, 2004; and Leon et al., 2009). In a rather amazing study conducted over many decades in Scotland, nearly everyone in the country born in 1921 completed an intelligence test in 1932, when they were 11 years old. A second cohort born in 1936 was also tested when they turned 11 years old, in 1947, yielding more than 150,000 original participants (Deary, Whalley, & Starr, 2009). Following up on health and death records of participants decades later, researchers found that individuals who scored one standard deviation (15 points) below the average (see Exploration Box 9.1 on measuring intelligence) were less likely to be alive at age 76 and more likely to have experienced stomach or lung cancers and cardiovascular or coronary heart disease. Stated another way, those children who scored in the top 25% on intelligence at age 11 were 2–3 times more likely to be alive 65 years later than those scoring in the bottom 25% (Deary et al., 2009). Similar results are emerging from a study in the United States that has tracked participants from adolescence to age 40 (Der, Batty, & Deary, 2009). Consistent with the Scotland research, higher intelligence in early adolescence is associated with fewer health problems at age 40.

A common explanation for this connection between IQ and health is socioeconomic status: smart people may have better jobs, giving them the resources to obtain better health care. But when living conditions are statistically controlled (that is, held constant), there is still a connection between intelligence and health (Gottfredson & Deary, 2004). Similarly, providing equal

access to health care reduces but does not eliminate the social-class differences in health (Steenland, Henley, & Thun, 2002).

So what else could be going on? Linda Gottfredson (2004) argues that good health takes more than access to material resources. It requires some of the abilities measured by intelligence tests, such as efficient learning and problem solving. In other words, successfully monitoring health and properly applying treatment protocols require a certain amount of intelligence. Consider the chronic illness diabetes. Successful management requires acquiring knowledge of the disease symptoms and course, identifying signs of inappropriate blood sugar levels, and making judgments about how to respond to blood sugar fluctuations. A patient's IQ predicts how much knowledge of diabetes she acquires during the year following diagnosis (Taylor et al., 2003). Other research shows that many people with diabetes who have limited literacy, which correlates with intelligence, do not know the signs of high or low blood sugar and do not know how to correct unhealthy levels (Williams et al., 1998). Research on relationships between IQ and health is relatively new and ongoing. But it suggests that IQ influences socioeconomic status, which in turn influences health, and that IQ also influences health directly. Smarter people are able to apply their intellectual skills to understanding and managing their health.

Changes in IQ with Age

Perhaps no question about adult development has been studied as thoroughly as that of how intellectual abilities change with age. We know that an individual's IQ score remains relatively stable from pre-adolescence (age 11) until well into older adulthood (Deary et al., 2004, 2009). Thus, where a person's IQ score falls within the spread of group scores is a good predictor of where this person's score will fall if retested with the same group later in life: high scorers tend to remain high scorers and low scorers tend to remain low scorers. But is there any pattern to the change of IQ scores for either the group as a whole or for individuals within the group?

Alan Kaufman (2001) examined cross sections of adults ranging in age from 16 to 89 who were tested with the Wechsler Adult Intelligence Scale. As ■ Figure 9.7 shows, IQs rise slightly

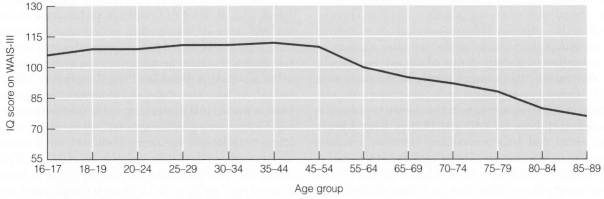

■ **FIGURE 9.7** IQ scores by age, showing a slow decline starting at about age 55.
SOURCE: Based on data from Kaufman (2001).

until the mid-40s and then decline, with the steepest declines starting around age 80. But recall the description of cross-sectional designs in Chapter 1. Cross-sectional studies compare people of different cohorts who have had different levels of education and life experiences because they were born at different times. Could the apparent declines in IQ with age reflect cohort differences?

Kaufman (2001) also studied the longitudinal performance of several cohorts of adults over a 17-year period. The results of this longitudinal study were similar to those obtained cross-sectionally. Over the 17-year period, there was a loss of about 5 IQ points among the 40-year-old cohort; losses of 7–8 points among the 50- and 60-year-old cohorts; and losses of about 10 points among the two oldest cohorts, who were 67 and 72 at the start of the study. Thus, the youngest cohort lost about 5 IQ points over a 17-year period and the oldest cohorts lost twice this—about 10 IQ points over the same period. Do intellectual abilities decline with age, as these data suggest? It depends on which abilities are examined. In both the cross-sectional and longitudinal studies, verbal IQ was essentially unchanged with age, at least until the person's 80s. In contrast, performance IQ peaked by ages 20–24, then steadily declined.

More data on changes in IQ with age come from a comprehensive sequential study directed by K. Warner Schaie (1996, 2005). Schaie's study began in 1956 with a sample of members of a health maintenance organization ranging in age from 22 to 70. They were given a revised test of primary mental abilities that yielded scores for five separate mental abilities: verbal meaning, spatial ability, reasoning, numerical ability, and word fluency. Seven years later, as many of them as could be found were retested. In addition, a new sample of adults ranging from their 20s to their 70s was tested. This design made it possible to determine how the performance of the same individuals changed over 7 years and to compare the performance of people who were 20 years old in 1956 with that of people who were 20 years old in 1963. This same strategy was repeated at regular intervals, giving the researchers a wealth of information about different cohorts, including longitudinal data on some people over a 45-year period.

Several findings have emerged from this important study. First, it seems that *when a person was born* has at least as much influence on intellectual functioning as age does. In other words, cohort or generational effects on performance exist. This evidence confirms the suspicion that cross-sectional comparisons of different age groups have usually yielded too grim a picture of declines in intellectual abilities during adulthood. Specifically, recently born cohorts (the youngest people in the study were born in 1973) tended to outperform earlier generations (the oldest were born in 1889) on most tests. Yet on the test of numerical ability, people born between 1903 and 1924 performed better than both earlier and later generations. Inductive reasoning scores have increased with every cohort tested since 1889. Scores on verbal meanings increased until 1952 but dropped off in the three most recently born cohorts (Schaie & Zanjani, 2006). So different generations may have a special edge in different areas of intellectual performance. Overall, though, judging from Schaie's findings, young and middle-aged adults today can look forward to

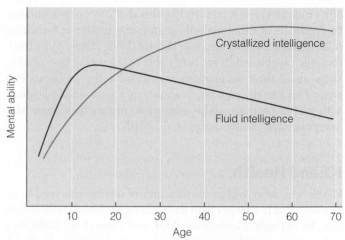

■ **FIGURE 9.8** What can you conclude about intelligence from "reading" this graph? SOURCE: From Cattell, R., *Intelligence: Its structure, growth, and action*, p. 206. Copyright © 1986. Reprinted by permission of Elsevier.

better intellectual functioning in old age than their grandparents experienced.

Another important message of Schaie's study, and of other research, is that patterns of aging differ for different abilities (■ **Figure 9.8**). Fluid intelligence (those abilities requiring active thinking and reasoning applied to novel problems, as measured by tests such as the primary mental abilities tests of reasoning and space) usually declines earlier and more steeply than crystallized intelligence (those abilities involving the use of knowledge acquired through experience, such as in answering the verbal meaning test used by Schaie). Consistently, adults lose some of their ability to grapple with new problems starting in middle age, but their crystallized general knowledge and vocabulary stay steady throughout middle and older adulthood (Rabbitt, Chetwynd, & McInnes, 2003; Singer et al., 2003). Some research even shows that knowledge, such as vocabulary, is greater among older adults than among younger adults (Field & Gueldner, 2001; Verhaeghen, 2003).

Why is this? Tests of performance and fluid IQ are often timed, and, as noted in Chapter 8, performance on timed tests declines more in old age than performance on untimed tests does. This may be linked to the slowing of central nervous system functioning that most people experience as they age (Salthouse, 1996; Sliwinski & Buschke, 1999; Zimprich & Martin, 2002). Indeed, we have seen that speed of information processing is related to intellectual functioning across the life span. Not only is rapid information processing in infancy associated with high IQ scores in childhood, but young adults with quick reaction times also outperform their more sluggish age-mates on IQ tests, and adults who lose information-processing speed in later life lose some of their ability to think through complex and novel problems (Jensen, 1993). It is not just that older adults cannot finish tests that have time limits; declines in performance intelligence occur in later life even on untimed tests (Kaufman & Kaufman,

1997). The problem is that the slower information processor cannot keep in mind and process simultaneously all relevant aspects of a complex problem.

You now have an overall picture of intellectual functioning in adulthood. Age group differences in performance suggest that older adults today are at a disadvantage on many tests compared with younger adults, partly because of deficiencies in the amount and quality of education they received early in life. But actual declines in intellectual abilities associated with aging are generally minor until people reach their late 60s or 70s. Even in old age, declines in fluid intelligence, performance intelligence, and performance on timed tests are more apparent than declines in crystallized intelligence, verbal intelligence, and performance on untimed tests. As you will soon see, declines in fluid intelligence can be reduced when adults remain cognitively stimulated through work or other activities (Weinert & Hany, 2003).

One last message of this research is worth special emphasis: Declines in intellectual abilities are not universal. Even among the 81-year-olds in Schaie's study, only about 30 to 40% had experienced a significant decline in intellectual ability in the previous 7 years (Schaie, 2005). Moreover, although few 81-year-olds maintained all five mental abilities, almost all retained at least one ability from testing to testing and about half retained four out of five (Schaie & Zanjani, 2006). The range of differences in intellectual functioning in a group of older adults is extremely large (Dixon, 2003). Anyone who stereotypes all elderly adults as intellectually limited is likely to be wrong most of the time.

Predictors of Decline

What is most likely to affect whether or not a person experiences declines in intellectual performance in old age? *Poor health*, not surprisingly, is one risk factor. People who have cardiovascular diseases or other chronic illnesses show steeper declines in mental abilities than their healthier peers (Schaie, 2005). Diseases (and most likely the drugs used to treat them) also contribute to a rapid decline in intellectual abilities within a few years of death (Johansson, Zarit, & Berg, 1992; Singer et al., 2003). This phenomenon has been given the depressing label **terminal drop**. Perhaps there is something, then, to the saying "Sound body, sound mind."

Why is it important to remain mentally and physically active across the life span?

A second factor in decline is an *unstimulating lifestyle*. Schaie and his colleagues found that the biggest intellectual declines were shown by elderly widows who had low social status, engaged in few activities, and were dissatisfied with their lives (Schaie, 1996). These women lived alone and seemed disengaged from life. Individuals who maintain their performance or even show gains tend to have above-average socioeconomic status, advanced education, intact marriages, intellectually capable spouses, and physically and mentally active lifestyles. Interestingly, married adults are affected by the intellectual environment they provide for each other. Their IQ test scores become more similar over the years, largely because the lower-functioning partner's scores rise closer to those of the higher-functioning partner (Gruber-Baldini, Schaie, & Willis, 1995; Weinert & Hany, 2003).

The moral is "Use it or lose it." This rule, applicable to muscular strength and sexual functioning, also pertains to intellectual functioning in later life. The plasticity of the nervous system throughout the life span enables elderly individuals to benefit from intellectual stimulation and training, to maintain the intellectual skills most relevant to their activities, and to compensate for the loss of less-exercised abilities (Dixon, 2003; Weinert & Hany, 2003; see also Application Box 9.1). There is still much to learn about how health, lifestyle, and other factors shape the individual's intellectual growth and decline. What is certain is that most people can look forward to many years of optimal intellectual functioning before some of them experience losses of some mental abilities in later life.

Potential for Wisdom

Many people believe—incorrectly, as you have seen—that intellectual decline is an inevitable part of aging. Yet many people also believe that old people are wise. Indeed, this belief has been expressed in many cultures throughout history. It is also featured in Erik Erikson's influential theory of life-span development. Erikson says that older adults often gain wisdom as they face the prospect of death and attempt to find meaning in their lives (see Chapter 11). Notice, too, that the word *wise* is rarely used to describe children, adolescents, or even young adults (unless perhaps it is to call one of them a *wise guy*). Is the association between wisdom and old age just a stereotype, or is there some truth to it?

People tend to believe that age brings wisdom. It can—but wisdom is rare even in later life. But first, what is wisdom, and how can researchers assess it? There is no consensus on these questions and, until recently, little research (Sternberg, 2003). Researchers do know that wisdom is not the same as high intelligence: there are many highly intelligent people who are not wise. Paul Baltes and his colleagues define **wisdom** as a constellation of rich factual knowledge about life combined with procedural knowledge such as strategies for giving advice and handling conflicts (Pasupathi, Staudinger, & Baltes, 2001). Similarly, Robert Sternberg (2003) defines a wise person as someone who can combine successful intelligence with creativity to solve problems that require balancing multiple interests or perspectives.

Can you teach old dogs new tricks? And can you reteach old dogs who have suffered declines in mental abilities the old tricks they have lost? K. Warner Schaie and Sherry Willis (1986; Willis & Schaie, 1986) sought to find out by training elderly adults in spatial ability and reasoning, two of the fluid mental abilities most likely to decline in old age. Within a group of older people ranging in age from 64 to 95 who participated in Schaie's longitudinal study of intelligence, they first identified individuals whose scores on one of the two abilities had declined over a 14-year period and individuals who had remained stable over the same period. The goal with the decliners would be to restore lost ability; the goal with those who had maintained their ability would be to improve it. Participants took pretests measuring both abilities, received 5 hours of training in either spatial ability or reasoning, and then were given post-tests on both abilities. The spatial training involved learning how to rotate objects in space, at first physically and then mentally. Training in reasoning involved learning how to detect a recurring pattern in a series of stimuli (for example, musical notes) and to identify what the next stimulus in the sequence should be.

The training worked. Both those who had suffered ability declines and those who had maintained their abilities before the study improved, although decliners showed significantly more improvement in spatial ability than nondecliners did. Schaie and Willis estimated that 40% of the decliners gained enough through training to bring them back to the level of performance they had achieved 14 years earlier, before decline set in. What is more, effects of the training among those who had experienced declines in performance were still evident 7 years later (Schaie, 1996). And, as noted in Chapter 8, the benefits of cognitive training with older adults extends beyond improving their performance on laboratory-type tests; their daily functioning improved as well (Willis et al., 2006).

Other research shows similar evidence for *neuroplasticity*, or restructuring the brain in response to training or experience, among older adults. Michelle Carlson and her colleagues (2009) conducted a pilot study with older women who were either trained and then served as volunteers in the Experience Corps program or were on a waitlist for future participation and served as the control group. Experience Corps volunteers spend 15 hours per week for 6 months in classrooms assisting kindergarten through third-graders with their learning. Their activities draw upon memory, literacy, and problem-solving skills. The researchers took a look inside their brains using functional magnetic resonance imaging (fMRI). The results, seen in the figure in this box, are striking: Women who volunteered in the classroom as part of the Experience Corps program showed significant gains in brain activity relative to the women who had not yet volunteered. Their activity changed the workings of their brains. Similar findings are emerging from similar programs, such as Senior Odyssey, that get older adults actively thinking (Stine-Morrow et al., 2007).

The larger messages? You can teach old dogs new tricks—and reteach them old tricks—in a short amount of time. This research does not mean that cognitive abilities can be restored in elderly people who have Alzheimer's disease or other brain disorders and have experienced significant neural loss. Instead, it suggests that many intellectual skills decline in later life because they are not used—and that these skills can be revived with a little coaching and practice. This research, combined with research on children, provides convincing evidence of the neuroplasticity of cognitive abilities over the entire life span (see Hertzog et al., 2009).

Group differences

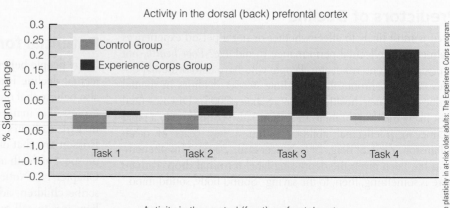

Activity in the dorsal (back) prefrontal cortex

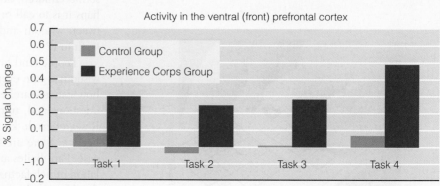

Activity in the ventral (front) prefrontal cortex

People tend to believe that age brings wisdom. It can—but wisdom is rare even in later life. Why is it difficult to attain wisdom?

Does wisdom typically increase with age, or are life experiences more important than age in determining whether or not a person is wise? Ursula Staudinger, Jacqui Smith, and Paul Baltes (1992) attempted to find out by interviewing young (ages 25–35) and elderly (ages 65–82) women who were clinical psychologists or similarly well-educated professionals in other fields. The goal was to assess the relative contributions of age and specialized experience to wisdom, based on the assumption that clinical psychologists gain special sensitivity to human problems from their professional training and practice.

These women were interviewed about a person named Martha, who had chosen to have a family but no career and who met an old friend who had chosen to have a career but no family. The women were asked to talk about how Martha might review and evaluate her life after this encounter. Answers were scored for qualities judged to be indicators of wisdom.

What was found? First, wisdom proved to be rare; it seems that only about 5% of the answers given by adults to problems such as these qualify as wise (Smith & Baltes, 1990). Second, expertise proved to be more relevant than age to the development of wisdom. That is, clinical psychologists, whether young or old, displayed more signs of wisdom than other women did. Older women were generally no wiser—or less wise—than younger women.

Age, then, does not predict wisdom. Yet the knowledge base that contributes to wisdom, like other crystallized intellectual abilities, holds up well later in life (Baltes et al., 1995).

Older adults, like younger adults, are more likely to display wisdom if they have life experiences (such as work as a clinical psychologist) that sharpen their insights into the human condition. The immediate social context also influences the degree to which wisdom is expressed; wiser solutions to problems are generated when adults have an opportunity to discuss problems with someone whose judgment they value and when they are encouraged to reflect after such discussions (Staudinger & Baltes, 1996). Thus, consulting with your fellow students and work colleagues and thinking about their advice may be the beginning of wisdom.

Finally, wisdom seems to reflect a particular combination of intelligence, personality, and cognitive style (Baltes & Staudinger, 2000). For example, individuals who have a cognitive style of comparing and evaluating relevant issues and who show tolerance of ambiguity are more likely to demonstrate wisdom than individuals without these characteristics. In addition, external factors influence the development of wisdom. Monika Ardelt (2000) found that a supportive social environment (loving family, good friends) during early adulthood was positively associated with wisdom 40 years later.

At this early stage in the study of wisdom, there is much disagreement about what it is, how it develops, and how it is related to other mental abilities. However, research on wisdom provides further evidence that different mental faculties develop and age differently over the adult years.

Creative Endeavors

Many studies of creativity during the adult years have focused on a small number of so-called eminent creators in such fields as art, music, science, and philosophy. A major question of interest has been this: When in adulthood are such individuals most productive and most likely to create their best works? Is it early in adulthood, when they can benefit from youth's enthusiasm and freshness of approach? Or is it later in adulthood, when they have fully mastered their field and have the experience and knowledge necessary to make a breakthrough in it? And what becomes of the careers of eminent creators in old age?

Early studies by Harvey Lehman (1953) and Wayne Dennis (1966) provided a fairly clear picture of how creative careers unfold (see also Runco, 2007; and Sternberg, 1999a). In most fields, creative production increases steeply from the 20s to the late 30s and early 40s, then gradually declines thereafter, although not to the same low levels that characterized early adulthood. Peak times of creative achievement also vary from field to field (Csikszentmihalyi & Nakamura, 2006). As ■ **Figure 9.9** shows, the productivity of scholars in the humanities (for example, historians and philosophers) continues well into old age and peaks in the 60s, possibly because creative work in these fields often involves integrating knowledge that has crystallized over years. By contrast, productivity in the arts (for example, music or drama) peaks in the 30s and 40s and declines steeply thereafter, perhaps because artistic creativity depends on a more fluid or innovative kind of thinking. Scientists seem to be intermediate, peaking in their 40s and declining only in their 70s. Even within

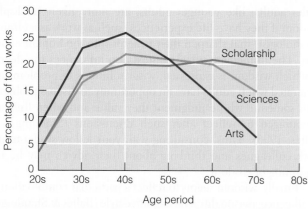

■ **FIGURE 9.9** Percentage of total works produced in each decade of the lives of eminent creators. The "scholarship" group includes historians and philosophers; the "sciences" category includes natural and physical scientists, inventors, and mathematicians; the "arts" creators include architects, musicians, dramatists, poets, and the like. SOURCE: Data from Dennis, W. (1966). Creative productivity between the ages of 20 and 80 years. *Journal of Gerontology, 21, 2.* Reprinted by permission.

the same general field, differences in peak times have been noted. For example, poets reach their peak before novelists do, and mathematicians peak before other scientists do (Dennis, 1966; Lehman, 1953).

Still, in many fields (including psychology), creative production rises to a peak in the late 30s or early 40s, and both the total number of works and the number of high-quality works decline thereafter (Simonton, 1990). This same pattern can be detected across different cultures and historical periods. Even so, the percentage of a creator's works that are significant changes little over the years (Simonton, 1999). This means that many creators are still producing outstanding works—sometimes their greatest works—in old age, not just rehashes of earlier triumphs. Michelangelo, for instance, was in his 70s and 80s when he worked on St. Peter's Cathedral, and Frank Lloyd Wright was 91 when he finished the blueprint for the Guggenheim Museum in New York City. Indeed, the most eminent among the eminent seem to start early and finish late (Simonton, 1999).

How can researchers account for changes in creative production over the adult years? One explanation, proposed long ago (Beard, 1874, in Simonton, 1984), is that creative achievement requires both enthusiasm and experience. In early adulthood, the enthusiasm is there, but the experience is not; in later adulthood, the experience is there, but the enthusiasm or vigor has fallen off. People in their 30s and 40s have it all.

Dean Simonton (1999) has offered another theory: Each creator may have a certain potential to create that is realized over the adult years; as the potential is realized, less is left to express.

According to Simonton, creative activity involves two processes: ideation (generating creative ideas) and elaboration (executing ideas to produce poems, paintings, or scientific publications). After a career is launched, some time elapses before any ideas are generated or any works are completed. This would explain the rise in creative achievement between the 20s and 30s. Also, some kinds of work take longer to formulate or complete than others, which helps explain why a poet (who can generate and carry out ideas quickly) might reach a creative peak earlier in life than, say, a historian (who may need to devote years to the research and writing necessary to complete a book once the idea for it is hatched).

Why does creative production begin to taper off? Simonton (1999) suggests that older creators may simply have used up much of their stock of potential ideas. They never exhaust their creative potential, but they have less of it left to realize. Simonton argues, then, that changes in creative production over the adult years have more to do with the nature of the creative process than with a loss of mental ability in later life. Creators who start their careers late are likely to experience the same rise and fall of creative output that others do, only later in life. And those lucky creators with immense creative potential to realize will not burn out; they will keep producing great works until they die.

What about mere mortals? Here, researchers have fallen back on tests designed to measure creativity. In one study, scores on a test of divergent thinking abilities decreased at least modestly after about age 40 and decreased more steeply starting around 70 (McCrae, Arenberg, & Costa, 1987). It seems that elderly adults do not differ much from younger adults in the originality of their ideas; the main difference is that they generate fewer of them (Jaquish & Ripple, 1981). Generally, then, these studies agree with the studies of eminent achievers: Creative behavior becomes less frequent in later life, but it remains possible throughout the adult years.

Checking Mastery

1. What do IQ scores predict during adulthood?

2. What are two factors that contribute to a decline in IQ scores among older adults?

3. How is wisdom different from intelligence?

Making Connections

1. As the administrator of a large health maintenance organization, would it be useful to collect information on intelligence from your clients? Why or why not?

2. In what ways are you smarter than your parents and grandparents and in what ways are these two older generations smarter or wiser than you? What are some factors that contribute to generational differences in intelligence and age differences in wisdom?

9.6 Factors That Influence IQ Scores

Now that we have surveyed changes in intellectual functioning over the life span, we will address a different question: Why do children or adults who are the same age differ in IQ? Part of the answer is that they differ in the kinds of motivational and situational factors that can affect performance on a given day. Yet there are real differences in underlying intellectual ability that need to be explained. As usual, the best explanation is that genetic and environmental factors interact to make us what we are.

Flynn Effect

Over the 20th century, average IQ scores have increased in all countries studied, a phenomenon called the **Flynn effect** after James Flynn (1987, 1998, 1999, 2007), who focused our attention on this phenomenon. In the United States, the increase has amounted to 3–4 IQ points per decade. So a group of adults born in, say, 1980, will score on average 3–4 points higher than a similar group of adults born in 1970 and 6–8 points higher than those born in 1960. ■ **Figure 9.10** illustrates the gains in intelligence over a period of more than 50 years. Full-scale IQ scores have increased 18 points over this time, with scores on some subscales increasing as much as 24 points (for example, simi-larities and Raven's Progressive Matrices), others increasing 10 points (such as comprehension), and some increasing a slight 2–3 points (for example, information, arithmetic, and vocabulary). Further, Flynn (2007) presents data that suggest these trends extend back more than 100 years, leading him to ask, "How can our recent ancestors have been so unintelligent compared to ourselves?" (p. 9). How indeed?

Most researchers argue that increases of this size cannot be caused by genetic evolution and therefore must have environmental causes (but see Mingroni, 2004). Flynn and others have suggested that improved nutrition and living conditions over the course of the 20th century have contributed to the rise in intellectual functioning (for example, Lynn, 2009). In addition, today's children grow up in smaller families where they have the opportunity to receive more focused attention from their parents than previous generations of children. Children today are also better educated than earlier generations; 85% today complete high school, compared with just 5% in 1895 (Greve, 2006).

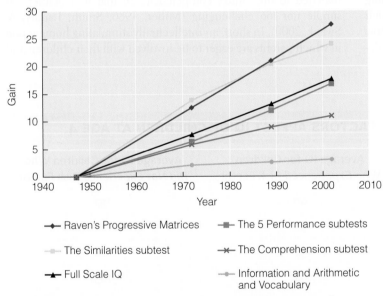

■ **FIGURE 9.10** Over a 50-year period, test scores on several measures of intelligence have risen substantially, illustrating the "Flynn effect." Are people really getting smarter? What factors might explain such a rise in intelligence test scores?

SOURCE: Flynn, J. R. (2007). *What is intelligence: Beyond the Flynn effect* (Figure 1, p. 8). Reprinted by permission of Cambridge University Press.

Genes and Environments

The pioneers of the IQ testing movement believed that individual differences in IQ exist simply because some people inherit better genes at conception than others do. This position is still held by hereditarians (for example, Herrnstein & Murray, 1994; and Jensen, 1998) who draw upon twin studies and other family research to demonstrate a genetic contribution to intelligence. As you saw in Chapter 3, identical twins obtain more similar IQ scores than fraternal twins do even when they have been raised apart (you might want to look again at Table 3.5). Moreover, the IQs of adopted children, once they reach adolescence, are more strongly correlated with those of their biological parents than with those of their adoptive parents. Overall, most researchers find that about half of the variation in IQ scores within a group of individuals is associated with genetic differences among them (Plomin & Spinath, 2004; van Leeuwen et al., 2008).

What exactly does it mean to conclude that there is a genetic influence on intelligence? First, we must make clear what it does *not* mean: Genetic influence, even if it is strong, does not mean that a trait, in this case intelligence, is "set in stone" or unresponsive to the environment (see Nisbett, 2009). Genetic factors may provide some upper and lower limits on what is possible, but environment can play a significant role in determining what and where, within these broad limits, behaviors fall. Genes need environments for expression. There are likely many genetic influences on intelligence. For example, one child might be predisposed to have a strong curiosity or openness to new experiences. As a result of this, the child asks more questions, picks up more books, works on more puzzles, accepts invitations to a variety of activities, goes on more trips, and so on. This creates an environment that may allow intelligence to bloom. So genetic factors are important, but they do not tell the entire story.

"The class genius, Warren, says it's the result of inherited faulty intelligence."

SOURCE: www.CartoonStock.com.

How, then, does the environment influence intelligence? Research by Arnold Sameroff and his colleagues (1993) provides a broad overview of some of the environmental factors that put children at risk for having low IQ scores—and, by implication, some of the factors associated with higher IQs. These researchers assessed the 10 risk factors shown in ● **Table 9.3** at age 4 and again at age 13. Every factor was related to IQ at age 4, and most predicted IQ at age 13. In addition, the greater the number of these risk factors affecting a child, the lower his IQ, a finding confirmed by other research (Lipina & Colombo, 2009). Which risk factors the child experienced was less important than how many he experienced. Clearly, it is not good for intellectual de-

velopment to grow up in a disadvantaged home with an adult unable to provide much intellectual nurturance.

In what ways do parents and the home influence children's intellectual development? A widely used assessment of the intellectual stimulation of the home environment is the **Home Observation for Measurement of the Environment (HOME) inventory** (Bradley et al., 2001). Sample items from the preschool version of a HOME inventory are shown in ● **Table 9.4**. Bradley and his colleagues (1989) have found that scores on the HOME can predict the IQs of African American and European American children at age 3, with correlations of about 0.50 (see also Cleveland et al., 2000). HOME scores continue to predict IQ scores between ages 3 and 6 (Espy, Molfese, & DiLalla, 2001). Gains in intellectual performance from age 1 to age 3, as measured by habituation and speed of processing, are likely to occur among children from stimulating homes, whereas children from families with low HOME scores often experience drops in performance over the same period. These findings are consistent across numerous countries and racial/ethnic groups, with a few exceptions (Farah et al., 2008; Lipina & Colombo, 2009).

What aspects of the home environment best predict high IQs? Studies using the HOME inventory indicate that the most important factors are parental involvement with the child and opportunities for stimulation (Gottfried et al., 1994). However, the amount of stimulation parents provide to their young children may not be as important as whether that stimulation is responsive to the child's behavior (a smile in return for a smile) and matched to the child's competencies so that it is neither too simple nor too challenging (Miller, 1986; Smith, Landry, & Swank, 2000). In short, an intellectually stimulating home is one in which parents are eager to be involved with their children and

● TABLE 9.3 HOW 10 ENVIRONMENTAL RISK FACTORS AFFECT IQ OF CHILDREN AT AGE 4

Risk Factor	Average IQ for Children Who *Experienced* Risk Factor	Average IQ for Children Who *Did Not Experience* Risk Factor
Child is member of minority group	90	110
Head of household is unemployed or low-skilled worker	90	108
Mother did not complete high school	92	109
Family has four or more children	94	105
Father is absent from family	95	106
Family experienced many stressful life events	97	105
Parents have rigid child-rearing values	92	107
Mother is highly anxious or distressed	97	105
Mother has poor mental health or diagnosed disorder	99	107
Mother shows little positive affect toward child	88	107

SOURCE: Adapted from Sameroff, A. J., Seifer, R., Baldwin, A., & Baldwin, C. (1993). Stability of intelligence from pre-school to adolescence: The influence of social and family risk factors. *Child Development, 64,* 80–97. Copyright © 1993 Blackwell Publishing. Reprinted with permission.

TABLE 9.4 SUBSCALES AND SAMPLE ITEMS FROM THE HOME INVENTORY

Subscale 1: Emotional and Verbal Responsivity of Parent (11 Items)

Sample Items	Parent responds verbally to child's vocalization or verbalizations.
	Parent's speech is distinct, clear, and audible.
	Parent caresses or kisses child at least once.

Subscale 2: Avoidance of Restriction and Punishment (8 Items)

Sample Items	Parent neither slaps nor spanks child during visit.
	Parent does not scold or criticize child during visit.
	Parent does not interfere with or restrict child more than three times during visit.

Subscale 3: Organization of Physical and Temporal Environment (6 Items)

Sample Items	Child gets out of house at least four times a week.
	Child's play environment is safe.

Subscale 4: Provision of Appropriate Play Materials (9 Items)

Sample Items	Child has a push or pull toy.
	Parent provides learning facilitators appropriate to age—mobile, table and chairs, highchair, playpen, and so on.
	Parent provides toys for child to play with during visit.

Subscale 5: Parental Involvement with Child (6 Items)

Sample Items	Parent talks to child while doing household work.
	Parent structures child's play periods.

Subscale 6: Opportunities for Variety in Daily Stimulation (5 Items)

Sample Items	Father provides some care daily.
	Child has three or more books of his or her own.

SOURCE: Adapted from Caldwell & Bradley, 1984.

are responsive to their developmental needs and behavior. This may help explain why some research on intelligence finds a connection to family size and birth order, with firstborns and children from small families scoring just slightly higher (about 2 points) on IQ tests than later-borns and children from large families (see, for example, Zajonc, 2001a, b; see also Sulloway, 2007).

Do differences in stimulation in the home really cause individual differences in IQ? Parents with greater intelligence are more likely than less intelligent parents to provide intellectually stimulating home environments for their children and to pass on to their children genes that contribute to high intelligence; that is, there is evidence of the gene–environment correlations described in Chapter 3. Maternal IQ, for example, is correlated with a child's IQ at 3 years and is also correlated with family income and quality of home environment (Bacharach & Baumeister, 1998). Although a mother's IQ is reliably associated with her children's IQ, a father's IQ is a less reliable predictor of his children's IQ.

So bright children are bright, not because of the genes they inherited *or* because of the home environment their bright parents provided. Instead, they are bright because genes and environments get combined in ways that allow children with particular genetic makeups to display high intelligence under some environmental conditions. Overall, intellectual development seems to go best when a motivated, intellectually capable child begging for intellectual nourishment is fortunate enough to get it from involved and responsive parents.

Poverty

Poverty is often defined by low family income, but **child poverty** involves more than parent income: it also includes low levels of meeting children's basic needs (see Lipina & Colombo, 2009). Thus, children who live in poverty often have inadequate health and dental care and nutrition; they live in overcrowded and unsafe neighborhoods; their families experience chronic stress; their relationships with parents are not as affectionate or supportive; and they lack opportunities for cognitive stimulation that are commonplace in other homes. Numerous studies with animals demonstrate that being raised in an impoverished environment has a direct impact on brain development (see, for example, Markham & Greenough, 2004; and Rosenzweig & Bennett, 1996). For example, rats raised in a large cage with a few other rats for company, wheels for exercising, and blocks to play with develop more neurons, more connections between neurons, and more glial cells supporting neurons than rats raised in isolation (Greenough, Black, & Wallace, 1987; Mohammed et al., 2002). The message is clear: the brain is influenced by the environment. So what happens when children are raised in impoverished environments?

Children who live in poverty average some 10–20 points below their middle-class age-mates on IQ tests. This is true in all racial and ethnic groups (Helms, 1997). Socioeconomic status affects IQ scores as well as children's rate of intellectual growth (Espy, Molfese, & DiLalla, 2001). Thus, their cognitive development is slower and their endpoint is lower—on average, they end up a full standard deviation below their age peers. What if socioeconomic conditions were to improve?

The brain is responsive to environmental change—it has *neuroplasticity*. So improving the economic conditions of children's homes can improve their IQs. For example, Sandra Scarr and Richard Weinberg charted the intellectual growth of African American and European American children adopted before their first birthday (Scarr & Weinberg, 1983; Weinberg, Scarr, & Waldman, 1992). Many of these children came from

Women walk by rundown apartments in an impoverished Connecticut neighborhood. How will these conditions affect the children who grow up here?

© Spencer Platt/Getty Images

disadvantaged family backgrounds and had biological parents who were poorly educated and somewhat below average in IQ. They were placed in middle-class homes with adoptive parents who were highly educated and above average in intelligence. Throughout childhood and adolescence, these adoptees posted average or above average scores on standardized IQ tests—higher scores than they would have obtained if they had stayed in the disadvantaged environments offered by their natural parents. Research with French children who were adopted later—around age 5—indicates that increases in IQ are much larger among children adopted into affluent homes with highly educated parents than among those adopted into disadvantaged homes (Duyme, Dumaret, & Tomkiewicz, 1999).

Race and Ethnicity

Most studies, using samples from numerous countries, find racial and ethnic differences in IQ scores, which has sparked much controversy (see Lynn, 2008a; 2008b). In the United States, for example, Asian American and European American children tend to score higher, on average, on IQ tests than African American, Native American, and Hispanic American children (Lynn, 2008b). Although some research suggests that racial differences on IQ tests have been shrinking in recent decades, other research shows little narrowing of the gap between, for example, black and white children on IQ tests (Dickens & Flynn, 2006; Murray, 2006; Yeung & Pfeiffer, 2009). Different subcultural groups sometimes show distinctive profiles of mental abilities; for example, black children often do well on verbal tasks, whereas Hispanic children, perhaps because of language differences, tend to excel on nonverbal items (Lynn, 2009; Taylor & Richards, 1991). It is essential to keep in mind that we are talking about *group averages*. Like the IQ scores of white children, those of minority children run the range from the mentally retarded to the gifted. Researchers certainly cannot predict an individual's IQ merely on the basis of racial or ethnic identity. Having said that, why do these average group differences exist? Consider the following hypotheses: bias in the tests, motivational factors, genetic differences among groups, and environmental differences among groups.

Biased Tests?

Racial differences in IQ tests may be attributable to culture bias in testing; that is, IQ tests may be more appropriate for children from white middle-class backgrounds than for those from other subcultural groups (Helms, 1992; Lopez, 1997). Low-income African American children who speak a dialect of English (such as Ebonics or Black English) different from that spoken by middle-class European American children, as well as Hispanic children who hear Spanish rather than English at home, may not understand some test instructions or items. What is more, their experiences may not allow them to become familiar with some of the information called for on the tests (for example, What is a 747? Who wrote *Hamlet?*).

Minority-group children often do not have as much exposure to the culture reflected in the tests as nonminority children

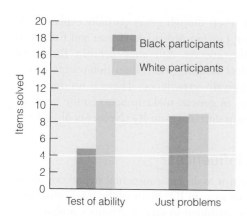

■ **FIGURE 9.11** African American students perform poorly on tests of mental abilities when they think they are taking a test that may result in their being stereotyped as unintelligent. Source: From Steele, C. M., & Aronson, J. (1995). Stereotype threat and the intellectual test performance of African Americans. *Journal of Personality and Social Psychology, 69*, 1995. Copyright © 1995 by the American Psychological Association. Reprinted by permission.

do. If IQ tests assess "proficiency in European American culture," minority children are bound to look deficient (Helms, 1992). Using IQ tests designed to be fair to all ethnic groups and introducing procedures to help minority children feel more comfortable and motivated can cut the usual IQ gap between African American and European American children in half (Kaufman, Kamphaus, & Kaufman, 1985). But even though standardized IQ test items sometimes have a white middle-class flavor, group differences in IQ probably cannot be traced solely to test bias. Culture-fair IQ tests include items that should be equally unfamiliar (or familiar) to people from all ethnic groups and social classes—for example, items that require completing a geometric design with a piece that matches the rest of the design. Still, racial and ethnic differences emerge on such tests (Jensen, 1980). In addition, IQ tests predict future school achievement as well for African Americans and other minorities as they do for European Americans (Neisser et al., 1996).

Motivational Differences?

Another possibility is that minority individuals are not motivated to do their best in testing situations because they are anxious or resist being judged by an examiner who is often of a different racial/ethnic background (Huang, 2009; Ogbu, 1994; Steele, 1997). Disadvantaged children score some 7–10 points higher when they are given time to get to know a friendly examiner or are given a mix of easy and hard items so that they do not become discouraged by a long string of difficult items (Zigler et al., 1982). Even though most children do better with a friendly examiner, it seems that African American children, even those from middle-class homes, are often less comfortable in testing situations than white middle-class children are (Moore, 1986). Minority children may be less likely to see value to themselves for performing well on a test (Okagaki, 2001). And their peers may accuse (or tease) them of "acting white" if they place too much emphasis on academic success and strong test scores, values that they may associate with white culture.

Claude Steele and his colleagues have argued that the performance of African Americans is especially likely to suffer whenever negative stereotypes of their group come into play (Steele, 1997, 1999; Steele & Aronson, 1995; see also Sackett, Hardison, & Cullen, 2004). In one study, female students at Stanford University were given difficult test items. Some students were told that they

were taking a test of verbal abilities and would get feedback about their strengths and weaknesses; others were told that they were going to do some verbal problems but that their ability would not be evaluated. As ■ **Figure 9.11** shows, African American students performed poorly when they were led to believe that the test would reveal their level of intellectual ability, but performed more like European American students when they did not think their ability would be judged. Even being asked to identify their race in a personal information section at the start of a test of intellectual ability can undermine the performance of African American college students (Steele & Aronson, 1995).

Why? Steele concluded that African Americans perform poorly on IQ tests partly because of **stereotype threat**—fear that they will be judged to have the qualities associated with negative stereotypes of African Americans (see also Aronson et al., 1999). It is not that African Americans have internalized stereotypes and believe they are intellectually inferior, according to Steele. Instead, they become anxious and unable to perform well in testing situations that arouse concerns about being negatively stereotyped.

Gregory Walton and Steven Spencer (2009) conducted two meta-analyses of the effects of stereotype threat on test performance of thousands of students. They found substantial effects on SAT

How does stereotype threat operate to potentially affect the test performance of this young African American woman?

scores, the standardized test taken by many college-bound high school students. Stereotype threat seems to account for 40 points of the score gap between majority (white) and non-majority (black and Hispanic) students. Thus, minority student performance is underestimated as a result of pervasive negative stereotypes.

On the positive side, other research has demonstrated that positive stereotypes about a group can increase the performance of members of that group. Margaret Shih and her colleagues (Shih, Pittinsky, & Ambady, 1999) gave Asian American women a math test under one of three conditions. In one, their identity as women was made noticeable; in another, their Asian American identity was made evident; and in a third condition, no identity was emphasized. Consistent with stereotypes, these women performed worse when their gender was emphasized and better when their ethnic background was emphasized, relative to the group that was not primed to think about either identity. So stereotypes can either hinder or enhance performance, depending on whether a person identifies with a group that is viewed negatively or positively on the dimension measured.

The effects of stereotype threat can be reduced by providing students with a mentor. Catherine Good, Joshua Aronson, and Michael Inzlicht (2003) had college students serve as mentors to seventh-graders likely to experience stereotype threat as a result of being female, impoverished, and a member of a minority group. The mentors encouraged students to interpret their academic troubles as a result of the transition to a new school for seventh grade. In addition, they talked about intelligence being flexible and responsive to new learning. Following such mentoring, the students performed better on standardized tests than students who did not receive mentoring. These findings provide a practical means for eliminating or reducing the negative influence of stereotype threat. Of course, eliminating the negative stereotypes that create the threat should also be a goal.

Genetic Factors?

We discussed the overall influence of genetic factors on intelligence, but is there any evidence that genetic differences *between* racial or ethnic groups account for different levels of performance? This is perhaps one of the most controversial ideas in psychology, and it has sparked much heated debate. Scholars such as Arthur Jensen (1969) and Herrnstein and Murray (1994) have suggested that IQ differences between European Americans and African Americans may be because of genetic differences between the races, and they have written books to present their positions.

However, most psychologists do not think the evidence that heredity contributes to *within-group* differences says much about the reasons for *between-group* differences. Consider this analogy from Richard Lewontin (1976): Suppose that corn seeds with different genetic makeups are randomly drawn from a bag and planted in two fields—one that has terrible soil with no nutrients and one that has rich, fertile soil. Because all the plants *within* each field were grown in the same soil, their differences in height would have to be because of differences in genetic makeup. A genetic explanation of differences would fit. But if the plants in the fertile field are generally taller than those in the non-fertile field, this *between-field* variation must be entirely because of en-

vironment. Similarly, even though genes partially explain individual differences in IQ *within* African American and European American groups, the average difference *between* the racial groups may still reflect nothing more than differences in the environments they typically experience. There is no direct evidence that differences in genetic makeup between the races account for average group differences in IQ (Neisser et al., 1996).

Environmental Influences?

It is time, then, to return to an environmental hypothesis about racial and ethnic differences in IQ. Many of the intellectual and academic differences attributed to race or ethnicity probably reflect racial and ethnic differences in socioeconomic status instead (Patterson, Kupersmidt, & Vaden, 1990). As noted earlier, placement in more advantaged homes has allowed lower-income African American children to equal or exceed the average IQ in the general population and to exceed the IQs of comparable African American children raised in more disadvantaged environments by 20 points (Moore, 1986; Scarr & Weinberg, 1983; Weinberg et al., 1992). This could not have happened if African American children were genetically deficient.

The major message of this research is that children, whatever their racial background, perform better on IQ tests when they grow up in intellectually stimulating environments with involved, responsive parents and are exposed to the "culture of the tests and the schools" (Scarr & Weinberg, 1983, p. 261). How much of the racial gap in IQ can be explained by racial differences in neighborhood and family socioeconomic conditions, mother's education, and qualities of the home environment? Jeanne Brooks-Gunn, Pamela Klebanov, and Greg Duncan (1996) used statistical procedures to correct for these environmental differences between African American and European American children so that they could estimate what the IQ difference would be if the two racial groups had been raised in similar environments. Without any controls for environmental differences, there was an IQ gap of 18 points. The gap narrowed to 8 points when family and neighborhood income levels were controlled and was reduced to 3 points, a trivial difference, when racial differences in the provision of a stimulating home environment (HOME scores) were also controlled. In short, that more African American than European American children live in poverty and have limited learning opportunities at home has a lot to do with racial difference in average IQ scores. Reducing poverty and offering more early developmental programs to offset the costs of impoverished home environments would go a long way toward eliminating racial differences in intellectual performance.

Checking Mastery

1. What is the Flynn effect?

2. How does home environment, as measured with the HOME Inventory, influence IQ scores?

3. What are several theories of why IQ tests yield racial/ethnic differences in scores?

Making Connections

1. The Maori are a socioeconomically disadvantaged group in New Zealand, a country colonized by the British long ago. Maori children typically score lower on IQ tests than children of British background. Knowing what you know about minorities in the United States, what are your top two hypotheses about why Maori children perform relatively poorly, and how might you test these hypotheses?

2. Considering material from this chapter as well as material from Chapter 3 on genetic influences, evaluate the relative contributions of nature and nurture to intelligence. Does one or the other have a greater contribution to intelligence? How do their effects combine? What evidence supports your position?

9.7 The Extremes of Intelligence

Although we have identified some of the factors that contribute to individual differences in intellectual performance, you cannot fully appreciate the magnitude of these differences without considering people at the extremes of the IQ continuum. Just how different are intellectually disabled and gifted individuals? And how different are their lives?

Intellectual Disability

Intellectual disability, or mental retardation as it was called for many decades, is defined as significantly below-average intellectual functioning with limitations in areas of adaptive behavior such as self-care and social skills, originating before age 18 (see AAIDD, 2010; Schalock et al., 2010). An IQ score of 70–75 or lower suggests a limitation in intellectual functioning. This, along with difficulties meeting age-appropriate expectations in important areas of everyday functioning, is indicative of intellectually disability. Thus, intellectual disability is not merely a deficiency within the person; rather, it is the product of the inter-

action between person and environment, strongly influenced by the type and level of supportive help the individual receives (Reiss, 1994). A person with an IQ score of 65 in a supportive environment that is structured in ways that allow the individual to fit in and flourish may not be considered disabled in this environment. However, in an environment with different expectations and support, this same individual may be viewed as disabled.

Individuals with intellectual disability differ greatly in their levels of functioning (● **Table 9.5**). An adult with an IQ in the range of about 55–70 is likely to have a mental age comparable to that of an 8- to 12-year-old child. Individuals with mild intellectual disability can learn both academic and practical skills in school, and they can potentially work and live independently as adults. Many of these individuals are integrated into regular classrooms, where they excel academically and socially relative to comparable individuals who are segregated into special classrooms (Freeman, 2000). At the other end of the continuum, individuals with IQs below 20–25 and mental ages below 3 years ("profoundly disabled") show major delays in all areas of development and require basic care, sometimes in institutional settings. However, they, too, can benefit considerably from training.

Intellectual disability has many causes. Those who are severely and profoundly disabled are often affected by "organic" conditions, meaning that their disability is because of some identifiable biological cause associated with hereditary factors, diseases, or injuries. Down syndrome, the condition associated with an extra 21st chromosome, and phenylketonuria (PKU) are familiar examples of conditions causing intellectual disability that are associated with genetic factors (Lovering & Percy, 2007; see also Chapter 3). Other forms of organic disability are associated with prenatal risk factors—an alcoholic mother, exposure to rubella, and so on (Nulman et al., 2007; see also Chapter 4). Because many such children are seriously delayed or have physical defects, they can often be identified at birth or during infancy and come from all socioeconomic levels.

● **TABLE 9.5 LEVELS AND CHARACTERISTICS OF INTELLECTUAL DISABILITY**

	Level			
	Mild	Moderate	Severe	Profound
Approximate Range of IQ Scores	52–70	35–51	20–34	Below 19
Degree of Independence	Usually independent	Some independence; needs some supervision	May be semi-independent with close supervision	Dependent; needs constant supervision
Educational Achievement	Can do some academic work—usually to sixth-grade level; focus is on career	Focus is on daily living skills rather than academics; some career training	Focus is on self-care (toileting, dressing, eating) and communication skills	Focus is on self-care, mobility, and basic communication education

SOURCE: From Barack, J. A., Hodapp, R. M., & Zigler E. (Eds.). (1998). *Handbook of mental retardation and development.* Copyright © 1998 Cambridge University Press. Reprinted with permission.

However, most cases of intellectual disability have no identifiable organic cause; they are characterized by milder symptoms and appear to result from some combination of genetic endowment and environmental factors (Batshaw, Shapiro, & Farber, 2007). Not surprisingly, then, these children often come from poor areas, have neglectful or abusive families, and frequently have a parent or sibling who is also disabled (Batshaw et al., 2007; Zigler, 1995).

Historically, about 3% of school-age children have been classified with intellectual disability, although this rate has decreased as fewer children today are diagnosed with mild disability (Patton, 2000). Oftentimes, these children have associated impairments, such as cerebral palsy, behavioral problems, physical impairments, or sensory disorders. As for children not diagnosed at birth, those with milder disabilities are typically diagnosed when as toddlers they fail to meet developmental milestones at a typical age. Once children are diagnosed, their parents experience complex reactions to their child and the disability itself (Boström, Broberg, & Hwang, 2010). Parents—mothers more so than fathers—of intellectually disabled children report higher levels of stress than parents of nondisabled children, but this stress is reduced where there are higher levels of marital and parenting satisfaction (Gerstein et al., 2009; Hill & Rose, 2009).

What becomes of these children as they grow up? Generally, they proceed along the same paths and through the same sequences of developmental milestones as other children do, although often at a slower rate (Zigler & Hodapp, 1991). Their IQs remain low because they do not achieve the same level of growth that others do. They, like nondisabled people, show signs of intellectual aging in later life, especially on tests that require speed (Devenny et al., 1996). Individuals with Down syndrome may experience even greater intellectual deterioration later in life because they are at risk for premature Alzheimer's disease (Lovering & Percy, 2007).

As for their outcomes in life, consider a series of follow-up studies with a group of individuals with intellectual disabilities known as the "Camberwell Cohort" for the region of England from where they were originally recruited (Beadle-Brown, Murphy, & Wing, 2005, 2006; Beadle-Brown, Murphy, & DiTerlizzi, 2009). In their 40s, about 50% lived in community group homes, 25% lived with their family, and 20% lived in a larger residential facility. Social skills, important to daily interactions with others, remained largely unchanged over the 25-year period of study. But for those who as children started out more socially impaired than others in the sample, social impairments tended to worsen with age, possibly because social demands increased in adulthood or because support in social situations was diminished. The combination of intellectual disability and social impairment led to a poor or fair overall outcome for most of the individuals in the cohort. Not surprisingly, those who were not as intellectually disabled and did not have associated impairments had more favorable outcomes.

The results from the Camberwell Cohort suggest that overall quality of life is lower for adults diagnosed with intellectual disability early in life. However, outcomes varied and were related to severity of the disability. Despite the relatively lackluster outcomes for these individuals, the findings also provide grounds for optimism. Only a minority of the group lived in what might be considered an institutional setting; most lived in the community, either in small group homes or with their family, and participated in typical community activities. This is a marked improvement from previous decades, when nearly everyone with any level of disability lived segregated from the mainstream of society.

Giftedness

The gifted child used to be identified solely by an IQ score—one that was at least 130. Programs for gifted children still focus mainly on those with very high IQs, but there is increased recognition that some children are gifted because they have special abilities—think again of Gardner's eight intelligences discussed at the beginning of this chapter—rather than because they have high general intelligence. Even high-IQ children are usually not equally talented in all areas; contrary to myth, they cannot just become anything they choose (Winner, 1996). More often, high-IQ children have exceptional talent in an area or two and otherwise are good, but not exceptional, performers (Achter, Benbow, & Lubinski, 1997). So today's definitions emphasize that **giftedness** involves having a high IQ or showing special abilities in areas valued in society, such as mathematics, the performing and visual arts, or even leadership.

Joseph Renzulli (1998) has long argued that giftedness emerges from a combination of above-average ability, creativity, and task commitment. According to this view, someone might have a high IQ and even creative ability, but Renzulli

Gifted children have either high IQ scores or special abilities. This young girl is performing with the Pacific Symphony of Orange County, California.

© Tony Freeman/PhotoEdit Inc.

questions whether they are truly gifted if they are not motivated to use this intelligence. Here we focus on individuals with exceptional IQs.

How early can intellectually gifted children be identified? Giftedness is usually apparent by toddlerhood, according to a longitudinal study by Allen Gottfried and his colleagues (1994). They tracked a large sample of children from age 1 to age 8, determined which children had IQs of 130 or above at age 8, and then looked for differences between these gifted children and other children earlier in life. The gifted children turned out to be identifiable as early as 18 months, primarily by their advanced language skills. Other recent research confirms that early language ability is a good, although not perfect, clue to later intellectual giftedness (Colombo et al., 2009). Gifted children were also highly curious and motivated to learn; they even enjoyed the challenge of taking IQ tests more than most children.

Linda Silverman and her colleagues at the Gifted Development Center have used the Characteristics of Giftedness Scale to identify gifted children (see Gifted Development Center, 2010). They have found that gifted children can be distinguished from average children in the following attributes:

- Rapid learning
- Extensive vocabulary
- Good memory
- Long attention span
- Perfectionism
- Preference for older companions
- Excellent sense of humor
- Early interest in reading
- Strong ability with puzzles and mazes
- Maturity
- Perseverance on tasks

Such early emergence of giftedness is consistent with research showing a strong genetic component for high intellect (see Brant et al., 2009; and Haworth et al., 2009). Still, prediction of giftedness is not perfect, although the prediction of *non*-giftedness is nearly so (Colombo et al., 2009). That is, experts are nearly always correct when they identify a child as not gifted; but among children identified early as gifted, some of these children drift out of this category as they get older (Colombo et al., 2009).

We get a richer understanding of the development of high-IQ children from a major longitudinal study launched in 1921 by Lewis Terman, developer of the Stanford-Binet test (Holahan & Sears, 1995; Oden, 1968; Terman, 1954). The participants were more than 1500 California schoolchildren who were nominated by their teachers as gifted and who had IQs of 140 or higher. It soon became apparent that these high-IQ children (who came to be called *Termites*) were exceptional in many other ways. For example, they had weighed more at birth and had learned to walk and talk sooner than most toddlers. They reached puberty somewhat earlier than average and had better-than-average health. Their teachers rated them as better adjusted and more morally mature than their less intelligent peers. And, although they were no more popular than their classmates, they were quick to take on leadership responsibilities. Taken together, these findings destroy the stereotype that most gifted children are frail, sickly youngsters who are socially inadequate and emotionally immature.

Another demonstration of the personal and social maturity of most gifted children comes from a study of high-IQ children who skipped high school and entered the University of Washington as part of a special program to accelerate their education (see Robinson Center, 2010). Contrary to the common wisdom that gifted children will suffer socially and emotionally if they skip grades and are forced to fit in with much older students, these youngsters showed no signs of maladjustment (see Noble et al., 1999). On several measures of psychological and social maturity and adjustment, they equaled their much older college classmates and similarly gifted students who attended high school. Many of them thrived in college, for the first time finding friends like themselves—friends who were like-minded rather than like-aged (Boothe, Sethna, & Stanley, 2000).

Most of Terman's gifted children remained as remarkable in adulthood as they had been in childhood. Fewer than 5% were rated as seriously maladjusted. Their rates of such problems as ill health, mental illness, alcoholism, and delinquent behavior were but a fraction of those observed in the general population (Terman, 1954), although they were no less likely to divorce (Holahan & Sears, 1995).

The occupational achievements of the men in the sample were impressive. In middle age, 88% were employed in professional or high-level business jobs, compared with 20% of men in the general population (Oden, 1968). As a group, they had taken out more than 200 patents and written some 2000 scientific reports, 100 books, 375 plays or short stories, and more than 300 essays, sketches, magazine articles, and critiques. These findings of notable accomplishment are echoed in recent follow-ups of other adults identified as gifted by age 13 (see Park, Lubinski, & Benbow, 2007). What about the gifted women in Terman's study? Because of the influence of gender-role expectations during the period covered by the study, gifted women achieved less than gifted men vocationally, often interrupting their careers or sacrificing their career goals to raise families. Still, they were more likely to have careers, and distinguished ones, than most women of their generation.

Finally, the Termites aged well. In their 60s and 70s, most of the men and women in the Terman study were highly active, involved, healthy, and happy people (Holahan & Sears, 1995). The men kept working longer than most men do and stayed involved in work even after they retired. The women too led exceptionally active lives. Contrary to the stereotype that gifted individuals burn out early, the Termites continued to burn bright throughout their lives.

Yet just as it is wrong to view intellectually gifted children as emotionally disturbed misfits, it is inaccurate to conclude that intellectually gifted children are models of good adjustment, perfect in every way. Some research suggests that children with IQs closer to 180 than 130 are often unhappy and socially isolated, perhaps because they are so out of step with their peers, and sometimes even have serious problems (Winner, 1996). In *Terman's Kids*, Joel Shurkin (1992) describes several less-than-happy life stories of some of Terman's Termites. A woman who graduated from Stanford at age 17 and was headed for success as a writer became a landlady; an emotionally disturbed boy took cyanide at age 18 after being rejected in love.

Even within this elite group, the quality of the individual's home environment was important. The most well-adjusted and successful adults had highly educated parents who offered them both love and intellectual stimulation (Tomlinson-Keasey & Little, 1990).

Checking Mastery

1. How is intellectual disability defined?
2. What characterizes the typical gifted person?

Making Connections

1. Should gifted, "regular," and intellectually disabled children be educated in the same classroom? What are some of the pros and cons of such integrated education for each of the three groups of children?

9.8 Integrating Cognitive Perspectives

Our account of cognitive development over the life span is now complete. We hope you appreciate that each of the major approaches to the mind that we have considered—the Piagetian cognitive developmental approach and Vygotsky's sociocultural theory described in Chapter 7, the information-processing approach explained in Chapter 8, and the psychometric, or testing, approach, and Sternberg's triarchic model covered here—offers something of value. ●**Table 9.6** lists how these approaches compare on their views of intelligence.

We can summarize the different approaches to cognitive development this way: Piaget has shown that comparing the thought of a preschooler with the thought of an adult is like comparing a caterpillar with a butterfly. Modes of thought change qualitatively with age. Vygotsky has highlighted the importance of culturally transmitted modes of thinking and interactions with others. The information-processing approach has helped researchers understand thinking processes and explain why the young child cannot remember as much information or solve problems as effectively as the adult can. The psychometric approach has told researchers that, if they look at the range of tasks to which the mind can be applied, they can recognize distinct mental abilities that each person consistently displays in greater or lesser amounts. Finally, Sternberg has pushed us to look beyond traditional psychometric tests of intelligence that emphasize analytic skills valued in the classroom to consider creative and practical intelligence alongside the analytical.

● **TABLE 9.6 COMPARISON OF APPROACHES TO INTELLIGENCE**

	Piagetian Cognitive-Developmental Theory	Vygotskian Sociocultural Theory	Information-Processing Approach	Psychometric Approach	Sternberg's Triarchic Model
What Is Intelligence?	Cognitive structures that help people adapt	Tools of culture	Attention, memory, and other mental processes	Mental abilities and scores on IQ tests	Components that allow people to succeed in their lives
What Changes with Age?	Stage of cognitive development	Ability to solve problems without assistance of others and with use of inner speech	Hardware (speed) and software (strategies) of the mind	Mental age (difficulty of problems solved)	Ability to respond to novel problems and automate familiar ones, adapt to current environmental demands, and select appropriate "mental tools" for solving problems
What Is of Most Interest?	Universal changes	Culturally influenced changes and processes	Universal processes	Individual differences	Adapting behavior to environmental challenges

You need not choose one approach and reject the others. Your understanding of the mind is likely to be richer if all four approaches continue to thrive. There are truly many intelligences, and it is foolish to think that a single IQ score can describe the complexities of human cognitive development.

Checking Mastery

1. How does the definition of intelligence vary across the various approaches presented in Chapters 7, 8, and 9?

Making Connections

1. Putting together material from Chapters 7, 8, and 9, how would you describe the cognitive functioning of a typical 70-year-old person? What are the greatest cognitive strengths of older adults, what are their greatest limitations, and how much can an individual do to optimize her functioning?

Chapter Summary

9.1 Defining Intelligence and Creativity

- The psychometric, or testing, approach to cognition defines intelligence as a set of traits that allows some people to think and solve problems more effectively than others. It can be viewed as a hierarchy consisting of a general factor (*g*), broad abilities such as fluid and crystallized intelligence, and many specific abilities.
- The Stanford-Binet and Wechsler scales are the most common intelligence tests and compare an individual's performance on a variety of cognitive tasks with the average performance of age-mates.
- Gardner's theory of multiple intelligences, with its focus on eight distinct forms of intelligence, offers an alternative view. His theory includes these types of intelligence: linguistic, logical–mathematical, musical, spatial, bodily-kinesthetic, interpersonal, intrapersonal, and naturalist.
- Sternberg's triarchic theory of intelligence proposes three components to intelligence. The practical component predicts that intelligent behavior will vary across different sociocultural contexts. According to the creative component, intelligent responses will vary depending on whether problems are novel or routine (automated). Finally, the analytical aspect of intelligence includes the critical thinking skills that a person brings to a problem-solving situation.
- Creativity is the ability to produce novel and socially valuable work. It involves divergent rather than convergent thinking and is often measured in terms of ideational fluency, the sheer number of different (including novel) ideas that a person can generate.

9.2 The Infant

- The Bayley scales include motor, mental, and behavior ratings to assess infant development. Although traditionally used as a measure of infant intelligence, they do not correlate well with later IQ scores.
- Infant measures that capture speed of information processing and preference for novelty are better at predicting later intelligence. Infants who can quickly process information are able to take in more information than those who are slower.

9.3 The Child

- During childhood, IQ scores become more stable so that scores at one point in time are generally consistent with scores obtained at a second point.
- Despite group stability, many individuals show wide variations in their IQ scores over time. Those who gain IQ points often have favorable home environments, whereas disadvantaged children often show a cumulative deficit.
- Creativity increases throughout early childhood but dips during elementary school, possibly in response to societal expectations to conform. Creativity is associated with playfulness, openness to new experiences, and originality but is largely independent of intelligence.

9.4 The Adolescent

- During adolescence, IQ scores are relatively stable and intellectual performance reaches near-adult level. IQ scores are useful at predicting academic achievement of adolescents.
- Levels of creativity rise somewhat in adolescence, although they vary considerably from one individual to another. Some adolescents conform to societal norms and express little creativity, and others show a great deal of innovation.
- Adolescents with exceptional talents or creativity have both talent and motivation on the nature side and environments that foster their talents and value independence on the nurture side.
- Tests of creativity do not always do a good job of predicting creative accomplishment in a specific field.

9.5 The Adult

- IQ scores are correlated with occupational status as well as health in adulthood.
- Both cross-sectional studies and longitudinal studies tend to show age-related decreases in IQ. Schaie's sequential study suggests that (1) date of birth (cohort) influences test performance, (2) no major declines in mental abilities occur until the late 60s or 70s, (3) some abilities (especially fluid ones) decline more than others (especially crystallized ones), and (4) not all people's abilities decline.
- A few adults display wisdom, or exceptional insight into complex life problems, which requires a rich knowledge base along with particular personality traits and cognitive styles and is influenced more by experience than age.
- Creative output increases sharply from early to middle adulthood, and although it then drops somewhat, it remains above the level where it started in young adulthood. Creativity varies from one field to another. Creative output may drop off in older adulthood because people have already generated and expressed their creative potential.

9.6 Factors That Influence IQ Scores

- The Flynn effect describes a global increase in IQ scores over the past century that is likely the result of better nutrition, living conditions, and education.
- Individual differences in IQ at a given age are linked to genetic factors and to intellectually stimulating qualities of the home environment such as parental involvement and responsive stimulation.
- Social class impacts IQ scores, raising the issue of middle-class testing bias. Children who are moved from low to higher socioeconomic status homes show an increase in IQ scores.
- Racial and ethnic differences in IQ also exist, with African American and Hispanic children typically scoring, on average, lower than European American children. Motivational differences, stereotype threat, genetic factors, and environment have all been considered as contributors.

9.7 The Extremes of Intelligence

- The extremes of intelligence are represented by intellectual disability at one end of the continuum and giftedness at the other end.
- Intellectual disability is defined by deficits in adaptive behavior with low IQ scores. Functioning varies by level of disability and is worse when accompanied by other conditions. Most intellectually disabled adults live in the community, either in group homes or with their families.
- Giftedness has most often been defined by high IQ scores, although more recent definitions recognize special talents not measured by traditional IQ tests. Life outcomes for gifted people are generally above average.

9.8 Integrating Cognitive Perspectives

- Five major approaches to cognitive development have been presented in Chapters 7, 8, and 9. These include Piaget's focus on qualitatively different stages of thought and Vygotsky's emphasis on culturally transmitted modes of thought. The information-processing approach reveals how memory and problem solving are influenced by characteristics of the person such as age and task factors such as complexity. The psychometric approach defines cognitive abilities in measurable ways, illustrating that people have more or less of distinct mental abilities. Sternberg's triarchic theory adds creative and practical intelligence to the more traditional analytic intelligence.

Checking Mastery Answers

For answers to Checking Mastery questions, visit **www.cengagebrain.com**

Key Terms

psychometric approach **289**
fluid intelligence **289**
crystallized intelligence **289**
mental age **290**
Stanford-Binet Intelligence Scale **290**
intelligence quotient (IQ) **290**
test norms **290**
Wechsler Scales **290**
normal distribution **290**
standard deviation **290**
savant syndrome **291**
triarchic theory of intelligence **291**
Sternberg's Triarchic Abilities Test (STAT) **292**
practical component **292**
creative component **292**
automatization **292**
culture bias **292**
analytic component **292**
successful intelligence **293**

creativity **293**
convergent thinking **294**
divergent thinking **294**
Bayley Scales of Infant Development **295**
developmental quotient (DQ) **296**
cumulative-deficit hypothesis **297**
terminal drop **305**
wisdom **305**
Flynn effect **309**
Home Observation for Measurement of the Environment (HOME) inventory **310**
child poverty **312**
stereotype threat **313**
intellectual disability **315**
giftedness **316**

Media Resources

Psychology CourseMate

Access an integrated eBook and chapter-specific learning tools including flashcards, quizzes, videos, and more. Go to **www.cengagebrain.com**

Classics in the History of Psychology: Binet on Intelligence

This page outlines Binet's conception of the Psychological Method and Measuring Scale of Intelligence. It also features a number of tests intended to measure different elements of intelligence. To access, see "web links" in Psychology CourseMate at www.cengagebrain.com

Free IQ Test

Check your IQ with this free online test. To access, see "web links" in Psychology CourseMate at www.cengagebrain.com

Understanding the DATA:
Exercises on the Web

www.cengagebrain.com

For additional insight on the data presented in this chapter, try out the exercises for these figures in Psychology CourseMate at

www.cengagebrain.com:

Figure 9.2 A normal distribution curve showing traditional intelligence testing scores in the classic bell shape around the average score of 100.

Figure 9.9 Percentage of total works produced in each decade of the lives of eminent creators. The "scholarship" group includes historians and philosophers; the "sciences" category includes natural and physical scientists, inventors, and mathematicians; the "arts" creators include architects, musicians, dramatists, poets, and the like.

Figure 9.10 Over a 50-year period, test scores on several measures of intelligence have risen substantially, illustrating the "Flynn effect." Are people really getting smarter? What factors might explain such a rise in intelligence test scores?

CengageNOW

www.cengagebrain.com

Go to www.cengagebrain.com to link to CengageNOW, your online study tool. First take the Pre-Test for this chapter to get your Personalized Study Plan, which will identify topics you need to review and direct you to online resources. Then take the Post-Test to determine what concepts you have mastered and what you still need work on.

Language Development and Education

As the cool stream gushed over one hand, she [Annie] spelled into the other the word water, first slowly, then rapidly. I stood still, my whole attention fixed upon the motions of her fingers. Suddenly I felt a misty consciousness as of something forgotten—a thrill of returning thought; and somehow the mystery of language was revealed to me. I knew then that W-A-T-E-R meant the wonderful cool something that was flowing over my hand. . . . I left the well-house eager to learn. Everything had a name, and each name gave birth to a new thought. As we returned to the house every object which I touched seemed to quiver with life (Keller, 1954, p. 15).

Ask Yourself This

1. How is it that a complex behavior such as language can emerge so early in life with little or no formal instruction?

2. What theories have been proposed to explain the emergence of language?

3. What are the neurobiological underpinnings that support the complex behavior of language?

4. What is the importance of achievement motivation and how does it emerge and change over the course of childhood and adolescence?

5. What can be done to foster healthy levels of achievement motivation over the life span?

6. Why do some children struggle with reading whereas others quickly become skilled readers?

7. What distinguishes an effective school from one that is less effective?

8. What does cross-cultural research suggest in terms of maximizing students' success in mathematics and science education?

Perhaps the most important milestone in development is mastering some type of language. Consider how the world changed for Helen Keller, deaf and blind from a young age, when she finally realized that every object, every person, every concept could be represented with a symbol. From this point on, she was able to communicate with the people around her and participate in the world in ways that were not available without a tool such as sign or spoken language. As you learned in Chapter 7, psychologist Lev Vygotsky argued that language is the primary vehicle through which adults pass culturally valued modes of thinking and problem solving to their children. He also believed that language is our most important tool of thinking.

In this chapter, we begin by examining the what, when, and how of language acquisition. Basic language skills become established largely through an informal education system consisting of parents, other grownups, peers, and even the media. We then consider formal education, which uses basic language skills to cultivate the reading, writing, thinking, and problem-solving skills that allow individuals to become fully functioning members of society. Getting the most out of education requires more than acquiring language and literacy skills, however. As Terrel Bell, former secretary of education, asserted: "There are three things to remember about education. The first one is motivation. The second one is motivation. The third one is motivation" (quoted in Maehr & Meyer, 1997, p. 372). Thus, we also examine achievement motivation and its relationship to education and educational outcomes.

10.1 Mastering Language

Although language is one of the most intricate forms of knowledge we will ever acquire, all normal children master a language early in life. Indeed, many infants are talking before they can walk. Can language be complex, then? It certainly can be. Linguists (scholars who study language) define **language** as a communication system in which a limited number of signals—sounds or letters (or gestures, in the case of the sign language used by deaf people)—can be combined according to agreed-upon rules to produce an infinite number of messages. Linguists have yet to fully describe the rules of English or of any of the other 6,000 or so languages that exist throughout the world. To master a spoken language such as English, a child must learn basic sounds, how sounds are combined to form words, how words are combined to form meaningful statements, what words and sentences mean, and how to use language effectively in social interactions. Let's look more closely at the pieces of this complex puzzle, addressing *what* must be mastered, *when* it is learned, and *how* it is accomplished.

What Must Be Mastered?

Every human language must have words (symbols) that represent the objects, people, ideas, and so on that are relevant to the community. In addition, there must be a system of rules to organize how the words are used and combined to facilitate communication among members of the community. Perhaps the most fundamental system involves **phonemes,** which are the basic units of *sound* that can change the meaning of a word. Substituting the phoneme /p/ for /b/ in the word *bit* changes the meaning of the word. Although there are 26 letters in the English alphabet, there are more phonemes than this because letters can be pronounced different ways. Trying to identify the precise number of phonemes in a language, though, is like trying to identify the exact number of colors that exist in a rainbow; there are numerous subtleties and interpretations. In addition to individual phonemes, languages also specify how phonemes can be combined. In English, for example, we can combine /b/ and /r/ to say "brat" but we cannot combine /b/ with /m/ to produce "bmat."

Languages also have a system for organizing the **morphemes,** the basic units of *meaning* that exist in a word. Some words consist of just one morpheme: *view*. But we can add another morpheme, *re*, and the meaning of the word changes (*review*). Add a different morpheme, *pre*, and the meaning changes again (*preview*). Morphemes are not the same as syllables: a word with multiple syllables, such as the three-syllable *crocodile*, can still consist of one morpheme if it cannot be further broken down into a smaller meaningful unit. To convey the meaning of what we intend when we say "crocodile," we have to include all three syllables.

An important step in language acquisition is mastering its **syntax,** the systematic rules for forming sentences. Consider these three sentences: (1) Fang Fred bit. (2) Fang bit Fred. (3) Fred bit Fang. The first violates the rules of English sentence structure or syntax, although this word order would be acceptable in German. The second and third are both grammatical English sentences, but their different word orders convey different meanings. Understanding these different meanings reflects the **semantics** of language. To understand the sentence "Sherry was green with jealousy," we must move beyond the literal meaning of each word, which would suggest that Sherry was the color green, to the meaning that is created when we combine these words into this particular sentence.

Finally, we must understand something of the **pragmatics** of language—rules for specifying how language is used appropriately in different social contexts. That is, children (and adults) have to learn when to say what to whom. They must learn to communicate effectively by taking into account who the listener is, what the listener already knows, and what the listener needs or wants to hear. "Give me that cookie!" may be grammatical English, but the child is far more likely to win Grandma's heart (not to mention a cookie) with a polite "May I please try one of your yummy cookies, Grandma?"

In addition to these features of language, producing meaningful speech also involves **prosody,** or *how* the sounds are produced (Patel & Brayton, 2009). Prosody has been called the "melody" of speech because it includes pitch or intonation, the stress or accentuation of certain syllables in a word or certain words in a sentence, and the duration or timing of speech. A child may say "dog" with little change in pitch, perhaps to make a statement meaning *There is a dog.* By raising his voice at the end of the word, though, the meaning is changed to a question, "Dog?" A parent may produce a loud, short, "NO!" to stop a child from running into the street, but produce a long "nooo" to perhaps sarcastically make a point with their teenager. Even young infants are sensitive to the prosody of speech and can distinguish between two languages based on their rhythms (Saffran, Werker, & Werner, 2006).

Thus, the "what" of language includes knowing the phonemes and morphemes and how these can be combined, the syntax for turning words into sentences, the semantics for understanding the meaning of words and sentences, and the pragmatics for how to best use language to suit the context and our conversational partner. With this understanding of the components of language, we can now turn our attention to the "when" of language acquisition.

When Does Language Develop?

For the first 10–13 months of life, infants are not yet capable of speaking meaningful words. But they are building up to that achievement by listening to the speech around them and by cooing and babbling.

Before the First Words

As you learned in Chapter 6, newborns seem to tune in to human speech immediately and show a preference for speech over nonspeech sounds and for their native language, which they listened to in the womb, over other languages (Gervain & Mehler, 2010; Kisilevsky et al., 2009). Very young infants can distinguish between phonemes such as /b/ and /p/ or /d/ and /t/ (Eimas, 1975a). Before they ever speak a word, infants are also becoming sensitive to the fact that pauses in speech fall between clauses, phrases, and words rather than in the middle of these important language units (Fisher & Tokura, 1996; Myers et al., 1996). By 7½ months, infants demonstrate **word segmentation** ability when they detect a target word in a stream of speech (see Gervain & Mehler, 2010). Thus, when they hear the sentence "The cat scratched the dog's nose," they understand that this is not one long word but a string of six words. Word segmentation is a formidable task, but infants seem to be sensitive to a number of cues marking the boundaries between words and this skill improves throughout the first 2 years of life (Saffran, Werker, & Werner, 2006).

A father draws his new infant into a "conversation." What does the infant gain from these sorts of interactions?

What about producing sounds? From birth, infants produce sounds—cries, burps, grunts, and sneezes. These sounds help exercise the vocal cords and give infants an opportunity to learn how airflow and different mouth and tongue positions affect sounds. By 5 months, infants realize that their sounds have an effect on their caregivers' behavior (Goldstein, Schwade, & Bornstein, 2009). Parents respond to as many as 50% of prelinguistic sounds as if they were genuine efforts to communicate (Goldstein et al., 2009; McCune et al., 1996). For instance, in response to her infant's hiccup sound, a mother replies, "My goodness! What's going on in there? Huh? Tell Mommy." The mother draws her infant into a sort of dialogue. Such prelinguistic sounds, and the feedback infants receive, eventually pave the way for meaningful speech sounds (Hoff, 2009).

The next milestone in vocalization, around 6–8 weeks of age, is **cooing**—repeating vowel-like sounds such as "oooooh" and "aaaaah." Babies coo when they are content and often in response to being spoken to in a happy voice. Do infants this age understand the words spoken to them? Not likely—they primarily respond to the intonation or "melody" of speech (Hirsh-Pasek, Golinkoff, & Hollich, 1999). Parents can say some rather nasty things to their young infants ("You're driving me nuts today!") as long as they say them with a happy voice, illustrating again, the importance of prosody.

Around 3–4 months, infants expand their vocal range considerably as they begin to produce consonant sounds. They enter a period of **babbling** between about 4 and 6 months, repeating consonant–vowel combinations such as "baba" or "dadadada," in what Jean Piaget would call a primary circular reaction—the repeating of an interesting noise for the pleasure of making it.

Up to about 6 months, infants all over the world, even deaf ones, sound pretty much alike, but the effects of experience soon become apparent. Without auditory feedback, deaf infants fall behind hearing infants in their ability to produce well-formed syllables (Oller & Eilers, 1988). By the time infants are about 8 months old, they babble with something of an accent; adults can often tell which language infants have been listening to from the sound of their babbling (Poulin-Dubois & Goodz, 2001). These advanced babblers increasingly restrict their sounds to phonemes in the language they are hearing, and they pick up the intonation patterns of that language (Hoff, 2009; Snow, 2006). Once these intonation patterns are added to an infant's babbles, the utterances sound a great deal like real speech until you listen closely and realize they are truly just babbles (Hoff, 2009).

As they attempt to master the semantics of language, infants come to understand many words before they can produce them. That is, *comprehension* (or reception) is ahead of *production* (or expression) in language development. Ten-month-olds can comprehend, on average, about 50 words but do not yet produce any of these (Golinkoff & Hirsh-Pasek, 2006). This early understanding of words is related to academic achievement in elementary school: 10-month-olds who understand more words are later the children who get better grades (Hohm et al., 2007).

Shortly before speaking their first true words, as they approach 1 year, infants really seem to understand familiar words. How do they figure out what words mean? When Mom points to a small, four-legged furry animal and says, "There's Furrball,"

how do infants learn that "Furrball" refers to this particular cat and not to its movement or to its tail or to a general category of furry animals? It turns out that infants and toddlers use a variety of cues in learning to connect words with their referents—the objects, people, or ideas represented by a name. At first, 10-month-old infants rely on attentional cues such as how important an object seems to be from their perspective (Pruden et al., 2006). Thus, if their attention is captured by the ball in front of them, they may assume that mom's verbalizations refer to this ball. By 12 months of age, though, their reliance on personal relevance is decreasing and infants begin to use social and linguistic cues to learn words. One important social cue is **joint attention,** or social eye gaze—two people looking at the same thing (Carpenter, Nagell, & Tomasello, 1998; Woodward & Markman, 1998). Infants listen to parents repeatedly labeling and pointing at objects, directing their gaze, and otherwise making clear the connection between words and their referents (Hollich, Hirsh-Pasek, & Golinkoff, 2000). If Mom says "cat" when both she and her child are looking at the furry animal, then this likely is the referent for the label.

Finally, children use the process of **syntactic bootstrapping** when they use the syntax of a sentence—that is, where a word is placed in a sentence—to determine the meaning of the word (Naigles & Swensen, 2010). In the earlier example, if mom had said, "There's *a* furrball" or "The cat is hacking up a furrball" instead of the original "There's Furrball," the syntactic placement—how *furball* was used in the sentence—would have changed the meaning of the word.

The First Words

An infant's first meaningful word, spoken around 1 year, is a special event for parents. First words have been called **holophrases** because a single word often conveys an entire sentence's worth of meaning. These single-word "sentences" can serve different communication functions depending on the way they are said and the context in which they are said (Tomasello, 2009). For example, 17-month-old Shelley used the word *ghetti* (spaghetti) in three different ways over a 5-minute period. First, she pointed to the pan on the stove and seemed to be asking, "Is that spaghetti?" Later, the function of her holophrase was to name the spaghetti when shown the contents of the pan, as in "It's spaghetti." Finally, there was little question that she was requesting spaghetti when she tugged at her companion's sleeve as he was eating and used the word in a whining tone.

Although there are limits to the meaning that can be packed into a single word and its accompanying intonation pattern and gestures, 1-year-olds in the holophrastic stage of language development seem to have mastered such basic language functions as naming, questioning, requesting, and demanding. When they begin to use words as symbols, they also begin to use nonverbal symbols—gestures such as pointing, raising their arms to signal "up," or panting heavily to say "dog" (Goldin-Meadow, 2009).

What do 1-year-olds talk about? They talk mainly about familiar objects and actions—those things that they encounter every day and are important to them (• **Table 10.1**). Katherine Nelson (1973) studied 18 infants as they learned their first

What is the likely content (that is, semantics) and form (that is, grammar or syntax) of this boy's language?

TABLE 10.1 EXAMPLES OF WORDS USED BY CHILDREN YOUNGER THAN 20 MONTHS

Category	Words
Sound effects	*baa baa, meow, moo, ouch, uh-oh, woof, yum-yum*
Food and drink	*apple, banana, cookie, cheese, cracker, juice, milk, water*
Animals	*bear, bird, bunny, dog, cat, cow, duck, fish, kitty, horse, pig, puppy*
Body parts and clothing	*diaper, ear, eye, foot, hair, hand, hat, mouth, nose, toe, tooth, shoe*
House and outdoors	*blanket, chair, cup, door, flower, keys, outside, spoon, tree, TV*
People	*baby, daddy, gramma, grampa, mommy, [child's own name]*
Toys and vehicles	*ball, balloon, bike, boat, book, bubbles, plane, truck, toy*
Actions	*down, eat, go, sit, up*
Games and routines	*bath, bye, hi, night-night, no, peek-a-boo, please, shhh, thank you, yes*
Adjectives and descriptors	*all gone, cold, dirty, hot*

SOURCE: From Jean Berko Gleason, *The development of language,* 6th ed., Table 4.1, p. 122. Copyright © 2005. Reprinted by permission of Pearson Education, Inc.

50 English words and found that nearly two-thirds of these early words were common nouns representing objects and people that the children interacted with daily *(mommy, kitty)*. These objects were nearly all things that the children could manipulate *(bottles, balls)* or that were capable of moving on their own *(animals, trucks)*. Children also acquire words that facilitate social interactions *(hello, bye-bye, no)*. Across quite diverse languages, researchers observe a noun bias in young children's early vocabularies (Bornstein & Cote, 2004). It may be easier for young children to decipher nouns and their referents in the language around them, and adults tend to use more nouns in their conversations with children (Pan & Uccelli, 2009).

Initial language acquisition proceeds literally one word at a time. Three or four months may pass before the child has a vocabulary of 10 words, slowly acquired one by one. Then, in what is called the **vocabulary spurt,** around 18 months of age, when the child has mastered about 30–50 words, the pace of word learning quickens dramatically (Bloom, 1998; Carroll, 2008). Steven Pinker (1995), an experimental psychologist who has studied and written extensively on all aspects of language development, estimates that a new word is acquired every 2 hours during this time (see also Tomasello, 2003)! At 20 months, children are producing an average of 150 words, and just 4 months later, this has doubled to 300 words (Camaioni, 2004). What changes? During the vocabulary spurt, toddlers seem to arrive at the critical realization, as Helen Keller did, that everything has a name and that by learning the names of things they can share what they are thinking with someone else and vice versa (Bloom & Tinker, 2001). The vocabulary spurt also seems to follow the switch from reliance on attentional cues to the more effective use of social cues such as joint attention (Golinkoff & Hirsh-Pasek, 2006).

With such a rapidly increasing vocabulary, it should come as no surprise that children sometimes make mistakes. Although they rarely get the meaning entirely wrong, they often use a word too broadly or too narrowly (Pan & Uccelli, 2009). One error is **overextension,** or using a word to refer to too wide a range of objects or events, as when a 2-year-old calls all furry, four-legged animals "doggie." The second, and opposite, error is **underextension,** as when a child initially uses the word *doggie* to refer only to basset hounds like the family pet. Notice that both overextension and underextension are examples of Piaget's concept of assimilation, using existing concepts to interpret new experiences. Getting semantics right seems to be mainly a matter of discriminating similarities and differences—for example, categorizing animals on the basis of size, shape, the sounds they make, and other perceptual features (Clark & Clark, 1977). By 2½–3 years of age, these sorts of semantic errors begin to disappear from children's conversations.

But might children know more about the world than their semantic errors suggest? Yes. Two-year-olds who say "doggie" when they see a cow will point to the cow rather than the dog when asked to find the cow (Naigles & Gelman, 1995; Thompson & Chapman, 1977). Children may overextend the meaning of certain words such as *doggie* not because they misunderstand word meanings but because they want to communicate, have only a small vocabulary with which to do so, and have not yet learned to call something a "whatchamacallit" when they cannot come up with the word for it (Naigles & Gelman, 1995).

You must be careful about applying these generalizations about early language acquisition to all children because they mask large individual differences in speaking style (Nelson, 2007). As ■ **Figure 10.1** shows, one 24-month-old may have a vocabulary of approximately 50 words, and another may be able to produce more than 500 words (Fenson et al., 1994). Some children use a referential style—lots of nouns referring to objects, such as "ball" and "truck." Others seem to treat language as a social tool; they use an expressive style of speaking with more personal pronouns and memorized social routines such as "bye-bye" and "I want it" (Nelson, 2007). Culture exerts some influence: infants learning English use many nouns and few verbs in their early speech, whereas infants learning Korean use more verbs (Gopnik & Choi, 1995). More important, differences in the daily language experiences of children contribute to the differences in their speech. Both quantity of speech (how many words the child hears in the home) and quality of speech (how sophisticated the speech is) affect young children's vocabularies (Hoff, 2009; Weizman & Snow, 2001). So individual differences in language acquisition are the norm rather than the exception.

Telegraphic Speech

The next step in language development, normally occurring at 18–24 months of age, is combining two words into a simple sentence. Toddlers all over the world use two-word sentences to express the same basic ideas (● **Table 10.2**). Early combinations of two, three, or more words are sometimes called **telegraphic speech** because, like telegrams, these sentences contain critical content words and omit frills such as articles, prepositions, and auxiliary verbs.

It is ungrammatical in adult English to say "No want" or "Where ball." However, these two-word sentences are not just random word combinations or mistakes; they reflect children's developing understanding of syntax. Psycholinguists such as Lois Bloom (1998) believe it is appropriate to describe children's early sentences in terms of a **functional grammar**—one that emphasizes the semantic relationships among words, the meanings being expressed, and the functions served by sentences (such as naming, questioning, or commanding). For example, young children often use the same word order to convey different meanings. "Mommy nose" might mean "That's Mommy's nose" in one context, but for one 22-month-old girl one afternoon it meant "Mommy, I've just wiped my runny nose the length of the living room couch." Word order sometimes does matter: "Billy hit" and "Hit Billy" may mean different things. Body language and tone of voice also communicate meanings, such as when a child points and whines to request ice cream, not merely to note its existence.

Between ages 2 and 5, children experience a dramatic increase in the number and type of sentences they produce. Consider 3-year-old Kyle's reply to his mother after she suggests that he release a bug:

After I hold him, then I'll take the bug back to his friends. Mommy, where did the bug go? Mommy, I didn't know where the bug go. Find it. Maybe Winston's on it [the family dog]. Winston, get off the bug! [Kyle spots the bug and picks it up. His mother again asks him to "let the bug go back to his friends."] He does not want to go to his friends. [Kyle drops the bug and squashes it, much to his mother's horror.] I stepped on it and it will not go to his friends.

Compared with a child in the telegraphic stage, Kyle's sentences are much longer and more grammatically complex, although not free of errors, and he is better able to participate in the give-and-take of conversation. Kyle has also begun to add the little function words such as articles and prepositions that are often missing in the earlier telegraphic sentences (Hoff, 2009).

How do people know when children are mastering new rules? Oddly enough, their progress sometimes reveals itself in new "mistakes." A child who has been saying "feet" and "went" may suddenly start to say "foots" and "goed." Does this represent a step backward? Not at all. The child was probably using the correct irregular forms at first by imitating adult speech with-

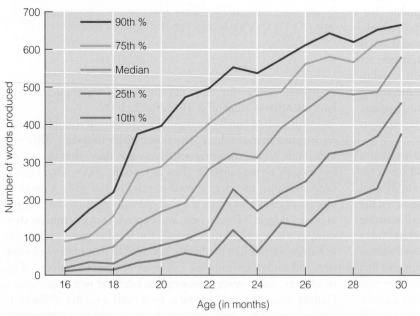

■ **FIGURE 10.1** The range of individual differences in vocabulary size from 16 to 30 months. Source: From Fenson L., et al., Variability in early communicative development. *Monographs of the Society for Research in Child Development, 59* (Serial No. 242). Copyright © 1994. Reprinted with permission of John Wiley & Sons, Inc.

TABLE 10.2 TWO-WORD SENTENCES SERVE SIMILAR FUNCTIONS IN DIFFERENT LANGUAGES

Function of Sentence	Language	
	English	German
To locate or name	*There book*	*Buch da* (book there)
To demand	*More milk*	*Mehr milch* (more milk)
To negate	*No wet*	*Nicht blasen* (not blow)
To indicate possession	*My shoe*	*Mein ball* (my ball)
To modify or qualify	*Pretty dress*	*Armer wauwau* (poor doggie)
To question	*Where ball*	*Wo ball* (where ball)

SOURCE: Adapted from Slobin, 1979.

out understanding the meaning of plurality or verb tense. The use of "foots" and "goed" is a breakthrough: the child has inferred the morphological rules of adding -*s* to pluralize nouns and adding -*ed* to signal past tense. At first, however, the youngster engages in **overregularization,** overapplying the rules to cases in which the proper form is irregular. When the child masters exceptions to the rules, she will say "feet" and "went" once more.

Children must also master rules for creating variations of the basic declarative sentence; that is, they must learn the rules for converting a basic idea such as "I am eating pizza" into such forms as questions ("Am I eating pizza?"), negative sentences ("I am not eating pizza"), and imperatives ("Eat the pizza!"). The prominent linguist Noam Chomsky (1968, 1975) drew attention to the child's learning of these rules by proposing that language be described in terms of a **transformational grammar,** or rules of syntax for transforming basic underlying thoughts into a variety of sentence forms.

How do young children learn to phrase the questions that they so frequently ask to fuel their cognitive growth? The earliest questions often consist of nothing more than two- or three-word sentences with rising intonation ("See kitty?"). Sometimes *wh-* words such as *what* or *where* appear ("Where kitty?"). During the second stage of question asking, children begin to use auxiliary, or helping, verbs, but their questions are of this form: "What Daddy is eating?" "Where the kitty is going?" Their understanding of transformation rules is still incomplete (Tager-Flusberg, 2005). Finally, they learn the transformation rule that calls for moving the auxiliary verb ahead of the subject (as in the adultlike sentence "What is Daddy eating?").

Later Language Development

School-age children improve their pronunciation skills, produce longer and more complex sentences, and continue to expand their vocabularies. The average first-grader starts school with a vocabulary of about 10,000 words and adds somewhere between 5 and 13 new words a day throughout the elementary-school years (Anglin, 1993; Bloom, 1998). During adolescence, with the help of formal operational thought, teens become better able to understand and define abstract terms such as ethics. They also become better able to infer meanings that are not explicitly stated (Beal, 1990).

School-age children also begin to think about and manipulate language in ways previously impossible (Ely, 2005; Klein, 1996). They can, for example, interpret passive sentences such as "Goofy was liked by Donald" and conditional sentences such as "If Goofy had come, Donald would have been delighted" (Boloh & Champaud, 1993; Sudhalter & Braine, 1985). Command of grammar continues to improve through adolescence; teenagers' spoken and written sentences become increasingly long and complex (Christie, 2002).

Throughout childhood and adolescence, advances in cognitive development are accompanied by advances in language and communication skills. For example, as children become less cognitively egocentric, they are more able to take the perspective of their listeners (Hoff, 2009). Middle childhood and adolescence also bring increased **metalinguistic awareness,** or knowledge of language as a system (Ely, 2005). Children with metalinguistic awareness understand the concept of words and can define words (semantics). Adolescents are increasingly able to define abstract words (such as *courage* or *pride*) but are still outperformed by adults on difficult words (such as *idleness* or *goodness*; Nippold et al., 1999). Development of metalinguistic awareness also means that children and adolescents can distinguish between grammatically correct and grammatically incorrect sentences (syntax) and can understand how language can be altered to fit the needs of the specific social context in which it is used (pragmatics).

What happens to language skills during adulthood? Adults simply hold onto the knowledge of the phonology they gained as children, although elders can have difficulty distinguishing speech sounds (such as /*b*/ from /*p*/) if they have hearing impairments or deficits in the cognitive abilities required to make out what they hear (Thornton & Light, 2006). Adults also retain their knowledge of grammar or syntax. Older adults tend to use less complex sentences than younger adults do, however. Also, those with memory difficulties may have trouble understanding sentences that are highly complex syntactically (for example, "The children warned about road hazards refused to fix the bicycle of the boy who crashed"); they may not be able to remember the beginning of the sentence by the time they get to the end (Kemtes & Kemper, 1997; Stine, Soederberg, & Morrow, 1996).

Meanwhile, knowledge of the semantics of language, of word meanings, often expands during adulthood, at least until people are in their 70s or 80s (Obler, 2005; Schaie, 1996). After all, adults gain experience with the world from year to year, so it is not surprising that their vocabularies continue to grow and that they enrich their understandings of the meanings of words. However, older adults more often have the "tip-of-the-tongue" experience of not being able to recall the name of an object (or especially a person's name) when they need it (Thornton & Light, 2006). This problem is a matter of not being able to retrieve information stored in memory rather than a matter of no longer knowing the words. In order to maintain fluency in the face of these retrieval problems, older adults speak a little more slowly and plan their choice of words further in advance than when they were younger (Spieler & Griffin, 2006).

Adults also refine their pragmatic use of language—adjusting it to different social and professional contexts (Obler, 2005). Physicians, for example, must develop a communication style that is effective with their patients. Partners who have been together for years often develop a unique way of communicating with one another that is distinctly different from how they communicate with others. Overall, command of language holds up well in later life unless the individual experiences major declines in cognitive functioning (Kemper & Mitzner, 2001; Stine et al., 1996).

How Does Language Develop?

We cannot help but be awed by the pace at which children master the fundamentals of language during their first 5 years of life, but we must also appreciate the continued growth that occurs in childhood and adolescence and the maintenance of language skills throughout the life span. In this section, we attempt to understand *how* these remarkable skills are acquired and maintained, first by examining the neurobiological underpinnings of language, and second by revisiting the nature–nurture issue as it relates to language development.

Neurobiology of Language

Until recently, our understanding of how the brain supported language function came from studying individuals who had the misfortune to sustain brain damage and an associated loss of some aspect of language (see Shafer & Garrido-Nag, 2009). From these studies, researchers concluded that language was largely a product of left hemisphere activity, with a region called Broca's area associated with speech production and another region called Wernicke's area associated with comprehension of language (■ **Figure 10.2**). Thanks to improved methodologies such as functional magnetic resonance imaging (fMRI) and event-related potentials (ERPs), we are beginning to craft a more precise picture of how neural activity relates to and supports language (Bookheimer, 2002; Friederici, 2009; Kuhl & Rivera-Gaxiola, 2008).

We have learned that human brains show remarkably consistent organization for language across the life span, with the left hemisphere showing increased activity when listening to speech and the right hemisphere active when processing the melody or rhythm of speech (Gervain & Mehler, 2010). Adults attempting to learn new words show different patterns of brain activity depending on whether they are successful or not: those who are successful show more connectivity between the left and right

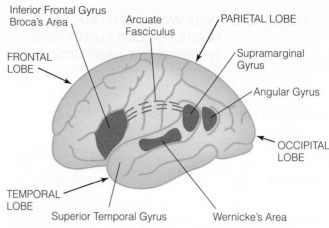

■ **FIGURE 10.2** Brain regions associated with language.

supramarginal gyrus, located in the parietal lobe, one of four main brain regions (Veroude et al., 2010). Studies using fMRI show that areas in both the left and right hemispheres are active in women's brains when processing language, whereas activity in men's brains is more typically localized in the left hemisphere (Shaywitz et al., 1995). We have also learned that Wernicke's area and Broca's area are connected with a band of fibers. Typically, incoming language is processed—comprehended—in Wernicke's area and then sent to Broca's area via these fibers (called the arcuate fasciculus) to be turned into speech. Damage to this band of fibers can cause a type of **aphasia,** or language disorder, in which the person might hear and understand linguistic input but be unable to vocally repeat the information. Finally, there is evidence that neurons in Broca's area are activated not only when producing speech but also when a person sees or hears another person speaking (Fogassi & Ferrari, 2007). This may facilitate language learning and suggests the presence of a mirror neuron system, which we discuss in more detail in Chapter 13.

What are the theoretical implications of these neurobiological findings? To some, they suggest that language is hard-wired and innate. Yet others believe that language acquisition intuitively seems more a matter of nurture: children imitate what they hear, receiving praise when they get it right and being corrected when they get it wrong. But consider what Steven Pinker (1995) concludes about the nature versus nurture of language acquisition:

> "All humans talk but no house pets or house plants do, no matter how pampered, so heredity must be involved in language. But a child growing up in Japan speaks Japanese whereas the same child brought up in California would speak English, so the environment is also crucial. Thus, there is no question about whether heredity or environment is involved in language, or even whether one or the other is "more important." Instead, language acquisition might be our best hope of finding out how heredity and environment interact." (p. 136)

So as we examine the learning, nativist, and interactionist positions in the next section, we do so not to determine *whether* each contributes to language but to understand *how* each contributes.

Nurture: the Contributions of the Environment and Learning

How does the environment influence language development? It is no accident that children learn the language their parents speak, down to the regional accent. Children learn the words they hear spoken by others—even when the words are not spoken directly to them (Floor & Akhtar, 2006). For example, 18-month-olds can learn object labels and verbs by "eavesdropping" on a conversation between two adults (so be careful about what you say within ear-shot of toddlers). In addition, young children are more likely to start using new words if they are reinforced for doing so than if they are not (Whitehurst & Valdez-Menchaca, 1988). Finally, children whose caregivers frequently encourage them to converse by asking questions, making requests, and the like are more advanced in early language development than those whose parents are less conversational (Bohannon & Bonvillian, 2009).

However, learning theorists, with their focus on environment, have had an easier time explaining the development of phonology and semantics than accounting for how syntactical rules are acquired. For example, after analyzing conversations between mothers and young children, Roger Brown, Courtney Cazden, and Ursula Bellugi (1969) discovered that a mother's approval or disapproval depended on the truth value or semantics of what was said, not on the grammatical correctness of the statement. Thus, when a child looking at a cow says, "Her cow" (accurate but grammatically incorrect), Mom is likely to provide reinforcement ("That's right, darling"), whereas if the child were to say, "There's a dog, Mommy" (grammatically correct but un-truthful), Mom would probably correct the child ("No, sweetie—that's a cow"). Similarly, parents seem just as likely to reward a grammatically primitive request ("Want milk") as a well-formed version of the same idea (Brown & Hanlon, 1970). Such evidence casts doubt on the idea that the major mechanism behind syntactic development is reinforcement.

Could imitation of adults account for the acquisition of syntax? You have already seen that young children produce many sentences they are unlikely to have heard adults using ("All gone cookie," overregularizations such as "It swimmed," and so on). These kinds of sentences are not imitations. Also, an adult is likely to get nowhere in teaching syntax by saying, "Repeat after me," unless the child already has at least some knowledge of the grammatical form to be learned (Baron, 1992; McNeill, 1970). Young children frequently imitate other people's speech, and this may help them get to the point of producing new structures. But it is hard to see how imitation and reinforcement alone can account for the learning of grammatical rules.

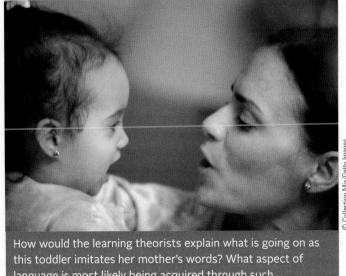

How would the learning theorists explain what is going on as this toddler imitates her mother's words? What aspect of language is most likely being acquired through such experiences?

Nature: the Contributions of Biology

On the nature side are the nativists who minimize the role of the language environment and focus instead on the role of the child's biologically programmed capacities to acquire language (see, for example, Chomsky, 1995; Pinker, 1999; see also Valian, 2009). Noam Chomsky (2000) proposed that humans have a unique genetic capacity to learn language. According to this view, humans are equipped with knowledge of a **universal grammar,** a system of common rules and properties for learning any of the world's languages. Universal grammar offers a limited number of possibilities for forming language. As many as 75% of the world's languages have the basic word order of subject-verb-object (SVO; English, for example) or subject-object-verb (SOV; Japanese, for example). Another 15% have a word order that begins with a verb, whereas word order that begins with an object is quite unusual (Goodluck, 2009). Thus, most of the world's languages are based on a grammatical system that starts with a subject, followed by a verb and then an object or by an object and then a verb.

Universal grammar provides the framework for acquiring a language, but it is not language specific. Exposure to language activates the areas of the brain collectively called the **language acquisition device (LAD),** which sifts through language, applies the universal rules, and begins tailoring the system to the specifics of the language spoken in the young child's environment (■ **Figure 10.3**). Infants listening to English determine that SVO

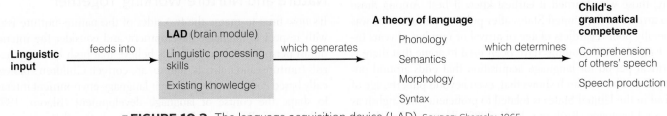

| Linguistic input | feeds into | **LAD** (brain module)

 Linguistic processing skills

 Existing knowledge | which generates | **A theory of language**

 Phonology

 Semantics

 Morphology

 Syntax | which determines | **Child's grammatical competence**

 Comprehension of others' speech

 Speech production |

■ **FIGURE 10.3** The language acquisition device (LAD). Source: Chomsky, 1965.

is the typical grammatical sequence, whereas infants listening to Japanese detect that SOV is typical. Thus, although nature may ensure that infants arrive "language ready," the environment determines what they end up with.

What evidence supports a nativist perspective on language development? First, there is what some have called the "learnability factor": children acquire an incredibly complex communication system rapidly and without formal instruction. For example, 18-month-olds show an understanding of syntax that they could not have acquired solely from information provided to them by others; they must have inferred rules of syntax on their own (Lidz, Waxman, & Freedman, 2003). Second, children all progress through the same sequences at roughly similar ages, and they even make the same kinds of errors, which suggests that language development is guided by a species-wide maturational plan. Third, these universal aspects of early language development occur despite cultural differences in the styles of speech that adults use in talking to young children. In some cultures, for example, parents believe that babies are incapable of understanding speech and do not even talk directly to them (Crago, Allen, & Hough-Eyamir, 1997).

Other evidence for the nativist position comes from studies of second-language learning. Much research shows that young children learn their native language with ease but often struggle later to learn a second language to the same level of proficiency. Does this mean that there is a critical period for language acquisition and that the brain becomes less responsive to language learning? Consider, first, research with deaf children, some of whom (especially those with hearing parents) do not have an opportunity to learn any language, oral or signed, in their early years. Rachel Mayberry (1994) studied language mastery in deaf college students exposed to American Sign Language (ASL) at different ages and found that the rule "the earlier, the better" applies (see also Mayberry, Lock, & Kazmi, 2002). Mastery of the syntax, and semantics of sign language was greatest among students exposed to it in infancy or early childhood. Those who learned sign later in their development (ages 9–16) mastered it better if they had had some exposure to English early in life than if they had not been exposed to any language system before they encountered sign language. Exploration Box 10.1 provides more details on how the language development of deaf children compares with that of hearing children.

Elissa Newport and her colleagues (Newport, 1991) uncovered similar evidence of a critical period for second-language learning. In one study (Johnson & Newport, 1989), native speakers of Korean or Chinese who had come to the United States between age 3 and age 39 were tested for mastery of English grammar. Among those who began learning English before puberty, those who learned it earliest knew it best. Among those who arrived in the United States after puberty, performance was generally poor regardless of age of arrival or number of years using English. Such findings have been used to argue that there is a critical period for language acquisition that ends around puberty. But other research shows that, even beyond puberty, age of arrival in the United States is related to proficiency in English as a second language (Birdsong, 1999, 2005). Thus, adults relocating at age 25 develop greater proficiency than adults relocating

at age 30, an advantage related more to age than to length of residence in the United States (Stevens, 1999). And although adults are generally less likely than children to ever attain nativelike proficiency in a second language—suggesting a critical period—some adults achieve such proficiency, usually through massive effort and exposure to the second language (Birdsong, 1999).

Young children may have advantages over adults when learning a second language. This does not necessarily mean that there is a critical period for language acquisition. Children are generally immersed in their second language through school and peer-group activities. This greater exposure may facilitate second-language acquisition partly by making the new language dominant in their lives. Adults, by contrast, may be more likely to continue using their native language as their dominant mode of communication, making second-language acquisition more difficult (Jia & Aaronson, 1999).

It is possible that the language-processing areas of the brain are shaped for a lifetime by early experience with language in ways that limit later learning of other languages. But it seems unlikely that there is a hard-and-fast critical period for language acquisition. Janet Werker and Richard Tees (2005) suggest that it is more accurate to say there is an "optimal period" during which languages are most easily and flawlessly acquired. And studies of brain architecture confirm that it is more appropriate to conclude that there may be a *sensitive* period for language acquisition (Fox, Levitt, & Nelson, 2010). Perhaps the main message is that young children are supremely capable of learning languages and advancing their cognitive development in the process. Meanwhile, college students learning a foreign language for the first time must appreciate that they may never speak it as well as someone who learned it as a young child.

Finally, there is evidence that the capacity for acquiring language has a genetic basis. Some of our linguistic competencies, including the ability to combine symbols to form short sentences, are shared with chimpanzees and other primates, suggesting that they arose during the course of evolution and are part of our genetic endowment as humans (Greenfield & Savage-Rumbaugh, 1993; Pinker, 1994). In humans, a gene called *FOXP2* has been identified in connection with the motor skills necessary for speech (Tomblin, 2009; Vargha-Khadem et al., 1995). Individuals whose *FOXP2* gene is damaged are unable to speak, although they may have no other limitations. We also know that identical twins score more similarly than fraternal twins on measures of verbal skills, and certain speech, language, and reading disorders run in families, indicating that individual heredity influences the course of language development (Tomblin, 2009).

Nature and Nurture Working Together

It's now time to merge the two sides of the nature–nurture issue with respect to language development and consider the interactionist perspective. Interactionists believe that both learning theorists (nurture) and nativists (nature) are correct: Children's biologically based competencies and their language environment interact to shape the course of language development (Bloom, 1998; Bohannon & Bonvillian, 2009). They emphasize that acquisition of language skills depends on and is related to the acquisition of

Language Acquisition among Deaf Children

Many deaf children gain their first exposure to language by learning American Sign Language (ASL). This is a true language. For example, signs are arbitrary symbols, not attempts to mimic objects and events, and they are used according to a system of grammatical rules that determines their ordering. You ought to be able to learn some interesting lessons about language acquisition in general, then, by studying language acquisition among deaf children.

On average, deaf children acquire sign language in much the same sequence and at much the same rate as hearing children acquire spoken language, and they make many of the same kinds of errors along the way (Bellugi, 1988; Masataka, 2000). Interestingly, deaf infants whose parents are deaf "babble" in sign language. They experiment with gestures in much the same way that hearing infants experiment with sounds in preparation for their first meaningful communications (Petitto & Marentette, 1991). They then sign their first meaningful single words around 12 months, use their first syntax (combinations of two signs) between 18 and 24 months, and master many rules of language, such as past tense formation, between 2 and 3 years (Meier, 1991). Just as hearing children have difficulty with the pronunciation of certain words and overgeneralize certain rules, deaf children make predictable errors in their signing (Meier, 1991). Moreover, for both deaf and hearing children, advances in language development are linked closely to advances in cognitive development; for example, putting signs or words together in sentences happens around the same age that children put sequences of actions together in their play (Spencer, 1996).

The language environment experienced by deaf infants is also far more similar to that of hearing infants than you would imagine. For example, deaf mothers sign in child-directed speech; they present signs at a slower pace, repeat signs more, and exaggerate their signing motions more when they talk to their infants than when they talk to their deaf friends (Holzrichter & Meier, 2000). Moreover, just as hearing babies prefer the exaggerated intonations of child-directed speech, deaf infants pay more attention and give more emotional response when they are shown videos of infant-directed signing than tapes of adult-directed signing.

Finally, it turns out that language areas of the brain develop much the same in deaf children exposed to sign as in hearing children exposed to speech. For example, Helen Neville and her colleagues (1997, 1998) examined brain activity during the processing of sentences by deaf and hearing ASL users, hearing individuals (interpreters) who acquired sign late in life, and hearing individuals who did not know ASL. Mostly, reliance on areas of the left hemisphere of the cortex to process sentences was as evident among those who acquired ASL early in life (that is, native signers) as among hearing individuals who acquired English early in life (native speakers). Reliance on the left hemisphere to process syntax was not as clear among individuals who acquired a language later in life (non-native signers or speakers). Some research, though, does show some right hemisphere activity during the perception of signing, perhaps because spatial skills based in the right hemisphere come into play in interpreting gestures (see Campbell, MacSweeney, & Waters, 2007). But in terms of production of sign and spoken language, the left hemisphere dominates.

As you have seen, language development is sometimes delayed among deaf children of hearing parents if they cannot hear well enough to understand spoken language but are not exposed to sign language (Mayberry, 1994). Overall, then, studies of language acquisition among deaf children suggest that young humans are biologically prepared to master language and will do so if given the opportunity, whether that language is signed or spoken and whether it involves visual–spatial skills or auditory ones (see Goldin-Meadow, 2003, 2005).

© Stephen McBrady/PhotoEdit Inc.

many other capacities: perceptual, cognitive, motor, social, and emotional. They point out that the capacity for acquiring language is not unique, as nativists who speak of universal grammar and the language acquisition device claim (Bates, O'Connell, & Shore, 1987). It is, instead, interrelated to other developments that are taking place concurrently with language acquisition. For example, young children first begin to use words as meaningful symbols when they begin to display nonlinguistic symbolic capacities, such as the ability to use gestures (waving bye-bye), and begin to engage in pretend play (treating a bowl as if it were a hat).

The interactionists' position is not unlike that taken by Piaget (1970). He believed that milestones in cognitive development pave the way for progress in language development and that maturation and environment interact to guide both cognitive development and language development. Like Piaget (but unlike learning theorists), many interactionists argue that language development depends on the maturation of cognitive abilities such as the capacity for symbolic thought. However, the interactionist position also emphasizes—as Vygotsky did but Piaget did not—ways in which social interactions with adults contribute to cognitive and linguistic development. Language is primarily a means of communicating—one that develops in the context of social interactions as children and their companions strive to get their messages across (Tomasello, 2009).

Long before infants use words, Jerome Bruner (1983) says, their caregivers show them how to take turns in conversations—even if the most these young infants can contribute when their turn comes is a laugh or a bit of babbling. As adults converse with young children, they create a supportive learning environment—a *scaffold*, in Bruner's terms, a *zone of proximal development* in Vygotsky's—that helps the children grasp the regularities of language (Bruner, 1983; Harris, 1992). For example, parents may go through their children's favorite picture books at bedtime and ask "What's this?" and "What's that?" This gives their children repeated opportunities to learn that conversing involves taking turns, that things have names, and that there are proper ways to pose questions and give answers. Soon the children are asking "What's this?" and "What's that?"

On a daily basis, toddlers in English-speaking homes hear between 5,000 and 7,000 utterances (Tomasello, 2006). As they gain new language skills, adults adjust their styles of communication accordingly. Language researchers use the term **child-directed speech** to describe the speech adults use with young children: short, simple sentences spoken slowly, in a high-pitched voice, often with much repetition, and with exaggerated emphasis on key words (usually words for objects and activities). For example, the mother trying to get her son to eat his peas might say, "Eat your *peas* now. Not the cracker. See those *peas*? Yes, eat the *peas*. Oh, such a good boy for eating your *peas*." Mothers also convey more exaggerated emotions (positive and negative) when speaking to their infants than when speaking to other adults (Kitamura & Burnham, 2003). From the earliest days of life, toddlers seem to pay more attention to the high-pitched sounds and varied intonational patterns of child-directed speech than to the speech adults use when communicating with one another (Cooper et al., 1997; Pegg, Werker, & McLeod, 1992). Importantly, caregivers' child-directed speech is dynamic—constantly changing in response to the child's utterances (Gros-Louis et al., 2006). Children learn best

Adults are not the only ones who use child-directed speech. Children also adjust their speech to their listener. How could this girl alter her speech to make it appealing and appropriate for her baby sister?

when parents engage them in conversation as opposed to merely "talking at them" (Zimmerman et al., 2009).

Would children learn language just as well if adults talked to them in an adultlike style? Perhaps not. The nativists seem to have underestimated the contributions of environment to language development. Mere exposure to speech is not enough; children must be actively involved in using language (Locke, 1997). Catherine Snow and her associates, for example, found that a group of Dutch-speaking children, although they watched a great deal of German television, did not acquire German words or grammar (Snow et al., 1976). True, there are cultural groups (the Kaluli of New Guinea, the natives of American Samoa, and the Trackton people of the Piedmont Carolinas) in which child-directed speech does not seem to be used. Children in these societies still seem to acquire their native language without noticeable delays (Ochs, 1982; Schieffelin, 1986). Yet even these children overhear speech and participate in social interactions in which language is used, and that is what seems to be required to master a human language (Lieven, 1994). Those parents who use child-directed speech further simplify the child's task of figuring out the rules of language (Harris, 1992; Kemler Nelson et al., 1989). They converse with children daily in attention-getting and understandable ways about the objects and events that have captured the youngsters' attention.

Adults speaking to young children also use certain communication strategies that foster language development. For example, if a child says, "Kitty goed," an adult may respond with an **expansion**—a more grammatically complete expression of the same thought ("Yes, the cat went in the car"). Adults use conversational techniques such as expansions mainly to improve communication, not to teach grammar (Penner, 1987). However, these techniques also serve as a subtle form of correction after children produce grammatically incorrect sentences and show children more grammatical ways to express the same ideas (Bohannon & Stanowicz, 1988; Saxton, 1997). It is not quite true, then, that adults provide no corrective feedback concerning children's grammatical errors, as nativists claim. True, they rarely say, "No, that's wrong; say it this way." Nevertheless, they provide subtle corrective feedback through their responses to children, and this feedback helps children grow linguistically (Bohannon & Bonvillian, 2009).

How can adults best facilitate young children's language learning? What cognitive capacities enable children to learn how language works? Much remains to be learned about language development, but it does seem to require the interaction of a biologically prepared child with at least one conversational partner, ideally one who tailors her own speech to the child's level of understanding.

Developing language competence may be our earliest and greatest learning challenge, but it is only the beginning. There is much more to be mastered during the school years and beyond. Language lays the foundation for acquiring reading, writing, and countless other skills. But unlike language, which seems to develop effortlessly in the absence of formal education, these other skills typically require directed education. In the following sections, we look at education across the life span, examining changes in motivation for learning and changes in educational environments as learners get older.

Checking Mastery

1. What are the basic components of language that children must master in order to communicate effectively?

2. Through what stages does early language acquisition progress?

3. Give an example of an overregularization of language.

4. What are the main features of the nativist and learning theories of language acquisition?

Making Connections

1. What should parents and early childhood educators look for (or listen for) to confirm that infants and toddlers are progressing typically with regard to their language acquisition at ages 1, 2, and 3?

2. Based on what we know about acquisition of language, how would you structure a child's world so that he has the best opportunity to become fluent in not just one but two languages?

10.2 The Infant

Before children begin their formal education, they are learning a great deal from the informal curriculum of their lives. As we have just discussed, they master language, and as we see next, they also learn to master their environments.

Mastery Motivation

Infants seem to be intrinsically motivated to master their environment. This **mastery motivation** can be seen clearly when infants struggle to open kitchen cabinets, take their first steps, or figure out how new toys work—and derive great pleasure from their efforts (Jennings & Dietz, 2003; Masten & Reed, 2002).

Much evidence supports the claim that infants are curious, active explorers constantly striving to understand and to exert control over the world around them. This, you should recall, was one of Piaget's major themes. A striving for mastery or competence appears to be inborn and universal and will display itself in the behavior of all normal infants without prompting from parents. Even so, some infants appear to be more mastery oriented than others. Given a new push toy, one baby may simply look at it, but another may mouth it, bang it, and push it across the floor (Jennings & Dietz, 2003). Why might some infants have a stronger mastery motive than others?

One possibility is that the goal itself may hold greater value to some infants: If that red ball looks highly appealing to Joanie, she may expend more time and energy to retrieve it than Naomi, who just doesn't judge it worthy of her attention (Kenward et al., 2009). Mastery motivation also seems higher when parents frequently provide sensory stimulation designed to arouse and amuse their babies—tickling them, bouncing them, playing games of pat-a-cake, giving them stimulating toys, and so on (Busch-Rossnagel, 1997). Mastery motivation flourishes when infants grow up in a responsive environment that provides plenty of opportunities to see for themselves that they can control their environments and experience successes (Maddux, 2002; Masten & Reed, 2002). Consider the toddler who, faced with the challenge of retrieving a cookie from the kitchen counter, struggles to maneuver a chair across the room and to climb up without tipping the chair or falling off. When Mom offers to help him, he shrieks, "Me do it!" And when he does it, he feels a sense of accomplishment that increases the likelihood he will tackle future challenges. Parents who return smiles and coos or respond promptly to cries show infants they can affect people around them. By contrast, the children of parents who are depressed show less interest in and persistence on challenging tasks, perhaps because their parents are not responsive to them (Redding, Harmon, & Morgan, 1990). As well, children who are raised by parents who constantly stifle their initiatives ("you will *not* move the chair across the room!") may be less likely to take on new tasks.

An infant's level of mastery motivation affects her later achievement behavior. Babies who actively attempt to master challenges at 6 and 12 months score higher on tests of mental development at 2 and 3 years than their less mastery-oriented peers (Jennings & Dietz, 2003; Messer et al., 1986). There is even some continued influence of early mastery motivation, measured at age 1, into adulthood, as measured at age 32, at least

Every day, infants and young children display their innate mastery motive.

for males (Jennings, Yarrow, & Martin, 1984). In short, infants are intrinsically motivated to master challenges, but parents may help strengthen this inborn motive by stimulating their infants appropriately and responding to their actions. What about infants and toddlers who spend considerable amounts of time away from their parents? Is their motivation influenced by time spent in preschool?

Early Education

As you have seen in previous chapters, babies learn a great deal in the first few years of life. But do infants and toddlers need specific educational experiences? Manufacturers of products such as *Baby Einstein* DVDs and *Baby Mozart* CDs hope that parents will buy into the idea that early stimulation is critical to infants' intellectual development (McCormick, 1998). Formal programs such as Bookstart, which promotes literacy early by providing 6- to 9-month-old infants and their parents with books and literacy information, have even been developed (Hall, 2001; Wade & Moore, 1998).

Despite its popular appeal, most experts dispute the idea that children need special educational experiences during their first 3 years (Bruer, 1999; Kagan, 1998). And some, such as David Elkind (1987), author of *Miseducation: Preschoolers at Risk*, fear that the push for earlier education may be going too far and that young children today are not given enough time simply to be children—to play and socialize as they choose. Elkind even worries that children may lose their self-initiative and intrinsic motivation to learn when their lives are orchestrated by parents who pressure them to achieve at early ages. Is there anything to these concerns?

Some research seems to confirm Elkind's fears. Dimitri Christakis and colleagues (2007) studied infants who watched *Baby Einstein* or *Brainy Baby* videos. They found, rather alarmingly, that for each hour spent watching videos, babies understood 6–8 fewer words than babies who did not watch videos. The research did not follow infants into childhood to determine if the

video-watching babies later caught up to the other babies, but the findings do raise a red flag, at least with respect to language abilities. If educational videos are not valuable, and may even be detrimental, what about educational infant and preschool programs?

In one study, 4-year-olds in preschools with strong academic thrusts gained an initial advantage in basic academic skills such as knowledge of letters and numbers but lost it by the end of kindergarten (Hyson, Hirsh-Pasek, & Rescorla, 1989). What is more, they proved to be less creative, more anxious in testing situations, and more negative toward school than children who attended preschool programs with a social rather than academic emphasis. Similarly, Deborah Stipek and her colleagues (1995) have found that highly academic preschool programs raise children's academic achievement test scores but decrease their expectancies of success and pride in accomplishment. So it may be possible to undermine achievement motivation by overemphasizing academics in the preschool years.

However, preschool programs that offer a healthy mix of play and academic skill-building activities can be beneficial to young children, especially disadvantaged ones (Barnett, 2002; Gottlieb & Blair, 2004). Although many children who attend preschool programs are no more or less intellectually advanced than those who remain at home, disadvantaged children who attend programs specially designed to prepare them for school experience more cognitive growth and achieve more success in school than disadvantaged children who do not attend such programs (Barnett, 2002). Consider again the Abecedarian Project, a full-time educational program from infancy (starting around 4–5 months) to age 5 for children from low-income families (Campbell et al., 2001; and see Chapter 9). Compared with children who did not participate, Abecedarian children showed impressive cognitive gains during and immediately after the program (■ **Figure 10.4**). Although their performance level compared with test norms decreased over the subsequent years, these children continued to show an advantage over children who did not receive this intensive early educational experience (Nelson, Westhues, & MacLeod, 2003).

An alternative type of program focuses on educating parents about the importance of the early environment and the types of experiences that can be beneficial to their children. It turns out that parent training pays off. In one such program, Born to Learn, children displayed higher levels of mastery motivation than nonparticipants by 36 months of age, or even earlier—24 months—if they were from disadvantaged families (Drotar et al., 2008).

Thus, early education can provide disadvantaged children with a boost that has lasting consequences, lending support to the basic idea of Head Start (a federally funded program aimed at preparing disadvantaged children for school) and similar programs. Positive effects on later school achievement are especially likely if the preschool experience not only stimulates children's cognitive growth but also gets parents more involved with their children's education and includes follow-up during elementary school (Nelson et al., 2003). More generally, preschool programs that build school readiness skills but also allow plenty of time for play and social interaction can help all children make a smooth transition to kindergarten and elementary school (Parker et al., 1999).

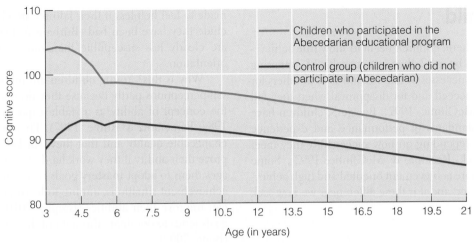

■ **FIGURE 10.4** Cognitive growth curves as a function of preschool treatment. SOURCE: From Campbell, F. A. et al., The development of cognitive and academic abilities: Growth curves from an early childhood educational experience, *Developmental Psychology, 37*, pp. 231–242. Copyright © 2001, American Psychological Association. Reprinted with permission.

What should preschools do to optimize development and maintain high levels of motivation among children?

Checking Mastery

1. What is mastery motivation?
2. What is one advantage and one potential disadvantage of early education programs for infants and toddlers?

Making Connections

1. Should preschool education be mandatory? At what age should formal education begin? Provide some evidence to support your answer.
2. How can parents and early childhood teachers foster mastery motivation in their children?

10.3 The Child

With infancy behind them, children begin to show true achievement motivation. Even by age 2, they seem capable of appraising their performances as successes or failures and look to others for approval when they succeed and for disapproval when they fail (Stipek, Recchia, & McClintic, 1992). By age 3, children have clearly internalized standards of performance and experience true pride or shame, depending on how successfully they meet those standards (Stipek, Recchia, & McClintic, 1992). Some children are clearly more achievement oriented and high achieving than others, however, and it is these differences we now seek to explain.

Achievement Motivation

All children occasionally experience failure in their efforts to master challenges and meet achievement standards. What are the differences between children who persist and triumph in the face of failure and those who give up? Carol Dweck and her colleagues (Dweck & Elliott, 1983; Dweck & Grant, 2008; Dweck & Master, 2008) find that high achievers tend to attribute their successes to internal and stable causes such as high ability. However, they blame their failures either on external factors beyond their control ("That test was impossibly hard," "That teacher's grading is biased") or—and this is even more adaptive—on internal causes that they can overcome (particularly insufficient effort). They do not blame the internal but stable factor of low ability ("I'm terrible at this and will never do any better"). Students with this healthy attributional style are said to have a **mastery orientation**; they thrive on challenges and persist in the face of failure, believing that their increased effort will pay off.

By contrast, children who tend to be low achievers often attribute their successes either to the internal cause of hard work or to external causes such as luck or the easiness of the task. Thus, they do not experience the pride and self-esteem that come from viewing themselves as highly capable. Yet they often attribute their failures to an internal and stable cause—namely, lack of ability. As a result, they have low expectancies of success and tend to give up. Dweck describes children with this attributional style as having a **helpless orientation**—a tendency to avoid challenges and to cease trying—to give up—when they experience failure, based on the belief that they can do little to improve.

Child Contributions

Several characteristics of the child contribute to achievement levels and motivation to succeed. First is the child's age or developmental level. Before age 7 or so, children tend to be unrealistic optimists who think they can succeed on almost any task (Stipek & Mac Iver, 1989). With age, children's perceptions of their academic abilities become more accurate (Wigfield et al., 1997). Even after repeated poor performances, young children often continue to think they have high ability and will do well, whereas older children tend to become helpless (Miller, 1985; Ruble, Eisenberg, & Higgins, 1994). Young children can be made to feel helpless if their failures are clear-cut and they conclude they have been bad (Burhans & Dweck, 1995), but they are clearly less susceptible than older children to a helpless orientation.

Why is this? Young children are protected from damaging self-perceptions partly because they do not yet fully understand the concept of ability as a stable capacity (Nicholls & Miller, 1984; Pomerantz & Ruble, 1997). They believe that ability is a changeable quality and that they can become smarter and improve their ability if they work hard. This view of ability encourages them to adopt **mastery goals** (also called learning goals) in achievement situations, aiming to learn new things so that they can improve their abilities (Brophy, 2010). A focus on mastery goals tends to dominate throughout the lower elementary grades (Bong, 2009).

As children age, they begin to see ability as a fixed trait that does not change much with effort. As a result, by late elementary and middle school, more of them adopt **performance goals** in school; they aim to *prove* their ability rather than to *improve* it and seek to be judged smart rather than dumb (Bong, 2009; Dweck & Leggett, 1988; Erdley et al., 1997; and see ● **Table 10.3**). These changes in the understanding of ability are probably caused both by cognitive development—especially an increased ability to analyze the causes of successes and failures and to infer enduring traits from behavior—and by an accumulation of feedback in school (Stipek, 1984).

Importantly, children who continue to focus on mastery or learning goals tend to do better in school than those who switch to performance goals (Butler, 1999; Covington, 2000; Stipek & Gralinski, 1996). Children focused on mastery goals do not become as disheartened by a low grade if they have nonetheless progressed in their understanding of the material. For these children, the *process* of learning is enjoyable; it helps quench their curiosity (Fisher, Marshal, & Nanayakkara, 2009). Their ability to enjoy the learning process may help explain why these children exhibit higher levels of achievement (Daniels et al., 2009; Pekrun, Elliot, & Maier, 2009). In contrast, children with a focus on performance goals are more discouraged because for them the *outcome*—the grade—was the goal, not the process of learning. These children are more likely to report anxiety and boredom, factors that are negatively associated with achievement (Daniels et al., 2009; Pekrun, Elliot, & Maier, 2009). The two groups of children—those with mastery or learning goals and those with performance goals—display different patterns of neurological activity in response to their performance outcomes, further evidence that these two groups are truly experiencing their successes and failures differently (Fisher et al., 2009). Importantly, the two types of goals are not mutually exclusive; that is, it is possible to be motivated by both mastery goals and performance goals (Darnon et al., 2010). What is important, though, is the predominant focus that students hold as they work to achieve their goals. As **Table 10.3** illustrates, when students believe that ability is primarily a fixed entity that they either have or do not have and conclude that they lack it, they set performance goals rather than learning goals; figuring that hard work will not pay off, they run the risk of becoming helpless in the classroom (Dweck & Leggett, 1988). Even gifted students can fall into this

TABLE 10.3 COMPARISON OF MASTERY AND PERFORMANCE GOALS

Mastery Goals	Performance Goals
• Ability as a changeable trait	• Ability as a fixed trait
• Ability to focus on increasing competence or knowledge ("I understand this material better than I did before")	• Ability to focus on increasing status relative to others ("I did better on this than the other students did")
• Self-regulated learning; ability to monitor understanding of material and adjust behavior (for example, effort) accordingly	• Other-regulated learning; ability to monitor performance relative to peers and increase effort (approach) to outperform them or decrease effort (avoidance) to save face (to say that failures are because of a lack of effort, not incompetence)
• Deep-level processing of material (for example, learning to understand)	• Superficial-level processing of material (for example, memorizing for a test)
• Feelings of pride and satisfaction associated with success, with failures indicating a need for more effort or different learning strategies	• Feelings of anxiety and shame associated with failure; boastful feelings associated with success

SOURCE: Adapted from Covington, 2000; Elliot & Church, 1997.

trap (Ablard & Mills, 1996). Evaluate your own motivation style with the exercise in Engagement Box 10.1.

In addition to their age, children's level of intelligence, not surprisingly, contributes to their success in academics (Spinath et al., 2006). But clearly level of intelligence is just a piece of the puzzle because some students with above average intelligence do not do particularly well in school and others exceed expectations based solely on their IQ scores. It turns out that both motivation and achievement levels are higher when children value a subject—when they believe that it is important (Spinath et al., 2006). Think of this in relation to your own learning and motivation and you will likely recognize that you try harder and perform better when something is important to you.

Parent Contributions

As you saw earlier, parents can foster mastery motivation in infancy by providing their babies with appropriate sensory stimulation, being responsive, and (as you will see in Chapter 14) building a secure attachment relationship. Parents can then strengthen their children's achievement motivation by stressing and reinforcing independence and self-reliance at an early age, encouraging children to do things on their own (Peterson & Steen, 2002). They can also emphasize the importance of doing things well, or meeting high standards of performance (Deci & Ryan, 1992). As children begin formal schooling, parents can help foster high levels of achievement motivation by getting involved with their child's education and emphasizing practices that stimulate curiosity and engagement in learning (Gottfried et al., 2009).

Finally, parents can provide a cognitively stimulating home environment (Gottfried, Fleming, & Gottfried, 1998). This includes having reading material in the home, engaging in intellectual discussions, attending lectures or cultural events, visiting museums, and holding high expectations for children's education. By doing these things, parents stimulate intellectual curiosity and a desire to learn. Children who are encouraged and supported in a positive manner are likely to enjoy new challenges and feel confident about mastering them. They are also unlikely to make the kinds of counterproductive attributions ("I'm dumb") that can cause them to lose interest in schoolwork (Glasgow et al., 1997). Children typically feel competent when their parents are satisfied with their performance (McGrath & Repetti, 2000). By contrast, parents can undermine a child's school performance and intrinsic motivation to learn if they are uninvolved and offer little guidance or if they are highly controlling, nag continually about homework, offer bribes for good grades, and criticize bad grades (Ginsburg & Bronstein, 1993; Gottfried et al., 2009). Over an 8-year interval from age 9 to age 17, children maintain higher levels of motivation when their parents initially focus on intrinsic goals (learning for the sake of learning) rather than extrinsic goals (learning to earn high grades or money; Gottfried et al., 2009).

In a fascinating new study, Harvard economist Roland Fryer, Jr. (see Ripley, 2010) spent millions of dollars to learn whether students could be bribed into earning higher standardized test scores. He enlisted school districts in four major cities and used a different set of incentives in each location. For example, in Chicago, ninth-graders could earn up to $2,000 per year (!) by getting paid $50 for each A test grade, $35 for each B grade, and $20 for each C grade. A similar scheme was used in New York City with younger students—fourth- and seventh-graders. In Washington, D.C., students were paid for such things as attendance and staying out of trouble. The Dallas program enlisted the youngest students in the study—second-graders—and paid them the least, $2 every time they read a book and completed a quiz on their reading.

The results may surprise you. The program was a bust in Chicago and New York City: students earned lots of money for getting good grades on tests throughout the year but showed no improvement on standardized tests given at the end of the school year. In Washington, the results were somewhat mixed,

Indicate whether you agree (A) or disagree (D) with each of the following statements, as they pertain to your typical approach or thoughts about learning and coursework.

___ 1. I read the chapter because the material was interesting to me.

___ 2. I read the chapter because the instructor said there would be a quiz on the material.

___ 3. I often look up some additional information related to the course material so that I can better understand what is discussed in class or presented in the textbook.

___ 4. I feel good when I am able to convey my understanding of the material on the exam.

___ 5. I need to earn a B+ or higher in this class to maintain my scholarship.

___ 6. I want to get an A on this test to show the professor that I'm good.

___ 7. I want to get an A on all the quizzes this semester because then I will be exempt from taking the final exam.

___ 8. As long as I pass this class, I'll be happy because I know I've learned something new from a really difficult professor.

___ 9. I like to see how others in the class score on the assignments so I can get an idea of how well I'm doing.

___10. I don't really care how other people in the class score because their performance is unrelated to my learning.

___11. I get bored and frustrated when the instructor spends time on easy material and quizzes us on stuff that seems obvious.

___12. I get frustrated when the instructor goes over difficult material that is going to be hard to study to earn a good grade.

___13. There is nothing I like more than a good challenging homework assignment that makes me think harder or differently.

___14. I like getting a homework assignment that is easy and fairly mindless to complete. I know I can get it done and the instructor will be happy with my answers.

___15. I usually find that I can master a task or material by working really hard on it.

___16. If I cannot solve a task right away, I usually stop working on it because I'm not going to be able to solve it.

Scoring: Count the number of "Agree" answers to these questions: 1, 3, 4, 8, 10, 11, 13, 15. Count the number of "Agree" answers to these questions: 2, 5, 6, 7, 9, 12, 14, 16. If the number of "Agree" answers to the first set (1, 3, 4, 8, 10, 11, 13, 15) is higher than the number of "Agree" answers to the second set (2, 5, 6, 7, 9, 12, 14, 16), then you focus more on learning or mastery goals. You are more interested in mastering material for the sake of learning and not for the sake of grades. If, on the other hand, the number of your "Agree" answers to the second set of questions is higher than the number of "Agree" answers to the first set, then you focus more on performance goals. You are motivated to perform well and earn good grades. According to the text, which of these motivation styles—mastery versus performance—ultimately leads to a deeper and richer understanding of material? What could you do to shift from one style to the other?

although promising in that standardized reading scores improved among children who were rewarded not for grades but for behaviors such as attendance throughout the school year. The program that proved to have the biggest bang for the bucks was the one that paid the least and targeted not grades but a behavior that all children could already perform and could control—their reading. Young students who were paid for reading books and answering quiz questions significantly improved their standardized reading comprehension scores. We still need to see how students in the various groups perform over time—and ensure that rewarding activities such as reading books does not eventually undermine intrinsic motivation for reading. But the results suggest that rewarding children not for the final products of their work (that is, the grades) but for the steps that contribute to the final product (such as reading and attendance) can have a positive effect on their performance. Fryer and others involved in the study found that students who had the opportunity to earn the most money for high test scores were very excited by this prospect but did not know how to go about achieving it. Instead of bribing students for the grades they earn, it might be better to encourage students to involve themselves in behaviors they can control that contribute to greater engagement with the course material. Ultimately, this is what will lead to greater achievement gains.

School Contributions

How do schools affect achievement? Nearly every school asserts that the major goal of classroom instruction is improvement of children's learning. Many of these same schools, however, are structured in ways that focus on the external rewards that students can earn (such as grades or stickers). As a result, they may encourage children, either deliberately or inadvertently, to set performance goals rather than mastery or learning goals (Covington, 2000). Many classrooms are competitive places where students try to outdo each other to earn the best grades and gain teacher recognition. Students receive a grade (good or bad), indicating their performance on a test or project, and that is the end of it. If they did not fully learn the material, they are given no opportunity to do so: They learn that the grade, not learning, is the goal.

Martin Covington (1998, 2000) believes that schools can foster children's academic motivation by downplaying the competitive race for the best grades in class. How might this work? Consider some research by Elaine Elliott and Carol Dweck (1988). They asked fifth-graders to perform a novel task. The students were led to believe that they had either low or high ability and were warned that they would soon be performing similar tasks that would prove difficult. Half the children worked under a performance goal (not unlike the goals emphasized in many classrooms): They were told that their performance would be compared with that of other children and evaluated by an expert. The remaining children were induced to adopt a learning or mastery goal: Although they would make some mistakes, they were told, working at the tasks would "sharpen the mind" and help them at school.

As expected, the only children who displayed the telltale signs of helplessness (that is, deteriorating performance and attribution of failure to low ability) were those who believed they had low ability and were pursuing a performance goal. For them, continuing to work on the difficult task meant demonstrating again that they were stupid. By contrast, even "low ability" students who pursued a mastery goal persisted despite their failures and showed remarkably little frustration, probably because they believed they could grow from their experience. Perhaps, then, teachers undermine achievement motivation by distributing gold stars and grades and frequently calling attention to how students compare with one another (Brophy, 2010). Children might be better off if teachers nurtured their intrinsic motivation to master challenges and structured their classrooms to emphasize mastery rather than performance goals (Murayama & Elliot, 2009). Then, slow learners could view their mistakes as a sign that they should change strategies to improve their competencies rather than as further proof that they lack ability.

Finally, the school climate can influence achievement. Academic achievement is greater when schools encourage family involvement and regular parent–teacher communication and when they develop a system that makes family involvement possible (Rimm-Kaufman & Pianta, 1999). Schools can also try to capture students' enthusiasm for learning from the start of schooling. Students who start out liking school are typically the ones who like school later; they also participate more in the classroom, which leads to higher levels of achievement (Ladd, Buhs, & Seid, 2000).

To recap what you have learned so far, children approach achievement tasks with either a mastery orientation or a helpless orientation, based on how they view their academic triumphs and disasters. As they age, children understand the concept of ability as a stable trait and shift from focusing on mastery goals to focusing on performance goals. These changes, brought about by both cognitive development and feedback in school, give them a more realistic picture of their own strengths and weaknesses but also make them more vulnerable to "failure syndrome" or helplessness, a tendency to give up at the first obstacle they encounter (Brophy, 2010). Yet some children remain far more motivated to succeed in school than others, and parents and schools have a lot to do with that.

Learning to Read

Perhaps the most important achievement in school is acquiring the ability to read. Mastery of reading paves the way for mastering other academic skills. Skilled readers consume more printed material than unskilled readers or nonreaders, giving them an advantage in other academic areas that increasingly rely on reading skills over the school years (Stanovich, 1986). Unlike language acquisition, a natural learning task that typically requires no formal education, reading acquisition is an "unnatural" task (Stanovich & Stanovich, 1999). Learning to read almost always requires direct instruction. How do children master this complex and important skill?

Mastering the Alphabetic Principle

Before children can read, they must understand the **alphabetic principle**—the idea that the letters in printed words represent the sounds in spoken words in a systematic way (Byrne, 1998; Treiman, 2000). According to Linnea Ehri (1999), this is a four-step process. First, children in the prealphabetic phase memorize selected visual cues to remember words. They can "read" text that they have memorized during previous readings. For instance, seeing a picture of a dinosaur on a page in a favorite book cues a child to recall the words she has often heard her mother read when they turned to this page. Or a child in the prealphabetic phase might recognize a word by its shape (physically, the printed word *bed* looks different than the word *egg*).

In the partial alphabetic phase, children learn the shapes and sounds of letters. For example, they recognize the curved shape of the letter C and begin to associate this with a particular sound. These children begin to connect at least one letter in a word—usually the first—to its corresponding sound. Not surprisingly, children typically recognize the initial letter of their first name before other letters (Treiman & Broderick, 1998).

Complete connections between written letters and their corresponding sounds are acquired during the full alphabetic phase. In this phase, children apply to the challenge of reading their **phonological awareness**—the sensitivity to the sound system of language that enables them to segment spoken words into sounds or phonemes (Carroll et al., 2003). Children who have phonological awareness can recognize that *cat* and *trouble* both have the phoneme /t/ in them, can tell you how many distinct sounds there are in the word *bark*, and can tell you what will be left if you take the /f/ sound out of *fat*. Children can decode words never before seen by applying their knowledge of phonetics. They can decipher the new word *mat* from their previous understanding of the word *cat* and the letter *m*.

In addition to decoding unfamiliar words, children in the full alphabetic phase use sight reading for familiar words. Sight reading is fast and works well for words that are hard to decode (such as those with unusual spellings) or frequently encountered. If you regularly run across the word *alligator* in your readings, you may initially read this by decoding it, or "unpacking" each sound then putting the sounds together. But after many encounters with this word, you can sight-read it, or recall it from memory, without having to decode every sound.

Finally, in the consolidated alphabetic phase, letters that regularly occur together are grouped as a unit. For instance, the letter sequence *ing*, which frequently appears at the end of verbs, is perceived as a single unit rather than as three separate letters. This grouping speeds the processing of the multisyllabic words that older children are increasingly exposed to in their books.

Thus, the basic components of literacy include mastering a language system, understanding connections between sounds and their printed symbols (the alphabetic principle), and discriminating phonemes that make up words (phonological awareness). How does the child pull all this together into reading?

Emergent Literacy

Several factors influence **emergent literacy**—the developmental precursors of reading skills in young children (Whitehurst & Lonigan, 1998). Emergent literacy includes knowledge, skills, and attitudes that will facilitate the acquisition of reading ability. Children with greater working memory and attention control demonstrate a higher degree of reading readiness than other children, suggesting that activities strengthening these skills can help foster reading achievement (Welsh et al., 2010). One way to do this is through reading storybooks to preschoolers (Evans & Shaw, 2008). Repetitious storybook reading enhances children's vocabulary and allows them to see the connection between printed and spoken words. Importantly, parents should read *with* their child rather than *to* their child, meaning they should actively involve their child in the activity rather than having the child remain the passive recipient (Phillips, Norris, & Anderson, 2008). With each successive reading, parents who ask increasingly complex questions about the text can move their child from a superficial to a deeper understanding (van Kleeck et al., 1997). Even older children benefit from reading the same book on multiple occasions (Faust & Glenzer, 2000) and from shared reading with a parent (Clarke-Stewart, 1998). Parents, with their greater mastery of reading, can help their fledgling readers develop an understanding of printed words. If you think of this in Vygotsky's framework, it is an example of parent and child operating in the zone of proximal development.

Rhyming stories and games can help foster phonological awareness. For this reason, listening to books with a rhyming structure (for example, Dr. Seuss's *The Cat in the Hat*) can benefit children. Young children's sensitivity to rhyme (for example, *cat–sat*) helps predict their later reading success (Bryant, 1998; Goswami, 1999).

How is pointing at an image in a picture book contributing to emergent literacy?

By assessing preschool children's emergent literacy skills, parents and early childhood educators can develop a fairly accurate idea of what children's later reading skills will be. In particular, differences among children in knowledge of letters (for example, knowing the alphabet), phonological awareness, and word segmentation skills predict later differences in their reading ability (Carroll et al., 2003; Kendeou et al., 2009). In addition, semantic knowledge as reflected in children's ability to retrieve words, provide word definitions, and assign meaning to the printed symbols that represent words predicts later reading ability (Kendeou et al., 2009; Roth, Speece, & Cooper, 2002). This suggests that parents can help children get a head start on reading by encouraging activities such as rhyming, repeating the ABCs, and defining words.

Skilled and Unskilled Readers

After children have received reading instruction, why are some children quick, advanced readers but others struggle to master the most basic reading material? For starters, skilled readers have a solid understanding of the alphabetic principle—the notion that letters must be associated with phonemes. Thus, when they see the letter *b*, they know the sound that it represents. A large body of research also confirms that reading ability is influenced by a child's level of phonological awareness (Adams, Treiman, & Pressley, 1998; Bus & van Ijzendoorn, 1999). Children with higher levels of phonological awareness usually become better readers than children with lower levels of phonological awareness (Schneider, Roth, & Ennemoser, 2000).

But there is more to being a skilled reader than connecting letters with sounds. Analyses of eye movement patterns show that unskilled readers skip words or parts of words, whereas skilled readers' eyes hit all the words (Perfetti, 1999). Skilled readers do not use context to help them identify words, although they may use context to help with comprehension. As noted previously, they rely on phonology to identify words, something most unskilled readers have trouble with.

Some children have serious difficulties learning to read, even though they have normal intellectual ability and no sensory impairments or emotional difficulties that could account for their problems. These children have **dyslexia,** or a reading disability. A minority have the kind of visual perception problem that used to be seen as the heart of dyslexia; they cannot distinguish between letters with similar appearances, or they read words backward (*top* might become *pot*). However, it is now clear that the difficulties of most dyslexic children involve auditory perception more than visual perception (see, for example, Temple et al., 2000).

Specifically, children who become dyslexic readers often show deficiencies in phonological awareness well before they enter school (Bruck, 1992; Vellutino et al., 1996). There is even evidence that the brains of dyslexic children respond differently than those of other children to speech sounds soon after birth, and functional imaging of the brain shows that distinctive patterns of neural activity persist in children with dyslexia (see, for example, Caylak, 2009; Shaywitz et al., 2001). This suggests that a perceptual deficit may develop during the prenatal period of

© UpperCut Images/Getty Images

decoding the words on the page that they have little attention to spare for interpreting and remembering what they have read. Dyslexic children continue to perform poorly on tests of phonological awareness and tests of word recognition as adolescents and adults, even if they have become decent readers (Bruck, 1990, 1992; Shaywitz et al., 1999). It is now clear that dyslexia is a lifelong disability, not just a developmental delay that is eventually overcome (Shaywitz et al., 1999).

How Should Reading Be Taught?

What does all this suggest about teaching children to read? For years a debate has raged over the merits of two broad approaches to reading instruction: the phonics approach and the whole-language approach (see, for example, Chall, 1967; Lemann, 1997). The phonics (or code-oriented) approach teaches children to analyze words into their component sounds; that is, it systematically teaches them letter–sound correspondence rules (Vellutino, 1991). By contrast, the whole-language (or look–say) approach emphasizes reading for meaning and teaches children to recognize specific words by sight or to figure out what they mean using clues in the surrounding context. It assumes that the parts of printed words (the letters) are not as meaningful as the whole words and that by focusing on whole words children can learn to read as effortlessly and naturally as they learn to understand speech.

Research strongly supports the phonics approach. To read well, children must somehow learn that spoken words are made up of sounds and that the letters of the alphabet correspond to these sounds (Foorman, 1995). Teaching phonological awareness skills can pay off in better reading skills (National Reading Panel, 1999). ● **Table 10.4** shows what happened when a third-grade boy with poor phonological awareness tried to read by the look–say method. He ended up with an incorrect interpretation and lost the intended meaning of the sentence. Better decoding skills (phonics) might have enabled him to read the sentence accurately.

With this in mind, several programs have been developed for at-risk and dyslexic children who have special difficulty discriminating speech sounds that are made rapidly, such as /b/, /d/, and /t/. By playing an entertaining computer game, children are able to practice discriminating pairs of these hard-to-

Repeatedly reading the same story fosters vocabulary and deepens children's understanding of the story content.

© Jack Hollingsworth/Getty Images

brain development. Because dyslexic children have difficulty analyzing the sounds in speech, they also have trouble detecting sound–letter correspondences, which in turn impairs their ability to recognize printed words automatically and effortlessly (Bruck, 1990; Vellutino, 1991). They must then devote so much effort to

---

● **TABLE 10.4 ONE BOY'S MISREADING OF THE SENTENCE "A BOY SAID, 'RUN, LITTLE GIRL.'"**

Words in Target Sentence	Strategies Employed by Reader	Words "Read"
A	Sight word known to reader	A
boy	Unknown; uses beginning *b* to guess *baby*	baby
said, "Run,	*Said* unknown; jumps to the next word (*run*), which he recognizes, then uses the *s* in *said* and his knowledge of syntax to generate *is running*	is running
little	Sight word known to reader	little
girl."	Unknown; uses beginning *g* to guess *go*	go

SOURCE: Adapted from Ely, 2001.

distinguish sounds, which are altered so that they are stretched in time and thereby made easier to perceive (Merzenich et al., 1996; Tallal et al., 1996). After only a month of such game playing, children's ability to recognize fast sequences of speech sounds and to understand language improves dramatically. These gains eventually pay off in improved reading performance as children become more able to sound out words on the page (Foorman et al., 1998). Despite the importance of phonological awareness, however, children must also make sense of what they are reading—they must be able to read for meaning. Thus, reading programs should use both phonics and whole-language instruction, teaching letter–sound correspondences but also helping children find meaning and enjoyment in what they read (Adams, 1990).

The debate over reading instruction and its effectiveness raises a broader question about just how well schools are doing at educating children. What factors contribute—or do not contribute—to effective schools?

Effective Schools

As a result of the federal No Child Left Behind Act in the United States (NCLB, 2002), schools are under increasing pressure to demonstrate their effectiveness with annual increases in the percentage of children scoring at or above the proficient level in reading/language arts and mathematics. Clearly, some schools seem to do a better job than others—they graduate a higher percentage of students or have a higher percentage of students at or above the proficient level in one or more subjects. Why? Is it something the schools are doing differently or does it simply reflect the different qualifications of the entering students? After all, families select schools by selecting neighborhoods, and neighborhood selection is based on numerous variables including socioeconomic status. Some schools may take in more successful students from the start. We'll keep this in mind as we review first the school factors that do not seem to matter a great deal and then the school factors that do influence students' performance.

Less Important Factors

Many people assume that pouring financial resources into schools will automatically increase school effectiveness. But the relationship between funding and student outcome is complex. Some research shows that as long as schools have reasonable resources, the precise amount of money spent per pupil plays only a minor role in determining student outcomes (Hanushek, 1997; Rutter, 1983). Other research suggests that increased resources, if applied directly to classroom instruction, can increase student achievement in the earlier grades (Wenglinsky, 1998). Thus, simply adding money to school budgets is unlikely to improve school effectiveness unless schools invest this money wisely.

Another factor that has relatively little to do with a school's effectiveness is average class size (Ehrenberg et al., 2001; Rutter & Maughan, 2002). Within a range of 18 to 40 students per class, reducing class sizes (from, say, 36 to 24 students) is unlikely to increase student achievement (Hanushek, 1997,

1998). Instead, tutoring students in the early grades (kindergarten through third), especially disadvantaged and low-ability ones, one-on-one or in small groups makes a big difference in their learning of reading and mathematics (Blatchford et al., 2002; Finn, 2002). However, more modest reductions in the student–teacher ratio do not seem to be worth the large amount of money they cost.

What about the amount of time spent in school? Most children go to school for 6 hours on about 180 days of each school year. Many people assume that schools could improve student outcomes if they lengthened the school day or year. But research shows that the modest increases in time that some schools have implemented have only minimal effects on achievement (Glass, 2002b). Thus, adding 30 minutes to each school day or lengthening the school year by 15, 20, or even 25 days has negligible effects on student outcomes. Similarly, redistributing school days so that they are evenly spread across the year (called *year-round schools*) rather than bunched between September and May does not improve student achievement.

Finally, it matters little whether or not a school uses **ability grouping,** in which students are grouped according to ability and then taught in classes or work groups with others of similar academic or intellectual standing. Grouping by ability has no clear advantage over mixed-ability grouping for most students (Glass, 2002a). It *can* be beneficial, especially to higher ability students, if it results in a curriculum more appropriate to students' learning needs (Glass, 2002a; Kulik & Kulik, 1989). Research with gifted students shows that they can benefit from being grouped with their gifted peers for a substantial part of the school day (Cornell et al., 1992; Kulik & Kulik, 1987). Such high-ability grouping allows these students to move through the curriculum at a faster rate and/or deeper levels. In contrast, low-ability students are unlikely to benefit from being grouped with like-ability peers and may suffer if they are denied access to the most effective teachers, taught less material than other children, and stigmatized as "dummies" (Mac Iver, Reuman, & Main, 1995; Mehan et al., 1996). Too often, this is what happens. As Hugh Mehan and his colleagues (1996) put it, "It is not that dumb kids are placed in slow groups or low tracks; it is that kids are made dumb by being placed in slow groups or low tracks" (p. 230). Exploration Box 10.2 takes a closer look at mixing students with different abilities and backgrounds.

These, then, are examples of school characteristics that do not seem to contribute a great deal to effective education. A school that has limited financial support (assuming it exceeds a basic minimum), places most students (except perhaps beginning readers) in relatively large classes, and combines students in mixed-ability learning groups or classes is often just as effective as a school that has ample financial resources, small classes, and ability grouping.

Factors That Matter

So what does influence how well children perform? To understand why some schools are more effective than others, you must consider characteristics of the students, characteristics of the teachers and school settings, and the interaction between student and environment.

First, a school's effectiveness depends in part on what it has to work with—the students it takes in and the teachers who provide the instruction. With respect to the children, genetic differences among children contribute to differences in aptitude among them (Rutter & Maughan, 2002). As you learned in Chapters 3 and 9, IQ scores have a genetic component, and children with higher IQs attain higher grades throughout their 12 years of school (Gutman, Sameroff, & Cole, 2003). Schools cannot eliminate these genetic differences among children, but they can influence (that is, raise) overall levels of academic achievement (Zvoch & Stevens, 2006). In addition, academic achievement, on average, tends to be higher in schools with a preponderance of economically advantaged students; children are better able to make academic progress in school when they come from homes that are stocked with computers, books, and intellectually stimulating toys (Portes & MacLeod, 1996). However, this does not mean that schools are only as good as the students they serve. Many schools that serve disadvantaged populations are highly effective at motivating students and preparing them for jobs or further education. To really determine a school's effectiveness, researchers need to look at how students change from before to after they receive instruction (Zvoch & Stevens, 2006). This is, in large part, the goal of *No Child Left Behind* (NCLB)—to show that children, regardless of how high or low they score at the start, improve their performance after each year of instruction.

Studies of the effects of schools provide another illustration of the interaction of nature and nurture. High-achieving parents pass their genes to their children, providing genetic potential for high achievement to their children (Rutter & Maughan, 2002). These same high-achieving parents are likely to select schools that have strong academic reputations, often by choosing to live in a neighborhood served by a "good" school district (Rutter & Maughan, 2002). This is an example of a passive gene–environment correlation, described in Chapter 3, in which children are influenced by their parent's genes directly through genetic transmission and indirectly through the environments their parents create for them.

As for the effects of teachers on school achievement, Andrew Wayne and Peter Youngs (2003) reviewed research on the relationship between teacher characteristics and student achievement. They found that student achievement scores rose with increases in the quality of their teachers' undergraduate institutions and their teachers' licensure examination scores. Perhaps the most intriguing findings about teacher effectiveness come from statistical analyses conducted by William Sanders, who concludes that "the answer to why children learn well or not isn't race, it isn't poverty, it isn't even per-pupil expenditure at the elementary level. It's teachers, teachers, teachers" (Sanders, 1999). He draws this conclusion after finding that students who are lucky enough to get the best teachers three years in a row achieve as much as 50 points higher on standardized tests than students who are unfortunate enough to get the worst teachers three years in a row (■ **Figure 10.5**; Sanders & Horn, 1995; Sanders & Rivers, 1996). What is an

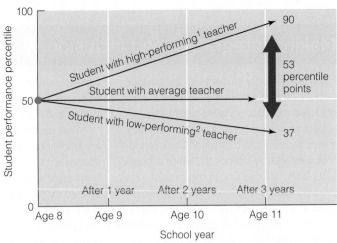

■ **FIGURE 10.5** Students who are fortunate to have high-performing teachers can increase their relative performance each year, whereas students with low-performing teachers actually lose ground, leading to a performance gap that increases each year students are with a high- or low-performing teacher.

1 Among the top 20% of teachers

2 Among the bottom 20% of teachers

SOURCE: Sanders and Rivers, "Cumulative and Residual Effects on Future Student Academic Achievement," 1996.

effective teacher? According to Sanders, effectiveness can be defined by how far teachers can advance their students each year. Eric Hanushek reaches a similar conclusion after finding that students with the best teachers advance 1.5 years in 1 school year with this teacher, compared with those students with the worst teachers, who advance only half a year over the course of the school year (see Hanushek, Rivkin, & Kain, 2005). These effects are cumulative and long-lasting: a student with the best teachers 2 years in a row progresses the equivalent of 3 years, whereas the student with the worst teachers 2 years in a row progresses just 1 year and will be 2 years behind the other student in achievement level.

What might be going on in the classrooms of the students who show the most progress each year? Basically, the effective school environment is a comfortable but businesslike setting in which teachers are involved with students, students are motivated to learn, and serious teaching takes place (Mac Iver et al., 1995; Phillips, 1997; Rutter, 1983). More specifically, in effective schools and classrooms, teachers:

- Strongly emphasize academics. They demand a lot from their students, expect them to succeed, regularly assign homework, and work hard to achieve their objectives in the classroom.
- Create a task-oriented but comfortable atmosphere. For example, they waste little time starting activities or dealing with distracting discipline problems, provide clear instructions and feedback, and encourage and reward good work.
- Manage discipline problems effectively. For example, they enforce the rules on the spot rather than sending offenders to

Making Integration and Inclusion Work

For many minority students of the past, especially African Americans, additional barriers to school success were created by school segregation. Black children in many states were forced to attend "black schools" that were clearly inferior to "white schools." In its landmark decision in the case of *Brown v. Board of Education of Topeka* in 1954, the Supreme Court ruled that segregated schools were "inherently unequal" and declared that they must be desegregated. More than 50 years have passed since this ruling. What has been learned about desegregation during this time?

In general, the effects of school **integration,** or teaching children of different racial/ethnic backgrounds in the same classroom, have been mixed (Gray-Little & Carels, 1997; Rumberger & Palardy, 2005). Some studies suggest that both African American and European American children tend to have higher self-esteem and higher achievement when they attend racially mixed schools, but the effects are often small (Gray-Little & Carels, 1997). Sadly, white prejudice toward black students often does not decrease much following integration. The self-esteem of black children in integrated schools is only sometimes higher than that of black children in racially homogeneous schools (Gray-Little & Carels, 1997). And although minority students sometimes achieve more in integrated schools, especially if they begin to attend them early in their academic careers, school integration often has little effect on achievement (Rossell, Armor, & Walberg, 2002).

What seems to be more important than a school's racial composition is the socioeconomic status of its students. Russell Rumberger and Gregory Palardy (2005) examined more than 14,000 students attending 913 different high schools to determine the school factors that affect students' academic achievement. They found that, regardless of a student's race or the ratio of different racial groups attending the school, students achieved at higher levels when they attended schools with students from higher socioeconomic backgrounds than when they attended with students from low socioeconomic backgrounds (see also Ryabov & van Hook, 2007). Such findings have led some school districts to use socioeconomic status as the basis for their integration programs rather than race or ethnicity (Kahlenberg, 2006).

The message from this research is not that integration has been unsuccessful. The message is that integration alone will not improve academic achievement if other issues are not addressed. For instance, school safety, availability of advanced courses, homework assignment, teacher expectations, and family support need to be addressed regardless of what is done to continue the 50-year-old struggle to desegregate schools and integrate students.

Children with developmental disabilities (mental retardation, learning disabilities, physical and sensory handicaps, and other special learning needs) have had a similar history (Ferri & Connor, 2005). They used to be placed in separate schools or classrooms—or, in some cases, rejected as unteachable by the public schools. But the Individuals with Disabilities Education Act requires schools to provide such children with a free and appropriate education that occurs "to the maximum extent appropriate. . . with children who are not disabled."

What has been achieved? Studies of developmentally disabled children integrated into regular classrooms through a practice called **inclusion** (formerly called *mainstreaming*)—to emphasize the philosophy that children with special learning needs should spend the entire school day rather than only parts of it in a regular classroom and truly be included in the normal educational process—have yielded mixed results. Compared with similar students who attend segregated special education classes, these mainstreamed youngsters sometimes fare better in terms of academic performance, self-esteem, and social adjustment but sometimes do not (Buysse & Bailey, 1993; Hunt & Goetz, 1997; Manset & Semmel, 1997). The outcome depends partly on the severity of the child's disability. The performance of higher-functioning disabled children often benefits from inclusion in the

the principal's office, and they avoid the use of physical punishment.

Effective schools also have supportive parents and supportive communities behind them (Comer, 1997). Students achieve more when their parents are interested in and value school and school achievement; participate in parent–teacher conferences, PTA meetings, and other school events; and participate in homework and other school-related activities at home (Hill & Craft, 2003; Hill & Taylor, 2004). Parents' involvement in school is also associated with better social skills and fewer behavioral problems among their children (Kohl et al., 2000; Marcon, 1999). Parents with less education are typically less involved in their children's education than highly educated parents are, yet they can have a greater effect on their children's grades if they become involved (Bogenschneider, 1997; Downey, 2002).

Finally, characteristics of the student and characteristics of the school environment often interact to affect student outcome. This is an example of the concept of goodness of fit—an appropriate match between the person's characteristics and her environment (see Chapter 11). Much educational research has been based on the assumption that one teaching method, organizational system, or philosophy of education will prove superior for regular classroom, whereas the performance of lower-functioning children is similar in integrated and segregated classrooms (Holahan & Costenbader, 2000). In terms of peer acceptance, it is the children with severe disabilities who are better accepted by their normally developing peers than the children with mild disabilities in regular classrooms. Those with more severe disabilities presumably stand out as different, prompting other students to adjust their expectations (Cook & Semmel, 1999). Children with mild disabilities may not stand out in the regular classroom and therefore do not achieve "special" status; these children are better accepted in heterogeneous classrooms that include a wide range of abilities including children with mild and moderate disabilities (Cook & Semmel, 1999). Overall, though, children with disabilities often remain stigmatized and invisible in the regular classroom (Books, 2007).

What researchers seem to be learning about both integration and inclusion is that simply putting diverse students into the same schools and classrooms accomplishes little. Instead, something special must be done to ensure that students of different ethnic backgrounds and ability levels interact in positive ways and learn what they are supposed to be learning.

One promising model uses **cooperative learning,** in which diverse students are assigned to work teams and are reinforced for performing well as a team. Consider research conducted by Uri Treisman with African Americans and Asian Americans enrolled in first-year calculus (see Fullilove & Treisman, 1990). The Asian Americans did well in the class, whereas the African Americans performed poorly. But this was not the only difference between the two groups of students. The African American students worked independently on work related to the class; the Asian Americans worked in small study groups and often combined studying with socializing, something the African American students rarely did. Treisman decided to see whether working together and receiving support from peers could boost the African American students' performance—it did (see also Duncan & Dick, 2000).

In cooperative learning classrooms, children of different races and ability levels interact in a context where, ideally, the efforts of even the least capable team members are important to the group's success. Typically developing elementary-school students like school better and learn more when they participate in cooperative learning groups than when they receive traditional instruction, although the brightest children may sometimes experience frustration if the ability range of the group is quite large (Johnson, Johnson, & Maruyama, 1983; O'Donnell & O'Kelly, 1994; Stevens & Slavin, 1995). Moreover, team members gain self-esteem from their successes, and minority students and students with developmental disabilities are more fully accepted by their peers. In short, racial integration and inclusion can succeed if educators deliberately design learning experiences that encourage students from different backgrounds to pool their efforts to achieve common goals. Interventions such as this are important if children are to be ready for the challenges of secondary school.

© Gabe Palmer/Corbis

all students, regardless of their ability levels, learning styles, personalities, and cultural backgrounds. This assumption is often wrong. Instead, many educational practices are highly effective with some kinds of students but ineffective with other students. The secret is to find an appropriate match between the learner and the teaching method.

In a good illustration of goodness of fit between learners and environments, highly achievement-oriented students adapt well to unstructured classrooms in which they have a good deal of choice, whereas less achievement-oriented students often do better with more structure (Peterson, 1977). Sometimes an alternative teaching method works as well as a traditional one for highly capable students but only one of these methods suits less capable students. In one study, for example, highly distractible students got more from computer-assisted instruction than from a teacher's presentation of the same material, whereas more attentive students benefited equally from both methods (Orth & Martin, 1994). Finally, students tend to have more positive outcomes when they and their teacher share similar backgrounds (Goldwater & Nutt, 1999). Evidence of the importance of the fit between student and classroom environment implies that educational programs are likely to be most effective when they are highly individualized—tailored to suit each student's developmental competencies and needs.

What factors will determine whether this student remains motivated and focused on mastery goals or shifts to performance goals and possibly becomes disinterested with school?

© Tom & Dee Ann McCarthy/Corbis

Checking Mastery

1. What is the difference between a mastery (or learning) goal and a performance goal?

2. What is one characteristic that differentiates a skilled reader from a less skilled reader?

3. What are two features of an effective school?

Making Connections

1. Using the material on effective schools, evaluate your high school and indicate ways it could improve to become a highly effective school.

2. Unlike most of his peers, Johnny, age 7, is not yet reading despite having the usual classroom instruction. What might account for Johnny's trouble with reading?

10.4 The Adolescent

Adolescents make critical decisions about such matters as how much time to devote to studying, whether to work part-time after school, whether to go to college, and what to be when they grow up. They become more capable of making these educational and vocational choices as their cognitive and social skills expand; in turn, the choices they make shape their development. But many of them lose interest in school when they leave elementary school.

Declining Levels of Achievement

You might think that adolescents would become more dedicated to academic success once they begin to realize that they need a good education to succeed in life. But consider what Deborah Stipek

(1984) concluded after reviewing studies on the development of achievement motivation from early childhood to adolescence:

> On the average, children value academic achievement more as they progress through school, but their expectations for success and self-perceptions of competence decline, and their affect toward school becomes more negative. Children also become increasingly concerned about achievement outcomes and reinforcement (e.g., high grades) associated with positive outcomes and less concerned about intrinsic satisfaction in achieving greater competence. (p. 153)

Many of the negative trends Stipek describes become especially apparent as young adolescents make the transition from elementary school to middle school (typically grades 6–8) or junior high school (grades 7–9). At this critical juncture, achievement motivation, self-esteem, and grades may all decline. ■ **Figure 10.6** shows the academic trajectories for four groups of students studied by Leslie Gutman and his colleagues: those with high and low IQ scores who had either many or few risk factors (Gutman, Sameroff, & Cole, 2003). Risk factors included minority group status, low maternal education and mental health, stressful life events, family size, and father absence. Students with more risk factors showed a steady decline in academic achievement throughout their schooling, regardless of whether they had high or low IQ scores to begin with. Students with few risk factors showed a slight increase in achievement until around grade 6 or 7, at which time achievement began to drop slowly. Boys show greater declines in motivation and school interest than girls (Dotterer, McHale, & Crouter, 2009).

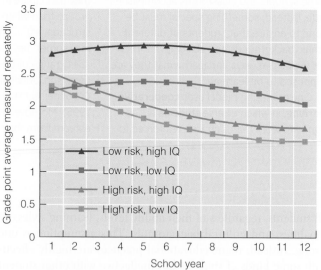

■ **FIGURE 10.6** Grade point average from 1st grade to 12th grade for students with high and low risk and IQ. SOURCE: From Gutman, L. M., Samereroff, A. J., & Cole, R. Academic growth curve trajectories from 1st grade to 12th grade: Effects of multiple social risk factors and preschool child factors, *Developmental Psychology, 39*, pp. 777–790. Copyright © 2003 by the American Psychological Association. Reprinted with permission.

By adolescence, some students have little motivation to achieve in the classroom. How can this be prevented?

© GoGo Images Corporation/Alamy

What might explain these discouraging trends? To answer this question, we'll first examine what is going on at the individual level, and then consider family and peer influences before ending with a look at the wider context of school and society.

At the individual level, children become increasingly capable of analyzing the causes of events, interpreting feedback from teachers, and inferring enduring traits such as high or low ability from their behavior (Stipek & Mac Iver, 1989). The result is that they view their strengths and weaknesses more realistically—and lose some of their high academic self-esteem and high expectancies of success (Stipek & Mac Iver, 1989; Wigfield et al., 1997). Those who manage to maintain an emphasis on mastery or learning goals attain higher grades in high school than those who do not (Gutman, 2006). Students who believe that success is a matter of luck have lower grades than students without this attributional style (House, 2006).

At the family level, several characteristics are associated with lower achievement and more absences from school. Being a member of a minority group, growing up in a single-parent family, and having a mother with less education or with mental health problems are potential academic risk factors (Gutman, Sameroff, & Cole, 2003; Gutman, Sameroff, & Eccles, 2002). In contrast, living in a small, caring family with at least one stable parent who uses consistent discipline can bolster school performance (Gutman, Sameroff, & Eccles, 2002). Mothers who talk to their middle-school children about assuming responsibility and making decisions have teens who are more likely to complete high school and continue their education (Tenenbaum et al., 2007). Adolescents who believe their parents are more involved in their schooling are generally more academically motivated than adolescents who believe their parents are less involved (Spera, 2006). Importantly, it is the students' *perceptions* of parental involvement and not actual involvement that is related to motivation levels.

The adolescent's achievement motivation is also affected by the increasing importance of the peer group, which at times can undermine parents' and teachers' efforts to encourage school achievement. Many years ago, when James Coleman (1961) asked high school students how they would like to be remembered, only 31% of the boys and 28% of the girls wanted to be remembered as bright students. They were more concerned with having the athletic and social skills that lead to popularity. Not much has changed. Tim Urdan and Miranda Mestas (2006) interviewed high school seniors about their reasons for pursuing performance goals. Many of the responses indicated that teens were motivated by a desire to avoid looking dumb or to look competent and make their parents proud. But some of the students specifically noted that they wanted to be average and not appear to be too smart. As one student said, "I just want to be normal, not the best. I don't want to be the worst but I just want to be normal" (p. 361).

Peer pressures that undermine achievement motivation tend to be especially strong for many lower-income males and for minority students (Véronneau et al., 2008). In particular, African American and Hispanic peer cultures in many low-income areas actively discourage academic achievement, whereas European American and especially Asian American peer groups tend to value and encourage it (Steinberg, Dornbusch, & Brown, 1992). High-achieving African American students in some inner-city schools risk being rejected by their African American peers if their academic accomplishments cause them to be perceived as "acting white" (Fordham & Ogbu, 1986). They may feel that they have to abandon their cultural group and racial identity to succeed in school, and this takes a psychological toll (Arroyo & Zigler, 1995; Ogbu, 2003). Some students may disengage from academics to preserve their cultural identity with a group that has historically not always been treated fairly by the educational system (Ogbu, 2003). Although African American parents are as likely as European American parents to value education and to provide the kind of authoritative parenting that encourages school achievement, their positive influences are sometimes canceled out by negative peer influences (Steinberg et al., 1992).

For those African American teens who belong to a supportive peer group, academic achievement is strengthened (Gutman et al., 2002). In addition, African American teens who strongly value their ethnic group membership and have positive beliefs about how society views African Americans tend to have more positive beliefs about education (Chavous et al., 2003). But even a strong ethnic identity may not be able to overcome the subtle and negative effects of discrimination still experienced by many minority students in the classroom, eroding their self-confidence and lowering their motivation (Thomas et al., 2009).

Finally, we must consider that some of the decline in the achievement motivation of adolescents may reflect a poor fit between person and environment. Adopting a goodness-of-fit explanation, Jacquelynne Eccles and her colleagues (Eccles, Lord, & Midgley, 1991; Eccles et al., 1993) argue that the transition to middle school or junior high school is likely to be especially difficult because young adolescents are often experiencing major physical and psychological changes at the time they are switching schools (see also Hill & Tyson, 2009). For example, girls who were reaching puberty when they were moving from sixth grade in an elementary school to seventh grade in a junior high school were more likely to experience drops in self-esteem and other negative changes than girls who remained in a K–8 school during this vulnerable period (Simmons & Blyth, 1987).

Could it be that more adolescents would remain interested in school if they did not have to change schools when they are experiencing pubertal changes? This idea became an important part of the rationale for shifting from junior high schools, in which students transitioned between the sixth and seventh grades, to middle schools where the transition occurs between the fifth and sixth grades. Yet Eccles and her colleagues (1991, 1993) have shown that students do not necessarily find the transition to middle school any easier than the transition to junior high school. These researchers suspect that *when* adolescents make a school change is less important than what their new school is like.

The transition to middle or junior high school often involves going from a small school with close student–teacher relationships, a good deal of choice regarding learning activities, and reasonable discipline to a larger, more bureaucratized environment in which student–teacher relationships are impersonal, good grades are more emphasized but harder to come by, opportunities for choice are limited, assignments are not as intellectually stimulating, and discipline is rigid—all when adolescents are seeking more rather than less autonomy and are becoming more rather than less intellectually capable (Hill & Tyson, 2009). Giving students a sense of ownership and some degree of control in their learning helps maintain their interest and motivation (Tsai et al., 2008; Valiente et al., 2008).

Eccles and her colleagues have demonstrated that the fit between developmental needs and school environment is an important influence on adolescent adjustment to school. In one study (Mac Iver & Reuman, 1988), the transition to junior high school brought about a decline in intrinsic motivation to learn mainly among students who wanted more involvement in classroom decisions but ended up with fewer such opportunities than they had in elementary school. In another study (Midgley, Feldlaufer, & Eccles, 1989), students experienced negative changes in their attitudes toward mathematics only when their move from elementary school to junior high resulted in less personal and supportive relationships with math teachers. For those few students whose junior high school teachers were more supportive than those they had in elementary school, interest in academics increased. Similarly, other research has shown that training staff members to understand and respond appropriately to the developmental needs of this age group helped students maintain a positive outlook on learning and perform better in school (Martin, 2008). Moreover, the middle school slump is largely avoided among students whose mothers display a high interest in academics and hold high expectations (Dotterer et al., 2009). Thus, here is something tangible that parents can do to help their children experience continued success in school.

The message? Declines in academic motivation and performance are not inevitable during early adolescence. Students may indeed form more realistic expectancies of success as their growing cognitive abilities allow them to use the increasingly informative feedback they receive from teachers. Experiencing pubertal changes at the same time as other stressful changes and needing to downplay academics to gain popularity may also hurt school achievement. However, educators can help keep adolescents engaged in school by creating school environments that provide a better fit to the developmental needs and interests of adolescents. Whether they are called middle schools or junior high schools, such schools should provide warm, supportive relationships with teachers, intellectual challenges, and increased opportunities for self-direction (Eccles et al., 1993). Parents can also help by remaining supportive and involved in their child's education throughout the middle school years rather than pulling back (Hill & Tyson, 2009).

Science and Mathematics Education

Elementary schools necessarily spend much time on reading and writing skills. But secondary-school teachers take these skills largely for granted and focus energy on other academic areas. More advanced skills of concrete-operational and then formal-operational thought enable children to tackle more challenging academic tasks. Much attention has been focused on mathematics and science, skills important for success in many industrialized nations. How well do secondary-school students perform in science and math? And how might achievement in these areas be optimized?

■ **Figure 10.7** and ■ **Figure 10.8** show average mathematics and science achievement test scores of eighth-grade students in various countries. Students in the United States score above the international average but significantly below achievement levels in nations such as Singapore, Japan, and Korea. When researchers looked at the best students—those in the top 10% of all eighth-graders surveyed in the 48 nations—only 6% of U.S. students met the criteria in math and only 10% met it in science. In comparison, 45% of Chinese Taipei eighth-graders scored in the top 10% in math and 32% of Singapore's eighth-graders scored at the top in science. What might account for these international differences in math and science achievement? Are students in some nations simply more intelligent than students in other nations?

Cross-cultural research conducted by Harold Stevenson and his colleagues (Chen & Stevenson, 1995; Stevenson & Lee, 1990; Stevenson, Chen, & Lee, 1993) shows that American schoolchildren perform about as well on IQ tests as their Asian counterparts when they enter school (Stevenson et al., 1985). They score at least as well as Japanese and Chinese students on tests of general information not typically covered in school (Stevenson et al., 1993). Instead, the achievement gap between American and Asian students seems to be rooted in cultural differences in attitudes concerning education and educational practices. Here is what some of this cross-cultural research on education and achievement shows:

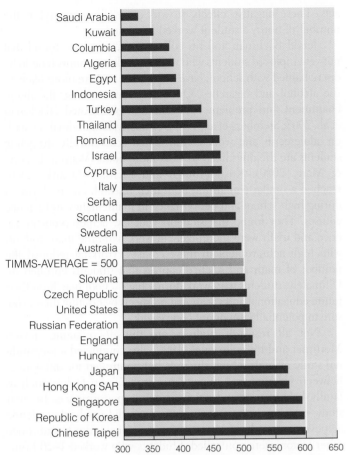

■ **FIGURE 10.7** International comparison of eighth-grade math performance. Source: Adapted from P. Gonzales, T. Williams, L. Jocelyn, S. Roey, D. Kastberg, and S. Brenwald. (2008). *Highlights from TIMSS 2007: Mathematics and Science Achievement of U.S. Fourth- and Eighth-Grade Students in an International Context* (NCES 2009–001 Revised). National Center for Education Statistics, Institute of Education Sciences, U.S. Department of Education. Washington, DC.

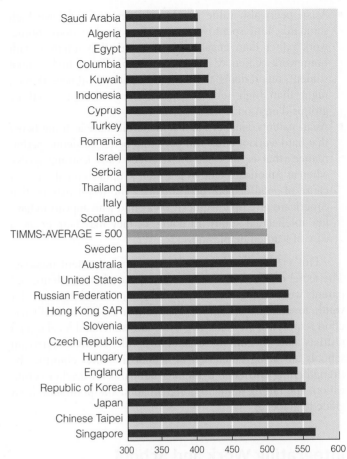

■ **FIGURE 10.8** International comparison of eighth-grade science performance. Source: Adapted from P. Gonzales, T. Williams, L. Jocelyn, S. Roey, D. Kastberg, and S. Brenwald. (2008). *Highlights from TIMSS 2007: Mathematics and Science Achievement of U.S. Fourth- and Eighth-Grade Students in an International Context* (NCES 2009–001 Revised). National Center for Education Statistics, Institute of Education Sciences, U.S. Department of Education. Washington, DC.

- Asian students spend more time being educated. Elementary-school teachers in Asian countries devote more class time to academics. The classroom is a businesslike place where little time is wasted; Asian students spend about 95% of their time "on task" (in activities such as listening to the teacher and completing assignments), whereas American students spend only about 80% of their time "on task" (Stigler, Lee, & Stevenson, 1987). Asian students also attend school for more hours per day and more days per year (Stevenson, Lee, & Stigler, 1986).

- Teachers have different approaches to instruction. For instance, in China, more time in the math classroom is spent on extended discourse in which the teacher continues to question and discuss students' correct answers (Schleppenbach et al., 2007). In contrast, teachers in U.S. math classrooms tend to move on to the next problem once a student has given a correct answer.

- Asian students, especially Japanese students, are assigned and complete considerably more homework than American students (Verma & Larson, 2003). When American students are working or socializing with friends, Asian students are hitting the books (Fuligni & Stevenson, 1995).

- Asian parents are strongly committed to the educational process. About 40% think their children should have 3 hours or more of homework each day (Ebbeck, 1996). Asian parents are rarely satisfied with how their children are doing in school or with the quality of education their children are receiving; American parents seem to settle for less (Mathews, 2003). Asian parents also receive frequent communications from their children's teachers in notebooks children carry to and from school each day. They find out how their children are progressing and follow teachers' suggestions for encouraging and assisting their children at home (Stevenson & Lee, 1990).

- Asian peers also value school achievement and have high standards; time spent with peers often involves doing homework rather than engaging in activities that interfere with homework (Chen & Stevenson, 1995). Asian high school students report doing about a half hour more homework each night than high school students from other racial/ethnic groups (Ferguson, 2002).
- Asian parents, teachers, and students all share a strong belief that hard work or effort will pay off in better academic performance (that is, they set what Dweck calls learning goals), whereas Americans tend to put more emphasis on ability as a cause of good or poor performance. The result may be that Americans give up too quickly on a child who appears to have low intellectual ability. In doing so, they may help create a case of learned helplessness.

This cross-cultural research carries an important message: The secret of effective education is to get teachers, students, and parents working together to make education the top priority for youth, to set high achievement goals, and to invest the day-by-day effort required to attain those goals. Many states and local school districts have begun to respond to evidence that American schools are being outclassed by schools in other countries by strengthening curricula, tightening standards for teacher certification, and raising standards for graduation and promotion from grade to grade.

Integrating Work and School

Unlike teens in many other industrialized nations, a sizable number (between one-third and one-half) of teens in the United States and Canada work part-time during their high school careers (Bachman et al., 2003; Thomas, 1998). How do these early work experiences affect their development and, in particular, their school achievement?

Laurence Steinberg and his associates have compared working and nonworking high school students in terms of such outcomes as autonomy from parents, self-reliance, self-esteem, sense of investment in school, academic performance, delinquency, and drug and alcohol use (Greenberger & Steinberg, 1986; Steinberg & Dornbusch, 1991; Steinberg, Fegley, & Dornbusch, 1993). Overall, this research offers more bad news than good. The good news is that working students seem to gain knowledge about work, consumer issues, and financial management and sometimes about greater self-reliance. However, high school students who worked 20 or more hours a week had lower grade-point averages than students who did not work or who worked only 10 or fewer hours per week (Steinberg & Dornbusch, 1991). Working students were also more likely than nonworkers to be disengaged from school—bored and uninvolved in class and prone to cut class and spend little time on homework.

In addition, the more adolescents worked, the more independent they were of parental control, the more likely they were to be experiencing psychological distress (anxiety, depression, and physical symptoms such as headaches), and the more frequently they used alcohol and drugs and engaged in delinquent

acts. These negative effects of work generally increased as the number of hours a student worked increased.

Jerald Bachman and his colleagues (2003) have found that not-yet-employed students who want to work long hours tend to be disenchanted with school, have low grades, and are more likely to use alcohol and cigarettes. Once they start working, the disenchantment and problem behaviors are exacerbated (Bachman et al., 2003; Steinberg et al., 1993). Similarly, longitudinal research on adolescents and work confirms that academically struggling students are the ones likely to work more hours (Warren, LePore, & Marc, 2000). Kusum Singh and Mehmet Ozturk (2000) reached a similar conclusion from their research on employment during high school and performance in mathematics and science courses. They found that students with low achievement in science and math were more likely to work part-time than students with high achievement in these courses. Working reduced the number of math and science courses that students enrolled in. Ultimately, students who work during high school may limit their future educational and vocational prospects by limiting their exposure to potentially important coursework.

Not all research findings are this discouraging. Jeylen Mortimer and his colleagues (1996) also conducted a longitudinal study of high school students but controlled for differences between working and nonworking students on factors such as family background and prior academic performance. In their study, working 20 hours or more a week did not hurt academic achievement, self-esteem, or psychological adjustment once other factors were controlled. Students who worked 1–20 hours a week actually earned better grades than either nonworkers or students who worked more than 20 hours a week. As in Steinberg's study, however, students who worked more than 20 hours used alcohol more frequently than students who were not employed.

When all the research is examined as a package, the findings suggest that working while attending high school is often more damaging than beneficial (Marsh & Kleitman, 2005). Much depends on the nature of the work adolescents do. Many teenagers work in food service jobs (pouring soft drinks behind the

Working in fast-food restaurants is not the kind of intellectually challenging job that can contribute positively to adolescent development. If a high school student does work during the school year, what guidelines would help ensure a healthy blend of work and academics?

counter at fast-food restaurants, scooping ice cream, and the like) or perform manual labor (especially cleaning or janitorial work). These routine and repetitive jobs offer few opportunities for self-direction or decision making and only rarely call on academic skills such as reading and mathematics (Greenberger & Steinberg, 1986). They are not the kinds of jobs that build character or teach new skills. Adolescents experience gains in mastery motivation and become less depressed over time when the work they do provides opportunities for advancement and teaches useful skills, but they lose mastery motivation and become more depressed when they hold menial jobs that interfere with their schooling (Call, Mortimer, & Shanahan, 1995; Shanahan et al., 1991). Thus, many adolescents who are flipping hamburgers might be better off postponing work or working only a limited number of hours if possible so that they can concentrate on obtaining a solid education and exploring their career options (Greenberger & Steinberg, 1986).

Pathways to Adulthood

The educational paths and attainments of adolescents are partially set long before they enter adolescence. Because many individuals' IQ test scores remain stable from childhood on, some children enter adolescence with more aptitude for schoolwork than others do (see Chapter 9). Moreover, some students have more achievement motivation than others. Clearly, a bright and achievement-oriented student is more likely to obtain good grades and go on to college and is less likely to drop out of school than a student with less ability and less need to achieve. By early elementary school, and sometimes even before they enter school, future dropouts are often identifiable by such warning signs as low IQ and achievement test scores, poor grades, aggressive behavior, low socioeconomic status, and troubled homes (Ensminger & Slusarcick, 1992; Gamoran et al., 1997).

This does not mean that adolescents' fates are sealed in childhood, however; experiences during adolescence clearly make a difference. Some teenagers make the most of their intellectual abilities, whereas others who have the ability to do well in school drop out or get poor grades. The quality of an adolescent's school, the extent to which her parents are authoritative and encourage school achievement, and the extent to which her peers value school can make a big difference (Brown et al., 1993; Rutter et al., 1979; Steinberg, Dornbusch, & Brown, 1992).

The stakes are high. Students who achieve good grades are more likely to complete high school; recently, 92% of European American students, 86% of African American students, 85% of Asian Americans, and an alarmingly low 70% of Hispanic students achieved this milestone (National Center for Education Statistics, 2007). They then stand a chance of being among the 30% of European Americans, 17% of African Americans, 49% of Asian Americans, and 11% of Hispanics who complete 4 years of college or more (U.S. Census Bureau, 2007). These youth, in turn, are likely to have higher career aspirations and to end up in higher status occupations than their peers who do not attend college or do not even finish high school (McCaul et al., 1992). If their grades are good, they are likely to perform well in those jobs

and advance far in their careers (Roth et al., 1996). In a real sense, then, individuals are steered along "high success" or "low success" routes starting in childhood. Depending on their own decisions and family, peer, and school influences, adolescents are more distinctly "sorted" in ways that will affect their adult lifestyles, income levels, and adjustment. Meanwhile, high school dropouts not only have less successful careers but also miss out on the beneficial effects that every year of schooling has on intellectual functioning (Ceci & Williams, 1997). In addition, they experience more psychological problems than those who stay in school (Kaplan, Damphousse, & Kaplan, 1994).

Checking Mastery

1. What are two reasons why achievement motivation may decline during adolescence?

2. Why might students in Asian schools outperform many other students in science and math?

3. What is one advantage and one disadvantage of working while in high school?

Making Connections

1. Research shows that achievement motivation and grades often drop as students move through middle school and high school. Develop a program to combat this trend, keeping in mind that students of different backgrounds may lose motivation for different reasons.

2. After finishing up ninth grade, your teenager says he wants to work for the next 3 years while in high school. What advice will you give him?

10.5 The Adult

The lives of adults are dominated by work—paid or unpaid, outside the home or within the home. What becomes of achievement motivation and literacy during the adult years? What educational options are available to adults, and what are the benefits of lifelong education?

Achievement Motivation

The level of achievement motivation that we acquire in childhood and adolescence carries into adulthood to influence our decisions and life outcomes (Wlodkowski, 1999). For instance, women who have a strong need to achieve are more likely than less achievement-oriented women to work outside the home (Krogh, 1985). Adults with strong achievement needs are also likely to be more competent workers than adults who have little concern with mastering challenges (Helmreich, Sawin, & Carsrud, 1986; Spence, 1985).

What happens to achievement motivation in later life? Is there any support for the common belief that older adults lose some of their drive to excel? Joseph Veroff, David Reuman, and Sheila Feld (1984) explored this question by analyzing motivational themes in stories that American adults told in response to pictures. Older men displayed only slightly lower levels of achievement motivation than young or middle-aged men did. Here, then, there is no support for the stereotyped idea that older adults are "unmotivated" or have ceased to pursue goals (Filipp, 1996; McAdams, de St. Aubin, & Logan, 1993).

Veroff and his associates (1984) did find that women's achievement motivation declined fairly steeply with age (see also Mellinger & Erdwins, 1985). However, this age trend pertained mainly to career-related motivation and an interest in striving for success in competitive situations. Women's motivation in other areas remains high. Many women have traditionally set aside career-achievement goals after they have children and make nurturing those children their priority (Krogh, 1985). However, highly educated women often regain a strong motive to achieve outside the home once their children are older and they can invest more energy in outside work. Apparently, then, women are especially likely to be motivated to achieve career success when they have the educational background that would allow them to pursue attractive career goals and when they are not pursuing family-related goals.

Overall, adults' achievement-related motives are far more affected by changes in work and family contexts than by the aging process (Filipp, 1996). Adults of different ages are often more alike than they are different, and different people tend to retain their characteristic levels of achievement motivation over the years, much as they retain many personality traits (Stevens & Truss, 1985). There is little evidence that elderly adults inevitably lose their motivation to pursue important goals. Moreover, those elders who have a strong sense of purpose and direction and feel they are achieving their goals enjoy greater physical and psychological well-being than those who do not (Hooker & Siegler, 1993; Rapkin &

Many older adults remain motivated to learn and seek challenging experiences.

Fischer, 1992; Reker, Peacock, & Wong, 1987). Throughout the life span, then, setting and achieving goals are important.

Literacy

Literacy is the ability to use printed information to function in society, achieve goals, and develop one's potential (National Center for Education Statistics, 2007). Few adults are completely illiterate, but many adults do not have functional literacy skills despite years of formal education. The National Adult Literacy Survey reports that about 14% of adults in the United States demonstrate the lowest level of literacy skills, which is roughly equivalent to a third-grade or lower reading ability. Such an adult could probably find an expiration date on a driver's license and sign a form but would have trouble filling out an application or reading a simple book to a child. Although one-quarter of this group consists of immigrants learning English as a second language, most individuals in this group are U.S.-born citizens and nearly two-thirds did not finish high school.

Another 29% of adults have just rudimentary, or basic, literacy skills, allowing them to perform simple literacy tasks such as using a television guide or comparing prices on two receipts, but limiting their abilities to consult reference information online or in texts (National Center for Education Statistics, 2007). Only 13% of adults demonstrate proficient levels of literacy. When the U.S. literacy rate is compared with rates in other countries, researchers find that the United States has one of the largest pockets of illiterate adults but also has some of the most highly literate adults (U.S. Department of Education, 1997). Thus, literacy in the United States is unevenly distributed.

Literacy contributes to economic security through occupational advancement. Nearly half of the adults with the lowest literacy scores live in poverty, whereas few adults with the highest literacy scores do (Bowen, 1999). Improving the literacy skills of impoverished adults, however, does not automatically raise them out of poverty. For many low-income and functionally illiterate adults, other obstacles must be overcome, including addiction, discrimination, and disabilities (Bowen, 1999).

Programs to raise the literacy level of adults are rarely successful. Several factors limit the success of such programs. For one thing, despite having limited literacy skills, many of these adults (75%) reported that they could read or write "well" or "very well"—attitudes that must make it difficult to motivate them to improve their literacy skills. Second, adults do not stay in literacy programs long enough to make improvements (Amstutz & Sheared, 2000). The dropout rate is as high as 70 to 80%, and many leave in the first weeks of the program (Quigley & Uhland, 2000). Adults who do not persist report that the programs are boring and do not meet their needs (Imel, 1996; Kerka, 1995; Quigley, 1997). Materials, for example, are often geared toward children, not adults who have families, jobs, and different interests than children do.

Continuing Education

Increasingly, adults are seeking education beyond basic literacy skills. Nearly 40% of college students are 25 years or older, representing 15 million adults enrolled in college (National Center

To help you appreciate the practical implications for school reform and school achievement of the material in Chapters 6 through 9, we provide the following recommendations based on the research and theories discussed in these chapters.

Piaget

- Provide opportunities for independent, hands-on interaction with the physical environment, especially for younger children.
- With the child's current level of understanding in mind, create some disequilibrium by presenting new information slightly above the child's current level. Children who experience disequilibrium—cognitive discomfort with their understanding (or lack of understanding)—will work to resolve it, achieving a higher level of mastery of the material.
- Encourage interaction with peers, which will expose children to other perspectives and give them an opportunity to reevaluate and revise their own view.

Vygotsky

- Provide opportunities for children to interact with others who have greater mastery of the material—an older peer, teacher, or parent. These more advanced thinkers can help "pull" children to a level of understanding they would be unable to achieve on their own.

- Encourage students, especially young ones, to talk to themselves as they work on difficult tasks. Such private speech can guide behavior and facilitate thought.
- Present challenging tasks, but do not expect students to complete such tasks successfully without guidance. With support, students can accomplish more difficult tasks than those they would be able to achieve independently.

Research on Information Processing

- Provide opportunities for rehearsal and other memory strategies to move information into long-term memory. Realize that young children do not spontaneously use memory strategies but often can use them when prompted.
- Structure assignments so that retrieval cues are consistent with cues present at acquisition to facilitate retrieval of information from long-term memory.
- Enable learners to develop a knowledge base and expertise in domains of study. When beginning a new lesson, start with and build on what students already know.
- Assess the knowledge and strategies required to solve assigned problems; then determine which aspects of a task pose difficulties for learners and target these for further instruction.

- Be aware that well-learned and frequently repeated tasks become automatized over time, freeing information-processing capacity for other tasks.

Research on Intelligence

- Realize that individual differences in intelligence have implications for the classroom. Students at both ends of the continuum may need special educational services to optimize their learning.
- Recognize that although IQ scores do a reasonably good job of predicting achievement in the classroom, such tests have weaknesses that limit their usefulness, especially in assessing members of minority groups.

Research on Sensory and Perceptual Abilities

- Test all children early and regularly for sensory and perceptual problems that might limit their ability to benefit from regular classroom instruction.
- Be aware of developmental differences in attention span. Clearly, a young child will not be able to attend to a task for as long as a teenager.
- Minimize distractions in the learning environment. Younger students have trouble "tuning out" background noise and focusing on the task at hand.

---

for Education Statistics, 1998). The number of "older" adults attending college is expected to increase as the overall population ages. Whether we call them adult learners, nontraditionals, returning students, mature students, or lifelong learners, these adults represent a diverse group. They bring different work and life experiences to the classroom, and they report a variety of reasons for enrolling in postsecondary education (Kopka & Peng, 1993).

Many "traditional" students (17- to 24-year-olds) are motivated to attend college by external expectations, but older students are often motivated by internal factors (Dinmore, 1997). Women are more likely to return to the classroom for personal enrichment or interest, whereas men are more likely to take classes required or recommended for their work (Sargant et al., 1997). The internal motivation of adult students often leads to deeper levels of processing information (Harper & Kember, 1986). In other words, returning students may put forth greater effort to truly understand material because they want to learn and want (or need) to use the material. Traditional students who do not have the benefit of experience may learn the material necessary to do well on an examination but may not process the material in ways that will lead to long-term retention.

Continued or lifelong education has its drawbacks. Mainly, it is often difficult for adults already busy with jobs and family to find the time to take classes. Successful continuing education programs must devise ways to schedule classes at convenient times and must be responsive to the lifestyles of their adult learners (Parnham, 2001). Yet the benefits of lifelong education typically outweigh drawbacks. For instance, continued education allows adults to remain knowledgeable and competitive in fields that change rapidly. Adults who return to school for bachelor's or master's degrees can also advance their careers, particularly if their education and work are closely related (Senter & Senter, 1997). Finally, higher education is associated with maintaining or improving physical and mental health (Fischer, Blazey, & Lipman, 1992).

In this and previous chapters, you have examined a great deal of material on thinking and learning across the life span. How can principles of cognitive development be used to improve education for all ages? Before closing this chapter, we summarize, in Application Box 10.1, what theorists Piaget and Vygotsky contribute to education and what research on information processing, intelligence, and perception suggests about optimal learning environments.

Checking Mastery

1. How might achievement motivation change during adulthood?

2. Why is literacy important to adults and are literacy programs successful?

Making Connections

1. If you find that one of your parents (or spouse) is going through a midlife "career slump," what might you do to foster a higher level of achievement motivation during this stage of their life?

2. Based on what you have learned in this and previous chapters about memory, thinking, problem solving, and language skills, how would you teach older adult students versus students of traditional high school or college age?

Chapter Summary

10.1 Mastering Language

- The complex process of language acquisition appears to occur effortlessly through an interaction of inborn readiness and a normal language environment.
- To acquire language, children must master phonology (sound), semantics (meaning), and syntax (sentence structure). They must also learn how to use language appropriately (pragmatics) and how to understand nonverbal communication.
- Infants are able to discriminate speech sounds and progress from crying, cooing, and babbling to one-word holophrases (at 12 months) and then to telegraphic speech (at 18 months).
- During the preschool years, language abilities improve dramatically, as illustrated by overregularizations and new transformation rules.

- School-age children and adolescents refine their language skills and become less egocentric communicators.
- Theories of language development include learning theories, nativist theories, and interactionist theories. These emphasize the child's biologically based capacities and experience conversing with adults who use child-directed speech and strategies such as expansion that simplify the language-learning task.

10.2 The Infant

- Precursors of achievement motivation can be seen among infants who strive to master their environments. Opportunities to succeed are important for children of all ages. Without such opportunities, children are at risk for developing a learned helplessness orientation.
- Early education can help prepare disadvantaged children for formal schooling, but an overemphasis on academics at the expense of other activities may hinder young children's development.

10.3 The Child

- During childhood, some children develop higher levels of achievement motivation than others; they tend to have mastery-oriented rather than helpless attribution styles, and they set learning goals rather than performance goals in the classroom.
- To read, children must master the alphabetic principle and develop phonological awareness so that they can grasp letter–sound correspondence rules. Emergent literacy activities such as listening to storybooks facilitate later reading. Compared with unskilled readers, skilled readers have better understanding of the alphabetic principle and greater phonological awareness.
- A school's effectiveness is not influenced much by financial support, class size, time spent in school, or use of ability grouping. Instead, students perform best when (1) they are intellectually capable and motivated; (2) their teachers create a motivating, comfortable, and task-oriented setting and involve parents in their children's schooling an effective learning environment; and (3) there is a good fit between children's characteristics and the kind of instruction they receive.

10.4 The Adolescent

- Achievement motivation and grades tend to drop during adolescence for a variety of reasons, including cognitive growth, family characteristics, peer pressure, and a poor fit between the student and the school.
- Middle school and high school include a greater focus on science and mathematics education. U.S. students score close to the international average but below several other countries in math and science. Cross-cultural research suggests that the success of Asian schools is rooted in more class time spent on academics, more homework, more parent involvement, more peer support, and a stronger belief that hard work pays off.

10.5 The Adult

- Level of achievement carries over from adolescence into adulthood. There may be some decline in achievement motivation among women who set aside career goals to raise children, but career goals reemerge as their children age, especially among women with higher levels of education.
- Some adults, despite years of education, have not acquired the skills of functional literacy. Literacy programs have had minimal success in improving literacy rates. Adults increasingly are seeking continued educational opportunities for both personal and work-related reasons.

Checking Mastery Answers

For answers to Checking Mastery questions, visit **www.cengagebrain.com**

Key Terms

language **324**
phonemes **324**
morphemes **324**
syntax **325**
semantics **325**
pragmatics **325**
prosody **325**
word segmentation **325**
cooing **326**
babbling **326**
joint attention **326**
syntactic bootstrapping **326**
holophrases **326**
vocabulary spurt **327**
overextension **327**
underextension **327**
telegraphic speech **328**
functional grammar **328**
overregularization **329**
transformational grammar **329**
metalinguistic awareness **329**
aphasia **330**
universal grammar **331**
language acquisition device (LAD) **331**
child-directed speech **334**
expansion **335**
mastery motivation **335**
mastery orientation **338**
helpless orientation **338**
mastery (learning) goal **338**
performance goal **338**
alphabetic principle **341**
phonological awareness **341**
emergent literacy **342**
dyslexia **342**
ability grouping **344**
integration **346**
inclusion **346**
cooperative learning **347**
literacy **354**

Media Resources

Psychology CourseMate

Find online quizzes, flash cards, animations, video clips, experiments, interactive assessments, and other helpful study aids for this text at **www.cengagebrain.com**. You can also connect directly to the following sites:

National Center on Adult Literacy

The National Center on Adult Literacy has been engaged for almost 30 years in cutting edge research and innovation in adult education and technology. This website is host to a number of articles and links to other resources. To access, see "web links" in Psychology CourseMate at www.cengagebrain.com

Speech and Language Milestones

This website is host to a timeline of Speech and Language Milestones for children up to age six. To access, see "web links" in Psychology CourseMate at www.cengagebrain.com

Understanding the Data: Exercises on the Web

www.cengagebrain.com
For additional insight on the data presented in this chapter, try out the exercises for these figures in Psychology CourseMate at
www.cengagebrain.com:

Figure 10.1 The range of individual differences in vocabulary size from 16 to 30 months.

Figure 10.6 Grade point average from 1st grade to 12th grade for students with high and low risk and IQ.

CengageNOW

www.cengagebrain.com
Go to www.cengagebrain.com to link to CengageNOW, your online study tool. First take the Pre-Test for this chapter to get your Personalized Study Plan, which will identify topics you need to review and direct you to online resources. Then take the Post-Test to determine what concepts you have mastered and what you still need work on.

The Conceptualization of Self and Personality

© DEX IMAGE/Getty Images

For Tom Cruise, childhood was a painful period. He was abused, at least psychologically, by his father; diagnosed as dyslexic; and regularly beaten up by bullies. A turning point in his life came when his mother finally stood up to his father and divorced him, teaching Cruise this lesson: "People can create their own lives," he said. "I saw how my mother created hers and so made it possible for us to survive. . . . And I decided that I'm going to create, for myself, who I am, not what other people say I should be" (Rader, 2006, p. 7). After contemplating the priesthood, Cruise took a role in a student production at his high school, set off for New York, and in 2 years, at age 21, became a star when the film *Risky Business* became a big success. Now a father and happy with Katie Holmes after two failed marriages, Cruise says he defines happiness this way: "It's being able to confront and overcome problems. It's not running away but trying to see life in its full glory" (Rader, 2006, p. 8).

1. How have developmentalists conceptualized the self and personality?

2. When in infancy can we see the emergence of self-awareness and the beginnings of a unique personality?

3. What influences how children perceive and evaluate themselves, and to what extent can we detect in them the personalities they will have as adults?

4. How do self-conceptions and self-esteem change in adolescence, and how do adolescents integrate their self-perceptions into a sense of identity?

5. How do self-conceptions and personality change and remain the same in adulthood as adults address Erik Erikson's psychosocial conflicts and progress through their careers to retirement?

Tom Cruise has constructed a life story in which he overcame dyslexia, life in an abusive family, and bullying by peers to become a successful movie star and family man.

Here is one human, Tom Cruise, putting together the life story that defines him as a unique person who overcame challenges to find out who he was. How would you tell your life story? Who are you, how have you changed over the years, and what do you think you will be like 20 years from now?

This chapter is about the self and the personality and the ways in which personalities, and perceptions of those personalities, change—and remain the same—over the life span. It is, in other words, about the issue of continuity (consistency or stability) and discontinuity (change) in human development (see Chapter 2). It is also about influences on and implications of our self-concepts and personalities.

11.1 Conceptualizing the Self and Personality

We begin our inquiry by clarifying some terms used in describing the personality and the self and then lay out some key theoretical perspectives.

Basic Concepts

Personality is often defined as an organized combination of attributes, motives, values, and behaviors unique to each individual. Most people describe personalities in terms of relatively enduring **dispositional traits** such as extraversion or introversion, independence or dependence, and the like. As Dan McAdams and Jennifer Pals (2006) note, though, at least two other aspects of personality deserve attention. People also differ in **characteristic adaptations**, more situation-specific and changeable ways in which people adapt to their roles and environments. Characteristic adaptations include motives, goals, plans, schemas, self-conceptions, stage-specific concerns, and coping mechanisms. We differ too in **narrative identities**, unique and integrative "life stories" that we construct about our pasts and futures to give ourselves an identity and our lives meaning (as Tom Cruise seems to have done, judging from the chapter opener). McAdams and Pals believe that both biological factors, including a "human nature" we share with our fellow humans, and cultural and situational influences help shape these three aspects of personality.

When you describe yourself, you may not be describing your personality so much as revealing your **self-concept**—your perceptions, positive or negative, of your unique attributes and traits as a person. We all know people who seem to have unrealistic self-conceptions—the fellow who thinks he is "God's gift to women" (who do not agree) or the woman who believes she is a dull plodder (but is actually brilliant). A closely related aspect of self-perception is **self-esteem**—your overall evaluation of your worth as a person, high or low, based on all the positive and negative self-perceptions that make up your self-concept. Self-concept is about "what I am," whereas self-esteem concerns "how good I am" (Harter, 1999). This chapter examines how self-concept and self-esteem change and remain the same over the life span. It also takes up the question of how adolescents pull together their various self-perceptions to form an **identity**—an overall sense of who they are, where they are heading, and where they fit into society.

Theories of Personality

Although these concepts give us a vocabulary for talking about the self and the personality, we also gain perspective on the nature of personality development and how to study it by considering these three major theoretical perspectives: psychoanalytic theory, trait theory, and social learning theory.

Psychoanalytic Theory

Psychoanalytic theorists generally use in-depth interviews, dream analysis, and similar techniques to get below the surface of the person and her behavior and to understand the inner dynamics of personality. As you will recall from Chapter 2, Sigmund Freud believed that children progressed through universal stages of psychosexual development, ending with the genital stage of adolescence. Freud did not see psychosexual growth continuing during adulthood. Indeed he believed that the personality was formed during the first 5 years of life and showed considerable continuity thereafter. Anxieties arising from harsh parenting, overindulgence, or other unfavorable early experiences, he said, would leave a permanent mark on the personality and reveal themselves in adult personality traits.

The psychosocial theory of personality development formulated by neo-Freudian Erik Erikson, also introduced in Chapter 2, will be highlighted in this chapter. Like Freud, Erikson concerned himself with the inner dynamics of personality and proposed that people undergo similar personality changes at similar ages as they confront the challenges associated with different stages of development (Erikson 1963, 1968, 1982). Compared with Freud, however, Erikson placed more emphasis on social influences such as peers, teachers, and cultures; the rational ego and its adaptive powers; possibilities for overcoming the effects of harmful early experiences; and the potential for growth during the adult years.

Trait Theory

The approach to personality that has most strongly influenced efforts to study it is trait theory, based on the psychometric approach that guided the development of intelligence tests (see Chapter 9). According to trait theorists, personality is a set of dispositional trait dimensions or continua along which people can differ (for example, sociable–unsociable, responsible–irresponsible). (You may want to complete the brief personality scale in Engagement Box 11.1 before reading further.) To identify distinct trait dimensions, researchers construct personality scales and use the statistical technique of factor analysis to identify groupings of personality scale items that are correlated with each other but not with other groupings of items. Trait theorists assume that personality traits are relatively enduring; like psychoanalytic theorists, they expect to see carryover in personality over the years. Unlike psychoanalytic theorists, however, they do not believe that the personality unfolds in a series of stages.

How many personality trait dimensions are there? Although scholars have disagreed for many years about this, a consensus has now formed that human personalities can best be described in terms of a five-factor model—with five major dimensions of personality that have come to be known as the **Big Five** (Digman, 1990; McCrae & Costa, 2003, 2008). These five personality dimensions—openness to experience, conscientiousness, extraversion, agreeableness, and neuroticism—are

described in ● **Table 11.1.** If you take and score the personality scale in Engagement Box 11.1, you will get a rough sense of where you fall on the Big Five trait dimensions.

All the Big Five trait dimensions in the five-factor model of personality appear to be genetically influenced and emerge fairly early in life, as we will see (Krueger, Johnson, & Kling, 2006; McCrae & Costa, 2008). The Big Five also seem to be universal; they capture the ways in which people all over the world describe themselves and other people (Heine & Buchtel, 2009; McCrae, 2004). This is true even though levels of Big Five traits differ from culture to culture (for example, Europeans appear to be more extroverted on average than Asians or Africans) and even though traits may be expressed differently in different cultures (as when a Chinese extravert smiles to convey happiness but an American one like Tom Cruise jumps up and down on the couch). You will soon learn more about these trait dimensions.

Social Learning Theory

Finally, social learning (or social cognitive) theorists such as Albert Bandura (1986; and see Chapter 2) and Walter Mischel (1973; Mischel & Shoda, 2008; Shoda & Mischel, 2000) not only reject the notion of universal stages of personality development but also question the existence of enduring personality traits that show themselves in a variety of situations and over long stretches of the life span. Instead, they emphasize that people change if their environments change. An aggressive boy can become a warm and caring man if his aggression is no longer reinforced but his caring behavior is. Similarly, that aggressive boy could learn to be nonaggressive in school even though he is aggressive at home. Walter Mischel and Yuichi Shoda (2008) argue that if there is consistency in personality it is often a matter of people behaving consistently in the same situation from occasion to occasion, not behaving consistently across different situations. We must, therefore, look at people in context to understand personality.

From the social learning perspective, personality boils down to a set of behavioral tendencies shaped by interactions with other people in specific social situations. Because social context is so powerful, consistency in personality over time is most likely if the person's social environment remains the same. Thus, if Rick the rancher continues to run the same ranch in the same small town for a lifetime, he might stay the "same old Rick." However, most of us experience new social environments as we grow older. Just as we behave differently when we are in a library than when we are in a bar, we become "different people" as we take on new roles, develop new relationships, or move to new locations. An example: Firstborns are often thought to be bossy, and they may well be when they tend younger siblings, but this trait does not necessarily carry over into situations in which they interact with peers who are similar in age and competence and cannot be pushed around as easily as younger brothers and sisters (Harris, 2000b, 2006). Different situation, different personality.

Armed with basic concepts and a sense of the strikingly different perspectives psychoanalytic, trait, and social learning theorists take on personality, we will now explore continuity and discontinuity in self-conceptions and personality traits across the life span.

engagement 11.1

A Brief Personality Scale

Here are several personality traits that may or may not apply to you. Write a number from 1–7 next to each statement to indicate the extent to which you agree or disagree with that statement. You should rate the extent to which the pair of traits applies to you, even if one characteristic applies more strongly than the other.

1 = Disagree strongly	5 = Agree a little
2 = Disagree moderately	6 = Agree moderately
3 = Disagree a little	7 = Agree strongly
4 = Neither agree nor disagree	

I see myself as:

1. _____ Extraverted, enthusiastic
2. _____ Critical, quarrelsome
3. _____ Dependable, self-disciplined
4. _____ Anxious, easily upset
5. _____ Open to new experiences, complex
6. _____ Reserved, quiet
7. _____ Sympathetic, warm
8. _____ Disorganized, careless
9. _____ Calm, emotionally stable
10. _____ Conventional, uncreative

To score yourself, reverse the scoring of items marked below with *R* so that a score of 1 becomes 7, 2 becomes 6, 3 becomes 5, 4 stays 4, 5 becomes 3, 6 becomes 2, and 7 becomes 1. Then add the pair of scores listed here for each of the Big Five personality dimensions:

Extraversion	Item 1 + item 6R =
Agreeableness	Item 2R + item 7 =
Conscientiousness	Item 3 + item 8R =
Low neuroticism (high emotional stability)	Item 4R + item 9 =
Openness to experience	Item 5 + item 10R =

To help you see roughly where you stand, mean scores (the sum of the 2 item scores divided by 2) for a sample of 1813 individuals tested by Samuel Gosling and colleagues (2003) were 4.44 for extraversion, 5.23 for agreeableness, 5.40 for conscientiousness, 4.83 for low neuroticism (high emotional stability), and 5.38 for openness to experience.

SOURCE: Reprinted from Gosling, Rentfrow, & Swann (2003). A very brief personality scale. *Journal of Research in Personality, 37,* 525, with permission from Elsevier, © 2003.

● **TABLE 11.1 THE BIG FIVE PERSONALITY DIMENSIONS**

Dimension	Basic Definition	Key Characteristics
Openness to experience	Curiosity and interest in variety vs. preference for sameness	Openness to fantasy, esthetics, feelings, actions, ideas, values
Conscientiousness	Discipline and organization vs. lack of seriousness	Competence, order, dutifulness, striving for achievement, self-discipline, deliberation
Extraversion	Sociability and outgoingness vs. introversion	Warmth, gregariousness, assertiveness, activity, excitement seeking, positive emotions
Agreeableness	Compliance and cooperativeness vs. suspiciousness	Trust, straightforwardness, altruism, compliance, modesty, tender-mindedness
Neuroticism	Emotional instability vs. stability	Anxiety, hostility, depression, self-consciousness, impulsiveness, vulnerability

As a mnemonic device, notice that the first letters of the five dimensions spell *ocean*.
SOURCE: Adapted from Costa & McCrae, 1992.

Checking Mastery

1. What is the difference between a dispositional trait and a characteristic adaptation?

2. What is the difference between self-esteem and self-concept?

3. Why do social learning theorists think trait theorists are wrong about personality?

Making Connections

1. Using the concepts of dispositional traits, characteristic adaptations, and narrative identities, as described by McAdams and Pals, do an analysis of the main features of your own personality. What are your prominent dispositional traits and characteristic adaptations, and what is the plot of your narrative identity or life story? Finally, what forces have shaped this personality, do you think?

2. Think about two people you know well and list for each of them five dispositional traits that you believe capture their personalities well. Now look at the Big Five dimensions in Table 11.1 and see if you can match the traits you saw in them to the Big Five dimensions and their key characteristics. Based on this analysis, do you agree that the Big Five dimensions capture the main ways in which humans differ—or do you believe that something is missing from the Big Five? Why?

11.2 The Infant

When do infants display an awareness that they exist and a sense of themselves as distinct individuals? We will explore this issue and then look at infants' unique "personalities."

The Emerging Self

Infants may be born without a sense of self, but they quickly develop an implicit, if not conscious, sense of self through their perceptions of their bodies and actions (Rochat & Striano, 2000; Thompson, 2006). The capacity to differentiate self from world becomes even more apparent in the first 2 or 3 months of life as infants discover that they can cause things to happen. For example, 2-month-old infants whose arms are connected by strings to audiovisual equipment delight in producing the sight of a smiling infant's face and the theme from *Sesame Street* by pulling the strings (Lewis, Alessandri, & Sullivan, 1990). When the strings are disconnected and the infants can no longer produce such effects, they pull harder and become frustrated and angry. Over the first 6 months of life, then, infants discover properties of their physical selves, distinguish between the self and the rest of the world, and appreciate that they can act upon other people and objects (Thompson, 2006).

In the second half of their first year, infants realize that they and their companions are separate beings with different perspectives, ones that can be shared (Thompson, 2006). This is illustrated by the phenomenon of *joint attention*, in which infants about 9 months or older and their caregivers share perceptual experiences by looking at the same object at the same time (Mitchell, 1997; Mundy & Acra, 2006). When an infant points at an object and looks toward her companions in an effort to focus their attention on the object, she shows awareness that self and other do not always share the same perceptions.

Around 18 months, infants recognize themselves visually as distinct individuals. To establish this, Michael Lewis and Jeanne Brooks-Gunn (1979) used an ingenious technique first used with chimpanzees to study **self-recognition**—the ability to recognize oneself in a mirror or photograph. Mother daubs a spot of blush or rouge on an infant's nose and then places the infant in front of a mirror. If the infant has some mental image of his own face and recognizes his mirror image as himself, he should soon notice the red spot and reach for or wipe his own nose rather than the nose of the mirror image.

When infants 9–24 months old were given this mirror test, the youngest infants showed no self-recognition: they seemed to treat the image in the mirror as if it were "some other baby" and sometimes touched the mirror. Some 15-month-olds recognized themselves, but only among 18- to 24-month-olds did most infants show clear evidence of self-recognition. They touched their noses rather than the mirror, apparently realizing that they had a strange mark on their faces that warranted investigation.

As babies develop, they also form a **categorical self**; that is, they classify themselves into social categories based on age, sex, and other visible characteristics, figuring out what is "like me" and what is "not like me." Before they are 18 months old, toddlers can tell themselves apart from toddlers of the other sex or from older individuals but are less able to distinguish between photos of themselves and photos of other infants of the same sex. As they approach age 2, they also master this task (Brooks-Gunn & Lewis, 1981; Lewis & Brooks-Gunn, 1979). By 18–24 months, then, most infants have an awareness of who they are—at least as a physical self with a unique appearance and as a categorical self belonging to specific age and gender categories. They even begin to use their emerging language skills to talk about themselves and to construct stories about events in their lives, past and present (Thompson, 2006).

What contributes to self-awareness in infancy? First, the ability to recognize the self depends on *cognitive development* (Bertenthal

Does this boy know that he is the fascinating tot in the mirror? Probably not if he is younger than 18 months, which is about when self-recognition is mastered by most toddlers.

© Joseph Pobereskin/Getty Images

& Fischer, 1978). Mentally retarded children are slow to recognize themselves in a mirror but can do so once they have attained a mental age of at least 18 months (Hill & Tomlin, 1981). Second, self-awareness depends on *social interaction*. Chimpanzees who have been raised without contact with other chimps fail to recognize themselves in a mirror as normal chimps do (Gallup, 1979). And human toddlers who have formed secure attachments to their parents are better able to recognize themselves in a mirror and know more about their names and genders than do toddlers whose relationships are less secure (Pipp, Easterbrooks, & Harmon, 1992).

It is clear that a sense of self grows out of social relationships. Through their actions and words, parents and other companions communicate to infants that they are babies and are either girls or boys. Later, social feedback helps children determine what they are like and what they can and cannot do well. Throughout life, we forge new self-concepts from the social feedback we receive, good and bad (Harter, 1999). Thus, the development of the self is closely related to both cognitive development and social interaction, beginning in infancy.

Achieving self-awareness at around 18–24 months of age is an exciting breakthrough that paves the way for other critical emotional and social developments. Toddlers who recognize themselves in the mirror are more able than those who do not to:

- Talk about themselves and to assert their wills (DesRosiers et al., 1999)
- Experience self-conscious emotions such as pride upon mastering a new toy or embarrassment if asked to show off by dancing in front of strangers (Lewis et al., 1989)
- Coordinate their own perspectives with those of other individuals—for example, communicate with their playmates by imitating their actions (Asendorpf, Warkentin, & Baudonnière, 1996); cooperate with peers to achieve common goals such as retrieving toys from containers (Brownell & Carriger, 1990); and empathize with peers in distress (Eisenberg, Spinrad, & Sadovsky, 2006)

Temperament

Although it takes infants some time to become aware of themselves as individuals, they have distinctive personalities from the first weeks of life. The study of infant personality has centered on dimensions of **temperament**—early, genetically based tendencies to respond in predictable ways to events that serve as the building blocks of personality (see Rothbart & Bates, 2006). Learning theorists have tended to view babies as "blank slates" who can be shaped in any number of directions by their experiences. However, it is now clear that babies differ from the start in basic response tendencies. Temperament has been defined and measured in several ways, each of which gives us insights into baby personality (Rothbart & Bates, 2006).

Easiness and Difficultness

One of the first attempts to characterize infant temperaments was the influential work of Alexander Thomas, Stella Chess, and their colleagues (Chess & Thomas, 1999; Thomas & Chess, 1986). These researchers gathered information about nine di-

mensions of infant behavior, including typical mood, regularity or predictability of biological functions such as feeding and sleeping habits, tendency to approach or withdraw from new stimuli, intensity of emotional reactions, and adaptability to new experiences and changes in routine. Based on the overall patterning of these temperamental qualities, most infants could be placed into one of three categories:

- **Easy temperament.** Easy infants are even tempered, typically content or happy, and open and adaptable to new experiences such as the approach of a stranger or their first taste of strained plums. They have regular feeding and sleeping habits, and they tolerate frustrations and discomforts.
- **Difficult temperament.** Difficult infants are active, irritable, and irregular in their habits. They often react negatively (and vigorously) to changes in routine and are slow to adapt to new people or situations. They cry frequently and loudly and often have tantrums when they are frustrated by such events as being restrained or having to live with a dirty diaper.
- **Slow–to–warm up temperament.** Slow–to–warm up infants are relatively inactive, somewhat moody, and only moderately regular in their daily schedules. Like difficult infants, they are slow to adapt to new people and situations, but they typically respond in mildly, rather than intensely, negative ways. For example, they may resist cuddling by looking away from the cuddler rather than by kicking or screaming. They eventually adjust, showing a quiet interest in new foods, people, or places.

Of the infants in Thomas and Chess's longitudinal study of temperament, 40% were easy infants, 10% were difficult infants, and 15% were slow–to–warm up infants. The remaining third could not be clearly placed in one category because they shared qualities of two or more categories. Thomas and Chess went on to study the extent of continuity and discontinuity in temperament from infancy to early adulthood (Chess & Thomas, 1984; Thomas & Chess, 1986). Difficult infants who had fussed when they could not have more milk often became children who fell apart if they could not work mathematics problems correctly. By adulthood, however, an individual's adjustment had little to do with her temperament during infancy, suggesting a good deal of discontinuity over this long time span (Guerin et al., 2003).

Behavioral Inhibition

Jerome Kagan and his colleagues identified another aspect of early temperament that they believe is highly significant— **behavioral inhibition,** or the tendency to be extremely shy, restrained, and distressed in response to unfamiliar people and situations (Kagan, 1994; Kagan et al., 2007; Kagan & Snidman, 2004). In the language of the Big Five personality dimensions, inhibited children could be considered low in extraversion with some neuroticism or anxiety thrown in (Muris et al., 2009). Kagan (1989) estimates that about 15% of toddlers have this inhibited temperament, whereas 10% are extremely uninhibited, exceptionally eager to jump into new situations.

At 4 months, behaviorally inhibited infants wriggle and fuss and fret more than most infants in response to novel stimuli such as a moving mobile (Fox et al., 2001; Moehler et al., 2008). At 21 months, they take a long time to warm up to a strange examiner, retreat from unfamiliar objects such as a large robot, and fret and cling to their mothers, whereas uninhibited toddlers readily and enthusiastically engage with strangers, robots, and all manner of new experiences (Kagan, 1994). As children, inhibited youngsters are shy in a group of strange peers and afraid to try a balance beam. And as adolescents, these individuals continue to be wary and cautious in new social situations (Kagan et al., 2007).

Kagan and his colleagues have concluded that behavioral inhibition is biologically rooted. Individuals with inhibited temperaments display strong brain responses and high heart rates in reaction to unfamiliar stimuli (Kagan et al., 2007; Schwartz et al., 2003), and twin studies suggest that this temperament is genetically influenced (DiLalla, Kagan, & Reznick, 1994). When it becomes ingrained, behavioral inhibition puts individuals at risk for later anxiety disorders (Fox et al., 2005).

Surgency, Negative Affect, and Effortful Control

Finally, Mary Rothbart and her colleagues (Rothbart, 2007; Rothbart, Ahadi, & Evans, 2000; Rothbart & Derryberry, 2002; Putnam, Gartstein, & Rothbart, 2006) have defined infant temperament in terms of emotional reactions and the control or regulation of such reactions. They have identified three dimensions of temperament, the first two evident from infancy, the last emerging more clearly in toddlerhood or early childhood:

Surgency/extraversion—the tendency to actively and energetically approach new experiences in an emotionally positive way (rather than to be inhibited and withdrawn).

Negative affectivity—the tendency to be sad, fearful, easily frustrated, and irritable (as opposed to laid back and adaptable).

Effortful control—the ability to focus and shift attention when desired, control one's behavior and plan a course of action, and regulate or suppress one's emotions.

● **Table 11.2** shows the different ways of describing infant temperaments. There are some clear similarities. Today, Rothbart's dimensions of temperament have become especially influential,

probably because they share similarities with the Big Five dimensions used to describe adult personality (Rothbart, 2007). Surgency/extraversion clearly matches up with extraversion (and perhaps agreeableness too), negative affectivity with neuroticism, and effortful control with conscientiousness. Accumulating evidence suggests that Rothbart and her colleagues are on the right track and that there are meaningful connections between temperament in infancy and early childhood and personality later in life (Saucier & Simonds, 2006; Shiner, 2006).

Goodness of Fit

Differences in temperament appear to be rooted in genetically based differences in levels of certain neurotransmitters and in the functioning of the brain (Ebstein, Benjamin, & Belmaker, 2003). However, environment helps determine how adaptive particular temperamental qualities are and whether they persist (Rothbart & Bates, 2006). Much may depend on what Thomas and Chess call the **goodness of fit** between child and environment—the extent to which the child's temperament is compatible with the demands and expectations of the social world to which she must adapt.

The case of Carl, one of the children studied by Thomas and Chess, illustrates the significance for later personality development of the match between a child's temperament and his social environment. Early in life, Carl was clearly a difficult child: "Whether it was the first bath or the first solid foods in infancy, the beginning of nursery and elementary school, or the first birthday parties or shopping trips, each experience evoked stormy responses, with loud crying and struggling to get away" (1984, p. 188). Carl's mother became convinced that she was a bad parent, but his father accepted and even delighted in Carl's "lusty" behavior. He patiently and supportively waited for Carl to adapt to new situations. As a result, Carl did not develop serious behavioral problems as a child and became a well-adjusted adult after weathering some adjustment problems when he started college.

If the fit between his difficult temperament and his parents' demands and expectations had been poor—for example, if his parents had been impatient, angry, and overly demanding instead of sensitive—research suggests Carl might have been headed for serious behavioral problems and poor adjustment (Guerin et al., 2003; Leerkes, Blankson, & O'Brien, 2009). Similarly, behaviorally inhibited children are likely to remain inhibited if their parents are either overprotective or angry and impatient, but can overcome their inhibition if their parents create a good fit by preparing them for potentially upsetting experiences and making reasonable but firm demands that they cope (Kagan, 1994).

The moral for parents is clear: get to know your baby as an individual, and allow for his personality quirks. Infants' temperaments and their parents' parenting behaviors reciprocally influence one another and interact over time to steer the direction of later personality development (Sanson, Hemphill, & Smart, 2004). Training parents of irritable, difficult babies in how to interpret their infants' cues and respond sensitively and appropriately to them can produce calmer infants who cry less and be-

● **TABLE 11.2 SUMMARY OF TEMPERAMENT CATEGORIES**

Researchers	Dimensions of Temperament
Thomas and Chess	Easy temperament Difficult temperament Slow-to-warm up temperament
Kagan	Behaviorally inhibited Uninhibited
Rothbart	Surgency/extraversion Negative affectivity Effortful control

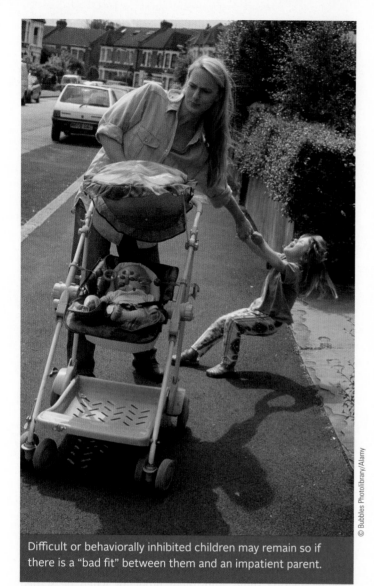
Difficult or behaviorally inhibited children may remain so if there is a "bad fit" between them and an impatient parent.

come less irritable preschoolers than temperamentally similar children whose parents do not receive training (van den Boom, 1995; Crockenberg & Leerkes, 2003).

Checking Mastery

1. What important development in the self happens at around 18 months of age, and what makes it possible?

2. In Rothbart's terms, Serena is low in surgency/extraversion, high in negative affectivity, and low in effortful control. How would (1) Thomas and Chess and (2) Kagan likely describe Serena?

Making Connections

1. The mirror test has become the main way of assessing self-awareness in infants. What do you see as the strengths and limitations of this approach? Can you think of other ways to assess infant self-awareness?

2. Gracie the toddler throws fits when her routines are changed, a stranger comes to visit, or she is asked to try something she has never tried before. Using two different systems for analyzing temperament, help her parents understand her temperament and, more importantly, what they can do to help her become as well-adjusted as possible.

11.3 The Child

Children's personalities continue to form, and children acquire much richer understandings of themselves as individuals, as they continue to experience cognitive growth and interact with other people during the preschool and school years.

Elaborating on a Sense of Self

Once toddlers begin to talk, they can and do tell us about their emerging self-concepts. By age 2, some toddlers are already using the personal pronouns *I, me, my,* and *mine* (or their names) when referring to the self and *you* when addressing a companion (Lewis & Brooks-Gunn, 1979; Stipek, Gralinski, & Kopp, 1990). Toddlers also show their emerging categorical selves when they describe themselves in terms of age and sex ("Katie big girl"). Parent–child conversations that focus on past experiences and the emotions associated with them help young children pull together what they know of themselves into a consistent self-concept (Bird & Reese, 2006).

The preschool child's emerging self-concept is concrete and physical (Damon & Hart, 1988; Harter, 2006). Asked to describe themselves, preschoolers describe their physical characteristics, possessions, physical activities and accomplishments, and preferences. One exuberant 3-year-old described herself this way:

> I'm 3 years old and I live in a big house with my mother and father and my brother, Jason, and my sister, Lisa. I have blue eyes and a kitty that is orange and a television in my own room. I know all of my ABC's, listen: A, B, C, D, E, F, G, H, J, L, K,O, M, P, Q, X, Z. I can run real fast. I like pizza and I have a nice teacher at preschool. I can count up to 100, want to hear me? I love my dog Skipper. (Harter, 1999, p. 37)

Few young children mention their psychological traits or inner qualities. At most, young children use global terms such as *nice* or *mean* and *good* or *bad* to describe themselves and others (Livesley & Bromley, 1973). However, their descriptions of their characteristic behavioral patterns and preferences ("I like to play by myself at school") may provide the foundation for their later personality trait descriptions ("I'm shy"; Eder, 1989).

Self-conceptions become more sophisticated around age 8, thanks in part to cognitive growth (Harter, 2003, 2006). Now psychological and social qualities become prominent in self-descriptions. First, children begin to describe their enduring qualities using personality trait terms such as *funny* and *smart* (Harter, 1999; Livesley & Bromley, 1973). Second, children form social identities, defining themselves as part of social units ("I'm a Kimball, a second-grader at Brookside School, a Brownie Scout"; Damon & Hart, 1988). Third, they become more capa-

Preschool children engage in less social comparison than school-aged children do and are not as devastated when they come out on the short end of a comparison.

cial adequacy (for example, their social acceptance). By mid–elementary school, children differentiate among five aspects of self-worth: scholastic competence (feeling smart or doing well in school); social acceptance (being popular or feeling liked); behavioral conduct (staying out of trouble); athletic competence (being good at sports); and physical appearance (feeling good-looking).

When Harter's scale was given to third- through ninth-graders, even third-graders showed that they had well-defined positive or negative feelings about themselves in each of these areas. As children get older, they integrate their self-perceptions in these distinct domains to form an overall, abstract sense of self-worth (Harter, 1999; Marsh & Ayotte, 2003). Now self-esteem is not only *multidimensional* but *hierarchical* in nature. ■ **Figure 11.1** shows the structure that results, with global self-worth at the top of the hierarchy and specific dimensions of self-concept below it.

The accuracy of children's self-evaluations increases steadily over the elementary-school years (Harter, 1999; Marsh, Craven, & Debus, 1999). Children as young as 5 already have some sense of whether they are worthy and lovable (Verschueren, Buyck, & Marcoen, 2001). However, the self-esteem scores of young children sometimes reflect their desires to be liked or to be good at various activities more than their true competencies (Harter, 2006). Around age 8, children's self-evaluations become more accurate—more consistent with objective indicators. For example, those with high scholastic self-esteem are more likely than those with low scholastic self-esteem to be rated as intellectually competent by their teachers, and those with high athletic self-esteem are frequently chosen by peers to be on sports teams (Harter, 1999).

At the same time, children are forming an ever grander sense of what they "should" be like—an **ideal self**. With age, the gap between the real self and the ideal self increases; older children therefore run a greater risk than younger children do of

ble of **social comparison**—of using information about how they compare with other individuals to characterize and evaluate themselves (Frey & Ruble, 1985; Pomerantz et al., 1995). The preschooler who said she could hit a baseball becomes the elementary-school child who says she is a better batter than her teammates.

Young children often seem oblivious to information about how they compare with others. They tend to believe that they are the greatest, even in the face of compelling evidence that they have been outclassed (Butler, 1990; but see Rhodes and Brickman, 2008, for evidence that even 4- and 5-year-olds can be crushed by failure experiences on some occasions—such as when they are outdone by a member of the other sex!). By first grade, children are very interested in social comparisons and more aware of their implications. They glance at each other's papers, ask "How many did you miss?" and say things like "I got more right than you did" (Frey & Ruble, 1985; Pomerantz et al., 1995).

Self-Esteem

As children amass a range of perceptions of themselves and engage in social comparisons, they begin to evaluate their worth. Susan Harter (1999, 2003, 2006) has developed self-perception scales for use across the life span and has found that self-esteem becomes more differentiated or *multidimensional* with age. Preschool children distinguish only two broad aspects of self-esteem: their competence (both physical and cognitive) and their personal and so-

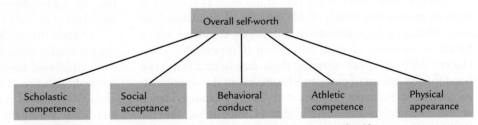

■ **FIGURE 11.1** The multidimensional and hierarchical nature of self-esteem. Source: From Harter, S. Historical roots of contemporary issues involving self-concepts. In Bracken B. A. (Ed.), *Handbook of self-concept: Developmental, social, and clinical considerations.* Copyright © 1996. Reprinted with permission of John Wiley & Sons, Inc.

thinking that they fall short of what they should be (Glick & Zigler, 1985; Oosterwegel & Oppenheimer, 1993). Social comparisons that do not always come out well, a widening gap between the real self and the ideal self, and a tendency for parents and teachers to "raise the bar" and give older children more critical feedback than they give younger children all contribute to a decrease in average self-esteem from early to middle childhood (Harter, 2006).

Influences on Self-Esteem

Why do some children develop higher self-esteem than others? Part of the answer lies in genes; like most human characteristics, self-esteem is a heritable trait (Kamakura, Ando, & Ono, 2007). Experiences also influence self-esteem, though: some children discover that they are more competent than other children, and, apart from their competence, some children receive more positive social feedback (Harter, 1999).

Children who are more capable and socially attractive than other children experience more success in areas important to them and come out better in social comparisons. Thus, for example, achievement in school has a positive effect on academic self-concept; a positive academic self-concept then contributes to future academic achievement (Guay, Marsh, & Boivin, 2003; Marsh & Craven, 2006).

Even when two children are equally competent and do equally well in social comparisons, social feedback from parents, teachers, and peers can make a big difference in their self-perceptions. Most notably, children with high self-esteem tend to be securely attached to parents who are warm and democratic (Arbona & Power, 2003; Coopersmith, 1967). Loving parents frequently communicate approval and acceptance rather than saying, through words, looks, or actions, "You're not important" or "Why can't you be more like your older brother?" (Doyle, Markiewicz, et al., 2000). Democratic parents enforce clearly stated rules of behavior but allow their children to express their opinions and participate in decision making. This gives children a firm basis for evaluating their behavior and tells them that their opinions are respected. The relationship between high self-esteem and a warm, democratic parenting style has been observed in a variety of ethnic groups in the United States as well as in other countries (Scott, Scott, & McCabe, 1991; Steinberg, Dornbusch, & Brown, 1992).

Once a child's level of self-esteem has been established, it tends to remain surprisingly stable over the elementary-school years. Moreover, high self-esteem is positively correlated with a variety of measures of good adjustment (Coopersmith, 1967; Harter, 1999). It is encouraging, then, that interventions can boost the self-esteem of children who are low in it in specific areas such as mathematics (O'Mara et al., 2006). Despite evidence of the importance and modifiability of self-esteem, though, William Damon (1994) and other observers believe that American parents and educators go overboard in trying to make all children feel good about themselves. Self-esteem, Damon maintains, means nothing unless it grows out of a child's real achievements. Moreover, he argues, children need opportunities to learn about their limitations as they progress through school; giving them an inflated and unrealistic sense of their worth will do more harm than good in the end. What we need to appreciate is that self-esteem and performance influence one another reciprocally (Marsh & Craven, 2006). From this perspective, it will not work in the long run to tell children they are the greatest when they can see for themselves that they are not. However, helping children succeed at important tasks can boost their self-esteem, and higher self-esteem can then help fuel future achievements.

The Developing Personality

The biologically based response tendencies called temperament are increasingly shaped, with the help of the individual's social experiences, into a predictable personality during childhood. Links between temperament in infancy and early childhood and later personality are only now being understood (Halverson et al., 2003; Sanson, Hemphill, & Smart, 2004; Shiner, 2006).

For example, in a longitudinal study of 1000 children in New Zealand, Avshalom Caspi and his colleagues (Caspi, 2000; Caspi et al., 2003) found long-term continuity in personality. Inhibited 3-year-olds who are shy and fearful, they found, tend to become teenagers who are cautious and unassertive and later become young adults who have little social support, tend to be depressed, and are barely engaged in life. By contrast, 3-year-olds who are difficult to control, irritable, and highly emotional tend to be difficult to manage later in childhood and end up as impulsive adolescents and adults who do not get along well with other people at home and on the job, are easily upset, get into scrapes with the law, and abuse alcohol. Finally, well-adjusted ("easy") 3-year-olds tend to remain well adjusted.

Links between dimensions of infant temperament and Big Five personality trait dimensions are also being discovered, although it is still not clear exactly how and when the Big Five personality dimensions emerge (John, Naumann, & Soto, 2008). For example, behavioral inhibition in the preschool period is predictive of low extraversion in middle childhood, and negative affectivity is related to later neuroticism (Hagekull & Bohlin, 1998; and see Shiner, 2006). Meanwhile, the ability of infants to exert effortful control over their attention and arousal (for example, to calm themselves) predicts later conscientiousness (Rothbart et al., 2000; Sanson et al., 2004).

Despite this evidence, we cannot accept Freud's view that the personality is mostly formed by age 5. Correlations between early childhood traits and adult traits are usually quite small. Some dimensions of personality do not seem to "gel" until the elementary-school years, when they begin to predict adolescent and adult personality and adjustment much better (Tackett et al., 2008). Other aspects of personality do not seem to stabilize until adolescence or even adulthood (Caspi & Roberts, 2001; McCrae & Costa, 2003). In sum, the older the individual, the more accurately personality traits predict later personality and adjustment.

Checking Mastery

1. What are three major ways in which the self-description of 9-year-old Alonzo might differ from that of his brother, 4-year-old Jamal?

2. What are three main reasons that Jenna may have developed high self-esteem?

3. Is it possible to predict adult personality from personality in childhood?

Making Connections

1. Some educators believe that nurturing high self-esteem in children is critical; they favor giving all children lots of positive feedback so that they feel competent in important ways. William Damon and others have criticized the "self-esteem movement" that grew out of this belief; they charge that giving children an inflated sense of their worth will do more harm than good in the long run. What is your view, and what evidence would you cite to support it?

2. Revisit the Big Five personality dimensions in Table 11.1. If you wanted to determine whether these trait dimensions are evident at age 2, how would you go about doing so?

11.4 The Adolescent

Perhaps no period of the life span is more important to the development of the self than adolescence. Adolescence is truly a time for "finding oneself," as research on adolescent self-conceptions, self-esteem, and identity formation illustrates.

Self-Conceptions

Raymond Montemayor and Marvin Eisen (1977) learned a great deal about the self-concepts of children and adolescents in grades 4–12 by asking students to write 20 different answers to the question "Who am I?" How would you describe the age differences evident in these answers given by a 9-year-old, an 11½-year-old, and a 17-year-old?

> 9-year-old: My name is Bruce C. I have brown eyes. I have brown hair…I have great! eye sight. I have lots! of friends. I live at. . . I have an uncle who is almost 7 feet tall. My teacher is Mrs. V. I play hockey! I'm almost the smartest boy in the class. I love! food . . . I love! school.

> 11½-year-old: My name is A. I'm a human being. . . a girl. . . a truthful person. I'm not pretty. I do so-so in my studies. I'm a very good cellist. I'm a little tall for my age. I like several boys. . . I'm old fashioned. I am a very good swimmer. . . I try to be helpful. . . Mostly I'm good, but I lose my temper.

> 17-year-old: I am a human being. . . a girl. . . an individual. . . I am a Pisces. I am a moody person. . . an indecisive person. . . an ambitious person. I am a big curious person. . . I am lonely. I am an American (God help me). I am a Democrat. I am a liberal person.

> I am a radical. I am conservative. I am a pseudoliberal. I am an Atheist. I am not a classifiable person (i.e., I don't want to be). (Montemayor & Eisen, 1977, pp. 317–318)

There are remarkable differences between the self-descriptions of children and adolescents (Damon & Hart, 1988; Harter, 1999, 2003). First, self-descriptions become *less physical and more psychological* as children age (contrast "I have brown eyes" with "I am lonely"). Second, self-portraits become *less concrete and more abstract*, thanks to cognitive development (contrast "I love! sports" with "I am a truthful person" or the even more abstract "I am a pseudoliberal").

Third, adolescents have a *more differentiated* self-concept than children. For example, the child's "social self," which reflects perceived acceptance by peers, splits into distinct aspects: acceptance by the larger peer group, acceptance by close friends, and acceptance by romantic partners (Harter, 1999). Fourth, older adolescents gain the ability to organize their self-perceptions into a *more integrated, coherent self-portrait.* Adolescents who at first do not recognize inconsistencies in their behavior—for example, that they are happy in some situations, grumpy in others—start to be bothered by such inconsistencies and then, in their later teens, integrate these discrepant self-perceptions, explaining that they are moody or that they are happier when they are around people who accept them as they are than when they are with people who criticize them (Harter & Monsour, 1992). Finally, adolescents are *more self-aware* and reflective about the self than children are (Selman, 1980). Indeed, they can become painfully self-conscious.

In sum, from childhood to adolescence and over the course of adolescence, self-understandings become more psychological, abstract, differentiated, and integrated and self-awareness increases. Many adolescents even become sophisticated personality theorists who reflect for hours upon the workings of their own personalities and those of their companions.

Self-Esteem

Self-esteem tends to decrease from childhood to early adolescence for a number of reasons. Adolescents become more knowledgeable and realistic about their strengths and weaknesses (Jacobs et al., 2002; Robins et al., 2002), can become temporarily unsure of themselves when they move from elementary school to middle school or junior high school (Cole et al., 2001), and often become unhappy with their changing bodies (Paxton et al., 2006). This dip in self-esteem affects only some teens, though. It is most common among white females, especially those facing multiple stressors—for example, entering middle school, coping with pubertal changes, beginning to date, and perhaps dealing with a family move all at the same time (Gray-Little & Hafdahl, 2000; Simmons et al., 1987).

Self-esteem can also be affected by the social context and the social comparisons it makes available. To illustrate, Herbert Marsh and Kit-Tai Hau (2003) studied more than 100,000 15-year-olds in 26 countries to better understand the **big fish–little pond effect.** Holding factors such as academic competence equal, a student's academic self-concept tends to be less positive when the average academic achievement level of her classmates is high (when she is a small fish in a big pond) than when her classroom or school's average academic achievement level is low (when she is a big fish in a little pond; see Seaton, Marsh, & Craven, 2009, for further evidence that this effect is evident in a variety of cultures).

This big fish–little pond effect suggests that making the transition from regular classes to classes for gifted students, or from an unselective high school to a selective college or university, could threaten adolescents' self-esteem by changing the social comparisons they make. Indeed, gifted children moved from regular classes into gifted programs sometimes do lose academic self-esteem (Marsh et al., 1995). Similarly, special education students tend to have higher academic self-esteem when they are placed in homogeneous special education classes than when they are placed in regular classes with higher-achieving classmates, despite other benefits that may come from including students with learning problems in the mainstream (Manning, Bear, & Minke, 2006; Marsh & Hau, 2003).

In the end, though, adolescence is not as hazardous to self-esteem as most people believe. Although some adolescents do experience drops in self-esteem in early adolescence, and some feel like tiny guppies in huge ponds, most emerge from this developmental period with higher self-esteem than they had at the onset (Donnellan, Trzesniewski, & Robins, 2006; Robins et al., 2002). Assuming that adolescents have opportunities to feel competent in areas important to them and to experience the approval and support of parents, peers, and other important people in their lives, they are likely to feel good about themselves (Harter, 1999). It matters: As adults, adolescents with low self-esteem tend to have poorer physical and mental health, poorer career and financial prospects, and higher levels of criminal behavior than adolescents with high self-esteem (Trzesniewski et al., 2006).

Adolescents sometimes experiment with a variety of looks in their search for a sense of identity.

Forging a Sense of Identity

Erik Erikson (1968) characterized adolescence as a critical period in the lifelong process of forming an identity as a person and proposed that adolescents experience the psychosocial conflict of **identity versus role confusion.** The concept of *identity*, as noted at the start of the chapter, refers to a definition of who you are, where you are going, and where you fit into society. To achieve a sense of identity, the adolescent must somehow integrate the many separate perceptions that are part of the self-concept into a coherent sense of self (van Hoof, 1999). The search for identity involves grappling with many important questions: What kind of career do I want? What religious, moral, and political values can I really call my own? Who am I as a man or woman and as a sexual being? Where do I fit into the world? What do I really want out of my life?

If you have struggled with such issues, you can appreciate the uncomfortable feelings that adolescents may experience when they cannot seem to work out a clear sense of who they are. Erikson believed that many young people in complex societies such as that of the United States experience a full-blown and painful "identity crisis." There are many reasons they might do so. First, their bodies are changing and they must revise their body images (a part of their self-concepts) and adjust to being sexual beings. Second, cognitive growth allows adolescents to think systematically about hypothetical possibilities, including possible future selves. Third, social demands are placed on them to "grow up"—to decide what they want to do in life and to get on with it. According to Erikson (1968), our society supports youths by allowing them a **moratorium period**—a time during the high school and college years when they are relatively free of responsibilities and can experiment with different roles to find themselves (see Arnett, 2006). But complex societies like ours also make establishing an identity hard by giving youths a huge number of options and encouraging them to believe they can be anything they want to be.

Developmental Trends

James Marcia (1966) expanded on Erikson's theory and stimulated much research on identity formation by developing an interview procedure to assess where an adolescent is in the process of identity formation. Adolescents are classified into one of four identity statuses based on their progress toward an identity in each of several domains (for example, occupational, religious, and political–ideological). The key questions are whether an individual has experienced a *crisis* (or has seriously grappled with identity issues and explored alternatives) and whether he has achieved a *commitment* (that is, resolved the questions raised). On the basis of crisis and commitment, the individual is classified into one of the four identity statuses shown in ■ **Figure 11.2.**

How long does it take to achieve a sense of identity? Philip Meilman's (1979) study of college-bound boys between 12 and 18, 21-year-old college males, and 24-year-old young men provides an answer (■ **Figure 11.3**). Most of the 12- and 15-year-olds were in either the identity diffusion status or the identity foreclosure status.

© Mark Azavedo/Alamy

Commitment?

	No Commitment Made	Commitment Made
No Crisis Experienced	**Diffusion Status** The individual has not yet thought about or resolved identity issues and has failed to chart directions in life. Example: "I haven't really thought much about religion, and I guess I don't know what I believe exactly."	**Foreclosure Status** The individual seems to know who he or she is but has latched onto an identify prematurely with little thought. Example: "My parents are Baptists, and I'm a Baptist; it's just the way I grew up."
Crisis Experienced	**Moratorium Status** The individual is experiencing an identity crisis, actively raising questions, and seeking answers. Example: "I'm in the middle of evaluating my beliefs and hope that I'll be able to figure out what's right for me. I've become skeptical about some of what I have been taught and am looking into other faiths for answers."	**Identity Achievement Status** The individual has resolved his/her identify crisis and made commitments to particular goals, beliefs, and values. Example: "I really did some soul-searching about my religion and other religions, too, and finally know what I believe and what I don't."

Crisis? (vertical label on left)

■ **FIGURE 11.2** The four identity statuses as they apply to religious identity.

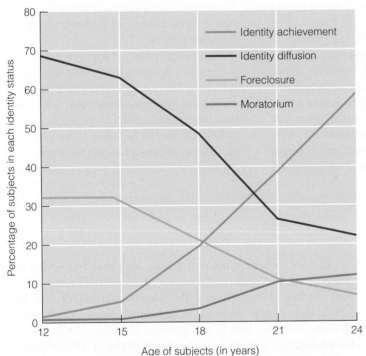

■ **FIGURE 11.3** Percentage of subjects in each of James Marcia's four identity statuses as a function of age. Note that only 4% of the 15-year-olds and 20% of the 18-year-olds had achieved a stable identity. Source: From Meilman, P. W. Cross-sectional age changes in ego identity status during adolescence. *Developmental Psychology, 15*, pp. 230–231. Copyright © 1979 American Psychological Association. Reprinted with permission.

At these ages, many adolescents simply have not yet thought about who they are—either they have no idea or they know that any ideas they do have are likely to change (the **diffusion status,** with no crisis and no commitment). Other adolescents have made commitments, may say things like "I'm going to be a doctor like my dad," and appear to have their acts together. However, it becomes apparent that they have never thought through on their own what suits them best and have simply accepted identities suggested to them by their parents or other people (the **foreclosure status,** involving a commitment without a crisis).

As Figure 11.3 indicates, progress toward identity achievement becomes more evident starting at age 18. Notice that diffusion drops off steeply and more individuals begin to fall into the **moratorium status.** Now they are experiencing a crisis or actively exploring identity issues; now they may be questioning their religious upbringing, experimenting with drugs, changing majors or relationships, or putting outrageous postings in Facebook, all to find themselves. Presumably, entering the moratorium status is a good sign; if the individual can not only raise questions but answer them, he will move to the **identity achievement status.** About 20% of the 18-year-olds, 40% of the college students, and slightly more than half of the 24-year-olds in Meilman's study had achieved a firm identity based on a careful weighing of alternatives.

Females progress toward achieving a clear sense of identity at about the same rate that males do. However, one reliable sex difference has been observed: Although college women are just as concerned about establishing a career identity as men are, they attach greater importance to and think more about the aspects of identity that center on sexuality, interpersonal relations,

Picture your life as a book that tells your life story from your birth to your death. Outline the major scenes, describing the high and low points, the turning points that really defined who you are, and your dreams and fears for the future.

As noted at the start of the chapter, McAdams and Pals (2006) believe that people construct narrative identities, or life stories, that reconstruct their personal histories and imagine their futures. These coherent, integrative stories give their lives meaning and purpose and are an important aspect of personality (McAdams & Pals, 2006; McAdams, 2008). What do these life stories look like, and how does the process of constructing a life story relate to the process of forming an identity in Erik Erikson's sense?

According to Dan McAdams (2005), a life story says "who I am, how I came to be, and where my life is going in the future" (p. 241). (Sounds like identity so far, doesn't it?) We start narrating our experiences at about age 2, with the help of parents, and learn how to structure a story so that it is more coherent and more in keeping with our culture's scripts for life stories as we get older (Bohn & Berntsen, 2008). Late adolescence or emerging adulthood (roughly age 18–29) appears to be the prime time, though, for creating a life story—as well as

for achieving a sense of identity. Life stories then become an important element of our personalities and are revised over the years and reflected upon in old age.

To study narrative identities, McAdams and other researchers ask people to do what you were invited to do at the start of this box—to talk or write about your past, present, and future. Life stories are then coded for such qualities as their coherence, tone, and themes. McAdams (2005) has become especially interested in "redemptive life stories" in which people overcome difficulties and build a better life (like Tom Cruise at the start of the chapter, who in his telling of it rises from abused and bullied child to successful and well-adjusted movie star and father). Adults who tell redemptive life stories tend to be more satisfied with their lives and to have a stronger sense of generativity or caring in Erikson's sense than other adults.

Kate McLean and Michael Pratt (2006) directly compared James Marcia's identity status approach and the narrative identity–life story approach. Questions about both were asked periodically beginning when the participants were 17-year-old high school students and concluding when they were age 23. The researchers coded "meaning making"—the extent to which individuals

derived personal meaning from turning points such as falling in love or landing a job and came to think differently about themselves as a result. Constructing a meaningful life story and making progress toward achieving identity were correlated.

Cultural influences on life stories have been detected. For example, Americans tend to tell of individual experiences, Chinese adults of significant others and social interactions (Wang & Conway, 2004, cited by McAdams, 2008). Social influences on life stories are evident too: Responsive friends who serve as good listeners when we tell our life stories can do a great deal to help us shape more meaningful tales (Pasupathi & Hoyt, 2009). Finally, personality is expressed in life stories: for example, people who score high on a measure of the Big Five trait of neuroticism tell negatively toned stories, whereas those who score high in agreeableness tell stories of caring (McAdams, 2008).

How people construct their life stories appears to influence not only their sense of well-being but also, by incorporating their aspirations, the choices they make and their later life outcomes (Birren & Schroots, 2006). We are just beginning to learn how to decipher the stories people tell about themselves.

and balancing career and family goals (Archer, 1992; Kroger, 2007). These concerns probably reflect the influence of traditional gender roles.

Judging from such research, identity formation takes a long time. Many young men and women move from the diffusion or the foreclosure status to the moratorium status and then achieve a sense of identity in their late teens or early 20s during the period of emerging adulthood (Kroger, 2007; Waterman, 1982). But this is by no means the end of the identity formation process. Some adults continue in a moratorium status for years; others reopen the question of who they are and recycle through the identity moratorium and achievement statuses after thinking they had all the answers earlier in life (Anthis & LaVoie, 2006; Kroger, 2007). Even in later adulthood, some adults are reworking and strengthening their sense of identity (Zucker, Ostrove, & Stewart, 2002).

Identity formation not only takes a long time but occurs at different rates in different domains of identity. For example, Sally Archer (1982) assessed the identity statuses of 6th- to 12th-graders in four domains: occupational choice, gender-role attitudes, religious beliefs, and political ideologies. Only 5% of the adolescents were in the same identity status in all four areas, and more than 90% were in two or three statuses across the four areas. Finally, identity formation is messy; rather than proceeding along one standard path, it often involves some backsliding and recycling through some of the identity statuses (Reis & Youniss, 2004).

In short, identity development is complex. It takes a long time, occurs at different rates in different domains, and often involves recycling through identity statuses. In Exploration Box 11.1, we look at an alternative approach to studying identity—the life story, or narrative identity, approach.

Developing a Positive Ethnic Identity

The process of identity development includes forging an **ethnic identity**—a sense of personal identification with an ethnic group and its values and cultural traditions (Phinney, 1996, 2006; Umaña-Taylor & Alfaro, 2006). Everyone has an ethnic and racial background, but members of minority groups tend to put more emphasis than white adolescents on defining who they are ethnically or racially. This is probably because majority group members often do not think of themselves as having an ethnicity, whereas minority group members become very aware of theirs (Bracey, Bamaca, & Umaña-Taylor, 2004; Laursen & Williams, 2002).

The process begins in infancy as babies notice differences among people; in one study, 3-month-old Caucasian infants already showed a preference for looking at other Caucasian babies rather than at babies from other ethnic backgrounds (Kelly et al., 2005). African babies show a similar preference for African faces, though not if they grow up among Caucasians, suggesting that babies form these preferences based on the faces they see most often (Bar-Haim et al., 2006).

During the preschool years, children learn more about different racial and ethnic categories and gradually become able to classify themselves correctly into one (Spencer & Markstrom-Adams, 1990). For example, Mexican American preschool children learn behaviors associated with their culture, such as how to give a Chicano handshake, but they often do not know until about age 8 what ethnic labels apply to them and what they mean, or that their ethnicity will last a lifetime (Bernal & Knight, 1997).

In forming a positive ethnic identity, adolescents seem to proceed through the same identity statuses as they do in forming a vocational or religious identity (Phinney, 1993; Seaton, Scottham, & Sellers, 2006). School-age children and young adolescents say either that they identify with their racial or ethnic group because their parents and others in their ethnic group influenced them to do so (foreclosure status) or that they have not given the matter much thought (diffusion status). In their mid- to late teens, many minority youths move into the moratorium and achievement statuses with respect to ethnic identity (Seaton et al., 2006). Others do not reflect on their ethnic identity until their 20s, especially if they have grown up in a homogenous environment and have had little interaction with other ethnic and racial groups (Phinney, 2006).

What are the ingredients of a positive ethnic identity? Youth are most likely to explore ethnic identity issues, establish a positive ethnic identity, and enjoy high self-esteem when their parents socialize them regarding their ethnicity by teaching them

Establishing a positive ethnic identity is more central for minority adolescents than for white ones.

© Mike Watson Images Limited/First Light

about their group's cultural traditions, preparing them to live in a culturally diverse society, and even preparing them to deal with prejudice, at least as long as it is done in a positive manner that does not breed anger and mistrust (Hughes et al., 2006; Neblett et al., 2008; Umaña-Taylor, Bhanot, & Shin, 2006).

Exploring and forging a positive ethnic identity can protect adolescents' self-concepts from the damaging effects of racial or ethnic discrimination (Wong, Eccles, & Sameroff, 2003), breed high overall self-esteem (Bracey et al., 2004; Umaña-Taylor, Gonzales-Backen, & Guimond, 2009), help promote academic achievement and good adjustment (Laursen & Williams, 2002; Rodriguez et al., 2009), and reduce depression symptoms (Mandara et al., 2009). Most minority adolescents cope well with the special challenges they face in identity formation. They settle their questions of ethnic identity, they resolve other identity issues around the same ages that European American youth do (Markstrom-Adams & Adams, 1995), and they wind up feeling at least as good about themselves (Gray-Little & Hafdahl, 2000).

Vocational Identity and Choice

> I wanted to be a firefighter, then I touched a spark. I'm too afraid. I wanted to be a teacher, then I babysat for a 4-year-old. I'm too impatient. I wanted to be a model, then I looked in the mirror. I'm too short.
>
> I know, I know—I can be anything I want when I am all grown up. But I am rapidly approaching all grown up and I see less of what I can be and more of what I cannot be. (Kelly Witte, *The Washington Post*, April 2, 2006, p. D1)

Vocational identity is a central aspect of identity with major implications for adult development. How do adolescents choose career paths? Children younger than about age 10 actively explore vocational possibilities but are not very realistic in their choices; they may want to be zookeepers, professional basketball players, firefighters, rock stars, or whatever else strikes them as glamorous and exciting (Ginzberg, 1972, 1984; Hartung, Porfeli, & Vondracek, 2005). Children make important progress, though, beginning to narrow their ideas about future careers to those consistent with their emerging self-concepts—as humans rather than as bunnies or ninja turtles, as males rather than as females, and so on (Gottfredson, 1996). As early as kindergarten, for instance, boys choose traditionally masculine occupations and girls choose traditionally female occupations, setting them on a path that leads to traditional gender-stereotyped careers (Hartung et al., 2005; Porfeli, Hartung, & Vondracek, 2008). Children also learn a lot about and are guided by the social status associated with different careers; they begin to prefer the idea of being a surgeon to the idea of being a butcher.

Like teenager Kelly Witte, quoted in the beginning of this section, adolescents age 11 to age 18 become more realistic, begin to weigh factors other than their wishes, and make preliminary vocational choices. According to theorist Eli Ginzberg (1972, 1984), they consider their *interests* ("Would I enjoy counseling people?"), their *capacities* ("Am I skilled at relating to people?"), and their *values* ("Is it really important to me to help people, or do I value power or money more?").

As they get still older, adolescents begin to take into account the realities of the job market and the physical and intellectual requirements for different occupations, and they begin serious preparation for their chosen occupations (Ginzberg, 1984; Hirschi & Vondracek, 2009; Walls, 2000). By late adolescence or emerging adulthood, they are in a good position to consider the availability of job openings in a field such as school counseling, the years of education required, the work conditions, and other relevant factors.

The main developmental trend evident in vocational choice, then, is *increasing realism with age*. As adolescents narrow career choices in terms of both personal factors (their own interests, capacities, and values) and environmental factors (the opportunities available and the realities of the job market), they seek the vocation that best suits them. According to vocational theorists such as John Holland (1985), vocational choice is just this: a search, often successful, for an optimal fit between one's self-concept and personality and an occupation (see also Ozer & Benet-Martinez, 2006; and Super, Savickas, & Super, 1996).

Adolescents from lower-income families, especially minority group members living in poverty and facing limited opportunities, discrimination, and stress, may have difficulty forming a positive vocational identity (Phillips & Pittman, 2003). They may aim high at first but, as they become more aware of constraints, lower their career aspirations and aim toward the jobs they think they are likely to get rather than the jobs that interest them most (Armstrong & Crombie, 2000; Hartung et al., 2005). Similarly, the vocational choices of females have been and continue to be constrained by traditional gender norms. Young women who have adopted traditional gender-role attitudes and expect to marry and start families early in adulthood sometimes set their educational and vocational sights low, figuring that they

cannot "have it all" (Mahaffy & Ward, 2002). Although more young women aspire toward high-status jobs now, many others, influenced by gender norms, do not seriously consider traditionally male-dominated jobs, doubt their ability to land such jobs, and aim instead toward feminine-stereotyped, and often lower-status and lower-paying, occupations (Armstrong & Crombie, 2000; Hartung et al., 2005).

Moreover, many teenagers, male and female, simply do not do as Erikson and vocational theorists would advise—explore a range of possible occupations, then make a choice. Almost 70% of the high school and university students in one study acknowledged that chance events had a lot to do with their career decisions (Bright, Pryor, & Harpham, 2005). Those adolescents who *do* investigate a range of options are more likely than those who do not to choose careers that fit their personalities (Grotevant & Cooper, 1986). A good fit between person and vocation, in turn, predicts greater job satisfaction and success (Spokane, Meir, & Catalano, 2000; Verquer, Beehr, & Wagner, 2003). The saving grace is that those who do not explore thoroughly as adolescents have plenty of opportunities to change their minds as adults.

Influences on Identity Formation

The adolescent's progress toward achieving identity in various domains is a product of at least five factors: (1) cognitive growth, (2) personality, (3) relationships with parents, (4) opportunities to explore, and (5) cultural context. *Cognitive development* enables adolescents to imagine and contemplate possible future identities. Adolescents who have achieved solid mastery of formal-operational thought, who think in complex and abstract ways, and who are self-directed and actively seek relevant information when they face decisions are more likely to raise and resolve identity issues than less cognitively advanced adolescents (Berzonsky & Kuk, 2000; Waterman, 1992). Second, *personality* is a factor; adolescents who explore and achieve identity have been found to be low in neuroticism and high in openness to experience and conscientiousness (Ozer & Benet-Martinez, 2006). That is, they are emotionally stable, curious, and responsible.

Third, adolescents' *relationships with parents* affect their progress in forging an identity (Emmanuelle, 2009; Kroger, 2007; Waterman, 1982). Youths who get stuck in the diffusion status of identity formation are more likely than those in the other categories to be neglected or rejected by their parents and to be emotionally distant from them. It can be difficult to forge an identity without first having the opportunity to identify with respected parental figures and to take on some of their desirable qualities. At the other extreme, adolescents in the foreclosure status appear to be extremely close to parents who are loving but overly protective and controlling. Because foreclosed adolescents love their parents and have little opportunity to make decisions on their own, they may never question parental authority or feel a need to forge a separate identity.

By comparison, students classified in the moratorium and identity achievement statuses generally appear to have a solid base of affection at home combined with encouragement of autonomy (Kroger, 2007). In family discussions, these adolescents experience a sense of closeness and mutual respect but also feel free to disagree with their parents (Grotevant & Cooper, 1986). Notice that this is the same warm and democratic parenting style that seems to help younger children gain a strong sense of self-esteem.

Opportunities to explore are a fourth influence on identity formation. For example, adolescents who attend college are exposed to diverse ideas and encouraged to think through issues independently. College provides the kind of moratorium period with freedom to explore that Erikson felt was essential to identity formation (Kroger, 2007).

Finally, identity formation is influenced by the broader *cultural context* in which it occurs—a point Erikson also emphasized. The notion that adolescents should forge a personal identity after carefully exploring many options may well be peculiar to modern industrialized Western societies (Coté & Levine, 1988; Flum & Blustein, 2000). As was true of adolescents in earlier eras, adolescents in many traditional societies today simply adopt the adult roles they are expected to adopt in their culture, without much soul-searching or experimentation. For many adolescents in traditional societies, identity foreclosure may be the most adaptive path to adulthood (Coté & Levine, 1988).

In Western industrialized societies, however, the adolescent who is able to raise serious questions about the self and answer them—that is, the individual who achieves identity—is likely to be better off for it. Identity achievement is associated with psychological well-being and high self-esteem, complex thinking about moral issues and other matters, a willingness to accept and cooperate with other people, and a variety of other psychological strengths (Kroger, 2007; Waterman, 1992).

Checking Mastery

1. How are 17-year-old Kwan's self-descriptions likely to differ from those of her 9-year-old sister Min?

2. College student Jack is in the foreclosure status with respect to vocational identity; his roommate Tim is in the diffusion status. What does each status mean, and what kind of parenting is associated with it?

3. What besides warm, democratic parenting is likely to foster identity achievement?

Making Connections

1. Write three brief descriptions of yourself to show how you might have answered the question "Who am I?" at age 4, age 8, and age 18. What developmental changes in self-conceptions do your self-descriptions illustrate?

2. In our culture, we assume that giving youth a long moratorium period in which to explore possible vocational identities is a good thing, so we send them to college and give them lots of time to experiment before they must take on adult responsibilities. More traditional societies simply ask youth to assume the adult roles specified for them and train them for those roles. What do you see as the pros and cons of these two approaches?

3. Analyze your own identity statuses in the areas of vocational, ethnic, religious, and sexual identity.

11.5 The Adult

We enter adulthood having gained a great deal of understanding of what we are like as individuals—but we are not done developing. How do self-conceptions change during adulthood, and to what extent are they shaped by the culture in which the person develops? How do personalities change and remain the same, and how are both self-concepts and personalities related to the changes adults experience as their careers unfold and end?

Self-Conceptions

It is clear that adults differ greatly from each other in their self-perceptions and levels of self-esteem. To what extent do age and cultural context help explain that variation?

Age Differences

In Western society, it is commonly believed that adults gain self-esteem as they cope successfully with the challenges of adult life but then lose it as aging, disease, and losses of roles and relationships take their toll in later life. Is there truth to this view? A large Internet survey of more than 300,000 people ages 9–90 conducted by Richard Robins and his colleagues (2002) suggests there is. Self-esteem tends to be relatively high in childhood, to drop in adolescence, to rise gradually through the adult years until the mid-60s, then to drop in late old age, as shown in ▪ Figure 11.4 (and see Robins, Tracy, & Trzesniewski, 2008). The same analysis showed that males generally have higher self-esteem than females except in childhood and very old age.

So there is some support for the idea that self-esteem increases during the adult years and drops in late adulthood, although only in the 70s and 80s. However, other work suggests that elderly adults are more like young- and middle-aged adults than different in both levels of self-esteem and in the ways in which they describe themselves (Helgeson & Mickelson, 2000; Ruth & Coleman, 1996). There is little truth, then, to the stereotyped view that most older adults suffer from a poor self-image, even though self-esteem drops for some adults in very old age. The interesting question becomes this: How do most elderly people manage to maintain positive self-images for so long, even as they experience some of the disabilities and losses that come with aging? Reducing the ideal–real self gap, changing standards of self-evaluation, making social comparisons to other old people, and avoiding self-stereotyping all play a role.

Reducing the Gap between Ideal and Real Self. Older people adjust their ideal selves to be more in line with their real selves. Carol Ryff (1991) asked young, middle-aged, and elderly adults to assess their ideal, likely future, present, and past selves with respect to various dimensions of well-being, including self-acceptance. ▪ Figure 11.5 shows the average scores on the self-acceptance scale. Ratings of the present self changed little across

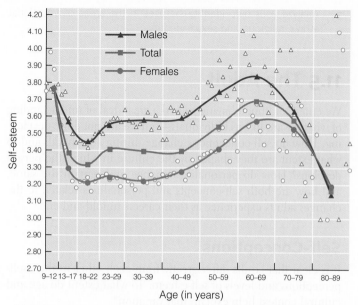

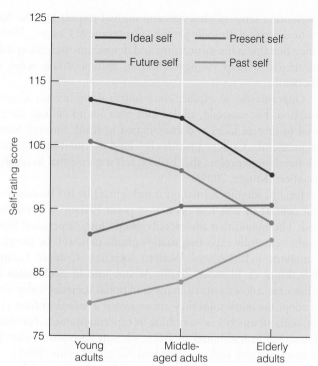

■ FIGURE 11.4 Self-esteem dips in early adolescence and rises during the adult years until it declines in very old age. Males have higher scores than females except in childhood and late old age. The lines graph mean or average self-esteem for the various age groups shown; the triangles (for males) and circles (for females) plot mean self-esteem at particular ages in the various studies summarized in this meta-analysis. SOURCE: From Robins, R. W., et al., J. Global self-esteem across the life span, *Psychology and Aging, 17*, pp. 423–434. Copyright © 2002 American Psychological Association. Reprinted with permission.

■ FIGURE 11.5 Favorability of ratings of their ideal, likely future, present (real), and past selves by young, middle-aged, and elderly adults. The gap between the ideal and the real self that widens during childhood and adolescence shrinks during adulthood, as indicated by the converging lines in the graph. As they age, adults become more comfortable with the idea of remaining as they are and as they have been. SOURCE: From Ryff, C. D. Possible selves in adulthood and old age: A tale of shifting horizons, *Psychology and Aging, 6*, pp. 286–295. Copyright © 1991 American Psychological Association. Reprinted with permission.

the adult years. However, older adults scaled down their visions of what they could ideally be and what they likely will be, possibly because they recognized that aging brings with it a loss of capacities. They also judged more positively what they had been. As a result, their ideal, future, present, and past selves converged. Notice, then, that the gap between the ideal self and the real self that widens during childhood and adolescence, and that gives us a sense of falling short, apparently closes again in later life, helping us maintain self-esteem.

Adjusting Goals and Standards of Self-Evaluation. People's goals and standards change with age so that what seem like losses or failures to a younger person may not be perceived as such by the older adult (Carstensen & Freund, 1994; Helgeson & Mickelson, 2000). A 40-year-old may be devastated at being passed over for a promotion, whereas a 60-year-old nearing retirement may not be bothered at all (Carstensen & Freund, 1994). For the older adult with a disability, walking a mile may be as much a triumph as running a mile might have been earlier in life (Rothermund & Brandtstädter, 2003b). As our goals and standards change over the life span, we apply different measuring sticks in evaluating ourselves and do not mind failing to achieve goals that are no longer important.

Comparing Self to Other Older Adults. Third, older adults are able to maintain self-esteem by making social comparisons primarily to other older adults (Brandtstädter & Greve, 1994; Helgeson & Mickelson, 2000). Older adults generally do not compare themselves with young adults but with people who have the same kinds of chronic diseases and impairments they have—or worse ones. Indeed, if they want to feel good about themselves, they may even strategically select worse-off peers to judge themselves against, making what are called downward social comparisons (Bauer, Wrosch, & Jobin, 2008; Frieswijk et al., 2004), as in, "I'm getting around much better than poor Bessie is." Indeed, some observers argue that stereotypes of aging in our society are so bleak that older adults can feel better about their own aging simply by conjuring up an image of the typical "old person" (Brandtstädter & Greve, 1994). As the next section illustrates, however, negative stereotypes of old age probably do more harm than good.

Not Internalizing Ageist Stereotypes. Finally, older adults are likely to maintain self-esteem if they can resist applying negative stereotypes of aging people to themselves. Becca Levy (2003) argues that stereotypes of old people learned in childhood often become self-stereotypes when people reach old age. She cites studies indicating that children learn early to take a dim view of elderly people, to stereotype them as sick, weak, forgetful, and incompetent (and see Hess, 2006). These negative stereotypes are reinforced over the years and are available to be applied to the self once people begin to think of themselves as "old." This may be why aging adults often go to great lengths to deny that they are old—a sign in itself that old age is negatively perceived in our society. But eventually they can deny no longer, apply the "old" label to themselves, and run the risk of negatively stereotyping themselves.

To demonstrate that aging self-stereotypes can negatively affect elderly adults, Levy and her associates (Hausdorff, Levy, & Wei, 1999) used a priming technique. Words reflecting either negative stereotypes of aging or positive stereotypes of aging were flashed rapidly on a computer screen to elderly participants in the study so that the words were perceived but below the level of awareness. After the priming experience, these adults were asked to walk down a hall wearing measuring devices on their feet that registered how rapidly they walked and how lightly they stepped (how long their feet were off the ground). Most people assume that a slow, shuffling gait in old age is caused by either biological aging or illness. This study demonstrated that social stereotypes can also slow people down. Older adults primed with positive stereotypes of aging clocked faster speeds and more spritely foot-off-the-floor time than older adults who were exposed to negative stereotypes and shuffled along like old people. As Chapter 8 revealed, Levy (1996) has also found that priming older adults with words such as *senile* results in poorer memory performance than priming them with words such as *wise*.

Levy and her colleagues (2002) have even found that middle-aged adults who have positive perceptions of their own aging (for example, who disagree with statements such as "Things keep getting worse as I get older") end up not only in better health in old age but live more than 7 years longer than adults who have less positive self-perceptions of aging. This was the case even when age, health, socioeconomic status, and other variables related to longevity were controlled. Similarly, adults who hold negative stereotypes of aging turn out to be at higher risk than those with more positive views of aging for cardiovascular events such as heart attacks over the next 38 years, even when other predictors of cardiovascular problems are controlled (Levy et al., 2009).

It sounds like ageist stereotypes are a hazard to old people, then, but to make sure Klaus Rothermund and Jochen Brandtstädter (2003a) tested three competing hypotheses about the relationship between aging stereotypes and self-perceptions in later life:

- Do aging stereotypes damage self-perceptions, as Levy (2003) argues?
- Alternatively, do aging stereotypes offer such a dismal view of old age that they give the self-concepts of aging adults a boost

by allowing them to compare themselves with worse-off others?
- Instead, might aging stereotypes reflect self-perceptions rather than shape them? That is, might adults experiencing the negative effects of aging begin to take a dim view of old people in general?

These researchers asked German adults aged 54–77 at the start of the study to rate a "typical old person" and to rate themselves on the same trait scales. The sample was then studied over 8 years so that relationships between earlier and later stereotyped beliefs about old people and self-perceptions could be assessed. The adults in this study clearly had a more positive view of themselves than they had of the typical old person (see also Ryan, Jin, & Anas, 2009). Moreover, the results supported Levy's view that aging stereotypes damage self-perceptions. Holding negative aging stereotypes at the outset of the study led to negative self-perceptions later, especially among the oldest adults studied. However, early self-perceptions did not affect later aging stereotypes. This study and others suggest that ageist stereotypes are indeed harmful to behavior, health, and self-esteem, especially among people who have come to identify themselves as "old" and apply ageist stereotypes to themselves (Hess, 2006; O'Brien & Hummert, 2006). Application Box 11.1 looks at what can be done to combat ageist stereotypes.

In sum, adults of different ages generally describe themselves in similar ways, but self-esteem appears to rise in early and middle adulthood and to drop off in late old age. Many older adults are able to maintain self-esteem, however, by perceiving a smaller gap than younger adults do between their real and ideal selves, adjusting their goals and standards of self-evaluation, making social comparisons with other older people, and resisting the tendency to internalize negative stereotypes of old people.

Cultural Differences

Self-conceptions show the imprint not only of individual experiences such as positive or negative feedback from parents, romantic partners, and bosses but also of broader cultural influences. In an **individualistic culture**, individuals define themselves primarily as individuals and put their own goals ahead of their social group's goals, whereas in a **collectivist culture**, people define themselves in terms of group memberships and give group goals higher priority than personal goals (Triandis, 1989, 1995). North American and Western European societies typically have an individualistic orientation, whereas many societies in Latin America, Africa, and East Asia are primarily collectivist.

How do self-conceptions differ in individualistic and collectivist cultures? Hazel Markus and her colleagues have carefully studied the meanings of self in the United States and Japan (Cross, 2000; Markus, 2004; Markus, Mullally, & Kitayama, 1997; and see Heine & Buchtel, 2009). They have found that being a person in the United States (an individualistic culture) means being your own person—independent and different from other people—whereas being a person in Japan (a collectivist culture) means being interdependent with others, embedded in society. Thus, when asked to describe themselves, American

Combating Negative Stereotypes of Aging

Although our society sometimes stereotypes older adults as wise, generous, and otherwise admirable, negative stereotypes of them abound—and as we have seen can have negative effects on self-perceptions, behavior, and even health and longevity if they are internalized and applied to the self. How might we combat ageist stereotypes and call attention to positive aspects of old age and aging?

Intervention might need to begin in childhood, as that is when we first learn ageist stereotypes (Hess, 2006). For example, intergenerational programs in which elderly adults work with children in the schools not only help children learn but also improve their attitudes toward old people (Cummings, Williams, & Ellis, 2003).

Interventions to combat ageism may also need to be aimed at elderly people, though. For example, Levy's (2003) work suggests that activating positive stereotypes of aging before elderly people perform cognitive tasks may boost their performance, at least temporarily. Organizations such as the Gray Panthers have also taken steps to help older adults resist the damaging effects of negative stereotypes of aging and of our society's emphasis on youth, self-reliance, and productivity (Cruikshank, 2009).

In a now classic study, Judith Rodin and Ellen Langer (1980) set out to demonstrate that changing the attributions aging adults make for problems they experience can make a difference. They discovered that 80% of elderly nursing home residents blamed physical aging for many of their difficulties in functioning and did not consider that the nursing home environment could be a source of their problems. In an experiment, Rodin and Langer exposed one group of nursing home residents to a new theory highlighting environmental causes of their limitations in functioning: That they had difficulty walking, for example, was attributed to the nursing home floors, which were tiled and therefore slippery for people of any age. Compared with an untreated control group and a group that received medical information that physical aging was not the major source of their difficulties, the group that learned to attribute everyday problems in functioning to the nursing home environment rather than to old age became more active, more sociable, and even more healthy.

Changing the orientations of helping professionals and helping professionals in training is also part of the solution. Few in or entering the health and mental health fields want to specialize in the care and treatment of the ever-growing elderly population; many professionals know little about aging, and many, products of their culture, hold ageist stereotypes. For example, a study of nursing students at four colleges showed that many held misconceptions about and negative attitudes toward older adults (Ferrario et al., 2008). One of the colleges decided to do something about it, using a vision of successful, healthy aging as an organizing theme for curriculum reform, developing the faculty's expertise in aging, and requiring more course work and practical experience with not only frail but also healthy older adults who illustrate that aging has a positive side. Although a carefully designed experiment was not conducted, preliminary results suggested that students exposed to the new curriculum had adopted more positive views of aging.

Ultimately, societal-level change may be needed. Some countries (China, for example) clearly have more positive views of old age than the United States does and grant elders a great deal of respect (Levy & Langer, 1994). Possibly our society can promote more positive views of aging across the life span by instituting new social policies and attitude-change programs (Braithwaite, 2002). Yet programs could backfire if they present too rosy a picture of aging, for then normal older adults may feel deficient when they compare themselves to the healthy, active elders they see in the media. At this point, older adults may be best off if they become more aware of negative stereotypes of old people, resist taking them to heart, and avoid blaming difficulties they encounter on the ravages of old age.

What stereotypes do we have of elderly women—and to what extent do they believe the stereotypes apply to them?

adults talk about their unique personal qualities but Japanese adults more often refer to their social roles and identities and mention other people (for example, "I try to make my parents happy").

In addition, Americans describe their generalizable personality traits—traits they believe they display in most situations and relationships. By contrast, Japanese adults describe their behavior in specific contexts such as home, school, or work and often describe themselves differently depending on the social situation or context they are talking about. Indeed, the Japanese language has no word to refer to *I* apart from social context (Cross, 2000). In short, Americans think like trait theorists and feel they have an inner self that is consistent across situations and over time, whereas Japanese people seem to adopt a social learning theory perspective on personality and see situational influences on behavior as powerful (Heine &Buchtel, 2009; Tafarodi et al., 2004).

Finally, Americans are obsessed with maintaining high self-esteem; most believe that they are above average in most respects. Japanese and other East Asian adults are more modest and self-critical. They readily note their inadequacies, seem reluctant to call attention to ways in which they are better than other members of their group, and do not seem as concerned with protecting and bolstering their self-esteem (Heine & Buchtel, 2009; also see ●Table 11.3 for a summary of these differences).

Interestingly, cultural differences in self-descriptions can be detected as early as age 3 or 4 by asking children to talk about themselves and their experiences (Wang, 2004, 2006). American children talk about their roles, preferences, characteristics, and feelings, whereas Chinese children describe themselves in terms of social roles and social routines such as family dinners. They

are a good deal more modest, too, saying things like "I sometimes forget my manners." Parents probably contribute to these cultural differences through everyday conversations with their children; for example, American mothers tell stories in which their children are the stars, whereas Chinese mothers talk about the experiences of the family as a group (Wang, 2004). Perhaps as a result, as American children enter adolescence, they put less emphasis on their relationships with their parents in their self-definitions, whereas Chinese students continue to keep their parents in a prominent role, as indicated by their responses to items like, "My relationships with my parents are an important part of who I am" (Pomerantz, Qin, Wang, & Chen, 2009).

Cross-cultural studies of individualistic and collectivist cultures challenge the Western assumption that a person cannot develop normally without individuating himself from others and coming to know his identity as an individual. In much of the world, it's about "self-in-relation-to-others," not about individuals with their own unique identities (Shweder et al., 2006). These studies also suggest that our methods for studying the self—asking people who they are, having them respond to personality scale items about how they *generally* behave across social contexts—may be culturally biased. It is wise to bear in mind, then, that self-conceptions are culturally defined.

Continuity and Discontinuity in Personality

How much continuity and how much change is there in personality over the adult years? Actually, we must ask two questions: Do individual adults retain their rankings on trait dimensions compared with others in a group over the years? Do average scores on personality trait measures increase, decrease, or remain the same as age increases?

Do People Retain Their Rankings?

Paul Costa, Robert McCrae, and their colleagues have closely studied personality change and continuity by giving adults from their 20s to their 90s personality tests and administering these tests repeatedly over the years (McCrae & Costa, 2003, 2008). Focusing on the Big Five dimensions of personality listed in Table 11.1, they have found a good deal of *consistency in rankings within a group*, as indicated by high correlations between scores on the same trait dimensions at different ages. In other words, the person who tends to be extraverted as a young adult is likely to be extraverted as an elderly adult, and the introvert is likely to remain introverted over the years. Similarly, the adult who shows high or low levels of neuroticism, conscientiousness, agreeableness, or openness to new experiences is likely to retain that ranking compared with that of peers years later. Correlations between personality trait scores on two occasions 20–30 years apart average about 0.60 across the five personality dimensions, suggesting consistency in personality over time but also room for change (McCrae & Costa, 2003; Morizot & Le Blanc, 2003).

The tendency to be consistent increases with age. In a meta-analysis of 152 studies in which personality was assessed on two

● TABLE 11.3	VIEWS OF THE SELF IN INDIVIDUALISTIC AND COLLECTIVIST CULTURES	
Individualistic (e.g., United States)	**Collectivist (e.g., Japan)**
Separate	Connected
Independent	Interdependent
Traitlike (personal qualities transcend specific situations and relationships)	Flexible (different in different social contexts)
Need for self-esteem results in seeing self as above average	Self-critical, aware of inadequacies
Emphasis on uniqueness	Emphasis on group memberships and similarities to others

SOURCE: Adapted from Markus, H. R., Mullally, P. R., & Kitayama, S. Diversity in modes of cultural participation. In U. Neisser & D. A. Jopling (Eds.), *The conceptual self in context, culture, experience, self-understanding.* Copyright © 1997 Cambridge University Press. Reprinted with permission.

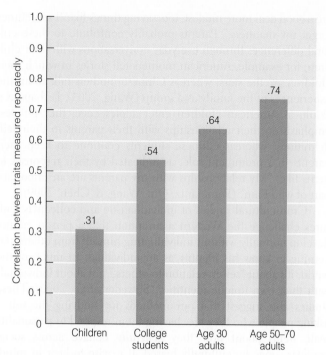

FIGURE 11.6 Rank-order consistency of personality trait measures at different ages. Consistency, as indicated by strong correlations between scores obtained 6–7 years apart, increases with age.

SOURCE: Data from Roberts, B. W., & DelVecchio, W. F. (2000). The rank-order consistency of personality traits from childhood to old age: A quantitative review of longitudinal studies. *Psychological Bulletin, 126,* 3–25.

changes. That tells us that people's personalities are affected by when they were born and by the experiences they had in their formative years (Roberts, Walton, & Viechtbauer, 2006; Schaie & Parham, 1976).

When age-group differences appear consistently in different cultures undergoing different social changes at different times, they are not likely to be because of cohort effects. McCrae, Costa, and their colleagues (2000) have examined age-group differences in scores on the Big Five personality dimensions in countries as diverse as Turkey, the Czech Republic, and Japan. From adolescence to middle age, they find, extraversion (especially excitement-seeking) and openness to experience decline modestly, whereas emotional stability (the opposite of neuroticism), agreeableness, and conscientiousness increase over this same age range. From adolescence or early adulthood to middle adulthood, then, we become less in need of stimulation and less open to new experiences but more psychologically mature—more emotionally stable, more cooperative and easy to get along with, and more disciplined and responsible. A major meta-analysis combining the results of longitudinal studies reinforced these general findings (Roberts et al., 2006). This evidence, coupled with evidence that the Big Five personality trait dimensions are genetically influenced (Krueger et al., 2006; Yamagata et al., 2006), has led McCrae and Costa (2003, 2008) to conclude that the Big Five are biologically based temperaments and that they undergo a universal process of maturational change.

What personality changes can people expect later—from middle age to old age? Activity level—the tendency to be energetic and action oriented, an aspect of extraversion—begins to decline in people's 50s and continues declining through the 80s and 90s (McCrae & Costa, 2003). Openness to experience also tends to decrease, whereas agreeableness increases (Roberts et al., 2006). Otherwise, most of us will not undergo similar personality changes as part of the aging experience. Either we will re-

or more occasions, Brent Roberts and Wendy DelVecchio (2000) found that the average correlation between scores at two testings an average of 6–7 years apart increased quite steadily from infancy and early childhood to late adulthood, as shown in ▪ Figure 11.6. Because they are still forming, personalities are unsettled in childhood and even in a person's teens and 20s; by around age 50 and beyond, they are quite consistent (Roberts & DelVecchio, 2000).

Do Mean Personality Scores Change?

Do most people change systematically in common directions over the years? You may be consistently more extraverted than your best friend over the years, and yet both of you could become less extraverted at age 70 than you were at age 20. This second major type of continuity in personality, *stability in the average level of a trait,* is relevant when we ask whether there is truth to stereotypes of older adults—for example, that they are more rigid, grumpy, depressed, or passive than younger adults.

Early cross-sectional studies suggested that younger and older adults have quite different personalities on average. However, some age-group differences have turned out to be generational, or cohort, differences rather than true maturational

Research on common changes in personality during adulthood suggests that this grandfather (left) and father (right) may be less open to experience and lower in activity level but more agreeable, conscientious, and emotionally stable than the young man of the family (center).

main much the same or we will change in response to life experiences in our own ways and at our own times (Helson, Jones, & Kwan, 2002).

Overall, most evidence points to (1) a good deal of cross-age consistency, more with age, in people's rankings compared with other people on Big Five personality trait dimensions; (2) cohort effects suggesting that the historical context in which people grow up affects their personality development; (3) personality growth from adolescence to middle adulthood highlighted by less excitement seeking and openness to experience but more maturity (emotional stability, conscientiousness, and agreeableness); and (4) little personality change from middle adulthood to later adulthood except for decreased activity level and openness to experience and increased agreeableness. In short, there is both continuity and discontinuity in personality during adulthood.

Why Do People Change or Remain the Same?

Having figured out that personality exhibits both continuity and change over the life span, developmentalists naturally want to know why people stay the same and why they change (see Roberts, Wood, & Caspi, 2008). What makes a personality stable? First, *heredity* is at work. As we have noted, genes contribute to individual differences in all five of the Big Five personality factors (Borkenau et al., 2001; Krueger & Johnson, 2008). Second, *lasting effects of childhood experiences* may contribute; you have seen, for example, that parents can either help a child overcome a difficult temperament or contribute to its becoming an enduring pattern of response. Third, traits may remain stable because people's *environments remain stable*; playing consistent social roles like mother or engineer may be especially important in creating consistency in personality (Roberts, Wood, & Caspi, 2008). Fourth, *gene–environment correlations* may promote continuity. That is, genetic endowment may influence the kinds of experiences we have, and those experiences, in turn, may strengthen our genetically based predispositions in a kind of snowball effect (Caspi, 1998; Roberts & Caspi, 2003; also see Chapter 3). Thus, an extravert's early sociability will elicit friendly responses from others, cause her to seek out social activities, and in the process strengthen her initial tendency to be extraverted—while the introvert seeks and experiences an environment that reinforces introversion.

What, then, might cause the significant changes in personality that some adults experience? *Biological factors* such as disease can contribute. The nervous system deterioration associated with Huntington's disease or Alzheimer's disease, for example, can cause affected individuals to become moody, irritable, and irresponsible (McCrae & Costa, 2003). Adults also change in response to *changes in the environment*, including major life events, changes in social and vocational roles, and therapy (Roberts et al., 2008; Maiden et al., 2003). For example, attaining a responsible position at work can result in increased social dominance (an aspect of extraversion), conscientiousness, and emotional stability (Roberts et al., 2008).

Finally, change is more likely when there is *a poor fit between person and environment* (Roberts & Robins, 2004). For example, Florine Livson (1976) discovered that independent

women who did not have traditionally feminine traits experienced more personality change during midlife than traditional women who fit the stereotypically feminine roles of wife and mother better. Bothered by the mismatch between their personalities and their traditionally feminine roles, the nontraditional women redirected their lives in their 40s, expressed their masculine sides, and experienced better psychological health by their 50s. Similarly, men who fit the traditional male role changed less over the years than nontraditional men who felt cramped by this role and who, after a crisis in their 40s, began to express their more feminine, emotional sides (Livson, 1981). For both men and women, then, a poor person–environment fit prompted personality change.

Thus, genes, lasting effects of early childhood experiences, stable environments, and gene–environment correlations all contribute to the considerable continuity seen in adult personality. Change in personality is clearly common too, though, and becomes more likely if people's biologies or environments change or if there is a poor fit between their personalities and their lifestyles. All things being equal, the forces for continuity are likely to be stronger than the forces for change, perhaps in part because we want to retain our identities as individuals and keep building the same niches for ourselves even when we move, change jobs, or make other life changes (Roberts et al., 2008).

When all is said and done, personality has a tremendous impact on life-span development. It clearly influences both physical health and psychological well-being, for example. Good health is strongly associated with conscientiousness, which probably encourages learning about and adopting good health practices (Hampson & Friedman, 2008). Good health is also linked to high extraversion and low neuroticism, which probably protect against the damaging effects of stressful life events on health (Hampson & Friedman, 2008). Similarly, psychological well-being is associated with high extraversion and low neuroticism; indeed, personality appears to be more important than objective life circumstances in determining a person's sense of well-being (Lucas & Diener, 2008). We will encounter more examples of the importance of personality throughout this book.

Eriksonian Psychosocial Growth

Researchers who conclude that adults change little over the years typically study personality by administering standardized personality scales. These tests were designed to assess enduring traits and probably reveal the most stable aspects of personality. Researchers who interview people in depth about their lives often detect considerably more change and growth (McCrae & Costa, 2003).

This is clear in research on Erikson's theory of psychosocial development through the life span. Erikson's eight stages of psychosocial development, listed in ● **Table 11.4,** will be reviewed briefly here in relation to changes in the self and with emphasis on their implications for development during adulthood (see also Chapter 2). Both maturational forces and social demands, Erikson believed, push humans everywhere through these eight psychosocial crises. Later conflicts may prove difficult to resolve

● TABLE 11.4 THE EIGHT STAGES OF ERIKSON'S PSYCHOSOCIAL THEORY

Stage	Age Range	Central Issue	Virtue or Strength
1. Trust vs. mistrust	Birth–1 year	Can I trust others?	Hope
2. Autonomy vs. shame and doubt	1–3 years	Can I act on my own?	Will
3. Initiative vs. guilt	3–6 years	Can I carry out my plans successfully?	Purpose
4. Industry vs. inferiority	6–12 years	Am I competent compared with others?	Competence
5. Identity vs. role confusion	12–20 years	Who am I?	Fidelity
6. Intimacy vs. isolation	20–40 years	Am I ready for a relationship?	Love
7. Generativity vs. stagnation	40–65 years	Have I left my mark?	Care
8. Integrity vs. despair	65 years and older	Has my life been meaningful?	Wisdom

if early conflicts were not resolved successfully. For development to proceed optimally, a healthy balance between the terms of each conflict must be struck; if this happens, the individual gains a particular "virtue," or psychosocial strength.

The Path to Adulthood

During Erikson's first psychosocial conflict, **trust versus mistrust,** infants learn to trust other people if their caregivers are responsive to their needs; otherwise, the balance of trust versus mistrust will tip in the direction of mistrust. Erikson believed that infants come to recognize that they are separate from their caregivers. Indeed, as you saw earlier in this chapter, infants begin to distinguish self from other (typically the mother) during the first 2 or 3 months of life.

Toddlers acquire an even clearer sense of themselves as individuals as they struggle with the psychosocial conflict of **autonomy versus shame and doubt.** According to Erikson, they develop a sense of themselves and assert that they have wills of their own. Consistent with this view, toddlers recognize themselves in a mirror and lace their speech with "me" and "no" around 18 months of age. Four- and five-year-olds who have achieved a sense of autonomy then enter Erikson's stage of **initiative versus guilt.** They develop a sense of purpose by devising bold plans and taking great pride in accomplishing the goals they set. As you have seen, preschoolers define themselves primarily in terms of their physical activities and accomplishments.

A sense of initiative, Erikson believed, paves the way for success when elementary-school children face the conflict of **industry versus inferiority** and focus on mastering important cognitive and social skills. As you have seen, elementary-school children seem intent on evaluating their competencies; they engage in more social comparison than younger children and are likely to acquire a sense of industry rather than one of inferiority if those comparisons turn out favorably.

According to Erikson, children who successfully master each of these childhood psychosocial conflicts gain new ego strengths. Moreover, they learn a good deal about themselves and position themselves to resolve the adolescent crisis of *identity versus role confusion,* Erikson's fifth stage, which was discussed in some detail earlier in this chapter. What happens to adolescents with newfound identities during the adult years? Erikson thought that stagelike changes in personality—and exciting possibilities for personal growth—continue during adulthood through psychosocial crises focused on intimacy versus isolation, generativity versus stagnation, and integrity versus despair.

Early Adult Intimacy

As Erikson saw it, early adulthood is a time for dealing with the psychosocial conflict of **intimacy versus isolation.** He theorized that a person must achieve a sense of individual identity before becoming able to commit himself to a shared identity with another person. The young adult who has no clear sense of self may be threatened by the idea of entering a committed, long-term relationship and being "tied down," or he may become overdependent on a romantic partner (or possibly a close friend) as a source of identity.

Does identity indeed pave the way for genuine intimacy? To find out, Susan Whitbourne and Stephanie Tesch (1985) measured identity status and intimacy status among college seniors and 24- to 27-year-old alumni from the same university. The researchers interviewed people about their closest relationships and placed each person in one of six "intimacy statuses." These included being a social isolate with no close relationships, being in a shallow relationship with little communication or involvement, being in a deep relationship but not yet being ready to make a long-term commitment to a partner, and being in a genuinely intimate relationship that has it all—involvement, open communication, and a long-term commitment. College graduates had progressed farther than college seniors in resolving intimacy issues; more of them were in long-term, committed relationships. In addition, the college graduates who had well-formed identities were more likely than those who did not to be capable of genuine and lasting intimacy.

Early adulthood is the time, according to Erik Erikson, for deciding whether to commit to a shared identity with another person—for resolving the conflict of intimacy versus isolation.

As Erikson theorized, then, we must know ourselves before we can truly love another person (see also Montgomery, 2005). Yet Erikson believed that women resolve identity questions when they choose a mate and fashion an identity around their roles as wife and mother-to-be. Is this rather sexist view correct? Only for some women (Kroger, 2007). Some women with feminine gender-role orientations tackle identity and intimacy issues simultaneously as Erikson envisioned, defining themselves primarily as wives and mothers (Dyk & Adams, 1990). Also influenced by traditional sex-role expectations, other women resolve intimacy issues before identity issues: they marry, raise children, and only after the children are more self-sufficient ask who they are as individuals (Hodgson & Fischer, 1979). However, still other women, those with more masculine gender-role orientations, tend to follow the identity-before-intimacy route that characterizes men, settling on a career first, thinking about a serious relationship next (Dyk & Adams, 1990). Overall, then, Erikson's theory seems to fit men better than it fits women because fewer women follow the hypothesized identity-then-intimacy path. Sex differences in routes to identity and intimacy are likely to diminish, however, as more women postpone marriage to pursue careers.

Midlife Generativity

Does psychosocial growth continue in middle age? George Vaillant (1977), a psychoanalytic theorist, conducted an in-depth longitudinal study of mentally healthy Harvard men from college to middle age and a similar longitudinal study of blue-collar workers (Vaillant, 1983; Vaillant & Milofsky, 1980). Vaillant found support for Erikson's view that the 20s are a time for intimacy issues. He found that in their 30s, men shifted their energies to advancing their careers and were seldom reflective or concerned about others. In their 40s, though, many men became concerned with Erikson's issue of **generativity versus stagnation.** This psychosocial conflict involves gaining the capacity to generate or produce something that outlives you and to care about the welfare of future generations through such activities as parenting, teaching, mentoring, and leading (De St. Aubin, McAdams, & Kim, 2004; Slater, 2003).

Vaillant's 40-something men expressed more interest in passing on something of value, either to their own children or to younger people at work. They were growing as individuals, often becoming more caring and self-aware as they entered their 50s. One of these men expressed the developmental progression Vaillant detected perfectly: "At 20 to 30, I think I learned how to get along with my wife. From 30 to 40, I learned how to be a success in my job. And at 40 to 50, I worried less about myself and more about the children" (1977, p. 195).

More recent studies of midlife generativity (see De St. Aubin et al., 2004) show, first, that middle-aged men and women are more likely than young adults to have achieved a sense of generativity (McAdams, Hart, & Maruna, 1998; Timmer, Bode, & Dittmann-Kohli, 2003). Moreover, those adults who have achieved a sense of identity and intimacy are more likely than other adults to achieve generativity as well, as Erikson predicted (Christiansen & Palkovitz, 1998). Although generativity is often thought of primarily in relation to successful parenting, it can be achieved by adults who do not have children too and is just as closely linked to well-being among adults without children as among parents (Rothrauff & Cooney, 2008). Overall, research on generativity supports Erikson's view that both women and men are capable of impressive psychosocial growth during middle adulthood.

Old Age Integrity

Elderly adults, according to Erikson, confront the psychosocial issue of **integrity versus despair.** They try to find a sense of meaning in their lives that will help them face the inevitability of death. If they constructed a life story or narrative identity during their early adult years, they may work on accepting it in old age as the only life they could have led (McAdams & Adler, 2006).

A sense of identity in early adulthood predicts both generativity and integrity in later life (James & Zarrett, 2005). Moreover, women in their 50s who display a high level of generativity and have resolved regrets about how their marriages and careers went (or have no such regrets) are more likely than other women to achieve a sense of integrity in their 60s (Torges, Stewart, & Duncan, 2008). A sense of integrity, in turn, is related to a high sense of psychological well-being and low levels of depression or despair (James & Zarrett, 2005).

Some years ago, gerontologist Robert Butler (1963) proposed that elderly adults engage in a process called **life review,** in which they reflect on unresolved conflicts of the past to come to terms with themselves, find new meaning and coherence in

Reminiscence and life review can help older adults achieve a sense of integrity.

their lives, and prepare for death (see also Haber, 2006; Webster & Haight, 2002). Elders who engage in life review display a stronger sense of integrity and better overall adjustment and well-being than those who do not reminisce much and those who mainly stew about unresolved regrets (Bohlmeijer, Roemer, Cuijpers, Smit, 2007; Wong & Watt, 1991; Wrosch, Bauer, & Scheier, 2005). Finding that life review can be beneficial, Butler and other gerontologists have turned it into a therapy approach in which elderly adults reconstruct and reflect on their life stories, sometimes with the help of photo albums and other memorabilia (Haight & Haight, 2007; Kunz & Soltys, 2007).

On balance, Erikson's view that humans experience psychosocial growth throughout the life span is supported by research. Although few studies have directly tested Erikson's childhood stages, his theorizing about the adolescent stage of identity versus role confusion has been tested extensively and is well supported. In addition, achieving a sense of identity in adolescence paves the way for forming a truly intimate relationship in early adulthood, gaining a sense of generativity in middle adulthood, and resolving the issue of integrity versus despair through life review in later adulthood.

Midlife Crisis?

> "Midlife is when you reach the top of the ladder and find that it was against the wrong wall." —Joseph Campbell, cited in Weiss (2008)

This quotation captures the essence of midlife crisis. But where in all the evidence of stability in personality traits over the adult years and of psychosocial growth through Erikson's stages is the midlife crisis that many people believe is a standard feature of personality development in middle age? Although Erikson, and Vaillant after him, saw few signs of a midlife crisis, another psychoanalytic theorist, Daniel Levinson (1986, 1996; Levinson et al., 1978) did. He proposed a stage theory of adult development based on intensive interviews with 40 men and later reported that it applied to a sample of women he interviewed as well (Levinson, 1996).

Levinson claimed that adults go through a repeated process of first building a "life structure," or pattern of living, and then questioning and altering it during a transition period every 7 years or so. He believed that the transition period from age 40 to age 45 is an especially significant time developmentally, a time of **midlife crisis** in which a person questions his life structure and raises unsettling issues about where he has been and where he is heading. Most middle-aged adults Levinson interviewed did not seek divorces, quit their jobs, buy red sports cars, or behave like lovesick adolescents, as popular images of the midlife crisis would have it, but most did seem to experience a crisis in their early 40s.

Many researchers agree that middle age is often a time when important issues arise, self-evaluations are made, and goals may change (Hermans & Oles, 1999; McAdams & Adler, 2006; Rosenberg, Rosenberg, & Farrell, 1999). What's more, some people experience midlife changes in personality in response to life events such as divorce, a job change, or the death of a parent. However, there is little support for Levinson's claim that most adults experience a genuine crisis in their early 40s (Hedlund & Ebersole, 1983; Vaillant, 1977). It seems sounder to call what many middle-aged adults experience midlife *questioning*, to recognize that it can occur in response to life events at a variety of ages, and to appreciate that it is usually not a true psychological crisis.

Vocational Development and Adjustment

Although Levinson's concept of midlife crisis is not well supported, he was right to emphasize that adults revise important life decisions as they develop. To illustrate, consider the important area of vocational development, which as we have already seen is an outgrowth of an individual's self-concept and personality (Judge & Bono, 2001). After much experimenting in early adulthood, people settle into chosen occupations in their 30s and strive for success. Ultimately, they prepare for the end of their careers, make the transition into retirement, and attempt to establish a satisfying lifestyle during their "golden years."

Establishing a Career

Early adulthood is a time for exploring vocational possibilities, launching careers, making tentative commitments, revising them if necessary, seeking advancement, and establishing yourself firmly in what you hope is a suitable occupation. Mentors can be of great help in getting young adults' careers launched (Kammeyer-Mueller & Judge, 2008; McDonald et al., 2007), but it often takes time and involves false starts.

To illustrate, Susan Phillips (1982), using data from a longitudinal study of males tracked from adolescence to age 36, examined whether men's decisions about jobs at different ages were tentative and exploratory (for example, "to see if I really liked that kind of work") or more final (for example, "to get started in a field I wanted [to enter]"). The proportions of decisions that were predominantly exploratory were 80% at age 21, 50% at age 25, and 37% at age 36. From age 21 to age 36, then, young adults progressed from wide-open exploration of different career possibilities to tentative or trial commitments to a stabilization of their choices. Even in their mid-30s, however, about a third of adults were still exploring what they wanted to be when they grew up! The average man held *seven* full-time jobs or training positions between age 18 and age 36 (Phillips, 1982). The picture for women is similar (Fuller, 2008; Jenkins, 1989).

After their relatively unsettled 20s and decision-making 30s, adults often reach the peaks of their careers in their 40s (Simonton, 1990). They often have major responsibilities and define themselves in terms of their work. The days of one employer or even one career for life are gone, though (Porfeli & Vondracek, 2009). Many workers, even in their 40s and beyond, find themselves recyling through the process of career exploration and choice and changing jobs.

Personality is an important influence on how careers go. Job performance is consistently correlated with the Big Five dimensions of conscientiousness, extraversion, and emotional stability (Ozer & Benet-Martinez, 2006). Person–environment fit can be critical, too: people tend to perform poorly and become open to changing jobs when the fit between their personality and aptitudes and the demands of their job or workplace is poor (Hoffman & Woehr, 2006).

Gender is another significant influence on vocational development. Although women are entering a much wider range of fields today than they were a few decades ago, most administrative assistants, teachers, and nurses are still women. U.S. women earn about 80 cents for every dollar men earn (Institute for Women's Policy Research, 2009). Why the gap? It is probably caused by both the influence of gender-role norms on the choices women make and by discrimination in the workplace.

Traditional gender-role norms have prompted many women to subordinate career goals to family goals. Women often interrupt their careers, drop down to part-time work, take less demanding jobs, and decline promotions that would involve transferring to a new location so that they can bear and raise children (Kirchmeyer, 2006; Moen, 1992). Both giving birth and moving to a new residence (sometimes in connection with having children) result in a drop in women's earnings for several years (Cooke et al., 2009). The hours mothers spend on homemaking and childcare tasks when their children are young often reduce their productivity at work; meanwhile, young fathers may become more productive at work in order to provide for their new families (Wallace & Young, 2008). In the process, women end up with lower odds of rising to higher paid, more responsible positions. Meanwhile, the women who make it to the top of the career ladder, especially in male-dominated fields, sometimes achieve this success by remaining single, divorcing, or limiting their childbearing (Jenkins, 1989). On average, women without children achieve more in their careers than women with children (Carr et al., 1998; Wilson, 2003). Women are also less likely than men to enjoy the career boost that comes from having a non-working partner supporting one's career (Kirchmeyer, 2006; Wallace & Young, 2008).

In addition to family taking priority over career, discrimination can limit women's vocational development. For example:

- Traditionally "female" jobs pay less than "male" jobs even when the intellectual demands of the work are similar (England, Reid, & Kilbourne, 1996).

- Women who enter jobs with the same management degrees and salaries as men, and receive equal performance ratings, still do not rise as far in the organization or earn as much as their male peers (Cox & Harquail, 1991).

- Women earn about 20% less than men even controlling for the tendency of women to work less, step out of the work force more, and enter lower-paying occupations (Associated Press, 2003).

So, although we make preliminary vocational choices as adolescents, we remain open to making new choices as young adults and take some time to settle on careers that fit our personalities and gender roles. The choices matter: for example, people whose work is complex and intellectually challenging are stretched by the intellectual stimulation they receive, becoming more able to handle intellectual problems adeptly and more self-confident (Kohn & Schooler, 1982; Schooler, Mulatu, & Oates, 1999). Perhaps most importantly, work becomes an important part of our identities. As a result, becoming unemployed, as happened to so many workers during the economic recession that began in 2008, can be a significant cause of family stress, depression, and other psychological problems (Paul & Moser, 2009).

The Aging Worker

Many people believe that adults become less able or less motivated to perform well on the job as they approach retirement. As it turns out, the job performance of workers in their 50s and 60s is largely similar overall to that of younger workers (Ng & Feldman, 2008; Rhodes, 1983). A recent meta-analysis of multiple studies looked at age differences in several aspects of vocational functioning (Ng & Feldman, 2008). Age was largely unrelated to quality of task performance and creativity on the job. Older workers actually outperformed younger workers in areas such as good citizenship and safety and had fewer problems with counterproductive behavior, aggression, substance use on the job, tardiness, and absenteeism. Older workers did not perform as well in training programs, possibly because many of them involved computer technology.

Why is the performance of older workers not hurt by some of the age-related physical and cognitive declines described in this book? First, these declines typically do not become significant until people are in their 70s and 80s, long after they have retired, and even then they do not affect everyone. The "older" workers in most studies are mainly middle-aged adults in their 40s, 50s, and 60s. Second, older workers have often accumulated a good deal of on-the-job expertise that helps them continue to perform well (Hansson et al., 1997).

Third and finally, the answer may lie in the strategies that aging adults use to cope with aging. Gerontologists Paul and Margaret Baltes (1990) have theorized that older people can best cope with aging, and people in general can best cope with the challenges of living, through the strategy they call **selective optimization with compensation,** or **SOC** (Baltes & Baltes, 1990; Baltes & Freund, 2003; Freund & Riediger, 2006; and see Chapter 8). Three processes are involved: *selection* (focus on a

Gender roles and career choices illustrated in *Doonesbury*.

limited set of goals and the skills most needed to achieve them), *optimization* (practice those skills to keep them sharp), and *compensation* (develop ways around the need for other skills). Using selective optimization with compensation, an overworked 60-year-old lawyer might, for example, avoid spreading herself too thin by focusing on her strongest specialty area and delegating other types of assignments to younger workers (selection); put a lot of time into staying up-to-date in her main area of specialization (optimization); and make up for her failing memory by taking more notes at meetings (compensation). For pianist Arthur Rubenstein, maintaining excellence in old age meant playing fewer different pieces (selection), practicing them more (optimization), and compensating for loss of speed by increasing the contrast between the slower and faster parts of a piece to make the faster parts sound faster (Baltes, Lindenberger, & Staudinger, 2006).

In one study of the SOC coping strategy (Abraham & Hansson, 1995), workers age 40 to age 69 completed scales measuring their reliance on selection, optimization, and compensation. Among older adults in the sample, especially those with highly stressful jobs, heavy reliance on selective optimization with compensation helped workers maintain a high level of performance and achieve their goals at work (see also Freund & Riediger, 2006).

The federal government seemed to have recognized that older workers are generally effective workers when it raised or eliminated mandatory retirement ages, increased the age of eligibility for receiving Social Security, and, through the Age Discrimination in Employment Act, protected older workers from age discrimination in hiring and retention (Hansson et al., 1997). But much remains to be done to understand the true strengths and limitations of older workers and to meet the needs of those who have the desire

and ability to continue working well into old age (see Hedge, Borman, & Lammlein, 2006).

Retirement

A century ago in North America, most working adults continued working as long as they were able, as people in many traditional societies today do. As late as 1930, more than half of all men age 65 or older in the United States were still working (Palmore et al., 1985). The introduction of Social Security in 1934, affluence, and increased availability of private pension plans changed that, making it financially possible for more men and women to retire and to do so earlier. And they have! As shown in ■ **Figure 11.7**, roughly half of adults are out of the labor force by age 62–64, two thirds are out by age 65–69, and about 90% are out by age 70 or older.

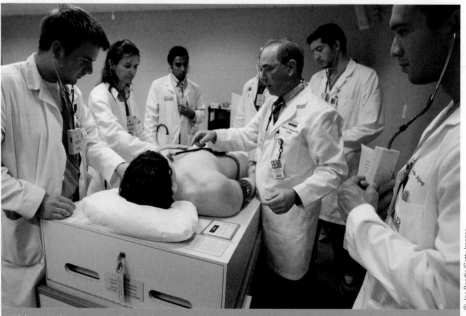

Older workers generally perform as well as younger ones, possibly because they use selective optimization with compensation to cope with aging.

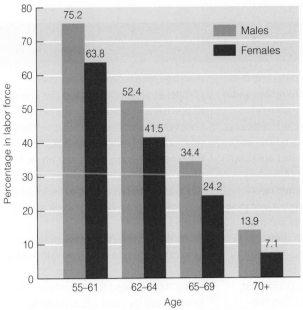

■ FIGURE 11.7 Labor force participation rates by age group for men and women in the United States. Most adults retire in their 60s. Many have been retiring in their early 60s, but the trend toward early retirement may be reversing.

Source: Modified from Federal Interagency Forum on Aging Related Statistics (2008). *Older Americans 2008: Key indicators of well-being.* Washington, DC: U.S. Government Printing Office. Available at: www.agingstats.gov. Accessed: September 20, 2009.

Men are still more involved in work than women, but the labor force participation rates of older men and women have become more similar since the 1960s as more women have spent more time in the work force and men have retired earlier (Federal Interagency Forum on Aging Related Statistics, 2008). Since the 1960s, the average age of retirement has dropped from over 67 to 62, although it appears to be inching up again as retiring baby boomers find that they need to continue working for financial reasons and as the age of eligibility for full Social Security benefits increases (Song & Manchester, 2009; Wilmoth & Longino, 2006).

Retirement is not a single event; it is a process that often plays out over a number of years. While some workers do retire "cold turkey" all at once, many others retire gradually, cutting back their work hours, becoming self employed, taking part-time "bridge" jobs, and sometimes cycling in and out of retirement multiple times before they settle into full retirement (Calvo, Haverstick, & Sass, 2009; Zissimopoulos & Karoly, 2009).

How do people adjust to the final chapter of the work life cycle? They face two main challenges: adjusting to the loss of their work role and developing a satisfying and meaningful lifestyle in retirement (van Solinge & Henkens, 2008). Robert Atchley (1976) proposed that adults progress through a series of

phases as they make the transition from worker to retiree. The process of adjustment begins with a *preretirement phase* in which workers nearing retirement gather information, talk about retirement, and plan for the future (Ekerdt, Kosloski, & DeViney, 2000). Discussing retirement with one's spouse and working out a financial plan during the pretirement phase are likely to pay off in greater well-being after retirement (Noone, Stephens, & Alpass, 2009). Deciding when to retire is an important part of the process; people can become worried in this phase about whether they will be able to retire when they want to and still be financially secure (van Solinge & Henkens, 2008). Although some workers choose to retire early, mainly because they have the means to live comfortably, others are forced to do so because of poor health or because they are pushed out of their jobs (Beehr et al., 2000; Hansson et al., 1997).

Just after they retire, according to Atchley, workers often experience a *honeymoon phase* in which they relish their newfound freedom; they head for the beach, golf course, or camp grounds and do all the projects they never had time to do while they worked. Then, according to Atchley, many enter a *disenchantment phase* as the novelty wears off; they feel aimless and sometimes unhappy. Finally, they move to a *reorientation phase* in which they begin to put together a realistic and satisfying lifestyle. Research supports this view. For example, David Ekerdt and his colleagues (Ekerdt, Bossé, & Levkoff, 1985) found that (1) men who had been retired only a few months were in a honeymoon period, highly satisfied with life and optimistic about the future, (2) men who had been retired 13–18 months were rather disenchanted, and (3) men who had been retired for longer periods were relatively satisfied.

Clearly, retirement takes getting used to. After retirees have adjusted, however, are they worse off than they were before they retired? Negative images of the retired person abound in our society; the retiree supposedly ends up feeling useless, old, bored, sickly, and dissatisfied with life. Yet research shows that retirement has surprisingly few effects on adults (Hansson et al., 1997; Palmore et al., 1985). Retirement's most consistent effect is to reduce the individual's income (Palmore et al., 1985). Retired people generally do not experience a decline in health simply because they retire. Poor health more often causes retirement than retirement causes poor health. Retirees' activity patterns and social lives do not change much either (Palmore et al., 1985). Retirement typically has no noticeable effect on the size of people's social networks, the frequency of their social contacts, or their satisfaction with the social support they receive. Finally, retirement generally does not reduce life satisfaction or damage mental health.

Overall, then, retirees are likely to experience an adjustment process involving preretirement then honeymoon, disenchantment, and reorientation phases. They usually adapt successfully to retirement and to the drop in income that it typically involves. Yet there are huge individual differences in adjustment. What makes for a favorable adjustment? The happiness of retirees does not seem to hinge on whether they retire suddenly or gradually (Calvo et al., 2009). Rather, adults who (1) retire voluntarily rather than involuntarily, (2) enjoy good physical and mental health, (3) have the financial resources to live comfortably, and

Janice, a 64-year-old public relations director, is not sure what to do about retirement. Her husband, Ron, hopes to retire next year and wants her to retire too so that they can travel and renovate their cabin at the lake, but she started her career late, loves her job, and isn't sure she's ready to leave it. She also isn't sure their savings and Social Security will be enough. She'd love it if she and Ron could do some of the things they've dreamed of doing before one or the other of them cannot, but she also wonders if they'd get on each other's nerves if they were both home all day.

Marriage is usually considered a positive influence on adult development and well-being, but it does complicate the retirement process. Now that most women work, many husbands and wives try to plan their retirements at the same time. In one study (Ho & Raymo, 2009), 42% of men and 39% of females age 50 or older in dual-career families who were still working expected to retire when their spouse did. However, only 24% of couples actually retired within a year of each other. Husbands and wives had equal influence on what happened—it was not just a matter of the man calling the shots—but for various reasons, including financial needs, many couples who wanted to retire at the same time could not.

Yet adjustment to retirement seems to go most smoothly when partners do retire together. Neither retired husbands nor retired wives are likely to be as happy if their spouse continues to work as if their spouse is also retired, especially if they feel their working spouse has more power in the relationship as a result (Szinovacz & Davey,

2005). Marital quality tends to decline temporarily after a husband or wife retires and it is especially likely to dip if the retiree's spouse still works (Moen, Kim, & Hofmeister, 2001). Two or more years into retirement, though, reports of marital conflict are down and marital satisfaction has improved.

Meanwhile, women who have been homemakers for years may find it irritating to have their retired husbands around the house all day, intruding in their worlds and disrupting their routines. A sample of women studied by Patricia Bushman and her colleagues (Bushfield, Fitzpatrick, & Vinick, 2008) cited "impingement" problems as the most difficult part of their husbands' retirement. When the researchers then developed an "impingement" scale and administered it to these women and to a second sample of women, they were surprised to find that women whose husbands had been retired for four or more years reported even more impingement problems than women whose husbands were only a year from retirement. Perceptions that their husbands were disrupting their lives were correlated with marital dissatisfaction.

Given the risk that retirement can strain a

marriage, one team of researchers (Trudel et al., 2008) tested the impact of marital and sexual therapy on retiring couples who wanted to improve their relationship (Trudel et al., 2008). Their preventive therapy approach proved effective, although differences in marital functioning between the experimental and control groups had shrunk after a year.

As these studies suggest, in retirement as in other life transitions people lead what Glen Elder (Elder & Shanahan, 2006) has called "linked lives." It is therefore critical to look at each person's adjustment to retirement in its family context.

© Hans Neleman/Photonica/Getty Images

(4) are married or otherwise have strong social support typically fare better than those who are forced to retire or who find themselves in poor health and with inadequate incomes and few social ties (Fouquereau et al., 2005; Palmore et al., 1985; Wong & Earl, 2009). Cultural context can be important, too: For example, Scandinavian countries generally have generous social welfare systems, but because the Chinese government has restricted families to one child, an increasing number of elders in China find themselves with no son to support them in the Chinese tradition and no pension either (Eberstadt, 2006).

Given these main influences on adjustment to retirement, we have reason to worry about women (Cruikshank, 2009). They may feel pressured to retire if their husbands retire or develop health problems; they move in and out of the work force more and do not earn as much as men and therefore often find themselves with no pension and an inadequate income in retirement; and they are likely to outlive their husbands and end up living alone. As Exploration Box 11.2 suggests, men and women have different experiences of retirement and we therefore need to consider the retirement transition in a family context.

Personality and Successful Aging

What lifestyle decisions make not only for a successful transition to retirement but also for a happy and fulfilling old age? Theories of successful aging have been offered for years to answer that question and help us all enjoy a satisfying old age.

Activity theory holds that aging adults will find their lives satisfying to the extent that they can maintain their previous lifestyles and activity levels, either by continuing old activities or by finding substitutes—for example, by replacing work with hobbies, volunteer work, or other stimulating pursuits (Fry, 1992; Havighurst, Neugarten, & Tobin, 1968). According to this view, psychological needs do not really change as people enter old age: most aging individuals continue to want an active lifestyle. This view is strongly promoted in our society by communications that youthfulness is valued and "...that *defying* aging is the primary way to *go about* aging" (Settersten & Trauten, 2009, p. 464).

By contrast, **disengagement theory** says that successful aging involves a withdrawal of the aging individual from society that is satisfying to both (Achenbaum & Bengtson, 1994; Cumming & Henry, 1961). The aging individual is said to have needs different from those she once had and to seek to leave old roles behind and reduce activity. Meanwhile, society both encourages and benefits from the older person's disengagement, which makes room for the younger generation.

Which is it? Throughout this text, you have seen evidence that individuals who remain active in old age benefit from their activity. Those who are physically active maintain their health longer (see Chapter 5), those who are physically and intellectually active maintain their cognitive functions longer (see Chapter 9), and those who remain involved in meaningful social relationships are likely to be more satisfied with their lives (see Chapter 14). In other words, there is more support for activity theory than for disengagement theory.

But before you conclude that activity theory explains all you need to know about successful aging, add three qualifications. First, the relationship between level of activity and life satisfaction or well-being is surprisingly weak (Fry, 1992). Apparently, many inactive individuals are nonetheless satisfied with their lives, and many busy individuals are nonetheless miserable. This suggests that quality of activity is probably more important than its quantity (Pinquart & Sorensen, 2000).

Second, some messages of disengagement theory have merit (Achenbaum & Bengtson, 1994). As our review of personality changes in later life revealed, for example, older adults sometimes do become less active than they were earlier in life. This can be viewed as a sign of disengagement. Moreover, most older people today do indeed withdraw voluntarily from certain roles and activities. Most notably, they choose to retire from work in their 60s, and society generally supports their doing so.

But third, neither activity theory nor disengagement theory says enough about the role of personality in influencing well-being in old age. Generally, for example, people who are highly extraverted, conscientious, and emotionally stable have a greater sense of well-being than other adults (Siegler & Brummett, 2000). Even more important, a good fit between the individual's lifestyle and the individual's needs, preferences, and personality may be the real secret to successful aging (Fry, 1992; Seleen, 1982). Energetic and outgoing Linda may want to maintain her active lifestyle in old age by being highly involved in church activities and family affairs, whereas Albert, who always found work to be stressful and annoying, may like nothing better than to disengage by fishing the day away. Linda might be happy but Albert might be miserable if made to participate in a retirement community's sing-alongs, dances, and skits.

Rather than remaining highly active or disengaging, some older adults find satisfaction by focusing on a few highly important roles, relationships, and personally meaningful projects, optimizing their competencies in those areas, and compensating for performance declines in other areas (Lawton et al., 2002; Turk-Charles & Carstensen, 1999). That is, they engage in *selective optimization with compensation*, which not only helps aging workers maintain good job performance but also works as a strategy for maintaining a sense of well-being in old age (Baltes & Carstensen, 2003; Freund & Riediger, 2006). In short, you cannot assume, as both activity theory and disengagement theory do, that what suits one suits all. Rather, you should again adopt an interactionist model of development that emphasizes the goodness of fit between person and environment. In the next chapter, we explore some fascinating interactions between biology and environment that contribute to differences between males and females in cognition, personality, and behavior.

Checking Mastery

1. What are two different meanings of continuity in personality from age 40 to age 50?

2. According to Erikson, when and how might an adult gain a sense of generativity?

3. Who theorizes that adults experience a midlife crisis in their early 40s, and what does research say about that?

4. What are three factors likely to make retirement a negative experience?

Making Connections

1. Costa and McCrae have argued that people's personalities are very stable by age 30 and hardly change thereafter. What evidence would you cite to refute them?

2. Aunt Rosalia is about to retire and wants to establish a satisfying lifestyle in old age. What would an activity theorist, a disengagement theorist, and a selective optimization with compensation theorist recommend that she do and why? Which option do you think will be best for her and why?

Chapter Summary

11.1 Conceptualizing the Self and Personality

- Personality is an organized combination of attributes unique to the individual. McAdams and Pals describe personality in terms of dispositional traits, more changeable characteristic adaptations, and unique narrative identities, as shaped by both biological and cultural and situational factors. Self-concept is an individual's perceptions of those attributes; self-esteem an overall evaluation of self-worth; and identity a coherent self-definition.
- Psychoanalytic theorists such as Erikson maintain that we all experience stagelike personality changes at similar ages; trait theorists believe that aspects of personality such as the Big Five trait dimensions are enduring, and social learning theorists maintain that people can change in any number of directions at any time if their social environments change.

11.2 The Infant

- Early in their first year, infants sense that they are separate from the world around them and can affect it; by 18–24 months, they display self-recognition and form a categorical self based on age and sex.
- Infants differ in temperament: in easy, difficult, and slow-to-warm-up temperaments (Thomas and Chess); behavioral inhibition (Kagan); and surgency/extraversion, negative affectivity, and effortful control (Rothbart). Temperament is influenced by genes and goodness of fit with the environment, and is only moderately related to later personality.

11.3 The Child

- Whereas the self-concepts of preschool children are focused on physical characteristics and activities, 8-year-olds describe their inner psychological traits and social ties and evaluate their competencies through social comparison.
- Children are most likely to develop high self-esteem when they are competent, fare well in social comparisons, and have warm, democratic parents.
- Links between early temperament and Big Five personality traits are evident, and some personality traits gel in childhood but others become even more consistent in adolescence and adulthood.

11.4 The Adolescent

- During adolescence, self-concepts become more psychological, abstract, differentiated, and integrated, and self-awareness increases; self-esteem dips for some but mainly increases.
- In resolving Erikson's conflict of identity versus role confusion, many college-age youths progress from diffusion or foreclosure to moratorium to identity achievement status, at different rates in different domains. Analyzing life stories, or narrative identities, is another approach to studying identity.

- Developing a positive ethnic identity is more central to minority than to majority group adolescents. Adolescents' vocational choices become increasingly realistic with age; the choices made by females and by low-income youth are sometimes constrained.
- Cognitive development, personality, parenting, opportunities to explore, and culture influence identity development.

11.5 The Adult

- Older adults maintain self-esteem until late old age by converging their ideal and real selves, changing goals and standards of self-evaluation, comparing themselves with other aging adults, and not internalizing ageist stereotypes. Self-conceptions differ in individualistic cultures and collectivist cultures.
- Individuals' rankings on Big Five dimensions of personality become more stable with age; excitement seeking, openness to experience, and, later, activity level typically decline, while maturity (emotional stability, conscientiousness, and agreeableness) increases over the adult years.
- Stability of personality may be caused by genes, early experience, stable environments, and gene–environment correlations; personality change may result from biological or environmental changes or a poor person–environment fit.
- Erikson's psychosocial theory is supported by evidence that resolution of conflicts centering on trust, autonomy, initiative, and industry paves the way for achieving a sense of identity in adolescence, intimacy in early adulthood, generativity in middle age, and integrity through life review in old age.
- Daniel Levinson's theory that adults question the life structures they build and experience a midlife crisis in their early 40s is not well supported, but young adults do engage in much career exploration and questioning before they settle down in their 30s and achieve peak success in their 40s. Older workers are generally as effective as younger workers, possibly because they use selective optimization with compensation to cope with aging.
- Retiring workers experience preretirement, honeymoon, disenchantment, and reorientation phases, and a drop in income, but little change in health or psychological well-being.
- In accounting for successful aging, neither activity theory nor disengagement theory places enough emphasis on person–environment fit and selective optimization with compensation.

Checking Mastery Answers

For answers to Checking Mastery questions, visit
www.cengagebrain.com

Key Terms

Media Resources

Psychology CourseMate

Find online quizzes, flash cards, animations, video clips, experiments, interactive assessments, and other helpful study aids for this text at **www.cengagebrain.com**. You can also connect directly to the following sites:

Big Five Quickstart: Introduction to the Five-Factor Model of Personality

This website provides a very detailed description of the Big Five trait theory and discusses ways of using the theory in business settings with individuals and teams. To access, see "web links" in Psychology CourseMate at www.cengagebrain.com

Great Ideas in Personality

This website could be subtitled, "Everything you wanted to know about personality theory, personality research, and more!" Covering most of the major personality theories, this website allows the visitor access to the historical development of each approach, a general overview of each approach, and most importantly links to other sites focusing on each theory. To access, see "web links" in Psychology CourseMate at www.cengagebrain.com

Understanding the DATA: Exercises on the Web

www.cengagebrain.com

For additional insight on the data presented in this chapter, try out the exercises for these figures in Psychology CourseMate at

www.cengagebrain.com:

Figure 11.3 Percentage of subjects in each of James Marcia's four identity statuses as a function of age. Note that only 4% of the 15-year-olds and 20% of the 18-year-olds had achieved a stable identity.

Figure 11.5 Favorability of ratings of their ideal, likely future, present (real), and past selves by young, middle-aged, and elderly adults. The gap between the ideal and the real self that widens during childhood and adolescence shrinks during adulthood, as indicated by the converging lines in the graph. As they age, adults become more comfortable with the idea of remaining as they are and as they have been.

Figure 11.7 Labor force participation rates by age group for men and women in the United States. Most adults retire in their 60s. Many have been retiring in their early 60s, but the trend toward early retirement may be reversing.

CengageNOW

www.cengagebrain.com

Go to www.cengagebrain.com to link to CengageNOW, your online study tool. First take the Pre-Test for this chapter to get your Personalized Study Plan, which will identify topics you need to review and direct you to online resources. Then take the Post-Test to determine what concepts you have mastered and what you still need work on.

Gender and Sexuality

© Cindy Karp/New York Times/Redux

Developmental psychologist Carole Beal (1994) learned an interesting lesson about the significance of being a girl or a boy when she was interviewing 9-year-olds:

> I had just finished one interview and was making some quick notes when the next child came into the office. I looked up, and an odd thing happened: I could not tell whether the child was a boy or a girl. The usual cues were not there: The child's hair was trimmed in a sort of pudding-bowl style, not really long but not definitively short either. The child was dressed in a gender-neutral outfit of jeans, sneakers, and a loose T-shirt, like most of the children at the school. The name on the interview permission slip was "Cory," which did not clarify matters much as it could be either a boy's or a girl's name. Still puzzled, I began the interview and found myself becoming increasingly frustrated at not knowing Cory's sex. I quickly realized how many unconscious assumptions I usually made about boys and girls. (p. 3)

Unlike Cory, most children are readily identified as girls or boys and treated accordingly. How much does it matter, in terms of development, whether a child is perceived and treated as a girl or as a boy? How much does it matter whether a child is a girl or a boy biologically? These are the kinds of questions we tackle in this chapter.

Ask Yourself This

1. How does biological sex set the stage for construction of gender?

2. How does gender influence how we experience our world and how we are perceived by others?

3. How does our understanding of gender change across the life span, and how is it different for boys/men and girls/women?

4. To what extent is "maleness" and "femaleness" determined by biological factors, and what environmental/cultural factors influence our expression of gender?

5. How are sexual behaviors typically expressed during childhood and adolescence? What gender differences are evident in sexual behaviors and sexual morality?

6. What factors seem to contribute to sexual orientation?

7. How does sexuality change throughout adulthood?

Gender matters. It used to be that the first question following a birth was whether the baby was a boy or girl. With today's technology, this question is often posed as soon as a pregnancy is announced. As children develop, girls discover that they are girls, and many acquire a taste for wearing pink clothes and playing with dolls, while boys discover that they are boys and often wrestle each other on the lawn. As an adult, you are probably keenly aware of being either a man or a woman and may define yourself partly in terms of roles or activities that highlight gender, such as mother, boyfriend, primary wage earner, and so on. In short, being female or male is a highly important aspect of the self throughout the life span. Before you read any further, try the quiz in Engagement Box 12.1 to see if you know which of the many beliefs we hold about males and females have some truth to them.

12.1 Sex and Gender

To what extent are you influenced by being a male or a female? Chances are good that sex and gender have influenced several characteristics that make you the unique person that you are, from your physical characteristics and abilities, to some of the roles you play in society, to some of your psychological characteristics. When we talk about your **biological sex,** we mean those physical characteristics that define male and female, whereas **gender** incorporates all those features that a society associates with or considers appropriate for being men and women. For example, women menstruate as a result of their hormonal and physiologic makeup, making this a component of their biological sex. Men typically have larger bones and muscle mass than women, another sex difference. Consider, though, that women as a group earn less money than men. This is not a sex difference but a gender difference be-

cause it arises from societal factors that have created different expectations and outcomes for males and females in the workforce. To understand how sex and gender might influence your life, we begin with some of the obvious physical differences before examining the psychological correlates of gender.

The physical differences between males and females are undeniable. A zygote that receives an X chromosome from each parent is a genetic (XX) female, whereas a zygote that receives a Y chromosome from the father is a genetic (XY) male. In rare cases of gender chromosome abnormalities (see Chapter 3), this is not the case; a girl may have only one X chromosome or a boy may have three chromosomes (XYY or XXY). Chromosomal differences result in different prenatal hormone balances in males and females, and hormone balances before and after birth are responsible for the facts that the genitals of males and females differ and that only females can bear children. Moreover, males typically grow to be taller, heavier, and more muscular than females, although females may be the hardier sex in that they live longer and are less susceptible to many physical disorders (Giampaoli, 2000). As you will see later in the chapter, some theorists argue that biological differences between males and females are responsible for psychological and social differences.

However, there is much more to being a man or woman than the biological features that define one's sex. Virtually all societies expect the two sexes to take on different **gender roles**—the patterns of behavior that females and males should adopt in a particular society (for example, the roles of wife, mother, and woman for females and of husband, father, and man for males). Characteristics and behaviors viewed as desirable for males or females are specified in *gender-role norms*—society's expectations or standards concerning what males and females *should be* like. Each society's norms generate **gender stereotypes,** overgeneralized and largely inaccurate beliefs about what males and females *are* like. For example, when trying to decide who should drive to a friend's house in an unfamiliar location, John may say to his new girlfriend, "I'll drive because you women always get lost," to which she replies, "Well, unlike you guys, at least women stop to ask for directions." They have both applied stereotypes about groups to an individual member of the groups. The reality is that this particular woman may be a superb navigator and John may be highly likely to stop and ask directions. Where did such gender stereotypes come from and is there any truth behind them?

Gender Roles and Stereotypes

Many stereotypes originate with a grain of truth, and in the case of gender stereotypes, the grain may be the physical makeup of males and females. One clear physical difference between the

Which of the following do you think are consistent sex differences that have been demonstrated in studies comparing males and females? Mark each statement true or false. Answers are printed upside down; they will be clarified in the main text.

_____ 1. Males are more aggressive than females.

_____ 2. Males are more active than females.

_____ 3. Females are more social than males.

_____ 4. Females have stronger verbal abilities than males.

_____ 5. Males have greater achievement motivation than females.

_____ 6. Males are more analytical than females.

_____ 7. Females are more suggestible and prone to conform than males.

_____ 8. Females are more emotionally unstable than males.

_____ 9. Males are more rational and logical than females.

_____ 10. Males have greater spatial and mathematical abilities than females.

Answers: 1-T, 2-T, 3-F, 4-T, 5-T, 6-F, 7-F, 8-F, 9-F, 10-T.

---

sexes is women's ability to bear and nurse children. As a result, women have adopted the role of childbearer and nurturer and this role has shaped the gender-role norms that prevail in many societies, including our own. At the heart of the nurturer gender role is **communality** (or communion) an orientation that emphasizes connectedness to others and includes traits of emotionality and sensitivity to others (Best & Williams, 1993; Rosenkrantz et al, 1968). Girls who adopt communal traits will presumably be

Take a look at this baby boy and write down a few adjectives describing what you think he might have been feeling or thinking at the time this photo was taken. Now suppose you learn that this "boy" is actually a girl. Do the adjectives still seem to fit? Do any of them reflect gender stereotyping?

© Turbo/Corbis

prepared to play the roles of wife and mother—to keep the family functioning and to raise children successfully. By contrast, the central aspect of the masculine gender role is **agency,** an orientation toward individual action and achievement that emphasizes traits of dominance, independence, assertiveness, and competitiveness. Boys have been encouraged to adopt agentic traits to fulfill the traditionally defined roles of husband and father, which involve providing for the family and protecting it from harm. Taking this one step further, Baron-Cohen (2003) claims that men's focus on work, achievement, and independence stems from the male brain's tendency to **systemize,** or analyze and explore how things work (see also Chapter 16). Communion and agency have long been viewed as two fundamental psychological dimensions of human nature (Abele, 2003; Bakan, 1966; Eagly, 2009) that are widespread across a variety of cultures (Abele et al., 2008; Williams & Best, 1990).

With gender-role norms in many cultures mandating that females play a communal role and males play an agentic role, stereotypes have arisen saying that females possess communal traits and males possess agentic traits (Williams & Best, 1990). If you are thinking that these stereotypes have disappeared as attention to women's rights has increased and as more women have entered the labor force, think again. Although some change has occurred, children, adolescents, and adults still endorse many traditional stereotypes about men and women (Botkin, Weeks, & Morris, 2000; Oswald & Lindstedt, 2006; Spence & Buckner, 2000). Boys are more likely than girls to endorse traditional stereotypes, perhaps because stereotypes about males (such as "independent") tend to be more positive than the stereotypes about females (for example, "dependent") (Rowley et al., 2007).

Moreover, males and females continue to describe themselves differently. When Jean Twenge (1997) analyzed studies conducted from 1970 to 1995 in which standard scales assessing gender-relevant traits had been administered, she found that men and women in the mid-1990s described themselves more similarly than men and women did 20 years previously, largely because modern women saw themselves as having more agentic traits. However, male and female personality profiles continued to differ in ways consistent with gender stereotypes.

Gender Differences or Similarities?

Much research has attempted to answer the question of whether there are meaningful gender differences in behavior. Although differences in some areas have been identified, other areas show no gender differences. Early research on gender seemed focused on trying to reveal differences of any size or value, and psychological differences between men and women were emphasized (see, for example, Tannen, 1991). More recently, Janet Hyde (2005) and others have proposed that it is more accurate to focus on gender similarities. They advance a **gender similarities hypothesis,** which states that "males and females are similar on most, but not all, psychological variables. That is, men and women, as well as boys and girls, are more alike than they are different" (Hyde, 2005, p. 581). As you review the following research on gender, try to evaluate for yourself whether there are more gender similarities or differences, and where there are differences, decide whether they are large and meaningful or negligible and unimportant. Also keep in mind that these are *group differences,* and even when research shows that women score higher (or lower) than men on average, there will be individual women who score lower (or higher) than individual men. With this in mind, here is what the research shows:

- *Females sometimes display greater verbal abilities than males, but on most verbal tasks the difference is small.* One verbal task where females consistently outperform males is reading (Organization for Economic Co-operation and Development [OECD], 2007). This difference is observed in many different countries, and the size of the difference is often quite large.

- *Males outperform females on many tests of spatial ability* (for example, arranging blocks in patterns or identifying the same figure from different angles; ■ **Figure 12.1**). Although some research suggests that these differences emerge only in adolescence (see Maccoby & Jacklin, 1974), differences on some tests—especially mental rotations—can be detected in childhood and persist across the life span (Choi & Silverman, 2003; Johnson & Bouchard, 2007; Kaufman, 2007; Nordvik & Amponsah, 1998). It should be noted that on a few tests of spatial ability, namely remembering object locations, females outperform males (Voyer et al., 2007). Further, training in the form of playing action video games can reduce or eliminate the gender difference on most spatial tasks (Feng, Spence, & Pratt, 2007).

- Historically, males outperformed females on standardized tests of mathematical ability, but this male advantage has all but disappeared in the United States and many other countries: *females and males perform similarly on most standardized math tests, and females obtain slightly higher math grades in the classroom than males* (Else-Quest, Hyde, & Linn, 2010; Kenney-Benson et al., 2006; Lachance & Mazzocco, 2006). In some countries (such as Austria, Chile, Germany, and Japan), there is a male advantage on math, perhaps reflecting different educational opportunities for males and females in these countries (OECD, 2007). In a handful of countries, females score higher than males (for example, Qatar and Jordan). Thus, in most cases there are not significant gender differences in math performance, but in those cases where there is a difference, it typically is in favor of males. Interestingly, males express more positive attitudes about math than do females, and this more positive outlook may create more opportunities for males to gain experience and comfort with math; for example, they may be more likely to sign up for higher level math classes than females (Else-Quest, Hyde, & Lin, 2010).

- *Girls display greater memory ability than boys.* Some studies show that this is a general or overall advantage (Johnson & Bouchard, 2007), whereas other research suggests that female's memory advantage is in specific areas. As noted earlier, there is a female advantage when it comes to remembering object locations, and other research shows females excel at recalling verbal information, as well as faces, particularly female faces (see Herlitz & Rehnman, 2008). Finally, listen to your female friends if they tell you something smells bad because women also show an advantage over men when it comes to recognizing familiar odors (Herlitz & Rehnman, 2008).

- *Males engage in more physical and verbal aggression than females, starting as early as 17 months* (Baillargeon et al., 2007; Burton, Hafetz, & Henninger, 2007; Buss & Perry, 1992). Across 21 diverse countries, teachers in nearly all the countries report that boys are more aggressive than girls (Rescorla et al., 2007; but see Kim, Kim, & Kamphaus, 2010). Sex differences are more obvious for physical aggression than for other forms of aggression. For example, at 17 months, for every girl who is physically aggressive there are five boys who display frequent physical aggression (Baillargeon et al., 2007). Males also commit more serious and more physically violent crimes (Barash, 2002). Some research shows that females tend to specialize in subtle, indirect, and relational forms of aggression such as gossiping about and excluding others (Crick & Bigbee, 1998; Murray-Close, Ostrov, & Crick, 2007; Ostrov & Godleski, 2010).

- Even before birth and throughout childhood, *boys are more physically active* than girls (Almli, Ball, & Wheeler, 2001); they fidget and squirm more as infants and run around more as children. In 19 out of 21 countries studied by Leslie Rescorla and colleagues (2007), teachers report that boys are more hyperactive than girls.

- *Boys are more developmentally vulnerable,* not only to prenatal and perinatal (birth-related) stress (for example, they die more often before birth) but also to several diseases and to disorders such as reading disabilities, speech defects, hyperactivity, emotional problems, and mental retardation (Henker & Whalen, 1989; Jacklin, 1989; Raz et al., 1994).

- *Girls are more tactful and cooperative, as opposed to being forceful and demanding, and are more compliant with requests from adults,* although they are no more likely than boys to give in to peers (Baron-Cohen, 2003; Maccoby, 1998).

- *Both males and females report that females are more nurturant and empathic; sex differences in behaviors are small but show females empathizing more than males* (Baron-Cohen, 2003; Deutsch, 1999; Feingold, 1994b). Females also take more interest in and are more responsive to infants (Reid & Trotter, 1993).

- *Females are more prone to develop anxiety disorders, depression, and phobias* (Pigott, 2002). *In contrast, males are more likely to display antisocial behaviors and drug and alcohol abuse* (Hicks et al., 2007).

- *Males use computers more than females and express greater confidence in their computer abilities* (Li & Kurkup, 2007). These findings do not tell us, though, whether there are gender differences in computer ability.

What have you concluded from this collection of research on gender? Are males and females different in meaningful ways or are any differences trivial, as would be predicted by the gender similarities hypothesis? To help answer this, consider that if we ordered people based on degree of aggressiveness from most aggressive to the least aggressive person in a group, only 5% of the observed differences could be attributed to whether a person is male or female (Hyde, 1984). It is worth repeating the point we made earlier: *Average* levels of a behavior such as aggression may be noticeably different for males and females, but within each sex there are both extremely aggressive and extremely nonaggressive individuals. Therefore it is impossible to predict accurately how aggressive a person is simply by knowing that person's biological sex. Gender differences in most other abilities and personality traits are similarly small.

If, as we have just seen, females and males are more psychologically similar than different, then why do unfounded stereotypes persist? Partly because we, as the holders of male–female stereotypes, are biased in our perceptions. We are more likely to notice and remember behaviors that confirm our beliefs than to notice and remember exceptions, such as independent behavior in a woman or emotional sensitivity in a man (Martin & Halverson, 1981).

In addition, Alice Eagly's (1987) **social-role hypothesis** suggests that differences in the roles that women and men play in society do a lot to create and maintain gender stereotypes. For example, men have traditionally occupied powerful roles in business and industry that require them to be dominant and forceful.

According to Alice Eagly's social-role hypothesis, this man would be perceived as nurturant, warm, and caring because he has assumed the role of caregiver.

Women have more often filled the role of homemaker and therefore have been called upon to be nurturant and sensitive to their children's needs. As a result, we begin to see men as dominant or agentic by nature and women as nurturant or communal by nature. We lose sight of the fact that the differences in the social roles they play cause men and women to behave differently; it is not all "by nature." Individuals even perceive themselves differently depending on which of their roles they are considering: more agentic when thinking of their work role and more communal when thinking of their family role (Uchronski, 2008). Might gender differences in behavior be minimized or reversed if women ran companies and men raised children?

Some research suggests that this may be the case. Both men and women rate male and female homemakers as equally communal (Bosak, Sczesny, & Eagly, 2008). Thus, men who are in the role of homemaker are perceived as being just as caring and affectionate as women in this role. Still, women presented in employee roles are not always judged as having equal agency as men in employee roles. This may be a result of the continued gender segregation of the workforce, with far more women in such occupations as nursing and teaching and far more men in occupations of plumber, corporate executive, and construction worker. Thus, conjuring up the role of employee for men and women may lead not to a single image of what this role involves but to multiple images based on existing gender patterns in the workforce (Bosak, Sczesny, & Eagly, 2008).

Although psychological gender differences are often small, it still makes a difference in society whether a person is male or female. First, gender norms and stereotypes, even when they are unfounded, affect how we perceive ourselves and other people. As long as people expect females to be less competent in math than males, for example, females may lack confidence in their abilities and perform less competently (Eccles, Jacobs, & Harold, 1990). That many stereotypes are unfounded does not make them less potent.

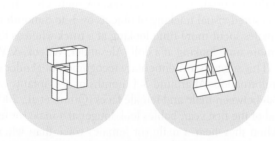

■ **FIGURE 12.1** A spatial ability task. Are the two figures alike or different? The task assesses the ability to mentally rotate visual information and is a task on which average differences between males and females are large. SOURCE: From Shepard, R. N. and Metzler, J., Mental rotation of three-dimensional objects, *Science, 17*, pp. 701–703. Copyright © 1971 by the American Association for the Advancement of Science. Reprinted with permission.

In addition, even though males and females are similar psychologically, they are steered toward different roles in society. In childhood, girls and boys conform to their gender roles by segregating themselves by biological sex and developing different interests and play activities (Maccoby, 1998). As adolescents and adults, males and females pursue different vocations and lifestyles. Although more women are entering male-dominated fields today than in the past, they are underrepresented in many traditionally male-dominated fields, and men rarely enter female-dominated fields (U.S. Department of Labor, 2010). Occupations remain highly gender segregated. For instance, the top five occupations held in 2009 by U.S. women were secretary, nurse, teacher, cashier, and nursing or health aide (U.S. Department of Labor, 2010). More men are sharing child-rearing and household responsibilities with their partners, but many couples still divide the labor along traditional lines, so that the woman is primarily responsible for child care and housework and the man is primarily responsible for income and money management (Perkins & DeMeis, 1996; Poortman & Van Der Lippe, 2009; Sayer, 2005). When we think about who asks whom out on a date, who stays home from work when a child has an ear infection, or who sews the buttons back on shirts, we must conclude that, despite significant social change, traditional gender roles are alive and well.

Checking Mastery

1. What is the central aspect of agency and of communion?

2. What are four differences between males and females, two that favor females and two that favor males?

3. How does Eagly's social-role hypothesis explain gender differences?

Making Connections

1. What roles do you play as a result of your biological sex? For example, are you a son or a daughter? How do these roles influence your behavior? Would you, for instance, behave any differently if you were a son rather than a daughter (or vice versa)?

2. Your grandmother strongly believes that boys and girls (and men and women) are quite different. Sometimes, she is even bothered by some of your behaviors because she doesn't believe you are behaving like a "proper" young woman or man. How did her thinking about gender become so entrenched, and what could be done to soften her views?

12.2 The Infant

At birth there are few differences, other than the obvious anatomical ones, between males and females. Male newborns tend to be somewhat more irritable than females, and female newborns are more alert than males (Boatella-Costa et al., 2007). But overall, differences between males and females at birth are small and inconsistent. Nonetheless, it does not take long after newborns are labeled as girls or boys for gender stereotypes to affect how they are perceived and treated—and for infants to notice that males and females are different.

Differential Treatment

When the baby is still in the hospital delivery room or nursery, parents tend to use masculine terms when talking to or about their infant son (such as "big guy" or "tiger") and to comment on the strength of his cries, kicks, and grasps. Girl infants are more likely to be labeled "sugar" or "sweetie" and to be described as soft, cuddly, and adorable (Maccoby, 1980). Even when objective examinations reveal no such differences between boys and girls at birth, adults perceive boys as strong, large featured, and coordinated and view girls as weaker, finer featured, and more awkward (Rubin, Provenzano, & Luria, 1974; see also Karraker, Vogel, & Lake, 1995). Soon boys and girls are decked out in either blue or pink and provided with "sex-appropriate" hairstyles, toys, and room furnishings (Pomerleau et al., 1990).

In an early study of the effects of gender stereotyping, college students watched a videotape of a 9-month-old infant who was introduced as either "Dana," a girl, or as "David," a boy (Condry & Condry, 1976). Students who saw "David" interpreted his strong reaction to a jack-in-the-box as anger, whereas students who watched "Dana" concluded that the same behavior was fear. A similar study found that college students rated babies introduced as males as stronger and more "masculine" than babies introduced as females (Burnham & Harris, 1992). Although stereotyping of boys and girls from birth could be partly the effect of differences between the sexes (Benenson, Philippoussis, & Leeb, 1999), it may also be a cause of such differences.

Early Learning

Yet infants are not merely the passive targets of other people's reactions to them; they are actively trying to get to know the social world around them and to get to know themselves. In a study that measured visual tracking of objects by 3- to 8-month old infants, males spent more time looking at a truck whereas females spent more time looking at a doll (Alexander, Wilcox, & Woods, 2009). This suggests a rudimentary recognition of gender stereotypic information. At around 3-4 months of age, infants can distinguish between male and female faces (Quinn et al., 2002). By the end of the first year, babies look longer at a male (or female) face when they hear a male (or female) voice than when they hear a voice that does not match the gender of the face, demonstrating cross-modal association of gender-related information (Fagot & Leinbach, 1993; Poulin-Dubois & Serbin, 2006). By 24 months, they look longer at males and females performing gender-inconsistent activities (such as a man putting on makeup) than those performing activities consistent with gender stereotypes (such as a man mowing the grass; Hill & Flom, 2007). Their response shows that they recognize something incongruent or odd about males and females engaged in activities inconsistent with gender stereotypes.

Which of these siblings, the brother or the sister, is likely to feel greater pressure to conform to gender stereotypes and play with toys that are thought to be gender-congruent? Why?

24-month-old toddlers are not interested in playing with toys regarded as appropriate for the opposite sex—even when there are no other toys to play with (Caldera, Huston, & O'Brien, 1989). As they approach age 2, then, infants are already beginning to behave in ways considered gender appropriate in our society.

Checking Mastery

1. What is gender identity, and what evidence shows understanding of this concept during infancy?

Making Connections

1. Think of someone who recently became a new parent. In what ways has this person's thinking, and the thinking of his or her surrounding social network, already been shaped by knowing the biological sex of the baby? What is the baby's world like—can you tell by looking at its room or clothes whether it is a boy or girl?

12.3 The Child

Much of the action in gender-role development takes place during the toddler and preschool years. Having already come to understand their basic gender identity, young children rapidly acquire gender stereotypes, or ideas about what males and females are supposedly like, and gender-typed behavioral patterns, or tendencies to favor "gender-appropriate" activities and behaviors over those typically associated with the other sex. Through the process of **gender typing**, children not only become aware that they are biological males or females but also acquire the motives, values, and patterns of behavior that their culture considers appropriate for members of their biological sex. Through the gender-typing process, for example, Susie may learn a gender-role norm stating that women should strive to be good mothers and gender-role stereotypes indicating that women are more skilled at nurturing children than men are. As an adult, Susan may then adopt the traditional communal role by switching from full-time to part-time work when her first child is born and devoting herself to the task of mothering.

It would be a mistake, then, to attribute any differences that we observe between girls and boys (or women and men) solely to biological causes. They could just as easily be caused by differences in the ways males and females are perceived and raised.

Acquiring Gender Stereotypes

Remarkably, young children begin to learn society's gender stereotypes around the time they become aware of their basic gender identities. Judith Blakemore (2003) showed pictures of toys to 3- to 11-year-olds and asked them whether boys or girls would usually play with each toy. Toys included masculine-stereotyped ones (for example, GI Joe dolls) and feminine-stereotyped ones (for example, Barbie dolls). Even the youngest children (3 years) knew that

As they begin to categorize other people as males and females, they also figure out which of these two significant social categories they belong to. By 18 months, most toddlers seem to have an emerging understanding that they are either like other males or like other females, even if they cannot verbalize it (Lewis & Weinraub, 1979). Girls as young as 24 months understand which activities are associated with males and which ones are more typical of females (Poulin-Dubois et al., 2002; see also Serbin, Poulin-Dubois, & Eichstedt, 2002). Boys, however, do not show the same understanding until at least 6 months later. Almost all children give verbal proof that they have acquired a basic sense of **gender identity**, or an awareness that they are either a boy or a girl, by age 2½ to age 3 (Levy, 1999; Warin, 2000).

As they acquire their gender identities, boys and girls also begin to behave differently. By the end of their second year, boys usually prefer trucks and cars to other playthings, whereas girls of this age would rather play with dolls and soft toys (Smith & Daglish, 1977; Wood, Desmarais, & Gugula, 2002). Many 18- to girls, but not boys, play with Barbie dolls and vice versa for GI Joes. They also recognized that boys and girls differ in clothes and hairstyles. By age 5, boys hold more gender-stereotypical toy preferences than girls (Cherney, Harper, & Winter, 2006).

Over the next several years, children acquire considerably more "knowledge" about the toys and activities considered appropriate for girls or boys (Blakemore, 2003; Serbin, Powlishta, & Gulko, 1993). For instance, Gary Levy and his associates (2000) asked 4- and 6-year-olds whether men or women would be better in two masculine-stereotyped occupations (car mechanic and airplane pilot) and two feminine-stereotyped occupations (clothes designer and secretary). Children believed that men would be more competent than women as mechanics and pilots, whereas women would make better designers and secretaries. Boys and girls also expressed positive emotions at the thought of growing up and holding gender-stereotypic occupations. They reacted negatively, however, when asked to consider holding gender-counterstereotypic occupations.

How seriously do children take the gender-role norms and stereotypes that they are rapidly learning? It depends on how old they are. Robin Banerjee and Vicki Lintern (2000) tested the rigidity of 4- to 9-year-olds' gender-stereotypic beliefs with four brief stories in which characters had either gender-stereotypic interests (for example, a boy named Tom who was best friends with another boy and liked playing with airplanes) or gender-counterstereotypic interests (for example, a boy named John who was best friends with a girl and liked playing with doll carriages). Children were then asked whether the target child would like to play with dolls, play football, skip, or play with toy guns. Younger children (4- and 6-year-olds) were considerably more rigid in their beliefs than older children; they did not believe that boys would want to play with dolls or skip (stereotypic girl activities)

or that girls would want to play with footballs or toy guns (stereotypic boy activities). Some children seem particularly offended when peers step outside of traditional gender-stereotypic behaviors and will act as "enforcers" of gender-stereotyped behaviors, telling boys, "You shouldn't be playing with that doll" or telling girls, "That game is for boys" (see Martin & Ruble, 2010). Consistent with earlier research (Damon, 1977), rigidity about gender stereotypes is especially high during the preschool years (around ages 4–7), but then decreases over the elementary school years (Ruble et al., 2007). Similar findings emerged from a longitudinal study of gender stereotypes. Hanns Trautner and his colleagues (2005) followed the same group of children from age 5 through age 10 to see if children who held rigid beliefs about gender stereotypes at age 5 remained unshakable in these beliefs over the next 5 years. As ■ **Figure 12.2** shows, peak levels of rigidity occurred between ages 5 and 7, followed by significant relaxation of beliefs from age 7 to age 10.

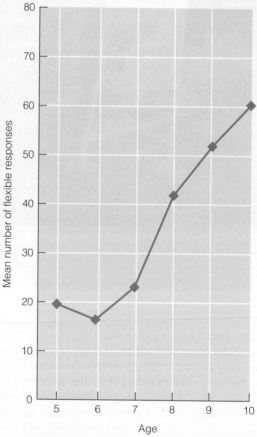

■ **FIGURE 12.2** Once gender identities are clearly established, usually by age 7, children become much more open about gender behaviors, as illustrated by the sharp increase in number of flexible responses after the age of 7. Source: From Trautner, H. M., et al., Rigidity and flexibility of gender stereotypes in childhood: Developmental or differential? *Infant and Child Development, 14*, p. 370. Copyright © 2005. Reprinted with permission of John Wiley & Sons, Inc.

What percent of boys versus girls are likely to receive boxing gloves to play with? Chances are good that most of these purchases are made for boys and not girls. What traits are likely to be encouraged by such play and what message is conveyed to children by such gendered gifts?

© Michael Greenberg/Corbis

Why? The younger children are in the process of acquiring a clear understanding that their biological sex will remain constant, making them intolerant of anyone who violates traditional gender-role standards. These norms now have the force of absolute moral laws and must be obeyed: boys must not play with dolls. Eleanor Maccoby (1998) suggests that young children may exaggerate gender roles to cognitively clarify these roles. However, once their gender identities are more firmly established, children can afford to be more flexible in their thinking about what is "for boys" and what is "for girls." They still know the stereotypes but no longer believe the stereotypes are "written in stone" (Martin, Ruble, & Szkrybalo, 2002). Other research suggests that children's rigidity about gender-role violations depends on how essential a behavior is to children's understanding of gender identity (Blakemore, 2003). Thus, children believe it would be bad for boys to wear dresses because dresses are strongly associated with the feminine gender role. But if boys wanted to play with a toy kitchen, this would not be too bad because, although the toy kitchen may be associated with the feminine gender role, it is not considered an essential aspect of the feminine gender role (Blakemore, 2003).

Gender-Typed Behavior

Finally, children rapidly come to behave in "gender-appropriate" ways. As you have seen, preferences for gender-appropriate toys are detectable in infancy. Apparently, babies establish preferences for "boys' toys" (such as action figures and building toys) or "girls' toys" (such as dolls and stuffed animals) even before they have established clear identities as males or females or can correctly label toys as "boy things" or "girl things" (Cherney & London, 2006; Fagot, Leinbach, & Hagan, 1986). In childhood, preference for gender-congruent toys is still evident, although occasionally both boys and girls choose "boys' toys" more than "girls' toys" (Cherney, 2005; Klinger, Hamilton, & Cantrell, 2001). Their leisure activities also differ, with boys spending more time playing sports and video/computer games than girls (Cherney & London, 2006).

Children begin to favor same-sex playmates as early as 30–36 months of age (see, for example, Howes, 1988; and Martin & Fabes, 2001). During the elementary-school years, boys and girls develop even stronger preferences for peers of their own sex and show increased **gender segregation,** separating themselves into boys' and girls' peer groups and interacting far more often with their own sex than with the other sex (Halim & Ruble, 2010). Gender segregation occurs in a variety of cultures, including Botswana, Kenya, India, and the Philippines, and it increases with age (Bock, 2005; Leaper, 1994; Whiting & Edwards, 1988). At age 4½, children in the United States spend 3 times more time with same-sex peers than with peers of the other sex; by age 6½, they spend 11 times more time (■ Figure 12.3; Maccoby & Jacklin, 1987). This is partly because of incompatibilities between boys' and girls' play styles. Boys are too rowdy, domineering, and unresponsive to suit the tastes of many girls, so girls gravitate toward other girls and develop a style of interacting among themselves different from the rather timid style they

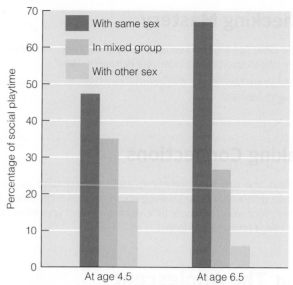

■ **FIGURE 12.3** Do children prefer playmates of their own sex? Apparently so. Both boys and girls spend more time playing with same-sex peers, especially at age 6. SOURCE: Reprinted from *Advances in child development and behavior,* Volume 20, edited by H. Reese. Copyright © 1987 with permission from Elsevier.

adopt in the company of boys (Maccoby, 1998; Pellegrini et al., 2007).

But there is more to gender segregation than different activity levels of boys and girls. Preschool girls who are just as active as boys often start the school year playing with boys but end up in gender-segregated groups as they progress through the year in preschool (Pellegrini et al., 2007). Socialization pressures seem to encourage these active girls to drift away from the boys and create their own playgroup, separate from the active boys and the less-active girls. Preschool boys also seem to experience some pressure to exclude girls from their group; thus, even boys and girls who might be good playmates are discouraged from mingling, at least in the presence of other children.

As it turns out, children who insist most strongly on clear boundaries between the sexes and avoid consorting with the opposite sex tend to be socially competent and popular, whereas children who violate gender segregation rules tend to be less well adjusted and run the risk of being rejected by their peers (Kovacs, Parker, & Hoffman, 1996; Sroufe et al., 1993). Boys face stronger pressures to adhere to gender-role expectations than girls do. This may be why they develop stronger gender-typed preferences at earlier ages (Banerjee & Lintern, 2000; O'Brien et al., 2000). Just ask your female classmates if they were tomboys when they were young; you are likely to find that about half were (Bailey, Bechtold, & Berenbaum, 2002). But we challenge you to find many male classmates who willingly admit they were "sissies" in their youth. The agentic role is clearly defined in our society, and boys are ridiculed and rejected if they do not conform to it (Halim & Ruble, 2010).

Checking Mastery

1. At what age are children likely to be most concerned about adhering to traditional gender role behaviors? Why?

2. What are two factors that contribute to gender segregation during childhood?

Making Connections

1. Boys and girls have sometimes been characterized as living in two different worlds. Thinking about your own childhood, how was your world similar or different from that of your other-sexed siblings (if any) and friends?

12.4 The Adolescent

After going their separate ways in childhood, boys and girls come together in the most intimate ways during adolescence. How do they prepare for the gender roles that will likely characterize their adulthood?

Adhering to Gender Roles

As you have just seen, young elementary-school children are highly rigid in their thinking about gender roles, whereas older children think more flexibly, recognizing that gender norms are not absolute, inviolable laws. Curiously, adolescents again seem to become highly intolerant of certain role violations and to become stereotyped in their thinking about the proper roles of males and females in adolescence. They are more likely than somewhat younger children to make negative judgments about peers who violate expectations by engaging in cross-sex behavior or expressing cross-sex interests (Alfieri, Ruble, & Higgins, 1996; Sigelman, Carr, & Begley, 1986).

Consider what Trish Stoddart and Elliot Turiel (1985) found when they asked children ages 5 to 13 questions about boys who wear a barrette in their hair or put on nail polish and about girls who sport a crew haircut or wear a boy's suit. Both the kindergartners and the adolescents judged these behaviors to be wrong, whereas third-graders and fifth-graders viewed them far more tolerantly. Like the elementary-school children, eighth-graders clearly understood that gender-role expectations are just social conventions that can easily be changed and do not necessarily apply in all societies. However, these adolescents had also begun to conceptualize gender-role violations as a sign of psychological abnormality and could not tolerate them.

Increased intolerance of deviance from gender-role expectations is tied to a larger process of **gender intensification,** in which gender differences may be magnified by hormonal changes associated with puberty and increased pressure to conform to gender roles (Boldizar, 1991; Galambos, Almeida, & Petersen, 1990). According to this process, boys begin to see themselves as more masculine and girls emphasize their feminine side. There is some support for this, at least in terms of

higher levels of "femininity" reported by teen girls than by boys (Priess, Lindberg, & Hyde, 2009). When it comes to "masculinity," though, teen boys and girls report roughly the same levels. When gender intensification does occur, it is largely related to peer influence and the growing importance of dating. Adolescents increasingly find that they must conform to traditional gender norms to appeal to the other sex. A girl who was a tomboy and thought nothing of it may find, as a teenager, that she must dress and behave in more "feminine" ways to attract boys and must give up her tomboyish ways (Burn, O'Neil, & Nederend, 1996; Carr, 2007). A boy may find that he is more popular if he projects a more sharply "masculine" image. Social pressures on adolescents to conform to traditional roles may even help explain why sex differences in cognitive abilities sometimes become more noticeable as children enter adolescence (Hill & Lynch, 1983; Roberts et al., 1990). It should be noted that the social pressure to conform to gender stereotypes does not need to be real—adolescents' *perceptions* of their peers' thoughts and expectations can affect behaviors and lead to gender intensification (Pettitt, 2004). Later in adolescence, teenagers again become more comfortable with their identities as men and women and more flexible in their thinking.

We have now surveyed some major milestones in gender-role development from infancy to adolescence—the development of basic gender identity in toddlerhood, gender segregation in childhood, and a return to rigid thinking about gender as part of gender intensification during adolescence. Now comes the most intriguing question about gender-role development in childhood and adolescence: How can it be explained?

Explaining Gender-Role Development

"Once there was a baby named Chris. . . [who] went to live on a beautiful island . . . [where] there were only boys and men; Chris was the only girl. Chris lived a very happy life on this island, but she never saw another girl or woman" (Taylor, 1996, p. 1559). Do you think Chris developed traditionally masculine or traditionally feminine characteristics? When Marianne Taylor (1996) asked children about Chris's toy preferences, occupational aspirations, and personality traits, she found that 4- to 8-year-olds took the nature side of the nature–nurture controversy: they expected Chris's biological status as a girl to determine her development. The 9- and 10-year-olds in the study emphasized the role of nurture in Chris's development, expecting her to be influenced by the masculinizing environment in which she was raised. Where do you come down in this debate, and why?

Several theories about the development of gender roles have been proposed. Some theories emphasize the role of biological differences between the sexes, whereas others emphasize social influences on children. Some emphasize what society does to children; others focus on what children do to themselves as they try to understand gender and all its implications. In Chapter 2, we learned that Freud believed that gender-role behaviors are shaped early, during the phallic stage, when children harbor a strong, biologically based love for the parent of the other sex; experience internal conflict and anxiety as a result of this incestuous desire; and resolve the conflict through a process of identification with the same-sex parent. Although Freud's views on gender sparked controversy and research, there is little support for this theory of gender-typing. Here, we will examine a biologically oriented theory and then consider the more "social" approaches offered by social learning theory, cognitive developmental theory, and gender schema theory.

Biosocial Theory

The **biosocial theory** of gender-role development proposed by John Money and Anke Ehrhardt (1972) calls attention to the ways in which biological events influence the development of boys and girls. But it also focuses on ways in which early biological developments influence how people react to a child and suggests that these social reactions have much to do with children's assuming gender roles.

Chromosomes, Hormones, and Social Labeling.

Money and Ehrhardt stress that the male (XY) or female (XX) chromosomes most of us receive at conception are merely a starting point in biological differentiation of the sexes. Several critical events affect a person's eventual preference for the masculine or feminine role (see also Breedlove, 1994):

1. If certain genes on the Y chromosome are present, a previously undifferentiated tissue develops into testes as the embryo develops; otherwise, it develops into ovaries.
2. The testes of a male embryo normally secrete more of the male hormone testosterone, which stimulates the development of a male internal reproductive system, and another hormone that inhibits the development of female organs. Without these hormones, the internal reproductive system of a female will develop from the same tissues.
3. Three to four months after conception, secretion of additional testosterone by the testes normally leads to the growth of a penis and scrotum. If testosterone is absent (as in normal females), or if a male fetus's cells are insensitive to the male sex hormones he produces, female external genitalia (labia and clitoris) will form.
4. The relative amount of testosterone alters the development of the brain and nervous system. For example, it signals the male brain to stop secreting hormones in a cyclical pattern so that males do not experience menstrual cycles at puberty.

Thus, fertilized eggs have the potential to acquire the anatomical and physiological features of either sex. Events at each critical step in the sexual differentiation process determine the outcome.

Once a biological male or female is born, social labeling and differential treatment of girls and boys interact with biological factors to steer development. Parents and other people label and begin to react to children on the basis of the appearance of their genitalia. If children's genitals are abnormal and they are mislabeled as members of the other sex, this incorrect label will affect their future development. For example, if a biological male were

Brothers, yet very different personalities, as reflected here in how they are dressed. According to the biosocial theory, what factors influence children's acquisition of gender-typed behaviors?

© Maria Teijeiro/Getty Images

consistently labeled and treated as a girl, he would, by about age 3, acquire the gender identity of a girl. Finally, biological factors reenter the scene at puberty when large quantities of hormones are released, stimulating the growth of the reproductive system and the appearance of secondary sex characteristics. These events, with a person's earlier self-concept as a male or female, provide the basis for adult gender identity and role behavior. The complex series of critical points in biological maturation and social reactions to biological changes that Money and Ehrhardt (1972) propose is diagrammed in ■ **Figure 12.4.** But how much is nature, and how much is nurture?

Evidence of Biological Influences.

Much evidence suggests that biological factors influence the development of males and females in many species of animals (Breedlove, 1994). Evolutionary psychologists notice that most societies socialize males to have agentic traits and females to have communal ones; they conclude that traditional gender roles may be a reflection of species heredity (Archer, 1996; Buss, 1995). In addition, individual differences in agency and communality may be partly genetic. Twin studies suggest that individual heredity accounts for 20% to 50% of the variation in the extent to which people describe themselves as having masculine and feminine psychological traits (Iervolino et al., 2005; Loehlin, 1992). In other words, experience does not explain everything.

Biological influences on development are also evident in studies of children exposed to the "wrong" hormones prenatally (Ehrhardt & Baker, 1974; Money & Ehrhardt, 1972). Before the consequences were known, some mothers who previously

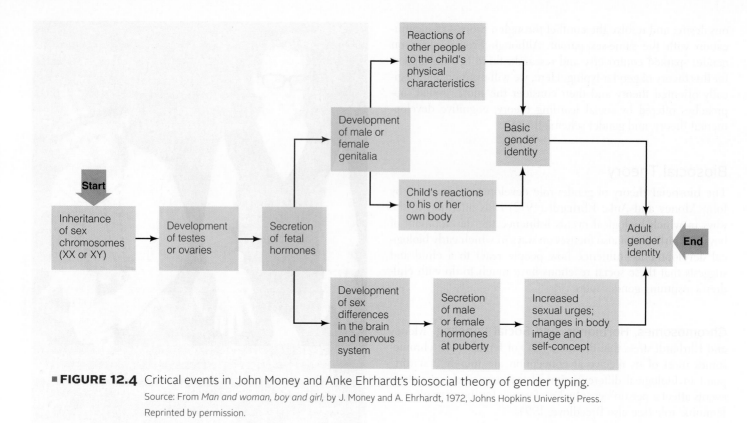

■ FIGURE 12.4 Critical events in John Money and Anke Ehrhardt's biosocial theory of gender typing.

Source: From *Man and woman, boy and girl,* by J. Money and A. Ehrhardt, 1972, Johns Hopkins University Press. Reprinted by permission.

had problems carrying pregnancies to term were given drugs containing progestins, which are converted by the body into the male hormone testosterone. These drugs had the effect of masculinizing female fetuses so that, despite their XX genetic endowment and female internal organs, they were born with external organs that resembled those of a boy (for example, a large clitoris that looked like a penis and fused labia that resembled a scrotum). Several of these **androgenized females** (girls prenatally exposed to excess androgens) were recognized as genetic females, underwent surgery to alter their genitals, and were then raised as girls. When Money and Ehrhardt compared them with their sisters and other girls, it became apparent that many more androgenized girls were tomboys and preferred boys' toys and vigorous activities to traditionally feminine pursuits (see also Meyer-Bahlburg et al., 2006). As adolescents, they began dating somewhat later than other girls and felt that marriage should be delayed until they had established their careers. A high proportion (37%) described themselves as homosexual or bisexual (Money, 1985; see also Dittman, Kappes, & Kappes, 1992). Androgenized females may also perform better than most other females on tests of spatial ability, further evidence that early exposure to male hormones has "masculinizing" effects on a female fetus (Kimura, 1992; Resnick et al., 1986; but see Malouf et al., 2006).

In addition, male exposure to testosterone and other male hormones may be part of the reason males are more likely than females to commit violent acts (Rubinow & Schmidt, 1996). Evidence from experiments conducted with animals is quite convincing. For example, female rhesus monkeys exposed pre-natally to the male hormone testosterone often threaten other monkeys, engage in rough-and-tumble play, and try to "mount" a partner as males do at the beginning of a sexual encounter (Young, Goy, & Phoenix, 1964; Wallen, 1996). Men with high testosterone levels tend to have high rates of delinquency, drug abuse, abusiveness, and violence, although nature interacts with nurture so that these links between testosterone and antisocial behavior are not nearly as evident among men high in socioeconomic status as among men low in socioeconomic status (Dabbs & Morris, 1990). Note, however, that these are correlational studies showing an association between testosterone and aggression, but they do not show us the direction of the relationship.

Biologist Robert Sapolsky (1998) has argued that being in an aggressive situation may raise testosterone levels. Because testosterone levels rise as a result of aggressive and competitive activities, it has been difficult to establish unambiguously that high concentrations of male hormones cause aggressive behavior in humans (Archer, 1991). Still, animal experiments show that early experiences can alter the developing nervous systems of males and females and, in turn, their behavior (Breedlove, 1994). Much evidence suggests that prenatal exposure to male or female hormones has lasting effects on the organization of the brain and, in turn, on sexual behavior, aggression, cognitive abilities, and other aspects of development (Rubinow & Schmidt, 1996). Yet biology does not dictate gender-role development. Instead, gender-role development evolves from the complex interaction of biology, social experience, and the individual's behavior.

Evidence of Social-Labeling Influences. We must also take seriously the social aspect of Money and Ehrhardt's biosocial theory. How a child is labeled and treated can considerably affect gender development. For instance, some androgenized females were labeled as boys at birth and raised as such until their abnormalities were detected. Money and Ehrhardt (1972) report that the discovery and correction of this condition (by surgery and relabeling as a girl) caused few adjustment problems if the sex change took place before 18 months. After age 3, sexual reassignment was exceedingly difficult because these genetic females had experienced prolonged masculine gender typing and had already labeled themselves as boys. These findings led Money and Ehrhardt to conclude that there is a critical period between 18 months and 3 years for the establishment of gender identity when the label society attaches to the child is likely to stick. Yet some studies in which infants are presented to some people as boys but to others as girls indicate that labeling has little effect on how people perceive and treat these infants (Stern & Karraker, 1989). And, as Exploration Box 12.1 on social labeling and biological destiny shows, biological males who are labeled as girls during the so-called critical period sometimes adopt a male gender identity later in life despite their early labeling and socialization, suggesting that we should refer to a sensitive rather than a critical period. Once again, then, we see both nature and nurture at work in development.

Social Learning Theory

According to social learning theorists, children learn masculine or feminine identities, preferences, and behaviors through two processes. First, through *differential reinforcement*, children are rewarded for sex-appropriate behaviors and are punished for behaviors considered more appropriate for members of the other sex. Second, through *observational learning*, children adopt the attitudes and behaviors of same-sex models. In this view, children's gender-role development depends on which of their behaviors people reinforce or punish and on what sorts of social models are available. Change the social environment and you change the course of gender-role development.

Differential Reinforcement. Parents use differential reinforcement to teach boys how to be boys and girls how to be girls (Lytton & Romney, 1991). By the second year of life, parents are already encouraging sex-appropriate play and discouraging cross-sex play, before children have acquired their basic gender identities or display clear preferences for male or female activities (Fagot & Leinbach, 1989). By 20–24 months, daughters are reinforced for dancing, dressing up (as women), following their parents around, asking for help, and playing with dolls; they are discouraged from manipulating objects, running, jumping, and climbing. By contrast, sons are not encouraged to pursue such "feminine" behavior as playing with dolls and seeking help and they receive more positive responses from their parents when they play with "masculine" toys such as blocks, trucks, and push-and-pull toys (Blakemore, 2003; Fagot, 1978; Fagot, Leinbach, & O'Boyle, 1992). Mothers and fathers may also discipline their

sons and daughters differently, with fathers more likely to use physical forms of discipline (such as spanking) than mothers and mothers more likely to use reasoning to explain rules and consequences (Conrade & Ho, 2001; Russell et al., 1998). In addition, boys end up on the receiving end of a spanking more often than girls do (Day & Peterson, 1998).

In research by Barbara Morrongiello and Kerri Hogg (2004), mothers were asked to imagine how they would react if their 6- to 10-year-old son or daughter misbehaved in some way that might be dangerous (for example, bicycling fast down a hill they had been told to avoid). Mothers reported that they would be angry with their sons but disappointed and concerned with their daughters for misbehaving and putting themselves in harm's way. Boys will be boys, they reasoned, but girls should know better. To prevent future risky behaviors, mothers said they would be more rule-bound with their daughters but would not do anything different with their sons. After all, they reasoned, there is no point in trying to prevent these risky behaviors in boys because it is "in their nature." Girls' behavior, on the other hand, can be influenced, so mothers may believe that it is worth enforcing an existing rule or instituting a new one. It's not just mothers: other research shows that fathers are more protective of their preschool-aged daughters than their preschool-aged sons (Hagan & Kuebli, 2007).

Does this "gender curriculum" in the home influence children? It certainly does. Parents who show the clearest patterns of differential reinforcement have children who are relatively quick to label themselves as girls or boys and to develop strongly sex-typed toy and activity preferences (Fagot & Leinbach, 1989; Fagot, Leinbach, & O'Boyle, 1992). Fathers play a central role in gender socialization; they are more likely than mothers to reward children's gender-appropriate behavior and to discourage behavior considered more appropriate for the other sex (Leve & Fagot, 1997; Lytton & Romney, 1991). Women who choose nontraditional professions are more likely than women in traditionally female fields to have had fathers who encouraged them to be assertive and competitive (Coats & Overman, 1992). Fathers, then, seem to be an especially important influence on the gender-role development of both sons and daughters.

Could differential treatment of boys and girls by parents also contribute to gender differences in ability? Possibly so. Jacquelynne Eccles and her colleagues (1990) have conducted several studies to determine why girls tend to shy away from math and science courses and are underrepresented in occupations that involve math and science (see also Benbow & Arjmand, 1990). They suggest that parental expectations about gender differences in mathematical ability become self-fulfilling prophecies. The plot goes something like this:

1. Parents, influenced by societal stereotypes about gender differences in ability, expect their sons to outperform their daughters in math and expect their sons will be more interested in math and science than their daughters (Tenenbaum & Leaper, 2003).

2. Parents attribute their sons' successes in math to ability but credit their daughters' successes to hard work. Perhaps as a result of this, fathers talk differently to their sons and

Is the Social Label Everything, or Is Biology Destiny?

When biological sex and social labeling conflict, which wins out? Consider the tragic case of a male identical twin, named Bruce at birth, whose penis was damaged beyond repair during a botched circumcision (Money & Tucker, 1975). On the advice of John Money, who at the time was considered the world's leading authority on gender identity, the parents agreed to a surgical procedure that removed what was left of the damaged penis and altered their 21-month-old boy's external genitals to appear feminine. From then on, they treated him like a girl. By age 5, Money reported that this boy-turned-girl, now named Brenda, was different from her genetically identical brother. According to Money and the team in charge of her treatment, Brenda clearly knew she was a girl; had developed strong preferences for feminine toys, activities, and apparel; and was far neater and daintier than her brother. This, then, was supposedly a vivid demonstration that the most decisive influence on gender-role development is how a child is labeled and treated during the critical period for such development. But there is much more to the story.

Milton Diamond and H. Keith Sigmundson (1997) followed up on this twin and found that the story had a very different and ultimately disastrous ending from what Money reported (see also Colapinto, 1997, 2000, 2004). Brenda was never comfortable with doll play and other traditionally feminine pursuits; she preferred to dress up in men's clothing, play with her twin brother's toys, and take things apart to see how they worked. She used the jumping rope she was given to whip people and tie them up; she was miserable when she was forced to make daisy chains and become a Girl Scout rather than a Boy Scout (Colapinto, 1997). Somewhere around age 10, she had the distinct feeling that she was not a girl: "I began to see how different I felt and was. . . . I thought I was a freak or something. . . but I didn't want to admit it. I figured I didn't want to wind up opening a can of worms" (Colapinto, 2000, pp. 299–300). Being rejected by other children because of her masculine looks and feminine dress and being called "cavewoman" and "gorilla" also

took their toll, as did continued pressure from psychiatrists to behave in a more feminine manner. Finally, at age 14 and after years of inner turmoil and suicidal thinking, Brenda had had it and simply refused to take the female hormones prescribed for her and pretend to be a girl any longer. When finally told that she was a chromosomal male and had started life as a normal baby boy, Brenda was relieved: "Suddenly it all made sense why I felt the way I did. I *wasn't* some sort of weirdo" (Colapinto, 1997, p. 92). She then received male hormone shots, a double mastectomy, and surgery to construct a penis and emerged as a nice young man who eventually dated girls, married at age 25, and for a time, seemed to settle into his hard-won identity as an adult male named David.

When he realized that his case was being used to justify sex change operations on other infants with injured or ambiguous genitals, he went public with his story and spoke out against this practice. David and his family struggled for years with the aftermath of the attempt to change his sex. His twin brother died of a drug overdose at age 36, and 2 years later David committed suicide.

This disturbing case study shows that we must back off from the conclusion that social learning is all that matters. Clearly, for Bruce/Brenda/David, gender identity was not as pliable as Money believed. And this is not the only case that illustrates that biology, along with social environment, matters when it comes to gender identity. Researchers studied a group of 18 biological males in the Dominican Republic who had a genetic condition that made their cells insensitive to the effects of male hormones (Imperato-McGinley et al., 1979; see also Herdt & Davidson, 1988). They had begun life with ambiguous genitals, were mistaken for girls, and so were labeled and raised as girls. However, under the influence of male hormones produced at puberty, they sprouted beards and became entirely masculine in appearance. How, in light of Money and Ehrhardt's critical-period hypothesis, could a person possibly adjust to becoming a man after leading an entire childhood as a girl?

© Reuters/Corbis

Amazingly, 16 of these 18 individuals seemed able to accept their late conversion from female to male and to adopt masculine lifestyles, including the establishment of heterosexual relationships. One retained a female identity and gender role, and the remaining individual switched to a male gender identity but still dressed as a female. This study also casts doubt on the notion that socialization during the first 3 years is critical to later gender-role development. Instead, it suggests that hormonal influences may be more important than social influences. It is possible, however, that Dominican adults, knowing that this genetic disorder was common in their society, treated these girls-turned-boys differently from other girls when they were young or that these youngsters recognized on their own that their genitals were not normal (Ehrhardt, 1985). As a result, these "girls" may never have fully committed themselves to being girls.

What studies such as these of individuals with genital abnormalities appear to teach us is this: We are predisposed by our biology to develop as males or females; the first 3 years of life are a sensitive period perhaps, but not a critical period, for gender-role development; and both biology and social labeling contribute to gender-role development.

daughters when discussing science with them (Tenenbaum & Leaper, 2003). With their sons, they use more scientific terms, provide more detailed explanations, and ask more abstract questions than with their daughters. These differences reinforce the belief that girls lack mathematical talent and turn in respectable performances only through plodding effort.

3. Children begin to internalize their parents' views, so girls come to believe that they are "no good" in math. Girls report that they are less competent and more anxious about their performance than boys (Pomerantz, Altermatt, & Saxon, 2002).

4. Thinking they lack ability, girls become less interested in math, are less likely to take math courses, and are less likely to pursue career possibilities that involve math after high school.

In short, parents who expect their daughters to have trouble with numbers may get what they expect. The negative effects of low parental expectancies on girls' self-perceptions are evident regardless of their performance. Indeed, girls feel less competent than do boys about math and science even when they outperform the boys (Pomerantz, Altermatt, & Saxon, 2002). Girls whose parents are nontraditional in their gender-role attitudes and behaviors do not show the declines in math and science achievement in early adolescence that girls from more traditional families display, so apparently the chain of events Eccles describes can be broken (Updegraff, McHale, & Crouter, 1996).

Peers, like parents, reinforce boys and girls differentially. As Beverly Fagot (1985) discovered, boys only 21–25 months of age belittle and disrupt each other for playing with "feminine" toys or with girls, and girls express their disapproval of other girls who choose to play with boys (see also Blakemore, 2003). Similarly, on the playground, preschoolers who engage in same-sex play are better liked by their peers than those who engage in play with the opposite sex (Colwell & Lindsey, 2005).

Observational Learning. Social learning theorists call attention to differential treatment of girls and boys by parents, peers, and teachers; they also emphasize that observational learning contributes in important ways to gender typing. Children see which toys and activities are "for girls" and which are "for boys" and imitate individuals of their own sex. Around age 6 or 7, children begin to pay much closer attention to same-sex models than to other-sex models; for example, they will choose toys that members of their own sex prefer even if it means passing up more attractive toys (Frey & Ruble, 1992). Children who see their mothers perform agentic tasks and their fathers perform household and child care tasks tend to be less aware of gender stereotypes and less gender typed than children exposed to traditional gender-role models at home (Sabattini & Leaper, 2004; Turner & Gervai, 1995). Similarly, boys with sisters and girls with brothers have less gender-typed activity preferences than children who grow up with same-sex siblings (Colley et al., 1996; Rust et al., 2000).

Not only do children learn by watching the children and adults with whom they interact, but they also learn from the media—radio, television, movies, video games—and even from their picture books and elementary-school texts. Although sexism in children's books has decreased over the past 50 years, male characters are still more likely than female characters to engage in active, independent activities such as climbing, riding bikes, and making things, whereas female characters are more often depicted as passive, dependent, and helpless, spending their time picking flowers, playing quietly indoors, and "creating problems that require masculine solutions" (Diekman & Murnen, 2004; Kortenhaus & Demarest, 1993). In an analysis of 200 popular children's picture books, David Anderson and Mykol Hamilton (2007) found that portrayals of fathers, but not mothers, were largely absent. In the few instances where fathers were portrayed, they were not engaged with their children, which conveys the message that it is still mothers who are the primary caretakers of children.

In recent decades, blatant gender stereotyping of television characters has decreased but not disappeared. Male characters still dominate on many children's programs, prime-time programs, and advertisements (Ganahl, Prinsen, & Netzley, 2003; Glascock, 2001; Oppliger, 2007). Even on shows with an equal number of male and female characters, the male characters assume more prominent roles (Ogletree et al., 2004). Typically, men are influential individuals who work at a profession, whereas many women—especially those portrayed as married—are passive, emotional creatures who manage a home or work at "feminine" occupations such as nursing (Signorielli & Kahlenberg, 2001). Women portrayed as single are often cast in traditionally male occupations. The message children receive is that men work regardless of their marital status and they do important business, but women only work at important jobs if they are single (Signorielli & Kahlenberg, 2001). Children who watch a large amount of television are more likely to choose gender-appropriate toys and to hold stereotyped views of males and females than their classmates who watch little television (Oppliger, 2007; Signorielli & Lears, 1992).

Perhaps the strongest traditional gender stereotypes are found in today's video games, which males play at a much higher rate than females (Ogletree & Drake, 2007). College students, both male and female, report that female video game characters are portrayed as helpless and sexually provocative, in contrast to male characters who are portrayed as strong and aggressive (Ogletree & Drake, 2007). Men do not find these stereotypes as offensive as do women, perhaps because men already hold more traditional gender stereotypes than women (Brenick et al., 2007).

To recap, there is much evidence that both differential reinforcement and observational learning contribute to gender-role development. However, social learning theorists often portray children as the passive recipients of external influences: parents, peers, television and video game characters, and others show them what to do and reinforce them for doing it. Perhaps this perspective does not put enough emphasis on what children contribute to their own gender socialization. Youngsters do not receive gender-stereotyped birthday presents simply because their parents choose these toys for them. Instead, parents tend to select gender-neutral and often educational toys for their children, but their boys ask for trucks and their girls request tea sets

(Alexander, 2003; Robinson & Morris, 1986; Servin, Bohlin, & Berlin, 1999).

Cognitive Theories

Some theorists have emphasized cognitive aspects of gender-role development, noting that as children acquire understanding of gender, they actively teach themselves to be girls or boys. Lawrence Kohlberg based his cognitive theory on Jean Piaget's cognitive developmental theory, whereas Carol Martin and Charles Halverson, Jr., based their theory on an information-processing approach to cognitive development.

Cognitive Developmental Theory. Kohlberg (1966a) proposed a cognitive theory of gender typing that is different from the other theories you have considered and that helps explain why boys and girls adopt traditional gender roles even when their parents do not want them to do so. Among Kohlberg's major themes are the following:

- Gender-role development depends on stagelike changes in cognitive development; children must acquire certain understandings about gender before they will be influenced by their social experiences.
- Children engage in self-socialization; instead of being the passive targets of social influence, they actively socialize themselves.

According to both psychoanalytic theory and social learning theory, children are influenced by their companions to adopt male or female roles before they view themselves as girls or boys and identify with (or habitually imitate) same-sex models. Kohlberg suggests that children first understand that they are girls or boys and then actively seek same-sex models and a range of information about how to act like a girl or a boy. To Kohlberg, it is not "I'm treated like a boy; therefore, I must be a boy." It is more like "I'm a boy, so now I'll do everything I can to find out how to behave like one."

What understandings are necessary before children will teach themselves to behave like boys or girls? Kohlberg believes that children everywhere progress through the following three stages as they acquire **gender constancy,** or an understanding of what it means to be a boy or girl, man or woman:

1. Basic gender identity is established by age 2 or 3, when children can recognize and label themselves as males or females (Campbell, Shirley, & Caygill, 2002; Zosuls et al., 2009).
2. Somewhat later, usually by age 4, children acquire **gender stability**—that is, they come to understand that gender identity is stable over time. They know that boys invariably become men and girls grow up to be women.
3. The gender concept is complete, somewhere between age 5 and age 7, when children achieve **gender consistency** and realize that their sex is also stable across situations. Now children know that their sex cannot be altered by superficial changes such as dressing up as a member of the other sex or engaging in cross-sex activities.

Children 3–5 years of age often do lack the concepts of gender stability and gender consistency; they often say that a boy could become a mommy if he really wanted to or that a girl could become a boy if she cut her hair and wore a hockey uniform (Warin, 2000). This changes over the kindergarten and early grade-school years (Ruble et al., 2007). As children enter Piaget's concrete-operational stage of cognitive development and come to grasp concepts such as conservation of liquids, they also realize that gender is conserved—remains constant—despite changes in appearance. Gender constancy is demonstrated by very few 3- to 5-year-olds, about half of 6- to 7-year-olds, and a majority of 8- to 9-year-olds (Trautner, Gervai, & Nemeth, 2003). In support of Kohlberg's theory, Jo Warin (2000) found that children who have achieved the third level of understanding display more gender-stereotypic play preferences than children who have not yet grasped gender consistency.

But not all research supports Kohlberg. In one study, children who had acquired only the first step in the process—using gender labels—began to engage in more gender-typed play, which, according to Kohlberg's model, shouldn't occur until after the third step (Zosuls et al., 2009). Other research similarly shows that children need not reach the concrete operations stage to understand gender stability and consistency if they have sufficient knowledge of male and female anatomy to realize that people's genitals make them male or female (Bem, 1989). Children who have younger siblings often arrive at this understanding earlier than children with only older siblings or those without siblings (Karniol, 2009). The most controversial aspect of Kohlberg's cognitive developmental theory, however, has been his claim that only when children fully grasp that their biological sex is unchangeable, around age 5 to age 7, do they actively seek same-sex models and attempt to acquire values, interests, and behaviors consistent with their cognitive judgments about themselves. Although some evidence supports some aspects of Kohlberg's theory, this chapter shows that children learn many gender-role stereotypes and develop clear preferences for same-sex activities and playmates long before they master the concepts of gender stability and gender consistency and then, according to Kohlberg, attend more selectively to same-sex models (Halim & Ruble, 2010). It seems that only a rudimentary understanding of gender is required before children learn gender stereotypes and preferences.

Gender Schema Theory. Martin and Halverson (1981, 1987) have proposed a somewhat different cognitive theory, an information-processing one that overcomes the key weakness of Kohlberg's theory. Like Kohlberg, they believe that children are intrinsically motivated to acquire values, interests, and behaviors consistent with their cognitive judgments about the self. However, Martin and Halverson argue that self-socialization begins as soon as children acquire a basic gender identity, around age 2 or age 3. According to their schematic-processing model, children acquire **gender schema** (plural: **schemata**)—organized sets of beliefs and expectations about males and females that influence the kinds of information they will attend to and remember.

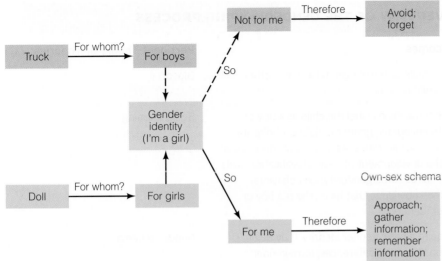

FIGURE 12.5 Gender schema theory in action. A young girl classifies new information according to an in-group–out-group schema as either "for boys" or "for girls." Information about boys' toys and activities is ignored, but information about toys and activities for girls is relevant to the self and is added to an even-larger own-sex schema. SOURCE: Adapted from Martin & Halverson, 1987.

ample, Martin and Halverson (1983) showed 5- and 6-year-olds pictures of children performing gender-consistent activities (for example, a boy playing with a truck) and pictures of children performing gender-inconsistent activities (for example, a girl sawing wood). A week later, the children easily recalled the sex of the actor performing gender-consistent activities; when an actor expressed gender-inconsistent behavior, however, children often distorted the scene to reveal gender-consistent behavior (for example, by saying that it was a boy, not a girl, who had sawed wood). This research gives some insight into why inaccurate gender stereotypes persist. The child who believes that women cannot be doctors may be introduced to a female doctor but may remember meeting a nurse instead and continue to state that women cannot be doctors. Even adults have trouble suppressing gender stereotypes and are influenced by their gender stereotypes when reading and interpreting text (Oakhill, Garnham, & Reynolds, 2005).

First, children acquire a simple in-group–out-group schema that allows them to classify some objects, behaviors, and roles as appropriate for males and others as appropriate for females (cars are for boys, girls can cry but boys should not, and so on). Then they seek more elaborate information about the role of their own sex, constructing an own-sex schema. Thus, a young girl who knows her basic gender identity might first learn that sewing is for girls and building model airplanes is for boys. Then, because she is a girl and wants to act consistently with her own self-concept, she gathers a great deal of information about sewing to add to her own-sex schema, largely ignoring any information that comes her way about how to build model airplanes (**Figure 12.5**).

Consistent with this schema-processing theory, children appear to be especially interested in learning about objects or activities that fit their own-sex schemata. In one study, 4- to 9-year-olds were given boxes of gender-neutral objects (hole punches, burglar alarms, and so on) and were told that some objects were "girl" items and some were "boy" items (Bradbard et al., 1986). Boys explored boy items more than girls did, and girls explored girl items more than boys did. A week later, the children easily recalled which items were for boys and which were for girls; they had apparently sorted the objects according to their in-group–out-group schemata. In addition, boys recalled more in-depth information about boy items than did girls, whereas girls recalled more than boys about these same objects if they had been labeled girl items. If children's information-gathering efforts are guided by their own-sex schemata in this way, you can easily see how boys and girls might acquire different stores of knowledge as they develop.

Once gender schemata are in place, children will distort new information in memory so that it is consistent with their schemata (Liben & Signorella, 1993; Martin & Halverson, 1983). For ex-

An Attempt at Integration

The biosocial, social learning, and cognitive perspectives all contribute to our understanding of sex differences and gender-role development (**Table 12.1**). The biosocial model offered by Money and Ehrhardt notes the importance of biological developments that influence how people label and treat a child. Yet socialization agents are teaching children how to be girls or boys well before they understand that they are girls or boys. Differences in social learning experiences may also help explain why, even though virtually all children form gender concepts and schemata, some children are far more gender typed than others in their preferences and activities (Serbin, Powlishta, & Gulko, 1993).

Kohlberg's cognitive developmental theory and Martin and Halverson's gender schema approach convince us that cognitive growth and self-socialization processes also contribute to gender-role development. Once children acquire a basic gender identity as a boy or a girl and form gender schemata, they become highly motivated to learn their appropriate roles. When they finally grasp, from age 5 to age 7, that their sex will never change, they become even more determined to learn their gender roles and pay special attention to same-sex models. Parents who want to avoid socializing their children into traditional gender roles are often amazed to see their children turn into traditional girls and boys on their own.

In short, children have a male or female biological endowment that helps guide their development, are influenced by other people from birth on to become "real boys" or "real girls," and actively socialize themselves to behave in ways that seem consistent with their understandings that they are either boys or girls. Most developmentalists today would agree that what children learn regarding how to be male or female depends on an

● TABLE 12.1 AN INTEGRATIVE OVERVIEW OF THE GENDER-TYPING PROCESS

Developmental Period	Events and Outcomes	Pertinent Theory or Theories
Prenatal period	The fetus develops male or female genitalia, which others will react to once the child is born.	Biosocial
Birth to 3 years	Parents and other companions label the child as a boy or a girl; they begin to encourage gender-consistent behavior and discourage cross-sex activities. As a result of these social experiences and the development of basic classification skills, the young child acquires some gender-typed behavioral preferences and the knowledge that he or she is a boy or a girl (basic gender identity).	Social learning
3 to 6 years	Once children acquire a basic gender identity, they begin to seek information about sex differences, form gender schemata, and actively try to behave in ways viewed as appropriate for their own sex.	Gender schema
7 to puberty	Children finally acquire the concepts of gender stability and consistency, recognizing that they will be males or females all their lives and in all situations. They begin to look closely at the behavior of same sex models to acquire attributes consistent with their firm self-categorization as male or female.	Cognitive developmental
Puberty and beyond	The biological changes of adolescence, with social pressures, intensify gender differences and stimulate formation of an adult gender identity.	Biosocial Social learning Gender schema Cognitive developmental

interaction between biological factors and social influences. Thus, we must respect the role of genes and hormones in gender-role development but also view this process from a contextual perspective and appreciate that the patterns of male and female development that we observe in society today are not inevitable. In another era, in another culture, the process of gender-role socialization could produce different kinds of boys and girls.

Checking Mastery

1. What are the main components of the biosocial theory of gender?
2. How do cognitive developmental theorists explain gender typing?
3. What are gender schemas, and what role do they play in gender typing?

Making Connections

1. Jen and Ben are fraternal twins whose parents are determined that they should grow up having no gender stereotypic attitudes or behaviors. Nonetheless, when the twins are only 4, Jen wants frilly dresses and loves to play with her Barbie doll, and Ben wants a machine gun and loves to pretend he's a football player and tackle people. Each seems headed for a traditional gender role. Which of the theories in this chapter do you think explains this best, which has the most difficulty explaining it, and why did you reach these conclusions?

2. Fewer women than men become architects. Drawing on the material in this chapter, explain the extent to which nature and nurture may be responsible for this, citing evidence.

12.5 The Adult

You might think that once children and adolescents have learned their gender roles, they simply play them out during adulthood. Instead, as people face the challenges of adult life and enter new social contexts, their gender roles and their concepts of themselves as men and women change.

Changes in Gender Roles

Although males and females fill their agentic or communal roles throughout their lives, the specific content of those roles changes considerably over the life span. The young boy may act out his agentic role by playing with trucks or wrestling with his buddies;

the grown man may play his role by holding down a job. Moreover, the degree of difference between male and female roles also changes. Children and adolescents adopt behaviors consistent with their "boy" or "girl" roles, but the two sexes otherwise adopt similar roles in society—namely, those of children and students. Even as they enter adulthood, males' and females' roles differ little because members of both sexes are often single and in school or working.

However, the roles of men and women become more distinct when they marry and especially when they have children. In most couples, for example, the wife typically does more housework than her husband, whether or not she is employed—about 17–18 hours per week for her compared with 10 hours for him (Bianchi et al., 2000). If this does not seem like a large discrepancy on a weekly basis, consider that over 1 year, wives contribute more than 400 hours to housework beyond the amount their husbands contribute. By their silver wedding anniversary, wives will have logged about 10,000 more hours than husbands have! Furthermore, specific tasks tend to be parceled out along traditional lines—she does the cooking, he takes out the garbage (Bianchi et al., 2000). The birth of a child tends to make even egalitarian couples divide their labors in more traditional ways than they did before the birth and migrate toward more traditional gender-role attitudes (Katz-Wise, Priess, & Hyde, 2010). She becomes primarily responsible for child care and household tasks; he tends to emphasize his role as breadwinner and center his energies on providing for the family. Even as men increase their participation in child care and housework, they tend to play a helper role and spend only two-thirds as much time with their children as women do (Bianchi, 2000).

What happens after the children are grown? The roles played by men and women often become more similar again starting in middle age, when the nest empties and child care responsibilities end. The similarity between gender roles continues to increase as adults enter old age; as retirees and grandparents, men and women lead similar lives. It would seem, then, that the roles of men and women are fairly similar before marriage, maximally different during the child-rearing years, and similar again later (Gutmann, 1997).

Androgyny?

Do the shifts in the roles played by men and women during adulthood affect them psychologically? For years, psychologists assumed that "being masculine" or having agentic traits and "being feminine" or having communal traits were at opposite ends of a single continuum and mutually exclusive. If a person possessed agentic traits, then that person must be non-communal, whereas being highly communal implied being non-agentic. This bipolar view was challenged with evidence that at least some individuals can be characterized by psychological **androgyny**—that is, by a balancing or blending of both agentic traits and communal traits (Spence, Helmreich, & Stapp, 1973). According to this perspective, then, agency and communion are two separate dimensions of

personality. A male or female who has many agentic traits and few communal ones is considered to have a stereotypic "masculine" gender type. A person who has many communal traits and few agentic traits is said to have a "feminine" gender type. The androgynous person possesses both agentic and communal traits, whereas the undifferentiated individual lacks both kinds of attributes.

Early research conducted in the 1970s indicated that about one-third of adults were androgynous and another third were traditionally gender-typed (Spence & Helmreich, 1978). Research conducted 20 years later revealed some shift in self-perceptions of agency, with men rating themselves higher than women on just 9 of 22 agentic traits (Spence & Buckner, 2000). In contrast, there has been no shift in self-perceptions of communal traits, with women rating themselves higher on 15 of 16 communal traits. Although men and women evaluate themselves much more similarly on agentic traits than in the past, they continue to hold traditional stereotypes of others (Spence & Buckner, 2000). For example, when asked to rate themselves on "acts as a leader," responses from men and women were nearly identical. But when asked whether "acts as a leader" characterizes women more than men or vice versa, both men and women agreed that it described men more than women.

If a person can be both assertive and sensitive, both independent and understanding, being androgynous sounds psychologically healthy. Is it? Most college students—both males and females—believe that the ideal person is androgynous (Slavkin & Stright, 2000). Bem (1975, 1978) demonstrated that androgynous men and women behave more flexibly than more gender-typed individuals. For example, androgynous people, like those with high levels of agentic traits, can display the "masculine" agentic trait of independence by resisting social pressure to conform to undesirable group activities. Yet they are as likely as individuals with communal traits to display nurturance by interacting positively with a baby. Androgynous people seem to be highly adaptable, able to adjust their behavior to the demands of the situation at hand (Shaffer, Pegalis, & Cornell, 1992). Perhaps this is why androgynous parents are viewed as warmer and more supportive than nonandrogynous parents (Witt, 1997). In addition, androgynous individuals appear to enjoy higher self-esteem and are perceived as better adjusted than their traditionally gender-typed peers, although this may be largely because of the agentic qualities they possess (Lefkowitz & Zeldow, 2006; Spence & Hall, 1996).

Before you jump to the conclusion that androgyny is a thoroughly desirable attribute, can you imagine any disadvantages of androgyny? During childhood, expressing too many of the traits considered more appropriate in the other biological sex can result in rejection by peers and low self-esteem (Lobel, Slone, & Winch, 1997). Among college students, being well-adjusted psychologically is associated with gender-congruent personality traits (that is, males displaying agentic traits and females expressing communal traits), agentic traits in general, and having flexible attitudes about gender (Didonato & Berenbaum, 2010). In addition, you may need to distinguish between the androgynous individual who possesses *positive* agentic and communal traits and the one who possesses *negative* agentic and communal traits (Woodhill & Samuels, 2003, 2004). People with positive androgyny score higher on measures of mental health and well-being than those with negative androgyny (Woodhill & Samuels, 2003). It may be premature, then, to conclude that it is better in all respects to be androgynous rather than either agentic or communal in orientation. Still, you can at least conclude that it is unlikely to be damaging for men to become a little more communal or for women to become a little more agentic than they have traditionally been. Now let's consider whether there are any systematic changes in gender-related traits throughout adulthood.

Changes with Age

David Gutmann (1987, 1997) has offered the intriguing hypothesis that gender roles and gender-related traits in adulthood are shaped by what he calls the **parental imperative**—the requirement that mothers and fathers adopt different roles to raise children successfully. Drawing on his own cross-cultural research and that of others, he suggests that in many cultures, young and middle-aged men must emphasize their "masculine" qualities to feed and protect their families, whereas young and middle-aged women must express their "feminine" qualities to nurture the young and meet the emotional needs of their families.

According to Gutmann, this changes dramatically starting in midlife, when men and women are freed from the demands of the parental imperative. Men become less active and more passive, take less interest in community affairs, and focus more on religious contemplation and family relationships. They also become more sensitive and emotionally expressive. Women, meanwhile, are changing in the opposite direction. After being passive, submissive, and nurturing in their younger years, they become more active, domineering, and assertive in later life. In many cultures, they take charge of the household after being the underlings of their mothers-in-law and become stronger forces in their communities. In short, Gutmann's parental imperative hypothesis states that over the course of adulthood, agentic men become communal men and communal women become agentic women—that the psychological traits of the two sexes flip-flop.

A somewhat different hypothesis is that adults experience a midlife **androgyny shift**. Instead of giving up traits they had as young adults, men and women retain their gender-typed qualities but add qualities traditionally associated with the other sex; that is, they become more androgynous. How have these ideas fared?

Shirley Feldman and her associates (Feldman, Biringen, & Nash, 1981) assessed individuals at eight different stages of the family life cycle on the traits that you assessed yourself on in Engagement Box 12.1. Consistent with Gutmann's notion of a parental imperative, taking on the role of parent seemed to lead men to perceive themselves as more agentic in personality and women to perceive themselves as having predominantly com-

What traits might we associate with this woman based on her agentic role in the workplace?

© Rainer Elstermann/Getty Images

munal traits. Among adults beyond their parenting years, especially among grandparents, sex differences in self-perceptions were smaller. Contrary to Gutmann's hypothesis, however, grandfathers did not replace their agentic traits with communal traits, and grandmothers did not become less communal and more agentic. Instead, both sexes appeared to experience an androgyny shift: Grandfathers retained their agentic traits and gained communal attributes; grandmothers retained their communal traits and took on agentic attributes (see also Wink & Helson, 1993). More recent research also suggests increased androgyny among older adults. Compared with younger age groups, men over the age of 70 are most likely to view androgyny positively and adopt androgynous traits (Strough et al., 2007). This finding is particularly interesting because today's older people should, if anything, be more traditionally gender typed than younger adults who have grown up in an era of more flexible

Changing Gender-Role Attitudes and Behavior

Some people believe that the world would be a better place if boys and girls were no longer socialized to adopt traditional masculine or feminine roles, interests, and behaviors. Children of both sexes would then have the freedom to be androgynous; women would no longer suffer from a lack of assertiveness in the world of work, and men would no longer be forced to suppress their emotions. Just how successful are efforts to encourage more flexible gender roles?

In several projects designed to change gender-role behavior, children have been exposed to nonsexist films, encouraged to imitate models of cross-sex behavior, reinforced by teachers for trying cross-sex activities, and provided with nonsexist educational materials (Katz, 1986; Katz & Walsh, 1991). For example, Rebecca Bigler and Lynn Liben (1990) reasoned that if they could alter children's gender stereotypes, they could head off the biased information processing that stereotypes promote. They exposed 6- to 11-year-olds to a series of problem-solving discussions emphasizing that (1) the most important considerations in deciding who could perform well in such traditionally masculine or feminine occupations as construction worker and beautician are the

person's interests and willingness to learn and (2) the person's gender is irrelevant. Compared with children who received no such training, program participants showed a clear decline in occupational stereotyping, especially if they had entered the study with firm ideas about which jobs are for women and which are for men. Moreover, this reduction in stereotyping brought about the predicted decrease in biased information processing: participants were more likely than nonparticipants to remember counterstereotypic information presented to them in stories (for example, recalling that the garbage collector in a story was a woman).

Yet many efforts at change that work in the short run fail to have lasting effects. Children encouraged to interact in mixed-sex groups revert to their preference for same-sex friends as soon as the program ends (Lockheed, 1986; Serbin, Tonick, & Sternglanz, 1977). Why is it so difficult to change children's thinking? Perhaps because children are groomed for their traditional gender roles from birth and are bombarded with traditional gender-role messages every day. A short-term intervention project may have little chance of succeeding in this larger context.

Other research shows that it is often difficult to change the gender schemata we have constructed. Farah Hughes and Catherine Seta (2003) gave fifth-graders descriptions of men and women behaving in ways inconsistent with traditional gender stereotypes. The children were then asked to rate the likelihood that another man or woman would behave in gender-inconsistent ways. Despite being exposed to a model of gender-stereotype inconsistent behavior, children believed that the other man (although not the other woman) would behave in a gender-consistent manner. The authors interpret this in terms of gender schema theory and children's desire to maintain their stereotypic gender schemata by countering an inconsistent piece of information with a highly consistent one. It also illustrates that simply exposing children to models of people who defy gender stereotypes is not going to miraculously lead to changes in the way children think about gender-stereotypic behavior: Men should still behave in masculine ways, women in feminine ways, although, consistent with other research presented in this chapter, Hughes and Seta found that women were given more flexibility than men to express both their feminine and masculine sides.

---

gender norms. To learn whether researchers have had any success in changing gender-role attitudes and behavior, check out the material in Application Box 12.1.

Checking Mastery

1. How do gender roles shift during adulthood?

2. What is androgyny? Is it beneficial to be androgynous?

Making Connections

1. The extent to which males and females differ changes from infancy to old age. When are gender differences in psychological characteristics and roles played in society most evident, and when are they least evident? How would you account for this pattern?

12.6 Sexuality Over the Life Span

A central part of the process of becoming a woman or a man is the process of becoming a sexual being, so it is appropriate that we examine sexual development here. It is a lifelong process that starts in infancy.

Are Infants Sexual Beings?

Sigmund Freud (see Chapter 2) made the seemingly outrageous claim that humans are sexual beings from birth onward. We are born, he said, with a reserve of sexual energy redirected toward different parts of the body as we develop. Freud may have been wrong about some things, but he was right that infants are sexual beings.

Babies are biologically equipped at birth with male or female chromosomes, hormones, and genitals. Moreover, young infants in Freud's oral stage of development appear to derive pleasure from sucking, mouthing, biting, and other oral activi-

Young children tend to be comfortable with their bodies and are curious about how they work and how they compare to other bodies. Most societies, though, impose restrictions on nakedness and discourage children from expressing too much curiosity about the body, which adults interpret as sexual expressions.

ties. But the clincher is this: Both male babies and female babies have been observed to touch and manipulate their genital areas, to experience physical arousal, and to undergo what appear to be orgasms (Hyde & DeLamater, 2011; Leung & Robson, 1993).

What should you make of these infant behaviors? Infants feel body sensations, but they are hardly aware that their behavior is "sexual" (Crooks & Baur, 2011). Infants are sexual beings primarily in the sense that their genitals are sensitive and their nervous systems allow sexual responses. They are also as curious about their bodies as they are about the rest of the world. They enjoy touching all parts of their body, especially those that produce pleasurable sensations, and are likely to continue touching themselves unless reprimands from parents or other grownups discourage this behavior, at least in public (Thigpen, 2009). From these early experiences, children begin to learn what human sexuality is about and how the members of their society regard it.

Childhood Sexuality

Although boys and girls spend much of their time in gender-segregated groups, most are nonetheless preparing for the day they will participate in sexual relationships with the other sex, although some will end up in same sex relationships. They learn a great deal about sexuality and reproduction, continue to be curious about their bodies, and begin to interact with the other sex in ways that will prepare them for dating in adolescence.

Knowledge of Sex and Reproduction

With age, children learn that sexual anatomy is the key differentiator between males and females, and they acquire a more correct and explicit vocabulary for discussing sexual organs (Gordon,

Schroeder, & Abrams, 1990). As Anne Bernstein and Philip Cowan (1975) have shown, children's understandings of where babies come from also change as they develop cognitively. Young children often seem to assume either that babies are just there all along or that they are somehow manufactured, much as toys might be. According to Jane, age 3½, "You find [the baby] at a store that makes it. . . . Well, they get it and then they put it in the tummy and then it goes quickly out" (p. 81). Another preschooler, interpreting what he could of an explanation about reproduction from his mom, created this scenario (author's files):

> The woman has a seed in her tummy that is fertilized by something in the man's penis. (How does this happen?) The fertilizer has to travel down through the man's body into the ground. Then it goes underground to get to the woman's body. It's like in our garden. (Does the fertilizer come out of his penis?) Oh no. Only pee-pee comes out of the penis. It's not big enough for fertilizer.

As these examples illustrate, young children construct their own understandings of reproduction well before they are told the "facts of life." Consistent with Piaget's theory of cognitive development, children construct their understanding of sex by assimilating and accommodating information into their existing cognitive structures. Children as young as age 7 know that sexual intercourse plays a role in the making of babies, but their understanding of just how this works is limited (Cipriani, 2002; Hyde & DeLamater, 2011). By age 12, most children have integrated information about sexual intercourse with information about the biological union of egg and sperm and can provide an accurate description of intercourse and its possible outcomes. Thus, as children mature cognitively and as they gain access to information, they are able to construct ever more accurate understandings of sexuality and reproduction.

Sexual Behavior

According to Freudian theory, preschoolers in the phallic stage of psychosexual development are actively interested in their genitals and seek bodily pleasure through masturbation, but school-age children enter a latency period during which they repress their sexuality and turn their attention instead to schoolwork and friendships with same-sex peers. It turns out that Freud was half right and half wrong.

Freud was correct that preschoolers are highly curious about their bodies, masturbate, and engage in both same-sex and cross-sex sexual play (see Kellogg, 2009). Between ages 2 and 5, interest increases and at least half of all children engage in sexual play (playing doctor or house), and sexual exploration such as looking at and touching genitals—their own, a peer's, or a younger sibling's (Kellogg, 2009; Larsson & Svedin, 2002). Freud was wrong, though, to believe that such activities occur infrequently among school-age children. Elementary school–age children in Freud's latency period may be more discreet about their sexual experimentation than preschoolers, but they have by no means lost their sexual curiosity. Surveys show, for example, that about two-thirds of boys and half of girls have masturbated by age 13 (Janus & Janus, 1993; Larsson & Svedin, 2002) and are beginning to engage in "light" sexual activities (holding hands, kissing) with other young teens (Williams, Connolly, & Cribbie, 2008).

Gilbert Herdt and Martha McClintock (2000) have gathered evidence that age 10 is an important point in sexual development, a time when many boys and girls experience their first sexual attraction (often to a member of the other sex if they later become heterosexual or to a member of their own sex if they later become gay or lesbian). This milestone in development appears to be influenced by the maturation of the adrenal glands (which produce male androgens). It comes well before the maturation of the sex organs during puberty and therefore challenges the view of Freud (and many of the rest of us) that puberty is the critical time in sexual development. As Herdt and McClintock note, our society does little to encourage fourth-graders to have sexual thoughts, especially about members of their own sex, so perhaps a hormonal explanation of early sexual attraction makes more sense than an environmental one (see also Halpern, 2006). The adrenal glands mature around age 6 to age 8 and produce low but increasing amounts of androgens (McClintock & Herdt, 1996).

Yet sexual development is also shaped by the social and cultural contexts in which children develop. For example, research shows that teens are less likely to use condoms if their friends report engaging in sex without condoms (Henry et al., 2007). Conversely, teens are more likely to use condoms if they believe their friends are using condoms. Examining the larger cultural context, Eric Widmer and his colleagues (Widmer, Treas, & Newcomb, 1998) found wide variations in sexual beliefs across the 24 countries that they studied. These prevailing cultural beliefs, whether conservative, permissive, or somewhere in the middle, influence how teens construct their individual sexual identities. Teens growing up in cultures that have more permissive attitudes about sexuality are likely to interpret their own behaviors differently than teens growing up in cultures with largely conservative beliefs. Thus, sexual behavior is not driven simply by the surge in hormones that accompanies puberty; it is mediated by social context and by the personal beliefs that are constructed in response to physical changes and cultural beliefs.

Childhood Sexual Abuse

Every day in this country, children, adolescents, and even infants are sexually abused by the adults closest to them. A typical scenario would be this: A girl age 12 or 13—although it happens to boys, too—is abused repeatedly by her father, stepfather, or another male relative or family friend (Freyd et al., 2005; Putnam, 2003). Estimates of the percentages of girls and boys who are sexually abused vary wildly, perhaps because so many cases go unreported and because definitions vary substantially. The Centers for Disease Control and Prevention (2010) surveyed nearly 10,000 women and 8000 men as part of the Adverse Childhood Experiences (ACE) Study, revealing that 25% of the women and 16% of the men reported having been sexually molested at some time (Centers for Disease Control and Prevention, 2010). Clearly, childhood sexual abuse is a serious and widespread social problem. Unfortunately, only one out of every four abused children tells someone about the abuse within the first 24 hours and one in four remains silent, never telling anyone about their painful experience (Kogan, 2004).

What is the effect of sexual abuse on the survivor? Kathleen Kendall-Tackett, Linda Williams, and David Finkelhor (1993) offer a useful account, based on their review of 45 studies. No single distinctive "syndrome" of psychological problems characterizes abuse survivors. Instead, they may experience any number of problems commonly seen in emotionally disturbed individuals, including anxiety, depression, low self-esteem, aggression, acting out, withdrawal, and school learning problems. Roughly 20% to 30% experience each of these problems, and boys seem to experience the same types and degrees of disturbance as girls do.

Many of these aftereffects boil down to lack of self-worth and difficulty trusting others (Freyd et al., 2005; Putnam, 2003). A college student who had been abused repeatedly by her father and other relatives wrote this about her experience (author's files):

> It was very painful, emotionally, physically, and psychologically. I wanted to die to escape it. I wanted to escape from my body. . . . I developed a "good" self and a "bad" self. This was the only way I could cope with the experiences. . . . I discovered people I trusted caused me harm. . . . It is difficult for me to accept the fact that people can care for me and expect nothing in return. . . . I dislike closeness and despise people touching me.

Two problems seem to be especially linked to being sexually abused. First, about a third of survivors engage in sexualized behavior, acting out sexually by putting objects in their vaginas, masturbating in public, behaving seductively, or if they are older, behaving promiscuously (Kendall-Tackett, Williams, & Finkelhor, 1993). One theory is that this sexualized behavior helps survivors master or control the traumatic events they experienced (Tharinger, 1990). Second, about a third of survivors display the symptoms of **posttraumatic stress disorder.** This clinical disorder, involving nightmares, flashbacks to the traumatizing events, and feelings of helplessness and anxiety in the face of danger, affects some soldiers who have experienced combat and other survivors of extreme trauma (Kendall-Tackett, Williams, & Finkelhor, 1993).

In a few children, sexual abuse may contribute to severe psychological disorders, yet about a third of children seem to experience no psychological symptoms (Kendall-Tackett, Williams, & Finkelhor, 1993; Putnam, 2003). Some of these symptomless children may experience problems in later years. Nevertheless, some children are less severely damaged and more able to cope than others are.

Which children have the most difficulty? The effects of abuse are likely to be most severe when the abuse involved penetration and force and occurred frequently over a long period, when the perpetrator was a close relative such as the father, and when the child's mother did not serve as a reliable source of emotional support (Beitchman et al., 1991; Kendall-Tackett, Williams, & Finkelhor, 1993; Trickett & Putnam, 1993). Children are likely to recover better if they have high-quality relationships with their mother and friends (Adams & Bukowski, 2007; Aspelmeier, Elliott, & Smith, 2007). Psychotherapy aimed at treating the anxiety and depression many survivors experience and teaching them coping and problem-solving skills so that they will not be revictimized can also contribute to the healing process (Cuevas et al., 2010; Finkelhor & Berliner, 1995).

Finally, not all sex abuse offenders fit the stereotype of an adult who is an obvious pervert. Some offenders are themselves juveniles taking advantage of peers or somewhat younger children (Finkelhor, 2009). With appropriate and timely intervention and education, they can learn acceptable behaviors that reduce the likelihood of continued offending. Education can also prepare children to respond to inappropriate advances in ways that derail the possibility of an offense occurring. This three-pronged approach—working with the survivors, the offenders, and all children on prevention of sexual abuse—may be behind a recent decline in reports of childhood abuse (Finkelhor et al., 2010).

Adolescent Sexuality

Although infants and children are sexual beings, sexuality assumes far greater importance once sexual maturity is achieved. Adolescents must incorporate into their identities as males or females concepts of themselves as sexual males or females. Moreover, they must figure out how to express their sexuality in relationships. As part of their search for identity, teenagers raise questions about their sexual attractiveness, their sexual values, and their goals in close relationships. They also experiment with sexual behavior—sometimes with good outcomes, sometimes with bad ones.

Sexual Orientation

Part of establishing a sexual identity, part of an individual's larger task of resolving Erikson's conflict of identity versus role confusion, is becoming aware of one's **sexual orientation**—that is, preference for sexual partners of the same or other sex, or both. Sexual orientation exists on a continuum; not all cultures categorize sexual preferences as ours does (Paul, 1993), but we commonly describe people as having primarily heterosexual, homosexual, or bisexual orientations. Most adolescents establish a heterosexual sexual orientation without much soul-searching. For youths attracted to members of their own sex, however, the process of accepting that they have a homosexual or bisexual orientation and establishing a positive identity in the face of negative societal attitudes can be a long and torturous one. Many have an initial awareness of their sexual preference before reaching puberty but do not accept being gay or lesbian, or gather the courage to "come out," until their mid-20s (Savin-Williams, 1995). Among 17- to 25-year-olds with same-sex attractions, fewer than half have told both their parents and about one-third have not told either parent about their sexual orientation (Savin-Williams & Ream, 2003). Those who have disclosed to one or both parents did so around age 19. By this age, most are out of high school and have achieved some independence from their parents, which may give them the confidence to share this information.

Experimentation with homosexual activity is fairly common during adolescence, but few adolescents become part of the estimated 5% to 6% of adults who establish an enduring homosexual or bisexual sexual orientation (Savin-Williams & Ream, 2007). Contrary to societal stereotypes of gay men as effeminate and lesbian women as masculine, gay and lesbian individuals have the same range of psychological and social attributes that hetero-

● TABLE 12.2 PERCENTAGE OF TWINS WHO ARE ALIKE FOR HOMOSEXUAL OR BISEXUAL SEXUAL ORIENTATION

	Identical Twins	Fraternal Twins
Both male twins are gay or bisexual if one is	52%	22%
Both female twins are lesbian or bisexual if one is	48%	16%

SOURCE: From J. M. Bailey & R. C. Pillard, A genetic study of male sexual orientation. *Archives of General Psychiatry, 48,* 1089–1096. Copyright © 1991 American Medical Association. Reprinted with permission.

NOTE: Higher rates of similarity for identical twin pairs than for fraternal twin pairs provide evidence of genetic influence on homosexuality. Less-than-perfect agreement points to the additional operation of environmental influences.

sexual adults do. Knowing that someone prefers same-sex romantic partners reveals no more about his personality than knowing that someone is heterosexual.

What influences the development of sexual orientation? Part of the answer lies in the genetic code. Twin studies have established that identical twins are more alike in sexual orientation than fraternal twins (Bailey et al., 1993; Bailey & Pillard, 1991). As ● **Table 12.2** reveals, however, in about half the identical twin pairs, one twin is homosexual or bisexual but the other is heterosexual. This means that environment contributes at least as much as genes to the development of sexual orientation (Bailey, Dunne, & Martin, 2000).

Research also shows that many gay men and lesbian women expressed strong cross-sex interests when they were young, despite being subjected to the usual pressures to adopt a traditional gender role (Bailey, Dunne, & Martin, 2000; LeVay, 1996). Richard Green (1987), for example, studied a group of highly feminine boys who did not just engage in cross-sex play now and then but who strongly and consistently preferred female roles, toys, and friends. He found that 75% of these boys (compared with 2% of a control group of gender-typical boys) were exclusively homosexual or bisexual 15 years later. Still, it is important to note that sexual orientation is every bit as heritable among gay men who were typically masculine boys and lesbian women who were typically feminine girls as among those who showed early cross-sex interests (Bailey & Pillard, 1991; Bailey et al., 1993). In longitudinal research with women, Lisa Diamond (2008) found that orientation as lesbian or bisexual was relatively enduring over a ten-year period, although women often defied attempts to be defined exclusively by a single sexual orientation. Many preferred to be unlabeled, perhaps reflecting an openness to changes in sexual orientation or an attraction to the person without regard to that person's biological sex (see Diamond, 2008). Although it might be tempting to infer sexual orientation from early childhood behaviors, all we really know is that *some* gay and lesbian adults knew from an early age that traditional gender-role expectations did not suit them, but others did not.

What environmental factors may help determine whether a genetic predisposition toward homosexuality is actualized? We do not know yet. The old psychoanalytic view that male homosexuality stems from having a domineering mother and a weak father has received little support (LeVay, 1996). Growing up with a gay or lesbian parent also seems to have little effect on later sexual orientation (Patterson, 2004). Nor is there support for the idea that homosexuals were seduced into a homosexual lifestyle by older individuals.

A more promising hypothesis is that hormonal influences during the prenatal period influence sexual orientation (Ellis et al., 1988; Meyer-Bahlburg et al., 1995). For example, androgenized females are more likely than other women to adopt a lesbian or bisexual orientation, suggesting that high prenatal doses of male hormones may predispose at least some females to homosexuality (Dittman et al., 1992; Money, 1988). Later-born males with older brothers may be more prone to a homosexual orientation because, according to one theory, their mother produces anti-male antibodies that accumulate over the course of each pregnancy with a male (see Blanchard & Lippa, 2007), but this does not explain why some firstborn males or males without older brothers develop a homosexual orientation (see Gooren, 2006). Another possibility is

that nature and nurture interact. Biological factors may predispose an individual to have certain psychological traits, which in turn influence the kinds of social experiences the person has, which in turn shape her sexual orientation (Byne, 1994). However, no one yet knows which factors in the prenatal or postnatal environment contribute, with genes, to a homosexual orientation (see Bailey, 2003; Kendler et al., 2000).

Sexual Morality

Whatever their sexual orientation, adolescents establish attitudes regarding what is and is not appropriate sexual behavior. The sexual attitudes of adolescents changed dramatically during the 20th century, especially during the 1960s and 1970s, yet many of the old values have endured (Caron & Moskey, 2002). Three generalizations emerge from the research on sexual attitudes.

First, many adolescents—approximately 3 out of 4—have come to believe that sex with affection in the context of a committed relationship is acceptable (Caron & Moskey, 2002). They no longer buy the traditional view that premarital intercourse is always morally wrong (● **Table 12.3**). However, they do not go so far as to approve of casual sex, although males have somewhat

● **TABLE 12.3 CHANGES IN SEXUAL BELIEFS AND BEHAVIORS OVER 50 YEARS: PERCENTAGE OF RESPONDENTS WHO AGREED WITH THE FOLLOWING STATEMENTS FROM THE CLASSES OF 1950, 1975, AND 2000**

	1950	1975	2000
Having sex as a teenager would go against my beliefs, even if in a serious relationship.	65%	27%	20%
I believe it is OK to have sex as a teenager.	24%	60%	70%
If I had sex as a teenager, it would have been OK with my parents.	6%	8%	33%
If I had sex as a teenager, it would have been OK with my friends.	15%	75%	81%
If I had sex with boyfriend/girlfriend, it would have made our relationship stronger.	14%	21%	37%
Based on your beliefs while in high school, when was it acceptable to have sex?			
Within the first month of dating	8%	18%	15%
After the relationship became serious	19%	72%	76%
Only after becoming married	73%	10%	9%
Respondents who had sex in high school			
	24%	65%	69%
Of those responents who had sex by the end of high school, their age at first sex:			
12–14 years	21%	15%	22%
15 years old	32%	10%	9%
16 years old	32%	30%	45%
17 years or older	15%	45%	24%

SOURCE: Adapted from Table 1 and Table 4, Sandra L. Caron and Eilean G. Moskey (2002). Changes over time in teenage sexual relationships: Comparing the high school class of 1950, 1975, and 2000. *Adolescence, 37,* 515-526.

more permissive attitudes about this than females. Most adolescents believe that partners should be in a long-term romantic relationship or feel a close emotional involvement with each other (Caron & Moskey, 2002). Most adolescents—both male and female—report that their first sexual relationship was with someone with whom they were romantically, not casually, involved (Ryan, Manlove, & Franzetta, 2003). On average, teens wait about 5 months before having sex with a romantic partner and about 1 in 4 of these teens have sex with this first partner only one time. For others, their first sexual relationship lasts 1–3 months (37%), 4–6 months (19%), or more than 6 months (20%). Thus, casual and frequent sex with multiple partners is not the norm among adolescents (Ryan, Manlove, & Franzetta, 2003).

A second finding is that the **double standard** has declined over the years. According to the double standard, sexual behavior that is viewed as appropriate for males is considered inappropriate for females; there is one standard for males, another for females. In the "old days," a young man was expected to sow some wild oats and obtain some sexual experience, and gained respect from peers for his sexual exploits ("he's a stud"). In contrast, a young woman was expected to remain a virgin until she married and was viewed negatively for engaging in sexual behaviors ("she's a slut"). Although the double standard has declined, it has not disappeared (Crawford & Popp, 2003; Peterson & Hyde, 2010). For instance, college students still tend to believe that a woman who has many sexual partners is more immoral than an equally promiscuous man (Blumberg, 2003; Crawford & Popp, 2003). In part, the double standard for male–female sexuality may persist because it fits entrenched societal expectations, even though actual sexual behaviors of males and females are more similar than different (Peterson & Hyde, 2010). For instance, among 11th-graders, 54% of females and 57% of males report having had sex, and among 12th-graders, 66% of females and 63% of males report at least one sexual encounter, indicating no significant male–female difference on this measure (Centers for Disease Control and Prevention [CDC], 2008).

A third generalization that emerges from research on sexual attitudes is that adolescents are confused about sexual norms. Adolescents continually receive mixed messages about sexuality (Ponton, 2001). They are encouraged to be popular and attractive to the other sex, and they watch countless television programs and movies that glamorize sexual behavior. Yet they are told to value virginity and to fear and avoid pregnancy, bad reputations, and AIDS and other sexually transmitted illnesses (STIs). Adults often tell teens that they are too young to engage in sexual activity, yet they make teens feel ashamed or embarrassed about masturbating (Halpern et al., 2000; Ponton, 2001). The standards for males and females are now more similar, and adolescents tend to agree that sexual intercourse in the context of emotional involvement is acceptable; but teenagers still must forge their own codes of behavior, and they differ widely in what they decide.

Sexual Behavior

If attitudes about sexual behavior have changed over the years, has sexual behavior itself changed? Yes, it has. Today's teenagers are involved in more intimate forms of sexual behavior at earlier ages than adolescents of the past were. Several themes emerge from the research on teens' sexual behavior:

- Rates of sexual activity climbed in the 1960s and continued to climb through the 1980s before leveling off and then declining somewhat from the mid-1990s on (CDC, 2008).
- The percentages of both males and females who have had intercourse increased steadily over the past century.
- Perhaps reflecting the decline of the double standard, the sexual behavior of females has changed more than that of males, and the difference in experience between the sexes has largely disappeared (CDC, 2008; Peterson & Hyde, 2010). As noted earlier, today's male and female teenagers begin having sex at about the same age.

The percentage of adolescents with sexual experience increases steadily over the adolescent years, although as ●Table 12.4 shows, this varies by the students' gender and race/ethnicity. By age 21 to age 24, 85% report having had sexual intercourse (Meschke et al., 2000). Of course, rates of sexual activity depend greatly on how sexual activity is defined. What constitutes "having sex"? Virtually all college students—both male and female—agree that penile–vaginal intercourse is having sex, but by 2007 only 20% of college students agreed that they had "had sex" when they engaged in oral–genital stimulation (Hans, Gillen, & Akande, 2010). Perhaps this is why there are higher rates of **oral sex** than intercourse among today's high school students (Prinstein, Meade, & Cohen, 2003). If their cognitive schema of having sex does not include oral sex (or anal sex for some teens), they can engage in oral sex without feeling they are really having sex. Consequently, as many as 40% of college students who label themselves virgins report giving or receiving oral sex, and some of these have had three or more oral sex partners (Chambers, 2007).

Interestingly, today's teens rate oral sex as less intimate than intercourse, the opposite of what many from their parent's generation believe (Chambers, 2007). This may help explain the rise in oral sex among teenagers. Another reason is teens' inaccurate perception that oral sex is safer than vaginal penetration. Although oral sex without intercourse may sharply reduce pregnancy rates, it does not prevent transmission of sexually transmitted infections (STIs) unless partners consistently use protection. Unfortunately, many teens lack knowledge about how to protect themselves during oral sex (Brady & Halpern-Fisher, 2007; Chambers, 2007). In addition to possible health consequences, there may be emotional consequences for teens who engage in oral sex. Teens who engage only in oral sex

●TABLE 12.4 PERCENTAGE OF HIGH SCHOOL STUDENTS WHO HAVE EVER HAD SEXUAL INTERCOURSE

	White	Black	Hispanic
Female	44	61	44
Male	42	75	58

SOURCE: Eaton et al., 2006.

(without intercourse) report less positive feelings about themselves and their relationship than other sexually active teens (Brady & Halpern-Fisher, 2007).

Becoming sexually active is a normal part of development, but parents and society often express concerns about teens becoming sexually active when they are too young because early sexual activity is associated with risky behaviors that can lead to unwanted pregnancies and sexually transmitted infections. Jessica Siebenbruner and her colleagues (2007) studied the antecedents of early sexual behavior among three groups of 16-year-olds who had previously been evaluated on a variety of measures at ages 6, 9, 12, and 13. The researchers distinguished among three groups on the basis of self-reported sexual behaviors at age 16: sexual abstainers who had not yet had sexual intercourse, low risk-takers who reported having five or fewer sexual partners and always using contraception, and high risk-takers who reported having six or more sexual partners and inconsistently using contraception. The researchers wanted to know whether they could predict which of these three groups a teen would end up in at age 16 based on information collected at the earlier ages.

Several findings emerged from this research. High-risk sexual behavior at age 16 seemed to be part of a general pattern of problem behavior that started at birth with a mother who was unmarried (Siebenbruner et al., 2007). Unwed mothers tend to be younger, less educated, and more likely to experience economic hardships. High-risk teens grew up in homes that were characterized as less emotionally responsive and they were rated by teachers as engaging in more externalizing behaviors at ages 9 and 12. In these respects, the high-risk teens were different from both the low-risk teens and the abstainers throughout childhood. In contrast, the low-risk teens and the abstainers were similar throughout childhood, yet began to diverge in early adolescence. At age 13, low-risk teens *looked* more mature than abstainers and were more involved in romantic relationships. They were also somewhat more likely to drink alcohol at age 16 than the abstainers. Their mature appearance may have led others to respond to them differently, leading them to romantic relationships, sexual involvement, and alcohol use at an earlier age than their peers who appeared less mature. These findings suggest that parents who are concerned about early involvement in sex should be on the alert for problem behaviors during childhood, provide an emotionally responsive home environment, and talk to their teens about how their appearance may influence how others perceive and treat them.

Some teens seem headed for engaging in riskier sexual behaviors than other teens. Lynne Cooper (2010) evaluated the sexual behaviors of nearly 2000 young adults and found that numerous factors, including within-person factors, situational factors, and interactions of the two, contribute to the chances of engaging in risky sex. Within-person factors associated with more risky sexual behaviors included low levels of impulse control and communality and high levels of adventuresomeness and negative emotionality (a tendency to feel anxious and depressed and react poorly to stressful situations). Situations involving sex with a new partner were associated with drinking more alcohol and choosing a riskier partner but also with greater likelihood of using a condom. Research consistently shows that alcohol use is associated with riskier sexual behaviors (see Cooper, 2002; Testa, Hoffman, & Livingston, 2010). Teens and young adults, especially those from minority groups and males, are most likely to engage in risky sex practices (see Espinosa-Hernandez & Lefkowitz, 2009; Lee & Hahm, 2010). The consequences can be long-lasting and devastating.

Although most adolescents seem to adjust successfully to becoming sexually active, there have also been some casualties among those who are psychologically unready for sex or who end up with an unintended pregnancy or an STI. Sexually active adolescent couples often fail to use contraception, partly because they are cognitively immature and do not take seriously the possibility that their behavior could have unwanted long-term consequences (Loewenstein & Furstenberg, 1991). Although condom use has increased over past decades, it is still lower than health-care professionals would like to see. Overall, more than one-third of sexually active teens did not use a condom during their last sexual intercourse (Eaton et al., 2006). Adolescent females report less frequent condom use than males, possibly because their sexual partners are often several years older and because condom use among males declines from mid to late adolescence (Eaton et al., 2006). This may reflect that adolescent couples who are in long-term, monogamous relationships stop using condoms because they no longer fear transmission of HIV or other STIs.

For the adolescent who gives birth, the consequences of teenage sexuality can include an interrupted education, a low income, and a difficult start for both her and her child (Furstenberg, Brooks-Gunn, & Chase-Lansdale, 1989). This young mother's life situation and her child's developmental status are likely to improve later, especially if she goes back to school and limits her family size, but she is likely to remain economically disadvantaged compared with her peers who postpone

There are numerous contraceptives available in most developed countries. Which one helps protect against STIs as well as unwanted pregnancies?

● TABLE 12.5 SEXUALLY TRANSMITTED ILLNESSES (STIS) WITH THEIR CAUSE, SYMPTOMS, AND TREATMENT

STI	Cause and Treatment	Symptoms and Side Effects
Chlamydia: Highest rates among 15- to 19-year-olds, followed by 20- to 24-year-olds	Caused by a bacteria; can be treated and cured with antibiotics	Few or no symptoms; when present, symptoms include slight discharge from vagina or penis, burning with urination, and lower abdominal pain. If left untreated, it can result in pelvic inflammatory disease, which is associated with infertility.
Trichomoniasis: Highest rates among women 30 and older	Caused by a parasite; can be treated and cured with antibiotics	Few or no symptoms; when present, symptoms include irritation or itching of the genital area, painful urination and intercourse, and possibly lower abdominal pain.
Gonorrhea: Highest rates among adolescents and young adults	Caused by bacteria; can be treated and usually cured with antibiotics although some strains have become resistant	Few or no symptoms; when present, symptoms include genital discharge and painful urination. Gonorrheal infections can also invade the mouth and throat through oral sex with an infected partner, or the anus and rectum through anal sex with an infected partner. Can lead to infertility if untreated.
Genital Herpes: Incidence increases across age groups, peaking in middle adulthood	Caused by herpes simplex virus; can be treated but not cured	Symptoms include genital discharge, itching or burning, and painful blisters in the genital and anal regions. Although blisters may disappear in 2–3 weeks, the underlying virus that causes genital herpes remains and can cause symptom recurrence at any time. On average, infected persons have four occurrences per year.
Genital Warts: Highest rates among those in their early 20s	Caused by human papillomavirus (HPV); can be treated with surgery or cauterization of warts but may recur if immune system does not completely eliminate virus	Symptoms include small painless bumps on the vagina, cervix, or vulva (females) and penis (males); the anus and mouth may also be affected. If left untreated, the growths can grow into a larger clump of warts resembling cauliflower. Some strains of HPV are associated with cervical cancer and a vaccine has been developed to prevent HPV.
Syphilis: Highest rates among 20-somethings	Caused by *Treponema pallidum* bacteria, which is highly contagious; can be treated in early stages with antibiotics	Symptoms emerge in stages: The first symptom is typically one or more ulcerlike sores around the genitals, although these sores, called chancres, can also appear in the mouth or anal area depending on point of contact with an infected person. This is followed by a body rash and flulike symptoms, which may last for several weeks. The underlying bacteria can remain dormant for years, or it can resurface in the lungs, heart, or brain. Can cause brain disease, dementia, or blindness if left untreated.

SOURCES: Adapted from Centers for Disease Control and Prevention (2009, November). *Sexually transmitted disease surveillance, 2008.* Atlanta: U.S. Department of Health and Human Services. Dunne, E. F., Unger, E. R., Sternberg, M., McQuillan, G., Swan, D. C., Patel, S. S., & Markowitz, L. E. (2007). Prevalence of HPV infection among females in the United States. *JAMA, 297,* 813–819. Guttmacher Institute (2009, June). *Facts on sexually transmitted infections in the United States.* Available at: www.guttmacher.org/pubs/FIB_STI_US.html. Accessed: April 20, 2010.

parenthood until their 20s or later (Furstenberg, Brooks-Gunn, & Morgan, 1987). Fortunately, after increasing for many years, rates of teenage pregnancy have begun to decline recently (Kost, Henshaw, & Carlin, 2010).

As mentioned, in addition to unplanned pregnancy, poorly planned sexual activity can have health consequences, namely STIs. ● **Table 12.5** provides an overview of STIs that can result from inconsistent or inadequate safe sex practices. Sadly, few adolescents are doing what they would need to do to protect themselves from STIs: abstaining from sex or using a condom *every* time. No wonder many educators are calling for stronger programs of sex education and distribution of free condoms at school. There is little chance of preventing the unwanted consequences of teenage sexuality unless more adolescents either postpone sex or practice safer sex.

One encouraging finding is that teens who feel close to their parents, especially their mothers, and who report having closer parental supervision are more likely to delay initiating sexual activity (L'Engle & Jackson, 2008). Parent–teen communication about sexuality can also delay age of first intercourse, particularly when mothers point out the negative consequences of having sex at an early age (Usher-Seriki, Bynum, & Callands, 2008). Unfortunately, many parents do not communicate clearly or regularly with their teens about matters of sexuality (Guilamo-Ramos et al., 2008). In a survey of mothers of at-risk urban middle-school students, those who thought that a conversation about sex would embarrass their teen or felt unsure of what to say or how to initiate such a conversation tended not to talk to their teen about sex. In contrast, mothers who thought that talking about sex would encourage their teen to think more maturely, believed it wouldn't be too embarrassing, thought they would be able to answer their teen's questions, and felt comfortable with themselves and with the idea of talking about sex were more likely to have such conversations (Guilamo-Ramos et al., 2008; Pluhar, DiIorio, & McCarty, 2008). This suggests that successful "sex education" programs need to reach out to parents and help educate parents as well as their teens.

Adult Sexuality

Adults' sexual lifestyles are as varied as their personalities and intellects. Some adults remain single—some of them actively seeking a range of partners, others having one partner at a time, and still others leading celibate lives. Almost 9 of 10 Americans marry, and most adults are married at any given time. Men have more sexual partners and report more sexual activity than women during their adult lives, but most members of both sexes have just one sexual partner at a time (Cherlin, 2009; Peterson & Hyde, 2010).

Among married couples, there is a small decline in quality of sex over the course of marriage (Liu, 2003). And married women report somewhat less satisfaction with their sex lives than do married men (Liu, 2003). On average, married middle-aged couples have sex about once a week and report that they would have sex more often if they were not so busy and tired from their jobs and raising kids (Deveny, 2003). Men's sexual satisfaction, more so than women's, is largely determined by the frequency of their sexual activity (McNulty & Fisher, 2007). Middle-aged women report more positive moods and lower stress levels on days following sexual behavior with a partner (Burleson, Trevathan, & Todd, 2007). This benefit may be due to sexual activity alone or in combination with the affection that many women reported with the sexual activity.

What becomes of people's sex lives as they age? Just as parents may be uncomfortable thinking of their teens as sexual beings, many young people struggle to conceive of their parents or—heaven forbid—their grandparents as sexual beings. We tend to stereotype older adults as sexless or asexual. But we are wrong: people continue to be sexual beings throughout the life span. For example, in a recent survey of more than 6000 adults ranging in age from 25 to 85, most adults reported being interested in sex and being sexually active (Lindau & Gavrilova, 2010). Gender differences were small among younger adults but became larger with age, leading to relatively large differences among the oldest

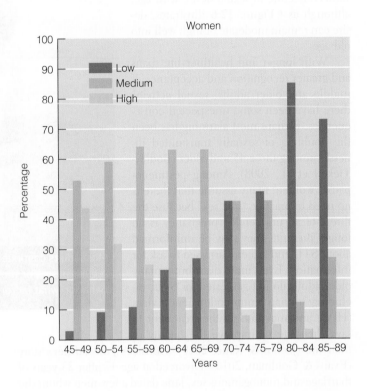

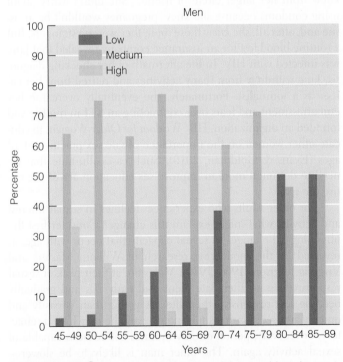

■ **FIGURE 12.6** Percentage of women (top graph) and men (bottom graph), by age, reporting low, moderate, and high levels of sexual desire. SOURCE: From DeLamater, J. S., & Sill, M., Sexual desire in later life, *Journal of Sex Research, 42,* pp. 138–149.

adults: 75- to 85-year-old men were twice as likely to be sexually active and four times as likely to express interest in sex as women the same age. Other research shows a decline in sexual desire with age, although as ■ **Figure 12.6** illustrates, desire can remain moderate or high well into old age.

With longer and healthier life spans and greater recognition and acceptance of middle and older adults' sexual activity, there have been some unexpected consequences. Perhaps most alarming has been the doubling of sexually transmitted illnesses among those 45 and older (Bodley-Tickell et al., 2008). Among postmenopausal women, many assume that there is no need to practice "safe sex" because the threat of an unintended pregnancy is no longer present. They may be uninformed about STIs and too embarrassed to ask for information. Even more disturbing, many older adults do not get tested for STIs, including human immunodeficiency virus (HIV), and may not get the treatment to save their life or improve the quality of their life (Jacobs & Kane, 2010). Consider Jane Fowler's story (Evans & Goldman, 2010): Divorced at age 47 after 23 years of marriage and monogamous sex, Jane dated a few men whom she knew from her larger circle of friends. She didn't worry about using condoms because she knew pregnancy wouldn't be an issue and, after all, she *knew* these men; they weren't strangers. But a routine blood test for an insurance company revealed that Jane was infected with HIV. In the aftermath of her shocking diagnosis, Jane withdrew from many activities and retired from her career as a journalist. Fortunately, she eventually overcame her embarrassment and fears over contracting an STI in midlife and founded an organization, *HIV Wisdom for Older Women*, to educate other women on the importance of safe sex practices at all ages (Evans & Goldman, 2010). Such cases illustrate that we need to do much more to improve sex education across the entire life span.

For older adults who experience declines in sexual interest and activity, what might explain this change? Consider first the physiological changes in sexual capacity that occur with age, as revealed by the pioneering research of William Masters and Virginia Johnson (1966, 1970). Males are at their peak of sexual responsiveness in their late teens and early 20s and gradually become less responsive thereafter. A young man is easily and quickly aroused; his orgasm is intense; and he may have a refractory, or recovery, period of only minutes before he is capable of sexual activity again. The older man is likely to be slower—slower to arouse, slower to ejaculate after being aroused, and slower to recover afterward. In addition, levels of male sex hormones decline gradually with age in many men. This may con-

Most adults continue to be interested in sex and engage in sexual behaviors on a regular basis. For those older adults who experience a decline in sexual desire or behavior, what factors might be behind the change?

© A. Green/Corbis

tribute to diminished sexual functioning among older men (Schiavi et al., 1991), although most researchers do not believe that hormonal factors fully explain the changes in sexual behavior that most men experience (Kaye, 1993).

Physiological changes in women are less dramatic. Females reach their peak of sexual responsiveness later than men do, often not until their mid-30s. Women are capable of more orgasms in a given time span than men are because they have little or no refractory period after orgasm, and this capacity is retained into old age. As noted in Chapter 5, menopause does not seem to reduce sexual activity or interest for most women. However, like older men, older women typically are slower to become sexually excited. Moreover, some experience discomfort associated with decreased lubrication that occurs as estrogen levels drop with menopause.

The physiological changes that men and women experience do not explain why many of them become less sexually active in middle and old age. Masters and Johnson concluded that both men and women are physiologically capable of sexual behavior well into old age. Women retain this physiological capacity even longer than men, yet they are less sexually active in old age.

Apparently, we must turn to factors other than biological aging to explain changes in sexual behavior. In summarizing these factors, Pauline Robinson (1983) quotes Alex Comfort (1974): "In our experience, old folks stop having sex for the same reason they stop riding a bicycle—general infirmity, thinking it looks ridiculous, and no bicycle" (p. 440).

Under the category of infirmity, diseases and disabilities, as well as the drugs prescribed for them, can limit sexual functioning (DeLamater & Sill, 2005). Older adults in good or excellent health not only report engaging in more frequent sex than their peers in poor or fair health, they also report more interest and greater satisfaction with their sexual activity (Lindau & Gavrilova, 2010). Poor health may be especially problematic for men, who may become impotent if they have high blood pressure, coronary disease, diabetes, or other health problems. Mental health problems are also important: Many cases of impotence among middle-aged and elderly men are attributable to psychological causes such as stress at work and depression rather than to physiological causes (Persson & Svanborg, 1992).

The second source of problems is social attitudes that view sexual activity in old age as ridiculous, or at least inappropriate. Old people are stereotyped as sexually unappealing and sexless (or as "dirty old men") and are discouraged from expressing sexual interests. These negative attitudes may be internalized by elderly people, causing them to suppress their sexual desires (Kaye, 1993; Purifoy, Grodsky, & Giambra, 1992). Older females may be even further inhibited by the double standard of aging, which regards aging in women more negatively than aging in men (Arber & Ginn, 1991).

Third, there is the "no bicycle" part of Comfort's analogy—the lack of a partner, or at least of a willing and desirable partner. Most older women are widowed, divorced, or single and face the reality that there just are not enough older men to go around. Moreover, most of the men who are around are married: 85% of men over the age of 85 are married, compared with 12% of women (Martinez et al., 2006). Lack of a partner, then, is the major problem for elderly women, many of whom continue to be interested in sex, physiologically capable of sexual behavior, and desirous of love and affection (DeLamater & Sill, 2005).

Perhaps we should add one more element to Comfort's bicycle analogy: lack of cycling experience. Masters and Johnson (1966, 1970) proposed a "use it or lose it" principle of sexual behavior to reflect two findings. First, an individual's level of sexual activity early in adulthood predicts his level of sexual activity in later life. The relationship is not necessarily causal, by the way; it could simply be that some people are more sexually motivated than others throughout adulthood. A second aspect of the use it or lose it rule may be causal, however: Middle-aged and elderly adults who experience a long period of sexual abstinence often have difficulty regaining their sexual capacity.

Checking Mastery

1. What do we know about the sexual beliefs of many of today's teens?

2. Are there differences in sexual behavior of males and females?

3. What are three consequences of childhood sexual abuse on the target of such abuse?

4. What factors likely contribute to one's sexual orientation?

Making Connections

1. What factors are likely to influence the age at which young people today become sexually active? If you wanted to delay the age of first intercourse, what would be some ways to do this?

Chapter Summary

12.1 Sex and Gender

- Differences between males and females can be detected in the physical, psychological, and social realms; gender differences arise from an interaction of biological influences and socialization into gender roles (including the learning of gender-role norms and stereotypes).
- Research comparing males and females indicates that the two sexes are far more similar than different psychologically. The average male is more aggressive and better at spatial and mathematical problem-solving tasks, but less adept at verbal tasks, than the average female. Males also tend to be more active, assertive, and developmentally vulnerable than females, who tend to be more compliant with adults' requests, tactful, nurturant, and anxious. Most sex differences are small, however, and some are becoming smaller.

12.2 The Infant

- During infancy, boys and girls are similar but adults treat them differently.
- By age 2, infants have often gained knowledge of their basic gender identity and display "gender-appropriate" play preferences.
- Because their sex is important to those around them, and because they see that males and females differ, infants begin to form categories of "male" and "female," establish a basic gender identity, and pursue "gender-appropriate" activities.

12.3 The Child

- Gender-role development proceeds with remarkable speed. By the time they enter school, children have long been aware of their basic gender identities, have acquired many stereotypes about how the sexes differ, and have come to prefer gender-appropriate activities and same-sex playmates.
- During middle childhood, their knowledge continues to expand as they learn more about gender-stereotyped psychological traits, but they also become more flexible in their thinking about gender roles. Their behavior, especially if they are boys, becomes even more gender typed, and they segregate themselves even more from the other sex.

12.4 The Adolescent

- Adolescents become intolerant in their thinking about gender-role deviations and, through gender intensification, show increased concern with conforming to gender norms.
- Theories of gender-role development include the biosocial theory proposed by Money and Ehrhardt, which emphasizes prenatal biological developments and stresses the importance of how a child is labeled and treated during a critical period for gender identity information.
- Social learning theorists focus on differential reinforcement and observational learning. Cognitive perspectives emphasize understanding of gender and active self-socialization.
- Kohlberg's cognitive developmental theory emphasizes that children master gender roles once they master the concepts of gender identity, gender stability, and gender consistency.

- Martin and Halverson's gender schema theory holds that children socialize themselves as soon as they have a basic gender identity and can construct gender schemata. Each theory has some support, but none is completely right.

12.5 The Adult

- Gender roles become more distinct when adults marry and have children, as men and women fulfill their roles as husband/wife and father/mother. Once children are grown, however, older adults often display greater flexibility in their behavior.
- Some adults display androgyny, a combination of both masculine-stereotypic and feminine-stereotypic traits. Some evidence suggests that androgyny is beneficial, but not at all ages or in all situations.

12.6 Sexuality over the Life Span

- We are sexual beings from infancy onward. School-age children engage in sex play and appear to experience their first sexual attractions around age 10. In adolescence, forming a positive sexual identity is an important task, one that can be difficult for those with a gay or lesbian sexual orientation.
- During the past century, we have witnessed increased endorsement of the view that sex with affection is acceptable, a weakening of the double standard, and increased confusion about sexual norms.
- Many older adults continue having sexual intercourse, and many of those who cease having it or have it less frequently continue to be sexually motivated. Elderly people can continue to enjoy an active sex life if they retain their physical and mental health, do not allow negative attitudes surrounding sexuality in later life to stand in their way, have a willing and able partner, and continue to "use" their capacity for sex.

Checking Mastery Answers

For answers to Checking Mastery questions, visit **www.cengagebrain.com**

Key Terms

Media Resources

Psychology CourseMate

Find online quizzes, flash cards, animations, video clips, experiments, interactive assessments, and other helpful study aids for this text at **www.cengagebrain.com**. You can also connect directly to the following sites:

APA Online: Aging and Human Sexuality Resource Guide

The APA website hosts a resource guide for Aging and Human Sexuality. Find articles, book chapters, and other pertinent resources here. To access, see "web links" in Psychology CourseMate at www.cengagebrain .com

Electronic Journal of Human Sexuality

Explore cutting edge research on sexuality by reviewing some of the research articles available free at this website. To access, see "web links" in Psychology CourseMate at www.cengagebrain.com

Understanding the DATA: Exercises on the Web

www.cengagebrain.com

For additional insight on the data presented in this chapter, try out the exercises for these figures in Psychology CourseMate at

www.cengagebrain.com:

Figure 12.3 Do children prefer playmates of their own sex? Apparently so. Both boys and girls spend more time playing with same-sex peers, especially at age 6.

Table 12.2 Percentage of twins who are alike for homosexual or bisexual sexual orientation.

Table 12.3 Changes in sexual beliefs and behaviors over 50 years: percentage of respondents who agreed with the following statements from the classes of 1950, 1975, and 2000.

CengageNOW

CENGAGENOW™

www.cengagebrain.com

Go to www.cengagebrain.com to link to CengageNOW, your online study tool. First take the Pre-Test for this chapter to get your Personalized Study Plan, which will identify topics you need to review and direct you to online resources. Then take the Post-Test to determine what concepts you have mastered and what you still need work on.

Social Cognitive and Moral Development

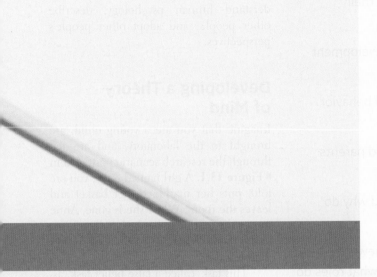

Certain campers one summer repeatedly pulled a prank on Edward. Edward was a small, uneven-legged, mildly retarded adult who was the basic maintenance staffer for the camp. He was kind, conscientious in his duties, and proud that he was earning his way in life. There was just one thing: At a point of frustration or moment of embarrassment, Ed would invariably unleash a torrent of profanities that was surprising and, to some campers, entertaining. Several campers had devised a way to set off this "entertainment." Ed worked hard mowing and doing other chores on the camp grounds and would sometimes take a nap during the day. His bed was located in the boys' wing of the campers' open barracks-style sleeping quarters. Seeing Ed asleep, the plotters would move in. They would gently sink one of Ed's hands into a pail of water. Ed would wet his pants in bed and awaken, swearing madly and running frantically after the hysterically laughing campers (Gibbs, 2010, p. 1).

1. How do we develop understandings of other people and of the role of mental states like emotions and beliefs in explaining their behavior?

2. What do different theories say about the nature and development of morality?

3. When do we first see signs of moral understanding and behavior in infancy?

4. How morally sophisticated are children, and what should parents do to raise moral children?

5. What moral growth takes place during adolescence, and why do some adolescents engage in antisocial behavior?

6. How does moral reasoning change in adulthood, what new perspectives on moral development are emerging, and what roles do religion and spirituality play in human development?

are like as individuals and about how males and females differ. Here we focus on developmental changes in the ability to understand human psychology, describe other people, and adopt other people's perspectives.

Developing a Theory of Mind

Imagine that you are a young child, are brought to the laboratory, and are led through the research scenario portrayed in ■ Figure 13.1. A girl named Sally, you are told, puts her marble in her basket and leaves the room. While she is gone, Anne moves the marble to her box. Sally returns to the room. Where will Sally look for her marble?

This task, called a **false belief task**, assesses the understanding that people can

John Gibbs (2010), author of the book *Moral Development and Reality*, attended the camp just described, watched the torment of Edward play out again and again, and feels guilty to this day that he did nothing to stop it, fearful of his fellow campers' reactions if he did. Many of you, we wager, can recall episodes like this when you and/or your peers did something hurtful to a nerdy or overweight classmate or to someone else who did not deserve it, when you failed to take the perspective of and empathize with an innocent victim. What might have stopped you from mistreating someone like Edward or prompted you to intervene to save him from abuse by others?

In this chapter, we continue our examination of the development of the self by exploring how we come to understand people and think through a variety of social issues, especially issues of right and wrong like those raised by the example Gibbs described, and how our thinking about other people is related to our social behavior. We begin with the broad topic of **social cognition**—thinking about the perceptions, thoughts, emotions, motives, and behaviors of self, other people, groups, and even whole social systems (Flavell, 1985; and see Harris, 2006). This includes learning to take the perspectives of other people, including victims like Edward. We then look closely at the social cognition involved in thinking through moral issues. We ask how humans acquire moral standards, how they decide what is right and wrong, how empathy and other emotions influence what they do, and how their moral decision making changes over the life span.

13.1 Social Cognition

We have already touched on some important aspects of social cognitive development in this book, seeing, for example, that older children think differently than younger children about what they

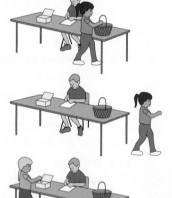

Sally places her marble in a basket.

Sally leaves the room.

The child being tested watches as Anne transfers Sally's marble to the box.

Sally returns.

The child being tested is asked the critical question: Where will Sally look for her marble?

■ **FIGURE 13.1** The false belief task involving Sally and Anne. The child who has developed a theory of mind should say that Sally will look in the basket based on her *false belief* that the marble is there. The child who fails this false belief task says that Sally will look in the box (where the child knows the marble has been moved).

Source: From Baron-Cohen, S., Leslie, A. M., & Frith, U., Does the Autistic Child Have a "Theory of Mind"?, *Cognition*, 21, pp. 37–46. Copyright © 1985. Reprinted with permission from Elsevier.

hold incorrect beliefs and that these beliefs, even though incorrect, can influence their behavior. The task was used in a pioneering study by Simon Baron-Cohen, Alan Leslie, and Uta Frith (1985) to determine whether young children, children with Down syndrome, and children with autism have a theory of mind. A **theory of mind** is the understanding that people have mental states such as desires, beliefs, and intentions and that these mental states guide (or cause, if you like) their behavior. We all rely on a theory of mind, also called mind-reading skills, to predict and explain human behavior. We refer to mental states every day, saying, for example, that people did what they did because they wanted to, intended to, or believed that doing so would have a desired effect.

Children who pass the false belief task in Figure 13.1, and therefore show evidence of having a theory of mind to explain human behavior, say that Sally will look for her marble in the basket (where she falsely believes it to be) rather than in the box (where it was moved without her knowledge). Children who have a theory of mind believe that Sally's behavior will be guided by her false belief about the marble's location. They are able to set aside their own knowledge of where the marble ended up after Anne moved it.

In the study by Baron-Cohen and his colleagues, about 85% of 4-year-olds of normal intelligence and older children with Down syndrome passed the false belief task about Sally and her marble. Yet despite mental ages greater than those of the children with Down syndrome, 80% of the children with autism failed. They incorrectly said Sally would look where they knew the marble to be (in the box) rather than where Sally had every reason to believe it was (in the basket).

This study served as the basis for hypothesizing that children with autism display severe social deficits because they lack a theory of mind and suffer from a kind of "mind blindness" (Baron-Cohen, 1995; and see Chapter 16). Imagine trying to understand and interact with people if you were unable to appreciate such fundamentals of human psychology as that people look for objects where they believe the objects are located, choose things that they want and reject things that they dislike, and sometimes attempt to plant false beliefs in others (that is, lie). Temple Grandin, a woman with autism who is intelligent enough to be a professor of animal sciences, describes what it is like to lack a theory of mind: she must create a memory bank of how people behave and what emotions they express in various situations and then "compute" how people might be expected to behave in similar situations (Sacks, 1993). Just as we cannot understand falling objects without employing the concept of gravity, we cannot hope to understand humans without invoking the concept of mental states and our theory of mind.

First Steps in Infancy

The idea that humans develop and rely on a theory of mind in understanding the world of people has stimulated exciting research on the nature and causes of autism and on when and how normal children develop the components of a theory of mind. Although children normally do not pass false belief tasks until about age 4, researchers have detected forerunners of a theory of mind in the first 2 years of life and believe that a theory of mind begins to form long before children pass false belief tasks (Doherty, 2009; Gopnik, Capps, & Meltzoff, 2000). They have also helped us appreciate that infants have far more sophisticated social cognitive skills than we suspected. Several abilities are considered important early signs of a theory of mind (see, for example, Charman, 2000; and Doherty, 2009); intriguingly, most of these skills are deficient in children with autism:

- Starting around 9 months, infants and their caregivers begin to engage in *joint attention*, both looking at the same object at the same time (see Chapter 10). At this age, infants sometimes point to toys and then look toward their companions, encouraging others to look at what they are looking at. By doing so, infants show awareness that other people have different perceptual experiences than they do—and that two people can share a perceptual experience. It turns out that an infant's ability to get involved in bouts of joint attention is a good predictor of later social competence (Van Hecke et al., 2007).
- In their first months of life, infants come to understand, partly from their own actions on the world, that other people have *intentions*, set goals, and act to achieve them (Woodward, 2009).
- When infants engage in their first simple *pretend play*, between 1 and 2 years, they show at least a primitive understanding of the difference between pretense (a kind of false belief) and reality (see Chapter 14). They show that they know the difference between a pretend tea party and a real one, for example, when they make exaggerated lip-smacking noises as they drink from a cup at a pretend tea party.
- *Imitation* of other people in the first year of life reveals an ability to mentally represent their actions—and very likely the goals or intentions behind them.
- *Emotional understanding*, as evidenced by comforting a playmate who is crying (see later section on infant empathy and prosocial behavior) or teasing a sibling in the second year of life, reflects an understanding that other people have emotions and that these emotions can be influenced for good or bad (Flavell, 1999).

Some researchers even claim that infants as young as 15 months understand that people can hold false beliefs. By simplifying the false belief task, Kristine Onishi and Renée Baillargeon (2005) found that infants this age are surprised (as indicated by looking longer) when an actor who was unable to see a toy moved from one box to another looks in the second box rather than in the first, where she should believe the toy is hidden (and see Scott & Baillargeon, 2009). By contrast, when infants observe that the actor can see the toy change locations, they are not surprised when she looks in the second box. Other researchers question whether this research demonstrates the kind of explicit, firm understanding of false mental states that is normally achieved by age 4. They suggest that the intuitions shown by infants may be achieved by reading situational and behavioral cues or by applying a simple rule that says people look where they last saw an object rather than where they *believe* an object to be (Doherty, 2009; Sodian & Thoermer, 2008).

Even 1-year-olds show awareness that other people can have mental states (perceptions) different from their own when they point at objects so that their companions and they can jointly attend to the same object.

The question of whether infants have an intuitive grasp of false beliefs is still being debated. In the meantime, it may serve us best to conclude that infants know more about the world of people than we used to give them credit for. Such achievements as joint attention, understanding of intentions, pretend play, imitation, and emotional understanding suggest that a theory of mind forms gradually, starting in infancy (Charman, 2000; Wellman, Phillips, & Rodriguez, 2000).

Desire and Belief–Desire Psychologies

We have even more solid evidence that children, starting at age 2, are developing theories of mind when they begin to refer to mental states in their speech (Bretherton & Beeghly, 1982). For example, Ross (at 2 years, 7 months) was asked why he kept asking why and replied, "I want to say 'why,'" explaining his behavior in terms of his desire; Adam (at 3 years, 3 months) commented about a bus, "I thought it was a taxi," showing awareness that he held a false belief about the bus (Wellman & Bartsch, 1994, p. 345). Children as young as 2½ years of age will even attempt to deceive other people; they will try to plant a false belief in an experimenter if they are shown how to erase telltale footprints leading toward the spot where a bag of gold coins and jewels is hidden and to lay new footprints heading in the wrong direction (Chandler, Fritz, & Hala, 1989).

Based on studies like these, Henry Wellman (1990) has theorized that children's theories of mind unfold in two phases. Around age 2 children develop a **desire psychology.** Toddlers talk about what they want and explain their own behavior and that of others in terms of wants or desires. This early desire psychology could be seen even among 18-month-olds in a clever study by Betty Repacholi and Alison Gopnik (1997). An experimenter tried two foods—Goldfish crackers and broccoli florets—and expressed happiness in response to one but disgust in response to the other. Because the toddlers almost universally preferred the crackers to the broccoli, the acid test was a scenario in which toddlers saw the experimenter express her liking for broccoli but her disgust at the crackers ("Eww! Crackers! I tasted crackers! Eww!"). When confronted with the two bowls of food and asked to give the experimenter some, would these toddlers give her broccoli or crackers? The 14-month-olds in the study either did not comply with the request or gave the experimenter crackers, despite her distaste for them. However, the 18-month-olds gave her broccoli (undoubtedly against their better judgment), showing that they were able to infer and honor her desire based on her previous emotional reactions to the two foods.

By age 4, children normally progress to a **belief–desire psychology.** They appreciate that people do what they do because they *desire* certain things and because they *believe* that certain actions will help them fulfill their desires. They now pass false belief tasks like the one about Sally and her marble, demonstrating an explicit understanding that beliefs, true or false, guide people's behavior just as desires do (Wellman, Cross, & Watson, 2001; Wellman & Liu, 2004).

Notice, then, that the 4-year-olds described by theory-of-mind researchers are more sophisticated students of psychology than the egocentric preschoolers described by Jean Piaget. However, it is better to think of a theory of mind as a set of understandings that children begin to develop well before age 4, and continue to refine and learn to use long afterward, than to view it as something children "have" at 4 years (Wellman & Liu, 2004). In late elementary school, for example, children are still mastering complex second-order belief statements such as, "Mary thinks that Jeff thinks that she hates him," in which people have beliefs about other people's beliefs (Harris, 2006; Keenan, 2003). Moreover, it is not until then that children grasp that different human minds construct different views of reality and that their interpretations of events are influenced by these views (Flavell, 1999).

Nature and Nurture

What roles do nature and nurture play in the development of theory of mind? On the nature side, evolutionary theorists argue that having a theory of mind proved adaptive to our ancestors and became part of our biological endowment as a species through natural selection (Bjorklund & Pellegrini, 2002). You can easily appreciate that theory-of-mind skills would help humans function as members of a social group, gain resources, and therefore survive. Social behaviors such as bargaining, conflict resolution, cooperation, and competition depend on understanding other people and predicting their behavior accurately.

Some support for an evolutionary perspective on theory-of-mind skills comes from studies of other primates. As it turns out, chimpanzees, gorillas, and other great apes share with humans basic, although not advanced, theory-of-mind skills. They can, for example, deceive others to get what they want (Hare, Call, & Tomasello, 2006; Tomasello, Call, & Hare, 2003). Yet human chil-

Recently neuroscientists, inspired by discoveries made by Italian scientist Giacomo Rizzolatti and his colleagues in research with monkeys, have been making fascinating and important discoveries about *mirror neurons,* neurons that are activated both when we perform an action and when we observe someone else perform the same action (Iacoboni, 2009; Oberman & Ramachandran, 2007; Pineda, 2009; Rizzolatti & Sinigaglia, 2008). Thus, observing someone grasp a ball activates the same neurons that fire when we grasp a ball ourselves, and mirror neuron systems may therefore facilitate imitation of what we see and hear. These neurons, evident in multiple areas of the brain, may also be critical in allowing us to quickly infer another person's internal state based on our own experiences of the same visible actions and facial expressions and corresponding internal states. For example, by watching a person reach for a Coke on a hot day, we readily infer that she's thirsty and wants a drink, and when she takes a sip, we readily infer from her facial expression, which we may even unconsciously and subtly imitate, that she's happy. Very simply, we make

sense of other people by drawing on what we know of ourselves. Mirror neuron systems make this possible through a mirroring process in which we simulate or reproduce within ourselves the actions, expressions of emotion, and other states we observe in other people and, through this process, come to understand them (Oberman & Ramachandran, 2007).

Mirror neurons have now been implicated not only in imitation, but in language, empathy, and theory of mind—all, interestingly, areas in which individuals with autism have difficulty (Iacoboni & Dapretto, 2006; Oberman & Ramachandran, 2007). Could it be, then, that mirror neuron systems do not work properly in people with autism? Possibly. Researchers have discovered that the mirror neurons of individuals with autistic disorder are not as active as those of nonautistic people when people are asked to observe or imitate others' actions; indeed, the less activity there is in mirror neuron areas of the brain, the more severe the autism (Dapretto et al., 2006). This difference is especially noticeable in the right temporoparietal area—one of the areas involved in processing information about

other people's beliefs and thoughts (Williams et al., 2006).

In addition, individuals with autism do not automatically and subtly mimic other people's facial expressions of emotion the way the rest of us do—as when we cringe while watching someone else in pain (McIntosh et al., 2006). Such mimicry, which involves mirror neurons, appears to help us recognize other people's emotions and empathize with them. Indeed, the amount of mirror neuron activity shown by nonautistic children while they observe and imitate facial expressions of emotion is correlated with measures of their interpersonal skills and empathic concern (Pfeifer et al., 2008).

This exciting research is helping us answer a baffling question about social cognition: How, when we have access only to what is going on in our own minds, do we read the minds of other people (Iacoboni, 2009). It is too simple to think that a particular "brain module" for social cognitive skills will be located; instead, whole systems of neurons spanning multiple areas of the brain are likely involved. Progress in the neuroscience of social cognition is spectacular—but much more remains to be learned.

dren have more advanced skills and are more successful than chimps at participating in games in which they must cooperate with others to achieve a goal (Warneken, Chen, & Tomasello, 2006).

In further support of the "nature" side of the nature—nurture issue, developing a theory of mind requires a certain level of biological maturation, especially neurological and cognitive development. This may be why children everywhere develop a theory of mind and progress from a desire psychology to a belief–desire psychology in the same manner at about the same age (Tardif & Wellman, 2000). Abnormal brain development in children with autism is suspected to be behind their great difficulty passing theory-of-mind tasks.

Are humans endowed with a specialized module in the brain devoted to understanding mental states, as some scholars maintain (Leslie, 1994; Scholl & Leslie, 2001)? The neuroscience of social cognition is a booming new field of study. Researchers are beginning to identify areas in the prefrontal cortex and temporoparietal areas of the brain that are uniquely involved in thinking about people's beliefs (Gallagher & Frith, 2003; Sabbagh, 2006; Saxe, Carey, & Kanwisher, 2004; Saxe & Powell, 2006). Using *functional magnetic resonance imaging*

(fMRI) to determine which areas of the brain are active while a person completes a task, for example, Rebecca Saxe and Nancy Kanwisher (2003) found that the areas of adults' brains that respond strongly during false belief tasks do not respond when people are asked questions about "false photographs" (for example, when they are shown a photo of chocolate in a green cupboard after the chocolate had been moved to a blue cupboard). Moreover, 4- to 6-year-old children who pass false belief tasks rely on the same area of the prefrontal cortex to think about others' beliefs as adults do, whereas children who fail these tasks use different brain areas (Liu et al., 2009; and see Saxe et al., 2009). Finally, while thinking about desires and thinking about beliefs rely on some of the same areas of the brain, thinking about beliefs calls on additional areas, supporting Wellman's distinction between an early desire psychology and a later developing belief–desire psychology (Liu, Meltzoff, & Wellman, 2009).

Neuropsychologists are currently very excited about the discovery of **mirror neurons** in several areas of the brain—neurons that are activated both when we perform an action and when we observe someone else perform the same action. As Exploration Box 13.1 illustrates, researchers believe mirror neuron systems are involved in imitation, theory-of-mind understandings, and empathy—all areas of difficulty for individuals with autism.

So "nature" has endowed human brains with a capacity for social cognition. On the "nurture" side of the nature–nurture issue, though, is evidence that acquiring a theory of mind, much like acquiring language, requires not only a normal human brain but also experience interacting with other humans and participating in a "community of minds" (Nelson et al., 2003). Children do not construct their theories of mind on their own; instead, they construct them jointly with others during conversations about mental states (Doherty, 2009; Thompson, 2006).

The evidence? Social interaction involving language seems to be critical to the development of a theory of mind. Deaf children of deaf parents, who can communicate with their companions using sign language, develop theory-of-mind skills right on schedule. However, deaf children of hearing parents, who usually do not have an opportunity to converse in sign language from an early age, achieve milestones in social cognitive development slowly, sometimes struggling with false belief tasks even at ages 8 to 10 (Peterson & Siegal, 1999; Peterson & Wellman, 2009; Peterson, Wellman, & Liu, 2005).

Conversations with siblings may also contribute to mind-reading skills, as children with siblings seem to grasp the elements of a theory of mind earlier than children without siblings (McAlister & Peterson, 2006). Engaging in pretend play with siblings may be especially instructive because the players must have shared beliefs about their pretend world (Taylor & Carlson, 1997; Youngblade & Dunn, 1995). In multichild families, there may also be more talk about mental states ("She thought you were done with your ice cream," "He didn't mean to step on your head").

Parents also contribute to the development of theory-of-mind skills. They do so by forming secure attachments with their children and being sensitive to their needs and perspectives (Symons & Clark, 2000; Thompson, 2006). Even more important may be a parent's "mind-mindedness." Mothers who talk in elaborated and appropriate ways about their children's mental states ("You were probably sad because you thought Grandma would stay with us longer") tend to have children with advanced theory-of-mind skills (Meins et al., 2002; Peterson & Slaughter, 2003). So do mothers who encourage their children to imagine what others may have thought or felt after the child misbehaved (Pears & Moses, 2003).

Finally, cultural influences are evident: Where there is not much talk about mental states, children are slow to develop theory-of-mind skills, though they generally develop such skills in the same order as other children. Among the Junin Quechua people of Peru, for example, adults rarely talk about beliefs and thoughts and have few words in their language for them. The result is that children as old as 8 years have trouble understanding that beliefs can be false (Vinden & Astington, 2000).

In sum, acquiring a theory of mind—the foundation for all later social cognitive development—begins in infancy and toddlerhood with first steps such as joint attention, understanding of intentions, pretend play, imitation, and emotional understanding and advances from a desire psychology to a belief–desire psychology universally. It is the product of both nature and nurture; that is, it is an evolved set of skills that relies on specialized

Deaf children who can communicate with their companions through sign language develop theory-of-mind skills on schedule.

areas of the brain and mirror neurons and that will not emerge without normal neurological and cognitive growth but that also will not develop normally without social experiences that involve talking about mental states with parents, siblings, and other companions.

Formulating a theory of mind has many important consequences for development. Children who have mastered theory-of-mind tasks generally tend to have more advanced social skills and better social adjustment than those who have not (Doherty, 2009; Keenan, 2003; Repacholi et al., 2003). They can understand that others' emotional responses might differ from their own (Harwood & Farrar, 2006), and, as you will see soon, they think more maturely about moral issues. However, theory-of-mind skills can be used for good or bad ends. Bullies and good liars often prove to be very adept at "mind reading" too (Repacholi et al., 2003; Talwar & Lee, 2008), so there is no guarantee that good "mind readers" will be socially well adjusted.

Describing and Evaluating Other People

Although research on theory of mind shows that even preschool children are budding psychologists, they still have a way to go to understand people in terms of their enduring personality traits and to predict how people will react and behave. Consider first how children of different ages describe people they know—parents, friends, disliked classmates, and so on.

As you discovered in Chapter 11, children younger than 7 or 8 describe themselves primarily in physical rather than psychological terms. They describe other people that way, too (Livesley & Bromley, 1973; Yuill, 1993). Thus, 4-year-old Evan says of his father, "He has one nose, one Mom, two eyes, brown hair." And 5-year-old Keisha says, "My daddy is big. He has hairy legs and eats mustard. Yuck! My daddy likes dogs—do you?" Not much of a personality profile there.

Young children perceive others in terms of their physical appearance, possessions, and activities. When they use psychological terms, the terms are often global, evaluative ones such as "nice" or "mean," "good" or "bad," rather than specific personality-trait labels (Ruble & Dweck, 1995). Moreover, they do not yet seem to understand traits as enduring qualities that predict how a person will behave in the future and explain why a person behaves as he does. The 5-year-old who describes a friend as "dumb" may be using this trait label only to describe that friend's recent "dumb" behavior; she may expect "smart" behavior tomorrow. As happens so often, though, recent research tells us that young children understand more than we used to appreciate. For example, 4- and 5-year-olds seem to be able to infer from examples of selfish behavior that a person has the trait of selfishness and to predict that a person who has the trait of selfishness will behave selfishly in the future; they just can't quite put these two insights together to predict future behavior from past behavior via an inference about the person's trait (Liu, Gelman, & Wellman, 2007).

Around age 7 or 8, children's descriptions of people show that they are more able to "get below the surface" and think about people in terms of enduring psychological traits. Thus, 10-year-old Juanita describes her friend Tonya: "She's funny and friendly to everyone, and she's in the gifted program because she's smart, but sometimes she's too bossy." As children reach age 11 or 12, they make more use of psychological traits to explain why people behave as they do, saying, for instance, that Mike pulled the dog's tail *because* he is cruel (Gnepp & Chilamkurti, 1988). Clearly, then, children become more psychologically minded as their emerging social cognitive abilities permit them to make inferences about enduring inner qualities from the concrete behavior they observe in the people around them.

When asked to describe people they know, adolescents offer personality profiles that are even more psychological than those provided by children (Livesley & Bromley, 1973). They see people as unique individuals with distinctive personality traits, interests, values, and feelings. Moreover, they are able to create more integrated, or organized, person descriptions, analyzing how an individual's often inconsistent traits fit together and make sense as a whole personality. Dan, for example, may notice that Noriko brags about her abilities at times but seems unsure of herself at other times, and he may integrate these seemingly discrepant impressions by concluding that Noriko is basically insecure and boasts to hide her insecurity. Some adolescents spend hours "psychoanalyzing" people, trying to figure out what makes them tick.

As was the case for self-descriptions, then, you can detect a progression in perceptions of other people from (1) physical descriptions and global evaluations of other people as good or bad during the preschool years to (2) more differentiated descriptions that refer to specific personality traits starting at age 7 or 8 and, finally, to (3) more integrated personality profiles during adolescence that show how even seemingly inconsistent traits fit together.

Social Perspective Taking

Another important aspect of social cognitive development involves outgrowing the egocentrism that characterizes young children and developing **social perspective-taking skills,** also called role-taking skills: the ability to adopt another person's perspective and understand her thoughts and feelings in relation to your own. Social perspective-taking skills are an example of theory of mind in action (Blair, 2003). They are essential in thinking about moral issues from different points of view, predicting the consequences of a person's actions for others, and empathizing with others (Gibbs, 2010). If the campers at the start of the chapter had taken Edward's perspective, perhaps they would have laid off him.

Robert Selman (1976, 1980; Yeates & Selman, 1989) contributed greatly to our understanding of role-taking abilities by asking children questions about interpersonal dilemmas like this one (Selman, 1976, p. 302):

> Holly is an 8-year-old girl who likes to climb trees. She is the best tree climber in the neighborhood. One day while climbing down from a tall tree, she falls. . . but does not hurt herself. Her father sees her fall. He is upset and asks her to promise not to climb trees anymore. Holly promises.
>
> Later that day, Holly and her friends meet Shawn. Shawn's kitten is caught in a tree and can't get down. Something has to be done right away or the kitten may fall. Holly is the only one who climbs trees well enough to reach the kitten and get it down but she remembers her promise to her father.

To assess how well a child understands the perspectives of Holly, her father, and Shawn, Selman asks: "Does Holly know how Shawn feels about the kitten? How will Holly's father feel if he finds out she climbed the tree? What does Holly think her father will do if he finds out she climbed the tree? What would you do in this situation?" Children's responses to these questions led Selman (1976) to conclude that social perspective-taking abilities develop in a stagelike manner:

- Consistent with Piaget's theory, children 3 to 6 years old tend to respond egocentrically to stories like this, assuming that others share their point of view. If young children like kittens, for example, they assume that Holly's father does, too, and therefore will be delighted if Holly saves the kitten. Just as they have trouble considering both the height and width of glasses in conservation of liquid problems, they have trouble coordinating the perspectives of both Holly and her father.

- By age 8 to age 10, as concrete-operational cognitive abilities solidify, children appreciate that two people can have different points of view even if they have access to the same information. Children are able to think about their own thoughts and about the thoughts of another person, and they realize that their companions can do the same. Thus, they can appreciate that Holly may think about her father's concern for her safety but conclude that he will understand her reasons for climbing the tree.

- Adolescents who have reached the formal-operational stage of cognitive development, at roughly age 12, become capable of mentally juggling multiple perspectives, including the perspective of the "generalized other," or the broader social group. The adolescent might consider how fathers in general react when children disobey them and consider whether Holly's father is similar to or different from the typical father. Adolescents thus become even better mental jugglers, keep-

Adolescents who have advanced role-taking, or social perspective-taking, skills are better able than those who do not to resolve conflicts with their parents (Selman et al., 1986). They are better able to adopt the perspectives of their parents (and parents in general) and to identify mutually acceptable solutions.

ing in the air their own perspective, that of another person, and that of an abstract "generalized other" representing a larger social group.

These advances in social cognition are more likely if parents are good models of social perspective taking, consider their children's feelings and thoughts, and rely on explanation rather than punishment in disciplining their children. This may be part of the reason why maltreated children and adolescents often prove to be less able to take others' perspectives than their peers (Burack et al., 2006).

Social perspective-taking skills have important implications for children's and adolescents' relationships. Experience interacting with peers seems to sharpen role-taking skills; sophisticated role-taking skills, in turn, help make children more sensitive and desirable companions. Children with advanced social perspective-taking skills are more likely than age-mates with less advanced skills to be sociable and popular and to enjoy close relationships with peers (Kurdek & Krile, 1982; LeMare & Rubin, 1987). Moreover, coaching in perspective taking can help improve the social behavior of disruptive children (Grizenko et al., 2000).

Social Cognition in Adulthood

As you saw in earlier chapters, nonsocial cognitive abilities, such as those used in remembering what you have read and solving scientific problems, tend to improve during early and middle adulthood and decline in later life. Do important social cognitive skills, such as the ability to think through advanced theory-of-mind problems or adopt other people's perspectives, also increase to a peak in middle age and decline later?

Social cognitive development during adulthood appears to involve more gains than losses (Blanchard-Fields, 1996; Hess, 1999). For example, Fredda Blanchard-Fields (1986) presented adolescents, young adults, and middle-aged adults with dilemmas that required them to engage in role taking and to integrate discrepant perspectives—for example, between a teenage boy and his parents regarding whether he must visit his grandparents with the family. Adults, especially middle-aged ones, were better able than adolescents to see both sides of the issues and to integrate the perspectives of both parties into a workable solution. Here, then, is evidence that the social cognitive skills of adults may continue to improve after adolescence.

Do elderly people continue to display the sophisticated social cognitive skills that middle-aged adults display? The evidence is mixed but, overall, social cognitive skills hold up quite well late in life. For example, Thomas Hess and his colleagues found that both middle-aged and elderly adults were more adept than young adults at reading a person's behavior to infer whether he possessed traits such as honesty or intelligence (Hess, Osowski, & Leclerc, 2005). Elderly adults perform as well as young and middle-aged adults on many social cognitive tasks, probably because they have accumulated expertise about the world of people (Blanchard-Fields & Kalinauskas, 2009; Hess, 1994; Pratt & Norris, 1999).

Yet some researchers detect deficiencies in the social cognitive skills of older adults (Blanchard-Fields, 1996; Pratt et al., 1996). Consider performance on adult-appropriate theory-of-mind tasks—tasks like the one in Engagement Box 13.1. A study of 50- to 90-year-olds found a decrease with age in performance on theory-of-mind tasks that could be accounted for by declines in fluid intelligence, executive functioning, and information-processing speed (Charlton et al., 2009; and see Sullivan and Ruffman, 2004). Others find that memory limitations hurt the performance of some older adults on these tasks (Happé, Winner, & Brownell, 1998; Keightley et al., 2006). Together, the findings suggest that declines in basic cognitive functions such as working memory and processing speed—declines that hurt the performance of older adults on certain nonsocial cognitive tasks—sometimes take a toll on their social cognitive performance as well (Hess, 1999).

Nonetheless, as mentioned, social cognitive abilities tend to hold up better than nonsocial cognitive abilities in later life (Blanchard-Fields & Kalinauskas, 2009; Keightley et al., 2006). One possible explanation is that the areas of the cortex that support social cognition and emotional understanding age more slowly than the areas that support nonsocial cognition (MacPherson, Phillips, & Della Sala, 2002). Another explanation has more to do with cognitive strategy than with neurological or cognitive deficits. It has been observed that in completing social cognitive tasks older adults tend to rely more than younger adults on simple rules of thumb and strongly held beliefs about people; this may be an adaptive strategy for avoiding more mentally taxing cognitive maneuvers (Blanchard-Fields & Kalinauskas, 2009). Finally, social cognitive skills may hold up well, especially in "real life" people-reading tasks, because they are used—exercised—every day (Charlton et al., 2009).

Possibly the most important research finding on social cognitive development in adulthood, though, is that older adults differ

Below is one of several tasks designed to test theory-of-mind skills in both school-aged children and adults (White et al., 2009). Try it and then score yourself using the scoring system developed by the researchers (printed upside down at the end of this box). Older adults sometimes have more difficulty than younger adults with these kinds of tasks; however, their difficulties may stem not from specific theory-of-mind deficits but from more general cognitive problems such as slower information processing or limited working memory.

> Late one night old Mrs. Peabody is walking home. She doesn't like walking home alone in the dark because she is always afraid that someone will attack her and rob her. She really is a very nervous person! Suddenly, out of the shadows comes a man. He wants to ask Mrs. Peabody what time it is, so he walks toward her. When Mrs. Peabody sees the man coming toward her, she starts to tremble and says, "Take my purse, just don't hurt me please!"

Q: Why did she say that? (White et al., 2009, pp. 1110–1111)

2 points—reference to her belief that he was going to mug her or her ignorance of his real intention

1 point—reference to her trait (she's nervous) or state (she's scared) or intention (so he wouldn't hurt her) without suggestion that fear was unnecessary

0 points—factually incorrect/irrelevant answers; reference to the man actually intending to attack her

greatly in their social cognitive abilities. Those who have the sharpest social cognitive skills tend to be socially active and involved in meaningful social roles such as spouse, grandparent, church member, and worker (Dolen & Bearison, 1982; Hess, Osowski, & Leclerc, 2005). It is mainly when elderly people become socially isolated or inactive that their social cognitive skills become rusty.

In sum, social cognition takes shape in infancy through precursors of a theory of mind such as joint attention and pretend play; a desire psychology at age 2; and then a belief–desire psychology at age 4, when children pass false belief tasks thanks to both nature (normal neurological functioning and cognitive maturation) and nurture (social interaction using language). Children's descriptions of other people progress from a focus on physical features and activities to a focus on inner traits to the integration of trait descriptions; and social perspective-taking skills improve with age. Social cognitive skills then often improve during early and middle adulthood and hold up well in old age if adults remain socially active.

Social cognitive skills hold up well when older adults remain socially active like Gwendolyn Connally, age 93, on the right, who is enjoying the beat of the disco song "Freak Out" during a dance competition at her senior center.

© AP Photo/Plain Dealer, Lisa DeJong

Having examined some important and dramatic changes in social cognition over the life span, we are well positioned to focus on an important area of development in which social cognitive skills play a crucial role: moral development. Along the way, we will see how theory-of-mind and social perspective-taking skills help shape thinking about right and wrong.

Checking Mastery

1. Sharon wonders if Baby Ben, age 18 months, is on his way to developing a theory of mind. What four developments in infancy can you point to as early precursors of a theory of mind?

2. If you were trying to make sure a deaf child, Luis, develops a theory of mind, what kinds of experiences would you try to provide him?

3. What breakthrough in social perspective-taking skills is achieved at about age 8 to age 10?

Making Connections

1. Eavesdrop on a conversation in which your friends talk about people, and write down any statements in which they refer to people's beliefs, desires, intentions, and the like in attempting to account for someone's behavior. What evidence do you see that your friends have and use a theory of mind?

2. Imagine what would have happened if you had started college without a theory of mind. Identify three possible problems that might have developed for you.

13.2 Perspectives on Moral Development

Although we could debate endlessly what **morality** is (see Gibbs, 2010; Turiel, 2006), most of us might agree that it involves the ability to distinguish right from wrong, to act on this distinction, and to experience pride when we do the right things and guilt or shame when we do not. Accordingly, three basic components of morality have been of interest to developmental scientists:

1. The *affective*, or emotional, component consists of the feelings (guilt, concern for others' feelings, and so on) that surround right or wrong actions and that motivate moral thoughts and actions.
2. The *cognitive* component centers on how we conceptualize right and wrong and make decisions about how to behave, drawing on social cognitive skills such as role taking.
3. The *behavioral* component reflects how we behave when, for example, we experience the temptation to cheat or are called upon to help a needy person.

Major theoretical perspectives on moral development focus on different aspects of morality. So in this section we look at what psychoanalytic theory and later perspectives emphasizing emotions say about moral affect, what cognitive developmental theory says about moral cognition or reasoning, and what social learning (or social cognitive) theory reveals about moral behavior. Then we examine morality from a broad, evolutionary perspective.

Moral Affect: Psychoanalytic Theory and Beyond

What kind of **moral affect,** or emotion related to matters of right and wrong, do you feel if you contemplate cheating or lying? Chances are you experience such negative feelings as shame, guilt, anxiety, and fear of being detected—feelings that keep you from doing what you know is wrong. You may also experience disgust or righteous anger when witnessing harmful acts and injustices (Tangney, Stuewig, & Mashek, 2007). Positive emotions, such as pride and self-satisfaction when you have done the right thing and admiration or gratitude when you witness moral acts, are also an important part of morality (Turiel, 2006). Moral emotions, both positive and negative, require being able to evaluate whether you or others have exceeded or fallen short of standards of behavior (Tangney, Stuewig, & Mashek, 2007). We are generally motivated to avoid negative moral emotions and to experience positive ones by acting in moral ways.

Empathy is the vicarious experiencing of another person's feelings (for example, smiling at another person's good fortune or experiencing another person's distress). Although it is not a specific emotion, it is an emotional process believed to be especially important in moral development by theorists such as Martin Hoffman, whom we will encounter later (Hoffman, 2000, 2008; Tangney, Stuewig, & Mashek, 2007). Empathizing with individuals who are suffering—not only taking their perspective but also feeling their pain—can motivate **prosocial behavior**—positive social acts, such as helping or sharing, that reflect concern for the welfare of others. Empathy can also keep us from harming others; if the campers in the chapter opener had really felt Edward's distress, they might have refrained from picking on him.

When do children begin to experience moral emotions? Sigmund Freud's (1960) psychoanalytic theory offered an answer (see Chapter 2). As you will recall, Freud believed that the *superego*, or conscience, has the important task of ensuring that any plans formed by the rational ego to gratify the id's selfish urges are morally acceptable. The superego is formed during the phallic stage (ages 3–6), when children are presumed to experience an emotional conflict over their love for the other-sex parent and resolve it by identifying with the same-sex parent, taking on the parent's moral standards as his or her own. Having a superego, then, is like having a parent inside your head—there, even when your parent is not, to tell you what is right or wrong and to arouse emotions such as shame and guilt if you so much as think about doing wrong. The only problem is that the specifics of Freud's theory are largely unsupported:

- Cold, threatening, and punitive parents who make their children anxious about losing their parents' love do not raise morally mature youngsters; instead, as modern psychoanalytic thinkers appreciate, children form strong consciences when they are securely attached to warm and responsive parents (Hoffman, 2000).
- Males do not appear to have stronger superegos than females, as Freud predicted they would based on their intense fear of castration and therefore stronger motivation to internalize parental values; if anything, females are more able to resist temptation (Silverman, 2003).
- Moral development begins well before the phallic stage and extends long after age 6 or 7.

Although the particulars of Freud's theory of moral development lack support, his main themes are taken very seriously today, as you will see shortly, because research has shown that: (1) moral emotions are an important part of morality and motivate of moral behavior, (2) early relationships with parents contribute to moral development, and (3) children must somehow internalize moral standards if they are to behave morally even

Learning to resist the temptation to break moral rules (here, one about taking turns) is an important part of moral development.

when no authority figure is present to detect and punish their misbehavior (Kochanska & Aksan, 2006; Turiel, 2006). As we will see later, Martin Hoffman (2000) is a modern theorist who emphasizes the emotional side of morality. He believes that even young infants show a capacity for empathy, which then becomes more sophisticated with age with the help of social cognitive development and serves as a major motivator of moral behavior.

Moral Reasoning: Cognitive Developmental Theory

Cognitive developmental theorists study morality by looking at the development of **moral reasoning**—the thinking process involved in deciding whether an act is right or wrong. These theorists assume that moral development depends on social cognitive development, particularly social perspective-taking skills that allow us to picture how our victims might react to our misdeeds or how people in distress must feel. These skills also allow us to get beyond our egocentrism to construct a concept of **reciprocity**, or equal give and take between the parties in a relationship that makes us ask whether what looks fair or just from our own point of view would look equally fair from other people's points of view (Gibbs, 2010).

Moral reasoning is said to progress through an invariant sequence—a fixed and universal order of stages, each of which represents a consistent way of thinking about moral issues that is different from the stage preceding or following it. To cognitive developmental theorists, what is of interest is *how* we decide what to do, not what we decide or what we actually do. A young child and an adult may both decide not to steal a pen, but the reasons they give for their decision may be entirely different. Jean Piaget paved the way for the influential theory of moral development put forth by Lawrence Kohlberg.

Piaget's View

Piaget (1965) studied children's concepts of rules by asking Swiss children about their games of marbles and explored children's concepts of justice by presenting them with moral dilemmas to ponder. For example, he told children about two boys: John, who accidentally knocked over a tray of 15 cups when coming to dinner as requested, and Henry, who broke only 1 cup when sneaking jam from the cupboard. The key question Piaget posed was which child was naughtier, and why.

Based on children's responses to such questions, Piaget formulated a theory of moral development that included a premoral period and two moral stages:

- **Premoral period.** During the preschool years, children show little awareness or understanding of rules and cannot be considered moral beings.
- **Heteronomous morality.** Children 6 to 10 years old take rules seriously, believing that they are handed down by parents and other authority figures and are sacred and unalterable (the term *heteronomous* means under the rule of another). They also judge rule violations as wrong based on the extent of damage done, not paying much attention to whether the violator had good or bad intentions.

Moral dilemma: Do you think a doctor should give a pain-ridden and terminal patient a drug that would hasten her death if she asks for it? Amelie Van Esbeen, pictured in her bed in a home for the elderly in Belgium, thought so. The 93-year-old went on a hunger strike when her request for mercy killing was denied. She had already tried to commit suicide.

© JORGE DIRKX/epa/Corbis

- **Autonomous morality.** At age 10 or 11, Piaget said, most children enter a final stage of moral development in which they begin to appreciate that rules are agreements between individuals—agreements that can be changed through a consensus of those individuals. In judging actions, they pay more attention to whether the person's intentions were good or bad than to the consequences of his act; thus, they see Henry, the misbehaving boy who broke 1 cup, as naughtier than John, the well-intentioned boy who broke 15.

Kohlberg's View

Inspired by Piaget's pioneering work, Lawrence Kohlberg (1963, 1981, 1984; Colby & Kohlberg, 1987) formulated a highly influential cognitive developmental theory of moral development. Kohlberg began his work by asking 10-, 13-, and 16-year-old boys questions about various moral dilemmas to assess how they thought about these issues. Careful analysis of the responses led Kohlberg to conclude that moral growth progresses through a universal and invariant sequence of three broad moral levels, each of which is composed of two distinct stages. Each stage grows out of the preceding stage and represents a more complex way of thinking about moral issues.

Stages of Moral Reasoning. Think about how you would respond to the following moral dilemma posed by Kohlberg and his colleagues (Colby et al., 1983, p. 79):

There was a woman who had very bad cancer, and there was no treatment known to medicine that would save her. Her doctor, Dr. Jefferson, knew that she had only about 6 months to live. She was in terrible pain, but she was so weak that a good dose of a pain killer like ether or morphine would make her die sooner. She was delirious and almost crazy with pain, and in her calm periods she would ask Dr. Jefferson to give her enough ether to kill her. She said she couldn't stand the pain and she was going to die in a few months anyway. Although he knows that mercy killing is against the law, the doctor thinks about granting her request.

Should Dr. Jefferson give her the drug that would make her die? Why or why not? Should the woman have the right to make the final decision? Why or why not? These are among the questions that people are asked after hearing the dilemma. You may want to answer them for yourself before reading further so that you can then analyze your own moral thinking. Remember, Kohlberg's goal is to understand how an individual thinks, not whether she is for or against providing the woman with the drug. Individuals at each stage of moral reasoning might endorse either of the alternative courses of action, but for different reasons. Following are Kohlberg's three levels of moral reasoning, and the two stages within each level.

Level 1: Preconventional Morality. At the level of **preconventional morality**, rules are external to the self rather than internalized. The child conforms to rules imposed by authority figures to avoid punishment or to obtain personal rewards. The perspective of the self dominates: What is right is what one can get away with or what is personally satisfying.

- *Stage 1: Punishment-and-Obedience Orientation.* The goodness or badness of an act depends on its consequences. The child will obey authorities to avoid punishment but may not consider an act wrong if it will not be punished. The greater the harm done or the more severe the punishment, the more "bad" the act is.
- *Stage 2: Instrumental Hedonism.* A person at the second stage of moral development conforms to rules to gain rewards or satisfy personal needs. There is some concern for the perspectives of others, but it is motivated by the hope of benefit in return. "You scratch my back and I'll scratch yours" and "an eye for an eye" are the guiding philosophies.

Level 2: Conventional Morality. At the level of **conventional morality**, the individual has internalized many moral values. He strives to obey the rules set by others (parents, peers, the government), at first to win their approval, later to maintain social order. The perspectives of other people are clearly recognized and given serious consideration.

- *Stage 3: "Good Boy" or "Good Girl" Morality.* What is right is now what pleases, helps, or is approved of by others. People are often judged by their intentions; "meaning well" is valued, and being "nice" is important. Other people's feelings, not just one's own, should be considered. At its best, Stage 3 thinking involves reciprocity—a simple Golden Rule morality of doing unto someone else what you would want done unto you.
- *Stage 4: Authority and Social Order–Maintaining Morality.* Now what is right is what conforms to the rules of legitimate authorities and is good for society as a whole. The principle of reciprocity becomes more abstract and is applied on a broader societal level. The reason for conforming is not so much a fear

of punishment as a belief that rules and laws maintain a social order worth preserving. Doing one's duty and respecting law and order are valued.

Level 3: Postconventional Morality. At the final level of moral reasoning, **postconventional morality**, the individual defines what is right in terms of broad principles of justice that have validity apart from the views of particular authority figures. The individual may distinguish between what is morally right and what is legal, recognizing that some laws—for example, the racial segregation laws that Dr. Martin Luther King, Jr., challenged—violate basic moral principles. Thus, the person transcends the perspectives of particular social groups or authorities and begins to take the perspective of *all* individuals.

- *Stage 5: Morality of Contract, Individual Rights, and Democratically Accepted Law.* At this "social contract" stage, there is an understanding of the underlying purposes served by laws and a concern that rules should be arrived at through a democratic consensus so that they express the will of the majority and maximize social welfare. Whereas the person at stage 4 is unlikely to challenge an established law, the moral reasoner at stage 5 might call for democratic change in a law that compromises basic rights.
- *Stage 6: Morality of Individual Principles of Conscience.* At this "highest" stage of moral reasoning, the individual defines right and wrong on the basis of self-generated principles that are broad and universal in application. The stage 6 thinker does not just make up whatever principles she chooses. She discovers, through reflection, abstract principles of respect for all individuals and for their rights that all religions or moral authorities would view as moral. Kohlberg (1981) described stage 6 thinking as a kind of "moral musical chairs" in which the person facing a moral dilemma is able to take the "chair," or perspective, of each person and group and social system that could potentially be affected by a decision and to arrive at a solution that would be regarded as just from every chair. Stage 6 is Kohlberg's vision of ideal moral reasoning, but it is so rarely observed that Kohlberg stopped attempting to measure its existence.

In ● **Table 13.1**, we present examples of how people at the preconventional, conventional, and postconventional levels might reason about the mercy-killing dilemma. As you can see, progress through Kohlberg's stages of moral reasoning depends partly on the development of social perspective-taking abilities. Specifically, as individuals become more able to consider perspectives other than their own, moral reasoning progresses from an egocentric focus on personal welfare at the preconventional level, to a concern with the perspectives of other people (parents, friends, and other members of society) at the conventional level, and to an ability to coordinate multiple perspectives and determine what is right from the perspective of all people at the postconventional level (Carpendale, 2000).

Influences on Moral Thinking. Whereas Freud emphasized the role of parents in moral development, Kohlberg, like Piaget before him, believed that the two main influences on moral de-

Give the Drug	Do Not Give the Drug
Preconventional Morality	**Preconventional Morality**
Stage 1: The doctor should give the terminally ill woman a drug that will kill her because there is little chance that he will be found out and punished. **Stage 2:** He should give her the drug; he might benefit from the gratitude of her family if he does what she wants. He should think of it as the right thing to do if it serves his purposes to be for mercy killing.	**Stage 1:** The doctor runs a big risk of losing his license and being thrown in prison if he gives her the drug. **Stage 2:** He has little to gain by taking such a big chance. If the woman wants to kill herself, that is her business, but why should he help her if he stands to gain little in return?
Conventional Morality	**Conventional Morality**
Stage 3: Most people would understand that the doctor was motivated by concern for the woman's welfare rather than by self-interest. They would be able to forgive him for what was essentially an act of kindness. **Stage 4:** The doctor should give the woman the drug because of the Hippocratic oath, which spells out a doctor's duty to relieve suffering. This oath is binding and should be taken seriously by all doctors.	**Stage 3:** Most people are likely to disapprove of mercy killing. The doctor would clearly lose the respect of his colleagues if he administered the drug. A good person simply would not do this. **Stage 4:** Mercy killing like this is against the laws that doctors are obligated to uphold. The Bible is another compelling authority, and it says, "Thou shalt not kill." The doctor simply cannot take the law into his own hands; rather, he has a duty to uphold the law.
Postconventional Morality	**Postconventional Morality**
Stage 5: Although most of our laws have a sound basis in moral principle, laws against mercy killing do not. The doctor's act is morally justified because it relieves the suffering of an agonized human without harming other people. Yet if he breaks the law in the service of a greater good, he should still be willing to be held legally accountable because society would be damaged if everyone simply ignored laws they do not agree with. **Stage 6:** We must consider the effects of this act on everyone concerned—the doctor, the dying woman, other terminally ill people, and all people everywhere. Basic moral principle dictates that all people have a right to dignity and self-determination as long as others are not harmed by their decisions. Assuming that no one else will be hurt, then, the dying woman has a right to live and die as she chooses. The doctor may be doing right if he respects her integrity as a person and saves her, her family, and all of society from needless suffering.	**Stage 5:** The laws against mercy killing protect citizens from harm at the hands of unscrupulous doctors and selfish relatives and should be upheld because they serve a positive function for society. If the laws were to be changed through the democratic process, that might be another thing. But right now the doctor can do the most good for society by adhering to them. **Stage 6:** If we truly adhere to the principle that human life should be valued above all else and all lives should be valued equally, it is morally wrong to "play God" and decide that some lives are worth living and others are not. Before long, we would have a world in which no life has value.

velopment are cognitive growth and social interactions with equals. Regarding cognitive growth, reaching the conventional level of moral reasoning and becoming concerned about living up to the moral standards of parents and society requires the ability to take other people's perspectives, and gaining the capacity for postconventional or "principled" moral reasoning requires still more cognitive growth—namely, a solid command of formal-operational thinking (Tomlinson-Keasey & Keasey, 1974; Walker, 1980; and see Chapter 7).

The social interactions that count involve taking the perspectives of others and experiencing growth-promoting cogni-tive disequilibrium when one's own ideas conflict with those of other people. Piaget and Kohlberg both maintained that interactions with peers or equals, in which we must work out differences between our own and others' perspectives through negotiation, contribute more to moral growth than one-sided interactions with adult authority figures in which children are expected to bow to the adult's power. Discussions of moral issues with peers *do* contribute to moral growth, especially when peers challenge our ideas, but Piaget and Kohlberg probably underestimated the importance of parents in moral development, as we will see (Walker, Hennig, & Krettenauer, 2000).

Growth-promoting social interaction also comes through advanced schooling. Going to college not only contributes to cognitive growth but also exposes students to diverse perspectives (Pratt et al., 1991). Finally, participating in a complex, diverse, and democratic society can stimulate moral development by encouraging people to weigh the opinions of many groups and appreciate that laws reflect a consensus of the citizens.

So Kohlberg maintained that progress from preconventional to conventional to postconventional moral reasoning is most likely to occur if the individual has acquired the necessary cognitive skills (particularly perspective-taking skills and, later, formal-operational thinking) and has appropriate social interactions, especially discussions with peers, involvement in higher education, and participation in democratic governance.

Moral Behavior: Social Learning Theory

Social learning theorists such as Albert Bandura (1991, 2002; Bandura et al., 2001), whose social cognitive theory was introduced in Chapter 2, have been primarily interested in the behavioral component of morality—in what we actually do when faced with temptation or with an opportunity to behave prosocially. These theorists say that moral behavior is learned in the same way that other social behaviors are learned: through observational learning and reinforcement and punishment principles. They also consider moral behavior to be strongly influenced by situational factors—for example, by how closely a professor watches exam takers, by whether jewelry items are on the counter or behind glass in a department store. Due to situational influences, what we do (moral performance) is not always reflective of our internalized values and standards (moral competence).

Applying his social cognitive perspective, Bandura goes on to emphasize that moral cognition is linked to moral action through *self-regulatory mechanisms* that involve monitoring and evaluating our own actions (or anticipated actions), disapproving of ourselves when we contemplate doing wrong, and approving of ourselves when we behave responsibly or humanely. By applying consequences to ourselves in this way, we become able to exert self-control, inhibit urges to misbehave, and keep our behavior in line with internalized standards of moral behavior. Sometimes this system of moral self-regulation can triumph over strong situational influences pushing us to do wrong. However, according to Bandura we have also devised mechanisms of **moral disengagement** that allow us to avoid condemning ourselves when we engage in immoral behavior, even though we know the difference between right and wrong. For example, a store clerk who feels underpaid and mistreated by his employer may convince himself that he is justified in pilfering items from the store, or people may disengage morally from the use of military force by their country by dehumanizing their foes (McAlister, Bandura, & Owen, 2006). Many of us learn the right moral standards, but some people hold themselves strictly to those standards while others find ways to disengage morally and slither out from under guilt. Those individuals who have perfected techniques of moral disengagement tend to be the ones who engage in the most antisocial and unethical behavior (Detert, Treviño, & Sweitzer, 2008; Paciello et al., 2008).

How many students in your class would admit to having cheated in high school? Fifty years ago, only about one in five college students admitted to it, but in recent surveys at least three in five, and often more, admit to having cheated in high school (Crary, 2008; Kleiner & Lord, 1999). Cheating is also rampant in college and graduate school; 56% of MBA students admit to cheating or plagiarizing in the past year (McCabe, Butterfield, & Trevino, 2006). Why do you think cheating is so rampant today?

The Functions of Morality: Evolutionary Theory

Finally, evolutionary theorists such as Dennis Krebs and others have contributed to our understanding of moral development (Fry, 2006; Gintis et al., 2008; Krebs, 2005, 2008). Their focus is on morality and human nature—on how moral thought, emotion, and behavior may have helped humans adapt to their environments over the course of evolution. Just as having a theory of mind helps humans get along with others and adapt to living in groups, prosocial behaviors such as cooperation and altruism may have evolved because our ancestors were better able to obtain food and protect themselves from harm if they worked together than if they went it alone. Similarly, mechanisms for controlling and inhibiting harm-doing may have evolved because they enhanced survival (Hauser, 2006). Recent studies of social animals like dogs and wolves suggest that they have "moral codes" that govern what is fair and what is not when they play together as pups and live together as adults (Pierce & Bekoff, 2009). Those who don't play by the rules become social outcasts and as a result do not live as long as their rule-abiding peers.

The phrase "survival of the fittest" implies raw selfishness, though. How can evolutionary theorists explain how humans evolved to be altruistic when altruists who sacrifice their lives for others die rather than pass on their genes? Evolutionary theorists have argued that it can be in our genetic self-interest to act altruistically toward kin because they will pass on the family's genes if we help them survive (Verbeek, 2006). Even helping nonrelatives may be adaptive if we have reason to believe that the help we give will be reciprocated. Cooperating with other people to obtain resources that the individual could not obtain alone also makes good genetic sense, as do abiding by society's rules in order to avoid punishment and punishing people who *do* violate society's rules (Krebs, 2008).

So, whereas Freud emphasized the dark, selfish side of human nature, Krebs (2008) and other evolutionary theorists argue that humans have an evolved genetic makeup that predisposes them not only to behave antisocially but also to empathize with their fellow humans and to behave prosocially and morally. Indeed, humans may be a uniquely altruistic species. Studies of chimpanzees suggest that they too show empathy for injured peers and engage in a variety of cooperative behaviors. However, they do not seem willing to benefit others at a cost to themselves as humans do (Silk et al., 2005). In further support of the evolutionary perspective, a primitive form of empathy is evident in humans from birth, as we will discover later.

To highlight differences among the four theoretical perspectives on moral development we have discussed, consider how different theorists might try to predict whether a teenager (call him Bart) will cheat on his upcoming math test. Freud would want to know whether Bart developed a strong superego and sense of guilt; Kohlberg would be more interested in the stage at which he typically reasons about moral dilemmas. Both the psychoanalytic perspective and the cognitive developmental perspective view morality as a traitlike quality that consistently influences an individual's judgments and actions.

By contrast, Bandura's social cognitive theory would see it this way: If Bart's parents have consistently reinforced moral behavior and punished misbehavior and have served as models of moral behavior, if he has well-developed self-regulatory mechanisms that cause him to take responsibility for his actions rather than to disengage morally, and if situational forces discourage cheating, Bart is likely to behave in morally acceptable ways.

Finally, evolutionary theorists like Krebs might look into the adaptive functions that cheating—or refraining from cheating—serve for the individual and his or her social group. Like Bandura, Krebs might look at the classroom environment and conclude that so much cheating is going on that it is almost in Bart's self-interest to cheat too—or that the professor and students in the class have developed good control systems to discourage cheating. Moral emotion, thought, and behavior would all be considered (see ● Table 13.2 for a comparison of theories).

We are now ready to trace the development of morality from infancy to old age. Our coverage charts the development of the self as a moral being, examining moral affect, cognition, and behavior over the life span.

Checking Mastery

1. What are the three components of morality, and what is a theory of moral development that emphasizes each?

2. What is the main difference between conventional and preconventional moral reasoning about why stealing is wrong?

3. How do evolutionary theorists differ from Freud regarding the nature of human beings?

● TABLE 13.2 COMPARISON OF THEORETICAL PERSPECTIVES ON MORAL DEVELOPMENT

Perspective	Theorist(s)	Focus	Message
Psychoanalytic theory	Freud	Moral emotion	Early parenting and emotional conflicts forge the superego and guilt.
Cognitive developmental theory	Piaget Kohlberg	Moral reasoning	Cognitive maturation and experience with peers bring stagelike changes in thinking about moral issues.
Social learning theory	Bandura	Moral behavior	Observational learning, reinforcement, self-regulation processes, and situational influences affect what we do.
Evolutionary theory	Krebs	Moral emotion, reasoning, and behavior	Humans have evolved so that either immoral or moral behavior can be in their genetic self-interest depending on the context.

Making Connections

1. A preconventional thinker, a conventional thinker, and a post-conventional thinker all face a moral dilemma the night before the final examination: A friend has offered them a key to the examination. Should they use it? Provide examples of the reasoning you might expect at each of the three main levels of moral development—one argument in favor of cheating and one against it at each level. Are any of these arguments especially easy or difficult to make? Why?

2. Jamal decides to become a kidney donor and live the rest of his life with only one kidney so that his brother Malcolm can live. How do you think Freud, Kohlberg, Bandura, and Krebs would explain his altruistic action?

13.3 The Infant

Do infants have a sense of right or wrong? If a baby takes a teddy bear that belongs to another child, would you label the act stealing? If an infant bashes another child on the head with a sippy cup, would you insist that the infant be put on trial for assault? Of course not. We tend to view infants as **amoral**—that is, lacking any sense of morality. We do not believe that infants are capable of evaluating their behavior in relation to moral standards, and so we do not hold them responsible for wrongs they commit (although we certainly attempt to prevent them from harming others). Nor do we expect them to be "good" when we are not around to watch them. Yet it is now clear that infants are predisposed to be empathic, prosocial beings and learn many important moral lessons during their first 2 years of life.

Early Moral Training

Moral socialization begins early. Roger Burton (1984) relates how his daughter Ursula, age 1, was so taken by the candy that she and her sisters had gathered on Halloween that she snatched some from her sisters' bags. The sisters immediately said, "No, that's mine," and conveyed their outrage in the strongest terms. A week later, the sisters again found some of their candy in Ursula's bag and raised a fuss, and it was their mother's turn to explain the rules to Ursula. The problem continued until finally Burton came upon Ursula looking at some forbidden candy. Ursula looked up and said, "No, this is Maria's, not Ursula's" (p. 199).

It is through such social learning experiences, accumulated over years, that children come to understand and internalize moral rules and standards. Infants begin to learn that their actions have consequences, some good, some bad; they learn a lot by watching their companions' reactions to their missteps (Thompson, Meyer, & McGinley, 2006). They also begin to learn to associate negative emotions with violating rules and to exert self-control, inhibiting their impulses when they are tempted to violate rules (Kochanska, 1993, 2002). By 18–24 months, children are already beginning to show visible

signs of distress such as anticipating disapproval when they break things, spill their drinks, or otherwise violate standards of behavior (Cole, Barrett, & Zahn-Waxler, 1992; Kagan, 1981). Made to think that they have caused a doll's head to fall off, some toddlers even show signs of guilt, as opposed to mere distress, as evidenced by frantic attempts to make amends (Kochanska, Casey, & Fukumoto, 1995). Amazingly, even younger infants seem capable of judging other people by their moral actions, as shown in Exploration Box 13.2.

Grazyna Kochanska and her colleagues have found that forming a secure parent–infant attachment is the best way to get moral socialization off to a good start (Kochanska, Barry, Stellern, & O'Bleness, 2009). When the parent–infant relationship is insecure at 15 months of age, parents' attempts to control the child through power assertion are met by resentment and opposition at age 4, which paves the way for aggressive, disruptive behavior by age 5. When infants are securely attached to their parents, they tolerate quite well even heavy-handed and coercive attempts by their parents to control them and do not develop conduct problems.

Kochanska (1997, 2002) maintains that the real secret to successful moral socialization is development of a **mutually responsive orientation** between caregiver and child—a close, emotionally positive, and cooperative relationship in which child and caregiver care about each other and are sensitive to each other's needs (Kochanska & Aksan, 2006). Such a relationship makes children trust their caregivers and want to comply with their rules and adopt their values and standards. These children then learn moral emotions such as guilt and empathy, develop the capacity for advanced moral reasoning, and become able to resist temptation even when no one is around to catch them.

Parents can also foster early moral development by discussing their toddlers' behavior in an open way, expressing their feelings, and evaluating their children's acts as good or bad (Laible & Thompson, 2000). By establishing a mutually responsive orientation, working toward mutual understandings of what is and is not acceptable, and discussing the emotional consequences of the child's behavior, parents help infants and toddlers develop a conscience (Emde et al., 1991; Thompson, Meyer, & McGinley, 2006).

Empathy and Prosocial Behavior

Not only are infants capable of internalizing rules of behavior, but they are not so selfish, egocentric, and unconcerned about other people as Freud, Piaget, Kohlberg, and many other theorists have assumed. Rather, some of their behavior supports Krebs's view that empathy and prosocial behavior are part of our evolutionary heritage (Tomasello, 2009).

Start at birth: even newborns display a primitive form of empathy, becoming distressed by the cries of other newborns (Hastings, Zahn-Waxler, & McShane, 2006; Hoffman, 2000; Martin & Clark, 1982). It is unlikely that young infants distinguish between another infant's distress and their own, however. From age 1 to age 2, according to Martin Hoffman (2000, 2008),

Are Infants Judging Us?

Although infants are too young to be held morally accountable when they harm others, do they recognize the difference between moral and immoral behavior in other people? J. Kiley Hamlin, Karen Wynn, and Paul Bloom (2007) set up a scenario in which a round block with eyes tried a couple of times to climb a hill and then on the third try was either helped up the hill by another block with eyes or pushed down the hill by another block with eyes, as shown in the drawing. Infants 6 and 10 months of age were then given an opportunity to reach for either the "helper" or the "hinderer."

A wopping 26 of 28 preferred the helper to the hinderer. These infants had apparently formed an impression of the block character based on its behavior toward the hill climber (and also must have understood the hill climber's intention to reach the summit). It was not just that infants pre-ferred seeing a push up the hill to seeing a push down the hill, either: They showed no preference for one direction of movement or the other when the blocks were just blocks—missing the eyes that made them look like people.

The researchers suggest that a capacity to evaluate other people's social behavior may be evident so early in life because it is part of our evolutionary heritage. It may have evolved because it helps us distinguish be-tween individuals who are likely to cooperate with us and individuals who may be out to get us. This capacity to size people up may also pave the way for judging the rightness or wrongness of peo-ple's actions later in life. We cannot be sure, of course, that reac-tions to block figures translate into reactions to real people. However, subsequent re-search suggests that 21-month-old infants are more likely to help an adult who intended to give them a toy (but failed) than one who pulled it out of their reach to tease them (Dunfield & Kuhlmeier, 2010). So to be on the safe side, watch what you do around in-fants: They may be judging you as a social partner!

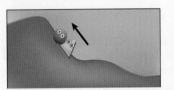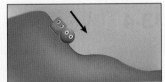

On the left, the climber (red circle) is pushed up the hill by the "helper" (yellow triangle); on the right, the climber (red circle) is pushed down the hill by the "hinderer" (blue square). Babies are more attracted to the helper than to the hinderer. SOURCE: Hamlin, J. K., Wynn, K., & Bloom, P. (2007). Social evaluation by preverbal infants. *Nature, 450,* 557–560.

infants become capable of a truer form of empathy that motivates helping and other forms of moral behavior. Toddlers begin to understand that someone else's distress is different from their own, and they try to comfort the person in distress. Consider some concrete examples described by Hoffman (2000). One 10-month-old, watching a peer cry, looked sad and buried her head in her mother's lap, as she often did when she was dis-tressed. A 2-year-old brought his own teddy bear to comfort a distressed friend; when that failed, he offered the friend's teddy instead, beginning to show an ability to take the perspective of the friend.

Carolyn Zahn-Waxler and her colleagues (1992) report that more than half of the 13- to 15-month-old infants they observed engaged in at least one act of prosocial behavior—helping, shar-ing, expressing concern, comforting, and so on. These behaviors became increasingly common from age 1 to age 2, when all but one child in the study acted prosocially. Similarly, when adults drop things on the floor, 18-month-olds normally help with the pickup (Tomasello, 2009). With age, according to Hoffman (2000, 2008), empathy becomes less egocentric and more sophis-ticated as cognitive processes, including the child's developing social perspective-taking skills, shape it into a variety of moral emotions such as guilt, sympathy, and eventually a sense of injus-tice (see also Eisenberg, Spinrad, & Sadovsky, 2006; Gibbs, 2010). Some children become more empathic and prosocial than others as a result of both genetic and environmental influ-ences (Knafo et al., 2008).

Before they are age 2, toddlers show evidence of early moral sensibilities when they attempt to comfort distressed peers.

Checking Mastery

1. What is Grazyna Kochanska's message to parents who want their infants to become moral beings?

2. According to Martin Hoffman, when is empathy first evident in infancy and how does it change thereafter?

Making Connections

1. Suppose you want to study how toddlers in a day care center react when their peers are upset. How might you distinguish between true empathy for a classmate and personal distress in reaction to the classmate's crying?

13.4 The Child

Research on moral development during childhood has explored how children of different ages think about moral issues and how parents can raise moral children. This research shows that children's moral thinking is more sophisticated than Piaget and Kohlberg believed and that parents can have a big impact on their children's moral development.

Thinking through Kohlberg's Dilemmas

As we saw earlier, Piaget believed that the shift from heteronomous to autonomous morality, and thus to a more complete understanding of rules and of the importance of assessing a wrongdoer's intentions, does not occur until age 10 or 11. The hypothetical moral dilemmas that Lawrence Kohlberg devised to assess stages of moral reasoning (for example, the mercy-killing dilemma presented earlier) were intended primarily for adolescents and adults; the youngest individuals Kohlberg studied were age 10.

As a result, Kohlberg did not have much to say about children except that they are mostly preconventional moral reasoners. They take an egocentric perspective on morality and define as right those acts that are rewarded and as wrong those acts that are punished (Colby et al., 1983). At best, older school-age children are beginning to make the transition to conventional moral reasoning by displaying a stage 3 concern with being a good boy or a good girl who takes others' perspectives and is concerned with others' approval. As we will now see, both Piaget and Kohlberg underestimated children. Other researchers have looked more closely at the moral reasoning of children and find that they engage in some sophisticated thinking about right and wrong from an early age.

Weighing Intentions

Consider Piaget's claim that young children (heteronomous moral thinkers) judge acts as right or wrong on the basis of their consequences, whereas older children (autonomous thinkers) judge on the basis of the intentions that guided the act. His

■ **FIGURE 13.2** Examples of drawings used by Sharon Nelson to convey a character's intentions to preschool children. Here you see negative intent and a negative consequence. SOURCE: From Nelson, S. A., Factors influencing young children's use of motives and outcomes as moral criteria, *Child Development, 51,* pp. 823–829. Copyright © 1980. Reprinted with permission of John Wiley & Sons, Inc.

moral-decision story about the two boys and the cups—asking whether a child who causes a small amount of damage in the service of bad intentions is naughtier than a child who causes a large amount of damage despite good intentions—was flawed in that it confounded goodness of intentions and amount of damage done.

Sharon Nelson (1980) overcame this flaw in an interesting experiment in which 3-year-olds listened to stories about a boy throwing a ball to a playmate. The boy's motive was described as *good* (his friend had nothing to play with) or *bad* (the boy was mad at his friend), and the consequences of his act were either *positive* (the friend caught the ball and was happy to play with it) or *negative* (the ball hit his friend in the head and made him cry). To make the task simpler, Nelson showed children drawings of what happened (see ■ **Figure 13.2** for an example).

Not surprisingly, the 3-year-olds in the study judged acts that had positive consequences more favorably than acts that caused harm. However, they also judged the well-intentioned child who had wanted to play more favorably than the child who intended to hurt his friend, regardless of the consequences of his actions. Apparently, then, even young children can base their moral judgments on both a person's intentions and the consequences of his act.

Overall, Piaget was correct to conclude that young children place less emphasis on the intentions behind actions than older children do (Lapsley, 2006). However, it is now clear that young children are capable of considering both intentions and consequences when they evaluate others' conduct.

Understanding Rules

Piaget also claimed that 6- to 10-year-old heteronomous children view rules as sacred prescriptions laid down by respected authority figures. These moral absolutes cannot be questioned or changed. However, Elliot Turiel (1978, 1983, 2006) has argued and observed that even young children distinguish sharply between different kinds of rules. Most importantly, they distinguish between **moral rules,** or standards that focus on the welfare and basic rights of individuals, and **social-conventional rules,** standards determined by social consensus that tell us what is appropriate in particular social settings. Moral rules include rules against hitting, stealing, lying, and otherwise harming others or violating their rights. Social-conventional rules are more like rules of social etiquette; they include the rules of games and school rules that forbid eating snacks in class or using the restroom without permission.

From their preschool years, children understand that moral rules are more compelling and unalterable than social-conventional rules (Smetana, 2006; Turiel, 2006). Judith Smetana (1981), for example, discovered that children as young as age 2 regard moral transgressions such as hitting, stealing, or refusing to share as more serious and deserving of punishment than social-conventional violations. Similarly, young children appreciate that hitting is wrong even if the teacher did not see it; even if the rules say hitting is okay; and whether it is done at home, at school, or in a faraway land with different laws. They also give the right reasons for their views, emphasizing the harm done by hitting (Killen & Smetana, 2008).

Piaget also claimed that 6- to 10-year-old children view any law laid down by adults as sacred. Instead, children appear to be quite capable of questioning adult authority (Tisak & Tisak, 1990). School-age children say it is fine for parents to enforce rules against stealing and other moral violations, but they believe that it can be inappropriate and unjustifiable for parents to arbitrarily restrict their children's friendship choices, which are viewed as a matter of personal choice. And they maintain that not even God can proclaim that stealing is morally right and make it so (Nucci & Turiel, 1993). In other words, school-age children will not blindly accept any dictate offered by an authority figure as legitimate.

Applying Theory of Mind

As you have probably guessed, children's moral thinking becomes quite a bit more sophisticated once they have the basics of a theory of mind down at about age 4. Showing that they understand that intentions matter, 4-year-old children who have a theory of mind and pass false belief tasks may cry, "I didn't mean it! I didn't mean it!" when they stand to be punished. Moreover, their understandings of a wrongdoer's beliefs at the time he committed a harmful act ("Spencer didn't know Lauren was in the box when he pushed it down the stairs!") influence their judgments about whether the act was intentional and therefore how bad it was (Chandler, Sokol, & Wainryb, 2000). Preschool children who pass theory-of-mind tasks are also more able than those who fail them to distinguish between lying (deliberately promoting false beliefs) and simply having one's facts wrong (Peterson & Siegal, 2002).

Theory-of-mind skills also help young children understand people's emotional reactions to behavior, an important consideration in judging right and wrong. At only 3 years, for example, children can use their emerging theory of mind to figure out that

Lewis, who likes tarantulas but fears puppies, will be upset if his friend gives him a puppy—and that it is therefore "bad" to give Lewis a puppy, even though it may be "nice" to give almost any other child a puppy (Helwig, Zelazo, & Wilson, 2001). Children who have mastered theory-of-mind tasks are also more attuned than those who have not to other people's feelings and welfare when they think through the morality of snatching a friend's toy or calling a friend a bad name (Dunn, Cutting, & Demetriou, 2000).

Overall, then, both Piaget and Kohlberg failed to appreciate how much moral growth takes place during early childhood. We now know that even preschool children are capable of judging acts as right or wrong according to whether the actor's intentions were good or bad; view only moral rules, not social-conventional rules, as absolute, sacred, and unchangeable; challenge adult authority when they believe it is illegitimate; and use their theories of mind to analyze the motives behind and the emotional consequences of actions.

Moral Socialization

How can parents best raise a child who can be counted on to behave morally in most situations? You have already seen that a secure attachment and a mutually responsive orientation between parent and child starting in infancy help. Social learning theorists like Bandura would also advise parents to reinforce moral behavior, punish immoral behavior (but mildly and with caution, as discussed in Chapter 2), and serve as models of moral behavior.

The important work of Martin Hoffman (2000) has provided additional insights into how to foster not only moral behavior but also moral thought and affect. As you saw earlier, Hoffman (2000) believes that empathy is a key motivator of moral behavior and that the key task in moral socialization, therefore, is to foster empathy. Many years ago, Hoffman (1970) reviewed the child-rearing literature to determine which approaches to discipline were associated with high levels of moral development. Three major approaches were compared:

1. **Love withdrawal.** Withholding attention, affection, or approval after a child misbehaves—in other words, creating anxiety by threatening a loss of reinforcement from parents.
2. **Power assertion.** Using power to threaten, chastise, administer spankings, take away privileges, and so on—in other words, using punishment.
3. **Induction.** Explaining to a child why the behavior is wrong and should be changed by emphasizing how it affects other people.

Suppose that little Angel has just put the beloved family cat through a cycle in the clothes dryer. Using love withdrawal, a parent might say, "How could you do something like that? I can't stand to look at you!" Using power assertion, a parent might say, "Get to your room this minute; you're going to get it." Using induction, a parent might say, "Angel, look how scared Fluffball is. You could have killed her, and you know how sad we'd be if she died." Induction, then, is a matter of providing rationales or ex-

A Case Study in Raising a Moral Child

It takes only a few observations at the day care center to see that Doug, father of 3-year-old Trina, has mastered everything developmental psychologists know about how to foster moral development. He is sensitive to his daughter's emotional needs, often staying when he drops her off in the morning until he is sure she is ready for him to leave. He asks her to look after the new teacher because it's her first day and she might need help. As they hug and kiss, he tells Trina how happy it makes him to get hugs and kisses from her.

One day, Doug witnessed a little boy grab an 18-month-old girl, causing her to cry. He separated the two children, comforted the girl, and explained to the boy that grabbing hurts and that the girl was crying because she was hurt. He asked the boy to say he was sorry and to give the girl a hug because it might make her feel better. Another day, he was telling some of the girls a story and told them how good it makes him feel to share with Trina's friends.

As you might predict, Trina is following in her father's footsteps. She frequently comforts children who cry when their mothers drop them off in the morning; regularly offers toys to children who are upset; often hugs and pats and holds the hand of a smaller, more timid girl; and cheerfully cleans up all the toys when play time is over. Her father has developed what Kochanska calls a mutually responsive orientation with her. He models and reinforces prosocial behavior, social perspective-taking skills, and empathy, talking about his feelings and those of other people and pointing out that antisocial behavior makes other people feel bad whereas prosocial behavior makes them feel good. Using the discipline technique that Martin Hoffman finds to be most effective, induction, he explains why hurtful behaviors are wrong by emphasizing their consequences for other people and fosters empathy in the process. And using proactive parenting strategies, he teaches his daughter about prosocial values. What might the world be like if it were full of model parents like Doug?

Martin Hoffman's formula for raising a moral child involves lots of induction and affection and only occasional power assertion.

planations that focus attention on the consequences of wrongdoing for other people (or cats).

Which approach best fosters moral development? Induction is more often positively associated with children's moral maturity than either love withdrawal or power assertion (Brody & Shaffer, 1982). In Hoffman's (2000) view, induction works well because it breeds empathy. Anticipating empathic distress if we contemplate harming someone keeps us from doing harm; empathizing with individuals in distress motivates us to help them.

Although expressing disappointment in a child's behavior can be effective on occasion, making a child worry that their parents' love can be withdrawn at any time usually is not effective (Patrick & Gibbs, 2007). The use of power assertion is more often associated with moral immaturity than with moral maturity. At the extreme, children whose parents are physically abusive feel less guilt and engage in more immoral behaviors such as stealing than other children (Koenig, Cicchetti, & Rogosch, 2004). But even frequent use of milder power tactics such as physical restraint and commands to keep young children from engaging in prohibited acts is generally ineffective (Kochanska, Aksan, & Nichols, 2003).

Despite evidence that power assertion interferes with the internalization of moral rules and the development of self-control and that physical punishment in particular can produce unwanted consequences such as anxiety and aggression, Hoffman (2000) concludes that mild power assertion tactics such as a forceful "No," a reprimand, or the taking away of privileges can be useful occasionally if they arouse some but not too much fear and motivate a child to pay close attention to the inductions that follow. Such careful uses of power assertion work best in the context of a loving and mutually responsive parent–child relationship. All in all, Hoffman's work provides a fairly clear picture of how parents can best contribute to the moral growth of their children. As he puts it, the winning formula is "a blend of frequent inductions, occasional power assertions, and a lot of affection" (Hoffman, 2000, p. 23).

Finally, effective parents use **proactive parenting strategies,** tactics designed to prevent misbehavior and therefore reduce the need for correction or discipline—techniques such as distracting young children from temptations and explicitly teaching older children values (Thompson, Meyer, & McGinley, 2006). In

Exploration Box 13.3, you can see in action a parent who illustrates several effective strategies for fostering moral growth.

Yet parents do not settle on one approach and use it all the time. Both the likelihood that a particular moral socialization technique will be used and its effectiveness depend on a host of factors such as the particular misdeed, child, parent, situation, and cultural context (Critchley & Sanson, 2006; Grusec, Goodnow, & Kuczynski, 2000). There is no one best discipline method for all occasions; instead, what may be most important is a parent's ability to maintain a high-quality relationship with his children and know which approach to use in which situation with which child (Grusec, 2006).

Consider just one example. A child's temperament turns out to be an important influence on how morally trainable she is and what motivates her to comply with parents' rules and requests (Thompson, Meyer, & McGinley, 2006). Grazyna Kochanska and her colleagues have found that children are likely to be easiest to socialize if (1) they are by temperament fearful or inhibited (see Chapter 11), and therefore are likely to experience guilt when they transgress, become appropriately distressed when they are disciplined, and want to avoid such distress in the future; and (2) they are capable of effortful control, and therefore are able to inhibit their urges to engage in wrongdoing (Kochanska, Barry, Jimenez, et al. 2009; Kochanska & Knaack, 2003; Kochanska, Murray, & Coy, 1997).

Fearful, inhibited children can be socialized through a gentle approach that capitalizes on their anxiety but does not terrorize them (Fowles & Kochanska, 2000). Children who are fearless or uninhibited do not respond to this gentle approach—but they do not respond to being treated harshly, either. Fearless children are most likely to learn to comply with rules and requests when the parent–child relationship is characterized by a mutually responsive orientation and the child is therefore motivated to please the parent and maintain a good relationship (Fowles & Kochanska, 2000; and see Kochanska, Aksan, & Joy, 2007). Here, then, is another example of the importance of the goodness of fit between a child's temperament and her social environment. Socialized in a way that suits their temperament, most children will internalize rules of conduct, experience appropriate moral emotions, and learn to regulate their behavior.

Checking Mastery

1. How is a moral rule different from a social-conventional rule and at what age can children tell the difference?

2. What capacities shown by preschool children contradict Piaget's view that they are limited moral thinkers?

3. Give an example of induction and explain why Martin Hoffman believes it is the best approach to discipline.

Making Connections

1. Ben, age 6, lies and steals frequently, bullies other children, and rarely complies with rules at home or at school. Using what you have learned about moral socialization and referring to appropri-

ate concepts and research, describe how ineffective parenting might have contributed to the development of this apparently immoral child.

2. What approaches to moral socialization did your parents use with you? If you have siblings, can you see any signs that your parents adopted different approaches to moral socialization with different children? Finally, do your parents' strategies seem sound in retrospect?

13.5 The Adolescent

As adolescents gain the capacity to think about abstract and hypothetical ideas, and as they begin to chart their future identities, many of them reflect on their values and moral standards and some make morality a central part of their identities. At the other extreme are the adolescents who end up engaging in serious antisocial behavior.

Changes in Moral Reasoning

Adolescence is a period of significant moral growth. Consider first the results of a 20-year longitudinal study by Kohlberg and his colleagues that involved repeatedly asking the 10-, 13-, and 16-year-old boys originally studied by Kohlberg to respond to moral dilemmas (Colby et al., 1983). ▪ Figure 13.3 shows the percentage of judgments offered at each age that reflected each of Kohlberg's six stages.

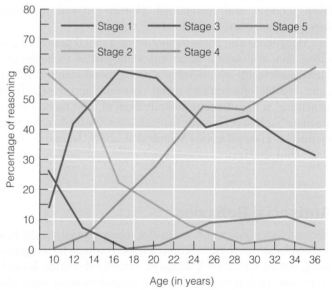

▪ FIGURE 13.3 Average percentage of moral reasoning at each of Lawrence Kohlberg's stages for males from age 10 to age 36. SOURCE: From A. Colby, L. Kohlberg, J. Gibbs, & M. Lieberman. A longitudinal study of moral judgment, *Monographs of the Society for Research in Child Development, 48,* (1–2, Serial No. 200). Copyright © 1983 Blackwell Publishing. Reprinted with permission.

Several interesting developmental trends can be seen here. Notice that the preconventional reasoning (stage 1 and 2 thinking) that dominates among 10-year-olds decreases considerably during the teen years. During adolescence, conventional reasoning (stages 3 and 4) becomes the dominant mode of moral thinking. So, among 13- to 14-year-olds, most moral judgments reflect either a stage 2 (instrumental hedonism) approach—"You scratch my back and I'll scratch yours"—or a stage 3 (good boy or good girl) concern with being nice and earning approval. More than half the judgments offered by 16- to 18-year-olds embody stage 3 reasoning, and about a fifth were scored as stage 4 (authority and social order–maintaining morality) arguments. These older adolescents were beginning to take a broad societal perspective on justice and were concerned about acting in ways that would help maintain the social system.

Gangs in inner-city areas are only part of the larger problem of youth violence.

© Paul Bradbury/OJO Images/Getty Images

In short, the main developmental trend in moral reasoning during adolescence is a shift from preconventional to conventional reasoning. During this period, most individuals begin to express a genuine concern with living up to the moral standards that parents and other authorities have taught them and ensuring that laws designed to make human relations just and fair are taken seriously and maintained. Postconventional reasoning does not emerge until adulthood—if at all.

Many teens also come to view being a moral person who is caring, fair, and honest as an important part of their identity. Those adolescents who develop a strong moral identity end up more capable of advanced moral reasoning and, especially if something in the situation reminds them of their moral values, are more likely to act morally than adolescents who do not define themselves in moral terms (Aquino et al., 2009; Aquino & Reed, 2002; Hart, 2005).

Antisocial Behavior

Although most adolescents internalize society's moral standards, a few youths are involved in serious antisocial conduct—muggings, rapes, armed robberies, knifings, or drive-by shootings. Indeed, crime rates peak during adolescence in most societies, especially for "hell-raising" crimes such as vandalism (Agnew, 2003).

Most severely antisocial adults start their antisocial careers in childhood and continue them in adolescence. The consequences of their early misbehavior cumulate, and they engage in **juvenile delinquency,** law breaking by a minor. They find themselves leaving school early, participating in troubled and sometimes abusive relationships, having difficulty keeping jobs, and engaging in lawbreaking as adults (Huesmann, Dubow, & Boxer, 2009; Maughan & Rutter, 2001). Some of these individuals qualify

as youth for psychiatric diagnoses such as **conduct disorder**—a persistent pattern of violating the rights of others or age-appropriate societal norms through such behaviors as fighting, bullying, and cruelty—and as adults for a diagnosis of antisocial personality disorder (see Dodge, Coie, & Lynam, 2006).

Yet most adolescents who engage in aggressive behavior and other antisocial acts do not grow up to be antisocial adults. There seem to be at least two subgroups of antisocial youths, then: an early-onset group that is recognizable in childhood through acts such as torturing animals and hitting other children and is persistently antisocial across the life span, and a larger, late-onset group that behaves antisocially mainly during adolescence, partly in response to peer pressures, and outgrows this behavior in adulthood (Moffitt & Caspi, 2001; Odgers et al., 2008; Quinsey et al., 2004).

What causes some youths to become menaces to society? Might adolescents who engage repeatedly in aggressive, antisocial acts be cases of arrested moral development who have not internalized conventional values? Juvenile delinquents are indeed more likely than nondelinquents to rely on preconventional moral reasoning (Gregg, Gibbs, & Basinger, 1994; Raaijmakers, Engels, & Van Hoof, 2005). Some juvenile offenders, then, lack a well-developed sense of right and wrong. Yet many delinquents are capable of conventional moral reasoning but commit illegal acts anyway. So to understand the origins of antisocial conduct, we must consider more than stage of moral reasoning (see Gibbs, 2010; Quinsey et al., 2004).

What about the moral emotions of antisocial youth? Adolescents who are aggressive or who are diagnosed with conduct disorders are less likely than other adolescents to show empathy and concern for others in distress, and they often feel little guilt and remorse about their acts (Blair, 2003; Gibbs, 2010; Lovett & Sheffield, 2007). Apparently their moral emotions have not been socialized in ways that would promote moral behavior.

As will now become clear, these adolescents also process social information differently than other adolescents do.

Dodge's Social Information-Processing Model

Kenneth Dodge and his colleagues have advanced our understanding by offering a social information-processing model of aggressive behavior (Crick & Dodge, 1994; Dodge, 1986). Imagine that you are walking down the aisle in a classroom, trip over a classmate's leg, and end up in a heap on the floor. As you fall, you are not sure what happened. Dodge and other social information-processing theorists believe that the individual's reactions to frustration, anger, or provocation depend not so much on the social cues in the situation as on the ways in which she processes and interprets this information.

An individual who is provoked (as by being tripped) progresses through six steps in information processing, according to Dodge:

1. *Encoding of cues:* Taking in information
2. *Interpretation of cues:* Making sense of this information and deciding what caused the other person's behavior
3. *Clarification of goals:* Deciding what to achieve in the situation
4. *Response search:* Thinking of possible actions to achieve the goal
5. *Response decision:* Weighing the pros and cons of these alternative actions
6. *Behavioral enactment:* Doing something

People do not necessarily go through these steps in precise order; we can cycle among them or work on two or more simultaneously (Crick & Dodge, 1994). And at any step, we may draw not only on information available in the immediate situation but also on a stored database that includes memories of previous social experiences and information about the social world. The skills involved in carrying out the six steps in social information processing improve with age (Dodge & Price, 1994; Mayeux &

Cillessen, 2003). For example, older children are more able than younger ones to encode and interpret all the relevant cues in a situation to determine why another person behaved as he did, generate a range of responses, and carry off intended behaviors skillfully. Why, then, are some children more aggressive than other children the same age?

Highly aggressive youths, including adolescents incarcerated for violent crimes, show deficient or biased information processing at every step (Dodge, 1993; Slaby & Guerra, 1988). For example, a highly aggressive adolescent who is tripped by a classmate is likely to proceed through the following mental steps (● Table 13.3):

1. Process relatively few of the available cues in the situation and show a bias toward information suggesting that the tripping was deliberate (for example, noticing a fleeting smirk on the classmate's face)
2. Make an "attribution of hostile intent," inferring that the classmate meant to cause harm
3. Set a goal of getting even (rather than a goal of smoothing relations)
4. Think of only a few possible ways to react, mostly aggressive ones
5. Conclude, after evaluating alternative actions, that an aggressive response will have favorable outcomes (or perhaps not think through the consequences)
6. Carry out the particular aggressive response selected

Many aggressive youths act impulsively, "without thinking"; they respond automatically based on their database of past experiences. These youths tend to see the world as a hostile place; they are easily angered and quickly attribute hostile intent to whoever harms them (Crick & Dodge, 1994; Orobio de Castro et al., 2002). Severely violent youths have often experienced abandonment, neglect, abuse, bullying, and other insults that may have given them cause to view the world as a hostile place and to feel little concern for others (Lansford et al., 2007; Margolin & Gordis, 2000). They can even feel morally justified in taking antisocial

● **TABLE 13.3** **THE SIX STEPS IN DODGE'S SOCIAL INFORMATION-PROCESSING MODEL AND SAMPLE RESPONSES OF AGGRESSIVE YOUTH**

Step	Behavior	Likely Response of Aggressive Youth
1. Encoding of cues	Search for, attend to, and register cues in the situation	Focus on cues suggesting hostile intent; ignore other relevant information
2. Interpretation of cues	Interpret situation; infer other's motive	Infer that provoker had hostile intent
3. Clarification of goals	Formulate goal in situation	Make goal to retaliate
4. Response search	Generate possible responses	Generate few options, most of them aggressive
5. Response decision	Assess likely consequences of responses generated; choose the best	See advantages in responding aggressively rather than nonaggressively (or fail to evaluate consequences)
6. Behavioral enactment	Carry out chosen response	Behave aggressively

Social information processors use a database of information about past social experiences, social rules, and social behavior at each step of the process and skip from step to step.

Source: From Crick, N. R., & Dodge, K. A. (1994). A review and reformulation of social information-processing mechanisms in children's social adjustment. *Psychological Bulletin, 115,* pp. 74–101. Copyright © 1994 American Psychological Association. Reprinted with permission.

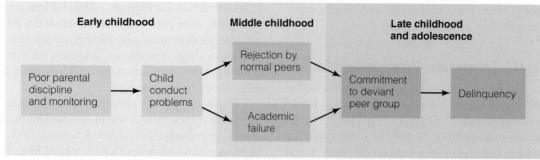

Early childhood   **Middle childhood**   **Late childhood and adolescence**

■ **FIGURE 13.4** Gerald Patterson's model of the development of antisocial behavior starts with poor discipline and coercive cycles of family influence. Source: Adapted from Patterson, G. R., DeBaryshe, B. D., & Ramsey, E., VA Developmental perspective on antisocial behavior, *American Psychologist*, 44, pp. 329–335. Copyright © 1989. American Psychological Association. Reprinted with permission.

action because they believe they are only retaliating against individuals who are "out to get them" (Coie et al., 1991; Gibbs, 2010; Smithmyer, Hubbard, & Simons, 2000).

Dodge's social information-processing model is helpful in understanding why children and adolescents might behave aggressively in particular situations. However, it leaves somewhat unclear the extent to which the underlying problem is *how one thinks* (how skilled the person is at processing social information), *what one thinks* (for example, whether the individual believes that other people are hostile), or *whether one thinks* (how impulsive the person is). The role of emotions also needs more attention. Children whose genetically influenced temperament makes them high in emotionality but low in emotional control are especially likely to show deficiencies in social information processing and to engage in problem behavior (Eisenberg et al., 1996; Lemerise & Arsenio, 2000). Finally, we need more research, like the work we describe next, to tell us why only some children develop the social information-processing styles associated with aggressive behavior.

Patterson's Coercive Family Environments

Gerald Patterson and his colleagues have found that highly antisocial children and adolescents often grow up in **coercive family environments** in which family members are locked in power struggles, each trying to control the others through negative, coercive tactics (Kiesner, Dishion, & Poulin, 2001; Patterson, 2008; Patterson, DeBaryshe, & Ramsey, 1989). Parents learn (through negative reinforcement) that they can stop their children's misbehavior, temporarily at least, by threatening, yelling, and hitting. Meanwhile, children learn (also through negative reinforcement) that they can get their parents to lay off them by ignoring requests, whining, throwing full-blown temper tantrums, and otherwise being difficult. As both parents and children learn to rely on coercive tactics, parents increasingly lose control over their children's behavior until even the loudest lectures and hardest spankings have little effect and the child's conduct problems spiral out of control. It is easy to see how a child who has grown up in a coercive family environment might attribute hostile intent to other people and rely on aggressive tactics to resolve disputes.

Growing up in a coercive family environment sets in motion the next steps in the making of an antisocial adolescent,

according to Patterson and his colleagues (■ **Figure 13.4**): The child, already aggressive and unpleasant to be around, ends up performing poorly in school and being rejected by other children. Having no better options, he becomes involved in a peer group made up of other low-achieving, antisocial, and unpopular youths, who positively reinforce one another's delinquency. Overall, there is much support for the view that ineffective parenting in childhood contributes to behavior problems, peer rejection, involvement with antisocial peers, and, in turn, antisocial behavior in adolescence (Dodge et al., 2008).

Nature and Nurture

In the final analysis, severe antisocial behavior is the product of a complex interplay between genetic predisposition and social learning experiences. We can start by putting aggression in an evolutionary context. For example, males are more aggressive overall than females and engage in three or four times as much crime. The male edge in aggression is evident in many cultures and in many species (Barash, 2002) and shows up as early as infancy (Baillargeon et al., 2007). It has been argued that aggression may have evolved in males because becoming dominant in the male peer group enables adolescent males to compete successfully for mates and pass their genes to future generations (Hilton, Harris, & Rice, 2000; Pellegrini & Long, 2003).

In addition, some individuals, male or female, are more genetically predisposed than others to have difficult, irritable temperaments; impulsive tendencies; and other response tendencies and personality traits that contribute to aggressive, delinquent, and criminal behavior (Baker et al., 2008; Rhee & Waldman, 2002; van Goozen et al., 2007). Genetic differences among us account for about 40% of individual differences in antisocial behavior and environmental influences for the remaining 60% of the variation (Rhee & Waldman, 2002).

Through the mechanism of *gene–environment interaction*, children with certain genetic predispositions may become antisocial if they also grow up in a dysfunctional family and receive poor parenting or, worse, are physically abused (Button et al., 2005; Dodge, 2009). For example, Kenneth Dodge (2009) has summarized research on the monoamine oxidase A (MAO-A) gene, a gene on the X chromosome that normally contributes to an ability to control our tempers when we are threatened or provoked. If children have a variant of this gene that results in low MAO-A activity *and* if they are abused or mistreated, they readily attribute hostile intentions to others if provoked, cannot control their anger, and lash out impulsively. They show higher levels of antisocial behavior as adults than both youth who were not mistreated and youth who were mistreated but have high levels of MAO-A activity and can therefore better control their rage (Caspi et al., 2002; and see Kim-Cohen et al., 2006).

Through the mechanism of *gene–environment correlation*, children who inherit a genetic predisposition to become aggressive may actually evoke the coercive parenting that Patterson and his colleagues find breeds aggression. This *evocative gene–environment correlation* effect is evident even when aggression-prone children grow up with adoptive parents rather than with their biological parents because these children bring out negativity in their adoptive parents. In the end, child antisocial behavior and negative parenting influence one another reciprocally over time: aggressive children evoke negative and coercive parenting, and negative, coercive parenting further strengthens their aggressive tendencies (Larsson et al., 2008; O'Connor et al., 1998).

Many other risk and protective factors in the environment can help determine whether a child genetically predisposed to be aggressive ends up on a healthy or unhealthy developmental trajectory (Guerra & Williams, 2006). The prenatal environment—for example, exposure to alcohol, opiate drugs, and lead poisoning—has been linked to conduct problems (Dodge & Pettit, 2003). Complications during delivery may also contribute, especially if the child later grows up in a deprived home (Arseneault et al., 2002).

Some cultural contexts are more likely to breed aggression than others. In Japan, a collectivist culture in which children are taught early to value social harmony, children are less angered by interpersonal conflicts and less likely to react to them aggressively than American children are (Zahn-Waxler et al., 1996). Similarly, Hispanic American youths who have been brought up with traditional Hispanic cultural values such as the importance of family are less likely than those who are more acculturated into American society to engage in antisocial behavior (Cota-Robles, 2003; Soriano et al., 2004). This could be partly because children in the United States are so heavily exposed to violence on television, a known contributor to aggression (Anderson et al., 2003; and see Chapter 1). More generally, the United States is a relatively violent country where corporal punishment of children is heavily used (Lansford & Dodge, 2008; Lim, Bond, & Bond, 2005).

Subcultural and neighborhood factors can also contribute to youth violence (Guerra & Williams, 2006). Rates of aggression and violent crime are two to three times higher in lower socioeconomic neighborhoods and communities, especially transient ones, than in middle-class ones (Elliott & Ageton, 1980; Maughan, 2001). For young African American and Hispanic males in gang-dominated inner-city neighborhoods, it may even be adaptive to be quick to detect others' hostile intentions and take defensive action (Hudley & Graham, 1993).

Finally, certain schools have higher rates of delinquency and aggression than others, even when socioeconomic factors are controlled (Maughan, 2001). **Bullying**, repeatedly inflicting harm through words or actions on weaker peers who often cannot defend themselves, can become something of an epidemic in certain schools. In these schools, neither teachers nor parents set high standards for achievement, bullies egg each other on, and other students reinforce the bullies or at least do not stop them (Barboza et al., 2009). Because bullies, victims of bullies, and children who are both bullies and victims are more likely than other youths to become involved in delinquent and self-harmful behaviors (Barker et al., 2008; Salmivalli & Peets, 2009), many schools take active steps to combat bullying instead of writing it off as normal child behavior (Beane, 2009; and see Chapter 14).

Kenneth Dodge and his colleagues have attempted to integrate all these influences into a biopsychosocial model of aggression that recognizes the contributions of biological predisposition, individual psychology, and social or contextual factors (Dodge & Pettit, 2003). They have also proposed a "dynamic cascade" model showing how various influences, playing out over childhood and adolescence, can result in chronic and serious violence in adolescence and beyond (Dodge et al., 2008). Biological factors such as genes and sociocultural context factors such as living in a disadvantaged, violence-prone neighborhood put certain children at risk from birth. Then a chain of causal events, along the lines of Patterson's model in Figure 13.4, plays out: experiences with harsh, inconsistent parenting in early childhood; poor readiness for school; early behavior problems; failure in elementary school (both academically and socially); lack of appropriate parental supervision in early adolescence; and affiliation with antisocial peers (Dodge et al., 2008). The more risk factors at work and interacting with each other over the years, the greater the odds of an aggressive adult. Then, unfortunately, this antisocial adult stands a good chance of contributing to the intergenerational transmission of aggression—of becoming the kind of negative and coercive parent who helps raise another generation of aggressive children, who then use the same coercive style with their own children (Conger et al., 2003; Dogan et al., 2007).

Prevention of antisocial behavior should clearly be a national priority, then. Many experts believe that prevention needs to start in infancy or toddlerhood with a strong emphasis on positive parenting (Dodge et al., 2006; Tremblay, 2000). Comprehensive, school-based prevention programs aimed at children who are at risk of becoming aggressive can also help. For instance, the Fast Track Program, designed by Kenneth Dodge and other members of the Conduct Problems Prevention Research Group (2007), began in first grade, extended over 10 years, and used a multipronged approach involving the teaching of social information-processing and social skills, efforts to improve academic skills, and behavior management training for parents. It has proven effective in reducing antisocial behavior and preventing diagnoses of conduct disorder and related psychiatric disorders. The program worked only with those children who were at highest risk initially and was very costly, however, suggesting the need to aim prevention programs more squarely at the children most in need of them (see also Wilson, Lipsey, & Derzon, 2003). As Application Box 13.1 suggests, helping youth who have already become seriously antisocial is even more challenging.

How can we put aggressive, antisocial adolescents on a more positive developmental path? We'll explore applications of three perspectives described in this chapter—Lawrence Kohlberg's theory of moral reasoning, Kenneth Dodge's social information-processing model, and Gerald Patterson's coercive family environment model.

Improving Moral Reasoning (Kohlberg)

If, as both Jean Piaget and Lawrence Kohlberg said, peers are especially important in stimulating moral growth, a sensible approach to moral training is to harness "peer power." Thus, several researchers have put youth in small groups to discuss hypothetical moral dilemmas or have created school-based character education programs, patterned after the "Just Community" approach that Kohlberg himself pioneered, in which students are actively engaged in the democratic process of making and enforcing school rules (Nucci, 2006; Power & Higgins-D'Alessandro, 2008; Snarey & Samuelson, 2008). The rationale is simple: Opportunities to take other people's perspectives and to hear moral reasoning more mature than one's own will create cognitive disequilibrium and spur moral growth.

Participation in group discussions of moral issues does produce more mature moral reasoning; the equivalent of about 4–5 years of natural development has been achieved in programs lasting only 3–12 weeks (Rest et al., 1999). And even institutionalized delinquents can benefit (Niles, 1986). However, fostering mature moral judgment alone is insufficient to cause delinquents to cease behaving like delinquents (Gibbs, 2010; Niles, 1986).

John Gibbs (2010) and his colleagues have had luck in reducing recidivism (relapse after release from a correctional facility) through a program called EQUIP. However, EQUIP does not stop at teaching social perspective-taking and moral reasoning skills. It also attempts to combat the self-serving cognitions that cause problems with anger control among delinquent youth and to teach them social skills such as how to register complaints constructively—all in the context of a mutual help group.

Building Social Information-Processing Skills (Dodge)

As you saw earlier, Dodge's social information-processing model identifies six steps at which highly aggressive youth display deficient or biased social information processing when provoked. Nancy Guerra and Ronald Slaby (1990) coached small groups of incarcerated and violent juveniles of both sexes to (1) look for situational cues other than those suggesting hostile intentions, (2) control their impulses so that they do not lash out without considering the consequences, and (3) generate more nonaggressive solutions to conflicts. After a 12-week intervention, these adolescents showed dramatic improvements in social information-processing skills, believed less strongly in the value of aggression, and behaved less aggressively in their interactions with authority figures and other inmates. Trained offenders were only somewhat less likely than untrained offenders (34% versus 46%) to violate their paroles after release, however.

Breaking Coercive Cycles (Patterson)

Gerald Patterson and his colleagues maintain that the secret to working with violent youths is to change the dynamics of interactions in their families so that the cycle of coercive influence is broken. In one study, Patterson and his team (Bank et al., 1991) randomly assigned adolescent boys who were repeat offenders to either a special parent-training intervention guided by learning theory or the services usually provided by the juvenile court. In the parent-training program, therapy sessions held with each family taught parents how to observe both prosocial and antisocial behaviors in their son, to gather and use teachers' reports on his performance and behavior at school, and to establish behavioral contracts detailing the reinforcement for prosocial behavior and the punishment (such as loss of privileges) for antisocial behavior their son can expect.

The parent-training intervention was judged at least a partial success. It improved family processes, although it did not fully resolve the problems these dysfunctional families had. Rates of serious crime among this group dropped and remained lower even 3 years after the intervention ended. The usual juvenile services program also reduced crime rates but took longer to take effect.

In sum, efforts to treat highly aggressive adolescents have included attempts to apply the work of Kohlberg (through group discussion of moral issues), Dodge (by teaching effective social information-processing skills), and Patterson (by replacing coercive cycles in the family with positive behavioral management techniques). It has not been easy. The most promising approaches today appear to recognize that a comprehensive strategy is needed. They seek to change not only the individual and his thinking but also his family, peers, school, and community (Curtis, Ronan, & Bourduin, 2004; Dodge et al., 2006).

© AP Photo/Steve Yeater

Discussion of moral dilemmas may increase complexity of moral reasoning but does not necessarily reduce delinquency.

Checking Mastery

1. What is the main change in moral reasoning during adolescence?

2. What are the main contributions of (1) Kenneth Dodge and (2) Gerald Patterson to understanding why some children are highly aggressive?

3. What is an example of the contribution of a gene–environment interaction to the development of aggression?

Making Connections

1. To demonstrate to yourself that Dodge's social information-processing model can be applied not only to antisocial behavior but to prosocial behavior, picture a situation in which you are one of the campers in the story at the beginning of this chapter and witness two other campers put the hand of Edward, the camp employee, in a bucket of water while he naps. Show how considerations at each of the six steps of Dodge's model (see Table 13.3) might contribute to your intervening to help Edward—and then how they might keep you from helping.

2. You pick up the newspaper and see that still another teenage boy has gone on a shooting rampage at his school. Drawing on material in this chapter, what factors besides coercive parenting would you identify to explain why he might have done what he did?

3. The Supreme Court has had to rule on the question of whether minors who commit capital offenses should face the death penalty. What is your view on this issue, and what theory and research in this chapter would you cite to support it?

13.6 The Adult

How does moral thinking change during adulthood, what can we conclude overall about moral development across the life span, and what roles do religiosity and spirituality play in adult lives, especially in late adulthood?

Changes in Moral Reasoning

Much research on moral development in adulthood has been guided by Kohlberg's theory. As you have discovered (see Figure 13.3), Kohlberg's postconventional moral reasoning appears to emerge only during the adult years (if it emerges). In Kohlberg's 20-year longitudinal study (Colby et al., 1983), most adults in their 30s still reasoned at the conventional level, although many of them had shifted from stage 3 to stage 4. A minority of individuals—one-sixth to one-eighth of the sample—had begun to use stage 5 postconventional reasoning, showing a deeper understanding of the basis for laws and distinguishing between just and unjust laws. Clearly there is opportunity for moral growth in early adulthood.

Do these growth trends continue into later adulthood? Most studies find no major age differences in complexity of moral reasoning, at least when relatively educated adults are studied and when the age groups compared have similar levels of educa-

tion (Pratt et al., 1991, 1996; Pratt & Norris, 1999). Older adults are also more likely than younger adults to feel that they have learned important lessons from moral dilemmas they have faced during their lives (Pratt & Norris, 1999). This, then, is further evidence that social cognitive skills hold up well across the life span.

Kohlberg's Theory in Perspective

Lawrence Kohlberg's theory of moral development has made a tremendous contribution to the field and has dominated the study of moral development for many years, but increasingly his perspective is being challenged. It is time to evaluate its strengths and weaknesses and then see how researchers are trying to move beyond it toward a more complete picture of moral development.

You have seen that children think about hypothetical moral dilemmas primarily in a preconventional manner, that adolescents adopt a conventional mode of moral reasoning, and that a minority of adults shift to a postconventional perspective. Kohlberg claimed that his stages form an invariant and universal sequence of moral growth, and longitudinal studies of moral growth in several countries support his view that at least the first three or four stages form an invariant sequence (Colby & Kohlberg, 1987; Gibbs, 2010; Rest et al., 1999).

However, as you saw earlier, young children are more sophisticated moral thinkers than either Piaget or Kohlberg appreciated. Moreover, while the idea that everyone progresses from preconventional to conventional reasoning is well supported, the idea that people continue to progress from conventional to post-conventional reasoning is not (Gibbs, 2010). In addition, it has been charged that the theory is biased against people who are non-Western, politically conservative, and female and that it slights moral emotion and behavior.

Charges of Bias

Questions have been raised about whether Kohlberg's theory is *culture biased*. Although support for the theory has been obtained in more than 20 countries (Gibbs et al., 2007), critics charge that Kohlberg's highest stages reflect a Western ideal of justice centered on individual rights and rule of law and that it is biased against people who live in non-Western societies (Shweder, Mahapatra, & Miller, 1990; Turiel, 2006). Indeed, cross-cultural studies suggest that postconventional moral reasoning emerges primarily in Western democracies (Snarey, 1985). People in *collectivist cultures*, which emphasize social harmony and place the good of the group ahead of the good of the individual, often look like stage 3 conventional moral thinkers in Kohlberg's system, yet may have sophisticated concepts of justice that focus on the individual's responsibility for others' welfare (Snarey, 1985; Tietjen & Walker, 1985).

Richard Shweder, Manamohan Mahapatra, and Joan Miller (1990), studying the moral judgments of children and adults in India and the United States, identified even more striking cultural differences in thinking about right and wrong. For example, Hindu children and adults rated a son's getting a haircut and eating chicken the day after his father's death as one of the most

Adults in traditional, rural societies may have no need for postconventional moral reasoning because they share the same moral perspective.

morally offensive of the 39 acts they were asked to rate, whereas Americans dismissed it as only a matter of breaking seemingly arbitrary social-conventional rules about appropriate mourning behavior. Meanwhile, Americans viewed a husband's beating of his "disobedient" wife for going to the movies without his permission as a serious moral violation, whereas Hindus viewed it as appropriate behavior. To orthodox Hindus, not showing proper respect for the dead violates a moral rule required by natural law, not an arbitrary social-conventional rule, and it is morally necessary for a man to beat his disobedient wife to uphold his obligations as head of the family.

Cross-cultural findings like this challenge the cognitive developmental position that important aspects of moral development are universal. Instead, they support a social learning or contextual perspective on moral development, suggesting that our moral judgments are shaped by the social context in which we develop. Possibly the resolution is this: Individuals all over the world think in more complex ways about moral issues as they get older, as Kohlberg claimed, but they also adopt different notions about what is right and what is wrong depending on what they are taught, as Shweder claims (Miller, 2006).

Critics also charge that Kohlberg's theory is *biased against political conservatives*. A person must hold liberal values—for example, opposing capital punishment or supporting civil disobedience in the name of human rights—to be classified as a postconventional moral reasoner, they say. Opposition to capital punishment may be a more valid moral position than support of capital punishment in that it involves valuing life (de Vries & Walker, 1986), but there is some truth to the idea that Kohlberg's theory favors people who support human rights and take liberal

positions on issues (Emler, Tarry, & St. James, 2007; Lapsley et al., 1984).

Finally, Kohlberg's theory has been accused of *gender bias*. Psychologist and feminist Carol Gilligan (1977, 1982, 1993) was disturbed that Kohlberg's stages were developed based on interviews with males only and that, in some studies, women seemed to reason at stage 3 when men usually reasoned at stage 4. Gilligan argued that boys, who traditionally have been raised to be independent, come to view moral dilemmas as conflicts between the rights of two or more parties and to view laws as necessary for resolving these inevitable conflicts (a perspective reflected in Kohlberg's stage 4 reasoning). Girls, Gilligan argued, are brought up to define their sense of "goodness" in terms of their concern for other people (a perspective that approximates stage 3 in Kohlberg's scheme). What this difference boils down to is two moralities: a "masculine" **morality of justice** (focused on laws and rules, individual rights, and fairness) and a "feminine" **morality of care** (focused on an obligation to be selfless and look after the welfare of other people), neither more "mature" than the other.

Despite the appeal of Gilligan's ideas, there is little support for her claim that Kohlberg's theory is systematically biased against females. In most studies, women reason just as complexly about moral issues as men do (Jaffee & Hyde, 2000; Walker, 2006). Moreover, most studies have found that males and females do not differ significantly in their approaches to thinking about morality. Instead, both men and women use care-based reasoning when they ponder dilemmas involving relationships and justice-based reasoning when issues of rights arise. Ultimately, then, although her charges of gender bias have not received much support, Gilligan's work has increased our awareness that both men and women often think about moral issues in terms of their responsibilities for the welfare of other people and that Kohlberg emphasized only one way—a legalistic and abstract way—of thinking about right and wrong (Brabeck, 1983).

Underemphasizing Emotion and Behavior

The biggest limitation of Kohlberg's perspective may be that it looks primarily at moral thinking and devotes little attention to moral emotions and moral behavior (Gibbs, 2010; Turiel, 2006). Although a person may decide to uphold or to break a law at any of Kohlberg's stages of moral reasoning, Kohlberg argued that more advanced moral reasoners are more likely to behave morally than less advanced moral reasoners are. For example, where the preconventional thinker might readily decide to cheat if the chances of being detected were small and the potential rewards were large, the postconventional thinker would be more likely to appreciate that cheating is wrong in principle, regardless of the chances of punishment or reward, because it infringes on the rights of others and undermines social order.

What does research tell us? Individuals determined to be at higher stages of moral reasoning are more likely than individuals at lower stages to behave prosocially (Gibbs, 2010), to do good through their involvement in social organizations (Matsuba & Walker, 2004), and to be helpful in everyday life (Midlarsky et al., 1999). They are also less likely to cheat and to engage in delinquent and criminal activity (Judy & Nelson, 2000; Rest et al., 1999). Yet relationships between stage of moral reasoning and moral behavior are usually weak, suggesting that other factors may be important in motivating and explaining behavior—factors like emotions (Hart, Atkins, & Donnelly, 2006; Walker, 2004).

In sum, Kohlberg's stage theory has a good deal of support, but he underestimated children's moral sophistication and his later stages are not as well supported as his early stages. In addition, his theory is to some extent biased against non-Westerners and political conservatives, is more focused on a morality of justice than on Gilligan's morality of care, and has more to say about moral thinking than about moral emotion and behavior. Today's researchers are moving in new directions.

New Approaches to Morality

Developmentalists today are trying to correct for Kohlberg's overemphasis on moral reasoning by exploring the emotional component of morality more fully, including a kind of thinking about moral issues that is far more intuitive and emotion-based than the rational deliberation Kohlberg studied. As you have seen already, Martin Hoffman (2000) and others have long highlighted the critical role of emotions and especially empathy in motivating moral action. Researchers have also been studying the emotions children and adults experience when they engage in moral or immoral behavior and how they learn to regulate these emotions (Eisenberg, 2000; Eisenberg, Spinrad, & Sadovsky, 2006; Gibbs, 2010).

In addition, a number of scholars are converging on the idea that gut emotional reactions and intuitions play an important role in morality (Gibbs, 2010; Greene, 2008; Haidt, 2008).

● TABLE 13.4 DUAL PROCESS MODELS OF MORALITY

Moral Cognition/Reasoning (Emphasized by Kohlberg)	Moral Emotion/Intuition (Emphasized by Haidt, Greene)
Rational thought	Intuition
Cold logic	Hot emotion
Controlled processes	Automatic processes
Impartiality	Empathy
Careful deliberation	Quick gut reaction

Think about whether you would eat your fellow passengers after a plane crash in the mountains if there were nothing else to eat. Most of us find this idea morally repugnant and immediately know in our gut, without the need for contemplation, that cannibalism is wrong. Jonathan Haidt (2001, 2008), influenced by evolutionary theory and research in neuroscience and social psychology, argues that we have evolved as a species to have such quick moral intuitions, which are often based in emotions like disgust and anger. He believes that these intuitions are far more important than deliberative reasoning in shaping moral decisions. If deliberate thought of the sort emphasized by Kohlberg plays a role at all, Haidt suggests, it is mainly to rationalize after the fact what we have already decided intuitively or to communicate our moral views to others.

Some scholars have now proposed **dual-process models of morality** in which *both* deliberate thought and emotion/intuition inform decisions about moral issues and motivate behavior (● Table 13.4; and see Gibbs, 2010). As Exploration Box 13.4 reveals, Joshua Greene has proposed one such dual-process model of morality and has tried to explain why we sometimes make judgments primarily based on quick emotion-based intuitions and other times make judgments using more deliberative cognitive processes. The message of his and other recent work is that we need to learn much more about moral emotions and intuitions, when they come into play, and how they interact with moral reasoning.

In the end, we do best recognizing that the moral reasoning of interest to Piaget and Kohlberg, the moral emotions and intuitions of interest to Freud and Hoffman and more recently Haidt and Greene, and the self-regulatory and moral disengagement processes highlighted by Albert Bandura—together with many other personal and situational factors—all help predict whether a person will behave morally or immorally when faced with an important moral choice.

Religion and Spirituality

Lawrence Kohlberg viewed moral development and religious development as distinct, but they are clearly interrelated for the many people whose religious values and beliefs guide their

Dual-Process Morality

In a well-known moral dilemma, a runaway trolley is heading toward five people. They can be saved if you hit a switch that will divert the trolley onto another track, where it will kill one person rather than five. Should you hit the switch to save five people at the expense of one?

And what do you think about this version of the trolley dilemma: As before, the trolley is heading toward and will kill five people. You are standing with a large stranger on a footbridge over the tracks and can save the five people if you push the stranger off the bridge and onto the tracks below, where he will be killed but his body will stop the trolley from killing the others. Should you push the stranger off the bridge?

Despite the similarities between these two scenarios, most people would hit the switch in the first scenario but would not push the stranger off the bridge in the second. Why do you think this is? Philosophers have struggled to explain it. Joshua Greene and his colleagues (2001) have proposed that it is because the second footbridge dilemma evokes a strong emotional response that the first scenario does not: we are appalled at the idea of directly killing a person with our own hands, probably because we have evolved to feel such revulsion. Using functional MRI techniques, Greene and his colleagues demonstrated that areas of the brain associated with emotion were more active when people deliberated dilemmas, such as the footbridge scenario, that were personally involving than they were when people considered more impersonal dilemmas like that involving the first trolley. By contrast, areas of the brain associated with rational cognition were more active when impersonal dilemmas were considered. The findings were consistent with Greene's (2008) concept of a dual-process model of morality involving: (1) an emotion-based intuitive process that prompts us, quickly and without awareness, to focus on (and abhor) the harm that would be done if a moral principle like respect for human life is violated (as in pushing the stranger off the footbridge); and (2) a more deliberative, cognitive approach in which we weigh the costs and benefits of an action in a cool and calculating manner (and conclude that it is more rational to sacrifice one life than to lose five).

Other evidence supports this dual-process model (Greene, 2009; Greene et al., 2008). Much remains to be learned about when we go with our gut reactions and when we rely on conscious deliberation in making moral decisions, though, and about what happens when the two processes in the dual-process model of morality pull in different directions. However, Greene's work, like that of Jonathan Haidt, makes clear that deliberate reasoning and quick, emotion-based intuition both play important but distinct roles in morality.

---

moral thinking and behavior (Nelson, 2009). Indeed, James Fowler (1981, Fowler & Dell, 1996) proposed stages in the development of religious faith from infancy to adulthood that parallel quite closely Kohlberg's stages of moral development. Fowler's stages lead from concrete images of God in childhood, to internalization of conventional faith in adolescence, to soul searching in early adulthood, and, for a few, progression to a more universal perspective on faith in middle age and beyond. Although the concept of universal stages of religious development has come into question, researchers continue to be interested in the roles religion and spirituality play in people's lives (Nelson, 2009).

We know that children often adopt the beliefs of their parents uncritically and that adolescence or emerging adulthood is often an important time for participating in religious institutions, exploring religious and spiritual issues as part of identity formation, and sometimes rejecting the religious beliefs one was taught as a child, undergoing a spiritual conversion, or developing one's own belief system (Good & Willoughby, 2008; Nelson, 2009). What happens during adulthood? Is old age a special time for religious and spiritual growth? What do religiosity and spirituality contribute to well-being in later life?

Religiosity or religiousness has generally been defined as sharing the beliefs and participating in the practices of an organized religion. **Spirituality** is harder to define but involves a quest for ultimate meaning and for a connection with something greater than oneself (see Nelson, 2009). It may be carried out within the context of a religion (some people are both religious and spiritual) or outside it (some people say they are spiritual but not religious).

Using interview data from a long-term longitudinal study of California adults born in the 1920s, Michelle Dillon and Paul Wink sought to understand changes over the years in both religiosity and spirituality, as well as the relationships of both to psychosocial functioning in old age (Dillon & Wink, 2007; Wink & Dillon, 2002, 2003). The researchers coded interviews for degree of religiousness (participating in traditional forms of religion practice) and degree of spirituality (seeking, in a more personal way, a relationship with a higher power, whether it be God, nature, or something else).

As shown in ■ **Figure 13.5**, Part A, religiosity proved to be strong in adolescence; decreased somewhat in middle age, possibly because people had many responsibilities and little time; and rose again closer to its earlier levels in people's late 60s and 70s. By comparison, spirituality (see Figure 13.5, Part B) was judged to be at lower levels than religiosity throughout adulthood and changed more dramatically with age, increasing significantly from middle age to later adulthood, especially among women (Dillon & Wink, 2007). These findings and others suggest that old age is indeed a time for reflecting on larger questions in life and finding meaning through a kind of spiritual life review (Atchley, 2009; Nelson, 2009).

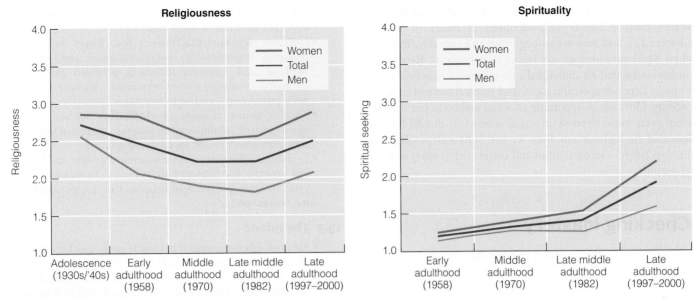

Religiousness

Spirituality

FIGURE 13.5 Changes over time in religiousness and spirituality among adults born in the 1920s. Levels of rated spirituality are lower than levels of religiousness but increase more dramatically in old age, especially among women.

SOURCE: Dillon, M., & Wink, P. (2007). *In the course of a lifetime: Tracing religious belief, practice, and change*, Figures 1 and 4. Reprinted by permission of the University of California Press.

Wink and Dillon (2003) have also found that individuals are highly consistent over the years in their degrees of religiosity and spirituality, probably because of their personalities. In terms of Big Five personality dimensions (see Chapter 11), highly religious people tend to be conscientious and (if they are women) agreeable, whereas highly spiritual people tend to be highly open to new experiences (Wink et al., 2007).

Both religiosity and spirituality contribute positively to psychosocial adjustment but in different ways (Greenfield, Vaillant, & Marks, 2009; Wink & Dillon, 2008). Religiosity in late adulthood is correlated with a sense of well-being stemming from positive relationships with other people, involvement in social and

community service activities, and the sympathetic and caring qualities associated with Erikson's concept of generativity (Wink & Dillon, 2003). Highly religious adults are very involved in their religious communities and act on their religious beliefs by serving others. Other research suggests that religious involvement, perhaps because it is associated with both a sense of meaning and a sense of being part of a caring community, is linked to good health, good mental health, and prosocial behavior (Nelson, 2009).

Wink and Dillon (2003) discovered that highly spiritual older adults have a different but also positive psychosocial profile. They too have a sense of well-being but it is derived from personal growth. Spiritual adults are highly involved in activities that allow them to express their creativity and build their knowledge and skills, and they display qualities associated with wisdom such as introspectiveness and insightfulness.

Religion and spirituality appear to be especially important to older adults in certain minority groups. For example, Robert Taylor and his colleagues (Taylor, Chatters, & Jackson, 2007) surveyed African Americans, Caribbean Blacks, and non-Hispanic Whites age 55 and older about their religiosity as expressed in organizational activities like church attendance, nonorganizational activities such as private prayer, and a subjective sense of being religious and seeing religion as an important part of one's life. Both African American and Caribbean Blacks reported more religious participation of various types, more use of prayer to cope with stress, and more spirituality than Whites did.

In sum, religiosity and spirituality are distinct, but both appear to be strongest in later life, especially among women, and both contribute positively to a sense of well-being, engagement in purposeful activities, and good physical and mental health.

We have now completed our series of chapters on the development of the self, or the person as an individual, having exam-

The church is at the center of the African American community and may have both health and mental health benefits for those elderly people who are highly involved in it.

ined the development of self-conceptions and distinctive personality traits (Chapter 11), identities as males or females (Chapter 12), and now social cognition and morality. But individual development does not occur in a vacuum. Repeatedly, you have seen that an individual's development may take different paths depending on the social and cultural context in which it occurs. Our task in upcoming chapters will be to put the individual even more squarely in social context. It should become clear that throughout our lives we are both independent and interdependent—separate from and connected to other developing persons.

Checking Mastery

1. Against what three groups is Kohlberg's theory said to be biased and for which of the three groups is the evidence of bias weakest?

2. What are the two processes in dual-process models of morality?

3. What is the main difference between a highly religious (but not spiritual) person and a highly spiritual (but not religious) person?

Making Connections

1. Play the part of Lawrence Kohlberg and defend yourself against charges that your theory is flawed, drawing on relevant evidence from throughout this chapter.

2. The members of the Supreme Court are generally elderly adults. What evidence in this chapter can you point to that would suggest that having elderly adults make difficult legal decisions is good for the country?

Chapter Summary

13.1 Social Cognition

- Social cognition (thinking about self and others) is involved in all social behavior, including moral behavior. Starting in infancy with milestones such as joint attention, understanding of intentional action, and pretend play, children develop a theory of mind—a desire psychology at age 2 and a belief–desire psychology by age 4 as evidenced by passing false belief tasks. Developing a theory of mind requires a normal brain (including mirror neuron systems) and appropriate social and communication experience.

- In characterizing other people, preschool children focus on physical features and activities, children 8 years and older on inner psychological traits, and adolescents on integrating trait descriptions to create personality profiles. With age, children also become more adept at social perspective taking. Social cognitive skills often improve during adulthood and hold up well but may decline late in life if a person is socially isolated.

13.2 Perspectives on Moral Development

- Morality has cognitive, affective, and behavioral components. Sigmund Freud's psychoanalytic theory emphasized the superego

and moral emotions, and Martin Hoffman has emphasized empathy as a motivator of moral behavior.

- Cognitive developmental theorist Jean Piaget distinguished premoral, heteronomous, and autonomous stages of moral thinking, and Lawrence Kohlberg proposed three levels of moral reasoning—preconventional, conventional, and postconventional—each with two stages.

- Social cognitive theorist Albert Bandura focused on how moral behavior is influenced by learning, situational forces, self-regulatory processes, and moral disengagement.

- Evolutionary theorists consider emotion, cognition, and behavior and maintain that humans have evolved to be moral beings because morality and prosocial behavior have proven adaptive for the human species.

13.3 The Infant

- Although infants are amoral in some respects, they begin learning about right and wrong through their early disciplinary encounters, internalize rules, and display empathy and prosocial behavior early in life. Their moral growth is facilitated by a secure attachment and what Grazyna Kochanska calls a mutually responsive orientation between parent and child.

13.4 The Child

- Kohlberg and Piaget underestimated the moral sophistication of young children (for example, their ability to consider intentions, to distinguish between moral and social-conventional rules, and to question adult authority); most children display preconventional moral reasoning.

- Reinforcement, modeling, the disciplinary approach of induction, and proactive parenting can foster moral growth, and a child's temperament interacts with the approach to moral training parents adopt to influence outcomes.

13.5 The Adolescent

- During adolescence, a shift from preconventional to conventional moral reasoning is evident, and many adolescents incorporate moral values into their sense of identity.

- Antisocial behavior can be understood in terms of Kenneth Dodge's social information-processing model, Gerald Patterson's coercive family environments and the negative peer influences they set in motion, and, more generally, a biopsychosocial model involving the interaction of genetic predisposition with psychological and social–environmental influences. Attempts to reduce youth violence have applied the work of Kohlberg, Dodge, and Patterson.

13.6 The Adult

- A minority of adults progress from the conventional to the postconventional level of moral reasoning; elderly adults typically reason as complexly as younger adults.

- Kohlberg's early stages of moral reasoning form an invariant sequence, although he underestimated children. It has been charged that Kohlberg's theory is biased against people from non-Western cultures, conservatives, and women and that it slights moral emotion and behavior.

- Today, researchers like Haidt and Greene emphasize that a full understanding of moral development requires attention to emotion and intuition as well as to the rational thought emphasized by Kohlberg and have proposed dual-process models of morality that include both deliberative reasoning and emotion-based intuitions.

- Religiosity and especially spirituality become stronger in later life and are associated with good physical and mental health and well-being.

Checking Mastery Answers

For answers to Checking Mastery questions, visit **www.cengagebrain.com**

Key Terms

social cognition, **428**
false belief task, **428**
theory of mind, **429**
desire psychology, **430**
belief–desire psychology, **430**
mirror neurons, **431**
social perspective-taking
   skills, **433**
morality, **435**
moral affect, **436**
empathy, **436**
prosocial behavior, **436**
moral reasoning, **437**
reciprocity, **437**
premoral period, **437**
heteronomous morality, **437**
autonomous morality, **437**
preconventional morality, **438**
conventional morality, **438**
postconventional morality, **438**
moral disengagement, **440**

amoral, **442**
mutually responsive
   orientation, **442**
moral rules, **445**
social-conventional rules, **445**
love withdrawal, **445**
power assertion, **445**
induction, **445**
proactive parenting
   strategies, **446**
juvenile delinquency, **448**
conduct disorder, **448**
coercive family
   environment, **450**
bullying, **451**
morality of justice, **454**
morality of care, **454**
dual-process model of
   morality, **455**
religiosity, **456**
spirituality, **456**

Media Resources

Psychology CourseMate

Find online quizzes, flash cards, animations, video clips, experiments, interactive assessments, and other helpful study aids for this text at **www.cengagebrain.com**. You can also connect directly to the following sites:

Moral Development: Answers.com

This Answers.com website provides a solid review of the major theories of moral development (for example, Piaget and Kohlberg). One special feature of the site is a built-in dictionary that allows the visitor to get a definition of a highlighted word with just a click. To access, see "web links" in Psychology CourseMate at www.cengagebrain.com

Parenting in America: Fostering Goodness

This website features material on facilitating children's moral development, covering topics such as parental influence and the psychological foundations of moral agency. To access, see "web links" in Psychology CourseMate at www.cengagebrain.com

Understanding the DATA: Exercises on the Web

(WWW)

www.cengagebrain.com
For additional insight on the data presented in this chapter, try out the exercises for these figures in Psychology CourseMate at
www.cengagebrain.com:

   Figure 13.3 Average percentage of moral reasoning at each of Lawrence Kohlberg's stages for males from age 10 to age 36.

   Figure 13.5 Changes in religiousness and spirituality among adults born in the 1920s. Levels of rated spirituality are lower than levels of religiousness but increase more dramatically in old age, especially among women.

CengageNOW

www.cengagebrain.com
Go to www.cengagebrain.com to link to CengageNOW, your online study tool. First take the Pre-Test for this chapter to get your Personalized Study Plan, which will identify topics you need to review and direct you to online resources. Then take the Post-Test to determine what concepts you have mastered and what you still need work on.

Human Development and Relationships

Mike Pohle was about to graduate and wanted to find a job close to his fiancée, Marcy Crevonis (Jones, 2007). He slept every night in a Phillies jersey she gave him, filled her dorm room with chocolate kisses on Valentine's Day, and had already named the five children they hoped to have. They were soulmates. As Marcy put it, "We were the same person. We shared the same thoughts. We finished each other's sentences" (Jones, 2007, p. C1).

Mike Pohle was one of the 32 victims of the mass murders at Virginia Tech University April 16, 2007. Marcy had walked him part of the way to his German class that morning and raced to find him when his class was to end but was blocked by the police. Told of Mike's death, she went back to his apartment, put on the Phillies jersey, and wept.

The shooter, Seung Hui Cho, had no soulmates. He was an unusually quiet child who did not respond to greetings; one high school classmate recalled the jokes about him: "We would just say, 'Did you see Seung say nothing again today?'" (Cho & Gardner, 2007, p. A8). Cho spent his lonely days writing stories of violence and death. He had been diagnosed and treated for social anxiety disorder and selective mutism as a child, but he never made this known to Virginia Tech and deteriorated in college (Schulte & Craig, 2007). As a result, he was almost completely isolated from the human community.

1. What do theorists say about the roles of relationships with parents and peers in development?

2. How do our emotional lives and later orientations toward close relationships take shape during infancy?

3. How do parent–child relationships change in childhood, and what roles do peers and friends play in child development?

4. How do parent and peer relationships evolve during adolescence?

5. How does attachment theory help us understand adult romantic relationships, and how do social relationships contribute to development and well-being over the adult years?

How did their developmental experiences prepare Mike and Marcy to fall in love? What kept Seung from developing close human relationships, and what made him so angry at his fellow humans? Think about Mike Pohle and Seung Hui Cho as you read this chapter. It concerns our closest emotional relationships across the life span and their implications for development. We should not have to work hard to convince you that close interpersonal relationships play a critical role in our lives and in development. The poet John Donne wrote, "No man is an island, entire of itself"; it seems equally true that no human can *become* entire without the help of other humans.

In this chapter, we ask what social relationships are especially important during different phases of the life span and what their character is. We explore how we develop the social competence it takes to interact smoothly with other people and to enter into intimate relationships with them, and we examine the developmental implications of being deprived of close relationships. We look too at how social relationships and emotional development are interrelated over the life span. We begin with some broad theoretical perspectives on social relationships.

14.1 Perspectives on Relationships

Relationships are important in human development for an endless range of reasons, but developmental theorists have disagreed about which relationships are most critical. Many noted theorists have argued that no social relationship is more important than the first: the bond between parent and infant. Sigmund Freud (1930) left no doubt about his opinion: a warm and stable mother–child relationship is essential for normal personality development. His follower Erik Erikson tended to agree, emphasizing the importance of responsive parenting to the development of trust in the parent–infant relationship. These theorists, in turn, influenced the architects of today's most influential theory of close human relationships, attachment theory, to emphasize the lasting significance of the parent–infant relationship. As you will

see later, though, other theorists believe that peers are at least as significant as parents in the developmental process.

Attachment Theory

Attachment theory was formulated by British psychiatrist John Bowlby (1969, 1973, 1980, 1988), and it was elaborated on by his colleague Mary Ainsworth, an American developmental psychologist (1989; Ainsworth et al., 1978). The theory was based primarily on ethological theory and therefore asked how attachment might have evolved (see Chapter 2). It also drew on concepts from psychoanalytic theory (Bowlby was a therapist trained in psychoanalytic thinking about the contribution of mother–child relationships to psychopathology and studied war orphans separated from their mothers) and cognitive theory (Bowlby called attention to expectations about self and other, as you will see).

According to Bowlby (1969), an **attachment** is a strong affectional tie that binds a person to an intimate companion. It is also a behavioral system through which humans regulate their emotional distress when under threat and achieve security by seeking proximity to another person. For most of us, the first attachment we form, around 6 or 7 months of age, is to a parent. How do we know when baby Alberto becomes attached to his mother? He will try to maintain proximity to her—crying, clinging, approaching, following, doing whatever it takes to maintain closeness to her and expressing his displeasure when he cannot. He will prefer her to other people, reserving his biggest smiles for her and seeking her when he is upset, discomforted, or afraid; she is irreplaceable in his eyes. He will also be confident about exploring his environment as long as he knows that his mother is there to provide the security he needs.

Notice that an infant attached to a parent is rather like an adult "in love" (like Mike or Marcy at the start of the chapter). True, close emotional ties are expressed in different ways, and serve different functions, at different points in the life span. Adults, for example, do not usually feel compelled to follow their mates around the house, and they look to their loved ones for more than comforting hugs and smiles. Nonetheless, there are basic similarities among the infant attached to a caregiver, the child attached to a best friend, and the adolescent or adult attached to a romantic partner. Throughout the life span, the objects of our attachments are special, irreplaceable people to whom we want to be close and from whom we derive a sense of security (Ainsworth, 1989).

Nature, Nurture, and Attachment

Drawing on ethological theory and research, Bowlby argued that both infants and parents are biologically predisposed to form attachments. As you saw in Chapter 2, ethologists and evolutionary theorists assume that all species, including humans, are born

Ethologist Konrad Lorenz demonstrated that goslings would become imprinted to him rather than to their mother if he was the first moving object they encountered during their critical period for imprinting. Human attachment is more complex.

with behavioral tendencies that have been built into their species over the course of evolution because they have contributed to survival. It makes sense to think, for example, that young birds tended to survive if they stayed close to their mothers so that they could be fed and protected from predators—but that they starved or were gobbled up, and therefore failed to pass their genes to future generations, if they strayed. Thus, chicks, ducks, and goslings may have evolved so that they engage in **imprinting,** an innate form of learning in which the young will follow and become attached to a moving object (usually the mother) during a critical period early in life.

Groundbreaking ethologist Konrad Lorenz (1937) observed imprinting in young goslings and noted that it is automatic (young fowl do not have to be taught to follow), it occurs only within a critical period shortly after the bird has hatched, and it is irreversible—once the gosling begins to follow a particular object, whether its mother or Lorenz, it will remain attached to that object. The imprinting response is considered a prime example of a species-specific and largely innate behavior that has evolved because it has survival value. However, subsequent research has shown that it is not quite as different from other learning as claimed, that the "critical" period is more like a "sensitive" period, that imprinting can be reversed, and that imprinting does not happen without the right interplay of biological and environmental factors (Spencer et al., 2009).

What about human infants? Babies may not become imprinted to their mothers, but they certainly form attachments in infancy and follow their love objects around. Bowlby argued that they come equipped with several other behaviors besides following, or proximity seeking, that help ensure adults will love them, stay with them, and meet their needs. Among these behaviors are sucking and clinging, smiling and vocalizing (crying, cooing, and babbling), and expressions of negative emotion (fretting and crying). Moreover, Bowlby argued, just as infants are programmed to respond to their caregivers, adults are biologically programmed to respond to an infant's signals. Indeed, it is difficult for an adult to ignore a baby's cry or fail to warm to a baby's grin. As Exploration Box 14.1 reveals, biology, as illustrated by the workings of the so-called love hormone **oxytocin,** plays an important role in facilitating parent–infant attachment as well as other social relationships. In short, both human infants and human caregivers have evolved in ways that predispose them to form close attachments and help ensure that infants will survive and thrive.

Just as the imprinting of goslings occurs during a critical period, human attachments form during what Bowlby viewed as a sensitive period for attachment, the first 3 years of life. But attachments do not form automatically. According to Bowlby, a responsive social environment is critical: an infant's preprogrammed signals to other people may eventually wane if caregivers are unresponsive to them. Ultimately, the security of an attachment relationship depends on the interaction over time between infant and caregiver and on the sensitivity of each partner to the other's signals.

Attachment, the product of nature and nurture interacting over many months, should be distinguished from **bonding,** a more biologically based process in which parent and infant form a connection in the first hours after birth, when a mother is likely to be exhilarated and her newborn highly alert. Marshall Klaus and John Kennell (1976) made much of the importance of this early bonding through skin-to-skin contact immediately after birth. Such early physical contact is pleasurable, may help a mother start on a path toward a secure attachment relationship with her baby, and may have other benefits for babies (see Chapter 4 on kangaroo care, for example). However, subsequent research has shown that early contact is not necessary for a secure attachment to form (witness adoptive parents and their children) and does not seem to have as much significance for later development as Klaus and Kennell believed (Goldberg, 1983).

Attachment and Later Development

Bowlby maintained that the quality of the early parent–infant attachment has lasting impacts on development, including the kinds of relationships people have with their friends, romantic partners, and children. He proposed that, based on their interactions with caregivers, infants construct expectations about relationships in the form of **internal working models**—cognitive representations of themselves and other people that guide their processing of social information and behavior in relationships (Bowlby, 1973; see also Bretherton, 1996). Securely attached infants who have received responsive care will form internal working models suggesting that they are lovable and that other people can be trusted to care for them. By contrast, insecurely attached infants subjected to insensitive, neglectful, or abusive care may conclude that they are difficult to love, that other people are unreliable, or both. These insecure infants would be expected to have difficulty participating in close relationships later in life. They may, for example, be wary of getting too close to anyone or become jealous and overly dependent partners if they do.

In sum, attachment theory, as developed by Bowlby and elaborated by Ainsworth, claims that (1) the capacity to form attachments is part of our evolutionary heritage; (2) attachments

Oxytocin: The Love Hormone

We think of social development and social interaction as influenced primarily by environmental influences—especially other people—but should not lose sight of biological factors. To illustrate, consider some fascinating research on oxytocin, a hormone produced primarily in the hypothalamus that affects the brain and plays important roles in love and attachment as well as in stress management (Hart, 2008).

Oxytocin is implicated in several ways in the formation and maintenance of social relationships. It affects the muscles that facilitate contractions during labor and the release of milk during breast feeding. It is also released in large quantities by both sexes during sexual intercourse, and it is released when women are distressed by their romantic relationships, probably because they feel a need for closeness (Taylor, Saphire-Bernstein, & Seeman, 2010). More generally, oxytocin is associated with feelings of friendship and the desire to affiliate (Hart, 2008). Even being gazed upon lovingly by your dog can raise your oxytocin level (Nagasawa et al., 2009)! In all these cases, the release of the hormone generates warm, calm, trusting feelings (Hart, 2008).

Because most knowledge of oxytocin has come from studies of animals, Ruth Feldman and her colleagues (2007) set out to determine whether oxytocin is involved in the attachment of human mothers to their infants. She and her colleagues measured both oxytocin and cortisol (a stress hormone negatively associated with oxytocin levels) in the blood of 62 pregnant women during their first and third trimesters and a month after they gave birth. The researchers also observed mother–infant interactions for 15 minutes, recording maternal attachment behaviors such as gazing at, touching affectionately, showing positive affect toward, and vocalizing to the baby. Finally, they assessed the extent to which mothers' thoughts focused on attachment and the frequency with which they checked on their infants.

Mothers with high levels of oxytocin before birth engaged in high levels of positive attachment behavior after the birth. They also thought more about their relationships with their infants and checked more often on their infants than other mothers. By contrast, high levels of the stress hormone cortisol were negatively correlated with maternal behaviors and thoughts.

Molecular genetics researchers are now focusing on a gene (OXTR) that affects oxytocin receptors in the brain. Mothers who have inefficient variants of the OXTR gene and of a serotonin transporter gene are less sensitive in interactions with difficult children than mothers with other genetic makeups (Bakermans-Kraneburg & van IJzendoorn, 2008).

Studies in which oxytocin is administered to adults suggest that this so-called love hormone calms people, reduces their feelings of anxiety and depression, and facilitates attachment by making it easier to enter into and enjoy close human relationships (Gordon et al., 2008; Hart, 2008). A dose of oxytocin administered nasally increases ratings of the trustworthiness and attractiveness of other people, suggesting that the hormone primes us to affiliate with others (Theodoridou et al., 2009). A spritz of oxytocin (versus a placebo) also makes couples interact more positively while discussing problems in their relationships (Ditzen et al., 2009). Lack of sufficient oxytocin is even being examined as a possible contributor to autism (Yamasue et al., 2009; Wu et al., 2005).

So oxytocin bears watching as more is learned about it. We must be cautious, though: Relationships between hormones and behavior are often bidirectional, hormone levels influencing behavior, but behavior also influencing hormone levels (Feldman, 2007). For now, we mainly hope you appreciate that a variety of hormonal and other biological influences on social relationships must be taken seriously.

---

unfold through an interaction of biological and environmental forces during a sensitive period early in life; (3) the first attachment relationship, the one between infant and caregiver, shapes later development and the quality of later relationships; and (4) internal working models of self and other are the mechanism through which early experience affects later development.

Peers and the Two Worlds of Childhood

A **peer** is a social equal, someone who functions at a similar level of behavioral complexity—often someone of similar age (Lewis & Rosenblum, 1975). Although the parent–infant relationship is undoubtedly important in development, some theorists argue that relationships with peers are at least as significant. In effect, they argue, there are "two social worlds of childhood"—one involving adult–child relationships, the other involving peer relationships—and these two worlds contribute differently to development (Harris, 1998, 2006; Youniss, 1980). From an evolutionary perspective, it makes sense to think that humans evolved to live as members of groups, just as they evolved to form close one-on-one attachments to parents.

As you saw in Chapter 13, Jean Piaget believed that because peers are equals rather than powerful authority figures, they help children learn that relationships are reciprocal, force them to hone their social perspective-taking skills, and contribute to their social cognitive and moral development in ways that parents cannot. Another theorist who believed in the power of peer relationships, especially friendships, was neo-Freudian theorist Harry Stack Sullivan (1953; see also Buhrmester & Furman, 1986). Sullivan stressed the importance of interpersonal relationships throughout life but argued that social needs change as we get older and are gratified through different kinds of social relationships at different ages.

The parent–child relationship is central up to about age 6 in providing tender care and nurturance, but then peers become increasingly important. At first children need playmates; then they need acceptance by the peer group; and then around age 9 to age 12 they begin to need intimacy in the form of a close friendship. Sullivan stressed the developmental significance of these **chumships,** or close childhood friendships. Having a close friend or chum not only teaches children to take others' perspectives but validates and supports children and can protect them from the otherwise harmful effects of a poor parent–child relationship or rejection by the larger peer group. Chumships also teach children how to participate in emotionally intimate relationships and pave the way for romantic relationships during adolescence. Research bears Sullivan out, as we will see as we now examine contributions of both parents and peers to human development (Bukowski, Motzoi, & Mayer, 2009).

Checking Mastery

1. How do ethological theorists explain why imprinting occurs in young goslings?

2. According to attachment theory, what is the mechanism through which early experience affects later social development, and what is the nature of this mechanism?

3. What two theorists would argue that peers are at least as important as parents as contributors to development?

Making Connections

1. Ethological theory, psychoanalytic theory, and cognitive psychology all influenced John Bowlby as he formulated attachment theory. Which elements of attachment theory do you think most reflect each of these three theoretical perspectives, and why?

2. Return to the chapter opener and analyze Marcy's and Mike's thoughts and behavior from the perspective of John Bowlby and other attachment theorists, using their language.

3. Who do you believe you are attached to, and what evidence would you cite that each such relationship is a true attachment?

14.2 The Infant

Human infants are social beings from the start, but their social relationships change dramatically once they form close attachments to caregivers and develop the social skills that allow them to coordinate their own activities with those of other infants. Because attachments involve strong emotions, both positive and negative, and because attachment figures are critical in shaping emotional development, we begin by setting the development of parent–infant attachment in the context of early emotional development.

Early Emotional Development

Emotions are complex phenomena that involve a subjective feeling ("I'm furious"), physiological changes (a pounding heart), and behavior (an enraged face). Carroll Izard (1982; Izard & Ackerman, 2000) and his colleagues maintain that basic emotions develop early and play critical roles in motivating and organizing behavior. By videotaping infants' responses to such events as having a toy taken away or seeing their mothers return after a separation, analyzing specific facial movements (such as the raising of the brows and the wrinkling of the nose), and asking raters to judge what emotion a baby's face reveals, Izard has established that very young infants express distinct emotions in response to different experiences and that adults can readily interpret which emotions they are expressing (see also Saarni et al., 2006). The work of Izard and others allows us to piece together an account of the early development of a number of so-called primary emotions (Lewis, 2000; ■ Figure 14.1).

At birth, babies show contentment (by smiling), interest (by staring intently at objects), and distress (grimaces in response to pain or discomfort). Within the first 6 months, more specific

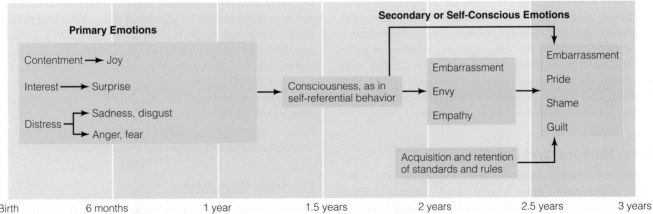

■ **FIGURE 14.1** The emergence of different emotions. Primary emotions emerge in the first 6 months of life; secondary or self-conscious emotions emerge starting from about 18 months to 2 years. Source: From Lewis, M., The emergence of human emotions. In M. Lewis & J. M. Haviland-Jones (Eds.), *Handbook of Emotions* (2nd ed.). Copyright © 2000. Reprinted with permission of Guilford Publications, Inc.

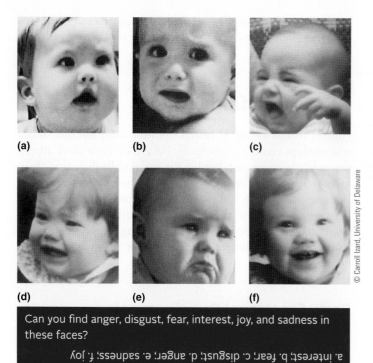

(a) **(b)** **(c)**

(d) **(e)** **(f)**

© Carroll Izard, University of Delaware

Can you find anger, disgust, fear, interest, joy, and sadness in these faces?

a. interest; b. fear; c. disgust; d. anger; e. sadness; f. joy

emotions evolve from these three. By 3 months of age or so, contentment becomes joy or excitement at the sight of something familiar such as a big smile in response to Mom's face. Interest becomes surprise, such as when expectations are violated in games of peekaboo. Distress soon evolves into a range of negative emotions, starting with disgust (in response to foul-tasting foods) and sadness. Angry expressions appear as early as 4 months—about the time infants acquire enough control of their limbs to push unpleasant stimuli away. Fear makes its appearance as early as 5 months.

Next, as Figure 14.1 also shows, come the so-called secondary or **self-conscious emotions**. These emotions, such as embarrassment, require an awareness of self and begin to emerge around 18 months of age, just when infants become able to recognize themselves in a mirror (see Chapter 11). At this age, they begin to show embarrassment when they are asked to perform for guests (Lewis, 2000). Then, when toddlers become able to judge their behavior against standards of performance at around age 2, they become capable of the self-conscious emotions of pride, shame, and guilt (Lewis, 2000). They can feel proud if they catch a ball because they know that's what you're supposed to do when a ball is tossed your way—or guilty if they spill their milk because they know you are not supposed to make messes.

Nature, Nurture, and Emotions

Primary or basic emotions such as interest and fear seem to be biologically programmed. They emerge in all normal infants at roughly the same ages and are displayed and interpreted similarly in all cultures (Izard, 1982; Malatesta et al., 1989). The timing of their emergence is tied to cognitive maturation; for example, babies cannot fear strangers until they are able to represent

mentally what familiar companions look like (Lewis, 2000). As Charles Darwin recognized long ago, basic emotions probably evolved in humans because they helped our ancestors appraise and respond appropriately to new stimuli and situations (Cole, Martin, & Dennis, 2004). As Bowlby emphasized, infants' emotional signals—whether expressions of joy or distress—also prompt their caregivers to respond to them (Kopp & Neufield, 2003).

Whether an infant tends to be predominantly happy and eager to approach new stimuli or irritable and easily distressed depends in part on his individual genetic makeup (Goldsmith, 2003). However, nurture also contributes to emotional development. Through the attachment relationship, caregivers help shape infants' predominant patterns of emotional expression. Observational studies of face-to-face interactions between mothers and infants suggest that young infants display a range of positive and negative emotions, changing their expressions with lightning speed (once every 7 seconds) while their mothers do the same (Malatesta et al., 1986; Malatesta et al., 1989). Mothers mainly display interest, surprise, and joy, thus serving as models of positive emotions and eliciting positive emotions from their babies. Mothers also respond selectively to their babies' expressions; over the early months, they become increasingly responsive to their babies' expressions of happiness, interest, and surprise and less responsive to their negative emotions. Through basic learning processes, then, infants are trained to show happy faces more often than unhappy, grumpy ones—and they do just that over time. They are beginning to learn what emotional expressions mean in their sociocultural environment and which are socially acceptable (Saarni, 1999; Sroufe, 1996).

At around 9 months of age, infants also begin to monitor their companions' emotional reactions in ambiguous situations and use this information to decide how they should feel and behave—a phenomenon called **social referencing** (Feinman, 1992). If their mothers are wary when a stranger approaches, so are they; if their mothers smile at the stranger, so may they. It is not just that 1-year-olds are imitating their parents' emotions. They are able to understand what triggered these emotions and to regulate their behavior accordingly. Infants are especially attentive to stimuli that provoke negative emotional reactions such as fear or anger in their caregivers, as if they know that these emotions are warning signals (Carver & Vaccaro, 2007). Parents also socialize their children's emotions by reacting (for example, sympathetically or critically) to their children's expressions of emotion and by talking about emotions in everyday conversations (Thompson & Meyer, 2007). Gradually, in the context of a secure parent–child relationship in which there is healthy emotional communication, infants and young children learn to understand emotions and express them appropriately.

Emotion Regulation

To conform to their culture's rules and their caregiver's rules about when and how different emotions should be expressed, and most importantly to keep themselves from being overwhelmed by their emotions, infants must develop strategies for

emotion regulation—the processes involved in initiating, maintaining, and altering emotional responses (Bridges & Grolnick, 1995; and see Calkins & Hill, 2007; Gross, 2007). Infants are active from the start in regulating their emotions, but at first they have only a few simple emotion regulation strategies.

Very young infants are able to reduce their negative arousal by turning from unpleasant stimuli or by sucking vigorously on a pacifier (Mangelsdorf, Shapiro, & Marzolf, 1995). By the end of the first year, infants can also regulate their emotions by rocking themselves or moving away from upsetting events. They also actively seek their attachment figures when they are upset because the presence of these individuals has a calming effect.

By 18–24 months, toddlers will try to control the actions of people and objects, such as mechanical toys, that upset them—for example, by pushing the offending person or object away (Mangelsdorf, Shapiro, & Marzolf, 1995). They are able to cope with the frustration of waiting for snacks and gifts by playing with toys and otherwise distracting themselves (Grolnick, Bridges, & Connell, 1996). They have been observed knitting their brows or compressing their lips in an attempt to suppress their anger or sadness (Malatesta et al., 1989). Finally, as children gain the capacity for symbolic thought and language, they become able to regulate their distress symbolically—for example, by repeating the words, "Mommy coming soon, Mommy coming soon," after Mom goes out the door (Thompson, 1994).

The development of emotion regulation skills is influenced by both an infant's temperament and a caregiver's behavior (Grolnick, McMenamy, & Kurowski, 2006). Attachment figures play critical roles in helping infants regulate their emotions and in teaching them how to do so on their own. When infants are very young and have few emotion regulation strategies of their own, they rely heavily on caregivers to help them—for example, by stroking them gently or rocking them when they are distressed (Calkins & Hill, 2007; Cole, Michel, & Teti, 1994). As infants age, they gain control of emotion regulation strategies first learned in the context of the parent–child relationship and can regulate their emotions on their own (for example, by rocking themselves rather than looking to be rocked). As you might guess, children who are not able to get a grip on their negative emotions tend to experience stormy relationships with both caregivers and peers and are at risk to develop behavior problems (Saarni et al., 2006).

Attachment figures also arouse powerful emotions, positive and negative, that need to be regulated. Infants can become uncomfortably overstimulated during joyful bouts of play with parents and highly distressed when their parents leave them. Finally, as we shall soon discover, infants develop their own distinct styles of emotional expression designed to keep attachment figures close (Bridges & Grolnick, 1995). One infant may learn to suppress negative emotions such as fear and anger to avoid angering an irritable caregiver, whereas another may learn to scream loud and long to keep an unreliable caregiver close. By being sensitive, responsive caregivers, parents can help keep fear, anger, and other negative emotions to a minimum (Pauli-Pott, Mertesacker, & Beckmann, 2004). Clearly, then, emotions and

emotion regulation develop in the context of attachment relationships and both affect and are affected by the quality of these relationships.

An Attachment Forms

Like any relationship, the parent–infant attachment is reciprocal. Parents become attached to their infants, and infants become attached to their parents.

The Caregiver's Attachment to the Infant

Parents often begin to form emotional attachments to their babies before birth. Moreover, as noted earlier, parents who have an opportunity for skin-to-skin contact with their babies during the first few hours after birth often feel a special bond forming, although such contact is neither crucial nor sufficient for the development of strong parent–infant attachments. Not only are newborns cute, but their early reflexive behaviors, such as sucking, rooting, and grasping, help endear them to their parents (Bowlby, 1969). Smiling is an especially important social signal. Although it is initially a reflexive response to almost any stimulus, it is triggered by voices at 3 weeks of age and by faces at 5 or 6 weeks (Bowlby, 1969; Wolff, 1963).

Smiling is one of the biologically based behaviors that help ensure adults will fall in love with babies.

© Michael Newman/PhotoEdit Inc.

Preventing Stranger Anxiety

It is not unusual for 1- or 2-year-olds meeting a new baby-sitter or being approached by a nurse or doctor at the doctor's office to break into tears. Stranger-wary infants often stare at the stranger for a moment, then turn away, whimper or cry, and seek the comfort of their parents. Occasionally, infants become terrified. Obviously it is in the interests of baby-sitters, health care professionals, and other "strangers" to be able to prevent such negative reactions. What might we suggest?

- *Keep familiar companions available.* Stranger anxiety is less likely to occur if an attachment figure is nearby to serve as a secure base. In one study, less than one-third of 6- to 12-month-olds were wary of an approaching stranger when they were seated on their mothers' laps, but two-thirds were visibly upset if their mothers were 4 feet away (Morgan & Ricciuti, 1969). A security blanket or beloved stuffed animal can have much the same calming effect as a parent's presence for some infants (Passman, 1977).
- *Arrange for the infant's companions to respond positively to the stranger.* As you have seen, infants about 9 months or older engage in social referencing, using other people's emotional reactions to guide their own responses. Infants are likely to respond favorably to a stranger's approach if their mothers or fathers greet the stranger warmly.
- *Make the setting more "familiar."* Stranger anxiety is less likely to occur in familiar settings than in unfamiliar ones (Sroufe, Waters, & Matas, 1974). Wariness is likely to be less evident if the baby-sitter comes to the child's home than if the child is taken to the baby-sitter's home or some other unfamiliar place. Yet an unfamiliar environment can become a familiar one if infants are given the time to get used to it: in one study (Sroufe, Waters, & Matas, 1974), more than 90% of 10-month-olds became upset if a stranger approached within 1 minute after they had been placed in an unfamiliar room, but only 50% did so when they were given 10 minutes to become accustomed to the room.
- *Be a sensitive, unobtrusive stranger.* Encounters with a stranger go best if the stranger initially keeps her distance and then approaches slowly while smiling, talking, and offering a familiar toy or suggesting a familiar activity (Bretherton, Stolberg, & Kreye, 1981; Sroufe, 1977). It also helps if the stranger, like any sensitive caregiver, takes her cues from the infant (Mangelsdorf, 1992). Babies prefer strangers they can control!
- *Try not to look any stranger than need be.* Finally, infants are most likely to be afraid of people who violate their mental schemas or expectations (Kagan, 1972). Baby-sitters who favor faddish clothes or unusual hairstyles and health care professionals who don surgical masks or stethoscopes, beware!

© Blend/Image Source

Babies are also endearing because they are responsive. Over the weeks and months, caregivers and infants develop **synchronized routines** much like dances, in which the partners take turns responding to each other's leads (Stern, 1977; Tronick, 1989). Note the synchrony as this mother plays peekaboo with her infant (Tronick, 1989, p. 112):

> The infant abruptly turns away from his mother as the game reaches its "peak" of intensity and begins to suck on his thumb and stare into space with a dull facial expression. The mother stops playing and sits back watching. . . . After a few seconds the infant turns back to her with an inviting expression. The mother moves closer, smiles, and says in a high-pitched, exaggerated voice, "Oh, now you're back!" He smiles in response and vocalizes. As they finish crowing together, the infant reinserts his thumb and looks away. The mother again waits. [Soon] the infant turns. . . . to her and they greet each other with big smiles.

Synchronized routines are likely to develop when caregivers are sensitive, providing social stimulation when a baby is alert and receptive but not pushing their luck when the infant's message is "Cool it—I need a break from all this stimulation." When parent–infant synchrony can be achieved, it contributes to a secure attachment relationship (Jaffe et al., 2001) as well as to later self-regulation and empathy (Feldman, 2007).

The Infant's Attachment to the Caregiver

Infants progress through the following phases in forming attachments (Ainsworth, 1973; Bowlby, 1969):

1. *Undiscriminating social responsiveness (birth to 2 or 3 months).* Very young infants are responsive to voices, faces, and other social stimuli, but any human interests them. They do not yet show a clear preference for one person over another.
2. *Discriminating social responsiveness (2 or 3 months to 6 or 7 months).* Infants begin to express preferences for familiar companions. They direct their biggest grins and most enthusiastic babbles toward those companions, although they are still friendly toward strangers.

3. *Active proximity seeking or true attachment (6 or 7 months to about 3 years).* Around 6 or 7 months, infants form their first clear attachments, most often to their mothers. Now able to crawl, an infant will follow her mother to stay close, protest when her mother leaves, and greet her mother warmly when she returns. Soon most infants become attached to other people as well—fathers, siblings, grandparents, and regular baby-sitters (Schaffer & Emerson, 1964).

4. *Goal-corrected partnership (3 years and older).* By about age 3, partly because they have more advanced social cognitive abilities, children can participate in a **goal-corrected partnership**, taking a parent's goals and plans into consideration and adjusting their behavior to achieve the all-important goal of maintaining optimal proximity to the attachment figure. Thus, a 1-year-old cries and tries to follow when Dad leaves the house to talk to a neighbor, whereas a 4-year-old probably understands where Dad is going and can control the need for his attention until Dad returns. This final, goal-corrected partnership phase lasts a lifetime.

Attachment-Related Fears

Infants no sooner experience the pleasures of love than they discover the agonies of fear. One form of fear is **separation anxiety:** once attached to a parent, a baby often becomes wary or fretful when separated from that parent. Separation anxiety normally appears when infants are forming their first genuine attachments, peaks between 14 and 18 months, and gradually becomes less frequent and less intense (Weinraub & Lewis, 1977). Still, even children and adolescents may become homesick and distressed when separated from their parents for a long time (Thurber, 1995).

A second fearful response that often emerges shortly after an infant becomes attached to someone is **stranger anxiety**—a wary or fretful reaction to the approach of an unfamiliar person (Schaffer & Emerson, 1964). Anxious reactions to strangers—often mixed with signs of interest—become common between 8 and 10 months, continue through the first year, and gradually decline in intensity over the second year (Sroufe, 1996).

Application Box 14.1 suggests how baby-sitters and health-care professionals can head off outbreaks of fear and trembling.

Exploratory Behavior

The formation of a strong attachment to a caregiver has another important consequence: It facilitates exploratory behavior. Ainsworth and her colleagues (1978) emphasized that an attachment figure serves as a **secure base** for exploration—a point of safety from which an infant can feel free to venture—as well as a safe haven to which she can return if frightened for some "emotional refueling" (Mercer, 2006). Thus Isabelle, a securely attached infant visiting a neighbor's home with Mom, may be comfortable cruising the living room as long as she can check occasionally to see that Mom is still on the couch but may freeze and fret and stop exploring if Mom disappears into the bathroom. Isabelle may also beat a quick retreat to the safe haven Mom provides if stressed by the doorbell or some other unexpected event.

Quality of Attachment

Ainsworth's most important contribution to attachment theory was to devise a way to assess differences in the quality of parent–infant attachments, making Bowlby's hypotheses testable (Thompson & Raikes, 2003). She and her associates created the **Strange Situation,** a now-famous procedure for measuring the quality of an attachment (Ainsworth et al., 1978). It consists of eight episodes that gradually escalate the amount of stress infants experience as they react to the approach of an adult stranger and the departure and return of their caregiver (● **Table 14.1**). On the basis of an infant's pattern of behavior across the episodes, the quality of his attachment to a parent can be characterized as one of four types: secure, resistant, avoidant, or disorganized–disoriented.

1. **Secure attachment.** About 60 to 65% of 1-year-olds in our society are securely attached to their mothers or primary caregivers (Colin, 1996). The securely attached infant actively explores the room when alone with his mother be-

● TABLE 14.1 THE EPISODES OF THE STRANGE SITUATION

Episode	Events	Attachment Behavior Observed
1	Experimenter leaves parent and baby to play	
2	Parent sits while baby plays	Use of parent as secure base
3	Stranger enters, talks to parent	Stranger anxiety
4	Parent leaves; stranger lets baby play, offers comfort if needed	Separation anxiety
5	Parent returns, greets baby, offers comfort if needed; stranger leaves	Reactions to reunion
6	Parent leaves	Separation anxiety
7	Stranger enters, offers comfort	Stranger anxiety; ability to be soothed by stranger
8	Parent returns, greets baby, offers comfort, lets baby return to play	Reactions to reunion

SOURCE: Modified from Ainsworth et al., 1978.

cause she serves as a secure base. The infant may be upset by separation but greets his mother warmly and is comforted by her presence when she returns. The securely attached child is outgoing with a stranger when his mother is present. As Cindy Hazan and her colleagues (Hazan, Campa, & Gur-Yaish, 2006) summarize the Bowlby–Ainsworth view, the securely attached infant "stays close and continuously monitors [the caregiver's] whereabouts (*proximity maintenance*), retreats to her for comfort if needed (*safe haven*), resists and is distressed by separations from her (*separation distress*), and explores happily as long as she is present and attentive (*secure base*)" (p. 190).

2. **Resistant attachment.** About 10% of 1-year-olds show a resistant attachment, an insecure attachment characterized by anxious, ambivalent reactions (and also called anxious/ ambivalent attachment). The resistant infant does not dare venture off to play even when her mother is present; she does not seem to serve as a secure base for exploration. Yet this infant becomes distressed when her mother departs, often showing stronger separation anxiety than the securely attached infant—perhaps because she is uncertain whether her mother will return. When her mother returns, the infant is ambivalent: she may try to remain near her but seems to resent her for having left, may resist if she tries to make physical contact, and may even hit and kick her in anger (Ainsworth et al., 1978). Resistant infants are also wary of strangers, even when their mothers are present. It seems, then, that resistant or ambivalent infants are never sure that the affection and comfort they so visibly crave will be forthcoming.

3. **Avoidant attachment.** Infants with avoidant attachments (up to 15% of 1-year-olds) seem uninterested in exploring, show little apparent distress when separated from their mothers, and avoid contact or seem indifferent when their mothers return. These insecurely attached infants are not particularly wary of strangers but sometimes avoid or ignore them, much as these babies avoid or ignore their mothers. Avoidant infants seem to have distanced themselves from their parents, almost as if they were denying their need for affection or had learned not to express their emotional needs.

4. **Disorganized–disoriented attachment.** Ainsworth's work initially focused on secure, resistant, and avoidant attachment styles, but some infants do not develop any of these consistent ways of coping with their need for proximity to their caregiver when they are stressed and seem confused. Up to 15% of infants—more in high-risk families—display what is now recognized as a fourth attachment classification, one that seems to be associated with later emotional problems (van IJzendoorn, Schuengel, & Bakermans-Kranenburg, 1999).

Reunited with their mothers after a separation, these infants may act dazed and freeze or lie on the floor immobilized—or they may seek contact but then abruptly move away as their mothers approach them, only to seek contact again (Main & Solomon, 1990). Infants with a disorganized–disoriented attachment have not been able to devise a consistent strategy for regulating negative emotions such as separation anxiety; they seem frightened of their parent and stuck between approaching and avoiding this frightening figure (Hesse & Main, 2006).

● **Table 14.2** summarizes the features of these four patterns of attachment, which have been the subject of considerable re-

● **TABLE 14.2 CHILD BEHAVIORS IN THE STRANGE SITUATION ASSOCIATED WITH ATTACHMENT TYPES AND RELATED PARENTING STYLES**

Behavior	Type of Attachment			
	Secure	Resistant	Avoidant	Disorganized– Disoriented
Child explores when caregiver is present to provide a secure base for exploration?	Yes, actively	No, clings	Yes, but play is not as constructive as that of secure infant	No
Child responds positively to stranger?	Yes, comfortable if caregiver is present	No, fearful even when caregiver is present	No, often indifferent, as with caregiver	No, confused responses
Child protests when separated from caregiver?	Yes, at least mildly distressed	Yes, extremely upset	No, seemingly unfazed	Sometimes; unpredictable
Child responds positively to caregiver at reunion?	Yes, happy to be reunited	Yes and no, seeks contact, but resents being left; ambivalent, sometimes angry	No, ignores or avoids caregiver	Confused; may approach or avoid caregiver or do both
Parenting style	Sensitive, responsive	Inconsistent, often unresponsive (e.g., depressed)	Rejecting– unresponsive or intrusive–overly stimulating	Frightened (e.g., overwhelmed) and frightening (e.g., abusive)

search. What determines which of these attachment patterns will characterize a parent–infant relationship? The caregiver, the infant, and the context all contribute.

The Caregiver's Contributions

According to Freud, infants in the oral stage of psychosexual development become attached to the individual who provides them with oral pleasure, and the attachment bond will be most secure if a mother is relaxed and generous in her feeding practices. Early learning theorists put it differently but also believed that infants learns positive emotional responses to their mother by associating her with food. In a classic study conducted by Harry Harlow and Robert Zimmerman (1959), the psychoanalytic and learning theory views dominant at the time were put to the test—and failed. Monkeys were reared with two surrogate mothers: a wire "mother" and a cloth "mother" wrapped in foam rubber and covered with terrycloth (see the photo below). Half the infants were fed by the cloth mother, and the remaining infants were fed by the wire mother. To which mother did these infants become attached? There was no contest: Infants strongly preferred the cuddly cloth mother, regardless of which mother had fed them. Even if their food came from the wire mother, they spent more time clinging to the cloth mother, ran to her when they were upset or afraid, and showed every sign of being attached to her.

The wire and cloth surrogate "mothers" used in Harlow's classic research. This infant monkey has formed an attachment to the cloth mother that provides "contact comfort," even though it must stretch to the wire mother in order to feed.

© Harlow Primate Laboratory, University of Wisconsin

Harlow's research demonstrated that **contact comfort,** the pleasurable tactile sensations provided by a soft and cuddly "parent," is a more powerful contributor to attachment in monkeys than feeding or the reduction of hunger. Contact comfort also promotes human attachments (Anisfeld et al., 1990). Moreover, many infants become attached to someone other than the adult who feeds them, and variations in feeding schedules and the age at which infants are weaned have little effect on the quality of infants' attachments (Schaffer & Emerson, 1964).

Styles of parenting strongly influence the infant attachment styles described in Table 14.2, however. Infants who enjoy *secure* attachments to their parents have parents who are sensitive and responsive to their needs and emotional signals, as Bowlby and Ainsworth proposed (Ainsworth et al., 1978; De Wolff & van IJzendoorn, 1997). Babies who show a *resistant* pattern of attachment often have parents who are inconsistent in their caregiving; they react enthusiastically or indifferently, depending on their moods, and are frequently unresponsive (Isabella, 1993; Isabella & Belsky, 1991). Mothers who are depressed, for example, often have difficulty responding sensitively to their babies' signals and do not provide the comforting that helps babies regulate their negative emotions (Dawson & Ashman, 2000). The infant copes with unreliable caregiving by trying desperately—through clinging, crying, and other attachment behaviors—to obtain emotional support and comfort, and then becomes saddened and resentful when these efforts fail. This resistant attachment style has been linked to the development of negative internal working models of self and parents as early as age 3 or 4 (Toth et al., 2009).

The parents of infants with an *avoidant* attachment tend to provide either too little or too much stimulation. Some are rejecting; they are impatient, unresponsive, and resentful when the infant interferes with their plans (Ainsworth, 1979; Isabella, 1993). Some of these parents find an infant's crying extremely aversive and are unresponsive as a result (Mills-Koonce et al., 2007). Others have been called "intrusive"; they are overzealous and provide high levels of stimulation even when their babies become uncomfortably aroused and need a break so that they can regain control of their emotions (Isabella & Belsky, 1991). Infants with an avoidant attachment style may learn to avoid and make few emotional demands on adults who seem to dislike their company or who bombard them with stimulation they cannot handle.

Finally, a *disorganized–disoriented* style of attachment is evident in as many as 80% of infants who have been physically abused or maltreated (Carlson et al., 1989; and see Baer & Martinez, 2006). It is also common among infants whose mothers are severely depressed or abuse alcohol and drugs (Beckwith, Rozga, & Sigman, 2002). The parents of infants with a disorganized attachment pattern have been described as frightening and frightened—as fragile and fearful adults who are not up to the challenge of caring for an infant and create an unpredictable, scary environment for their babies (Hesse & Main, 2006). Infants with a disorganized attachment are understandably confused about whether to approach or avoid a parent who can be loving one minute but angry and abusive or indifferent the next. Each of the four types of attachment, then, reflects a reasonable way of coping with a particular brand of parenting.

The Infant's Contributions

Do the infant's characteristics also have a bearing on the quality of the attachments that form? Cognitive developmental theorists emphasize that the ability to form attachments depends partly on the infant's cognitive development. For example, the infant must recognize that close companions continue to exist even when they are absent to experience separation anxiety when a caregiver leaves the room (Kohlberg, 1969; Lester et al., 1974). That is, infants will not form attachments until they have acquired some concept of person permanence, a form of Jean Piaget's object permanence concept (see Chapter 7).

An infant's temperament also matters: Attachments tend to be insecure when infants are by temperament fearful, irritable, or unresponsive (Beckwith, Rozga, & Sigman, 2002), and the caregiver's style of parenting and the infant's temperament often interact to determine the outcome. To illustrate, ◾ Figure 14.2 shows the percentages of 12-month-olds who tested as securely attached as a function of whether they were difficult-to-read infants born prematurely and whether their mothers were depressed (Poehlmann & Fiese, 2001). Only when a depressed mother was paired with a difficult-to-read, premature infant did the odds of a secure attachment become low. Similarly, the combination of a mother with a low sense of self-efficacy as a parent and an infant with colic who cries endlessly makes for an insecure attachment (Stifter, 2003). This means that a sensitive parent can do a lot to convert a difficult, distressed baby into a baby who has learned to regulate his emotions and is socially competent (Leerkes, Blankson, & O'Brien, 2009).

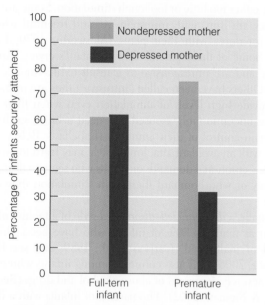

■ **FIGURE 14.2** The combination of a depressed mother and a premature infant means low odds that a secure attachment will form. Source: Data from J. Poehlmann & B. H. Fiese, The interaction of maternal and infant vulnerabilities on developing attachment relationships, *Development and Psychopathology, 13,* pp. 1–11. Copyright © 2001 Guilford. Reprinted by permission from Cambridge University Press.

Overall, the caregiver affects the quality of the attachment that forms more than the infant does (Goldberg et al., 1986; Vaughn et al., 1989). If the infant's temperament were the main influence on security of attachment, (1) we would not see so many infants securely attached to one parent but insecurely attached to the other (van IJzendoorn & De Wolff, 1997); (2) we would not have evidence that an infant's genes, although they do influence the infant's temperament, have relatively little influence on quality of attachment (Fearon et al., 2006; Roisman & Fraley, 2008); and (3) it would not be possible for caregivers who are patient and adjust to their baby's temperamental quirks to establish secure relationships with temperamentally difficult babies (Mangelsdorf et al., 1990).

Contextual Contributors

Finally, the broader social context surrounding caregiver and infant can affect how they react to each other. For example, the stresses associated with living in poverty or experiencing marital difficulties may make it difficult for parents to provide sensitive care and may contribute to insecure attachments (Howes & Markman, 1989; Murray et al., 1996). The cultural context in which caregiver and baby interact also colors their relationship. For instance, German parents strongly encourage independence and discourage clingy behavior, fearing that if they are too responsive to cries they will spoil their infants. This may explain why many German infants make few emotional demands on their parents and are often classified as avoidantly attached in the Strange Situation (Grossmann, Grossmann, & Keppler, 2005). The Strange Situation may underestimate the number of securely attached infants in Germany—and also among U.S. babies who regularly receive nonmaternal care and who learn not to be bothered much by separations (Clarke-Stewart, Goossens, & Allhusen, 2001). By contrast, Japanese babies, who are rarely separated from their mothers early in life and are encouraged to be dependent on their mothers, become highly distressed by separations such as those they must endure in the Strange Situation. As a result, they are more likely than American babies to be classified as resistantly attached (Takahashi, 1990; van IJzendoorn & Sagi, 1999).

Could findings like this mean that research on infant attachment is culturally biased? Fred Rothbaum and his colleagues (Rothbaum, Weisz et al., 2000; Rothbaum & Morelli, 2005) think so. They observe that in Western *individualistic cultures,* such as Germany, optimal development means becoming an autonomous being, whereas in Eastern *collectivist cultures,* such as Japan, the goal is to become integrated into the group, and this leads to differences in parenting and in the meaning of a secure attachment. Rothbaum appreciates that the main predictions of attachment theory—for example, the relationship between parental sensitivity and security of attachment—hold up well across cultures (see van IJzendoorn & Sagi-Schwartz, 2008). Still, characteristics of the caregiver (or in many cultures, caregivers), the baby, and the surrounding social environment all affect the quality of the emerging attachment, and what represents an adaptive attachment relationship in one culture may not be viewed as such in another.

Compared with American babies, Japanese infants become more anxious in the Strange Situation because they are rarely separated from their mothers.

Implications of Early Attachment

From Freud on, almost everyone has assumed that the parent–child relationship is critical in human development. Just how important is it? Several lines of research offer some answers: studies of socially deprived infants; studies of infants separated from their caregivers, including those who attend day care; and studies of the later development of securely and insecurely attached infants.

Social Deprivation

What happens to infants who never have an opportunity to form an attachment? It is better to have loved and lost than never to have loved at all, say studies of infants who grow up in deprived institutional settings and are never able to form attachments (MacLean, 2003; Rutter & O'Connor, 2004). In the 1990s, children from deprived institutions in Romania were adopted into homes in the United States, the United Kingdom, and Canada after the fall of the Romanian government (Gunnar, Bruce, & Grotevant, 2000). These adoptees reportedly spent their infancies in orphanages with 20–30 children in a room and only one caregiver for every 10–20 children; they spent most of their time rocking in their cribs with little human contact, much less hugs, bouts of play, and synchronous routines (Fisher et al., 1997). How have they turned out?

Infants who spent their first 6 months or more in deprived orphanages displayed eating problems and medical problems and showed delays in physical, cognitive, and social–emotional development (Fisher et al., 1997; Gunnar, Bruce, & Grotevant, 2000; MacLean, 2003). Rapid recovery was evident once the children were adopted, and some children overcame their developmental problems entirely (Judge, 2003). Yet many children institutionalized for more than 6 months never achieved normal levels of cognitive development, possibly because they lacked the intellectual stimulation necessary for normal brain development (Rutter & O'Connor, 2004).

Continuing problems in interpersonal relationships were evident, too. These children have tended to be emotionally with-

drawn, indiscriminately friendly, or both (Smyke, Dumitrescu, & Zeanah, 2002). For example, Thomas O'Connor and his colleagues (2003) compared attachment quality at age 4 among children who started their lives in deprived institutions in Romania and were adopted into British homes (either before 6 months or between 6 and 24 months of age) and British children who were adopted before 6 months of age. As ■ **Figure 14.3** shows, the longer the Romanian children had experienced early deprivation, the less likely they were to be securely attached and the more likely they were to show a disturbed pattern of behavior called **disinhibited attachment**, which is characterized by indiscriminate friendliness, lack of appropriate wariness of strangers, and difficulty participating in real, reciprocal social interactions.

The children with the disinhibited attachment pattern, half of those deprived for 6 months or more, were often indiscriminately friendly toward both a stranger and their parent in the Strange Situation test. They would eagerly approach the stranger in a coy or silly manner but then back off warily (rather than showing the normal pattern of wariness first and approach second). They could not sustain give-and-take social interactions. A meta-analysis of many studies of institutionalized and otherwise maltreated and neglected children concluded that those who are adopted before 1 year of age are likely to become as securely attached to their caregivers as nonadopted children, but that high

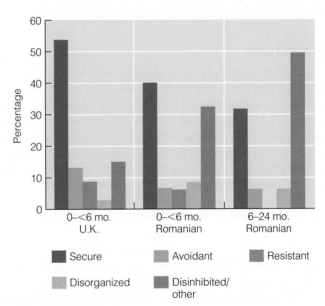

■ **FIGURE 14.3** Percentages of secure, avoidant, resistant, disorganized, and "disinhibited or other" attachments among nondeprived British children adopted before 6 months of age, deprived Romanian children adopted in the United Kingdom before 6 months, and deprived Romanian children adopted between 6 and 24 months. Notice the high percentage of disinhibited attachment in Romanian infants who spent a long time in a deprived institution. Source: From O'Connor, T. G., et al., Child-parent attachment following early institutional deprivation, *Development and Psychopathology*, 15, pp. 19–38. Copyright © 2003. Reprinted by permission of Cambridge University Press.

rates of insecure and disturbed attachment are observed in children adopted after their first birthday (van den Dries et al., 2009). This, then, supports Bowlby's claim that infancy is a sensitive period for the formation of attachments.

What is it about deprived early environments that damages development? Lack of proper nutrition, hygiene, and medical care; lack of stimulation; and lack of stable attachment relationships may all contribute (Gunnar, Bruce, & Grotevant, 2000). However, institutionalized children who are provided with good physical care and sensory and intellectual stimulation but lack a stable team of caregivers are still developmentally delayed and have long-lasting social and emotional difficulties (Hodges & Tizard, 1989). Nor is the problem lack of a single "mother figure." In adequately staffed institutions and communes, infants cared for by a few responsive caregivers turn out quite normal (Groark et al., 2005; Smyke, Dumitrescu, & Zeanah, 2002). Indeed, placing institutionalized children in small groups with a few, consistent caregivers who interact with the children caringly can prevent most of the negative effects of living in a large residential institution (St. Petersburg–USA Orphanage Research Team, 2008).

Apparently, then, normal development requires sustained interactions with responsive caregivers—whether one or a few. Apparently too, children are resilient, provided that they are given reasonable opportunities to socialize and to find someone to love. However, as Bowlby claimed, early social experiences can sometimes leave lasting marks on development.

Separations

Now consider babies who form an attachment but are separated from their caregivers as a result of illness, war, death, or other unforeseen circumstances. These infants go through a grieving process in which they are likely to be sad and anxious but normally recover once reunited with their loved one. One man described by Jean Mercer (2006) recalls being traumatized, though, because when he was growing up adults did not appreciate the need to prepare children for long separations: "His mother brought him to the hospital, handed him to a nurse, and then left, returning for him as instructed ten days later. He did not speak again for a year after this event" (p. 21).

Infants who are permanently separated from a caregiver normally recover if they are able to maintain or form an attachment with someone else (Bowlby, 1960, 1980; and see Chapter 17). The earlier the separation takes place, the better (van IJzendoorn & Juffer, 2006). It is children who experience a series of separations from caregivers, as happens to some infants and children in foster care, that we should worry about: they may be permanently marred by their repeated experiences of loving and losing (Colin, 1996; Ward, Munro, & Dearden, 2006).

Day Care

The daily separations from their parents that infants experience when they are placed in day care centers or in family care homes (in which caregivers take children into their homes) are unlikely to keep infants from forming or maintaining close relationships with their parents. Day care can have positive or negative effects,

depending on several factors, but it normally does not damage child development (Clarke-Stewart & Allhusen, 2005). This is good news for the more than 60% of mothers in the United States who work outside the home at least part-time.

A major longitudinal study supported by the National Institute of Child Health and Human Development and involving teams of researchers in 10 cities in the United States is our best source of evidence (NICHD Early Child Care Research Network [ECCRN], 1997, 2003, 2005, 2006; NICHD, 2006). Overall, infants in this national study who experienced routine care by someone other than their mothers were not much different than infants cared for almost exclusively by their mothers in the various developmental outcomes studied. Most notably, infants who received alternative forms of care, even more than 20 hours a week of it, were no less securely attached to their mothers overall than infants who were tended by their mothers (Friedman & Boyle, 2008; NICHD ECCRN, 1997). Quality of parenting was a much stronger influence on these infants' attachment security and development than day care experience.

Quality of day care, defined in terms of sensitive caregiving and cognitive and language stimulation, also had impacts. Children who spent a good deal of time in quality day care performed better than home-reared children on measures of cognitive and language skills and some measures of social skills. On the other hand, they tended to display more behavior problems (Belsky et al., 2007; NICHD ECCRN, 2006). Parents seeking quality day care should look for a reasonable child-to-caregiver ratio (up to three infants, four toddlers, or eight preschoolers per adult); caregivers who have been well trained and who are warm and responsive; little staff turnover so that children can become attached to their caregivers; and planned, age-appropriate stimulation activities (Burchinal et al., 2000; Clarke-Stewart & Allhusen, 2005).

Finally, the NICHD study showed that quality of the home environment interacts with quality of the day care environment to influence outcomes. For example, infants fared poorly if their

To be a high-quality, stimulating care setting, a day care center should generally have only about three infants per staff member. In this Baby Care Center in Beijing, mothers, grandmothers, nannies, and even fathers visit frequently to ensure that their babies receive plenty of social stimulation.

mothers were insensitive and unresponsive *and* they were subjected to poor-quality day care on top of it (NICHD ECCRN, 1997). Under these circumstances, about half the infants were insecurely attached to their mothers. By contrast, infants who received either good parenting or good day care were usually securely attached. In sum, infants and young children who spend time in day care do not turn out much different from infants and young children cared for at home—and are most likely to thrive when they interact with both sensitive and stimulating parents and sensitive and stimulating substitute caregivers.

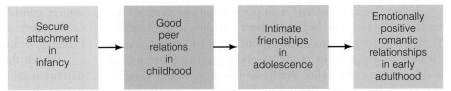

■ **FIGURE 14.4** Simpson et al. (2007) found that relationship quality at each step in development affects relationship quality at the next step. Source: From Simpson, J. A., Collins, W. A., Tran, S., & Haydon, K. C., Attachment and the experience and expression of emotions in romantic relationships: A developmental perspective, *Journal of Personality and Social Psychology, 92*, pp. 355–367. Copyright © 2007 American Psychological Association. Reprinted with permission.

Later Development of Securely and Insecurely Attached Infants

Finally, we can assess the importance of early attachment experiences by asking this: How much difference does having secure rather than insecure attachment to caregivers in infancy make later in life? According to Bowlby and Ainsworth's attachment theory, a secure attachment, once formed, allows exploration from a secure base. This implies that securely attached children should be more cognitively competent (because they will be curious, explore the environment freely, and not shy away from challenges) and more socially and emotionally competent (because they will explore the world of people freely, expect positive reactions from others because of the positive internal working models they form, and have learned in the parent–child relationship how to regulate their emotions). Does research support these predictions?

Indeed it does. Securely attached infants turn into preschool children whom teachers describe as curious, self-directed, and eager to learn, whereas insecurely attached children are less independent (Waters, Wippman, & Sroufe, 1979). Children who had been securely attached as infants are also more socially competent—more able to initiate play activities, more sensitive to the needs and feelings of other children, and more popular (see also Booth-LaForce & Kerns, 2009). Finally, secure attachment in infancy is linked to positive emotional development and the capacity to cope with stress and regulate emotions in childhood (Gunnar, 1998, 2000; Kochanska, 2001).

Do these effects of quality of attachment in infancy on intellectual curiosity, social competence, and emotional development last? In late childhood and adolescence, children who have enjoyed secure relationships with their parents continue to be well adjusted (Elicker, Englund, & Sroufe, 1992; Jacobsen & Hofmann, 1997). In a revealing longitudinal study, Jeffrey Simpson and his colleagues (2007) studied 78 individuals from infancy to their early 20s. These researchers were able to link secure attachment in the Strange Situation at 12 months of age to the quality of a child's peer relations in elementary school, which in turn predicted quality of friendships in adolescence, which in turn predicted the emotional quality of romantic relationships in early adulthood. Although quality of attachment during infancy and quality of romantic relationship in adulthood

were not directly linked, they were indirectly associated through a chain of influence in which the quality of relationships in each developmental period affects the quality of relationships in the next period, as shown in ■ Figure 14.4.

In sum, children are unlikely to develop normally if they never have the opportunity to form an attachment or if their first relationships in life are repeatedly severed. By contrast, a secure attachment during infancy has many positive implications for intellectual, social, and emotional development. Yet you must avoid concluding that infants who are securely attached to their mothers are forever blessed—or that infants who are insecurely attached to their mothers are doomed.

First, affectionate ties to fathers (or siblings or grandparents) can compensate for insecure mother–infant relationships (Main & Weston, 1981). Second, attachment quality changes, and early attachments may have no long-term consequences if they change later—if stressful life events such as divorce and illness convert secure attachments into insecure ones, or if positive life changes make insecure attachments more secure (Waters, Wippman, & Sroufe, 2000; Weinfield, Sroufe, & Egeland, 2000). Internal working models are just that—working models, subject to revision based on later social experiences (Sroufe et al., 2005).

All things considered, the Bowlby–Ainsworth attachment theory is well supported. Studies of the long-term consequences of early attachment support Bowlby's claim that internal working models formed early in life shape later relationships and development. Still, many of us learn new social skills and different attitudes toward relationships in our later interactions not only with parents but also with peers, friends, lovers, and spouses. It is time, then, to supplement this description of parent–child relations with a look at the "second world of childhood"—the world of peer relations.

First Peer Relations

Evolution seems to have equipped human infants not only with a capacity for forming attachments to caregivers but also with a capacity for establishing social relationships with peers (Hay, Caplan, & Nash, 2009; Rubin, Bukowski, & Parker, 2006). Infants show an interest in other babies from an early age and show capacities for sharing, cooperation, and sympathy in their first year.

Infants begin to interact with peers in earnest in about the middle of the first year; by then, infants will often smile or babble at their tiny companions, vocalize, offer toys, and gesture to one another, although many of their friendly gestures go unnoticed and unreciprocated (Hay, Nash, & Pedersen, 1983; Vandell, Wilson, & Buchanan, 1980). During their first year, they may share toys nicely at times but also get into squabbles over them, though they only rarely hit each other (Hay, Caplan, & Nash, 2009). During their first year, infants even show signs that they are biologically prepared for life in social groups: they can relate meaningfully in groups of three (Selby & Bradley, 2003).

By about 18 months, infants are able to engage in simple forms of reciprocal, complementary play with peers (Mueller & Lucas, 1975). They turn rounds of imitation into social games (Howes & Matheson, 1992). They can also adopt and reverse roles in their play. Thus, the toddler who receives a toy may immediately offer a toy in return, or the one who has been the chaser will become the chasee. Toward the end of the second year, infants have become proficient at this kind of turn-taking and reciprocal exchange, especially if they are securely attached to their parents (Fagot, 1997).

Some infants even form special, distinctive relationships with certain preferred playmates—friendships (Hay, Caplan, & Nash, 2009; Rubin, Bukowski, & Parker, 2006). On Israeli kibbutzim, where children are cared for in groups, Martha Zaslow (1980) discovered that many pairs of infants as young as 1 year became truly attached to each other. Hadara and Rivka, for in-

stance, consistently sought each other as playmates, mourned each other's absence, and disturbed everyone with their loud babbling "conversations" when they were confined to their cribs.

Clearly the caregiver–infant relationship is not the only important social relationship that develops during infancy; peer relations are well under way, too. Still under debate is whether through the caregiver–infant relationship children learn social skills that they later transfer to their peer relationships or whether infants develop social skills in the two relationships in parallel (Hay, Caplan, & Nash, 2009).

Checking Mastery

1. What is the difference between a primary emotion and a secondary, or self-conscious, emotion?

2. What are two phenomena that result when infants form their first attachments?

3. Compare how infants with a resistant attachment and infants with an avoidant attachment react to separations from their caregivers and the reunions that follow.

4. What is distinctive about the disinhibited attachment pattern seen in infants from deprived institutions?

Making Connections

1. Some years ago, a 2-year-old named Baby Jessica made news because she was taken suddenly from the parents who thought they had adopted her and awarded by the court to her biological parents. What would attachment theory and research on attachment predict about Jessica's development? Was she able to form close attachments to her biological parents? What kind of child did she become? Then speculate about why Jessica apparently turned into a happy, well-adjusted individual instead (Ingrassia & Springen, 1994).

2. Explain how infants with resistant attachments, avoidant attachments, and disorganized attachments are each trying to regulate their emotions as best they can given the parenting they receive.

Even before 1 year of age, infants seem ready to engage in social interactions, not only in dyads but in groups.

© Myrleen Ferguson Cate/PhotoEdit Inc.

14.3 The Child

How do relationships with parents and peers change from infancy to childhood as children become more involved in play activities and try to gain acceptance by their peers? And how do changing social relationships in childhood contribute to development?

Parent–Child Attachments

The parent–child attachment changes qualitatively during childhood. According to John Bowlby (1969), it becomes a goal-corrected partnership in which parent and child accommodate to each other's needs and the child becomes a more sensitive partner and grows more independent of the parent. Young preschool children want separations to be predictable and controllable and will negotiate with their parents to make sure that certain rituals such as the reading of a favorite book occur before bedtime or before parents go out for the evening (Mercer, 2006). Children continue to seek attention and approval from their parents, and they rush to their parents for safe haven when they are frightened or hurt, but they also become increasingly dependent on peers for social and emotional support (Furman & Buhrmester, 1992). The result during the elementary school years is that children continue to perceive their parents as available to them, and turn to them when they really need comfort, but rely on their parents less and less frequently as they get older (Kerns, Tomich, & Kim, 2006).

Peer Networks

From age 2 to age 12, children spend more time with peers and less time with adults; about 10% of social interactions in toddlerhood but 30% of those in middle childhood are with peers (Rubin, Bukowski, & Parker, 2006). Sharri Ellis and her colleagues (Ellis, Rogoff, & Cromer, 1981) observed 436 children playing in their homes and around the neighborhood. Youngsters of all ages spent less time with age-mates (defined as children whose ages were within 1 year of their own) than with children who were more than 1 year older or younger, suggesting that peer groups typically contain children of different levels of competence. In addition, even 1- to 2-year-olds played more often with same-sex companions than with other-sex companions. This gender segregation became increasingly strong with age (see Chapter 12), as it does in a variety of other cultures (Munroe & Romney, 2006).

Once in their sex-segregated worlds, boys and girls experience different kinds of social relationships and interactions (Munroe & Romney, 2006). For example, there seems to be truth to the saying that boys travel in packs, girls in pairs: boys spend more time than girls in groups, and girls spend more time than boys in dyads (Fabes, Martin, & Hanish, 2003). Overall, then, children spend an increasing amount of time with peers as they get older, typically same-sex children only roughly similar in age who enjoy the same sex-typed activities.

Play

Although some people think of play as anything children do, it is generally defined as activities that do not have an obvious or direct purpose or use (Pelligrini, 2009). Four types of children's play are generally recognized by scholars (Pelligrini, 2009): locomotor play (as in games of tag or ball), object play (stacking blocks, making crafts), social play (as in mutual imitation or playing board games), and pretend play (enacting roles). So important is play in the life of the child from age 2 to age 5 that these years are sometimes called *the play years*. This is when children hop about the room shrieking with delight, don capes and go off on dragon hunts, and whip up cakes and cookies made of clay, sand, or air. We can detect two major changes in play between infancy and age 5: it becomes more social, and it becomes more imaginative. After age

5 or so, the exuberant and fanciful play of the preschool years gives way to somewhat more serious play (Smith, 2005).

Play Becomes More Social

Years ago, Mildred Parten (1932) devised a method for classifying the types of play engaged in by preschool children of different ages. Her six categories of activity, arranged from least to most social, are as follows:

1. *Unoccupied play.* Children stand idly, look around, or engage in apparently aimless activities such as pacing.
2. *Solitary play.* Children play alone, typically with objects, and appear to be highly involved in what they are doing.
3. *Onlooker play.* Children watch others play, taking an active interest in and perhaps even talking to the players but not directly participating.
4. *Parallel play.* Children play next to one another, doing much the same thing, but they interact little (for example, two girls might sit near each other, both drawing pictures, without talking to each other to any extent).
5. *Associative play.* Children interact by swapping materials, conversing, or following each other's lead, but they are not united by the same goal (for example, the two girls may swap crayons and comment on each other's drawings as they draw).
6. *Cooperative play.* Children join forces to achieve a common goal; they act as a pair or group, dividing their labor and coordinating their activities in a meaningful way (for example, the two girls collaborate to draw a mural for their teacher).

The major message of Parten's study (and of others like it) is that play becomes increasingly social and socially skilled from age 2 to age 5 (Barnes, 1971; Smith, 1978). Unoccupied and onlooker activities are evident at all ages; solitary and parallel play become less frequent with age; and associative and cooperative play, the most social and complex of the types of play, become more frequent with age (■ Figure 14.5).

The picture is more complex than Parten's work suggests (Coplan & Abreau, 2009). Older children continue to engage in solitary play, often to build skills. They also work their way into play groups by first being onlookers and then playing in parallel with the other children before trying to join the ongoing activity (Rubin, Bukowski, & Parker, 2006). Thus, although there is an age trend toward more associative and cooperative play, all of Parten's forms of play can serve useful functions for children young and old depending on the occasion.

Play Becomes More Imaginative

The first **pretend play**—play in which one actor, object, or action symbolizes or stands for another—occurs around age 1, when an infant may raise an empty cup, or perhaps a forbidden treat, to her lips, smile, give a parent a knowing glance, and make loud lip-smacking sounds (Nicolich, 1977). The earliest pretend play is just like this: The infant performs actions that symbolize familiar activities such as eating, sleeping, and washing. By age 2, toddlers

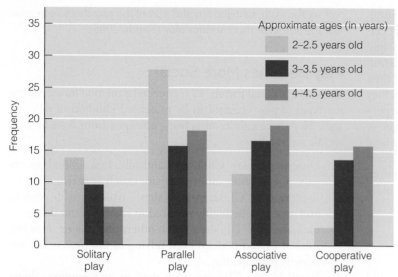

■ FIGURE 14.5 Frequency of activities engaged in by preschool children of different ages. With age, solitary and parallel play occur less frequently, whereas associative and cooperative play occur more frequently. SOURCE: Adapted from Barnes, 1971.

readily join in pretense; if you hand them a towel and suggest that they wipe up the imaginary tea you just spilled, they will (Harris & Kavanaugh, 1993)! Because there is no tea in sight, this willingness to clean it up is remarkable. It means that toddlers are capable of using their new symbolic capacity to construct a mental representation of a pretend event and of acting according to this representation.

Pretend play fully blossoms from age 2 to age 5, increasing in both frequency and sophistication (Howes & Matheson, 1992; Rubin, Bukowski, & Parker, 2006). As children age, they can depict heroes and heroines more different from themselves and can enact their dramas using fewer props. Most important, children combine their capacity for increasingly social play and their capacity for pretense to create **social pretend play,** play in which

Social pretend play during the preschool years contributes to intellectual, social, and emotional development.

children cooperate with caregivers or playmates to enact dramas (Howes & Matheson, 1992). Social pretend play episodes can become quite sophisticated and require a good deal of social competence, including the theory-of-mind or people-reading skills discussed in Chapter 13 (Doherty, 2009). Consider the following example, in which a 5-year-old (M) wants her partner (E), playing the role of a mother, to leave her babies and come to M's house. The two girls negotiate what will happen next, managing to stay in role and keep in mind the other's role as they do so (Garvey, 1990, p. 137):

> M: You come here. The babies are sleeping now and. . . (interrupted).
> E: No, they'll cry when I leave 'cause they'll hear the car.
> M: Nooo. The car's broken. I have the car.
> E: All right, but one baby will have to take care of these little babies.

Although social pretend play is universal, the quality and content of preschoolers' play are influenced by the culture in which they live (Haight et al., 1999). For example, U.S. children like to play superheroes and act out themes of danger and fantasy, whereas Korean children take on family roles and enact everyday activities (Farver & Lee-Shin, 1997). American children also talk a lot about their own actions, reject other children's ideas, and boss others around, whereas Korean children are more focused on their partners' activities and are more prone to make polite requests and agree with one another. Through their play, then, children in the United States (an individualistic culture) learn to assert their identities as individuals, whereas children in Korea (a collectivist culture) learn how to keep their egos and emotions under control to achieve group harmony.

Play Becomes More Rule-Governed

After they enter school, children engage less frequently in pretend play. Now they spend more of their time playing organized games with rules—board and computer games, games of tag or hide-and-seek, organized sports, and so on (Smith, 2005). They also develop individual hobbies, such as building model cars, collecting coins, or making scrapbooks, that help them acquire skills and knowledge.

According to Jean Piaget (1965), it is not until children enter the stage of concrete operations, around age 6 or 7, that they become capable of cooperating with other children to follow the rules of games. Older children—11- and 12-year-olds who are entering the stage of formal operations—gain a more flexible concept of rules, recognizing that rules are arbitrary agreements that can be changed as long as the players agree. Partly because of cognitive gains, then, the play of the school-age child is more organized and rule-governed—and less fanciful—than that of the preschool child.

What Good Is Play?

In 19th-century America, child's play was discouraged because it was viewed as a frivolous waste of time (Athey, 1984). Today's parents who program their children's lives in hopes of molding little Einsteins may also have lost sight of the important contributions of play to virtually all aspects of child development (Singer, Golinkoff, & Hirsh-Pasek, 2006). Indeed, that playful activity occurs among the young of so many species strongly suggests that play is an evolved behavior that helps the young adapt during childhood and prepare for adulthood (Coplan & Abreau, 2009; Pelligrini, 2009). It is easy to see how girls playing with dolls might be grooming themselves for traditional roles as mothers or how the rough-and-tumble play of boys, like the playful fights observed in young males of many species, might prepare them to compete with other males later in life. But because play allows children to experiment with new behaviors, it may also help humans learn to respond creatively to new challenges in their environments (Pelligrini, 2009).

Play fosters cognitive, motor, and social skills and helps children cope with emotional problems (Coplan & Abreau, 2009; Smith, 2005). Physical or locomotor play, from the leg kicking of infants to the soccer playing of children, contributes to neural maturation, increased bone density, and the development of motor skills (Pelligrini, 2009; Smith, 2005). Engaging in lots of pretend play has been linked to better performance on tests of cognitive development, language skills, and creativity (E. P. Fisher, 1992; Farver, Kim, & Lee-Shin, 2000). Engaging in social pretend play helps children construct their theories of mind, understand others' perspectives, and hone their social skills (Coplan & Abreau, 2009; Lillard, 2001). Perhaps as a result, preschoolers who engage in a lot of social pretend play tend to be more popular and socially skilled than children who do not (Connolly & Doyle, 1984; Farver, Kim, & Lee-Shin, 2000).

Finally, play contributes to healthy emotional development by providing opportunities to express bothersome feelings, regulate emotions, resolve emotional conflicts, and master challenges (Coplan & Abreau, 2009; Landreth & Homeyer, 1998). If Yoko, for example, has recently been scolded by her mother for drawing on the dining room wall, she may gain control of the situation by scolding her "child" for doing the same thing. And Jackie, an abused 5-year-old, apparently coped with his abuse by having an alligator puppet swallow a small child doll and then smashing the alligator with a mallet and burying it in the sandbox (Landreth & Homeyer, 1998).

Let it never be said, then, that play is useless; it is truly the child's work. Although children play because it is fun, not because it sharpens their skills, they contribute to their own development by doing so. And parents can support their children's development by becoming involved in the social give and take that play episodes require (Lindsey & Mize, 2000).

Peer Acceptance and Popularity

Being accepted by peers means having the opportunity to play and interact with other children and in the process to develop normally. Researchers study peer-group acceptance through **sociometric techniques**—methods for determining who is liked and who is disliked in a group (Cillessen, 2009). In a sociometric survey, children in a classroom may be asked to nominate several classmates whom they like and several whom they dislike or to rate all their classmates in terms of their desirability as companions. It is important to find out both who is liked and who is disliked; this allows children to be classified into the following distinct categories of social status (Coie, Dodge, & Coppotelli, 1982):

1. *Popular.* Well liked by most and rarely disliked.
2. *Rejected.* Rarely liked and often disliked.
3. *Neglected.* Neither liked nor disliked; these isolated children seem to be invisible to their classmates.
4. *Controversial.* Liked by many but also disliked by many; for example, the fun-loving child with leadership skills who also bullies peers and starts fights.
5. *Average.* In the middle on both the liked and disliked scales.

Why are some children more popular than others, and why are some children rejected by their peers? Popularity is affected by some personal characteristics that a child can do little to change. For instance, physically attractive children are usually more popular than physically unattractive children, and children who are relatively intelligent tend to be more socially accepted than those who are not (Bellanti, Bierman, & Conduct Problems Prevention Research Group, 2000). Social competence—the successful use of social cognitive skills in initiating social interactions, responding positively to peers, resolving interpersonal conflicts smoothly, and so on—strongly predicts popularity (Coie, Dodge, & Kupersmidt, 1990; Rubin, Bukowski, & Parker, 2006). Well-liked children are also able to regulate their emotions well (Graziano, Keane, & Calkins, 2007).

"Rejected" children are often highly aggressive, although some are socially isolated, submissive children who are overly sensitive to teasing and are seen by others as "easy to push around" (Parkhurst & Asher, 1992; Rubin, Bukowski, & Parker, 2006). Children who fall into the neglected category of sociometric status often have reasonably good social skills; they are usually nonaggressive and tend to be shy, withdrawn, and unassertive (Coie, Dodge, & Kupersmidt, 1990). As a result, no one really notices them. Controversial children are interesting: They often show good social skills and leadership qualities, like popular children, but they are also viewed as aggressive bullies, like many rejected children (DeRosier & Thomas, 2003; Miller-Johnson et al., 2003).

To appreciate how social skills contribute to popularity, consider what happens when children try to enter and gain acceptance in play groups (Dodge et al., 1990; Putallaz & Wasserman, 1989). When children who ultimately become popular want to join a group's activity, they first hold back and assess what is going on, then smoothly blend into the group, commenting pleasantly about whatever the other children are discussing. By contrast, children who are eventually rejected by their peers tend to be pushy and disruptive. Jimmy, for example, may sit beside two boys who are playing a computer game and distract them by talking about a TV program he saw the night before. Even worse, he may criticize the way the boys are playing, start pecking computer keys at random, or threaten to turn off the computer if he is not allowed to play. By contrast, children who end up being neglected by their peers often hover around the edges of a group without taking positive steps to initiate contact, and they shy away from peers who attempt to make contact with them.

Influences on popularity can vary depending on the cultural and historical context (Chen, Chung, & Hisao, 2009). For example, children who are shy have been found to be unpopular in Canada but popular in China, where being quiet and reserved has traditionally been regarded as socially desirable and has been associated with academic and social competence (Chen, Rubin, & Sun, 1992; Chen et al., 2006). This pattern may be changing, however, especially in urban areas, as China moves to a capitalistic economic system and parents want their children to be more assertive so that they will succeed in this new culture (Chen, Chung, & Hisao, 2009). In one study, shyness/sensitivity was positively associated with the peer acceptance and school adjustment of Chinese children in 1990 but had become associated with peer rejection, school problems, and symptoms of depression by 2002 (Chen et al., 2005).

In sum, popularity or peer acceptance is affected by many factors. It helps to have an attractive face and cognitive skills, but it is probably more important to behave in socially competent ways and to be able to regulate one's emotions. As you have seen, children who enjoy secure relationships with their parents as infants tend to become popular children because they have learned social and emotion-regulation skills that make for positive relationships with peers.

Do the outcomes of childhood popularity polls matter? Very much so, especially for the 10 to 15% of children who are rejected by their peers (Rubin, Bukowski, & Parker, 2006). Children who are neglected by peers often gain greater acceptance later (Bierman, 2004; Cillessen et al., 1992). An exception would be extremely socially withdrawn children like Seung Hui Cho, the Virginia Tech killer—children whose social anxiety keeps them from interacting with peers and exposes them to victimization by peers. Such children are at risk for a variety of negative outcomes (Rubin, Coplan, & Bowker, 2009). Children who are rejected, usually because of aggressive behavior, are likely to maintain their rejected status from grade to grade (Bierman, 2004; Cillessen et al., 1992). More significantly, rejected children may end up even more poorly adjusted as a result of the experience of being rejected (Wentzel, 2003). Their self-esteem suffers, they lose opportunities to learn social skills, they develop negative attitudes toward others, they are negatively influenced by the other antisocial children they end up hanging out with, and their academic performance suffers (Coie, 2004; Prinstein et al., 2009).

Some students who lose in sociometric polls manage to feel good about their social acceptance nonetheless and end up well adjusted, possibly because they have developed a niche outside of school where they are liked (McElhaney, Antonishak, & Allen, 2008). Moreover, children who are neglected or rejected by peers can benefit from social skills training and coaching programs that aim to improve their interaction skills and in turn their acceptance by peers (Bierman & Powers, 2009).

Friendships

Being accepted by the wider peer group and having close friends are distinct and serve different functions for children. True, popular children are more likely than unpopular children to have friends, but many unpopular children have at least one reciprocated friendship and many popular children do not. In one study of 7- and 8-year-olds, for example, 39% of children rejected by peers had at least one mutual or reciprocated friendship,

Chumships in late elementary school, said Harry Stack Sullivan, are a training ground for later intimate relationships.

whereas 31% of popular children lacked such a friendship (Gest, Graham-Bermann, & Hartup, 2001).

Having friends increases the odds that a child will be happy and socially competent and reduces the odds that a child will be lonely and depressed (Bukowski, Motzoi, & Meyer, 2009; Nangle et al., 2003). This is especially true if the friendships are with peers who are well adjusted and supportive; it may not be as true if the friends are antisocial or depressed (Vaughn et al., 2000; Vitario, Boivin, & Bukowski, 2009). As you learned earlier, psychoanalytic theorist Harry Stack Sullivan (1953) theorized that having a close friend or chum has many developmental benefits, and research bears him out (Bukowski, Motzoi, & Meyer, 2009). As we will see shortly, research also supports Sullivan's view that chumships pave the way for romantic relationships in adolescence. Friends also provide social support and comfort that can help children weather stressful events such as a divorce or the first day of kindergarten (Bukowski, Motzoi, & Meyer, 2009; Ladd, 1999). True friends become true attachment figures; maybe that is why having a secure attachment to a parent predicts having friends even better than it predicts being accepted by the wider peer group (Schneider, Atkinson, & Tardif, 2001).

Checking Mastery

1. How do the peer relations of boys and girls differ?

2. What are the two main trends in the development of play over the preschool years?

3. What are two important influences on sociometric status in childhood?

Making Connections

1. Addy's parents would like to help advance her physical, cognitive, and social development through play activities, but they do not know how to go about it. Give them some ideas of what they can do with a 1-, 4-, and 8-year-old to provide age-appropriate play experiences.

2. Darren's sociometric status is neglected, whereas Alonzo's is rejected. What training program might you design for each boy to help him become more popular and why?

14.4 The Adolescent

Although children are already highly involved in peer activities, adolescents spend even more time with peers and less time with parents. The quality of the individual's attachment to parents continues to be highly important throughout adolescence, but peers, including romantic partners, begin to rival or surpass parents as sources of intimacy and support (Furman & Buhrmester, 1992). Moreover, the quality of peer relations changes. Not only do adolescents begin to form boy–girl friendships and go on dates, but they also become more capable of forming deep and intimate attachments.

Attachments to Parents

Just as infants must have a secure base if they are to explore, adolescents seem to need the security, as well as the encouragement to explore, provided by supportive parents to become independent and autonomous individuals (Scharf, Mayseless, & Kivenson-Baron, 2004). Adolescents may feel conflicted as they seek greater autonomy from their parents yet continue to need their support, but a balance of exploration and attachment is the key to successful development at this age (Allen, 2008). Adolescents who enjoy secure attachment relationships with their parents generally have a stronger sense of identity, higher self-esteem, greater social competence, better emotional adjustment, and fewer behavioral problems than their less securely attached peers (Allen, 2008; Arbona & Power, 2003; Kenny & Rice, 1995).

For many youths in our society, going off to college qualifies as a "naturally occurring Strange Situation"—a potentially stressful separation that activates the attachment system (Kenny, 1987). Students who go home on weekends or talk to Mom or Dad on their cell phones every day during their first semester are engaging in attachment behavior just as surely as the infant who whimpers for his mommy. From an attachment theory perspective, experiencing separation anxiety in this situation is normal and adaptive. Preoccupation with parents typically decreases over the first semester and predicts adjustment problems only when it is extreme and prolonged (Berman & Sperling, 1991). In the end, college students who are securely attached to their parents display better psychological and social adjustment and academic performance during the potentially difficult transition to college than students who are insecurely attached (Lapsley, Rice, & FitzGerald, 1990; Larose, Bernier, & Tarabulsy, 2005; Mayseless, Danieli, & Sharabany, 1996).

Friendships

Friendships change qualitatively with age, being based on (1) enjoyment of common activities in early childhood, (2) mutual loyalty and caring in late childhood, and (3) intimacy and self-

Going to college is a "Strange Situation" that activates attachment behaviors, such as hugging and e-mailing, designed to maintain contact with attachment figures.

© Media Bakery

disclosure in adolescence (Collins & Madsen, 2006; Rubin, Bukowski, & Parker, 2006). Like children, teenagers form friendships with peers who are similar to themselves in observable ways. For example, most high school students choose friends of the same ethnic background (Hamm, 2000; Graham, Taylor, & Ho, 2009). However, adolescents increasingly choose friends whose psychological qualities—interests, attitudes, values, and personalities—match their own. In adolescence, friends are like-minded individuals who confide in each other.

Although same-sex friendships remain important throughout adolescence, teenagers increasingly form close cross-sex friendships too. Ruth Sharabany and her colleagues (Sharabany, Gershoni, & Hofman, 1981) asked 5th- to 11th-graders to assess their same-sex and cross-sex friendships in terms of such aspects of emotional intimacy as spontaneity, trust, loyalty, sensitivity to the other's feelings, and attachment. Same-sex friendships were highly intimate in most respects throughout this age range, whereas cross-sex friendships did not attain a high level of intimacy until 11th grade. These findings support Harry Stack Sullivan's view that children learn lessons about intimate attachments in their same-sex chumships that they later apply in their heterosexual relationships (Buhrmester & Furman, 1986). Finally, girls tended to report higher degrees of intimacy in their friendships than boys did, and they achieved emotional intimacy in their cross-sex relationships at earlier ages.

Intimate friendships may seem like a positive for girls, but there is a downside: In a study of third-, fifth-, seventh-, and ninth-graders followed over a 6-month period, Amanda Rose and her colleagues (Rose, Carlson, & Waller, 2007) found that when girls spend a lot of time engaging in **co-rumination**—excessive discussion of personal problems with a friend—they strengthen their friendships but also aggravate rather than relieve their symptoms of depression and anxiety. There is the potential for a snowball effect: The study also found that having more symptoms of distress in turn leads to more discussion of problems with friends. For boys, co-ruminating about problems had a positive effect on friendship without the negative effects of increased depression and anxiety.

Changing Social Networks

Most elementary-school children take interest in members of the other sex, talk at length about who likes whom, develop crushes, and in the process prepare themselves for heterosexual relationships (Thorne, 1993). Still, how do boys and girls who live in their own gender-segregated worlds arrive at the point of dating each other?

Some time ago, Dexter Dunphy (1963) offered a plausible account of how peer-group structures change during adolescence to pave the way for dating relationships. His five stages are still helpful today in understanding how peer relations lay the foundation for romantic attachments (see also Collins & Madsen, 2006; and Furman & Collins, 2009):

1. In late childhood, boys and girls become members of same-sex **cliques,** or small friendship groups, and have little to do with the other sex.
2. Boy cliques and girl cliques then begin to interact. Just as parents provide a secure base for peer relationships, same-sex cliques provide a secure base for romantic relationships. For an adolescent boy, talking to a girl at the mall with his friends and her friends there is far less threatening than doing so on his own.
3. The most popular boys and girls form a heterosexual clique.
4. As less popular peers also form mixed-sex cliques, a new peer-group structure, the **crowd,** completes its evolution. The crowd, a collection of several heterosexual cliques, is involved in arranging organized social activities—parties, outings to the lake or mall, and so on. Those adolescents who become members of a mixed-sex clique and a crowd (not all do) have many opportunities to get to know members of the other sex as both friends and romantic partners.
5. Couples form and the crowd disintegrates in late high school, having served its purpose of bringing boys and girls together.

High school crowds not only bring boys and girls together but give adolescents a social identity and a place in the social order. The names may vary, but every school has its crowds of, for example, "populars," "jocks," "druggies," and "losers," each consisting of adolescents who are similar in some way (Brown & Dietz, 2009; Brown, Mory, & Kinney, 1994). Everyone in high school seems to recognize these differences: "[The brains] all wear glasses and 'kiss up' to teachers and after school they all tromp uptown to the library" (Brown, Mory, & Kinney, 1994, p. 128), "The partiers goof off a lot more than the jocks do, but they don't come to school stoned like the burnouts do" (p. 133).

Which crowd or crowds an adolescent belongs to has important implications for her social identity and self-esteem; it is easier for her to feel good about herself if she is a "popular" or a "jock" than if she is a "dweeb," a "druggie," or a social isolate (like Seung Hui Cho of Virginia Tech) who does not belong to any crowd (Brown & Lohr, 1987). Indeed, self-perceived crowd membership in high school predicts adjustment in adulthood. In one study (Barber, Eccles, & Stone, 2001), "brains" tended to graduate from college and have high self-esteem at age 24; "basket cases" were more likely than their peers to have seen a psychologist and attempted suicide; "jocks" achieved financial success but shared with "criminals" a tendency to drink too much; and "criminals" were the least well adjusted. Crowd membership

The self-esteem and social identity of adolescents, as well as their development, often hinge on which cliques and crowds they belong to.

The Dark Side of Peer Relations

The 2004 film *Mean Girls* painted a vivid picture of the treacherous world of teenage peer relations. The film concerns the tribulations of Cady, a newcomer to North Shore High School who was homeschooled in Africa and has much to learn about her high school's social world. The center of this world is Regina George, the "queen bee" of a clique called the Plastics. Cady is told this about Regina by a classmate: "And evil takes a human form in Regina George. Don't be fooled, because she may seem like your typical selfish, back-stabbing slut-faced ho-bag, but in reality she's so much more than that." No one escapes the insults, vicious rumors, and betrayals that permeate this society of "mean girls."

Although appreciative of the positive contributions of peer acceptance and friendship to child and adolescent development, developmentalists also understand that peer relationships have a dark side (Hartup, 2006; Rubin, Bukowski, & Parker, 2006). One of your authors has only to conjure up memories of Sunday school bully Norma T. and her unprovoked pinches and kicks to appreciate the point! The kind of "relational aggression" at which Regina George excelled—subtle and indirect aggression such as gossiping about and ignoring and excluding others—has been studied by Amanda Rose and her colleagues (Rose, Swenson, & Waller, 2004). These researchers found that relational aggression works for girls (though not boys) in early adolescence (though not in middle childhood) to enhance their perceived popularity (Rose, Swenson, & Waller, 2004). Perceived popularity also predicts more use of relational aggression later for both males and females, suggesting that adolescents who become popular may discover that they can use their social power to exclude or hurt others—and do just that. Doing so serves the useful purpose of enforcing a group's norms and strengthening allegiance to the group (Killen, Rutland, & Jampol, 2009).

The dark side of peer relations is even clearer in bullying, which typically involves a quite socially competent child or adolescent intent on dominance repeatedly inflicting harm, physically or verbally, on a weaker peer (Olweus, 1993; Salmivalli & Peets, 2009; and see Chapter 13). And now we have cyberbullying, which enables bullies to spread rumors, insults, embarrassing photographs, and threats quickly and widely via computer or digital device (Smith et al., 2008; Surdin, 2009). A national survey of students in grades 6 to 10 indicates that self-reported rates of bullying or being bullied at least once in the last 2 months were approximately 21% for physical, 54% for verbal, 51% for social, and 14% for cyber forms of bullying, respectively (Wang, Iannotti, & Nansel, 2009). For some children and adolescents, being hounded by bullies can lead to becoming a bully, as well as to high rates of delinquency, depression, and self-harmful behavior, including suicide (Barker et al., 2008; Smetana, Campione-Barr, & Metzger, 2006).

Finally, we should not ignore enemy relationships in which two individuals express mutual dislike for one another on sociometric surveys (Hodges & Card, 2003). Figures vary greatly, but around 30% of children may be involved in enemyships (Hartup, 2006). Enemy relationships often start with conflict; sometimes they are friendships turned bad (Card, 2007). Children and adolescents who are rejected by peers are especially likely to have enemies (Rodkin & Hodges, 2003).

Being gossiped about or excluded by peers, victimized by bullies, and detested by enemies are all, it seems, part of the normal landscape of peer relations in childhood and adolescence. Nonetheless, we must still conclude that peer relations are an essential—and in the end mostly positive—force in human development.

partly reflects personality traits, abilities, and values that existed before the adolescent ever got involved with a particular crowd, but experiences in a crowd also help shape future development (Giordano, 2003).

A common misconception is that peers are typically a negative influence on adolescents. As it turns out, peers typically do more to foster positive behavior than to encourage antisocial behavior (Berndt & Murphy, 2002; Rubin, Bukowski, & Parker, 2006). True, much depends on the crowd to which an adolescent belongs: "brains" discourage drug use, for example, but "druggies" encourage it. Moreover, at around the age of 14 or 15 adolescents are quite dependent on their peers and may "go along with the crowd" and take risks when with friends that they would not take when alone (Berndt & Murphy, 2002; Gardner & Steinberg, 2005). Getting in trouble by conforming to peers is much less likely, though, among adolescents who have secure attachments to warm and authoritative parents who are neither too lax nor too strict (Brown et al., 1993; Goldstein, Davis-Kean, & Eccles, 2005). In sum, the influences of peers and friends on development are usually healthy but can be destructive, depending on which cliques and crowds adolescents belong to, how good their relationships with their parents are, and how much they need the security of peer acceptance. Although human development could not proceed normally without peers, developmentalists appreciate that there is also a dark side to peer relations, which we examine in Exploration Box 14.2.

Dating

As Dunphy's model tells us, the transition to dating takes place in the context of the larger peer group (Collins & Laursen, 2004; Rubin, Bukowski, & Parker, 2006). About 25% of 12-year-olds, 50% of 15-year-olds, and 70% of 18-year-olds say that they have been involved in a "special romantic relationship" in the past 18 months (Carver, Joyner, & Udry, 2003).

Dating relationships in early adolescence are more superficial and short lived than dating relationships in later adolescence

(Brown, Feiring, & Furman, 1999). In B. Bradford Brown's (1999) view, adolescent romantic relationships evolve through the following four phases:

1. *Initiation phase.* In early adolescence, the focus is on the self—specifically, on coming to see oneself as a person capable of relating to members of the other sex in a romantic way.
2. *Status phase.* In mid-adolescence, peer approval is what counts; having a romantic relationship, and having it with the "right kind" of partner, is important for the status it brings in the larger peer group.
3. *Affection phase.* In late adolescence, the focus is on the relationship rather than on self-concept or peer status. Romantic relationships become more personal and caring; they are set in the context of a small, mixed-sex clique rather than in the context of the larger crowd, with friends providing advice and emotional support.
4. *Bonding phase.* In the transition to early adulthood, the emotional intimacy achieved in the affection phase is coupled with a long-term commitment to create a lasting attachment.

Brown's phases were evident in an 8-year longitudinal study of German adolescents who were age 13 at the start of the study (Seiffge-Krenke, 2003). The 13-year-olds who had romantic relationships tended to have relatively low-quality and unstable, although emotionally intense, relationships that lasted an average of only about 3 months. With age, relationships lasted longer (an average of 21 months by age 21) and became more emotionally intimate and supportive. Moreover, having a committed romantic relationship at age 21 was associated with having a positive self-concept at age 13, supportive peer relationships at age 15, and a supportive romantic relationship at age 17. Parents contributed too; supportive relationships with both mother and father proved to be at least as important as supportive relationships with peers in predicting involvement in a love relationship in early adulthood (see also Furman & Collins, 2009; and Miller & Hoicowitz, 2004).

How does dating affect adolescent adjustment and development? Dating at an early age appears to have more negative than positive effects on social and emotional adjustment, either because troubled adolescents start dating early or because early daters get hurt or become involved in problem behavior such as drinking and drug use before their time (Collins, 2003; Compian, Gowen, & Hayward, 2004). Overall, though, dating typically has more positive than negative effects on development and can even compensate for a poor relationship with parents, as Sullivan theorized. Involvement in a steady relationship is good for self-esteem (although breakups hurt it and can lead to depression), and adolescents who date tend to be better adjusted overall than those who do not (Collins, 2003; Furman & Collins, 2009).

Adolescence is clearly an important time of change in attachment relationships. As adolescents get older, they look more to peers, both friends and romantic partners, to fulfill some of the attachment needs that parents fulfilled when they were younger—the needs for proximity, a secure base for exploration, and a safe haven in times of stress (Markiewicz et al., 2006). Even so, parents, especially mothers, remain a critical source of security throughout the adolescent years (Markiewicz et al., 2006).

Checking Mastery

1. According to Dunphy, what is the difference between a clique and a crowd?
2. Before they are capable of truly intimate romantic relationships, what two things do young teens seek from dating relationships, according to Brown?

Making Connections

1. Analyze the clique and crowd structure in your high school, where you fit in it, and how you might have been affected by your experience.
2. How well do Brown's account of four phases in adolescent dating relationships, and the related study of German adolescents by Seiffge-Krenke (2003), fit you? Where does your dating history differ, and why might that be?

14.5 The Adult

Relationships with family and friends are no less important during adulthood than they are earlier in life, but they take on different qualities. How do people's social networks change over the adult years and why, and what is the character of their romantic relationships and friendships?

Social Networks

Some years ago, Robert Kahn and Toni Antonucci (1980; and see Antonucci, Birditt, & Akiyama, 2009) proposed that each of us has a **social convoy**, a social network and support system that accompanies us during our life's journey, changing as we go. The social convoy provides social support in the form of aid, affection, and affirmation (validation of our values and goals). An infant's social convoy may consist only of parents. The convoy enlarges over the years as others (relatives, friends, supportive teachers, romantic partners, colleagues, and so on) join it, then typically shrinks in later life (Carstensen, Mikels & Mather, 2006; Levitt, Weber, & Guacci, 1993). As new members are added, some members drift away. Others remain in the convoy, but our relationships with them change, as when the infant son thoroughly dependent on his mother becomes the adolescent son clamoring for his independence—and later the middle-aged son on whom his aging mother depends for help when she needs it.

Social Interaction Patterns

With whom do adults of different ages interact, and how socially active are they? Young adults are busily forming romantic relationships and friendships. The trend toward greater intimacy with the other sex that began in adolescence continues (Reis et al., 1993). Young women also continue to form closer friendship ties than men do (Antonucci, Birditt, & Akiyama, 2009).

Young adults, especially single ones, tend to have more friends than middle-aged and older adults do. As adults marry, have children, take on increasing job responsibilities, and age, their social networks shrink (Antonucci, Birditt, & Akiyama, 2009; Fischer et al., 1989). The trend toward smaller social networks with age can be seen in many ethnic groups, but ethnic group differences are also evident. For example, from early adulthood on, African American adults' networks tend to be smaller, to be more dominated by kin, and to involve more frequent contact than those of European Americans (Ajrouch, Antonucci, & Janevic, 2001).

Socioemotional Selectivity

You may be guessing that the shrinking of the social convoy in later adulthood is the result of increased disease, disability, and social isolation. However, Laura Carstensen's (1992) **socioemotional selectivity theory** explains the shrinking social convoy quite differently—as a choice older adults make to better meet their emotional needs once they perceive the time left to them as short (also see Charles & Carstensen, 2007; Lang & Carstensen, 2002). The perception that one has little time left to live is critical in Carstensen's theory. It prompts older adults to put less emphasis on the goal of acquiring knowledge for future use and more emphasis on the goal of fulfilling current emotional needs. As a result, older adults actively choose to narrow their range of social partners to those who bring them emotional pleasure, usually family members and close friends, and they let other social relationships fall by the wayside. Whereas younger adults need the social stimulation and new information that contacts with strangers and acquaintances often provide—and are even willing to sacrifice some emotional well-being to have many social contacts—older adults put their emotional well-being first.

Does the evidence support socioemotional selectivity theory? It is clear that with age adults narrow their social networks to close family and friends and feel very emotionally close to these intimate companions (Carstensen, 1992; Lang & Carstensen, 1994). But is this due to perceiving little time left to live? In one study, cancer patients of various ages preferred familiar to unfamiliar social partners more than control adults who were not ill did (Pinquart & Silbereisen, 2006). Moreover, if their cancer therapy was successful, they showed increased interest in interacting with people they did not know, suggesting that perceived time left to live *is* important, as Carstensen theorizes.

Older adults' emotional lives appear to benefit from socioemotional selectivity, as Carstensen theorizes. She and her colleagues (2000) sampled the emotional experiences of African American and European American adults between age 18 and age 94 by paging them at random times over a 1-week period as they went about their lives and asking them to report their emotional state. Contrary to ageist stereotypes, older adults did not have more dismal, depressing emotional lives than younger adults. Younger and older adults differed little in the frequency with which they experienced positive emotions;

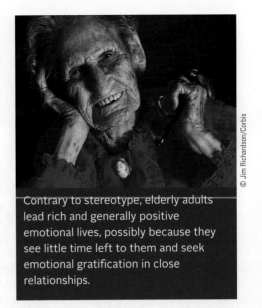

Contrary to stereotype, elderly adults lead rich and generally positive emotional lives, possibly because they see little time left to them and seek emotional gratification in close relationships.

and negative emotions were actually less common among older adults. Older adults also experienced longer-lasting positive emotions and more fleeting negative moods, suggesting that they are more able than younger adults to regulate their emotions, savoring the happy experiences while cutting short the sad and angry ones (see also Kliegel, Jager, & Phillips, 2007). So older adults lead rich and rewarding emotional lives and are able to experience and express their emotions fully and regulate them effectively (Carstensen, Mikels, & Mather, 2006; Magai et al., 2006; Mroczek, 2004). How do they do it? Older adults may achieve their emotional gratification goals in part through a so-called **positivity effect** in information processing: by paying more attention to, better remembering, and putting more priority on positive information than on negative information (Kennedy, Mather, & Carstensen, 2004; Kryla-Lighthall & Mather, 2009).

Whether it is because of socioemotional selectivity and the positivity effect or other factors, older adults end up at least as satisfied as young adults with their relationships (Lansford, Sherman, & Antonucci, 1998) and less likely to find them emotionally unpleasant (Akiyama et al., 2003). There is a downside, however: Older adults may be so intent on grabbing emotional enjoyment that their ability to gather and evaluate information in an unbiased way suffers. The positivity effect can mean zeroing in on positive information and ignoring or avoiding negative information when making decisions, even in areas of significance such as reviewing different physicians and health care plans (Löckenhoff & Carstensen, 2007).

Romantic Relationships

An important developmental task for young adults is to resolve Erikson's issue of intimacy versus isolation by finding a romantic partner and entering into a committed relationship. How do we choose partners, how does love develop, and how do the internal working models of self and others that we form starting in infancy affect our romantic relationships?

According to filter theories, we choose romantic partners mainly on the basis of homogamy or similarity—at first surface similarities such as belonging to the same ethnic group attract us to someone, but later we look for psychological similarities as well.

Mate Selection

Many models and schemes have been developed to answer the question of how people choose romantic partners (see Regan, 2008; Strong, DeVault, & Cohen, 2008). Evolutionary theorists have asked how certain preferences might optimize reproductive success (Buss, 2009; Buss & Schmitt, 1993). Their research tells us that although the two sexes generally look for similar traits in partners, men are more likely than women to emphasize physical attractiveness in a partner, whereas women put more emphasis than men on a potential mate's resources and social status. Attractiveness may have signaled our ancestors that a woman is healthy and able to reproduce and raise children; signs of wealth, dominance, and status in the community may signal that a man can support and protect a wife and children.

Filter theories of mate selection have envisioned it as a process in which we progress through a series of filters leading us from all possible partners to one partner in particular (see Regan, 2008; Strong, DeVault, & Cohen, 2008). Early in an acquaintance, similarities in physical appearance, race, education, socioeconomic status, religion, and the like serve as the first filters and provides a basis for dating. Then partners may disclose more about themselves and look for similarity in inner qualities such as values, attitudes, beliefs, and personality traits. If they continue to find themselves compatible, their relationship may survive; if not, it may end. There is little agreement, though, on how many such filters there might be; moreover, mate selection does not appear to unfold in a stagelike manner as filter theories imply (Regan, 2008).

Researchers agree, however, that the greatest influence on mate selection is similarity, or **homogamy** (Strong, DeVault, & Cohen, 2008). Once homogamy is assured, people may also prefer partners who complement them in some way, bringing strengths to the relationship that compensate for their own weaknesses. However, the saying "birds of a feather flock together" has far more validity than the saying "opposites attract"

when it comes to mate selection. Partner choice works similarly in gay and lesbian relationships as in heterosexual relationships (Diamond & Butterworth, 2009).

Love

Philosophers and poets have struggled for centuries to define love, but it is an elusive concept. Robert Sternberg (1988, 2006) gives us a starting point with his **triangular theory of love**, which identifies different types of love based on the strength of three components of love. As shown in ■ **Figure 14.6**, the three components are passion, intimacy, and decision/commitment:

- *Passion* involves sexual attraction, romantic feelings, and excitement. A 24-year-old woman in love expressed it well: "I get so excited when I know that I'm going to see him, and then when I do see him, I can't breathe I'm so full of want" (Regan, 2008, p. 142).
- *Intimacy* involves feelings of warmth, caring, closeness, trust, and respect in the relationship. It is about emotional togetherness, communication, and happiness.
- *Decision/commitment* involves first deciding that one loves the other person and then committing to a long-term relationship.

In our culture, couples often experience passion early in a dating relationship and then move on to greater intimacy and finally to decision/commitment as their relationship evolves. In cultures with arranged marriages, decision/commitment may come first, with the parents who arranged the marriage hoping that passion and intimacy will bloom later (Regan, 2008). If couples are lucky, they will enjoy high levels of passion, inti-

■ **FIGURE 14.6** The three components of love in Sternberg's triarchic theory of love. Think about each component being high or low and what the resulting quality of a relationship would be. For example, companionate love has high intimacy and decision/commitment but low passion; infatuation has high passion but low intimacy and decision/commitment. Source: Adapted from Sternberg, R. J. (1988). Triangulating love. In R. J. Sternberg & M. L. Barnes (Eds.), *The psychology of love.* New Haven, CT: Yale University Press.

macy, and decision/commitment—or what is called **consummate love**. Passion, that intense feeling of "being in love," may have evolved because it lures partners into relationships that will lead to mating and childbearing (Reis & Aron, 2008). However, it often wanes with time, changing a relationship characterized by passionate love into one characterized by **companionate love**, affectionate love defined by high intimacy and commitment but not much passion (Regan, 2008; Reis & Aron, 2008).

Sternberg identified other types of love that can result depending on whether each of the three dimensions of love are high or low, making the point that love can take a variety of forms. His work also suggests that relationships are likely to fare best if partners have similar balances of passion, intimacy, and decision/commitment; it can be problematic if one partner is passionate and the other is not, for example.

Attachment Styles

Intrigued by parallels between an infant's attachment to a parent figure and a young adult's love for a romantic partner, researchers like Phillip Shaver and his colleagues have been studying adult romantic relationships from the perspective of attachment theory (Fraley & Shaver, 2008; Mikulincer & Shaver, 2007). By any account, attachment is an important component of love relationships. The intimacy component of Sternberg's triangular theory of love, for example, reflects the formation of a caring attachment between romantic partners. Signs of attachment anxiety early in a dating relationship are at least as important as sexual desire in predicting the later development of a serious relationship (Eastwick & Finkel, 2008).

Like the infant who is attached to a parent, the adult who is in love experiences a strong emotional bond to her partner, wants to be close, takes comfort from the bond, and is upset by separations, as illustrated by the story of star-crossed lovers Mike and Marcy at the start of the chapter. Like parent–child attachment, attachment between romantic partners is also biologically adaptive; it increases the odds of having children and the odds that these children will have two parents to help them survive (Fisher, 2006). Perhaps it is not surprising, then, that the concept of romantic love is not just a Western phenomenon or a modern phenomenon, as some people incorrectly believe (Hatfield & Rapson, 2006). Romantic love has been documented in at least 88% of the world's cultures (Jankowiak & Fischer, 1992).

■ **Figure 14.7** shows a way of thinking about how the internal working models that we construct may affect the quality of our romantic relationships (Bartholomew & Horowitz, 1991; Crowell, Fraley, & Shaver, 1999). It describes the four attachment styles that result when view of the self is either positive or negative and view of other people is either positive or negative. Attachment styles can also be described in terms of two dimen-

MODEL OF SELF		
	POSITIVE	**NEGATIVE**
MODEL OF OTHER POSITIVE	**SECURE** *Secure attachment history* Healthy balance of attachment and autonomy; freedom to explore	**PREOCCUPIED** *Resistant attachment history* Desperate for love to feel worthy as a person; worry about abandonment; express anxiety and danger openly
MODEL OF OTHER NEGATIVE	**DISMISSING** *Avoidant attachment history* Shut out emotions; defend against hurt by avoiding intimacy, dismissing the importance of relationships, and being "compulsively self-reliant"	**FEARFUL** *Disorganized–disoriented attachment history* Need relationships but doubt own worth and fear intimacy; lack a coherent strategy for meeting attachment needs

■ **FIGURE 14.7** Internal working models of self and other people arising from early experiences in relationships. It is also possible to look at these four types of attachment in terms of anxiety and avoidance dimensions (Gallo, Smith, & Ruiz, 2003; Mikulincer & Shaver, 2003). The secure attachment type is low in both anxiety over relationships (fear of abandonment) and avoidance of relationships (discomfort over being intimate with and dependent on someone); the preoccupied type is high in anxiety but low in avoidance; the dismissing type is low in anxiety but high in avoidance; and the fearful type is high in both anxiety and avoidance. SOURCE: Adapted with permission from Bartholomew, K., & Horowitz, L. M., Attachment styles among young adults: A test of a four-category model, *Journal of Personality and Social Psychology*, 61, pp. 226–244. Copyright © 1991 American Psychological Association.

sions (Roisman, 2009): anxiety (extent of concern about the availability and responsiveness of partners) and avoidance (extent of discomfort being intimate with and depending on a partner).

Adults with a *secure* working model feel good about both themselves and others; they are not afraid of entering intimate relationships or of being abandoned once they do. People with a *preoccupied* internal working model have a positive view of other people but feel unlovable. Like resistantly attached infants, they crave closeness to others as a means of validating their self-worth and tend to become overly dependent on their partners, but are highly fearful of abandonment; thus, they are high in attachment anxiety but low in avoidance.

Adults with a *dismissing* style of attachment have a positive view of self but do not trust other people and dismiss the importance of close relationships (Beckwith, Cohen, & Hamilton, 1999). Like avoidantly attached infants, they defend themselves against hurt by not expressing their need for love or their fear of abandonment. They downplay the importance of their relationships, find it hard to trust partners, feel that others want them to be more intimate than they wish to be, and keep partners at a distance (that is, they are low in attachment anxiety but high in avoidance). Bowlby (1973) described dismissing or avoidant individuals as "compulsively self-reliant." Finally, adults with a *fearful* internal working model resemble infants with a disorganized–disoriented attachment; they take a dim view of both themselves and other people and display a confusing, unpredictable mix of neediness and fear of closeness.

An analysis of multiple samples of mothers (Bakermans-Kranenburg & van IJzendoorn, 2009) suggests that 58% can be classified as secure, 19% as preoccupied (resistant), and 23% as

Which of the internal working models of attachment in Figure 14.7—secure, dismissing, preoccupied, or fearful—is expressed in each of the following statements, and which working model best describes you (Bartholomew & Horowitz, 1991, p. 244; adapted from Hazan & Shaver, 1987)?

___1. "I want to be completely emotionally intimate with others, but I often find that others are reluctant to get as close as I would like. I am uncomfortable being without close relationships, but I sometimes worry that others don't value me as much as I value them."

___2. "I am somewhat uncomfortable getting close to others. I want emotionally close relationships, but I find it difficult to trust others completely or to depend on them. I sometimes worry that I will be hurt if I allow myself to become too close to others."

___3. "It is relatively easy for me to become emotionally close to others. I am comfortable depending on others and having others depend on me. I don't worry about being alone or having others not accept me."

___4. "I am comfortable without close emotional relationships. It is very important to me to feel independent and self-sufficient, and I prefer not to depend on others or have others depend on me."

Answers: 1. Preoccupied 2. Fearful 3. Secure 4. Dismissing

dismissing (avoidant); 18% were also coded as having an unresolved loss or trauma, which is sometimes associated with a fearful or disorganized–disoriented attachment. Distributions for men were similar. You may wish to see if you can identify the internal working models expressed by the statements in Engagement Box 14.1.

In a pioneering study, Cindy Hazan and Phillip Shaver (1987) demonstrated that adults' styles of attachment are related to the quality of their romantic relationships (see also Creasey & Jarvis, 2009). For example, adults with a secure attachment style experienced a good deal of trust and many positive emotions in their current love relationships, and their relationships tended to last longer than those of adults with insecure attachment styles. Avoidant lovers feared intimacy, whereas resistant individuals tended to be obsessed with their partners. A study in which engaged and married partners discussed problems in their relationships (Roisman, 2007) offers a similar picture: adults with a secure attachment style calmly shared their feelings and thoughts; avoidant-style adults showed physiological signs of shutting down or inhibiting their true feelings; and resistant-style adults became highly emotionally aroused, as indicated by high heart rates (see also Creasey & Jarvis, 2009).

The quality of the parent–child relationship that an adult experienced earlier in life predicts both adult attachment style and romantic relationship quality. In a longitudinal study spanning the years from infancy to adulthood, adults who had experienced sensitive maternal care in infancy had more positive mental representations of their romantic relationships than did other adults (Grossmann et al., 2002a). In addition, the quality of the parent–child attachment, especially after infancy, predicted the quality of an adult's romantic relationship. Similarly, and as we saw earlier, Jeffrey Simpson and his colleagues (2007) found that a secure attachment at 1 year of age was linked, in turn, to social competence in childhood, close friendships in adolescence, and an emotionally positive romantic relationship in early adulthood. So, as Bowlby theorized, internal working models of self and other formed on the basis of parent–child interactions affect the quality of later relationships (Fraley, 2002; Mayseless & Scharf, 2007).

Adults' internal working models predict a lot more, though. They predict the extent to which adults have the confidence and curiosity to explore and master their environments (Mikulincer & Shaver, 2003). A secure attachment style in adulthood is associated with strong achievement motivation and a focus on mastering challenges as opposed to avoiding failure (Elliot & Reis, 2003). Securely attached adults also enjoy their work and are good at it, whereas preoccupied (resistantly attached) adults want approval and grumble about not being valued enough, and dismissing (avoidantly attached) adults bury themselves in their work and do little socializing with coworkers (Hazan & Shaver, 1990).

Internal working models also affect an adult's capacity for caregiving—most importantly, for being a sensitive and responsive parent (Mikulincer & Shaver, 2003). Mothers and fathers who had secure relations with their parents tend to interact more sensitively with their children and form more secure attachment relationships with them than parents whose early attachments were insecure (van IJzendoorn, 1995). Mothers with a preoccupied style are anxious and behave irritably and intrusively with their infants, whereas mothers with a dismissing attachment style seem to derive little pleasure from their babies (Adam, Gunnar, & Tanaka, 2004). Attachment styles are even transmitted across multiple generations (Benoit & Parker, 1994).

Finally, attachment styles even have a bearing on adjustment in old age (Magai, 2008). Older adults who recall loving relationships with their parents during childhood tend to have better physical and mental health than those who recall unsupportive relationships (Shaw et al., 2004). Interestingly, Carol Magai and her colleagues (2001) found that most of the European American and African American elderly adults they studied fell in the dismissing–avoidant attachment category rather than the secure category; they expressed some discomfort with closeness and tended to be compulsively self-reliant (see also Magai, 2008). This may be the result of having to cope with the deaths of loved ones or with wanting to avoid dependency in old age—it's not clear. However, elderly adults with either a secure or a dismissive (avoidant) attachment style tend to be happier than those whose styles are preoccupied or fearful, suggesting that the independent, dismissive style may be adaptive in old age (Webster, 1998). Finally, attachment styles affect how older adults, and people of any age for that matter, react to loss of an attachment figure, bereaved people with a secure attachment style faring best, as we will see in Chapter 17 (and see Shaver & Fraley, 2008).

Overall, internal working models and attachment styles, past and present, have implications for the quality of romantic relationships, exploration and work, relationships with children, overall adjustment, and coping with loss. Research on secure, preoccupied, dismissing, and fearful styles of attachment in adulthood has taught us a good deal about adult relationships.

Friendships

Friendships are important across the life span but take on different characters at different ages (Blieszner & Roberto, 2004). Young adults typically have more friends than older adults do, but even very old adults usually have one or more close friends and are in frequent contact with their friends (Ueno & Adams, 2006). Men and women generally have similar expectations of friends, but women tend to place greater emphasis on these intimate relationships (Felmlee & Muraco, 2009).

Friendships can become strained as older adults begin to develop significant health problems and disabilities and one friend needs more aid than the other (Ueno & Adams, 2006). Social psychologists have long emphasized the influence of **equity,** or a balance of contributions and gains, on satisfaction in relationships (Walster, Walster, & Berscheid, 1978). A person who receives more from a relationship than he gives is likely to feel guilty; a person who gives a great deal and receives little in return may feel angry or resentful.

Consistent with equity theory, involvement in relationships in which the balance of emotional support given and received is unequal is associated with lower emotional well-being and more symptoms of depression than involvement in more balanced relationships (Keyes, 2002; Ramos & Wilmoth, 2003). Interestingly, overbenefited, or dependent, friends are often more distressed than underbenefited, or support-giving, friends (Roberto & Scott, 1986). Being able to help other people, or at least to reciprocate help, tends to boost the self-esteem and reduce the depressive symptoms of elderly adults (Krause & Shaw, 2000; Ramos & Wilmoth, 2003). Perhaps because of gender-role norms, men who have a strong desire to be independent react especially negatively to receiving help (Nagurney, Reich, & Newsom, 2004). Perhaps because inequity threatens friendships, older adults usually call on family before friends when they need substantial help (Felton & Berry, 1992; Kendig et al., 1988). To combat feelings of inequity, friends and family do best to provide help unobtrusively, so that the recipient of help is barely aware of it (Maisel & Gable, 2009).

Adult Relationships and Adult Development

We have emphasized throughout this chapter that close attachments to other people are essential to normal cognitive, social, and emotional development. It should not surprise you to learn, then, that adults are better off in many ways when they enjoy meaningful social relationships. Research tells us this: The quality rather than the quantity of an individual's social relationships is most closely related to that person's sense of well-being or life satisfaction (O'Connor, 1995; Pinquart & Sorensen, 2000). Similarly, perceived social support is more important than the social support actually received (Uchino, 2009). Just as people can feel lonely despite being surrounded by other people, adults can feel deprived of

Old friends are likely to be most satisfied with their relationship when it remains equitable.

© Gaby Gerster/laif/Redux

How might attachment theory be applied to help humans develop more satisfying intimate relationships across the life span? As you have seen, stressed parents who are likely to be insensitive caregivers and infants who have difficult temperaments are at risk for forming insecure attachments. In one study grounded in attachment theory (van den Boom, 1995), low-income mothers in Holland with irritable babies were given a series of three 2-hour training sessions designed to help them recognize, interpret, and respond appropriately to their infants' signals. Trained mothers became more sensitive caregivers, and their infants were more likely than those of mothers who received no training to be able to soothe themselves when upset, to be securely attached at age 1, and to remain securely attached at age 3. What is more, these children had more positive relationships with peers. Even parents who are depressed can be trained in only a few sessions to be more sensitive caregivers and, as a result, to build more secure attachments with even difficult infants (Berlin, 2005; Berlin, Zeanah, & Lieberman, 2008; van Doesum et al., 2008; Velderman et al., 2006).

Attachment theory has also guided treatment of adopted children with attachment problems, including those with **reactive attachment disorder,** a psychiatric diagnosis affecting socially deprived and maltreated children that involves either emotionally withdrawn behavior suggestive of a lack of attachment or the disinhibited attachment pattern we discussed earlier, in which children display indiscriminate interest in people and lack of appropriate wariness of strangers (Zeanah & Smyke, 2008).

Finally, attachment theory has become the basis for therapy with individual adults or couples experiencing relationship problems. The emotionally focused couples therapy developed by Susan Johnson (2008) is an example. This form of therapy helps partners understand their attachment-related emotions and see that it is okay to need one another and to be fearful of separation; to communicate their emotions, including painful ones about experiences of betrayal and unresponsiveness; and to collaborate to better meet one another's emotional needs and heal old wounds. This and other work suggests that insecure and troubled relationships can be converted into secure attachments that serve as secure bases for exploration, safe havens in times of stress, and foundations for healthy development across the life span.

social support even though they receive a lot of it—or they can have restricted social networks yet be highly satisfied with their relationships.

The size of an adult's social network is not nearly as important as whether it includes at least one **confidant**—a spouse, relative, or friend to whom the individual feels especially attached and with whom thoughts and feelings can be shared (de Jong-Gierveld, 1986; Levitt, 1991). For most married adults in our society, spouses are the most important confidants, and the quality of an adult's marriage is one of the strongest influences on overall satisfaction with life (Fleeson, 2004). Men are particularly dependent on their spouses; women rely more than men on friends, siblings, and children for emotional support (Gurung, Taylor, & Seeman, 2003). Of concern is evidence that the percentage of adults in the United States who say they have no one with whom to discuss important matters increased from 10% in 1985 to almost 25% in 2004 and the number of confidants the average person had dropped from about three to two over this same time span (McPherson, Smith-Lovin, & Brashears, 2006).

Also important to life satisfaction is whether interacting with close companions is rewarding or stressful (Krause, 1995). Perhaps because of their personality traits, people who have positive (or negative) interactions in one relationship tend to have similar experiences in other relationships, creating a constellation of supportive (or stressful) relationships (Krause & Rook, 2003). Relationships with spouses, children, or other significant companions can undermine rather than bolster emotional well-being if they involve mostly negative exchanges (Newsom et al., 2003).

So a small number of close, harmonious, and supportive relationships can improve the quality of an adult's life, whereas negative relationships (or none) can make life unpleasant. It is more than that, however: Social support, especially from family members, has positive effects on the cardiovascular, endocrine, and immune systems; improves the body's ability to cope with stress and illness; and contributes to better physical and cognitive functioning and a longer life, especially in old age (Cohen & Janicki-Deverts, 2009; Uchino, 2009). John Cacioppo (Cacioppo & Patrick, 2008) concludes that humans have evolved to be with other people and that isolation and loneliness wear the body down, affecting genes, stress hormones, and the brain in ways that speed the aging process. Special programs can help reduce the loneliness of socially isolated elderly adults—for example, home visitors who befriend them (Andrews et al., 2003) and senior centers that allow them to meet and form friendships with other elders (Aday, Kehoe, & Farney, 2006).

Whatever our ages, our well-being and development hinge considerably on the quality of our ties to our fellow humans—particularly on having a close emotional bond with at least one person. It is fitting, then, that we conclude this chapter by illustrating, in Application Box 14.2, how attachment theory has been applied to improve close relationships.

Checking Mastery

1. According to Carstensen's socioemotional selectivity theory, why do social networks shrink in later adulthood?

2. What qualities does a companionate love relationship have, according to Sternberg's triarchic theory?

3. How would you characterize people with a dismissing internal working model in terms of their (1) views of self and others and (2) position on the dimensions of attachment anxiety and avoidance?

4. Gus and Andy were great friends, but ever since Gus's heart attack the friendship has been strained. What concept helps explain this?

Making Connections

1. Laura Carstensen's socioemotional selectivity theory suggests that adults narrow their social networks with age to better meet their emotional needs. Develop some alternative hypotheses about why elderly adults have smaller social networks than young adults.

2. Analyze the internal working models that guide you and your partner in your current (or if you are not in a current relationship, most recent) romantic relationship. What are (were) the implications?

Chapter Summary

14.1 Perspectives on Relationships

- The developmental significance of early parent–child relationships is emphasized in the Bowlby–Ainsworth attachment theory, which argues that attachments are built into the human species, develop through an interaction of nature and nurture during a sensitive period, and affect later development by shaping internal working models of self and other.
- The second world of childhood, the peer world, was believed to be especially important by Jean Piaget, who emphasized the reciprocal nature of peer relations, and by Harry Stack Sullivan, who emphasized chumships as a source of social support and training ground for later intimate relationships.

14.2 The Infant

- Biologically based primary emotions such as anger and fear appear in the first year of life, secondary or self-conscious emotions in the second year. Attachment figures arouse strong emotions, socialize emotions, and help infants regulate their emotions until they can develop better emotion regulation strategies of their own.
- Parents typically become attached to infants before or shortly after birth, and parent and child quickly establish synchronized routines. Infants progress through phases of undiscriminating social responsiveness, discriminating social responsiveness, active proximity seeking, and goal-corrected partnership. The formation of a first attachment around 6 or 7 months is accompanied by separation anxiety and stranger anxiety, as well as by exploration from a secure base and retreat to the safe haven the caregiver provides.
- Research using Mary Ainsworth's Strange Situation classifies the quality of parent–infant attachment as secure, resistant, avoidant, or disorganized–disoriented. Harry Harlow demonstrated that contact comfort is more important than feeding in attachment; secure attachments are also associated with sensitive, responsive parenting, but infant characteristics such as temperament also contribute.
- Repeated long-term separations and social deprivation can make it difficult for an infant to form normal attachments, though recovery is evident. Attending day care normally does not disrupt parent–child attachments, although quality of care matters. Secure attachments contribute to later cognitive and social competence, but attachment quality often changes over time, and insecurely attached infants are not doomed to a lifetime of poor relationships.
- Infants are interested in peers and become increasingly able to coordinate their own activity with that of their small companions; by 18 months, they participate in reciprocal exchanges and form friendships.

14.3 The Child

- From ages 2 to 12, children participate in goal-corrected partnerships with their parents and spend increasing amounts of time with peers, especially same-sex ones, engaging in increasingly social and imaginative play, including social pretend play, and later in organized games and hobbies.
- Physical attractiveness, cognitive ability, social competence, and emotion regulation skills contribute to popular—rather than rejected, neglected, or controversial—sociometric status. Children who are rejected by their peers or who have no friends are especially at risk for future problems.

14.4 The Adolescent

- During adolescence, same-sex and cross-sex friendships increasingly involve emotional intimacy and self-disclosure, and a transition is made from same-sex cliques, to mixed-sex cliques and larger crowds, and finally to dating relationships, which at first meet self-esteem and status needs and later become more truly affectionate. Although susceptibility to negative peer pressure peaks around age 14 or 15, peers are more often a positive than a negative force in development, unless poor relationships with parents lead to association with an antisocial crowd.

14.5 The Adult

- Adult social networks shrink with age, possibly because of increased socioemotional selectivity.
- Evolved preferences and various filters may be involved in mate selection; choices are based mainly on homogamy, with complementarity a lesser consideration. According to Sternberg's triarchic theory, love involves passion, intimacy, and decision/commitment and different types of love differ in the proportions of each component.
- Adults have secure, preoccupied, dismissing, or fearful internal working models that appear to be rooted in their early attachment experiences and that affect their romantic relationships, approaches to work, attachments with their own children, and adjustment.
- Although adults are highly involved with their spouses or romantic partners, they continue to value friendships, especially long-lasting and equitable ones. Having at least one confidant has beneficial effects on life satisfaction, as well as on physical health and cognitive functioning.

Checking Mastery Answers

For answers to Checking Mastery questions, visit **www.cengagebrain.com**

Key Terms

attachment theory **462**
attachment **462**
imprinting **463**
oxytocin **463**
bonding **463**
internal working model **463**
peer **464**
chumship **465**
self-conscious emotion **466**
social referencing **466**
emotion regulation **467**
synchronized routines **468**
goal-corrected partnership **469**
separation anxiety **469**
stranger anxiety **469**
secure base **469**
Strange Situation **469**
secure attachment **469**
resistant attachment **470**
avoidant attachment **470**
disorganized–disoriented attachment **470**

contact comfort **471**
disinhibited attachment **473**
pretend play **477**
social pretend play **478**
sociometric techniques **479**
co-rumination **482**
clique **482**
crowd **482**
social convoy **484**
socioemotional selectivity theory **485**
positivity effect **485**
homogamy **486**
triangular theory of love **486**
consummate love **487**
companionate love **487**
equity **489**
reactive attachment disorder **490**
confidant **490**

Media Resources

Psychology CourseMate

Find online quizzes, flash cards, animations, video clips, experiments, interactive assessments, and other helpful study aids for this text at **www.cengagebrain.com**. You can also connect directly to the following sites:

Better Kid Care: Play is the Business of Kids

This site hosts material relating to the types, value, and importance of play in the development of children. Broken down into sections based on age groups. To access, see "web links" in Psychology CourseMate at www.cengagebrain.com

Types of Love

This site hosts material relating to the concept of love and the different forms it may take for different people. To access, see "web links" in Psychology CourseMate at www.cengagebrain.com

Understanding the DATA: Exercises on the Web

www

www.cengagebrain.com
For additional insight on the data presented in this chapter, try out the exercises for these figures in Psychology CourseMate at

www.cengagebrain.com:

> **Figure 14.3** Percentages of secure, avoidant, disorganized, and "disinhibited or other" attachments among nondeprived British children adopted before 6 months of age, deprived Romanian children adopted in the United Kingdom before 6 months, and deprived Romanian children adopted between 6 and 24 months. Notice the high percentage of disinhibited attachment in Romanian infants who spent a long time in a deprived institution.

> **Figure 14.5** Frequency of activities engaged in by preschool children of different ages. With age, solitary and parallel play occur less frequently, whereas associative and cooperative play occur more frequently.

CengageNOW

www.cengagebrain.com
Go to www.cengagebrain.com to link to CengageNOW, your online study tool. First take the Pre-Test for this chapter to get your Personalized Study Plan, which will identify topics you need to review and direct you to online resources. Then take the Post-Test to determine what concepts you have mastered and what you still need work on.

Human Development and the Family

© Larry Dale Gordon/The Image Bank/Getty Images

Think about America's first family —Barack, Michelle, Malia, and Sasha Obama: Do you view them as a traditional American family or a modern one? Barack was the son of a black father from Kenya and a white mother from Kansas. He experienced life in a single-mother home, the remarriage of his mother to an Indonesian businessman, and stints living in Hawaii and being raised by his maternal grandparents (Friesen, 2009). Michelle came from a two-parent working-class family descended from slaves.

The Obamas waited until after their careers were established—until they were 31 and 28, respectively—to marry, and they then became a very egalitarian, dual-career couple (Romano, 2009). Michelle was Barack's mentor at a law firm for a time. They had their marital strains over balancing work and family when Barack became immersed in Illinois politics and Michelle, left with the lion's share of child-rearing responsibility, realized that "marriage is hard" (Kantor, 2009, p. 1). When Barack left Chicago for the United States Senate, he did not see the family much. After he became President in 2009, however, they all moved into the White House, along with Michelle's mother, and saw more of each other than they had for many years. Barack and Michelle have "date nights" and the family watches movies and plays Scrabble for fun. It is clear that the Obamas are strongly committed to each other and to their children and continue to function as a team of equals (Kantor, 2009).

1. What does it mean to say that the family is a changing system in a changing world?

2. How do family systems concepts help us understand how infants are affected by their mothers and fathers?

3. How is child development affected by parenting styles and relationships with siblings?

4. How does the parent–child relationship change during adolescence?

5. How are adults affected by the events of the family life cycle, and how do family relationships change over the years?

6. How do family experiences differ in the diverse kinds of families that exist today?

7. Why does family violence occur, what are its effects on development, and what can be done to stop it?

The Obama family is clearly unique—but just as clearly it has undergone some of the same experiences that have affected many other American families. It is a traditional family in some ways but a modern one in others. Like the Obamas, we are all bound to and affected by our families. We are born into them, work our way toward adulthood in them, start our own as adults, and continue to be bound to them in old age. We are part of our families, and they are part of us. James Garbarino (1992) has gone so far as to call the family the "basic unit of human experience" (p. 7).

Are the Obamas a traditional or modern American family?

© AP Photo/Jae C. Hong

This chapter examines the family and its central roles in human development throughout the life span. How has the family changed in recent years? How do infants, children, and adolescents experience family life, and how are they affected by their relationships with parents and siblings? How is adult development affected by such family transitions as marrying, becoming a parent, watching children leave the nest, and becoming a grandparent? Finally, what are the implications of the immense diversity that characterizes today's families—and of such decisions as remaining childless or divorcing?

15.1 Understanding the Family

The family is a system—and a system within other systems. It is also a changing system—and a changing system in a changing world. We invite you to see how much you know about American family life by making the estimates called for in Engagement Box 15.1 before reading on.

The Family as a System within Systems

Debate rages in the United States today about whether marriage, the basis for most families, must be between a husband and wife or can be between two men or two women. This controversy illustrates that it may not be possible to define *family* in a way that applies across all cultures and eras; many forms of family life have worked and continue to work for humans (Coontz, 2000; Leeder, 2004). However we define it, proponents of **family systems theory** conceptualize a family as a system. This means that the family, like the human body, is truly a whole consisting of interrelated parts, each of which affects and is affected by every other part, and each of which contributes to the functioning of the whole (Bornstein & Sawyer, 2006; Parke & Buriel, 2006). Moreover, the family is a dynamic system—a self-organizing system that adapts itself to changes in its members and to changes in its environment (Maccoby, 2007). In the past, developmentalists did not adopt this family systems perspective. They typically focused almost entirely on the mother–child relationship, assuming that the only process of interest within the family was the mother's influence on the child's development.

The **nuclear family** typically consists of father, mother, and at least one child. Even a simple man, woman, and infant "system" can be complex. An infant interacting with her mother is already involved in a process of reciprocal influence: The baby's smile is greeted by a smile from Mom, and Mom's smile is reciprocated by the infant's grin. However, the presence of both parents means that we must consider husband–wife, mother–infant, and father–infant relationships (Belsky, 1981). Every individual

The family has changed dramatically over the past century, and we wonder how many of you have a good feel for characteristics of American family life today. Fill in the blanks below with a number you would guess is close to the correct percentage and then compare your answers with the statistics in A Changing System in a Changing World, on page 486. Read that section a bit more closely if your guesses are wildly different from the real percentages.

____ 1. What percentage of adults can be expected to marry at some point in their lives?

____ 2. What percentage of births are now to unmarried rather than married women?

____ 3. What percentage of women with children younger than age 6 work outside the home?

____ 4. What percentage of newly married couples can expect to divorce?

____ 5. What percentage of children live with two parents (whether biological, adoptive, or stepparents)?

____ 6. What percentage of women age 65 and older live alone?

---

and every relationship within the family affects every other individual and relationship through reciprocal influence.

Now think about how complex the family system becomes if we add another child (or two or six) to it. We must then understand the husband–wife relationship, the relationships between each parent and each of their children, and the relationships between siblings. The family now becomes a system with subsystems—in this case, marital, parent–child, and sibling subsystems (Parke & Buriel, 2006). In addition, researchers have begun to focus on another subsystem, **coparenting,** or the ways in which two parents coordinate their parenting and function well (or poorly) as a team in relation to their children (McHale et al., 2002; Parke & Buriel, 2006). Do they talk to each other about the children, are they consistent in the rules they set, do they back one another up—or do they contradict one another, compete for their children's affection, and undermine each other's parenting? Mutually supportive coparenting can make a big difference in development, beyond the impact of a close marital relationship. For example, it can head off behavior problems in children who by temperament are predisposed to develop them (Schoppe-Sullivan et al., 2009).

Now consider the complexity of an **extended family household,** in which parents and their children live with other kin— some combination of grandparents, siblings, aunts, uncles, nieces, and nephews. Extended family households (like the Obama White House, once Michelle's mother moved in) are common in many cultures (Ruggles, 1994). Indeed, it has been suggested that humans evolved to involve the whole "village," or at least many members of the extended family rather than just a mother and father, in raising children (Hrdy, 2005). In the United States, African Americans, Hispanic Americans, and other ethnic minorities tend to place more emphasis on extended family bonds than European Americans do (Parke & Buriel, 2006). For example, African-American single mothers often obtain needed help with child care and social support by living with their mothers (Burton, 1990; Oberlander, Black, & Starr, 2007). Even when members of the extended family live in

their own nuclear family households, they often interact frequently and share responsibility for raising children, often to the benefit of the children.

The family is also a *system within other systems;* whether it is of the nuclear or the extended type, it does not exist in a vacuum. Urie Bronfenbrenner's bioecological model, a systems theory introduced in Chapter 1, emphasizes nicely that the family is a system that is embedded in and interacts with larger social systems such as a neighborhood, a community, a subculture, and a broader culture (Bronfenbrenner & Morris, 2006). The family experience in our culture is different from that in cultures where new brides become underlings in the households of their mothers-in-law or where men can have several wives (Strong, DeVault, & Cohen, 2008). There is an almost infinite variety of family forms and family contexts in the world and a correspondingly wide range of developmental experiences within the family.

The Family as a Changing System

It would be difficult enough to study the family as a system if it kept the same members and continued to perform the same activities for as long as it existed. However, family membership changes as new children are born and as grown children leave the nest, as parents separate or die. Moreover, each family member is a developing individual, and the relationships between husband and wife, parent and child, and sibling and sibling change in systematic ways over the years. Changes in family membership and changes in any person or relationship within the family affect the dynamics of the whole system.

The earliest theories of family development featured the concept of a **family life cycle**—a sequence of changes in family composition, roles, and relationships from the time people marry until they die (Duvall, 1977; Hill & Rodgers, 1964). Family theorist Evelyn Duvall (1977), for example, outlined eight stages of the family life cycle, from the married couple without children through the family with children to the aging family, as shown in

TABLE 15.1 STAGES OF THE FAMILY LIFE CYCLE

Stage	Available Roles
1. Married couple without children	Wife Husband
2. Childbearing family (oldest child from birth to 30 months)	Wife–mother Husband–father Infant daughter or son
3. Family with preschool children (oldest child from 30 months to 6 years)	Wife–mother Husband–father Daughter–sister Son–brother
4. Family with school-age children (oldest child up to 12 years)	Wife–mother Husband–father Daughter–sister Son–brother
5. Family with teenagers (oldest child from 13 to 20 years)	Wife–mother Husband–father Daughter–sister Son–brother
6. Family launching young adults (First child gone to last child gone)	Wife–mother–grandmother Husband–father–grandfather Daughter–sister–aunt Son–brother–uncle
7. Family without children (empty nest to retirement)	Wife–mother–grandmother Husband–father–grandfather
8. Aging family (retirement to death)	Wife–mother–grandmother Husband–father–grandfather Widow or widower

SOURCE: Adapted from Duvall, 1977.

Table 15.1. Each stage has a particular set of family members, and family members play distinctive roles—husband, wife, daughter, and so on—and carry out distinctive developmental tasks—for example, establishing a satisfying relationship in the newlywed phase, adjusting to the demands of new parenthood in the childbearing phase, and adapting to the departure of children in the "launching" phase.

In this chapter, we look at the effect of these common family transitions on adults, and we examine how the child's experience of the family changes as she develops. You will see, however, that an increasing number of people do not experience all the phases of this traditional family life cycle or do not experience the phases in the same ways. Many adults enter into romantic relationships but remain single or childless, marry multiple times, or otherwise follow a different path than the one in which a man and woman form a nuclear family, raise children, and grow old together (Cherlin, 2009; Patterson &

Hastings, 2007). As a result, many family researchers find fault with early models of the family life cycle in which a nuclear family remains intact and moves through the phases in sequence (Strong, DeVault, & Cohen, 2008). They have expanded on the traditional family life cycle concept to describe a wider variety of family life cycles (see, for example, Carter & McGoldrick, 2005). They have also embraced the proposition developed by Glen Elder and his colleagues (Elder & Johnson, 2003; Elder & Shanahan, 2006) that we lead **linked lives**—that our development as individuals is intertwined with that of other family members. Finally, they have embraced the concept that families function as systems and that they, like the individuals in them, develop and change over the life span.

A Changing System in a Changing World

Not only is the family a system embedded within systems, and not only is it a developing system, but the world in which it is embedded is ever changing. During the second half of the 20th century, several dramatic social changes altered the makeup of the typical family and the quality of family experience. Drawing on analyses of U.S. Census Bureau data and other surveys, we will highlight some of these trends (see Bryant et al., 2006; Cherlin, 2009; Federal Interagency Forum on Child and Family Statistics, 2009; Teachman, 2000; U.S. Census Bureau, 2009; Whitehead & Popenoe, 2003; Wilmoth & Longino, 2006):

1. *More single adults.* More adults are living as singles today than in the past. Often they are living with a partner or a partner and children but are unmarried. Do not conclude that marriage is out of style; almost 90% of adults can still be expected to marry at some time in their lives (Cherlin, 2009). The percentage of the population that is married at any given time has been dropping, though (Schoen & Cheng, 2006).
2. *More postponed marriages.* The average age of first marriage decreased during the first half of the 20th century but then crept up in the late 20th and early 21st centuries so that by 2009 it was 26 for women and 28 for men (Bernstein, 2010). Most young adults still want to marry but, like the Obamas, they are waiting until they are older to do it.
3. *More unmarried parents.* Partly because marriage is being postponed, more and more females are giving birth without being married to their child's father. About 18% of births in 1980 but a whopping 40% of births in 2007 were to unmarried women (Federal Interagency Forum on Child and Family Statistics, 2009). Some of these women have concerns about the institution of marriage but most are simply delaying marriage while they pursue educational and career goals.
4. *Fewer children.* Today's adults are also having fewer children than women in the early 20th century did and therefore spend fewer years of their lives raising children. Increasing numbers of young women are also remaining childless. In 1980, 10% of women ages 40 to 44 were childless; by 1998 that percentage had climbed to 19% (Whitehead & Popenoe, 2003).

5. *More working mothers.* In 1950, 12% of married women with children younger than 6 years worked outside the home; by 2005 the figure had climbed to about 60%, a truly remarkable social change (U.S. Census Bureau, 2006).

6. *More divorce.* The divorce rate increased substantially over the 20th century. More than 4 in 10 newly married couples can expect to divorce (Schoen & Canudas-Romo, 2006), and up to half of children can expect to experience a divorce at some point in their development (Lansford, 2009).

7. *More single-parent families.* Because of more births to unmarried women and more divorce, more children live in single-parent families. In 1960, only 9% of children lived with one parent, usually a widowed one (Whitehead & Popenoe, 2003); in 2008, 70% of children younger than 18 years lived with two parents, 23% lived with their mothers only, and more than 3% lived with their fathers only (Federal Interagency Forum on Aging Related Statistics, 2009; and see ▪ **Figure 15.1**).

8. *More children living in poverty.* The higher number of single-parent families has affected the proportion of children living in poverty. About 18% of children in the United States live in poverty today (Federal Interagency Forum on Aging Related Statistics, 2009). Fully 35% of African American children and 29% of Hispanic American children, compared with 10% of nonhispanic white children, are poor. A greater percentage of children in female-headed families than children in families with married parents are poor—43% versus 9%.

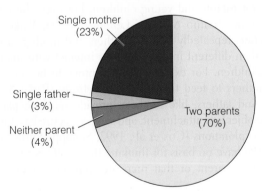

▪ **FIGURE 15.1** Percentage of children from birth to age 17 in various living arrangements. In all, 30% of children today do not live with two parents. A minority of two-parent families involve cohabiting couples or stepparents rather than two married biological or adoptive parents. In a minority of single-parent homes, the parent has a cohabiting partner. Most children living with neither parent live with grandparents. SOURCE: Data from Federal Interagency Forum on Child and Family Statistics. (2009). *America's children: Key national indicators of well-being, 2009.* Washington, DC: U. S. Government Printing Office, pp. 3, 92–95. Available at: http://childstats.gov. Accessed: January 9, 2010.

9. *More remarriages.* As more married couples have divorced, more adults have been remarrying. Often they form new, **reconstituted families**, also called blended families, that include at least a parent, a stepparent, and a child; sometimes they blend multiple children from two families into a new family.

10. *More years without children.* Because modern couples are compressing their childbearing into a shorter time span, because some divorced adults do not remarry, and mainly because people are living longer, adults today spend more of their later years as couples—or, especially if they are women, as single adults—without children in their homes. Men 65 and over are more likely than women 65 and over to live with spouses (73% vs. 42%), and older women are more likely than older men to live alone (39% vs. 19%), mainly because more women are widowed (Federal Interagency Forum on Aging Related Statistics, 2008).

11. *More multigenerational families.* As a result of these same trends, three- and even four-generation families became more common over the 20th century. More children today than in the past know their grandparents and even their great-grandparents, parent–child and grandparent–child relationships are lasting longer, and multigenerational bonds are becoming more important (Bengtson, 2001). Usually the different generations of a family do not live together; however, the economic woes of the early 21st century have forced an increasing number of Americans to live in multigenerational households out of economic necessity (St. George, 2010).

12. *Fewer caregivers for aging adults.* Smaller families with fewer children, increases in the numbers of adults living alone, increased longevity, increased geographic mobility, and the large Baby Boom generation now entering old age mean that more and more aging adults need care from relatives but have fewer children to provide it (Brody, 2004).

Clearly, many important changes in the family have been occurring. Some observers view these changes as evidence of a "decline of the family," noting the negative effects on children of increased births to unmarried parents, divorce, single-parent families, and poverty, and the problem of more elderly adults having fewer children to support them. Some observers also worry because most Americans now view marriage as an institution whose purpose is more to meet the emotional needs of adults than to nurture children (Whitehead & Popenoe, 2003). Family scholar Andrew Cherlin (2009) adds that American children today experience a dizzying "merry-go-round" of changes as their parents switch from one partner to another and from singlehood to cohabitation or marriage and back. He argues that Americans very much want to be married but also want the freedom to end relationships that are not self-fulfilling enough. The instability in family life that results from these conflicting desires, he feels, is not good for child development.

Other scholars, though, find good news with the bad in trends in family life (Connidis, 2010; Teachman, 2000; White & Rogers, 2000). For example, and as illustrated by the Obama family, postponing marriage improves its chances of success, men's and women's roles in the family are more equal than they used to be, more children have relationships with their grandparents and great-grandparents today, and families are better off financially with two wage earners than with only one. From this perspective, the family is not dying; it is just different. It can even be characterized as a highly "adaptable institution" in that it has survived despite many social changes that could have done it in (Amato et al., 2003).

Whether it is in decline or not, the American family is more diverse than ever before. Our stereotyped image of the family—the nuclear family with a married couple consisting of a breadwinner–husband/father, a full-time housewife/mother, plus children—has become just that: a stereotype. By one estimate, about 45% of families in 1960, but only 12% of families by 1995, were of this type (Hernandez, 1997). Clearly, we must broaden our image of the family to include the many dual-career, single-parent, reconstituted, childless, and other types of families that exist today. We must also avoid assuming that families that do not fit the stereotypical family pattern are deficient.

Fathers are just as capable as mothers of sensitive, responsive parenting.

© Ariel Skelley/Corbis

Checking Mastery

1. According to Duvall, what changes in the family as it moves through the phases of the family life cycle?

2. What are three changes over the 20th century that have resulted in fewer children living their childhoods in a stereotypical family with a married breadwinner father and homemaker mother?

Making Connections

1. What does it really mean to be a family? Bearing in mind the diversity of families today, offer a definition of "family" and justify it.

2. Returning to the Obama family, in what ways are their family experiences traditional and in what ways are they modern and reflective of the changes that have taken place in the family over the past few decades?

15.2 The Infant

We begin this look at family development by exploring relationships between parenting and the child's development in the family from infancy to adolescence. Later, we will adopt the perspective of this child's parents and see how the family life cycle looks to them.

Mother–Infant and Father–Infant Relationships

Once developmentalists took seriously the idea that the family is a system, they discovered the existence of fathers and began to look more carefully at how both mothers and fathers interact

with their children and at what each parent contributes to a child's development.

Gender stereotypes would suggest that fathers are not cut out to care for infants and young children; however, the evidence says they are (Lamb & Tamis-Lemonda, 2004; Parke, 1996). Researchers repeatedly find that fathers and mothers are more similar than different in the ways they interact with infants and young children. For example, fathers prove to be no less able than mothers to feed their babies effectively (Parke & Sawin, 1976). And fathers, like mothers, provide sensitive parenting, become objects of attachment, and serve as secure bases for their infants' explorations (Cox et al., 1992; Schoppe-Sullivan et al., 2006). We have no basis for thinking that mothers are uniquely qualified to parent or that men are hopelessly inept around babies.

However, that fathers are capable of sensitive parenting does not mean that they play the same roles as mothers in their children's lives. Fathers and mothers differ in both the quantity and the style of the parenting they provide (Lamb & Tamis-Lemonda, 2004; Marsiglio et al., 2000), and we can ask how nature and nurture contribute to these differences. Consider first differences in quantity: Mothers spend more time with children than fathers do (Bianchi, 2000). This gender difference is common across cultures, causing some to argue that it has been built into our genes during the course of evolution. True, fathers today are more involved with their children than ever (Marsiglio et al., 2000; Pleck & Masciadrelli, 2004). Some are even sharing responsibility for child care equally with their spouses rather than just "helping," especially if they hold egalitarian views about gender roles (Bulanda, 2004; Deutsch, 2001). Yet there is still a gap.

Mothers and fathers also differ in their typical styles of interacting with young children. When mothers interact with their babies, a large proportion of their time is devoted to caregiving: offering food, changing diapers, wiping noses, and so on. Fathers spend much of their time with children in playful interaction. They specialize in tickling, poking, bouncing, and surprising infants, whereas mothers hold, talk to, and play quietly with infants (Laflamme, Pomerleau, & Malcuit, 2002; Neville & Parke, 1997). Yet fathers are able to adopt a "motherlike" caregiver role if they have primary responsibility for their children, so their playful parenting may be more about being in the role of the "backup" parent than about being male rather than female (Phares, 1999). It seems, then, that both nature (evolution) and nurture (societal gender-role norms) contribute to mother–father differences in parental involvement and styles of interacting with young children.

In view of the roles that fathers play in their children's lives, what are their major contributions to child development? Fathers contribute to healthy development by supporting their children financially, whether they live with them or not (Marsiglio et al., 2000). They also contribute by being warm and effective parents, just as mothers do. Babies are likely to be more socially competent if they are securely attached to both parents than if they are securely attached to just one (Main & Weston, 1981). In addition, children whose fathers are warm and involved with them are more likely than other children to become high achievers in school (Cabrera et al., 2000). A father's tendency to challenge his young children during play, egging them on to take risks, may be particularly important, breeding a secure attachment style and an eagerness to explore later in life (Grossmann et al., 2002b). Finally, children generally have fewer psychological disorders and problems if their fathers are caring, involved, and effective parents than if they are not (Cabrera et al., 2000; Marsiglio et al., 2000). Overall, children fare better cognitively, socially, and emotionally if they have a supportive father in their lives than if they do not (Holden, 2010).

What does the fact that 40% of babies are now born to unmarried mothers mean for father involvement? Generally, unmarried fathers who do not live with their child's mother are not very involved parents. However, they can be under some conditions. A recent study of low-income, urban fathers over the first 3 years of their child's life suggests that much depends on the quality of the relationship between mother and father (Fagan et al., 2009). If they have a strong relationship, the father is likely to be involved with his child, whereas if he has lost interest in his partner or has moved on to another romantic relationship, the odds of his being an involved father are low. Another positive factor is moving into the same household with mother and child, as many unmarried fathers wind up doing. Finally, father involvement is greatest when young fathers move away from high-risk lifestyles involving drug use, unemployment, criminal activity, and the like and toward more conventional activities such as job training and religious participation. Finally, fathers who get involved before the birth are likely to stay involved afterward (Cabrera, Fagan, & Farrie, 2008; Fagan et al., 2009).

Unmarried mothers and their children clearly benefit when unmarried fathers become partners in child rearing; meanwhile, becoming an involved father seems to help some young men

mature and make positive changes in their lives (Fagan et al., 2009). Couples groups emphasizing parenting skills, couple communication, and effective coping strategies can help increase a father's engagement with his child, improve his relationship with his partner, and positively affect child development (Cowan et al., 2009).

Mothers, Fathers, and Infants: The System at Work

Now let's view the new family as a three-person system functioning in a social context (Bornstein & Sawyer, 2006). The mother–child relationship cannot be understood without considering the father; nor can the father–child relationship be understood without taking the mother into account. This is because parents have **indirect effects** on their children through their ability to influence the behavior of their spouses. More generally, indirect effects within the family are instances in which the relationship or interaction between two individuals is modified by the behavior or attitudes of a third family member.

Fathers indirectly influence the mother–infant relationship in many ways. For example, mothers who have close, supportive relationships with their husbands tend to interact more patiently and sensitively with their babies than do mothers who are experiencing marital tension and who feel that they are raising their children largely without help (Cox et al., 1992; Lamb & Tamis-Lemonda, 2004). Meanwhile, mothers indirectly affect the father–infant relationship. For example, fathers who have just had pleasant conversations with their wives are more supportive and engaged when they interact with their children than fathers who have just had arguments with their wives (Kitzmann, 2000). As you can imagine, infant development goes best when parents get along well and truly coparent, or work as a team (Parke & Buriel, 2006). When parents compete rather than cooperate—for example, when one parent tries to capture the child's attention while she is being engaged by the other parent—their infants may show signs of insecure attachment or may become securely attached to one parent but be blocked from enjoying close relationships with both parents (Caldera & Lindsey, 2006).

Checking Mastery

1. In terms of their parenting roles, what is one way in which fathers are similar to mothers and one way in which they are different?

2. Give an example of a negative indirect effect of a father on the mother–infant relationship.

Making Connections

1. Because of his wife's death during childbirth, Alex suddenly finds himself the sole parent of his infant son, Aaron. Given the material in this section, how do you think this will affect Aaron's development compared with what would have happened if Alex had been the one who died and his wife had to raise Aaron on her own?

15.3 The Child

As children reach age 2 or age 3, parents continue to be caregivers and playmates, but they also become more concerned with socializing their offspring in how (and how not) to behave, using some approach to child rearing and discipline. Siblings also serve as socialization agents and become an important part of the child's experience of the family.

Parenting Styles

How can I be a good parent? Certainly this question is uppermost in most parents' minds. You can go far in understanding which parenting styles are effective by considering just two dimensions of parenting: acceptance–responsiveness and demandingness–control (Darling & Steinberg, 1993; Holden, 2010; Maccoby & Martin, 1983; Schaefer, 1959).

Parental **acceptance–responsiveness** refers to the extent to which parents are supportive, sensitive to their children's needs, and willing to provide affection and praise when their children meet their expectations. Accepting, responsive parents are affectionate and often smile at, praise, and encourage their children, although they also let children know when they misbehave. Less accepting and responsive parents are often quick to criticize, belittle, punish, or ignore their children and rarely communicate to children that they are loved and valued.

Demandingness–control (sometimes called *permissiveness–restrictiveness*) refers to how much control over decisions lies with the parent as opposed to with the child. Controlling and demanding parents set rules, expect their children to follow them, and monitor their children closely to ensure that the rules are followed. Less controlling and demanding parents (often called *permissive parents*) make fewer demands and allow their children a great deal of autonomy in exploring the environment, expressing their opinions and emotions, and making decisions about their activities.

By crossing the acceptance and demandingness dimensions, we have four basic patterns of child rearing to consider, as shown in ■ Figure 15.2:

1. **Authoritarian parenting.** This is a restrictive parenting style combining high demandingness–control and low acceptance–responsiveness. Parents impose many rules, expect strict obedience, rarely explain why the child should comply with rules, and often rely on power tactics such as physical punishment to gain compliance.
2. **Authoritative parenting.** Authoritative parents are more flexible; they are demanding and exert control, but they are also accepting and responsive. They set clear rules and consistently enforce them, but they also explain the rationales for their rules and restrictions, are responsive to their children's needs and points of view, and involve their children in family decision making. They are reasonable and democratic in their approach; although it is clear that they are in charge, they communicate respect for their children.
3. **Permissive parenting.** This style is high in acceptance–responsiveness but low in demandingness–control. Permissive parents are indulgent; they have relatively few rules and make

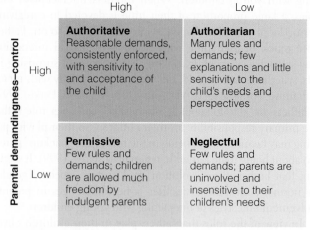

Parental acceptance–responsiveness

	High	Low
High (Parental demandingness–control)	**Authoritative** Reasonable demands, consistently enforced, with sensitivity to and acceptance of the child	**Authoritarian** Many rules and demands; few explanations and little sensitivity to the child's needs and perspectives
Low	**Permissive** Few rules and demands; children are allowed much freedom by indulgent parents	**Neglectful** Few rules and demands; parents are uninvolved and insensitive to their children's needs

■ **FIGURE 15.2** The acceptance–responsiveness and demandingness–control dimensions of parenting. Which combination best describes your parents' approach? Source: From E. E. Maccoby & J. A. Martin, Socialization in the context of the family: Parent–child interaction. In E. M. Hetherington (Ed.), P. H. Mussen (Ed. in Chief), *Handbook of child psychology: Vol.4, Socialization, personality, and social development* (4th ed.). Copyright © 1983 by Wiley. Reprinted with permission.

relatively few demands, encourage children to express their feelings and impulses, and rarely exert control over their behavior.

4. **Neglectful parenting.** Finally, parents who combine low demandingness–control and low acceptance–responsiveness are relatively uninvolved in their children's upbringing. They seem not to care much about their children and may even reject them—or else they are so overwhelmed by their own problems that they cannot devote sufficient energy to expressing love and setting and enforcing rules (Maccoby & Martin, 1983).

We assume that you have no difficulty deciding that parental acceptance and responsiveness are preferable to parental rejection and insensitivity (Holden, 2010). As you have seen in this book, warm, responsive parenting is associated with secure attachments to parents, academic competence, high self-esteem, good social skills, peer acceptance, a strong sense of morality, and many other virtues. By contrast, lack of parental acceptance and affection contributes to depression and other psychological problems (Ge et al., 1996).

The degree of demandingness and control shown by parents is also important. The authoritarian, authoritative, and permissive parenting styles were originally identified and defined by Diana Baumrind (1967, 1977, 1991). In a pioneering longitudinal study, Baumrind found that children raised by authoritative parents were the best adjusted: They were cheerful, socially responsible, self-reliant, achievement oriented, and cooperative with adults and peers. Children of authoritarian parents tended to be moody and seemingly unhappy, easily annoyed, relatively aimless, and unpleasant to be around. Children of permissive parents were often impulsive, aggressive, self-centered, rebellious, aimless, and low in independence and achievement. Note, however, that a warm, permissive style can be effective with older children and adolescents who have learned self-control.

Subsequent research has shown that the worst developmental outcomes are associated with the neglectful, uninvolved style of parenting. Children of neglectful parents display behavioral problems such as aggression and frequent temper tantrums as early as age 3 (Miller et al., 1993). They tend to become hostile and antisocial adolescents who abuse alcohol and drugs and get in trouble (Lamborn et al., 1991; Weiss & Schwarz, 1996). Parents who provide little guidance and communicate that they do not care breed children who are resentful and prone to strike back at their uncaring parents and other authority figures.

In short, children develop best when they have love and limits. If they are indulged or neglected and given little guidance, they will not learn self-control and may become selfish and lacking in direction. If they receive lots of guidance but little sensitivity to their needs and perspectives, as the children of authoritarian parents do, they will have few opportunities to learn self-reliance and may lack confidence in their own decision-making abilities. The link between authoritative parenting and positive developmental outcomes is evident in most ethnic groups and socioeconomic groups studied to date in the United States (Glasgow et al., 1997; Steinberg, 2001) and in a variety of other cultures (Scott, Scott, & McCabe, 1991; Vazsonyi, Hibbert, & Snider, 2003). Remembering one's parents as authoritative is associated with good adjustment even among middle-aged and elderly adults (Rothrauff, Cooney, & An, 2009). Still, the effectiveness of different parenting approaches can differ depending on the cultural or subcultural context in which they are used, as illustrated in Exploration Box 15.1.

Social Class, Economic Hardship, and Parenting

Middle-class and lower-class parents as groups have been found to pursue different socialization goals, emphasize different values, and rely on different parenting styles in raising children—

with some important implications. Compared with middle-class and upper-class parents, lower-class and working-class parents tend to stress obedience and respect for authority more. They are often more restrictive and authoritarian, reason with their children less frequently, and show less warmth and affection (Conger & Dogan, 2007; McLoyd, 1990). Although you will find a range of parenting styles in any social group, these average social-class differences in parenting help explain social-class differences in developmental outcomes such as school achievement, adjustment, and life success (Conger & Dogan, 2007).

Why might these socioeconomic differences in parenting styles and child outcomes exist? Let's consider socioeconomic status (SES) differences in financial stresses, resources invested in children, and socialization goals. One accepted explanation centers on the negative effects of financial stresses on parents (Conger & Dogan, 2007; McLoyd, 1990). Rand Conger and his associates (1992, 1995, 2002), for example, have shown that parents experiencing financial problems (economic pressure) tend to become depressed, which increases conflict between them. Marital conflict, in turn, disrupts each partner's ability to be a supportive, involved, and effective parent—another example of indirect effects within the family. This breakdown in parenting then contributes to negative child outcomes such as low self-esteem, poor school performance, poor peer relations, and adjustment problems such as depression and aggression, as summarized in ■ Figure 15.3. This basic model is useful in explaining the effects of other stressors on parents and in turn children—for example, the effects of living in a dangerous neighborhood or being an immigrant parent who does not speak English or understand the culture well (White et al., 2009).

Stresses are magnified for families living below the poverty line or moving in and out of poverty as a result of economic crises. Parents living in poverty tend to be restrictive, punitive, and inconsistent, sometimes to the point of being abusive and neglectful (Brooks-Gunn, Britto, & Brady, 1999; Seccombe, 2000). In high-crime poverty areas, parents may also feel the need to be more authoritarian and controlling to protect their children from danger (Laird et al., 2009; Taylor et al., 2000). In addition, both parenting and child development may suffer due to the stresses of coping with a physical environment characterized by pollution, noise,

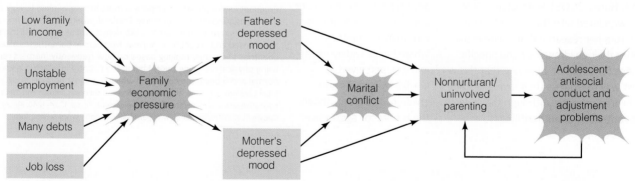

■ **FIGURE 15.3** A model of the relationship among family economic stress, patterns of parenting, and adolescent adjustment. Source: Adapted from Conger, R. D., Conger, K. J., Elder, G. H., Jr., Lorenz, F. O., Simons, R. L., & Whitbeck, L. B. (1992). A family process model of economic hardship and adjustment of early adolescent boys. *Child Development, 63*, 526–541.

Parenting in Cultural and Subcultural Context

Although much research tells us that an authoritative style of parenting is effective in a variety of cultural contexts, it remains important to interpret parenting in its cultural and subcultural context. Parents of different cultures and ethnic backgrounds are socialized to hold different beliefs about children and child rearing that shape their parenting practices and, in turn, their children's development (Holden, 2010; McLoyd et al., 2000; Parke & Buriel, 2006; Rothbaum & Trommsdorff, 2007). For example, American parents (influenced by the individualistic culture in which they live) emphasize the development of autonomy in children and, accordingly, encourage even babies to make their own choices, whereas Japanese parents (influenced by their collectivist culture) most want their children to have a sense of mutual dependence with others and emphasize closeness in the parent–child relationship and sensitivity to other people (Bornstein, 2009).

Parents in different cultures also differ in beliefs regarding how permissive or restrictive they should be (Holden, 2010). For example, some traditional Native American groups such as the Mayan and Navajo Indians believe strongly that the autonomy of young children must be respected and feel it is wrong to force children to do things (Rogoff, 2003). Their children seem to do fine with this relatively permissive parenting style. Meanwhile, Asian parents often rely on a more authoritarian approach to parenting than the authoritative approach favored in most research but get good results with it (Parke & Buriel, 2006). Ruth Chao (1994, 2000) wondered why this was. She concluded from her research that Chinese parents offer their children clear and specific guidelines for behavior, believing that this is the best way to express their love and train their children properly. Although the style seems controlling or authoritarian to

European American eyes, Chinese parents and children view it as warm, caring parenting and children respond well to it as a result (see also Grolnick & Pomerantz, 2009; Rothbaum & Trommsdorff, 2007).

Similarly, the use of physical, coercive discipline (short of abuse) is not as strongly linked to aggression and antisocial behavior among African American youths as it is among European Americans. Why? Probably because authoritarian parenting is common among African American parents and coercive discipline is viewed by African American children as a sign that their parents care rather than as a sign of hostility and rejection (Deater-Deckard et al., 1996; Deater-Deckard, Dodge, & Sorbring, 2005).

Is the acceptability of a parenting approach in a particular cultural context the key to its effects then? Jennifer Lansford and her colleagues (2005) interviewed mothers and children and adolescents in six countries to study the relationship between physical discipline and child outcomes as a function of how common the use of physical punishment was in the country (see also Gershoff et al., 2010). Receiving lots of physical punishment (spanking or slapping, grabbing or shaking, and beating up) was more closely associated with child behavior problems (aggression and anxiety) in countries where physical punishment was rare than in countries where it was widely used and was perceived as normal by parents and children. The graph shows the results for aggressive

behavior. When children view spanking as something that most parents do, it may not be as emotionally upsetting to them as being singled out for a practice that other children in their social world do not experience.

Note that frequent use of physical discipline was correlated to some extent with child aggression and anxiety in all the countries studied. As a result, we continue to recommend against heavy reliance on physical discipline. Similarly, the evidence makes us continue to recommend authoritative over authoritarian, highly controlling parenting in most settings (Pomerantz & Wang, 2009). Still, it is critical to appreciate that parenting practices can be more or less effective depending on how they are interpreted by those who use and experience them in a particular cultural context.

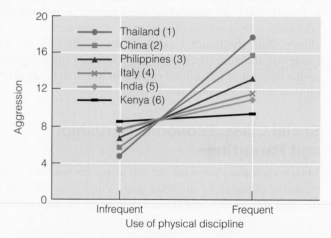

Frequent use of physical discipline is more strongly linked to high levels of child aggression in cultures like Thailand, where the use of physical discipline is rare, than in cultures like Kenya, where physical discipline is widely used and accepted as normal. Numbers in parentheses after the countries show their ranking based on how frequently mothers report using physical discipline (with 1 being the country in which it is least normal and 6 being the country in which it is most normal). Source: From Lansford, J. E., et al. Physical discipline and children's adjustment: Cultural normativeness as a moderator, *Child Development, 76*, pp. 1234–1246, Figure 6. Copyright © 2005. Reprinted with permission of John Wiley & Sons, Inc.

and crowded, unsafe living conditions and a social environment characterized by family instability and violence (Evans, 2004). The effects of poverty on child development include health problems, emotional and behavioral problems, and school failure (Bradley & Corwyn, 2002; Evans, 2004).

In addition to financial stress, a second explanation of social-class differences in parenting and child outcomes is that low-SES parents have fewer resources to invest in their children's development than high-SES parents do (Conger & Dogan, 2007). Wealthier parents can invest more money and time in getting their children a good education; providing books, computers, and other learning materials in the home; taking their children to cultural events; and otherwise stimulating their children's minds (Conger & Dogan, 2007).

Third and finally, high- and low-SES parents have different socialization goals in preparing their children for the world of work because they have had different work experiences (Conger & Dogan, 2007). As sociologist Melvin Kohn (1969) observed some time ago, parents from lower socioeconomic groups tend to be authoritarian and emphasize obedience to authority figures because that is what is required in jobs like their own. Middle-class and upper-class parents may reason with their children and foster initiative and creativity more because these are the attributes that count for business executives, professionals, and other white-collar workers.

So to summarize, low family socioeconomic status may be associated with poor developmental outcomes because of (1) economic stresses that result in authoritarian, non-nurturant, and inconsistent parenting; (2) limited investment of resources, financial and otherwise, in children's development; and (3) an orientation toward preparing children to obey a boss rather than be the boss.

Models of Influence in the Family

In thinking about influences within the family, we will bet that you, like most developmental scientists, think first about parents affecting children. But consider three different models of influence in the family: the parent effects, child effects, and transactional models.

Parent Effects Model

The study of human development has been guided through most of its history by a simple **parent effects model** of family influence (Holden, 2010; Maccoby, 2007). This model assumes that influences run one way, from parent (particularly mother) to child. You have just reviewed research demonstrating effects of parenting styles on child development. But what if you turn things around: Could it be that a child's behavior influences the style of parenting his parents adopt and that what appear to be parent effects are instead child effects?

Child Effects Model

A **child effects model** of family influence highlights the influences of children on their parents (Crouter & Booth, 2003; Sanson, Hemphill, & Smart, 2004). One good example of a child effect is the influence of a child's age and competence on the style of parenting used with that child. For example, infants in their first year of life require and elicit sensitive care, whereas older infants who are asserting their wills and toddling here and there force parents to provide more instruction and set more limits (Fagot & Kavanaugh, 1993). Normally parents then become less restrictive as their children mature and gradually, with parental guidance, become capable of making their own decisions. As children develop, then, parenting shifts from parent regulation of the child, to parent and child co-regulation of the child, to self-regulation by a now more capable child (Holden, 2010).

Now consider the possibility that a child's personality influences the parenting she receives. Is it not possible that easygoing, manageable children cause their parents to be warm and authoritative? Could not difficult, stubborn, and aggressive children help mold parents who are rejecting rather than accepting—and who either rule with an authoritarian iron hand or throw up their hands in defeat and become neglectful?

Recall the description in Chapter 13 of the discipline techniques of induction, power assertion, and love withdrawal. In a clever and convincing demonstration of child effects, Barbara Keller and Richard Bell (1979) had female college students attempt to convince 9-year-old girls to behave altruistically (for example, to spend more time sewing a pillow for a handicapped child than sewing a pillow for themselves). The girls had been coached to respond either attentively or inattentively. As expected, college students confronted with an attentive child used a great deal of induction, explaining how other children might feel if the child behaved selfishly. By contrast, college students who interacted with an inattentive child relied on power-assertion techniques such as promising rewards for altruism and threatening penalties for selfishness.

A study of budding juvenile delinquents from age 14 to age 16 revealed similar child effects on parents (Kerr & Stattin, 2003). In response to their delinquent child's difficult behavior at age 14, parents became less warm and emotionally supportive and less in control of their adolescents by the time the adolescents were 16. In contrast, this study yielded little evidence that the parenting these young delinquents received when they were 14 affected their behavior at age 16.

Transactional Model

As the research reviewed in Chapter 13 indicated, antisocial behavior most likely results when a child who is genetically predisposed to be aggressive behaves in ways that elicit negative, coercive parenting and when that parenting causes the child to become even more aggressive (Ge et al., 1996; O'Connor et al., 1998). When such a destructive family process develops, it becomes impossible to say who is more influential, parent or child. This scenario is best described by a **transactional model** of family influence, in which parent and child are seen as influencing one another reciprocally, as exemplified in Bronfenbrenner's bioecological model (Sameroff, 1975, 2009; and see ■ **Figure 15.4**). In the transactional model, child problems develop when *the relationship* between parent and child goes bad as the two

Parent effects model	$P \rightarrow C$
Child effects model	$C \rightarrow P$
Transactional model	$P \rightarrow C$ and $C \rightarrow P$

■ **FIGURE 15.4** Models of family influence.

interact over time. Optimal child development results when parent–child transactions evolve in more positive directions.

Demonstrations of child effects and transactional effects within the family are tremendously important. They mean that parents are not solely responsible for whether their children turn out "good" or "bad," even though they probably have somewhat more influence overall than children do on how the parent–child relationship unfolds (Holden, 2010; Kuczynski & Parkin, 2007). We must remind ourselves repeatedly that the family is a system in which family members lead linked lives and are influenced in reciprocal ways by both their genetic predispositions and the environments they create for one another.

Sibling Relationships

A family system consisting of mother, father, and child is changed by the arrival of a new baby and becomes a new—and considerably more complex—family system. How do children adapt to a new baby in the house, how does the sibling relationship change as children age, and what do brothers and sisters contribute to each other's development in the final analysis?

A New Baby Arrives

When Judy Dunn and Carol Kendrick (1982; see also Dunn, 1993, 2007) carefully studied young children's reactions to a new sibling, they found that mothers typically pay less attention to their firstborns after the new baby arrives than before. Partly for this reason, firstborns often find being "dethroned" a stressful experience. They become more difficult and demanding, or more dependent and clingy, and they often develop problems with their sleeping, eating, and toileting routines. Most of their battles are with their mothers, but a few firstborns are not above hitting, poking, and pinching their younger brothers or sisters. Secure attachments can become insecure, especially if firstborns are 2 years old or older and can fully appreciate how much they have lost (Teti et al., 1996). Although positive effects such as an increased insistence on doing things independently are also common, it is clear that many firstborns are not thrilled to have an attention-grabbing new baby in the house. They resent losing their parents' attention, and their own difficult behavior may alienate their parents further.

How can problems be minimized? Adjustment to a new sibling is easier if the marital relationship is good and if the first-born had secure relationships with both parents before the younger sibling arrived—and continues to enjoy close relationships with them afterward (Dunn, 2007; Teti et al., 1996). If parents continue providing love and attention to their firstborn and maintain the child's routines as much as possible, things are likely to go well. Increased involvement in parenting by the father helps (Volling, 2005). Parents can also encourage older children to become aware of the new baby's needs and feelings and to assist in her care (Dunn & Kendrick, 1982; Howe & Ross, 1990).

Ambivalence in Sibling Relationships

Fortunately, most older siblings adjust fairly quickly to having a new brother or sister. Yet even in the best of sibling relationships, **sibling rivalry**—the spirit of competition, jealousy, and resentment between brothers and sisters—is normal. It may be rooted in an evolutionary fact: Although siblings share half their genes

Sibling relationships are both close and rivalrous.

on average and are therefore more motivated to help one another than to help genetically unrelated individuals, siblings also compete with one another for their parents' time and resources to ensure their own survival and welfare (Bjorklund & Pellegrini, 2002). Siblings may also be at odds because they live in close proximity but lack mature social skills and because they feel they are treated differently by their parents (Holden, 2010). For all these reasons, perhaps, sibling relationships typically involve both closeness and conflict.

The number of skirmishes between very young siblings can be as high as 56 per hour (Dunn, 1993). Jealousies, bouts of teasing, shouting matches, and occasional kicks and punches continue to be part of the sibling relationship throughout childhood; squabbles are most often about possessions (McGuire et al., 2000). Each combatant, of course, feels that he is blameless and has been terribly wronged (Wilson et al., 2004). Thankfully, levels of conflict normally decrease after early adolescence as teenagers spend more time away from the family (Furman & Buhrmester, 1992; Larson et al., 1996).

Sibling relationships are friendlier and less conflicted if mothers and fathers get along well as a couple and if they respond warmly and sensitively to all their children rather than unfairly favoring one over another (Dunn, 2007). Children are able to accept that differences in treatment can be fair, and therefore not objectionable, if they are based on differences in the ages, competencies, and personalities of the siblings, but they resent seemingly unfair differences in treatment (Kowal et al., 2002).

Sibling Influences on Development

Despite sibling rivalry, the sibling relationship is generally close, interactions with siblings are mostly positive, and siblings play mostly positive roles in one another's development. One of the important positive functions of siblings is to provide *emotional support*. Brothers and sisters confide in one another, often more than they confide in their parents (Howe et al., 2000). They protect and comfort one another in rough times. Even preschoolers jump in to comfort their infant siblings when their mothers leave them or when strangers approach (Stewart & Marvin, 1984).

Second, older siblings often provide caregiving services for younger siblings; they babysit and tend young children. Indeed, in a study of 186 societies, older children were the principal caregivers for infants and toddlers in 57% of the cultures studied (Weisner & Gallimore, 1977). In many societies, children as young as 5 years are involved in meaningful ways in the care of infants and toddlers (Rogoff, 2003).

Older siblings also serve as teachers. Although older brothers and sisters are not always as skilled at teaching as parents are (Perez-Granados & Callanan, 1997), they clearly feel a special responsibility to teach, and younger siblings actively seek their guidance on any number of things.

Finally, siblings provide social experience. Although having a large number of siblings has negative implications for cognitive development, most likely because each child then receives less intellectual stimulation from adults, having at least one sibling to

In many societies, older siblings are major caregivers for young children.

interact with has positive effects on a child's social cognitive development and social skills (Dunn, 2007; McHale, Kim, & Whiteman, 2006; and see Chapter 13). In their interactions with siblings, especially all those skirmishes, children learn how to take others' perspectives, read others' minds, express their feelings, negotiate, and resolve conflicts.

So siblings provide emotional support, caregiving, teaching, and social experience. Interestingly, siblings can affect each other not only directly but also through the indirect effects they have on their parents. In an excellent illustration of the family as a system, Gene Brody (2003, 2004) discovered that if an older sibling is competent, this contributes positively to his mother's psychological functioning (possibly because she feels good about herself as a parent), which makes her more likely to provide supportive parenting to a younger sibling, which in turn increases the odds that the younger sibling will also be competent. By contrast, an incompetent older sibling can set in motion a negative chain of events involving less supportive parenting and less positive outcomes for the younger sibling.

Checking Mastery

1. Where does authoritative parenting fit on the dimensions of parental acceptance–responsiveness and demandingness–control?

2. What are two reasons that low-SES parents might use a more authoritarian and less warm and nurturing parenting style than high-SES parents do?

3. What is the main difference between the parent effects model and the transactional model of family influence?

4. How would you characterize the typical sibling relationship?

Making Connections

1. Alison, a 16-year-old teenager who was drunk at the time, plowed the family car into a Dairy Queen and is being held at the police station for driving under the influence. Her father must pick her up. What would you expect an authoritarian, authoritative, permissive, and neglectful father to say and do in this situation? What implications might these contrasting approaches to parenting have for this young woman's development?

2. How would you characterize the dominant parenting style of your parents, and to what extent do you think the research on the effects of that parenting style on development fits you?

3. If the child effects model of family influence were at work, what behavior by children do you think would be most likely to push parents to use each of the main parenting styles: authoritarian, authoritative, permissive, and neglectful?

15.4 The Adolescent

When you picture the typical relationship between a teenager and her parents, do you envision a teenager who is out all the time with friends, resents every rule and restriction, and talks back at every opportunity? Do you imagine parents wringing their hands in despair and wondering if they will survive their children's adolescent years? Many people believe that the period of the family life cycle during which parents have adolescents in the house is a particularly stressful time, with close parent–child relationships deteriorating into bitter tugs-of-war. How much truth is there to these characterizations?

Ripples in the Parent–Child Relationship

Although many people believe that the parent–child relationship deteriorates during adolescence, their beliefs are largely unfounded. Most parent–adolescent relationships are close, and most retain whatever quality they had in childhood (Collins & Laursen, 2006). It is rare for a parent–child relationship to suddenly turn bad at adolescence; more likely, a troubled parent–adolescent relationship has grown out of a troubled parent–child relationship and has been shaped by both the parent's parenting and the child's personality (Eisenberg et al., 2008).

Yet the parent–child relationship does change during adolescence. Time spent together decreases as adolescents become

Parent–child conflict escalates in early adolescence, but it is generally about minor issues.

more involved with peers, and this can make adolescents feel less involved with and supported by their parents (Collins & Laursen, 2006; De Goede, Branje, & Meeus, 2009). A modest increase in parent–child conflict is also common in early adolescence, around the onset of puberty (McGue et al., 2005; Shanahan et al., 2004). Young adolescents assert themselves, and they and their parents squabble more. The bickering is mainly about relatively minor matters such as disobedience, homework, household chores, and access to privileges, and the frequency of conflicts decreases from early to late adolescence (Collins & Laursen, 2006). These skirmishes in early adolescence alter the parent–child relationship, not so much its closeness as the balance of power between parents and adolescents, as we will now see.

Achieving Autonomy

A key developmental task of adolescence is achieving **autonomy**, or the capacity to make decisions independently and manage life tasks without being overly dependent on other people. If adolescents are to "make it" as adults, they cannot be rushing home for reassuring hugs after every little setback or depending on parents to get them to work on time or manage their checkbooks. Achieving autonomy is part of the larger task highlighted by Erik Erikson of establishing an identity separate from one's parents, and it prepares adolescents to leave the nest and fly on their own.

As children reach puberty and become more physically and cognitively mature and more capable of acting autonomously, they assert themselves more. As they do so, their parents give up some of their power, adolescents assume more control of their lives, and the parent–child relationship becomes more equal (De Goede, Branje, & Meeus, 2009; Steinberg, 2008). It is usually best for their development if adolescents maintain close attachments with their parents even as they are gaining autonomy (Allen, 2008; Lamborn & Steinberg, 1993). Gaining some separation from parents is healthy; becoming detached from them is not (Beyers et al., 2003). A blend of autonomy and attachment, or independence and interdependence, is most desirable.

How much autonomy adolescents want and parents grant differs from culture to culture. Studying different ethnic groups in the United States, Andrew Fuligni (1998) found that Filipino and Mexican American adolescents are more likely than European American adolescents to believe that they should not disagree with their parents, and Chinese Americans are less likely to expect the freedom to go to parties and to date at a young age. Adolescents in Japan are even more strongly socialized to expect limited autonomy. They remain closer to their mothers and fathers than American adolescents through the adolescent years, do not feel as much need to distance themselves from their parents, and spend less time with peers (Rothbaum et al., 2000). In collectivist Asian cultures, then, parents continue to impose many rules and the balance of power does not change as much, or at least as early, during adolescence as it does in the United States.

What can parents do to foster autonomy? Across cultures, adolescents are most likely to become autonomous, achievement oriented, and well adjusted if their parents consistently enforce a reasonable set of rules, involve their teenagers in decision making, recognize their need for greater autonomy, monitor their comings and goings, gradually loosen the reins, and continue to be warm, supportive, and involved throughout adolescence (Holden, 2010; Lamborn et al., 1991). In short, the winning approach is usually an authoritative style of parenting, although in some cultures and subcultures a more authoritarian style or a more permissive style can also achieve good outcomes (Garcia & Gracia, 2009; Steinberg et al., 1992).

Although you should remind yourself that children also affect their parents, an authoritative parenting style gives adolescents opportunities to strengthen their independent decision-making skills while retaining the benefit of their parents' guidance and advice. When parents are extremely strict and stifle autonomy, or when they are extremely lax and fail to guide and monitor their adolescents, teenagers are likely to become psychologically distressed, socialize with the wrong crowds, and get into trouble (Goldstein, Davis-Kean, & Eccles, 2005; Knoester, Haynie, & Stephens, 2006; Lamborn et al., 1991).

Checking Mastery

1. What do the parent–adolescent conflicts of early adolescence generally concern?
2. What parenting style is most likely to foster autonomy, and why?

Making Connections

1. At age 13, Miki moved from Japan to the United States with her family and now finds her relationship with her parents strained. Drawing on the material in this section, how would you analyze what is going on?
2. Brian, age 16, is very upset when he learns that his parents, who heard that some students at Brian's high school were becoming involved with hard drugs, have been checking his cell phone to find out whether he might be one of them. How does Brian see this situation? How do his parents see it? What do you recommend the parents do now?

15.5 The Adult

So far we have offered a child's-eye view of family life. How do adults experience the family life cycle? We will look at the establishment of a marriage, new parenthood, child rearing, empty nest, and grandparenthood phases of family life.

Establishing a Marriage

In U.S. society, almost 90% of adults choose to marry at some point in their lives (Cherlin, 2009). As we saw in Chapter 14, most choose partners who are similar to themselves and whom they love. Although love and marriage go together in most modern societies today, in many traditional societies marriages are not formed on the basis of love. They are arranged by leaders of kin groups who are concerned with acquiring property, allies, and the rights to any children the marriage produces (Ingoldsby & Smith, 1995; Regan, 2008). So in reading what follows, remember that the modern, Western way of establishing families is not the only way.

Marriage is a significant life transition for most adults: it involves taking on a new role (as husband or wife) and adjusting to life as a couple. We rejoice at weddings and view newlyweds as supremely happy beings. Indeed, they feel on top of the world, their self-esteem rises, and some develop a more secure orientation toward attachment relationships as a result of marrying (Crowell, Treboux, & Waters, 2002; Giarrusso et al., 2000). Yet individuals who have just been struggling to achieve autonomy and assume adult roles soon find that they must compromise with their partners and adapt to each other's personalities and preferences.

The honeymoon is great, but it often ends quickly.

Ted Huston and his colleagues have found that the honeymoon is short (Huston et al., 2001; Huston, McHale, & Crouter, 1986; Huston & Melz, 2004; also see Kurdek, 1999). In a longitudinal study of newlywed couples, these researchers discovered that perceptions of the marital relationship became less favorable and marital satisfaction declined during the first year after the wedding. Behavior changed as well: "One year into marriage, the average spouse says, 'I love you,' hugs and kisses their partner, makes their partner laugh, and has sexual intercourse about half as often as when they were newly wed" (Huston & Melz, 2004, p. 951). Although partners spend only slightly less time together, more of that time is devoted to getting tasks done and less to having fun or just talking.

Although most couples are far more satisfied than dissatisfied with their relationships after the "honeymoon" is over, adapting to marriage clearly involves strains. Blissfully happy relationships evolve into still happy but less idealized ones (Huston et al., 2001). Whether this happens because couples begin to see "warts" that they did not notice before marriage, stop trying to be on their best behavior, have run-ins as an inevitable part of living together, or start to take each other for granted, it is normal.

Does the quality of a couple's relationship early in their marriage have any implications for their later marital adjustment? It does. Huston and his colleagues (2001) assessed couples 2 months, 1 year, and 2 years into their marriages and again 13–14 years after the wedding. It is commonly believed that marriages crumble when negative feelings build up and conflicts escalate, but Huston's findings provide little support for this escalating conflict view. Compared with couples who were happily married after 13 years, couples who remained married but were unhappy had had relatively poor relationships all along. Even as newlyweds, and probably even before they married, these couples were less blissfully in love and more negative toward each other than were couples who stayed married and remained happy in their marriages. It is not the case that all marriages start out blissfully happy and then some turn sour; some start out sour and stay sour! Even couples who divorced did not usually experience escalating conflict over time; rather, they lost their positive feelings for each other.

So the establishment phase of the family life cycle involves some loss of enthusiasm for most couples. Some couples are already on a path to long-term marital satisfaction, whereas others are headed for divorce or for staying in a marriage that will continue to be less than optimal. Couples seem best off when they can maintain a high level of positive and supportive interactions to help them weather the conflicts that inevitably arise in any relationship (Fincham, 2003). Participating in a premarital education program can help (Stanley et al., 2006).

New Parenthood

How does the arrival of a new baby affect a wife, a husband, and their marital relationship? Some people believe that having children draws a couple closer together; others believe that children strain a relationship. Which is it?

On average, new parenthood is best described as a stressful life transition that involves both positive and negative changes (Cowan & Cowan, 2000; Nomaguchi & Milkie, 2003). On the positive side, parents claim that having a child brings them joy and fulfillment and contributes to their own growth as individuals (Emery & Tuer, 1993; Palkovitz, 2002). Barack Obama certainly felt that new parenthood was life changing: "And that night, knowing that there was this new life inside your house, in the little bassinet…and then feeling them lying on your chest after you've fed them and they are falling asleep….And you realize at that moment you will do anything for that child" (Milloy, 2009, p. B1).

But couples have added new roles (as mothers and fathers) to their existing roles (as spouses, workers, and so on), and new parents often find juggling work and family responsibilities challenging (as Michelle Obama did). They not only have a lot of new work to do as caregivers, but they also lose sleep, worry about their baby, find that they have less time to themselves, and sometimes face financial difficulties.

In addition, even egalitarian couples who previously shared household tasks often adopt more traditional gender-role attitudes and divide their labors along more traditional lines (as the Obamas did). She specializes in the "feminine" role by becoming the primary caregiver and housekeeper, often reducing her involvement in work outside the home and increasing her hours of labor inside the home, while he emphasizes his "masculine" role as provider and works harder in his job (Cowan & Cowan, 2000; Katz-Wise, Priess, & Hyde, 2010; Noller, 2006). This pattern is slowly changing in some countries, though; a study in Sweden showed that whereas new parenthood pulled parents toward a more traditional division of labor in 1990–1991, by 2000–2001 it affected the activity patterns of women and men more similarly (Dribe & Stanfors, 2009).

What are the effects of increased stress and of sharper gender-role differentiation? Marital satisfaction typically declines somewhat in the first year after a baby is born (Doss et al., 2009; Gottman & Notarius, 2000; Mitnick, Heyman, & Smith Slep, 2009). This decline is often steeper for women than for men, primarily because child care responsibilities typically fall more heavily on mothers and they may resent what they regard as an unfair division of labor (Levy-Shiff, 1994; Noller, 2006).

However, individuals vary widely in their adjustment to new parenthood. Some new parents experience the transition as a bowl of cherries, others as the pits—as a full-blown crisis in their lives. What might make this life event easier or harder to manage? Characteristics of the baby, the parent, and the social support the parent has available all count.

A baby who is difficult (for example, cries endlessly) creates more stresses and anxieties for parents than an infant who is quiet, sociable, responsive, and otherwise easy to love (Levy-Shiff, 1994; Meredith & Noller, 2003). An adopted baby can pose special challenges: parents who do not have a 9-month pregnancy during which to prepare are suddenly thrust into parenthood, often with only a few days notice that their baby is on her way (Weir, 2003).

Parent characteristics matter too. Parents who have good problem-solving and communication skills and find adaptive ways

New parenthood brings joy, but it is also a stressful transition involving new challenges.

to restructure and organize their lives to accommodate a new baby adjust well (Cox et al., 1999; Levy-Shiff, 1994). Similarly, parents who have realistic expectations about how parenthood will change their lives and about infants and children tend to adjust more easily than those who have an unrealistically rosy view (Kalmuss, Davidson, & Cushman, 1992; Mylod, Whitman, & Borkowski, 1997). Mentally healthy parents also fare better than parents who are experiencing mental health problems such as depression going into new parenthood (Cox et al., 1999).

Parents' attachment styles are also important. New parents who remember their own parents as warm and accepting are likely to experience a smoother transition to new parenthood than couples who recall their parents as cold or rejecting (Florsheim et al., 2003; van IJzendoorn, 1992). Mothers who have a preoccupied (resistant) style of romantic attachment—individuals who express a lot of anxiety about relationships—tend to have more difficulty than most mothers. They are at risk of becoming increasingly depressed after the birth and of becoming less satisfied with their marriages if they perceive that their husbands give them little support and are angry (Rholes et al., 2001; Simpson et al., 2003).

Finally, social support can make a great deal of difference to the new parent. Most important is partner support: as suggested already, things go considerably better for a new mother when she has a good relationship with the father, and when he shares the burden of child care and housework, than when she has no partner or an unsupportive one (Demo & Cox, 2000; Levy-Shiff, 1994). Social support from friends and relatives can also help new parents cope (Stemp, Turner, & Noh, 1986), as can interventions designed to help expecting mothers and fathers prepare

realistically for the challenges ahead and support each other as they deal with these challenges (Doherty, Erickson, & LaRossa, 2006; Schulz, Cowan, & Cowan, 2006).

In sum, parents who have an easy baby to contend with; who possess positive personal qualities and coping skills, including a secure attachment style; and who receive reliable support from their partners and other people are in the best position to cope adaptively with new parenthood, a transition normally both satisfying and stressful that can undermine marital satisfaction.

The Child-Rearing Family

The child-rearing family is the family with children in it. What can parents look forward to as they have additional children and as their children age? A heavier workload! The stresses and strains of caring for a toddler are greater than those of caring for an infant, and the arrival of a second child means additional stress (O'Brien, 1996). Parents must not only devote time to the new baby but also deal with their firstborn child's normal anxieties about this intruder. Mothers complain of the hassles of cleaning up food and toys, constantly keeping an eye on their children, and dealing with their perfectly normal but irritating demands for attention, failures to comply with requests, and bouts of whining (O'Brien, 1996). Because the workload increases, fathers often become more involved in child care after a second child is born (Dunn, 2007). However, the mother who is raising multiple children as a single parent or the mother whose partner is not very involved may find herself without a moment's rest as she tries to keep up with two or more active, curious, mobile, and dependent youngsters.

Additional challenges sometimes arise for parents when their children enter adolescence. As you saw earlier, parent–child conflicts become more frequent for a while as children enter adolescence. Moreover, parents' conflicts with each other over how to raise their adolescent children can stress their mar-

"Mrs. Millis, they can't ALL look like poopy diapers!"

riage and undermine their marital satisfaction (Cui & Donnellan, 2009). When the firstborn child in the family reaches puberty, marital love and satisfaction often decline (Whiteman, McHale, & Crouter, 2007).

In addition, there is intriguing evidence that living with adolescents who are becoming physically and sexually mature and beginning to date may cause parents to engage in more than the usual amount of midlife questioning about what they have done with their lives and what they can expect next (Silverberg & Steinberg, 1990). Middle-aged parents are also affected by how well adjusted their children are and have difficulty maintaining a sense of well-being if their children are experiencing trouble launching themselves successfully into adulthood (Greenfield & Marks, 2006). Here, then, may be another example of child effects within the family system. But it works the other way, too: when parents are unhappy or are experiencing marital problems, the parent–child relationship and parenting can deteriorate and teens can be at greater risk for problems such as delinquency, alcohol and drug use, anxiety, depression, and emotional distress (Chung, Flook, & Fuligni, 2009; Cui, Conger, & Lorenz, 2005).

Children clearly complicate their parents' lives by demanding everything from fresh diapers and close monitoring to college tuition. By claiming time and energy that might otherwise go into nourishing the marital relationship and by adding stresses to their parents' lives, children seem to have a negative—although typically only slightly negative—effect on marital satisfaction through the child-rearing years (Gorchoff, John, & Helson, 2008; Kurdek, 1999; Rollins & Feldman, 1970). Yet when parents are interviewed about the costs and benefits of parenthood, they generally emphasize the positives and feel that parenthood has contributed a great deal to their personal development, making them more responsible and caring people (Palkovitz, 2002).

The Empty Nest

As children reach maturity, the family becomes a "launching pad" that fires adolescents and young adults into the world to work and start their own families. The term **empty nest** describes the family after the departure of the last child—a phase of the family life cycle that became common only starting in the 20th century as people began to live longer but have fewer children (Fox, 2001). Clearly, the emptying of the nest involves changes in roles and lifestyle for parents, particularly for mothers who have centered their lives on child rearing. There can be moments of deep sadness (Span, 2000, p. 15):

> Pamela automatically started to toss Doritos and yucky dip into her cart—and then remembered. "I almost burst into tears," she recalls. "I wanted to stop some complete stranger and say, 'My son's gone away to college.' I had such a sense of loss."

Overall, however, parents react positively to the emptying of the nest. Whereas the entry of children into the family causes modest decreases in marital satisfaction, the departure of the last child seems to be associated with increases in marital satisfaction (Gorchoff, John, & Helson, 2008; White & Edwards, 1990). After the nest empties, women often feel that their marriages are more equitable and that their spouses are more accommodating

to their needs (Mackey & O'Brien, 1995; Suitor, 1991). Only a minority of parents find this transition disturbing.

Why are parents generally not upset by the empty nest? Possibly it is because they have fewer roles and responsibilities and therefore experience less stress and strain. As one mother put it, "Twenty years ago, we were in the battle of the children… today…[we] can enjoy one another for who we are" (Gorchoff, John, & Helson, 2008, p. 1199). Empty nest couples have more time to focus on their marital relationship and more money to spend on themselves. Moreover, parents are likely to view the emptying of the nest as evidence that they have done their job of raising children well and have earned what Erik Erikson called a sense of generativity. One 44-year-old mother put it well: "I have five terrific daughters who didn't just happen. It took lots of time to mold, correct, love, and challenge them. It's nice to see such rewarding results." Finally, most parents continue to enjoy a good deal of contact with their children after the nest empties, so it is not as if they are really losing the parent–child relationship (White & Edwards, 1990).

In recent years, an increasing number of adult children have been remaining in the nest, or leaving and then refilling it in a kind of "boomerang effect." These children are often unemployed, have limited finances, have divorced or separated, or have other difficulties getting their adult lives on track (Ward & Spitze, 1992; White & Rogers, 1997). Compared with emerging adults who leave the nest on time, those who stay put or leave only to return are less likely to have experienced a secure parent–child attachment that allowed them room to develop autonomy (Seiffge-Krenke, 2006). Parents can find having these adult children in the house distressing (Aquilino, 1991; Umberson, 1992). However, most empty nesters adapt, especially if their children are responsible young adults who are attending school or working rather than freeloading and who seem to be making progress toward greater independence (Aquilino, 2006; Ward & Spitze, 2004).

Grandparenthood

Although we tend to picture grandparents as white-haired, jovial elders who knit mittens and bake cookies, most adults become grandparents when they are middle-aged, not elderly, and when they are likely to be highly involved in work and community activities (Conner, 2000). Grandparenting styles are diverse, as illustrated by the results of a national survey of grandparents of teenagers conducted by Andrew Cherlin and Frank Furstenberg (1986). These researchers identified three major styles of grandparenting:

1. *Remote.* Remote grandparents (29% of the sample) were symbolic figures seen only occasionally by their grandchildren. Primarily because they were geographically distant, they were emotionally distant as well.
2. *Companionate.* This was the most common style of grandparenting (55% of the sample). Companionate grandparents saw their grandchildren frequently and enjoyed sharing activities with them. They only rarely played a parental role and liked it that way. As one companionate grandparent put

it, "It's great—I can enjoy them and send them home (Hayslip, 2009, p. 354).

3. *Involved.* Finally, 16% of the grandparents took on a parent-like role. Like companionate grandparents, they saw their grandchildren frequently and were playful with them, but unlike companionate grandparents, they often helped with child care, gave advice, and played other practical roles in their grandchildren's lives. Indeed some involved grandparents lived with and served as substitute parents for their grandchildren because their daughters or sons could not care for the children themselves. More and more grandparents today, especially in African American and Hispanic families, have custody of and are the primary parent figures for their grandchildren (Hayslip, 2009).

You can see, then, that grandparenting takes many forms but that most grandparents see at least some of their grandchildren frequently and prefer a companionate role that is high in enjoyment and affection but low in responsibility. Most grandparents find the role gratifying, especially if they *do* see their grandchildren frequently (Connidis, 2010; Reitzes & Mutran, 2004). Like grandparents, grandchildren report a good deal of closeness in the grandparent–grandchild relationship and only wish they could see their grandparents more (Block, 2000).

Grandparents have been called "the family national guard" because they must be ever ready to come to the rescue when there is a crisis in the family and they never know when they will be called (Hagestad, 1985). Grandmothers often help their daughters adjust to new parenthood and help with child care when their grandchildren are very young or step in to raise grandchildren when an unmarried teenage daughter gives birth or a son or daughter divorces or dies (Dunn, Fergusson, & Maughan, 2006). Yet grandparents may suddenly lose all access to their grandchildren if their child loses custody, causing them much anguish (Ahrons, 2007; Cooney & Smith, 1996).

Grandparents who do get "called to duty" sometimes make a real contribution to their grandchildren's development. A grandmother who mentors a teen mother and coparents with her

can help her gain competence as a parent (Oberlander, Black, & Starr, 2007). A close grandparent–grandchild relationship can protect the child of a depressed mother from becoming depressed (Silverstein & Ruiz, 2006). And although teenagers raised by single mothers tend to have low educational attainment and high rates of problem behavior on average, they resemble children raised by two parents if they are raised by a single mother and at least one grandparent (DeLeire & Kalil, 2002; and see Attar-Schwartz et al., 2009; Ruiz & Silverstein, 2007).

Involved grandparenting can take a toll on grandparents, however: They sometimes suffer from stress, depression, and deteriorating health when grandchildren move in with them and they must become the primary parents (Patrick & Goedereis, 2009; Szinovacz, DeViney, & Atkinson, 1999). In one study of African American grandparents raising grandchildren, 94% reported significant levels of stress (Ross & Aday, 2006). Although grandparents may also benefit from the intellectual challenges and emotional rewards that parenting brings (Ehrle, 2001), their development and well-being can suffer if they become overwhelmed by their responsibilities.

Changing Family Relationships

What becomes of relationships between spouses, siblings, and parents and children during the adult years? All family relationships develop and change with time.

Marital Relationships

As you have seen, marital satisfaction dips somewhat after the honeymoon period is over, dips still lower in the new-parenthood phase, continues to drop as new children are added to the family, and recovers only when the children leave the nest, especially for women. The character of marital relationships also changes over the years. Frequency of sexual intercourse decreases (see Chapter 12), but psychological intimacy often increases. The love relationship often changes from one that is passionate to one that is companionate, more like a best-friends relationship (Bierhoff & Schmohr, 2003). Elderly couples are often even more affectionate than middle-aged couples, have fewer conflicts, and are able to resolve their conflicts without as much venting of negative emotions (Carstensen, Levenson, & Gottman, 1995; Gagnon et al., 1999). Even when they disagree, elderly couples seem less upset than middle-aged couples by the negative behavior of their partners (Smith et al., 2009).

Overall, however, knowing what stage of the family life cycle an adult is in does not tell us much about how satisfied that person is with his marriage. Personality is far more important. Happily married people have more pleasant personalities than unhappily married people; for example, they are more emotionally stable and vent negative feelings less often (Robins, Caspi, & Moffitt, 2000). Moreover, in happy marriages, the personalities of marriage partners are similar and are likely to remain similar or even become more similar over the years, as each partner reinforces in the other the traits that brought them together (Caspi, Herbener, & Ozer, 1992; Gonzaga, Campos, & Bradbury, 2007).

Most grandparents prefer and adopt a companionate style of grandparenting.

© Leland Bobbé/Corbis

In the end, partners affect each other's development. For example, Denis Gerstorf and his colleagues studied older married couples averaging 75 years of age over a 10-year period. If a husband had good memory skills, his wife was less likely to suffer a decline in memory performance over the next 2 years. If a wife was depressed, her husband was likely to experience increased symptoms of depression and decreased memory performance. This and other studies show that we really do lead linked lives—that we influence and are influenced by our partners in close relationships. In addition, the marital relationship is affected by the other relationships partners have. Couples fare best when both partners can count on a good network of relatives and friends to support rather than to interfere with their relationship (Widmer et al., 2009).

The family life cycle ends with widowhood. By the time they reach age 65 or older, about 73% of men are married and live with their wives but only 42% of women are married and live with their husbands (Federal Interagency Forum on Aging Related Statistics, 2008). Marriages face new challenges when one of the partners becomes seriously ill or impaired and needs care. As our upcoming discussion of caregiver burden suggests, wives may suffer poor physical and mental health and feel socially isolated when they must care for a dying husband. However, they generally manage to cope with their spouse's death and rebuild their lives, often feeling afterward that they have grown (Connidis, 2010; Seltzer & Li, 2000; and see Chapter 17).

Without question, the marital relationship is centrally important in the lives and development of most adults. Overall, married adults tend to be "happier, healthier, and better off financially" than other adults and are likely to remain so if they can weather bad times in their marriages (Waite & Gallagher, 2000).

Sibling Relationships

The sibling relationship is typically the longest-lasting relationship we have, linking us to individuals who share many of our genes and experiences (Cicirelli, 1991; Connidis, 2010). It is a relationship that can be close, conflicted, or, for most of us, both. Today, of course, sibling relationships involve not only biological siblings but often half siblings, stepsiblings, and adoptive siblings (Connidis, 2010).

Relationships between siblings often change for the better once they no longer live together in the same home and once their age differences do not matter as much as they did in childhood. Conflict and rivalry diminish and relationships often become warmer and more equal in adulthood (Connidis, 2010; Scharf, Shulman, & Avigad-Spitz, 2005). Siblings often grow even closer in old age (Cicirelli, 1995; Connidis, 2010). Most adult siblings are in frequent contact and have positive feelings toward one another (Spitze & Trent, 2006). They do not often discuss intimate problems or help one another, but they usually feel that they can count on one another in a crisis (Cicirelli, 1982, 1995).

Some of the ambivalence that characterizes sibling relationships during childhood carries over into adulthood, however (Cicirelli, 1995; Connidis, 2010). Siblings may compete with

one another as they build their lives. And whereas siblings who enjoyed a close relationship during childhood are likely to be drawn closer after significant life events such as a parent's illness or death, siblings who had poor relationships during childhood may clash in response to the same life events—for example, bickering about who is doing more to help an ailing parent or how a deceased parent's estate should be divided (Lerner et al., 1991; Ross & Milgram, 1982). Parents can help forge close sibling relationships in adulthood by not favoring one child over another (Boll, Ferring, & Filipp, 2005; Suitor et al., 2008, 2009). Adult siblings who perceive that their parents played favorites when they were children or play favorites currently do not get along as well as those who believe their parents have treated them equitably (Suitor et al., 2009).

Parent–Child Relationships

Parent and child generations in most families are in close contact and enjoy affectionate give-and-take relationships throughout the adult years. When aging parents eventually need support, children are there to help.

Forging More Mutual Relationships. Parent–child relationships in adulthood take many forms—some are strained or conflictual, some are built more on obligation than love, and some are very close and friendlike (Van Gaalen & Dykstra, 2006). Usually the quality of a particular parent–child relationship stays much the same as adolescents become adults (Aquilino, 2006).

Even after emerging adults have left the nest, there are likely to be some tensions in most parent–adult child relationships. Parents can become stressed when their children have problems or when they are asked to help solve those problems; children can become irritated if their parents try to meddle in their lives or demand more of them than they want to give (Blieszner, 2006; Connidis, 2010). Parents and children are at different points in the life cycle, and parents may be more invested in maintaining a strong parent–child relationship than children who are building their own families are. Perhaps it is not surprising, then, that in one study 94% of parents and their adult children ages 22 to 49 reported at least some tension in their relationship, either concerning the relationship itself or the behavior of one or the other person (Birditt et al., 2009).

Yet adults have an opportunity to negotiate a new phase of their relationship with their parents in which they move beyond playing out roles as child and parent, see their parents as "real people, " understand them better, and become more like friends (Birditt et al., 2008; Lefkowitz, 2005). A more mutual, friendlike relationship is especially likely to develop if parents were supportive, authoritative parents earlier in the child's life (Belsky et al., 2001).

When children are middle-aged and their parents are elderly, the two generations typically continue to care about, socialize with, and help each other (Umberson & Slaten, 2000). Aging mothers enjoy closer relations and more contact with their children, especially their daughters, than aging fathers do (Umberson & Slaten, 2000). And Hispanic American, African

Many Hispanic American families benefit from close relationships and lots of mutual support across generations.

American, and other minority group elders often enjoy more supportive relationships with their families than European Americans typically do, especially when it comes to living together or near one another and providing mutual help (Bengtson, Rosenthal, & Burton, 1996; Sarkisian, Gerena, & Gerstel, 2007). Most elderly people in our society prefer to live close to but not with their children; they enjoy their independence and do not want to burden their children when their health fails (Connidis, 2010; Brody, 2004).

Typically, relationships between the generations are not only close and affectionate but equitable: each generation gives something, and each generation gets something in return (Conner, 2000; Markides, Boldt, & Ray, 1986). If anything, aging parents give more (Brody, 2004). It is rare for aging families to experience a "role reversal" in which the parent becomes the needy, dependent one and the child becomes the caregiver (Brody, 2004; Connidis, 2010). Only when parents reach advanced ages and begin to develop serious physical or mental problems does the parent–child relationship sometimes become lopsided like this.

Caring for Aging Parents. Elaine Brody (1985, 2004) uses the term **middle generation squeeze** (others call it the *sandwich generation* phenomenon) to describe the situation of middle-aged adults pressured by demands from both the younger and the older generations simultaneously (see also Grundy & Henretta, 2006). Imagine a 50-year-old woman caring for her daughter's children (and maybe even her granddaughter's children) as well as for her own ailing parents (and possibly her grandparents).

Adults with children increasingly find themselves caring for their aging parents (Gallagher & Gerstel, 2001); about one-third of women ages 55 to 69 report helping members of both the older and younger generations (Grundy & Henretta, 2006). Although spouses or partners are the first in line to care for frail elders, assuming they are alive and up to the challenge, most other caregivers of ailing elders are daughters or daughters-in-law in their 40s, 50s, and 60s. Daughters spend more time than sons providing emotional support to aging parents and in-laws, although sons are about as involved as daughters in providing help with practical tasks and financial assistance (Chesley & Poppie, 2009). The greater involvement of women in caregiving is partly because traditional gender-role norms call for women to be the "kinkeepers" of the family (Brody, 2004) and partly because women are less likely than men to have jobs that prevent them from helping (Sarkisian & Gerstel, 2004).

In many collectivist Asian societies, daughters-in-law have been the first choice as caregivers. Aging parents have often been taken in by a son, usually the oldest, and cared for by his wife (Youn et al., 1999). But this pattern of living with a son and his wife is changing as societies modernize. In China, for example, the government's former policy of only one child per family and rapid industrialization have meant that elders, especially those in rural areas whose children have moved to the cities, sometimes have no one to care for them (Zhang, 2009). Urban elders in China are faring better; although they do not as often live with children as they used to, most have pensions, medical care, and housing and more and more live together and provide one another with support.

In our individualistic society, most aging parents strongly resist having to live with and be dependent on their children. Thanks to greater financial independence for both elders and their adult children than in the era of family farms, adult children and their aging parents less often live together than they did in the 19th and early 20th centuries (Connidis, 2010; Ruggles, 2007). Families remain the major providers of care for the frail elderly today, however, and we see little support for the view that today's families have abandoned or failed to meet their responsibilities to their oldest members (Connidis, 2010; Stein, 2009).

Middle-aged adults who must foster their children's development while tending to their own development and caring for aging parents sometimes find their situation overwhelming. They may experience **caregiver burden**—psychological distress associated with the demands of providing care for someone with physical or cognitive impairments. Caring for a loved one with serious health problems can be rewarding and can even have beneficial effects on health and well-being in some cases (Brown et al., 2009). Yet many adult children providing such care experience emotional, physical, and financial strains and suffer for it (Hebert

& Schulz, 2006; Pinquart & Sorensen, 2006). A woman who is almost wholly responsible for a dependent elder may feel angry and resentful because she has no time for herself. She may experience role conflict between her caregiver role and her roles as wife, mother, and employee (Stephens et al., 2001, 2009). This can undermine her sense of well-being and put her at risk for depression.

Caregiver burden is likely to be perceived as especially weighty if the elderly parent engages in the disruptive and socially inappropriate behaviors often shown by people with dementia (Gaugler et al., 2000; Pinquart & Sorensen, 2003). The caregiver's motivations can matter: daughters who help out of love experience helping as less stressful and burdensome than those who help mainly out of a sense of duty or who are not very motivated by either love or duty (Cicirelli, 1993; Lyonette & Yardley, 2003). The caregiver's personality and coping abilities also makes a difference (Li, Seltzer, & Greenberg, 1999).

Cultural and contextual factors may enter in: for example, white caregivers devote fewer hours but feel more burdened than do African American caregivers, possibly because of differences in norms regarding elder care (Kosberg et al., 2007). Finally, strains are likely to be worse if a caregiving daughter is unmarried and therefore does not have a husband to lean on for practical and emotional support (Brody et al., 1992); if her marriage is an unsupportive one; or if her family life is otherwise conflict ridden (Scharlach, Li, & Dalvi, 2006; Stephens et al., 2009).

So the caregivers most likely to experience psychological distress are those who must care for parents or spouses with behavioral problems, who do not want to help or help out of duty rather than love, who lack personal resources such as good coping skills, and who lack social and cultural support for caregiving. What can be done for burdened caregivers? Behavior management training, anger management training, and cognitive behavioral therapy can help caregivers sharpen their caregiving skills, teach their aging parents self-care skills, learn to react less negatively to the difficult behavior often shown by elderly adults with dementia, and cope with the stress associated with their role and the conflicts that may arise between it and their other roles (Gallagher-Thompson & Coon, 2007; Hebert & Schulz, 2006; Zarit, 2009). Respite services that give caregivers a break now and then can also be tremendously important (Zarit, 2009).

Checking Mastery

1. If you were drawing a graph line to show changes in marital satisfaction over the family life cycle, what would it look like?

2. What are three factors that can make new parenthood a stressful transition?

3. Which of the three main grandparental roles do grandparents prefer, and what does it involve?

4. What are two factors that might increase the caregiver burden on a middle-aged woman taking care of her mother with Alzheimer's disease?

Making Connections

1. Martha has just married George and wonders how her experience of the events in the traditional family life cycle is likely to differ from his. Can you enlighten her?

2. You may want to ask your mother, but to what extent does the research on changes in the marital relationship and in parent–child relationships (relationships with parents and with children) apply to your mother? If there are differences, why do you think they arose?

15.6 Diverse Family Experiences

Useful as it is, the concept of the family life cycle, at least as originally conceived, does not capture the tremendous diversity of adult lifestyles and family experiences today. Many adults do not progress in an orderly way through the stages of the traditional family life cycle—marrying, having children, watching them leave the nest, and so on. Some never marry, and some of those live alone, whereas others cohabit with a romantic partner, heterosexual or homosexual, and in some cases raise children together. Some, married or not, never have children. Some continue working when their children are young, others stop or cut back. And an increasing number of adults change their family circumstances with some frequency—for example, marrying, divorcing, and cohabiting or remarrying. Let us examine some of these variations in family life (and see Cherlin, 2009; Patterson & Hastings, 2007).

Singles

It is nearly impossible to describe the "typical" single adult. This category includes not only young adults who have not yet married but also middle-aged and elderly people who experienced divorce or the death of a spouse or who never married. It is typi-

When we think of single adults, we may think of young professionals in their 20s, but many single adults are middle-aged or elderly.

cal to start adulthood as a single person, though; the large majority of adults ages 18 to 29 are unmarried (U.S. Census Bureau, 2009). Because adults have been postponing marriage, the number of young, single adults has been growing.

Cohabitation, living with a romantic partner without being married, is also on the rise (Amato et al., 2003). Many cohabiters have children; by one estimate, 4 out of 10 children will live in a family headed by a cohabiting couple sometime during childhood (Whitehead & Popenoe, 2003). Some never-married people live together as a matter of convenience—because they are in a romantic relationship and need an affordable living arrangement (Sassler, 2004). Other cohabiters see living together as a trial marriage. Still others have seen their marriages end and are looking for an alternative to marriage (Seltzer, 2000). This group includes many previously married older adults who want companionship but do not want to jeopardize their financial situation or upset their children by remarrying (Brown, Lee, & Bulanda, 2006; Connidis, 2010). Some older adults even decide to "live apart together," maintaining their own households but staying at each other's places with some frequency (Connidis, 2010).

It makes sense to think that couples who live together before marrying would have more opportunity than those who do not to determine whether they are truly compatible. Yet couples who live together and then marry tend to be more dissatisfied with their marriages and more likely to divorce overall than couples who do not live together before marrying. Why? Probably because they are less conventional in their family attitudes and less committed to marriage as an institution (Booth & Johnson, 1988). Marital problems are especially likely if partners have had multiple cohabitation experiences before they marry, live together before they make a commitment to each other by getting engaged, or have a child before they marry (Rhoades, Stanley, & Markman, 2009; Tach & Halpern-Meekin, 2009; Teachman, 2003).

What of the 10% or so of adults who never marry? Stereotypes suggest that they are miserably lonely and maladjusted. However, the stigma attached to being an "old maid" has lessened as more women have become "career women," and single adults often make up for their lack of spouse and children by forming close bonds with siblings, friends, or younger adults who become like sons or daughters to them (Connidis, 2010; Rubinstein et al., 1991). As "old-old" people in their 80s and 90s, never-married people do sometimes outlive their relatives and have no one to assist or care for them (Johnson & Troll, 1996). Yet it is divorced or widowed rather than never-married single adults who tend to be least happy with their singlehood in old age (Pudrovska, Schieman, & Carr, 2006).

Childless Married Couples

Many married couples who remain childless want children but cannot have them. However, a growing number of adults, especially highly educated adults with high-status, stable careers, voluntarily decide to delay having children or not have them at all (Keizer, Dykstra, & Jansen, 2008). One analysis of 2002 data indicated that 16% of women aged 35–44 in the United States were childless—7% voluntarily and, they said, permanently; 4%

involuntarily; and 5% temporarily, meaning that they expected to have children at a later time (Abma & Martinez, 2006).

How are childless couples faring while their peers are having, raising, and launching children? Generally, they are faring well. Although trying and failing to conceive a child is a difficult and demoralizing experience (Schwerdtfeger & Shreffler, 2009), the marital satisfaction of childless couples tends to be higher than that of couples with children during the child-rearing years (Kurdek, 1999). And middle-aged and elderly childless couples are no less satisfied with their lives than parents whose children have left the nest (Allen, Blieszner, & Roberto, 2000; Rempel, 1985) and in some studies have lower levels of depression than parents (Bures, Koropeckyj-Cox, & Loree, 2009). Children apparently do not guarantee happiness; nor does not having children doom people to an unhappy old age (Connidis, 2010). However, elderly women who find themselves without children and without a partner may have no one to help them when they develop health problems (Gray, 2009).

Dual-Career Families

Because of the huge increase over several decades in the numbers of mothers who work outside the home, developmental scientists have wondered how family life and child development are affected when a mother works outside the home rather than being a stay-at-home mother. Some have focused on the concept of **spillover effects**—ways in which events at work affect home life and events at home carry over into the workplace, whether good or bad. Most of their research has focused on negative spillover effects from work to home (Barnett, 1994; Crouter, 2006). After parents of either sex have stressful days at work, for example, they tend to be withdrawn from their spouse and children and angry and irritable if provoked (Repetti, Wang, & Saxbe, 2009); by contrast, a rewarding, stimulating job can have positive effects on a person's interactions within the family (Greenberger, O'Neil, & Nagel, 1994).

Despite the potential for negative spillover effects, dual-career families generally fare well (Gottfried & Gottfried, 2006). There is no indication that a mother's working, in itself, has damaging effects on child development. Children, especially girls, can even benefit from the positive role model a working mother provides; they may adopt less stereotyped views of men's and women's family and work roles and set higher educational and vocational goals for themselves (Hoffman, 1989; Riggio & Desrochers, 2005). The decision to work can have positive or negative effects, however, depending on the age of the child, its effects on parenting, and the family's circumstances (Gottfried & Gottfried, 2006; Holden, 2010). Living in a dual-career family is likely to be good for children when it means an increase in family income, when mothers are happy with the choice they have made and remain good parents, when fathers become more involved, and when children receive high quality day care or after-school care (Hoffman, 2000; Lerner & Noh, 2000). All these positive factors were at work for the Obamas. Having two working parents can be a negative experience, however, if the parents are unable to remain warm and involved and share "quality time" with their children (Beyer, 1995; Moorehouse, 1991; Parke & Buriel, 2006).

Dual-career families work best when partners share the workload.

Fortunately, most dual-career couples are able to stay involved with their children and enjoy the personal and financial benefits of working without compromising their children's development. They might be able to do so even more successfully if the United States, like other Western, industrialized nations, provided paid leave for parents and other family caregivers and did more to support families through flexible work hours, day care and preschool programs, after-school programs, and other support systems (Heymann, Penrose, & Earle, 2006).

Gay and Lesbian Families

What are the family experiences of gay men and lesbian women like? They are most notable for their diversity (Goldberg, 2009; Patterson & Hastings, 2007; Peplau & Fingerhut, 2007). In the United States, several million gay men and lesbian women are parents, most through previous heterosexual relationships, others through adoption, artificial insemination, or surrogacy. Some no longer live with their children, but others raise them as single parents and still others raise them in families that have two mothers or two fathers. Other gay men and lesbian women live as singles or as couples without children throughout their lives, some forming families that consist of a group of friends (Diamond & Butterworth, 2009).

Gay and lesbian families face special challenges, as suggested by the national controversy over whether gay and lesbian couples should be allowed to marry. These families are not fully recognized as families by society and are sometimes victims of discrimination (Peplau & Fingerhut, 2007). For example, a gay or lesbian person's life partner may not be embraced as a full

member of the family, allowed to make life-and-death decisions if their partner becomes ill, or given custody of the partner's children if the partner dies (Connidis, 2010). One study found that lesbian mothers in the United States were more worried about their legal status and possible discrimination and showed more symptoms of depression than lesbian mothers in Canada, a country that offers more protections to gay and lesbian citizens (Shapiro, Peterson, & Stewart, 2009).

Those gay and lesbian adults who live as couples debunk many stereotypes that associate homosexuality with unhappiness, loneliness, and difficulty sustaining romantic relationships (Peplau & Fingerhut, 2007). And contrary to myth, gay and lesbian couples usually do not have one adopt the traditional "husband" role and the other the "wife" role. Instead, relationships are usually egalitarian; partners share responsibilities equally and tend to work out a division of labor based on who is especially talented at or does not mind doing certain tasks (Huston & Schwartz, 1995). Even after the transition to parenthood, most couples report that their child has two equally involved parents (Goldberg & Perry-Jenkins, 2007). Generally, gay and lesbian relationships evolve through the same stages of development, are satisfying or dissatisfying for the same reasons, and are typically as rewarding as those of married or cohabiting heterosexuals (Kurdek, 1995, 2006; Peplau & Fingerhut, 2007).

What are the implications for children of being raised by gay or lesbian parents? Comparing lesbian mothers with heterosexual mothers in two-parent and single-parent homes, Susan Golombok and her colleagues (2003) found that lesbian mothers tend to hit children less and to engage in imaginative and domestic play more but are otherwise similar to heterosexual mothers. Moreover, children who lived with two parents of the same sex were better off in terms of developmental outcomes than chil-

Torin (age 2) climbs on Jessie Harris before going to bed while Zion (age 5) and Stacey Harris talk. Jessie gave birth to Torin after Zion was adopted by this lesbian couple, who married in Massachusetts in 2004 after same-sex marriage became legal there. Research tells us that the children of gay and lesbian parents generally turn out much like the children of heterosexual couples.

dren living with a single mother, and they were no different than children living with two heterosexual parents. This study and others suggest that gay and lesbian adults who raise children are as likely as heterosexual parents to produce competent and well-adjusted children (Goldberg, 2009; Patterson & Hastings, 2007). Moreover, contrary to what many people believe, their children are no more likely than the children of heterosexual parents to develop a homosexual or bisexual orientation.

Divorcing Families

Progress through the family life cycle is disrupted when a couple divorces. Divorce is not just one life event. Rather, it is a series of stressful experiences for the entire family that begins with marital difficulties before the divorce and includes a complex series of life changes as the marriage unravels and its members reorganize their lives (Amato, 2000; Demo & Fine, 2010; Hetherington & Kelly, 2002). Why do people divorce? What effects does divorce typically have on family members? And how can we explain why some adults and children thrive after a divorce whereas others experience persisting problems?

Before the Divorce

Scholars have pieced together a profile of the couples at highest risk for divorce (Demo & Fine, 2010; Kitson, 1992; Kitson, Babri, & Roach, 1985; Teachman, 2002). Generally they are young adults, in their 20s and 30s, who have been married for an average of 7 years and often have young children. Couples are especially likely to divorce if they married as teenagers, had a short courtship, conceived a child before marrying, or are low in socioeconomic status—all factors that might suggest an unreadiness for marriage and unusually high financial and psychological stress accompanying new parenthood. Personality problems and problem behaviors such as alcohol or drug abuse often play a role.

INTERESTING. WHAT ABOUT THAT, PHIL? HOW DO YOU FEEL ABOUT BECOMING SOMEONE ELSE ENTIRELY?

Nick Galifianakis "Interesting, What About That Phil? How Do You Feel About Becoming Someone Else Entirely?," for the *Washington Post.* Copyright © 2003, The *Washington Post* Writer's Group. Reprinted.

Couples typically divorce because they feel their marriages lack communication, emotional fulfillment, or compatibility. Wives tend to have longer lists of complaints than their husbands do and often have more to do with initiating the breakup (Hewitt, Western, & Baxter, 2006; Thompson & Amato, 1999). Whereas historically divorce was considered a drastic step taken only when adultery, desertion, abuse, or a similar crisis was involved, starting in the late 20th century it came to be viewed as more like a right—an action to be taken when people do not feel personally fulfilled in their marriage. Under no-fault divorce laws passed in most states after California passed such a law in 1969, either partner can cite irreconcilable differences and end the marriage simply because they want to (Cherlin, 2009). Still, most divorcing couples experience a few years of marital distress and often try separations before they make the final decision to divorce (Demo & Fine, 2010; Kitson, 1992).

After the Divorce

Most families going through a divorce experience it as a genuine crisis—a period of considerable disruption that often lasts at least 1–2 years—although there is tremendous variation in how it goes (Amato, 2000; Demo & Fine, 2010; Hetherington, 2006). The wife, who usually ends up as the primary caregiver for any children, is likely to be angry, depressed, and otherwise distressed, although often she is relieved as well. The husband is also likely to be distressed, particularly if he did not want the divorce and feels shut off from his children. Both individuals must revise their identities and their relationship. Both may feel isolated from former friends and unsure of themselves as they try out new romantic relationships. Divorced women with children are likely to face the added problem of getting by with considerably less money (Amato, 2000). In one study, the standard of living of custodial mothers declined by about a third on average, whereas the financial situation of their former husbands improved (Bianchi, Subaiya, & Kahn, 1999).

Because of all these stressors, divorced adults are at higher risk than married adults for depression and other forms of psychological distress, physical health problems, and even death (Amato, 2000; Lillard & Panis, 1996). Their adjustment is especially likely to be poor if they have little income, do not find a new relationship, take a dim view of divorce, and did not initiate the divorce (Wang & Amato, 2000).

As you might suspect, psychologically distressed adults do not make the best parents. Moreover, children going through a divorce do not make the best children because they too are suffering. They are often angry, fearful, depressed, and guilty, especially if they fear that they were somehow responsible for their parents' fighting or for the divorce (Buehler, Lange, & Franck, 2007; Hetherington, 1981). They are also likely to be whiny, dependent, disobedient, and disrespectful.

Mavis Hetherington and her associates (Hetherington, Cox, & Cox, 1982; Hetherington & Kelly, 2002) have found that stressed custodial mothers often become impatient and insensitive to their children's needs. In terms of the major dimensions of child rearing, they become less accepting and responsive, less authoritative, and less consistent in their discipline. They occasionally try to seize control of their children with a heavy-handed, authoritarian style of parenting, but more often they fail to carry through in enforcing rules and make few demands that their children behave maturely. Noncustodial fathers, meanwhile, are likely to be overly permissive, indulging their children during visitations (Amato & Sobolewski, 2004).

This is not the formula for producing well-adjusted, competent children. A vicious circle of the sort described by the transactional model of family influence can result: Children's behavioral problems make effective parenting difficult, and deterioration in parenting style aggravates children's behavioral problems. When this breakdown in family functioning occurs, children are likely to display not only behavioral problems at home but also strained relations with peers, low self-esteem, academic problems, and adjustment difficulties at school (Hetherington, 2006; Lansford, 2009).

Families typically begin to pull themselves back together about 2 years after the divorce, and by the 6-year mark most differences between children of divorce and children of intact families have disappeared (Hetherington & Kelly, 2002). Yet even after the crisis phase has passed and most children and parents have adapted, divorce can leave a residue of negative effects on at least some individuals that lasts years (Amato, 2006; Hetherington & Kelly, 2002). For example, as adolescents, children of divorce are less likely than other youth to perceive their relationships with their parents, especially their fathers, as close and caring, and many are still negative about what divorce has done to their lives (Emery, 1999; Woodward, Fergusson, & Belsky, 2000). About 20 to 25% of Hetherington's children of divorce still had emotional scars and psychological problems as young adults (Hetherington & Kelly, 2002). Adults whose parents divorced are also less likely than adults from intact families to marry (Maier & Lachman, 2000) and more likely to experience marital conflict and divorce if they do (Amato, 2006).

On a more positive note, not all families experience divorce as a major crisis, and of those that do, most parents and children rebound from their crisis period and adapt well in the long run, sometimes even undergoing impressive growth as a result of their experience (Demo & Fine, 2010; Hetherington & Kelly, 2002). Some adults feel better about themselves and their lives after extracting themselves from a bad marriage. And a conflict-ridden two-parent family is usually more detrimental to a child's development than a cohesive single-parent family (Amato, 2006), so it is not always wise to "stay together for the good of the children." Moreover, some of the problems we attribute to divorce are probably the result of parent conflict before the divorce (Lansford, 2009).

Influences on Adjustment

Perhaps the most important message of research on divorce is that the outcomes of this stressful experience vary widely (Demo & Fine, 2010; Lansford, 2009). Several factors can help facilitate a positive adjustment to divorce and prevent lasting damage:

1. *Adequate financial support.* Families fare better after a divorce if the noncustodial parent, usually the father, pays child support and the family has adequate finances (Amato & Sobolewski, 2004; Marsiglio et al., 2000). Adjustment is likely to be more difficult for mother-headed families that fall into poverty and must struggle to survive.

2. *Good parenting by the custodial parent.* If the custodial parent can manage to remain warm, authoritative, and consistent, children are far less likely to experience problems (Hetherington, 2006). Interventions for divorced parents can improve their parenting skills and, in turn, their children's adjustment (Forgatch & DeGarmo, 1999; see also Wolchik et al., 2000).

3. *Good parenting by the noncustodial parent.* Children may suffer when they lose contact with their noncustodial parent, as a quarter or more of children living with their mothers do (Demo & Cox, 2000). More important than amount of contact, however, is the quality of parenting provided (Amato & Sobolewski, 2004; King & Sobolewski, 2006).

4. *Minimal conflict between parents.* Children should be protected from continuing marital conflict after the divorce or, worse, efforts by parents to undermine each other in their children's eyes (Amato, 1993; Lansford, 2009). When parents can agree on joint custody, children's adjustment tends to be better than when custody is granted to one parent or the other (Bauserman, 2002). When the mother has custody, positive coparenting in which parents coordinate and cooperate helps keep fathers close to and involved with their children (Sobolewski & King, 2005).

5. *Additional social support.* Divorcing adults are less depressed if they have close confidants than if they do not (Menaghan & Lieberman, 1986). Children also benefit from having close friends (Lustig, Wolchik, & Braver, 1992) and from participating in peer-support programs in which they and other children of divorce can share their feelings and learn positive coping skills (Grych & Fincham, 1992).

6. *Minimal other changes.* Generally families do best if additional changes are kept to a minimum—for example, if parents do not have to move, get new jobs, cope with the loss of their children, and so on (Buehler et al., 1985–1986). It is easier to deal with a couple of stressors than a mountain of them.

7. *Personal resources.* Finally, personal resources such as intelligence, emotional stability, and good coping skills often put some individuals—even some members of the same family—on a more positive trajectory than others after a divorce (Demo & Fine, 2010; Lansford, 2009).

As Paul Amato (1993) concludes, adjustment to divorce will depend on the "total configuration" of stressors the individual faces and on the resources he has available to aid in coping, including both personal strengths and social supports.

Reconstituted Families

Within 3–5 years of a divorce, about 75% of single-parent families experience yet another major transition when a parent remarries and the children acquire a stepparent—and sometimes new siblings (Hetherington & Stanley-Hagan, 2000; and see

Most children adjust to being part of a reconstituted family, but it can be hard when both partners bring children to remarriage.

© Patrick Sheandell O'Carroll/PhotoAlto Agency

Checking Mastery

1. Why is cohabitation before marriage associated with later marital problems?

2. Is growing up in a dual-career family typically damaging to child development? Why or why not?

3. What is the typical effect of a custodial parent's remarriage after a divorce, and what kind of reconstituted family seems to have the most difficulty adjusting?

Making Connections

1. Three months after her divorce from Alex, Blanca has become depressed and increasingly withdrawn. Her son Carlos, age 7, has become a terror around the house and a discipline problem at school. From the perspective of (a) the parent effects model, (b) the child effects model, and (c) the transactional model of family influence, how would you explain what is going on in this single-parent family?

2. Suppose you are a counseling psychologist and Blanca comes to you for advice on how she and her family can deal most effectively with their divorce. What would you tell her based on research on factors affecting adjustment to divorce?

Teachman & Tedrow, 2008). Because about 60% of remarried couples divorce, an increasing number of adults and children today find themselves in recurring cycles of singlehood, cohabitation or marriage, conflict, and separation or divorce (Cherlin, 2009).

How do children fare when their custodial parent remarries? The first few years are a time of conflict and disruption as a new family system takes shape and new family roles and relationships are ironed out (Hetherington & Stanley-Hagan, 2000). Interviewed 20 years after their parents divorced, about one-third of the adults from one study recalled the remarriage as more stressful than the divorce (Ahrons, 2007).

The difficulties are likely to be worse if both parents bring children to the family than if only one parent does (Hetherington, 2006). Girls may have more trouble than boys, too; they are often so closely allied with their mothers that they may resent either a stepfather competing for their mother's attention or a stepmother attempting to play a substitute-mother role. Most children adapt with time, but on average adolescents in reconstituted families with children from more than one marriage, like children in single-parent families after a divorce, are less well adjusted and show more problems such as depression and antisocial behavior than adolescents who live in intact two-parent families (Hetherington, 2006). As Mavis Hetherington (2006) concludes, though, "It is family process rather than family structure that is critical to the well-being of children" (p. 232); in the final analysis, children and adolescents can thrive in any type of family if they receive good parenting.

15.7 The Problem of Family Violence

As this chapter makes clear, family relationships normally contribute positively to human development at every point in the life span. At the same time, families can be the cause of much anguish and of development gone astray. Nowhere is this more obvious than in cases of family violence (St. George, 2001, p. A20):

> From a young age, I have had to grow up fast. I see families that are loving and fathers who care for their children, and I find myself hating them. . . . I have nightmares pertaining to my father. I get angry and frustrated when family is around.

These sobering words were written by Sonyé Herrera, an abused adolescent who for years had been hit, threatened with guns, choked, and otherwise victimized—and had witnessed her mother abused—by an alcoholic father. The abuse continued even after the couple divorced. At age 15, unable to stand any more, Herrera had her father charged with assault, but he returned one afternoon, hit her, and shot and killed both her and her mother before turning his gun on himself (St. George, 2001, p. A21).

Child abuse, mistreating or harming a child physically, emotionally, or sexually, is perhaps the most visible form of family violence. Every day, infants, children, and adolescents are burned, bruised, beaten, starved, suffocated, sexually abused, or otherwise mistreated by their caretakers (Miller & Knudsen, 2007). Accurate statistics are hard to come by because much abuse goes unreported, but official statistics for the United States in 2007 suggest that 11 of every 1,000 children under age 18 were the victims of substantiated **child maltreatment**, a broad

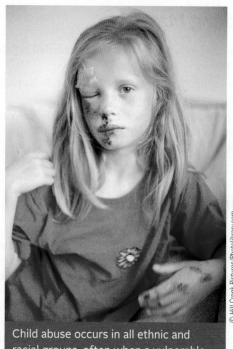

Child abuse occurs in all ethnic and racial groups, often when a vulnerable parent is overwhelmed by stress.

term that includes both abuse and neglect of the child's basic needs (Federal Interagency Forum on Child and Family Statistics, 2009). Of these victims, 71% were neglected, 16% physically abused, 9% sexually abused, and 7% emotionally or psychologically abused and 8% experienced other types of maltreatment. Many children experienced more than one of the preceding types; therefore the percentages add up to more than 100%.

Child abuse commands a good deal of attention and tugs at our heartstrings, but the potential for abuse exists in all possible relationships within the family (Tolan, Gorman-Smith, & Henry, 2006). Children and adolescents batter, and in rare cases kill, their parents (Agnew & Huguley, 1989). Siblings, especially brothers, abuse one another in countless ways, especially if there is violence elsewhere in the family (Hoffman, Kiecolt, & Edwards, 2005). And spousal or partner abuse, rampant in our society, appears to be the most common form of family violence worldwide. Globally it has been estimated that about one-third of women are beaten, coerced into sex, or emotionally abused by their partners (Murphy, 2003). In the United States, surveys suggest that 16% of married couples experience some form of marital violence in a year's time—often "only" a shove or a slap, but violence nonetheless—and that almost 6% experience at least one instance of severe violence such as kicking or beating (Straus & Gelles, 1986, 1990). Much "mild" spousal abuse is mutual. In more serious (and rarer) cases, the violence is one-sided: Men batter their female partners, usually in an attempt to control them (Johnson & Ferraro, 2000; Tolan, Gorman-Smith, & Henry, 2006). Worse, millions of children witness domestic violence (McDonald et al., 2006), and some get hurt themselves, intentionally or accidentally—sometimes while trying to protect their mothers (Mbilinyi et al., 2007).

Elderly adults are also targets of family violence. Frail or impaired older people are physically or psychologically mistreated, neglected, financially exploited, and stripped of their rights—most often by stressed adult children or spouses serving as their caregivers (Jayawardena & Liao, 2006; Nerenberg, 2008). Around 5% of elderly adults are probably neglected or abused in various ways (Tolan, Gorman-Smith, & Henry, 2006); all agree that elder abuse is especially hard to define and detect and that many cases go unreported (Nerenberg, 2008).

Family violence is not a pretty picture. Here is a social problem of major dimensions that causes untold suffering and harms the development of family members of all ages. What can be done to prevent it, or to stop it once it has started? To answer this question, we must understand why family violence occurs.

Why Does Family Violence Occur?

Various forms of family violence have many similarities, and the contributors are often similar (Tolan, Gorman-Smith, & Henry, 2006). Because child abuse has been studied the longest, we will look at what has been learned about how characteristics of the abuser and the abused and social context contribute to it.

The Abuser

Hard as it may be to believe, only about 1 child abuser in 10 appears to have a severe psychological disorder (Kempe & Kempe, 1978). Rather, the abusive parent is most often a young mother who tends to have many children, to live in poverty, to be unemployed, and to have no partner to share her load (U.S. Department of Health and Human Services, 2007; Wolfner & Gelles, 1993). Yet child abusers come from all races, ethnic groups, and social classes. Many of them appear to be fairly typical, loving parents—except for their tendency to become extremely irritated with their children and to do things they will later regret.

A few reliable differences between parents who abuse their children and those who do not have been identified. First, child abusers tend to have been abused as children. Although most maltreated children do not abuse their own children when they become parents, a relatively high percentage, 30%, do (Kaufman & Zigler, 1989). Abuse victims are prone to engage in other forms of family violence as well (Delsol & Margolin, 2004; Kwong et al., 2003). This cycle of abuse is not inevitable; it can be broken if abused individuals receive emotional support from parent substitutes, therapists, or spouses and are spared from severe stress as adults (Egeland, Jacobvitz, & Sroufe, 1988; Vondra & Belsky, 1993). Yet it happens and is an example of a broader phenomenon, the **intergenerational transmission of parenting,** or the passing down from generation to generation of parenting styles, abusive or otherwise. As Exploration Box 15.2 illustrates, we are beginning to get a clearer picture of how the intergenerational transmission of parenting works.

Second, abusive mothers are often battered by their partners (Coohey & Braun, 1997; McCloskey, Figueredo, & Koss, 1995). Adults are more likely to be in an abusive romantic relationship or marriage if they were abused or witnessed abuse as a child (Stith et al., 2000). Thus, abusive mothers may have learned

Do you think the way your parents raised you was influenced by the way your grandparents raised them, and that you will use the same parenting approach your parents used with you? Is abusive parenting handed down from generation to generation? A set of studies on the intergenerational transmission of parenting reported in the journal *Developmental Psychology* is revealing. As summarized by Rand Conger, Jay Belsky, and Deborah Capaldi (2009), the studies as a group suggest that both harsh parenting and positive parenting are transmitted across generations—but through different mechanisms.

A study by Tricia Neppl and her colleagues (2009), for example, looked at both harsh and positive parenting, focusing on 187 young adults, their mothers, and their preschool-age children as observed during family interaction tasks. There were indeed correlations, although modest ones, between the harshness of grandmothers' parenting styles with the mothers years earlier (for example, their hostility and coerciveness) and the harshness of their daughters' parenting styles with their preschoolers. Harsh parenting, the researchers found, leads to the development of conduct problems like aggression in children, and these behavior problems then contribute to

a harsh parenting style when these children become parents themselves.

There were also correlations between positive parenting (for example, good parental communication with and responsiveness to the child) in the two generations. Positive parenting fostered academic and social competencies, and those competencies then increased the odds that well-treated children would grow up to be effective parents (Neppl et al., 2009).

Stepping back, how do you think nature and nurture might contribute to the intergenerational transmission of parenting, especially harsh, abusive parenting? On the nature side of the issue, parents could affect the next generation's parenting styles through the direct effects of certain genes they pass to their children—or through gene–environment interactions and correlations involving these genes. We saw plenty of evidence in Chapter 13, for example, that aggressive behavior is influenced in part by genetic makeup.

On the nurture side of the issue, children could learn how to parent by watching their abusive parents—that is, through observational learning. Finally, we now believe *epi*genetic transmission of parenting across generations is possible. That is, nurture—being treated harshly or well early in life—

could affect the expression of genes that contribute to good or bad parenting later in life. As discussed in Chapter 3, research with rats reveals that early experience with a neglectful mother affects gene expression in ways that make offspring unable to cope effectively with stress and neglectful of their own offspring. Epigenetic effects on gene expression also help explain the transmission from mother to daughter of abusive parenting among monkeys (Maestripieri, Lindell, & Higley, 2007). And now analysis of the brain tissue of human suicide victims who were abused as children reveals patterns of gene expression similar to those observed in neglected and abused animals (McGowan et al., 2009).

So genetic makeup and its interplay with environmental factors, observational learning, and epigenetic effects of early experiences of abuse or neglect on gene expression could all help explain why harsh, abusive parenting runs in families. Studies of the intergenerational transmission of parenting not only tell us how parenting styles arise but also suggest that abusive and neglectful parents who seek help now in improving their parenting skills could well benefit not only their children but their grandchildren and perhaps even their great-grandchildren.

---

through their experiences both as children and as wives that violence is the way to solve problems, or they may take out some of their frustrations about being abused on their children.

Third, abusers are often insecure individuals with low self-esteem. Their unhappy experiences in insecure attachment relationships with their parents, reinforced by their negative experiences in romantic relationships, may lead them to formulate negative internal working models of themselves and others (Pianta, Egeland, & Erickson, 1989; and see Chapter 14). These adults often see themselves as victims, feel powerless as parents, and find the normal challenges of parenting stressful and threatening (Bugental, 2009; Bugental & Beaulieu, 2003).

Fourth, abusive parents often have unrealistic expectations about what children can do at different ages and have twisted perceptions of the normal behavior of infants and young children (Haskett, Johnson, & Miller, 1994). For example, when infants cry to communicate needs such as hunger, nonabusive mothers correctly interpret these cries as signs of discomfort, but

abusive mothers often infer that the baby is somehow criticizing or rejecting them (Egeland, 1979; Egeland, Sroufe, & Erickson, 1983). Similarly, one mother interpreted her three-month-old's babbling as "talking back" (Bugental, 2009). (See why the study of human development can be useful?)

In short, abusive parents tend to have been exposed to harsh parenting and abusive relationships themselves, to have low self-esteem, and to find caregiving more stressful and ego threatening than other parents do. Still, it has been difficult to identify a particular kind of person who is highly likely to turn into a child abuser. Could some children bring out the worst in parents?

The Abused

An abusive parent sometimes singles out only one child in the family as a target; this offers a hint that child characteristics might matter (Gil, 1970). No one is suggesting that children are to blame for being abused, but some children appear to be more at risk than others. For example, children who have medical problems or who have difficult temperaments are more likely to be abused than quiet, healthy, and responsive infants who are easier to care for (Bugental & Beaulieu, 2003). Yet many difficult children are not mistreated, and many seemingly cheerful and easygoing children are.

Just as characteristics of the caregiver cannot fully explain why abuse occurs, then, neither can characteristics of children. There is now intriguing evidence that the combination of a high-risk parent and a high-risk child spells trouble. For example, a mother who feels powerless to deal with children, and who must raise a child who has a disability or illness or is otherwise difficult, is prone to overreact emotionally when the child cannot be controlled and to use harsh discipline (Bugental, 2009). Such powerless parents experience higher levels of stress than most parents, as indicated by high cortisol levels and fast heart rates, when interacting with children who are unresponsive. Their uneasiness makes such children even less responsive, and this transactional chain of events provokes the use of power tactics by the parent (Bugental, 2009; Martorell & Bugental, 2006). However, even the match between child and caregiver may not be enough to explain abuse. We must, as always, consider the ecological context surrounding the family system (Cicchetti & Valentino, 2006).

The Context

Consistently, abuse is most likely to occur when a parent is under great stress and has little social support (Cano & Vivian, 2003; Egeland, Sroufe, & Erickson, 1983). Life changes such as the loss of a job or a move can disrupt family functioning and contribute to abuse or neglect (Wolfner & Gelles, 1993). Abuse rates are highest in deteriorating neighborhoods where families are poor, transient, socially isolated, and lacking in community services and informal social support—neighborhoods in which parents do not look after each other's children and the motto "It takes a village to raise a child" has little meaning (Korbin, 2001).

Finally, the larger macroenvironment is important. Ours is a violent society in which the use of physical punishment is common and the line between physical punishment and child abuse can be difficult to draw (Lansford & Dodge, 2008). Parents who believe strongly in the value of physical punishment are more at risk than those who do not to become abusive if they are under stress (Crouch & Behl, 2001). Child abuse is less common in societies that discourage physical punishment and advocate nonviolent ways of resolving interpersonal conflicts (Gilbert, 1997; Levinson, 1989).

As you can see, child abuse is a complex phenomenon with many causes and contributing factors. It is not easy to predict who will become a child abuser and who will not, but abuse seems most likely when a vulnerable individual faces overwhelming stress with insufficient social support. Much the same is true of spousal abuse, elder abuse, and other forms of family violence.

What Are the Effects of Family Violence?

As you might imagine, child abuse is not good for human development. Physically abused and otherwise maltreated children tend to have many problems, ranging from physical injuries, impaired brain development, and cognitive deficits to social, emotional, and behavioral problems and psychological disorders (Cicchetti & Valentino, 2006; Holden, 2010; Margolin & Gordis, 2000).

Intellectual deficits and academic difficulties are common among mistreated children (Malinosky-Rummell & Hansen, 1993; Shonk & Cicchetti, 2001). A particularly revealing study focused on 5-year-old identical and fraternal twins to rule out possible genetic influences on the association between exposure to domestic violence and intellectual development (Koenen et al., 2003). Children exposed to high levels of domestic violence had IQ scores 8 points lower, on average, than those of children who were not exposed to domestic violence, even taking genetic influences on IQ into account.

Social, emotional, and behavioral problems are also common among physically abused and other maltreated children (Flores, Cicchetti, & Rogosch, 2005). Some tend to be explosively aggressive youngsters, rejected by their peers for that reason (Bolger & Patterson, 2001). Their experience with an abusive parent makes them supersensitive to angry emotions; as a result, they may perceive anger in peers where there is none and lash out to protect themselves (Keil & Price, 2009; Reynolds, 2003). Even as adults, individuals who were abused as children also tend to have higher-than-average rates of depression, anxiety, and other psychological problems (Margolin & Gordis, 2000). Children who witness parental violence are prone to have psychological problems too (Maikovich et al., 2008; Sternberg et al., 2006).

One of the most disturbing consequences of physical abuse is a lack of normal empathy in response to the distress of others. When Mary Main and Carol George (1985) observed the responses of abused and nonabused toddlers to the fussing and crying of peers, they found that nonabused children typically attended carefully to the distressed child, showed concern, and attempted to provide comfort. Not one abused child showed appropriate concern in this situation. Instead, abused toddlers were likely to become angry and attack the crying child, reacting to the distress of peers much as their abusive parents react to their distress (Main & George, 1985, p. 410; see also Klimes-Dougan & Kistner, 1990):

> Martin (an abused boy of 32 months) tried to take the hand of the crying other child, and when she resisted, he slapped her on the arm with his open hand. He then turned away from her to look at the ground and began vocalizing very strongly, "Cut it out! CUT IT OUT!," each time saying it a little faster and louder. He patted her, but when she became disturbed by his patting, he retreated, hissing at her and baring his teeth. He then began patting her on the back again, his patting became beating, and he continued beating her despite her screams.

Remarkable as it may seem, though, many maltreated children are resilient and turn out fine. What distinguishes these

That family violence has many causes is discouraging. Where do we begin to intervene, and just how many problems must we correct before we can prevent or stop the violence? Despite the complexity of the problem, progress is being made (see Dodge & Coleman, 2009).

Consider the task of preventing violence before it starts. Daphne Bugental and her colleagues (Bugental, 2009; Bugental & Beaulieu, 2003; Bugental et al., 2002) have developed and evaluated an approach to prevention based on their findings that abuse results when parents who feel powerless face the challenge of raising a child who is unresponsive and difficult. One of their intervention studies (see Bugental & Beaulieu, 2003) targeted high-risk mothers who had recently emigrated from Mexico to California and who scored high on a measure of family stress. Some had infants who were high risk (who were born prematurely or scored low on the Apgar examination at birth and were therefore at risk for future health problems), and others had infants who were low risk. Bugental and her colleagues designed and evaluated a home visitation program aimed at empowering these mothers by teaching them to analyze the causes of caregiving problems without blaming either themselves or their children and to devise and try solutions to these caregiving problems. Families were randomly assigned to the empowerment program, another home visitation program without the empowerment training, or a control condition in which families were referred to regular community services.

After the intervention period, mothers in the empowerment training condition had a greater sense of power in the family than mothers in the other conditions did, and they reported fewer postpartum depression symptoms. The rate of physical abuse, including spanking and slapping, was only 4% in the empowerment group compared with 23% in the other home visitation group and 26% in the community referral group. Moreover, the children in the empowerment group were in better health and were better able to manage stress. Importantly, the benefits of the program were greatest for families with high-risk children. As the graph here shows, after empowerment training, harsh parenting was unlikely whether the child was at risk for health problems or not, whereas in the control conditions, children at risk were treated far more harshly than low-risk children, suggesting that they were headed for trouble developmentally.

What can be done for families where abuse has already occurred? Here the challenge is more difficult. In cases of serious abuse, it may be necessary to prosecute the abuser and protect the children from injury and death by removing them from the home, although courts are reluctant to take this step (Emery & Laumann-Billings,

1998). In most cases a comprehensive, ecological approach designed to convert a pathological family system into a healthy one is likely to be most effective. Abusive parents need emotional support and the opportunity to learn more effective parenting, problem-solving, and coping skills, and the victims of abuse need day care programs and developmental training to help them overcome cognitive, social, and emotional deficits caused by abuse (Malley-Morrison & Hines, 2004). Change is needed in families' neighborhoods and communities as well to ensure that families have the services and supports they need (Dodge et al., 2009).

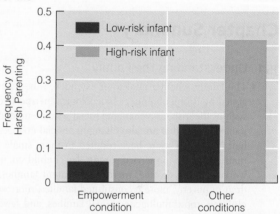

Empowerment training for low-income mothers under stress reduces harsh parenting practices, especially among mothers who are the most at risk of being abusive because their babies had medical problems or were born prematurely. Source: From *Advances in child development and behavior, Vol. 31.* Kail, Empowerment training for low-income mothers, page 252, Copyright 2003, with permission from Elsevier.

children from the ones who have long-term problems? First, there is evidence that they have genes that protect them from the negative psychological effects of abuse and possibly other negative life events (Kim-Cohen & Gold, 2009). For example, Avshalom Caspi and his colleagues (2003) found that maltreatment during childhood increases the likelihood of clinical depression among individuals with a genetic makeup that predisposes people to depression but not among individuals with a genetic makeup known to protect against depression. Some children's genes may make them stress resistant or equip them with personal resources—for example, intelligence, social

skills, or emotional stability—that allow them to demonstrate resilience in the face of adversity (Kim-Cohen & Gold, 2009). Environmental factors such as a close relationship with at least one nonabusive adult contribute to resilience too (Egeland, Jacobvitz, & Sroufe, 1988).

Knowing what we know about the causes and effects of abuse, what can be done to prevent it, stop it, and undo the damage? What would you propose? Application Box 15.1 offers some solutions. Meanwhile, we hope this examination of diverse family experiences has convinced you that the family is indeed centrally important in human development.

Checking Mastery

1. Identify one characteristic of the parent, one characteristic of the child, and one contextual factor that could contribute to child abuse.

2. What does Bugental's intervention to prevent child abuse involve?

Making Connections

1. Given what you now know about the roles of the abuser, the abused, and the context in child abuse, how do you think these three sets of factors enter into spousal violence?

2. Given the societal problems that stem from abuse and neglect of children, what do you think about the idea of licensing parents, much as we license drivers, to ensure that they have appropriate knowledge and skills and why? Licensing could involve pledging to support the child financially and to refrain from maltreating him; it could even involve being of a certain age and passing a parenting skills course (see Holden, 2010).

Chapter Summary

15.1 Understanding the Family

- The family, whether nuclear or extended, is best viewed, as suggested by Bronfenbrenner's bioecological perspective and family systems theorists, as a changing social system embedded in larger social systems that are also changing. Social changes in the past half century or more have resulted in more single adults, later marriage, more unmarried parents, fewer children, more women working, more divorce, more single-parent families, more children in poverty, more reconstituted families, more years without children, more multigenerational families, and fewer caregivers for aging adults.

15.2 The Infant

- Infants affect and are affected by their parents. Fathers are capable parents but are less involved in caregiving than mothers and specialize in challenging play. Developmental outcomes are likely to be positive when parents coparent and have positive indirect effects on development because of their positive influences on each other.

15.3 The Child

- Parenting styles can be described in terms of the dimensions of acceptance–responsiveness and demandingness–control; children are generally more competent when their parents adopt an authoritative style. Socioeconomic status, economic hardship, and culture all affect parenting styles.
- Research on the parent effects, child effects, and transactional models of family influence tells us that children's problem behaviors are not always solely caused by ineffective parenting.
- When a second child enters the family system, firstborns find the experience stressful; sibling relationships are characterized by ambivalence (both affection and rivalry), and siblings play important roles as providers of emotional support, caregiving, teaching, and social experience.

15.4 The Adolescent

- Parent–child relationships typically remain close in adolescence but involve increased conflict around puberty before they are renegotiated to become more equal.

15.5 The Adult

- Marital satisfaction declines somewhat as newlyweds adjust to each other and become parents, whereas the empty nest transition and a companionate style of grandparenthood are generally positive experiences. Marital satisfaction is more affected by personality than phase of the family life cycle, though.
- In adulthood, siblings have less contact but normally continue to feel both emotionally close and rivalrous. Young adults often establish more mutual relationships with their parents, and most middle-aged adults continue to experience mutually supportive relationships with their elderly parents until some experience middle generation squeeze and caregiver burden.

15.6 Diverse Family Experiences

- Inadequately described by the traditional family life cycle concept are single adults (some of whom cohabit with partners), childless married couples, dual-career families, and gay and lesbian families.
- Divorce creates a crisis in the family for 1 or 2 years; most adjust, but some children of divorce living in single-parent and reconstituted families experience long-lasting adjustment problems.

15.7 The Problem of Family Violence

- Parent characteristics such as being abused, child characteristics such as a difficult temperament, and contextual factors such as lack of social support all contribute to child abuse and must be considered in formulating prevention and treatment programs.

Checking Mastery Answers

For answers to Checking Mastery questions, visit **www.cengagebrain.com**

Key Terms

Media Resources

Psychology CourseMate

Find online quizzes, flash cards, animations, video clips, experiments, interactive assessments, and other helpful study aids for this text at **www.cengagebrain.com.** You can also connect directly to the following sites:

Families

From pregnancy and parenting to community and health, this website is host to a wealth of resources having to do with families. To access, see "web links" in Psychology CourseMate at www.cengagebrain .com

Foundation for Grandparenting

The Foundation for Grandparenting is a great resource for finding materials relevant to being a better grandparent and fostering community. To access, see "web links" in Psychology CourseMate at www .cengagebrain.com

Understanding the DATA: Exercises on the Web

(www)

www.cengagebrain.com

For additional insight on the data presented in this chapter, try out the exercises for these figures in Psychology CourseMate at

www.cengagebrain.com:

Parenting in Cultural and Subcultural Context Graph Frequent use of physical discipline is more strongly linked to high levels of child aggression in cultures like Thailand, where the use of physi-

cal discipline is rare, than in cultures like Kenya, where physical discipline is widely used and accepted as normal.

Battling Family Violence Graph Empowerment training for low-income mothers under stress reduces harsh parenting practices, especially among mothers who are the most at risk of being abusive because their babies had medical problems or were born prematurely.

CengageNOW

www.cengagebrain.com

Go to www.cengagebrain.com to link to CengageNOW, your online study tool. First take the Pre-Test for this chapter to get your Personalized Study Plan, which will identify topics you need to review and direct you to online resources. Then take the Post-Test to determine what concepts you have mastered and what you still need work on.

Human Development and Psychopathology

Peggy, a 17-year-old female, was referred by her pediatrician to a child psychiatry clinic for evaluation of an eating disorder. She had lost 10 pounds in 2 months and her mother was concerned. . . . At the clinic she stated that she was not trying to lose weight, had begun to sleep poorly about 2 months ago unless she had several beers, and that she and friends "got trashed" on weekends. Her relationship with her parents was poor; she had attempted suicide a year previously with aspirin and was briefly hospitalized. The day before this evaluation she had taken a razor to school to try to cut her wrists, but it was taken away by a friend. She admitted being depressed and wanting to commit suicide and finally told of discovering that she was pregnant 4 months earlier. Her boyfriend wanted her to abort, she was ambivalent, and then she miscarried spontaneously about 2 months after her discovery. After that, "It didn't really matter how I felt about anything" (Committee on Adolescence, 1996, pp. 71–72).

1. How do developmental psychopathologists define the line between normal and abnormal development and diagnose psychological disorders across the life span?

2. What are the implications of autism and depression for infant development?

3. How do nature and nurture contribute to problems in childhood and to what extent do childhood problems such as depression carry over into later life?

4. Is a heightened vulnerability to psychological disorder in adolescence evident when we consider eating disorders, substance abuse, and depression?

5. How does the prevalence of psychological disorders change over the adult years, and what special problems are faced by older adults who develop Alzheimer's disease or other severe cognitive impairments?

depression because it is so statistically common, but a more enduring, severe, and persistent case might be.

2. *Maladaptiveness.* Does the person's behavior interfere with adaptation or pose a danger to self or others? Psychological disorders disrupt functioning and create problems for the individual, other people, or both.

3. *Personal distress.* Does the behavior cause personal anguish or discomfort? Many psychological disorders involve personal suffering and are of concern for that reason alone.

Although these general guidelines provide a start at defining abnormal behavior, and we can see how each applies to Peggy at the start of the chapter, they are vague. We must identify specific forms of statistical deviation, maladaptiveness, and personal distress.

Does Peggy have any diagnosable psychological disorders? It would seem from this description that she may have diagnosable problems with substance abuse and depression and possibly even an eating disorder. However, her pregnancy and miscarriage may have provoked her symptoms: How do we differentiate between psychological disorders and normal responses to negative life events?

We do not all have as many problems as Peggy, but it is the rare person who makes it through the life span without having at least some difficulty adapting to the challenges of living. Each phase of life poses unique challenges, and some of us inevitably run into trouble mastering them. This chapter is about psychological disorder—about some of the ways in which human development can go awry. It is about how development influences psychopathology and how psychopathology influences development. By applying knowledge of life-span human development to the study of psychological disorders, we understand them better. And by learning more about abnormal patterns of development, we gain new perspectives on the forces that guide and channel—or block and distort—human development more generally.

16.1 What Makes Development Abnormal?

Clinical psychologists, psychiatrists, and other mental health professionals struggle to define the line between normal and abnormal behavior and diagnose psychological disorders, often thinking about three broad criteria in doing so:

1. *Statistical deviance.* Does the person's behavior fall outside the normal range of behavior? By this criterion, a mild case of the "blahs" or "blues" would not be diagnosed as clinical

DSM Diagnostic Criteria

Professionals who diagnose and treat psychological disorders use the more specific diagnostic criteria in the *Diagnostic and Statistical Manual of Mental Disorders*, published in 1994 by the American Psychiatric Association (with an update, or text revision, DSM-IV-TR, in 2000). The fourth edition of this manual, known as **DSM-IV**, spells out defining features and symptoms for the range of psychological disorders. It is to be replaced in 2013 by DSM-V (a draft of which is available at www.dsm5.org). Among other things, the drafters of DSM-V have proposed a single category of "autism spectrum disorders" rather than keeping the current subcategories (see the discussion of autism later in this chapter); use of the term *intellectual disability* in place of *mental retardation*; and use of *addiction and related disorders* to better distinguish compulsive drug seeking from the increased tolerance and the withdrawal symptoms associated with some prescribed medications (American Psychiatric Association, 2010). There will also be more attention to how gender and race or ethnicity may affect diagnoses.

Because we will be looking closely at depression in this chapter, we will use it here as an example of how DSM-IV-TR defines disorders. Depression is a family of several affective or mood disorders, some relatively mild and some severe. One of the most important is **major depressive disorder**, defined in DSM-IV-TR as at least one episode of feeling profoundly depressed, sad, and hopeless, and/or losing interest in and the ability to derive pleasure from almost all activities, for at least 2 weeks (American Psychiatric Association, 2000). To qualify as having a major depressive episode, the individual must experience at least five of the following symptoms, including one of the first two, persistently during a 2-week period:

1. Depressed mood (or irritable mood in children and adolescents) nearly every day

2. Greatly decreased interest or pleasure in all, or almost all, usual activities most of the day
3. Significant weight loss when not dieting or weight gain (or for children, failure to achieve expected weight gains)
4. Insomnia or sleeping too much
5. Psychomotor agitation or sluggishness/slowing of behavior observable by other people
6. Fatigue and loss of energy
7. Feelings of worthlessness or extreme guilt
8. Decreased ability to think or concentrate or indecisiveness
9. Recurring thoughts of death, recurring suicidal ideas, or a suicide attempt or specific plan to commit suicide

In addition, the manual calls for distinguishing major depressive disorder from certain other disorders and requires that the symptoms cause significant distress or impaired functioning and are not due to the direct effects of a substance (an abused drug or a medication) or a general medical condition. In addition, the symptoms should not better be described as reactions to bereavement; to qualify as major depressive disorder, grief reactions would need to persist for more than 2 months after a death and involve serious symptomatology. This requirement is likely to be dropped in DSM-V, though, as not only bereavement but other painful life events (like the miscarriage Peggy at the start of the chapter experienced?) can trigger a depressive episode and the real issue in diagnosis is the nature, frequency, and severity of the symptoms displayed, whatever life events may have precipitated them.

By these criteria, a man suffering from major depression might, for example, feel extremely discouraged, no longer seem to care about his job or even about sexual relations with his wife, lose weight or have difficulty sleeping, speak and move slowly as though lacking the energy to perform even the simplest actions, have trouble getting his work done, dwell on how guilty he feels about his many failings, and even begin to think he would be better off dead. Major depressive disorder would not be diagnosed if the individual is merely a little "down"; many more people experience depressive symptoms than qualify as having a clinically defined depressive disorder.

Some think DSM-IV-TR does not say enough about cultural and developmental considerations (Christensen, Emde, & Fleming, 2004; Doucette, 2002), but it does note that both should be taken into account in diagnosing major depressive disorder. For example, DSM-IV-TR indicates that Asians who are depressed tend to complain of **somatic symptoms** (body symptoms such as loss of appetite, tiredness, and disruption of normal sleep patterns) rather than talking about psychological symptoms such as guilt (American Psychiatric Association, 2000). And although DSM-IV-TR takes the position that depression in a child is fundamentally similar to depression in an adult, it points out that some depressed children express their depression by being irritable rather than sad.

Developmental Psychopathology

Psychologists and psychiatrists have long brought major theories of human development to bear in attempting to understand and treat psychological disorders. Freudian psychoanalytic theory once guided most thinking about psychopathology and clinical practice; behavioral theorists have applied learning principles to the understanding and treatment of behavioral problems; and cognitive psychologists have called attention to how individuals interpret their experiences and perceive themselves.

More recently, evolutionary psychologists have begun asking interesting questions about the adaptive functions of psychological disorders—about how they may have persisted rather than being eliminated through natural selection because they help people cope with abuse and other stressors (Keller, 2008; Mealey, 2005). For example, depression may be an adaptive response to loss, helping people conserve energy and avoid further stress (Mealey, 2005).

Psychologists have now forged a new field devoted to the study of abnormal behavior from a developmental perspective—**developmental psychopathology** (Cicchetti, 2006; Cicchetti & Toth, 2009; Cummings, Davies, & Campbell, 2000; Rutter & Sroufe, 2000; Sroufe, 2009). As defined by pioneers L. Alan Sroufe and Michael Rutter (1984), developmental psychopathology is the study of the origins and course of maladaptive behavior. Developmental psychopathologists appreciate the need to evaluate abnormal development in relation to normal development and to study the two in tandem. They want to know how disorders arise and how their expression changes as the individual develops, and they search for causal pathways and mechanisms involving genes, the nervous system, the person, and the social environment that lead to normal or abnormal adjustment (Rutter & Sroufe, 2000). In doing so, they bring life span, interdisciplinary, and systems perspectives to the study of abnormal behavior, looking at the interplay among biological, psychological, and social factors over the course of development.

Psychopathology as Development, Not Disease

Some developmental psychopathologists fault DSM-IV and similar diagnostic systems for being rooted in a medical or disease model of psychopathology that views psychological problems as diseaselike entities that people either have or do not have. Alan Sroufe (2009, p. 181) puts it this way:

> Psychopathology is not a condition that some individuals simply have or are born to have; rather, it is the outcome of a developmental process. It derives from the successive adaptations of individuals in their environment across time, each adaptation providing a foundation for the next.

■ **Figure 16.1** illustrates the concept of psychopathology as development. It portrays progressive branchings that lead development on either an optimal or a less-than-optimal course. Start with the assumption that typical human genes and typical human environments normally work to push development along a normal course and pull it back on course if it strays (Grossman et al., 2003). Some individuals—even some whose genes or experiences put them at risk to develop a disorder—manage to stay on a route to competence and good adjustment. Some start out poorly but get back on a more adaptive course later; others start off well but deviate later. Still others start on a maladaptive course due to genes and early experience and deviate further from developmental norms as they age because their early problems make it harder and harder for them to master later developmental tasks and challenges (Kendler, Gardner, & Prescott, 2002).

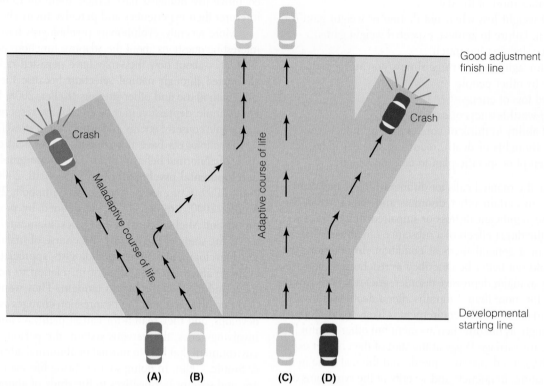

■ FIGURE 16.1 Developmental pathways leading to normal and abnormal outcomes. Some individuals start on a maladaptive course and deviate further from developmental norms as they age (route A); some start poorly but return to a more adaptive course later (route B); others stay on a route to competence and good adjustment all along (route C); and still others start off well but deviate later in life (route D). SOURCE: From Sroufe, L. A., Psychopathology as an outcome of development, *Development and Psychopathology*, Vol. 9, pp. 251–268. Copyright © Cambridge University Press. Reprinted with permission.

Now picture Figure 16.1 with many more roadways. In the developmental pathways model, change is possible at many points, and the lines between normal and abnormal development are blurred. A number of different pathways can lead to the same disorder, and the same risk factors can lead to a variety of different outcomes (Cicchetti & Toth, 2009). A model of this sort may seem complex, but it fits the facts of development.

More is being learned every day about relationships among genes, the brain, and behavior and about the role of the brain and its neurotransmitters in psychological disorders. As a result, some experts such as John March (2009) believe that psychological disorders now need to be viewed as life-span *neurodevelopmental* disorders. This neurodevelopmental perspective requires looking at normal and abnormal pathways of brain development and their implications for functioning, and intervening early with individuals who are at risk for various disorders to put them on healthier developmental trajectories.

Social Norms and Age Norms

Developmental psychopathologists appreciate that behaviors are abnormal or normal only within particular social and developmental contexts (Cummings et al., 2000; Lopez & Guarnaccia, 2000). **Social norms** are expectations about how to behave in a particular social context—whether a culture, a subculture, or an everyday setting. What is normal in one social context may be abnormal in another. For example, John Weisz and his colleagues (1997) have discovered that Thai children are more likely than American children to report (or to be reported by parents to have) symptoms of inner distress such as anxiety and depression and are less likely to engage in aggression and other forms of "acting out." One reason for the difference may be that the Thai culture places high value on emotional control and socializes children to internalize rather than vent their negative emotions (see also Weiss et al., 2009). As such findings hint, the definitions and meanings, the rates, and the developmental courses and correlates of abnormal behavior vary from culture to culture, from subculture to subculture, and from historical period to historical period (Serafica & Vargas, 2006). Although there are universal aspects of psychopathology too, it is shaped by its social context.

In addition, developmental psychopathologists recognize that abnormal behavior must be defined in relation to age norms—societal expectations about what behavior is appropriate or normal at various ages. The 4-year-old boy who frequently cries, acts impulsively, wets his bed, is afraid of the dark, and talks to his imaginary friend may be perceived as—and may be—normal. The 40-year-old who does the same things needs help! You simply

In Thailand, boys like this one are socialized to restrain their expressions of emotion rather than acting them out. As a result, children there are more prone to depression and anxiety but less aggressive than children in the United States.

cannot define abnormal behavior and development without having a solid grasp of normal behavior and development.

Developmental Issues

As they attempt to understand developmental pathways to adaptive or maladaptive functioning, developmental psychopathologists grapple with the same developmental issues that have concerned us throughout this book—most notably, the nature–nurture issue (Rutter, Moffitt, & Caspi, 2006) and the issue of continuity and discontinuity in development (Rutter, Kim-Cohen, & Maughan, 2006; and see Chapter 2). Addressing the nature–nurture issue involves asking important questions such as these:

- How do biological, psychological, and social factors interact over time to give rise to psychological disorders?
- What are the important risk factors for psychological disorders—and what are the protective factors that keep some individuals who are at risk from developing disorders?

Addressing the continuity–discontinuity issue means asking these sorts of questions:

- Are most childhood problems passing phases that have no bearing on adjustment in adulthood, or does poor functioning in childhood predict poor functioning later in life?

- How do expressions of psychopathology change as the developmental status of the individual changes?

The Diathesis–Stress Model

In their efforts to understand how nature and nurture contribute to psychopathology, developmental psychopathologists have found a **diathesis–stress model** of psychopathology useful (Coyne & Whiffen, 1995; Ingram & Price, 2001). This model proposes that psychopathology results from the interaction over time of a predisposition or vulnerability to psychological disorder (called a *diathesis*, which can involve a particular genetic makeup, physiology, set of cognitions, or personality or a combination of these) and the experience of stressful events.

Consider depression. We know that certain people are genetically predisposed to become depressed (Rice & Thapar, 2009). Genetic factors account for about 40% of the variation in a group of people in symptoms of major depressive disorder; environmental factors unique to the individual account for the rest (Glowinski et al., 2003). A genetic vulnerability to depression manifests itself as imbalances in serotonin and other key neurotransmitters that affect mood and in such characteristics as high emotional reactivity to stress, including high production of the stress hormone cortisol, and self-defeating patterns of thinking in the face of negative events (Garber & Flynn, 2001; Gotlib et al., 2006).

According to the diathesis–stress model, however, individuals predisposed to become depressed are not likely to do so unless they experience significant losses or other stressful events, as illustrated in ▪ **Figure 16.2.** One stressful life event (such as the death of a loved one or a divorce) is usually not enough to trigger major depression, but when negative events pile up or become chronic, a vulnerable person may succumb.

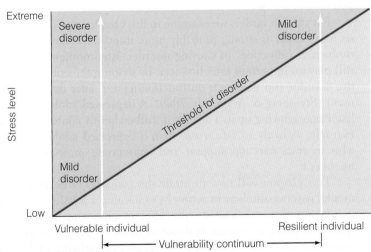

▪ **FIGURE 16.2** The diathesis–stress model. For a vulnerable individual, even mild stress can result in disorder. For an individual who is resilient and does not have a vulnerability or diathesis to disorder, it would take extremely high levels of stress to cause disorder; even then, the disorder might be only mild and temporary. SOURCE: Adapted from Ingram & Price, 2001.

Meanwhile, individuals who do not have a diathesis—a vulnerability to depression—may be able to withstand high levels of stress without becoming depressed.

Researchers can now pinpoint some of these diathesis–stress interactions. For example, inheriting a particular variant of a gene involved in controlling levels of the neurotransmitter serotonin and experiencing multiple stressful events in early adulthood results in an especially high probability of major depression (Caspi et al., 2003; and see Chapter 3). Among people with one or two of the high-risk genes, about 10% became depressed if they experienced no negative life events between ages 21 and 26, but 33% became depressed if they experienced four or more such events. By comparison, even when exposed to many stressful events, only 17% of individuals with two low-risk versions of the gene became depressed (and see Jokela et al., 2007).

Depressive disorders (and many other psychological disorders) often evolve from an interaction of diathesis and stress—or, to use familiar developmental terms, from an interaction between genes and environment. It is messier than Figure 16.2 suggests, though. For example, genes not only predispose some people to depression but also influence the extent to which they experience stressful life events (Rice, Harold, & Thapar, 2003). Moreover, the relationship between stress and disorder is reciprocal: Life stress aggravates disorder, but disorder also makes lives more stressful (Grant et al., 2004). Finally, in a person genetically predisposed to depression, a depressive episode early in life in response to intense stress may bring about changes in gene activity and in the neurobiology of the stress response system (the hypothalamic–pituitary–adrenal axis). These changes may lower the threshold for a future depressive episode (the diagonal line in Figure 16.2) so that later in life depression may reoccur even without major stressful events precipitating it (Grossman et al., 2003; Monroe & Reid, 2009).

For some disorders we examine in this chapter, the diathesis for disorder is strong, probably more important than environmental influences in causing disorder. Environment may still play an important role, however, by shaping the course of the disorder and its effects on functioning and later development (Steinberg & Avenevoli, 2000). A depressed adolescent like Peggy growing up in a hostile, disturbed family context, for example, is likely to fare worse than a depressed adolescent who receives parental support and appropriate professional treatment.

This chapter will now illustrate the concepts of developmental psychopathology in action by examining a few developmental problems associated with different phases of the life span—for example, autism to illustrate disorders arising in infancy; the concept of externalizing versus internalizing problems to illustrate childhood disorders; anorexia nervosa and substance abuse to illustrate disorders arising in adolescence; and Alzheimer's disease to illustrate disorders of old age. In addition, we look at depression in every developmental period to see how its symptoms and significance change over the life span.

Checking Mastery

1. What are two of the three broad criteria used in diagnosing psychological disorder?

2. Jake says psychological disorders are diseases that some people have and other people don't. What might a developmental psychopathologist tell Jake?

3. What is a diathesis?

Making Connections

1. What do you see as the strengths and weaknesses of the DSM-IV-TR definition of major depressive disorder (understanding that we have not quoted it in its entirety but have paraphrased its main points)?

2. How might you go about determining whether major depressive disorder, as we know it through DSM-IV's diagnostic criteria, is evident in a variety of cultures and at a variety of ages?

16.2 The Infant

Adults worry about infants who do not eat properly, who cry endlessly, or who seem overly withdrawn and timid. Because infant development is strongly channeled by biological maturation, few infants develop severe psychological problems. Yet psychological disorder exists in infancy, and its effects can be profound.

Autism

Jeremy, 3½ years old, has big brown eyes and a sturdy body. His mother carries him down the corridor toward the examiner, who greets them. Jeremy glances at the examiner's face but does not smile or say hello. They walk together into a playroom. Jeremy's mother puts him down, and he sits on the carpet in front of some toys. He picks up two blocks, bangs them together, and begins to stack the blocks, one on top of the other, not stopping until he has used the entire set. Jeremy does not look at the examiner or his mother while he works, nor when he finishes. And he does not make a sound. The examiner asks him to give her a red block. He does not respond. On their way out, Jeremy and his mother stop to look at a poster of a waterfall surrounded by redwood trees. "Yosemite Valley," Jeremy reads out—the name beneath the picture. His voice sounds automated, almost robotic. (Sigman & Capps, 1997, p. 1)

Autism, first identified and described by Leo Kanner in 1943, is a serious disorder that begins in infancy and is characterized by abnormal social development, impaired language and communication, and repetitive behavior. Picture the typical infant that we have described in this book: a social being who responds to others and forms close attachments starting at 6 or 7 months of age, a linguistic being who babbles and later uses one- and two-word sentences to converse with companions, and a curious explorer who is fascinated by new objects and experiences. Now consider the three defining features of autism highlighted in DSM-IV-TR (American Psychiatric Association, 2000; also see Bowler, 2007; Frith, 2003):

1. *Abnormal social development.* Autistic children have difficulty forming normal social relationships, responding appropriately to social cues, and sharing social experiences with other people. Like Jeremy, they seem to live in a world of their own, as though they find social contact aversive rather than pleasurable. They are far less likely than other infants to make eye contact, jointly attend to something with a social partner, seek other people for comfort, snuggle when held, and make friends. They also have great difficulty reading other people's minds and emotions, responding with empathy when others are distressed, and demonstrating self-awareness and self-conscious emotions such as embarrassment and guilt. Although many autistic children form secure attachments to their parents, many others display what Chapter 14 described as a disorganized–disoriented pattern of attachment (Sigman & Capps, 1997). Interestingly, Marinus van IJzendoorn and his colleagues (2007) have found that the parents of children with autism are no less sensitive than the parents of children without it, but that the usual relationship between sensitive parenting and secure attachment does not hold true for families with a child who has autism. Instead, the extent of the child's social deficits largely governs how secure the parent–child relationship can become.

2. *Impaired language and communicative skills.* Some autistic children are mute; others acquire language skills with some degree of success but still cannot communicate—that is, carry on a true conversation (Tager-Flusberg, 2000). As infants, autistic children often do not babble, gesture, or speak single words at the normal ages (Filipek et al., 2000). When they do speak, they may use a flat, robotlike tone; reverse pronouns (for example, use "you" to refer to the self); and engage in **echolalia** (a parroting of what someone else says).

3. *Repetitive, stereotyped behavior and restricted interests.* Autistic children seek sameness and repetition. They engage in stereotyped behaviors such as rocking, flapping their hands in front of their faces, or spinning toys; if they are more intellectually able, they may carry out elaborate rituals such as a particular sequence of getting-dressed activities. They also become obsessed with particular objects and interests and can become highly distressed when their physical environment is altered (as when a chair in the living room is moved a few feet).

It is important to recognize that individuals with autism vary greatly in the degree and nature, and probably the causes, of their deficits—so much so that some experts talk of "autisms" rather than autism (Jones & Klin, 2009). There is a whole family of autistic conditions, called **autism spectrum disorders (ASDs)**, within the DSM-IV category labeled "pervasive developmental disorders," which includes these and additional conditions that affect many aspects of functioning and have social and communication problems at their core (Bregman, 2005). Autism is an ASD; so is **Asperger syndrome,** in which the child has normal or

Many individuals with autism continue to function poorly as adolescents and adults, but some improve with age. One "improver," Jerry, described his childhood as a reign of "confusion and terror" in which "nothing seemed constant; everything was unpredictable and strange" (Bemporad, 1979, p. 192).

© Jan Sonnenmair/Aurora

above-average intelligence, good verbal skills, and a clear desire to establish social relationships but has seriously deficient social-cognitive and social-communication skills. Affected children are sometimes called "little professors" because they talk rather stiffly and formally, and at mind-numbing length, about the particular subjects that obsess them. They have been largely invisible until recently, although people around them tend to view them as odd and socially aloof.

Is There an Epidemic?

Rates of autism appear to be rising. Autism in the narrow sense affects about 20 of 10,000 children (Chakrabarti & Fombonne, 2005). According to the Centers for Disease Control and Prevention (CDC), autism in the broader sense of a spectrum of disorders affected almost 9 of 1000 8-year-olds in the United States in 2006—1 in 110, or almost 1%—more than in a previous study in 2002 (Autism and Developmental Disabilities Monitoring Network, 2009). There are four or five affected boys for every girl diagnosed with ASD.

Rates of autism have increased over the past few decades, and a debate has raged about why (Chakrabarti & Fombonne, 2005; Gillberg et al., 2006). You may have heard that either the measles virus or a mercury-based preservative in the vaccine infants receive for measles, mumps, and rubella is the culprit. The evidence simply does not support this charge, which unfortunately has made some parents fear having their children immunized. The main research study linking MMR vaccination to autism, authored by Andrew Wakefield and others, was retracted by the medical journal that published it after the General Medical Council of Great Britain found errors and irregularities in it (Editors of *The Lancet*, 2010). Rates of autism continued to climb after the mercury-based preservative (thimerosal) was removed from the vaccine in 1999 (Costello, Foley, & Angold, 2006; Vedantam, 2007). Still, because the vaccination is normally given to infants at about 15 months of age and children with autism often do not display their autistic symptoms until about that age, the vaccine myth has persisted.

Most researchers believe that increased rates of ASDs are mainly a result of increased awareness of autism, broader definitions of it to include the entire autistic spectrum (including mild cases), and better recognition and diagnosis of children who might previously have been diagnosed with language impairments or learning disabilities or simply considered as odd personalities (Benaron, 2009; Gillberg et al., 2006; Grinker, 2007). For example, autism was not added to a U. S. government list of disabilities eligible for special education services until 1991, and Asperger syndrome was not added to DSM-IV until 1994 (Grinker, 2007).

In sum, the recent rise in the prevalence of ASDs seems to be more about better detection of cases that were there all along than about new cases and causes. Still, the CDC is not quite ready to rule out the possibility that there has been a true increase in the prevalence of autism spectrum disorders (Autism and Developmental Disabilities Monitoring Network, 2009).

Characteristics

Autistic children are autistic before age 3 and probably from birth. However, because at first they often seem to be normal and exceptionally good babies, or because physicians are slow to make the diagnosis even when parents express concerns about their child's development, many autistic children have traditionally not been diagnosed until they are 5 or older and even now are usually not diagnosed until they are 2 or 3 (Benaron, 2009; Klin et al., 2004). Researchers are working furiously to improve early screening and detection because the earlier these children receive treatment, the more likely it is that they can be steered onto a more typical developmental pathway.

Autistic infants are given away by their lack of normal interest in and responsiveness to social stimuli and by their delayed language development—for example, by failure to display normal infant behaviors such as orientation to human voices, babbling, first words, preference for human over nonhuman stimuli, eye contact, visual focus on faces in a scene (autistic babies tend to focus on objects in the background), joint attention (a key precursor of theory-of-mind skills), and reciprocity or taking turns, as in mutual smiling and peekaboo games (Benaron, 2009; Klin et al., 2004; Zwaigenbaum et al., 2005). The longer they go undiagnosed, learning about the physical world but not about the social world, the more severe their social and communicative problems tend to become (Jones & Klin, 2009).

Many people believe that most autistic individuals are exceptionally intelligent. Some have average or above average IQs, but many have intellectual disabilities. Judging the intellectual functioning of individuals with autism is difficult, and their IQs have been underestimated in the past. For example, they perform considerably better on the Raven's Progressive Matrices test (a nonverbal test of fluid intelligence involving comparison of geometric patterns) than they do on the usual IQ tests, which require verbal skills and involve social interaction with a tester (Dawson et al., 2007). Moreover, because more higher functioning children are being diagnosed today, the percentage of children with autism who also show intellectual disability (an IQ of 70 or lower) is now less than 50% (Autism and Developmental Disabilities Monitoring Network, 2009). Meanwhile, some autistic individuals, whether their IQs are high or low, show special talents such as the ability to quickly calculate days of the week corresponding to dates on the calendar or to memorize incredible amounts of information about train schedules (see Heaton & Wallace, 2004; and the description of savant syndrome in Chapter 9).

Autism used to be viewed as a clear example of development that is qualitatively different from normal development. No more. The social impairment that defines autism is now viewed as the extreme end of a genetically influenced continuum of social responsiveness, quantitatively rather than qualitatively different from typical social behavior (Baron-Cohen, 2010; Constantino & Todd, 2003). In other words, many of us have some of the traits associated with autism to some degree, and the dividing line between normality and abnormality is arbitrary.

Suspected Causes

Interest in solving the mysteries of autism is intense, and some fascinating hypotheses have been put forward in recent years to explain why individuals with ASDs show the characteristics they do. Early theorists suggested that rigid and cold parenting by "refrigerator moms" caused autism, but this harmful myth has long been put to rest (Achenbach, 1982). It is now understood that interacting with an autistic child can easily cause parents to be tense and frustrated and that the parents of autistic children, the source of genes that contribute to autism, sometimes have mild autistic spectrum traits themselves. Bad parenting is not responsible for autism; rather, genes contribute strongly to autism (Curran & Bolton, 2009; Veenstra-Vanderweele & Cook, 2003). One research team found that if one identical twin was autistic, the other was autistic in 60% of the twin pairs studied; the concordance rate for fraternal twin pairs was 0% (Bailey et al., 1995). Moreover, when the broader spectrum of autism-related deficits was considered, 92% of the identical twins but only 10% of the fraternal twins were alike.

Many genes on several chromosomes, each with small effects, have been implicated (Benaron, 2009). Most likely, individuals with autism inherit several genes that put them at risk. It also appears that the three major impairments associated with autism—social impairments, communication disorders, and repetitive behaviors—have distinct genetic causes (Ronald et al., 2006).

In some cases genes related to neural communication appear to have been copied too many times or, more often, left out or copied too few times during meiosis; these "copy number variations" can be present in the parent and then inherited by the child, or they can arise as new errors (Autism Genome Project Consortium, 2007; Morrow et al., 2008). Autism occurs more often when the mother and especially the father are older; this is most likely because as we age, errors in DNA copying become more common (Gardener, Spiegelman, & Buka, 2009). When copy number errors occur, the normal process through which experience alters gene expression and guides the development of neural connections can be disrupted.

That one identical twin can develop autism but the other does not suggests that early environmental influences also contribute, although the precise mechanisms are a mystery. An environmental trigger such as a virus or chemicals in the environment could interact with a genetic predisposition to cause autism. Epigenetic influences that turn genes that guide brain development on or off are also being investigated (Benaron, 2009). Prenatal exposure to teratogens such as rubella, alcohol, and thalidomide can contribute to ASDs (Benaron, 2009). Autism also occurs more frequently when there is maternal bleeding or other complications during pregnancy (Gardener, Spiegelman, & Buka, 2009), so there are many possible environmental contributors.

Many autistic children display neurological abnormalities, and many of them have epilepsy (Volkmar et al., 2004). However, the neurological abnormalities are varied, and it is not yet clear which are most central to autism or how they arise. One leading hypothesis is that in children who later develop ASDs, neurons in the frontal cortex and certain other areas of the brain proliferate wildly during the early sensitive period for brain development in infancy; these neurons, however, do not become properly interconnected with other areas of the brain so that they can integrate brain signals from these other areas (Benaron, 2009; Courchesne, Carper, & Akshoomoff, 2003). This early brain overgrowth hypothesis has also focused on the amygdala, a part of the forebrain implicated in social and emotional behavior. Toddlers with autism have especially large amygdalas, and the extent of their social and communication impairments is correlated with the size of their amygdalas (Schumann et al., 2009).

Researchers also have been actively exploring a **mirror neuron hypothesis** of autism. This view holds that malfunctioning of mirror neuron systems located in a number of brain areas accounts for the deficits individuals with autism show in imitation, theory-of-mind skills, empathy, and language (Oberman & Ramachandran, 2007; and see Chapter 13). Mirror neuron systems allow us to make sense of other people's feelings and thoughts by reacting to them as though they were feelings and thoughts we have experienced ourselves. In one study (McIntosh et al., 2006), autistic and nonautistic adults watched pictures of happy and angry facial expressions so that the researchers could see if their faces automatically and subtly mimicked the expressions they saw—a good example of how mirror neurons allow us to simulate other people's emotions and relate them to our own. Although people with autistic disorders could mimic the faces they saw if asked to do so, they did not do so spontaneously—one example of accumulating evidence suggesting that their mirror neuron systems do not function properly (Oberman & Ramachandran, 2007).

It is too soon to say whether lack of connectedness between the frontal cortex and other brain areas, overgrowth of the amygdala, lack of properly functioning mirror neuron systems, and/or other neural impairments will prove to be at the heart of the problems children with ASDs display. It *is* clear that the disorder involves multiple cognitive impairments. Autistic individuals not only have social cognitive deficits but they have difficulty with certain **executive functions,** the higher level control functions based in the prefrontal cortex of the brain that allow us to plan, change flexibly from one course of action to another, and inhibit actions (Bowler, 2007; Frith, 2003). This may explain their repetitive behavior (they often become fixated on doing an activity again and again and are not able to switch to another activity). In addition, their tendency to focus on details, a strength on some tasks, is accompanied by difficulty integrating pieces of information to get "the big picture," or overall meaning (Bowler, 2007; Frith, 2003). One recent study suggests that difficulties both with executive functions and with integrating multiple pieces of information may underlie the difficulties children with ASDs have with social cognition, as reflected by their poor performance on theory-of-mind tasks (Pellicano, 2010).

To make the mystery of autism even more intriguing, Simon Baron-Cohen (2003) has put forth an **extreme male brain hypothesis** regarding autistic spectrum disorders, described in the Exploration Box 16.1. Perhaps it is not surprising that a number of cognitive and social deficits have been nominated as the "core" deficit in autism and a number of aspects of brain functioning are believed to be impaired; autism spectrum disorders are, after all, *pervasive* disorders, and most likely there are many such disorders with many different causes.

Developmental Outcomes and Treatment

What becomes of children with autism as they get older? The long-term outcome in the past has usually been poor, especially if autism is accompanied by intellectual disability. Most individuals with autism improve in functioning, but they are usually autistic for life (Howlin et al., 2004). Positive outcomes are most likely among those who have IQ scores above 70 and reasonably good communication skills by age 5.

Can treatment help autistic children overcome their problems? Some autistic children are given drugs to control behavioral problems such as hyperactivity or obsessive–compulsive behavior or drugs such as antipsychotics and antidepressants that help them benefit from educational programs but do not cure autism (Benaron, 2009; Volkmar, 2001). Nasal administration of oxytocin, the hormone discussed in Chapter 14 that facilitates social relationships, appears to improve attention to other people's eyes and social interest and understanding in high-functioning individuals with autism; however, since the effects of such doses are short-lived, it is not clear whether oxytocin would work as a long-term treatment (Andari et al., 2010). Researchers continue to search for drugs that will correct the suspected brain dysfunctions of these individuals, but there is probably no one "magic pill."

The most effective approach to treating autism is intensive and highly structured behavioral and educational programming,

Is Autism an Extreme Version of the Male Brain?

Simon Baron-Cohen (2003, 2010) has proposed an extreme male brain hypothesis about the origin of autism that attributes it to a brain that is strong in "masculine" but weak in "feminine" mental skills. In his book *The Essential Difference,* Baron-Cohen lays out evidence that females tend to excel in empathizing (identifying people's thoughts and emotions and responding to them with appropriate emotions), males in systemizing (analyzing things to figure out how they work, extracting rules that determine what leads to what, and understanding systems). So, for example, little girls tend to be more interested than little boys in faces and in interacting with people, and women tend to be more able than men to read facial expressions of emotions and more likely to enter the helping professions. Meanwhile, little boys are more likely than little girls to enjoy playing with cars and trucks and building blocks and are more likely as adults to go into math, science, and engineering fields where they can work with predictable systems of objects rather than with ever-unpredictable people.

Baron-Cohen is quick to note that not all women excel at empathizing and not all men excel at systemizing; there are simply average differences between the sexes, most likely caused by a combination of biological and environmental factors. Moreover, some people are strong at both or weak in both skills. Of interest to us here are the individuals who are extremely weak in empathizing and extremely strong in systemizing. They, Baron-Cohen argues, have the traits associated with autistic spectrum disorders. Much evidence suggests that individuals with autism and autism spectrum disorders have difficulty reading other people's mental

states and empathizing (Baron-Cohen, 2003; Golan et al., 2006). Moreover, their repetitive actions (spinning plates or dropping sand through their fingers for hours) could be interpreted as attempts to systemize, to figure out the rules, and their desire for sameness an attempt to keep the world orderly and rule governed.

Baron-Cohen's team (Auyeung et al., 2009a) has assessed empathizing and systemizing in both typically developing children and children with autism spectrum disorders. Among children ages 4 to 11, boys outscore girls in systemizing and girls outscore boys in empathizing, as expected. More interestingly, children with autistic spectrum disorders outperform typically developing boys in systemizing skills but do worse than typically developing boys in empathizing, regardless of their gender.

Baron-Cohen cites concrete cases of the extreme male brain at work. Richard, an award-winning mathematician, has Asperger syndrome. Despite his understanding of the mechanics of phones, he did not know how to begin or end a phone conversation or what to say in between. He much preferred dealing with people one at a time rather than in groups, because people were too unpredictable for him. Noting that Isaac Newton and Albert Einstein had some similar traits, Baron-Cohen points out that Asperger syndrome is common in families with many "male-brained" scientists and engineers. He and his colleagues are now offering preliminary evidence that high exposure to the male hormone testosterone prenatally is associated with autistic traits and may help explain why autism spectrum disorders are so much more common among males than among

Ann Cutting/Workbook Stock/Getty Images

females (see Auyeung, et al., 2009b; Ingudomnukul et al., 2007).

The extreme male brain hypothesis implies that autism, once thought to be a prime example of truly deviant human development, instead represents the extreme end of a continuum of intellectual functioning. The extreme male brain hypothesis also calls attention to the strengths of individuals with autism and suggests that if accommodations are made for their cognitive style, they can learn better and can be steered toward the kinds of mechanical and detail-oriented jobs that most suit them. Chances are that the extreme male brain hypothesis will not explain everything about autism, but it clearly merits further exploration.

---

beginning as early as possible, continuing throughout childhood, and involving the family (Koegel, Koegel, & McNerney, 2001; Simpson & Otten, 2005). The goal is to make the most of the plasticity of the young brain during its sensitive period for development. O. Ivar Lovaas and his colleagues pioneered the application of reinforcement principles to shape social and language skills in children with autism (Lovaas & Smith, 2003). In an early study, Lovaas (1987) compared a group that received intensive

treatment—more than 40 hours a week of one-on-one training for 2 or more years during their preschool years—with a control group of similarly disturbed children who, because of staff shortages or transportation problems, received treatment for only 10 or fewer hours a week.

Trained student therapists worked with the children using reinforcement principles to reduce their aggressive and self-stimulatory behavior and to teach them developmentally appropriate skills such as how to imitate others, play with toys and with peers, and use language. Parents were taught to use the same behavioral techniques at home. Lovaas reported astounding results—for example, IQ scores about 30 points higher in the treatment group than in the control group. Other researchers have criticized this study's design, however, because it was not a true experiment with random assignment to treatment and control groups.

Subsequent research indicates that early behavioral interventions usually do not convert children with autism into typically functioning children (Klinger & Williams, 2009; Volkmar et al., 2004). And although children with autism can be taught social scripts such as how to make eye contact, smile, and introduce themselves to another person, the training may not generalize easily to other situations—and there are many, many such social scripts to be taught (Klinger & Williams, 2009). Nonetheless, many children with autism, especially those who are young and do not have severe intellectual disabilities, make significant gains if they receive intensive cognitive and behavioral training and comprehensive family services starting early in life (Benaron, 2009; Lovaas & Smith, 2003). Training programs for the growing number of adults with autism and support services for their families are also advised.

Depression

Does it seem possible to you that an infant could experience major depressive disorder as defined in DSM-IV-TR? Infants are surely not capable of the negative cognitions common among depressed adults—the low self-esteem, guilt, worthlessness, hopelessness, and so on (Garber, 1984). After all, they have not yet acquired the capacity for symbolic thought or self-awareness that would allow them to reflect on their experience. Yet infants *can* exhibit some of the behavioral symptoms (such as loss of interest in activities or psychomotor slowing) and somatic, or body, symptoms of depression. Researchers are still debating whether true depressive disorders can occur in infancy, but it is clear that babies can and do experience depression-like states and symptoms (Cytryn & McKnew, 1996; Wasserman, 2006).

Depressive symptoms are most likely to be observed in infants who lack a secure attachment relationship or who experience a disruption of an all-important attachment (Boris & Zeanah, 1999; Lyons-Ruth, Zeanah, & Benoit, 2003). It has long been observed that infants permanently separated from their mothers between 6 and 12 months of age tend to become sad, weepy, listless, unresponsive, and withdrawn and to show delays in virtually all aspects of their development (Spitz, 1946). Infants who display a disorganized pattern of attachment, in which they do not seem to know whether to approach or avoid the attachment figure (see Chapter 14)—an attachment style common among abused children—are especially likely to show symptoms of depression (Egeland & Carlson, 2004; Lyons-Ruth, Zeanah, & Benoit, 2003).

Infants whose mothers—or fathers—are depressed are also at risk (Gotlib et al., 2006; Ramchandani et al., 2005). These babies adopt an interaction style that resembles that of their de-

pressed caregivers; they vocalize little and look sad, even when interacting with women other than their mothers, and show developmental delays (Field, 1995). They are at increased risk of becoming clinically depressed themselves later in life and of developing other psychological disorders. This may be because of a combination of genes and stressful experiences with their unpredictable mothers (that is, because of diathesis–stress). Stress early in life, it turns out, can produce children with an overactive stress-response system who are easily distressed, cannot regulate their negative emotions, and are more reactive to stress later in life (Gotlib et al., 2006; Gunnar & Quevedo, 2007; Wismer Fries, Shirtcliff, & Pollak, 2008). As we saw in Chapter 14, though, interventions can help depressed parents interact more sensitively with their babies.

Some infants who are neglected, abused, separated from attachment figures, or otherwise raised in a stressful or unaffectionate manner by a mother who may be stressed or de-

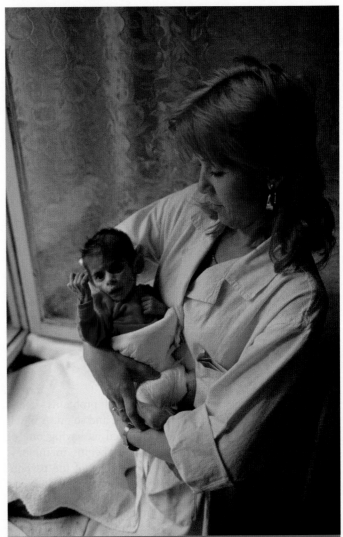

© Peter Turnley/Corbis

Failure to thrive can have either physical (organic) or emotional (nonorganic) causes. This Romanian boy has AIDS and is very ill.

pressed herself not only display depression-like symptoms but also may develop the life-threatening disorder called **failure to thrive** (Benoit & Coolbear, 2004; Chatoor & Ganiban, 2004). These youngsters fail to grow normally, lose weight, and become seriously underweight for their age—and are often developmentally delayed as a result. In some cases a physical cause such as a heart defect or swallowing problem can be identified, but in other cases, labeled nonorganic failure to thrive, the causes seem to be more emotional than physical (Chatoor & Ganiban, 2004; Lyons-Ruth, Zeanah, & Benoit, 2003; Stewart, 2007). Babies with nonorganic failure to thrive may gain weight and overcome their depression-like emotional symptoms quickly if they are removed from their homes but can relapse if they are returned to the insensitive care they were receiving (Bauchner, 1996). Intervening to change the family system—for example, to treat a stressed, abusive mother and help her parent more effectively—is therefore critical.

Checking Mastery

1. What three major characteristics would you expect to see in a child with autism?

2. If you were told that your son with autism has an "extreme male brain," what would that really mean?

3. Can an infant qualify as having major depressive disorder as defined in DSM-IV-TR?

Making Connections

1. How do you think the now discredited view that autism is caused by cold, "refrigerator" mothers arose, and how would you now characterize the parents of children with autism?

2. Why do you think the idea that autism can be caused by vaccinations, or a preservative that used to be put in vaccinations, has persisted so long despite a lack of solid evidence?

16.3 The Child

Many children experience developmental problems—fears, recurring stomachaches, temper tantrums, and so on. A much smaller proportion are officially diagnosed as having one of the psychological disorders that typically begins in infancy, childhood, or adolescence—or as having one of the psychological disorders (such as major depressive disorder) that can occur at a variety of ages. ● **Table 16.1** lists the major childhood disorders categorized in DSM-IV-TR. In a study assessing children longitudinally from age 9 to age 16 through detailed interviews with both parents and children, more than one-third of children were judged to have experienced at least one diagnosable psychological disorder by age 16 (Costello et al., 2003).

● **TABLE 16.1** **SOME PSYCHOLOGICAL DISORDERS USUALLY FIRST DIAGNOSED IN INFANCY, CHILDHOOD, OR ADOLESCENCE**

DSM-IV-TR Category	Major Examples
Mental retardation	Subaverage general intellectual functioning
Learning disorders	Reading, math, and writing difficulties
Motor skill disorder	Developmental coordination disorder (extreme clumsiness, lack of coordination)
Communication disorders	Expressive language disorder; stuttering
Pervasive developmental disorders	Autism; similarly severe conditions
Attention deficit and disruptive behavioral disorders	Attention deficit hyperactivity disorder; conduct disorders (persistent antisocial behavior); oppositional defiant disorder
Feeding and eating disorders	Pica (eating nonnutritive substances such as paint or sand)
Tic disorders	Tourette's disorder (involuntary grimaces, grunts, foul language)
Elimination disorders	Enuresis (inappropriate urination); encopresis (inappropriate defecation)

SOURCE: Based on *DSM-IV-TR*, American Psychiatric Association, 2000, Arlington, VA.

Externalizing and Internalizing Problems

Many developmental problems of childhood can be placed in one of two broad categories that reflect whether the child's behavior is out of control or overly controlled (Achenbach & Edelbrock, 1978). When children have **externalizing problems,** or undercontrolled disorders, they act out in ways that disturb other people and violate social expectations. They may be aggressive, disobedient, difficult to control, or disruptive (see the discussions of attention deficit hyperactivity disorder in Chapter 6 and of aggressive behavior and conduct disorder in Chapter 13). **Internalizing problems,** or overcontrolled disorders, involve inner distress; they are more disruptive to the child than to other people and include anxiety disorders (such as persistent worrying about separation from loved ones), phobias, severe shyness and withdrawal, and depression. Negative emotions are internalized, or bottled up, rather than externalized, or expressed.

Externalizing behaviors decrease from age 4 to age 18, whereas internalizing difficulties increase (Bongers et al., 2003). Externalizing problems are typically more common among boys, whereas internalizing problems are more prevalent among girls, and this is true across cultures (Crijnen, Achenbach, & Verhulst, 1997). Children from families with low socioeconomic status show more externalizing and internalizing problems than children with higher socioeconomic status do, partly because their environments are more stressful (Amone-P'Olak et al., 2009).

How do externalizing and internalizing problems arise, and to what extent do such problems in childhood spell trouble later in life? These questions concern the issues of nature–nurture and continuity–discontinuity in development.

Nature and Nurture

Most of us have a strong belief in the power of the social environment, particularly the family, to shape child development. This belief in a parent effects model (see Chapter 15) often leads us to blame parents—especially mothers—if their children are sad and withdrawn, uncontrollable and "bratty," or otherwise different from most children. Parents whose children develop problems often draw the same conclusion, feeling guilty because they assume they are at fault.

Instead, we must view developmental disorders from a family systems perspective and appreciate how emerging problems affect and are affected by family interactions. We should understand that problems are located not in an individual family member but in a whole family (Cowan & Cowan, 2006). From a family systems perspective, parents are important but they both influence and are influenced by their children, and the family also functions in a larger environment that influences it.

It is true that youngsters with depression, conduct disorder, and many other psychological disorders tend to come from problem-ridden families and to have insecure attachments to their parents (Graham & Easterbrooks, 2000). They are also more likely than other children to have mothers, fathers, or both who have histories of psychological disorder (Connell & Goodman, 2002; Ramchandani et al., 2005). But does this mean that children develop problems because they live in disturbed family environments with adults whose own psychological problems make it difficult for them to parent effectively, or are there other possibilities?

A child may have a genetically based predisposition to disorder that would be expressed even if the child were adopted into another home early in life (Plomin et al., 2008). In addition, "poor parenting" can be partly the effect of a child's disorder rather than its cause; children's problem behaviors can negatively affect their parents' moods, marital relationships, and parenting behaviors (Cowan & Cowan, 2006).

Unquestionably, stress on a family and the ineffective parenting that sometimes results from it contribute to and aggravate many childhood problems. To illustrate, Exploration Box 16.2 looks at how the stressful experiences associated with Hurricane Katrina gave rise to high rates of externalizing and internalizing problems in affected children and adolescents. There is also plenty of evidence that the children of parents who have psychological disorders may or may not develop disorders themselves depending on whether their parents are able to parent them effectively (Johnson et al., 2001) and that children with temperaments that predispose them to externalizing or internalizing problems can be protected from problems by warm, loving parents but hurt by rejecting ones (Sentse et al., 2009). As the diathesis–stress model suggests, then, disorders often arise from the toxic interaction of a genetic vulnerability and stressful experiences. Abnormal development, like normal development, is the product of both nature and nurture and of a history of complex transactions between person and environment in which each influences the other (Rutter, Moffitt, & Caspi, 2006).

Continuity and Discontinuity

The parents of children who develop psychological problems often want to know this: Will my child outgrow these problems, or will they persist? These parents are understandably concerned with the issue of continuity versus discontinuity in development. You have already seen that autism persists beyond childhood in most individuals, but what about the broader spectrum of childhood problems?

Avshalom Caspi and his colleagues (1996) used data from a longitudinal study in New Zealand to determine whether children's behavioral styles, or temperamental characteristics, at age 3 predicted their susceptibility to psychological disorders at age 21—a span of 18 years. Children who had externalizing problems (such as aggression) as young children and were described as irritable, impulsive, and rough were more likely than either inhibited, overcontrolled children or well-adjusted children to be diagnosed as having antisocial personality disorder and to have records of criminal behavior as young adults. Meanwhile, internalizers—inhibited children who were extremely shy, anxious, and upsettable at age 3—were more likely than other children to be diagnosed as depressed, although not suffering from anxiety disorder, as young adults. This study and others point to *continuity* in susceptibility to problems over the years and suggest that early problems tend to have significance for later development (Costello et al., 2003; Jokela, Ferrie, & Kivimäki, 2009; Mesman, Bongers, & Koot, 2001).

Relationships between early behavioral problems and later psychopathology tend to be weak, however, so there is also *discontinuity* in development. In Caspi's study, most children with temperaments that put them at risk did *not* have diagnosable problems as adults. Similarly, in a 14-year follow-up of children and adolescents with behavioral and emotional problems, about 40% still had significant problems in adulthood, but most did not (Hofstra, Van der Ende, & Verhulst, 2000). In short, having psychological problems as a child does not doom most individuals to a life of maladjustment.

Why might we see continuity of problem behavior in some children but discontinuity in others? If children have mild rather than severe psychological problems and receive help, their difficulties are likely to disappear. That means identifying children

Hurricane Katrina and Child Mental Health

In the years since Hurricane Katrina struck New Orleans and other parts of the Gulf Coast in 2005, researchers have been busily studying its impacts on the mental health of affected individuals. It has become clear that the hurricane has had negative and quite long-lasting effects on the mental health of both adults and children. In one study, adults who had experienced Katrina were compared to adults in the same area who had participated in a national study to detect psychological disorders 2–4 years before Katrina. Diagnosable disorders were detected in more than 30% of the adults interviewed after Katrina, almost double the 16% rate found in the adults interviewed before Katrina (Kessler et al., 2006). Several studies of children have also been conducted. In one (Roberts et al., 2010), children aged 11–18 were surveyed about their symptoms of depression, anxiety, and posttraumatic stress disorder 2 years after Katrina and were asked to recall their symptoms before Katrina and 1 year after it. Although this retrospective reporting approach has limitations, the prevalence of reported symptoms was 44% to 104% higher 2 years after Katrina than before Katrina, and respondents claimed most of their symptoms began after Katrina.

Other studies point to especially high rates of symptoms of posttraumatic stress disorder (PTSD) symptoms such as flashbacks, nightmares, and feelings of anxiety and helplessness. Howard Osofsky and his colleagues (2009) assessed 22 PTSD-related symptoms in children and adolescents in grade 4 through grade 12 (ages 7–19) and attempted to identify factors associated with high symptom scores. Most of these children saw their neighborhoods destroyed and had personal belongings destroyed or damaged; almost a third were separated from a caregiver or from a pet; and about 13% had a family member or friend killed. Moving was a common part of these children's experience too; they had lived in an average of three places after the hurricane, and fewer than half had returned to their original homes.

In all, 49% exceeded the cutoff score for referral to mental health services based on their posttraumatic stress symptoms in 2005–2006, and more than 41% still ex-

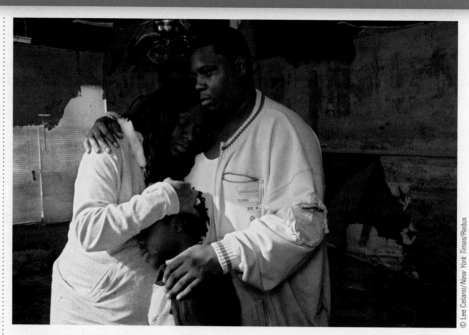

Jeralyn and Whitney Marcell stand with their son Rashad, age 10, in the home they had just bought in New Orleans after it was ravaged by Katrina. The family resettled in Atlanta. Hurricane Katrina was a tremendously stressful experience for affected families like the Marcells and raised rates internalizing and externalizing problems among children. Lessons from Katrina may be helpful in working with the families affected by the disastrous earthquakes in Haiti and Chile and disasters yet to come.

ceeded the cutoff a year later. (See also Moore & Varela, 2010, who found that 46% of fourth- to sixth-graders surveyed almost 3 years after the hurricane showed moderate to severe PTSD symptoms.) Which children were most affected? Those who showed significant posttraumatic stress problems tended to be those who had experienced previous traumas in their lives and who suffered the most trauma as a result of Katrina (especially property loss, separation from a caregiver or other significant personal losses, and life in a trailer or shelter).

Another team of researchers (McLaughlin et al., 2009), studying children and adolescents ages 4–17, also found associations between emotional problems and stressors such as losing a loved one or experiencing physical adversity. Parent psychopathology was another influential factor, whether because parent and child shared a genetically based vulnerability to psychological disorder, because parents with psychological problems tend to be ineffective parents, or both. Whether caregivers serve as caring, effective parents who can help their children cope with adversity, or have so

many posttraumatic stress symptoms of their own that they become unavailable and ineffective parents, has emerged as a critical factor in the adjustment of children to Katrina and other disasters (Gil-Rivas et al., 2010).

This research illustrates the importance of adopting an ecological or contextual perspective on development and seeing children's mental health as influenced by their sociocultural and historical environment. It testifies to the damaging effects of traumatic and stressful events on children but also sensitizes us to the need to look at a variety of factors to determine why some children are more vulnerable than others—factors such as the extent of exposure to traumatic events, preexisting characteristics of the child, the child's coping resources, and the child's family and community environment after the disaster (Silverman, Allen, & Ortiz, 2010). Fortunately, a variety of preventive interventions can reduce the psychological harm done by natural disasters like Katrina and other traumatic events (Silverman, Allen, & Ortiz, 2010; Wethington et al., 2008).

who are likely to have recurring internalizing and externalizing problems early and targeting them for treatment are critical (Essex et al., 2009). Some children also show remarkable resilience, functioning well despite exposure to risk factors for disorder or overcoming even severe early problems to become well adjusted (Garmezy, 1994; Small & Memmo, 2004). Resilient children appear to benefit from protective factors such as their own competencies (especially intellectual ability and social skills) and strong social support (especially a stable family situation with at least one caring parent figure). Let us look more closely at one childhood problem: depression, an internalizing disorder.

Depression

As you saw earlier, the depression-like symptoms displayed by deprived or traumatized infants probably do not qualify as major depressive disorder. When, then, can children experience true clinical depression? For years many psychologists and psychiatrists, especially those influenced by psychoanalytic theory, argued that young children simply could not be depressed. Feelings of worthlessness, hopelessness, and self-blame were not believed to be possible until the child was older (Garber, 1984). Besides, childhood is supposedly a happy, carefree time, right?

We now know that young children—as early as age 3—can meet the same criteria for major depressive disorder that are used in diagnosing adults (Garber & Flynn, 2001; Wasserman, 2006). Depression in children is rarer than depression in adolescents and adults, but an estimated 2% of children have diagnosable depressive disorders (Gotlib & Hammen, 1992). It used to be thought that depression in children was expressed in a "masked" manner as other problems. Many youngsters who show the key symptoms of depression do have other problems such as conduct

Even young children can experience a major depressive episode.

© Jose Luis Pelaez, Inc./Corbis

disorder, attention deficit hyperactivity disorder, and anxiety disorder. This co-occurrence of two or more psychiatric conditions in the same individual is called **comorbidity** and is very common throughout the life span. Disorders that are comorbid with depression in childhood are distinct diagnoses, though, not veiled symptoms of depression (Kaslow et al., 2000).

Developmentalists appreciate that depression expresses itself somewhat differently in a young child than in an adult, however (Weiss & Garber, 2003). Like depressed infants, depressed preschool children are more likely to display the behavioral and somatic symptoms of depression (losing interest in activities, eating poorly, and so on) than to display cognitive symptoms like hopelessness or to talk about being depressed (American Psychiatric Association, 2000; Kaslow et al., 2000). They are also prone to be anxious (Moffitt et al., 2007). Yet as early as age 3 children who are depressed sometimes express excessive shame or guilt—claiming, for example, that they are bad (Luby et al., 2009; Weiss & Garber, 2003)—and some act out themes of death and suicide in their play (Luby, 2004). Most important, depressed children are sad or irritable and show the same lack of interest in usually enjoyable activities that depressed adults do (Luby, 2004; Luby et al., 2006).

Children as young as age 2 or 3 are even capable of attempting suicide (Rosenthal & Rosenthal, 1984; Shaffer & Pfeffer, 2001). At age 3, Jeffrey repeatedly hurled himself down a flight of stairs and banged his head on the floor; upset by the arrival of a new brother, he was heard to say, "Jeff is bad, and bad boys have to die" (Cytryn & McKnew, 1996, p. 72). An 8-year-old, after writing her will, approached her father with a large rock and asked in all seriousness, "Daddy, would you crush my head, please?" (Cytryn & McKnew, 1996, pp. 69–70). Other children have jumped from high places, run into traffic, and stabbed themselves, often in response to abuse, rejection, or neglect. Moreover, children who attempt suicide once often try again (Shaffer & Pfeffer, 2001). The moral is clear: Parents, teachers, and human service professionals need to appreciate that childhood is not always a happy, carefree time and that children can develop serious depressive disorders and suicidal tendencies. Children's claims that they want to die should be taken dead seriously.

Do depressed children tend to have recurring bouts of depression, becoming depressed adolescents and adults? Most children make it through mild episodes of sadness, and carryover of depression problems from childhood to adulthood is not as strong as carryover from adolescence to adulthood (Rutter, Kim-Cohen, & Maughan, 2006). However, 5- and 6-year-olds who report many symptoms of depression are more likely than their peers to be depressed as adolescents, to think suicidal thoughts, to struggle academically, and to be perceived as in need of mental health services (Ialongo, Edelsohn, & Kellam, 2001). Moreover, it is estimated that half of children and adolescents diagnosed as having major depressive disorder have recurrences in adulthood (Kessler, Avenevoli, & Merikangas, 2001).

Fortunately, most depressed children—and children with other psychological disorders too—respond well to psychotherapy (Carr, 2009; Kazdin, 2003; Weisz & Weiss, 1993). **Cognitive behavioral therapy**, a well-established psychotherapy approach that identifies and changes distorted thinking and the maladaptive emotions and behavior that stem from it, has proved espe-

Challenges in Treating Children

The first challenge in treating children with psychological problems is getting them to treatment. According to the Surgeon General of the United States, fewer than one in five U.S. children with psychological disorders receives treatment (Shute, 2001). Sometimes the child does not think she has a problem and resists; sometimes parents cannot face reality. Other times, parents are dismissed by doctors or other professionals who say that that they are worrying too much or that their child is only going through "a phase" (Carter, Briggs-Gowan, & Davis, 2004). Cost factors also enter in.

Assuming children do enter treatment, the next challenge is to recognize that they are not adults and cannot be treated as such (Holmbeck, Greenley, & Franks, 2003; Kazdin, 2003). Because children are usually referred for treatment by parents who are disturbed by their behavior, therapists must view the child and her parents as the "client."

Children's therapeutic outcomes often depend greatly on the cooperation and involvement of their parents (Bailey, 2000; Heru, 2006), but not all parents cooperate.

Finally, children function at different levels of cognitive and emotional development than adults do, and this must be taken into consideration in both diagnosing and treating their problems—a point familiar to students of human development (Kazdin, 2000). For example, young children cannot easily participate in therapies that require them to verbalize their problems and gain insight into the causes of their behavior. A more developmentally appropriate approach for young children is play therapy, in which disturbed children are encouraged to act out concerns that they cannot easily express in words (see Schaefer, 2010). Behavioral approaches that do not require insight and verbal skills are also effective with young children.

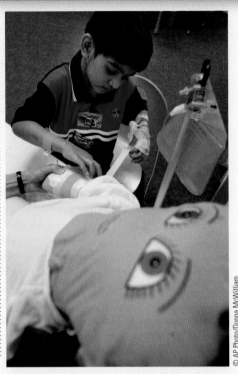

Play therapy can help young children who lack verbal skills express their feelings. Here it is used to help Ashwin Balaji, age 4, deal with his anxieties about his upcoming surgery.

cially effective, even though it requires more cognitive and verbal ability of the child than strictly behavioral treatments (Brent & Maalouf, 2009; Weisz, McCarty, & Valeri, 2006). Because children are not adults, though, treating children with depression and other psychological disorders poses several special challenges, as Application Box 16.1 reveals.

Many depressed children have also been treated with antidepressant drugs called selective serotonin reuptake inhibitors, such as Prozac (fluoxetine), that correct for low levels of the neurotransmitter serotonin in the brains of depressed individuals. However, these drugs do not appear to be as effective with children as with adults, and some research has suggested that they may increase the risk of suicidal thoughts and behavior among child and adolescent users; a warning regarding the possibility of increased suicidality in these patients was issued by the U.S. Food and Drug Administration in 2004 (Vedantam, 2006; Vitiello, Zuvekas, & Norquist, 2006). Antidepressants are still prescribed for seriously depressed youth who are likely to be at even greater risk of suicide if they are not treated with medication. However, they are prescribed less often and with more careful monitoring of the child's reactions (Nemeroff et al., 2007). A combination of Prozac and cognitive behavioral therapy appears to be the best treatment currently available for seriously de-

pressed children and adolescents (Brent & Maalouf, 2009). Because depressed children often have depressed parents, adopting a family systems approach and treating the depressed parent as well is likely to improve outcomes for depressed children even more (Brent & Maalouf, 2009).

Checking Mastery

1. What is another term for overcontrolled problems in childhood, and what are two examples of such problems?

2. What are two factors that might make it less likely that a childhood problem will carry over into adolescence and adulthood?

3. How does depression in childhood differ from depression in adulthood?

Making Connections

1. Why do you think some children exposed to stressful events like Hurricane Katrina develop externalizing problems, whereas others develop internalizing problems?

2. If your child were depressed, would you allow her to be treated with antidepressant medication? What do you see as the pros and cons?

16.4 The Adolescent

If any age group has a reputation for having problems and causing trouble, it is adolescents. This is supposedly the time when angelic children are transformed into emotionally unstable, unruly, problem-ridden delinquents. The view that adolescence is a time of emotional storm and stress was set forth by the founder of developmental psychology, G. Stanley Hall (1904). It has been with us ever since.

Storm and Stress?

Are adolescents really more likely than either children or adults to experience psychological problems? On one hand, adolescents have a worse reputation than they deserve. Most adolescents are not emotionally disturbed and do not develop serious problem behaviors such as drug abuse and chronic delinquency. Instead, significant mental health problems—real signs of storm and stress—characterize about 20% of adolescents, those like Peggy, described at the beginning of the chapter (Ford, Goodman, & Meltzer, 2003; Kazdin, 2000). Moreover, many of these adolescents were maladjusted before they reached puberty and continue to be maladjusted during adulthood (Reinherz et al., 1999).

Yet there is some truth in the storm-and-stress view. Adolescence is a period of risk taking, of problem behaviors such as substance abuse and delinquency, and of heightened vulnerability to some forms of psychological disorder (Cicchetti & Rogosch, 2002; Steinberg, 2008). The 20% rate of diagnosable psychological disorders at a given time among adolescents cited earlier is higher than an estimated rate of about 10% among children (Ford, Goodman, & Meltzer, 2003), although it is no higher than the rate for adults (Kazdin, 2000). Teenagers face greater stress than children; they must cope with physical maturation, changing brains and cognitive abilities, tribulations of dating, changes in family dynamics, moves to new and more complex school settings, societal demands to become more responsible and to assume adult roles, and more (Cicchetti & Rogosch, 2002; Hill, 1993). Most adolescents cope with these challenges remarkably well, maintain the level of adjustment they had when they entered adolescence, and undergo impressive psychological growth, although it is not unusual for them to feel depressed, anxious, and irritable occasionally. For a minority, a buildup of stressors during adolescence can precipitate serious psychopathology. Their problems should not be dismissed as adolescent moodiness and irritability.

Many adolescents of both sexes get themselves into trouble by overusing alcohol and drugs, having risky sex, engaging in delinquent behavior, and displaying other so-called adolescent problem behaviors. These behaviors, although common and often correlated with each other, usually do not reach the level of seriousness to qualify as psychological disorders (Boles, Biglan, &

Smolkowski, 2006; Jessor, 1998). Such problem behaviors may peak in adolescence in part because the normal timetable for brain development endows adolescents with strong sensation- and reward-seeking tendencies but immature self-regulatory capabilities (Spear, 2010; Steinberg, 2008; and see Chapter 5's discussion of risk taking and brain development). The result is sometimes impulsive pursuit of excitement and enjoyment without much self-control or thought of the consequences.

Here we focus on diagnosable disorders that clearly become more prevalent in adolescence. Eating disorders such as anorexia nervosa can make the adolescent period treacherous and even fatal; experimentation with alcohol and drugs can turn into substance abuse or dependence for some teens; and rates of depression increase dramatically from childhood to adolescence. These problems interfere with normal adolescent development; yet they become far more understandable when you view them in the context of this developmental period.

Eating Disorders

Perhaps no psychological disorders are more associated with adolescence than the eating disorders that disproportionately strike adolescent females, especially during the transition from childhood to adolescence or during the transition from adolescence to adulthood (Bryant-Waugh, 2007; le Grange, Eddy, & Hertzog, 2010). Eating disorders—anorexia nervosa, bulimia nervosa, and eating disorders not otherwise specified (plus, starting in DSM-V, binge eating disorder)—have become more common in several industrialized countries (Gordon, 2000; Milos et al., 2004). They are serious—indeed, potentially fatal—conditions that are difficult to cure.

Anorexia nervosa, which literally means "nervous loss of appetite," has been defined as a refusal to maintain a weight that is at least 85% of the expected weight for the person's height and age (American Psychiatric Association, 2000). Anorexic individuals are also characterized by a strong fear of becoming overweight, a distorted body image (a tendency to view themselves as fat even when they are emaciated), and, if they are females, an absence of regular menstrual cycles. Anorexia nervosa can be distinguished from **bulimia nervosa,** the so-called binge–purge syndrome, which involves recurrent episodes of consuming huge quantities of food followed by purging activities such as self-induced vomiting, use of laxatives, or rigid dieting and fasting (American Psychiatric Association, 2000; and see Pinhas et al., 2007).

The typical individual with anorexia may begin dieting soon after reaching puberty and simply continue, insisting, even when she weighs only 60 or 70 pounds and resembles a cadaver, that she is well nourished and could stand to lose a few more pounds (Hsu, 1990). Praised at first for losing weight, she becomes increasingly obsessed with dieting and exercising and gains a sense of control by resisting the urging of parents and friends to eat more (Levenkron, 2000).

Fewer than 3 in every 1,000 adolescent girls suffer from this condition, and there are about 11 female victims for every 1 male victim (van Hoeken, Seidell, & Hoek, 2003). The victims are getting younger; one third-grader was so severely affected that she

Anorexia can be life threatening.

considered five Cheerios a meal (Tyre, 2005). It is a myth that anorexia nervosa is restricted to European American females from upper-middle-class backgrounds. It is evident at all socio-economic levels (Gard & Freeman, 1996) and in all racial and ethnic groups, although African American females are less concerned than European American and Asian American females with being thin and with dieting and are more satisfied with their bodies (Franko & Goerge, 2009).

Suspected Causes

Both nature and nurture contribute to eating disorders. On the nurture side, cultural factors are significant and rates of eating disorders vary widely around the world, being highest in Western or Westernized countries and in urban areas within countries (Anderson-Fye, 2009). We live in a society obsessed with thinness as the standard of physical attractiveness that makes it hard for young women to feel good about themselves (Gordon, 2000; Keel & Klump, 2003). As the Western ideal of thinness has spread to other countries, rates of eating disorders in those countries have risen. Interestingly, exposure to television on the island of Fiji converted girls raised to view plump bodies as a status symbol associated with the generous sharing of food into girls who feel too fat and try to control their weight (Becker et al., 2002).

Well before they reach puberty, starting as early as pre-school, girls in our society begin to associate being thin with being attractive, fear becoming fat, and wish they were thinner (Hill, 2007; Ricciardelli & McCabe, 2001). Their desire to be thin and their feelings about themselves and their bodies are influenced by how much emphasis they think their peers place on thinness and how much television they watch focused on appearance (Dohnt & Tiggemann, 2006). Ultrathin Barbie dolls with unattainable body proportions also contribute to young girls' dissatisfaction with their bodies (Dittmar, Halliwell, & Ive, 2006). Perhaps all these cultural messages explain why about a fourth of

second-grade girls in one study dieted (Thelen et al., 1992; and see Hill, 2007).

As girls experience normal pubertal changes, they naturally gain fat and become, in their minds, less attractive; they have more reason than ever to be obsessed with controlling their weight (Murnen & Smolak, 1997). This may help explain why adolescence is prime time for the emergence of eating disorders. Concerns have even been raised that current efforts to combat obesity in the United States, as illustrated by Michelle Obama's campaign, may increase eating disorders unless strong emphasis is placed on eating healthy food and exercising rather than on being svelte (Schwartz & Henderson, 2009).

But why do relatively few adolescent females in our society develop anorexia, even though almost all of them experience social pressure to be thin? Genes, though we are not sure which ones, serve as a diathesis, predisposing certain individuals to develop eating disorders (Keel & Klump, 2003). Both twin studies and adoption studies suggest that more than half of the variation in risk for eating disorders is attributable to genes, with the remainder attributable to unique or nonshared environmental factors (Bulik et al., 2006; Klump et al., 2009). In a longitudinal study aimed at identifying early risk factors for the development of anorexia by age 30, feeding problems in infancy and a history of undereating were among the predictive factors, suggesting a biologically based and early-developing problem (Nicholls & Viner, 2009). A number of biochemical abnormalities have been found in individuals with anorexia (Klump & Culbert, 2007; Wilson, Becker, & Heffernan, 2003). For example, genes may contribute to low levels of the neurotransmitter serotonin, which is involved in both appetite and mood and has been linked to both eating disorders and mood disorders (Keel & Fulkerson, 2001; Klump & Culbert, 2007). The neurotransmitter dopamine has also been implicated because it is involved in the brain's reward system and some evidence suggests that eating disorders, like alcohol and drug addiction, involve compulsive behavior that is reinforcing (Halmi, 2009; and see Klump & Culbert, 2007). And perhaps genes also contribute to a personality profile that puts certain individuals at risk; females with anorexia tend to be highly anxious and obsessive perfectionists who are driven to control their eating (Halmi, 2009; Lilenfeld et al., 2006).

Yet anorexia still may not emerge unless a genetically predisposed girl living in a weight-conscious culture experiences stressful events—that is, unless genes and environment interact to produce a disorder (Keel & Fulkerson, 2001). Stress may strike early: there is evidence that prenatal problems and perinatal complications increase the risk of anorexia (Favaro, Tenconi, & Santonastaso, 2006). Girls who are overly concerned about their weight also tend to come from families preoccupied with weight where mothers may model disordered eating (Smolak, 2009; Strober et al., 2000). They are often insecurely attached to their parents and show extreme anxiety about separation from loved ones (O'Shaughnessy & Dallos, 2009; Sharpe et al., 1998). So family dynamics may contribute to anorexia (and to bulimia as well), although it is not always clear whether disturbed family dynamics are contributors to or effects of the condition (Gowers & Bryant-Waugh, 2004; Sim et al., 2009).

Ultimately, it may take a pileup of stressors to push a young woman over the edge. In anorexia nervosa, then, we have another clear example of the diathesis–stress model at work. A young woman who is at risk for it partly because of her genetic makeup may not develop anorexia unless she also grows up in a culture that overvalues thinness and in a family that makes it hard to forge a positive identity—and then faces an accumulation of stressful events.

Treatment

Effective therapies for individuals with anorexia start with behavior modification programs designed to bring their eating behavior under control, help them gain weight, and deal with any medical problems they may have, in a hospital or treatment facility if necessary (Patel, Pratt, & Greydanus, 2003). Then it is possible to move on to individual psychotherapy designed to help them understand and gain control of their problem, family therapy designed to change parent–child relationships and dynamics, and medication for depression and related psychological problems (see Grilo & Mitchell, 2010; Jaffa & McDermott, 2007).

The Maudsley approach to family therapy, named after the hospital in London where it originated, appears to be especially effective (Keel & Haedt, 2008; Loeb et al., 2007; Sperry, Roehrig, & Thompson, 2009). It focuses squarely on weight gain initially and views the family as part of the treatment team rather than the cause of the patient's problems, temporarily putting parents in charge of getting their daughter to eat, until she is ready to take over that responsibility herself. It requires gaining the cooperation of all family members (helping them to see the problem as serious but stop blaming themselves), assessing family interactions surrounding eating and the patient's symptoms, and helping the family respond more constructively to the patient's eating behavior in order to facilitate weight gain. Once sufficient weight is gained, control of eating is returned to the adolescent and any broader family issues such as the adolescent's need for more autonomy are addressed.

Individuals with anorexia are difficult to treat because they so strongly resist admitting that they have a problem. More success can be achieved if the problem is diagnosed and treated before age 18 than if it becomes chronic (Halmi, 2009). However, even many women who receive treatment overcome their eating disorders, or at least significantly improve (Gowers & Bryant-Waugh, 2004; Steinhausen, 2007).

Can eating disorders be prevented? Eric Stice and his colleagues have been testing the effectiveness of a dissonance-producing intervention called the Body Project (Stice et al., 2009; Stice & Presnell, 2007). It attempts to get adolescent girls who have body image concerns to stop viewing a thin body as ideal by having them critique the thin ideal in essays, role plays, and the like. The cognitive dissonance created by coming out against the thin ideal is expected to motivate these teens to stop pursuing thinness as their goal. In an intervention study with 306 adolescent girls who had body image concerns, the researchers compared a school-based dissonance program with an educational brochure on eating disorders. The program proved effective in reducing internalization of the thin body ideal and in turn reducing body dissatisfaction, dieting efforts, and eating disorder symptoms. Even Internet-based prevention programs based on cognitive behavioral principles have succeeded in reducing the risk of eating disorders among at-risk high school and college students (Heinicke et al., 2007; Taylor et al., 2006). Here, then, an ounce of prevention may be worth at least a pound of cure.

Substance Abuse Disorders

> She lost count of the vodka shots. It was New Year's Eve…, and for this high school freshman, it was time to party. She figured she'd be able to sleep it off—she'd done it before. But by the time she got home the next day, her head was still pounding, her mouth was dry, and she couldn't focus. This time, the symptoms were obvious even to her parents. After that night, she realized the weekend buzzes had gone from being a maybe to a must. (Aratani, 2008, p. C1)

One of the ways in which some adolescents explore their identities, strive for peer group acceptance, and reach toward adulthood is by experimenting with smoking, drinking, and drug use. For some, like this high school freshman and Peggy at the start of the chapter, substance use moves beyond experimentation to abuse and dependence. In DSM-IV language, *substance abuse* occurs when use of a substance has adverse consequences such as putting the person in physically dangerous situations, interfering with their performance in school or at work, or contributing to interpersonal problems. *Substance dependence* is worse, referring to continued use despite significant problems, as indicated by such signs as compulsive use, increased tolerance for the drug, withdrawal symptoms if use is terminated, and inability to quit.

The tolls of substance abuse and dependence on development can be heavy. As noted in Chapter 5, for example, teens under the influence of alcohol are likely to make additional risky choices that can have negative consequences for themselves or others: smoking, engaging in risky sex, driving under the influence, riding in cars with drivers who have been drinking, getting into physical fights, engaging in illegal behavior, and so on. Concerns also include possible toxic effects on the nervous system during a time of important brain development and negative impacts on academic achievement, occupational success, and interpersonal relationships (Colder et al., 2010). Moreover, much research indicates that use of alcohol or other substances in childhood or early adolescence predicts later problems with substance abuse and dependence (Dodge et al., 2009).

What do we know about substance use in adolescence, then? For years, the Monitoring the Future study based at the University of Michigan has tracked it. The percentages of adolescents in 2008 who reported that they had used various substances are listed in ■ **Figure 16.3**. These percentages are not as high as those reported in the 1970s and early 1980s, but they represent an increase since the early 1990s. For most substances, they also reveal a clear increase in use with age (Johnston et al., 2009). One exception is inhalants (glue, nail polish remover, solvents, and so on), which are used more by young teens than by older teens, probably because they are cheap and readily obtainable around the house and at stores. Overall, if inhalants are included

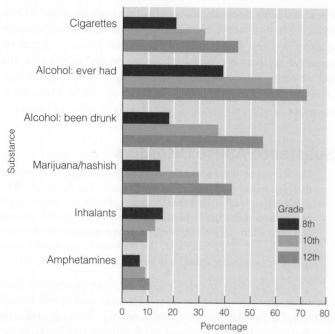

FIGURE 16.3 Percentages of adolescents in grades 8, 10, and 12 who report ever using various substances.

Source: Johnston, L. D., O'Malley, P. M., Bachman, J. G., & Schulenberg, J. E. (2009). *Monitoring the future: National results on adolescent drug use—overview of key findings, 2008.* Bethesda, MD: National Institute on Drug Abuse, U.S. Department of Health and Human Services. Available at: http://monitoringthefuture.org/pubs/monographs/overview2008.pdf. Accessed: March 1, 2010.

in the illicit drug category, more than a quarter of 8th-graders (13- to 14-year-olds) and half of 12th-graders (17- to 18-year-olds) have tried an illicit drug. As for alcohol, its use is widespread. Of even more concern is the finding that 8% of 8th-graders, 16% of 10th-graders, and almost 25% of 12th-graders had engaged in binge drinking (five or more drinks in a row) in the prior 2 weeks (Johnston et al., 2009). Binge drinking is an even more serious problem among college students (Grucza, Norberg, & Bierut, 2009).

Ethnic differences in substance use are evident: Native American youth have high rates of use, Hispanic white and non-Hispanic white youth have medium rates, and Asian American and African American youth have lower rates (Woo & Keatinge, 2008). Males have traditionally had higher rates of substance use and abuse than females, but the gap has been narrowing (Aratani, 2008; Woo & Keatinge, 2008).

It is now evident that the developmental pathway to adolescent substance use and abuse begins in childhood. A major study by Kenneth Dodge and others (2009) attempted to integrate what is known about contributors to the use of illicit drugs in adolescence in a **cascade model of substance use,** as shown in ▪Figure 16.4. This transactional, multifactor model envisions development as a flow of water over a series of waterfalls, gaining momentum as it goes as each influence along the way helps realize the previous factors and contributes to the next influence in the chain of influence. The cascade begins with (1) a child who

is at risk due to a difficult temperament (2) born into an adverse family environment characterized by such problems as poverty, stress, and substance use. The child is then (3) exposed to harsh parenting and family conflict; (4) develops behavior problems, especially aggression and conduct problems, as a result; and (5) is therefore rejected by peers and gets into more trouble at school, causing (6) parents, perhaps in frustration, to give up trying to monitor and supervise their now difficult-to-control adolescent child, which contributes to (7) involvement in a deviant peer group, where the adolescent is exposed to and reinforced for drug taking and other deviant behavior.

The model was tested in a longitudinal study following 585 children from prekindergarten through 12th grade through annual assessments. Substance use was measured in grade 7 to grade 12 as any use of marijuana, inhalants, cocaine, heroin, or another illicit drug. Use clearly increased with age, from 5% in grade 7 to 22% in grade 10 to 51% in grade 12. The seven groups of factors in the cascade model were correlated with one another and for the most part each predicted both the next step in the cascade and involvement in substance use. All in all, the model captures well the developmental concept that adolescent problem behaviors and psychological disorders do not spring out of nowhere; rather, they grow out of the accumulating effects of transactions among an individual and parents, peers, and other aspects of the social environment over many years. The model points to the possible value of substance abuse prevention programs targeting at-risk children long before adolescence. However, although it becomes harder to stop the cascade toward substance use as the years go by, there are new opportunities to intervene at each step. Similar cascade models have been formulated to help account for the development of internalizing and externalizing problems (Dodge et al., 2008; Masten et al., 2005; and see Chapter 13 on aggression).

What is missing from the cascade model? Other explanations of substance use and abuse put more emphasis on genetic contributors. Because of their genes, some individuals are more vulnerable to substance abuse and/or to the effects of the sorts of environmental influences described in the cascade model (Dick, Prescott, & McGue, 2009; Sartor et al., 2010; Woo & Keatinge, 2008). A case in point is a behavioral genetics study suggesting that peers may not be the major influence on substance use that everyone believes them to be—that instead, a genetic predisposition to drink alcohol may simply cause teens to associate with other peers who drink (Hill et al., 2008). In the end, alcohol and drug abuse are the developmental outcomes of interactions among many genes and many environmental factors.

A final point: Substance use disorders are often comorbid with other disorders such as depression and anxiety (Hawkins, 2009). Indeed, some of the same genes seem to contribute to both substance abuse and internalizing disorders like depression (Saraceno et al., 2009). Most likely, then, substance abuse develops as a way to cope with emotional problems through self-medication—but substance abuse then aggravates the person's mental health problems in a kind of vicious cycle (Colder et al., 2010). The good news is that preventive interventions to delay drinking and drug use in adolescence can head off problematic substance use in adulthood (Spoth et al., 2009; and see Sloboda, 2009).

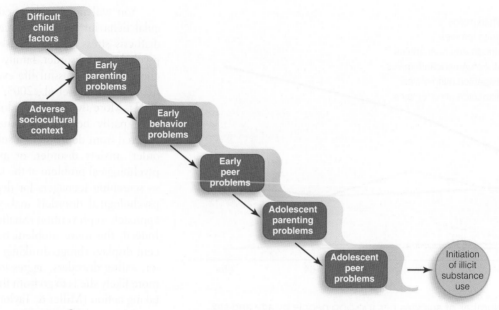

■ **FIGURE 16.4** A cascade model of substance use. Source: Dodge, K. A., et al., A dynamic cascade model of the development of substance-use onset, *Monographs of the Society for Research in Child Development, 74* (3, Serial No. 294), Figure 1. Reprinted by permission of John Wiley & Sons, Inc.

Depression and Suicidal Behavior

Before puberty, boys and girls have similarly low rates of depression; after puberty, rates climb, with the rate for girls becoming higher than that for boys (Wasserman, 2006). In one study of female adolescents, the rate of major depressive disorder at some time in the individual's life was 1% among girls younger than age 12 but 17% among young women age 19 and older—about 1 in 6 (Glowinski et al., 2003). Up to 35% of adolescents experience depressed moods at some time, and as many as 7% have diagnosable depressive disorders at any given time (Petersen et al., 1993). Symptoms are mostly like those displayed by depressed adults, although depressed adolescents sometimes act out and look more like delinquents than like victims of depression.

Factors in Depression

Why is adolescence a depressing period for some? For one thing, genetic influences on symptoms of depression seem to become stronger in adolescence than they were in childhood (Rutter, Kim-Cohen, & Maughan, 2006; Scourfield et al., 2003). Pubertal changes may be responsible or may provide another part of the answer: Being an early maturing female, especially one experiencing stressful relationships with peers, is associated with high levels of depression, whereas for boys being late maturing is more closely associated with depression (Conley & Rudolph, 2009; and see Ge et al., 2003).

In addition, teenagers, especially females, who have experienced family disruption and loss in childhood may be especially vulnerable to interpersonal stress after they reach puberty (Rudolph & Flynn, 2007). Girls are also more likely than males to experience a cumulation of stressful events in early adolescence (Ge et al., 1994; Nolen-Hoeksema & Girgus, 1994), and

stressful events—especially interpersonal ones such as divorce in the family and relationship breakups—predict increases in depressive symptoms (Ge, Natsuaki, & Conger, 2006). Girls are also more likely than boys to rely on **ruminative coping,** dwelling unproductively on their problems (Nolen-Hoeksema, 1990; Nolen-Hoeksema, Wisco, & Lyubomirsky, 2008; and see Chapter 14 on co-rumination by adolescent friends). Ruminative coping may make problems seem worse and does not usually result in active efforts to solve them. Indeed, ruminative coping predicts future depression and binge eating in adolescent girls, and those conditions in turn make ruminating about one's problems more likely, creating a vicious circle (Nolen-Hoeksema et al., 2007; and see Papadakis et al., 2006).

Suicidality

As depression becomes more common from childhood to adolescence, so do suicidal thoughts, suicide attempts, and actual suicides. Suicide is the third leading cause of death for 15- to 24-year-olds, far behind accidental injuries and just behind homicides; the yearly rate is 10 per 100,000 for this age group (National Center for Health Statistics, 2010). For every adolescent suicide, there are many unsuccessful attempts, and suicidal thoughts are even more common (Shaffer & Pfeffer, 2001). National data indicate that almost 12% of males and 22% of females in grades 9–12 had seriously considered suicide in the past year; 6% of males and almost 11% of females had attempted it (National Center for Health Statistics, 2006b).

Before you conclude that adolescence is the peak time for suicidal behavior, however, consider the suicide rates for different age groups shown in ■ **Figure 16.5.** It is clear that adults are more likely to commit suicide than adolescents are. The suicide

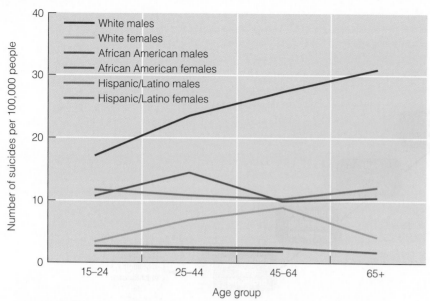

FIGURE 16.5 Number of suicides per 100,000 people by age and sex among European Americans, African Americans, and Hispanic Americans in the United States. Source: National Center for Health Statistics (2010). *Health, United States, 2009.* Hyattsville, MD: U.S. Department of Health and Human Services, Centers for Disease Control and Prevention, National Center for Health Statistics. Available at: www.cdc.gov.nchs/hus.htm. Accessed: March 18, 2010.

rate for females peaks in middle age, and the suicide rate for white males climbs throughout adulthood, making white men 65 and older the group most likely to commit suicide. Rates for minority groups, especially minority females, are very low by comparison.

Overall, males are more likely to commit suicide than females, by a ratio of at least three to one—a difference that holds up across most cultures studied (Girard, 1993; Shaffer & Pfeffer, 2001). When we look at suicide attempts, this ratio is reversed, with females leading males by a ratio of about three to one. Apparently, then, females attempt suicide more often than males do, but males more often commit suicide when they try, probably because they use more lethal techniques (especially guns).

If suicide rates are higher in adulthood than in adolescence, why do we hear so much about teenage suicide? Probably because adolescents attempt suicide more frequently than adults do. The typical adolescent suicide attempt has been characterized as a "cry for help"—a desperate effort to get others to notice and help resolve problems that have become unbearable (Berman & Jobes, 1991). The adolescent who attempts suicide often wants a better life rather than death (Lester, 1994). This by no means suggests that adolescent suicide attempts should be taken lightly. Their message is clear: "I've got serious problems; wake up and help me!" Indeed, even suicidal thoughts during adolescence should be taken seriously; adolescents who have such thoughts are more likely than those who do not to have attempted suicide, to have psychological disorders, and to display difficulties in functioning at age 30 (Reinherz et al., 2006).

You will not be surprised to learn that suicidal behavior in adolescence is the product of diathesis–stress. Four key risk factors are youth psychological disorder, family pathology and psychopathology, stressful life events, and access to firearms (Gould et al., 2003; and see Beautrais, 2003). More than 90% of adolescent suicide victims, partly because of genetic predisposition, suffered from depression, a substance-related disorder, anxiety disorder, or another diagnosable psychological problem at the time of their deaths, so screening teenagers for depression and other psychological disorders makes great sense as an approach to prevention (Shaffer & Pfeffer, 2001). Indeed, the more problem behaviors an adolescent displays (binge drinking, risky sexual behavior, eating disorders, aggression, and so on), the more likely she is to go from thinking suicidally to taking action (Miller & Taylor, 2005).

Many suicide attempters also have histories of troubled family relationships, and often psychopathology and even suicide run in the family. In the period leading up to a suicide attempt, the adolescent has often experienced a buildup of stressful life events that breeds a sense of helplessness—deteriorating relationships with parents and peers, academic and social failures, run-ins with the law (Berman & Jobes, 1991; Woo & Keatinge, 2008). The availability of firearms makes it easy to act on suicidal impulses. The adolescent who attempts suicide once may try again if he receives little help and continues to feel incapable of coping with problems; as a result, professional help is called for after an unsuccessful suicide attempt (Rotheram-Borus et al., 2000). Engagement Box 16.1 will help you to determine whether anyone you know may be planning to commit suicide and needs help.

Checking Mastery

1. What does the fact that about 20% of adolescents have significant mental health problems say for and against the notion that adolescence is a period of storm and stress?

2. What are three main factors that contribute to anorexia nervosa?

3. Judging from the cascade model of substance use, what are three factors you might look for if you wanted to identify children who are at risk for illicit drug use when they become adolescents?

Making Connections

1. How would you characterize your own mental health during adolescence? Consider whether the concept of "storm and stress," as well as the specific diagnoses we have discussed in this section, apply to you in any way.

Do you have any friends, relatives, or acquaintances who you think might be suicidal? If so, see if they show the following warning signs of suicidality in young people, compiled by the U.S. government's Substance Abuse and Mental Health Services Administration.

Look first, SAMHSA says, for signs of substance abuse or depression, then for the following words, actions, and feelings. Finally, take any warning signs seriously—seek advice, for example from your campus counseling center or by calling 1-800-273-TALK to find a local mental health crisis center.

Words

- Talks, writes, or otherwise expresses a preoccupation with suicide or death in general
- Complains of being a bad person or being "rotten inside"
- Gives verbal hints such as, "I'd be better off dead," "I won't be a problem for you much longer," "Nothing matters," "It's no use," and "I won't see you again"

Actions

- Withdraws from friends or family
- Significantly changes eating, sleeping, or appearance habits
- Experiences sudden drop in academic performance
- Puts his affairs in order; for example, gives away favorite toys, cleans his room, or throws away important belongings
- Acts in rash, hostile, or irrational ways; often expresses rage

Feelings

- Feels overwhelmingly hopeless, guilty, or ashamed
- Shows little interest in favorite activities or the future
- Becomes suddenly cheerful after a period of depression (perhaps feeling that she's found a "solution" to her problems)

SOURCE: Modified from *Know the warning signs—prevent suicide in young people.* (2007). U.S. Department of Health and Human Services, Substance Abuse and Mental Health Services Administration. Available at: http://family.samhsa.gov/get/suicidewarn.aspx. Accessed: March 16, 2010.

2. Peggy, the young woman described at the beginning of the chapter, attempted suicide. Using the material on suicide in this section, develop a theory of why she might have done so, showing how both diathesis and stress may have contributed.

16.5 The Adult

Let's remind ourselves that most adolescents, even though they may diet, drink, or think a depressive or even suicidal thought now and then, emerge from adolescence as well-adjusted and competent young adults. Still, stressful experiences in childhood and adolescence increase a person's chances of psychological disorder later in life (Turner & Lloyd, 2004). Psychological problems then emerge when a vulnerable individual faces overwhelming stress. As it turns out, adults typically experience the greatest number of life strains in early adulthood (McLanahan & Sorensen, 1985; Pearlin, 1980). Life strains decrease from early to middle adulthood, perhaps as adults settle into more stable lifestyles. And despite increased stress related to health problems, elderly adults report fewer hassles and strains overall than middle-aged adults do (Almeida & Horn, 2004; Martin, Grunendahl, & Martin, 2001). This may be because they have fewer roles and responsibilities to juggle or because they have learned to take more problems in stride.

Age differences in stressful experiences may help explain age differences in rates of psychological disorder. Diagnostic interviews with adults age 18 or older in the United States reveal that rates of affective disorders (major depression and related mood disorders), alcohol abuse and dependence, schizophrenia, anxiety disorders, and antisocial personality all decrease from early adulthood to late adulthood (Myers et al., 1984; Robins & Regier, 1991). The only category of disorder that increases with age is cognitive impairment, undoubtedly because some older adults develop Alzheimer's disease and other forms of dementia (to be described shortly). Overall, about one-fourth of American adults experienced a psychological disorder in the past year (Kessler, Chiu, et al., 2005).

With that as background, we can look more closely at one of the disorders to which young adults are especially susceptible, depression, and then turn to an examination of Alzheimer's disease and related cognitive impairments in later life.

Depression

Major depression and other affective disorders are among the most common psychological problems experienced by adults. Who gets depressed, and what does this reveal?

Age and Sex Differences

About 28% of Americans can expect to experience a diagnosable mood disorder by age 75 (Kessler, Berglund et al., 2005). The average age of onset of major depression is in the early 20s (Woo & Keatinge, 2008). Contrary to stereotypes of elderly people, older adults tend to be less vulnerable to major depression and other severe affective disorders than young or middle-aged adults are (Hybels, Blazer, & Hays, 2009). Unless older adults develop physical health problems that contribute to depression or experience increasing rather than decreasing levels of stress as they age, their mental health is likely to be good (Lynch & George, 2002; Wrosch, Schulz, & Heckhausen, 2004).

Still, there are good reasons to be concerned about depression in old age. First, we know that depressed elderly adults are more

Although few elderly adults have diagnosed depression, a sizable minority experiences at least some symptoms of depression.

© Mark Richards/PhotoEdit Inc.

likely than depressed adolescents to take their own lives. Second, reports of depression symptoms, if not diagnosable disorders, increase when people reach their 70s and beyond (Nguyen & Zonderman, 2006; Teachman, 2006). Although only about 1% to 2% of elderly adults have major depressive disorder at a given time, somewhere between 15% and 25% experience symptoms of depression (Hybels, Blazer, & Hays, 2009; Knight et al., 2006). Might some of the individuals who report symptoms of depression have a more serious but undiagnosed depressive disorder?

It's possible. Depression can be difficult to diagnose in later adulthood (Charney et al., 2003). Think about it: Symptoms of depression include fatigue and lack of energy, sleeping difficulties, cognitive deficits, and somatic (body) complaints. What if an elderly individual and/or her doctor note these symptoms but interpret them as nothing more than normal aging, as the result of the chronic illnesses so common in old age and medications for them, or as signs of dementia? A case of depression could easily be missed. To complicate matters, elderly adults sometimes deny that they are sad and report mainly their somatic symptoms (Nguyen & Zonderman, 2006).

So clinicians working with elderly adults need to be sensitive to the differences between normal aging, disease, and psychopathology. Moreover, the fact that relatively few elderly people suffer from severe, diagnosable depression should not blind us to the fact that a much larger number feel depressed or demoralized and could benefit from treatment (Lynch & George, 2002). This is especially true of very old women who are physically ill, poor, socially isolated, or a combination of these (Blazer, 1993; Falcon & Tucker, 2000).

Gender differences in depression are significant. Starting in adolescence, and in a variety of cultures, females are more likely than males to be diagnosed as depressed—by a margin of about two to one (Kuehner, 2003). This gender difference probably results from a variety of factors (Kuehner, 2003; Nolen-Hoeksema, 2002): hormones and biological reactions to stress; levels of stress

(including more exposure to interpersonal stressors among women); ways of expressing distress (women being more likely to express classic depression symptoms, men being more likely to become angry or overindulge in alcohol and drugs); and styles of coping with distress (especially the tendency for women to engage in more ruminative coping, overanalyzing their despair, whereas men distract themselves from problems and may be better off for it). In short, there is no simple explanation, but women are clearly more at risk than men for depression—at least until old age. Then, interestingly, male and female rates become more similar (Wasserman, 2006).

Treatment

One of the biggest challenges in treating adults with major depression and other psychological disorders is getting them to seek treatment; many eventually do, but they often go years without help (Wang et al., 2005). Elderly adults are especially likely to go undiagnosed and untreated, particularly if they are African American or other minority group members (Charney et al., 2003; Neighbors et al., 2007). Older adults and members of their families may believe, wrongly, that problems such as depression and anxiety are a normal part of getting older or becoming ill or that it is somehow shameful to have psychological problems or need help. Mental health professionals, meanwhile, may underdiagnose or misdiagnose the problems of elderly individuals or may view elderly adults as less treatable than younger adults (Graham et al., 2003; Meeks et al., 2009).

Despite these barriers, depressed elderly adults who seek psychotherapy benefit from it (Scogin et al., 2005). Moreover, those treated with antidepressant drugs not only overcome their depression in most cases but also show improved cognitive functioning (Blazer, 2003; Butters et al., 2000). As with many psychological problems, the most effective approach is often a combination of drug treatment and psychotherapy, especially cognitive behavioral therapy aimed at addressing carefully identified problems (Hollon, Thase, & Markowitz, 2002; March, 2009).

Aging and Dementia

Perhaps nothing scares us more about aging than the thought that we will become "senile." **Dementia**, the technical term for senility, is a progressive deterioration of neural functioning associated with cognitive decline—memory impairment, declines in tested intellectual ability, poor judgment, difficulty thinking abstractly, and often personality changes as well (see Lyketsos, 2009). Becoming "senile" is not a normal part of the aging process. Yet rates of dementia increase steadily with age. Overall, dementia affects 6% to 8% of elderly adults age 65 and older (Knight et al., 2006). Rates climb steeply with age, though—from less than 1% in the 60-to-64 age group to around 30% for people 85 and older (Ferri et al., 2005; Geldmacher, 2009).

Dementia is not a single disorder. Much damage can be done by labeling any older person with cognitive impairments as senile—or even as having Alzheimer's disease—and then assuming that he is a lost cause. Many different conditions can produce symptoms we associate with senility, and some of them are curable or reversible (Thompson, 2006). Let us look at Alzheimer's disease and other forms of dementia.

Alzheimer's Disease

With Alzheimer's disease, you just know you're going to forget things, and it's impossible to put things where you can't forget them because people like me can always find a place to lose things and we have to flurry all over the house to figure where in the heck I left whatever it was. . . . It's usually my glasses. . . . You've got to have a sense of humor in this kind of business, and I think it's interesting how many places I can find to lose things. . . . [People with Alzheimer's] want things like they used to be. And we just hate the fact that we cannot be what we used to be. It hurts like hell. (Cary Henderson, age 64, former history professor diagnosed with Alzheimer's disease at age 55; Rovner, 1994, pp. 12–13)

Alzheimer's disease, or *dementia of the Alzheimer's type* as it is termed in DSM-IV-TR, is the most common cause of dementia, accounting for about 70% of all cases, including former President Ronald Reagan's (Geldmacher, 2009; Qui & Fratiglioni, 2009; Tanzi & Parson, 2000). The disease can strike in middle age but becomes increasingly likely with advancing age. Because more people are living into advanced old age, more will end up with Alzheimer's disease unless ways of preventing it or slowing its progression are found.

Alzheimer's disease leaves two telltale signs in the brain (Selkoe, 1997): *senile plaques* (masses of dying neural material with a toxic protein called **beta-amyloid** at their core that injures neurons), and *neurofibrillary tangles* (twisted strands of neural fibers within the bodies of neural cells). Elderly adults without Alzheimer's disease have senile plaques and neurofibrillary tangles too; it is not only the number but their type and location that mark the difference between Alzheimer's disease and normal aging (Snowdon, 1997). The effects of Alzheimer's disease— deterioration of neurons, increasingly impaired mental function-

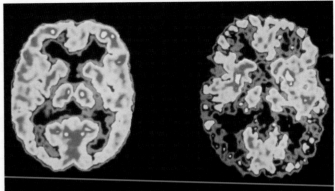

Positron emission tomography (PET scanning) shows metabolic activity in the brain and reveals areas of high brain activity (in red and yellow) and low brain activity (in blue or black). Here we see more activity in a normally functioning brain (left) than in the brain of a person with Alzheimer's disease (right).

ing, and personality changes—are progressive (and neither reversible nor curable).

Alzheimer's disease begins to affect the brain in early and middle adulthood, maybe even earlier, long before cognitive functioning is affected and even longer before the disease is diagnosed. The first noticeable signs of the disease, detectable 2–3 years before dementia can be diagnosed, are usually difficulties learning and remembering recently encountered verbal material such as names and phone numbers (Geldmacher, 2009; Howieson et al., 1997). As you saw in Chapter 8, mild cognitive impairment in some older adults is usually—but not always—an early warning that dementia will follow (Lyketsos, 2009; Tabert et al., 2006). It is more serious than the small declines in some aspects of memory performance that most aging adults experience. If all it took to warrant a diagnosis of mild cognitive impairment or dementia were occasional episodes of misplacing keys or being unable to remember someone's name, many young and middle-aged adults, not to mention textbook writers, would qualify!

In the early stages of Alzheimer's disease, free recall tasks are difficult but memory is good if cues to recall are provided; over time, individuals cannot recall even with the aid of cues and become increasingly frustrated (Grober & Kawas, 1997). As the disorder progresses, people with Alzheimer's may have trouble remembering not only recently acquired but old information, have more trouble coming up with the words they want during conversations, and forget what to do next midway through making a sandwich or getting ready for bed. If tested, they may be unable to answer simple questions about where they are, what the date is, and who the president of the United States is. Eventually they become incapable of caring for themselves; no longer recognize loved ones; lose all verbal abilities; and die, some earlier and some later, but on average about 8–10 years after onset (National Institute on Aging, 2000; and see ▪ **Figure 16.6**).

Not only do patients with Alzheimer's disease become increasingly unable to function, but they also often test the pa-

Ronald Reagan, who died in 1994 of complications of Alzheimer's disease, brought attention to the tragedy of the disease.

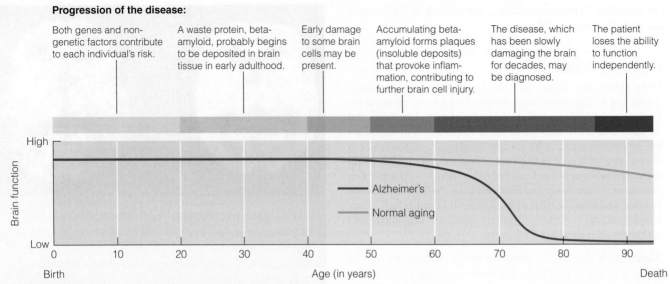

Progression of the disease:

Both genes and non-genetic factors contribute to each individual's risk.

A waste protein, beta-amyloid, probably begins to be deposited in brain tissue in early adulthood.

Early damage to some brain cells may be present.

Accumulating beta-amyloid forms plaques (insoluble deposits) that provoke inflammation, contributing to further brain cell injury.

The disease, which has been slowly damaging the brain for decades, may be diagnosed.

The patient loses the ability to function independently.

■ **FIGURE 16.6** Alzheimer's disease emerges gradually over the adult years; brain cells are damaged long before noticeable cognitive impairment results in old age. Changes in brain functioning are significantly different from those associated with normal aging. Source: Adapted from Okie, 2001.

tience of caregivers by forgetting they have left something cooking on the stove, wandering away and getting lost, accusing people of stealing the items they have misplaced, or taking off their clothes in public. Many become highly agitated and uncontrollable; large numbers suffer from depression and become apathetic; and some experience psychotic symptoms such as hallucinations (Geldmacher, 2009).

Causes and Contributors. What causes Alzheimer's disease? It has a genetic basis, but there is no single "Alzheimer's gene" (Gatz, 2007; Tanzi & Parson, 2000). Alzheimer's disease strikes repeatedly and early in some families. By analyzing blood samples from families with many Alzheimer's victims, genetic researchers made a big breakthrough when they located a gene for the disease on the 21st pair of chromosomes. Anyone who inherits just one of these apparently dominant genes will develop the disease. A couple of other genes of this sort associated with early-onset Alzheimer's disease have since been discovered, but these single-gene mutations account for only 2% of all cases of Alzheimer's disease (Gatz, 2007).

Genetic contributors to late-onset Alzheimer's disease, by far more common than the early-onset variety, are not as clear-cut or strong. Rather than making Alzheimer's disease inevitable, a number of genes only increase a person's risk slightly (Gatz, 2007). Overall, genes account for about 60% of the variation in Alzheimer's, with environmental factors accounting for the rest (Qui & Fratiglioni, 2009).

One variant of a gene on Chromosome 19 has proven to be especially important in late-onset Alzheimer's disease. It is responsible for the production of ApoE, a protein involved in processing cholesterol. Having two of the risk-inducing APOE4 variants of the gene means having up to 15 times the normal risk of Alzheimer's disease (Lyketsos, 2009). Having another specific variant of the

APOE gene means having a good chance of maintaining good cognitive functioning into very late adulthood (Riley et al., 2000).

Signs of brain atrophy can be detected in people with two APOE4 genes before they show cognitive impairment (Chen et al., 2007). It is believed that the APOE4 gene may increase the buildup of beta-amyloid—the damaging substance in senile plaques—and therefore speed the progression of Alzheimer's disease (National Institute on Aging, 2000). Yet not everyone with the APOE4 gene, or even a pair of them, develops Alzheimer's disease, and many people with Alzheimer's disease lack the gene; other genes and environmental factors apparently play a role.

It has not been easy to pinpoint gene–environment interactions, however (Gatz, 2007). Head injuries in earlier adulthood, such as those incurred by some boxers and football players, increase the risk of Alzheimer's disease (Plassman et al., 2000). Obesity and a diet that increases the odds of high blood pressure, high cholesterol, and cardiovascular disease also contribute (Nourhashemi et al., 2000; Savva & Brayne, 2009). Researchers are also becoming more aware of the importance of **cognitive reserve**—extra brain power or cognitive capacity that some people can fall back on as aging and disease begin to take a toll on brain functioning (Gatz et al., 2001). People who have advanced education and high intelligence and have been mentally, physically, and socially active over the years have more cognitive reserve than less active people and, as a result, are less likely to be impaired as Alzheimer's disease begins to damage their brains (Gatz et al., 2001; Savva & Brayne, 2009).

Prevention and Treatment

What is being done to prevent and treat Alzheimer's disease? Much attention is now focused on earlier detection in hopes that drugs can prevent or delay the changes in the brain associated with the disease. Because victims have a deficit in the neurotransmitter acetylcholine, which is essential for normal learning and memory, researchers have developed drugs to correct this problem and related problems in neural functioning. No pill to prevent or reverse Alzheimer's disease has yet been discovered, but some drugs are regularly prescribed (for example, Aricept [donepezil] and Namenda [memantine]). They modestly improve cognitive functioning, reduce behavioral problems, and slow the progression of the disease in some patients (Farlow & Boustani, 2009; Grossberg & Desai, 2003). More such drugs are in development.

Other approaches being investigated include drugs to combat the buildup and effects of beta-amyloid in the brain, including antioxidants such as vitamins E and C and statin drugs prescribed to combat high cholesterol; however, therapeutic effects have not yet been clearly demonstrated (Wilkinson, 2009). It does appear, however, that the same lifestyle factors that contribute to cardiovascular disease (eating too much and not getting enough exercise) contribute to dementia as well (Pope, Shue, & Beck, 2003; Underwood, 2004). Both physical exercise and mental exercise, including cognitive training programs, have been shown to delay cognitive decline in later life and may slow the progression of dementia as well (Hertzog et al., 2009; Larson et al., 2006).

Even if Alzheimer's disease cannot be prevented entirely, researchers are hopeful that its onset and progression can be slowed, especially if it is detected early (Weiner et al., 2009). And even though deterioration leading to death must be expected in today's Alzheimer's patients, a great deal can be done to make the disease more bearable through memory training and memory aids, the use of behavioral management techniques and medications to deal with behavioral problems, and educational programs and psychological interventions for both patients and their caregivers to help them understand and cope with dementia and function better (Grossberg & Desai, 2003; Kasl-Godley & Gatz, 2000).

Other Causes of Cognitive Impairment

The second most common type of dementia, often occurring in combination with Alzheimer's disease, is **vascular dementia** (Szoeke et al., 2009; Thompson, 2006). Also called multi-infarct dementia, most cases are caused by a series of minor strokes that cut off the blood supply to areas of the brain. Whereas Alzheimer's disease usually progresses slowly and steadily, vascular dementia often progresses in a steplike manner, with further deterioration after each small stroke. Whereas Alzheimer's disease impairs memory most, vascular dementia may do its greatest damage to executive functions or whatever functions are based in the brain area affected by the stroke or brain injury (Román, 2003; Szoeke et al., 2009). And whereas Alzheimer's disease is more strongly influenced by genes, vascular dementia is more closely associated with environmental risk factors for cerebrovascular diseases that affect blood flow in the brain—smoking, eating a fatty diet, and so on (Thompson, 2006). Huntington's disease (a genetic disorder described in Chapter 3), Parkinson's disease, AIDS, and multiple sclerosis are among the many other possible causes of dementia (Thompson, 2006; Zamrini & Quiceno, 2009).

Some cases of dementia—perhaps 10% or more—are not related to any of these causes and, more important, are reversible or curable (Gurland, 1991; Lipton & Weiner, 2003). Such problems as alcoholism, toxic reactions to medication, infections, metabolic disorders, and malnutrition can cause symptoms of dementia. If these problems are corrected—for example, if the individual is taken off a recently prescribed medicine or is placed on a nutritious diet—a once "senile" person can be restored to normal mental functioning. By contrast, if that same person is written off as senile or as a victim of Alzheimer's disease, a potentially curable condition may become a progressively worse and irreversible one.

Similarly, some elderly adults are mistakenly diagnosed as suffering from dementia when they are actually experiencing **delirium.** This treatable condition, which emerges more rapidly than dementia and comes and goes over the course of the day, is a disturbance of consciousness characterized by periods of disorientation, wandering attention, confusion, and hallucinations (American Psychiatric Association, 2000; Cole, 2004; Weiner et al., 2009). One 66-year-old woman with a history of seizures, for example, called 911 repeatedly because she believed burglars were in her home; in her agitated state, she even threatened her housemate with a knife (Weiner et al., 2009). After she was taken to the hospital, she continued to be highly agitated, moving and talking constantly, not trusting the staff. Her episode of delirium appeared to be the result of a urinary infection combined with early Alzheimer's disease, and she was able to return home after 5 days in the hospital.

Many hospital patients experience delirium in reaction to any number of stressors—illness, surgery, drug overdoses, interactions of different drugs, or malnutrition. It is essential to watch for signs of delirium, identify possible causes such as an incorrect drug prescription, and intervene to change them quickly (Flaherty & Morley, 2004). Unfortunately the condition often goes undetected or misdiagnosed. Elderly patients who experience delirium, are not identified, and are sent home from the hospital without treatment for it have high death rates (Kakuma et al., 2003; Moraga & Rodriguez-Pascual, 2007).

Finally, elderly adults who are depressed are sometimes misdiagnosed as suffering from dementia because depression is associated with cognitive impairments such as being forgetful and mentally slow (Butters et al., 2004). As you have seen, treatment with antidepressant drugs and psychotherapy can dramatically improve the functioning of such individuals. However, if their depression goes undetected and they are written off as senile, they may deteriorate further. A history of depression increases the risk of dementia and the two often co-occur (Ownby et al., 2006).

The moral is clear: It is critical to distinguish among irreversible dementias (notably, dementia of the Alzheimer's type and vascular dementia), reversible dementias, delirium, depression, and other conditions that may be mistaken for irreversible dementias—including old age itself. This requires a thorough assessment, including a medical history, physical and neurological examinations, and assessments of cognitive functioning (Thompson, 2006). Only after all other causes, especially potentially treatable ones, have been ruled out should a diagnosis of Alzheimer's disease be made.

So ends our tour of psychopathology across the life span. It can be discouraging to read about the countless ways in which genes and environment can conspire to make human development go awry and about the high odds that most of us will experience a psychological disorder sometime during our lives. Yet research provides an increasingly solid basis for attempting to prevent developmental psychopathology through a two-pronged strategy of eliminating risk factors (such as abusive parenting) and strengthening protective factors (such as effective parenting and social support). If prevention proves impossible, most psychological disorders and developmental problems can be treated successfully, enabling the individual to move onto a healthier developmental pathway.

Checking Mastery

1. In which adult age group and in which gender would you expect the highest rates of major depressive disorder?

2. What might make it difficult to detect a depressive disorder in an elderly adult?

3. How does Alzheimer's disease progress in terms of the timing of plaques and tangles in the brain, cognitive deficits, and diagnosable dementia?

4. What are two key differences between delirium and dementia?

Making Connections

1. So now that you have read this whole chapter, what do you think of the DSM-IV's position that major depressive disorder is basically the same from early childhood to old age? Argue for the DSM-IV position and then argue against it.

2. Grandpa Fred is starting to display memory problems; sometimes he asks questions that he just asked, forgets where he left his car keys, and cannot come up with the names of visiting grandchildren. Fred's son Will is convinced that his father has Alzheimer's disease and is a lost cause. What possibilities would you like to rule out before accepting that conclusion—and why?

Chapter Summary

16.1 What Makes Development Abnormal?

- To diagnose psychological disorders, clinicians consider statistical deviance, maladaptiveness, and personal distress and use DSM-IV criteria.
- Developmental psychopathology is concerned with the origins and course of maladaptive behavior; a diathesis–stress model has proved useful in understanding how nature and nurture contribute to psychological disorders.

16.2 The Infant

- Autism is characterized by deviant social responses, language and communication deficits, and repetitive behavior. It is genetically influenced, involves abnormalities in the development of brain connectivity and mirror neuron functioning, and responds to early behavioral training.
- Infants who have been maltreated or separated from attachment figures, infants whose parents are depressed, and infants suffering from failure to thrive display depression-like symptoms.

16.3 The Child

- Many childhood disorders can be categorized as externalizing (undercontrolled) or internalizing (overcontrolled) problems; they are often a product of diathesis–stress or gene–environment interactions, and they often persist, though mild problems tend to be more passing.
- Diagnosable depression, an internalizing disorder, and even suicidal behavior can occur during early childhood; it manifests itself somewhat differently at different ages, tends to recur, and can be treated.

16.4 The Adolescent

- Adolescents are more vulnerable than children but no more vulnerable than adults to psychological disorders; most do not experience storm and stress.
- Anorexia nervosa arises when a genetically predisposed female who lives in a society that strongly encourages dieting experiences stressful events.
- Substance abuse or dependence disorders can grow out of normal and widespread adolescent experimentation with substances; according to the cascade model, the developmental pathway toward illicit drug use begins in childhood.
- Risks of depression rise during adolescence, especially among females. Adolescents, in a cry for help, are more likely to attempt but less likely to commit suicide than adults, older white men being the group most likely to commit suicide.

16.5 The Adult

- Young adults experience both more life strains and more psychological disorders, including depression, than older adults.
- Diagnosing depression among older adults can be tricky if their symptoms are attributed to aging, chronic disease, or dementia; older adults have low rates of diagnosable depression but up to a quarter show some symptoms of depression.
- Dementia, a progressive deterioration in neural functioning associated with significant cognitive decline, increases with age. Alzheimer's disease, the most common cause of dementia, and vascular dementia, another irreversible dementia, must be carefully distinguished from correctible conditions such as dementia that has a reversible cause, delirium, and depression.

Checking Mastery Answers

For answers to Checking Mastery questions, visit
www.cengagebrain.com

Key Terms

Media Resources

Psychology CourseMate

Find online quizzes, flash cards, animations, video clips, experiments, interactive assessments, and other helpful study aids for this text at **www.cengagebrain.com**. You can also connect directly to the following sites:

Depression

This National Institute on Mental Health website on depression has a variety of useful and up-to-date information, as well as a link to another page on depression in childhood and adolescence. To access, see "web links" in Psychology CourseMate at www.cengagebrain.com

Dementia

Medline provides information relating to dementia. Topics covered include behavior and sleep problems, daily care, and mental status tests. To access, see "web links" in Psychology CourseMate at www .cengagebrain.com

Understanding the DATA: Exercises on the Web

www.cengagebrain.com
For additional insight on the data presented in this chapter, try out the exercises for these figures in Psychology CourseMate at

www.cengagebrain.com:

> **Figure 16.3** Percentages of adolescents in grades 8, 10, and 12 who report ever using various substances.

> **Figure 16.5** Number of suicides per 100,000 people by age and sex among European Americans, African Americans, and Hispanic Americans in the United States

CengageNOW

www.cengagebrain.com
Go to www.cengagebrain.com to link to CengageNOW, your online study tool. First take the Pre-Test for this chapter to get your Personalized Study Plan, which will identify topics you need to review and direct you to online resources. Then take the Post-Test to determine what concepts you have mastered and what you still need work on.

Death and Dying

Kelly Colasanti's husband Chris was one of the unlucky people working in the World Trade Center on September 11, 2001. The next morning, Kelly's 4-year-old daughter Cara stood outside her bedroom, and Kelly had to say something (Maraniss, Hull, & Schwartzman, 2001, p. A18):

Cara had not wanted to accept her mother's word at first. "Maybe Daddy fainted," she said hours after she had been told. "If he did faint," Kelly answered, "he also stopped breathing and died." She could not believe her own words, but if nothing else, Cara had to know the truth.

When the house emptied, Kelly gave Cara a bath, dressed her in pajamas and helped her into bed. She lay down in the adjoining trundle bed and started to tell a story that Chris loved to tell about his childhood—only she couldn't tell it so well. At the end of the story, the 4-year-old ordered her to leave and suggested that she go into the other room and read Harry Potter. Kelly was crushed; she wanted to sleep right there next to her daughter. She wandered across the hall and fell into bed, then got up and went to the closet for Chris's blue and green flannel bathrobe, the one he'd had forever. She took the robe to bed, burying her face in the cloth, again trying to smell him. Her chest went cold and her ribs ached and she opened her eyes, staring at the ceiling. "My husband is dead," she said. "I'm alone."

© Mike Kemp/Rubberball/Corbis

1. What is death, why do some people live longer than others, and why do all of us die?

2. How have theorists characterized the experiences of people who are dying and people who are bereaved?

3. How is the experience of death different in infancy, childhood, adolescence, and adulthood?

4. Why do some individuals cope more ably with death than others do?

5. What can be done to help dying and bereaved individuals?

The images of 9/11 have come to symbolize for many of us the horror of death. Whether we are 4, 34, or 84 when death strikes a loved one, death hurts. By adulthood, most of us have experienced a significant loss, even if it was "only" the death of a beloved pet. Even when death is not striking so closely, it is there, lurking somewhere in the background as we go about the tasks of living—in the newspaper, on television, fleeting through our minds. Some psychologists argue that much of human behavior and culture is an effort to defend against the terror of death (Pyszczynski, Solomon, & Greenberg, 2003; Greenberg, Solomon, & Arndt, 2008). Yet sooner or later we all face the ultimate developmental task: the task of dying.

This chapter explores death and its place in life-span human development, starting with a discussion of the meanings and causes of death. You will discover that death is part of the human experience throughout the life span, but that each person's experience of it depends on his level of development, personality, life circumstances, and sociocultural context.

17.1 Matters of Life and Death

What is death? When are we most vulnerable to it, and what kills us? And why is it that all of us eventually die of "old age" if we do not die earlier?

What Is Death?

There is a good deal of confusion and controversy in our society today about when life begins and when it ends. Proponents and opponents of legalized abortion argue vehemently about when life really begins. And we hear similarly heated debates about whether a person in an irreversible coma is truly alive and whether a terminally ill patient who is in agonizing pain should be kept alive with the help of life support machines or allowed to die naturally. Definitions of death as a biological phenomenon change; so do the social meanings attached to death.

Biological Definitions of Death

Biological death is hard to define because it is not a single event but a complex process. Different systems of the body die at different rates, and some individuals who have stopped breathing or who lack a heartbeat or pulse, and who would have been declared dead in earlier times, can now be revived before their brains cease to function. Moreover, basic body processes such as respiration and blood circulation can be maintained by life support machines in patients who have fallen into a coma and whose brains have ceased to function.

In 1968 a special committee of the Harvard Medical School offered a definition of biological death that has influenced modern legal definitions of death (Berger, 1993; Kastenbaum, 2009). The Harvard group defined biological death in terms of brain functioning and insisted that there be **total brain death**: an irreversible loss of functioning in the entire brain, both the higher centers of the cerebral cortex that are involved in thought and the lower centers of the brain that control basic life processes such as breathing. Specifically, to be judged dead a person must meet the following criteria:

1. Be totally unresponsive to stimuli, including painful ones
2. Fail to move for 1 hour and fail to breathe for 3 minutes after being removed from a ventilator
3. Have no reflexes (for example, no eye blink and no constriction of the eye's pupil in response to light)
4. Register a flat electroencephalogram, indicating an absence of electrical activity in the cortex of the brain.

As an added precaution, the testing procedure is repeated 24 hours later. Moreover, because a coma is sometimes reversible if the cause is either a drug overdose or an abnormally low body temperature, these conditions must be ruled out before a person in a coma is pronounced dead.

Ever since the Harvard committee's declaration, there has been much debate about which parts of the brain must cease to function for a person to be dead. In 1975 a young woman named Karen Ann Quinlan lapsed into a coma at a party, probably as the result of alcohol and drug consumption, and became a symbol of controversy over the meaning of death (Cantor, 2001; Urofsky, 1993). Quinlan was unconscious, but her bodily functioning was maintained with the aid of a ventilator and other life support systems. When a court finally granted her parents permission to turn off the respirator, Quinlan continued to breathe without it, much to everyone's surprise. She lived on in a "persistent vegetative state," lacking all consciousness and being fed through a tube, for 10 years.

More recently, the nation debated the question of whether the feeding and hydration of Terri Schiavo of Florida should be stopped (Cerminara, 2006; Preston & Kelly, 2006). In 1990 she had suffered a cardiac arrest, possibly as a result of an eating disorder, that caused irreversible and massive brain damage. Like

Karen Ann Quinlan, she was not dead by the Harvard criteria; part of her brain stem allowed her to breathe, swallow, and undergo sleep–wake cycles. Her husband wanted to remove her feeding tube as he believed she would have wanted, but her parents believed that she retained some awareness of her environment and fought a court decision to remove the tube. After the issue was debated at length in legislative bodies, courts (including the Supreme Court), and the media, the tube was removed when appeals of the court's decision failed. Ms. Schiavo died at the age of 41 in 2005.

These famous right-to-die cases highlight the different positions people can take on the issue of when a person is dead. The position laid out in the Harvard definition of total brain death (and in the laws of most states and nations) is quite conservative. By the Harvard criteria, neither Quinlan nor Schiavo was dead, even though both were in irreversible comas, because their brain stems were still functioning enough to support breathing and other basic body functions. Shouldn't we keep such seemingly hopeless patients alive in case we discover ways to revive them? A more liberal position is that a person should be declared dead when the cerebral cortex is irreversibly dead, even if some body functions are still maintained by the more primitive portions of the brain. After all, is a person really a person if she lacks any awareness and if there is no hope that conscious mental activity will be restored?

Defining life and death became more complicated still when Adrian Owen and his colleagues (2006) demonstrated that at least some people in comas or "vegetative states" may have more awareness than suspected. These researchers asked a young woman who had been in a vegetative state for 5 months as a result of a car accident to imagine playing tennis or visiting the rooms of her house. Brain imaging with functional MRI techniques showed that her brain responded exactly as healthy adults'

brains respond to these tasks, suggesting that she could understand and respond intentionally to instructions and implying that she had some degree of consciousness. A subsequent study found brain responses of this sort in 5 of 54 patients who were classified as in either a "vegetative" or "minimally conscious" state; one was even able to answer yes–no questions by willfully controlling his brain (Monti et al., 2010). Although most of the patients studied did not respond, this research opens up a new methodology for communicating with people who are in comas and determining whether they may still have cognitive capacities that would argue against a decision to stop providing them with food and water. Such research further complicates our understandings of the boundaries between life and death, but the Harvard standard of total brain death remains our society's official definition of biological death.

Life and Death Choices

Cases such as Quinlan's and Schiavo's raise issues concerning **euthanasia**—a term meaning "happy" or "good" death that usually refers to hastening the death of someone suffering from an incurable illness or injury. *Active euthanasia*, or "mercy killing," is deliberately and directly causing a person's death—for example, by administering a lethal dose of drugs to a pain-racked patient in the late stages of cancer or smothering a spouse with advanced Alzheimer's disease. *Passive euthanasia*, by contrast, means allowing a terminally ill person to die of natural causes—for example, by withholding extraordinary life-saving treatments (as happened when Terri Schiavo's feeding tube was removed). Between active euthanasia and passive euthanasia is **assisted suicide**—not killing someone, as in active euthanasia, but making available to a person who wishes to die the means by which she may do so. This includes physician-assisted suicide—for example, a doctor's writing a prescription for sleeping pills at the request of a terminally ill patient who has made known his desire to die, in full knowledge that he will probably take an overdose (Quill, 1993).

How do we as a society view these options? You can explore your own views in Engagement Box 17.1. There is overwhelming support among medical personnel and members of the general public for passive euthanasia (Shannon, 2006; Stillion & McDowell, 1996). And, surprisingly, more than 70% of U.S. adults appear to support a doctor's right to end the life of a patient with a terminal illness (Givens & Mitchell, 2009). African Americans and other minority group members are generally less accepting of actions to hasten death than European Americans, possibly because they do not trust the medical establishment or possibly for religious or philosophical reasons (Kwak & Haley, 2005; Werth et al., 2002).

Although active euthanasia is still viewed as murder in the United States and most countries, it is legal in most states to withhold extraordinary life-extending treatments from terminally ill patients and to "pull the plug" on life support equipment when that is the wish of the dying person or when the immediate family can show that the individual expressed, when she was able to do so, a desire to reject life support measures (Cantor, 2001). A **living will,** a type of advance directive, allows

Do you believe Terri Schiavo, who could breathe but suffered massive brain damage, should or should not have been taken off her feeding tube? Her husband Michael thought she should be taken off it but her parents fought him.

Imagine that you have terminal cancer and are told that there is no more that can be done for you and no hope of recovery. What would be your answers to the following questions? There are no right or wrong answers.

___ 1. Who would you want with you and what would you want to do with your last days or weeks?

___ 2. Would you want to spend your last days or weeks in a hospital, in a hospice facility for terminally ill people, or at home?

___ 3. Would you want the doctors to do all possible to keep you alive as long as possible in case a new treatment is discovered?

___ 4. Would you choose to take large doses of pain medicine even though it might limit your ability to think clearly and interact with people?

___ 5. Would you want the following applied to you to keep you alive: (a) resuscitation if your heart stops, (b) a respirator to keep you breathing if you stop breathing on your own, (c) a feeding tube inserted in your nose or abdomen to provide nourishment if you can no longer take food through your mouth?

___ 6. Would you want to be able to ask for and receive a drug with which you could end your own life if you desired?

___ 7. Would you want to be able to ask your doctor to give you a drug to end your life?

---

people to state that they do not want extraordinary medical procedures applied to them if they become hopelessly ill. Advance directives may also be prepared to specify who should make decisions if the dying person becomes unable to make them, whether organs should be donated, and what other instructions should be carried out after the person's death. (You can download state-specific advance directives and obtain other relevant information on death and dying at Caring Connections, a current link to which can be found at www.cengagebrain.com.)

In 1997, Oregon became the first state to legalize physician-assisted suicide; specifically, terminally ill adults with 6 or fewer months to live can request lethal medication from a physician, as patients in a few European countries such as the Netherlands can do. Few people in Oregon have taken this option (Wineberg & Werth, 2003); those who have have usually had terminal cancer and believed that they faced only hopeless pain and suffering and a loss of dignity with no chance of recovery (Georges et al., 2007). Only Washington State has since gone the way of Oregon; in fact, 40 states have enacted laws *against* assisted suicide (Glascock, 2009). This caution may be warranted. Terminally ill patients are sometimes in no shape to make life-or-death decisions, and others speaking for them may not always have their best interests at heart (Cantor, 2001; Mishara, 1999).

On many life-or-death issues, right-to-die advocates, who maintain that people should have a say in how they die, fight right-to-life advocates, who say that everything possible should be done to maintain life and that nothing should be done to cut it short. It makes sense to think through these issues now in case you must someday decide whether you or a loved one should live or die (see Shannon, 2006).

Social Meanings of Death

Death is not only a biological process but also a psychological and social one. The social meanings attached to death vary widely from historical era to historical era and from culture to culture (Rosenblatt, 2008). Indeed, you have just discovered that society defines who is dead and who is alive. True, people everywhere die, and people everywhere grieve deaths. Moreover, all societies have evolved some manner of reacting to this universal experience—of interpreting its meaning, disposing of corpses, and expressing grief. Beyond these universals, however, the similarities end.

As Phillippe Ariès (1981) has shown, the social meanings of death have changed over the course of history. In Europe during the Middle Ages, people were expected to recognize that their deaths were approaching so that they could bid their farewells and die with dignity surrounded by loved ones. Since the late 19th century, Ariès argues, Western societies have engaged in a "denial of death." We have taken death out of the home and put it in the hospital and funeral parlor to be managed by physicians and funeral directors; as a result, we have less direct experience with it than our ancestors did (Röcke & Cherry, 2002; Taylor, 2003). Right-to-die and death-with-dignity advocates have been arguing that we should return to the old ways, bringing death into the open, allowing it to occur more naturally, and making it again a normal life experience to be shared with family rather than a medical failure. As you will see later, this is just what the hospice movement has aimed to achieve. We are also witnessing a trend away from traditional funerals with caskets (which cost more than $7,000 in 2008, not counting the burial plot and marker); the percentage of deaths involving (much less expensive) cremation rather than burial has increased from 4% in the mid-1960s to more than 33% (Phillips, 2009).

The experience of dying also differs from culture to culture, anthropologists tell us. Societies take different stands, for example, on whether to support frail elders or speed their deaths. Anthony Glascock (2009) found that in 21 of 41 cultures he examined, practices that hastened the death of frail elderly people existed, whereas only 12 of the societies were entirely supportive of frail elders and had no death-hastening practices such as depriving frail elders of food, driving them from their homes, or stabbing them upon their request.

If we look at how people in other cultures grieve and mourn a death, we quickly realize that there are many alternatives to our Western ways and no single, biologically mandated grieving process (Klass, 2001; Rosenblatt, 2008). Depending on the society, "funerals are the occasion for avoiding people or holding parties, for fighting or having sexual orgies, for weeping or laughing, in a thousand different combinations" (Metcalf & Huntington, 1991, p. 24). In most societies, there is some concept of spiritual immortality. Yet here, too, there is much variety, from concepts of heaven and hell to the idea of reincarnation to a belief in ancestral ghosts who meddle in the lives of the living (Rosenblatt, 1993).

We need not look beyond North America to find considerable variation in the social meanings of death. Different ethnic and racial groups clearly have different rules for expressing grief. For example, it is customary among Puerto Ricans, especially women, to display intense, hysterical emotions after a death (Cook & Dworkin, 1992). Japanese Americans, by contrast, are socialized to restrain their grief—to smile so as not to burden others with their pain and to avoid the shame associated with losing self-control (Cook & Dworkin, 1992).

Different ethnic and racial groups also have different mourning practices. Irish Americans have traditionally believed that the dead deserve a good sendoff, a wake with food, drink, and jokes—the kind of party the deceased might have enjoyed (McGoldrick et al., 1991). African Americans tend to regard the funeral not as a time for rowdy celebration but as a forum for expressing grief, in some congregations by wailing and singing spirituals (McGoldrick et al., 1991; Perry, 1993). Jewish families are even more restrained; they quietly withdraw from normal activities for a week of mourning, called *shivah*, then honor the dead again at the 1-month and 1-year marks (Cytron, 1993).

In short, the experiences of dying individuals and of their survivors are shaped by the historical and cultural contexts in which death occurs. Death may be universal, and the tendency to react negatively to loss may be too (Parkes, 2000). Otherwise, death is truly what we humans make of it; there is no one "right" way to die or to grieve a death.

What Kills Us and When?

How long are we likely to live, and what is likely to kill us? In the United States the life expectancy at birth—the average number of years a newborn can be expected to live—is almost 78 years (National Center for Health Statistics, 2010). This average life expectancy disguises important differences between males and females, among racial and ethnic groups, and among social classes. The life expectancy for white males has risen to almost 76 years, the life expectancy for white females to almost 81 years. Female hormones seem to protect women from high blood pressure and heart problems, and they are less vulnerable than men to violent deaths and accidents and to the effects of smoking, drinking, and similar health hazards (Kajantie, 2008; Kaplan & Erickson, 2000). Women live longer than men in most other countries as well (United Nations, 2007). Meanwhile, life expectancies for African Americans, more of whom experience the health hazards associated with poverty, are a good deal lower than those for European Americans—70 years for males, 77 years for females—but the racial gap has been narrowing. Life expectancies are also lower in poor areas than in affluent areas (Malmstrom et al., 1999).

Life expectancies have increased steadily over the centuries, from 30 years in ancient Rome to around 80 years in modern affluent societies (Harman, 2001). Despite improvements in all regions of the world, however, life expectancies in some parts of the world lag behind life expectancies in others, as illustrated in

The dama funeral ceremony practiced by the Dogon people of Mali in western Africa involves a masquerade that leads the souls of the deceased to their final resting places. Mourning rituals differ considerably from culture to culture.

David Sutherland/Photographer's Choice/Getty Images

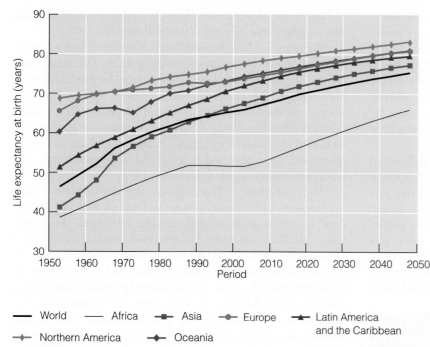

■ FIGURE 17.1 Life expectancy at birth for the world and the major areas, 1950–2050. SOURCE: From United Nations, Department of Economic and Social Affairs, Population Division 2007. *World population prospects: The 2006 revision, highlights,* Working Paper No. Esa/P/WP.201. Reprinted by permission.

■ Figure 17.1. In less developed countries plagued by malaria, famine, AIDS, and other such killers—in African countries such as Mozambique and Zambia, for example—the life expectancy barely exceeds 40 years (United Nations, 2007). The effect of AIDS in hard-hit countries in Africa has been to subtract about 30 years from the average life expectancy (Kinsella, 2005). By contrast, the life expectancy at birth is over 80 now in Asian countries such as Japan and China and in European countries such as Sweden and Switzerland (United Nations, 2007).

Death rates change over the life span, as illustrated by the "Total Deaths" statistics for different age groups in ● Table 17.1. Infants are relatively vulnerable; infant mortality in the United States has dropped considerably, however, and now stands at fewer than 7 out of 1,000 live births—lower for whites, higher for African Americans (U.S. Census Bureau, 2009). Assuming that we survive infancy, we have a relatively small chance of dying during childhood or adolescence. Death rates then climb steeply and steadily throughout adulthood.

What kills us? The leading causes of death change dramatically over the life span, as also shown in Table 17.1. Infant deaths are mainly associated with complications in the period surrounding birth and congenital abnormalities that infants bring with them to life. The leading cause of death among preschool and school-age children is unintentional injuries or accidents (especially car accidents but also poisonings, falls, fires, drownings, and so on). Adolescence and early adulthood are generally periods of good health. Accidents (especially car accidents), homicides, and suicides are the leading killers of adolescents.

Accidents and cancers kill young adults, and heart diseases also begin to take a toll. Starting in the 45-to-64 age group, cancers are the leading cause of death, followed by heart diseases, probably because certain individuals' genetic endowments, unhealthy lifestyles, or both put them at risk to develop these and other diseases prematurely (Horiuchi et al., 2003). The incidence of chronic diseases climbs steadily with age. Among adults 65 and older, heart diseases lead the list by far, accounting for more than a third of all deaths, followed by cancers and cerebrovascular diseases (strokes). By this age, general aging processes that affect all of us increase the odds that one disease or another will strike (Horiuchi et al., 2003).

● TABLE 17.1 LEADING CAUSES OF DEATH FOR DIFFERENT AGE GROUPS IN THE UNITED STATES

Age Group	Total Deaths, 2006	No. 1 Cause	No. 2 Cause	No. 3 Cause
Younger than 1 year	28,527	Congenital abnormalities	Short gestation, low birth weight	Sudden infant death syndrome
1–4 years	4,631	Unintentional injuries	Congenital abnormalities	Cancers
5–14 years	6,149	Unintentional injuries	Cancers	Homicide
15–24 years	34,887	Unintentional injuries	Homicide	Suicide
25–44 years	125,995	Unintentional injuries	Cancers	Heart diseases
45–64 years	466,432	Cancers	Heart diseases	Unintentional injuries
65 years and older	1,759,423	Heart diseases	Cancers	Cerebrovascular diseases

SOURCE: Based on data from National Center for Health Statistics (2010).

In sum, life expectancies are higher than ever. After we make it through the vulnerable period of infancy, we are at low risk of death through adolescence and are most likely to die suddenly because of an accident if we do die. As we age, we become more vulnerable to chronic diseases. But now a more fundamental question: Why is it that all of us die? Why does no one live to be 200 or 600?

Theories of Aging: Why Do We Age and Die?

There is no simple answer to the question of why we age and die. However, several theories have been proposed, and each of them says something important about the aging process. These theories can be divided into two main categories: **Programmed theories of aging** emphasize the systematic genetic control of aging processes; **damage theories of aging** call attention to more haphazard processes that cause errors in cells to accumulate and organ systems to deteriorate (Arking, 2006; Hayflick, 2004). The question, really, is whether aging and death are the result of a biological master plan or of random insults to the body while we live.

Programmed Theories

Humans, like other species, have a characteristic **maximum life span**—a ceiling on the number of years that anyone lives. The longest documented and verified life so far is that of Jeanne Louise Calment, a French woman who died in 1997 at age 122 (Willcox et al., 2009). She stopped smoking at age 119 when she could no longer see well enough to light a cigarette (Cruikshank, 2009). Nearly blind and deaf and confined to a wheelchair, she maintained her sense of humor to the end, attributing her longevity to everything from having a stomach "like an ostrich's" to being forgotten by God (Trueheart, 1997). Calment and others who live almost as long are the basis for setting the maximum human life span around 120 years. The maximum life span has not increased much, despite the fact that the average life expectancy increased 30 plus years during the 20th century and that more and more people today are living to be 100 (Kinsella, 2005).

Humans are long-lived compared with most species. The maximum life span for the mouse is 3½ years; for the dog, 20; for the chimpanzee, 50; and for the long-lived Galapagos tortoise, 150 (Walford, 1983). The fact that each species has its own characteristic maximum life span should convince us that species-wide genes influence how long people generally live.

Beyond that, the individual's genetic makeup, combined with environmental factors, influences how rapidly he ages and how long he lives compared with other humans. For example, genetic differences among us account for more than 50% of differences in the ability to stay free of major chronic diseases at age 70 or older (Reed & Dick, 2003) and for up to about a third of the variation in longevity (Melzer, Hurst, & Frayling, 2007). A fairly good way to estimate how long you will live is to average the longevity of your parents and grandparents (Medvedev, 1991).

It is not clear yet exactly how genes influence aging and longevity, though. Researchers are now able to identify specific genes that are expressed either more or less strongly from middle age to old age and that therefore may be implicated in the basic aging process (Ly et al., 2000). As it turns out, many of these genes regulate cell division. And many of the genes that become less active with age in normal adults are also inactive in children who have **progeria,** a premature aging disorder caused by a spontaneous (rather than inherited) mutation in a single gene. Babies with progeria appear normal at first but age prematurely and die on average just as they are entering their teens, often of heart disease or stroke (Eriksson et al., 2003; Hennekam, 2006).

There are almost certainly many genes involved in aging and dying (Arking, 2006; Melzer, Hurst, & Frayling, 2007). They include not only genes that affect susceptibility to the diseases that kill people but also genes that influence the human life span itself. Evolutionary theorists point to a puzzle, though: In the course of evolution, genes that act late in life to extend life will not be selected for, and genes that act late in life to shorten life will not be selected against, because they do not affect adaptation until after the person has reproduced (Arking, 2006). However, genes that

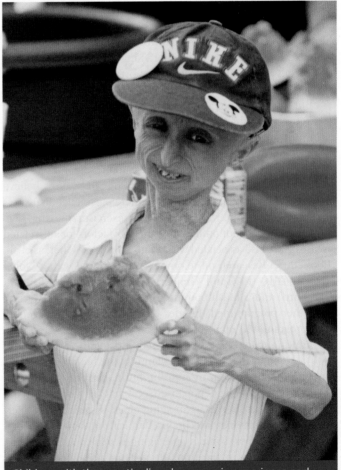

Children with the genetic disorder progeria experience early graying, wrinkling, and hair loss; cardiovascular problems; Alzheimer's disease; and death. They provide clues to the genetic basis of aging.

© Sunshine Foundation

proved adaptive to our ancestors early in life but have negative effects later in life *could* have become common in the species over time because they would be selected for (Martin, 2009; Olshansky & Carnes, 2004). For example, a gene that limits the creation of new cells through cell division could protect against the proliferation of cancer cells early in life but also contribute to cell aging later in life (Dumble et al., 2004; Ferbeyre & Lowe, 2002). Thus aging and death may prove to be the by-products of genes that served humans well during their reproductive years.

Biological researchers have also been exploring for some time the possibility that we are programmed with an "aging clock" in every cell of our bodies. Their work has built on that of Leonard Hayflick (1976, 1994), who discovered that cells from human embryos could divide only a certain number of times—50 times, plus or minus 10—an estimate referred to as the **Hayflick limit.** Hayflick also demonstrated that cells taken from human adults divide even fewer times, presumably because they have already used up some of their capacity for reproducing themselves. Moreover, the maximum life span of a species is related to the Hayflick limit for that species: The short-lived mouse's cells can go through only 14 to 28 doublings; the long-lived Galapagos tortoise's cells can manage 90 to 125.

The mechanism behind the cellular aging clock suggested by Hayflick's limit on cell division has turned out to be **telomeres**— stretches of DNA that form the tips of chromosomes and that shorten with every cell division (Effros, 2009; Epel, 2009; Wright & Shay, 2005). This progressive shortening of telomeres eventually makes cells unable to replicate and causes them to malfunction and die. Thus telomere length is a yardstick of biological aging.

But what determines how fast telomeres shorten? Fascinating research is revealing that chronic stress, such as that involved in caring for an ill child or a parent with dementia, is linked to shorter than normal white blood cell telomeres, which in turn are associated with heightened risk for cardiovascular disease and death (Epel, 2009; Epel et al., 2004, 2006). Many of us believe that stress ages people; now there is concrete evidence that stress speeds cellular aging. Moreover, lack of exercise, smoking, obesity, and low socioeconomic status—all risk factors for age-related diseases—are also associated with short telomeres (Cherkas et al., 2006, 2008). Research on telomeres was honored with a Nobel Prize in 2010 (to Carol Greider, Jack Szostak and Elizabeth Blackburn) and is mushrooming.

Other programmed theories of aging centering on genetically programmed changes in the neuroendocrine system and the immune system have been offered (Cristofalo, 1996; Knight, 2000). We know that the hypothalamus of the brain, guided by a genetic program, sets in motion the hormonal changes responsible for puberty and menopause (see Chapter 5). Possibly the hypothalamus also serves as an aging clock, systematically altering levels of hormones and brain chemicals in later life so that we die. Or perhaps, some argue, aging is related to genetically governed changes in the immune system, associated with the shortening of the telomeres of its cells. These changes could decrease the immune system's ability to defend against potentially life-threatening foreign agents such as infections, cause it to mistake normal cells for invaders (as in autoimmune diseases), and influence its effects on inflammation and disease (Effros,

2009; Wickens, 1998). All these examples of programmed theories of aging hold that aging and dying are the inevitable products of our biological endowment as humans, and all have some support.

Damage Theories

In contrast to programmed theories of aging, damage theories generally propose that wear and tear—an accumulation of haphazard or random damage to cells and organs over the years— ultimately causes death (Hayflick, 2004). Like cars, we may have a limited warranty and simply give out after a certain number of years of use and abuse (Olshansky & Carnes, 2004). Early in life, DNA strands and cells replicate themselves faithfully; later in life this fidelity is lost and cells become increasingly damaged. Damage theorists believe that biological aging is about random damage rather than genetically programmed change.

According to one leading damage theory, damage to cells that compromises their functioning is done by **free radicals,** which are toxic and chemically unstable by-products of metabolism, or the everyday chemical reactions in cells such as those involved in the breakdown of food (Harman, 2001; Shringarpure & Davies, 2009). Free radicals are produced when oxygen reacts with certain molecules in the cells. They have an extra, or "free," electron and react with other molecules in the body to produce substances that damage normal cells, including their DNA. Over time the genetic code contained in the DNA of more and more cells becomes scrambled, and the body's mechanisms for repairing such genetic damage simply cannot keep up with the chaos. More cells then function improperly or cease to function, and the organism eventually dies.

"Age spots" on the skin of older people are a visible sign of the damage free radicals can cause. Free radicals have also been implicated in some of the major diseases that become more common with age—most notably, cardiovascular diseases, cancer, and Alzheimer's disease (Harman, 2001). Moreover, they are implicated in the aging of the brain (Poon et al., 2004). However, the damage of most concern is damage to DNA because the result is more defective cells replicating themselves. Unfortunately, we cannot live and breathe without manufacturing free radicals. However, some experts conclude that free radicals alone cannot account for aging because there is no clear relationship between metabolic rate and longevity (Austad, 2009).

Nature and Nurture Conspiring

The theories just described are some of the most promising explanations of why we age and die. Programmed theories of aging generally say that aging and dying are as much a part of nature's plan as sprouting teeth or uttering first words and may be the by-products of genes that contributed to early growth, development, and reproduction. The maximum life span, the role of individual genetic makeup in longevity, the Hayflick limit on cell replication timed by telomeres, changes in the activity of certain genes as we age, and systematic changes in the neuroendocrine and immune systems all suggest that aging and dying are genetically controlled. By contrast, damage theories of aging hold that we eventually succumb to haphazard destructive processes, such as those caused by free radicals—processes that result in increasingly faulty DNA and abnormal cell functioning and ultimately a breakdown in bodily functioning.

Neither of these broad theories of aging has proved to be *the* explanation; instead, many interacting mechanisms involving both aging processes and disease processes are at work (Arking, 2006; Knight, 2000). For example, genes influence the capacity of cells to repair environmentally caused damage, and the random damage caused by free radicals alters genetic material. John Medina (1996) put it this way: "Toxic waste products accumulate because genes shut off. Genes shut off because toxic waste products accumulate" (p. 291). In short, nature and nurture, biological and environmental factors, interact to bring about aging and dying—just as they interact to produce development.

Extending Life?

What does research on the basic causes of aging and death say about our prospects for finding the long-sought fountain of youth, or extending the human life span? Aging baby boomers want to know, and in response a bustling field of anti-aging medicine has sprung forth, bringing with it hucksters offering magic diets, cosmetic changes, and countless pills of no proven value (Binstock, 2004).

It is not unthinkable that researchers might discover genetic mechanisms behind aging and dying and then devise ways of manipulating genes to increase longevity or even the maximum life span (Arking, 2006). Life spans of 200 to 600 years are probably not possible, but some think researchers could raise the average age of death to around 112 years and enable 112-year-olds to function more like 78-year-olds (Miller, 2004). For example, stem cell researchers may discover ways to replace aging cells or modify aging processes (Snyder & Loring, 2005). Researchers have also established that the enzyme telomerase can be used to prevent the telomeres from shortening and thus keep cells replicating and working longer; telomerase treatments could backfire, however, if they also make cancerous cells multiply more rapidly (Wang, 2010; Wright & Shay, 2005).

If aging is the result of random damage rather than a genetic program, or if many genetic and environmental factors contribute to it, the odds of long life through genetic engineering may be low; it will not be a simple matter of tinkering with a few "aging" genes. So some researchers are focusing on preventing the damage caused by free radicals. **Antioxidants** such as vitamins E and C (or foods high in them such as raisins, spinach, and blueberries) prevent oxygen from combining with other molecules to produce free radicals. At least when they are produced by the body or consumed in foods rather than taken in pill form, antioxidants may increase longevity, although not for long, by inhibiting free radical activity and in turn helping prevent age-related diseases (Meydani, 2001). Caution is advised, though: Taking exceptionally high doses of vitamin E may shorten rather than prolong life (Miller et al., 2005).

At present, the most successful life-extension technique is **caloric restriction**—a highly nutritious but severely restricted diet representing a 30% to 40% or more cut in normal total caloric intake (Arking, 2006; Casadesus et al., 2004; Roth, 2005).

Laboratory studies involving rats and primates suggest that caloric restriction extends both the average longevity and the maximum life span of a species and that it delays or slows the progression of many age-related diseases (Bodkin et al., 2003; Lane et al., 2001). By one estimate, a 40% reduction in daily calories results in a 40% decrease in body weight, a 40% increase in average longevity, and a 49% increase in the maximum life span of diet-restricted rats (Harman, 2001).

How does caloric restriction achieve these results? It clearly reduces the number of free radicals and other toxic products of metabolism. A restricted diet appears to alter gene activity and trigger the release of hormones that slow metabolism and protect cells against oxidative damage (Antebi, 2007; Arking, 2006). These changes help the half-starved organism hang on to life as long as possible.

However, we do not know whether caloric restriction works as well for humans as it apparently has for rats, what calorie counts and combinations of nutrients are optimal, or whether humans who have a choice would put up with being half-starved for most of their lives. We do know that exceptionally long-lived people are rarely obese (Willcox et al., 2009). We also have some intriguing evidence from four men and four women who lived for 2 years in Biosphere II, a sealed ecological dome in Arizona. Crop shortages had them eating as little as about 1800 calories a day for the first 6 months and then about 2000 calories a day for the rest of their stay, mostly vegetables they grew themselves (Walford et al., 2002). They underwent a 15% to 20% weight loss.

Measurements such as the one for cholesterol shown in ■ **Figure 17.2** indicated that these adults experienced significant improvements in several of the physiological indicators that also improve in calorie-restricted mice and monkeys. However, their

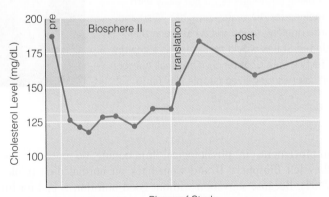

Phase of Study

■ **FIGURE 17.2** Cholesterol levels in eight adults before, during, and after their 2-year residence in Biosphere II, when they were on a low-calorie but high-nutrition diet. Many other physiological measures showed similarly dramatic change, but the benefits were lost when these adults resumed normal eating. Source: From Walford, Ray L., et al., Calorie restriction in biosphere 2: Alterations in physiologic, hematologic, hormonal, and biochemical parameters in humans restricted for a 2-year period, *Journal of Gerontology*, 57A, pp. B211–B224, 2002. Copyright © The Gerontological Society of America. Reproduced by permission of Oxford University Press.

A growing number of people around the world are **centenarians**—people who live to be 100 or older. What can we learn from them about the secrets to a long, healthy life? A study of centenarians living in Okinawa, Japan, is instructive (Willcox et al., 2009). Take Tsuru, a 110-year-old woman who does not take any medications. Standing about 5 feet tall and weighing less than 70 pounds, she was at 104 energetic as she walked through her neighborhood, tended her garden, and served as head of her family. Remarkably, she had never had a major illness until she developed pneumonia at age 105, which slowed her down and left her dependent on relatives for help.

Like most other centenarians and super-centenarians (those age 110 or over) in Okinawa, Tsuru is female. She was a teacher, has an extraverted and optimistic personality, and eats small amounts of nutritious food (mainly sweet potatoes, vegetables, fruits, and a little fish and pork). She has led an active lifestyle that includes meaningful and valued activities (weaving, for example, brings status to older women) and plenty of social interaction. Little smoking (although Tsuru got away with smoking for 40 years—until her 70s!) and little drinking round out what we in the United States would recognize as a healthy lifestyle (see Chapter 5). The small number of calories long-lived people like Tsuru

consume amounts to caloric restriction, a demonstrated life extender.

So the key to the fountain of youth may simply be a healthy lifestyle. Moreover, when Japanese people move to countries in which meat, sugar, and other unhealthy food choices are popular, their life expectancies drop and they develop the diseases of their new country (Willcox et al., 2009). Such evidence suggests that the secret to long life lies in nurture rather than nature. However, other evidence suggests that genes account for about one third of the variation in longev-

ity, so as usual we must see both nature and nurture as important (Willcox et al., 2009).

If you would like to calculate how long you can be expected to live based on information about your lifestyle, stress level, eating habits, and health status, try completing The Living to 100 Life Expectancy Calculator developed by Dr. Thomas Perls and available at www.livingto100.com; or calculate your life expectancy in Chapter 5's Engagement Box 5.1. You do not have to live in Okinawa or have super-centenarian genes to add quality years to your life.

© David McLain/Aurora

improvements in physiological functioning disappeared after they left Biosphere II and went back on normal diets (Coles, 2004). Because starvation without good nutrition is bad for humans (and no fun), experimenting with self-starvation before more evidence is in is unwise. Besides, researchers may develop drugs that would mimic the effects of caloric restriction so that we do not have to give up our beloved calories (Roth, 2005). One substance under investigation is resveratrol, a substance in red wine and peanuts.

Some think the search for the fountain of youth is misguided and will prove futile. Others worry about the social and economic consequences if average longevity were to be pushed up to 100, 110, or 120 years—about high health care expenses, overpopulation, bankruptcy of the Social Security system, and the like (Louria, 2005). For now, maybe it is best to concentrate

on reducing our chances of dying young by not smoking, drinking only in moderation, eating nutritious food, and exercising regularly, following the example of the long-lived people described in Exploration Box 17.1.

Checking Mastery

1. Why was Terry Schiavo not dead according to the Harvard definition of death?

2. What would be most likely to kill a 10-year-old? A 70-year-old?

3. What is the major difference between a programmed theory of aging and a damage theory of aging?

4. What is the most effective way discovered to date to extend the maximum life span?

Making Connections

1. What would you have decided about whether Terri Schiavo should have been taken off her feeding tube and why—and what does this imply about how you think death should be defined?

2. An 85-year-old British man and his 74-year-old wife, who was dying of terminal liver and pancreatic cancer, paid an organization in Switzerland to help them achieve an assisted suicide in which they both drank poison and lay down to die together (Gibbs, 2009). The husband had weak vision and hearing but no major health problems; he mainly did not want to go on living without his beloved wife. Do you believe that (1) the wife, and (2) the husband should be able to choose death in circumstances like these? Why or why not? How would you characterize your reasoning in terms of Kohlberg's preconventional, conventional, and postconventional levels of moral development, as described in Chapter 13?

3. What arguments would you make for and what arguments would you make against having the federal government invest heavily in research aimed at extending the human life span to 200?

17.2 The Experience of Death

People who die suddenly may be blessed, because those who develop life-threatening illnesses face the challenge of coping with the knowledge that they are seriously ill and are likely to die. What is it like to be dying, and how does the experience compare to the experience of losing a loved one to death?

Perspectives on Dying

Perhaps no one has done more to focus attention on the emotional needs and reactions of dying patients than psychiatrist Elisabeth Kübler-Ross, whose "stages of dying" are widely known and whose 1969 book *On Death and Dying* revolutionized the care of dying people. In interviews with terminally ill patients, Kübler-Ross (1969, 1974) detected a common set of emotional responses to the knowledge that one has a serious, and probably fatal, illness. She believed that similar reactions might occur in response to any major loss, so bear in mind that the family and friends of the dying person may experience similar emotional reactions during the loved one's illness and after the death.

Kübler Ross's Stages of Dying

Kübler-Ross's five "stages of dying" are as follows:

1. *Denial and isolation.* A common first response to dreadful news is to say, "No! It can't be!" Kelly's daughter Cara in the chapter opening story engaged in denial when she suggested that her father, a 9/11 victim, might have fainted rather than died. **Denial** is a defense mechanism in which anxiety-provoking thoughts are kept out of, or "isolated" from, conscious awareness. A woman who has just been diagnosed as having lung cancer may insist that the diagnosis is wrong—or accept that she is ill but be convinced that she will beat

the odds and recover. Denial can be a marvelous coping device: It can get us through a time of acute crisis until we are ready to cope more constructively. Yet even after dying patients face the facts and become ready to talk about dying, care providers and family members often engage in their own denial.

2. *Anger.* As the bad news begins to register, the dying person asks, "Why me?" Feelings of rage or resentment may be directed at anyone who is handy—doctors, nurses, or family members. Kübler-Ross advises those close to the dying person to be sensitive to this reaction so that they will not try to avoid this irritable person or become angry in return.

3. *Bargaining.* When the dying person bargains, he says, "Okay, me, but please. . . ." The bargainer begs for some concession from God, the medical staff, or family members—if not for a cure, perhaps for a little more time, a little less pain, or provision for his children.

4. *Depression.* As the dying person becomes even more aware of the reality of the situation, depression, despair, and a sense of hopelessness become the predominant emotional responses. Grief focuses on the losses that have already occurred (for example, the loss of functional abilities) and the losses to come (separation from loved ones, the inability to achieve dreams, and so on).

5. *Acceptance.* If the dying person is able to work through the emotional reactions of the preceding stages, she may accept the inevitability of death in a calm and peaceful manner. Kübler-Ross (1969) describes the acceptance stage this way: "It is almost void of feelings. It is as if the pain had gone, the struggle is over, and there comes a time for 'the final rest before the long journey,' as one patient phrased it" (p. 100).

In addition to these five stages of dying, Kübler-Ross emphasized a sixth response that runs throughout the stages: *hope*. She believed that it is essential for terminally ill patients to retain some sense of hope, even if it is only the hope that they can die with dignity. Sadly, Kübler-Ross spent her own dying days alone

Psychiatrist Elisabeth Kübler-Ross called on physicians to emphasize caring rather than curing.

and not too well tended, a prisoner in her armchair with the television for company (O'Rourke, 2010).

Problems with Kübler-Ross's Theory

Kübler-Ross deserves immense credit for sensitizing our society to the emotional needs of dying people. She convinced medical professionals to emphasize caring rather than curing in working with terminally ill people. At the same time, there are flaws in her account of the dying person's experience (Kastenbaum, 2009; Walter & McCoyd, 2009). Among the most important points made by critics are these: dying is not stagelike; the nature and course of an illness affects reactions to it; and individuals differ widely in their emotional responses to dying.

The major problem with Kübler-Ross's stages is that the dying process is simply not stagelike. Although dying patients often display symptoms of depression as death nears, the other emotional reactions Kübler-Ross describes seem to affect only minorities of dying people (Schulz & Aderman, 1974). Moreover, when these responses occur, they do not unfold in a standard order. It might have been better if Kübler-Ross had, from the start, described her stages simply as emotional reactions to dying. Unfortunately, some overzealous medical professionals have tried to push dying patients through the "stages" in order, believing incorrectly that their patients would never accept death unless they experienced the "right" emotions at the "right" times (Kastenbaum, 2009).

Edwin Shneidman (1973, 1980) offered an alternate view, arguing that dying patients experience a complex and ever-changing interplay of emotions, alternating between denial and acceptance of death. One day a patient may seem to understand that death is near; the next day she may talk of getting better and going home. Along the way many reactions—disbelief, hope, terror, bewilderment, rage, apathy, calm, anxiety, and others—come and go and are even experienced simultaneously. According to Shneidman, then, dying people experience many unpredictable emotional swings rather than distinct stages of dying. Research supports him (Chochinov & Schwartz, 2002).

A second major problem with Kübler-Ross's theory is that it does not allow for differences in emotional responses to dying associated with the disease and its course or trajectory and the specific events that occur along the way (Glaser & Strauss, 1968; Kastenbaum, 2009). When a patient is slowly and gradually worsening over time, the patient, family members, and staff can all become accustomed to the death that lies ahead, whereas when the path toward death is more erratic, emotional ups or downs are likely each time the patient's condition takes a turn for better or worse.

Finally, Kübler-Ross's approach overlooks the influences of personality on how a person experiences dying. People cope with dying much as they have coped with life (Schulz & Schlarb, 1987–1988). For example, cancer patients who previously faced life's problems directly and effectively, were satisfied with their lives, and maintained good interpersonal relationships before they became ill display less anger and are less depressed and withdrawn during their illnesses than patients who were not so well adjusted before their illnesses (Hinton, 1975). Depending on their predominant personality traits, coping styles, and social competencies, some dying people may deny until the bitter end, some may "rage against the dying of the light," some may quickly be crushed by despair, and still others may display incredible strength. Most will display combinations of these responses, each in his own unique way. There is no right way to die.

Perspectives on Bereavement

Most of us know more about the process of grieving a death than about the process of dying. To describe responses to the death of a loved one, we must distinguish among three terms: **Bereavement** is a state of loss, **grief** is an emotional response to loss, and **mourning** is a culturally prescribed way of displaying reactions to death. Thus, we can describe a bereaved person who grieves by experiencing such emotions as sadness, anger, and guilt and who mourns by attending the funeral and laying flowers on the grave each year.

Unless a death is sudden, relatives and friends, like the dying person, will experience many painful emotions before the death, from the initial diagnosis through the last breath (Grbich, Parker, & Maddocks, 2001). They, too, may alternate between acceptance and denial. They also may experience what has been termed **anticipatory grief**—grieving before death occurs for what is happening and for what lies ahead (Rando, 1986). Anticipatory grief can lessen later distress and improve outcomes of bereavement if it involves accepting the coming loss (Metzger & Gray, 2008). Yet no amount of preparation and anticipatory grief can entirely eliminate the need to grieve after the death occurs. How, then, do we grieve?

The Parkes/Bowlby Attachment Model

Pioneering research on the grieving process was conducted by Colin Murray Parkes and his colleagues in Great Britain (Parkes, 1991, 2006; Parkes & Prigerson, 2010; Parkes & Weiss, 1983). John Bowlby (1980), whose influential theory of attachment was outlined in Chapter 14, and Parkes have conceptualized grieving in the context of attachment theory as a reaction to separation from a loved one. As Parkes (2006) notes, "love and loss are two sides of the same coin. We cannot have one without risking the other" (p. 1). The grieving adult is very much like the infant who experiences separation anxiety when her mother disappears from view and tries to retrieve her. As humans, we have evolved not only to form attachments but also to protest their loss.

The **Parkes/Bowlby attachment model of bereavement** describes four predominant reactions. They overlap considerably and therefore should not be viewed as clear-cut stages even though the frequencies of different reactions change over time. These reactions are numbness, yearning, disorganization and despair, and reorganization (see also Jacobs et al., 1987–1988, and see ● **Table 17.2** to view this phase model of bereavement side by side with Kübler-Ross's stages of dying).

1. *Numbness.* In the first few hours or days after the death, the bereaved person is often in a daze—gripped by a sense of unreality and disbelief and almost empty of feelings. He may make plane reservations, call relatives, or order flowers—all

TABLE 17.2 MODELS OF DYING AND BEREAVEMENT

Kübler-Ross's Stages of Dying	The Parkes/Bowlby Attachment Model of Bereavement
1. Denial and isolation	1. Numbness
2. Anger	2. Yearning (including anger and guilt)
3. Bargaining	
4. Depression	3. Disorganization and despair
5. Acceptance	4. Reorganization

as if in a dream. Underneath this state of numbness and shock is a sense of being on the verge of bursting, and, occasionally, painful emotions break through. The bereaved person is struggling to defend himself against the full weight of the loss; the bad news has not fully registered.

2. *Yearning.* As the numbing sense of shock and disbelief diminishes, the bereaved person experiences more agony. Grief comes in pangs or waves that typically are most severe from 5 to 14 days after the death. The grieving person has feelings of panic, bouts of uncontrollable weeping, and physical aches and pains. She is likely to be extremely restless, unable to concentrate or to sleep, and preoccupied with thoughts of the loved one and of the events leading to the death. Most importantly, the bereaved person pines and yearns and searches for the loved one, longing to be reunited.

According to Parkes and Bowlby, it is these signs of separation anxiety—the distress of being parted from the object of attachment—that most clearly make grieving different from other kinds of emotional distress. A widow may think she heard her husband's voice or saw him in a crowd; she may sense his presence in the house and draw comfort from it; she may be drawn to his favorite chair—or, like Kelly in the chapter opener, try to recover him by smelling his bathrobe. Ultimately the quest to be reunited, driven by separation anxiety, fails.

Both anger and guilt are also common reactions during these early weeks and months of bereavement. Frustrated in their quest for reunion, bereaved people often feel irritable and sometimes experience intense rage—at the loved one for dying, at the doctors for not doing a better job, at almost anyone. They seem to need to pin blame somewhere. Unfortunately, they often find reason to blame themselves—to feel guilty. A father may moan that he should have spent more time teaching his son gun safety; the friend of a young man who dies of AIDS may feel that he was not a good enough friend. One of the London widows studied by Parkes felt guilty because she never made her husband bread pudding.

3. *Disorganization and despair.* As time passes, pangs of intense grief and yearning become less frequent, although they still occur. As it sinks in that a reunion with the loved one is impossible, depression, despair, and apathy increasingly predominate. During most of the first year after the death, and longer in many cases, bereaved individuals often feel apathetic and may have difficulty managing and taking interest in their lives.

4. *Reorganization.* Eventually, bereaved people begin to pull themselves together again as their pangs of grief and periods of apathy become less frequent. They invest less emotional energy in their attachment to the deceased and more in their attachments to the living. If they have lost a spouse, they begin to make the transition from being a wife or husband to being a widow or widower, revising their identities. They begin to feel ready for new activities and possibly for new relationships or attachments.

To test the Parkes-Bowlby phase model of grief, Paul Maciejewski and his colleagues (2007) assessed disbelief, yearning, anger, depression, and acceptance in 233 bereaved individuals from 1 to 24 months after their loss of a loved one to death from natural causes. The different emotional reactions peaked in the predicted order (disbelief, yearning, anger, and despair/depression), while acceptance steadily gained strength over time. Acceptance proved to be the strongest response, even in the early months, and yearning was the second strongest response; the remaining responses were relatively weak. ■ Figure 17.3 shows the changing mix of overlapping reactions predicted by attachment theory (Jacobs et al., 1987–1988). Although the worst of the grieving process is during the first 6 months after the loss, the process normally takes a year or more for widows and widowers and can take much longer (Parkes & Prigerson, 2010).

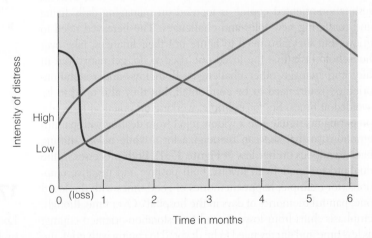

— Numbness and disbelief   — Separation anxiety   — Despair and depression

■ **FIGURE 17.3** The overlapping phases of grief in the Parkes-Bowlby attachment model of bereavement. Numbness and disbelief quickly give way to yearning and pining and then despair or depression (and, although not shown here, growing acceptance and reorganization).

SOURCE: Jacobs, S. C., et al., Attachment theory and multiple dimensions of grief. *Omega: Journal of Death and Dying, 18,* pp. 41-52, Figure 1. Reprinted by permission of Baywood Publishing Co., Inc.

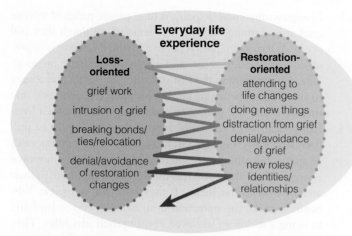

■ **FIGURE 17.4** The dual-process model of coping with bereavement. The bereaved oscillate between loss-oriented and restoration-oriented coping, both of which involve both positive and negative emotions. SOURCE: From Stroebe, M. S., & Schut, H. A. W. (1999). The dual process model of coping with bereavement. *Death Studies, 23,* pp. 197–224, Figure 1. Reprinted by permission of Taylor & Francis Group.

The Dual-Process Model of Bereavement

Like responses to dying, responses to bereavement have proven to be messy—messier than the Parkes/Bowlby phase model suggests (Röcke & Cherry, 2002). Recognizing this, Margaret Stroebe and Henk Schut have put forth a **dual-process model of bereavement** in which the bereaved oscillate between coping with the emotional blow of the loss and coping with the practical challenges of living, revising their identities, and reorganizing their lives (Stroebe & Schut, 1999; and see Hansson & Stroebe, 2007; and Stroebe, Schut, & Boerner, 2010). Loss-oriented coping involves dealing with one's emotions and reconciling oneself to the loss, whereas restoration-oriented coping is focused on managing daily living and mastering new roles and challenges. The bereaved need to grieve, but they also need to figure out their finances, take over household tasks that the loved one used to do, get reinvolved in life, and manage other challenges. Both loss- and restoration-oriented issues need to be confronted, but they also need to be avoided at times. So, for example, working on practical tasks like preparing taxes may give a widow relief from dealing with painful emotions so that she can reenergize for a while before shifting back to a focus on her loss (■ **Figure 17.4**). Both processes in the dual-process model can involve both positive and negative emotions (for example, happy memories of good times with the loved one, painful memories of days in the hospital). Over time, though, emphasis shifts from loss-oriented to restoration-oriented coping; as less time and energy need to be devoted to coping with grief, the balance of positive and negative emotions shifts in a positive direction (Hansson & Stroebe, 2007).

The dual-process model is somewhat like Schneidman's view that dying patients oscillate between acceptance and denial and suggests that adjustment to bereavement, like adjustment to dying, is not very stagelike or even phaselike. Most researchers agree that bereavement is a complex and multidimensional process that involves many ever-shifting emotions, varies greatly from person to person, and often takes a long time.

Meanwhile, the rest of us are sympathetic toward the bereaved immediately after a death—eager to help in any way we can—but we quickly grow weary of someone who is depressed, irritable, or preoccupied. We begin to think, sometimes after only a few days or weeks, that it is time for the bereaved person to cheer up and get on with life. We are wrong. To be of help to bereaved people, we must understand that their reactions of numbness and disbelief, yearning, and despair, and their needs to engage in both loss-oriented and restoration-oriented coping, may linger a long time.

We have now presented some of the major perspectives on how people experience dying and bereavement. However, these perspectives have been based primarily on the responses of adults. How do infants, children, and adolescents respond to death? What does death even mean to infants and young children? A life-span perspective on death and dying is needed (see Walter & McCoyd, 2009).

Checking Mastery

1. What are the roles of acceptance and denial in Kübler-Ross's stage theory and in Shneidman's view of emotional reactions to dying?

2. What are two main criticisms of Kubler-Ross's stage theory of dying?

3. How does attachment theory inform the Parkes/Bowlby model of bereavement?

4. What oscillates in the dual-process model of bereavement?

Making Connections

1. Look carefully at the five stages of dying that Elisabeth Kübler-Ross believes terminally ill patients experience and at the four phases of adjustment bereaved people experience according to Colin Murray Parkes and John Bowlby. What common themes do you see? How do these models differ?

2. If you worked in a hospital wing with terminally ill adults, how might you use Kübler-Ross's perspective to improve care? And how might you avoid misusing it?

17.3 The Infant

Looking at bereavement from an attachment theory perspective makes us wonder how infants understand and cope with the death of an attachment figure. Infants surely do not comprehend death as the cessation of life, but they do gain an understanding of concepts that pave the way for an understanding of death. Infants may, for example, grasp the concepts of being and nonbeing, here and "all gone," from such experiences as watching objects and people appear and disappear, playing peekaboo, and even going to sleep and "coming alive" again in the morning (Maurer, 1961). Possibly, infants first form a global category of things that are "all gone" and later divide it into subcategories,

Games of peekaboo help infants understand the concept of "all gone" and pave the way for an understanding of death.

figure most completely if they can rely on an existing attachment figure (for example, the surviving parent) or have the opportunity to attach themselves to someone new (Walter & McCoyd, 2009). Notice the similarities between these reactions and the yearning, disorganization and despair, and reorganization phases of the Parkes/Bowlby attachment model of bereavement.

Checking Mastery

1. What kinds of experiences in infancy may pave the way for an understanding of the concept of death?

2. When in infancy would you expect infants to show grief reactions if a parent were to die?

Making Connections

1. Baby Seth was a year old when his mother died in a car accident. How would you expect him to react, and how would his reactions compare to those of a bereaved adult, as described by the Parkes/Bowlby attachment model of bereavement?

one of which is "dead" (Kastenbaum, 2000). Infants lack the concept of death as permanent separation or loss, however, and the cognitive capacity to interpret what has happened.

The experience most directly relevant to an emerging concept of death is the disappearance of a loved one, and it is here that Bowlby's theory of attachment is helpful. After infants form their first attachments around 6 or 7 months, they begin to display signs of separation anxiety when their beloved caregivers leave them. According to Bowlby, they are biologically programmed to protest separations by crying, searching for their loved one, and attempting to follow, thereby increasing the chances that they will be reunited with the caregiver and protected from harm.

Bowlby (1980) observed that infants separated from their attachment figures display many of the same reactions that bereaved adults do. Infants first engage in vigorous *protest*—yearning and searching for the loved one and expressing outrage when they fail. One 17-month-old girl said only, "Mum, Mum, Mum" for 3 days after her mother died. She was willing to sit on a nurse's lap but would turn her back, as if she did not want to see that the nurse was not "Mum" (Freud & Burlingham, cited in Bowlby, 1980).

If, after some hours or days of protest, an infant has not succeeded in finding the loved one, he begins to *despair*, displaying depression-like symptoms. The baby loses hope, ends the search, and becomes apathetic and sad. Grief may be reflected in a poor appetite, a change in sleeping patterns, excessive clinginess, or regression to less mature behavior (Furman, 1984; Walter & McCoyd, 2009; and see the description of infant depression in Chapter 16). After some days—longer in some cases—the bereaved infant enters a *detachment* phase, in which he takes renewed interest in toys and companions and may begin to seek new relationships. Infants will recover from the loss of an attachment

17.4 The Child

Much as parents would like to shelter their children from unpleasant life experiences, children encounter death in their early years, if only of bugs and birds. How do they come to understand and cope with their experiences of death?

Grasping the Concept of Death

Contrary to what many adults would like to believe, young children are highly curious about death, think about it with some frequency, and can talk about it (Kastenbaum, 2009). Yet their beliefs about death often differ considerably from those of adults. In Western societies, a "mature" understanding of death has several components (Brent et al., 1996; Hoffman & Strauss, 1985; Kenyon, 2001; Slaughter, Jaakkola, & Carey, 1999). We see death as characterized by the following:

- *Finality.* It is the cessation of life and of all life processes, such as movement, sensation, and thought.
- *Irreversibility.* It cannot be undone.
- *Universality.* It is inevitable and happens to all living beings.
- *Biological causality.* It is the result of natural processes internal to the organism, even if external causes set off these internal changes.

Researchers have studied children's conceptions of death by asking them the sorts of questions contained in ● Table 17.3. Children between age 3 and age 5 have some understanding of death, especially of its universality (Brent et al., 1996). Rather than viewing death as a final cessation of life functions, however, many of them picture the dead as living under altered circumstances and retaining at least some of their capacities (Slaughter,

● TABLE 17.3 WESTERN CHILDREN'S CONCEPTS OF DEATH AND QUESTIONS PERTAINING TO THEM

Concept	Questions
Finality	Can a dead person move? Get hungry? Speak? Think? Dream? Do dead people know that they are dead?
Irreversibility	Can a dead person become a live person again? Is there anything that could make a dead animal come back to life?
Universality	Does everyone die at some time? Will your parents die someday? Your friends? Will you die?
Biological causality	What makes a person die? Why do animals die?

SOURCES: Adapted from Hoffman & Strauss, 1985; Florian & Kravetz, 1985; and other sources.

After the September 11, 2001 attack on the World Trade Center, the Sesame Workshop asked school-age children to draw pictures of their fears and worries. As one child wrote, "My worries is that terrist [sic] will harm my family, and I will be left with no family like the kids in New York" (Stepp, 2001, p. C4). Another child said: "I'm afraid we will be bombed again and it will be World War III. I hate technology" (Stepp, 2001, p. C1). Children's concepts of death are clearly affected by their sociocultural context and events like 9/11, the Southeast Asian tsunami, Hurricane Katrina, the Virginia Tech massacre, and the Haitian earthquake.

Jaakkola, & Carey, 1999). According to these preschoolers, the dead may have hunger pangs, wishes, and beliefs and may continue to love their moms (Bering & Bjorklund, 2004).

Some preschool-age children also view death as reversible rather than irreversible. They may liken it to sleep (from which a person can awaken) or to a trip (from which a person can return). With the right medical care, the right chicken soup, or a bit of magic, a dead person might be brought back to life (Speece & Brent, 1984). Finally, young children think death is caused by one external agent or another; one may say that people die because they eat aluminum foil; another may say the cause is eating a dirty bug or a Styrofoam cup (Koocher, 1974). They do not grasp the ultimate biological cause of death.

Children ages 5 to 7 make considerable progress in acquiring a mature concept of death. Most children this age understand that death is characterized by finality (cessation of life functions), irreversibility, and universality (Grollman, 1995; Speece & Brent, 1992). Even preschool children are capable of grasping these concepts if they understand that the function of the human body is to sustain life and that it needs food, air, and water to do so. They can then begin to infer that death is the opposite of life and that dead people no longer need to eat food or drink water (Bering & Bjorklund, 2004; Slaughter & Lyons, 2003).

Understanding the biological causality of death is the hardest concept of death for children to master but is typically mastered by about age 10 (Kenyon, 2001). Paula, age 12, had clearly mastered the concept that all deaths ultimately involve a failure of internal biological processes: "When the heart stops, blood stops circulating, you stop breathing and that's it. . . . there's lots of ways it can get started, but that's what really happens" (Koocher, 1974, pp. 407–408).

Children's understanding of death appears to be influenced by both their level of cognitive development and their cultural and life experiences. Major breakthroughs in the understanding of death occur in the 5-to-7 age range—when, according to Piaget's theory, children progress from the preoperational stage of cognitive development to the concrete-operational stage. A mature understanding of death is also correlated with IQ (Kenyon, 2001).

In addition, children's concepts of death are influenced by the cultural context in which they live and the specific cultural and religious beliefs to which they are exposed (Sagara-Rosemeyer & Davies, 2007; Stambrook & Parker, 1987). For example, Jewish and Christian children in Israel, who are taught our Western concept of death, provide more "mature" answers to questions about death than Druze children, who are taught to believe in reincarnation (Florian & Kravetz, 1985). Understandably, a child who is taught that dead people are reincarnated may not view death as an irreversible cessation of life processes.

Within any society, children's unique life experiences will also affect their understanding of death. Children who have life-threatening illnesses or who have encountered violence and death in their own lives sometimes grasp death sooner than other children (O'Halloran & Altmaier, 1996). How parents and others communicate with children about death can also make a difference. How is a young child to overcome the belief that death is temporary, for example, if parents and other adults claim that relatives who have died are "asleep"? And if a child is told that "Grandma has gone away," is it not logical to ask why she cannot hop a bus and return?

Experts on death insist that adults only make death more confusing and frightening to young children when they use such euphemisms. They point out that children often understand more than we think, as illustrated by the 3-year-old who, after her father explained that her long-ill and just deceased grandfather had "gone to live on a star in the sky," looked at him quizzically and said, "You mean he is dead?" (Silverman, 2000, pp. 2–3). Experts recommend that parents give children simple but honest answers to the many questions they naturally ask about death and capitalize on events such as the death of a pet to teach children about death and help them understand and express their emotions (Silverman, 2000). Developmentally appropriate educational programs can also help familiarize children with the concepts of life and death (Schonfeld & Kappelman, 1990; Slaughter & Lyons, 2003).

The Dying Child

Parents and doctors often assume that terminally ill children are unaware that they will die and are better off remaining so. Yet research shows that dying children are far more aware of what is happening to them than adults realize (Essa & Murray, 1994). Consider what Myra Bluebond-Langner (1977) found when she observed children ranging in age from 2 to 14 who had leukemia. Even many preschool children arrived, over time, at an understanding that they were going to die and that death is irreversible. Despite the secretiveness of adults, these children noticed changes in their treatments and subtle changes in the way adults interacted with them, and they paid close attention to what happened to other children who had the same disease and were receiving the same treatments. Over time, many of these ill children stopped talking about the long-term future and wanted to celebrate holidays such as Christmas early. A doctor trying to get one boy to cooperate with a procedure said, "I thought you would understand, Sandy. You told me once you wanted to be a doctor." Sandy threw an empty syringe at the doctor and screamed, "I'm not going to be anything!" (p. 59).

How do terminally ill children cope with the knowledge that they are dying? They are not all the models of bravery that some people suppose them to be. Instead, they experience many of the emotions that dying adults experience (Waechter, 1984). Preschool children may not talk about dying, but they may reveal their fears by having temper tantrums or portraying violent acts in their pretend play. School-age children understand more about their situation and can talk about their feelings if given an opportunity to do so. They want to participate in normal school and sports activities so that they will not feel inadequate compared with their peers, and they want to maintain a sense of control or mastery, even if the best they can do is take charge of deciding which finger should be pricked for a blood sample.

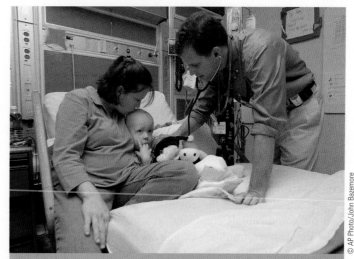

Jack, a three-year-old cancer patient, gets a kiss from his mother Jennifer as he is examined by his doctor. Children who are dying need to know they are loved and need opportunities to express their concerns and fears.

Children with terminal illnesses need the love and support of parents, siblings, and other significant individuals in their lives. In particular, they benefit from a strong sense that their parents are there to care for them (Worchel, Copeland, & Barker, 1987). In one study of Swedish families (Kreicbergs et al., 2004), about a third of parents of terminally ill children talked to their children about dying, and none regretted it. By comparison, 27% of the parents who did not talk with their children regretted not having done so, especially if they sensed their child was aware of dying (as over half the parents did). Perhaps the best advice to parents is to follow the child's lead, enabling children to talk about their feelings if they wish (Faulkner, 1997).

The Bereaved Child

Children's coping capacities are also tested when a parent, sibling, pet, or other loved one dies. Four major messages have emerged from studies of bereaved children: children grieve, they express their grief differently than adults do, they lack some of the coping resources that adults command, and they are vulnerable to long-term negative effects of bereavement (Osterweis, Solomon, & Green, 1984; Lieberman et al., 2003; Silverman, 2000).

Consider some of the reactions that have been observed in young children whose parents have died (Lewis & Lippman, 2004; Lieberman et al., 2003; Silverman, 2000). These children often misbehave or strike out in rage at their surviving parent; they can become unglued when favorite routines are not honored (Lieberman et al., 2003), as when Cara in the chapter opener became upset with her mother for not telling a bedtime story as well as her father used to. They ask endless questions: Where is Daddy? When is he coming back? Will I get a new Daddy? Anxiety about attachment and separation are common; more than half the bereaved children in one study reported being scared that other family members might die (Sanchez et al., 1994). Yet at other times bereaved children go about their activities as if nothing had happened, denying the loss or distracting themselves from it by immersing themselves in play. Alicia Lieberman and her colleagues (2003) characterize young children's responses as "cycles of intense distress, emotional withdrawal, anger, and emotional detachment" (p. 11). You can readily see how caregivers might be disturbed by some of these behaviors (although, as you may have noticed, they are not unlike the emotional swings that bereaved adults experience).

Because they lack the cognitive abilities and coping skills that older individuals command, it is natural that young children might have trouble grasping what has happened and attempt to deny and avoid emotions too overwhelming to face. Young children also have mainly behavioral or action coping strategies at their disposal (Skinner & Zimmer-Gembeck, 2007). For example, 2-year-old Reed found comfort by taking out a picture of his mother and putting it on his pillow at night, then returning it carefully to the photo album in the morning (Lieberman et al., 2003). Older children are able to use cognitive coping strategies such as conjuring up mental representations of their lost parents (Compas et al., 2001; Skinner & Zimmer-Gembeck, 2007).

Grief reactions differ greatly from child to child, but the preschooler's grief is likely to manifest itself in problems with sleeping, eating, toileting, and other daily routines (Oltjenbruns, 2001; Osterweis, Solomon, & Green, 1984). Negative moods, dependency, and temper tantrums are also common. Older children express their sadness, anger, and fear more directly, although somatic symptoms such as headaches and other physical ailments are also common (Worden & Silverman, 1996).

Well beyond the first year after the death, some bereaved children continue to display problems such as unhappiness, low self-esteem, social withdrawal, difficulty in school, and problem behavior (Osterweis, Solomon, & Green, 1984; Worden & Silverman, 1996). In a longitudinal study of school-age children, one in five children who had lost a parent had serious adjustment problems 2 years after the death (Worden & Silverman, 1996; see also Dowdney, 2000). Some children, though by no means all, even develop psychological problems that carry into adulthood— for example, over-reactivity to stress and stress-related health problems, depression and other psychological disorders, or insecurity in later attachment relationships (Harris & Bifulco, 1991; Luecken, 2008; Miralt, Bearor, & Thomas, 2001–2002).

However, most bereaved children—especially those who have effective coping skills and solid social support—adapt quite well. They are especially likely to fare well if they receive good parenting (Haine et al., 2006), if caregivers communicate that they will be loved and cared for (Lieberman et al., 2003), and if they have opportunities to talk about and share their grief (Lewis & Lippman, 2004, p. xii). Bereavement with the help of a caring and supportive caregiver is associated with adaptive responses to stress in adulthood, whereas bereaved children who perceive a lack of caring support after the death may have difficulty handling stress later in life (Luecken et al., 2009).

Checking Mastery

1. What are two factors that might help Jared develop a fuller understanding of death concepts than Jeremy at age 5?

2. What three concepts of death are children likely to master by age 5 to age 7?

3. What reactions on the part of bereaved children might irritate their caregivers?

Making Connections

1. How might you as a parent impede your children from developing a mature concept of death, and how might you facilitate their understanding?

2. If your child had untreatable cancer, would you talk to her about dying? Why or why not? Would the child's age affect your decision? How?

17.5 The Adolescent

Adolescents typically understand death as the irreversible cessation of biological processes and are able to think in more abstract ways about it as they progress from Piaget's concrete-operational stage to his formal-operational stage (Corr, 1995; Koocher, 1973). They use their new cognitive capacities to ponder the meaning of deaths they encounter and such hypotheticals as an afterlife (McCarthy, 2009; Noppe & Noppe, 1997). However, studies by Jesse Bering and David Bjorklund (2004) suggest that many adolescents and adults, although they clearly know that biological processes cease at death, share with young children a belief that psychological functions such as knowing, believing, and feeling continue even after bodily functions have ceased. This is because they have acquired a belief in an afterlife—a belief so common, these researchers suggest, that it could be a product of evolution.

Just as children's reactions to death and dying reflect their developmental capacities and needs, adolescents' reactions to becoming terminally ill are likely to reflect the themes of adolescence (Balk & Corr, 2009; Knapp et al., 2010; Stevens & Dunsmore, 1996). Concerned about their body images as they experience physical and sexual maturation, adolescents may be acutely disturbed if their illness brings hair loss, weight gain, amputation, loss of sexual attractiveness and responsiveness, or other such physical changes. Wanting to be accepted by peers, they may feel like "freaks" or become upset when friends who do not know what to say or do abandon them. Eager to become more autonomous, they may be distressed by having to depend on parents and medical personnel and may struggle to assert their will and maintain a sense of control. Wanting to establish their own identities and chart future goals, adolescents may be angry and bitter at having their dreams snatched from them.

Similarly, the reactions of adolescents to the deaths of family members and friends reflect the themes of the adolescent period (Balk & Corr, 2001; Tyson-Rawson, 1996). For example, still be-

The death of a friend can be a deeply affecting and transformational experience for adolescents.

ing dependent on their parents for emotional support and guidance, adolescents who lose a parent to death may carry on an internal dialogue with the dead parent for years (Silverman & Worden, 1993). And, given the importance of peers in this developmental period, it is not surprising that adolescents are often devastated when a close friend dies in a car accident, commits suicide, or succumbs to a deadly disease (Servaty-Seib, 2009). In one study, 32% of teenagers who lost a friend to suicide experienced clinical levels of depression during the month after the suicide (Bridge et al., 2003). Yet grief over the loss of a friend is often not taken as seriously as grief over the loss of a family member; parents, teachers, and friends may not appreciate how much the bereaved adolescent is hurting (Ringler & Hayden, 2000; Servaty-Seib, 2009).

Adolescents mostly grieve much as adults do. However, they are sometimes reluctant to express their grief for fear of seeming abnormal or losing control and may express their anguish instead through delinquent behavior and somatic ailments (Osterweis, Solomon, & Green, 1984; Walter & McCoyd, 2009). The adolescent who yearns for a dead parent may feel that he is being sucked back into the dependency of childhood and may therefore bottle up these painful feelings (Raphael, 1983, p. 176):

> "When my mother died I thought my heart would break," recalled Geoffrey, age 14. "Yet I couldn't cry. It was locked inside. It was private and tender and sensitive like the way I loved her. They said to me, 'You're cool man, real cool, the way you've taken it,' but I wasn't cool at all. I was hot—hot and raging. All my anger, all my sadness was building up inside me. But I just didn't know any way to let it out."

Checking Mastery

1. In what way do adolescents seem to "regress" to a less mature concept of death?

2. Why might bereaved adolescents be unable to express their grief?

Making Connections

1. Miki (age 3), Rosario (age 9), and Jasmine (age 16) have all been diagnosed with cancer. They have been given chemotherapy and radiation treatments for several months but seem to be getting worse rather than better. Write a short monologue for each child conveying how she understands death.

2. Think about Miki (3), Rosario (9), and Jasmine (16) again but this time write about each girl's major concerns and wishes based on what you know of normal development at each age.

17.6 The Adult

For adults, dealing with the loss of a spouse or partner and accepting their own mortality can be considered normal developmental tasks (Röcke & Cherry, 2002). We have already introduced models describing adults' experiences of dying and bereavement. Here we will elaborate by examining bereavement from a family systems perspective, then trying to define differences between normal and abnormal grief reactions.

Death in the Family Context

To fully understand bereavement, it is useful to adopt a family systems perspective and examine how a death alters relationships, roles, and patterns of interaction within the family, as well as interactions between the family and its environment (Shapiro, 2001; Silverman, 2000; Traylor et al., 2003). Consider the challenges associated with three kinds of death in the family: the loss of a spouse or partner, the loss of a child, and the loss of a parent.

The Loss of a Spouse or Partner

> How odd to smile during Richard's funeral. He was dead and I was smiling to myself. Grief does that. Laughter lies close in with despair, numbness near by acuity, and memory with forgetfulness. I would have to get used to it, but I didn't know this at the time. All I knew, as I sat in Thomas Jefferson's church next to Richard's coffin, was that memory had given pleasure first, and then cracking pain. (Jamison, 2009, pp. 126–127)

Most of what we know about bereavement is based on studies of widows and widowers. Experiencing the death of a spouse or partner becomes increasingly likely as we age; in heterosexual relationships, it is something most women can expect to endure because women tend both to live longer than men and to marry men who are older than they are. The marital relationship is a central one for most adults, and the loss of a marriage partner or other romantic attachment figure can mean the loss of a great deal. Moreover, the death of a partner often precipitates other changes—the need to move, enter the labor force or change jobs, assume responsibilities that the partner formerly performed, parent single-handedly, and so on. Bereaved partners must redefine their roles, identities, and basic assumptions about life in fundamental ways (Lopata, 1996; Parkes & Prigerson, 2010). If they are women, their income is also likely to decline substantially (Zick & Holden, 2000).

As noted earlier in this chapter, Colin Murray Parkes, in extensive research on widows and widowers younger than age 45, concluded that bereaved adults progress through overlapping phases of numbness, yearning, disorganization and despair, and reorganization. What tolls does this grieving process take on physical, emotional, and cognitive functioning? Widows and widowers are at risk for illness and physical symptoms such as loss of appetite and sleep disruption, and they tend to overindulge in alcohol, tranquilizers, and cigarettes (Parkes, 1996; also see Bonanno & Kaltman, 2000). Cognitive functions such as memory and decision making are often impaired, and emotional problems such as loneliness and anxiety are common. Most bereaved partners do not become clinically depressed, but many display increased symptoms of depression in the year after the death (Wilcox et al., 2003). Widows and widowers as a group have higher-than-average rates of death as well (Stroebe, 2001b).

An analysis of research on adjustment to bereavement by George Bonanno and Stacey Kaltman (2000) suggests that modest disruptions in cognitive, emotional, physical, and interpersonal functioning are common, that they usually last for a year, and that less severe, recurring grief reactions may then continue for several years. Although not captured in the Parkes/Bowlby attachment model, positive thoughts about the deceased, expressions of love, and feelings of gaining from the loss are also part of the typical picture, as in the quote at the beginning of this section.

Importantly, though, Bonanno and his colleagues have found much diversity in patterns of response to loss (Bonanno, Boerner, & Wortman, 2008). They studied adults who lost a partner from an average of 3 years before the death to 6 and 18 months afterward (Bonanno et al., 2002; Bonanno, Wortman, & Nesse, 2004). The sample was assessed again 4 years after their loss to examine the long-term implications of different patterns of grieving (Boerner, Wortman, & Bonanno, 2005; and see Ott et al., 2007). Gathering data both before and after the death of a partner revealed patterns of adjustment over time that had not been evident in studies focused only on adjustment after a loss. ■ Figure 17.5 shows the average depression symptom scores over time associated with the five most prevalent patterns of adjustment shown by widows and widowers:

- A resilient pattern in which distress is at low levels all along
- Common grief, with heightened and then diminishing distress after the loss
- Chronic grief in which loss brings distress and the distress lingers
- Chronic depression in which individuals who were depressed before the loss remain so after it
- A depressed–improved pattern in which individuals who were depressed before the loss become less depressed after the death

The biggest surprise in this study was that the resilient pattern of adjustment involving low levels of distress all along turned out to be the most common pattern of response, characterizing almost half the sample. The resilient grievers were not just cold, unfeeling people who did not really love their partners. Rather, as indicated by the data collected before their partners died, they seemed to be well-adjusted and happily married people with good coping resources (Bonanno et al., 2002). Nor was there any

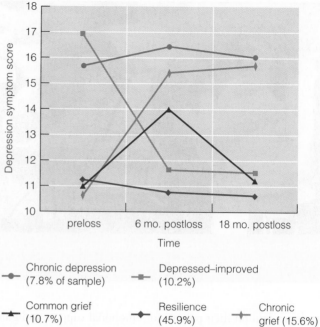

■ **FIGURE 17.5** Depression symptom scores of five subgroups of elderly widows and widowers an average of 3 years before, 6 months after, and 18 months after the death of their spouse. In parentheses are the percentages of the sample showing each pattern. Notice that resilience—a low level of depression all along—is the most common response, contrary to our belief that all bereaved people must go through a period of significant distress. From Bonanno, G. A., Wortman, C. B., & Neese, R. M., Prospective patterns of resilience and maladjustment during widowhood, *Psychology and Aging*, 19, pp. 260–271. Copyright © 2004 American Psychological Association. Reprinted with permission.

sign that they were defensively denying or avoiding painful feelings initially and would pay for it by having delayed grief reactions later (Boerner, Wortman, & Bonanno, 2005). Rather, although they experienced emotional pangs in the first months after the death, they were more comforted than most by positive thoughts of their partners and simply coped effectively with their loss. Other studies suggest that a surprisingly high proportion of bereaved people, from 15 to 50% depending on the study, can be described as resilient (Bonanno, 2004).

This study also helps us understand that some bereaved people who display symptoms of depression after a loss were depressed even before the death, whereas others become depressed in response to their loss. Those who are depressed before the loss tend to remain depressed even 4 years later and are in the most need of help. Those who become depressed in response to the loss often recover from their depression within a year or two; they show the "common grief" pattern, which is more common in some studies than in this one (Boerner, Wortman, & Bonanno, 2005; Bonanno, Wortman, & Nesse, 2004). Another 15% show chronic grief, becoming depressed after the loss and staying depressed for a long time.

The "depressed–improved" individuals in Bonanno's study who were depressed before the death but recovered quickly afterward are intriguing. Most likely they were experiencing caregiver burden (see Chapter 15) before the death and were relieved of stress after it. Richard Schulz and his colleagues (2003) have found that it is common among those who carry the burden of caring for family members with dementia to experience more depression before their partner's death than after; indeed, more than 70% admit that the death came as a relief to both themselves and their loved one.

Do the partners of gay men who die of AIDS experience similar patterns of bereavement? Bonanno and his colleagues (2005) wondered whether resilience would be as common in this group, as many of these men not only experienced the burden of caring for their dying partners but were HIV infected themselves and therefore stressed by their own illness and likely death. In a comparison sample of adults who lost marriage partners or children to death, about half proved to be resilient, showing levels of depression and other emotional symptoms within range of those of nonbereaved people. Among partners of gay men who died of AIDS, the same proportion—about half—showed resilience; whether they were HIV positive themselves did not seem to matter. So although most of these men experienced depression symptoms both before and after their partner's death, most showed considerable resilience.

This finding is all the more surprising because gay and lesbian partners sometimes experience what Kenneth Doka (1989, 2008) calls **disenfranchised grief**, grief that is not fully recognized or appreciated by other people and therefore may not receive much sympathy and support. Losses of ex-spouses, extramarital lovers, foster children, pets, and fetuses can also occasion disenfranchised grief, which is generally likely to be harder to cope with than socially recognized grief. Disenfranchised grief is likely when the relationship is not recognized (as when a gay relationship is in the closet), when the loss is not acknowledged (as when the loss of a pet is not viewed as a "real" loss), when the bereaved person is excluded from mourning activities (as happens sometimes to young children and cognitively impaired elders), and when the cause of death is stigmatized (as in suicides or drug overdoses) (Doka, 2008).

Overall, most bereaved individuals who experience significant grief begin to show signs of recovery a year or so after the death. It is normal, though, to continue to think and talk and have feelings about loved ones. Even 20 years after their loss, the widowed men and women in one study thought about their spouses once every week or two and continued to talk about and feel sad about the spouse now and then, especially on special dates such as the anniversary of the death (Carnelley et al., 2006).

For a minority, up to about 15%, significant grieving and psychological distress continue for many years (Bonanno, Wortman, & Nesse, 2004; Hansson & Stroebe, 2007). In such cases psychologists speak of **complicated grief**, grief that is unusually prolonged or intense and that impairs functioning (Parkes, 2006). People who have difficulty coping with loss are often diagnosed as having a depressive disorder or, if the death was traumatic, posttraumatic stress disorder. However, some experts have concluded that complicated grief, because it has unique symptoms such as intense yearning for the deceased, is distinct from these other conditions, has distinct effects on functioning, and should be considered a psychological disorder but a distinct one (Bonanno et al., 2007; Prigerson & Jacobs, 2001).

In sum, the loss of a spouse or partner is a painful and sometimes damaging experience. During the first weeks and months after the death, the psychological pain is typically most acute and the risks of developing physical or mental health problems or even dying are at a peak. Some widows and widowers experience emotional aftereffects for years, yet up to half of those who lose spouses or romantic partners show resilience and manage to cope without becoming highly distressed.

The Loss of a Child

> My child has died! My heart is torn to shreds. My body is screaming. My mind is crazed. The question is always present on my mind. Why? How could this possibly have happened? The anger is ever so deep, so strong, so frightening. (Bertman, 1991, p. 323, citing a mother's reflections on how she reacted to her 16-year-old daughter's death in a car accident after the initial numbness wore off.)

No loss seems more difficult for an adult than the death of a child (Murphy, 2008; Parkes, 2006). Even when there is forewarning, the loss of a child seems unexpected, untimely, and unfair. Understandably, parents experience a raging anger and often feel that they failed as parent and protector (Rando, 1991). In one study, only 12% of parents whose adolescent or young

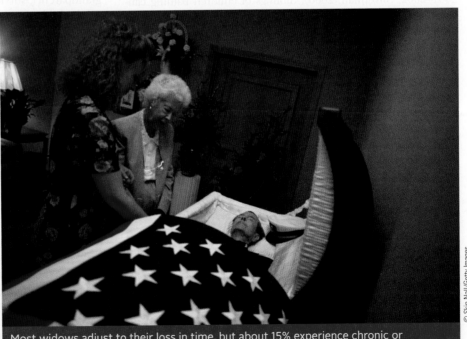

Most widows adjust to their loss in time, but about 15% experience chronic or complicated grief, showing significant distress even 2 years or more after their loss.

© Skip Nall/Getty Images

adult child died of an accident, suicide, or homicide had found meaning in the death 1 year later, and only 57% had found it 5 years later (Murphy, Johnson, & Lohan, 2003b). Being unable to make sense of a child's death is associated with more intense grief (Keesee, Currier, & Neimeyer, 2008). The age of the child who dies has little effect on the severity of the grief: parents, especially mothers, can experience severe grief reactions after a miscarriage, the loss of a premature baby, or the loss of a young infant to sudden infant death syndrome, as well as to the death of an adult child (Broen et al., 2004; Buchi et al., 2007; Walter & McCoyd, 2009).

The death of a child alters the family system, affecting the marital relationship, parenting, and the well-being of surviving siblings and grandparents. The marital relationship is likely to be strained because each partner grieves in a unique way and is not always able to provide emotional support for the other (Bohannon, 1990–1991). Strains are likely to be especially severe if the marriage was shaky before the death. The odds of marital problems and divorce tend to increase after the death of a child, although most couples stay together and some feel closer than ever (Dijkstra & Stroebe, 1998; Najman et al., 1993). Indeed, some help each other. One study guided by the dual-process model of bereavement found that parents who lost a child fared better if they focused more on restoration-oriented coping and less on loss-oriented coping and that men whose wives were restoration oriented and worked on rebuilding their lives were better adjusted than those whose wives focused mainly on the loss (Wijngaards-de Meij et al., 2008).

Grieving parents may have difficulty giving their surviving children the love and support they need to cope with their loss. Children are deeply affected when a brother or sister dies, but their grief is often not fully appreciated and their distraught parents may not be able to support them effectively (Lohan & Murphy, 2001–2002; Silverman, 2000). Siblings of children battling cancer, for example, may resent it if they are neglected by their par-

ents, may be anxious about their own health, may feel guilty about some of the unsavory feelings of rivalry they have, and may feel pressure to replace the lost child in their parents' eyes (Adams & Deveau, 1987). One 12-year-old boy whose brother died described his experience this way: "My dad can't talk about it, and my mom cries a lot. It's really hard on them. I pretend I'm O.K. I usually just stay in my room" (Wass, 1991, p. 29).

Finally, grandparents also grieve after the death of a child, both for their grandchild and for their child, the bereaved parent. As one grandparent said, "It's like a double whammy!" (DeFrain, Jakub, & Mendoza, 1991–1992, p. 178). Grandparents are likely to feel guilty about surviving their grandchildren and helpless to protect their adult children from pain (Fry, 1997). They may also experience disenfranchised grief, ignored while all the supportive attention focuses on the parents (Hayslip & White, 2008). Clearly, then, those who are attempting to help bereaved families need to include the whole family in their efforts.

The Loss of a Parent

Even if we escape the death of a child or spouse, the death of a parent is a normative life transition that most of us will experience. As noted already, some children experience long-lasting problems after the death of a parent. Fortunately, most of us do not have to face this event until we are in middle age. We are typically less dependent on our parents by then. Moreover, we expect that our parents will die someday and have prepared ourselves, at least to some degree.

Perhaps for all these reasons, adjusting to the death of a parent is usually not as difficult as adjusting to the death of a romantic partner or child (Parkes, 2006). Yet it can be a turning point in an adult's life, with effects on his identity and his relationships with his partner, children (who are grieving the loss of their grandparent), surviving parent, and siblings (Umberson, 2003). Adult children may feel vulnerable and alone in the world when their parents no longer stand between them and death (Walter & McCoyd, 2009). Guilt about not doing enough for the parent who died is also common (Moss et al., 1993). Compared with adults who are not bereaved, adults who have lost a parent in the past 3 years have higher rates of psychological distress, alcohol use, and health problems (Umberson, 2003).

Challenges to the Grief Work Perspective

It's time to step back and reflect. The view that has guided much research on bereavement has come to be called the **grief work perspective**—the view that to cope adaptively with death, bereaved people must confront their loss, experience painful emotions, work through those emotions, and move toward a detachment from the deceased (Stroebe, 2001a). This view, which grew out of Freudian psychoanalytic theory, is widely held in our society, not only among therapists but among people in general, and it influences what we view as an abnormal reaction to death (Wortman & Silver, 2001). From the grief work perspective, either a chronic grief that lasts longer and is more intense than usual, or both, or an absence, inhibition, or delay of grief, in which the bereaved never seems to confront and express painful

The death of a child can be devastating for parents.

© Oleg Popov/Reuters/Corbis

feelings, is viewed as pathological or complicated grief (see, for example, Raphael, 1983). This grief work perspective has now come under serious attack. Questions have been raised about its assumptions that there is a right way to grieve, that bereaved people must experience and work through intense grief to recover, and that they must sever their bonds with the deceased to move on with their lives (Bonanno, 2004; Wortman & Boerner, 2007).

First, cross-cultural studies reveal that there are many ways to grieve and suggest that the grief work model of bereavement may be culturally biased (Rosenblatt, 2008). An Egyptian mother may be conforming to her culture's norms of mourning if she sits alone, withdrawn and mute, for months or even years after a child's death. Likewise, a Balinese mother is following the rules of her culture if she is calm, composed, and even seemingly cheerful soon after a child's death (Wikan, 1988, 1991). We would be wrong to conclude, based on our own society's norms, that the Egyptian mother is suffering from chronic grief or the Balinese mother from absent or inhibited grief.

Second, there is surprisingly little support for the grief work perspective's assumption that bereaved individuals must confront their loss and experience painful emotions to cope successfully (Bonanno, 2004; Wortman & Silver, 2001). As you saw earlier, bereaved individuals who fail to show much emotional distress during the early months after the loss do not seem to pay for their lack of grief with a delayed grief reaction later, as the grief work model says they should. Delayed grief is extremely rare, and the individuals who adjust best to death are those very resilient ones who display relatively little distress at any point in their bereavement, experience many positive emotions and thoughts, and manage to carry on with life despite their loss (Bonanno, 2004; Bonanno & Field, 2001). In fact, there is growing evidence that too much "grief work" may, like ruminative coping that involves overanalyzing one's problems, backfire and *prolong* psychological distress rather than relieve it (Bonanno et al., 2005).

Finally, the grief work view that we must break our bonds to the deceased to overcome our grief is under attack. Freud believed that bereaved people had to let go in order to invest their psychic energy elsewhere. However, John Bowlby (1980) noticed that many bereaved individuals revise their internal working models of self and others and continue their relationships with their deceased loved ones on new terms (Bonanno & Kaltman, 1999). Recent research supports Bowlby, suggesting that many bereaved individuals maintain their attachments to the deceased indefinitely through **continuing bonds.** They reminisce and share memories of the deceased, derive comfort from the deceased's possessions, consult with the deceased and feel his or her presence, seek to make the deceased proud of them, and so on. Bereavement rituals in some cultures (in Japan and China, for instance) are actually designed to ensure a continued bond between the living and the dead (Klass, 2001).

Individuals who continue their bonds rather than severing them do not necessarily show poorer adjustment than those who do not. In fact, many benefit from the continuing, but redefined, attachment (Field et al., 1999; Waskowic & Chartier, 2003). Nigel Field and his colleagues (1999) tried to determine when continuing bonds are healthy and when they may not be. They

Is it pathological to maintain a relationship with a deceased parent for many years? Probably not. It is common practice in Japan to remember each morning during worship ancestors who have died, to leave them food and otherwise care for them, and to tell them about one's triumphs and disasters (Klass, 2001). A continuing bond with rather than detachment from the deceased is common in some cultural contexts and can have psychological benefits for the bereaved person.

investigated whether continuing attachment to a deceased spouse was positively or negatively related to levels of grief symptoms among widows and widowers at 6 months, 14 months, and 25 months after their loss. Those who expressed their continuing attachment by having and sharing fond memories of the deceased and by sensing that their loved one was watching over and guiding them experienced relatively low levels of distress. However, those who used their spouse's possessions to comfort themselves at the 6-month mark showed high levels of distress and little decrease in grief over the coming months.

Similarly, Field and Filanosky (2010) found that continuing bonds were helpful when they took the form of internal memories of the deceased that provided a "secure base" for becoming more independent but not when they involved hallucinations and illusions that reflected a continuing effort to reunite with the deceased. Apparently, then, maintaining continuing bonds is adaptive for some people but a sign of continued yearning and prolonged or complicated grief for others (Field, 2008). Cultural influences may also make a difference: in one study, for example, maintaining continuing bonds was related to better adjustment in China but poorer adjustment in the United States, possibly because continuing a relationship with the deceased is perceived as more appropriate in China (Lalande & Bonanno, 2006).

Overall, the traditional grief work perspective is flawed. First, norms for expressing grief vary widely across cultures, so there is no one "right" way to grieve. Second, there is little evidence that bereaved people must do intense "grief work" or that those who do not do it will pay later with a delayed grief reaction. And third, people do not need to sever their attachment to the deceased to adjust to a loss and sometimes benefit from continuing bonds. More fundamentally, researchers are now questioning the idea, embedded in the grief work model, that grief is a pathological process—like a disease that we catch, suffer from, and eventually get over (Bonanno, 2001). As you saw earlier, only about 15% of bereaved individuals experience complications of grief so severe that they can be described as pathological (Bonanno & Kaltman, 2000). What is more, it is common to experience positive emotions along with the negative ones and to feel in the end that one has benefited or grown from one's loss in some way (Davis & Nolen-Hoeksema, 2001; Folkman & Moskowitz, 2004). We must conclude that grief is more complex and less pathological than the grief work model implies.

Who Copes and Who Succumbs?

Even if it is difficult to find the line between normal grief and complicated grief, we can still ask what risk and protective factors distinguish people who cope well with loss from people who cope poorly. Coping with bereavement is influenced by the individual's personal resources, the nature of the loss, and the surrounding context of support and stressors.

Just as some individuals are better able to cope with their own dying than others are, some are better equipped to handle the stresses of bereavement due to their *personal resources.* *Attachment style* is one important resource (or liability). Bowlby's attachment theory emphasizes that early experiences in attachment relationships influence the internal working models we form of self and other, how we later relate to others, and how we handle losses of relationships. Colin Parkes (2006) has studied the internal working models of adults who seek help as they cope with bereavement. His research and other studies paint a picture consistent with attachment theory (see also Shaver & Fraley, 2008).

If infants and young children receive loving and responsive care, they form internal working models of self and others that tell them that they are lovable and that other people can be trusted, and they develop a secure attachment style (see Chapter 14). Having a secure attachment style is associated with coping relatively well with the death of a loved one (Fraley et al., 2006; Parkes, 2006; Stroebe et al., 2010; Waskowic & Chartier, 2003). Individuals who have developed a resistant (or preoccupied) style of attachment tend to be overly dependent and display extreme and chronic grief and anxiety after a loss, ruminating about the death and clinging to the loved one rather than revising their attachment bond (Stroebe et al., 2010). Those who have developed an avoidant (or dismissing) attachment style tend to have difficulty expressing their emotions or seeking comfort from other people; they may do little grieving and seem to disengage from or even devalue the person lost (Fraley & Bonanno, 2004; Parkes, 2006). Finally, those who have a disorganized attachment style rooted in unpredictable and anxiety-arousing parenting appear to be especially unequipped to cope with loss; they may turn inward, harm themselves, or abuse alcohol or drugs (Parkes, 2006).

Personality and coping style also influence how successfully people cope with death. For example, individuals who have difficulty coping tend to have low self-esteem (Lund et al., 1985–1986) and lack a sense that they are in control of their lives (Haas-Hawkings et al., 1985). They often score high on measures of neuroticism (Robinson & Marwit, 2006; Wijngaards-de-Meij et al., 2007), and many were experiencing chronic psychological problems such as depression before they were bereaved (Bonanno, Wortman, & Nesse, 2004). Many also rely on ineffective coping strategies such as denial and escape through alcohol and drugs (Murphy, Johnson, & Lohan, 2003a). By contrast, people who are optimistic, find positive ways of interpreting their loss, and use active coping strategies experience less intense grief reactions and are more likely to report personal growth after their losses than other bereaved adults (Riley et al., 2007).

Bereavement outcomes are influenced not only by the individual's personal resources but also by the nature of the loss. The closeness of the person's relationship to the deceased is a key factor. For example, spouses grieve especially hard if their relationship to the deceased was very close and if they were highly dependent on their partners; yet these same individuals often have a strong sense of personal growth later on as they find themselves capable of managing on their own (Carr, 2008; Johnson et al., 2007). The cause of death can also influence bereavement outcomes. One reason the death of a child is so painful is that children's deaths are often the result of "senseless" and violent events such as car accidents, homicides, and suicides (Parkes & Prigerson, 2010). Surprisingly, sudden deaths are not necessarily harder to cope with overall than expected deaths from illnesses, possibly because any advantages of being forewarned of death are offset by the stresses of caring for a dying loved one (Schulz, Boerner, & Hebert, 2008).

Finally, grief reactions are influenced positively by the presence of a strong social support system and negatively by additional life stressors (Parkes, 2006; Hansson & Stroebe, 2007). Social support is crucial at all ages. It is especially important for the child or adolescent whose parent dies to have good parenting (Haine et al., 2006). Brothers and sisters can help each other cope (Hurd, 2002). Indeed, family members of all ages recover best when the family is cohesive and family members can share their emotions (Traylor et al., 2003). There are also simple things that friends and colleagues can do to be supportive. Many of us are clueless about what to say or do that will be helpful, but it is not sage advice that bereaved individuals want and appreciate. Rather, they report that they are helped most by family and friends who say they are sorry to hear of the loss, make themselves available to serve as confidants, ask how things are going, and allow bereaved individuals to express painful feelings freely if and when they choose rather than trying to cheer them up and talk them out of their grief (Herkert, 2000; Hinds, 2007; Lehman, Ellard, & Wortman, 1986).

Just as social support helps the bereaved, additional stressors hurt. For example, outcomes tend to be poor for widows who must cope with financial problems after bereavement and for widowers who must manage household tasks without their wives (Lopata, 1996). Widows and widowers may have more than the usual difficulty adjusting if they must also single-handedly care

Sensitive social support can make all the difference to the bereaved.

for young children, find a new job, or move (Parkes, 1996; Worden & Silverman, 1993). These kinds of stressors all demand what the dual-process model of bereavement calls restoration-oriented coping; they take energy and resources that elderly widows in poor health, especially those living in poverty with little social support, may not have (Hansson & Stroebe, 2007).

By taking into account the person who has experienced a death, the nature of the death, and the context surrounding it, we can put together a profile of the individuals who are most likely to have long-term problems after bereavement. These individuals have had an unfortunate history of interpersonal relationships, perhaps suffering the death of a parent when they were young or experiencing insecurity in their early attachments. They have had previous psychological problems and generally have difficulty coping effectively with adversity. The person who died is someone whom they loved deeply and on whom they depended greatly, and the death was untimely and seemingly senseless. Finally, these high-risk individuals lack the kinds of social support that can aid them in overcoming their loss, and they are burdened by multiple stressors.

Bereavement and Human Development

The grief work perspective on bereavement has tended to put the focus on the negative side of bereavement, but as you have seen, psychologists are coming to appreciate that bereavement and other life crises also have positive consequences and sometimes foster personal growth (Davis & Nolen-Hoeksema, 2001; Tedeschi & Calhoun, 2004). Granted, it can be a painful way to grow, and we could hardly recommend it as a plan for optimizing human development. Still, the literature on death and dying is filled with testimonials about the lessons that can be learned, and there is evidence that finding benefit in losses has positive effects on not only mental but physical health (Bower, Moskowitz, & Epel, 2009).

Many bereaved individuals believe that they have become stronger, wiser, more loving, and more religious people with a

greater appreciation of life (Tedeschi & Calhoun, 2004). Many widows master new skills, become more independent, and emerge with new identities and higher self-esteem, especially those who depended heavily on their spouses and then discover that they can manage life on their own (Carr, 2004; Lopata, 1996). A mother whose infant died said it all: "Now I can survive anything" (DeFrain, Taylor, & Ernst, 1982, p. 57). So perhaps it is by encountering tragedy that we learn to cope with tragedy, and perhaps it is by struggling to find meaning in death that we come to find meaning in life.

Checking Mastery

1. What is the single most common pattern of adjustment observed in studies of widows and widowers?

2. What are three elements of the grief work perspective that have been challenged because the evidence does not support them?

3. How would individuals with a resistant (preoccupied) attachment style or orientation and those with an avoidant (or dismissing) style be expected to differ in their grief reactions?

Making Connections

1. Using the section "Who Copes and Who Succumbs," analyze your capacity to cope with death. If you have experienced a significant loss, analyze your actual success in coping and the factors that may have influenced it; if you have not experienced a significant loss, predict how you will respond to your first significant loss and why you think so.

2. Many people have misconceptions about what is normal and what is abnormal when it comes to grieving, as this chapter has illustrated. Identify two such misconceptions and, using relevant research, show why they are just that—misconceptions.

17.7 Taking the Sting Out of Death

What can be done to help children and adults who are dying or who are bereaved grapple with death and their feelings about it? Here is a sampling of strategies.

For the Dying

Dramatic changes in the care of dying people have occurred in the past few decades, thanks partly to the efforts of Elisabeth Kübler-Ross and others. The hospice movement is a prime example. A **hospice** is a program that supports dying people and their families through a philosophy of "caring" rather than "curing" (Connor, 2000; Knee, 2010; Saunders, 2002). One of the founders of the hospice movement and of St. Christopher's Hospice in London, Dr. Cicely Saunders (2002), put it this way: "I remain committed to helping people find meaning in the end of life and not to helping them to a hastened death" (p. 289).

The hospice concept spread quickly to North America, where hospices have been established in most communities to serve individuals with cancer, AIDS, and other life-threatening diseases. In many hospice programs today, however, dying patients stay at home and are visited by hospice workers. Hospice care is now part of a larger movement to provide **palliative care,** care aimed not at curing disease or prolonging life but at meeting the physical, psychological, and spiritual needs of patients with incurable illnesses (Shannon, 2006).

What makes hospice care different from hospital care? Whether hospice care is provided in a facility or at home, it entails these key features (Connor, 2000; Corr & Corr, 1992; Siebold, 1992):

- The dying person and his family—not the "experts"— decide what support they need and want.
- Attempts to cure the patient or prolong his life are deemphasized (but death is not hastened either).
- Pain control is emphasized.
- The setting for care is as normal as possible (preferably the patient's own home or a homelike facility that does not have the sterile atmosphere of many hospital wards).
- Bereavement counseling is provided to the family before and after the death.

Do dying patients and their families fare better when they spend their last days together receiving hospice care? Hospice leaders point to suggestive evidence that patients have less interest in physician-assisted suicide when they have access to hospice care and their pain is better controlled (Foley & Hendin, 2002). In one study, a third of individuals cared for by a home health care agency, nursing home, or hospital felt they received too little emotional support, whereas only about 20% of those receiving home hospice services felt this way (Teno et al., 2004). And an evaluation of hospice facility care, at-home hospice care, and conventional hospital care in Great Britain found that hospice patients spent more of their last days without pain, underwent fewer medical interventions and operations, and received nursing care that was more oriented to their emotional needs (Seale, 1991). Moreover, spouses and partners, parents, and other relatives of dying people who received hospice care appear to display fewer symptoms of grief and have a greater sense of well-being 1 to 2 years after the death than similar relatives who coped with a death without benefit of hospice care (Ragow-O'Brien, Hayslip, & Guarnaccia, 2000).

The hospice approach may not work for all, but for some it means an opportunity to die with dignity, free of pain and surrounded by loved ones. The next challenge may be to extend the hospice philosophy of caring rather than curing to more children (Davies et al., 2007; Kastenbaum, 2009). Many children who die of cancer die in a hospital where their pain is not adequately controlled, possibly because their doctors and parents cannot accept that the child is dying and so continue to treat the cancer aggressively (Stillion & Papadatou, 2002; Wolfe et al., 2000).

For the Bereaved

Most bereaved individuals do not need psychological interventions to help them cope with death; they deal with this normal life transition on their own and with support from significant others. At the same time, there are many treatment options for bereaved children, adolescents, and adults, ranging from counseling intended to prevent problems before they arise to interventions designed to treat serious psychological disorders precipitated by a loss (Kazak & Noll, 2004; Raphael, Minkov, & Dobson, 2001; Rosner, Kruse, & Hagl, 2010). Bereaved individuals at risk for complicated grief or depression—because of a history of losses, a history of psychological disorder, or other factors—can clearly benefit from therapy or counseling aimed at preventing or treating debilitating grief (Neimeyer & Currier, 2009; Zisook & Shuchter, 2001).

Because death takes place in a family context, family therapy often makes good sense (Kazak & Noll, 2004; Moore & Carr, 2000). Family therapy and other interventions designed for families can help bereaved parents and children communicate more openly and support one another. It can also help parents deal with their own emotional issues so that they can provide the warm and supportive parenting that can be so critical in facilitating their children's recovery, as illustrated by the Family Bereavement Program described in Application Box 17.1.

Another approach to helping the bereaved is the mutual support or self-help group (Goodkin et al., 2001; Silverman, 2000; Zisook & Shuchter, 2001). One such program is Compassionate Friends, serving parents whose children have died. Parents without Partners, THEOS (They Help Each Other Spiritually), the Widowed Persons Service, and similar groups bring widows and widowers and other bereaved partners together to offer everything from practical advice on such matters as settling finances to emotional support and friendship.

Participation in mutual support groups can be beneficial for bereaved parents, helping them find meaning in the death of their child (Murphy et al., 2003a). And compared with widows who do not participate in support groups, participants tend to be

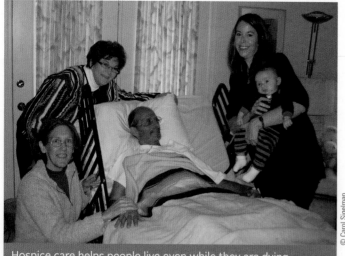

Hospice care helps people live even while they are dying. Lee Sigelman, husband of author Carol Sigelman, enjoyed many happy interactions with friends, family, and pets during his time in home hospice care, here meeting his grandnephew Gus.

© Carol Sigelman

The Family Bereavement Program

The Family Bereavement Program is a successful intervention for families in which a parent has died (Sandler et al., 2003, 2010; Schmiege et al., 2006). Children and adolescents ages 8 to 16 who had lost a parent and the surviving parent met for 14 sessions (2 individual and 12 group sessions for either parents, children, or adolescents). The aims of the program included helping children and adolescents interpret stressful events, use positive coping strategies, and find adaptive ways to express their grief and helping surviving parents deal with their mental health problems and maintain close parent–child relationships and effective discipline at home. A behavioral approach involving modeling and role-playing of target skills and homework assignments to apply skills was used. Among other things, survivors are taught that it is okay to feel sad and angry or to think they see the parent who died as they go about their lives and to maintain a relationship with this parent (Haine et al., 2008).

The intervention helped girls more than boys at the 1-year mark, allowing them to overcome their mental health and behavior problems faster than girls whose families were randomly assigned to a control treatment involving self-study of books about grief. Boys improved over the first year with or without treatment. A follow-up of participants indicated that they showed a greater reduction in problematic grief symptoms 6 years later than control youth did (Sandler et al., 2010). At the 6-year mark, interestingly, boys had shown more improvement than girls and girls were more likely to display prolonged grief.

The Family Bereavement Program was effective in part because it focused on the whole family. By fostering parent warmth, good parent-child communication, and effective discipline, it enabled surviving parents to do a better job of helping their children cope with their loss while also strengthening the ability of children and adolescents to help themselves (Haine et al., 2008).

---

less depressed and anxious, use less medication, and have a greater sense of well-being and self-esteem (Lieberman & Videka-Sherman, 1986). Perhaps this is because other bereaved people are in the best position to understand what a bereaved person is going through and to offer effective social support. One widow summed it up this way: "What's helpful? Why, people who are in the 'same boat'" (Bankoff, 1983, p. 230).

Taking Our Leave

We have reached the end not only of the life span but of this book and want to leave you with a few parting words. Notice that the book's inside back cover provides a chart summarizing key developments in different periods of the life span; it will help you put the "whole person" back together again and see at a glance relationships among the domains of physical, cognitive, personal, and social development. Also notice the appendix on Careers in Human Development—a resource for those of you who think you may want to make a life of studying development or intervening to optimize it.

Finally, we leave you with a reminder of some of the themes echoed throughout this book, many of them part of the life-span perspective on development formulated by Paul Baltes (Baltes, 1987; and see Chapter 1). We hope you can now think of many illustrations of each:

1. **Nature and Nurture Truly Interact in Development:** It's clear that both biology and environment, reciprocally influencing each other all the way, steer development.
2. **We Are Whole People throughout the Life Span:** Advances in one area of development (motor development, for example) have implications for other areas of development (cognitive development through exploration, for example); we must understand interrelationships among domains of development to understand whole human beings.
3. **Development Proceeds in Multiple Directions:** We experience gains and losses, along with changes that simply make us different than we were, at every age.

Newswoman Eleanor Clift, author of a memoir titled *Two Weeks of Life* about the death of her husband, Tom Brazaitis, took this away from her experience: "It's really a gift to help usher someone out of life. It's a moving experience, and I kept trying to be mindful of the fact that this is part of life....And if I could just somehow get through it and honor his memory and keep on living life as best I can and as normal as I can, that's what I would do" (Zanor, 2008, p. F4).

4. **There Is Both Continuity and Discontinuity in Development:** Each of us is at once "the same old person" and a new person, qualitatively different from the person who came before; development is also both gradual and stagelike.

5. **There Is Much Plasticity in Development:** We can change in response to experience at any age, getting off one developmental pathway and onto another.

6. **We Are Individuals, Becoming Even More Diverse with Age:** Developing humans are diverse from the start—and become even more diverse with age.

7. **We Develop in a Cultural and Historical Context:** Human development takes different forms in different times and cultures, in different socioeconomic and racial/ethnic groups, and in different social niches.

8. **We Are Active in Our Own Development:** We help create our environments, influence those around us, and, by doing so, contribute to our own development.

9. **Development Is a Lifelong Process:** We never stop developing, and behavior during any one phase of life is best understood in relation to what came before and what is to come.

10. **Development Is Best Viewed from Multiple Perspectives:** Many disciplines have something to contribute to a comprehensive understanding of human development—and we need them all.

We hope that you are intrigued enough by the mysteries of life-span human development to observe more closely your own development and that of those around you—or even to seek further course work and practical experience in the field. And we sincerely hope that you will use what you learn to steer your own and others' development in positive directions.

Checking Mastery

1. What are three key features of hospice care?

2. What are two approaches used to help bereaved individuals cope?

Making Connections

1. On what can proponents of assisted suicide (see the section "Life and Death Choices") and proponents of hospice care agree—and how do they differ?

2. Which of the life-span development themes illustrated throughout this book can you detect in this chapter on death and dying?

Chapter Summary

17.1 Matters of Life and Death

- In defining death as a biological process, the Harvard definition of total brain death has been influential. Many controversies surround issues of active and passive euthanasia and assisted suicide; meanwhile, the social meanings of death vary widely.

- The average life expectancy for a newborn in the United States has risen to 78 years, higher than that in less developed countries. Death rates decline after infancy but rise in adulthood as accidents give way to chronic diseases as the primary causes of death.

- Programmed theories of aging hold that aging is governed by species heredity, a telomere-controlled cellular aging clock, and individual heredity, whereas damage theories of aging focus on an accumulation of random damage caused by destructive free radicals and other agents.

- The most effective approach to life extension to date is caloric restriction, but its effects on humans have not fully been charted and we are best off for now living a healthy lifestyle and avoiding known health hazards.

17.2 The Experience of Death

- Elisabeth Kübler-Ross stimulated much concern for dying patients by describing five stages of dying, but, as Edwin Shneidman emphasized, dying people experience ever-changing emotions, depending on the course of their disease and on their personality.

- Bereavement precipitates grief and mourning, which are expressed, according to the Parkes/Bowlby attachment model, in overlapping phases of numbness, yearning, disorganization and despair, and reorganization.

- The dual-process model describes oscillation between loss-oriented coping and restoration-oriented coping, with a mix of positive and negative emotions.

17.3 The Infant

- Infants may not comprehend death but clearly grieve, protesting, despairing, and then detaching after separations.

17.4 The Child

- Children are curious about death and usually understand by age 5 to 7 that it is a final cessation of life functions that is irreversible and universal, later realizing that it is ultimately caused by internal biological changes.

- Terminally ill children often become very aware of their plight, and bereaved children often experience bodily symptoms, academic difficulties, and behavioral problems.

17.5 The Adolescent

- Adolescents understand death more abstractly, believe in an afterlife, and cope with dying and bereavement in ways that reflect the developmental themes of adolescence.

17.6 The Adult

- Although up to half show resilience, widows and widowers experience many physical, emotional, and cognitive symptoms and are at increased risk of dying; the death of a child is often even more difficult for an adult to bear, whereas the death of a parent is often easier because it is more expected.

- The grief work perspective has been challenged. What is normal depends on the cultural context. Many people display resilience, never doing "grief work" or suffering because they did not; and many people benefit from continuing rather than severing their attachment bonds.

- Complicated grief is especially likely among individuals who have insecure attachment styles, who have neurotic personalities and limited coping skills, who had close and dependent relationships with individuals who died violently and senselessly, and who lack social support or face additional stressors.

17.7 Taking the Sting Out of Death

- Successful efforts to take the sting out of death have included hospices and other forms of palliative care for dying patients and their families and individual therapy, family therapy, and mutual support groups for the bereaved.
- Themes of this book include many themes that are part of the life-span perspective on development formulated by Paul Baltes and introduced in Chapter 1.

Checking Mastery Answers

For answers to Checking Mastery questions, visit
www.cengagebrain.com

Key Terms

total brain death **560**	denial **569**
euthanasia **561**	bereavement **570**
assisted suicide **561**	grief **570**
living will **561**	mourning **570**
programmed theories	anticipatory grief **570**
of aging **565**	Parkes/Bowlby attachment
damage theories of aging **565**	model of bereavement **570**
maximum life span **565**	dual-process model
progeria **565**	of bereavement **572**
Hayflick limit **566**	disenfranchised grief **579**
telomere **566**	complicated grief **579**
free radicals **566**	grief work perspective **580**
antioxidants **567**	continuing bonds **581**
caloric restriction **567**	hospice **583**
centenarians **568**	palliative care **584**

Media Resources

Psychology CourseMate

Find online quizzes, flash cards, animations, video clips, experiments, interactive assessments, and other helpful study aids for this text at **www.cengagebrain.com**. You can also connect directly to the following sites:

Care of Terminally Ill Children

This website is host to a number of resources related to caring for terminally ill children. Topics covered include a child's concept of death, anticipatory grief, hospice, and others. To access, see "web links" in Psychology CourseMate at www.cengagebrain.com

Hospice Foundation of America

This is a great website for those interested in the hospice alternative to dying. Be sure to check out the sections on "Grief & Loss" and "End of Life Info." To access, see "web links" in Psychology CourseMate at www.cengagebrain.com

Understanding the DATA: Exercises on the Web

www.cengagebrain.com
For additional insight on the data presented in this chapter, try out the exercises for these figures in Psychology CourseMate at

www.cengagebrain.com:

Table 17.1 Leading causes of death for different age groups in the United States.

Figure 17.3 The overlapping phases of grief in the Parkes-Bowlby attachment model of bereavement.

Figure 17.5 Depression symptom scores of five subgroups of elderly widows and widowers an average of 3 years before, 6 months after, and 18 months after the death of their spouse.

CengageNOW

www.cengagebrain.com
Go to www.cengagebrain.com to link to CengageNOW, your online study tool. First take the Pre-Test for this chapter to get your Personalized Study Plan, which will identify topics you need to review and direct you to online resources. Then take the Post-Test to determine what concepts you have mastered and what you still need work on.

Appendix

Careers in Human Development

What career possibilities exist for students interested in understanding or optimizing human development? Being developmentalists ourselves, we would argue that *anyone* who works with people can benefit from an understanding of life-span human development. We are not alone in our belief: Preparation for many "people" professions—teaching, counseling, and nursing and other allied health professions—includes coursework in human development. Indeed, some of you are taking this course because it is required for your chosen career.

If you think you are interested in a career in human development, you might first ask yourself some basic questions:

- What *level of education* do you seek—bachelor's, master's, or doctoral?
- Are you interested in a particular *age group*—infants, children, adolescents, adults, elderly people?
- Are you interested in a particular *aspect of development*—physical, cognitive, or social development, normal or abnormal development?
- Are you most interested in *research, teaching, or practice* (work as a helping professional of some kind)?

We will sketch out some career possibilities within the broad areas of research, teaching, and professional practice, illustrating as we go how the level of education you seek and the age groups and aspects of development of interest to you come into play. Much information is drawn from the U. S. Bureau of Labor Statistics (2010) guide, *Occupational Outlook Handbook, 2010–11 edition*, available online; you may want to consult it to learn more about the employment outlook and average salaries in some of the professions discussed (see Resources at the end of this Appendix).

Research

Depending on what level of authority and responsibility you seek, you can conduct research on human development with a bachelor's degree, master's degree (typically 2 years of coursework and either a comprehensive examination or completion of a thesis), or doctoral degree (typically 5–7 years of work, including courses, a qualifying or comprehensive exam, and completion of a doctoral dissertation research project). Research on normal life-span development and aging, abnormal development, and genetic and environmental influences on development is conducted in a variety of settings: colleges and universities; medical schools, hospitals, and other health care facilities; government institutes and agencies (for example, the National Institutes of Health, including the National Institute of Child Health and Human Development and the National Institute on Aging, and state and local health and human services agencies), social research organizations (some of the larger ones that conduct research on children, families, aging, and social policy are Abt Associates, SRI International, Mathematica, MDRC, RAND, and Westat), and various for-profit and nonprofit organizations.

With a bachelor's degree, you could be hired as a research assistant, interviewer, or other member of a research team and might work on research tasks such as reviewing literature, conducting telephone surveys, testing children, observing and coding behavior, analyzing physiological data, and compiling tables and graphs. With additional work experience—or with a master's degree in a relevant field such as developmental psychology, including coursework in research methods and statistics—you would become eligible for positions of greater responsibility. For example, you might be hired as the project coordinator for an investigator's study, responsible for implementing the data collection plan and supervising the work of research assistants, or you might become a specialist in testing infants, administering tasks to elderly adults, or analyzing data.

Finally, with a doctor of philosophy (PhD) degree in developmental psychology or a related field, you would qualify to be a principal investigator and head a research team—to be the one who designs research projects, submits research proposals to the federal government or foundations to obtain funding, guides implementation of the study, supervises the research staff, analyzes data, writes up findings, and submits papers for publication in professional journals (publications that are then cited in textbooks like this one). Because research is conducted in so many settings, your options as a PhD include many besides becoming a college or university professor who combines teaching and research. And the topics you can study are as wide ranging as those in this book.

How can you get a start on a career in human development research now? You might ask professors at your college or university about graduate programs and job opportunities in areas of development that interest you. Seek as much research experience as you can get, too:

- Ask your professors whether they need help with their research and be on the lookout for notices about research projects that need student assistants on either a voluntary or paid basis.

- Sign up for an independent study course that would allow you to conduct a literature review or do a research project with guidance from a professor.
- Seek undergraduate research fellowships that might allow you to do a research project with financial support, possibly a summer living stipend; some colleges and universities offer such research fellowships to their own students or even to students from other universities (for example, through the National Science Foundation's Research Experiences for Undergraduates program).
- Do a senior thesis or capstone project if it is an option in your major.
- If you are seeking work, look for jobs that involve research, program evaluation, or policy analysis; even if the research is not directly related to human development, you may learn useful research skills.
- Attend professional conferences to gain exposure to researchers in your area of interest and hear about the latest research they are conducting.

- Use PsycInfo and other online databases to find out who is doing good research of interest to you and at what universities.

These sorts of activities will help you find out whether you like research and what aspects of it you like (or don't). They will also help you acquire research skills, get to know professors who can write reference letters for you and otherwise help you pursue your career plans, and demonstrate to graduate programs or employers that you are interested in research and have some familiarity with it. Increasingly, admission to doctoral programs requires experience assisting with research, presenting papers at professional conferences, or even publishing articles with professors.

Some students seek paid research staff positions after completing their bachelor's degree, do well, and work their way up to more responsible positions. Others work for a while and go on for an advanced degree after they have gained some experience. Others enter master's programs, and still others who are certain they want a research career apply directly to doctoral programs as college seniors. In most graduate programs, students gain hands-on experience by serving as research assistants for professors while they are taking courses; they then draw on this apprenticeship experience in designing and conducting a master's thesis or doctoral dissertation project of their own.

Teaching

Teachers clearly need to understand the developmental characteristics and learning capacities of their students to teach effectively and make a difference in their students' lives. As a result, coursework in human development is a required part of teacher training at the bachelor's and master's levels. Colleges of education offer teacher preparation programs in preschool or early childhood, kindergarten, elementary school, middle school, secondary school, and adult education; in the teaching of specific subjects such as English or science; and in special education (the teaching of students with developmental disabilities, behavior disorders, and other special learning needs). Teachers normally need to complete a teacher education program leading to a bachelor's or master's degree and then obtain certification from the state in which they will teach by demonstrating that they have taken the required coursework and passing a standardized teacher exam.

To teach at the college or university level, a doctoral degree, usually a doctor of philosophy (PhD) degree, is normally required. Much of what we said earlier about doctoral education for researchers applies to doctoral education for professors. Most PhD programs are highly research-oriented and involve both learning about the field through coursework and learning how to contribute to the field through research. Some community colleges hire professors with master's degrees in certain areas but more and more hire only PhDs. In schools of education, either a PhD or an EdD (doctor of education) can qualify an individual for a faculty position; the PsyD degree, discussed later, prepares people to be practicing psychologists and is not the right choice for those interested primarily in research and teaching positions.

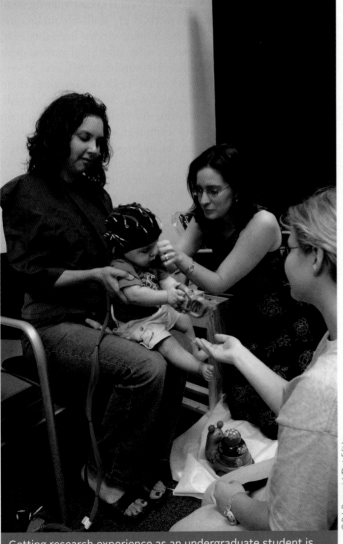

Getting research experience as an undergraduate student is good preparation for graduate school.

Students may get the impression that their professors do nothing but teach, but the job description of a faculty member often includes not only teaching and advising students but also conducting research and providing service to the college or university (for example, through committee work or involvement in university governance) as well as to the local community and profession (for example, by consulting with local nonprofit organizations or schools, by serving as a reviewer for a journal that publishes research in one's field, or as an officer in a professional organization). Specific responsibilities vary considerably depending on the type of institution; generally, teaching responsibilities are heavy and research responsibilities are light at a community college, whereas research may be the first and foremost responsibility of a professor at a large research university, who may teach only a course or two a semester. Large universities also appoint some PhDs as "research professors," who typically support their salaries by getting grants from the federal government and other sources and spend virtually all their time doing research.

If you are considering applying to doctoral programs, we strongly recommend that you do serious research to identify programs that are a good fit to your interests and qualifications. Doctoral-level training in human development can be found in a bewildering array of departments, schools, centers, and institutes within universities. The American Psychological Association's (2009) publication *Graduate Study in Psychology* is an excellent resource for students seeking a graduate program in developmental psychology (typically located in a psychology department), human development (typically an interdisciplinary program located in its own department or even school), family studies (also interdisciplinary, sometimes part of a larger "human development and family studies" or "family and consumer sciences" program), educational psychology (in either schools of education or psychology departments), or gerontology (also often interdisciplinary and sometimes based in a center or institute).

Most professors who teach human development or aging did their doctoral work in either psychology or education, but some departments of sociology and anthropology around the country also have strength in the study of families or aging. Moreover, graduate programs in biology often have faculty who specialize in developmental biology, and neuroscience and cognitive neuroscience programs often have specialists in developmental neuroscience, developmental disabilities, dementia, and other topics relevant to development and aging. The more you know about your specific research and teaching interests, the better; you will then be able to seek programs in the right field that have scholars whose interests match yours and can even apply to particular programs because you want to work with specific professors. Doctoral programs are competitive, but many doctoral students have their education paid for by fellowships and teaching and research assistantships.

Professional Practice

By *professional practice* we mean the application of knowledge of human development in order to optimize development. Opportunities for professional practice are even more varied than those for research and teaching.

Pre-Bachelor's– or Bachelor's-Level Positions

If you decide you want to enter one of the many helping professions, it makes sense to seek applied experience while you are completing your bachelor's degree or afterward—for example, through unpaid or paid internships or jobs in counseling centers, hospitals, human services agencies, treatment facilities for children or adolescents, or senior centers or nursing homes, depending on your interests. This is a great way to gauge your interests and abilities and develop skills. Some relevant jobs available to individuals with a bachelor's degree or less include:

- **Child care worker:** The pay is not good, but individuals who love working with children can, with a bachelor's degree or less, work in day care and preschool facilities, before- and after-school programs, camps and recreation programs, and residential programs for disturbed children (U. S. Bureau of Labor Statistics, 2010).
- **Social and human service assistant:** Countless entry-level positions in human services, mental health, and health care are available, carrying diverse titles such as case management aide, community outreach worker, life skills counselor, and gerontology aide. Social and human service assistants assist psychologists, nurses, social workers, and other professionals in hospitals, mental health centers and facilities, and government agencies, performing such tasks as assessing client needs, conducting intake interviews, keeping case records, processing paperwork, teaching life skills, supervising clients in residential facilities, and leading group or family sessions.
- **Social and community service manager:** A bachelor's degree, especially if combined with work experience, may qualify an individual to manage a social service program or community outreach organization, setting policies and practices, overseeing the budget, supervising staff, and so on (U. S. Bureau of Labor Statistics, 2010). Fundraising is often part of the job description in nonprofit organizations that depend on grants and donations for their survival.

Most of the following career options require graduate coursework in areas such as assessment and treatment approaches; practicum and internship experiences in which learning is put to practice; and the passing of an examination after completion of studies in order to be licensed or certified by a state to practice.

Applied Developmental Psychologist

If you want to be squarely in the field of human development and have a positive impact on development but do not want to become a therapist or counselor, you might look into master's or doctoral programs in applied developmental psychology, a fairly new subfield of psychology, or in the broader, multidisciplinary field of applied developmental science. Although many graduate programs in developmental psychology, human development, and family studies engage in real-world, policy-relevant research, applied developmental psychology programs make a point of it. Applied developmental psychologists may be trained to conduct research on practical problems such as improving early childhood

Some human service workers organize and lead activities at senior day care centers and residential facilities for elderly adults. Here an aide helps an elderly woman at the On Lok Senior Health Service in San Francisco.

© Ronnie Kaufman/Corbis

education, supporting at-risk families, or reducing childhood injuries; assess the developmental status of infants and children; design, implement, and evaluate interventions aimed at preventing or treating problems such as alcohol and drug abuse, aggression, or abusive parenting; and consult or serve as expert witnesses in juvenile court proceedings, custody hearings, and the like. After earning a doctorate, applied developmental psychologists may seek a license to practice as a scientist-practitioner; they must obtain the required supervised field experience and pass a licensure examination (Kuther & Morgan, 2010).

Counselor, Psychologist, or Therapist

Now consider some options if you want to provide counseling or psychotherapy to individuals or families as a state-licensed or certified psychologist. Wearing the title "psychologist" generally requires doctoral-level training in the United States. Individuals with master's degrees in fields such as clinical or counseling psychology are needed in mental health centers and facilities, but they are hired as "psychological assistants" or "psychological associates" and must be supervised by doctoral-level psychologists or psychiatrists (see U. S. Bureau of Labor Statistics, 2010). Here are three types of practicing psychologists:

Clinical Psychologist

Clinical psychologists are trained to diagnose and treat individuals with psychological disorders. Child clinical psychologists focus their practice and research on infants, children, and adolescents; pediatric psychologists, who sometimes obtain their degrees in health psychology programs, focus on child health care, often working in medical schools, hospitals, and other health care facilities; still other clinical psychologists specialize in treatment of elderly people.

Becoming a clinical psychologist normally requires earning a PhD or PsyD (the doctor of psychology degree, a more practice-oriented and less research-oriented degree than the PhD). You should look closely at the extent to which a program of interest is practice-oriented versus research-oriented and decide whether you want to be primarily a scientist, primarily a practitioner, or a scientist–practitioner who integrates the two roles. You should also understand that clinical psychology programs are extremely selective, requiring high grades, high scores on the Graduate Record Examinations (GREs), relevant experience, and excellent recommendations.

Counseling Psychologist

Counseling psychologists may earn a PhD, EdD, or PsyD. Like clinical psychologists, they qualify to be licensed as psychologists. Compared with clinical psychologists, though, they tend to emphasize optimizing mental health and more often work with everyday problems of adjustment (for example, as a counselor in a college or university, company, or community mental health center).

School Psychologist

After completing either an education specialist (EdS) degree (which requires about 3 years of study and a yearlong internship) or a PhD, EdD, or PsyD in school psychology, a school psychologist is prepared to use IQ tests and other assessment instruments to evaluate students believed to have learning disabilities or other special educational needs or to be gifted, consult with teachers and parents on how best to educate them, and provide other supportive psychological services in schools.

Now consider some additional possibilities for careers in counseling and therapy, some of which do not require doctoral-level education:

Psychiatrist

Becoming a psychiatrist involves earning a doctor of medicine (MD) degree and choosing psychiatry as one's specialty; job descriptions and employment opportunities are much like those of

Family therapy may be provided by clinical or counseling psychologists or by clinical social workers.

ing counseling and therapy. Clinical social workers with an MSW can practice independently, whereas psychologists must have a doctoral degree to do so.

Given the steady growth of the aging population, career opportunities for psychologists, counselors, and social workers with training in gerontology are likely to expand. A number of universities offer certificates or minors in gerontology that students can combine with any number of academic majors to position themselves to work with elderly people; other universities offer bachelor's, master's, and even doctoral programs in gerontology (see Association for Gerontology in Higher Education, 2009). Services for older adults are varied and are expanding, providing plenty of opportunities for individuals with bachelor's and master's degrees. Our society clearly needs more individuals in a variety of disciplines and professions who care about and have expertise in aging.

clinical psychologists, but psychiatrists can prescribe medications for psychological disorders.

Counselor

A wide range of counseling programs exist in psychology departments, schools of education, and human development and family studies programs, and many provide opportunities for independent practice after earning a master's degree and passing a state licensing examination. Subareas of counseling include school counseling (which may involve helping students who have academic or personal problems or, at the secondary school level, helping high school students plan their futures), career counseling, rehabilitation counseling (work in the vocational rehabilitation field helping adults with disabilities adapt to their disabilities and find appropriate jobs), substance abuse or addiction counseling, mental health or community counseling, marriage and family therapy, genetic counseling, gerontological (aging) counseling, and more (see U. S. Bureau of Labor Statistics, 2010, on Counselors).

Social Worker

Careers in social work normally require at least a master's degree in social work (MSW). Specialties include child, family, and school social work; medical and public health social work; and mental health or clinical social work (U. S. Bureau of Labor Statistics, 2010). Some social workers are employed by human services agencies as caseworkers who work with families on welfare, neglected or abused children and their families, or aging adults and their families; medical social workers are based in health care facilities and support patients and their families. Clinical social workers are trained in diagnosing personal and family problems and in provid-

Health Professionals

Let's briefly note that a wide range of careers in medicine and allied health professions offer opportunities to apply knowledge of human development and aging to practice. Physicians can focus their careers on newborns, children, adolescents, or elderly adults, as they choose, selecting specialties such as pediatrics or geriatrics in medical school and seeking positions that allow them to work with the age groups and health problems of greatest interest to them. Similarly, nurses can become hospice or palliative care nurses who work with terminally ill patients, developmental disabilities nurses, or psychiatric nurses—or can specialize in the care of a particular age group. Other allied health professions such as speech therapy, physical therapy, and occupational therapy also allow for specialization in particular age groups and type of problems.

Other Options

Finally, we need an "Other" category to say that individuals with training in developmental psychology, counseling, and other human development fields land in surprising places. Many people who enter the occupations we have discussed here advance by becoming administrators; for example, a teacher may become a principal, a psychologist, counselor, or social worker may become the director of a treatment facility or human service agency. Some of these helping professionals seek further education relevant to their administrative roles (for example, a master's degree in business administration, public administration, or heath care management); others simply take on higher administrative roles and learn on the job.

People with training in human development also find their way into business and industry. One may become a book editor in

TABLE A.1 SOME CAREER OPTIONS IN HUMAN DEVELOPMENT

Degree Required	Research	Teaching	Professional Practice
Bachelor's or master's degree	Research assistant Research staff member Project coordinator	Teacher's aide Teacher in preschool, elementary, secondary, or adult education	Child care worker Social and human services worker Psychological assistant or associate Social worker* School psychologist*
Doctoral degree	Research professor Principal investigator in university, hospital, health or mental health facility, research organization	Professor of developmental psychology, human development, family studies Professor of clinical psychology, counseling psychology, social work	Applied developmental psychologist Clinical psychologist Counseling psychologist Psychiatrist Counselor Health professional (medicine, allied health)

*Master's degree required.

a company that publishes books on psychology; another may test toys or other products for children; another may advise a company's employees on retirement issues; another may advise on architectural design for the elderly. Many also work as self-employed consultants, offering help to agencies, organizations, and businesses in areas in which they have expertise. ● Table A.1 summarizes some of the career options we have discussed.

We hope this is enough to get you thinking and dreaming—and, better yet, taking concrete steps now to gain the knowledge, skills, and experience that will help you formulate and realize your dream. We are confident that the need for individuals who understand the complexities and marvels of life-span human development and can steer it in healthy directions will remain strong as long as humans develop and age.

Resources

American Psychological Association. The APA website, www.apa.org, has information and publications about careers in psychology, including a short overview of the different types of jobs psychologists hold at: www.apa.org/careers/resources/guides/careers.aspx.

American Psychological Association. (2009). *Graduate Study in Psychology: 2010 Edition.* Washington, DC: American Psychological Association. This invaluable guide for students looking for appropriate graduate programs profiles more than 600 graduate programs in the United States and Canada, noting program emphases, admission standards, information about the employment of graduates, and the like.

Association for Gerontology in Higher Education (2009). *Directory of educational programs in gerontology and geriatrics* (8th ed.). Washington, DC: Author. Information on more than 750 for-credit and postdoctoral programs in 30 fields of study. The website of the Association for Gerontology in Higher

Education, www.aghe.org, also has information about careers in gerontology and geriatrics.

U. S. Bureau of Labor Statistics (2010). *Occupational Outlook Handbook, 2010–11.* A wonderful resource describing, for all major occupational fields, the nature of the work involved, working conditions, training and other qualifications, employment data, job prospects, and average earnings. Includes sections on Psychologists and Counselors. Available free at www.bls.gov/oco or as a book published by the U. S. Government Printing Office.

Careers in Aging. This website, www.careersinaging.com, orients students to career opportunities in gerontology and geriatrics.

GradSchools.com. This website allows you to search for graduate programs at the master's and doctoral levels in various fields and link to the web pages of those programs efficiently. The web address is http://GradSchools.com.

JobWeb.com. This site of the National Association of Colleges and Employers is aimed at new college graduates and provides useful guidance on resume preparation and job search strategies, as well as job listings. The web address is www.JobWeb.com.

Kuther, T. L. (2006). *The psychology major's handbook* (2nd ed.). Belmont, CA: Thomson Wadsworth. A good general guide to succeeding as a psychology major and preparing for graduate school and careers.

Kuther, T. L., & Morgan, R. D. (2010). *Careers in psychology: Opportunities in a changing world* (3rd ed.). Belmont, CA: Wadsworth Cengage Learning. A survey of opportunities in the various subfields of psychology, including developmental psychology.

Wegenek, A. R., & Buskist, W. (2010). *The insider's guide to the psychology major: Everything you need to know about the degree and profession.* Washington, DC: American Psychological Association. This guide can help psychology majors get the most out of their education and position themselves for careers in psychology.

Glossary

A-not-B error The tendency of 8- to 12- month-old infants to search for a hidden object in the place they last found it (A) rather than in its new hiding place (B).

ability grouping The practice in education of grouping students according to ability and educating them in classes with students of comparable academic or intellectual standing; also called ability tracking or simply tracking.

acceptance–responsiveness A dimension of parenting capturing the extent to which parents are supportive, sensitive to their children's needs, and willing to provide affection and praise when their children meet their expectations.

accommodation In Piaget's cognitive developmental theory, the process of modifying existing schemes to incorporate or adapt to new experiences. Contrast with *assimilation*. In vision, a change in the shape of the eye's lens to bring objects at differing distances into focus.

acquired immunodeficiency syndrome (AIDS) The life-threatening disease in which the human immunodeficiency virus (HIV) destroys the immune system and makes victims susceptible to rare, so-called opportunistic, infections that eventually kill them. AIDS is transmitted through sexual activity, drug needle sharing, and from mother to child before or during birth.

activity theory A perspective holding that aging adults will find satisfaction to the extent that they maintain an active lifestyle. Contrast with *disengagement theory*.

activity–passivity issue The issue in developmental theory centering on whether humans are active contributors to their own development or are passively shaped by forces beyond their control.

adaptation In Piaget's cognitive developmental theory, a person's inborn tendency to adjust to the demands of the environment, consisting of the complementary processes of *assimilation* and *accommodation*.

adolescence The transitional period between childhood and adulthood that begins with puberty and ends when the individual has acquired adult competencies and responsibilities.

adolescent egocentrism A characteristic of adolescent thought that involves difficulty differentiating between the person's own thoughts and feelings and those of other people; evident in the *personal fable* and *imaginary audience* phenomena.

adolescent growth spurt The rapid increase in physical growth that occurs during adolescence.

adoption study Method of studying genetic and environmental influence that involves determining whether adopted children are more similar to their biological parents (whose genes they share) or adoptive parents (who shaped their environment).

adrenarche A period of increased production of adrenal hormones, starting around 6–8 years of age, that normally precedes increased production of gonadal hormones associated with puberty.

age effects In developmental research, the effects of getting older or of developing. Contrast with *cohort effects* and *time of measurement effects*.

age grades Socially defined age groups or strata, each with different statuses, roles, privileges, and responsibilities in society.

age norms Expectations about what people should be doing or how they should behave at different points in the life span.

age of viability A point (around the 24th prenatal week) when a fetus may survive outside the uterus if the brain and respiratory system are well enough developed and if excellent medical care is available.

ageism Prejudice against elderly people.

agency An orientation toward individual action and achievement that emphasizes traits of dominance, independence, assertiveness, and competitiveness; considered masculine.

age-related macular degeneration Damage to cells in the retina responsible for central vision.

aging To most developmentalists, positive, negative, and neutral changes in the mature organism; different from *biological aging*.

allele One of the possible variants of a particular gene.

alphabetic principle The idea that the letters in printed words represent the sounds in spoken words.

Alzheimer's disease A pathological condition of the nervous system that results in an irreversible loss of cognitive capacities; the leading cause of dementia in later life.

amniocentesis A method of extracting amniotic fluid from a pregnant woman so that fetal body cells within the fluid can be tested for chromosomal abnormalities and other genetic defects.

amnion A watertight membrane that surrounds the developing embryo, regulating its temperature and cushioning it against injuries.

amoral Lacking any sense of morality; without standards of right and wrong.

analytic component In Sternberg's triarchic theory, the information-processing skills such as thinking critically and analytically.

androgenized female A genetic female who was exposed to male sex hormones during the prenatal period and therefore developed male-like external genitals and some masculine behaviors.

androgens Male hormones that help trigger the adolescent growth spurt and the development of the male sex organs, secondary sex characteristics, and sexual motivation.

androgyny A gender-role orientation in which the person blends both positive masculine-stereotyped and positive feminine-stereotyped personality traits.

androgyny shift A psychological change that begins in midlife, when parenting responsibilities are over, in which both men and women retain their gender-typed qualities but add to them qualities traditionally associated with the other sex, thus becoming more androgynous.

andropause The slower and less-dramatic male counterpart of *menopause*, characterized by decreasing levels of testosterone and symptoms that include low libido, fatigue and lack of energy, erection problems, memory problems, and loss of pubic hair.

anencephaly Condition in which the top of the neural tube fails to close and the main portion of the brain above the brain stem fails to develop properly.

anorexia nervosa A life-threatening eating disorder characterized by failure to maintain a normal weight, a strong fear of weight gain, and a distorted body image; literally, "nervous lack of appetite."

anoxia A lack of sufficient oxygen to the brain that may result in neurological damage or death.

anticipatory grief Grieving before death for what is happening and for what lies ahead.

antioxidant Vitamins C, E, and similar substances that may increase longevity, although not for long, by inhibiting the free radical activity associated with oxidation and in turn preventing age-related diseases.

Apgar test A test routinely used to assess a newborn's heart rate, respiration, color, muscle tone, and reflexes immediately after birth and 5 minutes later; used to identify high-risk babies.

aphasia A language disorder.

artificial insemination A method of conception that involves injecting sperm from a woman's partner or from a donor into the uterus.

Asperger syndrome An autistic spectrum disorder in which the child has normal or above-average intelligence, has good verbal skills, and wants to establish social relationships but has seriously deficient mindreading and social skills.

assimilation Piaget's term for the process by which children interpret new experiences in terms of their existing schemata. Contrast with *accommodation*.

assisted suicide Making available to individuals who wish to commit suicide the means by which they may do so, such as when a physician provides a terminally ill patient who wants to die with enough medication to overdose.

at risk Children who have a higher than normal chance of either short-term or long-term problems because of genetic defects, prenatal hazards, or perinatal damage.

attachment A strong affectional tie that binds a person to an intimate companion and is characterized by affection and a desire to maintain proximity.

attachment theory The theory of close relationships developed by Bowlby and Ainsworth and grounded in ethological theory (with psychoanalytic theory and cognitive theory); it says that close emotional bonds such as parent–child attachments are biologically based and contribute to species survival.

attention Focusing perception and cognition on something in particular.

attention deficit hyperactivity disorder (ADHD) A disorder characterized by atten-

tional difficulties, impulsive behavior, and overactive or fidgety behavior.

authoritarian parenting A restrictive style of parenting combining high demandingness–control and low acceptance–responsiveness in which adults impose many rules, expect strict obedience, and often rely on power tactics rather than explanations to elicit compliance.

authoritative parenting A flexible style of parenting combining high demandingness–control and high acceptance–responsiveness in which adults lay down clear rules but also grant a fair amount of autonomy to their children and explain the rationale for their restrictions.

autism A pervasive and severe developmental disorder that begins in infancy and is characterized by such problems as an aversion to social contact, deviant communication or mutism, and repetitive, stereotyped behavior.

autism spectrum disorders (ASDs) Also called pervasive developmental disorders because they affect many aspects of functioning, these disorders, which include autism, Asperger syndrome, Rett syndrome, and others, all involve social and communication problems.

autobiographical memory Memory of everyday events that the individual has experienced.

automatization The process by which information processing becomes effortless and highly efficient as a result of continued practice or increased expertise.

autonomous morality The most mature Piagetian stage of morality in which rules are viewed as agreements between individuals that can be changed through a consensus of those individuals and in which the older child or adolescent pays more attention to intentions than to consequences in judging actions. Contrast with *heteronomous morality*.

autonomy The capacity to make decisions independently, serve as one's own source of emotional strength, and otherwise manage life tasks without being overdependent on other people; an important developmental task of adolescence.

autonomy versus shame and doubt The psychosocial conflict in which toddlers attempt to demonstrate their independence from and control over other people; second of Erikson's stages.

avoidant attachment An insecure infant caregiver bond or other intimate relationship characterized by little separation anxiety and a tendency to avoid or ignore the attachment object upon reunion.

babbling An early form of vocalization that appears between 4 and 6 months of age and involves repeating consonant–vowel combinations such as "baba" or "dadada."

baby biographies Carefully recorded observations of the growth and development of children by their parents over a period; the first scientific investigations of development.

baby boom generation The huge generation of people born between 1946 (the close of World War II) and 1964.

Bayley Scales of Infant Development Standardized test to measure the mental, motor, and behavioral progress of infants and young children.

behavioral genetics The scientific study of the extent to which genetic and environmental differences among individuals are responsible for differences among them in traits such as intelligence and personality.

behavioral inhibition A temperamental characteristic reflecting a person's tendency to withdraw from unfamiliar people and situations.

behaviorism A school of thinking in psychology that holds that conclusions about human development should be based on controlled observations of overt behavior rather than on speculation about unconscious motives or other unobservable phenomena; the philosophical underpinning of early theories of learning.

belief–desire psychology The theory of mind reflecting an understanding that people's desires and beliefs guide their behavior and that their beliefs are not always an accurate reflection of reality; evident by age 4. Contrast with *desire psychology*.

bereavement A state of loss that provides the occasion for grief and mourning.

beta-amyloid A toxic protein that injures neurons and is located in the senile plaques associated with Alzheimer's disease.

Big Five The five major dimensions used to characterize people's personalities: neuroticism, extraversion, openness to experience, agreeableness, and conscientiousness.

big-fish–little-pond effect The phenomenon in which a student's academic self-concept and performance are likely to be more positive in an academically unselective school than in a highly selective one with many high-achieving students.

bioecological model Bronfenbrenner's model of development that emphasizes the roles of both nature and nurture as the developing person interacts with a series of environmental systems (microsystem, mesosystem, exosystem, and macrosystem).

biological aging The deterioration of organisms that leads inevitably to their death.

biological sex The physical characteristics that define male and female.

biosocial theory Money and Ehrhardt's theory of gender-role development that focuses on how biological events influence the development of boys and girls and how early biological developments influence how society reacts to children.

blastocyst A hollow sphere of about 100 to 150 cells that the zygote forms by rapid cell division as it moves through the fallopian tube.

body mass index (BMI) An indicator of body fat calculated from a person's height and weight.

bonding As distinguished from attachment, a more biologically-based process in which parent and infant form a connection through contact in the first hours after birth when both are highly alert.

breech presentation A delivery in which the fetus emerges feet first or buttocks first rather than head first.

bulimia nervosa A life-threatening eating disorder characterized by recurrent eating binges followed by purging activities such as vomiting.

bullying Repeatedly inflicting harm through words or actions on weaker peers who cannot or do not defend themselves.

caloric restriction A technique demonstrated to extend the life span of laboratory animals involving a highly nutritious but severely calorie-restricted diet.

caregiver burden The psychological distress associated with providing care for someone with physical, cognitive, or both types of impairment.

carrier In genetics, individuals who possesses a recessive gene associated with a disease and who, although they do not have the disease, can transmit the gene for it to offspring.

cascade model of substance use Transactional, multifactor model of substance use that envisions a chain of influences starting with a child with a difficult temperament born into troubled family and ending with involvement in a deviant adolescent peer group.

case study An in-depth examination of an individual (or a small number of individuals), typically carried out by compiling and analyzing information from a variety of sources such as observing, testing, and interviewing the person or people who know the individual.

cataracts A pathologic condition of the eye involving opacification (clouding) of the lens that can impair vision or cause blindness.

catch-up growth A phenomenon in which children who have experienced growth deficits will grow rapidly and catch up to the growth trajectory they are genetically programmed to follow.

categorical self A person's classification of the self along socially significant dimensions such as age and sex.

celiac disease An inherited digestive problem in which gluten (the proteins found in all wheat

products) triggers an immune response that damages a person's small intestine.

centenarian An individual who lives to be 100 years of age.

centration In Piaget's theory, the tendency to focus on only one aspect of a problem when two or more aspects are relevant.

cephalocaudal principle The principle that growth proceeds from the head (cephalic region) to the tail (caudal region).

cerebral palsy A neurological disability caused by anoxia that is associated with diffi- culty controlling muscle movements.

cesarean section A surgical procedure in which an incision is made in the mother's abdomen and uterus so that the baby can be removed through the abdomen.

characteristic adaptations Compared to traits, more situation-specific and changeable aspects of personality; ways in which people adapt to their roles and environments, including motives, goals, plans, schemas, selfconceptions, stage-specific concerns, and coping mechanisms.

child abuse Mistreating or harming a child physically, emotionally, or sexually, as distinguished from another form of child maltreatment, neglect of the child's basic needs.

child effects model A model of family influence in which children are believed to influence their parents rather than vice versa.

child maltreatment A broad term for inadequate care or harmful treatment of a child; encompasses both child abuse and child neglect.

child poverty A household climate that includes low income along with low levels of responsive to children's basic needs.

child-directed speech Speech used by adults speaking with young children, it involves short, simple sentences spoken slowly and in a high-pitched voice, often with much repetition and with exaggerated emphasis on key words.

childhood amnesia A lack of memory for the early years of a person's life.

chorion A membrane that surrounds the amnion and becomes attached to the uterine lining to gather nourishment for the embryo.

chorionic villus sampling (CVS) An alternative to amniocentesis in which a catheter is inserted through the cervix to withdraw fetal cells from the chorion for prenatal testing to detect genetic defects.

chromosome A threadlike structure made up of genes; in humans, there are 46 chromosomes in the nucleus of each cell.

chromosome abnormalities Conditions in which a child has too few, too many, or incomplete chromosomes because of errors in the formation of sperm or ova.

chronosystem In Bronfenbrenner's bioecological approach, the system that captures the way changes in environmental systems, such as social trends and life events, are patterned over a person's lifetime.

chumship According to neo-Freudian Harry Stack Sullivan, a close friendship in childhood that provides emotional support and teaches children how to participate in intimate relationships.

class inclusion The logical understanding that parts or subclasses are included in the whole class and that the whole is therefore greater than any of its parts.

classical conditioning A type of learning in which a stimulus that initially had no effect on the individual comes to elicit a response because of its association with a stimulus that already elicits the response.

clinical method An unstandardized interviewing procedure used by Piaget in which a child's response to each successive question (or problem) determines what the investigator will ask next.

clique A small friendship group that interacts frequently. See *crowd*.

cochlear implant A surgically implanted amplification device that stimulates the auditory nerve to provide the sensation of hearing to a deaf individual.

codominance In genetics, an instance in which two different but equally powerful genes produce a phenotype in which both genes are expressed.

coercive family environment A home in which family members are locked in power struggles, each trying to control the other through aggressive tactics such as threatening, yelling, and hitting.

cognition The activity of knowing and the processes through which knowledge is acquired (for example, attending, perceiving, remembering, and thinking).

cognitive behavioral therapy Well-established psychotherapy approach that involves identifying and changing distorted thinking and maladaptive emotions and behavior associated with it.

cognitive reserve The extra brain power or cognitive capacity that some people can fall back on as aging and diseases such as Alzheimer's begin to take a toll on brain functioning.

cohabitation When two single adults live together as an unmarried couple.

cohort A group of people born at the same time; a particular generation of people.

cohort effects In cross-sectional research, the effects on findings that the different age groups (cohorts) being compared were born at different times and had different formative experiences. Contrast with *age effects* and *time of measurement effects*.

collectivist culture A culture in which people define themselves in terms of group memberships, give group goals higher priority than personal goals, and socialize children to seek group harmony. Contrast with *individualistic culture*.

communality An orientation that emphasizes the well-being of others and includes traits of emotionality and sensitivity to others; considered feminine.

comorbidity The co-occurrence of two or more psychiatric conditions in the same individual.

companionate love In Sternberg's triangular theory of love, affectionate love characterized by high intimacy and commitment but low passion.

complicated grief An emotional response to a death that is unusually prolonged or intense and that impairs functioning; pathological grief.

conception The moment of fertilization, when a sperm penetrates an ovum, forming a zygote.

concordance rate The percentage of cases in which a particular attribute is present for both members of a pair of people (for example, twins) if it is present for one member.

concrete operations stage Piaget's third stage of cognitive development, lasting from about age 7 to age 11, when children are acquiring logical operations and can reason effectively about real objects and experiences.

conditioned response (CR) A learned response to a stimulus that was not originally capable of producing the response.

conditioned stimulus (CS) An initially neutral stimulus that elicits a particular response after it is paired with an unconditioned stimulus that always elicits the response.

conduct disorder A persistent pattern of behavior in which a child or adolescent violates the rights of others or age-appropriate societal norms, as through fighting, bullying, and cruelty.

confidant A spouse, relative, or friend to whom a person feels emotionally close and with whom that person can share thoughts and feelings.

congenital malformations Defects that are present at birth and are caused by genetic factors, prenatal events, or both.

conservation The recognition that certain properties of an object or substance do not change when its appearance is altered in some superficial way.

consolidation In information processing, the processing and organizing of information into a form suitable for long-term storage.

constitutional growth delay Children who are small for age (at or below the 5th percentile on a growth chart) and late entering puberty, but growing at a normal or near-normal pace.

constraint-seeking questions In the Twenty Questions task and similar hypothesis-testing tasks, questions that rule out more than one answer to narrow the field of possible choices rather than asking about only one hypothesis at a time.

constructivism The position taken by Piaget and others that humans actively create their own understandings of the world from their experiences, as opposed to being born with innate ideas or being programmed by the environment.

consummate love In Sternberg's triangular theory of love, love with high levels of all three components of love: passion, intimacy, and decision/commitment.

contact comfort The pleasurable tactile sensations provided by a parent or a soft, terry cloth mother substitute; believed to foster attachments in infant monkeys and possibly humans.

continuing bond Maintenance of attachment to a loved one after the person's death through reminiscence, use of the person's possessions, consultation with the deceased, and the like.

continuity–discontinuity issue The debate among theorists about whether human development is best characterized as gradual and continuous or abrupt and stagelike.

contour The amount of light–dark transition or boundary area in a visual stimulus.

conventional morality Kohlberg's term for the third and fourth stages of moral reasoning in which societal values are internalized and judgments are based on a desire to gain approval or uphold law and social order.

convergent thinking Thinking that involves "converging" on the one best answer to a problem; what IQ tests measure. Contrast with *divergent thinking*.

cooing An early form of vocalization that involves repeating vowel-like sounds.

cooperative learning Procedures that involve assigning students, usually of different races or ability levels, to work teams that are reinforced for performing well as teams and that encourage cooperation among teammates.

coordination of secondary schemes During Piaget's sensorimotor period, the infant's combining of actions to solve problems, using one scheme as a means to an end, as in batting aside a barrier in order to grasp a toy.

coparenting The extent and manner in which the two parents coordinate their parenting and function as a team in relation to their children.

correlation coefficient A measure, ranging from +1.00 to −1.00, of the extent to which two variables or attributes are systematically related to each other in either a positive or a negative way.

correlational method A research technique that involves determining whether two or more variables are related. It cannot indicate that one thing caused another, but it can suggest that a causal relationship exists or allow us to predict one characteristic from our knowledge of another.

co-rumination Excessive discussion and analysis of personal problems with a close friend.

couvade Sympathetic pregnancy, or the experiencing by fathers of some of the same physiological symptoms their pregnant partners experience (for example, bloating, weight gain, fatigue, insomnia, and nausea).

creative component In Sternberg's triarchic theory, the aspect of intelligence that varies with experience on a task.

creativity The ability to produce novel responses or works.

critical period A defined period in the development of an organism when it is particularly sensitive to certain environmental influences; outside this period, the same influences will have far less effect.

crossing over A process in which genetic material is exchanged between pairs of chromosomes during meiosis.

cross-modal perception The ability to use one sensory modality to identify a stimulus or a pattern of stimuli already familiar through another modality.

cross-sectional design A developmental research design in which different age groups are studied at the same point and compared.

crowd A network of heterosexual cliques that forms during adolescence and facilitates mixed-sex social activities. See *clique*.

crystallized intelligence Those aspects of intellectual functioning that involve using knowledge acquired through experience. Contrast with *fluid intelligence*.

cued recall memory Recollecting objects, events, or experiences in response to a hint or cue. Contrast with pure *recall memory* and *recognition memory*.

cultural evolution Change in a species achieved not through biological evolution but through learning and passing on from one generation to the next new ways of adapting to the environment.

culture A system of meanings shared by a population of people and transmitted from one generation to the next.

culture bias The situation that arises in testing when one cultural or subcultural group is more familiar with test items than another group and therefore has an unfair advantage.

cumulative-deficit hypothesis The notion that impoverished environments inhibit intellectual growth and that these inhibiting effects accumulate over time.

damage theories of aging Theories that emphasize several haphazard processes that cause cells and organ systems to deteriorate. Contrast with *programmed theories of aging*.

dark adaptation The process by which the eyes become more sensitive to light over time as they remain in the dark.

decentration The ability to focus on two or more dimensions of a problem at one time.

decontextualize To separate the demands of a task at hand from prior beliefs and knowledge.

defense mechanisms Mechanisms used by the ego to defend itself against anxiety caused by conflict between the id's impulses and social demands.

deferred imitation The ability to imitate a novel act after a delay.

delirium A clouding of consciousness characterized by alternating periods of disorientation and coherence.

demandingness–control A dimension of parenting reflecting the extent to which parents as opposed to children exert control over decisions and set and enforce rules; also called permissiveness-restrictiveness.

dementia A progressive loss of cognitive capacities such as memory and judgment that affects some aging individuals and that has a variety of causes.

denial A defense mechanism in which anxiety-provoking thoughts are kept out of, or isolated from, conscious awareness.

dependent variable The aspect of behavior measured in an experiment and assumed to be under the control of, or dependent on, the independent variable.

depression See *major depressive disorder*.

desire psychology The earliest theory of mind: an understanding that desires guide behavior (for example, that people seek things they like and avoid things they hate). Contrast with *belief–desire psychology*.

development Systematic changes in the individual occurring between conception and death; such changes can be positive, negative, or neutral.

developmental norm The age at which half of a large group of infants or children master a skill or display a behavior; the average age for achieving a milestone in development.

developmental psychopathology A field of study concerned with the origins and course of maladaptive or psychopathological behavior.

developmental quotient (DQ) A numerical measure of an infant's performance on a developmental test relative to the performance of other infants the same age.

developmental stage A distinct phase within a larger sequence of development; a period characterized by a particular set of abilities, motives, behaviors, or emotions that occur together and form a coherent pattern.

diabetes A metabolic disorder characterized by high levels of glucose or sugar in the blood leading to symptoms of thirst, excessive urination, fatigue, and problems involving eyes, kidneys, and other organs.

dialectical thinking An advanced form of thought that involves detecting paradoxes and inconsistencies among ideas and trying to reconcile them.

diathesis–stress model The view that psychopathology results from the interaction of a person's predisposition to psychological problems and the experience of stressful events.

differentiation In brain development, the progressive diversification of cells that results in their taking on different characteristics and functions.

difficult temperament Characteristic mode of response in which the individual is irregular in habits and adapts slowly, often with vigorous protest, to changes in routine or new experiences. Contrast with *easy temperament* and *slow-to-warm-up temperament*.

diffusion status Identity status characterizing individuals who have not questioned who they are and have not committed themselves to an identity.

disenfranchised grief Grief that is not fully recognized or appreciated by other people and therefore may not receive much sympathy and support, as in the loss of a gay partner.

disengagement theory A perspective that holds that successful aging involves a mutually satisfying withdrawal of the aging individual and society from each other. Contrast with *activity theory*.

disinhibited attachment A disturbed attachment pattern observed in socially deprived children that involves indiscriminate friendliness toward both parents and strangers, lack of appropriate wariness of strangers, and difficulty regulating emotions well enough to participate in real, reciprocal social interactions.

disorganized–disoriented attachment An insecure infant–caregiver bond, common among abused children, that combines features of the resistant and avoidant attachment styles and is characterized by the infant's dazed response to reunion and confusion about whether to approach or avoid the caregiver.

dispositional traits Relatively enduring dimensions or qualities of personality along which people differ (for example, extraversion, aloofness).

divergent thinking Thinking that requires coming up with a variety of ideas or solutions to a problem when there is no one right answer. Contrast with *convergent thinking*.

DNA Deoxyribonucleic acid, the double helix molecule whose chemical code makes up chromosomes and serves as our genetic endowment; it is made up of sequences of the chemicals (adenine), C (cytosine), G (guanine), and T (thymine).

dominant gene A relatively powerful gene that is expressed phenotypically and masks the effect of a less-powerful recessive gene.

double standard The view that sexual behavior appropriate for members of one gender is inappropriate for members of the other.

Down syndrome A chromosomal abnormality in which the child has inherited an extra 21st chromosome and is, as a result, mentally retarded; also called trisomy 21.

DSM-IV The fourth edition of the *Diagnostic and Statistical Manual of Mental Disorders*, which spells out defining features and symptoms for the range of psychological disorders.

dual process model of bereavement A theory of coping with bereavement in which the bereaved oscillate between loss-oriented coping in which they deal with their emotions, restoration-oriented coping in which they try to manage practical tasks and reorganize their lives, and periods of respite from coping.

dual process model of morality The view that *both* deliberate thought and more automatic emotion-based intuitions can inform decisions about moral issues and motivate behavior.

dynamic systems theory A perspective on development applied to motor development which proposes that more sophisticated patterns of motor behavior emerge over time through a "self-organizing" process in which children modify their motor behavior in adaptive ways on the basis of the sensory feedback they receive when they try different movements.

dyslexia Serious difficulties learning to read in children who have normal intellectual ability and no sensory impairments or emotional difficulties that could account for their learning problems.

easy temperament Characteristic mode of response in which the individual is even-tempered, content, and open and adaptable to new experiences. Contrast with *difficult temperament* and *slow-to-warm-up temperament*.

echolalia The repetition of sounds, such as when an autistic child parrots what someone else says.

eclectic In the context of science, an individual who recognizes that no single theory can explain everything but that each has something to contribute to our understanding.

effortful control Dimension of temperament pertaining to being able to sustain attention, control one's behavior, and regulate one's emotions (as opposed to unable to regulate one's arousal and stay calm and focused). See *negative affectivity* and *surgency/extraversion*.

ego Psychoanalytic term for the rational component of the personality.

egocentrism The tendency to view the world from the person's own perspective and fail to recognize that others may have different points of view.

elaboration A strategy for remembering that involves adding something to or creating meaningful links between the bits of information the person is trying to retain.

Electra complex Female version of the *Oedipus complex*, in which a 4- to 6-year-old girl is said to envy her father for possessing a penis and would choose him as a sex object in the hope of sharing this valuable organ that she lacks.

embryonic period Second phase of prenatal development, lasting from the third through the eighth prenatal week, during which the major organs and anatomical structures begin to develop.

emergent literacy The developmental precursors of reading skills in young children, including knowledge, skills, and attributes that will facilitate the acquisition of reading competence.

emerging adulthood Newly identified period of the life span extending from about age 18 to age 25, when young people are neither adolescents nor adults and are exploring their identities, careers, and relationships.

emotion regulation The processes involved in initiating, maintaining, and altering emotional responses.

empathy The vicarious experiencing of another person's feelings.

empty nest The term used to describe the family after the last child departs the household.

encoding The first step in learning and remembering something, it is the process of getting information into the information-processing system, or learning it, and organizing it in a form suitable for storing.

endocrine gland A type of gland that secretes chemicals called hormones directly into the bloodstream. Endocrine glands play critical roles in stimulating growth and regulating bodily functions.

environment Events or conditions outside the person that are presumed to influence and be influenced by the individual.

epigenesis The process through which nature and nurture, genes and environment, jointly bring forth development in ways that are difficult to predict at the outset, according to Gottlieb's epigenetic psychobiological systems perspective; in a more specific sense, epigenetic effects refer to ways in which environmental influences alter gene expression.

epigenetic psychobiological systems perspective Gilbert Gottlieb's view that development is the product of interacting biological and environmental forces that form a larger, dynamic system, both over the course of evolution and during the individual's life.

episodic memory A type of explicit memory consisting of specific episodes that one has experienced.

equilibration In Piaget's theory, the process of seeking a state of mental stability in which our thoughts (schemes) are consistent with the information we receive from the external world.

equity A balance of contributions and gains in a social relationship that results in neither partner feeling over- or underbenefited.

estrogen The female hormone responsible for the development of the breasts, the female sex organs, and secondary sex characteristics and for the beginning of menstrual cycles.

ethnic identity A sense of personal identification with the individual's ethnic group and its values and cultural traditions.

ethnicity A person's classification in or affiliation with a group based on common heritage or traditions.

ethnocentrism The belief that one's own cultural or ethnic group is superior to others.

ethology A discipline and theoretical perspective that focuses on the evolved behavior of different species in their natural environments.

euthanasia Literally, "good death"; specifically, hastening, either actively or passively, the death of someone suffering from an incurable illness or injury.

evidence-based practice Grounding what they do in research and ensuring that the curricula and treatments they provide have been demonstrated to be effective.

evolutionary psychology The application of evolutionary theory and its concept of natural selection to understanding why humans think and behave as they do.

executive control processes Processes that direct and monitor the selection, organization, manipulation, and interpretation of information in the information-processing system, including executive functions.

executive functions The planning and organizational functions that reside in the prefrontal cortex of the brain.

exosystem In Bronfenbrenner's bioecological approach, settings not experienced directly by individuals still influence their development (for example, effects of events at a parent's workplace on children's development).

expansion A conversational tactic used by adults in speaking to young children in which they respond to a child's utterance with a more grammatically complete expression of the same thought.

experiment A research strategy in which the investigator manipulates or alters some aspect of a person's environment to measure its effect on the individual's behavior or development.

experimental control The holding of all other factors besides the independent variable in an experiment constant so that any changes in the dependent variable can be said to be caused by the manipulation of the independent variable.

explicit memory Memory that involves consciously recollecting the past. Contrast with *implicit memory*.

extended family household A family unit composed of parents and children living with other kin such as grandparents, aunts and uncles, cousins, or a combination of these. Compare with *nuclear family*.

externalizing problem Childhood behavioral problem that involves "undercontrolled" behavior such as aggression or acting out difficulties that disturb other people. Contrast with *internalizing problem*.

extinction The gradual weakening and disappearance of a learned response when it is no longer reinforced.

extreme male brain hypothesis Baron-Cohen's theory that individuals with autism have brains that are more masculine, or skilled at systemizing, than feminine, or skilled at empathizing.

eyewitness memory Remembering and reporting events the person has witnessed or experienced.

failure to thrive A condition observed in infants who, because of either physical causes or emotional deprivation, are characterized by stunted growth, weight loss, and delays in cognitive and socioemotional development.

false belief task A research paradigm used to assess an important aspect of a theory of mind, mainly the understanding that people can hold incorrect beliefs and be influenced by them.

family life cycle The sequence of changes in family composition, roles, and relationships that occurs from the time people marry until they die.

family systems theory The conceptualization of the family as a whole consisting of interrelated parts, each of which affects and is affected by every other part, and each of which contributes to the functioning of the whole.

fetal alcohol syndrome (FAS) A group of symptoms commonly observed in the offspring of mothers who use alcohol heavily during pregnancy, including a small head, widely spaced eyes, and mental retardation.

fetal period The third phase of prenatal development, lasting from the ninth prenatal week until birth; during this period, the major organ systems begin to function effectively and the fetus grows rapidly.

fine motor skills Skills that involve precise movements of the hands and fingers or feet and toes. Contrast with *gross motor skills*.

fixation In psychoanalytic theory, a defense mechanism in which development is arrested and part of the libido remains tied to an early stage of development.

fluid intelligence Aspects of intelligence that involve actively thinking and reasoning to solve novel problems. Contrast with *crystallized intelligence*.

Flynn effect The rise in average IQ scores over the 20th century.

foreclosure status An identity status characterizing individuals who appear to have committed themselves to a life direction but who have adopted an identity prematurely, without much thought.

formal operations stage Piaget's fourth and final stage of cognitive development (from age 11 or 12), when the individual begins to think more rationally and systematically about abstract concepts and hypothetical ideas.

fragile X syndrome A chromosome abnormality in which one arm of the X chromosome is only barely connected to the rest of the chromosome; the most common hereditary cause of mental retardation.

fraternal twins Twins who are not identical and who result when a mother releases two ova at roughly the same time and each is fertilized by a different sperm.

free radicals Chemically unstable byproducts of metabolism that have an extra electron and react with other molecules to produce toxic substances that damage cells and contribute to aging.

functional grammar An analysis of the semantic relations (meanings such as naming and locating) that children express in their earliest sentences.

functional magnetic resonance imaging (fMRI) A brain-scanning technique that uses magnetic forces to measure the increase in blood flow to an area of the brain that occurs when that brain area is active. By having children and adults perform cognitive tasks while lying very still in an fMRI scanner, researchers can determine which parts of the brain are involved in particular cognitive activities.

fuzzy-trace theory The view that verbatim and general or gistlike accounts of an event are stored separately in memory.

gender A combination of all those features that a society associates with or considers appropriate for being a man and woman.

gender consistency The stage of gender typing in which children realize that their sex is stable across situations or despite changes in activities or appearance.

gender constancy A solid understanding of oneself as male-female, man-woman.

gender identity Individuals' basic awareness that they are either a male or a female.

gender intensification A magnification of differences between males and females during adolescence associated with increased pressure to conform to traditional gender roles.

gender role A pattern of behaviors and traits that defines how to act the part of a female or a male in a particular society.

gender schema (plural: schemata) Organized sets of beliefs and expectations about males and females that guide information processing.

gender segregation The formation of separate boys' and girls' peer groups during childhood.

gender similarities hypothesis The hypothesis that males and females are similar on most, but not all, psychological variables.

gender stability The stage of gender typing in which children realize that their sex remains the same over time.

gender stereotypes Overgeneralized and largely inaccurate beliefs about what males and females are like.

gender typing The process by which children become aware of their gender and acquire the motives, values, and behaviors considered appropriate for members of their biological sex.

gene A functional unit of heredity made up of DNA and transmitted from generation to generation.

gene expression The activation of particular genes in particular cells of the body at particular times in life.

gene therapy Interventions that involve substituting normal genes for the genes associated with a disease or disorder; otherwise altering a person's genetic makeup.

gene–environment correlation A systematic interrelationship between an individual's genes and that individual's environment; ways in which genes influence the kind of home environment provided by parents (passive gene–environment correlation), the social reactions to the individual (evocative gene–environment correlation), and the types of experiences the individual seeks (active gene–environment correlation).

gene–environment interaction The phenomenon in which the effects of people's genes depend on the kind of environment they experience and in which the effects of the environment depend on their genetic endowment.

general event representation Representations that people create over time of the typical sequence of actions related to an event; also called "scripts."

generativity versus stagnation The psychosocial conflict in which middle-aged adults must gain the sense that they have produced something that will outlive them and genuinely care for younger generations to avoid self-preoccupation; seventh of Erikson's stages.

genetic counseling A service designed to inform people about genetic conditions they or their unborn children are at risk of inheriting.

genotype The genetic endowment that an individual inherits. Contrast with *phenotype*.

germinal period First phase of prenatal development, lasting about 2 weeks from conception until the developing organism becomes attached to the wall of the uterus.

gerontology The study of aging and old age.

giftedness The possession of unusually high general intellectual potential or of special abilities in such areas as creativity, mathematics, or the arts.

glaucoma A condition in which increased fluid pressure in the eye damages the optic nerve and causes progressive loss of peripheral vision and ultimately blindness.

goal-corrected partnership In Bowlby's attachment theory, the most mature phase of attachment in which parent and child accommodate to each other's needs and the child becomes more independent.

goodness of fit The extent to which the child's temperament and the demands of the child's social environment are compatible or mesh, according to Thomas and Chess; more generally, a good match between person and environment.

grief The emotional response to loss. Contrast with *mourning*.

grief work perspective The view commonly held, but now challenged, that to cope adaptively with death bereaved people must confront their loss, experience painful emotions, work through these emotions, and move toward a detachment from the deceased.

gross motor skills Skills that involve large muscles and whole body or limb movements (for example, kicking the legs or drawing large circles). Contrast with *fine motor skills*.

growth The physical changes that occur from conception to maturity.

growth hormone Hormone produced by the pituitary gland that stimulates childhood physical growth and the adolescent growth spurt.

guided participation A process in which children learn by actively participating in culturally relevant activities with the aid and support of their parents and other knowledgeable individuals.

habituation A simple form of learning that involves learning not to respond to a repeated stimulus; learning to be bored by the familiar.

Hayflick limit The estimate that human cells can double only 50 times, plus or minus 10, and then will die.

helpless orientation An attribution style in which someone tends to avoid challenges and to cease trying—to give up—when they experience failure, based on the belief that they can do little to improve.

hemophilia A deficiency in the blood's ability to clot. It is more common among males than females because it is associated with a sex-linked gene on the X chromosome.

heritability The amount of variability in a population on some trait dimension that is attributable to genetic differences among those individuals.

heteronomous morality A term meaning subject to authority and referring to the childhood beliefs that rules are handed down by authority figures and are sacred and unalterable and that wrongness should be judged on the basis of consequences rather than intentions; typical of children ages 6 to 10, according to Piaget. Contrast with *autonomous morality*.

holophrase A single-word utterance used by an infant that represents an entire sentence's worth of meaning.

Home Observation for Measurement of the Environment (HOME) inventory A widely used instrument that allows an observer to determine how intellectually stimulating or impoverished a home environment is.

homogamy Mate selection or marriage on the basis of similarity in demographic and personal characteristics.

horizontal décalage A term used by Piaget to characterize that different cognitive skills related to the same stage of cognitive development emerge at different times.

hormone replacement therapy (HRT) Taking estrogen and progestin to compensate for hormone loss because of menopause in women.

hospice A program that supports dying persons and their families through a philosophy of caring rather than curing, either in a facility or at home.

hot flash A sudden experience of warmth and sweating, often followed by a cold shiver, that occurs in a menopausal woman.

human agency Ways in which humans deliberately exercise cognitive control over their environments and lives, according to Bandura.

Human Genome Project A massive, government-sponsored effort to decipher the human genetic code.

Huntington's disease A genetic disease caused by a single, dominant gene that strikes in middle age to produce a deterioration of physical and mental abilities and premature death.

hyperactivity See *attention deficit hyperactivity disorder (ADHD)*.

hypothesis A theoretical prediction about what will hold true if we observe a phenomenon.

hypothetical-deductive reasoning A form of problem solving in which a person starts with general or abstract ideas and deduces or traces their specific implications; "if–then" thinking.

id A psychoanalytic term for the inborn component of the personality that is driven by the instincts or selfish urges.

ideal self Idealized expectations of what one's attributes and personality should be like.

identical twins Monozygotic twins who develop from a single zygote that later divides to form two genetically identical individuals.

identification Freud's term for the individual's tendency to emulate, or adopt the attitudes and behaviors of, another person, particularly the same-sex parent.

identity A self-definition or sense of who one is, where one is going, and how one fits into society.

identity achievement status An identity status characterizing individuals who have carefully thought through identity issues and made commitments or resolved their identity issues.

identity versus role confusion The psychosocial conflict in which adolescents must form a coherent self-definition or remain confused about their life directions; fifth of Erikson's stages.

imaginary audience A form of adolescent egocentrism that involves confusing one's own thoughts with the thoughts of a hypothesized audience for behavior and concluding that others share these preoccupations.

imaginary companion A play companion invented by a child in the preoperational stage who has developed the capacity for symbolic thought.

implicit memory Memory that occurs unintentionally and without consciousness or awareness. Contrast with *explicit memory*.

imprinting An innate form of learning in which the young of certain species will follow and become attached to moving objects (usually their mothers) during a critical period early in life.

inclusion The educational practice of integrating handicapped students into regular classrooms rather than placing them in segregated special education classes; also called mainstreaming.

incomplete dominance A condition in which a stronger gene fails to mask all the effects of a weaker partner gene; a phenotype results that is similar but not identical to the effect of the stronger gene.

independent variable The aspect of the environment that a researcher deliberately changes or manipulates in an experiment to see its effect on behavior; a causal variable. Contrast with *dependent variable*.

indirect effect The instance in which the relationship between two individuals in a family is modified by the behavior or attitudes of a third family member.

individualistic culture A culture in which individuals define themselves as individuals and put their own goals ahead of their group's goals, and one in which children are socialized to be independent and self-reliant. Contrast with *collectivist culture*.

induction A form of discipline that involves explaining why a child's behavior is wrong and should be changed by emphasizing its effects on other people.

industry versus inferiority The psychosocial conflict in which school-aged children must master important cognitive and social skills or feel incompetent; fourth of Erikson's stages.

infertility A couple's inability to get pregnant after a year of trying to do so.

information-processing approach An approach to cognition that emphasizes the fundamental mental processes involved in attention, perception, memory, and decision making.

initiative versus guilt The psychosocial conflict in which preschool children must learn to initiate new activities and pursue bold plans or become self-critical; third of Erikson's stages.

instinct An inborn biological force assumed to motivate a particular response or class of responses.

integration Teaching children of different racial/ethnic backgrounds in the same classroom.

integrity versus despair The psychosocial conflict in which elderly adults attempt to find a sense of meaning in their lives and to accept the inevitability of death; eighth of Erikson's stages.

intellectual disability Significantly below-average intellectual functioning with limitations in areas of adaptive behavior such as self-care and social skills, originating before age 18 (previously known as mental retardation).

intelligence quotient (IQ) A numerical measure of a person's performance on an intelligence test relative to the performance of other examinees of the same age, typically with a score of 100 defined as average.

intergenerational transmission of parenting The passing down from generation to generation of parenting styles, abusive or otherwise.

internal working model In attachment theory, cognitive representation of self and other that children construct from their interactions with caregivers and that shape their expectations about relationships.

internalizing problem Childhood behavioral problem that represents an "overcontrolled" pattern of coping with difficulties and is expressed in anxiety, depression, and other forms of inner distress. Contrast with *externalizing problem*.

intimacy versus isolation The psychosocial conflict in which young adults must commit themselves to a shared identity with another person or remain aloof and unconnected to others; sixth of Erikson's stages.

intuitive theories Organized systems of knowledge, believed to be innate, that allow children to make sense of the world in areas such as physics and psychology.

in vitro fertilization (IVF) Procedure in which several eggs are removed from a woman's ovary, fertilized by sperm in a petri dish in the laboratory, then transferred to the woman's uterus in hopes that one will implant on the wall of the uterus.

joint attention The act of looking at the same object at the same time with someone else; a way in which infants share perceptual experiences with their caregivers.

juvenile delinquency Law-breaking by a minor.

kangaroo care Holding a young infant skin-to-skin on a parent's chest; often used with premature babies to help maintain body temperature, heart rate, and oxygen levels in the blood.

karyotype A chromosomal portrait created by staining chromosomes, photographing them under a high-power microscope, and arranging them into a predetermined pattern.

Klinefelter syndrome A sex chromosome abnormality in which males inherit two or more X chromosomes (XXY or XXXY); these males fail to develop secondary sex characteristics and often show deficiencies on tests of verbal abilities.

knowledge base A person's existing information about a content area, significant for its influence on how well that individual can learn and remember.

Lamaze method Prepared childbirth in which parents attend classes and learn mental exercises and relaxation techniques to ease delivery.

language A symbolic system in which a limited number of signals can be combined according to rules to produce an infinite number of messages.

language acquisition device (LAD) A set of linguistic processing skills that nativists believe to be innate; presumably the LAD enables a child to infer the rules governing others' speech and then use these rules to produce language.

latent learning Learning occurs but is not evident in behavior; children can learn from observation even though they do not imitate (perform) the learned responses.

lateralization The specialization of the two hemispheres of the cerebral cortex of the brain.

learning A relatively permanent change in behavior (or behavioral potential) that results from a person's experiences or practice.

learning goal A goal adopted by learners in which they seek to learn new things so that they can improve their abilities. Contrast with *performance goal*.

libido Freud's term for the biological energy of the sex instinct.

life expectancy The average number of years a newborn baby can be expected to live; now almost 78 years in the United States.

life review Process in which elderly adults reflect on unresolved conflicts of the past and evaluate their lives; it may contribute to a sense of integrity and readiness for death.

life-span perspective A perspective that views development as a lifelong, multidirectional process that involves gain and loss, is characterized by considerable plasticity, is shaped by its historical-cultural context, has many causes, and is best viewed from a multidisciplinary perspective.

linked lives The concept that the development of the individual is intertwined with the development of other family members.

literacy The ability to use printed information to function in society, achieve goals, and develop potential.

living will A document in which people state in advance that they do not wish to have extraordinary medical procedures applied if they are hopelessly ill.

locomotion The process of moving from one location to another.

longitudinal design A developmental research design in which one group of subjects is studied repeatedly over months or years.

long-term memory Memory store in which information that has been examined and interpreted is stored relatively permanently.

love withdrawal A form of discipline that involves withholding attention, affection, or approval after a child misbehaves.

low birth weight (LBW) A weight at birth of less than 2500 grams, or 5 ½ pounds, associated with increased risk of developmental problems.

macrosystem In Bronfenbrenner's bioecological approach, the larger cultural or subcultural context of development.

major depressive disorder An affective or mood disorder characterized by at least one episode of feeling profoundly sad and hopeless, losing interest in almost all activities, or both.

mastery (learning) goal In achievement situations, aiming to learn new things in order to learn or improve ability; contrast with performance goal.

mastery motivation An intrinsic motive to master and control the environment evident early in infancy.

mastery orientation A tendency to thrive on challenges and persist in the face of failure because of healthy attributions that lead to the belief that increased effort will pay off.

maternal blood sampling A noninvasive method of prenatal diagnosis involving testing for substances in maternal blood; more recently, analysis of fetal cells that have slipped through the placenta into the mother's blood.

maturation Developmental changes that are biologically programmed by genes rather than caused primarily by learning, injury, illness, or some other life experience.

maximum life span A ceiling on the number of years that any member of a species lives; 120 years for humans.

mediation deficiency The initial stage of mastery of memory strategies in which children cannot spontaneously use or benefit from strategies even if they are taught to use them.

meiosis The process in which a germ cell divides, producing sperm or ova, each containing half of the parent cell's original complement of chromosomes; in humans, the products of meiosis normally contain 23 chromosomes.

memory The ability to store and later retrieve information about past events.

menarche A female's first menstrual period.

menopause The ending of a woman's menstrual periods and reproductive capacity around age 51.

mental age A measure of intellectual development that reflects the level of age-graded problems that a child is able to solve; the age at which a child functions intellectually.

mental retardation See *intellectual disability*.

mesosystem In Bronfenbrenner's bioecological approach, interrelationships between microsystems or immediate environments (for example, ways in which events in the family affect a child's interactions at a day care center).

meta-analysis A research method in which the results of multiple studies addressing the same question are synthesized to produce overall conclusions.

metacognition Knowledge of the human mind and of the range of cognitive processes, including thinking about personal thought processes.

metalinguistic awareness Knowledge of language as a system.

metamemory A person's knowledge about memory and about monitoring and regulating memory processes.

microsystem In Bronfenbrenner's bioecological approach, the immediate settings in which the person functions (for example, the family).

middle generation squeeze The phenomenon in which middle-aged adults sometimes experience heavy responsibilities for both the younger and the older generations in the family.

midlife crisis A period of major questioning, inner struggle, and re-evaluation hypothesized to occur in an adult's early 40s.

mild cognitive impairment A level of memory loss between normal loss with age and pathological loss from disease.

mirror neuron hypothesis Theory of autism that holds that the malfunctioning of behavior-simulating mirror neuron systems accounts for the deficits individuals with autism show in imitation, theory of mind skills, empathy, and language.

mirror neurons Neural cells in several brain areas that are activated when we perform an action or observe someone else performing it.

miscarriage Loss of a pregnancy before survival of the baby outside the womb is possible.

mitosis The process in which a cell duplicates its chromosomes and then divides into two genetically identical daughter cells.

molecular genetics The analysis of particular genes and their effects, including the identification of specific genes that influence particular traits and the comparison of animals or humans who have these specific genes and those who do not.

moral affect The emotional component of morality, including feelings of guilt, shame, and pride regarding one's conduct.

moral disengagement According to Bandura, the ability to avoid self condemnation when engaged in immoral behavior by justifying, minimizing, or blaming others for one's actions.

moral reasoning The cognitive component of morality; the thinking that occurs when people decide whether acts are right or wrong.

moral rules Standards of conduct that focus on the basic rights and privileges of individuals. Contrast with *social-conventional rules*.

morality The ability to distinguish right from wrong, to act on this distinction, and to experience pride when doing something right and to experience guilt or shame when doing something wrong. Morality has affective, cognitive, and behavioral components.

morality of care Gilligan's term for what she says is the dominant moral orientation of females, in which the individual emphasizes concern and responsibility for the welfare of other people rather than abstract rights. Contrast with *morality of justice*.

morality of justice Gilligan's term for what she says is the dominant moral orientation of males, in which moral dilemmas are viewed as inevitable conflicts between the rights of two or more parties that must be settled by law. Contrast with *morality of care*.

moratorium period A period of time in high school or college when young adults are relatively free of responsibilities and can experiment with different roles to find their identities.

moratorium status Identity status characterizing individuals who are experiencing an identity crisis or actively exploring identity issues but who have not yet achieved an identity.

morphemes The basic units of meaning that exist in a word.

mourning Culturally prescribed ways of displaying reactions to a loss. Contrast with *grief*.

mutation A change in the structure or arrangement of one or more genes that produces a new phenotype.

mutually responsive orientation A close, affectively positive, and cooperative relationship in which child and parent are attached to each other and are sensitive to each other's needs; a contributor to moral development.

myelin A fatty sheath that insulates neural axons and thereby speeds the transmission of neural impulses.

myelination The depositing of a fatty sheath around neural axons that insulates them and thereby speeds the transmission of neural impulses.

narrative identities Unique and integrative "life stories" that we construct about our pasts and futures to give ourselves an identity and our lives meaning; an aspect of personality.

nativist An individual whose approach to human development emphasizes the contribution of genetic factors; specifically, a person who

believes that infants enter the world equipped with knowledge that allows them to perceive a meaningful world from the start. Contrast with *empiricist*.

natural selection The evolutionary principle that individuals who have characteristics advantageous for survival in a particular environment are most likely to survive and reproduce. Over many generations, this process of "survival of the fittest" will lead to changes in a species and the development of new species.

naturalistic observation A research method in which the scientist observes people as they engage in common everyday activities in their natural habitats. Contrast with *structured observation*.

nature–nurture issue The debate over the relative importance of biological predispositions (nature) and environmental influences (nurture) as determinants of human development.

negative affectivity Dimension of temperament that concerns the tendency to be sad, fearful, easily frustrated, and irritable (as opposed to laid back and adaptable). See *effortful control* and *surgency/extraversion*.

negative punishment The process in operant conditioning in which a response is weakened or made less probable when its consequence is the removal of a pleasant stimulus from the situation.

negative reinforcement The process in operant conditioning in which a response is strengthened or made more probable when its consequence is the removal of an unpleasant stimulus from the situation.

neglectful parenting A parenting style low in demandingness–control and low in acceptance–responsiveness; uninvolved parenting.

neonatal Pertaining to events or developments in the first month after birth.

neurogenesis The process of generating new neurons across the lifespan.

neuron The basic unit of the nervous system; a nerve cell.

neuroplasticity The brain's remarkable ability to change in response to experience throughout the life span, as when it recovers from injury or benefits from stimulating learning experiences.

nonshared environmental influences Experiences unique to the individual that are not shared by other members of the family and that tend to make members of the same family different. Contrast with *shared environmental influences*.

normal distribution A symmetrical (bell-shaped) curve that describes the variability of characteristics within a population. Most people fall at or near the average score; there are relatively few high or low scores.

nuclear family A family unit consisting of husband–father, wife–mother, and at least one child. Compare with *extended family household*.

obesity Condition of being overweight; specifically, being 20% or more above the "ideal" weight for one's height, age, and sex.

object permanence The understanding that objects continue to exist when they are no longer visible or otherwise detectable to the senses; fully mastered by the end of infancy.

observational learning Learning that results from observing the behavior of other people; emphasized in Bandura's social cognitive theory.

Oedipus complex Freud's term for the conflict that 4- to 6-year-old boys experience when they develop an incestuous desire for their mothers and a jealous and hostile rivalry with their fathers.

olfaction The sense of smell, made possible by sensory receptors in the nasal passage that react to chemical molecules in the air.

operant conditioning Also called instrumental conditioning, a form of learning in which freely emitted acts (or operants) become more or less probable depending on the consequences they produce.

oral sex Sexual activity involving contact between the mouth and genitals.

organization In Piaget's cognitive developmental theory, a person's inborn tendency to combine and integrate available schemes into more coherent and complex systems or bodies of knowledge; as a memory strategy, a technique that involves grouping or classifying stimuli into meaningful clusters.

organogenesis The process, occurring during the period of the embryo, in which every major organ takes shape in a primitive form.

orienting system An attentional system that that reacts to events in the environment; contrast with a focusing system that deliberately seeks out and maintains attention to events.

orthogenetic principle Werner's principle that development proceeds from global and undifferentiated states toward more differentiated and integrated patterns of response.

osteoarthritis A joint problem among older adults resulting from a gradual deterioration of the cartilage that cushions the bones and keeps them from rubbing together.

osteoporosis A disease affecting older adults in which bone tissue is lost, leaving bones fragile and easily fractured.

overextension The young child's tendency to use a word to refer to a wider set of objects, actions, or events than adults do (for example, using the word *car* to refer to all motor vehicles). Contrast with *underextension*.

overlapping waves theory Siegler's view that the development of problem-solving skills is not a matter of moving from one problemsolving approach to a better one with age but of knowing and using a variety of strategies at each age, becoming increasingly selective with experience about which strategies to use in particular situations, and adding new strategies to one's collection.

overregularization The overgeneralization of observed grammatical rules to irregular cases to which the rules do not apply (for example, saying *mouses* rather than *mice*).

oxytocin A hormone that plays important roles in facilitating parent-infant attachment as well as reducing anxiety and encouraging affiliation in other social relationships.

palliative care Care aimed not at curing but at meeting the physical, psychological, and spiritual needs of dying patients.

parent effects model A model of family influence in which parents (particularly mothers) are believed to influence their children rather than vice versa.

parental imperative The notion that the demands of parenthood cause men and women to adopt distinct roles and psychological traits.

Parkes/Bowlby attachment model of bereavement Model of grieving describing four predominant reactions to loss of an attachment figure: numbness, yearning, disorganization and despair, and reorganization.

peer A social equal; a person who functions at a level of behavioral complexity similar to that of the self, often someone of similar age.

perception The interpretation of sensory input.

perceptual salience Phenomenon in which the most obvious features of an object or situation have disproportionate influence on the perceptions and thought of young children.

performance goal A goal adopted by learners in which they attempt to prove their ability rather than to improve it. Contrast with *learning (or mastery) goal*.

perinatal environment The environment surrounding birth.

perinatologist A maternal-fetal specialist who focuses on high-risk pregnancies.

permissive parenting A lax style of parenting combining low demandingness–control and high acceptance–responsiveness in which adults love their children but make few demands on them and rarely attempt to control their behavior.

perseveration error Mistake made when an information processor continues to use the same strategy that was successful in the past over and over despite the strategy's lack of success in the current situation.

personal fable A form of adolescent egocentrism that involves thinking that oneself and one's thoughts and feelings are unique or special.

personality The organized combination of attributes, motives, values, and behaviors that is unique to each individual.

phenotype The way in which a person's genotype is expressed in observable or measurable characteristics.

phenylketonuria (PKU) A genetic disease in which the child is unable to metabolize phenylalanine; if left untreated, it soon causes hyperactivity and mental retardation.

phoneme One of the basic units of sound used in a particular spoken language.

phonological awareness The understanding that spoken words can be decomposed into some number of basic sound units, or phonemes; an important skill in learning to read.

pincer grasp A grasp in which the thumb is used in opposition to the fingers, enabling an infant to become more dexterous at lifting and manipulating objects.

pituitary gland The "master gland" located at the base of the brain that regulates the other endocrine glands and produces growth hormone.

placenta An organ, formed from the chorion and the lining of the uterus, that provides for the nourishment of the unborn child and the elimination of its metabolic wastes.

plasticity An openness of the brain cells (or of the organism as a whole) to positive and negative environmental influence; a capacity to change in response to experience.

polygenic trait A characteristic influenced by the action of many gene pairs rather than a single pair.

population A well-defined group that a researcher who studies a sample of individuals is interested in drawing conclusions about.

positive punishment The process in operant conditioning whereby a response is weakened when its consequence is an unpleasant event.

positive reinforcement The process in operant conditioning whereby a response is strengthened when its consequence is a pleasant event.

positivity effect The tendency of older adults to pay more attention to, better remember, and put more priority on positive information than on negative information; see also socioemotional selectivity theory.

postconventional morality Kohlberg's term for the fifth and sixth stages of moral reasoning, in which moral judgments are based on a more abstract understanding of democratic social contracts or on universal principles of justice that have validity apart from the views of particular authority figures.

postformal thought Proposed stages of cognitive development that lie beyond formal operations.

postpartum depression An episode of severe, clinical depression lasting for months in a woman who has just given birth; to be contrasted with milder cases of the "baby blues," in which a new mother is tearful and moody in the first days after birth.

posttraumatic stress disorder A psychological disorder involving flashbacks to traumatizing events, nightmares, and feelings of helplessness and anxiety in the face of danger experienced by victims of extreme trauma such as soldiers in combat and sexually abused children.

power assertion A form of discipline that involves the use of superior power to administer spankings, withhold privileges, and so on.

practical component In Sternberg's triarchic theory, the aspect of intelligence that varies from one sociocultural context to another.

pragmatics Rules specifying how language is to be used appropriately in different social contexts to achieve goals.

preconventional morality Kohlberg's term for the first two stages of moral reasoning, in which society's rules are not yet internalized and judgments are based on the punishing or rewarding consequences of an act.

preimplantation genetic diagnosis Prenatal diagnostic procedure in which a mother's eggs are fertilized in the laboratory using in vitro fertilization techniques, DNA tests are conducted on the first cells that result from mitosis of each fertilized egg, and only eggs that do not have chromosome abnormalities or genes associated with disorders are implanted in the uterus.

premenstrual syndrome (PMS) Several symptoms experienced shortly before each menstrual period that include having tender breasts, feeling bloated, and being irritable and moody.

premoral period According to Piaget, a period during the preschool years when children show little awareness or understanding of rules and cannot be considered to be moral beings.

prenatal environment The physical environment of the womb.

preoperational stage Piaget's second stage of cognitive development, lasting from about age 2 to age 7, when children think at a symbolic level but have not yet mastered logical operations.

presbycusis Problems of the aging ear, which commonly involve loss of sensitivity to high-frequency or high-pitched sounds.

presbyopia Problems of the aging eye, especially loss of near vision related to a decreased ability of the lens to accommodate to objects close to the eye.

pretend play Symbolic play in which one actor, object, or action symbolizes or stands for another.

primary circular reaction During Piaget's sensorimotor period, the infant's repetition of interacting acts centered on his or her own body (e.g., repeatedly kicking).

private speech Nonsocial speech, or speech for the self, commonly used by preschoolers to guide their activities and believed by Vygotsky to be the forerunner of inner speech, or silent thinking in words.

problem solving The use of the information-processing system to achieve a goal or arrive at a decision.

production deficiency A phase in the mastery of memory strategies in which children can use strategies they are taught but cannot produce them on their own.

progeria A genetic disorder caused by a single dominant gene that makes victims age prematurely and die early.

programmed theories of aging Theories that emphasize the systematic genetic control of aging processes. Contrast with *damage theories of aging*.

projection Defense mechanism that involves seeing in others the motives we fear we possess, as when a husband charges his wife with being the one who is jealous and insecure, not he.

prosocial behavior Positive actions toward other people such as helping and cooperating.

protective factors Influences that prevent the damaging effects of risk factors or help children overcome disadvantages.

proximodistal principle In development, the principle that growth proceeds from the center of the body (or the proximal region) to the extremities (or the distal regions).

psychoanalytic theory The theoretical perspective associated with Freud and his followers that emphasizes unconscious motivations for behavior, conflicts within the personality, and stages of psychosexual development.

psychometric approach The research tradition that spawned standardized tests of intelligence and that views intelligence as a trait or a set of traits that can be measured and that varies from person to person.

psychosexual stages Freud's five stages of development, associated with biological maturation and shifts in the libido: oral, anal, phallic, latency, and genital.

psychosocial stages Erikson's eight stages of development (trust, autonomy, initiative, industry, identity, intimacy, generativity, and integrity), emphasizing social influences more and biological urges less than Freud's psychosexual stages.

puberty The point at which a person reaches sexual maturity and is physically capable of conceiving a child.

quasi experiment An experiment-like study that evaluates the effects of different treatments but does not randomly assign individuals to treatment groups.

random assignment A technique in which research participants are placed in experimental conditions in an unbiased or random way so that the resulting groups are not systematically different.

random sample A sample formed by identifying all members of the larger population of interest and then selecting a portion of them in an unbiased or random way to participate in the study; a technique to ensure that the sample studied is representative or typical of the larger population of interest.

reaction formation Defense mechanism that involves expressing motives that are just the opposite of one's real motives, as when a woman who unconsciously wants to gratify her sexual urges instead takes up a crusade against all the sex on television.

reaction time The interval between the presentation of a stimulus and a response to it.

reactive attachment disorder A psychiatric diagnosis affecting socially deprived and maltreated children that involves either emotionally withdrawn behavior or "disinhibited" attachment that involves indiscriminate interest in people with lack of appropriate wariness of strangers.

recall memory Recollecting or actively retrieving objects, events, and experiences when examples or cues are not provided. Contrast with *cued recall memory* and *recognition memory*.

recessive gene A less powerful gene that is not expressed phenotypically when paired with a *dominant gene*.

reciprocal determinism The notion in social cognitive theory that the flow of influence between people and their environments is a two-way street; the environment may affect the person, but the person's characteristics and behavior will also influence the environment.

reciprocity The mutual give and take by both parties in a human relationship that forms an important basis for morality.

recognition memory Identifying an object or event as one that has been experienced before, such as when a person must select the correct answer from several options. Contrast with *cued recall memory* and *recall memory*.

reconstituted family A new family that forms after the remarriage of a single parent, sometimes involving the blending of two families into a new one.

reflex An unlearned and automatic response to a stimulus.

regression A defense mechanism that involves retreating to an earlier, less traumatic stage of development.

rehearsal A strategy for remembering that involves repeating the items the person is trying to retain.

relativistic thinking A form of postformal-operational thought in which it is understood that there are multiple ways of viewing a problem and that the solutions people arrive at will depend on their starting assumptions and perspective.

REM sleep A state of active, irregular sleep associated with dreaming; named for the rapid eye movements associated with it.

repression Removing unacceptable thoughts or traumatic memories from consciousness, as when a young woman who was raped has no memory at all of having been raped (or less drastically, engages in denial, knowing deep down that she was raped but not accepting the reality of it).

research ethics Standards of conduct that investigators are ethically bound to honor to protect their research participants from physical or psychological harm.

reserve capacity The ability of many organ systems to respond to demands for extraordinary output, such as when the heart and lungs work at maximal capacity.

resistant attachment An insecure infant-caregiver bond or other intimate relationship characterized by strong separation anxiety and a tendency to show ambivalent reactions to the attachment object upon reunion, seeking and yet resisting contact.

retinitis pigmentosa (RP) A group of hereditary disorders that involve gradual deterioration of the light-sensitive cells of the retina.

retrieval The process of retrieving information from long-term memory when it is needed.

reversibility In Piaget's theory, the ability to reverse or negate an action by mentally performing the opposite action.

rhythmic stereotypies Repetitive movements observed in infants shortly before a new motor skill emerges.

rite of passage A ritual that marks a person's "passage" from one status to another, usually in reference to rituals marking the transition from childhood to adulthood.

role-taking skills The ability to assume other people's perspectives and understand their thoughts, feelings, and behaviors. See *perspective-taking skills*.

rubella A disease that has little effect on a pregnant woman but may cause several serious birth defects, such as blindness, deafness, and mental retardation, in unborn children exposed in the first 3 to 4 months of gestation; German measles.

rule assessment approach Siegler's approach to studying the development of problem solving that determines what information about a problem children take in and what rules they then formulate to account for this information.

ruminative coping Way of managing stress that involves dwelling on problems and attempting to analyze them; may help explain higher rates of depression in females than in males.

sample The group of individuals chosen to be the subjects of a study.

savant syndrome The phenomenon in which extraordinary talent in a particular area is displayed by a person who is otherwise mentally retarded.

scaffolding Jerome Bruner's term for providing structure to a less skilled learner to encourage advancement.

scheme (or schema; plural: schemes or schemata) A cognitive structure or organized pattern of action or thought used to deal with experiences.

schizophrenia A serious form of mental illness characterized by disturbances in logical thinking, emotional expression, and interpersonal behavior.

school refusal behavior A reluctance or refusal to go to school or to remain there, sometimes called school phobia because it often involves intense anxiety.

scientific method An attitude or value about the pursuit of knowledge that dictates that investigators must be objective and must allow their data to decide the merits of their theorizing.

script A mental representation of a typical sequence of actions related to an event that is created in memory and that then guides future behaviors in similar settings.

secondary circular reaction During Piaget's sensorimotor period, the infant's repetition of interesting actions on objects (e.g., repeatedly shaking a rattle to make a noise).

secular trend A trend in industrialized society toward earlier maturation and greater body size.

secure attachment An infant–caregiver bond or intimate relationship in which the individual welcomes close contact, uses the attachment object as a source of comfort, and dislikes but can manage separations.

secure base A point of safety, represented by an infant's attachment figure, that permits exploration of the environment.

selective attention Deliberately concentrating on one thing and ignoring something else.

selective breeding A method of studying genetic influence that involves deliberately determining whether a trait can be bred in animals through selective mating.

selective optimization with compensation (SOC) The concept that older people cope with aging through a strategy that involves focusing on the skills most needed, practicing those skills, and developing ways to avoid the need for other skills.

self-concept People's perceptions of their unique attributes or traits.

self-conscious emotion A "secondary emotion" such as embarrassment or pride that requires an awareness of self; unlikely to emerge until about 18 months of age.

self-efficacy The belief that one can effectively produce desired outcomes in a particular area of life.

self-esteem People's overall evaluation of their worth as based on an assessment of the qualities that make up the self-concept.

self-recognition The ability to recognize oneself in a mirror or photograph, which occurs in most infants by 18 to 24 months of age.

semantic memory A type of explicit memory consisting of general facts.

semantics The aspect of language centering on meanings.

semenarche A boy's first ejaculation.

sensation The process by which information is detected by the sensory receptors and transmitted to the brain; the starting point in perception.

sensitive period As compared to a critical period, a period of life during which the developing individual is especially susceptible to the effects of experience or has an especially high level of plasticity.

sensorimotor stage Piaget's first stage of cognitive development, spanning the first 2 years of life, in which infants rely on their senses and motor behaviors in adapting to the world around them.

sensory register The first memory store in information processing in which stimuli are noticed and are briefly available for further processing.

sensory threshold The point at which low levels of stimulation can be detected.

separation anxiety A wary or fretful reaction that infants display when separated from their attachment objects.

sequential design A developmental research design that combines the cross-sectional approach and the longitudinal approach in a single study to compensate for the weaknesses of each.

seriation A logical operation that allows a person to mentally order a set of stimuli along a quantifiable dimension such as height or weight.

sex-linked characteristic An attribute determined by a gene that appears on one of the two types of sex chromosomes, usually the X chromosome.

sexual orientation A person's preference for sexual partners of the same or other sex, often characterized as primarily heterosexual, homosexual, or bisexual.

shared environmental influences Experiences that individuals living in the same home environment share and that work to make them similar. Contrast with *nonshared environmental influences*.

short-term memory The memory store in which limited amounts of information are temporarily held; called *working memory* when its active quality is being emphasized.

sibling rivalry A spirit of competition, jealousy, or resentment that may arise between two or more brothers or sisters.

sickle-cell disease A genetic blood disease in which red blood cells assume an unusual sickle shape and become inefficient at distributing oxygen throughout the body.

single gene-pair inheritance The genetic mechanism through which a characteristic is influenced by only one pair of genes, one gene from the mother and its partner from the father.

size constancy The tendency to perceive an object as the same size despite changes in its distance from the eyes.

slow-to-warm-up temperament A characteristic mode of response in which the individual is relatively inactive and moody and displays mild resistance to new routines and experiences but gradually adapts. Contrast with *easy temperament* and *difficult temperament*.

social clock A personal sense of when things should be done in life and when the individual is ahead of or behind the schedule dictated by age norms.

social cognition Thinking about the thoughts, feelings, motives, and behavior of the self and other people.

social cognitive theory Bandura's social learning theory, which holds that children and adults can learn novel responses merely by observing the behavior of a model, making mental notes on what they have seen, and then using these mental representations to reproduce the model's behavior; more broadly, a theory emphasizing the importance of cognitive processing of social experiences.

social comparison The process of defining and evaluating the self through comparisons with other people.

social convoy The changing cadre of significant people who serve as sources of social support to the individual during the life span.

social learning theory See *social cognitive theory*.

social norm A socially defined expectation about how people should behave in particular social contexts.

social perspective-taking skills The ability to assume other people's perspectives and understand their thoughts, feelings, and behaviors; role-taking skills.

social pretend play A form of play that involves both cooperation with playmates and pretend or symbolic activity.

social referencing Infants' monitoring of companions' emotional reactions in ambiguous situations and use of this information to decide how they should feel and behave.

social-conventional rules Standards of conduct determined by social consensus that indicate what is appropriate within a particular social setting. Contrast with *moral rules*.

social-role hypothesis Eagly's view that gender-role stereotypes are created and maintained by differences in the roles that men and women play in society rather than being inherent in males and females.

sociocultural perspective Vygotsky's contextual theory of development, which maintains that cognitive development is shaped by the sociocultural context in which it occurs and grows out of children's social interactions with members of their culture.

socioeconomic status (SES) The position people hold in society based on such factors as income, education, occupational status, and the prestige of their neighborhoods.

socioemotional selectivity theory Carstensen's notion that our needs change as we grow older and that we actively choose to narrow our range of social partners to those who can best meet our emotional needs.

sociometric techniques Methods for determining who is well liked and popular and who is disliked or neglected in a group.

somatic symptoms Physical or bodily signs of emotional distress such as loss of appetite or disruption of normal sleep patterns.

species heredity The genetic endowment that members of a particular species have in common; a contributor to universal species traits and patterns of maturation.

spillover effects Events at work affect home life, and events at home carry over into the work place.

spina bifida Condition in which the bottom of the neural tube fails to fully close during prenatal development and part of the spinal cord is not fully encased in the protective covering of the spinal column.

spirituality A search for ultimate meaning in life that may or may not be carried out in the context of religion.

standard deviation A measure of the dispersion or spread around the mean of a distribution of scores; in the case of IQ tests with a mean score of 100, the standard deviation is 15, meaning that about two-thirds of people taking the test have scores between 85 and 115.

Stanford–Binet Intelligence Scale One of the most widely used, individually administered intelligence tests, which yields an IQ score.

static thought In Piaget's theory, the thought characteristic of the preoperational period that is fixed on end states rather than on the changes that transform one state into another. Contrast with *transformational thought*.

stem cell Undifferentiated, primitive cells that have the ability both to multiply and to differentiate into a variety of specific cells.

stereotype threat An individual's fear of being judged to have the qualities associated with negative stereotypes of his or her social group.

Sternberg's Triarchic Abilities Tests (STAT) An intelligence test based on Sternberg's triarchic theory that uses a variety of question formats to assess practical, creative, and analytical components of intelligence.

stillbirth Fetal death that occurs late in pregnancy when survival outside womb would normally have been possible.

storage In information processing, the holding of information in the long-term memory store.

storm and stress Hall's term for the emotional ups and downs and rapid changes that he believed characterize adolescence.

Strange Situation A series of mildly stressful experiences involving the departure of the parent and exposure to a stranger to which infants are exposed to determine the quality of their attachments; developed by Ainsworth.

stranger anxiety A wary or fretful reaction that infants often display when approached by an unfamiliar person.

structured observation A research method in which scientists create special conditions designed to elicit the behavior of interest to achieve greater control over the conditions under which they gather behavioral data. Contrast with *naturalistic observation*.

successful intelligence Sternberg's concept that people are intelligent to the extent that they are able to succeed in life in their sociocultural context.

sudden infant death syndrome (SIDS) The death of a sleeping baby because of a failure of the respiratory system; linked to maternal smoking.

superego The psychoanalytic term for the component of the personality that consists of the individual's internalized moral standards.

surfactant A substance that aids breathing by preventing the air sacs of the lungs from sticking together.

surgency/extraversion Dimension of temperament that involves the tendency to actively and energetically approach new experiences in an emotionally positive way (rather than to be inhibited and withdrawn). See *negative affectivity* and *effortful control*.

symbolic capacity The capacity to use symbols such as words, images, or actions to represent or stand for objects and experiences; representational thought.

synapse The point at which the axon or dendrite of one neuron makes a connection with another neuron.

synchronized routine Harmonious, dancelike interaction between infant and caregiver in which each adjusts behavior in response to that of the other.

syntactic bootstrapping Using the syntax of a sentence—that is, where a word is placed in a sentence—to determine the meaning of the word.

syntax Rules specifying how words can be combined to form meaningful sentences in a language.

syphilis A common sexually transmitted disease that may cross the placental barrier in the middle and later stages of pregnancy, causing miscarriage or serious birth defects.

systemize The brain's ability to analyze and explore how things work.

systems theories Theories of development holding that changes over the life span arise from the ongoing interrelationships between a changing organism and a changing environment, both of which are part of a larger, dynamic system.

tabula rasa The idea that the mind of an infant is a "blank slate" and that all knowledge, abilities, behaviors, and motives are acquired through experience.

telegraphic speech Early sentences that consist primarily of content words and omit the less meaningful parts of speech such as articles, prepositions, pronouns, and auxiliary verbs.

telomere A stretch of DNA that forms the tip of a chromosome and that shortens after each cell division, possibly timing the death of cells.

temperament A genetically based pattern of tendencies to respond in predictable ways; building blocks of personality such as activity level, sociability, and emotionality.

teratogen Any disease, drug, or other environmental agent that can harm a developing fetus.

terminal drop A rapid decline in intellectual abilities that people within a few years of dying often experience.

tertiary circular reaction During Piaget's sensorimotor period, the infant's experimenting with actions to find new ways to solve problems or produce interesting effects.

test norms Standards of normal performance on psychometric instruments based on the average scores and range of scores obtained by a large, representative sample of test takers.

testosterone The most important of the male hormones, or androgens; essential for normal sexual development during the prenatal period and at puberty.

thalidomide A mild tranquilizer that, taken early in pregnancy, can produce a variety of malformations of the limbs, eyes, ears, and heart.

theory A set of concepts and propositions designed to organize, describe, and explain a set of observations.

theory of mind The understanding that people have mental states (feelings, desires, beliefs, intentions) and that these states underlie and help explain their behavior.

time of measurement effects In developmental research, the effects on findings of historical events occurring when the data for a study are being collected (for example, psychological changes brought about by an economic depression rather than as a function of aging). Contrast with *age effects* and *cohort effects*.

tinnitus Condition caused by exposure to high noise levels that involves ringing sounds in one or both ears and that can last for days, weeks, or indefinitely.

total brain death An irreversible loss of functioning in the entire brain, both the higher centers of the cerebral cortex that are involved in thought and the lower centers of the brain that control basic life processes such as breathing.

transactional model A model of family influence in which parent and child are believed to influence each other reciprocally.

transformational grammar Rules of syntax that allow a person to transform declarative statements into questions, negatives, imperatives, and other kinds of sentences.

transformational thought In Piaget's theory, the ability to conceptualize transformations, or processes of change from one state to another, which appears in the stage of concrete operations. Contrast with *static thought*.

transitivity The ability to recognize the necessary or logical relations among elements in a serial order (for example, that if A is taller than B, and B is taller than C, then A must be taller than C).

triangular theory of love Robert Sternberg's model describing types of love in terms of three components: passion, intimacy, and decision/commitment.

triarchic theory of intelligence An information-processing theory of intelligence that emphasizes three aspects of intelligent behavior: a practical component emphasizing the effect of context on what is intelligent; a creative component centering on whether a task is novel or familiar; and an analytic component focused on the cognitive processes used to solve a problem.

trust versus mistrust The psychosocial conflict of infancy in which infants must learn to trust others to meet their needs in order to trust themselves; first stage in Erikson's theory.

Turner syndrome A sex chromosome abnormality in which females inherit only one X chromosome (XO); they remain small in stature, fail to develop secondary sex characteristics, and may show some mental deficiencies.

twin study Method of studying genetic and environmental influence in which the similarity of identical twins is compared to that of (less genetically similar) fraternal twins, often in studies involving both twins reared together and twins reared apart.

ulnar grasp Holding objects by clamping them between the palm of hand and the fingers.

ultrasound Method of examining physical organs by scanning them with sound waves—for example, scanning the womb and thereby producing a visual outline of the fetus to detect gross abnormalities.

umami A taste sensation that roughly equates to "brothy" or "savory."

unconditioned response (UCR) The unlearned response elicited by an unconditioned stimulus.

unconditioned stimulus (UCS) A stimulus that elicits a particular response without prior learning.

unconscious motivation Freud's term for feelings, experiences, and conflicts that influence a person's thinking and behavior even though they cannot be recalled.

underextension The young child's tendency to use general words to refer to a smaller set of objects, actions, or events than adults do (for example, using *candy* to refer only to mints). Contrast with *overextension*.

universal grammar A system of common rules and properties of language that may allow infants to grow up learning any of the world's languages.

universality–context-specificity issue The debate over the extent to which developmental changes are common to everyone (universal, as in most stage theories) or different from person to person (particularistic).

utilization deficiency The third phase in mastery of memory strategies in which children fail to benefit from a memory strategy they are able to produce.

vascular dementia The deterioration of functioning and cognitive capacities caused by a series of minor strokes that cut off the blood supply to areas of the brain; also called multi-infarct dementia.

vicarious reinforcement In observational learning, the consequences experienced by models, because of their behavior, that affect the learner's likelihood of engaging in the behavior.

visual accommodation The ability of the lens of the eye to change shape to bring objects at different distances into focus.

visual acuity The ability to perceive detail in a visual stimulus.

visual cliff An elevated glass platform that creates an illusion of depth and is used to test the depth perception of infants.

vocabulary spurt A phenomenon occurring around 18 months of age when the pace of word learning quickens dramatically.

Wechsler Scales A set of widely used, individually administered intelligence tests that yield verbal, performance, and overall IQ scores.

wisdom A combination of rich factual knowledge about life and procedural knowledge such as strategies for giving advice and handling conflicts.

word segmentation In language development, the ability to break the stream of speech sounds into distinct words.

working memory A memory store, often referred to as a mental "scratch pad," that temporarily holds information when it is being actively operated upon; the active use of the short-term memory store.

X chromosome The longer of the two sex chromosomes; normal females have two X chromosomes, whereas normal males have only one.

Y chromosome The shorter of the two sex chromosomes; normal males have one Y chromosome, whereas females have none.

zone of proximal development Vygotsky's term for the difference between what a learner can accomplish independently and what a learner can accomplish with the guidance and encouragement of a more skilled partner.

zygote A single cell formed at conception from the union of a sperm and an ovum.

References

A

Aarnoudse-Moens, C., Weisglas-Kuperus, N., van Goudoever, J., & Oosterlaan, J. (2009). Meta-analysis of neurobehavioral outcomes in very preterm and/or very low birth weight children. *Pediatrics, 124,* 717–728.

Aarons, S. J., & Jenkins, R. R. (2002). Sex, pregnancy, and contraception-related motivators and barriers among Latino and African-American youth in Washington, DC *Sex Education, 2,* 5–30.

ABCNews (2010). He Never Forgets: Meet the Super-Memory Man. Available at: http://abcnews.go.com/Nightline/story?id=7075443&page=3. Accessed: February 9, 2010.

Abele, A. E. (2003). The dynamics of masculine-agentic and feminine-communal traits: Findings from a prospective study. *Journal of Personality and Social Psychology, 85,* 768–776.

Abele, A. E., Uchronski, M., Suitner, C., & Wojciszke, B. (2008). Towards an operationalization of the fundamental dimensions of agency and communion: Trait content ratings in five countries considering valence and frequency of word occurrence. *European Journal of Social Psychology, 38,* 1202–1217.

Ablard, K. E., & Mills, C. J. (1996). Implicit theories of intelligence and self-perceptions of academically talented adolescents and children. *Journal of Youth and Adolescence, 25,* 137–148.

Abma, J. C., & Martinez, G. M. (2006). Childlessness among older women in the United States: Trends and profiles. *Journal of Marriage and Family, 68,* 1045–1056.

Abraham, J. D., & Hansson, R. O. (1995). Successful aging at work: An applied study of selection, optimization, and compensation through impression management. *Journals of Gerontology: Psychological Sciences, 50,* P94–P103.

Achenbach, T. M. (1982). *Developmental psychopathology* (2nd ed.). New York: Wiley.

Achenbach, T. M., & Edelbrock, C. S. (1978). The classification of child psychopathology: A review and analysis of empirical efforts. *Psychological Bulletin, 85,* 1275–1301.

Achenbaum, W. A., & Bengtson, V. L. (1994). Re-engaging the disengagement theory of aging: On the history and assessment of theory development in gerontology. *Gerontologist, 34,* 756–763.

Achter, J. A., Benbow, C. P., & Lubinski, D. (1997). Rethinking multipotentiality among the intellectually gifted: A critical review and recommendations. *Gifted Child Quarterly, 41,* 5–15.

Ackerman, P. L. (2008). Knowledge and cognitive aging. In F. I. M. Craik & T. A. Salthouse (Eds.), *The handbook of aging and cognition* (3rd ed.). New York: Psychology Press.

Adachi, Y., Sato, C., & Hayama, J. (2008). Late bedtime after 22.00 hours affects daily weight gain in 4-month-old infants. *Sleep and Biological Rhythms, 6,* 50–52.

Adam, E. K., Gunnar, M. R., & Tanaka, A. (2004). Adult attachment, parent emotion, and observed parenting behavior: Mediator and moderator models. *Child Development, 75,* 110–122.

Adams, C. (1991). Qualitative age differences in memory for text: A life-span developmental perspective. *Psychology and Aging, 6,* 323–336.

Adams, D. W., & Deveau, E. J. (1987). When a brother or sister is dying of cancer: The vulnerability of the adolescent sibling. *Death Studies, 11,* 279–295.

Adams, M. J. (1990). *Beginning to read: Learning and thinking about print.* Cambridge, MA: MIT Press.

Adams, M. J., Treiman, R., & Pressley, M. (1998). Reading, writing, and literacy. In I. E. Sigel & K. A. Renninger (Vol. Eds.), W. Damon (Editor-in-Chief), *Handbook of child psychology: Vol. 4. Child psychology in practice* (5th ed.), 275–355. New York: Wiley.

Adams, R. E., & Bukowski, W. M. (2007). Relationships with mothers and peers moderate the association between childhood sexual abuse and anxiety disorders. *Child Abuse and Neglect, 31,* 645–656.

Aday, R. H., Kehoe, G. C., & Farney, L. A. (2006). Impact of senior center friendships on aging women who live alone. *Journal of Women & Aging, 18,* 57–73.

Adey, P. S., & Shayer, M. (1992). Accelerating the development of formal thinking in middle and high school students: II. Postproject effects on science achievement. *Journal of Research in Science Teaching, 29,* 81–92.

Adler, J. (2005, November 14). The Boomer Files: Hitting 60. *Newsweek,* 50–58.

Adolph, K. E. (2008). Learning to move. *Current Directions in Psychological Science, 17,* 213–218.

Adolph, K. E., & Avolio, A. M. (2000). Walking infants adapt locomotion to changing body dimensions. *Journal of Experimental Psychology: Human Perception and Performance, 26,* 1148–1166.

Adolph, K. E., & Berger, S. E. (2006). Motor Development. In D. Kuhn & R. Siegler (Vol. Eds.), *Handbook of child psychology: Cognition, perception, and language* (6th ed.). Hoboken, NJ: Wiley and Sons.

Adolph, K. E., Robinson, S. R., Young, J. W., Gill-Alvarez, F. (2008). What is the shape of developmental change? *Psychological Review, 115,* 527–543.

Agnew, R. (2003). An integrated theory of the adolescent peak in offending. *Youth & Society, 34,* 263–299.

Agnew, R., & Huguley, S. (1989). Adolescent violence toward parents. *Journal of Marriage and the Family, 51,* 699–711.

Aguiar, A., & Baillargeon, R. (1999). 2.5-month-old infants' reasoning about when objects should and should not be occluded. *Cognitive Psychology, 39,* 116–157.

Aguiar, A., & Baillargeon, R. (2002). Developments in young infants' reasoning about occluded objects. *Cognitive Psychology, 45,* 267–336.

Ahbe-Rappe, K. (2006). "I no longer believe": Did Freud abandon seduction theory? *Journal of the American Psychoanalytic Association, 54,* 171–199.

Ahluwalia, I. B., Morrow, B., & Hsia, J. (2006). Why do women stop breastfeeding? Findings from the pregnancy risk assessment and monitoring system. *Journal of the American Academy of Child and Adolescent Psychiatry, 45,* 699–700.

Ahrons, C. R. (2007). Family ties after divorce: Long-term implications for children. *Family Process, 46,* 53–65.

Ainscough, C. E. (1990). Premenstrual emotional changes: A prospective study of symptomatology in normal women. *Journal of Psychosomatic Research, 34,* 35–45.

Ainsworth, M. D. S. (1973). The development of infant–mother attachment. In B. M. Caldwell & H. N. Ricciuti (Eds.), *Review of child development research* (Vol. 3). Chicago: University of Chicago Press.

Ainsworth, M. D. S. (1979). Attachment as related to mother–infant interaction. In J. G. Rosenblatt, R. A. Hinde, C. Beer, & M. Busnel (Eds.), *Advances in the study of behavior* (Vol. 9). New York: Academic Press.

Ainsworth, M. D. S. (1989). Attachments beyond infancy. *American Psychologist, 44,* 709–716.

Ainsworth, M. D. S., Blehar, M., Waters, E., & Wall, S. (1978). *Patterns of attachment.* Hillsdale, NJ: Erlbaum.

Ajrouch, K. J., Antonucci, T. C., & Janevic, M. R. (2001). Social networks among blacks and whites: The interaction between race and age. *Journals of Gerontology: Psychological Sciences and Social Sciences, 56,* S112–S118.

Akiyama, H., Antonucci, T., Takahashi, K., & Langfahl, E. S. (2003). Negative interactions in close relationships across the life span. *Journals of Gerontology: Psychological Sciences and Social Sciences, 58,* P70–P79.

Aksglaede, L., Sørensen, K., Petersen, J. H., Skakkebaek, N. E., & Juul, A. (2009). Recent decline in age at breast development: the Copenhagen Puberty Study. *Pediatrics, 123,* e932–939.

Albers, L. L. (1999). The duration of labor in healthy women. *Journal of Perinatology, 19,* 114–119.

Albert, R. S. (1996). Some reasons why childhood creativity often fails to make it past puberty into the real world. In M. A. Runco (Ed.), *Creativity from childhood through adulthood: The developmental issues.* San Francisco: Jossey-Bass.

Aldwin, C. M., Spiro, A., & Park, C. L. (2006). Health, behavior, and optimal aging. In J. E. Birren & K. W. Schaie (Eds.), *Handbook of the psychology of aging.* Boston: Elsevier Academic Press.

Alexander, G. M. (2003). An evolutionary perspective of sex–typed toy preferences: Pink, blue, and the brain. *Archives of Sexual Behavior, 32,* 7–14.

Alexander, G. M., Wilcox, T., & Woods, R. (2009). Sex differences in infants' visual interest in toys. *Archives of Sexual Behavior, 38,* 427–433.

Alexander, P. A., Murphy, P. K., & Kulikowich, J. M. (2009). Expertise and the adult learner. A historical, psychological, and methodological exploration. In M. C. Smith (Ed.) & N. DeFrates-Densch (Asst. Ed.), *Handbook of research on adult learning and development.* New York: Routledge.

Alfieri, T., Ruble, D. N., & Higgins, E. T. (1996). Gender stereotypes during adolescence: Developmental changes and the transition to junior high school. *Developmental Psychology, 32,* 1129–1137.

Alford, J. R., Funk, C. L., & Hibbing, J. R. (2005). Are political orientations genetically transmitted? *American Political Science Review, 99,* 153–167.

Allen, J. P. (2008). The attachment system in adolescence. In J. Cassidy & P. R. Shaver (Eds.), *Handbook of attachment theory: Research, and clinical applications* (2nd ed.). New York: Guilford.

Allen, J. P., Seitz, V., & Apfel, N. H. (2007). The sexually mature teen as a whole person: New directions in prevention and intervention for teen pregnancy and parenthood. In J. L. Aber, S. J. Bishop-Josef, S. M. Jones, K. T. McLearn, & D. A. Phillips (Eds.), *Child development and social policy: Knowledge for action.* Washington, DC: American Psychological Association.

Allen, K. R., Blieszner, R., & Roberto, K. A. (2000). Families in the middle and later years: A review and critique of research in the 1990s. *Journal of Marriage and the Family, 62,* 911–926.

Allen, M. C., & Capute, A. J. (1986). Assessment of early auditory and visual abilities of extremely premature infants. *Developmental Medicine and Child Neurology, 28,* 458–466.

Alloway, T. P., Gathercole, S. E., & Pickering, S. J. (2006). Verbal and visuospatial short-term and working memory in children: Are they separable? *Child Development, 77,* 1698–716.

Allum, J. H., Greisiger, R., Straubhaar, S., & Carpenter, M. G. (2000). Auditory perception and speech identification in children with cochlear implants tested with the EARS protocol. *British Journal of Audiology, 34,* 293–303.

Almeida, D. M., & Horn, M. C. (2004). Is daily life more stressful during middle adulthood? In O. G. Brim, C. D. Ryff, & R. C. Kessler (Eds.), *How healthy are we? A national study of well-being at midlife.* Chicago: University of Chicago Press.

Almli, C. R., Ball, R. H., & Wheeler, M. E. (2001). Human fetal and neonatal movement patterns: Gender differences and fetal-to-neonatal continuity. *Developmental Psychobiology, 38,* 252–273.

Alwin, D. F. (2009). History, cohorts, and patterns of cognitive aging. In H. B. Bosworth & C. Hertzog (Eds.), *Aging and cognition: Research methodologies and empirical advances.* Washington, DC: American Psychological Association.

Amara, C. E., Rice, C. L., Koval, J. J., Paterson, D. H., Winter, E. M., & Cunningham, D. A. (2003). Allometric scaling of strength in an independently living population age 55–86 years. *American Journal of Human Biology, 15,* 48–60.

Amato, P. R. (1993). Children's adjustment to divorce: Theories, hypotheses, and empirical support. *Journal of Marriage and the Family, 55,* 23–38.

Amato, P. R. (2000). The consequences of divorce for adults and children. *Journal of Marriage and the Family, 62,* 1269–1287.

Amato, P. R. (2006). Marital discord, divorce, and children's well-being: Results from a 20-year longitudinal study of two generations. In A. Clarke-Stewart & J. Dunn (Eds.), *Families count: Effects on child and adolescent development.* New York: Cambridge University Press.

Amato, P. R., Johnson, D. R., Booth, A., & Rogers, S. J. (2003). Continuity and change in marital quality between 1980 and 2000. *Journal of Marriage and the Family, 65,* 1–22.

Amato, P. R., & Sobolewski, J. M. (2004). The effects of divorce on fathers and children: Nonresidential fathers and stepfathers. In M. E. Lamb (Ed.), *The role of the father in child development* (4th ed.). Hoboken, NJ: John Wiley & Sons.

American Academy of Pediatrics. (2000). Prevention and management of pain and stress in the neonate (RE9945). *Pediatrics, 105,* 454–461.

American Association on Intellectual and Developmental Disabilities (2010). *Definition of intellectual disability.* Available at: www.aaidd.org. Accessed: February 24, 2010.

American Psychiatric Association (2000). *Diagnostic and statistical manual of mental disorders DSM–IV–TR* (4th ed., text revision). Arlington, VA: American Psychiatric Association.

American Psychiatric Association (2010, February 10). *APA announces draft diagnostic criteria for DSM-5. New proposed changes posted for leading manual of mental disorders.* Available at: www.dsm5.org. Accessed: March 10, 2010.

Amone-P'Olak, K., Ormel, J., Huisman, M., Verhulst, F. C., Oldehinkel, A. J., & Burger, H. (2009). Life stressors as mediators of the relation between socio-economic position and mental health problems in early adolescence: The TRAILS study. *Journal of the American Academy of Child & Adolescent Psychiatry, 48,* 1031–1038.

Amsel, E., Klaczynski, P. A., Johnston, A., Bench, S., Close, J., Sadler, E., & Walker, R. (2008). A dual-process account of the development of scientific reasoning: The nature and development of meta-cognitive intercession skills. *Cognitive Development, 23,* 452–471.

Amstutz, D. D., & Sheared, V. (2000). The crisis in adult basic education. *Education and Urban Society, 32,* 155–166.

Anand, K. J., & Hickey, P. R. (1992). Halothane-morphine compared with high-dose sufentanil for anesthesia and postoperative analgesia in neonatal cardiac surgery. *New England Journal of Medicine, 326,* 1–9.

Anastasi, A. (1958). Heredity, environment, and the question, "how?" *Psychological Review, 65,* 197–208.

Andari, E., Duhamel, J., Zalla, T., Herbrecht, E., Leboyer, M., & Sirigu, A. (2010). Promoting social behavior with oxytocin in high functioning autism spectrum disorders. *Proceedings of the National Academy of Sciences, 107,* 4389–4394.

Anderson, A. N., Roncaroli, F., Hodges, A., Deprez, M., & Turkheimer, F. E. (2008). Chromosomal profiles of gene expression in Huntington's disease. *Brain, 131,* 381–388.

Anderson, C. A., & Bushman, B. J. (2002, March 29). The effects of media violence on society. *Science, 295,* 2377–2379.

Anderson, D. A., & Hamilton, M. (2007). Gender role stereotyping of parents in children's picture books: The invisible father. *Sex Roles, 52,* 145–151.

Anderson, S. E., Dallal, G. E., & Must, A. (2003). Relative weight and race influence average age at menarche: Results from two nationally representative surveys of US girls studied 25 years apart. *Pediatrics, 111,* 844–854.

Anderson, S. E. & Must, A. (2005). Interpreting the continued decline in the average age at menarche: results from two nationally representative surveys of U.S. girls studied 10 years apart. *The Journal of Pediatrics 147,* 753–760.

Anderson-Fye, E. (2009). Cross-cultural issues in body image among children and adolescents. In L. Smolak & J. K. Thompson (Eds.), *Body image, eating disorders, and obesity in youth.* Washington, DC: American Psychological Association.

Andersson, A. M., Carlsen, E., Petersen, J. H., & Skakkebaek, N. E. (2003). Variation in levels of serum inhibin B, testosterone, estradiol, luteinizing hormone, follicle-stimulating hormone, and sex hormone-ginding globulin in monthly samples from healthy men during a 17-month period: Possible effects of seasons. *Journal of Clinical Endocrinology and Metabolism, 88,* 932–937.

Andrade, J. Q., Bunduki, V., Curti, S. P., Figueiredo, C. A., de Oliveria, M. I., & Zugaib, M. (2006). Rubella in pregnancy: Intrauterine transmission and perinatal outcome during a Brazilian epidemic. *Journal of Clinical Virology: The Official Publication of the Pan American Society for Clinical Virology, 35,* 285–291.

Andrade, S. E., Gurwitz, J. H., Davis, R. L., Chan, K. A., Finkelstein, J. A., Fortman, K., McPhillips, H., Raebel, M.A., Roblin, D., Smith, D.H., Yood, M. U., Morse, A. N., Platt, R. (2004). Prescription drug use in pregnancy. *American Journal of Obstetrics and Gynecology, 191,* 398–407.

Andrews, G., Clark, M., & Luszcz, M. (2002). Successful aging in the Australian Longitudinal Study of Aging: Applying the MacArthur model cross-nationally. *Journal of Social Issues, 58,* 749–765.

Andrews, G. J., Gavin, N., Begley, S., & Brodie, D. (2003). Assisting friendships, combating loneliness: Users' views on a "befriending" scheme. *Ageing & Society, 23,* 349–362.

Anglin, J. M. (1993). Vocabulary development: A morphological analysis. *Monographs of the Society for Research in Child Development, 58* (Serial No. 10).

Anisfeld, E., Casper, V., Nozyce, M., & Cunningham, N. (1990). Does infant carrying promote attachment? An experimental study of the effects of increased physical contact on the development of attachment. *Child Development, 61,* 1617–1627.

Anstey, K. J., Hofer, S. M., & Luszcz, M. A. (2003). A latent growth curve analysis of late-life sensory and cognitive function over 8 years: Evidence for specific and common factors underlying change. *Psychology and Aging, 18,* 714–726.

Antebi, A. (2007). Ageing: When loss is more. *Nature, 447,* 536–537.

Anthis, K., & LaVoie, J. C. (2006). Readiness to change: A longitudinal study of changes in adult identity. *Journal of Research in Personality, 40,* 209–219.

Antonucci, T. C., Birditt, K. S., & Akiyama, H. (2009). Convoys of social relations: An interdisciplinary approach. In V. L. Bengtson, M. Silverstein, N. M. Putney, & D. Gans (Eds.), *Handbook of theories of aging* (2nd ed.). New York: Springer.

Aoki, K. (1986). A stochastic model of gene-culture coevolution suggested by the "culture historical hypothesis" for the evolution of adult lactose absorption in humans. *Proceedings of the National Academy of Sciences, 83,* 2929–2933.

Apgar, V., & Beck, J. (1974). *Is my baby all right?* New York: Pocket Books.

Appollonio, I., Carabellese, C., Frattola, L., & Trabucchi, M. (1996). Effects of sensory aids on the quality of life and mortality of elderly people: A multivariate analysis. *Age and Ageing, 25,* 89–96.

Aquilino, W. S. (1991). Predicting parents' experiences with coresident adult children. *Journal of Family Issues, 12,* 323–342.

Aquilino, W. S. (2006). Family relationships and support systems in emerging adulthood. In J. J. Arnett & J. L. Tanner (Eds.), *Coming of age in the 21st century.* Washington, DC: American Psychological Association.

Aquino, K., Freeman, D., Reed, A., II, Felps, W., & Lim, V. K. G. (2009). Testing a social-cognitive model of moral behavior: The interactive influence of situations and moral identity centrality. *Journal of Personality and Social Psychology, 97,* 123–141.

Aquino, K., & Reed, A. (2002). The self-importance of moral identity. *Journal of Personality & Social Psychology, 83,* 1423–1440.

Arana-Ward, M. (1997, May 11). As technology advances, a bitter debate divides the deaf. *The Washington Post,* A1.

Aratani, L. (2008, February 10). Catching up to the boys, in the good and the bad. *The Washington Post,* C1, C14.

Arber, S., & Ginn, J. (1991). *Gender and later life: A sociological analysis of resources and constraints.* London: Sage.

Arbona, C., & Power, T. G. (2003). Parental attachment, self-esteem, and antisocial behaviors among African American, European American, and Mexican American adolescents. *Journal of Counseling Psychology, 50,* 40–51.

Archer, J. (1991). The influence of testosterone on human aggression. *British Journal of Psychology, 82,* 1–28.

Archer, J. (1992). *Ethology and human development.* Hertfordshire, England: Harvester Wheatsheaf.

Archer, J. (1996). Sex differences in social behavior: Are the social role and evolutionary explanations compatible? *American Psychologist, 51,* 909–917.

Archer, S. L. (1982). The lower age boundaries of identity development. *Child Development, 53,* 1551–1556.

Archer, S. L. (1992). A feminist's approach to identity research. In G. R. Adams, T. P. Gullotta, & R. Montemayor (Eds.), *Adolescent identity formation: Vol. 4. Advances in adolescent development.* Newbury Park, CA: Sage.

Arck, P. C., Rücke, M., Rose, M., Szekeres-Bartho, J., Douglas, A. J., Pritsch, M., Blois, S. M., Pincus, M. K., Bärenstrauch, N., Dudenhausen, J. W., Nakamura, K., Sheps, S., & Klapp, B. F. (2008). Early risk factors for miscarriage: A prospective cohort study in pregnant women. *Reproductive BioMedicine Online, 17,* 101–113.

Ardelt, M. (2000). Antecedents and effects of wisdom in old age. *Research on Aging, 22,* 360–394.

Arendt, R., Singer, L., Angelopoulos, J., Bass-Busdiecker, O., & Mascia, J. (1998). Sensorimotor development in cocaine-exposed infants. *Infant Behavior and Development, 21,* 627–640.

Ariès, P. (1962). *Centuries of childhood.* New York: Knopf.

Ariès, P. (1981). *The hour of our death* (H. Weaver, Trans.). New York: Knopf. (Original work published 1977).

Arking, R. (2006). *The biology of aging: Observations and principles* (3rd ed.). New York: Oxford University Press.

Armstrong, P. I., & Crombie, G. (2000). Compromises in adolescents' occupational aspirations and expectations from grades 8 to 10. *Journal of Vocational Behavior, 56,* 82–98.

Armstrong, V. L., Brunet, P. M., He, C., Nishimura, M., Poole, H. L., & Spector, F. (2006). What is so critical?: A commentary on the reexamination of critical periods. *Developmental Psychobiology, 48,* 326–331.

Arnett, J. J. (1999). Adolescent storm and stress, reconsidered. *American Psychologist, 54,* 317–326.

Arnett, J. J. (2000). Emerging adulthood: A theory of development from the late teens through the twenties. *American Psychologist, 55,* 469–480.

Arnett, J. J. (2006). Emerging adulthood: Understanding the new way of coming of age. In J. J. Arnett & J. L. Tanner (Eds.), *Emerging adults in America: Coming of age in the 21st century.* Washington, DC: American Psychological Association.

Arnett, J. J., & Tanner, J. L. (Eds.) (2006). *Emerging adults in America: Coming of age in the 21st century.* Washington, DC: American Psychological Association.

Aronson, J., Lustina, M. J., Good, C., Keough, K., Steele, C. M., & Brown, J. (1999). When white men can't do math: Necessary and sufficient factors in stereotype threat. *Journal of Experimental Social Psychology, 35,* 29–46.

Arroyo, C. G., & Zigler, E. (1995). Racial identity, academic achievement, and the psychological well-being of economically disadvantaged adolescents. *Journal of Personality and Social Psychology, 69,* 903–914.

Arseneault, L., Tremblay, R. E., Boulerice, B., & Saucier, J. (2002). Obstetrical complications and violent delinquency: Testing two developmental pathways. *Child Development, 73,* 496–508.

Asbury, K., Dunn, J. F., & Plomin, R. (2006). Birthweight-discordance and differences in early parenting relate to monozygotic twin differences in behaviour problems and academic achievement at age 7. *Developmental Science, 9,* F22–F31.

Asendorpf, J. B., Warkentin, V., & Baudonnière, P. M. (1996). Self-awareness and other-awareness: 2. Mirror self-recognition, social contingency awareness, and synchronic imitation. *Developmental Psychology, 32,* 313–321.

Aspelmeier, J. E., Elliott, A. N., & Smith, C. H. (2007). Childhood sexual abuse, attachment, and trauma symptoms in college females: The moderating role of attachment. *Child Abuse and Neglect, 31,* 549–566.

Associated Press (2003, November 21). Women earn 20% less than men, GAO finds. *The Washington Post,* E4.

Atchley, R. C. (1976). *The sociology of retirement.* Cambridge, MA: Schenkman.

Atchley, R. C. (2009). *Spirituality and aging.* Baltimore: Johns Hopkins University Press.

Athey, I. (1984). Contributions of play to development. In T. D. Yawkey & A. D. Pellegrini (Eds.), *Child's play: Developmental and applied.* Hillsdale, NJ: Erlbaum.

Atkinson, R. C. & Shiffrin, R. M. (1968). Human memory: A proposed system and its control processes. In K. W. Spence & J. T. Spence (Eds.), *The psychology of learning and motivation: Advances in research and theory (Vol. 2).* New York: Academic Press.

Attar-Schwartz, S., Tan, J., Buchanan, A., Flouri, E., & Griggs, J. (2009). Grandparenting and adolescent adjustment in two-parent biological, lone-parent, and step-families. *Journal of Family Psychology, 23,* 67–75.

Austad, S. N. (2009). Making sense of biological theories of aging. In V. L. Bengtson, M. Silverstein, N. M. Putney, & D. Gans (Eds.), *Handbook of theories of aging* (2nd ed.). New York: Springer.

Austrian, S. (Ed.). (2008). *Developmental theories through the life cycle* (2nd ed.). New York: Columbia University Press.

Autism and Developmental Disabilities Monitoring Network Surveillance Year 2006 Principal Investigators (2009, December 18). Prevalence of autism spectrum disorders—Autism and Developmental Disabilities Monitoring Network, United States, 2006. *MMWR Surveillance Summaries, 58* (SS10), 1–20. Available at: www .cdc.gov/mmwr/preview/mmwrhtml/ss5810a1.htm. Accessed: February 26, 2010.

Autism Genome Project Consortium (2007). Mapping autism risk loci using genetic linage and chromosomal rearrangements. *Nature Genetics, 39,* 319–328.

Autti-Rämö, I. (2000). Twelve-year follow-up of children exposed to alcohol in utero. *Developmental Medicine & Child Neurology, 42,* 406–411.

Auyeung, B., Baron-Cohen, S., Ashwin, E., Knickmeyer, R., Taylor, K., & Hackett, G. (2009b). Fetal testosterone and autistic traits. *British Journal of Psychology, 100,* 1–22.

Auyeung, B., Wheelwright, S., Allison, C., Atkinson, M., Samarawickrema, N., & Baron-Cohen, S. (2009a). The children's empathy quotient and systemizing quotient: Sex differences in typical development and in autism spectrum conditions. *Journal of Autism and Developmental Disorders, 39,* 1509–1521.

Avert (2009). *Preventing mother-to-child transmission of HIV (PMTCT).* Available at: http://www.avert .org/motherchild.htm. Accessed: August 4, 2009.

Azmitia, M. (1992). Expertise, private speech, and the development of self-regulation. In R. M. Diaz & L. E. Berk (Eds.), *Private speech: From social interaction to self-regulation.* Hillsdale, NJ: Erlbaum.

B

Babai, R., & Levit-Dori, T. (2009). Several CASE lessons can improve students' control of variables reasoning scheme ability. *Journal of Science Education and Technology, 18,* 429–446.

Bacharach, V. R., & Baumeister, A. A. (1998). Direct and indirect effects of maternal intelligence, maternal age, income, and home environment on intelligence of preterm, low-birth-weight children. *Journal of Applied Developmental Psychology, 19,* 361–375.

Bachman, J. G., Safron, D. J., Sy, S. R., & Schulenberg, J. E. (2003). Wishing to work: New perspectives on how adolescents' part-time work intensity is linked to educational disengagement, substance use, and other problem behaviors. *International Journal of Behavioral Development, 27,* 301–315.

Bada, H. S., Das, A., Bauer, C. R., Shankaran, S., Lester, B. M., Gard, C. C., Wright, L. L., Lagasse, L. L., & Higgins, R. (2005). Low birth weight and preterm births: Etiologic fraction attributable to prenatal drug exposure. *Journal of Perinatology: Official Journal of the California Perinatal Association, 25,* 631–637.

Baddeley, A. (1986). *Working memory.* Oxford: Oxford University Press.

Baddeley, A. (1992). Working memory. *Science, 255,* 556–559.

Baer, J. C., & Martinez, C. D. (2006). Child maltreatment and insecure attachment: A meta-analysis. *Journal of Reproductive and Infant Psychology, 24,* 187–197.

Bahrick, H. P. (1984). Semantic memory content in permastore: Fifty years of memory for Spanish learned in school. *Journal of Experimental Psychology: General, 113,* 1–29.

Bahrick, H. P., Bahrick, P. O., & Wittlinger, R. P. (1975). Fifty years of memory for names and faces: A cross-sectional approach. *Journal of Experimental Psychology: General, 104,* 54–75.

Bailey, A., Lecouteur, A., Gottesman, I., Bolton, P., Simonoff, E., Yuzda, E. et al. (1995). Autism as a strongly genetic disorder: Evidence from a British twin study. *Psychological Medicine, 25,* 63–77.

Bailey, C. E. (Ed.) (2000). *Children in therapy: Using the family as a resource.* New York: W. W. Norton.

Bailey, H., Dunlosky, J., & Hertzog, C. (2009). Does differential strategy use account for age-related deficits in working-memory performance? *Psychology and Aging, 24,* 82–92.

Bailey, J. M. (2003). Biological perspectives on sexual orientation. In L. Garnets & D. Kimmel (Eds.), *Psychological perspectives on lesbian, gay, and bisexual experiences* (2nd ed.), 50–85. New York: Columbia University Press.

Bailey, J. M., Bechtold, K. T., & Berenbaum, S. A. (2002). Who are tomboys and why should we study them? *Archives of Sexual Behavior, 31,* 333–341.

Bailey, J. M., Dunne, M. P., & Martin, N. G. (2000). Genetic and environmental influences on sexual orientation and its correlates in an Australian twin sample. *Journal of Personality and Social Psychology, 78,* 524–536.

Bailey, J. M., & Pillard, R. C. (1991). A genetic study of male sexual orientation. *Archives of General Psychiatry, 48,* 1089–1096.

Bailey, J. M., Pillard, R. C., Neale, M. C., & Agyei, Y. (1993). Heritable factors influence sexual orientation in women. *Archives of General Psychiatry, 50,* 217–223.

Bailey, R. N., Indian, R. W., Zhang, X., Geiss, L. S., Duenas, M. R., & Saaddine, J. B. (2006). Visual impairment and eye care among older adults—five states. *Morbidity and Mortality Weekly Report, 55,* 1321–1345.

Baillargeon, R. (2002). The acquisition of physical knowledge in infancy: A summary in eight lessons.

In U. Goswami (Ed.), *Blackwell handbook of child cognitive development* (pp. 47–83). Oxford: Blackwell.

Baillargeon, R. H., Zoccolillo, M., Keenan, K., Côté, S., Pérusse, D., Wu, H., Boivin, M., & Tremblay, R. E. (2007). Gender differences in physical aggression: A prospective population-based survey of children before and after 2 years of age. *Developmental Psychology, 43*, 13–26.

Bajpai, A., Kabra, M., Gupta, A. K., & Menon, P. S. (2006). Growth pattern and skeletal maturation following growth hormone therapy in growth hormone deficiency: Factors influencing outcome. *Indian Pediatrics, 43*, 593–599.

Bakan, D. (1966). *The duality of human existence: Isolation and communion in Western man.* Boston: Beacon Press.

Baker, L. A., Raine, A., Liu, J., & Jacobson, K. C. (2008). Differential genetic and environmental influences on reactive and proactive aggression in children. *Journal of Abnormal Child Psychology, 36*, 1265–1278.

Baker, L., & Brown, A. L. (1984). Metacognitive skills and reading. In P. D. Pearson (Ed.), *A handbook of reading research.* New York: Longman.

Baker, T. B., McFall, R. M., & Shoham, V. (2009). Current status and future prospects of clinical psychology. Toward a scientifically principled approach to mental and behavioral health care. *Psychological Science in the Public Interest, 9*, 67–103.

Bakermans-Kranenburg, M. J., & van IJzendoorn, M. H. (2008). Oxytocin receptor (OXTR) and serotonin transporter (5-HTT) genes associated with observed parenting. *Social Cognitive and Affective Neuroscience, 3*, 128–134.

Bakermans-Kranenburg, M. J., & van IJzendoorn, M. H. (2009). The first 10,000 adult attachment interviews: Distributions of adult attachment representations in clinical and non-clinical groups. *Attachment and Human Development, 11*, 223–263.

Baker-Ward, L., Gordon, B. N., Ornstein, P. A., Larus, D. M., & Clubb, P. A. (1993). Young children's long-term retention of a pediatric examination. *Child Development, 64*, 1519–1533.

Baker-Ward, L., Ornstein, P. A., & Holden, D. J. (1984). The expression of memorization in early childhood. *Journal of Experimental Child Psychology, 37*, 555–575.

Balk, D. E., & Corr, C. A. (2001). Bereavement during adolescence: A review of research. In M. S. Stroebe, R. O. Hansson, W. Stroebe, & H. Schut (Eds.), *Handbook of bereavement research: Consequences, coping, and care.* Washington, DC: American Psychological Association.

Balk, D. E., & Corr, C. A. (Eds.) (2009). *Adolescent encounters with death, bereavement, and coping.* New York: Springer.

Baltes, P. B. (1987). Theoretical propositions of life-span developmental psychology: On the dynamics between growth and decline. *Developmental Psychology, 23*, 611–626.

Baltes, P. B., & Baltes, M. M. (1990). Psychological perspectives on successful aging: The model of selective optimization with compensation. In P. B. Baltes & M. M. Baltes (Eds.), *Successful aging: Perspectives from the behavioral sciences.* New York: Cambridge University Press.

Baltes, P. B., & Carstensen, L. L. (2003). The process of successful aging: Selection, optimization and compensation. In U. M. Staudinger & U. Lindenberger (Eds.), *Understanding human development: Dialogues with life-span psychology.* Dordecht, Netherlands: Kluwer Academic Press.

Baltes, P. B., & Freund, A. M. (2003). Human strengths as the orchestration of wisdom and selective optimization with compensation. In L. G. Aspinwall & U. M. Staudinger (Eds.),

A psychology of human strengths: Fundamental questions and future directions for a positive psychology. Washington, DC: American Psychological Association.

Baltes, P. B., & Lindenberger, U. (1997). Emergence of a powerful connection between sensory and cognitive functions across the adult life span: A new window to the study of cognitive aging? *Psychology and Aging, 12*, 12–21.

Baltes, P. B., Lindenberger, U., & Staudinger, U. M. (1998). Life-span theory in developmental psychology. In R. M. Lerner (Vol. Ed.), W. Damon (Editor-in-Chief), *Handbook of child psychology: Vol. 1. Theoretical models of human development* (5th ed.). New York: Wiley.

Baltes, P. B., Lindenberger, U., & Staudinger, U. M. (2006). Life span theory in developmental psychology. In W. Damon & R. M. Lerner (Eds. in Chief) & R. M. Lerner (Vol. Ed.), *Handbook of child psychology: Vol. 1. Theoretical models of human development* (6th ed.). Hoboken, NJ: Wiley.

Baltes, P. B., Smith, J., & Staudinger, U. M. (1992). Wisdom and successful aging. In T. B. Sonderegger (Ed.), *Nebraska Symposium on Motivation: Vol. 39. Psychology and aging.* Lincoln: University of Nebraska Press.

Baltes, P. B., & Staudinger, U. M. (2000). Wisdom: A metaheuristic (pragmatic) to orchestrate mind and virtue toward excellence. *American Psychologist, 55*, 122–136.

Baltes, P. B., Staudinger, U. M., Maercker, A., & Smith, J. (1995). People nominated as wise: A comparative study of wisdom-related knowledge. *Psychology and Aging, 10*, 155–166.

Banai, K., Ortiz, J., Oppenheimer, J. D., & Wright, B. A. (2010). Learning two things at once: Differential constraints on the acquisition and consolidation of perceptual learning. *Neuroscience, 165*, 436–444.

Bandura, A. (1965). Influence of models' reinforcement contingencies on the acquisition of imitative responses. *Journal of Personality and Social Psychology, 1*, 589–595.

Bandura, A. (1977). *Social learning theory.* Englewood Cliffs, NJ: Prentice-Hall.

Bandura, A. (1986). *Social foundations of thought and action: A social cognitive theory.* Englewood Cliffs, NJ: Prentice-Hall.

Bandura, A. (1989). Social cognitive theory. In R. Vasta (Ed.), *Annals of child development: Vol. 6. Theories of child development: Revised formulations and current issues.* Greenwich, CT: JAI Press.

Bandura, A. (1991). Social cognitive theory of moral thought and action. In W. M. Kurtines & J. L. Gewirtz (Eds.), *Handbook of moral behavior and development: Vol. 1. Theory.* Hillsdale, NJ: Erlbaum.

Bandura, A. (2000). Social cognitive theory: An agentic perspective. *Annual Review of Psychology, 52*, 1–26.

Bandura, A. (2002). Selective moral disengagement in the exercise of moral agency. *Journal of Moral Education, 31*, 101–119.

Bandura, A. (2006). Toward a psychology of human agency. *Perspectives on Psychological Science, 1*, 164–180.

Bandura, A., Caprara, G. V., Barbaranelli, C., Pastorelli, C., & Regalia, C. (2001). Sociocognitive self-regulatory mechanisms governing transgressive behavior. *Journal of Personality & Social Psychology, 80*, 125–135.

Banerjee, R., & Lintern, V. (2000). Boys will be boys: The effect of social evaluation concerns on gender-typing. *Social Development, 9*, 397–408.

Banerjee, T. D., Middleton, F., & Faraone, S. V. (2007). Environmental risk factors for attention-deficit hyperactivity disorder. *Acta Paediatrica, 96*, 1269–1274.

Bank, L., Marlowe, J., Reid, J., Patterson, G., & Weinrott, M. (1991). A comparative evaluation

of parent-training interventions for families of chronic delinquents. *Journal of Abnormal Child Psychology, 19*, 15–33.

Bankoff, E. A. (1983). Aged parents and their widowed daughters: A support relationship. *Journal of Gerontology, 38*, 226–230.

Banks, M. S., & Ginsburg, A. P. (1985). Infant visual preferences: A review and new theoretical treatment. In H. W. Reese (Ed.), *Advances in child development and behavior* (Vol. 19). Orlando, FL: Academic Press.

Banks, M. S., & Salapatek, P. (1983). Infant visual perception. In M. M. Haith & J. J. Campos (Eds.) & P. H. Mussen (Gen Ed.), *Handbook of child psychology: (Vol 2). Infancy and developmental psychobiology* (4th ed.), New York: Wiley.

Banks, M. S., & Shannon, E. (1993). Spatial and chromatic visual efficiency in human neonates. In C. E. Granrud (Ed.), *Visual perception and cognition in infancy.* Hillsdale, NJ: Erlbaum.

Barash, D. P. (2002, May 24). Evolution, males, and violence. *The Chronicle of Higher Education,* B7–B9.

Barash, D. P. (2006, April 7). The case for evolution, in real life. *The Chronicle of Higher Education, 52*(31), B10.

Barbeau, E. B., Mendrek, A., & Mottron, L. (2009). Are autistic traits autistic? *British Journal of Psychology, 100*, 23–28.

Barber, B. L., Eccles, J. S., & Stone, M. R. (2001). Whatever happened to the jock, the brain, and the princess? Young adult pathways linked to adolescent activity involvement and social identity. *Journal of Adolescent Research, 16*, 429–455.

Barboza, G. E., Schiamberg, L. B., Oehmke, J., Korzeniewski, S. J., Post, L. A., & Heraux, C. G. (2009). Individual characteristics and the multiple contexts of adolescent bullying: An ecological perspective. *Journal of Youth and Adolescence, 38*, 101–121.

Barclay, L., & Lupton, D. (1999). The experiences of new fatherhood: A socio-cultural analysis. *Journal of Advanced Nursing, 29*, 1013–1020.

Bargh, J. A., & Morsella, E. (2008). The unconscious mind. *Perspectives on Psychological Science, 3*, 73–79.

Bar-Haim, Y., Ziv, T., Lamy, D., & Hodes, R. M. (2006). Nature and nurture in own-race face processing. *Psychological Science, 17*, 159–163.

Barker, D. J. P. (1998). *Mothers, babies, and disease in later life* (2nd ed.). New York: Churchill Livingstone.

Barker, E. D., Arseneault, L., Brendgen, M., Fontaine, N., & Maughan, B. (2008). Joint development of bullying and victimization in adolescence: Relations to delinquency and self-harm. *Journal of the American Academy of Child and Adolescent Psychiatry, 47*, 1030–1038.

Barkley, R. A. (1997). Behavioral inhibition, sustained attention, and executive functions: Constructing a unifying theory of ADHD. *Psychological Bulletin, 121*, 65–94.

Barkley, R. A. (2000). Genetics of childhood disorders: XVII. ADHD, Part 1: The executive functions and ADHD. *Journal of the American Academy of Child and Adolescent Psychiatry, 39*, 1064–1068.

Barkley, R. A., Fischer, M., Smallish, L., & Fletcher, K. (2006). Young adult outcome of hyperactive children: Adaptive functioning in major life activities. *Journal of the American Academy of Child and Adolescent Psychiatry, 45*, 192–202.

Barnes, D. E., Yaffe, K., Satariano, W. A., & Tager, I. B. (2003). A longitudinal study of cardiorespiratory fitness and cognitive function in healthy older adults. *Journal of the American Geriatrics Society, 51*, 459–465.

Barnes, K. E. (1971). Preschool play norms: A replication. *Developmental Psychology, 5*, 99–103.

Barnet, L. M., Van Beurden, E., Morgan, P.J., Brooks, L.O., & Beard, J. R. (2008). Does childhood motor skill proficiency predict adolescent fitness? *Medicine and Science in Sports & Exercise, 40,* 2137–2144.

Barnett, R. C. (1994). Home-to-work spillover revisited: A study of full-time employed women in dual-earner couples. *Journal of Marriage and the Family, 56,* 647–656.

Barnett, W. S. (2002). Early childhood education. In A. Molnar (Ed.), *School reform proposals: The research evidence,* 1–26. Greenwich, CT: Information Age Publishing.

Barnett, W. S., Brown, K. C., Finn-Stevenson, M., & Henrich, C. (2007). From visions to systems of universal prekindergarten. In J. L. Aber, S. J. Bishop-Josef, S. M. Jones, K. T. McLearn, & D. A. Phillips (Eds.), *Child development and social policy: Knowledge for action.* Washington, DC: American Psychology Association.

Baron, N. S. (1992). Growing up with language: How children learn to talk. Reading, MA: Addison-Wesley.

Baron-Cohen, S. (1995). *Mindblindness: An essay on autism and theory of mind.* Cambridge, MA: MIT Press.

Baron-Cohen, S. (2003). *The essential difference: The truth about the male and female brain.* New York: Basic Books.

Baron-Cohen, S. (2010). Autism and the empathizing-systemizing (E-S) theory. In P. D. Zelazo, M. Chandler, & E. Crone (Eds.), *Developmental social cognitive neuroscience.* New York: Psychology Press.

Baron-Cohen, S., Leslie, A. M., & Frith, U. (1985). Does the autistic child have a "theory of mind"? *Cognition, 21,* 37–46.

Barr, R., Dowden, A., & Hayne, H. (1996). Developmental changes in deferred imitation by 6- to 24-month-old infants. *Infant Behavior & Development, 19,* 159–170.

Barrett, T. R., & Wright, M. (1981). Age-related facilitation in recall following semantic processing. *Journal of Gerontology, 36,* 194–199.

Barrett, T.M., & Needham, A. (2008). Developmental differences in infants' use of an object's shape to grasp it securely. *Developmental Psychobiology, 50,* 97–106.

Bartholomew, K., & Horowitz, L. M. (1991). Attachment styles among young adults: A test of a four-category model. *Journal of Personality and Social Psychology, 61,* 226–244.

Bartlett, D. (1997). Primitive reflexes and early motor development. *Journal of Developmental and Behavioral Pediatrics, 18,* 151–157.

Basseches, M. (1984). Dialectical thinking and adult development. Norwood, NJ: Ablex.

Basseches, M. (2005). The development of dialectical thinking as an approach to integration. *Integral Review, 1,* 47–63.

Bates, E., O'Connell, B., & Shore, C. (1987). Language and communication in infancy. In J. D. Osofsky (Ed.), *Handbook of infant development* (2nd ed.). New York: Wiley.

Batshaw, M. L., Shapiro, B., & Farber, M. L. Z. (2007). Developmental delay and intellectual disability, 245–261. In M. L. Batshaw, L. Pellegrino & N. J. Roizen (Eds.), *Children with disabilities* (6th ed.). Baltimore: Paul H. Brookes.

Bau, A. M., Ernert, A., Schenk, L., Wiegand, S., Martus, P., Grüters, A., & Krude, H. (2009). Is there a further acceleration in the age at onset of menarche? A cross-sectional study in 1840 school children focusing on age and bodyweight at the onset of menarche. *European Journal of Endocrinology, 160,* 107–113.

Bauchner, H. (1996). Failure to thrive. In R. E. Behrman, R. M. Kliegman, & A. M. Arvin (Eds.), *Nelson textbook of pediatrics* (15th ed.). Philadelphia: W. B. Saunders.

Baudouin, A., Clarys, D., Vanneste, S., & Isingrini, M. (2009). Executive functioning and processing speed in age-related differences in memory: Contribution of a coding task. *Brain and Cognition, 71,* 240–245.

Bauer, I., Wrosch, C., & Jobin, J. (2008). I'm better off than most other people: The role of social comparisons for coping with regret in young adulthood and old age. *Psychology and Aging, 23,* 800–811.

Bauer, P. J. (1996). What do infants recall of their lives? Memory for specific events by one- to two-year-olds. *American Psychologist, 51,* 29–41.

Bauer, P. J. (2007). *Remembering the times of our lives: Memory in infancy and beyond.* Mahwah, NJ: Lawrence Erlbaum.

Bauer, P. J. (2008). Toward a neuro-developmental account of the development of declarative memory. *Developmental Psychobiology, 50,* 19–31.

Bauer, P. J. (2009). The cognitive neuroscience of the development of memory. In M. L. Courage & N. Cowan (Eds.), *The development of memory in infancy and childhood,* 115-144. New York, NY: Psychology Press.

Bauer, P. J., Burch, M. M., Scholin, S. E., & Güler, O. E. (2007). Using cue words to investigate the distribution of autobiographical memories in childhood. *Psychological Science, 18,* 910–916.

Bauer, P. J., Wenner, J. A., Dropik, P. L., & Wewerka, S. S. (2000). Parameters of remembering and forgetting in the transition from infancy to early childhood. *Monographs of the Society for Research in Child Development, 65* (Serial No. 263).

Baumrind, D. (1967). Child care practices anteceding three patterns of preschool behavior. *Genetic Psychology Monographs, 75,* 43–88.

Baumrind, D. (1977, March). *Socialization determinants of personal agency.* Paper presented at the biennial meeting of the Society for Research in Child Development, New Orleans.

Baumrind, D. (1991). Effective parenting during the early adolescent transition. In P. A. Cowan & M. Hetherington (Eds.), *Family transitions.* Hillsdale, NJ: Erlbaum.

Bauserman, R. (2002). Child adjustment in joint-custody versus sole-custody arrangements: A meta-analytic review. *Journal of Family Psychology, 16,* 91–102.

Baydar, N., Greek, A., & Brooks-Gunn, J. (1997). A longitudinal study of the effects of the birth of a sibling during the first 6 years of life. *Journal of Marriage and the Family, 59,* 939–956.

Bayley, N. (1993). *Bayley scales of infant development* (2nd ed.). San Antonio: Psychological Corporation.

Beadle-Brown, J., Murphy, G., & DiTerlizzi, M. (2009). Quality of life for the Camberwell cohort. *Journal of Applied Research in Intellectual Disabilities, 22, 4,* 380–390.

Beadle-Brown, J., Murphy, G., & Wing, L. (2005). Long-term outcome for people with severe intellectual disabilities: Impact of social impairment. *American Journal on Mental Retardation, 110,* 1–12.

Beadle-Brown, J., Murphy, G., & Wing, L. (2006). The Camberwell cohort 25 years on: Characteristics and changes in skills over time. *Journal of Applied Research in Intellectual Disabilities, 19,* 317–329.

Beal, C. R. (1990). The development of text evaluation and revision skills. *Child Development, 61,* 247–258.

Beal, C. R. (1994). *Boys and girls: The development of gender roles.* New York: McGraw-Hill.

Beane, A. L. (2009). *Bullying prevention for schools: A step-by-step guide to implementing a successful anti-bullying program.* San Francisco: Jossey-Bass.

Beauchamp, G. K. (2009). Sensory and receptor responses to umami: An overview of pioneering work. *American Journal of Clinical Nutrition, 90,* 723S–727S.

Beauchamp, G. K, & Mennella, J. A. (2009). Early flavor learning and its impact on later feeding behavior. *Journal of Pediatric Gastroenterology and Nutrition, 48,* S25–S30.

Beautrais, A. L. (2003). Life course factors associated with suicidal behaviors in young people. *American Behavioral Scientist, 46,* 1137–1156.

Becker, A. E., Burwell, R. A., Herzog, D. B., Hamburg, P., & Gilman, S. E. (2002). Eating behaviours and attitudes following prolonged exposure to television among ethnic Fijian adolescent girls. *British Journal of Psychiatry, 180,* 509–514.

Beckwith, L., Cohen, S. E., & Hamilton, C. E. (1999). Maternal sensitivity during infancy and subsequent life events relate to attachment representation at early adulthood. *Developmental Psychology, 35,* 693–700.

Beckwith, L., Rozga, A., & Sigman, M. (2002). Maternal sensitivity and attachment in atypical groups. In R. V. Kail (Ed.), *Advances in child development and behavior* (Vol. 30). San Diego: Academic Press.

Beehr, T. A., Glazer, S., Nielson, N. L., & Farmer, S. J. (2000). Work and nonwork predictors of employee's retirement age. *Journal of Vocational Behavior, 57,* 206–225.

Beemsterboer, S. N., Homburg, R., Gorter, N. A., Schats, R., Hompes, P. G., & Lambalk, C. B. (2006). The paradox of declining fertility but increasing twinning rates with advancing maternal age. *Human Reproduction, 21,* 1531–1532.

Behrend, D. A., Rosengren, K., & Perlmutter, M. (1989). A new look at children's private speech: The effects of age, task difficulty, and parent presence. *International Journal of Behavioral Development, 12,* 305–320.

Beilin, H. (1992). Piaget's enduring contribution to developmental psychology. *Developmental Psychology, 28,* 191–204.

Beitchman, J. H., Zucker, K. J., Hood, J. E., daCosta, G. A., & Akman, D. (1991). A review of the short-term effects of child sexual abuse. *Child Abuse & Neglect, 15,* 537–556.

Bell, E. F. (2009). *What to look for in a neonatal intensive care unit.* Available at: www.uihealthcare.com/ topics/medicaldepartments/pediatrics/ neonatalintensivecareunit/index.html#LookForQ. Accessed: August 25, 2009.

Bell, J. H., & Bromnick, R. D. (2003). The social reality of the imaginary audience: A grounded theory approach. *Adolescence, 38,* 205–219.

Bell, M. A., & Wolfe, C. D. (2007). Changes in brain functioning from infancy to early childhood: Evidence from EEG power and coherence working memory tasks. *Developmental Neuropsychology, 31,* 21–38.

Bell, M. F. (2007). Infections and the fetus. In M. L. Batshaw, L. Pellegrino, & N. J. Roizen (Eds.), *Children with disabilities,* 6th ed. (pp. 71–82). Baltimore: Paul H. Brookes.

Bellanti, C. J., Bierman, K. L., & Conduct Problems Prevention Research Group (2000). Disentangling the impact of low cognitive ability and inattention on social behavior and peer relationships. *Journal of Clinical Child Psychology, 29,* 66–75.

Belloc, S., Cohen-Bacrie, P., Benkhalifa, M., Cohen-Bacrie, M., DeMouzon, J., Hazout, A., & Ménéza, Y. (2008). Effect of maternal and paternal age on pregnancy and miscarriage rates after intrauterine insemination. *Reproductive BioMedicine Online, 17,* 392–397. Available at: www.rbmonline.com/Article/3526.

Bellugi, U. (1988). The acquisition of a spatial language. In F. S. Kessel (Ed.), *The development of language and language researchers: Essays in honor of Roger Brown.* Hillsdale, NJ: Erlbaum.

Belsky, J. (1981). Early human experience: A family perspective. *Developmental Psychology, 17,* 3–23.

Belsky, J., Burchinal, M., McCartney, K., Vandell, D. L., Clarke-Stewart, K. A., Owen, M. T., & NICHD Early Child Care Research Network

(2007). Are there long-term effects of early child care? *Child Development, 78,* 681–701.

Belsky, J., Jaffee, S., Hsieh, K., & Silva, P. A. (2001). Child-rearing antecedents of intergenerational relations in young adulthood: A prospective study. *Developmental Psychology, 37,* 801–813.

Belsky, J., Steinberg, L. D., Houts, R. M., Friedman, S.L., DeHart, G. Cauffman, E., Roisman, G.I., Halpern-Felsher, B.L., & Susman, E. (2007). Family rearing antecedents of pubertal timing. *Child Development, 78,* 1302–1321.

Belsky, J., Vandell, D. L., Burchinal, M., Clark-Stewart, K. A., McCartney, K., & Owen, M. T. (2007). Are there long-term effects of early child care? *Child Development, 78,* 681–701.

Bem, S. L. (1975). Sex-role adaptability: One consequence of psychological androgyny. *Journal of Personality and Social Psychology, 31,* 634–643.

Bem, S. L. (1978). Beyond androgyny: Some presumptuous prescriptions for a liberated sexual identity. In J. A. Sherman & F. L. Denmark (Eds.), *The psychology of women: Future directions in research.* New York: Psychological Dimensions.

Bem, S. L. (1989). Genital knowledge and gender constancy in preschool children. *Child Development, 60,* 649–662.

Bemporad, J. R. (1979). Adult recollections of a formerly autistic child. *Journal of Autism and Developmental Disorders, 9,* 179–197.

Benaron, L. D. (2009). *Autism.* Westport, CT: Greenwood Press.

Benbow, C. P., & Arjmand, O. (1990). Predictors of high academic achievement in mathematics and science by mathematically talented students: A longitudinal study. *Journal of Educational Psychology, 82,* 430–441.

Benenson, J. F., Philippoussis, M., & Leeb, R. (1999). Sex differences in neonates' cuddliness. *Journal of Genetic Psychology, 160,* 332–342.

Benes, F. M. (1998). Human brain growth spans decades. *American Journal of Psychiatry, 155,* 1489.

Bengtson, V., Rosenthal, C., & Burton, L. (1996). Paradoxes of families and aging. In R. H. Binstock, L. K. George, V. W. Marshall, G. C. Myers, & J. H. Schulz (Eds.), *Handbook of aging and the social sciences* (4th ed.). San Diego: Academic Press.

Bengtson, V. L. (2001). Beyond the nuclear family: The increasing importance of multigenerational bonds. *Journal of Marriage and Family, 63,* 1–16.

Benjet, C., & Kazdin, A. E. (2003). Spanking children: The controversies, findings, and new directions. *Clinical Psychology Review, 23,* 197–224.

Benn, P. A., & Chapman, A. R. (2009). Practical and ethical considerations of noninvasive prenatal diagnosis. *JAMA, 301,* 2154–2156.

Benoit, D., & Coolbear, J. (2004). Disorders of attachment and failure to thrive. In L. Atkinson & S. Goldberg (Eds.), *Attachment issues in psychopathology and intervention.* Mahwah, NJ: Erlbaum.

Benoit, D., & Parker, K. C. (1994). Stability and transmission of attachment across three generations. *Child Development, 65,* 1444–1456.

Berg, C. A., & Klaczynski, P. A. (1996). Practical intelligence and problem solving: Searching for perspectives. In F. Blanchard-Fields & T. M. Hess (Eds.), *Perspectives on cognitive change in adulthood and aging.* New York: McGraw-Hill.

Bergen, D. (2008). *Human development. Traditional and contemporary theories.* Upper Saddle River, NJ: Pearson.

Berger, A. S. (1993). *Dying and death in law and medicine: A forensic primer for health and legal professionals.* Westport, CT: Praeger.

Berger, S. E., & Adolph, K. E. (2003). Infants use handrails as tools in locomotor task. *Developmental Psychology, 39,* 594–605.

Berger, S. E., Adolph, K. E., & Lobo, S. A. (2005). Out of the toolbox: Toddlers differentiate wobbly and wooden handrails. *Child Development, 76,* 1294–1307.

Bergman, K., Sarkar, P., O'Connor, T. G., Modi, N., & Glover, V. (2007). Maternal stress during pregnancy predicts cognitive ability and fearfulness in infancy. *Journal of the American Academy of Child Psychiatry, 46,* 1454–1463.

Bering, J. M., & Bjorklund, D. F. (2004). The natural emergence of reasoning about the afterlife as a developmental regularity. *Developmental Psychology, 40,* 217–233.

Berk, L. E. (1992). Children's private speech: An overview of theory and the status of research. In R. M. Diaz & L. E. Berk (Eds.), *Private speech: From social interaction to self-regulation.* Hillsdale, NJ: Erlbaum.

Berk, L. E., & Landau, S. (1993). Private speech of learning disabled and normally achieving children in classroom academic and laboratory contexts. *Child Development, 64,* 556–571.

Berk, L. E., & Winsler, A. (1995). *Scaffolding children's learning: Vygotsky and early childhood education.* Washington, DC: National Association for the Education of Young Children.

Berkowitz, G., Wolff, M., Janevic, T., Holzman, I., Yehunda, R., & Landrigan, P. (2003). The World Trade Center disaster and intrauterine growth restriction. *Journal of the American Medical Association, 290,* 595–596.

Berlin, L. J. (2005). Interventions to enhance early attachments. The state of the field today. In L. J. Berlin, Y. Ziv, L. Amaya-Jackson, & M. T. Greenberg (Eds.), *Enhancing early attachments: Theory, research, intervention, and policy.* New York: Guilford.

Berlin, L. J., Ispa, J. M., Fine, M. A., Malone, P. S., Brooks-Gunn, J., Brady-Smith, C., Ayoub, C., & Bai, Y. (2009). Correlates and consequences of spanking and verbal punishment for low-income White, African American, and Mexican American toddlers. *Child Development, 80,* 1403–1420.

Berlin, L. J., Zeanah, C. H., & Lieberman, A. F. (2008). Prevention and intervention programs for supporting early attachment security. In J. Cassidy & P. R. Shaver (Eds.), *Handbook of attachment: Theory, research, and clinical applications* (2nd ed.). New York: Guilford.

Berman, A. L., & Jobes, D. A. (1991). *Adolescent suicide: Assessment and intervention.* Washington, DC: American Psychological Association.

Berman, W. H., & Sperling, M. B. (1991). Parental attachment and emotional distress in the transition to college. *Journal of Youth and Adolescence, 20,* 427–440.

Bernal, M. E., & Knight, G. P. (1997). Ethnic identity of Latino children. In J. G. Garcia & M. C. Zea (Eds.), *Psychological interventions and research with Latino populations.* Boston: Allyn & Bacon.

Berndt, T. J., & Murphy, L. M. (2002). Influences of friends and friendships: Myths, truths, and research recommendations. In R. V. Kail (Ed.), *Advances in child development and behavior* (Vol. 30). San Diego: Academic Press.

Berney, T. (2009). Ageing in Down syndrome. In G. O'Brien, L. Rosenbloom, G. O'Brien, & L. Rosenbloom (Eds.), *Developmental disability and ageing.* London: Mac Keith Press.

Bernstein, A. C., & Cowan, P. A. (1975). Children's concepts of how people get babies. *Child Development, 46,* 77–91.

Bernstein, R. (2010, January 15). Census Bureau reports families with children increasingly face unemployment. *U. S. Census Bureau News.* Available at: www.census.gov/PressRelease/www/releases/archives/families_households/014540. Accessed: February 1, 2010.

Berry, J. W., Poortinga, Y. H., Segall, M., & Dasen, P. R. (1992). *Cross-cultural psychology: research and applications.* Cambridge, England: Cambridge University Press.

Berson, E. L. (2000). Nutrition and retinal degenerations. *International Ophthalmology Clinic, 40,* 93–111.

Bertenthal, B. I., & Fischer, K. W. (1978). Development of self-recognition in the infant. *Developmental Psychology, 14,* 44–50.

Berthier, N. E., & Keen, R. (2006). Development of reaching in infancy. *Experimental Brain Research, 169,* 507–518.

Bertman, S. L. (1991). Children and death: Insights, hindsights, and illuminations. In D. Papadatou & C. Papadatos (Eds.), *Children and Death.* New York: Hemisphere.

Berzoff, J. (2008). Psychosocial ego development: The theory of Erik Erikson. In J. Berzoff, L. M. Flanagan, L. Melano, & P. Hertz (Eds.), *Inside out and outside in: Psychodynamic clinical theory and psychopathology in contemporary multicultural contexts* (2nd ed.). Lanham, MD: Jason Aronson.

Berzonsky, M. D., & Kuk, L. S. (2000). Identity status, identity processing style, and the transition to university. *Journal of Adolescent Research, 15,* 81–98.

Best, D. L., & Williams, J. E. (1993). A cross-cultural viewpoint. In A. E. Beall & R. J. Sternberg (Eds.), *The psychology of gender,* 215–248. New York: Guilford Press.

Betts, J., McKay, J., Maruff, P., & Anderson, V. (2006). The development of sustained attention in children: The effect of age and task load. *Child Neuropsychology, 12,* 205–221.

Beyer, S. (1995). Maternal employment and children's academic achievement: Parenting styles as mediating variable. *Developmental Review, 15,* 212–253.

Beyers, J. M., Bates, J. E., Pettit, G. S., & Dodge, K. A. (2003). Neighborhood structure, parenting processes, and the development of youths' externalizing behaviors: A multilevel analysis. *American Journal of Community Psychology, 31,* 35–53.

Bhatara, V., Loudenberg, R., & Ellis, R. (2006). Association of attention deficit hyperactivity disorder and gestational alcohol exposure: An exploratory study. *Journal of Attention Disorders, 9,* 515–522.

Bianchi, S. M. (2000). Maternal employment and time with children: Dramatic change or surprising continuity? *Demography, 37,* 401–414.

Bianchi, S. M., Milkie, M. A., Sayer, L. C., & Robinson, J. P. (2000). Is anyone doing the housework? Trends in the gender division of household labor. *Social Forces, 79,* 191–228.

Bianchi, S. M., Subaiya, L., & Kahn, J. R. (1999). The gender gap in economic well-being of nonresident fathers and custodial mothers. *Demography, 36,* 195–203.

Bick, D. P., & Lau, E. C. (2006). Preimplantation genetic diagnosis. *Pediatric Clinics of North America, 53,* 559–577.

Bierhoff, H., & Schmohr, M. (2003). Romantic and marital relationships. In F. R. Lang & K. L. Fingerman (Eds.), *Growing together. Personal relationships across the life span.* Cambridge, UK: Cambridge University Press.

Bierman, K. L. (2004). *Peer rejection: Developmental processes and intervention strategies.* New York: Guilford.

Bierman, K. L., & Powers, C. J. (2009). Social skills training to improve peer relations. In K. H. Rubin, W. M. Bukowski, & B. Laursen (Eds.), *Handbook of peer interactions, relationships, and groups.* New York: Guilford.

Bigler, R. S., & Liben, L. S. (1990). The role of attitudes and interventions in gender-schematic processing. *Child Development, 61,* 1440–1452.

Billing, L., Eriksson, M., Jonsson, B., Steneroth, G., & Zetterstrom, R. (1994). The influence of environmental factors on behavioral problems in 8-year-old children exposed to amphetamine during fetal life. *Child Abuse and Neglect, 18,* 3–9.

Binstock, R. H. (2004). The search for prolongevity: A contentious pursuit. In S. G. Post & R. H.

Binstock (Eds.), *The fountain of youth: Cultural, scientific, and ethical perspectives on a biomedical goal.* New York: Oxford University Press.

Bird, A., & Reese, E. (2006). Emotional reminiscing and the development of an autobiographical self. *Developmental Psychology, 42,* 613–626.

Birditt, K. S., Fingerman, K. L., Lefkowitz, E. S., & Dush, C. M. K. (2008). Parents perceived as peers: Filial maturity in adulthood. *Journal of Adult Development, 15,* 1–12.

Birditt, K. S., Miller, L. M., Fingerman, K. L., & Lefkowitz, E. S. (2009). Tensions in the parent and adult child relationship: Links to solidarity and ambivalence. *Psychology and Aging, 24,* 287–295.

Birdsong, D. (1999). Introduction: Whys and why nots of the critical period hypothesis for second language acquisition. In D. Birdsong (Ed.), *Second language acquisition and the critical period hypothesis.* Mahwah, NJ: Erlbaum.

Birdsong, D. (2005). Interpreting age effects in second language acquisition. In J. Kroll & A. de Groot (Eds.), *Handbook of bilingualism: Psycholinguistic approaches.* New York: Oxford University Press.

Birren, J. E., Butler, R. N., Greenhouse, S. W., Sokoloff, L., & Yarrow, M. R. (Eds.). (1963). *Human aging: A biological and behavioral study.* Washington, DC: U.S. Government Printing Office.

Birren, J. E., & Fisher, L. M. (1995). Aging and speed of behavior: Possible consequences for psychological functioning. *Annual Review of Psychology, 46,* 329–353.

Birren, J. E., & Schroots, J. J. F. (2006). Autobiographical memory and the narrative self over the life span. In J. E. Birren & K. W. Schaie (Eds.), *Handbook of the psychology of aging* (6th ed.). Burlington, MA: Elsevier Academic Press.

Bishop, J. A., & Cooke, L. M. (1975). Moths, melanism and clean air. *Scientific American, 232,* 90–99.

Bishop, J. E., & Waldholz, M. (1990). *Genome. The story of the most astonishing scientific adventure of our time: The attempt to map all the genes in the human body.* New York: Simon & Schuster.

Bivens, J. A., & Berk, L. E. (1990). A longitudinal study of the development of elementary school children's private speech. *Merrill-Palmer Quarterly, 36,* 443–463.

Bjork, J. M., Knutson, B., Fong, G. W., Caggiano, D. M., Bennett, S. M., & Hommer, D. W. (2004). Incentive-elicited brain activation in adolescents: Similarities and differences from young adults. *The Journal of Neuroscience, 24,* 1793–1802.

Bjork, R. A., & Bjork, E. L. (Eds.) (1998). *Memory.* New York: Academic Press.

Bjorklund, D. F. (1985). The role of conceptual knowledge in the development of organization in children's memory. In C. J. Brainerd & M. Pressley (Eds.), *Basic processes in memory development: Progress in cognitive development research.* New York: Springer-Verlag.

Bjorklund, D. F. (1995). *Children's thinking: Developmental function and individual differences.* Pacific Grove, CA: Brooks/Cole.

Bjorklund, D. F., Brown, R. D., & Bjorklund, B. R. (2002). Children's eyewitness memory: Changing reports and changing representations. In P. Graf & N. Ohta (Eds.), *Life-span development of human memory* (pp. 101–126). Cambridge, MA: Massachusetts Institute of Technology.

Bjorklund, D. F., Dukes, C., & Brown, R. D. (2009). The development of memory strategies. In M. L. Courage & N. Cowan (Eds.), *The development of memory in infancy and childhood* (pp. 145–176). New York, NY: Psychology Press.

Bjorklund, D. F., Miller, P. H., Coyle, T. R., & Slawinski, J. L. (1997). Instructing children to use memory strategies: Evidence of utilization deficiencies in memory training studies. *Developmental Review, 17,* 411–441.

Bjorklund, D. F., & Pellegrini, A. D. (2002). *The origins of human nature.* Washington, DC: American Psychological Association.

Black, J. E., Isaacs, K. R., & Greenough, W. T. (1991). Usual vs. successful aging: Some notes on experiential factors. *Neurobiology of Aging, 12,* 325–328.

Blackburn, J. A. (1984). The influence of personality, curriculum, and memory correlates on formal reasoning in young adults and elderly persons. *Journal of Gerontology, 39,* 207–209.

Blackburn, J. A., & Papalia, D. E. (1992). The study of adult cognition from a Piagetian perspective. In R. J. Sternberg & C. A. Berg (Eds.), *Intellectual development.* New York: Cambridge University Press.

Blair, R. J. R. (2003). Did Cain fail to represent the thoughts of Abel before he killed him? The relationship between theory of mind and aggression. In B. Repacholi & V. Slaughter (Eds.), *Individual differences in theory of mind: Implications for typical and atypical development.* New York: Psychology Press.

Blakemore, J. E. O. (2003). Children's beliefs about violating gender norms: Boys shouldn't look like girls, and girls shouldn't act like boys. *Sex Roles, 49,* 411–420.

Blanchard, R., & Lippa, R. A. (2007). Birth order, sibling sex ratio, handedness, and sexual orientation of male and female participants in a BBC internet research project. *Archives of Sexual Behavior, 36,* 163–176.

Blanchard-Fields, F. (1986). Reasoning on social dilemmas varying in emotional saliency: An adult developmental perspective. *Psychology and Aging, 1,* 325–333.

Blanchard-Fields, F. (1996). Social cognitive development in adulthood and aging. In F. Blanchard-Fields & T. M. Hess (Eds.), *Perspectives on cognitive change in adulthood and aging.* New York: McGraw-Hill.

Blanchard-Fields, F., Chen, Y., & Norris, L. (1997). Everyday problem solving across the adult life span: Influence of domain specificity and cognitive appraisal. *Psychology and Aging, 12,* 684–693.

Blanchard-Fields, F., & Kalinauskas, A. (2009). Theoretical perspectives on social context, cognition, and aging. In V. L. Bengtson, M. Silverstein, N. M. Putney, & D. Gans (Eds.), *Handbook of theories of aging* (2nd ed.). New York: Springer.

Blatchford, P., Moriarty, V., Edmonds, S., & Martin, C. (2002). Relationships between class size and teaching: A multimethod analysis of English infant schools. *American Educational Research Journal, 39,* 101–132.

Blazer, D. G. (1993). *Depression in late life.* St. Louis: Mosby.

Blazer, D. G. (2003). Depression in late life: Review and commentary. *Journal of Gerontology: Medical Sciences, 58A,* 249–265.

Blieszner, R. (2006). A lifetime of caring: Dimensions and dynamics in late-life close relationships. *Personal Relationships, 13,* 1–18.

Blieszner, R., & Roberto, K. A. (2004). Friendship across the life span: Reciprocity in individual and relationship development. In F. R. Lang & K. L. Fingerman (Eds.), *Growing together: Personal relationships across the life span.* Cambridge, UK: Cambridge University Press.

Block, C. E. (2000). Dyadic and gender differences in perceptions of the grandparent–grandchild relationship. *International Journal of Aging and Human Development, 51,* 85–104.

Bloom, L. (1998). Language acquisition in its developmental context. In D. Kuhn & R. S. Siegler (Vol. Eds.), W. Damon (Editor-in-Chief), *Handbook of child psychology: Vol. 2. Cognition, perception, and language* (5th ed., pp. 309–370). New York: Wiley.

Bloom, L., & Tinker, E. (2001). The intentionality model and language acquisition: Engagement, effort, and the essential tension. *Monographs of the Society for Research in Child Development, 66* (Serial No. 267).

Bluebond-Langner, M. (1977). Meanings of death to children. In H. Feifel (Ed.), *New meanings of death.* New York: McGraw-Hill.

Blumberg, E. S. (2003). The lives and voices of highly sexual women. *The Journal of Sex Research, 40,* 146–157.

Boatella-Costa, E., Costas-Moragas, C., Botet-Mussons, F., Fornieles-Deu, A., & De Cáceres-Zurita, M. L. (2007). Behavioral gender differences in the neonatal period according to the Brazelton scale. *Early Human Development, 83,* 91–97.

Bock, J. (2005). Farming, foraging, and children's play in the Okavango Delta, Botswana. In A. D. Pellegrini & P. K. Smith (Eds.), *The nature of play: Great apes and humans.* New York: Guilford Press.

Bode, M. M., D'Eugenio, D. B., Forsyth, N., Coleman, J., Gross, C. R, & Gross, S. J. (2009). Outcome of extreme prematurity: A prospective comparison of 2 regional cohorts born 20 years apart. *Pediatrics, 124,* 866–874.

Bodkin, N. L., Alexander, T. M., Ortmeyer, H. K., Johnson, E., & Hansen, B. C. (2003). Morbidity and mortality in laboratory-maintained rhesus monkeys and effects of long-term dietary restriction. *Journal of Gerontology: Biological Sciences, 58A,* 212–219.

Bodley-Tickell, A. T., Olowokure, B., Bhaduri, S., White, D. J., Ward, D., Ross, J. D., Smith, G., Duggal, H. V., & Goold, P. (2008). Trends in sexually transmitted infections (other than HIV) in older people: Analysis of data from an enhanced surveillance system. *Sexually Transmitted Infections, 84,* 312–317.

Bodrova, E., & Leong, D. J. (1996). *Tools of the mind: The Vygotskian approach to early childhood education.* Englewood Cliffs, NJ: Prentice Hall.

Boerner, K., Wortman, C. B., & Bonanno, G. A. (2005). Resilient or at risk? A 4-year study of older adults who initially showed high or low distress following conjugal loss. *Journal of Gerontology: Psychological Sciences, 60B,* P67–P73.

Bogenschneider, K. (1997). Parental involvement in adolescent schooling: A proximal process with transcontextual validity. *Journal of Marriage and the Family, 59,* 718–733.

Bogoch, I. I., House, R. A., & Kudla, I. (2005). Perceptions about hearing protection and noise-induced hearing loss of attendees of rock concerts. *Canadian Journal of Public Health, 96,* 69–72.

Bohannon, J. N., & Bonvillian, J. D. (2009). Theoretical approaches. In J. B. Gleason & N. B. Ratner (Eds.), *The development of language,* 7th ed. Boston: Allyn & Bacon.

Bohannon, J. N., & Stanowicz, L. (1988). The issue of negative evidence: Adult responses to children's language errors. *Developmental Psychology, 24,* 684–689.

Bohannon, J. R. (1990–1991). Grief responses of spouses following the death of a child: A longitudinal study. *Omega: Journal of Death and Dying, 22,* 109–121.

Bohlmeijer, E., Roemer, M., Cuijpers, P., & Smit, F. (2007). The effects of reminiscence on psychological well-being in order adults: A meta-analysis. *Aging & Mental Health, 11,* 291–300.

Bohn, A., & Berntsen, D. (2008). Life story development in childhood: The development of life story abilities and the acquisition of cultural life scripts from late middle childhood to adolescence. *Developmental Psychology, 44,* 1135–1147.

Boldizar, J. P. (1991). Assessing sex-typing and androgyny in children: The children's sex-role inventory. *Developmental Psychology, 27,* 505–515.

Boles, S., Biglan, A., & Smolkowski, K. (2006). Relationships among negative and positive behaviours in adolescence. *Journal of Adolescence, 29,* 33–52.

Bolger, K. E., & Patterson, C. J. (2001). Developmental pathways from child maltreatment to peer rejection. *Child Development, 72,* 549–568.

Boll, T., Ferring, D., & Filipp, S. (2005). Effects of parental differential treatment on relationship quality with siblings and parents: Justice evaluations as mediators. *Social Justice Research, 18,* 155–182.

Bollag, B. (2006). The debate over deaf education. *The Chronicle of Higher Education, 52,* A18–A21.

Boloh, Y., & Champaud, C. (1993). The past conditional verb form in French children: The role of semantics in late grammatical development. *Journal of Child Language, 20,* 169–189.

Bombard, Y., Veenstra, G., Friedman, J. M., Creighton, S., Currie, L., Paulsen, J. S., Bottorff, J. L., & Hayden, M. R. (2009). Perceptions of genetic discrimination among people at risk for Huntington's disease: A cross sectional survey. *BMJ: British Medical Journal, 338* (7708).

Bonanno, G. A. (2001). Introduction. New direction in bereavement research and theory. *American Behavioral Scientist, 44,* 718–725.

Bonanno, G. A. (2004). Loss, trauma, and human resilience: Have we underestimated the human capacity to thrive after extremely aversive events? *American Psychologist, 59,* 20–28.

Bonanno, G. A., Boerner, K., & Wortman, C. B. (2008). Trajectories of grieving. In M. S. Stroebe, R. O. Hansson, H. Schut, & W. Stroebe (Eds.), *Handbook of bereavement research and practice. Advances in theory and intervention.* Washington, DC: American Psychological Association.

Bonanno, G. A., & Field, N. P. (2001). Examining the delayed grief hypothesis across 5 years of bereavement. *American Behavioral Scientist, 44,* 798–816.

Bonanno, G. A., & Kaltman, S. (1999). Toward an integrative perspective on bereavement. *Psychological Bulletin, 125,* 760–776.

Bonanno, G. A., & Kaltman, S. (2000). The varieties of grief experience. *Clinical Psychology Review, 21,* 705–734.

Bonanno, G. A., Neria, Y., Mancini, A., Coifman, K.G., Litz, B., & Insel, B. (2007). Is there more to complicated grief than depression and posttraumatic stress disorder? A test of incremental validity. *Journal of Abnormal Psychology, 116,* 342–351.

Bonanno, G. A., Papa, A., Lalande, K., Zhang, N., & Noll, J. G. (2005). Grief processing and deliberate grief avoidance: A prospective comparison of bereaved spouses and parents in the United States and the People's Republic of China. *Journal of Consulting and Clinical Psychology, 73,* 86–98.

Bonanno, G. A., Wortman, C. B., Lehman, D. R., Tweed, R. G., Haring, M., Sonnega, J., et al. (2002). Resilience to loss and chronic grief: A prospective study from preloss to 18 months postloss. *Journal of Personality and Social Psychology, 83,* 1150–1164.

Bonanno, G. A., Wortman, C. B., & Nesse, R. M. (2004). Prospective patterns of resilience and maladjustment during widowhood. *Psychology and Aging, 19,* 260–271.

Bong, M. (2009). Age-related differences in achievement goal differentiation. *Journal of Educational Psychology, 101,* 879–896.

Bongers, I. L., Koot, H. M., van der Ende, J., & Verhulst, F. C. (2003). The normative development of child and adolescent problem behavior. *Journal of Abnormal Psychology, 112,* 179–192.

Boodman, S. G. (2006, June 13). Too much information. Results of home DNA tests can shock, misinform some users. *The Washington Post,* F1, F4.

Bookheimer, S. (2002). Functional MRI of language: New approaches to understanding the cortical organization of semantic priming. *Annual Review of Neuroscience, 22,* 151–188.

Books, S. (Ed.) (2007). *Invisible children in the society and its schools* (3rd ed.). Mahwah, NJ: Lawrence Erlbaum Associates.

Booth, A., & Johnson, D. (1988). Premarital cohabitation and marital success. *Journal of Family Issues, 9,* 255–272.

Boothe, D., Sethna, B. W., & Stanley, J. C. (2000). Special educational opportunities for able high school students: A description of residential early-college-entrance programs. *Journal of Secondary Gifted Education, 26.*

Booth-LaForce, C., & Kerns, K. A. (2009). Child-parent attachment relationships, peer relationships, and peer-group functioning. In K. H. Rubin, W. M. Bukowski, & B. Laursen (Eds.), *Handbook of peer interactions, relationships, and groups.* New York: Guilford.

Borders, A. E., Grobman, W. A., Amsden, L. B., Holl, J. L. (2007). Chronic stress and low birth weight neonates in a low-income population of women. *Obstetrics and Gynecology, 109,* 331–338.

Boris, N. W., & Zeanah, C. H. (1999). Disturbances and disorders of attachment in infancy: An overview. *Infant Mental Health Journal, 20,* 1–9.

Borkenau, P., Riemann, R., Angleitner, A., & Spinath, F. M. (2001). Genetic and environmental influences on observed personality: Evidence from the German Observational Study of Adult Twins. *Journal of Personality and Social Psychology, 80,* 655–668.

Bornstein, E., Lenchner, E, Donnenfeld, A., Barnhard, Y., Seubert, D., & Divon, M. Y. (2009). Advanced maternal age as a sole indication for genetic amniocentesis: risk-benefit analysis based on a large database reflecting the current common practice. *Journal of Perinatal Medicine, 37,* 99–102.

Bornstein, M. H. (2009). Toward a model of culture — parent — child transactions. In A. Sameroff (Ed.), *The transactional model of development: How children and contexts shape each other.* Washington, DC: American Psychological Association.

Bornstein, M. H., & Bradley, R. H. (2003). *Socioeconomic status, parenting, and child development.* Mahwah, NJ: Erlbaum.

Bornstein, M. H., Cote, L. R., Maital, S., Painter, K., Sung-Yun, P., Pascual, L., Pêcheux, M-G., Ruel, J., Venuti, P., & Vyt, A. (2004). Cross-linguistic analysis of vocabulary in young children: Spanish, Dutch, French, Hebrew, Italian, Korean, and American English. *Child Development, 75,* 1115–1139.

Bornstein, M. H., & Sawyer, J. (2006). Family systems. In K. McCartney & D. Phillips (Eds.), *Blackwell handbook of early childhood development.* Malden, MA: Blackwell.

Borradaile, K. E., Sherman, S., Vander Veur, S., McCoy, T., Sandoval, B., Nachmani, J., Karpyn, A., & Foster, G. D. (2009). Snacking in children: The role of urban corner stores. *Pediatrics, 124,* 1292–1297.

Bosak, J., Sczesny, S., & Eagly, A. H. (2008). Communion and agency judgments of women and men as a function of role information and response format. *European Journal of Social Psychology, 38,* 1148–1155.

Bosch, A.M., Willekens, F.J., Baqui, A.H., Van Ginneken, J. K., & Hutter, I. (2008). Association between age at menarche and early-life nutritional status in rural Bangladesh. *Journal of Biosocial Science, 40,* 223–237.

Boston Retinal Implant Project (2009). Available at: http://www.bostonretinalimplant.org/. Accessed: November 15, 2009.

Boström, P. K., Broberg, M., & Hwang, P. (2010). Parents' descriptions and experiences of young children recently diagnosed with intellectual disability. *Child: Care, Health and Development, 36,* 93–100.

Botkin, D. R., Weeks, M. O., & Morris, J. E. (2000). Changing marriage role expectations: 1961–1996. *Sex Roles, 42,* 933–942.

Bouchard, T. J., Jr. (1984). Twins reared together and apart: What they tell us about human diversity. In S. W. Fox (Ed.), *Individuality and determinism: Chemical and biological bases.* New York: Plenum.

Bouchard, T. J., Jr. (2004). Genetic influence on human psychological traits: A survey. *Current Directions in Psychological Science, 13,* 148–151.

Bouchard, T. J., Jr., Lykken, D. T., McGue, M., Segal, N. L., & Tellegen, A. (1990). Sources of human psychological differences: The Minnesota Study of Twins Reared Apart. *Science, 250,* 223–228.

Bouchard, T. J., Jr., & McGue, M. (1981). Family studies of intelligence: A review. *Science, 212,* 1055–1059.

Bouchard, T. J., Jr., & Pedersen, N. (1999). Twins reared apart: Nature's double experiment. In M. C. LaBuda & E. L. Grigorenko (Eds.), *On the way to individuality: Methodological issues in behavioral genetics.* Commack, NY: Nova Science Publishers.

Bouldin, P. (2006). An investigation of fantasy predisposition and fantasy style of children with imaginary companions. *The Journal of Genetic Psychology, 167,* 17–29.

Bowen, B. A. (1999). Four puzzles in adult literacy: Reflections on the national adult literacy survey. *Journal of Adolescent & Adult Literacy, 42,* 314–323.

Bower, J. E., Moskowitz, J. T., & Epel, E. (2009). Is benefit finding good for your health? *Current Directions in Psychological Science, 18,* 337–341.

Bower, T. G. R., Broughton, J. M., & Moore, M. K. (1970). The coordination of vision and tactile input in infancy. *Perception and Psychophysics, 8,* 51–53.

Bowlby, J. (1960). Separation anxiety. *International Journal of Psychoanalysis, 41,* 89–113.

Bowlby, J. (1969). *Attachment and loss: Vol. 1. Attachment.* New York: Basic Books.

Bowlby, J. (1973). *Attachment and loss: Vol. 2. Separation.* New York: Basic Books.

Bowlby, J. (1980). *Attachment and loss: Vol. 3. Loss, sadness and depression.* New York: Basic Books.

Bowlby, J. (1988). *A secure base: Parent–child attachment and healthy human development.* New York: Basic Books.

Bowler, D. (2007). *Autism spectrum disorders: Psychological theory and research.* West Sussex, UK: Wiley.

Boxer, P., Huesmann, L. R., Bushman, B. J., Moceri, D., & O'Brien, M. (2009). The role of violent media preference in cumulative developmental risk for violence and general aggression. *Journal of Youth and Adolescence, 38,* 417–428.

Boyce, P. M. (2003). Risk factors for postnatal depression: A review and risk factors in Australian populations. *Archives of Women's Mental Health, Supplement 2,* S43–S50.

Brabeck, M. (1983). Moral judgment: Theory and research on differences between males and females. *Developmental Review, 3,* 274–291.

Brabyn, J. (2000). Visual function in the oldest old. Papers from the 15th Biennial Eye Research Seminar. New York: *Research to Prevent Blindness.* Available at: http://www. rpbusa.org/new/pdf/jbrabyn1.pdf.

Bracey, J. R., Bamaca, M. Y., & Umaña-Taylor, A. J. (2004). Examining ethnic identity and self-esteem among biracial and monoracial adolescents. *Journal of Youth and Adolescence, 33,* 123–132.

Bradbard, M. R., Martin, C. L., Endsley, R. C., & Halverson, C. F. (1986). Influence of sex stereotypes on children's exploration and memory: A competence versus performance distinction. *Developmental Psychology, 22,* 481–486.

Bradley, R. H., Caldwell, B. M., Rock, S. L., Ramey, C. T., Barnard, K. E., Gray, C., et al. (1989). Home environment and cognitive development in the first 3 years of life: A collaborative study involving six sites and three ethnic groups in North America. *Developmental Psychology, 25,* 217–235.

Bradley, R. H., Convyn, R. F., Burchinal, M., McAdoo, H. P., & Coll, C. G. (2001). The home environments of children in the United States, Part II: Relations with behavioral development through age thirteen. *Child Development, 72,* 1868–1886.

Bradley, R. H., & Corwyn, R. F. (2002). Socioeconomic status and child development. *Annual Review of Psychology, 53,* 371–399.

Bradshaw, C. P., Zmuda, J. K., Kellam, S. G., & Ialongo, N. S. (2009). Longitudinal impact of two universal preventive interventions in first grade on educational outcomes in high school. *Journal of Educational Psychology, 101,* 926–937.

Brady, S. S., & Halpern-Fisher, B. L. (2007). Adolescents' reported consequences of having oral sex versus vaginal sex. *Pediatrics, 119,* 229–236.

Brainerd, C. J., & Gordon, L. L. (1994). Development of verbatim and gist memory for numbers. *Developmental Psychology, 30,* 163–177.

Brainerd, C. J., & Reyna, V. F. (1993). Domains of fuzzy trace theory. In M. L. Howe & R. Pasnak (Eds.), *Emerging themes in cognitive development: Vol. 1. Foundations.* New York: Springer-Verlag.

Braithwaite, V. (2002). Reducing ageism. In T. D. Nelson (Ed.), *Ageism: Stereotyping and prejudice against older persons.* Cambridge, MA: The MIT Press.

Brandt, J., Aretouli, E., Neijstrom, E., Samek, J., Manning, K., Albert, M. S., & Bandeen-Roche, K. (2009). Selectivity of executive function deficits in mild cognitive deficit. *Neuropsychology, 23,* 607–618.

Brandtstädter, J., & Greve, W. (1994). The aging self: Stabilizing and protective processes. *Developmental Review, 14,* 52–80.

Brant, A. M., Haberstick, B. C., Corley, R. P., Wadsworth, S. J., DeFries, J. C., & Hewitt, J. K. (2009). The developmental etiology of high IQ. *Behavior Genetics, 39,* 393–405.

Brassett-Harknett, A., & Butler, N. (2007). Attention-deficit/hyperactivity disorder: An overview of the etiology and a review of the literature relating to the correlates and lifecourse outcomes for men and women. *Clinical Psychology Review, 27,* 188–210.

Bratberg, G. H., Nilsen, T. I., Holmen, T. L., & Vatten, L. J. (2005). Sexual maturation in early adolescence and alcohol drinking and cigarette smoking in late adolescence: A prospective study of 2,129 Norwegian girls and boys. *European Journal of Pediatrics, 164,* 621–625.

Braude, P. (2006, August 10). Preimplantation diagnosis for genetic susceptibility. *New England Journal of Medicine, 355,* 541–543.

Braver, E. R., & Trempel, R. E. (2004). Are older drivers actually at higher risk of involvement in collisions resulting in deaths or non-fatal injuries among their passengers and other road users? *Injury Prevention, 10,* 27–32.

Bray, N. W., Hersh, R. E., & Turner, L. A. (1985). Selective remembering during adolescence. *Developmental Psychology, 21,* 290–294.

Brazelton, T. B. (1979). Behavioral competence of the newborn infant. *Seminars in Perinatology, 3,* 35–44.

Breedlove, S. M. (1994). Sexual differentiation of the human nervous system. *Annual Review of Psychology, 45,* 389–418.

Bregman, J. D. (2005). Definitions and characteristics of the spectrum. In D. Zager (Ed.), *Autism spectrum disorders: Identification, education, and treatment* (3rd ed.). Mahwah, NJ: Erlbaum.

Brehmer, Y., Li, S., Müller, V., von Oertzen, T., Lindenberger, U. (2007). Memory plasticity across the life-span: Uncovering children's latent potential. *Developmental Psychology, 43,* 465–478.

Bremner, J. D., & Narayan, M. (1998). The effects of stress on memory and the hippocampus through-out the life cycle: Implications for childhood development and aging. *Development and Psychopathology, 10,* 871–886.

Bremner, J. G., Johnson, S. P., Slater, A., Mason, U., Foster, K., Cheshire, A., & Spring, J. (2005). Conditions for young infants' perception of object trajectories. *Child Development, 76,* 1029–1043.

Brenick, A., Henning, A., Killen, M., O'Connor, A., & Collins, M. (2007). Social evaluations of stereotypic images in video games: Unfair, legitimate, or 'just entertainment'? *Youth & Society, 38,* 395–419.

Brent, D. A., & Maalouf, F. T. (2009). Pediatric depression: Is there evidence to improve evidence-based treatments? *Journal of Child Psychology and Psychiatry, 50,* 143–152.

Brent, S. B., Speece, M. W., Lin, C. G., Dong, Q., & Yang, C. M. (1996). The development of the concept of death among Chinese and U.S. children 3–17 years of age: From binary to "fuzzy" concepts? *Omega: Journal of Death and Dying, 33,* 67–83.

Bretherton, I. (1996). Internal working models of attachment relationships as related to resilient coping. In G. G. Noam, & K. W. Fischer (Eds.), *Development and vulnerability in close relationships.* Mahwah, NJ: Erlbaum.

Bretherton, I., & Beeghly, M. (1982). Talking about internal states: The acquisition of an explicit theory of mind. *Developmental Psychology, 18,* 906–921.

Bretherton, I., Stolberg, U., & Kreye, M. (1981). Engaging strangers in proximal interaction: Infants' social initiative. *Developmental Psychology, 17,* 746–755.

Brewster, K. L., & Padavic, I. (2000). Changes in gender-ideology, 1977–1996: The contributions of intracohort change and population turnover. *Journal of Marriage and the Family, 62,* 477–487.

Bridge, J. A., Day, N. L., Day, R., Richardson, G. A., Birmaher, B., & Brent, D. A. (2003). Major depressive disorder in adolescents exposed to a friend's suicide. *Journal of the American Academy of Child and Adolescent Psychiatry, 42,* 1294–1300.

Bridges, L. J., & Grolnick, W. S. (1995). The development of emotional self-regulation in infancy and early childhood. In N. Eisenberg (Ed.), *Social development: Vol. 15. Review of personality and social psychology.* Thousand Oaks, CA: Sage.

Briefel, R. R., Crepinsek, M. K., Cabili, C., Wilson, A., & Gleason, P. M. (2009). School food environments and practices affect dietary behaviors of U.S. public school children. *Journal of the American Dietetic Association, 109,* S91–107.

Briefel, R. R., Wilson, A., & Gleason, P. M. (2009). Consumption of low-nutrient, energy-dense foods and beverages at school, home, and other locations among school lunch participants and non-participants. *Journal of the American Dietetic Association, 109,* S79–90.

Bright, J. E. H., Pryor, R. G. L., & Harpham, L. (2005). The role of chance events in career decision making. *Journal of Vocational Behavior, 66,* 561–576.

Brody, E. B., & Brody, N. (1976). *Intelligence: Nature, determinants, and consequences.* New York: Academic Press.

Brody, E. M. (1985). Parent care as a normative family stress. *Gerontologist, 25,* 19–29.

Brody, E. M. (2004). *Women in the middle: Their parent care years* (2nd ed.). New York: Springer.

Brody, E. M., Litvin, S. J., Hoffman, C., & Kleban, M. H. (1992). Differential effects of daughters' marital status on their parent care experiences. *Gerontologist, 32,* 58–67.

Brody, G. H. (2003). Parental monitoring: Action and reaction. In A. C. Crouter, & A. Booth (Eds.), *Children's influence on family dynamics: The neglected side of family relationships.* Mahwah, NJ: Erlbaum.

Brody, G. H. (2004). Siblings' direct and indirect contributions to child development. *Current Directions in Psychological Science, 13,* 124–126.

Brody, G. H., Beach, S. R. H., Philibert, R. A., Chen, Y., & Murry, V. M. (2009). Prevention effects moderate the association of 5-HTTLPR and youth risk behavior initiation: Gene x environment hypotheses tested via a randomized prevention design. *Child Development, 80,* 645–661.

Brody, G. H., & Shaffer, D. R. (1982). Contributions of parents and peers to children's moral socialization. *Developmental Review, 2,* 31–75.

Brody, J. A., Grant, M. D., Frateschi, L. J., Miller, S. C., & Zhang, H. (2000). Reproductive longevity and increased life expectancy. *Age and Ageing, 29,* 75–78.

Broen, A. N., Moum, T., Bodtker, A. S., & Ekeberg, O. (2004). Psychological impact on women of miscarriage versus induced abortion: A 2-year follow-up study. *Psychosomatic Medicine, 66,* 265–271.

Bronfenbrenner, U. (1979). *The ecology of human development: Experiments by nature and design.* Cambridge, MA: Harvard University Press.

Bronfenbrenner, U. (1989). Ecological systems theory. In R. Vasta (Ed.), *Annals of child development: Vol. 6. Theories of child development: Revised formulations and current issues.* Greenwich, CT: JAI Press.

Bronfenbrenner, U., & Morris, P. A. (2006). The bioecological model of human development. In W. Damon & R. M. Lerner (Eds. in Chief) & R. M. Lerner (Vol. Ed.), *Handbook of child psychology: Vol. 1. Theoretical models of human development* (6th ed.). Hoboken, NJ: Wiley.

Brooks-Gunn, J., Britto, P. R., & Brady, C. (1999). Struggling to make ends meet: Poverty and child development. In M. E. Lamb (Ed.), *Parenting and child development in "nontraditional" families.* Mahwah, NJ: Erlbaum.

Brooks-Gunn, J., Klebanov, P. K., & Duncan, G. J. (1996). Ethnic differences in children's intelligence test scores: Role of economic deprivation, home environment, and maternal characteristics. *Child Development, 67,* 396–408.

Brooks-Gunn, J., & Lewis, M. (1981). Infant social perception: Responses to pictures of parents and strangers. *Developmental Psychology, 17,* 647–649.

Brophy, J. (2010). *Motivating students to learn* (3rd ed.). New York: Routledge.

Broughton, J. M. (1984). Not beyond formal operations, but Beyond Piaget. In M. L. Commons, F. A. Richards, & C. Armon (Eds.), *Beyond formal operations: Late adolescent and adult cognitive development,* 395–411. New York: Praeger.

Brown, A. L., & Smiley, S. S. (1978). The development of strategies for studying text. *Child Development, 49,* 1076–1088.

Brown, A. M. & Lindsey, D. T. (2009). Contrast insensitivity: The critical immaturity in infant visual performance. *Optometry and Vision Science, 86,* 572–576.

Brown, B. B. (1999). "You're going out with who?" Peer group influences on adolescent romantic relationships. In W. Furman, B. B. Brown, & C. Feiring (Eds.), *The development of romantic relationships in adolescence.* Cambridge, England: Cambridge University Press.

Brown, B. B., & Dietz, E. L. (2009). Informal peer groups in middle childhood and adolescence. In K. H. Rubin, W. M. Bukowski, & B. Laursen (Eds.), *Handbook of peer interactions, relationships, and groups.* New York: Guilford.

Brown, B. B., Feiring, C., & Furman, W. (1999). Missing the love boat. Why researchers have shied away from adolescent romance. In W. Furman, B. B. Brown, & C. Feiring (Eds.), *The development of romantic relationships in adolescence.* Cambridge, England: Cambridge University Press.

Brown, B. B., & Lohr, M. J. (1987). Peer-group affiliation and adolescent self-esteem: An integration of ego–identity and symbolic-interaction theories. *Journal of Personality and Social Psychology, 52,* 47–55.

Brown, B. B., Mory, M. S., & Kinney, D. (1994). Casting adolescent crowds in a relational perspective: Caricature, channel, and context. In R. Montemayor, G. R. Adams, & T. P. Gulotta (Eds.), *Personal relationships during adolescence.* Thousand Oaks, CA: Sage.

Brown, B. B., Mounts, N., Lamborn, S. D., & Steinberg, L. (1993). Parenting practices and peer group affiliation in adolescence. *Child Development, 64,* 467–482.

Brown, D. (2005, September 5). Study suggests 'Y' the male chromosome will endure. *The Washington Post,* A13.

Brown, J. D., L'Engle, K. D., Pardun, C. J., Guang, G., Kenneavy, K., & Jackson, C. (2006). Sexy media matter: Exposure to sexual content in music, movies, television, and magazines predicts black and white adolescents' sexual behavior. *Pediatrics, 117,* 1018–1027.

Brown, J. E., & Satin, A. J. (2007). Having a baby: The birth process. In M. L. Batshaw, L. Pellegrino, & N. J. Roizen (Eds.), *Children with Disabilities,* 6th ed. (pp. 35–46). Baltimore, MD: Paul H. Brookes.

Brown, R., Cazden, C., & Bellugi, U. (1969). The child's grammar from I to III. In J. P. Hill (Ed.), *Minnesota Symposia on child psychology* (Vol. 2). Minneapolis: University of Minnesota Press.

Brown, R., & Hanlon, C. (1970). Derivational complexity and order of acquisition. In J. R. Hayes (Ed.), *Cognition and the development of language.* New York: Wiley.

Brown, S. L., Lee, G. R., & Bulanda, J. R. (2006). Cohabitation among older adults: A national portrait. *Journals of Gerontology: Psychological Sciences and Social Sciences, 61B,* S71–S79.

Brown, S. L., Smith, D. M., Schulz, R., Kabeto, M. U., Ubel, P. A., Poulin, M., Yi, J., Kim, C., & Langa, K. M. (2009). Caregiving behavior is associated with decreased mortality risk. *Psychological Science, 20,* 488–494.

Brown, S. M. (with contributions by J. G. Hay & H. Ostrer) (2003). *Essentials of medical genomics.* Hoboken, NJ: Wiley-Liss.

Brownell, C. A., & Carriger, M. S. (1990). Changes in cooperation and self/other differentiation during the second year. *Child Development, 61,* 1164–1174.

Bruck, M. (1990). Word recognition skills of adults with childhood diagnoses of dyslexia. *Developmental Psychology, 26,* 439–454.

Bruck, M. (1992). Persistence of dyslexics' phonological awareness deficits. *Developmental Psychology, 28,* 874–886.

Bruer, J. T. (1999). The myth of the first three years: A new understanding of early brain development and lifelong learning. New York: Free Press.

Brundin, P., Winkler, J. & Masliah, E. (2008). Adult neurogenesis in neurodegenerative diseases. In F. H. Gage, G. Kempermann, & H. Song (Eds.), *Adult Neurogenesis,* 503–533. NY: Cold Spring Harbor Laboratory Press.

Bruner, J. S. (1983). *Child's talk: Learning to use language.* New York: Norton.

Bruner, J. S. (1997). Celebrating divergence: Piaget and Vygotsky. *Human Development, 40,* 63–73.

Bryant, C. M., Bolland, J. M., Burton, L. M., Hurt, T., & Bryant, B. M. (2006). The changing social context of relationships. In P. Noller & J. A. Feeney (Eds.), *Close relationships: Functions, forms, and processes.* New York: Psychology Press.

Bryant, P. (1998). Sensitivity to onset and rhyme does predict young children's reading: A comment on Muter, Hulme, Snowling, and Taylor (1997). *Journal of Experimental Child Psychology, 71,* 39–44.

Bryant-Waugh, R. (2007). Anorexia nervosa in children and adolescents. In T. Jaffa & B. McDermott (Eds.), *Eating disorders in children and adolescents.* Cambridge, UK: Cambridge University Press.

Brynie, F. H. (2009). *Brain sense: The science of the senses and how we process the world around us.* New York: AMACOM.

Buchanan, C. M., Eccles, J. S., & Becker, J. B. (1992). Are adolescents the victims of raging hormones? Evidence for activational effects of hormones on moods and behavior at adolescence. *Psychological Bulletin, 111,* 62–107.

Buchanan, D., Fisher, C. B., & Gable, L. (Eds.). (2009). *Research with high-risk populations: Balancing science, ethics, and law.* Washington, DC: American Psychological Association.

Buchi, S., Morgeli, H., Schnyder, U., Jenewein, J., Hepp, U., Jina, E., Neuhaus, R., Fauchere, J., Bucher, H. U., & Sensky, T. (2007). Grief and post-traumatic growth in parents 2–6 years after the death of their extremely premature baby. *Psychotherapy and Psychosomatics, 76,* 106–114.

Buckhalt, J. A., Wolfson, A. R., El-Sheikh, M. (2009). Children's sleep and school psychology practice, *School Psychology Quarterly, 24,* 60–69.

Bucur, B., Madden, D.J., Spaniol, J., Provenzale, J.M., Cabeza, R., White, L.E., Huettel, S.A. (2008). Age-related slowing of memory retrieval: contributions of perceptual speed and cerebral white matter integrity. *Neurobiological Aging, 29,* 1070–1079.

Buehler, C., Lange, G., & Franck, K. L. (2007). Adolescents' cognitive and emotional responses to marital hostility. *Child Development, 78,* 775–789.

Buehler, C. A., Hogan, M. J., Robinson, B. E., & Levy, R. J. (1985–1986). The parental divorce transition: Divorce-related stressors and well-being. *Journal of Divorce, 9,* 61–81.

Bugental, D. (2009). Predicting and preventing child maltreatment: A biocognitive transactional approach. In A. Sameroff (Ed.), *The transactional model of development. How children and contexts shape each other.* Washington, DC: American Psychological Association.

Bugental, D. B., & Beaulieu, D. A. (2003). A bio-social-cognitive approach to understanding and promoting the outcomes of children with medical and physical disorders. In R. V. Kail (Ed.), *Advances in child development and behavior* (Vol. 31). San Diego: Academic Press.

Bugental, D. B., Ellerson, P. C., Lin, E. K., Rainey, B., Kokotovic, A., & O'Hara, N. (2002). A cognitive approach to child abuse prevention. *Journal of Family Psychology, 16,* 243–258.

Buhrmester, D., & Furman, W. (1986). The changing functions of friends in childhood: A neo-Sullivanian perspective. In V. J. Derlega & B. A. Winstead (Eds.), *Friendship and social interaction.* New York: Springer-Verlag.

Bukowski, W. M., Motzoi, C., & Meyer, F. (2009). Friendship as process, function, and outcome. In K. H. Rubin, W. M. Bukowski, & B. Laursen (Eds.), *Handbook of peer interactions, relationships, and groups.* New York: Guilford.

Bulanda, R. E. (2004). Paternal involvement with children: The influence of gender ideologies. *Journal of Marriage and Family, 66,* 40–45.

Bulcroft, R. A. (1991). The value of physical change in adolescence: Consequences for the parent–adolescent exchange relationship. *Journal of Youth and Adolescence, 20,* 89–105.

Bulik, C. M., Sullivan, P. F., Tozzi, F., Furberg, H., Lichtenstein, P., & Pedersen, N. L. (2006). Prevalence, heritability, and prospective risk factors for anorexia nervosa. *Archives of General Psychiatry, 63,* 305–312.

Bullock, M., Sodian, B., & Koerber, S. (2009). Doing experiments and understanding science: Development of scientific reasoning from childhood to adulthood. In W. Schneider & M. Bullock (Eds.). *Human development from early childhood to early adulthood: Findings from a 20-year longitudinal study,* 173–197. New York: Psychology Press.

Burack, J. A., Enns, J. T., Iarocci, G., & Randolph, B. (2000). Age differences in visual search for compound patterns: Long- versus short-range grouping. *Developmental Psychology, 36,* 731–740.

Burack, J. A., Flanagan, T., Peled, T., Sutton, H. M., Zygmuntowicz, C., & Manly, J. T. (2006). Social perspective-taking skills in maltreated children and adolescents. *Developmental Psychology, 42,* 207–217.

Burchinal, M. R., Roberts, J. E., Riggins, R., Zeisel, S. A., Neebe, E., & Bryant, D. (2000). Relating quality of center-based child care to early cognitive and language development longitudinally. *Child Development, 71,* 339–357.

Bures, R. M., Koropeckyj-Cox, T., & Loree, M. (2009). Childlessness, parenthood, and depressive symptoms among middle-aged and older adults. *Journal of Family Issues, 30,* 670–687.

Burgess, R. L., & MacDonald, K. (Eds.). (2005). *Evolutionary perspectives on human development.* Thousand Oaks, CA: Sage.

Burhans, K. K., & Dweck, C. S. (1995). Helplessness in early childhood: The role of contingent worth. *Child Development, 66,* 1719–1738.

Burke, T. M., Abramovitch, R., & Zlotkin, S. (2005). Children's understanding of the risks and benefits associated with research. *Journal of Medical Ethics, 31,* 715–720.

Burleson, M. H., Trevathan, W. R., & Todd, M. (2007). In the mood for love or vice versa? Exploring the relations among sexual activity, physical affection, affect, and stress in the daily lives of mid-aged women. *Archives of Sexual Behavior, 36,* 357–368.

Burn, S., O'Neil, A. K., & Nederend, S. (1996). Childhood tomboyishness and adult androgyny. *Sex Roles, 34,* 419–428.

Burnham, D. K., & Harris, M. B. (1992). Effects of real gender and labeled gender on adults' perceptions of infants. *Journal of Genetic Psychology, 153,* 165–183.

Burns, G. W., & Bottino, P. J. (1989). *The science of genetics* (6th ed.). New York: Macmillan.

Burt, C. D. B., Kemp, S., & Conway, M. A. (2003). Themes, events, and episodes in autobiographical memory. *Memory & Cognition, 31,* 317–325.

Burt, S. A. (2009). Rethinking environmental contributions to child and adolescent psychopathology: A meta-analysis of shared environmental influences. *Psychological Bulletin, 135,* 608–637.

Burt, S. A., McGue, M., DeMarte, J. A., Krueger, R. F., & Iacono, W. G. (2006). Timing of menarche and the origins of conduct disorder. *Archives of General Psychiatry, 63,* 890–896.

Burton, L. (2007). Childhood adultification in economically disadvantaged families: A conceptual model. *Family Relations, 56,* 329–345.

Burton, L. A., Hafetz, J., & Henninger, D. (2007). Gender differences in relational and physical aggression. *Social Behavior and Personality, 35,* 41–50.

Burton, L. M. (1990). Teenage childrearing as an alternative life-course strategy in multigenerational black families. *Human Nature, 1,* 123–143.

Burton, R. V. (1984). A paradox in theories and research in moral development. In W. M. Kurtines & J. L. Gewirtz (Eds.), *Morality, moral behavior, and moral development.* New York: Wiley.

Bus, A. G., & van IJzendoorn, M. H. (1999). Phonological awareness and early reading: A meta-analysis of experimental training studies. *Journal of Educational Psychology, 91,* 403–414.

Busch-Rossnagel, N. A. (1997). Mastery motivation in toddlers. *Infants and Young Children, 9,* 1–11.

Bush Foundation (2010). *Teacher effectiveness initiative.* Available at: www.bushfoundation.org/Education/TEInitiative.asp. Accessed: April 10, 2010.

Bushfield, S. Y., Fitzpatrick, T. R., & Vinick, B. H. (2008). Perception of 'impingement' and marital satisfaction among wives of retired husbands. *Journal of Women & Aging, 20,* 199–213.

Bushnell, E. W., & Baxt, C. (1999). Children's haptic and cross-modal recognition with familiar and unfamiliar objects. *Journal of Experimental Psychology: Human Perception and Performance*, 25, 1867–1881.

Buss, A. H., & Perry, M. (1992). The aggression question. *Journal of Personality and Social Psychology*, 63, 452–459.

Buss, D. M. (1995). Psychological sex differences: Origins through sexual selection. *American Psychologist*, 50, 164–168.

Buss, D. M. (2008). *Evolutionary psychology: The new science of the mind*. Boston: Pearson/Allyn & Bacon.

Buss, D. M. (2009). The great struggles of life. Darwin and the emergence of evolutionary psychology. *American Psychologist*, 64, 140–148.

Buss, D. M., & Schmitt, D. P. (1993). Sexual strategies theory: An evolutionary perspective on human mating. *Psychological Review*, 100, 204–232.

Butcher, L. M., Davis, O. S. P., Craig, I. W., & Plomin, R. (2008). Genome-wide quantitative trait locus association scan of general cognitive ability using pooled DNA and 500K single nucleotide polymorphism microarrays. *Genes, Brain & Behavior*, 7, 435–446.

Butcher, L. M., & Plomin, R. (2008). The nature of nurture: A genomewide association scan for family chaos. *Behavior Genetics*, 38, 361–371.

Butcher, P. R., Kalverboer, A. F., & Geuze, R. H. (2000). Infants' shifts of gaze from a central to a peripheral stimulus: A longitudinal study of development between 6 and 26 weeks. *Infant Behavior & Development*, 23, 3–21.

Butler, R. (1990). The effects of mastery and competitive conditions on self-assessment at different ages. *Child Development*, 61, 201–210.

Butler, R. (1999). Information seeking and achievement motivation in middle childhood and adolescence: The role of conceptions of ability. *Developmental Psychology*, 35, 146–163.

Butler, R. N. (1963). The life review: An interpretation of reminiscence in the aged. *Psychiatry*, 26, 65–76.

Butters, M. A., Becker, J. L., Nebes, R. D., Zmuda, M. D., Mulsant, B. H., Pollock, B. G., et al. (2000). Changes in cognitive functioning following treatment of late-life depression. *American Journal of Psychiatry*, 157, 1949–1954.

Butters, M. A., Whyte, E. M., Nebes, R. D., Begley, A. E., Dew, M. A., Mulsant, B. H., et al. (2004). The nature and determinants of neuropsychological functioning in late-life depression. *Archives of General Psychiatry*, 61, 587–595.

Button, T. M. M., Scourfield, J., Martin, N., Purcell, S., & McGuffin, P. (2005). Family dysfunction interacts with genes in the causation of antisocial symptoms. *Behavior Genetics*, 35, 115–120.

Buysse, V., & Bailey, D. B. (1993). Behavioral and developmental outcomes in young children with disabilities in integrated and segregated settings: A review of comparative studies. *Journal of Special Education*, 26, 434–461.

Bybee, R. W. (1995). Science curriculum reform in the United States. In R. W. Bybee & J. D. McInerney (Eds.), *Redesigning the science curriculum*. Colorado Springs, CO: Biological Sciences Curriculum Study.

Byne, W. (1994). The biological evidence challenged. *Scientific American*, 270, 50–55.

Byrne, B. (1998). *The foundation of literacy: The child's acquisition of the alphabetic principle*. East Sussex, UK: Psychology Press.

Byrnes, J. P. (1996). *Cognitive development and learning in instructional contexts*. Boston: Allyn & Bacon.

C

Cabrera, N. J., Fagan, J., & Farrie, D. (2008). Explaining the long reach of fathers? Prenatal involvement on later paternal engagement. *Journal of Marriage and Family*, 70, 1094–1107.

Cabrera, N. J., Tamis-LeMonda, C. S., Bradley, R. H., Hofferth, S., & Lamb, M. E. (2000). Fatherhood in the twenty-first century. *Child Development*, 71, 127–136.

Cacioppo, J. T., & Patrick, B. (2008). *Loneliness: Human nature and the need for social connection*. New York: W. W. Norton.

Cairns, R. B., & Cairns, B. (2006). The making of developmental psychology. In W. Damon & R. M. Lerner (Eds. in Chief) & R. M. Lerner (Vol. Ed.), *Handbook of child psychology: Vol. 1. Theoretical models of human development* (6th ed.). Hoboken, NJ: Wiley.

Caldera, Y. M., Huston, A. C., & O'Brien, M. (1989). Social interactions and play patterns of parents and toddlers with feminine, masculine, and neutral toys. *Child Development*, 60, 70–76.

Caldera, Y. M., & Lindsey, E. W. (2006). Coparenting, mother–infant interaction, and infant–parent attachment relationships in two-parent families. *Journal of Family Psychology*, 20, 275–283.

Caldwell, B. M., & Bradley, R. H. (1984). *Manual for the home observation for measurement of the environment*. Little Rock: University of Arkansas.

Calkins, S. D., & Hill, A. (2007). Caregiver influences on emerging emotion regulation: Biological and environmental transactions in early development. In J. J. Gross (Ed.), *Handbook of emotion regulation*. New York: Guilford.

Call, K. T., Mortimer, J. T., & Shanahan, M. (1995). Helpfulness and the development of competence in adolescence. *Child Development*, 66, 129–138.

Callaghan, W. M., MacDorman, M. F., Rasmussen, S. A., Qin, C., Lackritz, E. M. (2006). The contribution of preterm birth to infant mortality rates in the United States. *Pediatrics*, 118, 1566–1573.

Calvert, S. L., & Wilson, B. J. (Eds.). (2008). *The handbook of children, media, and development*. Malden, MA: Blackwell Publishing.

Calvo, E., Haverstick, K., & Sass, S. A. (2009). Gradual retirement, sense of control, and retirees' happiness. *Research on Aging*, 31, 112–135.

Camaioni, L. (2004). Early language. In G. Bremner & A. Fogel (Eds.), *Blackwell handbook of infant development* (pp. 404–426). Malden, MA: Blackwell Publishing.

Camp, C. J., Foss, J. W., O'Hanlon, A. M., & Stevens, A. B. (1996). Memory interventions for persons with dementia. *Applied Cognitive Psychology*, 10, 193–210.

Camp, C. J., & McKitrick, L. A. (1992). Memory interventions in Alzheimer's-type dementia populations: Methodological and theoretical issues. In R. L. West & J. D. Sinnott (Eds.), *Everyday memory and aging: Current research and methodology* 155–172. New York: Springer-Verlag.

Campbell, A., Shirley, L., & Caygill, L. (2002). Sex-typed preferences in three domains: Do two-year-olds need cognitive variables? *British Journal of Psychology*, 93, 203–217.

Campbell, F. A., Pungello, E. P., Miller-Johnson, S., Burchinal, M., & Ramey, C. T. (2001). The development of cognitive and academic abilities: Growth curves from an early childhood educational experiment. *Developmental Psychology*, 37, 231–242.

Campbell, F. A., & Ramey, C. T. (1995). Cognitive and school outcomes for high-risk African-American students at middle adolescence: Positive effects of early intervention. *American Educational Research Journal*, 32, 743–772.

Campbell, R., MacSweeney, M., & Waters, D. (2007). Sign language and the brain: A review. *Journal of Deaf Studies and Deaf Education*, 131, 3–20.

Campbell, V. A., Crews, J. E., Moriarty, D. G., Zack, M. M., & Blackman, D. K. (1999). Surveillance for sensory impairment, activity limitation, and health-related quality of life among older adults: United States, 1993–1997. *CDC MMWR Surveillance Summaries*, 48 (SS08), 131–156.

Campos, J. J., Bertenthal, B. I., & Kermoian, R. (1992). Early experience and emotional development: The emergence of wariness of heights. *Psychological Science*, 3, 61–64.

Campos, J. J., Langer, A., & Krowitz, A. (1970). Cardiac responses on the visual cliff in prelocomotor human infants. *Science*, 170, 196–197.

Campos, M., Bravo, E., & Eugenin, J. (2009, May 19). Respiratory dysfunctions induced by prenatal nicotine exposure. *Clinical and Experimental Pharmacology & Physiology*.

Canfield, R. L., Henderson, C. R., Cory-Slechta, D. A., Cox, C., Jusko, T. A., & Lanphaer, B. P. (2003). Intellectual impairment in children with blood lead concentrations below 10 microg per deciliter. *New England Journal of Medicine*, 348, 1517–1526.

Cannon, M., Kendell, R., Susser, E., & Jones, P. (2003). Prenatal and perinatal risk factors for schizophrenia. In R. M. Murray, P. B. Jones, E. Susser, J. van Os, & M. Cannon (Eds.), *The epidemiology of schizophrenia*. Cambridge, UK: Cambridge University Press.

Cano, A., & Vivian, D. (2003). Are life stressors associated with marital violence? *Journal of Family Psychology*, 17, 302–314.

Cantor, N. L. (2001). Twenty-five years after Quinlan: A review of the jurisprudence of death and dying. *Journal of Law, Medicine, and Ethics*, 29, 182–196.

Caplan, L. J., & Schooler, C. (2001). Age effects on analogy-based memory for text. *Experimental Aging Research*, 27, 151–165.

Card, N. A. (2007). "I hated her guts!": Emerging adults' recollections of the formation, maintenance, and termination of antipathetic relationships during high school. *Journal of Adolescent Research*, 22, 32–57.

Card, N. A., Stucky, B. D., Sawalani, G. M., & Little, T. D. (2008). Direct and indirect aggression during childhood and adolescence: A meta-analytic review of gender differences, intercorrelations, and relations to maladjustment. *Child Development*, 79, 1185–1229.

CARE Study Group (2008). Maternal caffeine intake during pregnancy and risk of fetal growth restriction: A large prospective observational study. *British Medical Journal*, 337, a2332.

Carlson, M. C., Erickson, K. I., Kramer, A. F., Voss, M. W., Bolea, N., Mielke, M., McGill, S., Rebok, G. W., Seeman, T., & Fried, L. P. (2009). Evidence for neurocognitive plasticity in at-risk older adults: The Experience Corps Program. *Journals of Gerontology A: Biological Sciences and Medical Sciences*, 64, 1275–1282.

Carlson, V., Cicchetti, D., Barnett, D., & Braunwald, K. (1989). Disorganized/disoriented attachment relationships in maltreated infants. *Developmental Psychology*, 25, 525–531.

Carmichael, M. (2004, May 10). Have it your way: Redesigning birth. *Newsweek*, 70–72.

Carmichael, S. L., Shaw, G. M., Schaffer, D. M, Laurent, C., & Selvin, S. (2003). Dieting behaviors and risk of neural tube defects. *American Journal of Epidemiology*, 158, 1127–1131.

Carnelley, K. B., Wortman, C. B., Bolger, N., & Burke, C. T. (2006). The time course of grief reactions to spousal loss: Evidence from a national probability sample. *Journal of Personality and Social Psychology*, 91, 476–492.

Carnethon, M., Gulati, M., & Greenland, P. (2005). Prevalence and cardiovascular disease correlates of low cardiorespiratory fitness in adolescents and adults. *Journal of the American Medical Association*, 294, 2981–2988.

Caron, S. L., & Moskey, E. G. (2002). Changes over time in teenage sexual relationships: Comparing the high school class of 1950, 1975, and 2000. *Adolescence*, 37, 515–526.

Carpendale, J. I. M. (2000). Kohlberg and Piaget on stages and moral reasoning. *Developmental Review, 20,* 181–205.

Carpenter, M., Nagell, K., & Tomasello, M. (1998). Social cognition, joint attention, and communicative competence from 9 to 15 months of age. *Monographs of the Society for Research in Child Development, 63* (Serial No. 255).

Carr, A. (2009). *What works with children, adolescents and adults? A review of research on the effectiveness of psychotherapy.* New York: Routledge/Taylor & Francis Group.

Carr, C. L. (2007). Where have all the tomboys gone? Women's accounts of gender in adolescence. *Sex Roles, 56,* 439–448.

Carr, D. (2004). Gender, preloss marital dependence, and older adults' adjustment to widowhood. *Journal of Marriage and Family, 66,* 220–235.

Carr, D. (2008). Factors that influence late-life bereavement: Considering data from the Changing Lives of Older Couples Study. In M. S. Stroebe, R. O. Hansson, H. Schut, & W. Stroebe (Eds.), *Handbook of bereavement research and practice. Advances in theory and intervention.* Washington, DC: American Psychological Association.

Carr, P. L., Ash, A. S., Friedman, R. H., Scaramucci, A., Barnett, R. C., Szalacha, L., et al. (1998). Relation of family responsibilities and gender to the productivity and career satisfaction of medical faculty. *Annals of Internal Medicine, 129,* 532–538.

Carrera, M., Kaye, J. W., Philliber, S., & West, E. (2000). Knowledge about reproduction, contraception, and sexually transmitted infections among young adolescents in American cities. *Social Policy, 30,* 41–50.

Carroll, D. W. (2008). *Psychology of language* (5th ed.). Belmont, CA: Wadsworth.

Carroll, J. B. (1993). *Human cognitive abilities: A survey of factor–analytic studies.* Cambridge, England: Cambridge University Press.

Carroll, J. M., Snowling, M. J., Hulme, C., & Stevenson, J. (2003). The development of phonological awareness in preschool children. *Developmental Psychology, 39,* 913–925.

Carstensen, L. L. (1992). Social and emotional patterns in adulthood: Support for socio-emotional selectivity theory. *Psychology and Aging, 7,* 331–338.

Carstensen, L. L., & Freund, A. M. (1994). Commentary: The resilience of the aging self. *Developmental Review, 14,* 81–92.

Carstensen, L. L., Levenson, R. W., & Gottman, J. M. (1995). Emotional behavior in long-term marriages. *Psychology and Aging, 10,* 140–149.

Carstensen, L. L., Mikels, J. A., & Mather, M. (2006). Aging and the intersection of cognition, motivation, and emotion. In J. E. Birren & K. W. Schaie (Eds.), *Handbook of the psychology of aging* (6th ed.). Burlington, MA: Elsevier Academic Press.

Carstensen, L. L., Pasupathi, M., Mayr, U., & Nesselroade, J. R. (2000). Emotional experience in everyday life across the adult life span. *Journal of Personality and Social Psychology, 79,* 644–655.

Carter, A. S., Briggs-Gowan, M. J., & Davis, N. O. (2004). Assessment of young children's social-emotional development and psychopathology: Recent advances and recommendations for practice. *Journal of Child Psychology and Psychiatry and Allied Disciplines, 45,* 109–134.

Carter, B., & McGoldrick, M. (Eds.) (2005). *The expanded family life cycle: Individual, family, and social perspectives.* New York: Pearson Allyn & Bacon.

Carter, R., Jaccard, J., Silverman, W. K., & Pina, A. A. (2009). Pubertal timing and its link to behavioral and emotional problems among 'at-risk' African American adolescent girls. *Journal of Adolescence, 32,* 467–481.

Carver, K., Joyner, K., & Udry, J. R. (2003). National estimates of adolescent romantic relationships. In P. Florsheim (Ed.), *Adolescent romantic relations and sexual behavior: Theory, research, and practical implications.* Mahwah, NJ: Erlbaum.

Carver, L. J., & Vaccaro, B. G. (2007). 12-month-old infants allocate increased neural resources to stimuli associated with negative adult emotion. *Developmental Psychology, 43,* 54–69.

Casadesus, G., Perry, G., Joseph, J. A., & Smith, M. A. (2004). Eat less, eat better, and live longer: Does it work and is it worth it? The role of diet in aging and disease. In S. G. Post & R. H. Binstock (Eds.), *The fountain of youth: Cultural, scientific, and ethical perspectives on a biomedical goal.* New York: Oxford University Press.

Case, R. (1985). *Intellectual development: Birth to adulthood.* Orlando, FL: Academic Press.

Case, R. (1998). The development of conceptual structures. In D. Kuhn & R. S. Siegler (Vol. Eds.), W. Damon (Editor-in-Chief), *Handbook of child psychology: Vol. 2. Cognition, perception, and language* (5th ed.), 745–800. New York: Wiley.

Case, T. I., Repacholi, B. M., & Stevenson, R. J. (2006). My baby doesn't smell as bad as yours: The plasticity of disgust. *Evolution and Human Behavior, 27,* 357–365.

Casey, B. M., McIntire D. D., & Leveno, K. J. (2001). The continuing value of the Apgar score for the assessment of newborn infants. *New England Journal of Medicine, 344,* 467–471.

Caspi, A. (1998). Personality development across the life course. In R. M. Lerner (Vol. Ed.), W. Damon (Editor-in-Chief), *Handbook of child psychology: Vol. 1. Theoretical models of human development* (5th ed.). New York: Wiley.

Caspi, A. (2000). The child is father of man: Personality continues from childhood to adulthood. *Journal of Personality and Social Psychology, 78,* 158–172.

Caspi, A., Harrington, H., Milne, B., Amell, J. W., Theodore, R. F., & Moffitt, T. E. (2003). Children's behavioral styles at age 3 are linked to their adult personality traits at age 26. *Journal of Personality, 71,* 495–513.

Caspi, A., Herbener, E. S., & Ozer, D. J. (1992). Shared experiences and the similarity of personalities: A longitudinal study of married couples. *Journal of Personality and Social Psychology, 62,* 281–291.

Caspi, A., McClay, J., Moffitt, T., Mill, J., Martin, J., Craig, I. W., Taylor, A., & Poulton, R. (2002). Role of genotype in the cycle of violence in maltreated children. *Science, 297,* 851–854.

Caspi, A., Moffitt, T. E., Newman, D. L., & Silva, P. A. (1996). Behavioral observations at age 3 years predict adult psychiatric disorders: Longitudinal evidence from a birth cohort. *Archives of General Psychiatry, 53,* 1033–1039.

Caspi, A., & Roberts, B. W. (2001). Personality development across the life course: The argument for change and continuity. *Psychological Inquiry, 12,* 49–66.

Caspi, A., Sugden, K., Moffitt, T. E., Taylor, A., Craig, I. W., Harrington, H., McClay, J., Mill, J., Martin, J., Braithwaite, A., & Poulton, R. (2003, July 18). Influence of life stress on depression: Moderation by a polymorphism in the 5-HTT gene. *Science, 301,* 386–389.

Cassia, V. M., Kuefner, D., Westerlund, A., & Nelson, C. A. (2006). A behavioural and ERP investigation of 3-month-olds' face preferences. *Neuropsychologia, 44,* 2113–2125.

Cassia, V. M., Turati, C., & Simion, F. (2004). Can a nonspecific bias toward top-heavy patterns explain newborns' face preference? *Psychological Science, 15,* 379–383.

Cassidy, T. (2006). *Birth: The surprising history of how we are born.* New York: Atlantic Monthly Press.

Cattell, R. B. (1963). Theory of fluid and crystallized intelligence: A critical experiment. *Journal of Educational Psychology, 54,* 1–22.

Cavanaugh, J. C. (1996). Memory self-efficacy as a moderation of memory change. In F. Blanchard-Fields & T. M. Hess (Eds.), *Perspectives on cognitive change in adulthood and aging.* New York: McGraw-Hill.

Cavanaugh, J. C., Grady, J. G., & Perlmutter, M. (1983). Forgetting and use of memory aids in 20 to 70 year olds' everyday life. *International Journal of Aging and Human Development, 17,* 113–122.

Caylak, E. (2009). Neurobiological approaches on brains of children with dyslexia: Review, *Academic Radiology, 16,* 1003–1024.

CDC (2009a). Child health. Available at: http://www.cdc.gov/nchs/fastats/children.htm. Accessed: October 24, 2009.

CDC (2009b). Differences in Prevalence of Obesity Among Black, White, and Hispanic Adults—United States, 2006–2008. *MMWR Weekly, 58,* 740–748. Available at: http://www.cdc.gov/mmwr/preview/mmwrhtml/mm5827a2.htm. Accessed: October 15, 2009.

CDC (2009c). How much physical activity do children need? Available at: http://www.cdc.gov/physicalactivity/everyone/guidelines/children.html. Accessed: October 24, 2009.

CDC (2009d). Recommended Community Strategies and Measurements to Prevent Obesity in the United States. *MMW, 58* (No. RR-7), 1–32.

CDC (2009e). Youth Violence: National Statistics. Five Leading Causes of Deaths Among Persons Ages 10-24 Years, United States, 2005. Available at: http://www.cdc.gov/ViolencePrevention/youthviolence/stats_at-a_glance/lcd_10-24.html. Accessed: October 15, 2009.

CDC/NCHS (2008). Physical activity and strength training. *Health, United States,* Figure 8. Data from the National Health Interview Survey.

Ceci, S. J., & Williams, W. M. (1997). Schooling, intelligence, and income. *American Psychologist, 52,* 1051–1058.

Cecil-Karb R. & Grogan-Kaylor, A. (2009). Childhood body mass index in community context: neighborhood safety, television viewing, and growth trajectories of BMI. *Health & Social Work 34,* 169–177.

Celgene Corporation (2010). Proposed changes to approved Thalomid® package insert. Available at: http://www.accessdata.fda.gov/drugsatfda_docs/label/2006/021430lbl.pdf. Accessed: May 24, 2010.

Centers for Disease Control and Prevention (2006a). Improved national prevalence estimates for 18 selected major birth defects—United States, 1999–2001. *MMWR Weekly, 54*(51 & 52), 1301–1305.

Centers for Disease Control and Prevention (2006b). *Percentage of births attended by midwives in the United States.* Available at: www.cdc.gov/nchs/births.htm. Accessed: September 6, 2006.

Centers for Disease Control and Prevention (2007). *Possible health effects of radiation exposure on unborn babies.* Available at: www.bt.cdc.gov/radiation/prenatal.asp. Accessed: February 14, 2007.

Centers for Disease Control and Prevention (2008). Youth risk behavior surveillance—United States, 2007, surveillance summaries. *MMWR, 57* (No. SS-4).

Centers for Disease Control and Prevention (2009). *Fetal alcohol spectrum disorders.* Available at: www.cdc.gov/ncbddd/fasd/data.html. Accessed: September 24, 2009.

Centers for Disease Control and Prevention (2010). *Adverse Childhood Experiences Study.* Available at: www.cdc.gov/nccdphp/ace/prevalence.htm. Accessed: April 20, 2010.

Centers for Disease Control and Prevention, American Society for Reproductive Medicine, Society for Assisted Reproductive Technology (2008). *2006 Assisted reproductive technology success rates: National summary and fertility clinic reports.* Atlanta: U.S. Department of Health and Human Services, Centers for Disease Control and Prevention.

Cerminara, K. L. (2006). Theresa Marie Schiavo's long road to peace. *Death Studies, 30,* 101–112.

Cernoch, J. M., & Porter, R. H. (1985). Recognition of maternal axillary odors by infants. *Child Development, 56,* 1593–1598.

Cervera, T. C., Soler, M. J., Dasi, C., & Ruiz, J. C. (2009). Speech recognition and working memory capacity in young-elderly listeners: Effects of hearing sensitivity. *Canadian Journal of Experimental Psychology, 63,* 216–226.

Chakrabarti, S., & Fombonne, E. (2001). Pervasive developmental disorders in preschool children. *Journal of the American Medical Association, 285,* 3093–3099.

Chakrabarti, S., & Fombonne, E. (2005). Pervasive developmental disorders in preschool children: Confirmation of high prevalence. *American Journal of Psychiatry, 162,* 1133–1141.

Chall, J. S. (1967). *Learning to read: The great debate.* New York: McGraw-Hill.

Chambers, W. C. (2007). Oral sex: Varied behaviors and perceptions in a college population. *Journal of Sex Research, 44,* 28–42.

Champagne, F. A. & Mashoodh, R. (2009). Genes in context. Gene—environment interplay and the origins of individual differences in behavior. *Current Directions in Psychological Science, 18,* 127–131.

Chandler, M., Fritz, A. S., & Hala, S. (1989). Small-scale deceit: Deception as a marker of two-, three-, and four-year-olds' early theories of mind. *Child Development, 60,* 1263–1277.

Chandler, M. J., Sokol, B. W., & Wainryb, C. (2000). Beliefs about truth and beliefs about rightness. *Child Development, 71,* 91–97.

Chandler, S., & Field, P. A. (1997). Becoming a father: First-time fathers' experience of labor and delivery. *Journal of Nurse-Midwifery, 42* 17–24.

Chandra, A., Martino, S. C., Collins, R. L., Elliott, M. N., Berry, S. H., Kanouse, D. E., & Miu, A. (2008). Does watching sex on television predict teen pregnancy? Findings from a national longitudinal survey of youth. *Pediatrics, 122,* 1047–1054.

Chang, S., & Chen, K. (2008). Age at menarche of three-generation families in Taiwan. *Annals of Human Biology, 35,* 394–405.

Chao, R. K. (1994). Beyond parental control and authoritarian parenting style: Understanding Chinese parenting through the cultural notion of training. *Child Development, 65,* 1111–1119.

Chao, R. K. (2000). Cultural explanations for the role of parenting in the school success of Asian American children. In R. D. Taylor & M. C. Wang (Eds.), *Resilience across contexts: Family, work, culture, and community.* Mahwah, NJ: Erlbaum.

Chapman, L. L. (2000). Expectant fathers and labor epidurals. *American Journal of Maternity and Child Nursing, 25,* 133–138.

Chapman, M., & Lindenberger, U. (1988). Functions, operations, and décalage in the development of transitivity. *Developmental Psychology, 24,* 542–551.

Charles, S. T., & Carstensen, L. L. (2007). Emotion regulation and aging. In J. J. Gross, J. J. (Ed.), *Handbook of emotion regulation.* New York: Guilford.

Charles, S. T., Mather, M., & Carstensen, L. L. (2003). Aging and emotional memory: The forgettable nature of negative images for older adults. *Journal of Experimental Psychology: General, 132,* 310–324.

Charlton, R. A., Barrick, T. R., Markus, H. S., & Morris, R. G. (2009). Theory of mind associations with other cognitive functions and brain imaging in normal aging. *Psychology and Aging, 24,* 338–348.

Charman, T. (2000). Theory of mind and the early diagnosis of autism. In S. Baron-Cohen, H. Tager-Flusberg, & D. J. Cohen (Eds.), *Understanding other minds. Perspectives from developmental cognitive neuroscience* (2nd ed.). Oxford: Oxford University Press.

Charney, D. S., Reynolds, C. F., Lewis, L., Lebowitz, B. D., Sunderland, T., Alexopoulos, G. S. et al. (2003). Depression and Bipolar Support Alliance consensus statement on the unmet needs in diagnosis and treatment of mood disorders in late life. *Archives of General Psychiatry, 60,* 664–672.

Chatoor, I., & Ganiban, J., (2004). The diagnostic assessment and classification of feeding disorders. In R. DelCarmen-Wiggins & A. Carter (Eds.), *Handbook of infant, toddler, and preschool mental health assessment.* New York: Oxford University Press.

Chavous, T. M., Bernat, D. H., Schmeelk-Cone, K., Caldwell, C. H., Kohn-Wood, L., & Zimmerman, M. A. (2003). Racial identity and academic attainment among African American adolescents. *Child Development, 74,* 1076–1090.

Chen, A. (2007). Learning to map: Strategy discovery and strategy change in young children. *Developmental Psychology, 43,* 386–403.

Chen, C., & Stevenson, H. W. (1995). Motivation and mathematics achievement: A comparative study of Asian-American, Caucasian-American, and East Asian high school students. *Child Development, 66,* 1214–1234.

Chen, D. (1996). Parent–infant communication: Early intervention for very young children with visual impairment or hearing loss. *Infants and Young Children, 9,* 1–12.

Chen, E., Martin, A. D., & Matthews, K. A. (2006). Understanding health disparities: The role of race and socioeconomic status in children's health. *American Journal of Public Health, 96,* 702–708.

Chen, J. Q., & Gardner, H. (1997). Alternative assessment from a multiple intelligences theoretical perspective. In D. P. Flanagan, J. Genshaft, & P. L. Harrison (Eds.), *Contemporary intellectual assessment: Theories, tests, and issues.* New York: Guilford.

Chen, K., Reiman, E. M., Alexander, G. E., Caselli, R. J., Gerkin, R., Bandy, D., Domb, A., Osborne, D., Fox, N., Crum, W. R., Saunders, A. M., & Hardy, J. (2007). Correlations between apolipoprotein E 4 gene dose and whole brain atrophy rates. *American Journal of Psychiatry, 164,* 916–921.

Chen, L. C., Metcalfe, J. S., Jeka, J. J., & Clark, J. E. (2007). Two steps forward and one back: Learning to walk affects infants' sitting posture. *Infant Behavioral Development, 30,* 16–25.

Chen, X., Cen, G., Li, D., & He, Y. (2005). Social functioning and adjustment in Chinese children: The imprint of historical time. *Child Development, 76,* 182–195.

Chen, X., Chung, J., & Hisao, C. (2009). Peer interactions and relationships from a cross-cultural perspective. In K. H. Rubin, W. M. Bukowski, & B. Laursen (Eds.), *Handbook of peer interactions, relationships, and groups.* New York: Guilford.

Chen, X., DeSouza, A. T., Chen, H., & Wang, L. (2006). Reticent behavior and experiences in peer interactions in Chinese and Canadian children. *Developmental Psychology, 42,* 656–665.

Chen, X., Rubin, K. H., & Sun, Y. (1992). Social reputation in Chinese and Canadian children: A cross-cultural study. *Child Development, 63,* 1336–1343.

Chen, X-K., Wen, S. W., Krewski, D., Fleming, N., Yang, O., & Walker, M. C. (2008). Paternal age and adverse birth outcomes: Teenager or 40+, who is at risk? *Human Reproduction, 23,* 1290–1296.

Cheng, A. K., Rubin, H. R., Powe, N. R., Mellon, M. K., Francis, H. W., & Niparko, J. K. (2000). Cost–utility analysis of the cochlear implant in children. *Journal of the American Medical Association, 284,* 850–856.

Cherkas, L. F., Aviv, A., Valdes, A. M., Hunkin, J. L., Gardner, J. P., Surdulescu, G. L., Kimura, M., & Spector, T. D. (2006). The effects of social status on biological aging as measured by white-blood-cell telomere length. *Aging Cell, 5,* 361–365.

Cherkas, L. F., Hunkin, J. L., Kato, B. S., Richards, J. B., Gardner, J. P., Surdulescu, G. L., Kimura, M., Lu, X., Spector, T. D., & Aviv, A. (2008). The association between physical activity in leisure time and leukocyte telomere length. *Archives of Internal Medicine, 168,* 154–158.

Cherlin, A. J. (2009). *The marriage-go-round. The state of marriage and the family in America today.* New York: Knopf Doubleday Publishing Group.

Cherlin, A. J., & Furstenberg, F. F., Jr. (1986). *The new American grandparent: A place in the family, a life apart.* New York: Basic Books.

Cherney, I. D. (2005). Children's and adults' recall of sex-stereotyped toy pictures: Effects of presentation and memory task. *Infant and Child Development, 14,* 11–27.

Cherney, I. D., Harper, H. J., & Winter, J. A. (2006). Nouveaux jouets: Ce que les enfants identifient comme 'jouets de garçons' et 'jouets de filles.' *Enfance, 58,* 266–282.

Cherney, I. S., & London, K. (2006). Gender-linked differences in the toys, television shows, computer games, and outdoor activities of 5- to 13-year-old children. *Sex Roles, 54,* 717–726.

Cherry, K. E., & LeCompte, D. C. (1999). Age and individual differences influence prospective memory. *Psychology and Aging, 14,* 60–76.

Cherry, K. E., & Morton, M. R. (1989). Drug sensitivity in older adults: The role of physiologic and pharmacokinetic factors. *International Journal of Aging and Human Development, 28,* 159–174.

Cherry, K. E., & Smith, A. D. (1998). Normal memory aging. In M. Hersen & V. B. Van Hasselt (Eds.), *Handbook of clinical geropsychology* (pp. 87–110). New York: Plenum.

Chesley, N., & Poppie, K. (2009). Assisting parents and in-laws: Gender, type of assistance, and couples' employment. *Journal of Marriage and Family, 71,* 247–262.

Chess, S., & Thomas, A. (1984). *Origins and evolution of behavior disorders: From infancy to early adult life.* New York: Brunner/Mazel.

Chess, S., & Thomas, A. (1999). *Goodness of fit: Clinical applications from infancy through adult life.* Ann Arbor, MI: Edwards Brothers.

Chi, M. T. H. (1978). Knowledge structures and memory development. In R. Siegler (Ed.), *Children's thinking: What develops?* Hillsdale, NJ: Erlbaum.

Chia, E. M., Wang, J. J., Rochtchina, E., Smith, W., Cumming, R. R., & Mitchell, P. (2004). Impact of bilateral visual impairment on health-related quality of life: The Blue Mountains Eye Study. *Investigations in Ophthalmology & Visual Science, 45,* 71–76.

Child Trends Databank (undat ed.). *Attitudes toward spanking.* Available at www.childtrendsdatabank .org/indicators/51AttitudesTowardsSpanking.cfm. Accessed: May 31, 2007.

Childbirth Connection (2010). Cesarean Section. Available at: www.childbirthconnection.org/article .asp?ck=10456&ClickedLink=274&area=27. Accessed: May 25, 2010.

Chimpanzee Sequencing and Analysis Consortium (2005). Initial sequence of the chimpanzee genome and comparison with the human genome. *Nature, 437,* 69–87.

Chisholm, J. S., Quinlivan, J. A., Petersen, R. W., & Coall, D. A. (2005). Early stress predicts age at menarche and first birth, adult attachment, and expected lifespan. *Human Nature, 16,* 233–265.

Chiu, S., & Alexander, P. A. (2000). The motivational function of preschoolers' private speech. *Discourse Processes, 30,* 133–152.

Cho, D., & Gardner, A. (2007, April 21). Virginia Tech killer: An isolated boy in a world of strangers. *The Washington Post,* A1, A8.

Cho, G. J., Park, H. T., Shin, J. H., Hur, J. Y., Kim, Y.T., Kim, S. H., Lee, K. W., & Kim, T. (2009,

June 7). Age at menarche in a Korean population: secular trends and influencing factors. *European Journal of Pediatrics*. Epub ahead of print.

Chochinov, H. M., & Schwartz., L. (2002). Depression and the will to live in the psychological landscape of terminally ill patients. In K. Foley, & H. Hendin (Eds.), *The case against assisted suicide: For the right to end-of-life care*. Baltimore: The Johns Hopkins Press.

Choi, J., & Silverman, I. (2003). Processes underlying sex differences in route-learning strategies in children and adolescents. *Personality and Individual Differences, 34*, 1153–1166.

Chomsky, N. (1965). *Aspects of the theory of syntax*. Cambridge: MIT Press.

Chomsky, N. (1968). *Language and mind*. New York: Harcourt Brace & World.

Chomsky, N. (1975). *Reflections on language*. New York: Pantheon Books.

Chomsky, N. (1995). *The minimalist program*. Cambridge: MIT Press.

Chomsky, N. (2000). *New horizons in the study of language and mind*. Cambridge: Cambridge University Press.

Christensen, M., Emde, R., & Fleming, C. (2004). Cultural perspectives for assessing infants and young children. In R. DelCarmen-Wiggins & A. Carter (Eds.), *Handbook of infant, toddler, and preschool mental health assessment*. New York: Oxford University Press.

Christiansen, S. L., & Palkovitz, R. (1998). Exploring Erikson's psychosocial theory of development: Generativity and its relationship to parental identity, intimacy, and involvement with others. *Journal of Men's Studies, 7*, 133–156.

Christianson, A., Howson, C. P., & Modell, B. (2006). *March of Dimes Global report on birth defects: The hidden toll of dying and disabled children*. White Plains, NY: March of Dimes Birth Defects Foundation.

Christie, F. (2002). The development of abstraction in adolescence in subject English. In M. J. Schleppegrell & Colombi, M. C. (Eds.), *Developing advanced literacy in first and second languages: Meaning with power*, 45–66. Mahwah, NJ: Lawrence Erlbaum Associates.

Chronis, A. M., Jones, H. A., & Raggi, V. L. (2006). Evidence-based psychosocial treatments for children and adolescents with attention-deficit/hyperactivity disorder. *Clinical Psychology Review, 26*, 486–502.

Chumlea, W. C., Schubert, C. M., Roche, A. F., Kulin, H. E., Lee, P. A., Himes, J. H., et al. (2003). Age at menarche and racial comparisons in US girls. *Pediatrics, 111*, 110–113.

Chung, G. H., Flook, L., & Fuligni, A. J. (2009). Daily family conflict and emotional distress among adolescents from Latin American, Asian, and European backgrounds. *Developmental Psychology, 45*, 1406–1415.

Chung, J. H., Des Roches, C. M., Meunier, J., & Eavey, R. D. (2005). Evaluation of noise-induced hearing loss in young people using a web-based survey technique. *Pediatrics, 115*, 861–867.

Church, J. A., Coalson, R. S., Lugar, H. M., Petersen, S. E., & Schlaggar, B. L. (2008). A developmental fMRI study of reading and repetition reveals changes in phonological and visual mechanisms over age. *Cerebral Cortex, 18*, 2054–2065.

Chyi, L. J., Lee, H. C., Hintz, S. R., Gould, J. B., Sutcliffe, T. (2008). School outcomes of late preterm infants: Special needs and challenges for infants born at 32 to 36 weeks gestation. Journal of Pediatrics, 153, 25–31.

CIA (2009). *The world fact book*. Available at: www.cia.gov/library/publications/the-world-factbook/rankorder/2091rank.html. Accessed: October 1, 2009.

Cicchetti, D. (2006). Development and psychopathology. In D. Cicchetti & D. J. Cohen (Eds.).

Developmental psychopathology: Vol. 1. Theory and method (2nd ed.). Hoboken, NJ: Wiley.

Cicchetti, D., & Rogosch, F. A. (2002). A developmental psychopathology perspective on adolescence. *Journal of Consulting and Clinical Psychology, 70*, 6–20.

Cicchetti, D., & Toth, S. L. (2009). The past achievements and future promises of developmental psychopathology: The coming of age of a discipline. *Journal of Child Psychology and Psychiatry, 50*, 16–25.

Cicchetti, D., & Valentino, K. (2006). An ecological–transactional perspective on child maltreatment: Failure of the average expectable environment and its influence on child development. In D. Cicchetti & D. J. Cohen (Eds.), *Developmental psychopathology: Vol. 3. Risk, disorder, and adaptation* (2nd ed.). Hoboken, NJ: Wiley.

Cicirelli, V. G. (1982). Sibling influence throughout the life span. In M. E. Lamb & B. Sutton-Smith (Eds.), *Sibling relationships: Their nature and significance across the life-span*. Hillsdale, NJ: Erlbaum.

Cicirelli, V. G. (1991). Sibling relationships in adulthood. *Marriage and Family Review, 16*, 291–310.

Cicirelli, V. G. (1993). Attachment and obligation as daughters' motives for caregiving behavior and subsequent effect on subjective burden. *Psychology and Aging, 8*, 144–155.

Cicirelli, V. G. (1995). *Sibling relationships across the life span*. New York: Plenum.

Cillessen, A. H., Van IJzendoorn, H. W., Van Lieshout, C. F., & Hartup, W. W. (1992). Heterogeneity among peer-rejected boys: Subtypes and stabilities. *Child Development, 63*, 893–905.

Cillessen, A. H. N. (2009). Sociometric methods. In K. H. Rubin, W. M. Bukowski, & B. Laursen (Eds.), *Handbook of peer interactions, relationships, and groups*. New York: Guilford.

Cipriani, N. (2002, November 1). What kids should know when. *Parenting, 16*, 150.

Clark, D. O., & Maddox, G. L. (1992). Racial and social correlates of age-related changes in functioning. *Journal of Gerontology: Social Sciences, 47*, S222–S232.

Clark, H. H., & Clark, E. V. (1977). *Psychology and language: An introduction to psycholinguistics*. New York: Harcourt Brace Jovanovich.

Clark, M. A. & Fox, M. K. (2009). National quality of the diets of U.S. public school children and the role of the school meal programs. *Journal of the American Dietetic Association, 109*, S44–56.

Clarke-Stewart, A., & Allhusen, V. D. (2005). *What we know about child care*. Cambridge, MA: Harvard University Press.

Clarke-Stewart, K. A. (1998). Reading with children. *Journal of Applied Developmental Psychology, 19*, 1–14.

Clarke-Stewart, K. A., Goossens, F. A., & Allhusen, V. D. (2001). Measuring infant-mother attachment: Is the strange situation enough? *Social Development, 10*, 143–169.

Clarkson, M. G., & Berg, W. K. (1983). Cardiac orienting and vowel discrimination in newborns: Crucial stimulation parameters. *Child Development, 54*, 162–171.

Claxton, A. F., Pannells, T. C., & Rhoads, P. A. (2005). Developmental trends in the creativity of school-age children. *Creativity Research Journal, 17*, 327–335.

Cleary-Goldman, J., Malone, F. D., Vidaver, J., Ball, R. H., Nyberg, D. A., Comstock, C. H., Saade, G. R., Eddleman, K. A., Klugman, S., Dugoff, L., Timor-Tritsch, E. I., Craigo, S. D., Carr. S. R., Wolfe, H. M., Bianchi, D. W., & D'Alton, M. for the First and Second Trimester Evaluation of Risk (FASTER) Trial Research Consortium. (2005). Impact of maternal age on obstetric outcome. *Obstetrics & Gynecology, 105*, 983–990.

Cleckner-Smith, C. S., Doughty, A. S., & Grossman, J. A. (1998). Premenstrual symptoms: Prevalence and severity in an adolescent sample. *Journal of Adolescent Health, 22*, 403–408.

Cleveland, E. S. & Reese, E. (2008). Children remember early childhood: Long-term recall across the offset of childhood amnesia. *Applied Cognitive Psychology, 22*, 127–142.

Cleveland, H. H., Jacobson, K. C., Lipinski, J. J., & Rowe, D. C. (2000). Genetic and shared environmental contributions to the relationship between the home environment and child and adolescent achievement. *Intelligence, 28*, 69–86.

Coats, P. B., & Overman, S. J. (1992). Childhood play experiences of women in traditional and nontraditional professions. *Sex Roles, 26*, 261–271.

Cobb, R. W., & Coughlin, J. F. (1998). Are elderly drivers a road hazard? Problem definition and political impact. *Journal of Aging Studies, 12*, 411–420.

Codipietro, L., Ceccarelli, M., & Ponzone, A. (2008). Breastfeeding or oral sucrose solution in term neonates receiving heel lance: A randomized, controlled trial. *Pediatrics, 122*, 716–721.

Coe, C. L., & Lubach, G. R. (2008). Fetal programming: Prenatal origins of health and illness. *Current Directions in Psychological Science, 17*, 36–41.

Cohen, B. B., Friedman, D. J., Zhang, A., Trudeau, E. B., Walker, D. K., Anderka, M., et al. (1999). Impact of multiple births on low birth weight: Massachusetts, 1989–1996. *Morbidity & Mortality Weekly Report, 48*, 289–293.

Cohen, G. D. (2005). *The mature mind: The positive power of the aging brain*. New York: Basic Books.

Cohen, L. B., & Cashon, C. H. (2006). Infant cognition. In D. Kuhn & R. Siegler (Vol. Eds.), *Handbook of child psychology: Cognition, perception, and language*. Hoboken, NJ: Wiley.

Cohen, M. (1996). Preschoolers' practical thinking and problem solving: The acquisition of an optimal solution strategy. *Cognitive Development, 11*, 357–373.

Cohen, S., & Janicki-Deverts, D. (2009). Can we improve our physical health by altering our social networks? *Perspectives on Psychological Science, 4*, 375–378.

Coie, J. D. (2004). The impact of negative social experiences on the development of antisocial behavior. In J. B. Kupersmidt & K. A. Dodge (Eds.), *Children's peer relations: From development to intervention*. Washington, DC: American Psychological Association.

Coie, J. D., Dodge, K. A., & Coppotelli, H. (1982). Dimensions and types of social status: A cross-age perspective. *Developmental Psychology, 18*, 557–570.

Coie, J. D., Dodge, K. A., & Kupersmidt, J. B. (1990). Peer group behavior and social status. In S. R. Asher & J. D. Coie (Eds.), *Peer rejection in childhood*. Cambridge, England: Cambridge University Press.

Coie, J. D., Dodge, K. A., Terry, R., & Wright, V. (1991). The role of aggression in peer relations: An analysis of aggression episodes in boys' play groups. *Child Development, 62*, 812–826.

Colapinto, J. (1997, December 11). The true story of John Joan. *Rolling Stone*, 54–97.

Colapinto, J. (2000). *As nature made him: The boy who was raised as a girl*. New York: Harper Collins.

Colapinto, J. (2004, June 3). What were the real reasons behind David Reimer's suicide? Available at: www.slate.com/id/2101678. Accessed: August 25, 2007.

Colburn, D. (2000, October 3). Wired for sound. *The Washington Post—Health*, 13–18.

Colby, A., & Kohlberg, L. (1987). *The measurement of moral judgment. Vol. 1: Theoretical foundations and research validation*. Cambridge, England: Cambridge University Press.

Colby, A., Kohlberg, L., Gibbs, J., & Lieberman, M. (1983). A longitudinal study of moral judgment. *Monographs of the Society for Research in Child Development*, 48 (1–2, Serial No. 200).

Colcombe, S. J., Kramer, A. F., Erickson, K. I., Scalf, P., McAuley, E., Cohen, N. J., Webb, A., Jerome, G. J., Marquez, D. X., & Elavsky, S. (2004). Cardiovascular fitness, cortical plasticity, and aging. *Proceedings of the National Academy of Sciences, 101*, 3316–3321.

Colder, C. R., Chassin, L., Lee, M. R., & Villatta, I. K. (2010). Developmental perspectives: Affect and adolescent substance use. In J. D. Kassel (Ed.), *Substance abuse and emotion*. Washington, DC: American Psychological Association.

Cole, D. A., Maxwell, S. E., Martin, J. M., Peeke, L. G., Seroczynski, A. D., Tram, J. M., et al. (2001). The development of multiple domains of child and adolescent self-concept: A cohort sequential longitudinal design. *Child Development, 72*, 1723–1746.

Cole, M. G. (2004). Delirium in elderly patients. *American Journal of Geriatric Psychiatry, 12*, 7–21.

Cole, P. M., Barrett, K. C., & Zahn-Waxler, C. (1992). Emotion displays in two-year-olds during mishaps. *Child Development, 63*, 314–324.

Cole, P. M., Martin, S. E., & Dennis, T. A. (2004). Emotion regulation as a scientific construct: Methodological challenges and directions for child development research. *Child Development, 75*, 317–333.

Cole, P. M., Michel, M. K., & Teti, L. O. (1994). The development of emotion regulation and dysregulation: A clinical perspective. In N. Fox (Ed.), *The development of emotion regulation: Biological and behavioral considerations. Monographs of the Society for Research in Child Development, 59* (Nos. 2–3, Serial No. 240).

Coleman, J. (1961). *The adolescent society*. New York: Free Press.

Coles, L. S. (2004). Demography of human supercentenarians. *Journal of Gerontology: Biological Sciences, 59A*, 579–586.

Colin, V. (1996). *Human attachment*. New York: McGraw-Hill.

Colley, A., Griffiths, D., Hugh, M., Landers, K., & Jaggli, N. (1996). Childhood play and adolescent leisure preferences: Associations with gender typing and the presence of siblings. *Sex Roles, 35*, 233–245.

Collins, W. A. (2003). More than myth: The developmental significance of romantic relationships during adolescence. *Journal of Research on Adolescence, 13*, 1–24.

Collins, W. A., & Laursen, B. (2004). Changing relationships, changing youth: Interpersonal contexts of adolescent development. *Journal of Early Adolescence, 24*, 55–62.

Collins, W. A., Maccoby, E. E., Steinberg, L., Hetherington, E. M., & Bornstein, M. H. (2000). Contemporary research on parenting. The case for nature and nurture. *American Psychologist, 55*, 218–232.

Collins, W. A., & Madsen, S. D. (2006). Personal relationships in adolescence and early adulthood. In A. L. Vangelisti & D. Perlman (Eds.), *The Cambridge handbook of personal relationships*. New York: Cambridge University Press.

Colombo, J. (2001). The development of visual attention in infancy. *Annual Review of Psychology, 52*, 337–367.

Colombo, J., Shaddy, D. J., BLaga, O. M., Anderson, C. J., & Kannass, K. N. (2009). High cognitive ability in infancy and early childhood. In F. D. Horowitz, R. F. Subotnik, & D. J. Matthews (Eds.), *The development of giftedness and talent across the life span*. Washington, DC: American Psychological Association.

Colombo, J. (1993). *Infant cognition: Predicting later intellectual functioning*. Newbury Park, CA: Sage.

Colwell, M. J., & Lindsey, E. W. (2005). Preschool children's pretend and physical play and sex of play partner: Connections to peer competence. *Sex Roles, 52*, 497–509.

Comer, J. P. (1997). *Waiting for a miracle: Why schools can't solve our problems—and how we can*. New York: Plume.

Committee on Adolescence (1996). Adolescent suicide (Group for the Advancement of Psychiatry, Report No. 140). Washington, DC: American Psychiatric Press.

Committee on Environmental Health (2009). The built environment: Designing communities to promote physical activity in children. *Pediatrics, 123*, 1591–1598.

Commons, M. L., & Richards, F. A. (2003). Four postformal stages. In J. Demick & C. Andreoletti (Eds.), *Handbook of adult development* (pp. 199–220). New York: Plenum.

Commons, M. L., & Ross, S. N. (2008). What postformal thought is, and why it matters. *World Futures, 64*, 321–329.

Compas, B. E., Connor-Smith, J. K., Saltzman, H., Thomsen, A. H., & Wadsworth, M. E. (2001). Coping with stress during childhood and adolescence: Problems, progress, and potential in theory and research. *Psychological Bulletin, 127*, 87–127.

Compian, L., Gowen, L. K., & Hayward, C. (2004). Peripubertal girls' romantic and platonic involvement with boys: Associations with body image and depression symptoms. *Journal of Research on Adolescence, 14*, 23–47.

Condon, E. M., Crepinsek, M. K., & Fox, M. K. (2009). School meals: Types of foods offered to and consumed by children at lunch and breakfast. *Journal of the American Dietetic Association, 109*, S67–78.

Condon, J. T. (1993). The premenstrual syndrome: A twin study. *British Journal of Psychiatry, 162*, 481–486.

Condon, J. T., Boyce, P., & Corkindale, C. J. (2004). The first-time fathers study: A prospective study of the mental health and wellbeing of men during the transition to parenthood. *Australia Psychiatry, 38*, 56–64.

Condry, J., & Condry, S. (1976). Sex differences: A study in the eye of the beholder. *Child Development, 47*, 812–819.

Conduct Problems Prevention Research Group (2007). Fast Track randomized controlled trial to prevent externalizing psychiatric disorders: Findings from grades 3 to 9. *Journal of the American Academy of Child and Adolescent Psychiatry, 46*, 1250–1262.

Conger, R. D., Belsky, J., & Capaldi, D. M. (2009). The intergenerational transmission of parenting: Closing comments for the special section. *Developmental Psychology, 45*, 1276–1283.

Conger, R. D., Conger, K. J., Elder, G. H., Jr., Lorenz, F. O., Simons, R. L., & Whitbeck, L. B. (1992). A family process model of economic hardship and adjustment of early adolescent boys. *Child Development, 63*, 526–541.

Conger, R. D., & Dogan, S. J. (2007). Social class and socialization in families. In J. E. Grusec & P. D. Hastings (Eds.), *Handbook of socialization theory and research*. New York: Guilford.

Conger, R. D., & Donnellan, M. B. (2007). An interactionist perspective on the socioeconomic context of human development. *Annual Review of Psychology, 58*, 175–199.

Conger, R. D., Neppl, T., Kim, K. J., & Scaramella, L. (2003). Angry and aggressive behavior across three generations: A prospective, longitudinal study of parents and children. *Journal of Abnormal Child Psychology, 31*, 143–160.

Conger, R. D., Patterson, G. R., & Ge, X. (1995). It takes two to replicate: A mediational model for the impact of parents' stress on adolescent adjustment. *Child Development, 66*, 80–97.

Conger, R. D., Wallace, L. E., Sun, Y., Simons, R. L., McLoyd, V. C., & Brody, G. H. (2002). Economic pressure in African American families: A replication and extension of the family stress model. *Developmental Psychology, 38*, 179–193.

Congressional Budget Office (2008, April 17). Growing disparities in life expectancy. *Economic and Budget Issue Brief*, pp. 1–6.

Conklin, H. M., Luciana, M., Hooper, C. J., & Yarger, R. S. (2007). Working memory performance in typically developing children and adolescents: Behavioral evidence of protracted frontal lobe development. *Developmental Neuropsychology, 31*, 103–128.

Conley, C. S., & Rudolph, K. D. (2009). The emerging sex difference in adolescent depression: Interacting contributions of puberty and peer stress. *Development and Psychopathology, 21*, 593–620.

Connell, A. M., & Goodman, S. H. (2002). The association between psychopathology in fathers versus mothers and children's internalizing and externalizing behavior problems: A meta-analysis. *Psychological Bulletin, 128*, 746–773.

Conner, K. A. (2000). *Continuing to care. Older Americans and their families*. New York: Falmer Press.

Connidis, I. A. (2010). *Family ties and aging* (2nd ed.). Thousand Oaks, CA: Pine Forge Press.

Connolly, J. A., & Doyle, A. B. (1984). Relation of social fantasy play to social competence in preschoolers. *Developmental Psychology, 20*, 797–806.

Connor, S. R. (2000). Hospice care and the older person. In A. Tomer (Ed.), *Death attitudes and the older adult: Theories, concepts, and applications*. Philadelphia, PA: Brunner-Routledge.

Conrade, G., & Ho, R. (2001). Differential parenting styles for fathers and mothers: Differential treatment for sons and daughters. *Australian Journal of Psychology, 53*, 29–35.

Constantino, J. N., & Todd, R. D. (2003). Autistic traits in the general population: A twin study. *Archives of General Psychiatry, 60*, 524–530.

Conway, M. A., Cohen, G., & Stanhope, N. (2006). Very long-term memory for knowledge acquired at school and university. *Applied Cognitive Psychology, 6*, 467–482.

Coohey, C., & Braun, N. (1997). Toward an integrated framework for understanding child physical abuse. *Child Abuse and Neglect, 21*, 1081–1094.

Cook, A. S., & Dworkin, D. S. (1992). *Helping the bereaved. Therapeutic interventions for children, adolescents, and adults*. New York: Basic Books.

Cook, B. G., & Semmel, M. I. (1999). Peer acceptance of included students with disabilities as a function of severity of disability and classroom composition. *Journal of Special Education, 33*, 50–61.

Cooke, T. J., Boyle, P., Couch, K., & Feijten, P. (2009). A longitudinal analysis of family migration and the gender gap in earnings in the United States and Great Britain. *Demography, 46*, 147–167.

Cooney, T. M., & Smith, L. A. (1996). Young adults' relations with grandparents following recent parental divorce. *Journal of Gerontology: Social Sciences, 51B*, S91–S95.

Coontz, S. (2000). Historical perspectives on family diversity. In D. H. Demo, K. R. Allen, & M. A. Fine (Eds.), *Handbook of family diversity*. New York: Oxford University Press.

Cooper, M. L. (2002). Alcohol use and risky sexual behavior among college students and youth: Evaluating the evidence. *Journal of Studies on Alcohol, 14*(Suppl.), 101–117.

Cooper, M. L. (2010). Toward a person x situation model of sexual risk-taking behaviors: Illuminating the conditional effects of traits across sexual situations and relationship contexts. *Journal of Personality and Social Psychology, 98*, 319–341.

Cooper, P. J., & Murray, L. (1998). Postnatal depression. *British Medical Journal, 316,* 1884–1886.

Cooper, R. P., Abraham, J., Berman, S., & Staska, M. (1997). The development of infants' preference for motherese. *Infant Behavior and Development, 20,* 477–488.

Coopersmith, S. (1967). *The antecedents of self-esteem.* San Francisco: W. H. Freeman.

Coplan, R. J., & Abreau, K. A. (2009). Peer interactions and play in early childhood. In K. H. Rubin, W. M. Bukowski, & B. Laursen (Eds.), *Handbook of peer interactions, relationships, and groups.* New York: Guilford.

Cornelius, S. W., & Caspi, A. (1987). Everyday problem solving in adulthood and old age. *Psychology and Aging, 2,* 144–153.

Cornell, D., Delcourt, M., Goldberg, M., & Bland, L. (1992). Characteristics of elementary students entering gifted programs: The Learning Outcomes Project at the University of Virginia. *Journal for the Education of the Gifted, 15,* 309–331.

Corr, C. A. (1995). Entering into adolescent understanding of death. In E. A. Grollman (Ed.), *Bereaved children and teens.* Boston: Beacon Press.

Corr, C. A., & Corr, D. M. (1992). Children's hospice care. *Death Studies, 16,* 431–449.

Correa-Chavez, M., & Rogoff, B. (2009). Children's attention to interactions directed to others: Guatemalan Mayan and European American patterns. *Developmental Psychology, 45,* 630–641.

Corwin, J., Loury, M., & Gilbert, A. N. (1995). Workplace, age, and sex as mediators of olfactory function: Data from the National Geographic Smell Survey. *Journals of Gerontology Series B: Psychological Sciences and Social Sciences, 50,* 179–186.

Costa, P. T., Jr., & McCrae, R. R. (1992). Trait psychology comes of age. In T. B. Sonderegger (Ed.), *Nebraska symposium on motivation: Vol 39. Psychology and aging.* Lincoln, NE: University of Nebraska Press.

Costello, E. J., Foley, D. L., & Angold, A. (2006). 10-year research update review: The epidemiology of child and adolescent psychiatric disorders: II. Developmental epidemiology. *Journal of the American Academy of Child and Adolescent Psychiatry, 45,* 8–25.

Costello, E. J., Mustillo, S., Erkanli, A., Keeler, G., & Angold, A. (2003). Prevalence and development of psychiatric disorders in childhood and adolescence. *Archives of General Psychiatry, 60,* 837–844.

Cota-Robles, S. (2003, April). *Traditional Mexican cultural values and the reduced risk for delinquency: Acculturation, familism and parent–adolescent process.* Poster presented at the biennial meeting of the Society for Research in Child Development, Tampa, FL.

Cote, J. E., & Levine, C. (1988). A critical examination of the ego identity status paradigm. *Developmental Review, 8,* 147–184.

Courage, M. L., & Cowan, N. (Eds.) (2009). *The development of memory in infancy and childhood.* New York, NY: Psychology Press.

Courage, M. L., Reynolds, G. D., & Richards, J. E. (2006). Infants' attention to patterned stimuli: Developmental change from 3 to 12 months of age. *Child Development, 77,* 680–695.

Courage, M. L., & Setliff, A. E. (2009). Debating the impact of television and video material on very young children: Attention, learning, and the developing brain. *Child Development Perspectives, 3,* 72–78.

Courchesne, E., Carper, R., & Akshoomoff, N. (2003). Evidence of brain overgrowth in the first year of life in autism. *Journal of the American Medical Association, 290,* 337–344.

Courchesne E., Chisum, H. J., Townsend, J., Cowles, A., Covington, J., Egaas, B., et al. (2000). Normal brain development and aging: Quantitative analysis at in vivo MR imaging in healthy volunteers. *Radiology, 216,* 672–682.

Covington, M. V. (1998). *The will to learn.* New York: Cambridge University Press.

Covington, M. V. (2000). Goal theory, motivation, and school achievement: An integrative review. *Annual Review of Psychology, 51,* 171–200.

Cowan, C. P., & Cowan, P. A. (2000). *When partners become parents: The big life change for couples.* Mahwah, NJ: Erlbaum.

Cowan, N., & Alloway, T. (2009). Development of working memory in childhood. In M. L. Courage & N. Cowan (Eds.), *The development of memory in infancy and childhood* (pp. 303-342). New York, NY: Psychology Press.

Cowan, N., Morey, C. C., AuBuchon, A. M., Zwilling, C. E., & Gilchrist, A. L. (2010). Seven-year-olds allocate attention like adults unless working memory is overloaded. *Developmental Science, 13,* 120–133.

Cowan, P. A., & Cowan, C. P. (2006). Developmental psychopathology from family systems and family risk factors perspectives: Implications for family research, practice, and policy. In D. Cicchetti & D. J. Cohen (Eds.), *Developmental psychopathology: Vol. 1. Theory and method* (2nd ed.). Hoboken, NJ: Wiley.

Cowan, P. A., Cowan, C. P., Pruett, M. K., Pruett, K., & Wong, J. J. (2009). Promoting fathers' engagement with children: Preventive interventions for low-income families. *Journal of Marriage and Family, 71,* 663–679.

Cox, M. J., Owen, M. T., Henderson, V. K., & Margand, N. A. (1992). Prediction of infant-father and infant-mother attachment. *Developmental Psychology, 28,* 474–483.

Cox, M. J., Paley, B., Burchinal, M., & Payne, C. C. (1999). Marital perceptions and interactions across the transition to parenthood. *Journal of Marriage and the Family, 61,* 611–625.

Cox, T. H., & Harquail, C. V. (1991). Career paths and career success in the early career stages of male and female MBAs. *Journal of Vocational Behavior, 39,* 54–75.

Coyne, J. C., & Whiffen, V. E. (1995). Issues in personality as diathesis for depression: The case of sociotropy dependency and autonomy self-criticism. *Psychological Bulletin, 118,* 358–378.

Crago, M. B., Allen, S. E., & Hough-Eyamir, W. P. (1997). Exploring innateness through cultural and linguistic variation. In M. Gopnik (Ed.), *The inheritance and innateness of grammars* (pp. 70–90). New York: Oxford University Press.

Crary, D. (2008, December 1). Survey finds growing deceit among teens. *The Washington Post,* A6.

Crawford, M., & Popp, D. (2003). Sexual double standards: A review and methodological critique of two decades of research, *The Journal of Sex Research, 40,* 13–26.

Creasey, G., & Jarvis, P. (2009). Attachment and marriage. In M. C. Smith (Ed.) & N. DeFrates-Densch (Asst. Ed.), *Handbook of research on adult learning and development.* New York: Routledge.

Creasey, G. L. (2006). *Research methods in life span development.* Boston, MA: Pearson Education.

Crepinsek, M. K., Gordon, A. R., McKinney, P. M., Condon, E. M., & Wilson, A. (2009). Meals offered and served in U.S. public schools: Do they meet nutrient standards? *Journal of the American Dietetic Association, 109,* S31–43.

Creusere, M. A. (1999). Theories of adults' understanding and use of irony and sarcasm: Applications to and evidence from research with children. *Developmental Review, 19,* 213–262.

Crews, F. (1996). The verdict on Freud (Review of *Freud evaluated: The completed arc*). *Psychological Science, 7,* 63–68.

Crick, N. R., & Bigbee, M. (1998). Relational and overt forms of peer victimization: A multiinformant approach. *Journal of Consulting and Clinical Psychology, 66,* 337–347.

Crick, N. R., & Dodge, K. A. (1994). A review and reformulation of social information-processing mechanisms in children's social adjustment. *Psychological Bulletin, 115,* 74–101.

Crijnen, A. A. M., Achenbach, T. M., & Verhulst, F. C. (1997). Comparisons of problems reported by parents of children in 12 cultures: Total problems, externalizing, and internalizing. *Journal of the American Academy of Child and Adolescent Psychiatry, 36,* 1269–1277.

Cristofalo, V. J. (1996). Ten years later: What have we learned about human aging from studies of cell cultures? *Gerontologist, 36,* 737–741.

Critchley, C. R., & Sanson, A. V. (2006). Is parent disciplinary behavior enduring or situational? A multilevel modeling investigation of individual and contextual influences on power assertive and inductive reasoning behaviors. *Journal of Applied Developmental Psychology, 27,* 370–388.

Crockenberg, S., & Leerkes, E. (2003). Infant negative emotionality, caregiving, and family relationships. In A. C. Crouter & A. Booth (Eds.), *Children's influence on family dynamics. The neglected side of family relationships.* Mahwah, NJ: Erlbaum.

Crooks, R. L., & Baur, K. (2011). *Our sexuality* (11th ed.). Belmont, CA: Cengage Learning.

Cross, S. E. (2000). What does it mean to "know thyself" in the United States and Japan? The cultural construction of the self. In T. J. Owens (Ed.), *Self and identity through the life course in cross-cultural perspective.* Stamford, CT: JAI Press.

Crouch, J. L., & Behl, L. E. (2001). Relationships among parental beliefs in corporal punishment, reported stress, and physical child abuse potential. *Child Abuse and Neglect, 25,* 413–419.

Crouter, A. C. (2006). Mothers and fathers at work: Implications for families and children. In A. Clarke-Stewart & J. Dunn (Eds.), *Families count: Effects on child and adolescent development.* New York: Cambridge University Press.

Crouter, A. C., & Booth, A. (Eds.) (2003). *Children's influence on family dynamics. The neglected side of family relationships.* Mahwah, NJ: Erlbaum.

Crowell, J. A., Fraley, R. C., & Shaver, P. R. (1999). Measurement of individual differences in adolescent and adult attachment. In J. Cassidy & P. R. Shaver (Eds.), *Handbook of attachment: Theory, research, and clinical applications.* New York: Guilford.

Crowell, J. A., Treboux, D., & Waters, E. (2002). Stability of attachment representations: The transition to marriage. *Developmental Psychology, 38,* 467–479.

Crozier, S. R., Robinson, S. M., Borland, S. E., Godfrey, K. M., Cooper, C., Inskip, H. M., & SWS Study Group. (2009). Do women change their health behaviours in pregnancy? Findings from the Southampton Women's Survey. *Paediatric and Perinatal Epidemiology, 23,* 446–453.

Cruickshanks, K. J., Nondahl, D. M., Tweed, T. S., Wiley, T. L., Klein, B. E., Klein, R., Chappell, R., Dalton, D. S., & Nash, S. D. (2010). Education, occupation, noise exposure history and the 10-yr cumulative incidence of hearing impairment in older adults. *Hearing Research, 264,* 3–9. Epub ahead of print.

Cruikshank, M. (2009). *Learning to be old: Gender, culture, and aging* (2nd ed.). Lanham, MD: Rowman & Littlefield.

Csikszentmihalyi, M., & Nakamura, J. (2006). Creativity through the life span from an evolutionary systems perspective. In C. Hoare (Ed.), *Handbook of adult development and learning.* New York: Oxford University Press.

Cuevas, C. A., Finkelhor, D., Clifford, C., Ormrod, R. K., & Turner, H. A. (2010). Psychological distress as a risk factor for re-victimization in children. *Child Abuse & Neglect, 34,* 235–243.

Cui, M., Conger, R. D., & Lorenz, F. O. (2005). Predicting change in adolescent adjustment from change in marital problems. *Developmental Psychology, 41,* 812–823.

Cui, M., & Donnellan, M. B. (2009). Trajectories of conflict over raising adolescent children and marital satisfaction. *Journal of Marriage and Family, 71,* 478–494.

Cumming, E., & Henry, W. E. (1961). *Growing old, the process of disengagement.* New York: Basic Books.

Cummings, E. M., Davies, P. T., & Campbell, S. B. (2000). *Developmental psychopathology and family process. Theory, research, and clinical implications.* New York: Guilford.

Cummings, S. M., Williams, M. M., & Ellis, R. A. (2003). Impact of an intergenerational program on 4th graders' attitudes toward elders and school behaviors. *Journal of Human Behavior in the Social Environment, 6,* 91–107.

Cunningham, H. (1996). The history of childhood. In C. P. Hwang, M. E. Lamb, & I. E. Sigel (Eds.), *Images of childhood.* Mahwah, NJ: Erlbaum.

Curran, S., & Bolton, P. (2009). Genetics of autism. In Y. Kim (Ed.), *Handbook of behavior genetics.* New York: Springer.

Curtis, N. M., Ronan, K. R., & Bourduin, C. M. (2004). Multisystemic treatment: A meta-analysis of outcome studies. *Journal of Family Psychology, 18,* 411–419.

Cytron, B. D. (1993). To honor the dead and comfort the mourners: Traditions in Judaism. In D. P. Irish, K. F. Lundquist, & V. J. Nelson (Eds.), *Ethnic variations in dying, death, and grief: Diversity in universality.* Washington, DC: Taylor & Francis.

Cytryn, L., & McKnew, D. H., Jr. (1996). *Growing up sad: Childhood depression and its treatment.* New York: W. W. Norton.

D

Dabbs, J. M., & Morris, R. (1990). Testosterone, social class, and antisocial behavior in a sample of 4462 men. *Psychological Science, 1,* 209–211.

Dahl, R. E. (1999). The consequences of insufficient sleep for adolescents: Links between sleep and emotional regulation. *Phi Delta Kappan, 80,* 354–359.

Daley, A. J. (2009). Can exergaming contribute to improving physical activity levels and health outcomes in children? *Pediatrics, 124,* 763–771.

Damon, W. (1977). *The social world of the child.* San Francisco: Jossey-Bass.

Damon, W. (1994). *Greater expectations: Overcoming the culture of indulgence in America's homes and schools.* New York: Free Press.

Damon, W., & Hart, D. (1988). *Self-understanding in childhood and adolescence.* New York: Cambridge University Press.

Dang-Vu, T. T., Desseilles, M., Peigneux, P., & Maquet, P. (2006). A role for sleep in brain plasticity. *Pediatric Rehabilitation, 9,* 98–118.

Daniels, L. M., Stupnisky, R. H., Pekrun, R., Haynes, T. L., Perry, R. P., & Newall, N. E. (2009). A longitudinal analysis of achievement goals: From affective antecedents to emotional effects and achievement outcomes. *Journal of Educational Psychology, 101,* 948–963.

Daniluk, J. C. (2001). Reconstructing their lives: A longitudinal, qualitative analysis of the transition to biological childlessness for infertile people. *Journal of Counseling Development, 79,* 439–449.

Dapretto, M., Davies, M. S., Pfeifer, J. H., Scott, A. A., Sigman, M., Bookheimer, S. Y., & Iacoboni, M. (2006). Understanding emotions in others: Mirror neuron dysfunction in children with autism spectrum disorders. *Nature Neuroscience, 9,* 28–30.

Darling, N., & Steinberg, L. (1993). Parenting style as context: An integrative model. *Psychological Bulletin, 113,* 487–496.

Darnon, C., Dompnier, B., Gilliéorn, O., & Butera, F. (2010). The interplay of mastery and performance goals in social comparison: A multiple-goal perspective. *Journal of Educational Psychology, 102,* 212–222.

Darwin, C. (1859). *The origin of species.* New York: Modern Library.

Darwin, C. A. (1877). A biographical sketch of an infant. *Mind, 2,* 285–294.

Davidson, P. W., & Myers, G. F. (2007). Environmental toxins. In M. L. Batshaw, L. Pellegrino & N. J. Roizen (Eds.), *Children with disabilities,* 6th ed., 61–70. Baltimore: Paul H. Brookes.

Davidson, R. G. (2002). *PDQ medical genetics.* Hamilton, ONT: B. C. Decker.

Davies, B., Collins, J., Steele, R., Cook, K., Distler, V., & Brenner, A. (2007). Parents' and children's perspectives of a children's hospice bereavement program. *Journal of Palliative Care, 23,* 14–23.

Davila, S. L., DiClemente, R. J., Wingood, G. M., Harrington, K. F., Crosby, R. A., & Sionean, C. (2003). Pregnancy desire among disadvantaged African American adolescent females. *American Journal of Health Behavior, 27,* 55–62.

Davila, E. P., Caban-Martinez, A. J., Muennig, P., Lee, D. J., Fleming, L. E., Ferraro, K. F., LeBlanc, W. G., Lam, B. L., Arheart, K. L., McCollister, K. E., Zheng, D., & Christ, S. L. (2009). Sensory impairment among older US workers. *American Journal of Public Health, 99,* 1378–1385.

Davis, C. G., & Nolen-Hoeksema, S. (2001). Loss and meaning: How do people make sense of loss? *American Behavioral Scientist, 44,* 726–741.

Davis, E., Glynn, L. J., Schetter, C. D., Hobel, C., Chicz-Demet, A., & Sandman, C. A. (2007). Prenatal exposure to maternal depression and cortisol influences infant temperament. *Journal of the American Academy of Child & Adolescent Psychiatry, 46,* 737–746.

Davis, N., Gross, J., & Hayne, H. (2008). Defining the boundary of childhood amnesia. *Memory, 16,* 465–474.

Dawood, K., Bailey, J. M., & Martin, N. G. (2009). Genetic and environmental influences on sexual orientation. In Y. Kim (Ed.), *Handbook of behavior genetics.* New York: Springer.

Dawson, G., & Ashman, S. B. (2000). On the origins of a vulnerability to depression: The influence of the early social environment on the development of psychobiological systems related to risk for affective disorder. In C. A. Nelson (Ed.), *Minnesota Symposium on Child Psychology: Vol. 31. The effects of early adversity on neurobe-havioral development.* Mahwah, NJ: Erlbaum.

Dawson, M., Soulieres, I., Gernsbacher, M. A., & Mottron, L. (2007). The level and nature of autistic intelligence. *Psychological Science, 18,* 657–662.

Day, R. D., & Peterson, G. W. (1998). Predicting spanking of younger and older children by mothers and fathers. *Journal of Marriage & the Family, 60,* 79–92.

De Goede, I. H. A., Branje, S. J. T., & Meeus, W. H. J. (2009). Developmental changes in adolescents' perceptions of relationships with their parents. *Journal of Youth and Adolescence, 38,* 75–88.

de Jong-Gierveld, J. (1986). Loneliness and the degree of intimacy in interpersonal relationships. In R. Gilmour & S. Duck (Eds.), *The emerging field of personal relationships.* Hillsdale, NJ: Erlbaum.

de St. Aubin, E., McAdams, D. P., & Kim, T. (2004). The generative society: An introduction. In E. de St. Aubin, D. P. McAdams, & T. Kim (Eds.), *The generative society: Caring for future generations.* Washington, DC: American Psychological Association.

de Vries, B., & Walker, L. J. (1986). Moral reasoning and attitudes toward capital punishment. *Developmental Psychology, 22,* 509–513.

de Weerth, C., van Hees, Y. H., & Buitelaar, J. K. (2003). Prenatal maternal cortisol levels and infant behavior during the first 5 months. *Early Human Development, 74,* 139–151.

De Wolff, M. S., & van IJzendoorn, M. H. (1997). Sensitivity and attachment: A meta-analysis on parental antecedents of infant attachment. *Child Development, 68,* 571–591.

Deary, I. J., Strand, S., Smith, P., & Fernandes, C. (2007). Intelligence and educational achievement. *Intelligence, 35,* 13–21.

Deary, I. J., Whalley, L. J., & Starr, J. M. (2009). *A lifetime of intelligence: Follow-up studies of the scottish mental surveys of 1932 and 1947.* Washington, DC: American Psychological Association.

Deary, I. J., Whiteman, M. C., Starr, J. M., Whalley, L. J., & Fox, H. C. (2004). The impact of childhood intelligence on later life: Following up the Scottish Mental Surveys of 1932 and 1947. *Journal of Personality and Social Psychology, 86,* 130–147.

Deater-Deckard, K., Dodge, K. A., & Sobring, E. (2005). Cultural differences in the effects of physical punishment. In M. Rutter & M. Tienda (Eds.), *Ethnicity and causal mechanisms.* New York: Cambridge University Press.

Deater-Deckard, K., Dodge, K. A., Bates, J. E., & Pettit, G. S. (1996). Physical discipline among African-American and European American mothers: Links to children's externalizing behaviors. *Developmental Psychology, 32,* 1065–1072.

DeCasper, A. J., & Fifer, W. P. (1980). Of human bonding: Newborns prefer their mothers' voices. *Science, 208,* 1174–1176.

DeCasper, A. J., & Spence, M. J. (1986). Prenatal maternal speech influences newborns' perception of speech sounds. *Infant Behavior and Development, 9,* 133–150.

Deci, E. L., & Ryan, R. M. (1992). The initiation and regulation of intrinsically motivated learning and achievement. In A. K. Boggiano & T. S. Pittman (Eds.), *Achievement and motivation: A social developmental perspective* (pp. 9–36). New York: Cambridge University Press.

DeFrain, J. D., Jakub, D. K., & Mendoza, B. L. (1991–1992). The psychological effects of sudden infant death on grandmothers and grandfathers. *Omega: Journal of Death and Dying, 24,* 165–182.

DeFrain, J., Taylor, J., & Ernst, L. (1982). *Coping with sudden infant death.* Lexington, MA: Lexington Books.

Del Giudice, M. (2009). Sex, attachment, and the development of reproductive strategies. *Behavioral Brain Science, 32,* 1–21; 21–67.

DeLamater, J. D., & Sill, M. (2005). Sexual desire in later life. *The Journal of Sex Research, 42,* 138–149.

Delaunay-El Allam, M., Marlier, L., & Schaal, B. (2006). Learning at the breast: Preference formation for an artificial scent and its attraction against the odor of material milk. *Infant Behavioral Development, 29,* 308–321.

DeLeire, T. C., & Kalil A. (2002). Good things come in threes: Single-parent multigenerational family structure and adolescent adjustment. *Demography, 39,* 393–413.

DeLoache, J. S., Cassidy, D. J., & Brown, A. L. (1985). Precursors of mnemonic strategies in very young children's memory. *Child Development, 56,* 125–137.

DeLoache, J. S., Miller, K. F., & Pierroutsakos, S. L. (1998). Reasoning and problem solving. In D. Kuhn & R. Siegler (Vol. Eds.), W. Damon (Editor-in-Chief), *Handbook of child psychology: Vol. 2. Cognition, perception, and language* (5th ed.), 801–850. New York: Wiley.

Delsol, C., & Margolin, G. (2004). The role of family-of-origin violence in men's marital-violence perpetration. *Clinical Psychology Review, 24,* 99–122.

DeMarie, D., & Ferron, J. (2003). Capacity, strategies, and metamemory: Tests of a three-factor model of memory development. *Journal of Experimental Child Psychology, 84,* 167–193.

DeMarie, D., Norman, A., & Abshier, D. W. (2000). Age and experience influence different verbal and nonverbal measures of children's scripts for the zoo. *Cognitive Development, 15,* 241–262.

Demo, D. H., & Cox, M. J. (2000). Families with young children: A review of research in the 1990s. *Journal of Marriage and the Family, 62,* 876–895.

Demo, D. H., & Fine, M. A. (2010). *Beyond the average divorce.* Los Angeles: Sage.

Denney, N. W. (1982). Aging and cognitive changes. In B. B. Wolman (Ed.), *Handbook of developmental psychology.* Englewood Cliffs, NJ: Prentice-Hall.

Denney, N. W. (1989). Everyday problem solving: Methodological issues, research findings, and a model. In L. W. Poon, D. C. Rubin, & B. A. Wilson (Eds.), *Everyday cognition in adulthood and late life.* Cambridge, England: Cambridge University Press.

Denney, N. W., & Pearce, K. A. (1989). A developmental study of practical problem solving in adults. *Psychology and Aging, 4,* 438–442.

Dennis, N. A., & Cabeza, R. (2008). Neuroimaging of healthy cognitive aging. In F. I. M. Craik & T. A. Salthouse (Eds.), *The handbook of aging and cognition* (3rd ed.). New York: Psychology Press.

Dennis, W. (1966). Creative productivity between the ages of 20 and 80 years. *Journal of Gerontology, 21,* 1–8.

Denworth, L. (2006, April 10). The sun has finally come out for Alex. *Newsweek,* p. 26.

Der, G., Batty, G. D., & Deary, I. J. (2009). The association between IQ in adolescence and a range of health outcomes at 40 in the 1979 US National Longitudinal Study of Youth. *Intelligence, 37,* 573–580.

Dere, E., Easton, A., Nadel, L., & Huston, J. (Eds.) (2008). *Handbook of episodic memory.* The Netherlands: Elsevier.

DeRosier, M. E., & Thomas, J. M. (2003). Strengthening sociometric prediction: Scientific advances in the assessment of children's peer relations. *Child Development, 74,* 1379–1392.

DESAction (2007). *DES Daughters.* Available at: www.desaction.org/desdaughers.htm. Accessed: June 9, 2007.

Desrochers, S. (2008). From Piaget to specific Genevan developmental models. *Child Development Perspectives, 2,* 7–12.

DesRosiers, F., Vrsalovic, W. T., Knauf, D. E., Vargas, M., & Busch-Rossnagel, N. A. (1999). Assessing the multiple dimensions of the self-concept of young children: A focus on Latinos. *Merrill-Palmer Quarterly, 45,* 543–566.

Detert, J. R., Treviño L. K., & Sweitzer, V. L. (2008). Moral disengagement in ethical decision making: A study of antecedents and outcome. *Journal of Applied Psychology, 93,* 374–391.

Deutsch, F. M. (1999). *Having it all: How equally shared parenting works.* Cambridge, MA: Harvard University Press.

Deutsch, F. M. (2001). Equally shared parenting. *Current Directions in Psychological Science, 10,* 25–28.

Devenny, D. A., Silverman, W. P., Hill, A. L., Jenkins, E., Sersen, E. A., & Wisniewski, K. E. (1996). Normal ageing in adults with Down's syndrome: A longitudinal study. *Journal of Intellectual Disability Research, 40,* 208–221.

Deveny, K. (2003, June 30). We're not in the mood. *Newsweek,* 40–46.

Devlin, B., Daniels, M., & Roeder, K. (1997). The heritability of IQ. *Nature, 388(6641),* 468–471.

DeVries, R. (2000). Vygotsky, Piaget, and education: A reciprocal assimilation of theories and educational practices. *New Ideas in Psychology, 18,* 187–213.

Dewar, R. E., Kline, D. W., & Swanson, H. A. (1995). Age differences in the comprehension of traffic sign symbols. *Transportation Research Record, 1456,* 1–10.

Dews, S., Winner, E., Kaplan, J., Rosenblatt, E., Hunt, M., Lim, K., Mcgovern, A., Qualter, A., & Smarsh, B. (1996). Children's understanding of the meaning and functions of verbal irony. *Child Development, 67,* 3071–3085.

Dewsbury, D. A. (2009). Charles Darwin and psychology at the bicentennial and sesquicentennial: An Introduction. *American Psychologist, 64,* 67–74.

Diamond, L. (2008). Female bisexuality from adolescence to adulthood: Results from a 10-year longitudinal study. *Developmental Psychology, 44,* 5–14.

Diamond, L. M., & Butterworth, M. (2009). The close relationships of sexual minorities. Partners, friends, and family. In M. C. Smith (Ed.) & N. DeFrates-Densch (Asst. Ed.), *Handbook of research on adult learning and development.* New York: Routledge.

Diamond, M., & Sigmundson, H. K. (1997). Sex reassignment at birth: Long-term review and clinical implications. *Archives of Pediatric and Adolescent Medicine, 151,* 298–304.

Diaz, J. (1997). *How drugs influence behavior: A neurobehavioral approach.* Upper Saddle River, NJ: Prentice-Hall.

Dick, D. M., Prescott, C., & McGue, M. (2009). The genetics of substance use and substance use disorders. In Y. Kim (Ed.), *Handbook of behavior genetics.* New York: Springer.

Dickens, W. T., & Flynn, J. R. (2006). Black Americans reduce the racial IQ gap: Evidence from standardization samples. *Psychological Science, 17,* 913–920.

Dickinson, J. E., Paech, M. J., McDonald, S. J., & Evans, S. F. (2002). The impact of intrapartum analgesia on labour and delivery outcomes in nulliparous women. *Department of Obstetrics and Gynaecology, 42,* 59–66.

Didonato, M. D., & Berenbaum, S. A. (2010, April 3). The benefits and drawbacks of gender typing: How different dimensions are related to psychological adjustment. *Archives of Sexual Behavior.*

Diego, M. A., Field, T., & Hernandez-Reif, M. (2005). Vagal activity, gastric motility, and weight gain in massaged preterm neonates. *The Journal of Pediatrics, 147,* 50–55.

Diekelmann, S., & Born, J. (2010). The memory function of sleep. *NatureReviews. 11,* 114-126.

Diekelmann, S., Wilhelm, I., & Born, J. (2009). The whats and whens of sleep-dependent memory consolidation. *Sleep Medicine Reviews, 13(5),* 309–321.

Diekman, A. B., & Murnen, S. K. (2004). Learning to be little women and little men: The inequitable gender equality of nonsexist children's literature. *Sex Roles, 50,* 373–385.

Digman, J. M. (1990). Personality structure: Emergence of the 5-factor model. *Annual Review of Psychology, 41,* 417–440.

Dijkstra, I. C., & Stroebe, M. S. (1998). The impact of a child's death on parents: A myth (not yet) disproved? *Journal of Family Studies, 4,* 159–185.

DiLalla, L. F., Kagan, J., & Reznick, S. J. (1994). Genetic etiology of behavioral inhibition among 2-year-old children. *Infant Behavior and Development, 17,* 405–412.

Dillon, M., & Wink, P. (2007). *In the course of a lifetime: Tracing religious belief, practice, and change.* Ewing, NJ: University of California Press.

DiMatteo, M. R., Morton, S. C., Lepper, H. S., & Damush, T. M. (1996). Cesarean childbirth and psychosocial outcomes: A meta-analysis. *Health Psychology, 15,* 303–314.

Dimmock, P. W., Wyatt, K. M., Jones, P. W., & O'Brien, P. M. S. (2000). Efficacy of selective serotonin-reuptake inhibitors in premenstrual syndrome: A systematic review. *Lancet, 356,* 1131–1136.

Dinmore, I. (1997). Interdisciplinarity and integrative learning: An imperative for adult education. *Education, 117,* 452–468.

DiPietro, J. A., Bornsetin, M. H., Hahn, C., Costigan, K., & Achy-Brou, A. (2007). Fetal heart rate and variability: Stability and prediction to developmental outcomes in early childhood. *Child Development, 78,* 1788–1798.

DiPietro, J. A., Costigan, K. A., & Gurewitsch, E. D. (2003). Fetal response to induced maternal stress. *Early Human Development, 74,* 125–138.

DiPietro, J. A., Hodgson, D. M., Costigan, K. A., Hilton, S. C., & Johnson, T. R. B. (1996a). Fetal antecedents of infant temperament. *Child Development, 67,* 2568–2583.

DiPietro, J. A., Hodgson, D. M., Costigan, K. A., Hilton, S. C., & Johnson, T. R. B. (1996b). Fetal neurobehavioral development. *Child Development, 67,* 2553–2567.

DiPietro, J. A., Novak, M. F. S. X., Costigan, K., A., Atella, L. D., & Reusing, S. P. (2006). Maternal psychological distress during pregnancy in relation to child development at age two. *Child Development, 77,* 573–587.

Dirix, C. E. H., Nijhuis, J. G., Jongsma, H. W., & Hornstra, G. (2009). Aspects of fetal learning and memory. *Child Development, 80,* 1251–1258.

Dittman, R. W., Kappes, M. E., & Kappes, M. H. (1992). Sexual behavior in adolescent and adult females with congenital adrenal hyperplasia. *Psychoneuroendocrinology, 17,* 153–170.

Dittmar, H., Halliwell, E., & Ive, S. (2006). Does Barbie make girls want to be thin? The effect of experimental exposure to images of dolls on the body image of 5- to 8-year-old girls. *Developmental Psychology, 42,* 283–292.

Ditzen, B., Schaer, M., Gabriel, B., Bodenmann, G., Ehlert, U., & Heinrichs, M. (2009). Intranasal oxytocin increases positive communication and reduces cortisol levels during couple conflict. *Biological Psychiatry, 65,* 728–731.

Dixon, R. A. (1992). Contextual approaches to adult intellectual development. In R. J. Sternberg & C. A. Berg (Eds.), *Intellectual development.* New York: Cambridge University Press.

Dixon, R. A. (2003). Themes in the aging of intelligence: Robust decline with intriguing possibilities. In R. J. Sternberg, J. Lautrey, & T. I. Lubart (Eds.), *Models of intelligence: International perspectives* (pp. 151–167). Washington, DC: American Psychological Association.

Dodge, K. A. (1986). A social information processing model of social competence in children. In M. Perlmutter (Ed.), *Minnesota Symposia on Child Psychology* (Vol. 18). Hillsdale, NJ: Erlbaum.

Dodge, K. A. (1993). Social-cognitive mechanisms in the development of conduct disorder and depression. *Annual Review of Psychology, 44,* 559–584.

Dodge, K. A. (2009). Mechanisms of gene-environment interaction effects in the development of conduct disorder. *Perspectives on Psychological Science, 4,* 408–414.

Dodge, K. A., & Coleman, D. L. (Eds.) (2009). *Preventing child maltreatment. Community approaches.* New York: Guilford.

Dodge, K. A., Coie, J. D., & Lynam, D. (2006). Aggression and antisocial behavior in youth. In N. Eisenberg (Vol. Ed.), & W. Damon & R. M. Lerner (Eds. in Chief), *Handbook of child psychology: Vol. 3. Social, emotional, and personality development* (6th ed.). Hoboken, NJ: Wiley.

Dodge, K. A., Coie, J. D., Pettit, G. S., & Price, J. M. (1990). Peer status and aggression in boys' groups: Developmental and contextual analysis. *Child Development, 61,* 1289–1309.

Dodge, K. A., Dishion, T. J., & Lansford, J. E. (Eds.) (2006). *Deviant peer influences in programs for youth: Problems and solutions.* New York: Guilford.

Dodge, K. A., Greenberg, M. T., Malone, P. S., & Conduct Problems Prevention Research Group (2008). Testing an idealized dynamic cascade model of the development of serious violence in adolescence. *Child Development, 79,* 1907–1927.

Dodge, K. A., Malone, P. S., Lansford, J. E., Miller, S., Pettit, G. S., & Bates, J. E. (2009). A dynamic cascade model of the development of substance-use onset. *Monographs of the Society for Research in Child Development, 74* (3, Serial No. 294).

Dodge, K. A., Murphy, R., O'Donnell, K., & Christopoulos, C. (2009). Community-level prevention of child maltreatment. The Durham Family Initiative. In K. A. Dodge & D. L. Coleman (Eds.), *Preventing child maltreatment. Community approaches.* New York: Guilford.

Dodge, K. A., & Pettit, G. S. (2003). A biopsychosocial model of the development of chronic conduct problems in adolescence. *Developmental Psychology, 39,* 349–371.

Dodge, K. A., & Price, J. M. (1994). On the relation between social information processing and socially competent behavior in early school-aged children. *Child Development, 65,* 1385–1397.

Dodson, C. S., Bawa, S., & Krueger, L. E. (2007). Aging, metamemory, and high-confidence errors: A misrecollection account. *Psychological Aging, 22,* 122–133.

Dogan, S. J., Conger, R. D., Kim, K. J., & Masyn, K. E. (2007). Cognitive and parenting pathways in the transmission of antisocial behavior from parents to adolescents. *Child Development, 78,* 335–349.

Doherty, M. J. (2009). *Theory of mind. How children understand others' thoughts and feelings.* New York: Psychology Press.

Doherty, W. J., Erickson, M. F., & LaRossa, R. (2006). An intervention to increase father involvement and skills with infants during the transition to parenthood. *Journal of Family Psychology, 20,* 438–447.

Dohnt, H., & Tiggemann, M. (2006). The contribution of peer and media influences to the development of body satisfaction and self-esteem in young girls: A prospective study. *Developmental Psychology, 42,* 929–936.

Doidge, N. (2007). *The brain that changes itself. Stories of personal triumph from the frontiers of brain science.* New York: Viking.

Doka, K. J. (1989). *Disenfranchised grief: Recognizing hidden sorrow.* Lexington, MA: Lexington Books.

Doka, K. J. (2008). Disenfranchised grief in historical and cultural perspective. In M. S. Stroebe, R. O. Hansson, H. Schut, & W. Stroebe (Eds.), *Handbook of bereavement research and practice. Advances in theory and intervention.* Washington, DC: American Psychological Association.

Dolen, L. S., & Bearison, D. J. (1982). Social interaction and social cognition in aging. *Human Development, 25,* 430–442.

Domjan, M. J. (1993). *Principles of learning and behavior* (3rd ed.). Pacific Grove, CA: Brooks/Cole.

Donnellan, M. B., Trzesniewski, K. H., & Robins, R. W. (2006). Personality and self-esteem development in adolescence. In D. K. Mroczek & T. D. Little (Eds.), *Handbook of personality development.* Mahwah, NJ: Erlbaum.

Donnelly, N., Cave, K., Greenway, R., Hadwin, J. A., Stevenson, J., & Sonuga-Barke, E. (2007). Visual search in children and adults: top-down and bottom-up mechanisms. *Quarterly Journal of Experimental Psychology, 60,* 120–136.

Dorn, L. D., Susman, E. J., & Ponirakis, A. (2003). Pubertal timing and adolescent adjustment and behavior: Conclusions vary by rater. *Journal of Youth and Adolescence, 32,* 157–167.

Doss, B. D., Rhoades, G. K., Stanley, S. M., & Markman, H. J. (2009). The effect of the transition to parenthood on relationship quality: An eight-year prospective study. *Journal of Personality and Social Psychology, 96,* 601–619.

Dotterer, A. M., McHale, S. J., & Crouter, A. C. (2009). The development and correlates of academic interests from childhood through adolescence. *Journal of Educational Psychology, 101,* 509–519.

Doty, R. L., & Cameron, E. L. (2009). Sex differences and reproductive hormone influences on human odor perception. *Physiological Behavior, 97,* 213–228.

Doucette, A. (2002). Child and adolescent diagnosis: The need for a model-based approach. In L. E. Beutler & M. L. Malik (Eds.), *Rethinking the DSM: A psychological perspective.* Washington, DC: American Psychological Association.

Dougherty, T. M., & Haith, M. M. (1997). Infant expectations and reaction time as predictors of childhood speed of processing and IQ. *Developmental Psychology, 33,* 146–155.

Dowda, M., Brown, W. H., McIver, K. L., Pfeiffer, K. A., O'Neill, J. R., Addy, C. L., & Pate, R. R. (2009). Policies and characteristics of the preschool environment and physical activity of young children. *Pediatrics, 123,* e261–e266.

Dowdney, L. (2000). Annotation: Childhood bereavement following parental death. *Journal of Child Psychology and Psychiatry and Allied Disciplines, 41,* 819–830.

Dowling, G.J., Weiss, S.R., & Condon, T.P. (2008). Drugs of abuse and the aging brain. *Neuropsychopharmacology, 33,* 209–218.

Down syndrome prevalence at birth—United States, 1983-1990 (1994, August 26). *Mortality and Morbidity Weekly Reports, 43,* 617–622.

Downey, D. B. (2002). Parental and family involvement in education. In A. Molnar (Ed.), *School reform proposals: The research evidence,* 113–134. Greenwich, CT: Information Age Publishing.

Downey, J., Elkin, E. J., Ehrhardt, A. A., Meyer-Bahlburg, H. F., Bell, J. J., & Morishima, A. (1991). Cognitive ability and everyday functioning in women with Turner syndrome. *Journal of Learning Disabilities, 24,* 32–39.

Doyle, A. B., Markiewicz, D., Brendgen, M., Lieberman, M., & Voss, K. (2000). Child attachment security and self-concept: Associations with mother and father attachment style and marital quality. *Merrill-Palmer Quarterly, 46,* 514–539.

Doyle, L. W., & Anderson, P. J. (2005). Improved neurosensory outcome at 8 years of age of extremely low birthweight children born in Victoria over three distinct years. *Archives of Disease in Childhood–Fetal and Neonantal Edition, 90,* 484–488.

Draper, J. (2002). It's the first scientific evidence: A man's experience of pregnancy confirmation. *Journal of Advanced Nursing, 39,* 563–570.

Drenowatz, C., Eisenmann, J. C., Pfeiffer, K.A,, Wickel, E.E., Gentile, D., & Walsh, D. (2009). Maturity-related differences in physical activity among 10- to 12-year-old girls. *American Journal of Human Biology.* Epub ahead of print.

Dribe, M., & Stanfors, M. (2009). Does parenthood strengthen a traditional household division of labor? *Journal of Marriage and Family, 71,* 33–45.

Drotar, D., Robinson, J., Jeavons, L., & Kirchner, H. L. (2008). A randomized, controlled evaluation of early intervention: the Born to Learn curriculum. *Child: Care, Health, and Development, 35,* 643–649.

Dubas, J. S., Graber, J. A., & Petersen, A. C. (1991). The effects of pubertal development on achievement during adolescence. *American Journal of Education, 99,* 444–460.

Dublin, L. I., & Lotka, A. J. (1936). *Length of life. A study of the life table.* New York: Ronald Press.

Dubois, L., Farmer, A., Girard, M., & Peterson, K. (2007). Regular sugar-sweetened beverage consumption between meals increases risk of overweight among preschool-aged children. *Journal of the American Dietetic Association, 107,* 924–934.

Dumble, M., Gatza, C., Tyner, S., Venkatachalam, S., & Donehower, L. A. (2004). Insights into aging obtained from p53 mutant mouse models. *Annals of the New York Academy of Sciences, 1019,* 171–177.

Duncan, H., & Dick, T. (2000). Collaborative workshops and student academic performance in introductory college mathematics courses: A study of a Treisman model math excel program. *School Science and Mathematics, 100,* 365–373.

Duncan, R. M., & Pratt, M. W. (1997). Microgenetic change in the quantity and quality of preschoolers' private speech. *International Journal of Behavioral Development, 20,* 367.

Dunfield, K. A., & Kuhlmeier, V. A. (2010). Intention-mediated selective helping in infancy. *Psychological Science, 21,* 523–527.

Dunn, J. (1993). *Young children's close relationships. Beyond attachment.* Newbury Park, CA: Sage.

Dunn, J. (2007). Siblings and socialization. In J. E. Grusec & P. D. Hastings (Eds.), *Handbook of socialization: Theory and research.* New York: Guilford.

Dunn, J., Cutting, A. L., & Demetriou, H. (2000). Moral sensibility, understanding others, and children's friendship interactions in the preschool period. *British Journal of Developmental Psychology, 18,* 159–177.

Dunn, J., Fergusson, E., & Maughan, B. (2006). Grandparents, grandchildren, and family change in contemporary Britain. In A. Clarke-Stewart & J. Dunn (Eds.), *Families count: Effects on child and adolescent development.* New York: Cambridge University Press.

Dunn, J., & Kendrick, C. (1982). *Siblings: Love, envy, and understanding.* Cambridge, MA: Harvard University Press.

Dunn, J., & Plomin, R. (1990). *Separate lives. Why siblings are so different.* New York: Basic Books.

Dunphy, D. C. (1963). The social structure of urban adolescent peer groups. *Sociometry, 26,* 230–246.

DuPaul, G. J., & Stoner, G. (2003). *ADHD in the schools. Assessment and intervention strategies* (2nd ed.). New York: Guilford.

Durik, A. M., Hyde, J. S., & Clark, R. (2000). Sequelae of cesarean and vaginal deliveries: Psychosocial outcomes for mothers and infants. *Developmental Psychology, 36,* 251–260.

Dustman, R. E., Emmerson, R. Y., Steinhaus, L. A., Shearer, D. E., & Dustman, T. J. (1992). The effects of videogame playing on neuropsychological performance of elderly individuals. *Journal of Gerontology, 47,* 168–171.

Dustman, R. E., Ruhling, R. O., Russell, E. M., Shearer, D. E., Bonekat, H. W., Shigeoka, J. W., Wood, J. S., & Bradford, D. C. (1989). Neurobiology of aging. In A. C. Ostrow (Ed.), *Aging and motor behavior.* Indianapolis: Benchmark Press.

Duvall, E. M. (1977). *Marriage and family development* (5th ed.). Philadelphia: J. B. Lippincott.

Duyme, M., Dumaret, A., & Tomkiewicz, S. (1999). How can we boost IQs of "dull children"? A late adoption study. *Proceedings of the National Academy of Sciences of the United States of America, 96,* 8790–8794.

Dweck, C. S., & Elliott, E. S. (1983). Achievement motivation. In P. H. Mussen (Gen. Ed.) & E. M. Hetherington (Vol Ed.), Handbook of Child Psychology: Vol. IV. Social and personality development, 643–691. New York: Wiley.

Dweck, C. S., & Grant, H. (2008). Self-theories, goals, and meaning. In J. Shah & W. Gardner (Eds.), *The handbook of motivational science.* New York: Guilford.

Dweck, C. S., & Leggett, E. L. (1988). A social-cognitive approach to motivation and personality. *Psychological Review, 95,* 256–273.

Dweck, C. S., & Master, A. (2008). Self-theories motivate self-regulated learning. In D. Schunk & B. Zimmerman (Eds), *Motivation and self-regulated learning: Theory, research, and applications.* Mahwah, NJ: Erlbaum.

Dyk, P. H., & Adams, G. R. (1990). Identity and intimacy: An initial investigation of three theoretical models using cross-lag panel correlations. *Journal of Youth and Adolescence, 19,* 91–110.

E

Eagly, A. H. (1987). *Sex differences in social behavior: A social-role interpretation.* Hillsdale, NJ: Erlbaum.

Eagly, A. H. (2009). The his and hers of prosocial behavior: An examination of the social psychology of gender. *American Psychologist, 64,* 644–658.

Earles, J. L., & Salthouse, T. A. (1995). Interrelations of age, health, and speed. *Journal of Gerontology: Psychological Sciences and Social Sciences, 50,* 33–41.

Easterbrook, M. A., Kisilevsky, B. S., Muir, D. W., & Laplante, D. P. (1999). Newborns discriminate schematic faces from scrambled faces. *Canadian Journal of Experimental Psychology, 53,* 231–241.

Eastwick, P. W., & Finkel, E. J. (2008). The attachment system in fledgling relationships: An activating role for attachment anxiety. *Journal of Personality and Social Psychology, 95,* 628–647.

Eaton, D. K., Kann, L., Kinchen, S., Ross, J., Hawkins, J., Harris, W. A., Lowry, R., McManus, T., Chyen, D., Shanklin, S., Lim, C., Grunbaum, J. A., & Wechsler, H. (2006, June 9). Youth risk behavior surveillance—United States, 2005. *Morbidity and Mortality Weekly Report, 55,* 1–108.

Eaton, W. O., & Ritchot, K. F. M. (1995). Physical maturation and information-processing speed in middle childhood. *Developmental Psychology, 31,* 967–972.

Eaves, L., Martin, N., Heath, A., Schieken, R., Meyer, J., Silberg, J., Neale, M., & Corey, L. (1997). Age changes in the causes of individual differences in conservatism. *Behavior Genetics, 27,* 121–124.

Ebbeck, M. (1996). Parents' expectations and child rearing practices in Hong Kong. *Early Child Development and Care, 119,* 15–25.

Eberstadt, N. (2006). Growing old the hard way: China, Russia, India. *Policy Review, 136.* Available at: www.policyreview.org/136/eberstadt.html. Accessed: July 22, 2006.

Ebstein, R. P., Benjamin, J., & Belmaker, R. H. (2003). Behavioral genetics, genomics, and personality. In R. Plomin, J. C. DeFries, I. W. Craig, & P. McGuffin (Eds.), *Behavioral genetics in the postgenomic era.* Washington, DC: American Psychological Association.

Eccles, J. S., Jacobs, J. E., & Harold, R. D. (1990). Gender role stereotypes, expectancy effects, and parents' socialization of gender differences. *Journal of Social Issues, 46,* 183–201.

Eccles, J. S., Lord, S., & Midgley, C. (1991). What are we doing to early adolescents? The impact of educational contexts on early adolescents. *American Journal of Education, 99,* 521–542.

Eccles, J. S., Midgley, C., Wigfield, A., Buchanan, C. M., Reuman, D., Flanagan, C., & Mac Iver, D. (1993). Development during adolescence: The impact of stage–environment fit on young adolescents' experiences in schools and in families. *American Psychologist, 48,* 90–101.

Ecklund-Flores, L., & Turkewitz, G. (1996). Asymmetric headturning to speech and nonspeech in human newborns. *Developmental Psychobiology, 29,* 205–217.

Eddleman, K. A., Malone, F. D., Sullivan, L., Dukes, K., Berkowitz, R. L., Kharbutli, Y., Porter, F., Luthy, D. A., Comstock, C. H., Saade, G. R., Klugman, S., Dugoff, L., Craigo, S. D., Timor-Tritsch, I. E., Carr, S. R., Wolfe, H. M., &

D'Alton, M. E., for the First and Second Trimester Evaluation of Risk (FASTER) Trial Research Consortium. (2006). Pregnancy loss rates after midtrimester amniocentesis. *Obstetrics & Gynecology, 108,* 1067–1072.

Eder, R. A. (1989). The emergent personologist: The structure and content of 3½-, 5½-, and 7½-year-olds' concepts of themselves and other persons. *Child Development, 60,* 1218–1228.

Editors of *The Lancet* (2010, February 2). Retraction—Ileal-lymphoid-nodular hyperplasia, non-specific colitis, and pervasive developmental disorder in children. Available at: www.thelancet.com. Accessed: February 26, 2010.

Effros, R. B. (2009). The immunological theory of aging revisited. In V. L. Bengtson, M. Silverstein, N. M. Putney, & D. Gans (Eds.), *Handbook of theories of aging* (2nd ed.). New York: Springer.

Egeland, B. (1979). Preliminary results of a prospective study of the antecedents of child abuse. *International Journal of Child Abuse and Neglect, 3,* 269–278.

Egeland, B., & Carlson, E. A. (2004). Attachment and psychopathology. In L. Atkinson & S. Goldberg (Eds.), *Attachment issues in psychopathology and intervention.* Mahwah, NJ: Erlbaum.

Egeland, B., Jacobvitz, D., & Sroufe, L. A. (1988). Breaking the cycle of abuse. *Child Development, 59,* 1080–1088.

Egeland, B., Sroufe, L. A., & Erickson, M. (1983). The developmental consequences of different patterns of maltreatment. *International Journal of Child Abuse and Neglect, 7,* 459–469.

Ehrenberg, R. G., Brewer, D. J., Gamoran, A., & Willms, J. D. (2001). Class size and student achievement. *Psychological Science in the Public Interest, 2,* 1–30.

Ehrhardt, A. A. (1985). The psychobiology of gender. In A. S. Rossi (Ed.), *Gender and the life course.* New York: Aldine.

Ehrhardt, A. A., & Baker, S. W. (1974). Fetal androgens, human central nervous system differentiation, and behavioral sex differences. In R. C. Friedman, R. M. Rickard, & R. L. Van de Wiele (Eds.), *Sex differences in behavior.* New York: Wiley.

Ehri, L. C. (1999). Phases of development in learning to read words. In J. Oakhill & R. Beard (Eds.), *Reading development and the teaching of reading* (pp. 79–108). Oxford: Blackwell.

Ehrle, G. M. (2001). Grandchildren as moderator variables in the family, social, physiological, and intellectual development of grandparents who are raising them. In E. L. Grigorenko & R. J. Sternberg (Eds.), *Family environment and intellectual functioning: A life-span perspective.* Mahwah, NJ: Erlbaum.

Eiger, M. S., & Olds, S. W. (1999). *The complete book of breastfeeding* (3rd ed.). New York: Workman Publishing & Bantam Books.

Eimas, P. D. (1975a). Auditory and phonetic cues for speech: Discrimination of the (r–l) distinction by young infants. *Perception and Psychophysics, 18,* 341–347.

Eimas, P. D. (1975b). Speech perception in early infancy. In L. B. Cohen & P. Salapatek (Eds.), *Infant perception: From sensation to cognition.* New York: Academic Press.

Eimas, P. D. (1985). The perception of speech in early infancy. *Scientific American, 252,* 46–52.

Eisenberg, N. (2000). Emotion, regulation, and moral development. *Annual Review of Psychology, 51,* 665–697.

Eisenberg, N., Fabes, R. A., Guthrie, I. K., Murphy, B. C., Maszk, P., Holmgren, R., & Suh, K. (1996). The relations of regulation and emotionality to problem behavior in elementary school children. *Development and Psychopathology, 8,* 141–162.

Eisenberg, N., Hofer, C., Spinrad, T. L., Gershoff, E. T., Valiente, C., Losoya, S., Zhou, Q.,

Cumberland, A., Liew, J., Reiser, M., & Maxon, E. (2008). Understanding mother-adolescent conflict discussions: Concurrent and across-time prediction from youths' dispositions and parenting. *Monographs of the Society for Research in Child Development, 73* (2, Serial No. 290).

Eisenberg, N., Spinrad, T. L., & Sadovsky, A. (2006). Empathy-related responding in children. In M. Killen & J. G. Smetana (Eds.), *Handbook of moral development.* Mahwah, NJ: Erlbaum.

Ekerdt, D. J., Bossé, R., & Levkoff, S. (1985). Empirical test for phases of retirement: Findings from the Normative Aging Study. *Journal of Gerontology, 40,* 95–101.

Ekerdt, D. J., Kosloski, K., & DeViney, S. (2000). The normative anticipation of retirement by older adults. *Research on Aging, 22,* 3–22.

Elbourne, D., & Wiseman, R. A. (2000). Types of intra-muscular opioids for maternal pain relief in labor. *Cochrane Database Systems Review 2000* (CD001237).

Elder, G., Jr., & Johnson, M. K. (2003). The life course and aging: Challenges, lessons and new directions. In R. Settersten, Jr. (Ed.), *Invitation to the life course: Toward new understandings of later life.* Amityville, NY: Baywood.

Elder, G. H., Jr. (1998). The life course as developmental theory. *Child Development, 69,* 1–12.

Elder, G. H., Jr., Liker, J. K., & Cross, C. E. (1984). Parent–child behavior in the Great Depression: Life course and intergenerational influences. In P. B. Baltes & O. G. Brim Jr. (Eds.), *Life-span development and behavior* (Vol. 6). Orlando, FL: Academic Press.

Elder, G. H., Jr., & Shanahan, M. J. (2006). The life course and human development. In W. Damon & R. M. Lerner (Eds. in Chief) & R. M. Lerner (Vol. Ed.), *Handbook of child psychology: Vol. 1. Theoretical models of human development* (6th ed.). Hoboken, NJ: Wiley.

Elicker, J., Englund, M., & Sroufe, L. A. (1992). Predicting peer competence and peer relationships in childhood from early parent–child relationships. In R. D. Parke & G. W. Ladd (Eds.), *Family-peer relationships: Modes of linkage.* Hillsdale, NJ: Erlbaum.

Elkind, D. (1967). Egocentrism in adolescence. *Child Development, 38,* 1025–1034.

Elkind, D. (1987). *Miseducation: Preschoolers at risk.* New York: Knopf.

Elkind, D. (1992, May/June). The future of childhood. Waaah!! Why kids have a lot to cry about. *Psychology Today,* 38–41, 80–81.

Elkind, D., & Bowen, R. (1979). Imaginary audience behavior in children and adolescents. *Developmental Psychology, 15,* 38–44.

Elliot, A. J., & Church, M. A. (1997). A hierarchical model of approach and avoidance achievement motivation. *Journal of Personality and Social Psychology, 72,* 218–232.

Elliot, A. J., & Reis, H. T. (2003). Attachment and exploration in adulthood. *Journal of Personality & Social Psychology, 85,* 317–331.

Elliott, D. S., & Ageton, S. S. (1980). Reconciling race and class differences in self-reported and official estimates of delinquency. *American Sociological Review, 45,* 95–110.

Elliott, E. S., & Dweck, C. S. (1988). Goals: An approach to motivation and achievement. *Journal of Personality and Social Psychology, 54,* 5–12.

Elliott, J. G. (1999). School refusal: Issues of conceptualization, assessment, and treatment. *Journal of Child Psychology and Psychiatry, 40,* 1001–1012.

Ellis, B. J., & Bjorklund, D. F. (Eds.). (2005). *Origins of the social mind.* New York: Guilford.

Ellis, B. J., & Garber, J. (2000). Psychosocial antecedents of variation in girls' pubertal timing: Maternal depression, stepfather presence, and marital and family stress. *Child Development, 71,* 485–501.

Ellis, L., Ames, M. A., Peckham, W., & Burke, D. M. (1988). Sexual orientation in human offspring may be altered by severe emotional distress during pregnancy. *Journal of Sex Research, 25,* 152–157.

Ellis, S., Rogoff, B., & Cromer, C. C. (1981). Age segregation in children's social interactions. *Developmental Psychology, 17,* 399–407.

Ellison, P. T. (2002). Puberty. In N. Cameron (Ed.), *Human growth and development,* 65–84. New York: Academic Press.

Else-Quest, N. M., Hyde, J. S., & Linn, M. C. (2010). Cross-national patterns of gender differences in mathematics: A meta-analysis. *Psychological Bulletin, 136,* 103–127.

Ely, R. (1997). Language and literacy in the school years. In J. K. Gleason (Ed.), *The development of language* (4th ed.). Boston: Allyn & Bacon.

Ely, R. (2001). Language and literacy in the school years. In J. B. Gleason (Ed.), *The development of language* (5th ed.). Boston: Allyn & Bacon.

Ely, R. (2005). Language development in the school years. In J. B. Gleason (Ed.), *The development of language* (6th ed.). Boston: Allyn & Bacon.

Emde, R. N., Biringen, Z., Clyman, R. B., & Oppenheim, D. (1991). The moral self of infancy: Affective core and procedural knowledge. *Developmental Review, 11,* 251–270.

Emery, R. E. (1999). Post divorce family life for children. An overview of research and some implications for policy. In R. A. Thompson & P. R. Amato (Eds.), *The post divorce family. Children, parenting, & society.* Thousand Oaks, CA: Sage.

Emery, R. E., & Laumann-Billings, L. (1998). An overview of the nature, causes, and consequences of abusive family relationships: Toward differentiating maltreatment and violence. *American Psychologist, 53,* 121–135.

Emery, R. E., & Tuer, M. (1993). Parenting and the marital relationship. In T. Luster & L. Okagaki (Eds.), *Parenting. An ecological perspective.* Hillsdale, NJ: Erlbaum.

Emler, N., Tarry, H., & St. James, A. (2007). Post-conventional moral reasoning and reputation. *Journal of Research in Personality, 41,* 76–89.

Emmanuelle, V. (2009). Inter-relationships among attachment to mother and father, self-esteem, and career indecision. *Journal of Vocational Behavior, 75,* 91–99.

Endara, S.M., Ryan, M.A., Sevick, C.J., Conlin, A.M., Macera, C.A., & Smith, T.C. (2009). Does acute maternal stress in pregnancy affect infant health outcomes? Examination of a large cohort of infants born after the terrorist attacks of September 11, 2001. *BMC Public Health, 9,* 252.

England, P., Reid, L. L., & Kilbourne, B. S. (1996). The effect of the sex composition of jobs on starting wages in an organization: Findings from the NLSY. *Demography, 33,* 511–521.

Englander-Golden, P., Sonleitner, F. J., Whitmore, M. R., & Corbley, G. J. M. (1986). Social and menstrual cycles: Methodological and substantive findings. In V. L. Olesen & N. F. Woods (Eds.), *Culture, society, and menstruation.* Washington, DC: Hemisphere.

Enright, R., Lapsley, D., & Shukla, D. (1979). Adolescent egocentrism in early and late adolescence. *Adolescence, 14,* 687–695.

Ensminger, M. E., & Slusarcick, A. L. (1992). Paths to high school graduation or dropout: A longitudinal study of a first-grade cohort. *Sociology of Education, 65,* 95–113.

Entringer, S., Kunsta, R., Hellhammer, D. H., Wadhwa, P. D., & Wüst, S. (2009). Prenatal exposure to maternal psychosocial stress and HPA axis regulation in young adults. *Hormones and Behavior, 55,* 292–298.

Epel, E. S. (2009). Telomeres in a life-span perspective: A new "psychobiomarker"? *Current Direction in Psychological Science, 18,* 6–10.

Epel, E. S., Blackburn, E. H., Lin, J., Dhabhar, F. S., Adler, N. E., Morrow, J. D., & Cawthon, R. M. (2004). Accelerated telomere shortening in response to life stress. *Proceedings of the National Academy of Sciences, 101,* 17312–17315.

Epel, E. S., Lin, J., Wilhelm, F. H., Wolkowitz, O. M., Cawthon, R., Adler, N. E., Dolbier, C., Mendes, W. B., & Blackburn, E. H. (2006). Cell aging in relation to stress arousal and cardiovascular disease risk factors. *Psychoneuroendocrinology, 31,* 277–287.

Eppler, M. A. (1995). Development of manipulatory skills and the deployment of attention. *Infant Behavior & Development, 18,* 391–405.

Erber, J. T. (2005). *Aging and older adulthood.* Belmont, CA: Wadsworth.

Erdley, C. A., Loomis, C. C., Cain, K. M., & Dumas-Hines, F. (1997). Relations among children's social goals, implicit personality theories, and responses to social failure. *Developmental Psychology, 33,* 263–272.

Ericsson, K. A. (1996). The acquisition of expert performance: An introduction to some of the issues. In K. A. Ericsson (Ed.), *The road to excellence: The acquisition of expert performance in the arts and sciences, sports, and games.* Mahwah, NJ: Erlbaum.

Ericsson, K. A., Chase, W. G., & Faloon, S. (1980). Acquisition of a memory skill. *Science, 208,* 1181–1182.

Ericsson, K. A., & Kintsch, W. (1995). Long-term working memory. *Psychological Review, 102,* 211–245.

Erikson, E. H. (1963). *Childhood and society* (2nd ed.). New York: Norton.

Erikson, E. H. (1968). *Identity: Youth and crisis.* New York: Norton.

Erikson, E. H. (1982). *The life cycle completed: A review.* New York: Norton.

Eriksson, M., Brown, W. T., Gordon, L. B., Glynn, M. W., Singer, J., Scott, L., Erdos, M. R., Robbins, C. M., Moses, T. Y., Berglund, P., Dutra, A., Pak, E., Durkin, S., Csoka, A. B., Boehnke, M., Glover, T. W., & Collins, F. S. (2003). Recurrent *de novo* point mutations in lamin A cause Hutchinson-Gilford progeria syndrome. *Nature, 423,* 239–298.

Eriksson, M., Rasmussen, F., & Tynelius, P. (2006). Genetic factors in physical activity and the equal environment assumption: The Swedish young male twins study. *Behavior Genetics, 36,* 238–247.

Escalona, S. (1968). *The roots of individuality: Normal patterns of individuality.* Chicago: Aldine.

Eskritt, M., & Lee, K. (2002). "Remember where you last saw that card": Children's production of external symbols as a memory aid. *Developmental Psychology, 38,* 254–266.

Espinosa-Hernandez, G., & Lefkowitz, E. S. (2009). Sexual behaviors and attitudes and ethnic identity during college. *Journal of Sex Research, 46,* 471–482.

Espy, K. A., Molfese, V. J., & DiLalla, L. F. (2001). Effects of environmental measures on intelligence in young children: Growth curve modeling of longitudinal data. *Merrill-Palmer Quarterly, 47,* 42–73.

Essa, E. L., & Murray, C. I. (1994). Young children's understanding and experience with death. *Young Children, 49,* 74–81.

Essex, M. J., Kraemer, H. C., Slattery, M., Burk, L. R., Boyce, W. T., Woodward, H. R., & Kupfer, D. J. (2009). Screening for childhood mental health problems: Outcomes and early identification. *Journal of Child Psychology and Psychiatry, 50,* 562–570.

Etgen, T., Sander, D., Huntgeburth, U., Poppert, H., Förstl, H., & Bickel, H. (2010). Physical activity and incident cognitive impairment in elderly persons. *Archives of Internal Medicine, 170,* 186–193.

Evans, D., & Goldman, B. (2010). First person: Jane Fowler. *The Body: The Complete HIV/AIDS Resource, HIV/AIDS Resource Center for Women.* Available at: http://www.thebody.com/content/art45791.html. Accessed: May 5, 2010.

Evans, G. W. (2004). The environment of childhood poverty. *American Psychologist, 59,* 77–92.

Evans, G. W. (2006). Child development and the physical environment. *Annual Review of Psychology, 57,* 423–451.

Evans, J. R. (2001). Risk factors for age-related macular degeneration. *Progress in Retinal and Eye Research, 20,* 227.

Evans, J. R., Fletcher, A. E., Wormald, R. P., Ng, E. S., Stirling, S., Smeeth, L., Breeze, E., Bulpitt, C. J., Nunes, M., Jones, D., & Tulloch, A. (2002). Prevalence of visual impairment in people aged 75 years and older in Britain: Results from the MRC trial of assessment and management of older people in the community. *Ophthalmology,* 795–800.

Evans, M. A., & Shaw, D. (2008). Home grown for reading: Parental contributions to young children's emergent literacy and word recognition. *Canadian Psychology, 49,* 89–95.

F

Faber, C. E., & Grontved, A. M. (2000). Cochlear implantation and change in quality of life. *Acta Otolaryngology Supplement, 543,* 151–153.

Fabes, R. A., Martin, C. L., & Hanish, L. D. (2003). Young children's play qualities in same-, other-, and mixed-sex peer groups. *Child Development, 74,* 921–932.

Fagan, J., & Palkovitz, R. (2007). Unmarried, nonresident fathers' involvement with their infants: A risk and resilience perspective. *Journal of Family Psychology, 21,* 479–489.

Fagan, J., Palkovitz, R., Roy, K., & Farrie, D. (2009). Pathways to paternal engagement: Longitudinal effects of risk and resilience on nonresident fathers. *Developmental Psychology, 45,* 1389–1405.

Fagot, B. I. (1978). The influence of sex of child on parental reactions to toddler children. *Child Development, 49,* 459–465.

Fagot, B. I. (1985). Beyond the reinforcement principle: Another step toward understanding sex-role development. *Developmental Psychology, 21,* 1097–1104.

Fagot, B. I. (1997). Attachment, parenting, and peer interactions of toddler children. *Developmental Psychology, 33,* 489–499.

Fagot, B. I., & Kavanaugh, K. (1993). Parenting during the second year: Effects of children's age, sex, and attachment classification. *Child Development, 64,* 258–271.

Fagot, B. I., & Leinbach, M. D. (1989). The young child's gender schema: Environmental input, internal organization. *Child Development, 60,* 663–672.

Fagot, B. I., & Leinbach, M. D. (1993). Gender-role development in young children: From discrimination to labeling. *Developmental Review, 13,* 205–224.

Fagot, B. I., Leinbach, M. D., & Hagan, R. (1986). Gender labeling and the adoption of sex-typed behaviors. *Developmental Psychology, 22,* 440–443.

Fagot, B. I., Leinbach, M. D., & O'Boyle, C. (1992). Gender labeling, gender stereotyping, and parenting behaviors. *Developmental Psychology, 28,* 225–230.

Falcon, L. M., & Tucker, K. L. (2000). Prevalence and correlates of depressive symptoms among Hispanic elders in Massachusetts. *Journal of Gerontology: Social Sciences, 55,* S108–S116.

Fantz, R. L., & Fagan, J. F. (1975). Visual attention to size and number of pattern details by term and preterm infants during the first six months. *Child Development, 46,* 3–18.

Farah, M. J., Betancourt, L., Shera, D. M., Savage, J. H., Giannetta, J. M., Brodsky, N. L., Malmud, E. K., & Hurt, H. (2008). Environmental stimulation, parental nurturance and cognitive development in humans. *Developmental Science, 11,* 793–801.

Farber, N. (2003). *Adolescent pregnancy. Policy and prevention services.* New York: Springer.

Farlow, M. R., & Boustani, M. (2009). Pharmacological treatment of Alzheimer disease and mild cognitive impairment. In M. F. Weiner & A. M. Lipton (Eds.), *The American Psychiatric Publishing Textbook of Alzheimer disease and other dementias.* Washington, DC: American Psychiatric Publishing.

Farroni, T., Johnson, M. H., Menon, E., Zulian, L., Faraguna, D., & Csibra, G. (2005). Newborns' preference for face-relevant stimuli: Effects of contrast polarity. *Proceedings of the National Academy of Sciences, 102,* 17245–17250.

Farver, J. A. M., Kim, Y. K., & Lee-Shin, Y. (2000). Within cultural differences: Examining individual differences in Korean American and European American preschoolers' social pretend play. *Journal of Cross-Cultural Psychology, 31,* 583–602.

Farver, J. A. M., & Lee-Shin, Y. (1997). Social pretend play in Korean and Anglo American preschoolers. *Child Development, 68,* 544–556.

Faulkner, D., Joiner, R., Littleton, K., Miell, D., & Thompson, L. (2000). The mediating effect of task presentation on collaboration and children's acquisition of scientific reasoning. *European Journal of Psychology of Education, 15,* 417–430.

Faulkner, K. W. (1997). Talking about death with a dying child. *American Journal of Nursing, 97,* 64, 66, 68–69.

Faust, M. A., & Glenzer, N. (2000). "I could read those parts over and over": Eighth graders rereading to enhance enjoyment and learning with literature. *Journal of Adolescent and Adult Literacy, 44,* 234–239.

Favaro, A., Tenconi, E., & Santonastaso, P. (2006). Perinatal factors and the risk of developing anorexia nervosa and bulimia nervosa. *Archives of General Psychiatry, 63,* 82–88.

Favilla, M. (2006). Reaching movements in children: Accuracy and reaction time development. *Journal of Experimental Brain Research, 169,* 122–125.

Fearon, R. M., P., van IJzendoorn, M. H., Fonagy, P., Bakermans-Kranenburg, M. J., Schuengel, C., & Bokhorst, C. L. (2006). In search of shared and nonshared environmental factors in security of attachment: A behavior-genetic study of the association between sensitivity and attachment security. *Developmental Psychology, 42,* 1026–1040.

Federal Interagency Forum on Aging Related Statistics (2008). *Older Americans 2008: Key indicators of well-being.* Washington, DC: U. S. Government Printing Office. Available at: www.agingstats.gov. Accessed: September 20, 2009.

Federal Interagency Forum on Child and Family Statistics (2009). *America's children: Key national indicators of well-being, 2009.* Washington, DC: U. S. Government Printing Office. Available at: http://childstats.gov. Accessed: January 9, 2010.

Fehlings, D., Hunt, C., & Rosenbaum, P. (2007). Cerebral palsy, 279–286. In I. Brown & M. Percy (Eds.), *A comprehensive guide to intellectual & developmental disabilities.* Baltimore, MD: Paul H. Brookes.

Feingold, A. (1994). Gender differences in personality: A meta-analysis. *Psychological Bulletin, 116,* 429–456.

Feinman, S. (1992). *Social referencing and the social construction of reality in infancy.* New York: Plenum.

Feldman, D. H. (1986). Nature's gambit: Child prodigies and the development of human potential. New York: Basic Books.

Feldman, D. H., & Fowler, R. C. (1997). The nature(s) of developmental change: Piaget, Vygotsky, and the transition process. *New Ideas in Psychology, 3,* 195–210.

Feldman, R. (2007). Parent-infant synchrony. Biological foundations and developmental outcomes. *Current Directions in Psychological Science, 16,* 340–345.

Feldman, R., & Eidelman, A. I. (2003). Skin-to-skin contact (kangaroo care) accelerates autonomic and neurobehavioral maturation in preterm infants. *Developmental Medicine and Child Neurology, 45,* 274–281.

Feldman, R., & Eidelman, A. I. (2006). Neonatal state organization, neuromaturation, mother–infant interaction, and cognitive development in small-for-gestational-age premature infants. *Pediatrics, 118,* 869–879.

Feldman, R., Weller, A., Sirota, L., & Eidelman, A. (2003). Testing a family intervention hypothesis: The contribution of mother–infant skin-to-skin contact (kangaroo care) to family interaction, proximity, and touch. *Journal of Family Psychology, 17,* 94–107.

Feldman, R., Weller, A., Zagoory-Sharon, O., & Levine, A. (2007). Evidence for a neuroendocrinological foundation of human affiliation. *Psychological Science, 18,* 965–970.

Feldman, R. D. (1982). *Whatever happened to the Quiz Kids? Perils and profits of growing up gifted.* Chicago: Chicago Review Press.

Feldman, S. S., Biringen, Z. C., & Nash, S. C. (1981). Fluctuations of sex-related self-attributions as a function of stage of family life cycle. *Developmental Psychology, 17,* 24–35.

Felmlee, D., & Muraco, A. (2009). Gender and friendship norms among older adults. *Research on Aging, 31,* 318–344.

Felton, B. J., & Berry, C. A. (1992). Do the sources of the urban elderly's social support determine its psychological consequences? *Psychology and Aging, 7,* 89–97.

Feng, J., Spence, I., & Pratt, J. (2007). Playing an action video game reduces gender differences in spatial cognition. *Psychological Science, 18,* 850–855.

Fenson, L., Dale, P. S., Reznick, J. S., Bates, E., Thal, D. J., & Pethick, S. J. (1994). Variability in early communicative development. *Monographs of the Society for Research in Child Development, 59* (Serial No. 242).

Ferbeyre, G., & Lowe, S. W. (2002). Ageing: The price of tumour suppression? *Nature, 415,* 26–27.

Ferguson., R. F. (2002). *What doesn't meet the eye: Understanding and addressing racial disparities in high-achieving suburban schools.* Oakbrook, IL: North Central Regional Educational Laboratory. Available at: http://www.tripodproject.org/uploads/file/What_doesnt_meet_the_eye.pdf. Accessed: November 2, 2007.

Fernald, A. (2004). Auditory development in -infancy. In G. Bremner, & A. Fogel (Eds.), *Blackwell handbook of infant development,* 35–70. Malden, MA: Blackwell Publishing.

Ferrario, C. G., Freeman, F. J., Nellett, G., & Scheel, J. (2008). Changing nursing students' attitudes about aging: An argument for the successful aging paradigm. *Educational Gerontology, 34,* 51–66.

Ferri, B., & Connor, D. J. (2005). Tools of exclusion: Race, disability, and (re)segregated education. *Teachers College Record, 107,* 453–474.

Ferri, C. P., Prince, M., Brayne, C., Brodaty, H., Fratiglioni, L., Ganguli, M., Hall, K., Hasegawa, K., Hendrie, H., Huang, Y., Jorm, A., Mathers, C., Menezes, P. R., Rimmer, E., & Scazufca, M. (2005). Global prevalence of dementia: A Delphi consensus study. *Lancet, 366,* 2112–2117.

Field, D. (1981). Can preschool children really learn to conserve? *Child Development, 52,* 326–334.

Field, D., & Gueldner, S. H. (2001). The oldest-old: How do they differ from the old-old? *Journal of Gerontological Nursing, 27,* 20–27.

Field, J., Muir, D., Pilon, R., Sinclair, M., & Dodwell, P. (1980). Infants' orientation to lateral sounds from birth to three months. *Child Development, 51,* 295–298.

Field, N. P. (2008). Whether to relinquish or maintain a bond with the deceased. In M. S. Stroebe, R. O. Hansson, H. Schut, & W. Stroebe (Eds.), *Handbook of bereavement research and practice. Advances in theory and intervention.* Washington, DC: American Psychological Association.

Field, N. P., & Filanosky, C. (2010). Continuing bonds, risk factors for complicated grief, and adjustment to bereavement. *Death Studies, 34,* 1–29.

Field, N. P., Nichols, C., Holen, A., & Horowitz, M. J. (1999). The relation of continuing attachment to adjustment in conjugal bereavement. *Journal of Consulting & Clinical Psychology, 67,* 212–218.

Field, T., Diego, M. A., Hernandez-Reif, M., Deeds, O., & Figuereido, B. (2006). Moderate versus light pressure massage therapy leads to greater weight gain in preterm infants. *Infant Behavior and Development, 2006,* 574–578.

Field, T. M. (1990). *Infancy.* Cambridge, MA: Harvard University Press.

Field, T. M. (1995). Infants of depressed mothers. *Infant Behavior and Development, 18,* 1–13.

Fifer, W. P., Monk, C. E.,. & Grose-Fifer, J. (2004). Prenatal development and risk. In G. Bremner, & A. Fogel (Eds.), *Blackwell handbook of infant development,* 505–542. Malden, MA: Blackwell Publishing.

Filipek, P. A., Accardo, P. J., Ashwal, S., & Baranek, G. T. (2000). Practice parameter: Screening and diagnosis of autism: Report of the Quality Standards Subcommittee of the American Academy of Neurology and the Child Neurology Society. *Neurology, 55,* 468–479.

Filipp, S. H. (1996). Motivation and emotion. In J. E. Birren, K. W. Schaie, R. P. Abeles, M. Gatz, & T. A. Salthouse (Eds.), *Handbook of the psychology of the aging* (4th ed.). San Diego: Academic Press.

Fincham, F. D. (2003). Marital conflict: Correlates, structure, and context. *Current Directions in Psychological Science, 12,* 23–27.

Finitzo, T., Gunnarson, A. D., & Clark, J. L. (1990). Auditory deprivation and early conductive hearing loss from otitis media. *Topics in Language Disorders, 11,* 29–42.

Finkel, D., Pedersen, N. L., Reynolds, C. A., Berg, S., de Faire, U., & Svartengren, M. (2003). Genetic and environmental influences on decline in biobehavioral markers of aging. *Behavior Genetics, 33,* 107–123.

Finkelhor, D. (2009). The prevention of childhood sexual abuse. *Future Children, 19,* 169–194.

Finkelhor, D., & Berliner, L. (1995). Research on the treatment of sexually abused children: A review and recommendations. *Journal of the American Academy of Child and Adolescent Psychiatry, 34,* 1408–1423.

Finkelhor, D., Turner, H., Ormrod, R., & Hamby, S. L. (2010). Trends in childhood violence and abuse exposure: Evidence from two national surveys. *Archives of Pediatric & Adolescent Medicine, 164,* 238–242.

Finkelstein, J. A., & Schiffman, S. S. (1999). Workshop on taste and smell in the elderly: An overview. *Physiological Behavior, 66,* 173–176.

Finn, J. D. (2002). Class-size reduction in grades K–3. In A. Molnar (Ed.), *School reform proposals: The research evidence,* 27–48. Greenwich, CT: Information Age Publishing.

Fisch, H., Hyun, G., Golder, R., Hensle, T. W., Olsson, C. A., & Liberson, G. L. (2003). The influence of paternal age on Down syndrome. *Journal of Urology, 169*, 2275–2278.

Fischer, J. L., Sollie, D. L., Sorell, G. T., & Green, S. K. (1989). Marital status and career stage influences on social networks of young adults. *Journal of Marriage and the Family, 51*, 521–534.

Fischer, J. S. (2000, February 14). Best hope or broken promise? After a decade, gene therapy goes on trial. *U.S. News and World Report, 46*.

Fischer, K. W. (1980). A theory of cognitive development: The control and construction of hierarchies of skills. *Psychological Review, 87*, 477–531.

Fischer, K. W., & Bidell, T. (1991). Constraining nativist inferences about cognitive capacities. In S. Carey & Gelman (Eds.), The epigenesis of mind: Essays on biology and cognition. Hillsdale, NJ: Erlbaum.

Fischer, K. W., Kenny, S. L., & Pipp, S. L. (1990). How cognitive processes and environmental conditions organize discontinuities in the development of abstractions. In C. N. Alexander & E. J. Langer (Eds.), *Higher stages of human development: Perspectives on adult growth*. New York: Oxford University Press.

Fischer, P., Jungwirth, S., Zehetmayer, S., Weissgram, S., Hoenigschnabl, S., Gelpi, E., Krampla, W., & Tragl, K. H. (2007). Conversion from subtypes of mild cognitive impairment to Alzheimer dementia. *Neurology, 68*, 288–291.

Fischer, R. B., Blazey, M. L., & Lipman, H. T. (1992). *Students of the third age*. New York: Macmillan.

Fisher, C., & Tokura, H. (1996). Acoustic cues to grammatical structure in infant-directed speech: Cross-linguistic evidence. *Child Development, 67*, 3192–3218.

Fisher, E. P. (1992). The impact of play on development: A meta-analysis. *Play and Culture, 5*, 159–181.

Fisher, H. (2006). The drive to love: The neural mechanism for mate selection. In R. J. Sternberg & K. Weis (Eds.), *The new psychology of love*. New Haven, CT: Yale University Press.

Fisher, K. R., Marshall, P. J., & Nanayakkara, A. R. (2009). Motivational orientation, error monitoring, and academic performance in middle childhood: A behavioral and electrophysiological investigation. *Mind, Brain, and Education, 3*, 56–62.

Fisher, L., Ames, E. W., Chisholm, K., & Savoie, L. (1997). Problems reported by parents of Romanian orphans adopted to British Columbia. *International Journal of Behavioral Development, 20*, 67–82.

Fisher, S., & Greenberg, R. P. (1977). *The scientific credibility of Freud's theories and therapy*. New York: Basic Books.

Fitzgerald, J. M. (1999). Autobiographical memory and social cognition: Development of the remembered self in adulthood. In T. M. Hess & F. Blanchard-Fields (Eds.), *Social cognition and aging* (pp. 143–171). San Diego: Academic Press.

Fivush, R. (2009). Sociocultural perspectives on autobiographical memory. In M. L. Courage & N. Cowan (Eds.), *The Development of Memory in Infancy and Childhood* (pp. 283–302). New York, NY: Psychology Press.

Fivush, R., Gray, J. T., & Fromhoff, F. A. (1987). Two-year-olds talk about the past. *Cognitive Development, 2*, 393–409.

Flaherty, J. H., & Morley, J. E. (2004). Delirium: A call to improve current standards of care. *Journal of Gerontology: Medical Sciences, 59A*, M341–M343.

Flavell, J. H. (1963). *The developmental psychology of Jean Piaget*. New York: Van Nostrand Reinhold.

Flavell, J. H. (1985). *Cognitive development* (2nd ed.). Englewood Cliffs, NJ: Prentice Hall.

Flavell, J. H. (1996). Piaget's legacy. *Psychological Science, 7*, 200–203.

Flavell, J. H. (1999). Cognitive development: Children's knowledge about the mind. *Annual Review of Psychology, 50*, 21–45.

Flavell, J. H., Beach, D. R., & Chinsky, J. M. (1966). Spontaneous verbal rehearsal in a memory task as a function of age. *Child Development, 37*, 283–299.

Flavell, J. H., Everett, B. H., Croft, K., & Flavell, E. R. (1981). Young children's knowledge about visual perception: Further evidence for the level 1–level 2 distinction. *Developmental Psychology, 17*, 99–103.

Flavell, J. H., Miller, P. H., & Miller, S. A. (1993). *Cognitive development*. Englewood Cliffs, NJ: Prentice Hall.

Flavell, J. H., & Wellman, H. M. (1977). Metamemory. In R. V. Kail & J. W. Hagen (Eds.), *Perspectives on the development of memory and cognition*. Hillsdale, NJ: Erlbaum.

Fleeson, W. (2004). The quality of American life at the end of the century. In O. G. Brim, C. D. Ryff, & R. C. Kessler (Eds.), *How healthy are we? A national study of well-being at midlife*. Chicago: University of Chicago Press.

Fletcher, K. L., & Bray, N. W. (1996). External memory strategy use in preschool children. *Merrill-Palmer Quarterly, 42*, 379–396.

Flieller, A. (1999). Comparison of the development of formal thought in adolescent cohorts aged 10 to 15 years (1967–1996 and 1972–1993). *Developmental Psychology, 35*, 1048–1058.

Flook, L., & Fuligni, A. J. (2008). Family and school spillover in adolescents' daily lives. *Child Development, 79*, 776–787.

Floor, P., & Akhtar, N. (2006). Can 18-month-old infants learn words by listening in on conversations? *Infancy, 9*, 327–339.

Flores, E., Cicchetti, D., & Rogosch, F. A. (2005). Predictors of resilience in maltreated and non-maltreated Latino children. *Developmental Psychology, 41*, 338–351.

Florian, V., & Kravetz, S. (1985). Children's concepts of death. A cross-cultural comparison among Muslims, Druze, Christians, and Jews in Israel. *Journal of Cross-Cultural Psychology, 16*, 174–189.

Florsheim, P., Sumida, E., McCann, C., Winstanley, M., Fukui, R., Seefeldt, T., & Moore, D. (2003). The transition to parenthood among young African American and Latino couples: Relational predictors of risk for parental dysfunction. *Journal of Family Psychology, 17*, 65–79.

Flum, H., & Blustein, D. L. (2000). Reinvigorating the study of vocational research. *Journal of Vocational Behavior, 56*, 380–404.

Flynn, J. R. (1987). Massive IQ gains in 14 nations: What IQ tests really measure. *Psychological Bulletin, 101*, 171–191.

Flynn, J. R. (1998). IQ gains over time: Toward finding the causes. In U. Neisser (Ed.), *The rising curve: Long-term gains in IQ and related measures*. Washington, DC: American Psychological Association.

Flynn, J. R. (1999). Search for justice: The discovery of IQ gains over time. *American Psychologist, 54*, 5–20.

Flynn, J. R. (2007). *What is intelligence?* New York: Cambridge University Press.

Fogassi, L., & Ferrari, P. F. (2007). Mirror neurons and the evolution of embodied language. *Current Directions in Psychological Science, 17*, 136–141.

Fogel, A., King, B. J., & Shanker, S. G. (Eds.). (2008). *Human development in the twenty-first century. Visionary ideas from systems scientists*. New York: Cambridge University Press.

Fogg, P. (2008, July 18). When generations collide. Colleges try to prevent age-old culture clashes as four distinct groups meet in the workplace. *The Chronicle of Higher Education*, B18–B20.

Foley, K., & Hendin, H. (2002). Conclusion: Changing the culture. In K. Foley, & H. Hendin (Eds.), *The case against assisted suicide: For the right to end-of-life care*. Baltimore: The Johns Hopkins Press.

Folkman, S., & Moskowitz, J. T. (2004). Coping: Pitfalls and promise. *Annual Review of Psychology, 55*, 745–774.

Fonagy, P., & Target, M. (2000). The place of psychodynamic theory in developmental psychopathology. *Development and Psychopathology, 12*, 407–425.

Foorman, B. R. (1995). Research on "The Great Debate": Code-oriented versus whole language approaches to reading instruction. *School Psychology Review, 24*, 376–392.

Foorman, B. R., Francis, D. J., Fletcher, J. M., Schatschneider, C., & Mehta, P. (1998). The role of instruction in learning to read: Preventing reading failure in at-risk children. *Journal of Educational Psychology, 90*, 37–55.

Foos, P. W., & Sarno, S. J. (1998). Adult age differences in semantic and episodic memory. *Journal of Genetic Psychology, 159*, 297–312.

Ford, T., Goodman, R., & Meltzer, H. (2003). The British child and adolescent mental health survey 1999: The prevalence of DSM-IV disorders. *Journal of the American Academy of Child and Adolescent Psychiatry, 42*, 1203–1211.

Fordham, S., & Ogbu, J. U. (1986). Black students' school success: Coping with the "burden of 'acting white.'" *Urban Review, 18*, 176–206.

Forgatch, M. S., & DeGarmo, D. S. (1999). Parenting through change: An effective prevention program for single mothers. *Journal of Consulting and Clinical Psychology, 67*, 711–724.

Foster, J. D. (2008). Beauty is mostly in the eye of the beholder: Olfactory versus visual cues of attractiveness. *Journal of Social Psychology, 148*, 765–773.

Fouquereau, E., Fernandez, A., Fonseca, A. M., Paul, M. C., & Uotinen, V. (2005). Perceptions of and satisfaction with retirement: A comparison of six European Union countries. *Psychology and Aging, 20*, 524–528.

Fowler, J. W. (1981). *Stages of faith: The psychology of human development and the quest for meaning*. San Francisco: Harper & Row.

Fowler, J., & Dell, M. (2006). Stages of faith from infancy through adolescence: Reflections on three decades of faith development theory. In E. Roehlkepartain, P. King, L. Wagener, & P. Benson (Eds.), *The handbook of spiritual development in childhood and adolescence*. Thousand Oaks, CA: Sage.

Fowles, D. C., & Kochanska, G. (2000). Temperament as a moderator of pathways to conscience in children: The contribution of electrodermal activity. *Psychophysiology, 37*, 788–795.

Fox, B. (2001). As times change: A review of trends in personal and family life. In B. J. Fox (Ed.), *Family patterns, gender relations* (2nd ed.). Don Mills, Ont.: Oxford University Press.

Fox, M. K., Dodd, A. H., Wilson, A., & Gleason, P. M. (2009). Association between school food environment and practices and body mass index of U.S. public school children. *Journal of the American Dietetic Association, 109*, S108–117.

Fox, N. A., Henderson, H. A., Marshall, P. J., Nichols, K. E., & Ghera, M. M. (2005). Behavioral inhibition: Linking biology and behavior within a developmental framework. *Annual Review of Psychology, 56*, 235–262.

Fox, N. A., Henderson, H. A., Rubin, K. H., Calkins, S. D., & Schmidt, L. A. (2001). Continuity and discontinuity of behavioral inhibition and exuberance: Psychophysiological and behavioral influences across the first four years of life. *Child Development, 72*, 1–21.

Fox, S. E., Levitt, P., & Nelson, C. A. (2010). How the timing and quality of early experiences influence the development of brain architecture. *Child Development, 81*, 28–40.

Fozard, J. L., & Gordon-Salant, T. (2001). Changes in vision and hearing with aging. In J. E. Birren & K. W. Schaie (Eds.), *Handbook of the psychology of aging, 5th ed* (pp. 241-266). San Diego: Academic Press.

Fraga, M. F., Ballestar, E., Paz, M. F., Ropero, S., Setien, F., Ballestar, M. L., Heine-Suner, D., Cigudosa, J. C., Urioste, M., Benitez, J., Boix-Chormet, M., Sanchez-Aguilera, A., Ling, C., Carlsson, E., Poulsen, P., Vaag, A., Stephan, Z., Spector, T. D., Wu, Y.-Z., Plass, C., & Esteller, M. (2005). Epigenetic differences arise during the lifetime of monozygotic twins. *Proceedings of the National Academy of Sciences, 102,* 10604–10609.

Fraley, R. C. (2002). Attachment stability from infancy to adulthood: Meta-analysis and dynamic modeling of developmental mechanisms. *Personality and Social Psychology Review, 6,* 123–151.

Fraley, R. C., & Bonanno, G. A. (2004). Attachment and loss: A test of three competing models on the association between attachment-related avoidance and adaptation to bereavement. *Personality and Social Psychology Bulletin, 30,* 878–890.

Fraley, R. C., Fazzari, D. A., Bonanno, G. A., & Dekel, S. (2006). Attachment and psychological adaptation in high exposure survivors of the September 11th attack on the World Trade Center. *Personality and Social Psychology Bulletin, 32,* 538–551.

Fraley, R. C., & Shaver, P. R. (2008). Attachment theory and its place in contemporary personality theory. In O. P. John, R. W. Robins, & L. A. Pervin (Eds.), *Handbook of personality theory and research* (3rd ed.). New York: Guilford.

Francis, D., Diorio, J., Liu, D., & Meaney, M. J. (1999). Nongenomic transmission across generations of maternal behavior and stress responses in the rat. *Science, 286* (5442), 1155–1158.

Francis, K. L., & Spirduso, W. W. (2000). Age differences in the expression of manual asymmetry. *Experimental Aging Research, 26,* 169–180.

Frank, D., Brown, J., Johnson, S., & Cabral, H. (2002a). Forgotten fathers: An exploratory study of mothers' report of drug and alcohol problems among fathers of urban newborns. *Neurotoxicology and Teratology, 24,* 339–347.

Frank, D., Jacobs, R. R., Beeghly, M., Augustyn, M., Bellinger, D., Cabral, H., & Heeren, T. (2002b). Level of prenatal cocaine exposure and scores on the Bayley Scales of Infant Development: modifying effects of caregiver, early intervention, and birth weight. *Pediatrics, 110,* 1143–1152.

Frank, S. M., Raja, S. N., Bulcao, C., & Goldstein, D. S. (2000). Age-related thermoregulatory differences during core cooling in humans. *American Journal of Physiological Regulation, Integration, and Comparative Physiology, 279,* R349-354.

Franke, B., Neale, B. M., & Faraone, S. V. (2009). Genome-wide association studies in ADHD. *Human Genetics, 126,* 13–50.

Frankenburg, W. K., Dodds, J. B., Archer, P., Shapiro, H., & Bresnick, B. (1992). The Denver II: A major revision and restandardization of the Denver Development Screening Test. *Pediatrics, 89,* 91–97.

Franklin, C., & Corcoran, J. (2000). Preventing adolescent pregnancy: A review of programs and practices. *Social Work, 45,* 40–52.

Franklin, Z., Pilling, M., & Davies, I. (2005). The nature of infant color categorization: Evidence from eye movements on a target detection task. *Journal of Experimental Child Psychology, 91,* 227–248.

Franko, D. L., & Goerge, J. B. E. (2009). Overweight, eating behaviors, and body image in ethnically diverse youth. In L. Smolak & J. K. Thompson (Eds.), *Body image, eating disorders, and obesity in youth.* Washington, DC: American Psychological Association.

Fraser, M. W. (2004). The ecology of childhood: A multisystems perspective. In M. W. Fraser (Ed.), *Risk and resilience in childhood: An ecological perspective, 2nd ed.,* 1–9. Washington, D. C. NASW Press.

Frattarelli, J. L., Miller, K. A., Miller, B. T., Elkind-Hirsch, K., & Scott, R. T. (2008). Male age negatively impacts embryo development and reproductive outcome in donor oocyte assisted reproductive technology cycles. *Fertility and Sterility, 90,* 97–103.

Frawley, W. (1997). *Vygotsky and cognitive science: Language and the unification of the social and computational mind.* Cambridge, MA: Harvard University Press.

Frederick, D. A., Peplau, L. A., & Lever, J. (2006). The swimsuit issue: Correlates of body image in a sample of 52,677 heterosexual adults. *Body Image, 3,* 413–419.

Fredriksen, K., Rhodes, J., Reddy, R., & Niobe, W. (2004). Sleepless in Chicago: Tracking the effects of adolescent sleep loss during the middle school years. *Child Development, 75,* 84–95.

Freeman, S. F. N. (2000). Academic and social attainments of children with mental retardation in general education and special education settings. *Remedial and Special Education, 21,* 3–19.

Fremont, W. P. (2003). School refusal in children and adolescents. *American Family Physician, 68,* 1555–1560.

Freud, S. (1930). *Three contributions to the theory of sex.* New York: Nervous and Mental Disease Publishing Company. (Original work published 1905).

Freud, S. (1933). *New introductory lectures in psychoanalysis.* New York: Norton.

Freud, S. (1960). *A general introduction to psychoanalysis.* New York: Washington Square Press. (Original work published 1935).

Freud, S. (1964). An outline of psychoanalysis. In J. Strachey (Ed.), *The standard edition of the complete psychological works of Sigmund Freud* (Vol. 23). London: Hogarth Press. (Original work published 1940).

Freund, A., & Riediger, M. (2006). Goals as building blocks of personality and development in adulthood. In D. K. Mroczek & T. D. Little (Eds.), *Handbook of personality development.* Mahwah, NJ: Erlbaum.

Freund, L. S. (1990). Maternal regulation of children's problem solving behavior and its impact on children's performance. *Child Development, 61,* 113–126.

Frey, K. S., & Ruble, D. N. (1985). What children say when the teacher is not around: Conflicting goals in social comparison and performance assessment in the classroom. *Journal of Personality and Social Psychology, 48,* 550–562.

Frey, K. S., & Ruble, D. N. (1992). Gender constancy and the cost of sex-typed behavior: A test of the conflict hypothesis. *Developmental Psychology, 28,* 714–721.

Freyd, J. J., Putnam, F. W., Lyon, T. D., Becker-Blease, K. A., Cheit, R. E., Siegel, N. B., & Pezdek, K. (2005). The Science of Child Sexual Abuse, *Science, 308,* 501.

Friebe, A., & Arck, P. (2008). Causes for spontaneous abortion: What the bugs "gut" to do with it? *The International Journal of Biochemistry & Cell Biology, 40,* 2348–2352.

Friederici, A. D. (2009). Neurocognition of language development. In E. L. Bavin (Ed.), *The Cambridge handbook of child language,* 51–68. New York: Cambridge University Press.

Friedman, L. J. (1999). *Identity's architect: A biography of Erik H. Erikson.* New York: Scribner.

Friedman, S. L., & Boyle, D. E. (2008). Attachment in US children experiencing nonmaternal care in the early 1990s. *Attachment and Human Development, 10,* 225–261.

Friedrich, L. K., & Stein, A. H. (1973). Aggressive and prosocial television programs and the natural behavior of preschool children. *Monographs of the Society for Research in Child Development, 38* (4, Serial No. 51).

Friesen, J. (2009, January 23). A family, yes, and a tapestry too; for perhaps the first time in history, a president's extended family reflects the diversity of the country he leads. *The Globe and Mail,* A3.

Frieswijk, N., Buunk, B. P., Steverink, N., & Slaets, J. P. J. (2004). The effect of social comparison information on the life satisfaction of frail older persons. *Psychology and Aging, 19,* 183–190.

Frith, Uta. (2003). *Autism: Explaining the enigma* (2nd ed.). Malden, MA: Blackwell.

Froehlich, T. E., Lanphear, B. P., Epstein, J. N., Barbaresi, W. J., Katusic, S. K., & Kahn, R. S. (2007). Prevalence, recognition, and treatment of attention-deficit/hyperactivity disorder in a national sample of US children. *Archives of Pediatric & Adolescent Medicine, 161,* 857–864.

Fry, C. L. (1985). Culture, behavior, and aging in the comparative perspective. In J. E. Birren & K. W. Schaie (Eds.), *Handbook of the psychology of aging* (2nd ed.). New York: Van Nostrand Reinhold.

Fry, C. L. (2009). Out of the armchair and off the veranda: Anthropological theories and the experiences of aging. In V. L. Bengtson, M. Silverstein, N. M. Putney, & D. Gans (Eds.), *Handbook of theories of aging* (2nd ed.). New York: Springer.

Fry, D. P. (2006). Reciprocity: The foundation stone of morality. In M. Killen & J. G. Smetana (Eds.), *Handbook of moral development.* Mahwah, NJ: Erlbaum.

Fry, P. S. (1992). Major social theories of aging and their implications for counseling concepts and practice: A critical review. *Counseling Psychologist, 20,* 246–329.

Fry, P. S. (1997). Grandparents' reactions to the death of a grandchild: An exploratory factor analytic study. *Omega: Journal of Death and Dying, 35,* 119–140.

Fryauf-Bertschy, H., Tyler, R. S., Kelsay, D. M. R., Gantz, B. J., & Woodworth, G. G. (1997). Cochlear implant use by prelingually deafened children: The influence of age at implant and length of device use. *Journal of Speech, Language, and Hearing Research, 40,* 183–199.

Fryer, S. L., McGee, C. L., Matt, G. E., Riley, E. P., and Mattson, S. N. (2007). Evolution of psychopathological conditions in children with heavy prenatal alcohol exposure. *Pediatrics, 119,* E733–E741.

Fuligni, A. J. (1998). Authority, autonomy, and parent–adolescent conflict and cohesion: A study of adolescents from Mexican, Chinese, Filipino, and European backgrounds. *Developmental Psychology, 34,* 782–792.

Fuligni, A. J., & Stevenson, H. W. (1995). Time use and mathematics achievement among American, Chinese, and Japanese high school students. *Child Development, 66,* 830–842.

Fuller, S. (2008). Job mobility and wage trajectories for men and women in the United States. *American Sociological Review, 73,* 158–183.

Fullilove, R. E., & Treisman, E. M. (1990). Mathematics achievement among African American undergraduates at the University of California, Berkeley: An evaluation of the mathematics workshop. *Journal of Negro Education, 59,* 463–478.

Furman, E. (1984). Children's patterns in mourning the death of a loved one. In H. Wass & C. A. Corr (Eds.), *Childhood and death.* Washington, DC: Hemisphere.

Furman, W., & Buhrmester, D. (1992). Age and sex differences in perceptions of networks of personal relationships. *Child Development, 63,* 103–115.

Furman, W., & Collins, W. A. (2009). Adolescent romantic relationships and experiences. In K. H. Rubin, W. M. Bukowski, & B. Laursen (Eds.),

Handbook of peer interactions, relationships, and groups. New York: Guilford.

Furstenberg, F. F. (2005). Non-normative life course transitions: Reflections on the significance of demographic events on lives. In R. Levy, P. Ghisletta, J. Le Goff, D. Spini, & E. Widmer (Eds.), *Advances in life course research: Vol. 10. Towards an interdisciplinary perspective on the life course.* Amsterdam: Elsevier.

Furstenberg, F. F., Jr. (2000). The sociology of adolescence and youth in the 1990s: A critical commentary. *Journal of Marriage and the Family, 62,* 896–910.

Furstenberg, F. F., Jr., Brooks-Gunn, J., & Chase-Lansdale, L. (1989). Teenage pregnancy and childbearing. *American Psychologist, 44,* 313–320.

Furstenberg, F. F., Jr., Brooks-Gunn, J., & Morgan, S. P. (1987). *Adolescent mothers in later life.* New York: Cambridge University Press.

Furstenberg, F. F., Jr., Kennedy, S., McLoyd, V. C., Rumbaut, R. G., & Settersten, R. A., Jr. (2004). Growing up is harder to do. *Contexts, 3*(3), 33–41.

G

Gable, S., & Lutz, S. (2000). Household, parent, and child contributions to childhood obesity. *Family Relations, 49,* 293–300.

Gabriel, K., Hofmann, C., Glavas, M., & Weinberg, J. (1998). The hormonal effects of alcohol use on the mother and fetus. *Alcohol Health & Research World, 22,* 170–177.

Gage, F. H., Song, H., & Kempermann, G. (2008a). Adult neurogenesis: A prologue. In F. H. Gage, G. Kempermann, & H. Song (Eds.), *Adult neurogenesis,* 1–6. NY: Cold Spring Harbor Laboratory Press.

Gage, F. H., Song, H., & Kempermann, G. (Eds.) (2008b). *Adult neurogenesis.* NY: Cold Spring Harbor Laboratory Press.

Gagne, J. R., Vendlinski, M. K., & Goldsmith, H. H. (2009). The genetics of childhood temperament. In Y. Kim (Ed.), *Handbook of behavior genetics.* New York: Springer.

Gagnon, M. D., Hersen, M., Kabacoff, R. I., & Vanhasselt, V. B. (1999). Interpersonal and psychological correlates of marital dissatisfaction in late life: A review. *Clinical Psychology Review, 19,* 359–378.

Galambos, N. L., Almeida, D. M., & Petersen, A. C. (1990). Masculinity, femininity, and sex role attitudes in early adolescence: Exploring gender intensification. *Child Development, 61,* 1905–1914.

Galdo-Alvarez, S., Lindin, M., & Diaz, F. (2009). Age-related prefrontal over-recruitment in semantic memory retrieval: Evidence from successful face naming and the tip-of-the-tongue state. *Biological Psychology, 82,* 89–96.

Gallagher, H. L., & Frith, C. D. (2003). Functional imaging of "theory of mind." *Trends in Cognitive Sciences, 7,* 77–83.

Gallagher, S. K., & Gerstel, N. (2001). Connections and constraints: The effects of children on caregiving. *Journal of Marriage and the Family, 63,* 265–275.

Gallagher-Thompson, D., & Coon, D. W. (2007). Evidence-based psychological treatments for distress in family caregivers of older adults. *Psychology and Aging, 22,* 37–51.

Gallup, G. G., Jr. (1979). Self-recognition in chimpanzees and man: A developmental and comparative perspective. In M. Lewis & L. A. Rosenblum (Eds.), *Genesis of behavior: Vol. 2. The child and its family.* New York: Plenum.

Galupo, M. P., Cartwright, K. B. & Savage, L. S. (2009, December 16). Cross-category friendships and postformal thought among college students. *Journal of Adult Development.* Springer Netherlands: Published online.

Galvan, A., Hare, T., Voss, H., Gover, G., & Casey, B. J. (2007). Risk-taking and the adolescent brain: Who is at risk? *Developmental Science, 10,* F8–F14.

Gamé, F., Carchon, I., & Vital-Durand, F. (2003). The effect of stimulus attractiveness on visual tracking in 2- to 6-month-old infants. *Infant Behavior & Development, 26,* 135–150.

Gamoran, A., Porter, A. C., Smithson, J., & White, P. A. (1997). Upgrading high school mathematics instruction: Improving learning opportunities for low-achieving, low-income youth. *Educational Evaluation and Policy Analysis, 19,* 325–338.

Ganahl, D. J., Prinsen, T. J., & Netzley, S. B. (2003). A content analysis of prime time commercials: A contextual framework of gender representation. *Sex Roles, 49,* 545–551.

Gannon, L., & Ekstrom, B. (1993). Attitudes toward menopause: The influence of sociocultural paradigms. *Psychology of Women Quarterly, 17,* 275–288.

Garbarino, J. (1992). *Children and families in the social environment* (2nd ed.). New York: Aldine de Gruyter.

Garber, J. (1984). The developmental progression of depression in female children. In D. Cicchetti & K. Schneider-Rosen (Eds.), *Childhood depression* (New Directions for Child Development, No. 26). San Francisco: Jossey-Bass.

Garber, J., & Flynn, C. (2001). Vulnerability to depression in childhood and adolescence. In R. E. Ingram & J. M. Price (Eds.), *Vulnerability to psychopathology. Risk across the life-span.* New York: Guilford.

Garces, E., Thomas, D., & Currie, J. (2002). Longer term effects of Head Start. *American Economic Review, 92,* 999–1102.

Garcia, F., & Gracia, E. (2009). Is always authoritative the optimum parenting style? Evidence from Spanish families. *Adolescence, 44,* 101–131.

Garciaguirre, J. S., Adolph, K. E., & Shrout, P. E. (2007). Baby carriage: Infants walking with loads. *Child Development, 78,* 664–680.

Gard, M. C. E., & Freeman, C. P. (1996). The dismantling of a myth: A review of eating disorders and socioeconomic status. *International Journal of Eating Disorders, 20,* 1–12.

Gardener, H., Spiegelman, D., & Buka, S. L. (2009). Prenatal risk factors for autism: Comprehensive meta-analysis. *British Journal of Psychiatry, 195,* 7–14.

Gardner, H. (1982). *Art, mind, and brain: A cognitive approach to creativity.* New York: Basic Books.

Gardner, H. (1993). *Creating minds: An anatomy of creativity as seen through the lives of Freud, Einstein, Picasso, Stravinsky, Eliot, Graham, and Gandhi.* New York, NY: Basic Books.

Gardner, H. (1993). *Frames of mind: The theory of multiple intelligences* [Tenth anniversary edition]. New York: Basic Books.

Gardner, H. (1999/2000). *Intelligence reframed: Multiple intelligences for the 21st century.* New York: Basic Books.

Gardner, M., & Steinberg, L. (2005). Peer influence on risk taking, risk preference, and risky decision making in adolescence and adulthood: An experimental study. *Developmental Psychology, 41,* 625–635.

Garmezy, N. (1994). Reflections and commentary on risk, resilience, and development. In R. J. Haggerty, L. R. Sherrod, N. Garmezy, & M. Rutter (Eds.), *Stress, risk and resilience in children and adolescents: Processes, mechanisms, and interventions.* Cambridge, England: Cambridge University Press.

Garvey, C. (1990). *Play* (enlarged ed.). Cambridge, MA: Harvard University Press.

Gatz, M. (2007). Genetics, dementia, and the elderly. *Current Directions in Psychological Science, 16,* 123–127.

Gatz, M., Reynolds, C. A., Fratiglioni, L., Johansson, B., Mortimer, J. A., Berg, S., Fiske, A., & Pedersen, N. L. (2006). Role of genes and environments for explaining Alzheimer disease. *Archives of General Psychiatry, 63,* 168–174.

Gatz, M., Svedberg, P., Pedersen, N. L., Mortimer, J. A., Berg, S., & Johansson, B. (2001). Education and the risk of Alzheimer's disease: Findings from the study of dementia in Swedish twins. *Journal of Gerontology: Psychological Sciences, 56B,* 292–300.

Gaugler, J. E., Davey, A., Pearlin, L. I., & Zarit, S. H. (2000). Modeling caregiver adaptation over time: The longitudinal impact of behavior problems. *Psychology and Aging, 15,* 437–450.

Gauvain, M., & Rogoff, B. (1989). Collaborative problem-solving and children's planning skills. *Developmental Psychology, 25,* 139–151.

Gazzaniga, M. S. (1998). The split brain revisited. *Scientific American, 279,* 50–55.

Ge, X., Best, K. M., Conger, R. D., & Simons, R. L. (1996). Parenting behaviors and the occurrence and co-occurrence of adolescent depressive symptoms and conduct problems. *Developmental Psychology, 32,* 717–731.

Ge, X., Jin, R., Natsuaki, M. N., Gibbons, F. X., Brody, G. H., Cutrona, C.E., & Simons, R. L. (2006). Pubertal maturation and early substance use risks among African American children. *Psychology of Addictive Behaviors, 20,* 404–414.

Ge, X., Kim, I. J., Brody, G. H., Conger, R. D., Simons, R. L., Gibbons, F. X., & Cutrona, C. E. (2003). It's about timing and change: Pubertal transition effects on symptoms of major depression among African American youths. *Developmental Psychology, 39,* 430–439.

Ge, X., Lorenz, F. O., Conger, R. D., Elder, G. H., Jr., & Simons, R. L. (1994). Trajectories of stressful life events and depressive symptoms during adolescence. *Developmental Psychology, 30,* 467–483.

Ge, X., Natsuaki, M. N., & Conger, R. D. (2006). Trajectories of depressive symptoms and stressful life events among male and female adolescents in divorced and nondivorced families. *Development and Psychopathology, 18,* 253–273.

Geithner, C. A., Satake, T., Woynarowska, B., & Malina, R. M. (1999). Adolescent spurts in body dimensions: Average and modal sequences. *American Journal of Human Biology, 11,* 287–295.

Geldmacher, D. S. (2009). Alzheimer disease. In M. F. Weiner & A. M. Lipton (Eds.), *The American Psychiatric Publishing textbook of Alzheimer disease and other dementias.* Washington, DC: American Psychiatric Publishing.

Gelman, R. (1978). Cognitive development. *Annual Review of Psychology, 29,* 297–332.

Gelman, S. A. (1996). Concepts and theories. In R. Gelman & T. K. Au (Eds.), *Perceptual and cognitive development.* San Diego: Academic Press.

Genc, M., & Ledger, W. J. (2000). Syphilis in pregnancy. *Sexual Transmission Information, 76,* 73–79.

George, L., Granath, F., Johansson, A. L., Annerén, G., & Cnattinguis, S. (2006). Environmental tobacco smoke and risk of spontaneous abortion. *Epidemiology, 17,* 500–505.

Georges, J., Onwuteaka-Philipsen, B. D., Muller, M. T., van der Wal, G., van der Heide, A., & van der Maas, P. J. (2007). Relatives' perspective on the terminally ill patients who died after euthanasia or physician-assisted suicide: A retrospective cross-sectional interview study in the Netherlands. *Death Studies, 31,* 1–15.

Gershoff, E. T. (2002). Corporal punishment by parents and associated child behaviors and experiences: A meta-analytic and theoretical review. *Psychological Bulletin, 128,* 539–579.

Gershoff, E. T., Grogan-Kaylor, A., Lansford, J. E., Chang, L., Zelli, A., Deater-Deckard, K., & Dodge, K. A. (2010). Parent discipline practices in an international sample: Associations with child behaviors and moderation by perceived normativeness. *Child Development, 81,* 487–502.

Gerstein, E. D., Crnic, K. A., Blacher, J., & Baker, B. L. (2009). Resilience and the course of daily parenting stress in families of young children with intellectual disabilities. *Journal of Intellectual Disability Research, 53,* 981–997.

Gerstorf, D., Hoppmann, C. A., Kadlec, K. M., & McArdle, J. J. (2009). Memory and depressive symptoms are dynamically linked among married couples: Longitudinal evidence from the AHEAD study. *Developmental Psychology, 45,* 1595–1610.

Gervain, J., & Mehler, J. (2010). Speech perception and language acquisition in the first year of life. *Annual Review of Psychology, 61,* 191–218.

Gest, S. D., Graham-Bermann, S. A., & Hartup, W. W. (2001). Peer experience: Common and unique features of number of friendships, social network centrality, and sociometric status. *Social Development, 10,* 23–40.

Getzels, J. W., & Jackson, P. W. (1962). Creativity and intelligence: Explorations with gifted children. New York: Wiley.

Gfroerer, J., Penne, M., Pemberton, M., & Folsom, R. (2003). Substance abuse treatment need among older adults in 2020: the impact of the aging baby-boom cohort. *Drug And Alcohol Dependence 69,* 127–135.

Ghaly, I., Hussein F.H., Abdelghaffar, S., Anwar G, Seirvogel, R.M. (2008). Optimal age of sexual maturation in Egyptian children. *East Mediterranean Health Journal, 14,* 1391–1399.

Gharravi, A. M., Gharravi, S., Marjani, A., Moradi, A., & Golalipour, M. J. (2008). Correlation of age at menarche and height in Iranian student girls living in Gorgan—northeast of Iran. *The Journal of the Pakistan Medical Association, 58,* 426–429.

Ghetti, S., Lyons, K. E., & Cornoldi, C. (2008). The development of metamemory monitoring during retrieval: The case of memory strength and memory absence. *Journal of Experimental Child Psychology, 99,* 157–181.

Giampaoli, S. (2000). Epidemiology of major age-related diseases in women compared to men. *Aging, 12,* 93–105.

Giarrusso, R., Feng, D., Silverstein, M., & Bengtson, V. L. (2000). Self in the context of the family. In K. W. Schaie & J. Hendrick (Eds.), *The evolution of the aging self. The societal impact on the aging process.* New York: Springer.

Gibbs, J. C. (2010). *Moral development and reality. Beyond the theories of Kohlberg and Hoffman* (2nd ed.). Boston, MA: Allyn & Bacon.

Gibbs, J. C., Basinger, K. S., Grime, R. L., & Snarey, J. R. (2007). Moral judgment development across cultures: Revisiting Kohlberg's universality claims. *Developmental Review, 27,* 443–500.

Gibbs, N. (2009, August 3). Dying together. An elderly British couple's suicide pact is a beautifully romantic act—and a troubling one. *Time,* 64.

Gibson, D. G., Glass, J. I., Lartigue, C., Noskov, V. N., Chuang, R., Algire, M. A., Benders, G. A., et al. (2010, May 20). Creation of a bacterial cell controlled by a chemically synthesized genome. *Science.*

Gibson, E. J. (1988). Exploratory behavior in the development of perceiving, acting, and the acquiring of knowledge. *Annual Review of Psychology, 39,* 1–41.

Gibson, E. J., & Pick, A. D. (2000). *An ecological approach to perceptual learning and development.* New York: Oxford University Press.

Gibson-Davis, C. M., & Brooks-Gunn, J. (2006). Couples' immigration status and ethnicity as determinants of breastfeeding. *American Journal of Public Health, 96,* 4684–4689.

Giedd, J. N. (2004). Structural magnetic resonance imaging of the adolescent brain. *Annals of the New York Academic of Sciences, 1021,* 77–85.

Gifted Development Center (2010). *Characteristics of giftedness and characteristics of giftedness scale.*

Available at: www.gifteddevelopment.com/What_is_Gifted/characgt.htm. Accessed: March 1, 2010.

Gil, D. G. (1970). *Violence against children.* Cambridge, MA: Harvard University Press.

Gilbert, N. (1997). *Combating child abuse: International perspectives and trends.* New York: Oxford University Press.

Gillberg, C., Cederlund, M., Lamberg, K., & Zeijlon, L. (2006). "The autism epidemic." The registered prevalence of autism in a Swedish urban area. *Journal of Autism and Developmental Disorders, 36,* 429–435.

Gilligan, C. (1977). In a different voice: Women's conceptions of self and morality. *Harvard Educational Review, 47,* 481–517.

Gilligan, C. (1982). *In a different voice: Psychological theory and women's development.* Cambridge, MA: Harvard University Press.

Gilligan, C. (1993). Adolescent development reconsidered. In A. Garrod (Ed.), *Approaches to moral development: New research and emerging themes.* New York: Teachers College Press.

Gil-Rivas, V., Kilmer, R. P., Hypes, A. W., & Roof, K. A. (2010). The caregiver–child relationship and children's adjustment following Hurricane Katrina. In R. P. Kilmer, V. Gil-Rivas, R. G. Tedeschi, & L. G. Calhoun (Eds.), *Helping families and communities recover from disaster: Lessons learned from Hurricane Katrina and its aftermath.* Washington, DC: American Psychological Association.

Ginsburg, G. S., & Bronstein, P. (1993). Family factors related to children's intrinsic/extrinsic motivational orientation and academic performance. *Child Development, 64,* 1461–1474.

Ginsburg, H. P., & Opper, S. (1988). *Piaget's theory of intellectual development* (3rd ed.). Upper Saddle River, NJ: Prentice-Hall.

Gintis, H., Bowles, S., Boyd, R., & Fehr, E. (2008). Gene-culture coevolution and the emergence of altruistic behavior in humans. In C. Crawford & D. Krebs (Eds.), Foundations of evolutionary psychology. New York: Taylor & Francis/Lawrence Erlbaum.

Ginzberg, E. (1972). Toward a theory of occupational choice: A restatement. *Vocational Guidance Quarterly, 20,* 169–176.

Ginzberg, E. (1984). Career development. In D. Brown, L. Brooks, & Associates (Eds.), *Career choice and development.* San Francisco: Jossey-Bass.

Giordano, P. C. (2003). Relationships in adolescence. *Annual Review of Sociology, 29,* 257–281.

Girard, C. (1993). Age, gender, and suicide: A cross-national analysis. *American Sociological Review, 58,* 553–574.

Givens, J. L., & Mitchell, S. L. (2009). Concerns about end-of-life care and support for euthanasia. *Journal of Pain and Symptom Management, 38,* 167–173.

Glascock, A. (2009). Is killing necessarily murder? Moral questions surrounding assisted suicide and death. In J. Sokolovsky (Ed.), *The cultural context of aging* (3rd ed.). Westport, CT: Praeger.

Glascock, J. (2001). Gender roles on prime-time network television: Demographics and behaviors. *Journal of Broadcasting & Electronic Media, 45,* 656–669.

Glaser, R., & Chi, M. T. H. (1988). Overview. In M. T. H. Chi, R. Glaser, & M. Farr (Eds.), *The nature of expertise.* Hillsdale, NJ: Erlbaum.

Glasgow, K. L., Dornbusch, S. M., Troyer, L., Steinberg, L., & Ritter, P. L. (1997). Parenting styles, adolescents' attributions, and educational outcomes in nine heterogeneous high schools. *Child Development, 68,* 507–529.

Glass, G. V. (2002a). Grouping students for instruction. In A. Molnar (Ed.), *School reform proposals: The research evidence,* 95–112. Greenwich, CT: Information Age Publishing.

Glass, G. V. (2002b). Teacher characteristics. In A. Molnar (Ed.), *School reform proposals: The research evidence,* 155–174. Greenwich, CT: Information Age Publishing.

Glass, G. V., McGaw, B., & Smith, M. L. (1981). *Meta-analysis in social research.* Beverly Hills, CA: Sage.

Gleason, J. B., & Ratner, N. B. (2009). *The development of language* (7th ed.). Boston: Allyn & Bacon.

Gleason, P. M., & Dodd, A. H. (2009). School breakfast program but not school lunch program participation is associated with lower body mass index. *Journal of the American Dietetic Association, 109,* S118–S128.

Glick, J. C. (1975). Cognitive development in cross-cultural perspective. In F. Horowitz (Ed.), *Review of child development research* (Vol. 1). Chicago: University of Chicago Press.

Glick, M., & Zigler, E. (1985). Self-image: A cognitive developmental approach. In R. L. Leahy (Ed.), *The Development of the self.* Orlando, FL: Academic Press.

Gloth, F. M. (2000). Geriatric pain: Factors that limit pain relief and increase complications. *Geriatrics, 55,* 51–54.

Glowinski, A. L., Madden, P. A. F., Bucholz, K. K., Lynskey, M. T., & Heath, A. C. (2003). Genetic epidemiology of self-reported lifetime DSM-IV major depressive disorder in a population-based twin sample of female adolescents. *Journal of Child Psychology and Psychiatry and Allied Disciplines, 44,* 988–996.

Gluckman, P. D., & Hanson, M. A. (2006). Evolution, development and timing of puberty. *Trends in Endocrinology and Metabolism, 17,* 7–12.

Gnepp, J., & Chilamkurti, C. (1988). Children's use of personality attributions to predict other people's emotional and behavioral reactions. *Child Development, 59,* 743–754.

Godar, S. P., Grieco, T. M., & Litovsky, R. Y. (2007, April). *Emergence of bilateral abilities in children who transition from using one to two cochlear implants.* Presented at the 11th International Cochlear Implant Conference, Charlotte, NC.

Goertzel, V., & Goertzel, M. G. (1962). *Cradles of eminence.* Boston: Little, Brown.

Gohlke, B., & Woelfle, J. (2009). Growth and puberty in German children: Is there still a positive secular trend? *Deutsches Ärzteblatt International, 106,* 377–382.

Golan, O., Baron-Cohen, S., Hill, J. J., & Golan, Y. (2006). The "Reading the Mind in Films" task: Complex emotion recognition in adults with and without autism spectrum conditions. *Social Neuroscience, 1,* 111–123.

Goldberg, A. E. (2009). *Lesbian and gay parents and their children: Research on the family life cycle.* Washington, DC: American Psychological Association.

Goldberg, A. E., & Perry-Jenkins, M. (2007). The division of labor and perceptions of parental roles: Lesbian couples across the transition to parenthood. *Journal of Social and Personal Relationships, 24,* 297–318.

Goldberg, A. P., & Hagberg, J. M. (1990). Physical exercise in the elderly. In E. L. Schneider & J. W. Rowe (Eds.), *Handbook of the biology of aging* (3rd ed.). San Diego: Academic Press.

Goldberg, G. R., & Prentice, A. M. (1994). Maternal and fetal determinants of adult diseases. *Nutrition Reviews, 52,* 191–200.

Goldberg, S. (1983). Parent-infant bonding: Another look. *Child Development, 54,* 1355–1382.

Goldberg, S., Perrotta, M., Minde, K., & Corter, C. (1986). Maternal behavior and attachment in low–birth-weight twins and singletons. *Child Development, 57,* 34–46.

Golden, J. (2005). *Message in a bottle: The making of fetal alcohol syndrome.* Cambridge, MA: Harvard University Press.

Goldenberg, R. L., & Culhane, J. F. (2007). Low birth weight in the United States. *The American Journal of Clinical Nutrition, 85,* 584–590.

Goldhaber, D. E. (2000). *Theories of human development. Integrative perspectives.* Mountain View, CA: Mayfield.

Goldin-Meadow, S. (2003). *The resilience of language: What gesture creation in deaf children can tell us about how all children learn language.* New York: Psychology Press.

Goldin-Meadow, S. (2005). What language creation in the manual modality tells us about the foundations of language. *Linguistic Review, 22,* 199–225.

Goldin-Meadow, S. (2009). From gesture to word. In E. L. Bavin (Ed.), *The Cambridge handbook of child language,* 145–160. New York: Cambridge University Press.

Goldman, S. (2008). Neurogenesis in the adult songbird: A model for inducible striatal neuronal addition. In F. H. Gage, G. Kempermann, & H. Song (Eds.), *Adult Neurogenesis,* 593–617. NY: Cold Spring Harbor Laboratory Press.

Goldsmith, H. H. (2003). Genetics of emotional development. In R. J. Davidson, K. R. Scherer, & H. H. Goldsmith (Eds.), *Handbook of affective sciences.* New York: Oxford University Press.

Goldstein, E. B. (2007). *Sensation and perception* (7th ed.). Belmont, CA: Wadsworth.

Goldstein, M. H., Schwade, J. A., & Bornstein, M. H. (2009). The value of vocalizing: Five-month-old infants associate their own noncry vocalizations with responses from caregivers. *Child Development, 80,* 636–644.

Goldstein, S. E., Davis-Kean, P. E., & Eccles, J. S. (2005). Parents, peers, and problem behavior: A longitudinal investigation of the impact of relationship perceptions and characteristics on the development of adolescent problem behavior. *Developmental Psychology, 41,* 401–413.

Goldwater, O. D., & Nutt, R. L. (1999). Teachers' and students' work-culture variables associated with positive school outcome. *Adolescence, 34,* 653–664.

Golinkoff, R. M., & Hirsh-Pasek, K. (2006). Baby wordsmith: From associationist to social sophisticate. *Current Directions in Psychological Science, 15,* 30–33.

Golombok, S., Perry, B., Burston, A., Murray, C., Mooney-Somers, J., Stevens, M., & Golding, J. (2003). Children with lesbian parents: A community study. *Developmental Psychology, 39,* 20–33.

Gomez, V., Krings, F., Bangerter, A., & Grob, A. (2009). The influence of personality and life events on subjective well-being from a life span perspective. *Journal of Research in Personality, 43,* 345–354.

Gonzaga, G. C., Campos, B., & Bradbury, T. (2007). Similarity, convergence, and relationship satisfaction in dating and married couples. *Journal of Personality and Social Psychology, 93,* 34–48.

Gonzales, P., Williams, T., Jocelyn, L., Roey, S., Kastberg, D., & Brenwald, S. (2008). Highlights from TIMSS 2007: Mathematics and science achievement of U.S. fourth- and eighth-grade students in an international context (NCES 2009–001 Revis ed.). Washington, DC: National Center for Education Statistics, Institute of Education Sciences, U.S. Department of Education.

Good, C., Aronson, J., & Inzlicht, M. (2003). Improving adolescents' standardized test performance: An intervention to reduce the effects of stereotype threat. *Journal of Applied Developmental Psychology, 24,* 645–662.

Good, M., & Willoughby, T. (2008). Adolescence as a sensitive period for spiritual development. *Child Development Perspectives, 2,* 32–37.

Goodkin, K., Baldewicz, T. T., Blaney, N. T., Asthana, D., Kumar, M., Shapshak, P., Leeds, B., Burkhalter, J. E., Rigg, D., Tyll, M. D., Cohen, J.,

& Zheng, W. L. (2001). Physiological effects of bereavement and bereavement support group interventions. In M. S. Stroebe & R. O. Hansson (Eds.), *Handbook of bereavement research: Consequences, coping, and care.* Washington, DC: American Psychological Association.

Goodluck, H. (2009). Formal and computational constraints on language development. In E. Hoff & M. Shatz (Eds.), *Blackwell handbook of language development* (pp. 46–67). Malden, MA: Wiley-Blackwell.

Goodman, S. H. (2002). Depression and early adverse experiences. In I. H. Gotlib & C. L. Hammen (Eds.), *Handbook of depression.* New York: Guilford.

Gooren, L. (2006). The biology of human psychosexual differentiation. *Hormonal Behavior, 50,* 589–601.

Gopnik, A. (1996). The post-Piaget era. *Psychological Science, 7,* 221–225.

Gopnik, A., Capps, L., & Meltzoff, A. N. (2000). Early theories of mind: What the theory can tell us about autism. In S. Baron-Cohen, H. Tager-Flusberg, & D. J. Cohen (Eds.), *Understanding other minds. Perspectives from developmental cognitive neuroscience* (2nd ed.). Oxford: Oxford University Press.

Gopnik, A., & Choi, S. (1995). Names, relational words, and cognitive development in English and Korean speakers: Nouns are not always learned before verbs. In M. Tomasello & W. E. Merriman (Eds.), *Beyond names for things: Young children's acquisition of verbs* (pp. 83–90). Hillsdale, NJ: Erlbaum.

Gorchoff, S. M., John, O. P., & Helson, R. (2008). Contextualizing change in marital satisfaction during middle age. *Psychological Science, 19,* 1194–1200.

Gordon, B. N., Schroeder, C. S., & Abrams, J. M. (1990). Children's knowledge of sexuality: A comparison of sexually abused and nonabused children. *American Journal of Orthopsychiatry, 60,* 250–257.

Gordon, I., Zagoory-Sharon, O., Schneiderman, I., Leckman, J. F., Weller, A., & Feldman, R. (2008). Oxytocin and cortisol in romantically unattached young adults: Associations with bonding and psychological distress. *Psychophysiology, 45,* 349–352.

Gordon, R. A. (2000). *Eating disorders. Anatomy of a social epidemic* (2nd ed.). Oxford, England: Blackwell.

Gosling, S. D., Rentfrow, P. J., & Swann, W. B. (2003). A very brief measure of the Big-Five personality domains. *Journal of Research in Personality, 37,* 504–528.

Gostin, L. O. (2001). National health information privacy: Regulations under the Health Insurance Portability and Accountability Act. *Journal of the American Medical Association, 23,* 3015–3021.

Goswami, U. (1999). Causal connections in beginning reading: The importance of rhyme. *Journal of Research in Reading, 22,* 217–241.

Gotlib, I. H., & Hammen, C. L. (1992). *Psychological aspects of depression. Toward a cognitive-interpersonal integration.* Chichester, England: John Wiley & Sons.

Gotlib, I. H., & Hammen, C. L. (2002). Introduction. In I. H. Gotlib & C. L. Hammen (Eds.), *Handbook of depression.* New York: Guilford.

Gotlib, I. H., Joormann, J., Minor, K. L., & Cooney, R. E. (2006). Cognitive and biological functioning in children at risk for depression. In T. Canli (Ed.), *Biology of personality and individual differences.* New York: Guilford.

Gottesman, I. I. (1991). *Schizophrenia genesis: The origins of madness.* New York: W. H. Freeman.

Gottesman, I. I., & Hanson, D. R. (2005). Human development: Biological and genetic processes. *Annual Review of Psychology, 56,* 263–286.

Gottfredson, L., & Saklofske, D. H. (2009). Intelligence: Foundations and issues in assessment. *Canadian Psychology, 50,* 183–195.

Gottfredson, L. S. (1997). Why g matters: The complexity of everyday life. *Intelligence, 24,* 79–132.

Gottfredson, L. S. (2002). G: Highly general and highly practical. In R. J. Sternberg & E. L. Grigorenko (Eds.), *The general factor in intelligence: How general is it?* Mahwah, NJ: Erlbaum.

Gottfredson, L. S. (2004). Intelligence: Is it the epidemiologists' elusive "fundamental cause" of social class inequalities in health? *Journal of Personality and Social Psychology, 86,* 174–199.

Gottfredson, L. S., & Deary, I. (2004). Intelligence predicts health and longevity, but why? *Current Directions in Psychological Science, 13,* 1–4.

Gottfried, A. E., Fleming, J. S., & Gottfried, A. W. (1998). Role of cognitively stimulating home environment in children's academic intrinsic motivation: A longitudinal study. *Child Development, 69,* 1448–1460.

Gottfried, A. E., & Gottfried, A. W. (2006). A long-term investigation of the role of maternal and dual-earner employment in children's development: The Fullerton Longitudinal Study. *American Behavioral Scientist, 49,* 1310–1327.

Gottfried, A. E., Marcoulides, G. A., Gottfried, A. W., & Oliver, P. H. (2009). A latent curve model of parental motivational practices and developmental decline in math and science academic intrinsic motivation. *Journal of Educational Psychology, 101,* 729–739.

Gottfried, A. W., Gottfried, A. E., Bathurst, K., & Guerin, D. W. (1994). *Gifted IQ: Early developmental aspects: The Fullerton Longitudinal Study.* New York: Plenum.

Gottlieb, G. (1991). Experiential canalization of behavioral development: Theory. *Developmental Psychology, 27,* 4–13.

Gottlieb, G. (1992). *Individual development and evolution: The genesis of novel behavior.* New York: Oxford University Press.

Gottlieb, G. (2000). Environmental and behavioral influences on gene activity. *Current Directions in Psychological Science, 9,* 93–97.

Gottlieb, G. (2002). Developmental-behavioral initiation of evolutionary change. *Psychological Review, 109,* 211–218.

Gottlieb, G., & Blair, C. (2004). How early experience matters in intellectual development in the case of poverty. *Prevention Science, 5,* 245–252.

Gottlieb, G., & Halpern, C. T. (2008). Individual development as a system of coactions: implications for research and policy. In A. Fogel, B. J. King, & S. G. Shanker (2008). *Human development in the twenty-first century. Visionary ideas from systems scientists.* New York: Cambridge University Press.

Gottlieb, G., Wahlsten, D., & Lickliter, R. (2006). The significance of biology for human development: A developmental psychobiological systems view. In W. Damon & R. M. Lerner (Eds. in Chief) & R. M. Lerner (Vol. Ed.), *Handbook of child psychology: Vol. 1. Theoretical models of human development* (6th ed.). Hoboken, NJ: Wiley.

Gottman, J. M., & Notarius, C. I. (2000). Decade review: Observing marital interaction. *Journal of Marriage and the Family, 62,* 927–947.

Goubet, N., Rochat, P., Maire-Leblond, C., & Poss, S. (2006). Learning from others in 9–18-month-old infants. *Infant and Child Development, 15,* 161–177.

Gould, D. C., Petty, R., & Jacobs, H. S. (2000). The male menopause—does it exist? *British Medical Journal, 320,* 858–861.

Gould, M. S., Greenberg, T., Velting, D. M., & Shaffer, D. (2003). Youth suicide risk and preventive interventions: A review of the past 10 years.

Journal of the American Academy of Child and Adolescent Psychiatry, 42, 386–405.

Gowers, S., & Bryant-Waugh, R. (2004). Management of child and adolescent eating disorders: The current evidence base and future directions. *Journal of Child Psychology and Psychiatry and Allied Disciplines, 45,* 63–83.

Grabe, S., & Shibley Hyde, J. (2006). Ethnicity and Body Dissatisfaction Among Women in the United States: A Meta-Analysis *Psychological Bulletin, 132,* 622–640.

Graber, J. A., Lewinsohn, P. M., Seeley, J. R., & Brooks-Gunn, J. (1997). Is psychopathology associated with the timing of pubertal development? *Journal of the American Academy of Child and Adolescent Psychiatry, 36,* 1768–1776.

Graf, D. L., Pratt, L. V., Hester, C. N., & Short, K. R. (2009). Playing active video games increases energy expenditure in children. *Pediatrics, 124,* 534–540.

Graf, P., Squire, L. R., & Mandler, G. (1984). The information that amnesic patients do not forget. *Journal of Experimental Psychology: Learning, Memory, and Cognition, 10,* 164–178.

Graham, C. A., & Easterbrooks, M. A. (2000). School-aged children's vulnerability to depressive symptomatology: The role of attachment security, maternal depressive symptomatology, and economic risk. *Development and Psychopathology, 12,* 201–213.

Graham, N., Lindesay, J., Katona, C., Bertolote, J. M., Camus, V., Copeland, J. R. M., de Mendonca Lima, C. A., Gaillard, M., Nargeot, M. C. G., Gray, J., Jacobsson, L., Kingma, M., Kuhne, N., O'Loughlin, A., Rutz, W., Saraceno, B., Taintor, Z., & Wancata, J. (2003). Reducing stigma and discrimination against older people with mental disorders: A technical consensus statement. *International Journal of Geriatric Psychiatry, 18,* 670–678.

Graham, S., Taylor, A. Z., & Ho, A. Y. (2009). Race and ethnicity in peer relations research. In K. H. Rubin, W. M. Bukowski, & B. Laursen (Eds.), *Handbook of peer interactions, relationships, and groups.* New York: Guilford.

Granrud, C. E. (2006). Size constancy in infants: 4-month-olds' responses to physical versus retinal image size. *Journal of Experimental Psychology: Human Perception and Performance, 32,* 1398–1404.

Grant, D. (2009). Physician financial incentives and cesarean delivery: New conclusions from the healthcare cost and utilization project, *Journal of Health Economics, 28,* 244–250.

Grant, K. E., Compas, B. E., Thurm, A. E., McMahon, S. D., & Gipson, P. Y. (2004). Stressors and child and adolescent psychopathology: Measurement issues and prospective effects. *Journal of Clinical Child and Adolescent Psychology, 33,* 412–425.

Graves, L., Stratton, G., Ridgers, N. D., & Cable, N. T. (2008). Energy expenditure in adolescents playing new generation computer games. *British Journal of Sports Medicine, 42,* 592–594.

Gray, A. (2009). The social capital of older people. *Ageing & Society, 29,* 5–31.

Gray, S. W., Ramsey, B. K., & Klaus, R. A. (1982). *From 3 to 20: The Early Training Project.* Baltimore: University Park Press.

Gray, W. M., & Hudson, L. M. (1984). Formal operations and the imaginary audience. *Developmental Psychology, 20,* 619–627.

Gray-Little, B., & Carels, R. A. (1997). The effect of racial dissonance on academic self-esteem and achievement in elementary, junior high, and high school students. *Journal of Research on Adolescence, 7,* 109–131.

Gray-Little, B., & Hafdahl, A. R. (2000). Factors influencing racial comparisons of self-esteem: A quantitative review. *Psychological Bulletin, 126,* 26–54.

Graziano, P. A., Keane, S. P., & Calkins, S. D. (2007). Cardiac vagal regulation and early peer status. *Child Development, 78,* 264–278.

Grbich, C., Parker, D., & Maddocks, I. (2001). The emotions and coping strategies of caregivers of family members with a terminal cancer. *Journal of Palliative Care, 17,* 30–36.

Green, C. R. (2001). *Total memory workout: 8 easy steps to maximum memory fitness.* New York: Bantam Doubleday.

Green, R. (1987). *The "sissy boy syndrome" and the development of homosexuality.* New Haven, CT: Yale University Press.

Green, R. E., Krause, J., Ptak, S. E., Briggs, A. W., Ronan, M. T., Egholm, J., Rothberg, J. M., Paunovic, M., & Pääbo, S. (2006). Analysis of one million base pairs of Neanderthal DNA. *Nature, 444,* 330–336.

Greenberg, J., Solomon, S., & Arndt, J. (2008). A basic but uniquely human motivation: Terror management. In J. Y. Shah & W. L. Gardner (Eds.), *Handbook of motivation science.* New York: Guilford.

Greenberger, E., O'Neil, R., & Nagel, S. K. (1994). Linking workplace and homeplace: Relations between the nature of adults' work and their parenting behaviors. *Developmental Psychology, 30,* 990–1002.

Greenberger, E., & Steinberg, L. (1986). When teenagers work: The psychological and social costs of adolescent employment. New York: Basic Books.

Greene, J. D. (2008). The secret joke of Kant's soul. In W. Sinnott-Armstrong (Ed.), *Moral psychology: The neuroscience of morality: Emotion, brain disorders, and development.* Cambridge, MA: MIT Press.

Greene, J. D. (2009). Dual-process morality and the personal/impersonal distinction: A reply to McGuire, Langdon, Coltheart, and MacKenzie. *Journal of Experimental Social Psychology, 45,* 581–584.

Greene, J. D., Morelli, S. A., Lowenberg, K., Nystrom, L. E., & Cohen, J. D. (2008). Cognitive load selectively interferes with utilitarian moral judgment. *Cognition, 107,* 1144–1154.

Greene, J. D., Sommerville, R. B., Nystrom, L. E., Darley, J. M., & Cohen, J. D. (2001). An fMRI investigation of emotional engagement in moral judgment. *Science, 293,* 2105–2108.

Greene, J. G. (1984). *The social and psychological origins of the climacteric syndrome.* Hants, England & Brookfield, VT: Gower.

Greene, K., Rubin, D. L., Hale, J. L., & Walters, L. H. (1996). The utility of understanding adolescent egocentrism in designing health promotion messages. *Health Communication, 8,* 131–152.

Greenfield, E. A., & Marks, N. F. (2006). Linked lives: Adult children's problems and their parents' psychological and relational well-being. *Journal of Marriage and Family, 68,* 442–454.

Greenfield, E. A., Vaillant, G. E., & Marks, N. E. (2009). Do formal religious participation and spiritual perceptions have independent linkages with diverse dimensions of psychological well-being? *Journal of Health and Social Behavior, 50,* 196–212.

Greenfield, P. M. (2009). Linking social change and developmental change: Shifting pathways of human development. *Developmental Psychology, 45,* 401–418.

Greenfield, P. M., & Savage-Rumbaugh, E. S. (1993). Comparing communicative competence in child and chimp: The pragmatics of repetition. *Journal of Child Language, 20,* 1–26.

Greenhalgh, R., Slade, P., & Spiby, H. (2000). Fathers' coping style, antenatal preparation, and experiences of labor and the postpartum. *Birth, 27,* 177–184.

Greenough, W. T., Black, J. E., & Wallace, C. S. (1987). Experience and brain development. *Child Development, 58,* 539–559.

Gregg, V., Gibbs, J. C., & Basinger, K. S. (1994). Patterns of developmental delay in moral judgment by male and female delinquents. *Merrill-Palmer Quarterly, 40,* 538–553.

Gregory, A. M., Rijsdijk, F. V., & Eley, T. C. (2006). A twin-study of sleep difficulties in school-aged children. *Child Development, 77,* 1668–1679.

Greve, F. (2006, Feb 3). Rise in average IQ scores makes kids today exceptional by earlier standards. *Knight Ridder Washington Bureau.*

Griesenbach, U., Geddes, D. M., & Alton, E. W. (2006). Gene therapy progress and prospects: Cystic fibrosis. *Gene Therapy, 13,* 1061–1067.

Grilo, C. M., & Mitchell, J. E. (Eds.) 2010. *The treatment of eating disorders: A clinical handbook.* New York: Guilford.

Grilo, C. M., & Pogue-Geile, M. F. (1991). The nature of environmental influences on weight and obesity: A behavior genetic analysis. *Psychological Bulletin, 110,* 520–531.

Grinker, R. R. (2007). *Unstrange minds: Remapping the world of autism.* New York: Basic Books.

Grizenko, N., Zappitelli, M., Langevin, J. P., Hrychko, S., El-Messidi, A., Kaminester, D., Pawliuk, N., & Stepanian, M. T. (2000). Effectiveness of a social skills training program using self/other perspective-taking: A nine-month follow-up. *American Journal of Orthopsychiatry, 70,* 501–509.

Groark, C. J., Muhamedrahimov, R. J., Palmov, O. I., Nikiforova, N. V., & McCall, R. B. (2005). Improvements in early care in Russian orphanages and their relationship to observed behaviors. *Infant Mental Health Journal, 26,* 96–109.

Grober, E., & Kawas, C. (1997). Learning and retention in preclinical and early Alzheimer's disease. *Psychology and Aging, 12,* 183–188.

Grollman, E. A. (1995). Explaining death to young children: Some questions and answers. In E. A. Grollman (Ed.), *Bereaved children and teens.* Boston: Beacon Press.

Grolnick, W. S., Bridges, L. J., & Connell, J. P. (1996). Emotion regulation in two-year-olds: Strategies and emotional expression in four contexts. *Child Development, 67,* 928–941.

Grolnick, W. S., McMenamy, J. M., & Kurowski, C. O. (2006). Emotional self-regulation in infancy and toddlerhood. In L. Balter & C. S. Tamis-LeMonda (Eds.), *Child psychology: A handbook of contemporary issues* (2nd ed.). New York: Psychology Press.

Grolnick, W. S., & Pomerantz, E. M. (2009). Issues and challenges in studying parental control: Toward a new conceptualization. *Child Development Perspectives, 3,* 165–170.

Gros-Louis, J., West, M. J., Goldstein, M. H., & King, A. P. (2006). Mothers provide differential feedback to infants' prelinguistic sounds. *International Journal of Behavioral Development, 30,* 509–516.

Gross, J. J. (Ed.) (2007). *Handbook of emotion regulation.* New York: Guilford.

Grossberg, G. T., & Desai, A. K. (2003). Management of Alzheimer's disease. *Journal of Gerontology: Medical Sciences, 58A,* 331–353.

Gross-Loh, C. (2006). Caring for your premature baby: Find out why breastfeeding and skin-to-skin contact are key components in making sure your premature infant thrives. *Mothering, 135,* 38–47.

Grossman, A. W., Churchill, J. D., McKinney, B. C., Kodish, I. M., Otte, S. L., & Greenough, W. T. (2003). Experience effects on brain development: Possible contributions to psychopathology. *Journal of Child Psychology and Psychiatry and Allied Disciplines, 44,* 33–63.

Grossmann, K., Grossmann, K. E., Fremmer-Bombik, E., Kindler, H., Scheuerer-Englisch, H., & Zimmermann, P. (2002b). The uniqueness of the child-father attachment relationship: Fathers' sensitive and challenging play as a pivotal variable in a 16-year longitudinal study. *Social Development, 11,* 307–331.

Grossmann, K. E., Grossmann, K., & Keppler, A. (2005). Universal and culture-specific aspects of human behavior: The case of attachment. In W. Friedlmeier, P. Chakkarath, & B. Schwarz (Eds.), *Culture and human development. The importance of cross-cultural research for the social sciences.* New York: Psychology Press.

Grossmann, K. E., Grossmann, K., Winter, M., & Zimmermann, P. (2002a). Attachment relationships and appraisal of partnership: From early experience of sensitive support to later relationship representation. In L. Pulkkinen & A. Caspi (Eds.), Paths to successful development: Personality in the life course. Cambridge, UK: Cambridge University Press.

Grotevant, H. D., & Cooper, C. R. (1986). Individuation in family relations. A perspective on individual differences in the development of identity and role-taking skills in adolescence. *Human Development, 29,* 82–100.

Gruber-Baldini, A. L., Schaie, K. W., & Willis, S. L. (1995). Similarity in married couples: A longitudinal study of mental abilities and rigidity–flexibility. *Journal of Personality and Social Psychology, 69,* 191–203.

Grucza, R. A., Norberg, K. E., & Bierut, L. J. (2009). Binge drinking among youths and young adults in the United States: 1979–2006. *Journal of the American Academy of Child & Adolescent Psychiatry, 48,* 692–702.

Grundy, E., & Henretta, J. C. (2006). Between elderly parents and adult children: A new look at the intergenerational care provided by the 'sandwich generation.' *Ageing and Society, 26,* 707–722.

Grusec, J. E. (2006). The development of moral behavior and conscience from a socialization perspective. In M. Killen & J. G. Smetana (Eds.), *Handbook of moral development.* Mahwah, NJ: Erlbaum.

Grusec, J. E., Goodnow, J. J., & Kuczynski, L. (2000). New directions in analyses of parenting contributions to children's acquisition of values. *Child Development, 71,* 205–211.

Grych, J. H., & Fincham, F. D. (1992). Interventions for children of divorce: Toward greater integration of research and action. *Psychological Bulletin, 111,* 434–454.

Guay, F., Marsh, H. W., & Boivin, M. (2003). Academic self-concept and academic achievement: Developmental perspectives on their causal ordering. *Journal of Educational Psychology, 95,* 124–136.

Guerin, D. W., Gottfried, A. W., Oliver, P. H., & Thomas, C. W. (2003). *Temperament: Infancy through adolescence: The Fullerton Longitudinal Study.* New York: Kluwer Academic/Plenum Publishers.

Guerra, N. G., & Slaby, R. G. (1990). Cognitive mediators of aggression in adolescent offenders: 2. Intervention. *Developmental Psychology, 26,* 269–277.

Guerra, N. G., & Williams, K. R. (2006). Ethnicity, youth violence, and the ecology of development. In N. G. Guerra, & E. P. Smith (Eds.), *Preventing youth violence in a multicultural society.* Washington, DC: American Psychological Association.

Guilamo-Ramos, V., Jaccard, J., Dittus, P., & Collins, S. (2008). Parent-adolescent communication about sexual intercourse: An analysis of maternal reluctance to communicate. *Health Psychology, 27,* 760–769.

Gundersen, C., Lohman, B. J., Garasky, S., Stewart, S., & Eisenmann, J. (2008). Food security, maternal stressors, and overweight among low-income US children: Results from the National Health and Nutrition Examination Survey (1999–2002). *Pediatrics, 122,* e529–e540.

Gunnar, M. R. (1998). Quality of early care and buffering of neuroendocrine stress reactions: Potential effects on the developing human brain. *Preventive Medicine, 27,* 208–211.

Gunnar, M. R. (2000). Early adversity and the development of stress reactivity and regulation. In C. A. Nelson (Ed.), *Minnesota Symposium on Child Psychology: Vol. 31. The effects of early adversity on neurobehavioral development.* Mahwah, NJ: Erlbaum.

Gunnar, M. R., Bruce, J., & Grotevant, H. D. (2000). International adoption of institutionally reared children: Research and policy. *Development and Psychopathology, 12,* 677–693.

Gunnar, M., & Quevedo, K. (2007). The neurobiology of stress and development. *Annual Review of Psychology, 58,* 145–153.

Gurba, E. (2005). On the specific character of adult thought: Controversies over post-formal operations. *Polish Psychological Bulletin, 36,* 175–185.

Gurland, B. (1991). Epidemiology of psychiatric disorders. In J. Sadavoy, L. W. Lazarus, & L. F. Jarvik (Eds.), *Comprehensive review of geriatric psychiatry.* Washington, DC: American Psychiatric Press.

Gurung, R. A. R., Taylor, S. E., & Seeman, T. E. (2003). Accounting for changes in social support among married older adults: Insights from the MacArthur Studies of Successful Aging. *Psychology and Aging, 18,* 487–496.

Gutman, L. (2006). How student and parent goal orientations and classroom goal structures influence the math achievement of African Americans during the high school transition. *Contemporary Educational Psychology, 31,* 44–63.

Gutman, L. M., Sameroff, A. J., & Cole, R. (2003). Academic growth curve trajectories from 1st grade to 12th grade: Effects of multiple social risk factors and preschool child factors. *Developmental Psychology, 39,* 777–790.

Gutman, L. M., Sameroff, A. J., & Eccles, J. S. (2002). The academic achievement of African American students during early adolescence: An examination of multiple risk, promotive, and protective factors. *American Journal of Community Psychology, 39,* 367–399.

Gutmann, D. (1987). *Reclaimed powers: Toward a new psychology of men and women in later life.* New York: Basic Books.

Gutmann, D. (1997). *The human elder in nature, culture, and society.* Boulder, CO: Westview.

Guttmacher Institute (2006). Facts on American teens' sexual and reproductive health. Available at: www.guttmacher.org/pubs/fb_ATSRH.html. Accessed: August 2, 2009.

H

Haas-Hawkings, G., Sangster, S., Ziegler, M., & Reid, D. (1985). A study of relatively immediate adjustment to widowhood in later life. *International Journal of Women's Studies, 8,* 158–166.

Habek, D., Habek, J. C., Ivanisevic, M., & Djelmis, J. (2002). Fetal tobacco syndrome and perinatal outcome. *Fetal Diagnosis and Therapy, 17,* 367–371.

Haber, D. (2006). Life review: Implementation, theory, research, and therapy. *International Journal of Aging & Human Development, 63,* 153–171.

Hack, M., & Fanaroff, A. A. (1999). Outcomes of children of extremely low birth weight and gestational age in the 1990's. *Early Human Development, 53,* 193–218.

Haegerstrom-Portnoy, G., Schneck, M. E., & Brabyn, J. A. (2000). Seeing into old age: Vision function beyond acuity. *Optometry and Vision Science, 76,* 141–158.

Haffner, W. H. F. (2007). Development before birth. In M. L. Batshaw, L. Pellegrino, & N. J. Roizen (Eds.), *Children with disabilities,* 6th ed., 23–34. Baltimore: Paul H. Brookes.

Hagan, L. K., & Kuebli, J. (2007). Mothers' and fathers' socialization of preschoolers' physical risk taking. *Journal of Applied Developmental Psychology, 28,* 2–14.

Hagekull, B., & Bohlin, G. (1998). Preschool temperament and environmental factors related to the five-factor model of personality in middle childhood. *Merrill-Palmer Quarterly, 44,* 194–215.

Hagen, E. W., Palta, M., Albanese, A., & Sadek-Badawi, M. (2006). School achievement in a regional cohort of children born very low birthweight. *Developmental & Behavioral Pediatrics, 27,* 112–119.

Hagestad, G. O. (1985). Continuity and connectedness. In V. L. Bengtson & J. F. Robertson (Eds.), *Grandparenthood.* Beverly Hills, CA: Sage.

Haidt, J. (2001). The emotional dog and its rational tail: A social intuitionist approach to moral judgment. *Psychological Review, 108,* 814–834.

Haidt, J. (2008). Morality. *Perspectives on Psychological Science, 3,* 65–72.

Haight, B. K., & Haight, B. S. (2007). *The handbook of structured life review.* Baltimore: Health Professions Press.

Haight, W. L., Wong, X., Fung, H. H., Williams, K., & Mintz, J. (1999). Universal, developmental, and variable aspects of young children's play: A cross-cultural comparison of pretending at home. *Child Development, 70,* 1477–1488.

Haine, R. A., Ayers, T. S., Sandler, I. N., & Wolchik, S. A. (2008). Evidence-based practices for parentally bereaved children and their families. *Professional Psychology: Research and Practice, 39,* 113–121.

Haine, R. A., Wolchik, S. A., Sandler, I. N., & Milsap, R. E. (2006). Positive parenting as a protective resource for parentally bereaved children. *Death Studies, 30,* 1–28.

Hainline, L. (1998). The development of basic visual abilities. In A. Slater (Ed.), *Perceptual development: Visual, auditory and speech perception in infancy* (pp. 37–44). Hove, East Sussex, UK: Psychology Press.

Hainline, L., & Abramov, I. (1992). Assessing visual development: Is infant vision good enough? *Advances in Infancy Research, 7,* 39–102.

Haith, M. M., & Benson, J. B. (1998). Infant cognition. In D. Kuhn & R. S. Siegler (Vol. Eds.), W. Damon (Editor-in-Chief), *Handbook of child psychology: Vol. 2. Cognition, perception, and language,* 5th ed., 199–254. New York: Wiley.

Halim, M. L. & Ruble, D. (2010). Gender identity and stereotyping in early and middle childhood. In J. C. Chrisler & D. R. McCeary (Eds.), Handbook of Gender Research in Psychology, 495-525. New York: Springer.

Hall, C. S. (1954). *A primer of Freudian psychology.* New York: New American Library.

Hall, E. (2001). Babies, books and "impact": Problems and possibilities in the evaluation of a Bookstart project. *Educational Review, 53,* 57–64.

Hall, G. S. (1891). The contents of children's minds on entering school. *Pedagogical Seminary, 1,* 139–173.

Hall, G. S. (1904). *Adolescence* (2 vols.). New York: Appleton.

Hall, G. S. (1922). *Senescence: The last half of life.* New York: Appleton.

Hallett, V. (2009, August 11). Brothers don't need sleep suits to reel in swimming medals. *The Washington Post,* E5.

Hallgren, A., Kihlgren, M., Forslin, L., & Norberg, A. (1999). Swedish fathers' involvement in and experiences of childbirth preparation and childbirth. *Midwifery, 15,* 6–15.

Halligan, S. L., Herbert, J., Goodyer, I. M., & Murray, L. (2004). Exposure to postnatal depression predicts elevated cortisol in adolescent offspring. *Biological Psychiatry, 55,* 376–381.

Halmi, K. A. (2009). Perplexities and provocations of eating disorders. *Journal of Child Psychology and Psychiatry, 50,* 163–169.

Halpern, C. J. T., Udry, J. R., Suchindran, C., & Campbell, B. (2000). Adolescent males' willingness to report masturbation. *Journal of Sex Research* [Special Issue], 37, 327–332.

Halpern, C. T. (2006). Integrating hormones and other biological factors into a developmental systems model of adolescent female sexuality. *New Directions for Child and Adolescent Development, 112*, 9–22.

Halpern, S. H., Leighton, B. L., Ohlsson A., Barrett, J. F., & Rice, A. (1998). Effect of epidural vs. parenteral opioid analgesia on the progress of labor: A meta-analysis. *Journal of the American Medical Association, 280*, 2105–2110.

Halverson, C. F., Havill, V. L., Deal, J., Baker, S. R., Victor, J. B., Pavlopoulous, V., Besevegis, E., & Wen, L. (2003). Personality structure as derived from parental ratings of free descriptions of children: The Inventory of Child Individual Differences. *Journal of Personality, 71*, 995–1026.

Hamer, R. D. (2009). *What can my baby see?* San Francisco: Smith-Kettlewell Eye Research Institute. Available at: www.ski.org/Vision/babyvision.html. Accessed: November 23, 2009.

Hamilton, B. E., Martin, J. A., & Ventura, S. J. (2009, March 18). Births: Preliminary data for 2007. *National Vital Statistics Reports, 57* (12).

Hamlin, J. K., Wynn, K., & Bloom, P. (2007). Social evaluation by preverbal infants. *Nature, 450*, 557–560.

Hamm, J. V. (2000). Do birds of a feather flock together? The variable bases for African American, Asian American, and European American adolescents' selection of similar friends. *Developmental Psychology, 36*, 209–219.

Hampson, S. E., & Friedman, H. S. (2008). Personality and health. A lifespan perspective. In O. P. John, R. W. Robins, & L. A. Pervin (Eds.), *Handbook of personality theory and research* (3rd ed.). New York: Guilford.

Han, B., Gfroerer, J. C., Colliver, J. D., & Penne, M. A. (2009). Substance use disorder among older adults in the United States in 2020. *Addiction, 104*, 88-96.

Hanawalt, B. A. (2003). The child in the Middle Ages and Renaissance. In W. Koops & M. Zuckerman. (Eds.), *Beyond the century of the child. Cultural history and developmental psychology.* Philadelphia: University of Pennsylvania Press.

Hans, J. D., Gillen, M., & Akande, K. (2010, June). Sex redefined: The reclassification of oral-genital contact. *Perspectives on Sexual and Reproductive Health, 42.*

Hansen, D., Lou, H. C., & Olsen, J. (2001). Serious life events and congenital malformations: A national study with complete follow-up. *Obstetrical and Gynecological Survey, 56*, 68–69.

Hansson, R. O., DeKoekkoek, P. D., Neece, W. M., & Patterson, D. W. (1997). Successful aging at work: Annual review, 1992–1996: The older worker and transitions to retirement. *Journal of Vocational Behavior, 51*, 202–233.

Hansson, R. O., & Stroebe, M. S. (2007). *Bereavement in late life: Coping, adaptation, and developmental influences.* Washington, DC: American Psychological Association.

Hanushek, E. A. (1997). Assessing the effects of school resources on student performance: An update. *Educational Evaluation and Policy Analysis, 19*, 141–164.

Hanushek, E. A. (1998). The evidence on class size: Occasional paper. ERIC: 443158.

Hanushek, E., Rivkin, S., & Kain, J. (2005). Teachers, schools and academic achievement. *Econometrica, 73*, 417–458.

Harden, K. P., Turkheimer, E., & Loehlin, J. C. (2007). Genotype by environment interaction in adolescents' cognitive aptitude. *Behavior Genetics, 37*, 273–283.

Hare, B., Call, J., & Tomasello, M. (2006). Chimpanzees deceive a human competitor by hiding. *Cognition, 101*, 495–514.

Harlow, H. F., & Zimmerman, R. R. (1959). Affectional responses in the infant monkey. *Science, 130*, 421–432.

Harman, D. (2001). Aging: An overview. In S. C. Park, E. S. Hwang, H. Kim, & W. Park (Eds.), *Annals of the New York Academy of Sciences: Vol. 928. Molecular and cellular interactions in senescence.* New York: The New York Academy of Sciences.

Harman, S. M., & Talbert, G. B. (1985). Reproductive aging. In C. E. Finch & E. L. Schneider (Eds.), *Handbook of the biology of aging* (2nd ed.). New York: Van Nostrand Reinhold.

Harper, G., & Kember, D. (1986). Approaches to study of distance education students. *British Journal of Educational Technology, 17*, 211–212.

Harrington, D. M., Block, J. H., & Block, J. (1987). Testing aspects of Carl Rogers's theory of creative environments: Child-rearing antecedents of creative potential in young adolescents. *Journal of Personality and Social Psychology, 52*, 851–856.

Harris, J. R. (1998). *The nurture assumption. Why children turn out the way they do.* New York: Free Press.

Harris, J. R. (2000). Context-specific learning, personality, and birth order. *Current Directions in Psychological Science, 9*, 174–177.

Harris, J. R. (2006). *No two alike: Human nature and human individuality.* New York: W. W. Norton.

Harris, J. R., Pedersen, N. L., McClearn, G. E., Plomin, R., & Nesselroade, J. R. (1992). Age differences in genetic and environmental influences for health from the Swedish Adoption/Twin Study of Aging. *Journal of Gerontology: Psychological Sciences, 47*, 213–220.

Harris, M. (1992). Language experience and early language development: From input to uptake. Hove, UK: Erlbaum.

Harris, M. A., Prior, J. C., Koehoorn, M. (2008). Age at menarche in the Canadian population: Secular trends and relationship to adulthood BMI. *Journal of Adolescent Health, 43*, 548–554.

Harris, P. L. (2006). Social cognition. In D. Kuhn & R. S. Siegler (Eds.), & W. Damon & R. M. Lerner (Eds. in Chief), *Handbook of child psychology: Vol. 2. Cognition, perception, and language* (6th ed.). Hoboken, NY: Wiley.

Harris, P. L., & Kavanaugh, R. D. (1993). Young children's understanding of pretense. *Monographs of the Society for Research in Child Development, 58* (1, Serial No. 181).

Harris, P. L., Pasquini, E. S., Duke, S., Asscher, J. J., & Pons, F. (2006). Germs and angels: The role of testimony in young children's ontology. *Developmental Science, 9*, 76–96.

Harris, T., & Bifulco, A. (1991). Loss of parent in childhood, attachment style, and depression in adulthood. In C. M. Parkes, J. Stevenson-Hinde, & P. Marris (Eds.), *Attachment across the life cycle.* London: Tavistock/Routledge.

Harrison, R. V., Gordon, K. A., & Mount, R. J. (2005). Is there a critical period for cochlear implantation in congenitally deaf children? Analyses of hearing and speech perception performance after implantation. *Developmental Psychobiology, 46*, 252–261.

Hart, D. (2005). The development of moral identity. *Nebraska Symposium on Motivation, 51*, 165–196.

Hart, D., Atkins, R., & Donnelly, T. M. (2006). Community service and moral development. In M. Killen & J. G. Smetana (Eds.), *Handbook of moral development.* Mahwah, NJ: Erlbaum.

Hart, M. A., & Foster, S. N. (1997). Couples' attitudes toward childbirth participation: Relationship to evaluation of labor and delivery. *Journal of Perinatal & Neonatal Nursing, 11*, 10–20.

Hart, S. (2008). *Brain, attachment, and personality. An introduction to neuroaffective development.* London: Karmac.

Harter, S. (1996). Historical roots of contemporary issues involving self-concept. In B. A. Bracken (Ed.), *Handbook of self-concept: Developmental, social, and clinical considerations.* New York: Wiley.

Harter, S. (1999). *The construction of the self. A developmental perspective.* New York: Guilford.

Harter, S. (2003). The development of self-representations during childhood and adolescence. In M. R. Leary & J. P. Tangney (Eds.), *Handbook of self and identity.* New York: Guilford.

Harter, S. (2006). The self. In N. Eisenberg (Ed.) & W. Damon & R. M. Lerner (Series Ed.), *Handbook of child psychology: Vol. 3. Social, emotional, and personality development* (6th ed.). Hoboken, NJ: Wiley.

Harter, S., & Monsour, A. (1992). Development analysis of conflict caused by opposing attributes in the adolescent self-portrait. *Developmental Psychology, 28*, 251–260.

Hartley, A. (2006). Changing role of the speed of processing construct in the cognitive psychology of human aging. In J. E. Birren & K. W. Schaie (Eds.), *Handbook of the psychology of aging.* Boston: Elsevier Academic Press.

Hartung, P. J., Porfeli, E. J., & Vondracek, F. W. (2005). Child vocational development: A review and reconsideration. *Journal of Vocational Behavior, 66*, 385–419.

Hartup, W. W. (2006). Relationships in early and middle childhood. In A. L. Vangelisti & D. Perlman (Eds.), *The Cambridge handbook of personal relationships.* New York: Cambridge University Press.

Harwood, M. D., & Farrar, M. J. (2006). Conflicting emotions: The connection between affective perspective taking and theory of mind. *British Journal of Developmental Psychology, 24*, 401–418.

Haskett, M. E., Johnson, C. A., & Miller, J. W. (1994). Individual differences in risk of child abuse by adolescent mothers: Assessment in the perinatal period. *Journal of Child Psychology and Psychiatry and Allied Disciplines, 35*, 461–476.

Hastings, P. D., Zahn-Waxler, C., & McShane, K. (2006). *Empathy, emotions, and aggression: Biological bases of concern for others.* Mahwah, NJ: Erlbaum.

Hatfield, E., & Rapson, R. L. (2006). Passionate love, sexual desire, and mate selection: Cross-cultural and historical perspectives. In P. Noller & J. A. Feeney (Eds.), *Close relationships: Functions, forms, and processes.* New York: Psychology Press.

Hatta, A., Nishihira, Y., Kim, S.R., Kaneda, T., Kida, T., Kamijo, K., Sasahara, M. and Haga, S. (2005) Effects of habitual moderate exercise on response processing and cognitive processing in older adults. *Japanese Journal of Physiology 555*, 29–36.

Hattie, J., Biggs, J., & Purdie, N. (1996). Effects of learning skills interventions on student learning: A meta-analysis. *Review of Educational Research, 66*, 99–136.

Haught, P. A., Hill, L. A., Nardi, A. H., & Walls, R. T. (2000). Perceived ability and level of education as predictors of traditional and practical adult problem solving. *Experimental Aging Research, 26*, 89–101.

Hauser, M. D. (2006). Moral ingredients: How we evolved the capacity to do the right thing. In S. C. Levinson & J. Pierre (Eds.), *Evolution and culture: A Fyssen Foundation symposium.* Cambridge, MA: MIT Press.

Havighurst, R. J., Neugarten, B. L., & Tobin, S. S. (1968). Disengagement and patterns of aging. In B. L. Neugarten (Ed.), *Middle age and aging.* Chicago: University of Chicago Press.

Hawkins, E. H. (2009). A tale of two systems: Co-occurring mental health and substance abuse disorders treatment for adolescents. *Annual Review of Psychology, 60*, 197–227.

Hawkley, L. C., Thisted, R. A. & Caciappo, J. T. (2009). Loneliness predicts reduced physical activity: Cross-sectional & longitudinal analyses. *Health Psychology, 28,* 354-363.

Hawley, R. S., & Mori, C. A. (1999). *The human genome. A user's guide.* San Diego: Academic Press.

Haworth, C. M. A., Wright, M. J., Martin, N. W., Martin, N. G., Boomsma, D. I., Bartels, M., Posthuma, D., Davis, O. S. P., Brant, A. M., Corley, R. P., Hewitt, J. K., Iacono, W. G., McGue, M., Lee A. Thompson, L. A., Hart, S. A., Petrill. S. A., Lubinski, D., & Plomin, R. (2009). A twin study of the genetics of high cognitive ability selected from 11,000 twin pairs in six studies from four countries. *Behavior Genetics, 39,* 359–370.

Hay, D. F., Caplan, M., & Nash, A. (2009). The beginnings of peer relations. In K. H. Rubin, W. M. Bukowski, & B. Laursen (Eds.), *Handbook of peer interactions, relationships, and groups.* New York: Guilford.

Hay, D. F., Nash, A., & Pedersen, J. (1983). Interaction between six-month-old peers. *Child Development, 54,* 557–562.

Hay, D. F., Pawlby, S., Angold, A., Harold, G. T., & Sharp, D. (2003). Pathways to violence in the children of mothers who were depressed postpartum. *Developmental Psychology, 39,* 1083–1094.

Hayatbakhsh, M.R., Najman, J.M., McGee, T.R., Bor, W., & O'Callaghan, M.J. (2009). Early pubertal maturation in the prediction of early adult substance use: a prospective study. *Addiction, 104,* 59–66.

Hayflick, L. (1976). The cell biology of human aging. *New England Journal of Medicine, 295,* 1302–1308.

Hayflick, L. (1994). *How and why we age.* New York: Ballantine.

Hayflick, L. (2004). "Anti-aging" is an oxymoron. *Journal of Gerontology: Biological Sciences, 59A,* 573–578.

Hayne, H., & Simcock, G. (2009). Memory development in toddlers. In M. L. Courage & N. Cowan (Eds.), *The Development of Memory in Infancy and Childhood* (pp. 43–68). New York, NY: Psychology Press.

Hayslip, B., Jr. (2009). Ethnic and cross-cultural perspectives on custodial grandparenting. In J. Sokolovsky (Ed.), *The cultural context of aging* (3rd ed.). Westport, CT: Praeger.

Hayslip, B., Jr., & White, D. L. (2008). The grief of grandparents. In M. S. Stroebe, R. O. Hansson, H. Schut, & W. Stroebe (Eds.), *Handbook of bereavement research and practice. Advances in theory and intervention.* Washington, DC: American Psychological Association.

Hazan, C., Campa, M., & Gur-Yaish, N. (2006). Attachment across the lifespan. In P. Noller & J. A. Feeney (Eds.), *Close relationships: Functions, forms, and processes.* New York: Psychology Press.

Hazan, C., & Shaver, P. (1987). Romantic love conceptualized as an attachment process. *Journal of Personality and Social Psychology, 52,* 511–524.

Hazan, C., & Shaver, P. (1990). Love and work: An attachment-theoretical perspective. *Journal of Personality and Social Psychology, 59,* 270–280.

He, F. J., Marrero, N. M., & MacGregor, G. A. (2008). Salt intake is related to soft drink consumption in children and adolescents: A link to obesity? *Hypertension, 51,* 629–634.

Heaton, P., & Wallace, G. L. (2004). Annotation: The savant syndrome. *Journal of Child Psychology and Psychiatry, 45,* 899–911.

Hebert, R. S., & Schulz, R. (2006). Caregiving at the end of life. *Journal of Palliative Medicine, 9,* 1174–1187.

Hedge, J. W., Borman, W. C., & Lammlein, S. E. (Eds.) (2006). *The aging workforce: Realities, myths, and implications for organizations.* Washington, DC: American Psychological Association.

Hedlund, B., & Ebersole, P. (1983). A test of Levinson's midlife reevaluation. *Journal of Genetic Psychology, 143,* 189–192.

Heh, S. S. (2003). Relationship between social support and postnatal depression. *Kaohsiung Journal of Medical Science, 19,* 491–496.

Heine, S. J., & Buchtel, E. E. (2009). Personality: The universal and the culturally specific. *Annual Review of Psychology, 60,* 369–394.

Heinicke, B. E., Paxton, S. J., McLean, S. A., & Wertheim, E. H. (2007). Internet-delivered targeted group intervention for body dissatisfaction and disordered eating in adolescent girls: A randomized controlled trial. *Journal of Abnormal Child Psychology, 35,* 379–391.

Helderman, R. S. (2003, June 13). Inseparable sisters say a first goodbye. *The Washington Post,* B5.

Helgeson, V. S., & Mickelson, K. (2000). Coping with chronic illness among the elderly: Maintaining self-esteem. In S. B. Manuck, R. Jennings, B. S. Rabin, & A. Baum (Eds.), *Behavior, health, and aging.* Mahwah, NJ: Erlbaum.

Hellemans, K. G., Sliwowska, J. H., Verma, P., & Weinberg, J. (2009, June 21). Prenatal alcohol exposure: Fetal programming and later life vulnerability to stress, depression and anxiety disorders. *Neuroscience and Biobehavioral Reviews.* Epub ahead of print.

Helmreich, R. L., Sawin, L. L., & Carsrud, A. L. (1986). The honeymoon effect in job performance: Temporal increases in the predictive power of achievement motivation. *Journal of Applied Psychology, 71,* 185–188.

Helms, J. E. (1992). Why is there no study of cultural equivalence in standardized cognitive-ability testing? *American Psychologist, 47,* 1083–1101.

Helms, J. E. (1997). The triple quandary of race, culture, and social class in standardized cognitive ability testing. In D. P. Flanagan, J. Genshaft, & P. L. Harrison (Eds.), *Contemporary intellectual assessment: Theories, tests, and issues.* New York: Guilford.

Helms, J. E., Jernigan, M., & Mascher, J. (2005). The meaning of race in psychology and how to change it. *American Psychologist, 60,* 27–36.

Helson, R., Jones, C., & Kwan, V. S. Y. (2002). Personality change over 40 years of adulthood: Hierarchical linear modeling analyses of two longitudinal samples. *Journal of Personality and Social Psychology, 83,* 752–766.

Helwig, C. C., Zelazo, P. D., & Wilson, M. (2001). Children's judgments of psychological harm in normal and noncanonical situations. *Child Development, 72,* 66–81.

Henderson, J., Hockley, C., Petrou, S., Goldacre, M., & Davidson, L. (2004). Economic implications of multiple births: Inpatient hospital cost in the first 5 years of life. *Archives of Disease in Childhood Fetal and Neonatal Edition, 89,* 542–545.

Henig, R. M. (2000). The monk in the garden: The lost and found genius of Gregor Mendel, the father of genetics. Boston: Houghton Mifflin.

Henker, B., & Whalen, C. K. (1989). Hyperactivity and attention deficits. *American Psychologist, 44,* 216–223.

Hennekam, R. C. (2006). Hutchinson-Gilford progeria syndrome: Review of the phenotype. *American Journal of Medical Genetics A, 140,* 2603–2624.

Henrich, C. C., Brookmeyer, K. A., Shrier, L. A., & Shahar, G. (2006). Supportive relationships and sexual risk behavior in adolescence: An ecological–transactional approach. *Journal of Pediatric Psychology, 31,* 286–297.

Henry, D. B., Schoeny, M. E., Deptula, D. P., & Slavick, J. T. (2007). Peer selection and socialization effects on adolescent intercourse without a condom and attitudes about the costs of sex. *Child Development, 78,* 825–838.

Henry, J. D., MacLeod, M. S., Phillips, L. H., & Crawford, J. R. (2004). A meta-analytic review of prospective memory and aging. *Psychology and Aging, 19,* 27–39.

Heo, S., Prakash, R. S., Voss, M. W., Erickson, K. L., Ouyang. C., Sutton, B. P., & Kramer, A. F. (2010). Resting hippocampal blood flow, spatial memory and aging. *Brain Research, 1315,* 119–127.

Herdt, G., & Davidson, J. (1988). The Sambia "turnim-man": Sociocultural and clinical aspects of gender formation in male pseudohermaphrodites with 5-alpha-reductase deficiency in Papua New Guinea. *Archives of Sexual Behavior, 17,* 33–56.

Herdt, G., & McClintock, M. (2000). The magical age of 10. *Archives of Sexual Behavior, 29,* 587–606.

Herkert, B. M. (2000). Communicating grief. *Omega: Journal of Death and Dying, 41,* 93–115.

Herlitz, A., & Rehnman, J. (2008). Sex differences in episodic memory. *Current Directions in Psychological Science, 17,* 52–56.

Herman-Giddens, M. E., Slora, E. J., Wasserman, R. C., Bourdony, C. J., Bhapkar, M. V., Koch, G. G., & Hasemeier, C. M. (1997). Secondary sexual characteristics and menses in young girls seen in office practice: A study from the Pediatric Research in Office Settings network. *Pediatrics, 99,* 505–512.

Hermans, H. J., & Oles, P. K. (1999). Midlife crisis in men: Affective organization of personal meanings. *Human Relations, 52,* 1403–1426.

Hermelin, B. (with foreword by M. Rutter). (2001). *Bright splinters of the mind: A personal story of research with autistic savants.* London: Jessica Kingsley Publishers, Ltd.

Hernandez, D. J. (1997). Child development and the social demography of childhood. *Child Development, 68,* 149–169.

Herrnstein, R. J., & Murray, C. (1994). *The bell curve: Intelligence and class structure in American life.* New York: Free Press.

Hertzog, C., Kramer, A. F., Wilson, R. S., & Lindenberger, U. (2009). Enrichment effects on adult cognitive development: Can the functional capacity of older adults be preserved and enhanced? *Psychological Science in the Public Interest, 9,* 1–65.

Heru, A. M. (2006). Family psychiatry: From research to practice. *American Journal of Psychiatry, 163,* 962–968.

Hess, T., Hinson, J. T., & Hodges, E. A. (2009). Moderators of and mechanisms underlying stereotype threat effects on older adults' memory performance. *Experimental Aging Research, 35,* 153–177.

Hess, T. M. (1994). Social cognition in adulthood: Age-related changes in knowledge and processing mechanisms. *Developmental Review, 14,* 373–412.

Hess, T. M. (1999). Cognitive and knowledge-based influences on social representations. In T. M. Hess & F. Blanchard-Fields (Eds.), *Social cognition and aging.* San Diego: Academic Press.

Hess, T. M. (2006). Attitudes toward aging and their effects on behavior. In J. E. Birren & K. W. Schaie (Eds.), *Handbook of the psychology of aging* (6th ed.). Burlington, MA: Elsevier Academic Press.

Hess, T. M., Osowski, N. L., & Leclerc, C. M. (2005). Age and experience influences on the complexity of social inferences. *Psychology and Aging, 20,* 447–459.

Hesse, E., & Main, M. (2006). Frightened, threatening, and dissociative parental behavior in low-risk samples: Description, discussion, and interpretations. *Development and Psychopathology, 18,* 309–343

Heston, L. L. (1970). The genetics of schizophrenia and schizoid disease. *Science, 167,* 249–256.

Hetherington, E. M. (1981). Children and divorce. In R. W. Henderson (Ed.), *Parent–Child Interaction:*

Theory, Research and Prospects. New York: Academic Press.

Hetherington, E. M. (2006). The influence of conflict, marital problem solving and parenting on children's adjustment in nondivorced, divorced and remarried families. In A. Clarke-Stewart & J. Dunn (Eds.), *Families count: Effects on child and adolescent development.* New York: Cambridge University Press.

Hetherington, E. M., Cox, M., & Cox, R. (1982). Effects of divorce on parents and children. In M. E. Lamb (Ed.), *Nontraditional families.* Hillsdale, NJ: Erlbaum.

Hetherington, E. M., & Kelly, J. (2002). *For better or for worse: Divorce reconsidered.* New York: Norton.

Hetherington, E. M., & Stanley-Hagen, M. (2000). Diversity among stepfamilies. In D. H. Demo, K. R. Allen, & M. A. Fine (Eds.), *Handbook of family diversity.* New York: Oxford University Press.

Hewitt, B., Western, M., & Baxter, J. (2006). Who decides? The social characteristics of who initiates marital separation. *Journal of Marriage and Family, 68,* 1165–1177.

Hewlett, B.S. (1996). Diverse contexts of human infancy. In C. Ember & M. Ember (Eds.), *Cross-Cultural Research for Social Science, 287–297.* Englewood Cliffs, NJ: Prentice Hall.

Heymann, S. J., Penrose, K., & Earle, A. (2006). Meeting children's needs: How does the United States measure up? *Merrill-Palmer Quarterly, 52,* 189–215.

Heyne, D., King, N. J., & Tonge, B. (2004). School refusal. In T. H. Ollendick & J. S. March (Eds.), *Phobic and anxiety disorders in children and adolescents: A clinician's guide to effective psychosocial and pharmacological interventions.* New York: Oxford University Press.

Heys, M., Schooling, C. M., Jiang, C., Cowling, B. J., Lao, X., Zhang, W., Cheng, K. K., Adab, P., Thomas, G. N., Lam, T. H., & Leung, G. M. (2007). Age of menarche and the metabolic syndrome in China. *Epidemiology, 18,* 740–746.

Hicks, B. M., Blonigen, D. M., Kramer, M. D., Krueger, R. F., Patrick, C. J., Iacono, W. G., & McGue, M. (2007). Gender differences and developmental change in externalizing disorders from late adolescence to early adulthood: A longitudinal twin study. *Journal of Abnormal Psychology, 116,* 433–447.

Hilgard, E. R., & Loftus, E. F. (1979). Effective interrogation of the eyewitness. *International Journal of Clinical and Experimental Psychology, 27,* 342–357.

Hill, A. J. (2007). The development of children's shape and weight concerns. In T. Jaffa & B. McDermott (Eds.), *Eating disorders in children and adolescents.* Cambridge, UK: Cambridge University Press.

Hill, C., & Rose, J. (2009). Parenting stress in mothers of adults with an intellectual disability: Parental cognitions in relation to child characteristics and family support. *Journal of Intellectual Disability Research, 53,* 969–980.

Hill, J., Emery, R. E., Harden, K. P., Mendle, J., & Turkheimer, E. (2008). Alcohol use in adolescent twins and affiliation with substance using peers. *Journal of Abnormal Child Psychology, 36,* 81–94.

Hill, J. B., & Haffner, W. H. J. (2002). Growth before birth. In M. L. Batshaw (Ed.), *Children with disabilities* (5th ed.). Baltimore: Paul H. Brookes.

Hill, J. P., & Lynch, M. E. (1983). The intensification of gender-related role expectations during early adolescence. In J. Brooks-Gunn & A. C. Petersen (Eds.), *Girls at puberty: Biological and psychosocial perspectives.* New York: Plenum.

Hill, N. E., & Craft, S. A. (2003). Parent–school involvement and school performance: Mediated pathways among socioeconomically comparable African American and Euro-American families. *Journal of Educational Psychology, 95,* 74–83.

Hill, N. E., & Taylor, L. C. (2004). Parent–school involvement and children's academic achievement: Pragmatics and issues. *Current Directions in Psychological Science, 13,* 161–164.

Hill, N. E., & Tyson, D. F. (2009). Parental involvement in middle school: A meta-analytic assessment of the strategies that promote achievement. *Developmental Psychology, 45,* 740–763.

Hill, P. (1993). Recent advances in selected aspects of adolescent development. *Journal of Child Psychology and Psychiatry and Allied Disciplines, 34,* 69–99.

Hill, R., & Rodgers, R. H. (1964). The developmental approach. In H. Christensen (Ed.), *Handbook of marriage and the family.* Chicago: Rand-McNally.

Hill, S. D., & Tomlin, C. (1981). Self-recognition in retarded children. *Child Development, 52,* 145–150.

Hill, S. E., & Flom, R. (2007). 18- and 24-month-olds' discrimination of gender-consistent and inconsistent activities. *Infant Behavior & Development, 30,* 168–173.

Hillard, P. J. A. (2008). Menstruation in adolescents: what's normal, what's not. *Annals of the New York Academy of Sciences, 1135,* 29–35.

Hilton, N. Z., Harris, G. T., & Rice, M. E. (2000). The functions of aggression by male teenagers. *Journal of Personality and Social Psychology, 79,* 988–994.

Hinde, R. A. (1983). Ethology and child development. In M. M. Haith & J. J. Campos (Vol. Eds.), P. H. Mussen (Editor-in-Chief), *Handbook of child psychology: Vol. 2. Infancy and developmental psychobiology* (4th ed.). New York: Wiley.

Hinds, J. D. (2007, May 28). 'I'm sorry' shouldn't be the hardest words. *Newsweek,* 20.

Hine, T. (1999). *The rise and fall of the American teenager.* New York: Bard.

Hines, J. C., Touron, D. R., & Hertzog, C. (2009). Metacognitive influences on study time allocation in an associative recognition task: An analysis of adult age differences. *Psychology and Aging, 24,* 462–275.

Hinton, J. (1975). The influence of previous personality on reactions to having terminal cancer. *Omega: Journal of Death and Dying, 6,* 95–111.

Hirschi, A., & Vondracek, F. W. (2009). Adaptation of career goals to self and opportunities in early adolescence. *Journal of Vocational Behavior, 75,* 120–128.

Hirsh-Pasek, K., Golinkoff, R. M., & Hollich, G. (1999). Trends and transitions in language development: Looking for the missing piece. *Developmental Neuropsychology, 16,* 139–162.

Ho, J., & Raymo, J. M. (2009). Expectations and realization of joint retirement among dual-worker couples. *Research on Aging, 31,* 153–179.

Hoare, C. H. (2005). Erikson's general and adult developmental revisions of Freudian thought: "Outward, forward, upward." *Journal of Adult Development, 12,* 19–31.

Hobbs, F. B. (with B. L. Damon). (1996). *65 in the United States.* Washington, DC: U.S. Bureau of the Census.

Hodges, E. V. E., & Card, N. A. (Eds.). (2003). *Enemies and the darker side of peer relations.* San Francisco: Jossey-Bass.

Hodges, J., & Tizard, B. (1989). IQ and behavioral adjustment of exinstitutional adolescents. *Journal of Child Psychology and Psychiatry, 30,* 53–75.

Hodgson, J. W., & Fischer, J. L. (1979). Sex differences in identity and intimacy development in college youth. *Journal of Youth and Adolescence, 8,* 37–50.

Hodnett, E. D., & Osborn, R. W. (1989). A randomized trial of the effects of monitrice support during labor: Mothers' views two to four weeks postpartum. *Birth, 16,* 177–183.

Hodnett, E. D., Gates, S., Hofmeyr, G. J., & Sakala, C. (2003). Continuous support for women during childbirth. *Cochrane Database System Review:* CD003766.

Hoegg, J., & Alba, J. W. (2007, March). Taste perception: More than meets the tongue. *Journal of Consumer Research, 33,* 490–498.

Hof, P., & Mobbs, C. (2001). *Functional neurobiology of aging.* Academic Press.

Hofer, S. M., Christensen, H., MacKinnon, A. J., Korten, A. E., Jorm, A. F., Henderson, A. S., & Easteal, S. (2002). Change in cognitive functioning associated with ApoE genotype in a community sample of older adults. *Psychology and Aging, 17,* 194–208.

Hoff, E. (2009). *Language development* (4th ed). Belmont, CA: Wadsworth.

Hoff, E. V. (2005a). A friend living inside me—The forms and functions of imaginary companions. *Imagination, Cognition, and Personality, 24,* 151–189.

Hoff, E. V. (2005b). Imaginary companions, creativity, and self-image in middle childhood. *Creativity Research Journal, 17,* 167–180.

Hoffman, K. L., Kiecolt, K. J., & Edwards, J. N. (2005). Physical violence between siblings: A theoretical and empirical analysis. *Journal of Family Issues, 26,* 1103–1130.

Hoffman, L. W. (1989). Effects of maternal employment in the two-parent family. *American Psychologist, 44,* 283–292.

Hoffman, L. W. (2000). Maternal employment: Effects of social context. In R. D. Taylor & M. C. Wang (Eds.), *Resilience across contexts: Family, work, culture, and community.* Mahwah, NJ: Erlbaum.

Hoffman, M. L. (1970). Moral development. In P. H. Mussen (Ed.), *Carmichael's manual of child psychology* (Vol. 2). New York: Wiley.

Hoffman, M. L. (2000). *Empathy and moral development: Implications for caring and justice.* Cambridge, UK: Cambridge University Press.

Hoffman, M. L. (2008). Empathy and prosocial behavior. In M. Lewis, J. M. Haviland-Jones, & L. F. Barrett (Eds.), *Handbook of emotions* (3rd ed.). New York: Guilford.

Hoffman, S. D., & Maynard, R. A. (Eds.) (2008). *Kids having kids. Economic costs and social consequences of teen pregnancy.* Washington, DC: Urban Institute.

Hoffman, S. I., & Strauss, S. (1985). The development of children's concepts of death. *Death Studies, 9,* 469–482.

Hofstra, M. B., Van der Ende, J., & Verhulst, F. C. (2000). Continuity and change of psychopathology from childhood into adulthood. *Journal of the American Academy of Child & Adolescent Psychiatry, 39,* 850–858.

Hogan, D. P., & Park, J. M. (2000). Family factors and social support in the developmental outcomes of very low-birth weight children. *Clinical Perinatology, 27,* 433–459.

Hohm, E., Jennen-Steinmetz, C., Schmidt, M. H., Laucht, M. (2007). Language development at ten months: Predictive of language outcome and school achievement ten years later? *European Child & Adolescent Psychiatry, 16,* 149–156.

Holahan, A., & Costenbader, V. (2000). A comparison of developmental gains for preschool children with disabilities in inclusive and self-contained classrooms. *Topics in Early Childhood Special Education, 20,* 224–235.

Holahan, C., & Sears, R. (1995). *The gifted group in later maturity.* Stanford, CA: Stanford University Press.

Holden, G. W. (2010). *Parenting. A dynamic perspective.* Thousand Oaks, CA: Sage.

Holland, J. L. (1985). *Making vocational choices: A theory of vocational personalities and work environments* (2nd ed.). Englewood Cliffs, NJ: Prentice-Hall.

Hollich, G. J., Hirsh-Pasek, K., & Golinkoff, R. M. (2000). Breaking the language barrier: An emergentist coalition model for the origins of word learning. *Monographs of the Society for Research in Child Development*, 65 (No. 262).

Hollon, S. D., Thase, M. E., & Markowitz, J. C. (2002). Treatment and prevention of depression. *Psychological Science in the Public Interest*, 3, 39–77.

Holmbeck, G. N., Crossman, R. E., Wandrei, M. L., & Gasiewski, E. (1994). Cognitive development, egocentrism, self-esteem, and adolescent contraceptive knowledge, attitudes, and behavior. *Journal of Youth and Adolescence*, 23, 169–193.

Holmbeck, G. N., Greenley, R. N., & Franks, E. A. (2003). Developmental issues and considerations in research and practice. In A. E. Kazdin (Ed.), *Evidence-based psychotherapies for children and adolescents*. New York: Guilford Press.

Holowka, S., & Petitto, L. A. (2002). Left hemisphere cerebral specialization for babies while babbling. *Science*, 297, 1515.

Holt, J. K. (2009). Analyzing change in adulthood with multilevel growth models. Selected measurement, design, and analysis issues. In M. C. Smith (Ed.) & N. DeFrates-Densch (Asst. Ed.), *Handbook of research on adult learning and development*. New York: Routledge.

Holt, R. I. & Sönksen, P.H. (2008). Growth hormone, IGF-I and insulin and their abuse in sport. *British Journal of Pharmacology*, 154, 542–556.

Holzrichter, A. S., & Meier, R. P. (2000). Child-directed signing in American Sign Language. In C. Chamberlain, J. P. Morford, & R. Mayberry (Eds.), *Language acquisition by eye*. Mahwah, NJ: Lawrence Erlbaum.

Honzik, M. P. (1983). Measuring mental abilities in infancy: The value and limitations. In M. Lewis (Ed.), *Origins of intelligence: Infancy and early childhood* (2nd ed.). New York: Plenum.

Hooker, K., & Siegler, I. C. (1993). Life goals, satisfaction, and self-rated health: Preliminary findings. *Experimental Aging Research*, 19, 97–110.

Hooper, F. H., Hooper, J. O., & Colbert, K. K. (1985). Personality and memory correlates of intellectual functioning in adulthood: Piagetian and psychometric assessments. *Human Development*, 28, 101–107.

Hopfer, C. J., Crowley, T. J., & Hewitt, J. K. (2003). Review of twin and adoption studies of adolescent substance use. *Journal of the American Academy of Child and Adolescent Psychiatry*, 42, 710–719.

Hopkins, M. (2006, July 3). 'Miracle recovery' shows brain's resilience. Available at: http://www.bioe-donline.org/news/news.cfm?art=2630. Accessed: October 10, 2009.

Horiuchi, S., Finch, C. E., Mesle, F., & Vallin, J. (2003). Differential patterns of age-related mortality increase in middle age and old age. *Journal of Gerontology: Biological Sciences*, 58A, 495–507.

Horn, J. L., & Cattell, R. B. (1967). Age differences in fluid and crystallized intelligence. *Acta Psychologica*, 26, 107–129.

Horn, J. L., & Noll, J. (1997). Human cognitive capabilities: Gf-Gc theory. In D. P. Flanagan, J. Genshaft, & P. L. Harrison (Eds.), *Contemporary intellectual assessment: Theories, tests, and issues*. New York: Guilford.

Horswill, M. S., Marrington, S. A., McCullough, C. M., Wood, J., Pachana, N. A., McWilliam, J., & Raikos, M. K. (2008). The hazard perception ability of older drivers. *The Journals of Gerontology, Series B: Psychological Sciences and Social Sciences*, 63, P212–P218.

Hosny, L. A., El-Ruby, M. O., Zaki M. E, Aglan, M. S., Zaki, M. S., El Gammal, M. A., & Mazen, I. M. J. (2005). Assessment of pubertal development in Egyptian girls. *Pediatric Endocrinology Metabolism*. 18, 577–584.

House, J. D. (2006). Mathematics beliefs, instructional strategies, and algebra achievement of adolescent students in Japan: Results from the TIMSS 1999 Assessment. *International Journal of Instructional Media*, 33, 443–462.

Houston, D. M., Pisoni, D. B., Kirk, K. I., Ying, E. A., & Miyamoto, R. T. (2005). Speech perception skills of deaf infants following cochlear implantation: A first report. *International Journal of Pediatric Otorhinolaryngology*, 67, 1479–1495.

Houx, P. J., Vreeling, F. W., & Jolles, J. (1991). Rigorous health screening reduces age effect on memory scanning task. *Brain and Cognition*, 15, 246–260.

Howe, M. (2006). Developmental invariance in distinctiveness effects in memory. *Developmental Psychology*, 42, 1193–1205.

Howe, M. L. (2000). *The fate of early memories: Developmental science and the retention of childhood experiences*. Washington, DC: American Psychological Association.

Howe, M. L., Courage, M. L., & Rooksby, M. (2009). In M. L. Courage & N. Cowan (Eds.), *The development of memory in infancy and childhood*, pp. 177–196. New York, NY: Psychology Press.

Howe, N., Aquan-Assee, J., Bukowski, W. M., Rinaldi, C. M., & Lehoux, P. M. (2000). Sibling self-disclosure in early adolescence. *Merrill-Palmer Quarterly*, 46, 653–671.

Howe, N., & Ross, H. S. (1990). Socialization, perspective-taking, and the sibling relationship. *Developmental Psychology*, 26, 160–165.

Howell, K. K., Lynch, M. E., Platzman, K. A., Smith, G. H., & Coles, C. D. (2006). Prenatal alcohol exposure and ability, academic achievement, and school functioning in adolescence: A longitudinal follow-up. *Journal of Pediatric Psychology*, 31, 116–126.

Howes, C. (1988). Same- and cross-sex friends: Implications for interaction and social skills. *Early Childhood Research Quarterly*, 3, 21–37.

Howes, C., & Matheson, C. C. (1992). Sequences in the development of competent play with peers: Social and social pretend play. *Developmental Psychology*, 28, 961–974.

Howes, P., & Markman, H. J. (1989). Marital quality and child functioning: A longitudinal investigation. *Child Development*, 60, 1044–1051.

Howieson, D. B., Dame, A., Camicioli, R., Sexton, G., Payami, H., & Kaye, J. A. (1997). Cognitive markers preceding Alzheimer's dementia in the healthy oldest old. *Journal of the American Geriatrics Society*, 45, 584–589.

Howieson, N. (1981). A longitudinal study of creativity: 1965–1975. *Journal of Creative Behavior*, 15, 117–134.

Howlin, P., Goode, S., Hutton, J., & Rutter, M. (2004). Adult outcome for children with autism. *Journal of Child Psychology and Psychiatry*, 45, 212–229.

Hoyer, W. J., & Verhaeghen, P. (2006). Memory aging. In J. E. Birren & K. W. Schaie (Eds.), *Handbook of the psychology of aging*. Boston: Elsevier Academic Press.

Hrdy, S. B. (2005). On why it takes a village. Cooperative breeders, infant needs, and the future. In R. L. Burgess & K. MacDonald (Eds.), *Evolutionary perspectives on human development*. Thousand Oaks, CA: Sage.

Hsia, Y., Neubert, A. C., Rani, F., Viner, R. M., Hindmarsh, P. C., & Wong, I. C. (2009). An increase in the prevalence of type 1 and 2 diabetes in children and adolescents: Results from prescription data from a UK general practice database. *British Journal of Clinical Pharmacology*, 67, 242–249.

Hsu, L. K. G. (1990). *Eating disorders*. New York: Guilford Press.

Huang, M. (2009). Race of the interviewer and the black-white test score gap. *Social Science Research*, 38, 29–38.

Hubbard, J. A., Smithmyer, C. M., Ramsden, S. R., Parker, E. H., Flanagan, K. D., Dearing, K. F., Relyea, N., & Simons, R. F. (2002). Observational, physiological, and self-report measures of children's anger: Relations to reactive versus proactive aggression. *Child Development*, 73, 1101–1118.

Hubel, D. H., & Wiesel, T. N. (1970). The period of susceptibility to the physiological effects of unilateral eye-closure in kittens. *Journal of Physiology*, 206, 419–436.

Hudley, C., & Graham, S. (1993). An attributional intervention to reduce peer-directed aggression among African American boys. *Child Development*, 64, 124–138.

Hudson, J. A., & Mayhew, E. M. Y. (2009). The development of memory for recurring events. In M. L. Courage & N. Cowan (Eds.), *The Development of Memory in Infancy and Childhood* (pp. 69-92). New York, NY: Psychology Press.

Huesmann, L. R., Dubow, E. F., & Boxer, P. (2009). Continuity of aggression from childhood to early adulthood as a predictor of life outcomes: Implications for the adolescent-limited and life-course-persistent models. *Aggressive Behavior*, 35, 136–149.

Huesmann, L. R., Moise-Titus, J., Podolski, C., & Eron, L. D. (2003). Longitudinal relations between children's exposure to TV violence and their aggressive and violent behavior in young adulthood: 1977–1992. *Developmental Psychology*, 39, 201–221.

Huesmann, L. R., & Taylor, L. D. (2006). The role of media violence in violent behavior. *Annual Review of Public Health*, 27, 393–415.

Hughes, D., Rodriguez, J., Smith, E. P., Johnson, D. J., Stevenson, H. C., & Spicer, P. (2006). Parents' ethnic socialization practices: A review of research and directions for future study. *Developmental Psychology*, 42, 747–770.

Hughes, D., & Simpson, L. (1995). The role of social change in preventing low birth weight. *The Future of Children*, 5, 87–102.

Hughes, F. M., & Seta, C. E. (2003). Gender stereotypes: Children's perceptions of future compensatory behavior following violations of gender roles. *Sex Roles*, 49, 685–691.

Huijbregts, S. C. J., Seguin, J. R., Zelazo, P. D., Parent, S., Japel, C., & Tremblay, R. E. (2006). Interrelations between maternal smoking during pregnancy, birth weight, and sociodemographic factors in the prediction of early cognitive abilities. *Infant and Child Development*, 15, 593–607.

Huizink, A. C., Bartels, M., Rose, R. J., Pulkkinen, L., Eriksson, C. J. P., & Kaprio, J. (2008). Chernobyl exposure as stressor during pregnancy and hormone levels in adolescent offspring. *Journal of Epidemiology and Community Health*, 62, e5.

Hultsch, D. F., Hammer, M., & Small, B. J. (1993). Age differences in cognitive perfor-mance in later life: Relationships to self-reported health and activity life style. *Journal of Gerontology: Psychological Sciences*, 48, 1–11.

Hummel, T., Kobal, G., Gudziol, J., & Mackay-Sim, A. (2007). Normative data for the "Sniffin' Sticks" including tests of odor identification, odor discrimination, and olfactory thresholds: An upgrade based on a group of more than 3,000 subjects. *European Archives of Otorhinolaryngology*, 264, 237–243.

Hunt, P., & Goetz, L. (1997). Research on inclusive educational programs, practices, and outcomes for students with severe disabilities. *Journal of Special Education*, 31, 3–29.

Hurd, L. C. (1999). "We're not old!" Older women's negotiation of aging and oldness. *Journal of Aging Studies*, 13, 419–439.

Hurd, R. C. (2002). Sibling support systems in childhood after a parent dies. *Omega: Journal of Death and Dying*, 45, 299–320.

Huston, M., & Schwartz, P. (1995). The relationships of lesbians and gay men. In J. T. Wood & S. Duck (Eds.), *Under-studied relationships: Off the beaten track.* Thousand Oaks, CA: Sage.

Huston, T. L., Caughlin, J. P., Houts, R. M., Smith, S. E., & George, L. J. (2001). The connubial crucible: Newlywed years as predictors of marital delight, distress, and divorce. *Journal of Personality and Social Psychology, 80,* 237–252.

Huston, T. L., McHale, S. M., & Crouter, A. C. (1986). When the honeymoon's over: Changes in the marriage relationship over the first year. In R. Gilmour & S. Duck (Eds.), *The emerging field of personal relationships.* Hillsdale, NJ: Erlbaum.

Huston, T. L., & Melz, H. (2004). The case for (promoting) marriage: The devil is in the details. *Journal of Marriage and Family, 66,* 943–958.

Hybels, C. F., Blazer, D. G., & Hays, J. C. (2009). Demography and epidemiology of psychiatric disorders in late life. In D. G. Blazer & D. C. Steffens (Eds.), *The American Psychiatric Publishing textbook of geriatric psychiatry* (4th ed.). Washington, DC: American Psychiatric Publishing.

Hyde, J. S. (1984). How large are gender differences in aggression? A developmental meta-analysis. *Developmental Psychology, 20,* 722–736.

Hyde, J. S. (2005). The gender similarities hypothesis. *American Psychologist, 60,* 581–592.

Hyde, J. S., & DeLamater, J. D. (2011). *Understanding human sexuality* (11th ed.). McGraw-Hill.

Hyson, M. C., Hirsh-Pasek, K., & Rescorla, L. (1989). *Academic environments in early childhood: Challenge or pressure?* Summary report to the Spencer Foundation.

I

Iacoboni, M. (2009). Imitation, empathy, and mirror neurons. *Annual Review of Psychology, 60,* 653–670.

Iacoboni, M., & Dapretto, M. (2006). The mirror neuron system and the consequences of its dysfunction. *Nature Reviews Neuroscience, 7,* 942–951.

Ialongo, N. S., Edelsohn, G., & Kellam, S. G. (2001). A further look at the prognostic power of young children's reports of depressed mood. *Child Development, 72,* 736–747.

Iervolino, A. C., Hines, M., Golombok, S. E., Rust, J., & Plomin, R. (2005). Genetic and environmental influences on sex-typed behavior during the preschool years. *Child Development, 76,* 826–840.

Imel, S. (1996). Adult literacy education: Emerging directions in program development. ERIC Digest No. 179.

Imperato-McGinley, J., Peterson, R. E., Gautier, T., & Sturla, E. (1979). Androgens and the evolution of male gender identity among male pseudohermaphrodites with 5a-reductase deficiency. *New England Journal of Medicine, 300,* 1233–1237.

Ingoldsby, B. B., & Smith, S. (1995). *Families in multicultural perspective.* New York: Guilford.

Ingram, R. E., & Price, J. M. (2001). The role of vulnerability in understanding psychopathology. In R. E. Ingram & J. M. Price (Eds.), *Vulnerability to psychopathology: Risk across the lifespan.* New York: Guilford.

Ingrassia, M., & Springen, K. (1994, March 21). She's not baby Jessica anymore. *Newsweek, 123,* 60–66.

Ingudomnukul, E., Baron-Cohen, S., Wheelwright, S., & Knickmeyer, R. (2007). Elevated rates of testosterone-related disorders in women with autism spectrum conditions. *Hormones and Behavior, 51,* 597–604.

Inhelder, B. (1966). Cognitive development and its contribution to the diagnosis of some phenomena of mental deficiency. *Merrill-Palmer Quarterly, 12,* 299–319.

Inhelder, B., & Piaget, J. (1958). *The growth of logical thinking from childhood to adolescence: An essay on the construction of formal operational structures* (A. Parsons & S. Milgram, Trans.). New York: Basic Books.

Inhelder, B., & Piaget, J. (1964). Early growth of logic in the child: Classification and seriation. New York: Harper & Row.

Institute for Women's Policy Research (2010, September). The gender wage gap: 2009. Fact Sheet, IWPR #C350. Available at: www.iwpr.org/pdf/C350.pdf. Accessed: October 13, 2010.

Insurance Institute for Highway Safety (2009). *Fatality facts 2008: Older people.* Available at: www.iihs.org/research/fatality_facts_2008/olderpeople.html. Accessed: December 5, 2009.

International Human Genome Sequencing Consortium (2004, October 21). Finishing the euchromatic sequence of the human genome. *Nature, 431,* 931–945.

Ip, S., Chung, M., Raman, G., Chen, P., Magula, N., DeVine, D., Trikalinos, T., & Lau, J. (2007). Breastfeeding and maternal and infant health outcomes in developed countries. Rockville, MD: US Department of Health and Human Services. Available at: http://www.ahrq.gov/downloads/pub/evidence/pdf/brfout/brfout.pdf.

Isabella, R. A. (1993). Origins of attachment: Maternal interactive behavior across the first year. *Child Development, 64,* 605–621.

Isabella, R. A., & Belsky, J. (1991). Interactional synchrony and the origins of infant-mother attachment: A replication study. *Child Development, 62,* 373–384.

Isles, A. R., & Wilkinson, L. S. (2008). Epigenetics: What is it and why is it important to mental disease? *British Medical Bulletin, 85,* 35–45.

Izard, C. E. (1982). *Measuring emotions in infants and children.* New York: Cambridge University Press.

Izard, C. E., & Ackerman, B. P. (2000). Motivational, organizational, and regulatory functions of discrete emotions. In M. Lewis & J. M. Haviland-Jones (Eds.), *Handbook of emotions* (2nd ed.). New York: Guilford.

J

Jack, F. & Hayne, H. (2007). Eliciting adults' earliest memories: Does it matter how we ask the question? *Memory, 15,* 647–663.

Jack, F., MacDonald, S., Reese, E., & Hayne, H. (2009). Maternal reminiscing style during early childhood predicts the age of adolescents' earliest memories. *Child Development, 80,* 496–505.

Jacklin, C. N. (1989). Male and female: Issues of gender. *American Psychologist, 44,* 127–133.

Jacobs, J. E., & Klaczynski, P. A. (2002). The development of judgment and decision making during childhood and adolescence. *Current Directions in Psychological Science, 11,* 145–149.

Jacobs, J. E., Lanza, S., Osgood, D. W., Eccles, J. S., & Wigfield, A. (2002). Changes in children's self-competence and values: Gender and domain differences across grades one through twelve. *Child Development, 73,* 509–527.

Jacobs, R. J., & Kane, M. N. (2010). HIV-related stigma in midlife and older women. *Social Work Health Care, 49,* 68–89.

Jacobs, S. C., Kosten, T. R., Kasl, S. V., Ostfeld, A. M., Berkman, L., & Charpentier, P. (1987–1988). Attachment theory and multiple dimensions of grief. *Omega: Journal of Death and Dying, 18,* 41–52.

Jacobsen, L. K. (2007, November 6). *Prenatal marijuana and nicotine exposure linked to teen neurologic deficits.* Presented at the 54th Annual Meeting of the American Academy of Child and Adolescent Psychiatry, Boston.

Jacobsen, T., & Hofmann, V. (1997). Children's attachment representations: Longitudinal relations to school behavior and academic competency in middle childhood and adolescence. *Developmental Psychology, 33,* 703–710.

Jacobson, J. L., & Jacobson, S. W. (1999). Drinking moderately and pregnancy: Effects on child development. *Alcohol Research and Health, 25,* 25–30.

Jacobson, J. L., Jacobson, S. W., Sokol, R. J., Martier, S. S., Ager, J. W., & Kaplan-Estrin, M. G. (1993). Teratogenic effects of alcohol on infant development. *Alcoholism: Clinical and Experimental Research, 17,* 174–183.

Jaffa, T., & McDermott, B. (Eds.) (2007). *Eating disorders in children and adolescents.* Cambridge, UK: Cambridge University Press.

Jaffe, J., Beebe, B., Feldstein, S., Crown, C. L., & Jasnow, M. D. (2001). Rhythms of dialogue in infancy: Coordinated timing in development. *Monographs of the Society for Research in Child Development, 66* (2, Serial No. 265).

Jaffee, S., & Hyde, J. S. (2000). Gender differences in moral orientation: A meta-analysis. *Psychological Bulletin, 126,* 703–726.

James, J. B., & Zarrett, N. (2005). Ego integrity in the lives of older women: A follow-up of mothers from the Sears, Maccoby, and Levin (1951) Patterns of Child Rearing Study. *Journal of Adult Development, 12,* 155–167.

Jamison, K. R. (2009). *Nothing was the same.* New York: Alfred A. Knopf.

Jankowiak, W. R., & Fischer, E. F. (1992). A cross-cultural perspective on romantic love. *Ethnology, 31,* 149–155.

Janus, J. S., & Janus, C. L. (1993). *The Janus report on sexual behavior.* New York: Wiley.

Jaquish, G. A., & Ripple, R. E. (1981). Cognitive creative abilities and self-esteem across the adult lifespan. *Human Development, 24,* 110–119.

Jastrzembski, T. S., Charness, N., & Vasyukova, C. (2006). Expertise and age effects on knowledge activation in chess. *Psychology and Aging, 21,* 401–405.

Jayawardena, K. M., & Liao, S. (2006). Elder abuse at the end of life. *Journal of Palliative Medicine, 9,* 127–136.

Jedrychowski, W., Jankowski, J., Flak, E., Skarupa, A., Mroz, E., Sochacka-Tatara, E., Lisowska-Miszczyk, I., Szpanowska-Wohn, A., Rauh, V., Skolicki, Z., Kaim, I., & Perera, F. (2006). Effects of prenatal exposure to mercury in cognitive and psychomotor function in one-year-old infants: Epidemiologic cohort study in Poland. *Annals of Epidemiology, 16,* 439–447.

Jedrychowski, W., Perera, F. P., Jankowski, J., Mrozek-Budzyn, D., Mroz, E., Flak, E., Edwards, S., Skarupa, A., & Lisowska-Miszczyk, I. (2009). Very low prenatal exposure to lead and mental development of children in infancy and early childhood: Krakow Perspective Cohort Study. *Neuroepidemiology, 32,* 270–278.

Jeffery, R., & Jeffery, P. M. (1993). Traditional birth attendants in rural north India: The social organization of childbearing. In S. Lindenbaum & M. Lock (Eds.), *Knowledge, power and practice: The anthropology of medicine and everyday life.* Berkeley: University of California Press.

Jelliffe-Pawlowski, L. L., Miles, S. Q., Courtney, J. G., Materna, B., & Charlton, V. (2006). Effect of magnitude and timing of maternal pregnancy blood lead (Pb) levels on birth outcomes. *Journal of Perinatology, 26,* 154–162.

Jenkins, S. R. (1989). Longitudinal prediction of women's careers: Psychological, behavioral, and social-structural influences. *Journal of Vocational Behavior, 34,* 204–235.

Jennings, K. D., & Dietz, L. J. (2003). Mastery motivation and goal persistence in young children. In M. H. Bornstein & Davidson, L. (Eds.), *Well-being: positive development across the life course,* 295–309. Mahwah, NJ: Lawrence Erlbaum.

Jennings, K. D., Yarrow, L. J., & Martin, P. D. (1984). Mastery motivation and cognitive development: A longitudinal study from infancy to 3 and 1/2 years of age. *International Journal of Behavioral Development, 7,* 441–461.

Jensen, A. R. (1969). How much can we boost IQ and scholastic achievement? *Harvard Educational Review, 39,* 1–123.

Jensen, A. R. (1977). Cumulative deficit in the IQ of blacks in the rural South. *Developmental Psychology, 13,* 184–191.

Jensen, A. R. (1980). *Bias in mental testing.* New York: Free Press.

Jensen, A. R. (1993). Why is reaction time correlated with psychometric g? *Current Directions in Psychological Science, 2,* 53–56.

Jensen, A. R. (1998). The g factor: The science of mental ability. Westport, CN: Praeger.

Jensen, P. S., Arnold, L. E., Swanson, J. M., Vitiello, B., Abikoff, H. B., Greenhill, L. L., Hechtman, L., Hinshaw, S. P., Pelham, W. E., Wells, K. C., Conners, C. K., Elliott, G. R., Epstein, J. N., Hoza, B., March, J. S., Molina, B. S., Newcorn, J. H., Severe, J. B., Wigal, T., Gibbons, R. D., & Hur, K. (2007). 3-year follow-up of the NIMH MTA study. *Journal of the American Academy of Child & Adolescent Psychiatry, 46,* 989–1002.

Jensen, P. S., Hinshaw, S. P., Swanson, J. M., Greenhill, L. L., Conners, C. K., Arnold, L. E., Abikoff, H. B., Elliott, G., Hechtman, L., Hoza, B., March, J. S., Newcorn, J. H., Severe, J. B., Vitiello, B., Wells, K., & Wigal, T. (2001). Findings from the NIMH Multimodal Treatment Study of ADHD (MTA): Implications and applications for primary care providers. *Journal of Developmental and Behavioral Pediatrics, 22,* 60–73.

Jessberger, S. & Parent, J. M. (2008). Epilepsy and adult neurogenesis. In F. H. Gage, G. Kempermann, & H. Song (Eds.), *Adult Neurogenesis,* 535-547. NY: Cold Spring Harbor Laboratory Press.

Jessor, R. (Ed.) (1998). *New perspectives on adolescent risk behavior.* Cambridge, England: Cambridge University Press.

Jia, G., & Aaronson, D. (1999). Age differences in second language acquisition: The dominant language switch and maintenance hypothesis. In A. Greenhill, H. Littlefield, & C. Tano (Eds.), *Proceedings of the 23rd Annual Boston University Conference on Language Development,* 301–312. Somerville, MA: Cascadilla Press.

Joh, A. S., & Adolph, K. E. (2006). Learning from falling. *Child Development, 77,* 89–102.

Johanson, R. B., & Menon, B. K. (2000). Vacuum extraction versus forceps for assisted vaginal delivery. *Cochrane Database System Review,* 2:CD000224.

Johansson, B., Zarit, S. H., & Berg, S. (1992). Changes in cognitive functioning of the oldest old. *Journal of Gerontology: Psychological Sciences, 47,* P75–P80.

Johansson, T., & Ritzén, E. M. (2005). Very long-term follow-up of girls with early and late menarche. *Endocrine Development, 8,* 126–136.

John, O. P., Naumann, L. P., & Soto, C. J. (2008). Paradigm shift to the integrative Big Five trait taxonomy. History, measurement, and conceptual issues. In O. P. John, R. W. Robins, & L. A. Pervin (Eds.), *Handbook of personality theory and research* (3rd ed.). New York: Guilford.

Johnson, C. L., & Troll, L. (1996). Family structure and the timing of transitions from 70 to 103 years of age. *Journal of Marriage and the Family, 58,* 178–187.

Johnson, H. M. (2005). *Developmental cognitive neuroscience.* Malden, MA: Blackwell Publishing.

Johnson, J., & Newport, E. (1989). Critical period effects in second language learning: The influence of maturational state on the acquisition of English as a second language. *Cognitive Psychology, 21,* 60–99.

Johnson, J. G., Cohen, P., Kasen, S., Smailes, E., & Brook, J. (2001). Association of maladaptive parental behavior with psychiatric disorder among parents and their offspring. *Archives of General Psychology, 58,* 453–460.

Johnson, J. G., Zhang, B., Greer, J. A., & Prigerson, H. G. (2007). Parental control, partner dependency, and complicated grief among widowed adults in the community. *Journal of Nervous and Mental Disease, 195,* 26–30.

Johnson, M., & de Haan, M. (2001). Developing cortical specialization for visual-cognitive function: The case of face recognition. In J. L. McClelland & R. S. Siegler (Eds.), *Mechanisms of cognitive development: Behavioral and neural perspectives,* 253–270. Mahwah, NJ: U Sum Associates Publishers.

Johnson, M. H. (1997). *Developmental cognitive neuroscience.* Cambridge, MA: Blackwell.

Johnson, M. P., & Ferraro, K. J. (2000). Research on domestic violence in the 1990s: Making distinctions. *Journal of Marriage and the Family, 62,* 948–963.

Johnson, S., Fawke, J., Hennessy, E., Rowell, V., Thomas, S., Wolke, D., & Marlow, N. (2009). Neurodevelopmental disability through 11 years of age in children born before 26 weeks gestation. *Pediatrics, 124,* e249–e257.

Johnson, S., Ring, W., Anderson, P., Marlow, N. (2005). Randomised trial of parental support for families with very preterm children: Outcome at 5 years. *Archives of Disease in Childhood, 90,* 909–915.

Johnson, S. M. (2008). Couple and family therapy. An attachment perspective. In J. Cassidy & P. R. Shaver (Eds.), *Handbook of attachment: Theory, research, and clinical applications* (2nd ed.). New York: Guilford.

Johnson, S. P., & Aslin, R. N. (1995). Perception of object unity in 2-month-old infants. *Developmental Psychology, 31,* 739–745.

Johnson, S. P., Bremner, J. G., Slater, A. M., & Mason, U. (2000). The role of good form in young infants' perception of partly occluded objects. *Journal of Experimental Child Psychology, 76,* 1–25.

Johnson, W., & Bouchard, T. J. (2007). Sex differences in mental abilities: g masks the dimensions on which they lie. *Intelligence, 35,* 23–39.

Johnson, W., Turkheimer, E., Gottesman, I. I., & Bouchard, T. J., Jr. (2009). Beyond heritability. Twin studies in behavioral research. *Current Directions in Psychological Science, 18,* 217–220.

John-Steiner, V. (1992). Private speech among adults. In R. M. Diaz & L. E. Berk (Eds.), *Private speech: From social interaction to self-regulation,* 285–296. Hillsdale, NJ: Erlbaum.

Johnston, L. D., O'Malley, P. M., Bachman, J. G., & Schulenberg, J. E. (2009). *Monitoring the future. National Results on Adolescent Drug Use. Overview of key findings,* 2008. Bethesda, MD: National Institute on Drug Abuse, U.S. Department of Health and Human Services. Available at: http://monitoringthefuture.org/pubs/monographs/overview2008.pdf. Accessed: March 1, 2010.

Johnston, T. D. (2008). Genes, experience, and behavior. In A. Fogel, B. J. King, & S. G. Shanker (Eds.), *Human development in the twenty-first century. Visionary ideas from systems scientists.* New York: Cambridge University Press.

Johnston, T. D., & Edwards, L. (2002). Genes, interactions, and the development of behavior. *Psychological Review, 109,* 26–34.

Joint Committee on Infant Hearing (2000). Year 2000 position statement: Principles and guidelines for early hearing detection and intervention programs. *Pediatrics, 106,* 798–817.

Jokela, M., Ferrie, J., & Kivimäki, M. (2009). Childhood problem behaviors and death by

midlife: The British National Child Development Study. *Journal of the American Academy of Child & Adolescent Psychiatry, 48,* 19–24.

Jokela, M., Keltikangas-Jarvinen, L., Kivimaki, M., Puttonen, S., Elovainio, M., Rontu, R., & Lehtimaki, T. (2007). Serotonin receptor 2A gene and the influence of childhood maternal nurturance on adulthood depressive symptoms. *Archives of General Psychiatry, 64,* 356–360.

Jones, L. L., Griffiths, P. L., Norris, S. A., Pettifor, J. M., Cameron, N. (2009). Is puberty starting earlier in urban South Africa? *American Journal of Human Biology, 21,* 395–397.

Jones, M., & Larson, E. (2003). Length of normal labor in women of Hispanic origin. *Journal of Midwifery, 48,* 2–9.

Jones, M. C. (1924). A laboratory study of fear: The case of Peter. *Pedagogical Seminary, 31,* 308–315.

Jones, S. S. (1996). Imitation or exploration? Young infants' matching of adults' oral gestures. *Child Development, 67,* 1952–1969.

Jones, T. (2007, April 18). A tragedy beyond the imagination. *The Washington Post,* C1, C4.

Jones, W., & Klin, A. (2009). Heterogeneity and homogeneity across the autism spectrum: The role of development. *Journal of the American Academy of Child & Adolescent Psychiatry, 48,* 471–473.

Judge, S. (2003). Developmental recovery and deficit in children adopted from Eastern European orphanages. *Child Psychiatry and Human Development, 34,* 49–62.

Judge, T. A., & Bono, J. E. (2001). Relationship of core self-evaluation traits—self-esteem, generalized self-efficacy, locus of control, and emotional stability—with job satisfaction and job performance: A meta-analysis. *Journal of Applied Psychology, 86,* 80–92.

Judge, T. A., Klinger, R. L., & Simon, L. W. (2010). Time is on my side: Time, general mental ability, human capital, and extrinsic career success. *Journal of Applied Psychology, 95,* 92–107.

Judy, B., & Nelson, E. S. (2000). Relationship between parents, peers, morality, and theft in an adolescent sample. *High School Journal, 83,* 31–42.

Junaid, K. A., & Fellowes, S. (2006). Gender differences in the attainment of motor skills on the Movement Assessment Battery for Children. *Physical and Occupational Therapy in Pediatrics, 26,* 5–11.

Jungblut, P. R., Ostorne, J. A., Quigg, R. J., McNeal, M. A., Clauser, J., Muster, A. J., & McPherson, D. D. (2000). Echocardiographic Doppler evaluation of left ventricular diastolic filling in older, highly trained male endurance athletes. *Echocardiography, 17,* 7–16.

Juola, J. F., Koshino, H., Warner, C. B., McMickell, M., & Peterson, M. (2000). Automatic and voluntary control of attention in young and older adults. *American Journal of Psychology, 113,* 159–178.

Justice, E. M., Bakerward, L., Gupta, S., & Jannings, L. R. (1997). Means to the goal of remembering: Developmental changes in awareness of strategy use–performance relations. *Journal of Experimental Child Psychology, 65,* 293–314.

Juul, A., Teilmann, G., Scheike, T., Hertel, N.T., Holm, K., Laursen, E.M/, Main, K.M., & Skakkebaek, N.E. (2006). Pubertal development in Danish children: Comparison of recent European and US data. *International Journal of Andrology, 29,* 247–255.

K

Kabir, A. A., Pridjian, G., Steinmann, W. C., Herrera, E. A., & Khan, M. M. (2005). Racial differences in cesareans: An analysis of U.S. 2001 national in-patient sample data. *Obstetrics & Gynecology, 105,* 710–718.

Kaffman, A., & Meaney, M. J. (2007). Neurodevelopmental sequelae of postnatal maternal care in rodents: Clinical and research implications of molecular insights. *Journal of Child Psychology and Psychiatry, 48,* 224–244.

Kagan, J. (1972). Do infants think? *Scientific American, 226,* 74–82.

Kagan, J. (1981). *The second year: The emergence of self-awareness.* Cambridge, MA: Harvard University Press.

Kagan, J. (1989). Temperamental contributions to social behavior. *American Psychologist, 44,* 668–674.

Kagan, J. (1994). *Galen's prophecy: Temperament in human nature.* New York: Basic Books.

Kagan, J. (1998). *Three seductive ideas.* Cambridge, MA: Harvard University Press.

Kagan, J., & Snidman, N. (2004). *The long shadow of temperament.* Cambridge, MA: The Belknap Press of Harvard University Press.

Kagan, J., Snidman, N., Kahn, V., & Towsley, S. (2007).The preservation of two infant temperaments into adolescence. *Monographs of the Society for Research in Child Development, 72,* 1–75.

Kahlenberg, R. D. (2006). *A new way on school integration.* The Century Foundation. Available at: www.tcf.org/publications/education/schoolintegration.pdf. Accessed: April 10, 2010.

Kahn, R. L., & Antonucci, T. C. (1980). Convoys over the life course: Attachment, roles, and social support. In P. B. Baltes & O. G. Brim Jr. (Eds.), *Lifespan development and behavior* (Vol. 3). New York: Academic Press.

Kail, R. (1991). Developmental change in speed of processing during childhood and adolescence. *Psychological Bulletin, 109,* 490–501.

Kail, R., & Bisanz, J. (1992). The information-processing perspective on cognitive development in childhood and adolescence. In R. J. Sternberg & C. A. Berg (Eds.), *Intellectual development.* New York: Cambridge University Press.

Kail, R., & Salthouse, T. A. (1994). Processing speed as a mental capacity. *Acta Psychologica, 86,* 199–225.

Kaiser Permanente Division of Research (2008, January 22). Caffeine is linked to miscarriage risk, new study shows. *ScienceDaily.* Available at: www.sciencedaily.com/releases/2008/01/080121080402.htm. Accessed: August 22, 2009.

Kajantie, E. (2008). Physiological stress response, estrogen, and the male-female mortality gap. *Current Directions in Psychological Science, 17,* 348–352.

Kakuma, R., duFort, G. G., Arsenault, L., Perrault, A., Platt, R. W., Monette, J., Moride, Y., & Wolfson, C. (2003). Delirium in older emergency department patients discharged home: Effect on survival. *Journal of the American Geriatrics Society, 51,* 443–450.

Kalmuss, D., Davidson, A., & Cushman, L. (1992). Parenting expectancies, experiences, and adjustment to parenthood: A test of the violated expectations framework. *Journal of Marriage and the Family, 54,* 516–526.

Kaltiala-Heino, R., Kosunen, E., & Rimpelä, M. (2003). Pubertal timing, sexual behaviour and self-reported depression in middle adolescence. *Journal of Adolescence, 26,* 531–545.

Kaltiala-Heino, R., Marttunen, M., Rantanen, P., & Rimpela, M. (2003). Early puberty is associated with mental health problems in middle adolescence. *Social Science Medicine, 57,* 1055–1064.

Kamakura, T., Ando, J., & Ono, Y. (2007). Genetic and environmental effects on stability and change in self-esteem during adolescence. *Personality and Individual Differences, 42,* 181–190.

Kameguchi, K. (2004). Empowering the spousal relationship in the treatment of Japanese families with school refusal children. In J. R. Ancis (Ed.), *Culturally responsive interventions: Innovative approaches to working with diverse populations.* New York: Brunner-Routledge.

Kameguchi, K., & Murphy-Shigematsu, S. (2001). Family psychology and family therapy in Japan. *American Psychologist, 56,* 65–70.

Kammeyer-Mueller, J. D., & Judge, T. A. (2008). A quantitative review of mentoring research: Test of a model. *Journal of Vocational Behavior, 72,* 269–283.

Kandel, E. R., & Jessell, T. (1991). Early experience and the fine tuning of synaptic connections. In E. R. Kandel, J. H. Schwartz, & T. Jessell (Eds.), *Principles of neural science* (3rd ed., pp. 945–958). Norwalk, CT: Appleton & Lange.

Kane, H. D., & Brand, C. R. (2006). The variable importance of general intelligence (g) in the cognitive abilities of children and adolescents. *Educational Psychology, 26,* 751–767.

Kanellopoulos, T. A., Varvarigon, A. A., Karatza, A. A., & Beratis, N. G. (2007). Course of growth during the first 6 years in children exposed in utero to to-bacco smoke. *European Journal of Pediatrics, 166,* 685–692.

Kang, M., Cannon, B., Remond, L., & Quine, S. (2009). 'Is it normal to feel these questions ...?': a content analysis of the health concerns of adolescent girls writing to a magazine. *Family Practitioner, 26,* 196–203.

Kang, M. J., Hsu, M., Krajbich, I. M., Loewenstein, G., McClure, S. M., Wang, J. T., & Camerer, C. F. (2009). The wick in the candle of learning: Epistemic curiosity activates reward circuitry and enhances memory. *Psychological Science, 20,* 963–973.

Kannass, K. N., & Colombo, J. (2007). The effects of continuous and intermittent distractors on cognitive performance and attention in preschoolers. *Journal of Cognition and Development, 8,* 63–77.

Kantor, J. (2009, October 31). A private partnership, for all to see. *The International Herald Tribune,* 1.

Kaplan, D. S., Damphousse, K. R., & Kaplan, H. B. (1994). Mental health implications of not graduating from high school. *Journal of Experimental Education, 62,* 105–123.

Kaplan, R. M., & Erickson, J. (2000). Quality adjusted life expectancy for men and women in the United States. In S. B. Manuck, R. Jennings, B. S. Rabin, & A. Baum (Eds.), *Behavior, health, and aging.* Mahwah, NJ: Erlbaum.

Karasik, L. B., Tamis-LeMonda, C. S., Adolph, K. E.; Dimitropoulou, K. A. (2008). How mothers encourage and discourage infants' motor actions. *Infancy, 13,* 366–392.

Karlawish, J., Rubright, J., Casarett, D., Cary, M., Ten Have, T., & Sankar, P. (2009). Older adults' attitudes toward enrollment of noncompetent subjects participating in Alzheimer's research. *American Journal of Psychiatry, 166,* 182–188.

Karniol, R. (2009). Israeli kindergarten children's gender constancy for others' counter-stereotypic toy play and appearance: the role of sibling gender and relative age. *Infant and Child Development, 18,* 73–94.

Karpov, Y. V. (2005). *The Neo-Vygotskian approach to child development.* New York: Cambridge University Press.

Kart, C. S., Metress, E. K., & Metress, S. P. (1992). *Human aging and chronic disease.* Boston: Jones and Bartlett.

Kashani, H. H., Kavosh, M. S., Keshteli, A. H., Montaze, M., Rostampour, N., Kelishadi, R., Shariatnejad, K., Memar-Ardestani, P., Hosseini, S. M., Abdeyazdan, Z., Hashemipour, M. (2009). Age of puberty in a representative sample of Iranian girls. *World Journal of Pediatrics, 5,* 132–135.

Kasl-Godley, J., & Gatz, M. (2000). Psychosocial interventions for individuals with dementia: An integration of theory, therapy, and a clinical understanding of dementia. *Clinical Psychology Review, 20,* 755–782.

Kaslow, N., Mintzer, M. B., Meadows, L. A., & Grabill, C. M. (2000). A family perspective on assessing and treating childhood depression. In C. E. Bailey (Ed.), *Children in therapy. Using the family as a resource.* New York: W. W. Norton.

Kastenbaum, R. (2000). *The psychology of death.* New York: Springer.

Kastenbaum, R. J. (2009). *Death, society, and human experience* (10th ed.). Boston: Allyn & Bacon.

Kasworm, C. E., & Medina, R. A. (1990). Adult competence in everyday tasks: A cross-sectional secondary analysis. *Educational Gerontology, 16,* 27–48.

Katz, P. A. (1986). Modification of children's gender-stereotyped behavior: General issues and research considerations. *Sex Roles, 14,* 591–602.

Katz, P. A., & Walsh, P. V. (1991). Modification of children's gender-stereotyped behavior. *Child Development, 62,* 338–351.

Katz-Wise, S. L., Priess, H. A., & Hyde, J. S. (2010). Gender-role attitudes and behavior across the transition to parenthood. *Developmental Psychology, 46,* 18–28.

Kaufman, A. S. (2001). WAIS-III IQs, Horn's theory, and generational changes from young adulthood to old age. *Intelligence, 29,* 131–167.

Kaufman, A. S., Kamphaus, R. W., & Kaufman, N. L. (1985). New directions in intelligence testing: The Kaufman Assessment Battery for Children (K-ABC). In B. B. Wolman (Ed.), *Handbook of intelligence.* New York: Wiley.

Kaufman, A. S., & Kaufman, N. L. (1997). The Kaufman Adolescent and Adult Intelligence Test. In D. P. Flanagan, J. L. Genshaft, & P. L. Harrison (Eds.), *Contemporary intellectual assessment: Theories, tests, and issues.* New York: Guilford.

Kaufman, A. S., & Kaufman, N. L. (2003). Kaufman Assessment Battery for Children (2nd ed). San Antonio, TX: Pearson.

Kaufman, J., & Zigler, E. (1989). The intergenerational transmission of child abuse. In D. Cicchetti & V. Carlson (Eds.), *Child maltreatment. Theory and research on the causes and consequences of child abuse and neglect.* New York: Cambridge University Press.

Kaufman, R. H., Adam, E., Hatch, E. E., Noller, K., Herbst, A. L., Palmer, J. R., & Hoover, R. N. (2000). Continued follow-up of pregnancy outcomes in diethylstilbestrol-exposed offspring. *Obstetric Gynecology, 96,* 483–489.

Kaufman, S. B. (2007). Sex differences in mental rotation and spatial visualization ability: Can they be accounted for by differences in working memory capacity? *Intelligence, 35,* 211–223.

Kavsek, M., & Yonas, A. (2006). The perception of moving subjective contours by 4-month-old infants. *Perception, 35,* 215–227.

Kaye, R. A. (1993). Sexuality in the later years. *Aging and Society, 13,* 415–426.

Kayed, N. S., & van der Meer, A. L. (2007). Infants' timing strategies to optical collisions: A longitudinal study. *Infant Behavior and Development, 30,* 50–59.

Kazak, A. E., & Noll, R. B. (2004). Child death from pediatric illness: Conceptualizing intervention from a family/systems and public health perspective. *Professional Psychology: Research and Practice, 35,* 219–226.

Kazdin, A. E. (2000). *Psychotherapy for children and adolescents : Directions for research and practice.* New York: Oxford University Press.

Kazdin, A. E. (2003). Psychotherapy for children and adolescents. *Annual Review of Psychology, 54,* 253–276.

Kearney, A. J. (2008). *Understanding applied behavior analysis: An introduction to ABA for parents, teachers, and professionals.* Philadelphia: Jessica Kingsley.

Kearney, C. A. (2008). School absenteeism and school refusal behavior in youth: A contemporary review. *Clinical Psychology Review, 28,* 451–471.

Keel, P. K., & Fulkerson, J. A. (2001). Vulnerability to eating disorders in childhood and adolescence. In R. E. Ingram & J. M. Price (Eds.), *Vulnerability to psychopathology. Risk across the lifespan.* New York: Guilford.

Keel, P. K., & Haedt, A. (2008). Evidence-based psychosocial treatments for eating problems and eating disorders. *Journal of Clinical Child & Adolescent Psychology, 37,* 39–61.

Keel, P. K., & Klump, K. L. (2003). Are eating disorders culture-bound syndromes? Implications for conceptualizing their etiology. *Psychological Bulletin, 129,* 747–769.

Keenan, T. (2003). Individual differences in theory of mind. The preschool years and beyond. In B. Repacholi & V. Slaughter (Eds.), *Individual differences in theory of mind: Implications for typical and atypical development.* New York: Psychology Press.

Keesee, N. J., Currier, J. M., & Neimeyer, R. A. (2008). Predictors of grief following the death of one's child: The contribution of finding meaning. *Journal of Clinical Psychology, 64,* 1145–1163.

Keeton, C. P., Perry-Jenkins, M., & Sayer, A. G. (2008). Sense of control predicts depressive and anxious symptoms across the transition to parenthood. *Journal of Family Psychology, 22,* 212–221.

Keightley, M. L., Winocur, G., Burianova, H., Hongwanishkul, D., & Grady, C. L. (2006). Age effects on social cognition: Faces tell a different story. *Psychology and Aging, 21,* 558–572.

Keil, V., & Price, J. M. (2009). Social information-processing patterns of maltreated children in two social domains. *Journal of Applied Developmental Psychology, 30,* 43–52.

Keither, J. (1985). Age in anthropological research. In R. H. Binstock & E. Shanas (Eds.), Handbook of aging and the social sciences (2nd ed.). New York: Van Nostrand Reinhold.

Keizer, R., Dykstra, P. A., & Jansen, M. D. (2008). Pathways into childlessness: Evidence of gendered life course dynamics. *Journal of Biosocial Science, 40,* 863–878.

Kelemen, W. L. (2000). Metamemory cues and monitoring accuracy: Judging what you know and what you will know. *Journal of Educational Psychology, 92,* 800–810.

Keller, B. B., & Bell, R. Q. (1979). Child effects on adult's method of eliciting altruistic behavior. *Child Development, 50,* 1004–1009.

Keller, H. (1954). *The story of my life.* New York: Doubleday.

Keller, K. L., Kirzner, J., Pietrobelli, A., St-Onge, M. P., & Faith, M. S. (2009). Increased sweetened beverage intake is associated with reduced milk and calcium intake in 3- to 7-year-old children at multi-item laboratory lunches. *Journal of the American Dietetic Association, 109,* 497–501.

Keller, M. C. (2008). The evolutionary persistence of genes that increase mental disorders risk. *Current Directions in Psychological Science, 17,* 395–399.

Kelley-Buchanan, C. (1988). *Peace of mind during pregnancy: An A–Z guide to the substances that could affect your unborn baby.* New York: Facts on File.

Kellman, P. J., & Arterberry, M. E. (2006). Infant visual perception. In D. Kuhn & R. Siegler (Vol. Eds.), *Handbook of child psychology: Cognition, perception, and language.* Hoboken, NJ: Wiley.

Kellman, P. J., & Spelke, E. S. (1983). Perception of partly occluded objects in infancy. *Cognitive Psychology, 15,* 483–524.

Kellogg, N. D. (2009). Clinical report—the evaluation of sexual behaviors in children. *Pediatrics, 124,* 992–998.

Kelly, D. J., Quinn, P. C., Slater, A. M., Lee, K., Gibson, A., Smith, M., Ge, L. Z., & Pascalis, O. (2005). Three-month-olds, but not newborns, prefer own-race faces. *Developmental Science, 8,* F31–F36.

Kelsall, D. C., Shallop, J. K., & Burnelli, T. (1995). Cochlear implantation in the elderly. *American Journal of Otology, 16,* 609–615.

Kemler Nelson, D. G., Hirsh-Pasek, K., Jusczyk, P. W., & Cassidy, K. W. (1989). How the prosodic cues in motherese might assist in language learning. *Journal of Child Language, 16,* 55–68.

Kempe, R. S., & Kempe, C. H. (1978). *Child abuse.* Cambridge, MA: Harvard University Press.

Kempen, G. I. J. M., Jelicic, M., & Ormel, J. (1997). Personality, chronic medical morbidity, and health-related quality of life among older persons. *Health Psychology, 16,* 539–546.

Kemper, S., & Mitzner, T. L. (2001). Production and comprehension. In J. E. Birren & K. W. Schaie (Eds.), *Handbook of the psychology of aging* (5th ed.). San Diego, CA: Academic Press.

Kemtes, K. A., & Kemper, S. (1997). Younger and older adults' on-line processing of syntactically ambiguous sentences. *Psychology and Aging, 12,* 362–371.

Kendall-Tackett, K. A., Williams, L. M., & Finkelhor, D. (1993). Impact of sexual abuse on children: A review and synthesis of recent empirical studies. *Psychological Bulletin, 113,* 164–180.

Kendeou, P., van den Broek, P., White, M. J., & Lynch, J. S. (2009). Predicting reading comprehension in early elementary school: The independent contributions of oral language and decoding skills. *Journal of Educational Psychology, 101,* 765–778.

Kendig, H. L., Coles, R., Pittelkow, Y., & Wilson, S. (1988). Confidants and family structure in old age. *Journal of Gerontology: Social Sciences, 43,* S31–S40.

Kendler, K. S. (2003). Of genes and twins. *Psychological Medicine, 33,* 763–768.

Kendler, K. S., Gardner, C. O., & Prescott, C. A. (2002). Toward a comprehensive developmental model for major depression in women. *American Journal of Psychiatry, 159,* 1133–1145.

Kendler, K. S., Neale, M., Kessler, R., Heath, A., & Eaves, L. (1993). A twin study of recent life events and difficulties. *Archives of General Psychiatry, 50,* 789–796.

Kendler, K. S., Silberg, J. L., Neale, M. C., Kessler, R. C., Heath, A. C., & Eaves, L. J. (1992). Genetic and environmental factors in the aetiology of menstrual, premenstrual and neurotic symptoms: A population-based twin study. *Psychological Medicine, 22,* 85–100.

Kendler, K.S., Thornton, L. M., Gilman, S. E., & Kessler, R. C. (2000). Sexual orientation in a U.S. national sample of twin and nontwin sibling pairs. *American Journal of Psychiatry, 157,* 1843–1846.

Keniston, K. (1970). Youth: A "new" stage of life. *American Scholar, 39,* 631–654.

Kennedy, Q., Mather, M., & Carstensen, L. L. (2004). The role of motivation in the age-related positivity effect in autobiographical memory. *Psychological Science, 15,* 208–214.

Kennell, J., Klaus, M., McGrath, S., Robertson, S., & Hinkley, C. (1991). Continuous emotional support during labor in a US hospital: A randomized controlled trial. *Journal of the American Medical Association, 265,* 2197–2201.

Kenney-Benson, G. A., Pomerantz, E. M., Ryan, A. M., & Patrick, H. (2006). Sex differences in math performance: The role of children's approach to schoolwork. *Developmental Psychology, 42,* 11–26.

Kenny, M. E. (1987). The extent and function of parental attachment among first-year college students. *Journal of Youth and Adolescence, 16,* 17–29.

Kenny, M. E., & Rice, K. G. (1995). Attachment to parents and adjustment in late adolescent college students: Current status, applications, and future considerations. *The Counseling Psychologist, 23,* 433–456.

Kensinger, E. A., & Choi, E. S. (2009). When side matters: Hemispheric processing and the visual specificity of emotional memories. *Journal of Experimental Psychology: Learning, Memory, and Cognition, 35,* 247–253.

Kenward, B., Folke, S., Holmberg, J., Johansson, A., & Gredebäck, G. (2009). Goal directedness and decision making in infants. *Developmental Psychology, 45,* 809–819.

Kenyon, B. L. (2001). Current research in children's conceptions of death: A critical review. *Omega: Journal of Death and Dying, 43,* 63–91.

Keough, J., & Sugden, D. (1985). *Movement skill development.* New York: Macmillan.

Kerka, S. (1995). Adult learner retention revisited. ERIC Clearinghouse on Adult, Career, and Vocational Education, Digest No. 166.

Kerns, K. A., Tomich, P. L., & Kim, P. (2006). Normative trends in children's perceptions of availability and utilization of attachment figures in middle childhood. *Social Development, 15,* 1–22.

Kerr, M., & Stattin, H. (2003). Parenting of adolescents: Action or reaction? In A. C. Crouter, & A. Booth (Eds.), *Children's influence on family dynamics: The neglected side of family relationships.* Mahwah, NJ: Erlbaum.

Kessler, R., Galea, S., Jones, R., & Parker, H. (2006). Mental illness and suicidality after Hurricane Katrina. *Bulletin of the World Health Organization, 84,* 930–939.

Kessler, R. C., Adler, L., Barkley, R., Biederman, J., Conners, C. K., Demler, O., Faraone, S. V., Greenhill, L. L., Howes, M. J., Secnik, K., Spencer, T., Ustun, T. B., Walters, E. E., & Zaslavsky, A. M. (2006). The prevalence and correlates of adult ADHD in the United States: Results from the National Comorbidity Survey Replication. *American Journal of Psychiatry, 163,* 716–723.

Kessler, R. C., Avenevoli, S., & Merikangas, K. R. (2001). Mood disorders in children and adolescents: An epidemiologic perspective. *Biological Psychiatry, 49,* 1002–1014.

Kessler, R. C., Berglund, P., Demler, O., Jin, R., & Walters, E. E. (2005). Lifetime prevalence and age-of-onset distributions of DSM-IV disorders in the National Comorbidity Survey Replication. *Archives of General Psychiatry, 62,* 593–602.

Kessler, R. C., Chiu, W. T., Demler, O., & Walters, E. E. (2005). Prevalence, severity, and comorbidity of 12-month DSM–IV disorders in the National Comorbidity Survey Replication. *Archives of General Psychiatry, 62,* 617–627.

Kett, J. F. (1977). *Rites of passage. Adolescence in America 1790 to the present.* New York: Basic Books.

Kettlewell, H. B. D. (1959). Darwin's missing evidence. *Scientific American, 200* (3), 48–53.

Keyes, C. L. M. (2002). The exchange of emotional support with age and its relationship with emotional well-being by age. *Journals of Gerontology: Psychological Sciences and Social Sciences, 57,* 518–525.

Kiesner, J., Dishion, T. J., & Poulin, F. (2001). A reinforcement model of conduct problems in children and adolescents: Advances in theory and intervention. In J. Hill & B. Maughan (Eds.), *Conduct disorders in childhood and adolescence.* New York: Cambridge University Press.

Killen, M., Rutland, A., & Jampol, N. S. (2009). Social exclusion in childhood and adolescence. In K. H. Rubin, W. M. Bukowski, & B. Laursen (Eds.), *Handbook of peer interactions, relationships, and groups.* New York: Guilford Press.

Killen, M., & Smetana, J. (2008). Moral judgment and moral neuroscience: Intersections, definitions, and issues. *Child Development Perspectives, 2*, 1–6.

Kim, K., & Spelke, E. J. (1992). Infants' sensitivity to effects of gravity on visible object motion. *Journal of Experimental Psychology: Human Perception and Performance, 18*, 385–393.

Kim, S., Kim, S., & Kamphaus, R. W. (2010). Is aggression the same for boys and girls? Assessing measurement invariance with confirmatory factor analysis and item response theory. *School Psychology Quarterly, 25*, 45–61.

Kim, S. Y. H., Appelbaum, P. S., Jeste, D. V., & Olin, J. T. (2004). Proxy and surrogate consent in geriatric neuropsychiatric research: Update and recommendations. *American Journal of Psychiatry, 161*, 797–806.

Kim, Y. (Ed.) (2009). *Handbook of behavior genetics.* New York: Springer.

Kim-Cohen, J., & Gold, A. L. (2009). Measured gene—environment interactions and mechanisms promoting resilient development. *Current Directions in Psychological Science, 18*, 138–142.

Kim-Cohen, J., Caspi, A., Taylor, A., Williams, B., Newcombe, R., Craig, I. W., & Moffitt, T. E. (2006). MAOA, maltreatment, and gene-environment interaction predicting children's mental health: New evidence and a meta-analysis. *Molecular Psychiatry, 11*, 903–913.

Kimura, D. (1992). Sex differences in the brain. *Scientific American, 267*, 119–125.

King, A. C., Castro, C., Wilcox, S., Eyler, A. A., Sallis, J. F., & Brownson, R. C. (2000). Personal and environmental factors associated with physical inactivity among different racial-ethnic groups of U.S. middle-aged and older-aged women. *Health Psychology, 19*, 354–364.

King, S. M., Forbes, J., Singer, J., Lapointe, N., Samson, L., Embree, J., & Vaudry, W. (2002, July). *Survival of perinatally HIV-infected children in Canada.* Presented at: XIV International AIDS Conference, Barcelona.

King, V., & Sobolewski, J. M. (2006). Nonresident fathers' contributions to adolescent well-being. *Journal of Marriage and Family, 68*, 537–557.

Kingston, H. M. (2002). ABC of clinical genetics (3rd ed.). London: BMJ Books.

Kinsella, K. (2009). Global perspectives on the demography of aging. In J. Sokolovsky (Ed.), *The cultural context of aging* (3rd ed.). Westport, CT: Praeger.

Kinsella, K. G. (2005). Future longevity—Demographic concerns and consequences. *Journal of the American Geriatrics Society, 53*, S299–S303.

Kirby, D., & Laris, B. A. (2009). Effective curriculum-based sex and STD/HIV education programs for adolescents. *Child Development Perspectives, 3*, 21–29.

Kirchhoff, B. A., & Buckner, R.L. (2006). Functional-anatomic correlates of individual differences in memory. *Neuron, 51*, 263–274.

Kirchmeyer, C. (2006). The different effects of family on objective career success across gender: A test of alternative explanations. *Journal of Vocational Behavior, 68*, 323–346.

Kirkpatrick, R. M., McGue, M., & Iacono, W. G. (2009). Shared-environmental contributions to high cognitive ability. *Behavior Genetics, 39*, 406–416.

Kirsh, S. J. (2006). *Children, adolescents, and media violence.* Thousand Oaks, CA: Sage.

Kisilevsky, B. S., Hains, S. M., Lee, K., Xie, X., Huang, H., Ye, H. H., Zhang, K., & Wang, Z. (2003). Effects of experience on fetal voice recognition. *Psychological Science, 14*, 220–224.

Kisilevsky, B. S., Hains, S. M. J., Brown, C. A., Lee, C. T., Cowperthwaite, B., Stutzman, S. S., Swansburg, M. L., Lee, K., Xie, X., Huang, H., Ye, H. H., Zhang, K., & Wang, Z. (2009). Fetal sensitivity to properties of maternal speech and language. *Infant Behavior & Development, 32*, 59–71.

Kisilevsky, B. S., & Muir, D. W. (1984). Neonatal habituation and dishabituation to tactile stimulation during sleep. *Developmental Psychology, 20*, 367–373.

Kitamura, C., & Burnham, D. (2003). Pitch and communicative intent in mother's speech: Adjustments for age and sex in the first year. *Infancy, 4*, 85–110.

Kitson, G. C. (1992). *Portrait of divorce: Adjustment to marital breakdown.* New York: Guilford.

Kitson, G. C., Babri, K. B., & Roach, M. J. (1985). Who divorces and why. A review. *Journal of Family Issues, 6*, 255–293.

Kitzmann, K. M. (2000). Effects of marital conflict on subsequent triadic family interactions and parenting. *Developmental Psychology, 36*, 3–13.

Klaczynski, P. A. (2000). Motivated scientific reasoning biases, epistemological beliefs, and theory polarization: A two-process approach to adolescent cognition. *Child Development, 71*, 1347–1366.

Klaczynski, P. A. (2001). Analytic and heuristic processing influences on adolescent reasoning and decision-making. *Child Development, 72*, 844–861.

Klaczynski, P. A. (2009). Cognitive and social cognitive development: Dual-process research and theory. In J. S. B. T. Evans & K. Frankish (Eds.), *In two minds: Dual processes and beyond* (pp. 265–292). New York: Oxford University Press.

Klaczynski, P. A., & Gordon, D. H. (1996a). Everyday statistical reasoning during adolescence and young adulthood: Motivational, general ability, and developmental influences. *Child Development, 67*, 2873–2892.

Klaczynski, P. A., & Gordon, D. H. (1996b). Self-serving influences on adolescents' evaluations of belief-relevant evidence. *Journal of Experimental Child Psychology, 62*, 317–339.

Klass, D. (2001). Continuing bonds in the resolution of grief in Japan and North America. *American Behavioral Scientist, 44*, 742–763.

Klaus, H. M., & Kennell, J. H. (1976). *Maternal–infant bonding.* St. Louis: C. V. Mosby.

Klein, P. J., & Meltzoff, A. N. (1999). Long-term memory, forgetting, and deferred imitation in 12-month-old infants. *Developmental Science, 2*, 102–113.

Klein, R., Klein, B. E., Lee, K. E., Cruickshanks, K. J., & Chappell, R. J. (2001). Changes in visual acuity in a population over a 10-year period: The Beaver Dam Eye Study. *Ophthalmology, 108*, 1757–1766.

Klein, W. (1996). Language acquisition at different ages. In D. Magnusson (Ed.), *The lifespan development of individuals: Behavioral, neurobiological, and psychosocial perspectives: A synthesis.* Cambridge, England: Cambridge University Press.

Kleiner, C., & Lord, M. (1999, November 22). The cheating game. 'Everyone's doing it,' from grade school to graduate school. *U.S. News & World Report*, 54–66.

Kliegel, M., Jager, T., & Phillips, L. H. (2007). Emotional development across adulthood: Differential age-related emotional reactivity and emotion regulation in a negative mood induction procedure. *International Journal of Aging and Human Development, 64*, 217–244.

Klimes-Dougan, B., & Kistner, J. (1990). Physically abused preschoolers' responses to peers' distress. *Developmental Psychology, 26*, 599–602.

Klin, A., Chawarska, K., Rubin, E., & Volkmar F. (2004). Clinical assessment of young children at risk for autism. In R. DelCarmen-Wiggins & A. Carter (Eds.), *Handbook of infant, toddler, and preschool mental health assessment.* New York: Oxford University Press.

Kline, D. W., & Scialfa, C. T. (1996). Visual and auditory aging. In J. E. Birren & K. W. Schaie (Eds.), *Handbook of the psychology of aging* (4th ed.). San Diego: Academic Press.

Klineberg, O. (1963). Negro–white differences in intelligence test performance: A new look at an old problem. *American Psychologist, 18*, 198–203.

Klinger, L. G., & Williams, A. (2009). Cognitive-behavioral interventions for students with autism spectrum disorders. In M. J. Mayer, R. Van Acker, J. E. Lochman, & F. M. Gresham (Eds.), *Cognitive-behavioral interventions for emotional and behavioral disorders.* New York: Guilford.

Klinger, L. J., Hamilton, J. A., & Cantrell, P. J. (2001). Children's perceptions of aggressive and gender-specific content in toy commercials. *Social Behavior and Personality, 29*, 11–20.

Klump, K. L., & Culbert, K. M. (2007). Molecular genetic studies of eating disorders. Current status and future directions. *Current Directions in Psychological Science, 16*, 37–41.

Klump, K. L., McGue, M., & Iacono, W. G. (2003). Differential heritability of eating attitudes and behaviors in prepubertal versus pubertal twins. *International Journal of Eating Disorders, 33*, 287–292.

Klump, K. L., Suisman, J. L., Burt, S. A., McGue, M., & Iacono, W. G. (2009). Genetic and environmental influences on disordered eating: An adoption study. *Journal of Abnormal Psychology, 118*, 797–805.

Knafo, A., Zahn-Waxler, C., Van Hulle, C., Robinson, J. L., & Rhee, S. H. (2008). The developmental origins of a disposition toward empathy: Genetic and environmental contributions. *Emotion, 8*, 737–752.

Knapp, C., Quinn, G. P., Murphy, D., Brown, R., & Madden, V. (2010). Adolescents with life-threatening illnesses. *American Journal of Hospice and Palliative Care, 27*, 139–144.

Knecht, S., Deppe, M., Drager, B., Bobe, L., Lohmann, H., Ringelstein, E., & Henningsen, H. (2000). Language lateralization in healthy right-handers. *Brain, 123*, 74–81.

Knee, D. O. (2010). Hospice care for the aging population in the United States. In J. C. Cavanaugh & C. K. Cavanaugh (Eds.), *Aging in America: Vol 3. Societal issues.* Santa Barbara, CA: Praeger/ABC-CLIO.

Knight, B. G., Kaskie, B., Shurgot, G. R., & Dave, J. (2006). Improving mental health of older adults. In J. E. Birren & K. W. Schaie (Eds.), *Handbook of the psychology of aging* (6th ed.). Burlington, MA: Elsevier Academic Press.

Knight, J. A. (2000). The biochemistry of aging. *Advances in Clinical Chemistry, 35*, 1–62.

Knightley, P., Evans, H., Potter, E., & Wallace, M. (1979). *Suffer the children: The story of thalidomide.* NY: Viking Press.

Knoester, C., Haynie, D. L., & Stephens, C. M. (2006). Parenting practices and adolescents' friendship networks. *Journal of Marriage and Family, 68*, 1247–1260.

Knopik, V. S., Jacob, T., Haber, J.R., Swenson, L. P., & Howell D. N. (2009). Paternal alcoholism and offspring ADHD problems: A children of twins design. *Twin Research & Human Genetics, 12*, 53–62.

Kochanska, G. (1993). Toward a synthesis of parental socialization and child temperament in early development of conscience. *Child Development, 64*, 325–347.

Kochanska, G. (1997). Mutually responsive orientation between mothers and their young children: Implications for early socialization. *Child Development, 68*, 94–112.

Kochanska, G. (2001). Emotional development in children with different attachment histories: The first three years. *Child Development, 72*, 474–490.

Kochanska, G. (2002). Mutually responsive orientation between mothers and their young children: A context for the early development of conscience. *Current Directions in Psychological Science, 11*(6), 191–195.

Kochanska, G., & Aksan, N. (2006). Children's conscience and self-regulation. *Journal of Personality, 74*, 1587–1617.

Kochanska, G., Aksan, N., & Joy, M. E. (2007). Children's fearfulness as a moderator of parenting in early socialization: Two longitudinal studies. *Developmental Psychology, 43,* 222–237.

Kochanska, G., Aksan, N., & Nichols, K. E. (2003). Maternal power assertion in discipline and moral discourse contexts: Commonalities, differences, and implications for children's moral conduct and cognition. *Developmental Psychology, 39,* 949–963.

Kochanska, G., Barry, R. A., Jimenez, N. B., Hollatz, A. L., & Woodard, J. (2009). Guilt and effortful control: Two mechanisms that prevent disruptive developmental trajectories. *Journal of Personality and Social Psychology, 97,* 322–333.

Kochanska, G., Barry, R. A., Stellern, S. A., & O'Bleness, J. J. (2009). Early attachment organization moderates the parent—child mutually coercive pathway to children's antisocial conduct. *Child Development, 80,* 1288–1300.

Kochanska, G., Casey, R. J., & Fukumoto, A. (1995). Toddlers' sensitivity to standard violations. *Child Development, 66,* 643–656.

Kochanska, G., & Knaack, A. (2003). Effortful control as a personality characteristic of young children: Antecedents, correlates, and consequences. *Journal of Personality, 71,* 1087–1112.

Kochanska, G., Murray, K., & Coy, K. C. (1997). Inhibitory control as a contributor to conscience in childhood: From toddler to early school age. *Child Development, 68,* 263–277.

Kodama, K., Mabuchi, K., & Shigematsu, I. (1996). A long-term cohort study of the atomic-bomb survivors. *Journal of Epidemiology, 6,* S95–S105.

Kodish, E. (2005). Ethics and research with children: An introduction. In E. Kodish (Ed.), *Ethics and research with children: A case-based approach.* Cary, NC: Oxford University Press.

Koegel, R. L., Koegel, L. K., & McNerney, E. K. (2001). Pivotal areas in intervention for autism. *Journal of Clinical Child Psychology, 30,* 19–32.

Koenen, K. C., Moffitt, T. E., Caspi, A., Taylor, A., & Purcell, S. (2003). Domestic violence is associated with environmental suppression of IQ in young children. *Development and Psychopathology, 15,* 297–311.

Koenig, A. L., Cicchetti, D., & Rogosch, F. A. (2004). Moral development: The association between maltreatment and young children's prosocial behaviors and moral transgressions. *Social Development, 13,* 97–106.

Koff, E., & Rierdan, J. (1995). Early adolescent girls' understanding of menstruation. *Women and Health, 22,* 1–19.

Kogan, N. (1983). Stylistic variation in childhood and adolescence: Creativity, metaphor, and cognitive styles. In J. H. Flavell & E. H. Markman (Eds.), *Handbook of child psychology: Vol. 3. Cognitive development* (4th ed.). New York: Wiley.

Kogan, S. M. (2004). Disclosing unwanted sexual experiences: Results from a national sample of adolescent women. *Child Abuse & Neglect, 28,* 147–165.

Kohl, G. O., Lengua, L. J., McMahon, R. J., & the Conduct Problems Prevention Research Group (2000). Parent involvement in school: Conceptualizing multiple dimensions and their relations with family and demographic risk factors. *Journal of School Psychology, 38,* 501–523.

Kohlberg, L. (1963). The development of children's orientations toward a moral order: I. Sequence in the development of moral thought. *Vita Humana, 6,* 11–33.

Kohlberg, L. (1966a). A cognitive-developmental analysis of children's sex-role concepts and attitudes. In E. E. Maccoby (Ed.), *The development of sex differences.* Stanford, CA: Stanford University Press.

Kohlberg, L. (1966b). Cognitive stages and preschool education. *Human Development, 9,* 5–17.

Kohlberg, L. (1969). Stage and sequence: The cognitive developmental approach to socialization. In D. A. Goslin (Ed.), *Handbook of socialization theory and research.* Chicago: Rand McNally.

Kohlberg, L. (1981). *Essays on moral development: Vol. 1. The philosophy of moral development.* San Francisco: Harper & Row.

Kohlberg, L. (1984). *Essays on moral development: Vol. 2. The psychology of moral development.* San Francisco: Harper & Row.

Kohn, M. L. (1969). *Class and conformity: A study of values.* Homewood, IL: Dorsey Press.

Kohn, M. L., & Schooler, C. (1982). Job conditions and personality: A longitudinal assessment of their reciprocal effects. *American Journal of Sociology, 87,* 1257–1286.

Kojima, H. (2003). The history of children and youth in Japan. In W. Koops & M. Zuckerman. (Eds.), *Beyond the century of the child. Cultural history and developmental psychology.* Philadelphia: University of Pennsylvania Press.

Kolb, B., & Wishaw, I. Q. (2008). *Fundamentals of Human Neuropsychology,* 6th ed. Worth Publishers. Hoboken, NJ: Wiley.

Kolev, V., Falkenstein, M., & Yordanova, J. (2006). Motor-response generation as a source of aging-related behavioural slowing in choice-reaction tasks. *Neurobiological Aging, 27,* 1719–1730.

Kolstad, V., & Aguiar, A. (1995, March). *Means–end sequences in young infants.* Paper presented at the biennial meeting of the Society for Research in Child Development, Indianapolis.

Koocher, G. P. (1973). Childhood, death, and cognitive development. *Developmental Psychology, 9,* 369–375.

Koocher, G. P. (1974). Talking with children about death. *American Journal of Orthopsychiatry, 44,* 404–411.

Koops, W. (2003). Imaging childhood. In W. Koops & M. Zuckerman. (Eds.), *Beyond the century of the child. Cultural history and developmental psychology.* Philadelphia: University of Pennsylvania Press.

Kopasz, M., Loessi, H. M., Riemann, D., Nissen, C., Piosczyk, H., & Voderholzer, U. (2010). Sleep and memory in healthy children and adolescents—A critical review. *Sleep Medicine Reviews.* EPub ahead of print.

Kopka, T. L. C., & Peng, S. S. (1993). *Adult education: Main reasons for participating.* Statistics in Brief NCES-93-451. Washington, DC: National Center for Education Statistics.

Kopp, C. B., & Krakow, J. B. (1982). *The child: Development in a social context.* Reading, MA: Addison-Wesley.

Kopp, C. B., & Neufield, S. J. (2003). Emotional development during infancy. In R. J. Davidson, K. R. Scherer, & H. H. Goldsmith (Eds.), *Handbook of affective sciences.* New York: Oxford University Press.

Korbin, J. E. (2001). Context and meaning in neighborhood studies of children and families. In A. Booth, & A. C. Crouter (Eds.), *Does it take a village? Community effects on children, adolescents, and families.* Mahwah, NJ: Erlbaum.

Koriat, A., Goldsmith, M., & Pansky, A. (2000). Toward a psychology of memory accuracy. *Annual Review of Psychology, 51,* 481–538.

Kortenhaus, C. M., & Demarest, J. (1993). Gender role stereotyping in children's literature: An update. *Sex Roles, 28,* 219–232.

Kosberg, J. I., Kaufman, A. V., Burgio, L. D., Leeper, J. D., & Sun, F. (2007). Family caregiving to those with dementia in rural Alabama: Racial similarities and differences. *Journal of Aging and Health, 19,* 3–21.

Kost, K., Henshaw, S., & Carlin, L. (2010). *U.S. teenage pregnancies, births and abortions: National and state trends and trends by race and ethnicity.* Available at: www.guttmacher.org/pubs/USTPtrends.pdf. Accessed: June 17, 2010.

Kothare, S. V., & Kaleyias, J. (2007). The adverse effects of antiepileptic drugs in children *Expert Opinion On Drug Safety, 6,* 251–65.

Kotilahti, K., Nissilä, I., Näsi, T., Lipiäinen, L., Noponen, T., Meriläinen, P., Huotilainen, M., & Fellman, V. (2009, September 29). Hemodynamic responses to speech and music in newborn infants. *Human Brain Mapping,* Epub ahead of print.

Kotler, L. A., Cohen, P., Davies, M., Pine, D. S., & Walsh, B. T. (2001). Longitudinal relationships between childhood, adolescent, and adult eating disorders. *Journal of the American Academy of Child and Adolescent Psychiatry, 40,* 1434–1440.

Kottak, C. P. (2009). *Cultural anthropology* (13th ed.). New York: McGraw Hill.

Koutstaal, W., Schacter, D. L., Johnson, M. K., Angell, K. E., & Gross, M. S. (1998). Post-event review in older and younger adults: Improving memory accessibility of complex everyday events. *Psychology and Aging, 13,* 277–296.

Kovacs, D. M., Parker, J. G., & Hoffman, L. W. (1996). Behavioral, affective, and social correlates of involvement in cross-sex friendships in elementary school. *Child Development, 67,* 2269–2286.

Kowal, A., Kramer, L., Krull, J. L., & Crick, N. R. (2002). Children's perceptions of the fairness of parental preferential treatment and their socioemotional well-being. *Journal of Family Psychology, 16,* 297–306.

Krafft, K. C., & Berk, L. E. (1998). Private speech in two preschools: Significance of open-ended activities and make-believe play for verbal self-regulation. *Early Childhood Research Quarterly, 13,* 637–658.

Kramer, D. A. (1989) A developmental framework for understanding conflict resolution processes. In J. D. Sinnott (Ed.), *Everyday problem solving in adulthood* (pp. 133–152). New York: Praeger.

Kramer, D. A., & Melchior, J. (1990). Gender, role conflict, and the development of relativistic and dialectical thinking. *Sex Roles, 23,* 553–575.

Kramer, L., & Kowal, A. K. (2005). Sibling relationship quality from birth to adolescence: The enduring contributions of friends. *Journal of Family Psychology, 19,* 503–511.

Krause, N. (1995). Negative interaction and satisfaction with social support among older adults. *Journal of Gerontology: Psychological Sciences, 50B,* 59–73.

Krause, N., & Rook, K. S. (2003). Negative interaction in late life: Issues in the stability and generalizability of conflict across relationships. *Journals of Gerontology: Psychological Sciences and Social Sciences, 58,* 88–99.

Krause, N., & Shaw, B. A. (2000). Role-specific feelings of control and mortality. *Psychology and Aging, 15,* 617–626.

Krebs, D. (2005). An evolutionary reconceptualization of Kohlberg's model of moral development. In R. L. Burgess & K. MacDonald (Eds.), *Evolutionary perspectives on human development.* Thousand Oaks, CA: Sage.

Krebs, D. L. (2008). Morality. An evolutionary account. *Perspectives on Psychological Science, 3,* 149–172.

Kreicbergs, U., Valdimarsdottir, U., Onelov, E., Henter, J., & Steineck, G. (2004). Talking about death with children who have severe malignant disease. *New England Journal of Medicine, 351,* 1175–1186.

Kroger, J. (2007). *Identity development. Adolescence through adulthood* (2nd ed.). Thousand Oaks, CA: Sage.

Krogh, K. M. (1985). Women's motives to achieve and to nurture in different life stages. *Sex Roles, 12,* 75–90.

Kron-Sperl, V., Schneider, W., & Hasselhorn, M. (2008). The development and effectiveness of memory strategies in kindergarten and elementary school: Findings from the Würzburg and Göttingen longitudinal memory studies. *Cognitive Development, 23,* 79–104.

Krucoff, C. (2000, May 16). Good to the bone. *The Washington Post—Health,* 8.

Krueger, R. F., & Johnson, W. (2008). Behavioral genetics and personality. A new look at the integration of nature and nurture. In O. P. John, R. W. Robins, & L. A. Pervin (Eds.), *Handbook of personality theory and research* (3rd ed.). New York: Guilford.

Krueger, R. F., Johnson, W., & Kling, K. C. (2006). Behavior genetics and personality development. In D. K. Mroczek & T. D. Little (Eds.), *Handbook of personality development.* Mahwah, NJ: Erlbaum.

Krueger, R. F., Markon, K. E., & Bouchard, T. J., Jr. (2003). The extended genotype: The heritability of personality accounts for the heritability of recalled family environments in twins reared apart. *Journal of Personality, 71,* 809–833.

Kryla-Lighthall, N., & Mather, M. (2009). The role of cognitive control in older adults' emotional well-being. In V. L. Bengtson, M. Silverstein, N. M. Putney, & D. Gans (Eds.). *Handbook of theories of aging* (2nd ed.). New York: Springer.

Ku, S. Y., Kang, J. W., Kim, H., Kim Y. D., Jee, B. C., Suh, C. S., Choi, Y. M., Kim, J. G. Moon, S. Y., & Kim, S. H. (2006). Age at menarche and its influencing factors in North Korean female refugees. *Human Reproduction, 21,* 833–836.

Kübler-Ross, E. (1969). *On death and dying.* New York: Macmillan.

Kübler-Ross, E. (1974). *Questions and answers on death and dying.* New York: Macmillan.

Kuczynski, L., & Parkin, C. M. (2007). Agency and bi-directionality in socialization. Interactions, transactions, and relational dialectics. In J. E. Grusec & P. D. Hastings (Eds.), *Handbook of socialization: Theory and research.* New York: Guilford.

Kuebli, J., & Fivush, R. (1994). Children's representation and recall of event alternatives. *Journal of Experimental Child Psychology, 58,* 25–45.

Kuehner, C. (2003). Gender differences in unipolar depression: An update of epidemiological findings and possible explanations. *Acta Psychiatrica Scandinavia, 108,* 163–174.

Kuhl, P. K., & Rivera-Gaxiola, M. (2008). Neural substrates of early language acquisition. *Annual Review of Neuroscience, 31,* 511–534.

Kuhl, P. K., Stevens, E., Hayashi, A., Deguchi, T., Kiritani, S., & Iverson, P. (2006). Infants show a facilitation effect for native language phonetic perception between 6 and 12 months. *Developmental Science, 9,* F13–F21.

Kuhn, D. (1993). Connecting scientific and informal reasoning. *Merrill-Palmer Quarterly, 39,* 74–103.

Kuhn, D. (2008). Formal operations from a twenty-first century perspective. *Human Development, 51,* 48–55.

Kuhn, D., & Franklin, S. (2006). The second decade: What develops (and how)? In D. Kuhn & R. Siegler (Eds.), *Handbook of child psychology, vol. 2: Cognitive, perception, and language* (6th ed., pp. 953–994). New York: Wiley.

Kuhn, D., Pease, M., & Wirkala, C. (2009). Coordinating the effects of multiple variables: A skill fundamental to scientific thinking. *Journal of Experimental Child Psychology, 103,* 268–284.

Kulik, J. A., & Kulik, C. C. (1992). Meta-analytic findings on grouping programs. *Gifted Child Quarterly, 36,* 73–77.

Kulik, J. A., and C.-L. Kulik. (1989). Effects of Ability Grouping on Student Achievement. *Equity and Excellence, 23,* 22–30.

Kuncel, N. R., Hezlett, S. A., & Ones, D. S. (2004). Academic performance, career potential, creativity, and job performance: Can one construct predict them all? *Journal of Personality and Social Psychology, 86,* 148–161.

Kunz, J. A., & Soltys, F. G. (Eds.). (2007). *Transformational reminiscence: Life story work.* New York: Springer.

Kurdek, L. A. (1995). Lesbian and gay couples. In A. R. Augelli & C. J. Patterson (Eds.), *Lesbian and gay identities over the life span: Psychological perspectives on personal, relational, and community processes.* New York: Oxford University Press.

Kurdek, L. A. (1999). The nature and predictors of the trajectory of change in marital quality for husbands and wives over the first 10 years of marriage. *Developmental Psychology, 35,* 1283–1296.

Kurdek, L. A. (2006). Differences between partners from heterosexual, gay, and lesbian cohabiting couples. *Journal of Marriage and Family, 68,* 509–528.

Kurdek, L. A., & Krile, D. (1982). A developmental analysis of the relation between peer acceptance and both interpersonal understanding and perceived social self-competence. *Child Development, 53,* 1485–1491.

Kurjak, A., Stanojevic, M., Andonotopo, W., Salihagic-Kadic, A., Carrera, J., & Azumendi, G. (2004). Behavioral pattern continuity from prenatal to postnatal life—a study by four-dimensional (4D) ultrasonography. *Journal of Perinatal Medicine, 32,* 346–353, 2004.

Kvaavik, E., Klepp, K., Tell, G. S., Meyer, H. E., & Batty, G. D. (2009). Physical fitness and physical activity at age 13 years as predictors of cardiovascular disease risk factors at ages 15, 25, 33, and 40 years: Extended follow-up of the Oslo Youth Study. *Pediatrics, 123,* e80–e86.

Kwak, J., & Haley, W. E. (2005). Current research findings on end-of-life decision making among racially and ethnically diverse groups. *Gerontologist, 45,* 634–641.

Kwong, M. J., Bartholomew, K., Henderson, A. J. Z., & Trinke, S. J. (2003). The inter-generational transmission of relationship violence. *Journal of Family Psychology, 17,* 288–301.

L

Labouvie-Vief, G. (1985). Intelligence and cognition. In J. E. Birren & K. W. Schaie (Eds.), *Handbook of the psychology of aging* (2nd ed.). New York: Van Nostrand Reinhold.

Labouvie-Vief, G., Adams, C., Hakim-Larson, J., & Hayden, M. (1983, April). *Contexts of logic: The growth of interpretation from pre-adolescence to mature adulthood.* Paper presented at the biennial meeting of the Society for Research in Child Development, Detroit.

Lachance, J. A., & Mazzocco, M. M. (2006). A longitudinal analysis of sex differences in math and spatial skills in primary school age children. *Learning and Individual Differences, 16,* 195–216.

Ladd, G. W. (1999). Peer relationships and social competence during early and middle childhood. *Annual Review of Psychology, 50,* 333–359.

Ladd, G. W., Buhs, E. S., & Seid, M. (2000). Children's initial sentiments about kindergarten: Is school liking an antecedent of early classroom participation and achievement? *Merrill-Palmer Quarterly, 46,* 255–279.

Laflamme, D., Pomerleau, A., & Malcuit, G. (2002). A comparison of fathers' and mothers' involvement in childcare and stimulation behaviors during free-play with their infants at 9 and 15 months. *Sex Roles, 47,* 507–518.

LaFranchi, S. H., Haddow, J. E., & Hollowell, J. G. (2005). Is thyroid inadequacy during gestation a risk factor for adverse pregnancy and developmental outcomes? *Thyroid, 15,* 60–71.

Laible, D. J., & Thompson, R. A. (2000). Mother–child discourse, attachment security, shared positive affect, and early conscience development. *Child Development, 71,* 1424–1440.

Laird, R. D., Criss, M. M., Pettit, G. S., Bates, J. E., & Dodge, K. A. (2009). Developmental trajectories and antecedents of distal parental supervision. *Journal of Early Adolescence, 29,* 258–284.

Lakatta, E. G. (1990). Heart and circulation. In E. L. Schneider & J. W. Rowe (Eds.), *Handbook of the biology of aging* (3rd ed.). San Diego: Academic Press.

Lalande, K. L., & Bonanno, G. A. (2006). Culture and continuing bonds: A prospective comparison of bereavement in the United States and the People's Republic of China. *Death Studies, 30,* 303–324.

Lamaze, F. (1958). *Painless childbirth: Psychoprophylactic method.* London: Burke.

Lamb, M. E., & Tamis-Lemonda, C. S. (2004). The role of the father: An introduction. In M. E. Lamb (Ed.), *The role of the father in child development* (4th ed.). Hoboken, NJ: John Wiley & Sons.

Lambert, S. R., & Drack, A. V. (1996). Infantile cataracts. *Survey of Ophthalmology, 40,* 427–458.

Lambert, S. R., Lynn, M. J., Reeves, R., Plager, D. A., Buckley, E. G., & Wilson, M. E. (2006). Is there a latent period for the surgical treatment of children with dense bilateral congenital cataracts? *Journal of the American Association for Pediatric Ophthalmology and Strabismus, 10,* 30–36.

Lamborn, S. D., & Steinberg, L. (1993). Emotional autonomy redux: Revisiting Ryan and Lynch. *Child Development, 64,* 483–499.

Lamborn, S. D., Mounts, N. S., Steinberg, L., & Dornbusch, S. M. (1991). Patterns of competence and adjustment among adolescents from authoritative, authoritarian, indulgent, and neglectful families. *Child Development, 62,* 1049–1065.

Lampinen, P., Heikkinen, R., & Ruoppila, I. (2000). Changes in intensity of physical exercise as predictors of depressive symptoms among older adults: An eight-year follow-up. *Preventive Medicine, 30,* 371–380.

Lampl, M., & Thompson, A. L. (2007). Growth chart curves do not describe individual growth biology. *American Journal of Human Biology, 19,* 643–653.

Lamy, P. P. (1986). The elderly and drug interactions. *Journal of the American Geriatrics Society, 34,* 586–592.

Landon, M. B., Hauth, J. C., Leveno, K. J., Spong, C. Y., Leindecker, S., Varner, M. W., Moawad, A. H., Caritis, S. N., Harper, M., Wapner, R. J., Sorokin, Y., Miodovnik, M., Carpenter, M., Peaceman, A. M., O'Sullivan, M. J., Sibai, B., Langer, O., Thorp, J. M., Ramin, S. M., Mercer, B. M., Gabbe, S. G., & the National Institute of Child Health and Human Development Maternal–Fetal Medicine Units Network (2004). Maternal and perinatal outcomes associated with a trial of labor after prior cesarean delivery. *New England Journal of Medicine, 351,* 2581–2589.

Landreth, G., & Homeyer, L. (1998). Play as the language of children's feelings. In D. P. Fromberg & D. Bergen (Eds.), *Play from birth to twelve and beyond.* New York: Garland.

Lane, M. A., Black, A., Handy, A., Tilmont, E. M., Ingram, D. K., & Roth, G. S. (2001). Caloric restriction in primates. In S. C. Park, E. S. Hwang, H. Kim, & W. Park (Eds.), *Annals of the New York Academy of Sciences: Vol. 928. Molecular and cellular interactions in senescence.* New York: The New York Academy of Sciences.

Lang, F. R., & Carstensen, L. L. (1994). Close emotional relationships in late life: Further support for proactive aging in the social domain. *Psychology and Aging, 9,* 315–324.

Lang, F. R., & Carstensen, L. L. (2002). Time counts: Future time perspective, goals, and social relationships. *Psychology and Aging, 17,* 125–139.

Lange, G., & Pierce, S. H. (1992). Memory-strategy learning and maintenance in preschool children. *Developmental Psychology, 28,* 453–462.

Langley-Evans, A. J., & Langley-Evans, S. C. (2003). Relationship between maternal nutrient intakes in early and late pregnancy and infants' weight and proportions at birth: Prospective cohort study.

Journal of Research in Social Health, 123, 210–216.

Langlois, J. A., Keyl, P. M., Guralnik, J. M., Foley, D. J., Marottoli, R. A., & Wallace, R. B. (1997). Characteristics of older pedestrians who have difficulty crossing the street. *American Journal of Public Health, 87,* 393–397.

Lansford, J. E. (2009). Parental divorce and children's adjustment. *Perspectives on Psychological Science, 4,* 140–152.

Lansford, J. E., & Dodge, K. A. (2008). Cultural norms for adult corporal punishment of children and societal rates of endorsement and use of violence. *Parenting: Science and Practice, 8,* 257–270.

Lansford, J. E., Chang, L., Dodge, K. A., Malone, P. S., Oburu, P., Palmerus, K., Bacchini, D., Pastorelli, C., Bombi, A. S., Zelli, A., Tapanya, S., Chaudhary, N., Deater-Deckard, K., Manke, B., & Quinn, N. (2005). Physical discipline and children's adjustment: Cultural normativeness as a moderator. *Child Development, 76,* 1234–1246.

Lansford, J. E., Miller-Johnson, S., Berlin, L. J., Dodge, K. A., Bates, J. E., & Pettit, G. S. (2007). Early physical abuse and later violent delinquency: A prospective longitudinal study. *Child Maltreatment, 12,* 233–245.

Lansford, J. E., Sherman, A. M., & Antonucci, T. C. (1998). Satisfaction with social networks: An examination of socioemotional selectivity theory across cohorts. *Psychology and Aging, 13,* 544–552.

Laplante, D. P., Barr, R. G., Brunet, A., Fort, G., Meaney, M. L., Saucier, J., Zelazo, P. R., King, S. (2004). Stress during pregnancy affects general intellectual and language functioning in human toddlers. *Pediatric Research, 56,* 400–410.

Laplante, D. P., Brunet, A., Schmitz, N., Ciampi, A., & King, S. (2008). Project ice storm: Prenatal maternal stress affects cognitive and linguistic functioning in 5 1/2-year-old children. *Journal of the American Academy of Child & Adolescent Psychiatry, 47,* 1063–1072.

Lapsley, D. K. (2006). Moral stage theory. In M. Killen & J. G. Smetana (Eds.), *Handbook of moral development.* Mahwah, NJ: Erlbaum.

Lapsley, D. K., Harwell, M. R., Olson, L. M., Flannery, D., & Quintana, S. M. (1984). Moral judgment, personality, and attitude toward authority in early and late adolescence. *Journal of Youth and Adolescence, 13,* 527–542.

Lapsley, D. K., Milstead, M., Quintana, S. M., Flannery, D., & Buss, R. R. (1986). Adolescent egocentrism and formal operations: Tests of a theoretical assumption. *Developmental Psychology, 22,* 800–807.

Lapsley, D. K., Rice, K. G., & FitzGerald, D. P. (1990). Adolescent attachment, identity, and adjustment to college: Implications for the continuity of adaptation hypothesis. *Journal of Counseling and Development, 68,* 561–565.

Larose, S., Bernier, A., & Tarabulsy, G. M. (2005). Attachment state of mind, learning dispositions, and academic performance during the college transition. *Developmental Psychology, 41,* 281–289.

Larson, E. B., Wang, L., Bowen, J. D., McCormick, W. C., Teri, L., Crane, P., & Kukull, W. (2006). Exercise is associated with reduced risk for incident dementia among persons 65 years of age and older. *Annuals of Internal Medicine, 144,* 73–81.

Larson, R. W., Richards, M. H., Moneta, G., Holmbeck, G., & Duckett, E. (1996). Changes in adolescents' daily interactions with their families from ages 10 to 18: Disengagement and transformation. *Developmental Psychology, 32,* 744–753.

Larsson, H., Viding, E., Rijsdijk, F. V., & Plomin, R. (2008). Relationships between parental negativity and childhood antisocial behavior over time: A bidirectional effects model in a longitudinal geneti-

cally informative design. *Journal of Abnormal Child Psychology, 36,* 633–645.

Larsson, I. & Svedin, C. (2002). Sexual experiences in childhood: Young adults' recollections. *Archives of Sexual Behavior, 31,* 263–273.

Larsson, M., Öberg-Blåvarg, C., & Jönsson, F. U. (2009). Bad odors stick better than good ones: Olfactory qualities and odor recognition. *Experimental Psychology, 56,* 375–380.

Laucht, M., Skowronek, M. H., Becker, K., Schmidt M. H., Esser, G., Schulze, T. G., & Rietschel, M. (2007). Interacting effects of the dopamine transporter gene and psychosocial adversity on attention-deficit/hyperactivity disorder symptoms among 15-year-olds from a high-risk community sample. *Archives of General Psychiatry, 64,* 585–590.

Laughon, M., O'Shea, M. T., Allred, E. N., Bose, C., Kuban, K., van Marter, L. J., Ehrenkranz, R. A., Leviton, A., & ELGAN Study Investigators. (2009). Chronic lung disease and developmental delay at 2 years of age in children born before 28 weeks' gestation. *Pediatrics, 124,* 637–648.

Laumann, E. O., Paik, A., & Rosen, R. C. (1999). Sexual dysfunction in the United States: Prevalence and predictors. *Journal of the American Medical Association, 281,* 537–544.

Laursen, B., & Williams, V. (2002). The role of ethnic identity in personality development. In L. Pulkkinen & A. Caspi (Eds.), *Paths to successful development. Personality in the life course.* Cambridge, UK: Cambridge University Press.

Lavigne, J. V., Arend, R., Rosenbaum, D., Smith, A., Weissbluth, M., Binns, H. J., & Christoffel, K. K. (1999). Sleep and behavior problems among preschoolers. *Journal of Developmental and Behavioral Pediatrics, 20,* 164–169.

Law, K. L., Stroud, L. R., LaGasse, L. L., Niaura, R., Liu, J., & Lester, B. M. (2003). Smoking during pregnancy and newborn neurobehavior. *Pediatrics, 111,* 1318–1323.

Lawrence, E., Rothman, A. D., Cobb, R. J., Rothman, M. T., & Bradbury, T. N. (2008). Marital satisfaction across the transition to parenthood. *Journal of Family Psychology, 22,* 41–50.

Lawton, M. P., Moss, M. S., Winter, L., & Hoffman, C. (2002). Motivation in later life: Personal projects and well-being. *Psychology and Aging, 17,* 539–547.

le Grange, D., Eddy, K. T., & Hertzog, D. (2010). In Dulcan, M. K. (Ed.), Anorexia nervosa and bulimia nervosa. *Dulcan's textbook of child and adolescent psychiatry.* Arlington, VA: American Psychiatric Publishing.

Leaper, C. (1994). *Childhood gender segregation: Causes and consequences* (New Directions for Child Development, Vol. 65). San Francisco: Jossey-Bass.

Lederman, S.A., Rauh, V., Weiss, L., Stein, J.L., Hoepner, L.A., Becker, M., Perera, F.P. (2004). The effects of the World Trade Center event on birth outcomes among term deliveries at three lower Manhattan hospitals. *Environmental Health Perspectives, 112,* 1772–1778.

Lee, J. M., Appugliese, D., Kaciroti, N., Corwyn, R. F., Bradley, R. H., & Lumeng, J. C. (2007). Weight status in young girls and the onset of puberty. *Pediatrics, 119,* E624–E630.

Lee, J., & Hahm, H. C. (2010). Acculturation and sexual risk behaviors among Latina adolescents transitioning to young adulthood. *Journal of Youth and Adolescence, 39,* 414–427.

Lee, K., Ng, E. L., & Ng, S. F. (2009). The contributions of working memory and executive functioning to problem representation and solution generation in algebraic word problems. *Journal of Educational Psychology, 101,* 373–387.

Leeder, E. J. (2004). *The family in global perspective. A gendered journey.* Thousand Oaks, CA: Sage.

Leerkes, E. M., Blankson, A. N., & O'Brien, M. (2009). Differential effects of maternal sensitivity to infant distress and nondistress on social-

emotional functioning. *Child Development, 80,* 762–775.

Lefkowitz, E. S. (2005). "Things have gotten better": Developmental changes among emerging adults after the transition to university. *Journal of Adolescent Research, 20,* 40–63.

Lefkowitz, E. S., & Zeldow, P. B. (2006). Masculinity and femininity predict optimal mental health: A belated test of the androgyny hypothesis. *Journal of Personality Assessment, 87,* 95–101.

Lehman, D. R., Ellard, J. H., & Wortman, C. B. (1986). Social support for the bereaved: Recipients' and providers' perspectives on what is helpful. *Journal of Consulting and Clinical Psychology, 54,* 438–446.

Lehman, H. C. (1953). *Age and achievement.* Princeton, NJ: Princeton University Press.

Lehn, H., Derks, E. M., Hudziak, J. J., Heutink, P., van Beijsterveldt, T. C. E. M., & Boomsma, D. I. (2007). Attention problems and attention-deficit/hyperactivity disorder in discordant and concordant monozygotic twins: Evidence of environmental mediators. *Journal of the American Academy of Child and Adolescent Psychiatry, 46,* 83–91.

Leichtman, M. D., & Ceci, S. J. (1993). The problem of infantile amnesia: Lessons from fuzzy-trace theory. In M. L. Howe & R. Pasnak (Eds.), *Emerging themes in cognitive development: Vol. 1. Foundations.* New York: Springer-Verlag.

Lejarraga, H. (2002). Growth in infancy and childhood: A pediatric approach. In N. Cameron (Ed.), *Human growth and development* (pp. 21–44). New York: Academic Press.

Lemann, N. (1997, November). The reading wars. *Atlantic Monthly,* 128–134.

LeMare, L. J., & Rubin, K. H. (1987). Perspective taking and peer interaction: Structural and developmental analyses. *Child Development, 58,* 306–315.

Lemerise, E. A., & Arsenio, W. F. (2000). An integrated model of emotion processes and cognition in social information processing. *Child Development, 71,* 107–118.

L'Engle, K. L., & Jackson, C. (2008). Socialization influences on early adolescents' cognitive susceptibility and transition to sexual intercourse. *Journal of Research on Adolescence, 18,* 353–378.

Leon, D. A., Lawlor, D. A., Clark, H., Batty, G. D., & Macintyre, S. (2009). The association of childhood intelligence with mortality risk from adolescence to middle age: Findings from the Aberdeen children of the 1950s cohort study. *Intelligence, 37,* 520–528.

Leonard, K. E., & Das Eiden, R. (2002). Cognitive functioning among infants of alcoholic fathers. *Drug and Alcohol Dependence, 67,* 139–147.

Lerner, J. V., & Noh, E. R. (2000). Maternal employment influences on early adolescent development: A contextual view. In R. D. Taylor & M. C. Wang (Eds.), *Resilience across contexts: Family, work, culture, and community.* Mahwah, NJ: Erlbaum.

Lerner, M. J., Somers, D. G., Reid, D., Chiriboga, D., & Tierney, M. (1991). Adult children as caregivers: Egocentric biases in judgments of sibling contributions. *Gerontologist, 31,* 746–755.

Lerner, R. M. (2003). What are SES effects effects of?: A developmental systems perspective. In M. H. Bornstein & R. H. Bradley (Eds.), *Socioeconomic status, parenting, and child development.* Mahwah, NJ: Erlbaum.

Lerner, R. M. (2006). Developmental science, developmental systems, and contemporary theories of human development. In W. Damon & R. M. Lerner (Eds. in Chief) & R. M. Lerner (Vol. Ed.), *Handbook of child psychology: Vol. 1. Theoretical models of human development* (6th ed.). Hoboken, NJ: Wiley.

Leslie, A. M. (1994). ToMM, ToBy, and agency: Core architecture and domain specificity in cognition and culture. In L. Hirschfeld & S. Gelman (Eds.), *Mapping the mind: Domain specificity in cognition* and culture. New York: Cambridge University Press.

Lester, B. M., Kotelchuck, M., Spelke, E., Sellers, M. J., & Klein, R. E. (1974). Separation protest in Guatemalan infants: Cross-cultural and cognitive findings. *Developmental Psychology, 10,* 79–85.

Lester, D. (1994). Are there unique features of suicide in adults of different ages and developmental stages. *Omega: Journal of Death and Dying, 29,* 337–348.

Lettre, G. (2009). Genetic regulation of adult stature. *Current Opinion in Pediatrics, 21,* 515–422.

Leung, A. K. C., & Robson, W. L. M. (1993). Childhood masturbation. *Clinical Pediatrics, 32,* 238–241.

Leutwyler, B. (2009). Metacognitive learning strategies: Differential development patterns in high school. *Metacognition Learning, 4,* 111–123.

LeVay, S. (1996). *Queer science: The use and abuse of research into homosexuality.* Cambridge, MA: MIT Press.

Leve, L. D., & Fagot, B. I. (1997). Gender-role socialization and discipline processes in one- and two-parent families. *Sex Roles, 36,* 1–21.

Levenkron, S. (2000). *Anatomy of anorexia.* New York: W. W. Norton.

Levinson, D. (1989). *Family violence in cross-cultural perspective.* Newbury Park, CA: Sage.

Levinson, D. J. (1986). A conception of adult development. *American Psychologist, 41,* 3–13.

Levinson, D. J. (in collaboration with J. D. Levinson) (1996). *The seasons of a woman's life.* New York: Alfred A. Knopf.

Levinson, D. J., Darrow, C. N., Klein, E. B., Levinson, M. H., & McKee, B. (1978). *The seasons of a man's life.* New York: Ballantine Books.

Levitt, M. J. (1991). Attachment and close relationships: A life-span perspective. In J. L. Gewirtz & W. M. Kurtines (Eds.), *Intersections with attachment.* Hillsdale, NJ: Erlbaum.

Levitt, M. J., Weber, R. A., & Guacci, N. (1993). Convoys of social support: An intergenerational analysis. *Psychology and Aging, 8,* 323–326.

Levy, B. (1996). Improving memory in old age through implicit self-stereotyping. *Journal of Personality and Social Psychology, 71,* 1092–1107.

Levy, B., & Langer, E. (1994). Aging free from negative stereotypes: Successful memory in China and among the American deaf. *Journal of Personality and Social Psychology, 66,* 989–997.

Levy, B. R. (2003). Mind matters: Cognitive and physical effects of aging self-stereotypes. *Journals of Gerontology: Psychological Sciences & Social Sciences, 58,* 203–211.

Levy, B. R., Slade, M. D., & Kasl, S. V. (2002). Longitudinal benefit of positive self-perceptions of aging on functional health. *Journals of Gerontology: Psychological Sciences and Social Sciences, 57,* 409–417.

Levy, B. R., Zonderman, A. B., Slade, M. D., & Ferrucci, L. (2009). Age stereotypes held earlier in life predict cardiovascular events in later life. *Psychological Science, 20,* 296–298.

Levy, G. D. (1999). Gender-typed and non-gender-typed category awareness in toddlers. *Sex Roles, 41,* 851–873.

Levy, G. D., Sadovsky, A. L., & Troseth, G. L. (2000). Aspects of young children's perceptions of gender-typed occupations. *Sex Roles, 42,* 993–1006.

Levy-Shiff, R. (1994). Individual and contextual correlates of marital change across the transition to parenthood. *Developmental Psychology, 30,* 591–601.

Lew, A. R., Hopkins, B., Owen, L. H., & Green, M. (2007, March 1). Postural change effects on infants' AB task performance: Visual, postural, or spatial? *Journal of Experimental Psychology, 97,* 1–13.

Lewis, D. A., Sesack, S. R., Levey, A. I., & Rosenberg, D. R. (1998). Dopamine axons in primate prefrontal cortex: Specificity of distribution, synaptic targets, and development. *Advances in Pharmacology, 42,* 703–706.

Lewis, M. (2000). The emergence of human emotions. In M. Lewis & J. M. Haviland-Jones (Eds.), *Handbook of emotions* (2nd ed.). New York: Guilford.

Lewis, M., & Brooks-Gunn, J. (1979). *Social cognition and the acquisition of self.* New York: Plenum.

Lewis, M., & Rosenblum, M. A. (1975). *Friendship and peer relations.* New York: Wiley.

Lewis, M., Sullivan, M. W., Stanger, C., & Weiss, M. (1989). Self-development and self-conscious emotions. *Child Development, 60,* 146–156.

Lewis, M., & Weinraub, M. (1979). Origins of early sex-role development. *Sex Roles, 5,* 135–153.

Lewis, P. G., & Lippman, J. G. (2004). *Helping children cope with the death of a parent. A guide for the first year.* Westport, CT: Praeger.

Lewis, T. L., & Maurer, D. (2005). Multiple sensitive periods in human visual development: Evidence from visually deprived children. *Developmental Psychobiology, 46,* 163–183.

Lewis, T. L., & Maurer, D. (2009). Effects of early pattern deprivation on visual development. *Optometry and Vision Science, 86,* 640–646.

Lewontin, R. C. (1976). Race and intelligence. In N. J. Block & G. Dworkin (Eds.), *The IQ controversy.* New York: Pantheon.

Li, K. Z. H., Lindenberger, U., Freund, A. M., & Baltes, P. B. (2001). Walking while memorizing: Age-related differences in compensatory behavior. *Psychological Science, 12,* 230–237.

Li, L. W., Seltzer, M. M., & Greenberg, J. S. (1999). Change in depressive symptoms among daughter caregivers: An 18-month longitudinal study. *Psychology and Aging, 14,* 206–219.

Li, N., & Kirkup, G. (2007). Gender and cultural differences in Internet use: A study of China and the UK. *Computers & Education, 48,* 301–317.

Li, S. (2003). Biocultural orchestration of developmental plasticity across levels: The interplay of biology and culture in shaping the mind and behavior across the life span. *Psychological Bulletin, 129,* 171–194.

Liben, L. S., & Signorella, M. L. (1993). Gender-schematic processing in children: The role of initial interpretations of stimuli. *Developmental Psychology, 29,* 141–149.

Lidz, J., Waxman, S., & Freedman, J. (2003). What infants know about syntax but couldn't have learned: Experimental evidence for syntactic structure at 18 months. *Cognition, 89,* B65–B73.

Lie, E., & Newcombe, N. S. (1999). Elementary school children's explicit and implicit memory for faces of preschool classmates. *Developmental Psychology, 35,* 102–112.

Lieberman, A. F., Compton, N. C., Van Horn, P., & Ippen, C. G. (2003). *Losing a parent to death in the early years. Guidelines for the treatment of traumatic bereavement in infancy and early childhood.* Washington, DC: Zero to Three Press.

Lieberman, M. A., & Videka-Sherman, L. (1986). The impact of self-help groups on the mental health of widows and widowers. *American Journal of Orthopsychiatry, 56,* 435–449.

Liégeois, F., Cross, J.H., Polkey, C., Harkness, W., & Vargha-Khadem F. (2008). Language after hemispherectomy in childhood: contributions from memory and intelligence. *Neuropsychologia, 46,* 3101–3107.

Lieven, E. V. M. (1994). Crosslinguistic and crosscultural aspects of language addressed to children. In C. Gallaway & B. J. Richards (Eds.), *Input and interaction in language acquisition.* Cambridge, England: Cambridge University Press.

Light, L. L. (1991). Memory and aging: Four hypotheses in search of data. *Annual Review of Psychology, 42,* 333–376.

Lilenfeld, L. R. R., Wonderlich, S., Riso, L. P., Crosby, R., & Mitchell, J. (2006). Eating disorders and personality: A methodological and empirical review. *Clinical Psychology Review, 26,* 299–320.

Lillard, A. (2001). Pretend play as twin earth: A social-cognitive analysis. *Developmental Review, 21,* 495–531.

Lillard, A. S. (2005). *Montessori: The science behind the genius.* Oxford, UK: Oxford University Press.

Lillard, L. A., & Panis, C. W. A. (1996). Marital status and mortality: The role of health. *Demography, 33,* 313–327.

Lim, F., Bond, M. H., & Bond, M. K. (2005). Linking societal and psychological factors to homicide rates across nations. *Journal of Cross-Cultural Psychology, 36,* 515–536.

Lim, S., Zoellner, J. M., Lee, J. M., Burt, B. A., Sandretto, A. M., Sohn, W., Ismail, A. I., & Lepkowski, J. M. (2009). Obesity and sugar-sweetened beverages in African-American preschool children: a longitudinal study. *Obesity, 17,* 1262–1268.

Lima, S. D., Hale, S., & Myerson, J. (1991). How general is general slowing? Evidence from the lexical domain. *Psychology and Aging, 6,* 416–425.

Lindau, S. T., & Gavrilova, N. (2010). Sex, health, and years of sexually active life gained due to good health: Evidence from two US population based cross sectional surveys of ageing. *British Medical Journal, 340,* C810. Available at: www.bmj.com/cgi/content/full/340/mar09_2/c810. Accessed: June 17, 2010.

Lindenberger, U., Marsiske, M., & Baltes, P. B. (2000). Memorizing while walking: Increase in dual-task costs from young adulthood to old age. *Psychology and Aging, 15,* 417–436.

Lindsey, E. W., & Mize, J. (2000). Parent–child physical and pretense play: Links to children's social competence. *Merrill-Palmer Quarterly, 46,* 565–591.

Lindvall, O., & Kokaia, Z. (2008). Neurogenesis following stroke affecting the adult brain. In F. H. Gage, G. Kempermann, & H. Song (Eds.), *Adult Neurogenesis* (pp. 549–570). NY: Cold Spring Harbor Laboratory Press.

Lipina, S. J., & Colombo, J. A. (2009). *Poverty and brain development during childhood: An approach from cognitive psychology and neuroscience.* Washington, DC: American Psychological Association.

Lipsey, M. W., & Wilson, D. B. (2001). *Practical meta-analysis.* Thousand Oaks, CA: Sage.

Lipton, A. M., & Weiner, M. F. (2003). Differential diagnosis. In M. F. Weiner & A. M. Lipton (Eds.), *The dementias. Diagnosis, treatment, and research.* Washington, DC: American Psychiatric Publishing.

Little, J., Cardy, A., & Munger, R. G. (2004). Tobacco smoking and oral clefts: A meta-analysis. *Bulletin of the World Health Organization, 82,* 213–218.

Liu, C. (2003). Does quality of marital sex decline with duration? *Archives of Sexual Behavior, 32,* 55–60.

Liu, D., Gelman, S. A., & Wellman, H. M. (2007). Components of young children's trait understanding: Behavior-to-trait inferences and trait-to-behavior predictions. *Child Development, 78,* 1543–1558.

Liu, D., Meltzoff, A., & Wellman, H. M. (2009). Neural correlates of belief- and desire-reasoning. *Child Development, 80,* 1163–1171.

Liu, D., Sabbagh, M. A., Gehring, W. J., & Wellman, H. M. (2009). Neural correlates of children's theory of mind development. *Child Development, 80,* 318–326.

Livesley, W. J., & Bromley, D. B. (1973). *Person perception in childhood and adolescence*. London: Wiley.

Livson, F. B. (1976). Patterns of personality in middle-aged women: A longitudinal study. *International Journal of Aging and Human Development, 7,* 107–115.

Livson, F. B. (1981). Paths to psychological health in the middle years: Sex differences. In D. H. Eichorn, J. A. Clausen, N. Haan, M. P. Honzik, & P. H. Mussen (Eds.), *Present and past in middle life.* New York: Academic Press.

Lloyd, M. E., Doydum, A. O., & Newcombe, N. S. (2009). Memory binding in early childhood: Evidence for a retrieval deficit. *Child Development, 80,* 1321–1328.

Lobel, T., Slone, M., & Winch, G. (1997). Masculinity, popularity, and self-esteem among Israeli preadolescent girls. *Sex Roles, 36,* 395–408.

LoBue, V., & DeLoache, J. S. (2008). Detecting the snake in the grass. Attention to fear-relevant stimuli by adults and young children. *Psychological Science, 19,* 284–289.

Locke, J. L. (1997). A theory of neurolinguistic development. *Brain and Language, 58,* 265–326.

Löckenhoff, C. E., & Carstensen, L. L. (2007). Aging, emotion, and health-related decision strategies: Motivational manipulations can reduce age differences. *Psychology and Aging, 22,* 134–146.

Lockheed, M. E. (1986). Reshaping the social order: The case of gender segregation. *Sex Roles, 14,* 617–628.

Lockl, K., & Schneider, W. (2007). Knowledge about the mind: Links between theory of mind and later metamemory. *Child Development, 78,* 148–167.

Loeb, K. L., Walsh, B. T., Lock, J., leGrange, D., Jones, J., Marcus, S., Weaver, J., & Dobrow, I. (2007). Open trial of family-based treatment for full and partial anorexia nervosa in adolescence. *Journal of the American Academy of Child & Adolescent Psychiatry, 46,* 792–800.

Loehlin, J. C. (1985). Fitting heredity–environment models jointly to twin and adoption data from the California Psychological Inventory. *Behavior Genetics, 15,* 199–221.

Loehlin, J. C. (1992). *Genes and environment in personality development (Individual Differences and Development Series, Vol. 2).* Newbury Park, CA: Sage.

Loehlin, J. C., McCrae, R. R., Costa, P. T., Jr., & John, O. P. (1998). Heritabilities of common and measure-specific components of the Big Five personality factors. *Journal of Research in Personality, 32,* 431–453.

Loewenstein, G., & Furstenberg, F. (1991). Is teenage sexual behavior rational? *Journal of Applied Social Psychology, 21,* 957–986.

Lohan, J. A., & Murphy, S. A. (2001–2002). Parents' perceptions of adolescent sibling grief responses after an adolescent or young adult child's sudden, violent death. *Omega: Journal of Death and Dying, 44,* 77–95.

Loovis, E. M., & Butterfield, S. A. (2000). Influence of age, sex, and balance on mature skipping by children in grades K–8. *Perceptual and Motor Skills, 90,* 974–978.

Lopata, H. Z. (1996). *Current widowhood: Myths and realities.* Thousand Oaks, CA: Sage.

Lopez, E. C. (1997). The cognitive assessment of limited English proficient and bilingual children. In D. P. Flanagan, J. Genshaft, & P. L. Harrison (Eds.), *Contemporary intellectual assessment: Theories, tests, and issues.* New York: Guilford.

Lopez, S. R., & Guarnaccia, P. J. J. (2000). Cultural psychopathology: Uncovering the social world of mental illness. *Annual Review of Psychology, 51,* 571–598.

Lorenz, K. Z. (1937). The companion in the bird's world. *Auk, 54,* 245–273.

Lorsbach, T. C., & Reimer, J. F. (1997). Developmental changes in the inhibition of previously relevant information. *Journal of Experimental Child Psychology, 64,* 317–342.

Lourenco, O., & Machado, A. (1996). In defense of Piaget's theory: A reply to 10 common criticisms. *Psychological Review, 103,* 143–164.

Louria, D. B. (2005). Extraordinary longevity: Individual and societal issues. *Journal of the American Geriatrics Society, 53,* S317–S319.

Lovaas, O. I. (1987). Behavioral treatment and normal educational and intellectual functioning in young autistic children. *Journal of Consulting and Clinical Psychology, 55,* 3–9.

Lovaas, O. I., & Smith, T. (2003). Early and intensive behavioral intervention in autism. In A. E. Kazdin & J. R. Weisz (Eds.), *Evidence-based psychotherapies for children and adolescents.* New York: Guilford.

Lovering, J. S., & Percy, M. (2007). Down syndrome. In I. Brown & M. Percy (Eds.), *A comprehensive guide to intellectual & developmental disabilities.* Baltimore: Paul H. Brookes.

Lovett, B. J., & Sheffield, R. A. (2007). Affective empathy in aggressive children and adolescents: A critical review. *Clinical Psychology Review, 27,* 1–13.

Luby, J., Belden, A., Sullivan, J., Hayen, R., McCadney, A., & Spitznagel, E. (2009). Shame and guilt in preschool depression: Evidence for elevations in self-conscious emotions in depression as early as age 3. *Journal of Child Psychology and Psychiatry, 50,* 1156–1166.

Luby, J. L. (2004). Affective disorders. In R. DelCarmen-Wiggins & A. Carter (Eds.), *Handbook of infant, toddler, and preschool mental health assessment.* New York: Oxford University Press.

Luby, J. L., Sullivan, J., Belden, A., Stalets, M., Blankenship, S., & Spitznagel, E. (2006). An observational analysis of behavior in depressed preschoolers: Further validation of early-onset depression. *Journal of the American Academy of Child and Adolescent Psychiatry, 45,* 203–212.

Lucas, R. E., & Diener, E. (2008). Personality and subjective well-being. In O. P. John, R. W. Robins, & L. A. Pervin (Eds.), *Handbook of personality theory and research* (3rd ed.). New York: Guilford.

Lucassen, P. J., Meerlo, P., Naylor, A.S., van Dam, A. M., Dayer, A. G., Fuchs, E., Oomen, C. A., & Czéh, B. (2009). Regulation of adult neurogenesis by stress, sleep disruption, exercise and inflammation: Implications for depression and antidepressant action. *European Journal of Neuropsycho-pharmacology.* Epub ahead of print.

Luciana, M., Conklin, H. M., Hooper, C. J., & Yarger, R. S. (2005). The development of nonverbal working memory and executive control processes in adolescents. *Child Development, 76,* 697–712.

Ludwig, J., & Phillips, D. A. (2008). Long-term effects of Head Start on low-income children. *Annals of the New York Academy of Science, 1136,* 257–268.

Luecken, L. J. (2008). Long-term consequences of parental death in childhood: Psychological and physiological manifestations. In M. S. Stroebe, R. O. Hansson, H. Schut, & W. Stroebe (Eds.), *Handbook of bereavement research and practice: Advances in theory and intervention.* Washington, DC: American Psychological Association.

Luecken, L. J., Kraft, A., Appelhans, B. M., & Enders, C. (2009). Emotional and cardiovascular sensitization to daily stress following childhood parental loss. *Developmental Psychology, 45,* 296–302.

Lund, D. A., Dimond, M. F., Caserta, M. S., Johnson, R. J., Poulton, J. L., & Connelly, J. R. (1985–1986). Identifying elderly with coping difficulties after two years of bereavement. *Omega: Journal of Death and Dying, 16,* 213–224.

Lundström, J. N., McClintock, M. K., & Olsson, M. J. (2006). Effects of reproductive state on olfactory sensitivity suggest odor specificity. *Biological Psychology, 71,* 244–247.

Lundy, B. L., Jones, N. A., Field, T., Nearing, G., Davalos, M., Pietro, P. A., Schanberg, S., & Kuhn, C. (1999). Prenatal depression effects on neonates. *Infant Behavior and Development, 22,* 119–129.

Luo, Y., & Johnson, S. C. (2009). Recognizing the role of perception in action at 6 months. *Developmental Science, 12,* 142–149.

Luo, Y., Waite, L. J. (2005). The impact of childhood and adult SES on physical, mental, and cognitive well-being in later life. *Journals of Gerontology: Social Sciences, 60B,* S93–S101.

Lupsakko, T. A., Kautiainen, H. J., & Sulkava, R. (2005). The non-use of hearing aids in people aged 75 years and over in the city of Kuopio in Finland. *European Archives of Oto-Rhino-Laryngology, 262,* 165–169.

Luria, A. R. (1974/1976). *Cognitive development: Its cultural and social foundations.* Cambridge, MA: Harvard University Press.

Lustig, J. L., Wolchik, S. A., & Braver, S. L. (1992). Social support in chumships and adjustment in children of divorce. *American Journal of Community Psychology, 20,* 393–399.

Ly, D. H., Lockhart, D. J., Lerner, R. A., & Schultz, P. G. (2000). Mitotic misregulation and human aging. *Science, 287,* 2486–2492.

Lyketsos, C. G. (2009). Dementia and milder cognitive syndromes. In D. G. Blazer & D. C. Steffens (Eds.), *The American Psychiatric Publishing textbook of geriatric psychiatry* (4th ed.). Washington, DC: American Psychiatric Publishing.

Lykken, D. T., Tellegen, A., & Iacono, W. G. (1982). EEG spectra in twins: Evidence for a neglected mechanism of genetic determination. *Physiological Psychology, 10,* 60–65.

Lyman, S., Ferguson, S. A., Braver, E. R. , & Williams, A. F. (2002). Older driver involvements in police reported crashes and fatal crashes: Trends and projections. *Injury Prevention, 8,* 116–120.

Lynch, M. P., Eilers, R. E., Oller, D. K., & Urbano, R. C. (1990). Innateness, experience, and music perception. *Psychological Science, 1,* 272–276.

Lynch, S. M., & George, L. K. (2002). Interlocking trajectories of loss-related events and depressive symptoms among el-ders. *Journal of Gerontology: Social Sciences, 57B,* S117–S125.

Lynn, R. (2008a). Race differences in intelligence, creativity and creative achievement. *Mankind Quarterly, 48,* 157–168.

Lynn, R. (2008b). *The global bell curve: Race, IQ, and inequality worldwide.* Augusta, GA: Washington Summit Publishers.

Lynn, R. (2009). Fluid intelligence but not vocabulary has increased in Britain, 1979–2008. *Intelligence, 37,* 249–255.

Lynn, R. (2010). In Italy, north-south differences in IQ predict differences in income, education, infant mortality, stature, and literacy. *Intelligence, 38,* 93–100.

Lynne, S. D., Graber, J. A., Nichols, T. R., Brooks-Gunn, J., & Botvin, G. J. (2007). Links between pubertal timing, peer influences, and externalizing behaviors among urban students followed through middle school. *Journal of Adolescent Health, 40,* 181.e7–181.e13.

Lyonette, C., & Yardley, L. (2003). The influence on carer wellbeing of motivations to care for older people and the relationship with the care recipient. *Ageing & Society, 23,* 487–506.

Lyons, M. J., York, T. P., Franz, C. E., Grant, M. D., Eaves, L. J., Jacobson, K. C., Schaie, K. W., Panizzon, M. S., Boake, C., Xian, H., Toomey, R., Eisen, S. A., & Kremen, W. S. (2009). Genes determine stability and the environment determines change in cognitive ability during 35 years of adulthood. *Psychological Science, 20,* 1146–1152.

Lyons-Ruth, K., Zeanah, C. H., & Benoit, D. (2003). Disorder and risk for disorder during infancy and toddlerhood. In E. J. Mash & R. A. Barkley (Eds.), *Child psychopathology* (2nd ed.). New York: Guilford Press.

Lytton, H., & Romney, D. M. (1991). Parents' differential socialization of boys and girls: A meta-analysis. *Psychological Bulletin, 109,* 267–296.

M

Ma, H. H. (2006). A synthetic analysis of the effectiveness of single components and packages in creativity training programs. *Creativity Research Journal, 18,* 435–446.

Ma, H. M., Du, M. L., Luo, X. P., Chen, S. K., Liu, L., Chen, R. M., Zhu, C., Xiong, F., Li, T., Wang, W., & Liu, G. L. (2009). Onset of breast and pubic hair development and menses in urban Chinese girls. *Pediatrics, 124,* e269–77.

Mac Iver, D. J. & Reuman, D. A. (1988, April). *Decision-making in the classroom and early adolescents' valuing of mathematics.* Paper presented at the annual meeting of the American Educational Research Association, New Orleans.

Mac Iver, D. J., Reuman, D. A., & Main, S. R. (1995). Social structuring of the school: Studying what is, illuminating what could be. *Annual Review of Psychology, 46,* 375–400.

Macario, A., Scibetta, W. C., Navarro, J., & Riley, E. (2000). Analgesia for labor pain: A cost model. *Anesthesiology, 92,* 643–645.

Maccoby, E. E. (1980). *Social development.* New York: Harcourt Brace Jovanovich.

Maccoby, E. E. (1998). *The two sexes: Growing up apart, coming together.* Cambridge, MA: Harvard University Press.

Maccoby, E. E. (2007). Historical overview of socialization research and theory. In J. E. Grusec & P. D. Hastings (Eds.), *Handbook of socialization theory and research.* New York: Guilford.

Maccoby, E. E., & Jacklin, C. N. (1974). *The psychology of sex differences.* Stanford, CA: Stanford University Press.

Maccoby, E. E., & Jacklin, C. N. (1987). Gender segregation in childhood. In H. W. Reese (Ed.), *Advances in child development and behavior* (Vol. 20). Orlando, FL: Academic Press.

Maccoby, E. E., & Martin, J. A. (1983). Socialization in the context of the family: Parent–child interaction. In E. M. Hetherington (Vol. Ed.), P. H. Mussen (Editor-in-Chief), *Handbook of child psychology: Vol. 4. Socialization, personality, and social development* (4th ed.). New York: Wiley.

MacDonald, K., & Hershberger, S. L. (2005). Theoretical issues in the study of evolution and development. In R. L. Burgess & K. MacDonald (Eds.), *Evolutionary perspectives on human development.* Thousand Oaks, CA: Sage.

MacDorman, M. F., & Kirmeyer, S. (2009, April). *The challenge of fetal mortality* (NCHS Data Brief No. 16). Hyattsville, MD: U. S. Department of Health and Human Services: Centers for Disease Control and Prevention.

MacDorman, M. F., & Mathews, T. J. (2008, October). *Recent trends in infant mortality in the United States.* NCHS Data Brief, no. 9. Hyattsville, MD: National Center for Health Statistics.

Maciejewski, P. K., Zhang, B., Block, S. D., & Prigerson, H. G. (2007). An empirical examination of the stage theory of grief. *JAMA, 297,* 716–723.

MacKenzie, G., & Donaldson, D. I. (2009). Examining the neural basis of episodic memory: ERP evidence that faces are recollected differently from names. *Neuropsychologia, 47,* 2756–2765.

Mackey, R. A., & O'Brien, B. A. (1995). *Lasting marriages: Men and women growing together.* Westport, CT: Praeger.

Mackinlay, R. J., Kliegel, M., Mäntylä, T., & Kliegel, M. (2009). Predictors of time-based prospective memory in children. *Journal of Experimental Child Psychology, 102,* 251–264.

MacLean, K. (2003). The impact of institutionalization on child development. *Development and Psychopathology, 15,* 853–884.

MacPherson, S. E., Phillips, L. H., & Della Sala, S. (2002). Age, executive function and social decision making: A dorsolateral prefrontal theory of cognitive aging. *Psychology and Aging, 17,* 598–609.

Madden, D. J. (2007). Aging and visual attention. *Current Directions in Psychological Science, 16,* 70–74.

Madden, D. J., Gottlob, L. R., & Allen, P. A. (1999). Adult age differences in visual search accuracy: Attentional guidance and target detectability. *Psychology and Aging, 14,* 683–694.

Madden, D. J., & Langley, L. K. (2003). Age-related changes in selective attention and perceptual load during visual search. *Psychology and Aging, 18,* 54–67.

Maddux, J. E. (2002). Self-efficacy: The power of believing you can. In C. R. Snyder & S. J. Lopez (Eds.), *Handbook of positive psychology* (pp. 277–287). New York: Oxford University Press.

Maehr, M., & Meyer, H. (1997). Understanding motivation and schooling: Where we've been, where we are, and where we need to go. *Educational Psychology Review, 9,* 371–409.

Maestripieri, D., Lindell, S. G., & Higley, J. D. (2007). Intergenerational transmission of maternal behavior in rhesus macaques and its underlying mechanisms. *Developmental Psychobiology, 49,* 165–171.

Magai, C. (2008). Attachment in middle and later life. In J. Cassidy & P. R. Shaver (Eds.), *Handbook of attachment: Theory, research, and clinical applications* (2nd ed.). New York: Guilford.

Magai, C., Cohen, C., Milburn, N., Thorpe, B., McPherson, R., & Peralta, D. (2001). Attachment styles in older European American and African American adults. *Journals of Gerontology: Psychological Sciences and Social Sciences, 56,* S28–S35.

Magai, C., Consedine, N. S., Krivoshekova, Y. S., Kudadjie-Gyamfi, E., & McPherson, R. (2006). Emotion experience and expression across the adult life span: Insights from a multimodal assessment study. *Psychology and Aging, 21,* 303–317.

Magnusson, D. (1995). Individual development: A holistic, integrated model. In P. Moen & G. H. Elder, Jr. (Eds.), *Examining lives in context: Perspectives on the ecology of human development.* Washington, DC: American Psychological Association.

Magoni, M., Bassani, L., Okong, P., Kituuka, P., Germinario, E. P., Giuliano, M., & Vella, S. (2005). Mode of infant feeding and HIV infection in children in a program for prevention of mother-to-child transmission in Uganda. *AIDS, 19,* 433–437.

Mahaffy, K. A., & Ward, S. K. (2002). The gendering of adolescents' childbearing and educational plans: Reciprocal effects and the influence of social context. *Sex Roles, 46,* 403–417.

Maiden, R. J., Peterson, S. A., Caya, M., & Hayslip, B. (2003). Personality changes in the old-old: A longitudinal study. *Journal of Adult Development, 10,* 31–39.

Maier, E. H., & Lachman, M. E. (2000). Consequences of early parental loss and separation for health and well-being in midlife. *International Journal of Behavioral Development, 24,* 183–189.

Maikovich, A. K., Jaffee, S. R., Odgers, C. L., & Gallup, J. (2008). Effects of family violence on psychopathology symptoms in children previously exposed to maltreatment. *Child Development, 79,* 1498–1512.

Maikovich-Fong, A. K., & Jaffee, S. R. (2010). Sex differences in childhood sexual abuse characteristics and victims' emotional and behavioral problems: Findings from a national sample of youth. *Child Abuse & Neglect, 34,* 429–437.

Main, M., & George, C. (1985). Responses of abused and disadvantaged toddlers to distress in agemates: A study in the day-care setting. *Developmental Psychology, 21,* 407–412.

Main, M., & Solomon, J. (1990). Procedures for identifying infants as disorganized/disoriented during the Ainsworth Strange Situation. In M. T. Greenberg, D. Cicchetti, & E. M. Cummings (Eds.), *Attachment in the preschool years: Theory, research, and intervention.* Chicago: University of Chicago Press.

Main, M., & Weston, D. R. (1981). The quality of the toddler's relationship to mother and to father: Related to conflict and the readiness to establish new relationships. *Child Development, 52,* 932–940.

Maioli, F., Coveri, M., Pagni, P., Chiandetti, C., Marchetti, C., Ciarrocchi, R., Ruggero, C., Nativio, V., Onesti, A., D'Anastasio, C., & Pedone, V. (2007). Conversion of mild cognitive impairment to dementia in elderly subjects: A preliminary study in a memory and cognitive disorder unit. *Archives of Gerontology and Geriatrics, 44,* 233–241.

Maiorana, A., & Cianfarani, S. (2009). Impact of growth hormone therapy on adult height of children born small for gestational age. *Pediatrics.* Epub ahead of print.

Maisel, N. C., & Gable, S. L. (2009). The paradox of received social support: The importance of responsiveness. *Psychological Science, 20,* 928–932.

Malaspina, D., Corcoran, C., Kleinhaus, K. R., Perrin, M. C., Fennig, S., Nahon, D., Friedlander, Y., & Harlap, S. (2008). Acute maternal stress in pregnancy and schizophrenia in offspring: A cohort prospective study. *BMC Psychiatry, 8,* 71.

Malatesta, C. Z., Culver, C., Tesman, J. R., & Shepard, B. (1989). The development of emotion expression during the first two years of life. *Monographs of the Society for Research in Child Development, 54* (1–2, Serial No. 219).

Malatesta, C. Z., Grigoryev, P., Lamb, C., Albin, M., & Culver, C. (1986). Emotional socialization and expressive development in preterm and full-term infants. *Child Development, 57,* 316–330.

Malinosky-Rummell, R., & Hansen, D. J. (1993). Long-term consequences of childhood physical abuse. *Psychological Bulletin, 114,* 68–79.

Malley-Morrison, K., & Hines, D. A. (2004). *Family violence in a cultural perspective. Defining, understanding, and combating abuse.* Thousand Oaks, CA: Sage.

Malmstrom, M., Sundquist, J., Bajekal, M., & Johansson, S. E. (1999). Ten-year trends in all-cause mortality and coronary heart disease mortality in socioeconomically diverse neighbourhoods. *Public Health, 113,* 279–284.

Malouf, M. A., Migeon, C. J., Carson, K. A., Petrucci, L., & Wisniewski, A. B. (2006). Cognitive outcome in adult women affected by congenital adrenal hyperplasia due to 21-hydroxylase deficiency. *Hormone Research, 65,* 142–150.

Mandara, J., Gaylord-Harden, N. K., Richards, M. H., & Ragsdale, B. L. (2009). The effects of changes in racial identity and self-esteem on changes in African-American adolescents' mental health. *Child Development, 80,* 1660–1675.

Mandoki, M. W., Sumner, G. S., Hoffman, R. P., & Riconda, D. L. (1991). A review of Klinefelter's syndrome in children and adolescents. *Journal of the American Academy of Child and Adolescent Psychiatry, 30,* 167–172.

Mangelsdorf, S. C. (1992). Developmental changes in infant-stranger interaction. *Infant Behavior and Development, 15,* 191–208.

Mangelsdorf, S. C., Gunnar, M., Kestenbaum, R., Lang, S., & Andreas, D. (1990). Infant proneness-to-distress temperament, maternal personality, and mother–infant attachment: Associations and goodness of fit. *Child Development, 61,* 820–831.

Mangelsdorf, S. C., Shapiro, J. R., & Marzolf, D. (1995). Developmental and temperamental differences in emotion regulation in infancy. *Child Development, 66,* 1817–1828.

Manning, M. A., Bear, G. G., & Minke, K. M. (2006). Self-concept and self-esteem. In G. G. Bear & K. M. Minke (Eds.), *Children's needs. Vol. 3: Development, prevention, and intervention.* Washington, DC: National Association of School Psychologists.

Manset, G., & Semmel, M. I. (1997). Are inclusive programs for students with mild disabilities effective? A comparative review of model programs. *Journal of Special Education, 31,* 155–180.

Mansi, G., Raimondi, F., Pichini, S., Campasso, L., Sarno, M., Zuccaro, P., Pacifici, R., Garcia-Algar, O., Romano, A., & Paludetto, R. (2007). Neonatal urinary cotinine correlates with behavioral alterations in newborns prenatally exposed to tobacco smoke. *Pediatric Research, 61,* 257–261.

Maraniss, D., Hull, A., & Schwartzman, P. (2001, September 30). The days after. *The Washington Post,* A1, A18.

Marceau, J. R., Murray, H., & Nanan, R. K. (2009). Efficacy of oral sucrose in infants of methadone-maintained mothers. *Neonatology, 97,* 67–70.

March, J. S. (2009). The future of psychotherapy for mentally ill children and adolescents. *Journal of Child Psychology and Psychiatry, 50,* 170–179.

Marchand, H. (2002). Some reflections on postformal thought. *The Genetic Epistemologist, 29,* 2–9.

Marcia, J. E. (1966). Development and validation of ego identity status. *Journal of Personality and Social Psychology, 3,* 551–558.

Marcon, R. A. (1999). Positive relationships between parent school involvement and public school inner-city preschoolers' development and academic performance. *School Psychology Review, 28,* 395–412.

Marcovitch, S., & Zelazo, D. (1999). The A-not-B error: Results from a logistic meta-analysis. *Child Development, 70,* 1297–1313.

Marean, G. C., Werner, L. A., & Kuhl, P. K. (1992). Vowel categorization by very young infants. *Developmental Psychology, 28,* 396–405.

Margolin, G., & Gordis, E. B. (2000). The effects of family and community violence on children. *Annual Review of Psychology, 51,* 445–479.

Marini, Z., & Case, R. (1994). The development of abstract reasoning about the physical and social world. *Child Development, 65,* 147–159.

Markham, J. A., & Greenough, W. T. (2004). Experience-driven brain plasticity: Beyond the synapse. *Neuron and Glia Biology, 1,* 351–363.

Markides, K. S., Boldt, J. S., & Ray, L. A. (1986). Sources of helping and intergenerational solidarity: A three-generations study of Mexican Americans. *Journal of Gerontology, 41,* 506–511.

Markiewicz, D., Lawford, H., Doyle, A. B., & Haggart, N. (2006). Developmental differences in adolescents' and young adults' use of mothers, fathers, best friends, and romantic partners to fulfill attachment needs. *Journal of Youth and Adolescence, 35,* 127–140.

Marklein, E., Negriff, S., & Dorn, L.D. (2009). Pubertal timing, friend smoking, and substance use in adolescent girls. *Preventive Science, 10,* 141–150.

Markstrom-Adams, C., & Adams, G. R. (1995). Gender, ethnic group, and grade differences in psychosocial functioning during middle adolescence. *Journal of Youth and Adolescence, 24,* 397–417.

Markus, H. R. (2004). Culture and personality: Brief for an arranged marriage. *Journal of Research in Personality, 38,* 75–83.

Markus, H. R., Mullally, P. R., & Kitayama, S. (1997). Self-ways: Diversity in modes of cultural participation. In U. Neisser & D. A. Jopling (Eds.), *The conceptual self in context. Culture, experience, self-understanding.* Cambridge, UK: Cambridge University Press.

Marlier, L., & Schaal, B. (2005). Human newborns prefer human milk: Conspecific milk odor is attractive without postnatal exposure. *Child Development, 76,* 155–168.

Marottoli, R. A. (2007). Enhancement of driving performance among older drivers. Washington, DC: AAA Foundation for Traffic Safety. Available at: www.aaafoundation.org/pdf/EnhancingSeniorDrivingPerfReport.pdf. Accessed: December 4, 2009.

Marschark, M. (1993). *Psychological development of deaf children.* New York: Oxford University Press.

Marsh, H. W., Chessor, D., Craven, R., & Roche, L. (1995). The effect of gifted and talented programs on academic self-concept: The big fish strikes again. *American Educational Research Journal, 32,* 285–319.

Marsh, H. W., & Craven, R. G. (2006). Reciprocal effects of self-concept and performance from a multidimensional perspective: Beyond seductive pleasure and unidimensional perspectives. *Perspectives on Psychological Science, 1,* 133–163.

Marsh, H. W., Craven, R., & Debus, R. (1999). Separation of competency and affect components of multiple dimensions of academic self-concept: A developmental perspective. *Merrill-Palmer Quarterly, 45,* 567–701.

Marsh, H. W., & Hau, K. (2003). Big fish-little pond effect on academic self-concept: A cross-cultural (26-country) test of the negative effects of academically selective schools. *American Psychologist, 58,* 364–376.

Marsh, H. W., & Kleitman, S. (2005). Consequences of employment during high school: Character building, subversion of academic goals, or a threshold? *American Educational Research Journal, 42,* 331–470.

Marshall, W. A., & Tanner, J. M. (1969). Variations in the pattern of pubertal changes in girls. *Archives of Disease in Childhood, 44,* 291–303.

Marshall, W. A., & Tanner, J. M. (1970). Variations in the pattern of pubertal changes in boys. *Archives of Disease in Childhood, 45,* 13–23.

Marsiglio, W., Amato, P., Day, R. D., & Lamb, M. E. (2000). Scholarship on fatherhood in the 1990s and beyond. *Journal of Marriage and the Family, 62,* 1173–1191.

Marsiske, M., & Margrett, J. A. (2006). Everyday problem solving and decision making. In J. E. Birren & K. W. Schaie (Eds.), *Handbook of the psychology of aging.* Boston: Elsevier Academic Press.

Marsiske, M., & Willis, S. L. (1995). Dimensionality of everyday problem solving in older adults. *Psychology and Aging, 10,* 269–283.

Martin, A. (2008). Enhancing student motivation and engagement: The effects of a multidimensional intervention. *Contemporary Educational Psychology, 33,* 239–269.

Martin, C. L. & Ruble, D. N. (2010). Patterns of gender development. *Annual Review of Psychology, 61,* 353–381.

Martin, C. L., & Fabes, R. A. (2001). The stability and consequences of young children's same-sex peer interactions. *Developmental Psychology, 37,* 431–446.

Martin, C. L., & Halverson, C. F., Jr. (1981). A schematic processing model of sex typing and stereotyping in children. *Child Development, 52,* 1119–1134.

Martin, C. L., & Halverson, C. F., Jr. (1983). The effects of sex-typing schemas on young children's memory. *Child Development, 54,* 563–574.

Martin, C. L., & Halverson, C. F., Jr. (1987). The roles of cognition in sex-roles and sex-typing. In D. B. Carter (Ed.), *Current conceptions of sex roles and sex-typing: Theory and research.* New York: Preager.

Martin, C. M. (2008). Prescription drug abuse in the elderly. *The Consultant Pharmacist, 23,* 930–934, 936, 941–942.

Martin, F. N., & Clark, J. G. (2002). *Introduction to audiology* (8th ed.). New York: Allyn & Bacon.

Martin, G. B., & Clark, R. D., III. (1982). Distress crying in neonates: Species and peer specificity. *Developmental Psychology, 18,* 3–9.

Martin, G. M. (2009). Modalities of gene action predicted by the classical evolutionary theory of aging. In V. L. Bengtson, M. Silverstein, N. M. Putney, & D. Gans (Eds.), *Handbook of theories of aging* (2nd ed.). New York: Springer.

Martin, J. A., Hamilton, B. E., Sutton, P. D., Ventura, S. J., Menacker, F., & Munson, M. L. (2005). *Births: Final data for 2003.* National Vital Statistics Reports, 54. Hyattsville, MD: National Center for Health Statistics. Available at: www.cdc.gov/nchs/data/nvsr/nvsr54/nvsr54_02.pdf. Accessed: February 14, 2007.

Martin, M., Grunendahl, M., & Martin, P. (2001). Age differences in stress, social resources, and well-being in middle and old age. *Journal of Gerontology: Psychological Sciences, 56,* 214–222.

Martin, M., & Lantos, J. (2005). Bioethics meets the barrio: Community-based research involving children. In E. Kodish (Ed.), *Ethics and research with children: A case-based approach.* Cary, NC: Oxford University Press.

Martin, R. A. (2007). *The psychology of humor: An integrative approach.* Burlington, MA: Elsevier Academic Press.

Martlew, M., & Connolly, K. J. (1996). Human figure drawings by schooled and unschooled children in Papua New Guinea. *Child Development, 67,* 2743–2762.

Martorano, S. C. (1977). A developmental analysis of performance on Piaget's formal operations tasks. *Developmental Psychology, 13,* 666–672.

Martorell, G. A., & Bugental, D. B. (2006). Maternal variations in stress reactivity: Implications for harsh parenting practices with very young children. *Journal of Family Psychology, 20,* 641–647.

Masataka, N. (2000). The role of modality and input in the earliest stage of language acquisition: Studies of Japanese sign language. In C. Chamberlain, J. Morford, & Mayberry, R. I. (Eds.), *Language acquisition by eye,* 3–24. Mahwah, NJ: Lawrence Erlbaum.

Masson, J. M. (1984). *The assault on truth: Freud's suppression of the seduction theory.* New York: Farrar, Straus, and Giroux.

Masten, A. S., & Reed, M. J. (2002). Resilience in development. In C. R. Snyder & S. J. Lopez (Eds.), *Handbook of positive psychology,* 74–88. New York: Oxford University Press.

Masten, A. S., Roisman, G. I., Long, J. D., Burt, K. B., Obradovic, J., Riley, J. R., Boelcke-Stennes, K., & Tellegen, A. (2005). Developmental cascades: Linking academic achievement and externalizing and internalizing symptoms over 20 years. *Developmental Psychology, 41,* 733–746.

Masters, W. H., & Johnson, V. E. (1966). *Human sexual response.* Boston: Little, Brown.

Masters, W. H., & Johnson, V. E. (1970). *Human sexual inadequacy.* Boston: Little, Brown.

Mathews, F., Youngman, L, & Neil, A. (2004). Maternal circulating nutrient concentrations in pregnancy: Implications for birth and placental weights of term infants. *American Journal of Clinical Nutrition, 79,* 103–110.

Mathews, J. (2003, October 1). Not quite piling on the homework. *The Washington Post,* A1, A4.

Matsuba, M. K., & Walker, L. J. (2004). Extraordinary moral commitment: Young adults involved in social organizations. *Journal of Personality, 72,* 413–436.

Matusov, E., & Hayes, R. (2000). Sociocultural critique of Piaget and Vygotsky. *New Ideas in Psychology, 18,* 215–239.

Maughan, B. (2001). Conduct disorder in context. In J. Hill & B. Maughan (Eds.), *Conduct disorders in childhood and adolescence.* New York: Cambridge University Press.

Maughan, B., & Rutter, M. (2001). Antisocial children grown up. In J. Hill & B. Maughan (Eds.), *Conduct disorders in childhood and adolescence.* New York: Cambridge University Press.

Maurer, A. (1961). The child's knowledge of nonexistence. *Journal of Existential Psychiatry, 2,* 193–212.

Maurer, D., & Maurer, C. (1988). *The world of the newborn.* New York: Basic Books.

Maurer, D., Lewis, T. L., Brent, H. P., & Levin, A. V. (1999). Rapid improvement in the acuity of infants after visual input. *Science, 286,* 108–110.

Maurer, D., Mondloch, C. J., & Lewis, T. L. (2007). Sleeper effects. *Developmental Science, 10,* 40–47.

Maurer, D., Stager, C. L., & Mondloch, C. J. (1999). Cross-modal transfer of shape is difficult to demonstrate in one-month-olds. *Child Development, 70,* 1047–1057.

May, P. A., Fiorentiono, D., Gossage, P. J., Kalberg, W. O., Hoyme, E. H., Robinson, L. K., Coriale, G., Jones, K. L., del Campo, M., Tarani, L., Romeo, M., Kodituwakku, P. W., Deiana, L., Buckley, D., & Ceccanti, M. (2005). Epidemiology of FASD in a province in Italy: Prevalence and characteristics of children in a random sample of schools. *Alcoholism, Clinical and Experimental Research, 30,* 1562–1575.

Mayberry, R. I. (1994). The importance of childhood to language acquisition: Evidence from American Sign Language. In J. C. Goodman & H. C. Nusbaum (Eds.), *The development of speech perception: The transition from speech sounds to spoken words.* Cambridge, MA: MIT Press.

Mayberry, R. I., & Eichen, E. B. (1991). The long-lasting advantage of learning sign language in childhood: Another look at the critical period for language acquisition. *Journal of Memory and Language, 30,* 486–512.

Mayberry, R. I., Lock, E., & Kazmi, H. (2002). Linguistic ability and early language exposure. *Nature, 417,* 38.

Mayer, M. J., Van Acker, R., Lochman, J. E., & Gresham, F. M. (Eds.). (2009). *Cognitive-behavioral interventions for emotional and behavioral disorders.* New York: Guilford.

Mayes, R., Bagwell, C., & Erkulwater, J. (2009). *Medicating children: ADHD and pediatric mental health.* Cambridge, MA: Harvard University Press.

Mayeux, L., & Cillessen, A. H. N. (2003). Development of social problem solving in early childhood: Stability, change, and associations with social competence. *Journal of Genetic Psychology, 164,* 153–173.

Mayo Clinic (2009). *Attention-deficit/hyperactivity disorder (ADHD) in children.* Available at: www.mayoclinic.com/health/adhd/DS00275/. Accessed: November 16, 2009.

Mayseless, O., Danieli, R., & Sharabany, R. (1996). Adults' attachment patterns: Coping with separations. *Journal of Youth and Adolescence, 25,* 667–690.

Mayseless, O., & Scharf, M. (2007). Adolescents' attachment representations and their capacity for intimacy in close relationships. *Journal of Research on Adolescence, 17,* 23–50.

Mbilinyi, L. F., Edleson, J. L., Hagemeister, A. K., & Beeman, S. K. (2007). What happens to children when their mothers are battered? Results from a four city anonymous telephone survey. *Journal of Family Violence, 22,* 309–317.

McAdams, D. P. (2005). Studying lives in time: A narrative approach. In R. Levy, P. Ghisletta, J. Le Goff, D. Spini, & E. Widmer (Eds.), *Advances in life course research. Vol. 10: Towards an interdisciplinary perspective on the life course.* Amsterdam: Elsevier.

McAdams, D. P. (2008). Personal narratives and the life story. In O. P. John, R. W. Robins, & L. A. Pervin (Eds.), *Handbook of personality theory and research* (3rd ed.). New York: Guilford.

McAdams, D. P., & Adler, J. M. (2006). How does personality develop? In D. K. Mroczek & T. D. Little (Eds.), *Handbook of personality development.* Mahwah, NJ: Erlbaum.

McAdams, D. P., Hart, H. M., & Maruna, S. (1998). The anatomy of generativity. In D. P. McAdams & E. de St. Aubin (Eds.), *Generativity and adult development: How and why we care for the next generation.* Washington, DC: American Psychological Association.

McAdams, D. P., & Pals, J. L. (2006). A new Big Five: Fundamental principles for an integrative science of personality. *American Psychologist, 61,* 204–217.

McAdams, P. P., de St. Aubin, E., & Logan, R. L. (1993). Generativity among young, middle, and older adults. *Psychology and Aging, 8,* 221–230.

McAlister, A., & Peterson, C. C. (2006). Mental playmates: Siblings, executive functioning and theory of mind. *British Journal of Developmental Psychology, 24,* 733–751.

McAlister, A. L., Bandura, A., & Owen, S. V. (2006). Mechanisms of moral disengagement in support of military force: The impact of Sept. 11. *Journal of Social and Clinical Psychology, 25,* 141–165.

McCabe, L. L., & McCabe, E. R. B. (2008). *DNA: Promise and peril.* Berkeley: University of California Press.

McCall, R. B. (1977). Challenges to a science of developmental psychology. *Child Development, 48,* 333–344.

McCall, R. B. (1981). Nature–nurture and the two realms of development: A proposed integration with respect to mental development. *Child Development, 52,* 1–12.

McCall, R. B. (1983). A conceptual approach to early mental development. In M. Lewis (Ed.), *Origins of intelligence: Infancy and early childhood* (2nd ed.). New York: Plenum.

McCall, R. B. (2009). Evidence-based programming in the context of practice and policy. *Social Policy Report, 23*(3), 3–11, 15–18.

McCall, R. B., Applebaum, M. I., & Hogarty, P. S. (1973). Developmental changes in mental test performance. *Monographs of the Society for Research in Child Development, 38* (3, Serial No. 150).

McCall, R. B., & Carriger, M. S. (1993). A meta-analysis of infant habituation and recognition memory performance as predictors of later IQ. *Child Development, 64,* 57–79.

McCarthy, J. R. (2009). Young people making meaning in response to death and bereavement. In D. E. Balk & C. A. Corr (Eds.), *Adolescent encounters with death, bereavement, and coping.* New York: Springer.

McCartney, K. (2003). On the meaning of models: A signal amidst the noise. In A. C. Crouter & A. Booth (Eds.), *Children's influence on family dynamics. The neglected side of family relationships.* Mahwah, NJ: Erlbaum.

McCartney, K., Harris, M. J., & Bernieri, F. (1990). Growing up and growing apart: A developmental meta-analysis of twin studies. *Psychological Bulletin, 107,* 226–237.

McCarton, C. M., Brooks-Gunn, J., Wallace, I. F., Bauer, C. R., Bennett, F. C., Bernbaum, J. C., Broyles, S., Casey, P. H., McCormick, M. C., Scott, D. T., Tyson, J., Tonascia, J., & Meinert, C. L. (1997). Results at age 8 years of early intervention for low-birth-weight premature infants. *Journal of the American Medical Association, 277,* 126–132.

McCaul, E. J., Donaldson, G. A., Coladarci, T., & Davis, W. E. (1992). Consequences of dropping out of school: Findings from high school and beyond. *Journal of Educational Research, 85,* 198–207.

McClintock, M. K., & Herdt, G. (1996). Rethinking puberty: The development of sexual attraction. *Current Directions in Psychological Science, 5,* 178–183.

McCloskey, L. A., Figueredo, A. J., & Koss, M. P. (1995). The effects of systematic family violence on children's mental health. *Child Development, 66,* 1239–1261.

McConkie-Rosell, A., Finucane, B., Cronister, A., Abrams, L., Bennett, R. L., & Pettersen, B. J. (2005). Genetic counseling for Fragile X syndrome: Updated recommendations of the National Society of Genetic Counselors. *Journal of Genetic Counseling, 14,* 249–270.

McCormick, M. (1998). Mom's "BABY" vids sharpen new minds. *Billboard, 110,* 72–73.

McCormick, M. C., Brooks-Gunn, J., Buka, S. L., Goldman, J., Yu, J., Salganik, M., Scott, D. T., Bennett, F. C., Kay, L. L., Bernbaum, J. C., Bauer, C. R., Martin, C., Woods, E. R., Martin, A., & Casey, P. H. (2006). Early intervention in low birth weight infants: Results at 18 years of age for the Infant Health and Developmental Program. *Pediatrics, 117,* 771–780.

McCowan, L. & Horgan, R. P. (2009, July 13). Risk factors for small for gestational age infants. *Best Practices and Research: Clinical Obstetrics & Gynaecology.* Epub ahead of print.

McCrae, R. R. (2004). Human nature and culture: A trait perspective. *Journal of Research in Personality 38,* 3–14.

McCrae, R. R., Arenberg, D., & Costa, P. T., Jr. (1987). Declines in divergent thinking with age: Cross-sectional, longitudinal, and cross-sequential analyses. *Psychology and Aging, 2,* 130–137.

McCrae, R. R., & Costa, P. T., Jr. (2003). *Personality in adulthood: A five-factor theory perspective* (2nd ed.). New York: Guilford Press.

McCrae, R. R., & Costa, P. T., Jr. (2008). *The five-factor theory of personality.* In O. P. John, R. W. Robins, & L. A. Pervin (Eds.), *Handbook of personality theory and research* (3rd ed.). New York: Guilford.

McCrae, R. R., Costa, P. T., Jr., Ostendorf, F., Angleitner, A., Hrebickova, M., Avia, M. D., Sanz, J., Sanchez-Bernardos, M. L., Kusdil, M. E., Woodfield, R., Saunders, P. R., & Smith, P. B. (2000). Nature over nurture: Temperament, personality, and life span development. *Journal of Personalty and Social Psychology, 78,* 173–186.

McCune, L., Vihman, M. M., Roug-Hellichius, L. Delery, D. B., & Gogate, L. L. (1996). Grunt communication in human infants (*Homo sapiens*). *Journal of Comparative Psychology, 110,* 27–27.

McDonald, R., Jouriles, E. N., Ramisetty-Mikler, S., Caetano, R., & Green, C. E. (2006). Estimating the number of American children living in partner-violent families. *Journal of Family Psychology, 20,* 137–142.

McDonald, S., Erickson, L. D., Johnson, M. K., & Elder, G. H. (2007). Informal mentoring and young adult employment. *Social Science Research, 36,* 1328–1347.

McDowell, M.A., Brody, D.J., & Hughes, J.P. (2007). Has age at menarche changed? Results from the National Health and Nutrition Examination Survey (NHANES) 1999–2004. *The Journal of Adolescent Health, 40,* 227–231.

McElhaney, K. B., Antonishak, J., & Allen, J. P. (2008). "They like me, they like me not":

Popularity and adolescents' perceptions of acceptance predicting social functioning over time. *Child Development, 79*, 720–731.

McFarlane, J. A., & Williams, T. M. (1990). The enigma of premenstrual syndrome. *Canadian Psychology, 31*, 95–108.

McGabe, M. P. & Ricciardelli, L. A. (2004). A longitudinal study of pubertal timing and extreme body change behaviors among adolescent boys and girls. *Adolescence, 39*.

McGee, C. L., Bjorkquist, O. A., Price, J. M., Mattson, S. N., & Riley, E. P. (2009). Social information processing skills in children with histories of heavy prenatal alcohol exposure. *Journal of Abnormal Child Psychology, 37*, 817–830.

McGhee, P. E. (1979). *Humor: Its origin and development.* San Francisco: Freeman.

McGoldrick, M., Almeida, R., Hines, P. M., Garcia-Preto, N., Rosen, E., & Lee, E. (1991). Mourning in different cultures. In F. Walsh & M. McGoldrick (Eds.), *Living beyond loss: Death in the family.* New York: W. W. Norton.

McGowan, P. O., Meaney, M. J., & Szyf, M. (2008). Diet and the epigenetic (re)programming of phenotypic differences in behavior. *Brain Research, 1237*, 12–24.

McGowan, P. O., Sasaki, A., D'Alessio, A.C., Dymov, S., Labonté, B., Szyf, M., Turecki, G. & Meaney, M. J. (2009). Epigenetic regulation of the glucocorticoid receptor in human brain associates with childhood abuse. *Nature Neuroscience, 12*, 342–348.

McGrath, E. P., & Repetti, R. L. (2000). Mothers' and fathers' attitudes toward their children's academic performance and children's perceptions of their academic competence. *Journal of Youth and Adolescence, 29*, 713–723.

McGue, M., Bouchard, T. J., Jr., Iacono, W. G., & Lykken, D. T. (1993). Behavioral genetics of cognitive ability: A life-span perspective. In R. Plomin & G. E. McClearn (Eds.), *Nature, nurture, and psychology.* Washington, DC: American Psychological Association.

McGue, M., & Johnson, W. (2008). Genetics of cognitive aging. In F. I. M. Craik & T. A. Salthouse (Eds.), *The handbook of aging and cognition* (3rd ed.). New York: Psychology Press.

McGue, M., Elkins, I., Walden, B., & Iacono, W. G. (2005). Perceptions of the parent–adolescent relationship: A longitudinal investigation. *Developmental Psychology, 41*, 971–984.

McGue, M., Keyes, M., Sharma, A., Elkins, I., Legrand, L., Johnson, W., & Iacono, W. (2007). The environments of adopted and non-adopted youth: Evidence on range restriction from the Sibling Interaction and Behavior Study (SIBS). *Behavior Genetics, 37*, 449–462.

McGuire, S., Manke, B., Eftekhari, A., & Dunn, J. (2000). Children's perceptions of sibling conflict during middle childhood: Issues and sibling (dis)similarity. *Social Development, 9*, 173–190.

McHale, J., Khazan, I., Erera, P., Rotman, T., DeCourcey, W., & McConnell, M. (2002). Coparenting in diverse family systems. In M. H. Bornstein (Ed.), *Handbook of parenting: Vol. 3. Being and becoming a parent* (2nd ed.). Mahwah, NJ: Erlbaum.

McHale, S. M., Kim, J., & Whiteman, S. D. (2006). Sibling relationships in childhood and adolescence. In P. Noller & J. A. Feeney (Eds.), *Close relationships: Functions, forms, and processes.* New York: Psychology Press.

McIntosh, D. N., Reichmann-Decker, A., Winkielman, P., & Wilbarger, J. L. (2006). When the social mirror breaks: Deficits in automatic, but not voluntary, mimicry of emotional facial expressions in autism. *Developmental Science, 9*, 295–302.

McIntosh, G. C., Olshan, A. F., & Baird, P. A. (1995). Paternal age and the risk of birth defects in offspring. *Epidemiology, 6*, 282–288.

McKay, K. E., Halperin, J. M., Schwartz, S. T., & Sharma, V. (1994). Developmental analysis of three aspects of information processing: Sustained attention, selective attention, and response organization. *Developmental Neuropsychology, 10*, 121–132.

McKusick, V. A. (1990). *Mendelian inheritance in man* (9th ed.) Baltimore: Johns Hopkins Press.

McLanahan, S. S., & Sorensen, A. B. (1985). Life events and psychological well-being over the life course. In G. H. Elder Jr. (Ed.), *Life course dynamics: Trajectories and transitions, 1968–1980.* Ithaca, NY: Cornell University Press.

McLaughlin, K. A., Fairbank, J. A., Gruber, M. J., Jones, R. T., Lakoma, M. D., Pfefferbaum, B., Sampson, N. A., & Kessler, R. C. (2009). Serious emotional disturbance among youths exposed to Hurricane Katrina 2 years postdisaster. *Journal of the American Academy of Child and Adolescent Psychiatry, 48*, 1069–1078.

McLean, K. C., & Pratt, M. W. (2006). Life's little (and big) lessons: Identity statuses and meaning-making in the turning point narratives of emerging adults. *Developmental Psychology, 42*, 714–722.

McLoyd, V. C. (1990). The impact of economic hardship on black families and children: Psychological distress, parenting, and socioemotional development. *Child Development, 61*, 311–346.

McLoyd, V. C., Cauce, A. M., Takeuchi, D., & Wilson, L. (2000). Marital processes and parental socialization in families of color: A decade review of research. *Journal of Marriage and the Family, 62*, 1070–1093.

McNeill, D. (1970). *The acquisition of language.* New York: Harper & Row.

McNulty, J. K. & Fisher, T. D. (2007, July 20). Gender differences in response to sexual expectancies and changes in sexual frequency: A short-term longitudinal study of sexual satisfaction in newly married couples. *Archives of Sexual Behavior* (in press).

McPherson, M., Smith-Lovin, L., & Brashears, M. E. (2006). Social isolation in America: Changes in core discussion networks over two decades. *American Sociological Review, 71*, 353–375.

Meadows, S. (2006). *The child as thinker: The development and acquisition of cognition in childhood* (2nd ed.). New York: Routledge.

Meadows-Orlans, K. P., & Orlans, H. (1990). Responses to loss of hearing in later life. In D. F. Moores & K. P. Meadows-Orlans, (Eds.), *Educational and developmental aspects of deafness.* Washington, DC: Gallaudet University Press.

Mealey, L. (2005). Evolutionary psychopathology and abnormal development. In R. L. Burgess & K. MacDonald (Eds.), *Evolutionary perspectives on human development.* Thousand Oaks, CA: Sage.

Medina, J. J. (1996). *The clock of ages: Why we age—how we age—winding back the clock.* Cambridge, England: Cambridge University Press.

Medvedev, Z. A. (1991). The structural basis of aging. In F. C. Ludwig (Ed.), *Life span extension: Consequences and open questions.* New York: Springer.

Meeks, T. W., Lanouette, N., Vahia, I., Dawes, S., Jeste, D. V., & Lebowitz, B. (2009). Psychiatric assessment and diagnosis in older adults. *Focus, 7*, 3–16.

Mehan, H., Villanueva, I., Hubbard, L., & Lintz, A. (1996). *Constructing school success: The consequences of untracking low-achieving students.* New York: Cambridge University Press.

Meier, R. P. (1991). Language acquisition by deaf children. *American Scientist, 79*, 69–70.

Meijer, J., & Elshout, J. J. (2001). The predictive and discriminant validity of the zone of proximal development. *British Journal of Educational Psychology, 71*, 93–113.

Meilman, P. W. (1979). Cross-sectional age changes in ego identity status during adolescence. *Developmental Psychology, 15*, 230–231.

Meilman, P. W. (1979). Cross-sectional age changes in ego identity status during adolescence. *Developmental Psychology, 15*, 230–231.

Meins, E., Fernyhough, C., Wainwright, R., Gupta, M., Fradley, E., & Tuckey, M. (2002). Maternal mind-mindedness and attachment security as predictors of theory of mind understanding. *Child Development, 73*, 1715–1726.

Mellinger, J. C., & Erdwins, C. J. (1985). Personality correlates of age and life roles in adult women. *Psychology of Women Quarterly, 9*, 503–514.

Meltzoff, A. N. (2004). Imitation as a mechanism of social cognition: Origins of empathy, theory of mind, and the representation of action. In U. Goswami (Ed.), *Blackwell handbook of childhood cognitive development*, 6–25. Malden, MA: Blackwell Publishing.

Meltzoff, A. N., & Moore, M. K. (1997). Explaining facial imitation: Theoretical model. *Early Development and Parenting, 6*, 179–192.

Melzer, D., Hurst, A. J., & Frayling, T. (2007). Genetic variation and human aging: Progress and prospects. *Journal of Gerontology: Medical Sciences, 62A*, 301–307.

Memon, A., & Vartoukian, R. (1996). The effects of repeated questioning on young children's eyewitness testimony. *British Journal of Psychology, 87*, 403–415.

Menaghan, E. G., & Lieberman, M. A. (1986). Changes in depression following divorce: A panel study. *Journal of Marriage and the Family, 48*, 319–328.

Mennella, J. A., Forestell, C. A., Morgan, L. K., & Beauchamp, G. K. (2009). Early milk feeding influences taste acceptance and liking during infancy. *American Journal of Clinical Nutrition, 90*, 780S–788S.

Mennella, J. A., Giffin, C. E., & Beauchamp, G. K. (2004). Flavor programming during infancy. *Pediatrics, 113*, 840–845.

Mennella, J. A., Kennedy, J. M., & Beauchamp, G. K. (2006). Vegetable acceptance by infants: Effects of formula flavors. *Early Human Development, 82*, 463–368.

Mennella, J. A., Pepino, M. Y., & Reed, D. R. (2005). Genetic and environmental determinants of bitter perception and sweet preferences. *Pediatrics, 115*, E216–222.

Ment, L. R., Vohr, B., Allan, W., Katz, K. H., Schneider, K. C., Westerveld, M., Duncan, C. C., & Makuch, R. W. (2003). Change in cognitive function over time in very low-birth-weight infants. *Journal of the American Medical Association, 289*, 705–711.

Mercer, J. (2006). *Understanding attachment: Parenting, child care, and emotional development.* Westport, CT: Praeger.

Meredith, P., & Noller, P. (2003). Attachment and infant difficultness in postnatal depression. *Journal of Family Issues, 24*, 668–686.

Merrick, J., Merrick, E., Morad, M., & Kandel, I. (2006). Fetal alcohol syndrome and its long-term effects. *Minerva Pediatrica, 58*, 211–218.

Merzenich, M. M., Jenkins, W. M., Johnston, P., Schreiner, C., Miller, S. L., & Tallal, P. (1996). Temporal processing deficits of language-learning impaired children ameliorated by training. *Science, 271*, 77–81.

Meschke, L. L., Zweig, J. M., Barber, B. L., & Eccles, J. S. (2000). Demographic, biological, psychological, and social predictors of the timing of first intercourse. *Journal of Research on Adolescence, 10*, 315–338.

Mesman, J., Bongers, I. L., & Koot, H. M. (2001). Preschool developmental pathways to preadolescent internalizing and externalizing problems. *Journal of Child Psychology and Psychiatry and Allied Disciplines, 42*, 679–689.

Messer, D. J., McCarthy, M. E., McQuiston, S., MacTurk, R. H., Yarrow, L. J., & Vietze, P. M. (1986). Relation between mastery behavior in infancy and competence in early childhood. *Developmental Psychology, 22,* 366–372.

Messinger-Rapport, B. J. (2003). Assessment and counseling of older drivers: A guide for primary care physicians. *Geriatrics, 58,* 16.

Metcalf, P., & Huntington, R. (1991). *Celebrations of death. The anthropology of mortuary ritual* (2nd ed.). Cambridge, England: Cambridge University Press.

Metzger, P. A., & Gray, M. J. (2008). End-of-life communication and adjustment: Pre-loss communication as a predictor of bereavement-related outcomes. *Death Studies, 32,* 301–325.

Meulenbroek, O., Kessels, R. P. C., de Rover, M., Petersson, M., Rikkert, M.G., Rijpkema, M., & Fernández, G. (2010). Age-effects on associative object-location memory. *Brain Research, 22,* 100–110.

Meydani, M. (2001). Nutrition interventions in aging and age-associated disease. In S. C. Park, E. S. Hwang, H. Kim, & W. Park (Eds.), *Annals of the New York Academy of Sciences: Vol. 928. Molecular and cellular interactions in senescence.* New York: The New York Academy of Sciences.

Meyer, S., Raisig, A., Gortner, L., Ong, M. F., Bücheler, M., & Tutdibi, E. (2009, June 26). In utero tobacco exposure: The effects of heavy and very heavy smoking on the rate of SGA infants in the Federal State of Saarland, Germany. *European Journal of Obstetrics, Gynecology, and Reproductive Biology, 146,* 37–40.

Meyer-Bahlburg, H. F., Dolezal, C., Baker, S. W., Ehrhardt, A. A., & New, M. I. (2006). Gender development in women with congenital adrenal hyperplasia as a function of disorder severity. *Archives of Sexual Behavior, 35,* 667–684.

Meyer-Bahlburg, H. F. L., Ehrhardt, A. A., Rosen, L. R., & Gruen, R. S. (1995). Prenatal estrogens and the development of homosexual orientation. *Developmental Psychology, 31,* 12–21.

Midgley, C., Feldlaufer, H., & Eccles, J. S. (1989). Student/teacher relations and attitudes toward mathematics before and after the transition to junior high school. *Child Development, 60,* 981–992.

Midlarsky, E., Kahana, E., Corley, R., Nemeroff, R., & Schonbar, R. A. (1999). Altruistic moral judgment among older adults. *International Journal of Aging and Human Development, 49,* 27–41.

Mikulincer, M., & Shaver, P. R. (2003). The attachment behavioral system in adulthood: Activation, psychodynamics, and interpersonal processes. In M. P. Zanna (Eds.), *Advances in experimental social psychology* (Vol. 35). San Diego: Academic Press.

Mikulincer, M., & Shaver, P. R. (2007). *Attachment in adulthood. Structure, dynamics, and change.* New York: Guilford.

Miller, A. (1985). A developmental study of the cognitive basis of performance impairment after failure. *Journal of Personality and Social Psychology, 49,* 529–538.

Miller, E. R., III, Pastor-Barriuso, R., Dalal, D., Riemersma, R. A. Appel, L. J., & Guallar, E. (2005). Meta-analysis: High-dosage vitamin E supplementation may increase all-cause mortality. *Annals of Internal Medicine, 142,* 37–46.

Miller, J., & Knudsen, D. D. (2007). *Family abuse and violence: A social problems perspective.* Lanham, MD: AltaMira Press.

Miller, J. A. (1995). Strictest diet avoids subtle detriments of PKU. *Bioscience, 45,* 244–245.

Miller, J. B., & Hoicowitz, T. (2004). Attachment contexts of adolescent friendship and romance. *Journal of Adolescence, 27,* 191–206.

Miller, J. G. (2006). Insight into moral development from cultural psychology. In M. Killen & J. G.

Smetana (Eds.), *Handbook of moral development.* Mahwah, NJ: Erlbaum.

Miller, N. B., Cowan, P. A., Cowan, C. P., Hetherington, E. M., & Clingempeel, W. G. (1993). Externalizing in preschoolers and early adolescents: A cross-study replication of a family model. *Developmental Psychology, 29,* 3–18.

Miller, P. H. (1990). The development of strategies of selective attention. In D. F. Bjorklund (Ed.), *Children's strategies: Contemporary views of cognitive development.* Hillsdale, NJ: Erlbaum.

Miller, P. H. (1994). Individual differences in children's strategic behavior: Utilization deficiencies. *Learning and Individual Differences, 6,* 285–307.

Miller, P. H. (2002). *Theories of developmental psychology* (4th ed.). New York: Worth.

Miller, P. H. (2010). *Theories of developmental psychology* (5th ed.). New York: Worth.

Miller, P. H., & Seier, W. S. (1994). Strategy utilization deficiencies in children: When, where and why. In H. W. Reese (Ed.), *Advances in Child Development and Behavior* (Vol. 25, pp. 107–156). New York: Academic Press.

Miller, P. H., & Weiss, M. G. (1981). Children's attention allocation, understanding of attention, and performance on the incidental learning task. *Child Development, 52,* 1183–1190.

Miller, R. A. (2004). Extending life: Scientific prospects and political obstacles. In S. G. Post & R. H. Binstock (Eds.), *The Fountain of Youth: Cultural, scientific, and ethical perspectives on a biomedical goal.* New York: Oxford University Press.

Miller, S. A. (1986). Parents' beliefs about their children's cognitive abilities. *Developmental Psychology, 22,* 276–284.

Miller, T. R., & Taylor, D. M. (2005). Adolescent suicidality: Who will ideate, who will act? *Suicide and Life-Threatening Behavior, 35,* 425–435.

Miller-Johnson, S., Costanzo, P. R., Coie, J. D., Rose, M. R., Browne, D. C., & Johnson, C. (2003). Peer social structure and risk-taking behaviors among African American early adolescents. *Journal of Youth and Adolescence, 32,* 375–384.

Miller-Loncar, C., Lester, B. M., Seifer, R., Lagasse, L. L., Bauer, C. R., Shankaran, S., Bada, H. S., Wright, L. L., Smeriglio, V. L., Bigsby, R., & Liu, J. (2005). Predictors of motor development in children prenatally exposed to cocaine. *Neurotoxicology and Teratology, 27,* 213–220.

Milloy, C. (2009, June 22). Obama leads conversation on fathering by example. *The Washington Post,* B1, B3.

Mills-Koonce, W. R., Gariepy, J., Propper, C., Sutton, K., Calkins, S., Moore, G., & Cox, M. (2007). Infant and parent factors associated with early maternal sensitivity: A caregiver-attachment systems approach. *Infant Behavior and Development, 30,* 114–126.

Milos, G., Spindler, A., Schnyder, U., Martz, J., Hoek, H. W., & Willi, J. (2004). Incidence of severe anorexia nervosa in Switzerland: 40 years of development. *International Journal of Eating Disorders, 35,* 250–258.

Mineka, S., & Zinbarg, R. (2006). A contemporary learning theory perspective on the etiology of anxiety disorders. *American Psychology, 61,* 10–26.

Ming, G. L. & Song, H. (2005). Adult neurogenesis in the mammalian central nervous system. *Annual Review of Neuroscience. 28,* 223–250.

Mingroni, M. A. (2004). The secular rise in IQ: Giving heterosis a closer look. *Intelligence, 32,* 65–83.

Minnes, S., Singer, L. T., Arendt, R., & Satayathum, S. (2005). Effects of prenatal cocaine/polydrug use on maternal–infant feeding interactions during the first year of life. *Journal of Developmental and Behavioral Pediatrics, 26,* 194–200.

Miralt, G., Bearor, K., & Thomas, T. (2001–2002). Adult romantic attachment among women who

experienced childhood maternal loss. *Omega: Journal of Death and Dying, 44,* 97–104.

Mischel, W. (1973). Toward a cognitive social learning reconceptualization of personality. *Psychological Review, 80,* 252–283.

Mischel, W., & Shoda, Y. (2008). Toward a unified theory of personality: Integrating dispositions and processing dynamics within the cognitive–affective processing system. In O. P. John, R. W. Robins, & L. A. Pervin (Eds.), *Handbook of personality theory and research* (3rd ed.). New York: Guilford.

Mishara, B. L. (1999). Synthesis of research and evidence on factors affecting the desire of terminally ill or seriously chronically ill persons to hasten death. *Omega: Journal of Death and Dying, 39,* 1–70.

Mishori, R. (2006, January 10). Increasingly, wired for sound. *The Washington Post,* F1, F5.

Mitchell, P. (1997). *Introduction to theory of mind: Children, autism, and apes.* London: Arnold.

Mitnick, D. M., Heyman, R. E., & Smith Slep, A. M. (2009). Changes in relationship satisfaction across the transition to parenthood: A meta-analysis. *Journal of Family Psychology, 23,* 848–852.

Miyamoto, R. T., Houston, D. M., & Bergeson, T. (2005). Cochlear implantation in deaf infants. *Laryngoscope, 115,* 1376–1380.

Miyawaki, K., Strange, W., Verbrugge, R., Liberman, A. M., Jenkins, J. J., & Fujimura, D. (1975). An effect of linguistic experience: The discrimination of [r] and [l] by native speakers of Japanese and English. *Perception and Psychophysics, 18,* 331–340.

Moehler, E., Kagan, J., Oelkers-Ax, R., Brunner, R., Poustka, L., Haffner, J., & Resch, F. (2008). Infant predictors of behavioural inhibition. *British Journal of Developmental Psychology, 26,* 145–150.

Moen, P. (1992). *Women's two roles: A contemporary dilemma.* New York: Auburn House.

Moen, P., Kim, J. E., & Hofmeister, H. (2001). Couples' work/retirement transitions, gender, and marital quality. *Social Psychology Quarterly, 64,* 55–71.

Moen, P., & Wethington, E. (1999). Midlife development in a life course context. In S. L. Willis & J. D. Reid (Eds.), *Life in the middle. Psychological and social development in middle age.* San Diego: Academic Press.

Moffitt, T. E., & Caspi, A. (2001). Childhood predictors differentiate life-course persistent and adolescence-limited antisocial pathways among males and females. *Development and Psychopathology, 13,* 355–375.

Moffitt, T. E., Harrington, H., Caspi, A., Kim-Cohen, J., Goldberg, D., Gregory, A. M., & Poulton, R. (2007). Depression and generalized anxiety disorder: Cumulative and sequential comorbidity in a birth cohort followed prospectively to age 32 years. *Archives of General Psychiatry, 64,* 651–660.

Mohammed, A. H., Zhu, S. W., Darmopil, S., Hjerling-Leffler, J., Ernfors, P., Winblad, B. Diamond, M. C., Eriksson, P. S., & Bogdanovic, N. (2002). Environmental enrichment and the brain. *Progress in Brain Research, 138,* 109–133.

Mohr, P. E., Feldman, J. J., Dunbar, J. L., McConkey-Robbins, A., Niparko, J. K., Rittenhouse, R. K., & Skinner, M. W. (2000). The societal costs of severe to profound hearing loss in the United States. *International Journal of Technology and Assessment of Health Care, 16,* 1120–1135.

Mojet, J., Christ-Hazelhof, E., & Heidema, J. (2001). Taste perception with age: Generic or specific losses in threshold sensitivity to the five basic tastes? *Chemical Senses, 26,* 845–860.

Molina, B. S. G., & Chassin, L. (1996). The parent–adolescent relationship at puberty: Hispanic ethnicity and parent alcoholism as moderators. *Developmental Psychology, 32,* 675–686.

Molyneux, C. S., Wassenaar, D. R., Peshu, N., & Marsh, K. (2005). 'Even if they ask you to stand by a tree all day, you will have to do it (laughter)...!': Community voices on the notion and practice of informed consent for biomedical research in developing countries. *Social Science and Medicine, 61,* 443–454.

Money, J. (1985). Pediatric sexology and hermaphroditism. *Journal of Sex and Marital Therapy, 11,* 139–156.

Money, J. (1988). *Gay, straight, and in-between: The sexology of erotic orientation.* New York: Oxford University Press.

Money, J., & Ehrhardt, A. (1972). *Man and woman, boy and girl.* Baltimore: Johns Hopkins University Press.

Money, J., & Tucker, P. (1975). *Sexual signatures: On being a man or a woman.* Boston: Little, Brown.

Monroe, S. M., & Reid, M.W. (2008). Gene-environmental interactions in depression research. *Psychological Science, 19,* 947–956.

Monroe, S. M., & Reid, M. W. (2009). Life stress and major depression. *Current Directions in Psychological Science, 18,* 68–72.

Montemayor, R., & Eisen, M. (1977). The development of self-conceptions from childhood to adolescence. *Developmental Psychology, 13,* 314–319.

Montgomery, M. J. (2005). Psychosocial intimacy and identity: From early adolescence to emerging adulthood. *Journal of Adolescent Research, 20,* 346–374.

Monti, M. M., Vanhaudenhuyse, A., Coleman, M. R., Boly, M., Pickard, J. D., Tshibanda, L., Owen, A. M., & Laureys, S. (2010). Willful modulation of brain activity in disorders of consciousness. *New England Journal of Medicine, 362,* 579–589.

Moore, E. G. J. (1986). Family socialization and the IQ test performance of traditionally and transracially adopted black children. *Developmental Psychology, 22,* 317–326.

Moore, K. L. (1988). *The developing human.* Philadelphia: W. B. Saunders.

Moore, K. W., & Varela, R. E. (2010). Correlates of long-term posttraumatic stress symptoms in children following Hurricane Katrina. *Child Psychiatry and Human Development, 41,* 239–250.

Moore, M., & Carr, A. (2000). Depression and grief. In A. Carr (Ed.), *What works with children and adolescents?: A critical review of psychological interventions with children, adolescents, and their families.* Florence, KY: Taylor & Francis/Routledge.

Moore, S. M. (1995). Girls' understanding and social constructions of menarche. *Journal of Adolescence, 18,* 87–104.

Moorehouse, M. J. (1991). Linking maternal employment patterns to mother–child activities and children's school competence. *Developmental Psychology, 27,* 295–303.

Moraga, A. V., & Rodriguez-Pascual, C. (2007). Accurate diagnosis of delirium in elderly patients. *Current Opinion in Psychiatry, 20,* 262–267.

Morgan, G. A., & Ricciuti, H. N. (1969). Infants' responses to strangers during the first year. In B. M. Foss (Ed.), *Determinants of infant behavior* (Vol. 4). London: Methuen.

Morin, R. (2003, January 9). Words matter. *The Washington Post,* B5.

Morizot, J., & Le Blanc, M. (2003). Continuity and change in personality traits from adolescence to midlife: A 25-year longitudinal study comparing representative and adjudicated men. *Journal of Personality, 71,* 705–755.

Morrell, R. W., Park, D. C., & Poon, L. W. (1989). Quality of instructions on prescription drug labels: Effects on memory and comprehension in young and old adults. *Gerontologist, 29,* 345–354.

Morrongiello, B. A., Fenwick, K. D., Hillier, L., & Chance, G. (1994). Sound localization in newborn human infants. *Developmental Psychobiology, 27,* 519–538.

Morrongiello, B. A., & Hogg, K. (2004). Mothers' reactions to children misbehaving in ways that can lead to injury: Implications for gender differences in children's risk taking and injuries. *Sex Roles, 50,* 1003–1118.

Morrow, D., Leirer, V., Altieri, P., & Fitzsimmons, C. (1994). When expertise reduces age differences in performance. *Psychology and Aging, 9,* 134–148.

Morrow, E. M., Yoo, S., Flavell, S. W., Kim, T., Lin, Y., Hill, R. S., Mukaddes, N. M., Balkhy, S., Gascon, G., Hashmi, A., Al-Saad, S., Ware, J., Joseph, R. M., Greenblatt, R., Gleason, D., Ertelt, J. A., Apse, K. A., Bodell, A., Partlow, J. N., Barry, B., Yao, H., Markianos, K., Ferland, R. J., Greenberg, M. E., & Walsh, C. A. (2008). Identifying autism loci and genes by tracing recent shared ancestry. *Science, 321,* 218–223.

Morse, C. A., Dudley, E., Guthrie, J., & Dennerstein, L. (1998). Relationships between premenstrual complaints and perimenopausal experiences. *Journal of Psychosomatic Obstetrics and Gynecology, 19,* 182–191.

Mortimer, J. T., Finch, M. D., Ryu, S., Shanahan, M. J., & Call, K. T. (1996). The effects of work intensity on adolescent mental health, achievement, and behavioral adjustment: New evidence from a prospective study. *Child Development, 67,* 1243–1261.

Moss, M. S., Moss, S. Z., Rubinstein, R., & Resch, N. (1993). Impact of elderly mother's death on middle age daughters. *International Journal of Aging and Human Development, 37,* 1–22.

Mroczek, D. K. (2004). Positive and negative affect at midlife. In O. G. Brim, C. D. Ryff, & R. C. Kessler (Eds.), *How healthy are we? A national study of well-being at midlife.* Chicago: University of Chicago Press.

Mueller, E., & Lucas, T. (1975). A developmental analysis of peer interactions among toddlers. In M. Lewis & L. Rosenblum (Eds.), *Friendship and peer relations.* New York: Wiley.

Mundy, P. C., & Acra, C. F. (2006). Joint attention, social engagement, and the development of social competence. In P. J. Marshall & N. A. Fox (Eds.), *The development of social engagement: Neurobiological perspectives.* Oxford, NY: Oxford University Press.

Munroe, R. L., Hulefeld, R., Rodgers, J. M., Tomeo, D. L., & Yamazaki, S. K. (2000). Aggression among children in four cultures. *Cross-Cultural Research, 34,* 3–25.

Munroe, R. L., & Romney, A. K. (2006). Gender and age differences in same-sex aggregation and social behavior: A four-culture study. *Journal of Cross-Cultural Psychology, 37,* 3–19.

Murayama, K., & Elliot, A. J. (2009). The joint influence of personal achievement goals and classroom goal structures on achievement-relevant outcomes. *Journal of Educational Psychology, 101,* 432–447.

Muris, P., Bos, A. E. R., Mayer, B., Verkade, R., Thewissen, V., & Dell'Avvento, V. (2009). Relations among behavioral inhibition, Big Five personality factors, and anxiety disorder symptoms in non-clinical children. *Personality and Individual Differences, 46,* 525–529.

Murnen, S. K., & Smolak, L. (1997). Femininity, masculinity and disordered eating: A meta-analytic review. *International Journal of Eating Disorders, 22,* 231–242.

Murphy, C. (1985). Cognitive and chemosensory influences on age-related changes in the ability to identify blended foods. *Journal of Gerontology, 40,* 47–52.

Murphy, C., Nordin, S., & Acosta, L. (1997). Odor learning, recall, and recognition memory in young and elderly adults. *Neuropsychology, 11,* 126–137.

Murphy, D. R., Craik, F. I. M., Li, K. Z. H., & Schneider, B. A. (2000). Comparing the effects of aging and background noise on short-term memory performance. *Psychology and Aging, 15,* 323–334.

Murphy, D. R., Daneman, M., & Schneider, B. A. (2006). Why do older adults have difficulty following conversations? *Psychology and Aging, 21,* 49–61.

Murphy, E. M. (2003). Being born female is dangerous for your health. *American Psychologist, 58,* 205–210.

Murphy, S. A. (2008). The loss of a child: Sudden death and extended illness perspectives. In M. S. Stroebe, R. O. Hansson, H. Schut, & W. Stroebe (Eds.), *Handbook of bereavement research and practice. Advances in theory and intervention.* Washington, DC: American Psychological Association.

Murphy, S. A., Johnson, C., & Lohan, J. (2003a). The effectiveness of coping resources and strategies used by bereaved parents 1 and 5 years after the violent deaths of their children. *Omega: Journal of Death and Dying, 47,* 25–44.

Murphy, S. A., Johnson, C., & Lohan, J. (2003b). Finding meaning in a child's violent death: A five-year prospective analysis of parents' personal narratives and empirical data. *Death Studies, 27,* 381–404.

Murray, C. (2006). Changes over time in the black–white difference on mental tests: Evidence from the children of the 1979 cohort of the National Longitudinal Survey of Youth. *Intelligence, 34,* 527–540.

Murray, L., Fiori-Cowley, A., Hooper, R., & Cooper, P. (1996). The impact of postnatal depression and associated adversity on early mother–infant interactions and later infant outcome. *Child Development, 67,* 2512–2526.

Murray, L., Sinclair, D., Cooper, P., Ducournau, P., Turner, P., & Stein, A. (1999). The socio-emotional development of 5-year-old children of postnatally depressed mothers. *Journal of Child Psychology and Psychiatry, 40,* 1259–1271.

Murray-Close, D., Ostrov, J. M., & Crick, N. R. (2007). A short-term longitudinal study of growth of relational aggression during middle childhood: Associations with gender, friendship intimacy, and internalizing problems. *Development and Psychopathology, 19,* 187–203.

Must, A., Jacques, P. F., Dallal, G. E., Bajema, C. J., & Dietz, W. H. (1992). Long-term morbidity and mortality of overweight adolescents: A follow-up of the Harvard Growth Study of 1922 to 1935. *New England Journal of Medicine, 327,* 1350–1355.

Mwamwenda, T. S. (1999). Undergraduate and graduate students' combinatorial reasoning and formal operations. *Journal of Genetic Psychology, 160,* 503–506.

Mwamwenda, T. S., & Mwamwenda, B. A. (1989). Formal operational thought among African and Canadian college students. *Psychological Reports, 64,* 43–46.

Myers, J., Jusczyk, P. W., Nelson, D. G. K., Charles-Luce, J., Woodward, A. L., & Hirsh-Pasek, K. (1996). Infants' sensitivity to word boundaries in fluent speech. *Journal of Child Language, 23,* 1–30.

Myers, J. K., Weissman, M. M., Tischler, G. L., Holzer, C. E., III, Leaf, P. J., & Orvaschel, H. (1984). Six-month prevalence of psychiatric disorders in three communities. *Archives of General Psychiatry, 41,* 959–967.

Myers, K. P., & Sclafani, A. (2006). Development of learned flavor preferences. *Developmental Psychobiology, 48,* 380–388.

Mylod, D. E., Whitman, T. L., & Borkowski, J. G. (1997). Predicting adolescent mothers' transition to adulthood. *Journal of Research on Adolescence, 7,* 457–478.

N

Nagasawa, M., Kikusui, T., Onaka, T., & Ohta, M. (2009). Dog's gaze at its owner increases owner's urinary oxytocin during social interaction. *Hormones and Behavior, 55*, 434–441.

Nagumey, A. J., Reich, J. W., & Newsom, J. (2004). Gender moderates the effects of independence and dependence desires during the social support process. *Psychology and Aging, 19*, 215–218.

Naigles, L. G., & Gelman, S. A. (1995). Over-extensions in comprehension and production revisited: Preferential-looking in a study of dog, cat, and cow. *Journal of Child Language, 22*, 19–46.

Naigles, L. R., & Swensen, L. D. (2007). Syntactic supports for word learning (pp. 212–231). In E. Hoff & M. Shatz (Eds.), *Blackwell handbook of language development*. Malden Blackwell Publishing.

Najman, J. M., Vance, J. C., Boyle, F., Embleton, G., Foster, B., & Thearle, J. (1993). The impact of a child death on marital adjustment. *Social Science and Medicine, 37*, 1005–1010.

Najman, J. M., Williams, G. M., Nikles, J., Spence, S., Bor, W., O'Callaghan, M., Le Brocque, R., & Andersen, M. J. (2000). Mothers' mental illness and child behavior problems: Cause–effect association or observation bias? *Journal of the American Academy of Child and Adolescent Psychiatry, 39*, 592–602.

Nakajima, S., Saijo, Y., Kato, S., Sasaki, S., Uno, A., Kanagami, N., Hirakawa, H., Hori, T., Tobiishi, K., Todaka, T., Nakamura, Y., Yanagiya, S., Sengoku, Y., Iida, T., Sata, F., & Kishi, R. (2006). Effects of prenatal exposure to polychlorinated biphenyls and dioxins on mental and motor development in Japanese children at 6 months of age. *Environmental Health Perspectives, 114*, 773–778.

Nanez, J. E., & Yonas, A. (1994). Effects of luminance and texture motion on infant defensive reactions to optical collision. *Infant Behavior and Development, 17*, 165–174.

Nangle, D. W., Erdley, C. A., Newman, J. E., Mason, C. A., & Carpenter, E. M. (2003). Popularity, friendship quantity, and friendship quality: Interactive influences on children's loneliness and depression. *Journal of Clinical Child and Adolescent Psychology, 32*, 546–555.

National Academy of Sciences (2000). *Sleep needs, patterns and difficulties of adolescents: Summary of a workshop*. Available at: http://www.nap.edu/openbook/030907177/html/3.html.

National Adult Literacy Survey. Available at: http://nces.ed.gov/naal/nals_products.asp. Accessed: October 11, 2010.

National Center for Education Statistics (1998). National Household Education Survey (NHES), "Adult Education Interview," 1991, 1995, 1999; Projections of Education Statistics to 2008 (NCES 98-016).

National Center for Education Statistics (2007). *Dropout rates in the United States: 2005*. Available at: http://nces.ed.gov/pubs2007/dropout05/tables/table_11.asp. Accessed: July 19, 2007.

National Center for Health Statistics (2006). *Health, United States, 2006, with chartbook on trends in the health of Americans*. Hyattsville, MD: U.S. Government Printing Office.

National Center for Health Statistics (2007). *Clinical growth charts*. Available at: www.cdc.gov/nchs/about/major/nhanes/growthcharts/clinical_charts.htm. Accessed: March 1, 2007.

National Center for Health Statistics (2009). *Health, United States, 2008 with chartbook*. Hyattsville, MD: U.S. Government Printing Office. Available at: http://www.cdc.gov/nchs/hus.htm. Accessed: July 2009.

National Center for Health Statistics (2010). *Health, United States, 2009*. Hyattsville, MD: U.S. Department of Health and Human Services, Centers for Disease Control and Prevention, National Center for Health Statistics. Available at:

www.cdc.gov/nchs/hus.htm. Accessed: March 18, 2010.

National Institute on Aging (2000). *Progress report on Alzheimer's disease 2000. Taking the next steps* (NIH Publication No. 00-4859). Available at: www.alzheimers.org/pubs/prog00.htm.

National Institutes of Health (2000). Phenylketonuria (PKU): Screening and management. *NIH Consensus Statement 2000 October 16–18, 17(3),* 1–33.

National Institutes of Health (2006). *Newborn hearing screening*. Available at: www.nih.gov/about/researchresultsforthepublic/Newborn.pdf. Accessed: April 15, 2007.

National Reading Panel (1999). *Teaching children to read: An evidence-based assessment of the scientific literature on reading and its implications for reading instruction*. Washington, DC: National Institute of Child Health & Human Development.

National Sleep Foundation (2009). Sleep Topics. Available at: http://www.sleepfoundation.org/articles/sleep-topics. Accessed: October 30, 2009.

Neale, M. C., & Martin, N. G. (1989). The effects of age, sex, and genotype on self-report drunkenness following a challenge dose of alcohol. *Behavior Genetics, 19*, 63–78.

Neblett, E. W. Jr., White, R. L.; Ford, K. R., Philip, C. L., Nguyên, H. X., & Sellers, R. M.(2008). Patterns of racial socialization and psychological adjustment: Can parental communications about race reduce the impact of racial discrimination? *Journal of Research on Adolescence, 18*, 477–515.

Neighbors, H. W., Caldwell, C., Williams, D. R., Nesse, R., Taylor, R. J., Bullard, K. M., Torres, M., & Jackson, J. S. (2007). Race, ethnicity, and the use of services for mental disorders: Results from the National Survey of American Life. *Archives of General Psychiatry, 64*, 485–494.

Neimark, E. D. (1975). Longitudinal development of formal operations thought. *Genetic Psychology Monographs, 91*, 171–225.

Neimark, E. D. (1979). Current status of formal operations research. *Human Development, 22*, 60–67.

Neimeyer, R. A., & Currier, J. M. (2009). Grief therapy. Evidence of efficacy and emerging directions. *Current Directions in Psychological Science, 18*, 352–356.

Neisser, U., Boodoo, G., Bouchard, T. J., Jr., Boykin, A. W., Brody, N., Ceci, S. J., Halpern, D. F., Loehlin, J. C., Perloff, R., Sternberg, R. J., & Urbina, S. (1996). Intelligence: Knowns and unknowns. *American Psychologist, 51*, 77–101.

Nelson, C. A., Thomas, K. M., & de Haan, M. (2006). Neural bases of cognitive development. In D. Kuhn & R. Siegler (Vol. Eds.), *Handbook of child psychology: Vol. 2. Theoretical models of human development* (6th ed.). Hoboken, NJ: Wiley.

Nelson, E. A., & Dannefer, D. (1992). Aged heterogeneity: Fact or fiction? The fate of diversity in gerontological research. *Gerontologist, 32*, 17–23.

Nelson, G., Westhues, A., & MacLeod, J. (2003). A meta-analysis of longitudinal research on preschool prevention programs for children. *Prevention & Treatment, 6*. Available at: http://journals.apa.org/prevention/volume6/toc-dec18-03.html.

Nelson, J. M. (2009). *Psychology, religion, and spirituality*. New York: Springer Science + Business Media.

Nelson, K. (1973). Structure and strategy in learning to talk. *Monographs of the Society for Research in Child Development, 38* (Serial No. 149).

Nelson, K. (1986). *Event knowledge: Structure and function in development*. Hillsdale, NJ: Erlbaum.

Nelson, K. (1997). Event representations then, now, and next. In P. W. van den Broek & P. J. Bauer (Eds.), *Developmental spans in event comprehension and representation: Bridging fictional and actual events*, 1–26. Mahwah, NJ: Erlbaum.

Nelson, K. (2007). *Young minds in social worlds: Experience, meaning, and memory*. Cambridge, MA: Harvard University Press.

Nelson, K., & Hudson, J. (1988). Scripts and memory: Functional relationship in development. In F. E. Weinert & M. Perlmutter (Eds.), *Memory development: Universal changes and individual differences*. Hillsdale, NJ: Erlbaum.

Nelson, K., Skwerer, D. P., Goldman, S., Henseler, S., Presler, N., & Walkenfeld, F. F. (2003). Entering a community of minds: An experiential approach to "theory of mind." *Human Development, 46*, 24–46.

Nelson, L. J., Padilla-Walker, L. M., Carroll, J. S., Madsen, S. D., Barry, C. M., & Badger, S. (2007). "If you want me to treat you like an adult, start acting like one!" Comparing the criteria that emerging adults and their parents have for adulthood. *Journal of Family Psychology, 21*, 665–674.

Nelson, S. A. (1980). Factors influencing young children's use of motives and outcomes as moral criteria. *Child Development, 51*, 823–829.

Nemeroff, C. B., Kalai, A., Keller, M. B., Charney, D. S. Lenderts, S. E., Cascade, E. F., Stephenson, H., & Schatzberg, A. F. (2007). Impact of publicity concerning pediatric suicidality data on physician practice patterns in the United States. *Archives of General Psychiatry, 64*, 466–472.

Neppl, T. K., Conger, R. D., Scaramella, L. V., & Ontai, L. L. (2009). Intergenerational continuity in parenting behavior: Mediating pathways and child effects. *Developmental Psychology, 45*, 1241–1256.

Nerenberg, L. (2008). *Elder abuse prevention. Emerging trends and promising strategies*. New York: Springer.

Nes, S. L. (2003). Using paired reading to enhance the fluency skills of less-skilled readers. *Reading Improvement, 40*, 179–193.

Nettelbeck, T., & Young, R. (1996). Intelligence and savant syndrome: Is the whole greater than the sum of the fragments? *Intelligence, 22*, 49–68.

Neugarten, B. L. (1968). Adult personality: Toward a psychology of the life cycle. In B. L. Neugarten (Ed.), *Middle age and aging: A reader in social psychology*. Chicago: University of Chicago Press.

Neugarten, B. L., Moore, J. W., & Lowe, J. C. (1965). Age norms, age constraints, and adult socialization. *American Journal of Sociology, 70*, 710–717.

Neville, B., & Parke, R. D. (1997). Waiting for paternity: Interpersonal and contextual implications of the timing of fatherhood. *Sex Roles, 37*, 45–59.

Neville, H. J., Bavelier, D., Corina, D., Rauschecker, J., Karni, A., & Lalwani, A. (1998). Cerebral organization for language in deaf and hearing subjects: Biological constraints and effects of experience. *Proceedings of the National Academy of Sciences of the United States of America, 95*, 922–929.

Neville, H. J., Coffey, S. A., Lawson, D. S., Fischer, A., Emmorey, K., & Bellugi, U. (1997). Neural systems mediating American Sign Language: Effects of sensory experience and age of acquisition. *Brain and Language, 57*, 285–308.

Newbold, R. R., Padilla-Banks, E., Jefferson, W. N., & Heindel, J. J. (2009) Environmental estrogens and obesity. *Molecular and Cellular Endocrinology, 304*, 84–89.

Newell, A., & Simon, H. A. (1961). Computer simulation of human thinking. *Science, 134*, 2011–2017.

Newell, K. M., Vaillancourt, D. E., & Sosnoff, J. J. (2006). Aging, complexity, and motor performance. In J. E. Birren & K. W. Schaie (Eds.), *Handbook of the psychology of aging*. Boston: Elsevier Academic Press.

Newell, M. L. (2003). Antenatal and perinatal strategies to prevent mother-to-child transmission of HIV infection. *Transactions of the Royal Society of Tropical Medicine and Hygiene, 97*, 22–24.

Newport, E. L. (1991). Contrasting conceptions of the critical period for language. In S. Carey & R.

Gelman (Eds.), *The epigenesis of mind: Essays on biology and cognition.* Hillsdale, NJ: Erlbaum.

Newsom, J. T., Nishishiba, M., Morgan, D. L., & Rook, K. S. (2003). The relative importance of three domains of positive and negative social exchanges: A longitudinal model with comparable measures. *Psychology and Aging, 18,* 746–754.

Ng, T. W. H., & Feldman, D. C. (2008). The relationship of age to ten dimensions of job performance. *Journal of Applied Psychology, 93,* 392–423.

Nguyen, H. T., & Zonderman, A. B. (2006). Relationship between age and aspects of depression: Consistency and reliability across two longitudinal studies. *Psychology and Aging, 21,* 119–126.

Nguyen, S., Choi, H. K., Lustig, R. H., & Hsu, C. Y. (2009). Sugar-sweetened beverages, serum uric acid, and blood pressure in adolescents. *Journal of Pediatrics, 154,* 807–813.

NICHD (2006). *The NICHD study of early child care and youth development: Findings for children up to age 4 ½ years.* Available at: www.nichd.nih.gov/publications/pubs.cfm.

NICHD Early Child Care Research Network (1997). The effects of infant child care on infant-mother attachment security: Results of the NICHD Study of Early Child Care. *Child Development, 68,* 860–879.

NICHD Early Child Care Research Network (2003). Does quality of child care affect child outcomes at age 4 ½? *Developmental Psychology, 39,* 451–469.

NICHD Early Child Care Research Network (2005). *Child care and child development: Results from the NICHD study of early child care and youth development.* New York: Guilford.

NICHD Early Child Care Research Network (2006). Child-care effect sizes for the NICHD Study of Early Child Care and Youth Development. *American Psychologist, 61,* 99–116.

Nicholls, D. E., & Viner, R. M. (2009). Childhood risk factors for lifetime anorexia nervosa by age 30 in a national birth cohort. *Journal of the American Academy of Child and Adolescent Psychiatry, 48,* 791–799.

Nicholls, J. G., & Miller, A. T. (1984). Reasoning about the ability of self and others: A developmental study. *Child Development, 55,* 1990–1999.

Nicolich, L. M. (1977). Beyond sensorimotor intelligence: Assessment of symbolic maturity through analysis of pretend play. *Merrill-Palmer Quarterly, 23,* 89–99.

NIDA (2009a). *Prenatal exposure to drugs of abuse: An update from the National Institute on Drug Abuse.* Available at: www.nida.nih.gov/tib/prenatal.html. Accessed: July 23, 2009.

NIDA (2009b). *Tobacco and nicotine research: An update from the National Institute on Drug Abuse.* Available at: www.nida.nih.gov/tib/tobnico.html. Accessed: July 23, 2009.

Niles, W. (1986). Effects of a moral development discussion group on delinquent and predelinquent boys. *Journal of Counseling Psychology, 33,* 45–51.

Nilsson, L., Adolfsson, R., Bäckman, L., Cruts, M., Edvardsson, H., Nyberg, L., & Van Broeckhoven, C. (2002). Memory development in adulthood and old age: The Betula prospective-cohort study. In P. Graf & N. Ohta (Eds.), *Lifespan development of human memory* (pp. 185–204). Cambridge, MA: Massachusetts Institute of Technology.

Nilsson, M., Perfilieva, E., Johansson, U., Orwar, O., & Eriksson, P. S. (1999). Enriched environment increases neurogenesis in the adult rat dentate gyrus and improves spatial memory. *Journal of Neurobiology, 39,* 569–578.

Nippold, M. A., Hegel, S. L., Sohlberg, M. M., & Schwarz, I. E. (1999). Defining abstract entities: Development in pre-adolescents, adolescents, and young adults. *Journal of Speech, Language, and Hearing Research, 42,* 473–481.

Nisbett, R. E. (2009). *Intelligence and how to get it: Why schools and cultures count.* New York: W. W. Norton & Company.

Nishitani, S., Miyamura, T., Tagawa, M., Sumi, M., Takase, R., Doi, H., Moriuchi, H., & Shinohara, K. (2009). The calming effect of a maternal breast milk odor on the human newborn infant. *Neuroscience Research, 63,* 66–71.

No Child Left Behind Act of 2002 (U.S. Public Law 107–110).

Noble, K. D., Arndt, T., Nicholson, T., Sletten, T., & Zamora, A. (1999). Different strokes: Perceptions of social and emotional development among early college entrants. *Journal of Secondary Gifted Education, 10,* 77–84.

Nolen-Hoeksema, S. (1990). *Sex differences in depression.* Stanford, CA: Stanford University Press.

Nolen-Hoeksema, S. (2002). Gender differences in depression. In I. H. Gotlib & C. L. Hammen (Eds.), *Handbook of depression.* New York: Guilford.

Nolen-Hoeksema, S., & Girgus, J. S. (1994). The emergence of gender differences in depression during adolescence. *Psychological Bulletin, 115,* 424–443.

Nolen-Hoeksema, S., Stice, E., Wade, E., & Bohon, C. (2007). Reciprocal relations between rumination and bulimic, substance abuse, and depressive symptoms in female adolescents. *Journal of Abnormal Psychology, 116,* 198–207.

Nolen-Hoeksema, S., Wisco, B. E., & Lyubomirsky, S. (2008). Rethinking rumination. *Perspectives on Psychological Science, 3,* 400–424.

Noller, P. (2006). Marital relationships. In P. Noller & J. A. Feeney (Eds.), *Close relationships: Functions, forms, and processes.* New York: Psychology Press.

Nomaguchi, K. M., & Milkie, M. A. (2003). Costs and rewards of children: The effects of becoming a parent on adults' lives. *Journal of Marriage and the Family, 65,* 356–374.

Noone, J. H., Stephens, C., & Alpass, F. M. (2008). Preretirement planning and well-being in later life. A prospective study. *Research on Aging, 31,* 295–317.

Noppe, I. C., & Noppe, L. D. (1997). Evolving meanings of death during early, middle, and later adolescence. *Death Studies, 21,* 253–275.

Nordin, S., Razani, L. J., Markison, S., & Murphy, C. (2003). Age-associated increases in intensity discrimination for taste. *Experimental Aging Research, 29,* 371–381.

Nordstrom, B. B., Sood, B. G., Sokol, R. J., Ager, J., Janisse, J., Hannigan, J. H., Covington, C., & Delaney-Black, V. (2005). Gender and alcohol moderate prenatal cocaine effects on teacher-report of child behavior. *Neurotoxicology and Teratology, 27,* 181–190.

Nordvik, H., & Amponsah, B. (1998). Gender differences in spatial abilities and spatial activity among university students in an egalitarian educational system. *Sex Roles, 38,* 1009–1023.

Norenzayan, A., & Heine, S. J. (2005). Psychological universals: What are they and how can we know? *Psychological Bulletin, 131,* 763–784.

Nourhashemi, F., Gillette-Guyonnet, S., Andrieu, S., Ghisolfi, A., Ousset, P. J., Grandjean, H., Grand, A., Pous, J., Vellas, B., & Albarede, J. L. (2000). Alzheimer disease: Protective factors. *American Journal of Clinical Nutrition, 71,* 643s–649s.

Nsamenang, A. B. (1992). *Human development in cultural context: A third world perspective.* Newbury Park, CA: Sage.

NSDUH (2008, September 11). *The NSDUH Report: Alcohol use among pregnant women and recent mothers: 2002–2007.* Rockville, MD: Substance Abuse and Mental Health Services Administration, Office of Applied Studies.

Nucci, L. (2006). Education for moral development. In M. Killen & J. G. Smetana (Eds.), *Handbook of moral development.* Mahwah, NJ: Erlbaum.

Nucci, L., & Turiel, E. (1993). God's word, religious rules, and their relation to Christian and Jewish children's concepts of morality. *Child Development, 64,* 1475–1491.

Nulman, I., Ickowicz, A., Koren, G., & Knittel-Keren, D. (2007). Fetal alcohol spectrum disorder. In I. Brown & M. Percy (Eds.), *A comprehensive guide to intellectual & developmental disabilities.* Baltimore, MD: Paul H. Brookes.

Nyborg, H., & Jensen, A. R. (2001). Occupation and income related to psychometric g. *Intelligence, 29,* 45–55.

O

Oakhill, J., Garnham, A., & Reynolds, D. (2005). Immediate activation of stereotypical gender information. *Memory and Cognition, 33,* 972–983.

Oberlander, S. E., Black, M. M., & Starr, R. H., Jr. (2007). African American adolescent mothers and grandmothers: A multigenerational approach to parenting. *American Journal of Community Psychology, 39,* 37–46.

Oberman, L. M., & Ramachandran, V. S. (2007). The simulated social mind: The role of the mirror neuron system and simulation in the social and communicative deficits of autism spectrum disorders. *Psychological Bulletin, 133,* 310–327.

Obler, L. K. (2005). Language in adulthood. In J. B. Gleason (Ed.), *The development of language* (6th ed.). Boston: Allyn & Bacon.

O'Brien, L. T., & Hummert, M. L. (2006). Memory performance of late middle-aged adults: Contrasting self-stereotyping and stereotype threat accounts of assimilation to age stereotypes. *Social Cognition, 24,* 338–358.

O'Brien, M. (1996). Child-rearing difficulties reported by parents of infants and toddlers. *Journal of Pediatric Psychology, 21,* 433–446.

O'Brien, M., Peyton, V., Mistry, R., Hruda, L., Jacobs, A., Caldera, Y., Huston, A., & Roy, C. (2000). Gender-role cognition in three-year-old boys and girls. *Sex Roles, 42,* 1007–1025.

Ochs, E. (1982). Talking to children in western Samoa. *Language in Society, 11,* 77–104.

Ochse, R. (1990). *Before the gates of excellence: The determinants of creative genius.* Cambridge, England: Cambridge University Press.

O'Connell, A., Gavin, A., Kelly, C., Molcho, M., & Nic Gabhainn, S. (2009). The mean age at menarche of Irish girls in 2006. *Irish Medical Journal, 102,* 76–79.

O'Connor, B. P. (1995). Family and friend relationships among older and younger adults: Interaction motivation, mood, and quality. *International Journal of Aging and Human Development, 40,* 9–29.

O'Connor, B. P., & Nikolic, J. (1990). Identity development and formal operations as sources of adolescent egocentrism. *Journal of Youth and Adolescence, 19,* 149–158.

O'Connor, M. J., & Whaley, S. E. (2003). Alcohol use in pregnant low-income women. *Journal of Studies in Alcohol, 64,* 773–783.

O'Connor, T. G., Deater-Deckard, K., Fulker, D., Rutter, M., & Plomin, R. (1998). Genotype-environment correlations in late childhood and early adolescence: Antisocial behavioral problems and coercive parenting. *Developmental Psychology, 34,* 970–981.

O'Connor, T. G., Marvin, R. S., Rutter, M., Olrick, J. T., & Britner, P. A. (2003). Child–parent attachment following early institutional deprivation. *Development and Psychopathology, 15,* 19–38.

O'Dempsey, T. J. D. (1988). Traditional belief and practice among the Pokot people of Kenya with particular reference to mother and child health: 2. Mother and child health. *Annals of Tropical Pediatrics, 8,* 125.

Oden, M. H. (1968). The fulfillment of promise: 40-year follow-up of the Terman gifted group. *Genetic Psychology Monographs, 77,* 3–93.

Odendaal, H. J., Steyn, D. W., Elliott, A., & Burd, L. (2009). Combined effects of cigarette smoking and alcohol consumption on perinatal outcome. *Gynecologic and Obstetric Investigation, 67,* 1–8.

Odgers, C. L., Moffitt, T. E., Broadbent, J. M., Dickson, N., Hancox, R. J., Harrington, H., Poulton, R., Sears, M. R., Thomson, W. M., & Caspi, A. (2008). Female and male antisocial trajectories: From childhood origins to adult outcomes. *Development and Psychopathology, 20,* 673–716.

O'Donnell, A. M., & O'Kelly, J. (1994). Learning from peers: Beyond the rhetoric of positive results. *Educational Psychology Review, 6,* 321–349.

O'Donnell, W. T., & Warren, S. T. (2002). A decade of molecular studies of fragile X syndrome. *Annual Review of Neuroscience, 25,* 315–338.

Ogbu, J. U. (1981). Origins of human competence: A cultural–ethological perspective. *Child Development, 52,* 413–429.

Ogbu, J. U. (1994). From cultural differences to differences in cultural frames of reference. In P. M. Greenfield & R. R. Cocking (Eds.), *Cross-cultural roots of minority child development.* Hillsdale, NJ: Erlbaum.

Ogbu, J. U. (2003). *Black American students in an affluent suburb: A study of academic disengagement.* Lawrence Erlbaum.

Ogbuanu, I., U., Karmaus, W., Arshad, S. H., Kurukulaaratchy, R. J., & Ewart, S. (2008). Effect of breastfeeding duration on lung function at age 10 years: A prospective birth cohort study, *Thorax, 64,* 62–66.

Ogletree, S. M., & Drake, R. (2007). College students' video game participation and perceptions: Gender differences and implications. *Sex Roles, 56,* 537–542.

Ogletree, S. M., Martinez, C. N., Turner, T. R., & Mason, B. (2004). Pokemon: Exploring the role of gender. *Sex Roles, 50,* 851–859.

O'Halloran, C. M., & Altmaier, E. M. (1996). Awareness of death among children: Does a life-threatening illness alter the process of discovery? *Journal of Counseling and Development, 74,* 259–262.

Ohman, A., & Mineka, S. (2003). The malicious serpent: Snakes as a prototypical stimulus for an evolved module of fear. *Current Directions in Psychological Science, 12,* 5–9.

Okagaki, L. (2001). Triarchic Model of Minority Children's School Achievement. *Educational Psychologist, 36,* 9–20.

Okie, S. (2001, May 8). Confronting Alzheimer's. Promising vaccine targets ravager of minds. *The Washington Post,* A1, A4.

Oller, D. K., & Eilers, R. E. (1988). The role of audition in infant babbling. *Child Development, 59,* 441–449.

Olshan, A. F., Schnitzer, P. G., & Baird, P. A. (1994). Paternal age and the risk of congenital heart defects. *Teratology, 50,* 80–84.

Olshansky, S. J., & Carnes, B. A. (2004). In search of the holy grail of senescence. In S. G. Post & R. H. Binstock (Eds.), *The fountain of youth: Cultural, scientific, and ethical perspectives on a biomedical goal.* New York: Oxford University Press.

Olson, J. M., Vernon, P. A., Harris, J. A., & Jang, K. L. (2001). The heritability of attitudes: A study of twins. *Journal of Personality and Social Psychology, 80,* 845–860.

Oltjenbruns, K. A. (2001). Developmental context of childhood: Grief and regrief phenomena. In M. S. Stroebe, R. O. Hansson, W. Stroebe, & H. Schut (Eds.), *Handbook of bereavement research. Consequences, coping, and care.* Washington, DC: American Psychological Association.

Olweus, D. (1993). *Bullying at school.* Oxford, UK: Blackwell.

O'Mara, A. J., Marsh, H. W., Craven, R. G., & Debus, R. L. (2006). Do self-concept interventions make a difference? A synergistic blend of construct validation and meta-analysis. *Educational Psychologist, 41,* 181–206.

O'Mathúna, D. P. (2006). Human growth hormone for improved strength and increased muscle mass in athletes. *Alternative Medicine Alert, 8,* 97–101.

Ong, K.K., Emmett, P., Northstone, K., Golding, J., Rogers, I., Ness, A.R., Wells, J.C., Dunger, D.B., Papadimitriou, A., Fytanidis, G., Douros, K., Bakoula, C., Nicolaidou, P., & Fretzayas, A. (2009). Infancy weight gain predicts childhood body fat and age at menarche in girls. *The Journal of Clinical Endocrinology & Metabolism, 94,* 1527–1532.

Onishi, K. H., & Baillargeon, R. (2005). Do 15-month-old infants understand false beliefs? *Science, 308,* 255–258.

Oosterwegel, A., & Oppenheimer, L. (1993). *The self-system: Developmental changes between and within self-concepts.* Hillsdale, NJ: Erlbaum.

Oppliger, P. A. (2007). Effects of gender stereotyping on socialization. In R. W. Preiss, B. Mae, N. Burrell, M. Allen, J. Bryant (Eds.), *Mass media effects research: Advances through meta-analysis* (pp. 199–214). Mahwah, NJ: Lawrence Erlbaum.

Organization for Economic Co-operation and Development (2007). *Executive summary PISA 2006: Science competencies for tomorrow's world.* The Programme for International Student Assessment. Available at: http://www.oecd.org/document/2/0,3343,en_32252351_32236191_39718850_1_1_1_1,00.html#ES. Accessed: July 12, 2010.

Orobio de Castro, B., Veerman, J. W., Koops, W., Bosch, J. D., & Monshouwer, H. J. (2002). Hostile attribution of intent and aggressive behavior: A meta-analysis. *Child Development, 73,* 916–934.

O'Rourke, M. (2010, February 1). Good grief. Is there a better way to be bereaved? *The New Yorker,* 66–72.

Orth, L. C., & Martin, R. P. (1994). Interactive -effects of student temperament and instruction method on classroom behavior and achievement. *Journal of School Psychology, 32,* 149–166.

O'Shaughnessy, E. S., Berl, M. M., Moore, E. N., & Gaillard, W. D. (2008). Pediatric functional magnetic resonance imaging (fMRI): Issues and applications. *Journal of Child Neurology, 23,* 791–801.

O'Shaughnessy, R., & Dallos, R. (2009). Attachment research and eating disorders: A review of the literature. *Clinical Child Psychology and Psychiatry, 14,* 559–574.

Osofsky, H. J., Osofsky, J. D., Kronenberg, M., Brennan, A., & Hansel, T. C. (2009). Posttraumatic stress symptoms in children after Hurricane Katrina: Predicting the need for mental health services. *American Journal of Orthopsychiatry, 79,* 212–220.

Osterweis, M., Solomon, F., & Green, M. (Eds.). (1984). *Bereavement: Reactions, consequences, and care.* Washington, DC: National Academy Press.

Ostrov, J. M., & Godleski, S. A. (2010). Toward an integrated gender-linked model of aggression subtypes in early and middle childhood. *Psychological Review, 117,* 233–242.

Oswald, D. L., & Lindstedt, K. (2006). The content and function of gender self-stereotypes: An exploratory investigation. *Sex Roles, 54,* 447–458.

Ott, C. H., Lueger, R. J., Kelber, S. T., & Prigerson, H. G. (2007). Spousal bereavement in older adults: Common, resilient, and chronic grief with defining characteristics. *Journal of Nervous and Mental Disease, 195,* 332–341.

Otte, E., & van Mier, H. I. (2006). Bimanual interference in children performing a dual motor task. *Human Movement Science, 25,* 678–693.

Owen, A. M., Coleman, M. R., Boly, M., Davis, M. H., Laureys, S., & Pickard, J. D. (2006). Detecting awareness in the vegetative state. *Science, 313*(5792), 1402.

Owen, M. J., & O'Donovan, M. C. (2003). Schizophrenia and genetics. In R. Plomin, J. C. DeFries, I. W. Craig, & P. McGuffin (Eds.), *Behavioral genetics in the postgenomic era.* Washington, DC: American Psychological Association.

Owens, J., Spirito, A., McGuinn, M., & Nobile, C. (2000). Sleep habits and sleep disturbance in elementary school-aged children. *Journal of Developmental and Behavioral Pediatrics, 21,* 27–36.

Ownby, R. L., Crocco, E., Acevedo, A., John, V., & Loewenstein, D. (2006). Depression and risk for Alzheimer disease: Systematic review, meta-analysis, and metaregression analysis. *Archives of General Psychiatry, 63,* 530–538.

Ozer, D. J., & Benet-Martinez, V. (2006). Personality and the prediction of consequential outcomes. *Annual Review of Psychology, 57,* 401–421.

P

Paciello, M., Fida, R., Tramontano, C., Lupinetti, C., & Caprara, G. V. (2008). Stability and change of moral disengagement and its impact on aggression and violence in late adolescence. *Child Development, 79,* 1288–1309.

Page, T. (1996, December 22). "Shine," brief candle. *The Washington Post,* G1, G10–G11.

Paikoff, R. L., & Brooks-Gunn, J. (1991). Do parent–child relationships change during puberty? *Psychological Bulletin, 110,* 47–66.

Palkovitz, R. (2002). *Involved fathering and men's adult development: Provisional balances.* Mahwah, NJ: Erlbaum.

Palmore, E. B., Burchett, B. M., Fillenbaum, G. G., George, L. K., & Wallman, L. M. (1985). *Retirement. Causes and consequences.* New York: Springer.

Pan, B. A. & Uccelli, P. (2009). Semantic Development. In J. B. Gleason & N. B. Ratner (Eds.), *The Development of Language,* 7th ed. Allyn & Bacon.

Papadakis, A. A., Prince, R. P., Jones, N. P., & Strauman, T. J. (2006). Self-regulation, rumination, and vulnerability to depression in adolescent girls. *Development and Psychopathology, 18,* 815–829.

Papadimitriou, A., Fytanidis, G., Douros, K., Bakoula, C., Nicolaidou., P. & Andreas. F. (2008). Age at menarche in contemporary Greek girls: Evidence for levelling-off of the secular trend. *Acta Paediatrica, 97,* 812–815.

Park, A. (2009, February 9). The quest resumes. After eight years of political ostracism, stem-cell scientists like Harvard's Douglas Melton are coming back into the light—and making discoveries that may soon bring lifesaving breakthroughs. *Time,* 36–43.

Park, D. C., Lautenschlager, G., Hedden, T., Davidson, N. S., Smith, A. D., & Smith, P. K. (2002). Models of visuospatial and verbal memory across the adult life span. *Psychological Aging, 17,* 299–320.

Park, D. C., Morrell, R. W., Frieske, D., & Kincaid, D. (1992). Medication adherence behaviors in older adults: Effects of external cognitive supports. *Psychology and Aging, 7,* 252–256.

Park, F., & Gow, K. W. (2006). Gene therapy: Future or flop. *Pediatric Clinics of North America, 53,* 621–638.

Park, G., Lubinski, D., & Benbow, C. P. (2007). Contrasting intellectual patterns predict creativity in the arts and sciences. *Psychological Science, 18,* 948–952.

Parke, R. D. (1996). *Fatherhood*. Cambridge, MA: Harvard University Press.

Parke, R. D., & Buriel, R. (2006). Socialization in the family: Ethnic and ecological perspectives. In N. Eisenberg (Ed.), W. Damon & R. M. Learner (Eds. in Chief), *Handbook of child psychology: Vol. 3. Social, emotional, and personality development*. Hoboken, NJ: Wiley.

Parke, R. D., & Sawin, D. B. (1976). The father's role in infancy: A reevaluation. *Family Coordinator*, 25, 365–371.

Parke, R. D., Ornstein, P. A., Rieser, J. J., & Zahn-Waxler, C. (1994). The past as prologue: An overview of a century of developmental psychology. In R. D. Parke, P. A. Ornstein, J. J. Rieser, & C. Zahn-Waxler (Eds.), *A century of developmental psychology*. Washington, DC: American Psychological Association.

Parker, E. S., Cahill, L., & McGaugh, J. L. (2006). A case of unusual autobiographical remembering. *Neurocase*, 12, 35–49.

Parker, F. L., Boak, A. Y., Griffin, K. W., Ripple, C., & Peay, L. (1999). Parent–child relationship, home learning environment, and school readiness. *School Psychology Review*, 28, 413–425.

Parker, L. O. (2008, August 17). Marathon men. The Washington Post, W10ff.

Parkes, C. M. (1991). Attachment, bonding, and psychiatric problems after bereavement in adult life. In C. M. Parkes, J. Stevenson-Hinde, & P. Marris (Eds.), *Attachment across the life cycle*. London: Tavistock/Routledge.

Parkes, C. M. (1996). *Bereavement: Studies of grief in adult life* (3rd ed.). London: Routledge.

Parkes, C. M. (2000). Comments on Dennis Klass' article "Developing a cross-cultural model of grief." *Omega: Journal of Death and Dying*, 41, 323–326.

Parkes, C. M. (2006). *Love and loss. The roots of grief and its complications*. London: Routledge.

Parkes, C. M., & Prigerson, H. G. (2010). *Bereavement. Studies of grief in adult life* (4th ed.). New York: Routledge.

Parkes, C. M., & Weiss, R. S. (1983). *Recovery from bereavement*. New York: Basic Books.

Parkhurst, J. T., & Asher, S. R. (1992). Peer rejection in middle school: Subgroup differences in behavior, loneliness, and interpersonal concerns. *Developmental Psychology*, 28, 231–241.

Parnham, J. (2001). Lifelong learning: A model for increasing the participation of non-traditional adult learners. *Journal of Further and Higher Education*, 25, 57–65.

Parten, M. B. (1932). Social participation among preschool children. *Journal of Abnormal and Social Psychology*, 27, 243–269.

Passman, R. H. (1977). Providing attachment objects to facilitate learning and reduce distress: Effects of mothers and security blankets. *Developmental Psychology*, 13, 25–28.

Pasupathi, M., & Hoyt, T. (2009). The development of narrative identity in late adolescence and emergent adulthood: The continued importance of listeners. *Developmental Psychology*, 45, 558–574.

Pasupathi, M., Staudinger, U. M., & Baltes, P. B. (2001). Seeds of wisdom: Adolescents' knowledge and judgment about difficult life problems. *Developmental Psychology*, 37, 351–361.

Patel, D. R., Pratt, H. D., & Greydanus, D. E. (2003). Treatment of adolescents with anorexia nervosa. *Journal of Adolescent Research*, 18, 244–260.

Patel, R., & Brayton, J. T. (2009). Identifying prosodic contrasts in utterances produced by 4-, 7-, and 11-year-old children. *Journal of Speech, Language, and Hearing Research*, 52, 790–801.

Patrick, J. H., & Goedereis, E. A. (2009). The importance of context and the gain-loss dynamic for understanding grandparent caregivers. In K. Shifren (Ed.), *How caregiving affects development. Psychological implications for child, adolescent, and adult caregivers*. Washington, DC: American Psychological Association.

Patrick, R. B., & Gibbs, J. C. (2007). Parental expression of disappointment: Should it be a factor in Hoffman's model of parental discipline? *Journal of Genetic Psychology*, 168, 131–145.

Patterson, C. J. (2004). Gay fathers. In M. E. Lamb (Ed.), *The role of the father in child development* (4th ed.). Hoboken, NJ: John Wiley & Sons.

Patterson, C. J., & Hastings, P. D. (2007). Socialization in the context of family diversity. In J. E. Grusec & P. D. Hastings (Eds.), *Handbook of socialization: Theory and research*. New York: Guilford.

Patterson, C. J., Kupersmidt, J. B., & Vaden, N. A. (1990). Income level, gender, ethnicity, and household composition as predictors of children's school-based competence. *Child Development*, 61, 485–494.

Patterson, G. R. (2008). A comparison of models for interstate wars and for individual violence. *Perspectives on Psychological Science*, 3, 203–223.

Patterson, G. R., DeBaryshe, B. D., & Ramsey, E. (1989). A developmental perspective on antisocial behavior. *American Psychologist*, 44, 329–335.

Patterson, P. H. (2007, October 26). Maternal effects on schizophrenia risk. *Science*, 318, 576–577.

Patton, J. R. (2000). Educating students with mild mental retardation. *Focus on Autism and Other Developmental Disabilities*, 15, 80–89.

Paul, J. P. (1993). Childhood cross-gender behavior and adult homosexuality: The resurgence of biological models of sexuality. *Journal of Homosexuality*, 24, 41–54.

Paul, K. I., & Moser, K. (2009). Unemployment impairs mental health: Meta-analyses. *Journal of Vocational Behavior*, 74, 264–282.

Pauli-Pott, U., Mertesacker, B., & Beckmann, D. (2004). Predicting the development of infant emotionality from maternal characteristics. *Development and Psychopathology*, 16, 19–42.

Paulson, J. F., Dauber, S., & Leiferman, J. A. (2006). Individual and combined effects of postpartum depression in mothers and fathers on parenting behavior. *Pediatrics*, 118, 659–668.

Paxton, S. J., Neumark-Sztainer, D., Hannan, P. J., Eisenberg, M. E. (2006). Body dissatisfaction prospectively predicts depressive mood and low self-esteem in adolescent girls and boys. *Journal of Clinical Child and Adolescent Psychology*, 35, 539–549.

Paz-Alonso, P. E., Larson, R. P., Castelli, P., Alley, D., & Goodman, G. (2009). In M. L. Courage & N. Cowan (Eds.), The Development of Memory in Infancy and Childhood, 197–240. New York, NY: Psychology Press.

Pearce, K. A., & Denney, N. W. (1984). A lifespan study of classification preference. *Journal of Gerontology*, 39, 458–464.

Pearlin, L. I. (1980). Life strains and psychological distress among adults. In N. J. Smelser & E. H. Erikson (Eds.), *Themes of work and love in adulthood*. Cambridge, MA: Harvard University Press.

Pears, K. C., & Moses, L. J. (2003). Demographics, parenting, and theory of mind in preschool children. *Social Development*, 12, 1–19.

Pearson, J. D., Morell, C. H., Gordon-Salant, S., Brant, L. J., Metter, E. J., Klein, L., & Fozard, J. L. (1995). Gender differences in a longitudinal study of age-associated hearing loss. *Journal of the Acoustical Society of America*, 97, 1196–1205.

Pedersen, N. L., McClearn, G. E., Plomin, R., & Friberg, L. (1985). Separated fraternal twins: Resemblance for cognitive abilities. *Behavior Genetics*, 15, 407–419.

Pedula, K. L., Coleman, A. L., Hillier, T. A., Ensrud, K. E., Nevitt, M. C., Hochberg, M. C., Mangione, C. M., & Study of Osteoporotic Fractures Research Group. (2006). Visual acuity, contract sensitivity, and mortality in older women: Study of osteoporotic fractures. *Journal of American Geriatric Society*, 54, 1871–1877,

Pegg, J. E., Werker, J. F., & McLeod, P. J. (1992). Preference for infant-directed over adult-directed speech: Evidence from 7-week-old infants. *Infant Behavior and Development*, 15, 325–345.

Peirano, P. D. & Algarín, C.R. (2007). Sleep in brain development. *Biological Research*, 40, 471–478.

Pekrun, R., Elliot, A. J., & Maier, M. A. (2009). Achievement goals and achievement emotions: Testing a model of their joint relations with academic performance. *Journal of Educational Psychology*, 101, 115–135.

Pelham, W., Chacko, A., & Wymbs, B. (2004). Diagnostic and assessment issues in ADHD in the young child. In R. DelCarmen-Wiggins & A. Carter (Eds.), *Handbook of infant, toddler, and preschool mental health assessment*. New York: Oxford University Press.

Pellegrini, A. D. (1996). *Observing children in their natural worlds: A methodological primer*. Mahwah, NJ: Erlbaum.

Pellegrini, A. D., & Long, J. D. (2003). A sexual selection theory longitudinal analysis of sexual segregation and integration in early adolescence. *Journal of Experimental Child Psychology*, 85, 257–278.

Pellegrini, A. D., Long, J. D., Roseth, C. J., Bohn, C. M., & Van Ryzin, M. (2007). A short-term longitudinal study of preschoolers' (*Homo sapiens*) sex segregation: The role of physical activity, sex, and time. *Journal of Comparative Psychology*, 121, 282–289.

Pellicano, E. (2010). Individual differences in executive function and central coherence predict developmental changes in theory of mind in autism. *Developmental Psychology*, 46, 530–544.

Pelligrini, A. D. (2009). Research and policy on children's play. *Child Development Perspectives*, 3, 131–136.

Penner, S. G. (1987). Parental responses to grammatical and ungrammatical child utterances. *Child Development*, 58, 376–384.

Peplau, L. A., & Fingerhut, A. W. (2007). The close relationships of lesbians and gay men. *Annual Review of Psychology*, 58, 405–424.

Pepper, S. C. (1942). *World hypotheses: A study in evidence*. Berkeley, CA: University of California Press.

Percy, M. (2007). Factors that cause or contribute to intellectual and developmental disabilities. In I. Brown & M. Percy (Eds.), *A comprehensive guide to intellectual & developmental disabilities*. Baltimore, MD: Paul H. Brookes.

Percy, M., Lewkis, S. Z., & Brown, I. (2007). Introduction to genetics and development. In I. Brown & M. Percy (Eds.), *A comprehensive guide to intellectual & developmental disabilities*. Baltimore, MD: Paul H. Brookes.

Pereira, A. C., Huddleston, D. E., Brickman, A. M., Sosunov, A. A., Hen, R., McKhann, G. M., Sloan, R., Gage, F. H., Brown, T. R., & Small, S. A. (2007). An *in vivo* correlate of exercise-induced neurogenesis in the adult dentate gyrus. *Proceedings of the National Academy of Sciences*, 104, 5638–5643.

Perera, F. P., Tang, D., Rauh, V., Tu, Y. H., Tsai, W. Y., Becker, M., Stein, J. L., King, J., Del Priore, G., & Lederman SA. (2007). Relationship between polycyclic aromatic hydrocarbon-DNA adducts, environmental tobacco smoke, and child development in the World Trade Center cohort. *Environmental Health Perspectives*, 115, 1497–502.

Perez-Granados, D. R., & Callanan, M. A. (1997). Conversations with mothers and siblings: Young children's semantic and conceptual development. *Developmental Psychology*, 33, 120–134.

Perfetti, C. A. (1999). Cognitive research and the misconceptions of reading education. In J. Oakhill & R. Beard (Eds.), *Reading development and the teaching of reading*, 42–58. Malden, MA: Blackwell.

Perkins, H. W., & DeMeis, D. K. (1996). Gender and family effects on the "second-shift" domestic activity of college educated young adults. *Gender & Society, 10*, 78–93.

Perlmutter, M. (1986). A life-span view of memory. In P. B. Baltes, D. L. Featherman, & R. M. Lerner (Eds.), *Life-span development and behavior* (Vol. 7). Hillsdale, NJ: Erlbaum.

Perry, D. G., & Parke, R. D. (1975). Punishment and alternative response training as determinants of response inhibition in children. *Genetic Psychology Monographs, 91*, 257–279.

Perry, H. L. (1993). Mourning and funeral customs of African Americans. In D. P. Irish, K. F. Lundquist, & V. J. Nelson (Eds.), *Ethnic variations in dying, death, and grief: Diversity in universality.* Washington, DC: Taylor and Francis.

Perry, W. G., Jr. (1970). *Forms of intellectual and ethical development in the college years: A scheme.* New York: Holt, Rinehart & Winston.

Persson, G., & Svanborg, A. (1992). Marital coital activity in men at the age of 75: Relation to somatic, psychiatric, and social factors at the age of 70. *Journal of the American Geriatrics Society, 40*, 439–444.

Peters, A. (2002). The effects of normal aging on myelin and nerve fibers: A review. *Journal of Neurocytology, 31*, 581–593.

Petersen, A. C., Compas, B. E., Brooks-Gunn, J., Stemmler, M., Ey, S., & Grant, K. E. (1993). Depression in adolescence. *American Psychologist, 48*, 155–168.

Petersen, R. C., Smith, G. E., Waring, S. C., & Ivnik, R. J. (1997). Aging, memory, and mild cognitive impairment. *International Psycho-geriatrics, 65* (Supplement).

Petersen, R. C., Stevens, J. C., Ganguli, M., Tangalos, E. G., Cummings, J. L., & DeKosky, S. T. (2001). Early detection of dementia: Mild cognitive impairment. *Neurology, 56*, 1133–1142.

Peterson, C. & Steen, T. A. (2002). Optimistic explanatory style. In C. R. Snyder & S. J. Lopez (Eds.) *Handbook of positive psychology*, 244–256. New York: Oxford University Press.

Peterson, C. C., & Rideout, R. (1998). Memory for medical emergencies experienced by 1 and 2-year-olds. *Developmental Psychology, 34*, 1059–1072.

Peterson, C. C., & Siegal, M. (1999). Representing inner worlds: Theory of mind in autistic, deaf, and normal hearing children. *Psychological Science, 10*, 126–129.

Peterson, C. C., & Siegal, M. (2002). Mind reading and moral awareness in popular and rejected preschoolers. *British Journal of Developmental Psychology, 20*, 205–224.

Peterson, C. C., & Slaughter, V. (2003). Opening windows into the mind: Mothers' preferences for mental state explanations and children's theory of mind. *Cognitive Development, 18*, 399–429.

Peterson, C. C., & Wellman, H. M. (2009). From fancy to reason: Scaling deaf and hearing children's understanding of theory of mind and pretense. *British Journal of Developmental Psychology, 27*, 297–310.

Peterson, C. C., Wellman, H. M., & Liu, D. (2005). Steps in theory-of-mind development for children with deafness or autism. *Child Development, 76*, 502–517.

Peterson, J. L., & Hyde, J. S. (2010). A meta-analytic review of research on gender differences in sexuality, 1993–2007. *Psychological Bulletin, 136*, 21–38.

Peterson, P. L. (1977). Interactive effects of student anxiety, achievement orientation, and teacher behavior on student achievement and attitude. *Journal of Educational Psychology, 69*, 779–792.

Petitto, L. A., & Marentette, P. F. (1991). Babbling in the manual mode: Evidence for the ontogeny of language. *Science, 251*, 1493–1496.

Pettitt, L. M. (2004). Gender intensification of peer socialization during puberty. *New Directions for Child and Adolescent Development, 106*, 23–34.

Pfeifer, J. H., Iacoboni, M., Mazziotta, J. C., & Dapretto, M. (2008). Mirroring others' emotions related to empathy and interpersonal competence in children. *Neuroimage, 39*, 2076–2085.

Phares, V. (1999). *"Poppa" psychology. The role of fathers in children's mental well-being.* Westport, CT: Praeger.

Phillips, L. M., Norris, S. P., & Anderson, J. (2008). Unlocking the door: Is parents' reading to children the key to early literacy development? *Canadian Psychology, 49*, 82–88.

Phillips, M. (1997). What makes schools effective? A comparison of the relationships of communitarian climate and academic climate to mathematics achievement and attendance during middle school. *American Educational Research Journal, 34*, 633–662.

Phillips, M. (2009, March 16). Where death comes cheap. *Newsweek*, 45–46.

Phillips, S. D. (1982). Career exploration in adulthood. *Journal of Vocational Behavior, 20*, 129–140.

Phillips, T. M., & Pittman, J. F. (2003). Identity processes in poor adolescents: Exploring the linkages between economic disadvantage and the primary task of adolescence. *Identity, 3*, 115–129.

Phinney, J. S. (1993). A three-stage model of ethnic identity development in adolescence. In M. E. Bernal, & G. P. Knight (Eds.), *Ethnic identity: Formation and transmission among Hispanics and other minorities.* Albany, NY: State University of New York Press.

Phinney, J. S. (1996). When we talk about American ethnic groups, what do we mean? *American Psychologist, 51*, 918–927.

Phinney, J. S. (2006). Ethnic identity exploration in emerging adulthood. In J. J. Arnett, & J. L. Tanner (Eds.), *Emerging adults in America: Coming of age in the 21st century.* Washington, DC: American Psychological Association.

Phipps, M. G., Blume, J. D., & DeMonner, S. M. (2002). Young maternal age associated with increased risk of postneonatal death. *Obstetrics and Gynecology, 100*, 481–486.

Piaget, J. (1926). *The child's conception of the world.* New York: Harcourt, Brace & World.

Piaget, J. (1950). *The psychology of intelligence.* New York: Harcourt, Brace & World.

Piaget, J. (1952). *The origins of intelligence in children.* New York: International Universities Press.

Piaget, J. (1965). *The moral judgment of the child.* New York: Free Press. (Original work published 1932).

Piaget, J. (1970). Piaget's theory. In P. H. Mussen (Ed.), *Carmichael's manual of child psychology* (Vol. 1). New York: Wiley.

Piaget, J. (1971). *Biology and knowledge.* Edinburgh, UK: Edinburgh University Press.

Piaget, J. (1972). Intellectual evolution from adolescence to adulthood. *Human Development, 15*, 1–12.

Piaget, J. (1977). The role of action in the development of thinking. In W. F. Overton & J. M. Gallagher (Eds.), *Knowledge and development* (Vol. 1). New York: Plenum.

Piaget, J. (1978). *The development of thought: Equilibration of cognitive structures.* Oxford, UK: Blackwell.

Piaget, J. (1985). *The equilibration of cognitive structures: The central problem of intellectual development* (T. Brown & K. J. Thampy, Trans.). Chicago: University of Chicago Press.

Piaget, J., & Inhelder, B. (1956). *The child's conception of space.* New York: Norton.

Piaget, J., & Inhelder, B. (1969). *The psychology of the child* (H. Weaver, Trans.). New York: Basic Books. (Original work published 1966).

Pianta, R., Egeland, B., & Erickson, M. F. (1989). The antecedents of maltreatment: Results of the Mother–child Interaction Research Project. In D. Cicchetti & V. Carlson (Eds.), *Child maltreatment: Theory and research on the causes and consequences of child abuse and neglect.* Cambridge, England: Cambridge University Press.

Pickens, J. (1994). Perception of auditory-visual distance relations by 5-month-old infants. *Developmental Psychology, 30*, 537–544.

Pickett, K. E., Wood, C., Adamson, J., DeSouzs, L., & Wakschlag, L. S. (2008). Meaningful differences in maternal smoking behaviour during pregnancy: implications for infant behavioural vulnerability. *Journal of Epidemiology and Community Health, 62*, 318–324.

Pierce, J., & Bekoff, M. (2009, October 18). Moral in tooth and claw. *The Chronicle of Higher Education*, B10–B11.

Pigott, T. A. (2002). Anxiety disorders. In S. G. Kornstein & A. H. Clayton (Eds.), *Women's mental health: A comprehensive textbook* (pp. 195–221). New York: The Guilford Press.

Pimple, K. D. (Ed.). (2008). *Research ethics.* Burlington, VT: Ashgate.

Pina, A. A., Zerr, A. A., Gonzales, N. A., & Ortiz, C. D. (2009). Psychosocial interventions for school refusal behavior in children and adolescents. *Child Development Perspectives, 3*, 11–20.

Pineda, J. A. (Ed.). (2009). *Mirror neuron systems: The role of mirroring processes in social cognition.* Totowa, NJ: Humana Press.

Pinhas, L., Katzman, D. K., Dimitropoulos, G., & Woodside, D. B. (2007). Bingeing and bulimia nervosa in children and adolescents. In T. Jaffa & B. McDermott (Eds.), *Eating disorders in children and adolescents.* Cambridge, UK: Cambridge University Press.

Pinker, S. (1994). *The language instinct.* New York: Harper Collins.

Pinker, S. (1995). Language acquisition. In L. R. Gleitman, M. Liberman, & D. N. Osherson (Eds.), *An invitation to cognitive science: Vol. 1. Language* (2nd ed.), 135–182. Cambridge, MA: MIT Press.

Pinker, S. (1999). *Words and rules: The ingredients of language.* New York: HarperCollins.

Pinker, S. (2002). *The blank slate. The modern denial of human nature.* New York: Viking.

Pinquart, M., & Silbereisen, R. K. (2006). Socioemotional selectivity in cancer patients. *Psychology and Aging, 21*, 419–423.

Pinquart, M., & Sorenson, S. (2000). Influences of socioeconomic status, social network, competence, or subjective competence in later life: A meta-analysis. *Psychology and Aging, 15*, 187–224.

Pinquart, M., & Sorensen, S. (2003). Associations of stressors and uplifts of caregiving with caregiver burden and depressive mood: A meta-analysis. *Journal of Gerontology: Psychological Sciences, 58B*, 112–128.

Pinquart, M., & Sorensen, S. (2006). Gender differences in caregiver stressors, social resources, and health: An updated meta-analysis. *Journals of Gerontology: Psychological Sciences, 61B*, P33–P45.

Pipe, M. & Salmon, K. (2009). Memory development in the forensic context. In M. L. Courage & N. Cowan (Eds.), *The development of memory in infancy and childhood*, pp. 241-282. New York, NY: Psychology Press.

Pipe, M. E., Thierry, K., & Lamb, M-E. (2007). The development of event memory: Implications for child witness testimony. In M.P. Toglia, J.D. Read, D.F. Ross, & R.C.L. Lindsay (Eds.), *Handbook of eyewitness psychology. Volume 1: Memory for Events.* Mahwah NJ: Lawrence Erlbaum.

Pipp, S., Easterbrooks, M. A., & Harmon, R. J. (1992). The relation between attachment and knowledge of self and mother in one-year-old infants to three-year-old infants. *Child Development, 63,* 738–750.

Pitts, S. C., Prost, J. H., & Winters, J. J. (2005). Quasi-experimental designs in developmental research: Design and analysis considerations. In D. M. Teti (Ed.), *Handbook of research methods in developmental science.* Malden, MA: Blackwell Publishing.

Plassman, B. L., Havlik, R. J., Steffens, D. C., Helms, M. J., Newman, T. N., Drosdick, D., Phillips, C., Gau, B. A., Welsh-Bohmer, K. A., Burke, J. R., Guralnik, J. M., & Breitner, J. C. (2000). Documented head injury in early childhood and risk of Alzheimer's disease and other dementias. *Neurology, 55,* 1158–1166.

Plassman, B. L., Langa, K. M., Fisher, G. G., Heeringa, S. G., Weir, D. R., Ofstedal, M. B., Burke, J. R., Hurd, M. D., Potter, G. G., Rodgers, W. L., Steffens, D. C., McArdle, J. J., Willis, R. J., & Wallace, R. B. (2008). Prevalence of cognitive impairment without dementia in the United States. *Annals of Internal Medicine, 148,* 427–434.

Pleck, J. H., & Masciadrelli, B. P. (2004). Paternal involvement by U.S. residential fathers: Levels, sources, and consequences. In M. E. Lamb (Ed.), *The role of the father in child development* (4th ed.). Hoboken, NJ: John Wiley & Sons.

Plomin, R. (1990). *Nature and nurture. An introduction to human behavioral genetics.* Pacific Grove, CA: Brooks/Cole.

Plomin, R., & Bergeman, C. S. (1991). The nature of nurture: Genetic influence on environmental measures. *Behavioral and Brain Sciences, 14,* 373–385.

Plomin, R., Corley, R., DeFries, J. C., & Fulker, D. W. (1990). Individual differences in television viewing in early childhood: Nature as well as nurture. *Psychological Science, 1,* 371–377.

Plomin, R., & Davis, O. S. P. (2009). The future of genetics in psychology and psychiatry: Microarrrays, genome-wide association, and non-coding RNA. *Journal of Child Psychology and Psychiatry, 50,* 63–71.

Plomin, R., DeFries, J. C., & Loehlin, J. C. (1977). Genotype–environment interaction and correlation in the analysis of human behavior. *Psychological Bulletin, 84,* 309–322.

Plomin, R., DeFries, J. C., McClearn, G. E., & McGuffin, P. (2008). *Behavioral genetics* (5th ed.). New York: Worth.

Plomin, R., Pedersen, N. L., McClearn, G. E., Nesselroade, J. R., & Bergeman, C. S. (1988). EAS temperaments during the last half of the life span: Twins reared apart and twins reared together. *Psychology and Aging, 3,* 43–50.

Plomin, R., & Spinath, F. M. (2004). Intelligence, genetics, genes, and genomics. *Journal of Personality and Social Psychology, 86,* 112–129.

Ploughman, M. (2008). Exercise is brain food: the effects of physical activity on cognitive function. *Developmental Neurorehabilitation, 11,* 236–240.

Pluhar, E. I., DiIorio, C. K., & McCarty, F. (2008). Correlates of sexuality communication among mothers and 6- to 12-year-old children. *Child: Care, Health and Development, 34,* 283–290.

Poehlmann, J., & Fiese, B. H. (2001). The interaction of maternal and infant vulnerabilities on developing attachment relationships. *Development and Psychopathology, 13,* 1–11.

Polakowski, L. L., Akinbami, L. J., & Mendola, P. (2009, August). Prenatal smoking cessation and the risk of delivering preterm and small-for-gestational-age newborns. *Obstetrics & Gynecology, 114,* 318–325.

Polanczyk, G., deLima, M. S., Horta, B. L., Biederman, J., & Rohde, L. A. (2007). The world wide prevalence of ADHD: A systematic review and metaregression analysis. *American Journal of Psychiatry, 164,* 942–948.

Pomerantz, E. M., Altermatt, E. R., & Saxon, J. L. (2002). Making the grade but feeling distressed: Gender differences in academic performance and internal distress. *Journal of Educational Psychology, 94,* 396–404.

Pomerantz, E. M., Qin, L., Wang, Q., & Chen, H. (2009). American and Chinese early adolescents' inclusion of their relationships with their parents in their self-construals. *Child Development, 80,* 792–807.

Pomerantz, E. M., Ruble, D. N., Frey, K. S., & Grenlich, F. (1995). Meeting goals and confronting conflict: Children's changing perceptions of social comparison. *Child Development, 66,* 723–738.

Pomerantz, E. M., & Ruble, D. N. (1997). Distinguishing multiple dimensions of conceptions of ability: Implications for self-evaluation. *Child Development, 68,* 1165–1180.

Pomerantz, E. M., & Wang, Q. (2009). The role of parental control in children's development in Western and East Asian countries. *Current Directions in Psychological Science, 18,* 285–289.

Pomerleau, A., Bolduc, D., Malcuit, G., & Cossette, L. (1990). Pink or blue: Environmental gender stereotypes in the first two years of life. *Sex Roles, 22,* 359–367.

Ponton, L. (2001). *The sex lives of teenagers: Revealing the secret world of adolescent boys and girls.* New York: Plume.

Poon, H. F., Calabrese, V., Scapagnini, G., & Butterfield, D. A. (2004). Free radicals: Key to brain aging and heme oxygenase as a cellular response to oxidative stress. *Journal of Gerontology: Medical Science, 59A,* 478–493.

Poortman, A., & Van Der Lippe, T. (2009). Attitudes toward housework and child care and the gendered division of labor. *Journal of Marriage & the Family, 71,* 526–541.

Pope, S. K., Shue, V. M., & Beck, C. (2003). Will a healthy lifestyle help prevent Alzheimer's disease? *Annual Review of Public Health, 24,* 111–132.

Porfeli, E. J., Hartung, P. J., & Vondracek, F. W. (2008). Children's vocational development: A research rationale. *Career Development Quarterly, 57,* 25–37.

Porfeli, E. J., & Vondracek, F. W. (2009). Career development, work, and occupational success. In M. C. Smith (Ed.) & N. DeFrates-Densch (Asst. Ed.), *Handbook of research on adult learning and development.* New York: Routledge.

Porter, R. H. (1999). Olfaction and human kin recognition. *Genetica, 104,* 259–263.

Porter, R. H., Makin, J. W., Davis, L. B., & Christensen, K. M. (1992). Breast-fed infants respond to olfactory clues from their own mother and unfamiliar lactating females. *Infant Behavior and Development, 15,* 85–93.

Portes, A., & MacLeod, D. (1996). Educational progress of children of immigrants: The roles of class, ethnicity, and school context. *Sociology of Education, 69,* 255–275.

Potter, J., Bouyer, J., Trussell, J., Moreau, C. (2009). Premenstrual syndrome prevalence and fluctuation over time: results from a French population-based survey. *Journal of Women's Health, 18,* 31–39.

Poulin-Dubois, D., & Goodz, N. (2001). Language differentiation in bilingual infants: Evidence from babbling. In J. Cenoz & F. Genesee (Eds.) *Trends in bilingual acquisition* (pp. 95–106). Amsterdam: Netherlandsing Company.

Poulin-Dubois, D., & Serbin, L. A. (2006). Infants' knowledge about gender stereotypes and categories. *Enfance, 58,* 283–310.

Poulin-Dubois, D., Serbin, L. A., Eichstedt, J. A., Sen, M. G., & Beissel, C. F. (2002). Men don't put on make-up: Toddlers' knowledge of the gender stereotyping of household activities. *Social Development, 11,* 166–181.

Powell, K. E., Roberts, A. M., Ross, J. G., Phillips, M. A., Ujamaa, D. A., & Zhou, M. (2009). Low physical fitness among fifth- and seventh-grade students, Georgia, 2006. *American Journal of Preventive Medicine, 36,* 304–310.

Power, F. C., & Higgins-D'Alessandro, A. (2008). The Just Community approach to moral education and the moral atmosphere of the school. In L. P. Nucci & D. Narvaez (Eds.), *Handbook of moral and character education.* New York: Routledge.

Pratt, M. W., Diessner, R., Hunsberger, B., Pancer, S. M., & Savoy, K. (1991). Four pathways in the analysis of adult development and aging: Comparing analyses of reasoning about personal-life dilemmas. *Psychology and Aging, 4,* 666–675.

Pratt, M. W., Diessner, R., Pratt, A., Hunsberger, B., & Pancer, S. M. (1996). Moral and social reasoning and perspective taking in later life: A longitudinal study. *Psychology and Aging, 11,* 66–73.

Pratt, M. W., & Norris, J. E. (1999). Moral development in maturity. Life-span perspectives on the processes of successful aging. In T. M. Hess & F. Blanchard-Fields (Eds.), *Social cognition and aging.* San Diego: Academic Press.

Pressley, M., & Hilden, K. (2006). Cognitive strategies. In D. Kuhn & R. Siegler (Vol. Eds.), *Handbook of child psychology: Cognition, perception, and language: Vol. 2.* Hoboken, NJ: Wiley and Sons.

Pressley, M., Levin, J. R., & Ghatala, E. S. (1984). Memory strategy monitoring in adults and children. *Journal of Verbal Learning and Verbal Behavior, 23,* 270–288.

Preston, T., & Kelly, M. (2006). A medical ethics assessment of the case of Terri Schiavo. *Death Studies, 30,* 121–133.

Price, D. W. W., & Goodman, G. S. (1990). Visiting the wizard: Children's memory for a recurring event. *Child Development, 61,* 664–680.

Price, J., with B. Davis (2008). *The woman who can't forget.* Simon and Schuster.

Priess, H. A., Lindberg, S. M., & Hyde, J. S. (2009). Adolescent gender-role identity and mental health: Gender intensification revisited. *Child Development, 80,* 1531–1544.

Prigerson, H., & Jacobs, S. (2001). Traumatic grief as a distinct disorder: A rationale, consensus criteria, and a preliminary empirical test. In M. S. Stroebe, R. O. Hansson, W. Stroebe, & H. Schut (Eds.), *Handbook of bereavement research: Consequences, coping, and care.* Washington, DC: American Psychological Association.

Prinstein, M. J., Meade, C. S., & Cohen, G. L. (2003). Adolescent oral sex, peer popularity, and perceptions of best friends' sexual behavior. *Journal of Pediatric Psychology, 28,* 243–249.

Prinstein, M. J., Rancourt, D., Guerry, J. D., & Browne, C. R. (2009). Peer reputations and psychological adjustment. In K. H. Rubin, W. M. Bukowski, & B. Laursen (Eds.), *Handbook of peer interactions, relationships, and groups.* New York: Guilford.

Pritchard, D. J., & Korf, B. R. (2008). *Medical genetics at a glance* (2nd ed.). Malden, MA: Blackwell.

Proctor, R. M. J., & Burnett, P. C. (2004). Measuring cognitive and dispositional characteristics of creativity in elementary students. *Creativity Research Journal, 16,* 421–429.

Proffitt, J. B., Coley, J. D., & Medin, D. L. (2000). Expertise and category-based induction. *Journal of Experimental Psychology: Learning, Memory, and Cognition, 26,* 811–828.

Pruden, S. M., Hirsh-Pasek, K., Golinkoff, R. M., & Hennon, E. A. (2006). The birth of words: Ten-month-olds learn words through perceptual salience. *Child Development, 77,* 266–280.

Pudrovska, T., Schieman, S., & Carr, D. (2006). Strains of singlehood in later life: Do race and gender matter? *Journals of Gerontology: Social Sciences, 61B,* S315–S322.

Pujol, J. Soriano-Mas, C., Ortiz, H., Sebastián-Gallés, N., Losilla, J. M., Deus, J. (2006). Myelination of language-related areas in the developing brain. *Neurology, 66,* 339–343.

Purifoy, F. E., Grodsky, A., & Giambra, L. M. (1992). The relationship of sexual daydreaming to sexual activity, sexual drive, and sexual attitudes for women across the life-span. *Archives of Sexual Behavior, 21,* 369–385.

Putallaz, M., & Wasserman, A. (1989). Children's naturalistic entry behavior and sociometric status: A developmental perspective. *Developmental Psychology, 25,* 297–305.

Putnam, F. W. (2003). Ten-year research update review: Child sexual abuse. *Journal of the American Academy of Child and Adolescent Psychiatry, 42,* 269–278.

Putnam, S. P., Gartstein, M. A., & Rothbart, M. K. (2006). Measurement of fine-grained aspects of toddler temperament: The Early Childhood Behavior Questionnaire. *Infant Behavior and Development, 29,* 386–401.

Pyszczynski, T., Solomon, S., & Greenberg, J. (2003). *In the wake of 9/11: The psychology of terror.* Washington, DC: American Psychological Association.

Q

Qui, C., & Fratiglioni, L. (2009). Epidemiology of Alzheimer's disease. In G. Waldemar & A. Burns (Eds.), *Alzheimer's disease.* Oxford: Oxford University Press.

Quigley, B. A. (1997). Rethinking literacy education: The critical need for practice-based change. San Francisco: Jossey-Bass.

Quigley, B. A., & Uhland, R. L. (2000). Retaining adult learners in the first three critical weeks: A quasi-experimental model for use in ABE programs. *Adult Basic Education, 10,* 55–68.

Quill, T. E. (1993). *Death and dignity: Making choices and taking charge.* New York: W. W. Norton.

Quinn, P.C., Yahr, J., Kuhn, A., Slater, A.M., & Pascalis, O. (2002). Representation of the gender of human faces by infants: A preference for female. *Perception, 31,* 1109–1121.

Quinsey, V. L. Skilling, T. A., Lalumiere, M. L., & Craig, W. M. (2004). *Juvenile delinquency. Understanding the origins of individual differences.* Washington, DC: American Psychological Association.

R

Raaijmakers, Q. A. W., Engels, R. C. M. E., & Van Hoof, A. (2005). Delinquency and moral reasoning in adolescence and young adulthood. *International Journal of Behavioral Development, 29,* 247–258.

Rabbani, A., Khodal, S., Mohammad, K., Sotoudeh, A., Karbakhsh, M., Nouri, K., Salavati, A., & Parvaneh, N. (2008). Pubertal development in a random sample of 4.020 urban Iranian girls. *Journal of Pediatric Endocrinology & Metabolism, 21,* 681–687.

Rabbitt, P., Chetwynd, A., & McInnes, L. (2003). Do clever brains age more slowly? Further exploration of a nun result. *British Journal of Psychology, 94,* 63–71.

Rader, D. (2006, April 9). After a painful childhood, Tom Cruise now believes… "I can create who I am." *Parade,* 6–8.

Ragland, D. R., Satariano, W. A., & MacLeod, K. E. (2004). Reasons given by older people for limitation or avoidance of driving. *Gerontologist, 44,* 237–244.

Ragow-O'Brien, D., Hayslip, B., & Guarnaccia, C. A. (2000). The impact of hospice on attitudes toward funerals and subsequent bereavement adjustment.

Omega: Journal of Death and Dying, 41, 291–305.

Ramchandani, P., Stein, A., Evans, J., O'Connor, T. G., & the ALSPAC Study Team (2005). Paternal depression in the postnatal period and child development: A prospective population study. *The Lancet, 365*(9478), 2201–2205.

Ramey, C. T., & Ramey, S. L. (1992). Effective early intervention. *Mental Retardation, 30,* 337–345.

Ramos, M., & Wilmoth, J. (2003). Social relationships and depressive symptoms among older adults in southern Brazil. *Journals of Gerontology: Psychological Sciences and Social Sciences, 58,* S253–S261.

Rando, T. A. (1986). A comprehensive analysis of anticipatory grief: Perspectives, processes, promises, and problems. In T. A. Rando (Ed.), *Loss and anticipatory grief.* Lexington, MA: Lexington Books.

Rando, T. A. (1991). Parental adjustment to the loss of a child. In D. Papadatou & C. Papadatos (Eds.), *Children and death.* New York: Hemisphere.

Rantanen, T., Guralnik, J. M., Foley, D., Masaki, K., Leveille, S., Curb, J. D., & White, L. (1999). Midlife Hand Grip Strength as a Predictor of Old Age Disability. *Journal of the American Medical Association, 281,* 558–560.

Raphael, B. (1983). *The anatomy of bereavement.* New York: Basic Books.

Raphael, B., Minkov, C., & Dobson, M. (2001). Psychotherapeutic and pharmacological intervention for bereaved persons. In M. S. Stroebe, & R. O. Hansson (Eds.), *Handbook of bereavement research: Consequences, coping, and care.* Washington, DC: American Psychological Association.

Rapkin, B. D., & Fischer, K. (1992). Personal goals of older adults: Issues in assessment and prediction. *Psychology and Aging, 7,* 127–137.

Rasmussen, F. (2006). Paternal age, size at birth, and size in young adulthood—risk factors for schizophrenia. *European Journal of Endocrinology, 155,* S65–S69.

Rattaz, C., Goubet, N., & Bullinger, A. (2005). The calming effect of a familiar odor on full-term newborns. *Journal of Developmental and Behavioral Pediatrics, 26,* 86–92.

Raz, S., Goldstein, R., Hopkins, T. L., Lauterbach, M. D., Shah, F., Porter, C. L., Riggs, W. W., Magill, L. H., & Sander C. J. (1994). Sex differences in early vulnerability to cerebral injury and their neurodevelopmental implications. *Psychobiology, 22,* 244–253.

Rebacz, E. (2009). Age at menarche in schoolgirls from Tanzania in light of socioeconomic and sociodemographic conditioning. *Collegium Antropologicum, 33,* 23–29.

Rebordosa, Kogevinas, Bech, B. H., Sørensen, H. T., & Olsen, J. (2009). Use of acetaminophen during pregnancy and risk of adverse pregnancy outcomes. *International Journal of Epidemiology, 38,* 706–714.

Redding, R. E., Harmon, R. J., & Morgan, G. A. (1990). Maternal depression and infants' mastery behaviors. *Infant Behavior and Development, 13,* 391–395.

Reder, L. M., Wible, C., & Martin, J. (1986). Differential memory changes with age: Exact retrieval versus plausible inference. *Journal of Experimental Psychology: Learning, Memory, and Cognition, 12,* 72–81.

Reed, R. (1996). Birthing fathers. *Mothering,* 50–55.

Reed, T., & Dick, D. M. (2003). Heritability and validity of healthy physical aging (wellness) in elderly male twins. *Twin Research, 6,* 227–234.

Rees, M. (1993). Menarche when and why? *Lancet, 342,* 1375–1376.

Reese, E., Hayne, H., & MacDonald, S. (2008). Looking back to the future: Mäori and Pakeha mother-child birth stories. *Child Development, 79,* 114-125.

Reese, H. W., & Overton, W. F. (1970). Models of development and theories of development. In L. R. Goulet & P. B. Baltes (Eds.), *Life-span developmental psychology: Research and theory.* New York: Academic Press.

Regan, P. C. (2008). *The mating game* (2nd ed.). Thousand Oaks, CA: Sage.

Reid, P. T., & Trotter, K. H. (1993). Children's self-presentations with infants: Gender and ethnic comparisons. *Sex Roles, 29,* 171–181.

Reinhardt, J. P., Boerner, K., & Horowitz, A. (2009). Personal and social resources and adaptation to chronic vision impairment over time. *Aging & Mental Health, 13,* 367–375.

Reinherz, H. Z., Giaconia, R. M., Hauf, A. M. C., Wasserman, M. S., & Silverman, A. B. (1999). Major depression in the transition to adulthood: Risks and impairments. *Journal of Abnormal Psychology, 108,* 500–510.

Reinherz, H. Z., Tanner, J. L., Berger, S. R., Beardslee, W. R., & Fitzmaurice, G. M. (2006). Adolescent suicidal ideation as predictive of psychopathology, suicidal behavior, and compromised functioning at age 30. *American Journal of Psychiatry, 163,* 1226–1232.

Reis, H. T., & Aron, A. (2008). Love: What is it, why does it matter, and how does it operate? *Perspectives on Psychological Science, 3,* 80–86.

Reis, H. T., Lin, Y., Bennett, M. E., & Nezlek, J. B. (1993). Change and consistency in social participation during early adulthood. *Developmental Psychology, 29,* 633–645.

Reis, O., & Youniss, J. (2004). Patterns of identity change and development in relationships with mothers and friends. *Journal of Adolescent Research, 19,* 31–44.

Reiss, D. (2005). The interplay between genotypes and family relationships. Reframing concepts of development and prevention. *Current Directions in Psychological Science, 14,* 139–143.

Reiss, D. (with J. M. Neiderhiser, E. M. Hetherington, & R. Plomin). (2000). *The relationship code. Deciphering genetic and social influences on adolescent development.* Cambridge, MA: Harvard University Press.

Reiss, D., & Neiderhiser, J. M. (2000). The interplay of genetic influences and social processes in developmental theory: Specific mechanisms are coming into view. *Development and Psychopathology, 12,* 357–374.

Reiss, D., Neiderhiser, J. M., Hetherington, E. M., & Plomin, R. (2000). *The relationship code: Deciphering genetic and social influences on adolescent development.* Cambridge, MA: Harvard University Press.

Reiss, S. (1994). Issues in defining mental retardation. *American Journal of Mental Retardation, 99,* 1–7.

Reiter, E. O., Price, D. A., Wilton, P., Albertsson-Wikland, K., & Ranke, M. B. (2006). Effect of growth hormone (GH) treatment on the near-final height of 1258 patients with idiopathic GH deficiency: Analysis of a large international database. *The Journal of Clinical Endocrinology and Metabolism, 91,* 2147–2054.

Reitzes, D. C., & Mutran, E. J. (2004). Grandparenthood: Factors influencing frequency of grandparent–grandchildren contact and grandparent role satisfaction. *Journal of Gerontology: Social Sciences, 59B,* S9–S16.

Reker, G. T., Peacock, E. J., & Wong, P. T. P. (1987). Meaning and purpose in life and well-being: A life-span perspective. *Journal of Gerontology, 42,* 44–49.

Rempel, J. (1985). Childless elderly: What are they missing? *Journal of Marriage and the Family, 47,* 343–348.

Rende, R., & Waldman, I. (2006). Behavioral and molecular genetics and developmental psychopathology. In D. Cicchetti & D. J. Cohen (Eds.),

Developmental psychopathology: Vol 2. Developmental neuroscience. Hoboken, NJ: Wiley.

Renzulli, J. S. (1998). The three-ring conception of giftedness. In S. M. Baum, S. M. Reis, & L. R. Maxfield (Eds.), *Nurturing the gifts and talents of primary grade students.* Mansfield Center, CT: Creative Learning Press.

Repacholi, B., Slaughter, V., Pritchard, M., & Gibbs, V. (2003). Theory of mind, Machiavellianism, and social functioning in childhood. In B. Repacholi & V. Slaughter (Eds.). *Individual differences in theory of mind: Implications for typical and atypical development.* New York: Psychology Press.

Repacholi, B. M., & Gopnik, A. (1997). Early reasoning about desires: Evidence from 14- and 18-month-olds. *Developmental Psychology, 33,* 12–21.

Repetti, R., Wang, S., & Saxbe, D. (2009). Bringing it all back home. How outside stressors shape families' everyday lives. *Current Directions in Psychological Science, 18,* 106–111.

Rescorla, L. A., Achenbach, T. M., Ginzburg, S., Ivanova, M., Dumenci, L., Almqvist, F., Bathiche, M., Bilenberg, N., Bird, H., Domuta, A., Erol, N., Fombonne, E., Fonseca, A., Frigerio, A., Kanbayashi, Y., Lambert, M. C., Liu, X., Leung, P., Minaei, A., Roussos, A., Simsek, Z., Weintraub, S., Weisz, J., Wolanczyk, T., Zubrick, S. R., Zukauskiene, R., & Verhulst, F. (2007). Consistency of teacher-reported problems for students in 21 countries. *School Psychology Review, 36,* 91–110.

Resnick, S. M. (2000). One-year age changes in MRI brain volumes in older adults. *Cerebral Cortex, 10,* 464–472.

Resnick, S. M., Berenbaum, S. A., Gottesman, I. I., & Bouchard, T. J., Jr. (1986). Early hormonal influences on cognitive functioning in congenital adrenal hyperplasia. *Developmental Psychology, 22,* 191–198.

Rest, J., Narvaez, D., Bebeau, M. J., & Thoma, S. J. (1999). *Postconventional moral thinking. A neo-Kohlbergian approach.* Mahwah, NJ: Erlbaum.

Resta, R., Biesecker, B. B., Bennett, R. L., Blum, S., Hahn, S. E., Strecker, M. N., & Williams, J. L. (2006). A new definition of genetic counseling: National Society of Genetic Counselors' Task Force Report. *Journal of Genetic Counseling, 15,* 77–83.

Reuben, D. B., Walsh, K., Moore, A. A., Damesyn, M., & Greendale, G. A. (1998). Hearing loss in community-dwelling older persons: National prevalence data and identification using simple questions. *Journal of the American Geriatric Society, 46,* 1008–1011.

Reuter-Lorenz, P. A. & Cappell, K. A. (2008). Neurocognitive aging and the compensation hypothesis. *Current Directions in Psychological Science, 17,* 177–182.

Reyna, V.F., Brainerd, C.J. (1995). Fuzzy-trace theory: An interim synthesis. *Learning and Individual Differences. 7,* 1–75.

Reynolds, T. (2003, October). Understanding emotion in abused children. *APS Observer, 16,* 1, 31–33.

Reznick, J. S. (2009). Working memory in infants and toddlers. In M. L. Courage & N. Cowan (Eds.), *The Development of Memory in Infancy and Childhood,* 343–366. New York: Psychology Press.

Reznikoff, M., Domino, G., Bridges, C., & Honeyman, M. (1973). Creative abilities in identical and fraternal twins. *Behavior Genetics, 3,* 365–377.

Rhee, S. H., & Waldman, I. D. (2002). Genetic and environmental influences on antisocial behavior: A meta-analysis of twin and adoption studies. *Psychological Bulletin, 128,* 490–529.

Rhoades, G. K., Stanley, S. M., & Markman, H. J. (2009). The pre-engagement cohabitation effect: A replication and extension of previous findings. *Journal of Family Psychology, 23,* 107–111.

Rhodes, M., & Brickman, D. (2008). Preschoolers' responses to social comparisons involving relative failure. *Psychological Science, 19,* 968–972.

Rhodes, S. R. (1983). Age-related differences in work attitudes and behavior: A review and conceptual analysis. *Psychological Bulletin, 93,* 328–367.

Rholes, W. S., Simpson, Jeffry A., Campbell, L., & Grich, J. (2001). Adult attachment and the transition to parenthood. *Journal of Personality and Social Psychology, 81,* 421–435.

Ribeiro, F., de Mendonca, A., & Guerreiro, M. (2006). Mild cognitive impairment: Deficits in cognitive domains other than memory. *Dementia and Geriatric Cognitive Disorders, 21,* 284–290.

Ricciardelli, L. A., & McCabe, M. P. (2001). Children's body image concerns and eating disturbance: A review of the literature. *Clinical Psychology Review, 21,* 325–344.

Ricco, R. B. (1990). Necessity and the logic of entailment. In W. Overton (Eds.), *Reasoning, necessity, and logic: Developmental perspectives* (pp. 45–66). Hillsdale, NJ: Lawrence Earlbaum.

Rice, F., Harold, G. T., & Thapar, A. (2003). Negative life events as an account of age-related differences in the genetic aetiology of depression in childhood and adolescence. *Journal of Child Psychology and Psychiatry and Allied Disciplines, 44,* 977–987.

Rice, F., Harold, G. T., Boivin, J., Hay, D. F., van den Bree, M., & Thapar, A. (2009). Disentangling prenatal and inherited influences in humans with an experimental design. *Proceedings of the National Academy of Sciences, 106,* 2464–2467.

Rice, F., & Thapar, A. (2009). Depression and anxiety in childhood and adolescence: Developmental pathways, genes and environment. In Y. Kim (Ed.), *Handbook of behavior genetics.* New York: Springer.

Richard, J. F., Normandeau, J., Brun, V., & Maillet, M. (2004). Attracting and maintaining infant attention during habituation: Further evidence of the importance of stimulus complexity. *Infant and Child Development, 13,* 277–286.

Richards, R. (1996). Beyond Piaget: Accepting divergent, chaotic, and creative thought. In M. A. Runco (Ed.), *Creativity from childhood through adulthood: The developmental issues.* San Francisco: Jossey-Bass.

Riediger, M., Li, S., & Lindenberger, U. (2006). Selection, optimization, and compensation as developmental mechanisms of adaptive resource allocation: Review and preview. In J. E. Birren & K. W. Schaie (Eds.), *Handbook of the psychology of aging.* Boston: Elsevier Academic Press.

Riegel, K. F. (1973). Dialectic operations: The final period of cognitive development. *Human Development, 16,* 346–370.

Rieser, J., Yonas, A., & Wilkner, K. (1976). Radial localization of odors by human newborns. *Child Development, 47,* 856–859.

Rieser, J. P. & Underwood, L. E. (2002). *Growing Children: A Parent's Guide* (4th ed.) San Francisco, CA: Genentech, Inc. Available at: http://www.nutropin.com/pdf/05628_gene_grow_child_fa_cr.pdf.

Riggio, H. R., & Desrochers, S. (2005). The influence of maternal employment on the work and family expectations of offspring. In D. F. Halpern & S. E. Murphy (Eds.), *From work-family balance to work-family interaction: Changing the metaphor.* Mahwah, NJ: Erlbaum.

Riley, K. P., Snowdon, D. A., Saunders, A. M., Roses, A. D., Mortimer, J. A., & Nanayakkara, N. (2000). Cognitive function and apolipoprotein E in very old adults: Findings from the Nun Study. *Journal of Gerontology: Psychological Sciences & Social Sciences, 55B,* S69–S75.

Riley, L. P., LaMontagne, L. L., Hepworth, J. T., & Murphy, B. A. (2007). Parental grief responses and personal growth following the death of a child. *Death Studies, 31,* 277–299.

Rilling, M. (2000). John Watson's paradoxical struggle to explain Freud. *American Psychologist, 55,* 301–312.

Rimm-Kaufman, S., & Pianta, R. C. (1999). Patterns of family–school contact in preschool and kindergarten. *School Psychology Review, 28,* 426–438.

Ringler, L. L., & Hayden, D. C. (2000). Adolescent bereavement and social support: Peer loss compared to other losses. *Journal of Adolescent Research, 15,* 209–230.

Ripley, A. (2010, April 8). Should kids be bribed to do well in school? *Time.* Available at: www.time.com/time/printout/0,8816,1978589,00.html. Accessed: July 6, 2010.

Ristic, J., & Kingstone, A. (2009). Rethinking attentional development: Reflexive and volitional orienting in children and adults. *Developmental Science, 12,* 289–296.

Rivera-Gaxiola, M., Silva-Pereyra, J., & Kuhl, P. K. (2005). Brain potentials to native and non-native speech contrasts in 7- and 11-month-old American infants. *Developmental Science, 8,* 162–172.

Riviere, J., & Lecuyer, R. (2003). The C-not-B error: A comparative study. *Cognitive Development, 18,* 285–297.

Rizzolatti, G., & Sinigaglia, C. (2008). *Mirrors in the brain: How our minds share actions, emotions* (F. Anderson, Trans.). Oxford, NY: Oxford University Press. (Original work published 2006).

Roberto, K. A., & Scott, J. P. (1986). Equity considerations in the friendships of older adults. *Journal of Gerontology, 41,* 241–247.

Roberts, B. W., & Caspi, A. (2003). The cumulative continuity model of personality development: Striking a balance between continuity and change in personality traits across the life course. In U. M. Staudinger & U. Lindenberger (Eds.), *Understanding human development: Dialogues with life-span psychology.* Dordrecht, Netherlands: Kluwer Academic.

Roberts, B. W., & Robins, R. W. (2004). Person–environment fit and its implications for personality development: A longitudinal study. *Journal of Personality, 72,* 89–110.

Roberts, B. W., Walton, K. E., & Viechtbauer, W. (2006). Patterns of mean-level change in personality traits across the life course: A meta-analysis of longitudinal studies. *Psychological Bulletin, 132,* 1–25.

Roberts, B. W., Wood, Dustin, & Caspi, A. (2008). The development of personality traits in adulthood. In O. P. John, R. W. Robins, & L. A. Pervin (Eds.), *Handbook of personality theory and research* (3rd ed.). New York: Guilford.

Roberts, D., & Foehr, U. (2004). *Kids & media in America.* Cambridge, MA: University Press.

Roberts, J. E., Mankowski, J. B., Sideris, J., Goldman, B. D., Hatton, D. D., Mirrett, P. L., Baranek, G. T., Reznick, J., Long, A. C. J., & Bailey, D. B. (2009). Trajectories and predictors of the development of very young boys with fragile X syndrome. *Journal of Pediatric Psychology, 34,* 827–836.

Roberts, L. R., Sarigiani, P. A., Petersen, A. C., & Newman, J. L. (1990). Gender differences in the relationship between achievement and self image during early adolescence. *Journal of Early Adolescence, 10,* 159–175.

Roberts, Y. H., Mitchell, M. J., Witman, M., & Taffaro, C. (2010). Mental health symptoms in youth affected by Hurricane Katrina. *Professional Psychology: Research and Practice, 41,* 10–18.

Robins, L. N., & Regier, D. A. (Eds.). (1991). *Psychiatric disorders in America. The Epidemiologic Catchment Area Study.* New York: The Free Press.

Robins, R. W., Caspi, A., & Moffitt, T. E. (2000). Two personalities, one relationship: Both partners' personality traits shape the quality of their relationship. *Journal of Personality and Social Psychology, 79,* 251–259.

Robins, R. W., Tracy, J. L., & Trzesniewski, K. H. (2008). Naturalizing the self. In O. P. John, R. W. Robins, & L. A. Pervin (Eds.), *Handbook of personality theory and research* (3rd ed.). New York: Guilford.

Robins, R. W., Trzesniewski, K. H., Tracy, J. L., Gosling, S. D., & Potter, J. (2002). Global self-esteem across the life span. *Psychology and Aging, 17,* 423–434.

Robinson, C. C., & Morris, J. T. (1986). The gender-stereotyped nature of Christmas toys received by 36-, 48-, and 60-month-old children: A comparison between nonrequested vs. requested toys. *Sex Roles, 15,* 21–32.

Robinson Center (2010). *The Halbert and Nancy Robinson Center for Young Scholars.* Available at: http://depts.washington.edu/cscy. Accessed: February 24, 2010.

Robinson, P. K. (1983). The sociological perspective. In R. B. Weg (Ed.), *Sexuality in the later years: Roles and behavior.* New York: Academic Press.

Robinson, T., & Marwit, S. J. (2006). An investigation of the relationship of personality, coping, and grief intensity among bereaved mothers. *Death Studies, 30,* 677–696.

Roccella, M., & Testa, D. (2003). Fetal alcohol syndrome in developmental age: Neuropsychiatric aspects. *Minerva Pediatrics, 55,* 63–69.

Rochat, P., & Striano, T. (2000). Perceived self in infancy. *Infant Behavior and Development, 23,* 513–530.

Röcke, C., & Cherry, K. E. (2002). Death at the end of the 20th century: Individual processes and developmental tasks in old age. *International Journal of Aging and Human Development, 54,* 315–333.

Rodin, J., & Langer, E. (1980). Aging labels: The decline of control and the fall of self-esteem. *Journal of Social Issues, 36,* 12–29.

Rodkin, P. C., & Hodges, E. V. E. (2003). Bullies and victims in the peer ecology: Four questions for psychological and school professionals. *School Psychology Review, 32,* 384–401.

Rodriguez, A., Olsen, J., Kotimaa, A. J., Kaakinen, M., Moilanen, I., Henriksen, T. B., Linnet, K. M., Miettunen, J., Obel, C., Taanila, A., Ebeling, H., & Järvelin, M. R. (2009). Is prenatal alcohol exposure related to inattention and hyperactivity symptoms in children? Disentangling the effects of social adversity. *Journal of Child Psychology and Psychiatry, 50,* 1073–1083.

Rodriguez, J., Umaña-Taylor, A., Smith, E. P., & Johnson, D. J. (2009). Cultural processes in parenting and youth outcomes: Examining a model of racial-ethnic socialization and identity in diverse populations. *Cultural Diversity and Ethnic Minority Psychology, 15,* 106–111.

Rogan, W. J., & Ware, J. H. (2003). Exposure to lead in children: How low is low enough? *New England Journal of Medicine, 384,* 1515–1516.

Rogler, L. H. (2002). The case of the Great Depression and World War II. *American Psychologist, 57,* 1013–1023.

Rogoff, B. (1998). Cognition as a collaborative process. In D. Kuhn & R. S. Siegler (Vol. Eds.), W. Damon (Editor-in-Chief), *Handbook of child psychology: Cognition, perception, and language* (5th ed.). New York: Wiley.

Rogoff, B. (2003). *The cultural nature of human development.* New York: Oxford University Press.

Rogoff, B., Paradise, R., Arauz, R. M., Correa-Chavez, M., & Angelillo, C. (2003). Firsthand learning through intent participation. *Annual Review of Psychology, 54,* 175–203.

Roid, G. (2003). *Stanford-Binet Intelligence Scales* (5th ed.). Itasca, IL: Riverside Publishing.

Roisman, G. I. (2007). The psychopathology of adult attachment relationships: Autonomic reactivity in marital and premarital interactions. *Developmental Psychology, 43,* 39–53.

Roisman, G. I. (2009). Adult attachment. Toward a rapprochement of methodological cultures. *Current Directions in Psychological Science, 18,* 122–126.

Roisman, G. I., & Fraley, R. C. (2008). A behavior-genetic study of parenting quality, infant attachment security, and their covariation in a nationally representative sample. *Developmental Psychology, 44,* 831–839.

Roizen, N. J., & Patterson, D. (2003). Down's syndrome. *Lancet, 361,* 1281–1289.

Rollins, B. C., & Feldman, H. (1970). Marital satisfaction over the family life cycle. *Journal of Marriage and the Family, 32,* 20–28.

Rolls, B. J. (1999). Do chemosensory changes influence food intake in the elderly? *Physiological Behavior, 66,* 193–197.

Rolls, E. T. (2009). Functional neuroimaging of umami taste: What makes umami pleasant? *American Journal of Clinical Nutrition, 90,* 804S–813S.

Román, G. C. (2003). Neurological aspects of vascular dementia: Basic concepts, diagnosis, and management. In P. A. Lichtenberg, D. L. Murman, & A. M. Mellow (Eds.), *Handbook of dementia. Psychological, neurological, and psychiatric perspectives.* Hoboken, NJ: John Wiley & Sons.

Romano, A. (2009, February 23). Our model marriage. The Obamas have the kind of relationship millennials aspire to. *Newsweek, 59.*

Romo, A., Carceller, R., & Tobajas, J. (2009, February 6). Intrauterine growth retardation (IUGR): Epidemiology and etiology. *Pediatric Endocrinology Review, Suppl 3,* 332–336.

Ronald, A., Happé, F., Bolton, P., Butcher, L. M., Price, T. S., Wheelright, S., Baron-Cohen, S., & Plomin, R. (2006). Genetic heterogeneity between the three components of the autism spectrum: A twin study. *Journal of the American Academy of Child and Adolescent Psychiatry, 45,* 691–699.

Rönnlund, M., Nyberg, L., Bäckman, L., & Nillson, L-G. (2005). Stability, growth, and decline in adult life span development of declarative memory: Cross-sectional and longitudinal data from a population-based study. *Psychology and Aging, 20,* 3–18.

Rose, A. J., Carlson, W., & Waller, E. M. (2007). Prospective associations of co-rumination with friendship and emotional adjustment: Considering the socioemotional trade-offs of co-rumination. *Developmental Psychology, 43,* 1019–1031.

Rose, A. J., Swenson, L. P., & Waller, E. M. (2004). Overt and relational aggression and perceived popularity: Developmental differences in concurrent and prospective relations. *Developmental Psychology, 40,* 378–387.

Rose, S. A., & Feldman, J. F. (1997). Memory and speed: Their role in the relation of infant information processing to later IQ. *Child Development, 68,* 630–641.

Rose, S. A., Feldman, J. F., & Jankowski, J. J. (2003). Infant visual recognition memory: Independent contributions of speed and attention. *Developmental Psychology, 39,* 563–571.

Rose, S. A., Feldman, J. F., Jankowski, J. J., & Rossem, R. (2005). Pathways from prematurity and infant abilities to later cognition. *Child Development, 76,* 1172–1184.

Rose, S. A., Feldman, J. F., Wallace, I. F., & McCarton, C. (1989). Infant visual attention: Relation to birth status and developmental outcome during the first 5 years. *Developmental Psychology, 25,* 560–576.

Rosenberg, H. G. (2009). Complaint discourse, aging, and caregiving among the Ju/'hoansi of Botswana.

In J. Sokolovsky (Ed.), *The cultural context of aging* (3rd ed.). Westport, CT: Praeger.

Rosenberg, J. (2001). Exposure to multiple risk factors linked to delivery of underweight infants. *Family Planning Perspectives, 33,* 238.

Rosenberg, K. D., Eastham, C., Kasehagen, L. J., & Sandoval, A. P. (2008). Infant formula marketing through hospitals: impact of commercial hospital discharge packs on breastfeeding. *American Journal of Public Health, 98,* 290–295.

Rosenberg, S. D., Rosenberg, H. J., & Farrell, M. P. (1999). The midlife crisis revisited. In S. L. Willis & J. D. Reid (Eds.), *Life in the middle. Psychological and social development in middle age.* San Diego: Academic Press.

Rosenblatt, P. C. (1993). Cross-cultural variation in the experience, expression, and understanding of grief. In D. P. Irish, K. F. Lundquist, & V. J. Nelson (Eds.), *Ethnic variations in dying, death, and grief: Diversity in universality.* Washington, DC: Taylor and Francis.

Rosenblatt, P. C. (2008). Grief across cultures: A review and research agenda. In M. S. Stroebe, R. O. Hansson, H. Schut, & W. Stroebe (Eds.), *Handbook of bereavement research and practice. Advances in theory and intervention.* Washington, DC: American Psychological Association.

Rosenbloom, C., & Bahns, M. (2006). What can we learn about diet and physical activity from master athletes? *Holistic Nursing Practice, 20,* 161–167.

Rosenkrantz, P., Vogel, S., Bee, H., Broverman, I., & Broverman, D. M. (1968). Sex-role stereotypes and self-concepts in college students. *Journal of Consulting and Clinical Psychology, 32,* 287–295.

Rosenthal, P. A., & Rosenthal, S. (1984). Suicidal behavior by preschool children. *American Journal of Psychiatry, 141,* 520–525.

Rosenzweig, M. R., & Bennett, E. L. (1996). Psychobiology of plasticity: Effects of training and experience on brain and behavior. *Behavioral Brain Research, 78,* 57–65.

Rosner, R., Kruse, J., & Hagl, M. (2010). A meta-analysis of interventions for bereaved children and adolescents. *Death Studies, 34,* 99–136.

Ross, E. E. T., & Aday, L. A. (2006). Stress and coping in African American grandparents who are raising their grandchildren. *Journal of Family Issues, 27,* 912–932.

Ross, H. G., & Milgram, J. I. (1982). Important variables in adult sibling relationships: A qualitative study. In M. E. Lamb & B. Sutton-Smith (Eds.), *Sibling relationships: Their nature and significance across the lifespan.* Hillsdale, NJ: Erlbaum.

Ross, L. A., Clay, O. J., Edwards, J. D., Ball, K. K., Wadley, V. G., Vance, D. E., Cissell, G. M., Roenker, D. L., & Joyce, J. J. (20009). Do older drivers at-risk for crashes modify their driving over time? *Journal of Gerontology, Series B: Psychological Sciences and Social Sciences, 64,* 163–170.

Ross, M. T., et al. (2005). The DNA sequence of the human X chromosome. *Nature, 434,* 325–337.

Rossell, C. H., Armor, D. J., & Walberg, H. J. (Eds.) (2002). *School desegregation in the 21st century.* Westport, CT: Praeger.

Roth, F. P., Speece, D. L., & Cooper, D. H. (2002). A longitudinal analysis of the connection between oral language and early reading. *Journal of Educational Research, 95,* 259–272.

Roth, G. S. (2005). Caloric restriction and caloric restriction mimetics: Current status and promise for the future. *Journal of the American Geriatrics Society, 53,* S280–S283.

Roth, P. L., Bevier, C. A., Switzer, F. S., & Schippmann, J. S. (1996). Meta-analyzing the relationship between grades and job performance. *Journal of Applied Psychology, 81,* 548–556.

Rothbart, M. K. (2007). Temperament, development, and personality. *Current Directions in Psychological Science, 16,* 207–212.

Rothbart, M. K., Ahadi, S. A., & Evans, D. E. (2000). Temperament and personality: Origins and outcomes. *Journal of Personality and Social Psychology, 78,* 122–135.

Rothbart, M. K., & Bates, J. E. (2006). Temperament. In N. Eisenberg (Vol. Ed.) & W. Damon & R. M. Lerner (Eds. in Chief), *Handbook of child psychology: Vol. 3. Social, emotional, and personality development* (6th ed.). Hoboken, NJ: Wiley.

Rothbart, M. K., & Derryberry, D. (2002). Temperament in children. In C. von Hofsten & L. Backman (Eds.), *Psychology at the turn of the millennium: Vol. 2. Social, developmental, and clinical perspectives.* New York: Taylor & Francis.

Rothbaum, F., & Morelli, G. (2005). Attachment and culture: Bridging relativism and universalism. In W. Friedlmeier, P. Chakkarath, & B. Schwarz (Eds.), *Culture and human development: The importance of cross-cultural research for the social sciences.* New York: Psychology Press.

Rothbaum, F., & Trommsdorff, G. (2007). Do roots and wings complement or oppose one another? The socialization of relatedness and autonomy in cultural context. In J. E. Grusec & P. D. Hastings (Eds.), *Handbook of socialization: Theory and research.* New York: Guilford.

Rothbaum, F., Weisz, J., Pott, M., Miyake, K., & Morelli, G. (2000). Attachment and culture: Security in the United States and Japan. *American Psychologist, 55,* 1093–1104.

Rothbaum, R., Pott, M., Azuma, H., Miyake, K., & Weisz, J. (2000). The development of close relationships in Japan and the United States: Paths of symbiotic harmony and generative tension. *Child Development, 71,* 1121–1142.

Rotheram-Borus, M. J., Piacentini, J., Cantwell, C., Belin, T. R., & Song, J. W. (2000). The 18-month impact of an emergency room-intervention for adolescent female suicide-attempters. *Journal of Consulting and Clinical Psychology, 68,* 1081–1093.

Rothermund, K., & Brandtstädter, J. (2003a). Age stereotypes and self-views in later life: Evaluating rival assumptions. *International Journal of Behavioral Development, 27,* 549–554.

Rothermund, K., & Brandtstädter, J. (2003b). Coping with deficits and losses in later life: From compensatory action to accommodation. *Psychology and Aging, 18,* 896–905.

Rothrauff, T., & Cooney, T. M. (2008). The role of generativity in psychological well-being: Does it differ for childless adults and parents? *Journal of Adult Development, 15,* 148–159.

Rothrauff, T. C., Cooney, T. M., & An, J. S. (2009). Remembered parenting styles and adjustment in middle and late adulthood. *Journals of Gerontology: Psychological Sciences and Social Sciences, 64B,* 137–146.

Rovee-Collier, C. (2001). Information pick-up by infants: What is it, and how can we tell? *Journal of Experimental Child Psychology, 78,* 35–49.

Rovee-Collier, C., & Barr, R. (2004). Infant learning and memory. In G. Bremner & A. Fogel (Eds.), *Blackwell handbook of infant development* (pp. 139–168). Malden, MA: Blackwell Publishing.

Rovee-Collier, C., & Cuevas, K. (2009a). Multiple memory systems are unnecessary to account for infant memory development: An ecological model. *Developmental Psychology, 45,* 160–174.

Rovee-Collier, C., & Cuevas, K. (2009b). The development of infant memory. In M. L. Courage & N. Cowan (Eds.), *The Development of Memory in Infancy and Childhood,* 11-42. New York, NY: Psychology Press.

Rovner, S. (1994, March 29). An Alzheimer's journal. *The Washington Post—Health,* 12–15.

Rowe, D. C. (1994). *The limits of family influence: Genes, experience, and behavior.* New York: Guilford.

Rowe, D. C. (2003). Assessing genotype-environment interactions and correlations in the postgenomic era. In R. Plomin, J. C. DeFries, I. W. Craig, & P. McGuffin (Eds.), *Behavioral genetics in the postgenomic era.* Washington, DC: American Psychological Association.

Rowe, D. C., & Jacobson, K. C. (1999). In the mainstream. Research in behavioral genetics. In R. A. Carson & M. A. Rothstein (Eds.), *Behavioral genetics. The clash of culture and biology.* Baltimore: Johns Hopkins University Press.

Rowe, J. W., & Kahn, R. L. (1998). *Successful aging.* New York: Pantheon.

Rowley, S. J., Jurtz-Costes, B., Mistry, R., & Feagans, L. (2007). Social status as a predictor of race and gender stereotypes in late childhood and early adolescence. *Social Development, 16,* 150–156.

Rubin, C., Maisonet, M., Kieszak, S., Monteilh, C., Holmes, A., Flanders, D., Heron, J., Golding, J., McGeehin, M., & Marcus, M. (2009). Timing of maturation and predictors of menarche in girls enrolled in a contemporary British cohort. *Paediatric and Perinatal Epidemiology, 23,* 492–504.

Rubin, D. C. (2002). Autobiographical memory across the lifespan. In P. Graf & N. Ohta (Eds.), *Lifespan development of human memory* (pp. 159–184). Cambridge, MA: Massachusetts Institute of Technology.

Rubin, D. C., Rahhal, T. A., & Poon, L. W. (1998). Things learned in early adulthood are remembered best. *Memory and Cognition, 26,* 3–19.

Rubin, J. Z., Provenzano, F. J., & Luria, Z. (1974). The eye of the beholder: Parents' views on sex of newborns. *American Journal of Orthopsychiatry, 44,* 512–519.

Rubin, K. H., Bukowski, W. M., & Parker, J. G. (2006). Peer interactions, relationships, and groups. In N. Eisenberg (Vol. Ed.), & W. Damon & R. M. Lerner (Eds. in Chief), *Handbook of child psychology: Vol. 3. Social, emotional, and personality development* (6th ed.). Hoboken, NJ: Wiley.

Rubin, K. H., Coplan, R. J., & Bowker, J. C. (2009). Social withdrawal in childhood. *Annual Review of Psychology, 60,* 141–171.

Rubinow, D. R., & Schmidt, P. J. (1996). Androgens, brain, and behavior. *American Journal of Psychiatry, 153,* 974–984.

Rubinstein, R. L., Alexander, R. B., Goodman, M., & Luborsky, M. (1991). Key relationships of never married, childless older women: A cultural analysis. *Journal of Gerontology: Social Sciences, 46,* S270–S277.

Ruble, D. N., & Dweck, C. S. (1995). Self-conceptions, person conceptions, and their development. In N. Eisenberg (Ed.), *Social development.* Thousand Oaks, CA: Sage.

Ruble, D. N., Eisenberg, R., & Higgins, E. T. (1994). Developmental changes in achievement evaluation: Motivational implications of self–other differences. *Child Development, 65,* 1095–1110.

Ruble, D. N., Taylor, L. J., Cypers, L., Greulich, F. K., Lurye, L. E., & Shrout, P. E. (2007). The role of gender constancy in early gender development. *Child Development, 78,* 1121–1136.

Ruchlin, H. S., & Lachs, M. S. (1999). Prevalence and correlates of exercise among older adults. *Journal of Applied Gerontology, 18,* 341–356.

Rudolph, K. D., & Flynn, M. (2007). Childhood adversity and youth depression: Influence of gender and pubertal status. *Development and Psychopathology, 19,* 497–521.

Ruff, H. A., & Capozzoli, M. C. (2003). Development of attention and distractibility in the first 4 years of life. *Developmental Psychology, 39,* 877–890.

Ruff, H. A., & Lawson, K. R. (1990). Development of sustained, focused attention in young children during free play. *Developmental Psychology, 26,* 85–93.

Ruff, H. A., & Rothbart, M. K. (1996). *Attention in early development: Themes and variations.* New York: Oxford University Press.

Ruff, H. A., Saltarelli, L. M., Coppozzoli, M., & Dubiner, K. (1992). The differentiation of activity in infants' exploration of objects. *Developmental Psychology, 27,* 851–861.

Ruffman, T., Slade, L., & Redman, J. (2005). Young infants' expectations about hidden objects. *Cognition, 97,* 835–843.

Ruffman, T., Slade, L., Sandino, J. C., & Fletcher, A. (2005). Are A-Not-B errors caused by a belief about object location? *Child Development, 76,* 122–136.

Ruffman, T. K., & Olson, D. R. (1989). Children's ascriptions of knowledge to others. *Developmental Psychology, 25,* 601–606.

Ruggles, S. (1994). The origins of African-American family structure. *American Sociological Review, 59,* 136–151.

Ruggles, S. (2007). The decline of intergenerational coresidence in the United States, 1850 to 2000. *American Sociological Review, 72,* 964–989.

Ruiz, S. A., & Silverstein, M. (2007). Relationships with grandparents and the emotional well-being of late adolescence and young adult grandchildren. *Journal of Social Issues, 63,* 793–808.

Rumberger, R. W., & Palardy, G. J. (2005). Does segregation still matter? The impact of student composition on academic achievement in high school. *Teachers College Record, 107,* 1999–2045.

Runco, M. A. (1992). Children's divergent thinking and creative ideation. *Developmental Review, 12,* 233–264.

Runco, M. A. (2006). Information, experience, and divergent thinking: An empirical test. *Creativity Research Journal, 18,* 269–277.

Runco, M. A. (2007). *Creativity—Theories and themes: Research, development, and practice.* Burlington, MA: Elsevier Academic Press.

Russ, S. W. (1996). Development of creative processes in children. In M. A. Runco (Ed.), *Creativity from childhood through adulthood: The developmental issues.* San Francisco: Jossey-Bass.

Russell, A., Aloa, V., Feder, T., Glover, A., Miller, H., & Palmer, G. (1998). Sex-based differences in parenting styles in a sample with preschool children. *Australian Journal of Psychology, 50,* 89–99.

Rust, J., Golombok, S., Hines, M., Johnston, K., & Golding, J. (2000). The role of brothers and sisters in the gender development of preschool children. *Journal of Experimental Child Psychology, 77,* 292–303.

Ruth, J. E., & Coleman, P. (1996). Personality and aging: Coping and management of the self in later life. In J. E. Birren, K. W. Schaie, R. P. Abeles, M. Gatz, & T. A. Salthouse (Eds.), *Handbook of the psychology of aging* (4th ed.). San Diego: Academic Press.

Rutherford, A. (2009). *Beyond the box: B. F. Skinner's technology of behavior from laboratory to life, 1950s–1970s.* Toronto: University of Toronto Press.

Rutledge, P. C., Park, A., & Sher, K. J. (2008). 21st birthday drinking: Extremely extreme. *Journal of Consulting and Clinical Psychology, 76,* 511–516.

Rutter, M. (1983). School effects on pupil progress: Research findings and policy implications. *Child Development, 54,* 1–29.

Rutter, M. (2006). *Genes and behavior. Nature-nurture interplay explained.* Malden, MA: Blackwell.

Rutter, M., Kim-Cohen, J., & Maughan, B. (2006). Continuities and discontinuities in psychopathology between childhood and adult life. *Journal of Child Psychology and Psychiatry, 47,* 276–295.

Rutter, M., & Maughan, B. (2002). School effectiveness findings 1979–2002. *Journal of School Psychology, 50,* 451–475.

Rutter, M., Maughan, B., Mortimore, P., Ouston, J., & Smith, A. (1979). *Fifteen thousand hours: Secondary schools and their effects on children.* Cambridge, MA: Harvard University Press.

Rutter, M., Moffitt, T. E., & Caspi, A. (2006). Gene–environment interplay and psychopathology: Multiple varieties but real effects. *Journal of Child Psychology and Psychiatry, 47,* 226–261.

Rutter, M., & O'Connor, T. G. (2004). Are there biological programming effects for psychological development? Findings from a study of Romanian adoptees. *Developmental Psychology, 40,* 81–94.

Rutter, M., & Sroufe, L. A. (2000). Developmental psychopathology: Concepts and challenges. *Development and Psychopathology, 12,* 265–296.

Ruusuvirta, T., Huotilainen, M., Fellman, V., & Naatanen, R. (2003). The newborn human brain binds sound features together. *Neuroreport, 14,* 2117–2119.

Ryabov, I., & Van Hook, J. (2007). School segregation and academic achievement among Hispanic children. *Social Science Research, 36,* 767–788.

Ryan, A. S., & Zhou, W. (2006). Lower breastfeeding rates persist among the special supplemental nutrition program for women, infants, and children participants, 1978–2003. *Pediatrics, 117,* 1136–1146.

Ryan, E. B., Jin, Y., & Anas, A. P. (2009). Cross-cultural beliefs about memory and aging for self and others: South Korea and Canada. *International Journal of Aging and Human Development, 68,* 185–194.

Ryan, R. M., & Kuczkowski, R. (1994). The imaginary audience, self-consciousness, and public individuation in adolescence. *Journal of Personality, 62,* 219–238.

Ryan, S., Manlove, J., & Franzetta, K. (2003). *The first time: Characteristics of teens' first sexual relationships* (Pub. no. 2003-16). Washington, DC: Child Trends.

Rybash, J. M. (1999). Aging and autobiographical memory: The long and bumpy road. *Journal of Adult Development, 6,* 1–10.

Ryff, C. D. (1991). Possible selves in adulthood and old age: A tale of shifting horizons. *Psychology and Aging, 6,* 286–295.

Ryff, C. D., & Singer, B. (2009).Understanding healthy aging: Key components and their integration. In V. L. Bengtson, M. Silverstein, N. M. Putney, & D. Gans (Eds.), *Handbook of theories of aging* (2nd ed.). New York: Springer.

Rypma, B., Prabhakaran, V., Desmond, J. E., & Gabrieli, J. D. E. (2001). Age differences in prefrontal cortical activity in working memory. *Psychology and Aging, 16,* 371–384.

S

Saarni, C. (1999). *The development of emotional competence.* New York: Guilford Press.

Saarni, C., Campos, J. J., Camras, L. A., & Withington, D. (2006). Emotional development: Action, communication, and understanding. In N. Eisenberg (Vol. Ed.), & W. Damon & R. M. Lerner (Eds. in Chief), *Handbook of child psychology: Vol. 3. Social, emotional, and personality development* (6th ed.). Hoboken, NJ: Wiley.

Sabattini, L., & Leaper, C. (2004). The relation between mothers' and fathers' parenting styles and their division of labor in the home: Young adults' retrospective reports. *Sex Roles, 50,* 217–225.

Sabbagh, M. A. (2006). Neurocognitive bases of preschoolers' theory-of-mind development: Integrating cognitive neuroscience and cognitive development. In P. J. Marshall & N. A. Fox (Eds.), *The development of social engagement: Neurobiological perspectives.* New York: Oxford University Press.

Sackett, P. R., Hardison, C. M., & Cullen, M. J. (2004). On interpreting stereotype threat as ac-counting for African American-White differences on cognitive tests. *American Psychologist, 59,* 7–13.

Sacks, O. (1993, December 27). A neurologist's notebook: An anthropologist on Mars. *The New Yorker,* 106–125.

Sadeh, A. (1994). Assessment of intervention for infant night waking: Parental reports and activity-based home monitoring. *Journal of Consulting and Clinical Psychology, 62,* 63–68.

Sadeh, A. (1996). Evaluating night wakings in sleep-disturbed infants: A methodological study of parental reports and actigraphy. *Sleep, 19,* 757–762.

Sadeh, A., Gruber, R., & Raviv, A. (2003). The effects of sleep restriction and extension on school-age children: What a difference an hour makes. *Child Development, 74,* 444–455.

Sadler, T. W. (2010). *Langman's Medical Embryology* (11th ed.). Baltimore: Lippincott Williams & Wilkins.

Saffran, J. R., Werker, J. F., & Werner, L. A. (2006). The infant's auditory world: Hearing, speech, and the beginnings of language. In D. Kuhn & R. Siegler (Vol. Eds.), *Handbook of child psychology: Cognition, perception, and language: Vol. 2* (6th ed.). Hoboken, NJ: Wiley.

Sagara-Rosemeyer, M., & Davies, B. (2007). The integration of religious traditions in Japanese children's view of death and afterlife. *Death Studies, 31,* 223–247.

Sai, F. Z. (2005). The role of the mother's voice in developing mother's face preference: Evidence for intermodal perception at birth. *Infant and Child Development, 14,* 9–50.

Saigal, S., Stoskopf, B., Boyle, M., Paneth, N., Pinelli, J., Streiner, D., & Godderis, J. (2007). Comparison of current health, functional limitations, and health care use of young adults who were born with extremely low birth weight and normal birth weight. *Pediatrics, 119,* e562–e573.

Salapatek, P. (1975). Pattern perception in early infancy. In L. B. Cohen & P. Salapatek (Eds.), *Infant perception: From sensation to cognition, Vol 1.* New York: Academic Press.

Salihu, H. M., Shumpert, M. N., Slay, M., Kirby, R. S., & Alexander, G. R. (2003). Childbearing beyond maternal age 50 and fetal outcomes in the United States. *Obstetrics and Gynecology, 102,* 1006–1014.

Salmivalli, C., & Peets, K. (2009). Bullies, victims, and bully-victim relationships in middle childhood and early adolescence. In K. H. Rubin, W. M. Bukowski, & B. Laursen (Eds.), *Handbook of peer interactions, relationships, and groups.* New York: Guilford.

Salmon, D. P., & Bondi, M. W. (2009). Neuropsychological assessment of dementia. *Annual Review of Psychology, 60,* 257–282.

Salthouse, T. A. (1990). Cognitive competence and expertise in aging. In J. E. Birren & K. W. Schaie (Eds.), *The handbook of the psychology of aging* (3rd ed.). San Diego: Academic Press.

Salthouse, T. A. (1993). Speed and knowledge as determinants of adult age differences in verbal tasks. *Journal of Gerontology: Psychological Sciences, 48,* 29–36.

Salthouse, T. A. (1996). General and specific speed mediation of adult age differences in memory. *Journals of Gerontology: Psychological Sciences and Social Sciences, 51B,* 30–42.

Salthouse, T. A. (2000). Aging and measures of processing speed. *Biological Psychology, 54,* 35–54.

Salthouse, T. A., Hancock, H. E., Meinz, E. J., & Hambrick, D. Z. (1996). Interrelations of age, visual acuity, and cognitive functioning. *Journals of Gerontology: Psychological Sciences and Social Sciences, 51,* 317–330.

Sameroff, A. (1975). Early influences on development: Fact or fancy? *Merrill-Palmer Quarterly, 21,* 263–294.

Sameroff, A. (2009). The transactional model. In A. Sameroff (Ed.), *The transactional model of development. How children and contexts shape each other.* Washington, DC: American Psychological Association.

Sameroff, A. J., Seifer, R., Baldwin, A., & Baldwin, C. (1993). Stability of intelligence from preschool to adolescence: The influence of social and family risk factors. *Child Development, 64,* 80–97.

Samson, M. M., Meeuwsen, I. B. A. E., Crowe, A., Dessens, J. A. G., Duursma, S. A., & Verhaar, H. J. J. (2000). Relationships between physical performance measures, age, height and body weight in healthy adults. *Age and Ageing, 29,* 235–242.

Sanchez, L., Fristad, M., Weller, R. A., Weller, E. B., & Moye, J. (1994). Anxiety in acutely bereaved prepubertal children. *Annals of Clinical Psychiatry, 6,* 39–43.

Sanders, W. (1999, September 1). Teachers, teachers, teachers! *DLC: Blueprint Magazine.* Available at: www.dlc.org/ndol_ci.cfm?contentid=1199&kaid=110&subid=135. Accessed: April 10, 2010.

Sanders, W. L., & Horn, S. P. (1995). The Tennessee value-added assessment system: (TVAAS): Mixed model methodology in educational assessment. In A. J. Shrinkfield & D. Stufflebeam (Eds.), Teacher Evaluation: Guide to Effective Practice (pp. 337–350). Boston, MA: Kluwer.

Sanders, W. L., & Rivers, J. C. (1996, November). *Cumulative and residual effects of teachers on future student academic achievement.* Research Progress Report. Knoxville, TN: University of Tennessee Value-Added Research and Assessment Center.

Sandler, I. N., Ayers, T. S., Wolchik, S. A., Tein, J., Kwok, O., Haine, R. A., Twohey-Jacobs, J., Suter, J., Lin, K., Padgett-Jones, S., Weyer, J. L., Cole, E., Kriege, G., & Griffin, W. A. (2003). The Family Bereavement Program: Efficacy evaluation of a theory-based prevention program for parentally-bereaved children and adolescents. *Journal of Consulting and Clinical Psychology, 71,* 587–600.

Sandler, I. N., Ma, Y., Tein, J., Ayers, T. S., Wolchik, S., Kennedy, C., & Millsap, R. (2010). Long-term effects of the family bereavement program on multiple indicators of grief in parentally bereaved children and adolescents. *Journal of Consulting and Clinical Psychology, 78,* 131–143.

Sanson, A., Hemphill, S. A., & Smart, D. (2004). Connections between temperament and social development: A review. *Social Development, 13,* 142–170.

Santos, L. L., Magalhaes, M. C., Januario, J. N., Aguiar, M. J., & Carvalho, M. R. (2006). The time has come: A new scene for PKU treatment. *Genetics & Molecular Research, 5,* 33–44.

Sapolsky, R. (1998). *The trouble with testosterone and other essays on the biology of the human predicament.* New York: Scribner.

Saraceno, L., Munafo, M., Heron, J., Craddock, N., & van den Bree, M. B. M. (2009). Genetic and non-genetic influences on the development of co-occurring alcohol problem use and internalizing symptatology in adolescence: A review. *Addiction, 104,* 1100–1121.

Sargant, N., Field, J., Francis, H., Schuller, T., & Tuckett, A. (1997). *The learning divide.* Brighton, UK: National Organisation for Adult Learning.

Sarkisian, N., Gerena, M., & Gerstel, N. (2007). Extended family integration among Euro and Mexican Americans: Ethnicity, gender, and class. *Journal of Marriage and Family, 69,* 40–54.

Sarkisian, N., & Gerstel, N. (2004). Explaining the gender gap in help to parents: The importance of employment. *Journal of Marriage and Family, 66,* 431–451.

Sartor, C. E., Grant, J. D., Bucholz, K. K., Madden, P. A. F., Heath, A. C., Agrawal, A., Whitfield, J. B., Statham, D. J., Martin, N. G., & Lynskey, M. T. (2010). Common genetic contributions to alcohol and cannabis use and dependence symptomatology. *Alcoholism: Clinical and Experimental Research, 34,* 545–554.

Sassler, S. (2004). The process of entering into cohabiting unions. *Journal of Marriage and Family, 66,* 491–505.

Satariano, W. A. (2006). *Epidemiology of aging: An ecological approach.* Sudbury, MA: Jones & Bartlett.

Saucier, G., & Simonds, J. (2006). The structure of personality and temperament. In D. K. Mroczek & T. D. Little (Eds.), *Handbook of personality development.* Mahwah, NJ: Erlbaum.

Saudino, K. J. & Zapfe, J. A. (2009). Genetic influences on activity level in early childhood: Do situations matter? *Child Development, 79,* 930–943.

Saunders, C. (2002). A hospice perspective. In K. Foley, & H. Hendin (Eds.), *The case against assisted suicide: For the right to end-of-life care.* Baltimore: The Johns Hopkins Press.

Savage, J. S. (2001). Birth stories: A way of knowing in childbirth education. *Journal of Perinatal Education, 10,* 3–7.

Savin-Williams, R. C. (1995). An exploratory study of pubertal maturation timing and self-esteem among gay and bisexual male youths. *Developmental Psychology, 31,* 56–64.

Savin-Williams, R. C., & Ream, G. L. (2003). Sex variations in the disclosure to parents of same-sex attractions. *Journal of Family Psychology, 17,* 429–438.

Savin-Williams, R. C., & Ream, G. L. (2007). Prevalence and stability of sexual orientation components during adolescence and young adulthood. *Archives of Sexual Behavior, 36,* 385–394.

Savva, G. M., & Brayne, C. (2009). Epidemiology and impact of dementia. In M. F. Weiner & A. M. Lipton (Eds.), *The American Psychiatric Publishing textbook of Alzheimer disease and other dementias.* Washington, DC: American Psychiatric Publishing.

Saxe, R., Carey, S., & Kanwisher, N. (2004). Understanding other minds: Linking developmental psychology and functional neuroimaging. *Annual Review of Psychology, 55,* 87–124.

Saxe, R., & Kanwisher, N. (2003). People thinking about thinking people: The role of the temporo-parietal junction in "theory of mind." *NeuroImage, 19,* 1835–1842.

Saxe, R., & Powell, L. J. (2006). It's the thought that counts: Specific brain regions for one component of theory of mind. *Psychological Science, 17,* 692–699.

Saxe, R. R., Whitfield-Gabrieli, S., Scholz, J., & Pephrey, K. A. (2009). Brain regions for perceiving and reasoning about other people in school-aged children. *Child Development, 80,* 1197–1209.

Saxton, M. (1997). The contrast theory of negative input. *Journal of Child Language, 24,* 139–161.

Sayal, K., Heron, J., Golding, J., Alati, R., Smith, G. D., Gray, R., & Emond, A. (2009). Binge pattern of alcohol consumption during pregnancy and childhood mental health outcomes: Longitudinal population-based study. *Pediatrics, 123,* e289–e296.

Sayal, K., Heron, J., Golding, J., & Emond, A. (2007). Prenatal alcohol exposure and gender differences in childhood mental health problems: A longitudinal population-based study. *Pediatrics, 119,* e426–e434.

Sayer, L. C. (2005). Gender, time and inequality: Trends in women's and men's paid work, unpaid work and free time. *Social Forces, 84,* 285–303.

Sayre, N. E., & Gallagher, J. D. (2001). *The young child and the environment.* Boston: Allyn & Bacon.

Scafidi, F. A., Field, T., & Schanberg, S. M. (1993). Factors that predict which preterm infants benefit most from massage therapy. *Journal of Developmental and Behavioral Pediatrics, 14,* 176–180.

Scarr, S., & McCartney, K. (1983). How people make their own environments: A theory of genotype → environment effects. *Child Development, 54,* 424–435.

Scarr, S., & Weinberg, R. A. (1978). The influence of family background on intellectual attainment. *American Sociological Review, 43,* 674–692.

Scarr, S., & Weinberg, R. A. (1983). The Minnesota adoption studies: Genetic differences and malleability. *Child Development, 54,* 260–267.

Schaal, B., Barlier, L., & Soussignan, R. (1998). Olfactory function in the human fetus: Evidence from selective neonatal responsiveness to the odor of amniotic fluid. *Behavioral Neuroscience, 112,* 1438–1449.

Schacter, D. L. (1996). *Searching for memory: The brain, the mind, and the past.* New York: Basic Books.

Schaefer, C. E. (Ed.) (2010). *Play therapy for pre-school children.* Washington, DC: American Psychological Association.

Schaefer, E. S. (1959). A circumplex model for maternal behavior. *Journal of Abnormal and Social Psychology, 59,* 226–235.

Schaffer, H. R., & Emerson, P. E. (1964). The development of social attachments in infancy. *Monographs of the Society for Research in Child Development, 29* (3, Serial No. 94).

Schaie, K. W. (1994). Developmental designs revisited. In S. H. Cohen & H. W. Reese (Eds.), *Life-span developmental psychology: Methodological contributions.* Hillsdale, NJ: Erlbaum.

Schaie, K. W. (1996). *Intellectual development in adulthood: The Seattle Longitudinal Study.* Cambridge, England: Cambridge University Press.

Schaie, K. W. (2000). The impact of longitudinal studies on understanding development from young adulthood to old age. *International Journal of Behavioral Development, 24,* 257–266.

Schaie, K. W. (2005). *Developmental influences on adult intelligence: The Seattle Longitudinal Study.* New York: Oxford University Press.

Schaie, K. W., & Caskie, G. I. L. (2005). Methodological issues in aging research. In D. M. Teti (Ed.), *Handbook of research methods in developmental science.* Malden, MA: Blackwell Publishing.

Schaie, K. W., & Parham, I. A. (1976). Stability of adult personality traits: Fact or fable? *Journal of Personality and Social Psychology, 34,* 146–158.

Schaie, K. W., & Willis, S. L. (1986). Can decline in adult intellectual functioning be reversed? *Developmental Psychology, 22,* 223–232.

Schaie, K. W., & Zanjani, F. A. K. (2006). Intellectual development across adulthood. In C. Hoare (Ed.), *Handbook of adult development and learning.* New York: Oxford University Press.

Schalock, R. L., Borthwick-Duffy, S. A., Bradley, V. J., Buntinx, W. H. E., Coulter, D. L., Craig, E. M., Gomez, S. C., Lachapelle, Y., Luckasson, R. Reeve, A., Shogren, K. A., Snell, M. E., Spreat, S. Tassé, M. J., Thompson, J. R., Verdugo-Alonso, M. A., Wehmeyer, M. L., & Yeager, M. H. (2010). *Intellectual disability: Definition, classification, and systems of supports,* 11th ed. Washington, DC: American Association on Intellectual and Developmental Disabilities.

Schalock, R. L., Shogren, K. A., Luckasson, R., Borthwick-Duffy, S., Buntinx, W. H. E., Coulter, D., Craig, E. M., Gomez, S., Lachapelle, Y., Reeve, A., Snell., M. E., Spreat, S., Tassé, M. J., Thompson, J. R., Verdugo, M. A., Wehmeyer, M. L., & Yeager, M. H. (2007). Understanding the change to the term intellectual disability. *Intellectual and Developmental Disabilities, 45,* 2, 116–124.

Schank, R. C., & Abelson, R. P. (1977). *Scripts, plans, goals, and understanding.* Hillsdale, NJ: Erlbaum.

Scharf, M., Mayseless, O., & Kivenson-Baron, I. (2004). Adolescents' attachment representations and developmental tasks in emerging adulthood. *Developmental Psychology, 40,* 430–444.

Scharf, M., Shulman, S., & Avigad-Spitz, L. (2005). Sibling relationships in emerging adulthood and in adolescence. *Journal of Adolescent Research, 20,* 64–90.

Scharlach, A., Li, W., & Dalvi, T. B. (2006). Family conflict as a mediator of caregiver strain. *Family Relations, 55,* 625–635.

Scheffler, R. M., Brown, T. T., Fulton, B. D., Hinshaw, S. P., Levine, P., Stone, S. (2009, May). Positive association between attention deficit/hyperactivity disorder medication use and academic achievement during elementary school. *Pediatrics, 123,* 1273–1279.

Schell, L. M., Gallo, M. V., Denham, M., & Ravenscroft, J. (2006). Effects of pollution on human growth and development: An introduction. *Journal of Physiological Anthropology, 25,* 103–112.

Schery, T. K., & Peters, M. L. (2003). Developing auditory learning in children with cochlear implants. *Topics in Language Disorders, 23,* 4–15.

Schiavi, R. C., Schreiner-Engel, P., White, D., & Mandeli, J. (1991). The relationship between pituitary-gonadal function and sexual behavior in healthy aging men. *Psychosomatic Medicine, 53,* 363–374.

Schieffelin, B. B. (1986). *How Kaluli children learn what to say, what to do, and how to feel.* New York: Cambridge University Press.

Schiff, A. R., & Knopf, I. J. (1985). The effect of task demands on attention allocation in children of different ages. *Child Development, 56,* 621–630.

Schiffman, H. R. (2000). *Sensation and perception* (5th ed.) New York: Wiley.

Schiffman, S. S. (1977). Food recognition by the elderly. *Journal of Gerontology, 32,* 586–592.

Schiffman, S. S. (2009). Effects of aging on the human taste system. *Annals of the New York Academy of Sciences, 1170,* 725–729.

Schiffman, S. S., & Warwick, Z. S. (1993). Effect of flavor enhancement of foods for the elderly on nutritional status: Food intake, biochemical indices, and anthropometric measures. *Physiological Behavior, 53,* 395–402.

Schindl, M., Birner, P., Reingrabner, M., Joura, E., Husslein, P., & Langer, M. (2003). Elective cesarean section vs. spontaneous delivery: A comparative study of birth experience. *Acta Obstetrics and Gynecology of Scandinavia, 82,* 834–840.

Schleppenbach, M., Perry, M., Miller, K. F., Sims, L., & Fang, G. (2007). The answer is only the beginning: Extended discourse in Chinese and U.S. mathematics classrooms. *Journal of Educational Psychology, 99,* 380–396.

Schmidt, F. L., & Hunter, J. E. (1998). The validity and utility of selection methods in personnel psychology: Practical and theoretical implications of 85 years of research findings. *Psychological Bulletin, 124,* 262–274.

Schmidt, F. L., & Hunter, J. E. (2004). General mental ability in the world of work: Occupational attainment and job perfor-mance. *Journal of Personality and Social Psychology, 86,* 162–173.

Schmidt, P. J., Nieman, L. K., Danaceau, M. A., Adams, L. F., & Rubinow, D. R. (1998). Differential behavioral effects of gonadal steroids in women with and in those without premenstrual syndrome. *New England Journal of Medicine, 338,* 209–216.

Schmidt, S., & Petermann, F. (2009). Developmental psychopathology: Attention deficit hyperactivity disorder (ADHD). *BMC Psychiatry, 9,* 58.

Schmiege, S. J., Khoo, S. T., Sandler, I. N., Ayers, T. S., Wolchik, S. A. (2006). Symptoms of internalizing and externalizing problems: Modeling recovery curves after the death of a parent. *American Journal of Preventive Medicine, 31*(6, Suppl 1), S152–S160.

Schmitt, S. K., Sneed, L., & Phibbs, C. S. (2006). Costs of newborn care in California: A population-based study. *Pediatrics, 117*, 154–160.

Schneider, B. H., Atkinson, L., & Tardif, C. (2001). Child–parent attachment and children's peer relations: A quantitative review. *Developmental Psychology, 37*, 86–100.

Schneider, W. (2004). Memory development in childhood. In U. Goswami (Ed.), *Blackwell handbook of childhood cognitive development*, 236–256. Malden, MA: Blackwell Publishing.

Schneider, W., & Bjorklund, D. F. (1998). Memory. In D. Kuhn & R. S. Siegler (Vol. Eds.), W. Damon (Editor-in-Chief), *Handbook of child psychology: Vol. 2. Cognition, perception, and language* (5th ed.), 467–522. New York: Wiley.

Schneider, W., Bjorklund, D. F., & Maier-Bruckner, W. (1996). The effects of expertise and IQ on children's memory: When knowledge is, and when it is not enough. *International Journal of Behavioral Development, 19*, 773–796.

Schneider, W., & Bullock, M. (Eds.) (2009). *Human development from early childhood to early adulthood*. New York: Psychology Press.

Schneider, W., Gruber, H., Gold, A., & Opwis, K. (1993). Chess expertise and memory for chess positions in children and adults. *Journal of Experimental Child Psychology, 56*, 328–349.

Schneider, W., Kron-Sperl, V. & & Hünnerkopf, M. (2009). The development of young children's memory strategies: Evidence from the Wurzburg Longitudinal Memory Study. *European Journal of Developmental Psychology, 6*, 70-99.

Schneider, W., & Pressley, M. (1997). *Memory development between two and 20* (2nd ed.). Mahwah, NJ: Erlbaum.

Schneider, W., Roth, E., & Ennemoser, M. (2000). Training phonological skills and letter knowledge in children at risk for dyslexia: A comparison of three kindergarten intervention programs. *Journal of Educational Psychology, 92*, 284–295.

Schneider, W., & Sodian, B. (1988). Metamemory-memory behavior relationships in young children: Evidence from a memory-for-location task. *Journal of Experimental Child Psychology, 45*, 209–233.

Schoemaker, J. A., & Schoemaker, P. J. H., (2010). *Chips, clones, and living beyond 100*. Upper Saddle River, NJ: Pearson Education.

Schoen, R., & Canudas-Romo, V. (2006). Timing effects on divorce: 20th century experience in the United States. *Journal of Marriage and Family, 68*, 749–758.

Schoen, R., & Cheng, Y. A. (2006). Partner choice and the differential retreat from marriage. *Journal of Marriage and Family, 68*, 1–10.

Scholl, B. J., & Leslie, A. M. (2001). Minds, modules, and meta-analysis. *Child Development, 72*, 696–701.

Schonfeld, D. J., & Kappelman, M. (1990). The impact of school-based education on the young child's understanding of death. *Developmental and Behavioral Pediatrics, 11*, 247–252.

Schooler, C., Mulatu, M. S., & Oates, G. (1999). The continuing effects of substantively complex work on the intellectual functioning of older workers. *Psychology and Aging, 14*, 483–506.

Schoppe-Sullivan, S. J., Diener, M. L., Mangelsdorf, S. C., Brown, G. L., & McHale, J. L. (2006). Attachment and sensitivity in family context: The roles of parent and infant gender. *Infant and Child Development, 15*, 367–385.

Schoppe-Sullivan, S. J., Weldon, A. H., Cook, J. C., Davis, E. F., & Buckley, C. K. (2009). Coparenting behavior moderates longitudinal relations between effortful control and preschool children's externaliz-

ing behavior. *Journal of Child Psychology and Psychiatry, 50*, 698–706.

Schott, J. M., & Rossor, M. N. (2003). The grasp and other primitive reflexes. *Journal of Neurology and Neurosurgical Psychiatry, 74*, 558–560.

Schulte, B., & Craig, T. (2007, August 27). Unknown to Va. Tech, Cho had a disorder. Fairfax helped student cope with anxiety. *The Washington Post*, A1, A8.

Schulz, J. H., & Binstock, R. H. (2006). *Aging nation. The economics and politics of growing older in America*. Baltimore: Johns Hopkins University Press.

Schulz, M. S., Cowan, C. P., & Cowan, P. A. (2006). Promoting healthy beginnings: A randomized controlled trial of a preventive intervention to preserve marital quality during the transition to parenthood. *Journal of Consulting and Clinical Psychology, 74*, 20–31.

Schulz, R., & Aderman, D. (1974). Clinical research and the stages of dying. *Omega: Journal of Death and Dying, 5*, 137–143.

Schulz, R., Belle, S. H., Czaja, S. J., Gitlin, L. N., Wisniewski, S. R., & Ory, M. G. (2003). Introduction to the special section on Resources for Enhancing Alzheimer's Caregiver Health (REACH). *Psychology and Aging, 18*, 357–360.

Schulz, R., Boerner, K., & Hebert, R. S. (2008). Caregiving and bereavement. In M. S. Stroebe, R. O. Hansson, H. Schut, & W. Stroebe (Eds.), *Handbook of bereavement research and practice. Advances in theory and intervention*. Washington, DC: American Psychological Association.

Schulz, R., & Schlarb, J. (1987–1988). Two decades of research on dying: What do we know about the patient? *Omega: Journal of Death and Dying, 18*, 299–317.

Schumann, C. M., Barnes, C. C., Lord, C., & Courchesne, E. (2009). Amygdala enlargement in toddlers with autism related to severity of social and communication impairments. *Biological Psychiatry, 66*, 942–949.

Schunn, C. D., & Anderson, J. R. (1999). The generality/specificity of expertise in scientific reasoning. *Cognitive Science, 23*, 337–370.

Schwartz, C. E., Wright, C. I., Shin, L. M., Kagan, J., & Rauch, S. L. (2003). Inhibited and uninhibited infants "grown up": Adult amygdalar response to novelty. *Science, 300*, 1952–1953.

Schwartz, M. B., & Henderson, K. E. (2009). Does obesity prevention cause eating disorders? *Journal of the American Academy of Child and Adolescent Psychiatry, 48*, 784–786.

Schweinhart, L. J., Montie, J., Xiang, Z., Barnett, W. S., Belfield, C. R., & Nores, M. (2005). *Lifetime effects: The High Scope Perry Preschool Study through age 40*. Ypsilanti, MI: High Scope Educational Research Foundation.

Schwenck, C., Bjorklund, D. F., & Schneider, W. (2007). Factors influencing the incidence of utilization deficiencies and other patterns of recall/strategy-use relations in a strategic memory task. *Child Development 78*, 1771–1787.

Schwenck, C., Bjorklund, D. F., & Schneider, W. (2009). Developmental and individual differences in young children's use and maintenance of a selective memory strategy, *Developmental Psychology, 45*, 1034–1050.

Schwerdtfeger, K. L., & Shreffler, K. M. (2009). Trauma of pregnancy loss and infertility among mothers and involuntarily childless women in the United States. *Journal of Loss and Trauma, 14*, 211–227.

Schwitzgebel, E. (1999). Gradual belief change in children. *Human Development, 42*, 283–296.

Scialfa, C. T., Esau, S. P., & Joffe, K. M. (1998). Age, target–distracter similarity, and visual search. *Experimental Aging Research, 24*, 337–358.

Scogin, F., Walsh, D., Hanson, A., Stump, J., & Coates, A. (2005). Evidence-based psychotherapies

for depression in older adults. *Clinical Psychology: Science and Practice, 12*, 222–237.

Scott, G., Leritz, L. E., & Mumford, M. D. (2004). The effectiveness of creativity training: A quantitative review. *Creativity Research Journal, 16*, 361–388.

Scott, K. D., Klaus, P. H., & Klaus, M. H. (1999). The obstetrical and postpartum benefits of continuous support during childbirth. *Journal of Women's Health and Gender Based Medicine, 8*, 1257–1264.

Scott, R. M., & Baillargeon, R. (2009). Which penguin is this? Attributing false beliefs about object identity at 18 months. *Child Development, 80*, 1172–1196.

Scott, W. A., Scott, R., & McCabe, M. (1991). Family relationships and children's personality: A cross-cultural, cross-source comparison. *British Journal of Social Psychology, 30*, 1–20.

Scourfield, J., Rice, F., Thapar, A., Harold, G. T., Martin, N., & McGuffin, P. (2003). Depressive symptoms in children and adolescents: Changing etiological influences with development. *Journal of Child Psychology and Psychiatry and Allied Disciplines, 44*, 968–976.

Seale, C. (1991). A comparison of hospice and conventional care. *Social Science and Medicine, 32*, 147–152.

Seaton, E. K., Scottham, K. M., & Sellers, R. M. (2006). The status model of racial identity development in African American adolescents: Evidence of structure, trajectories, and well-being. *Child Development, 77*, 1416–1426.

Seaton, M., Marsh, H. W., & Craven, R. G. (2009). Earning its place as a pan-human theory: Universality of the big-fish-little-pond effect across 41 culturally and economically diverse countries. *Journal of Educational Psychology, 101*, 403–419.

Sebby, R., & Papini, D. (1994). Postformal reasoning during adolescence and young adulthood: The influence of problem relevancy, *Adolescence, 29*, 389–400.

Seccombe, K. (2000). Families in poverty in the 1990s: Trends, causes, consequences, and lessons learned. *Journal of Marriage and the Family, 62*, 1094–1113.

Segal, N. L. (2005). Evolutionary studies of cooperation, competition, and altruism. A twin-based approach. In R. L. Burgess & K. MacDonald (Eds.), *Evolutionary perspectives on human development*. Thousand Oaks, CA: Sage.

Segal, N. L., & Johnson, W. (2009). Twin studies of general mental ability. In Y. Kim (Ed.), *Handbook of behavior genetics*. New York: Springer.

Seger, J. Y., & Thorstensson, A. (2000). Muscle strength and electromyogram in boys and girls followed through puberty. *European Journal of Applied Physiology, 81*, 54–61.

Segovia, C., Hutchinson, I., Laing, D. G., & Jinks, A. L. (2002). A quantitative study of fungiform papillae and taste pore density in adults and children. *Developmental Brain Research, 138*, 135–146.

Seidman, L. J. (2006). Neuropsychological functioning in people with ADHD across the lifespan. *Clinical Psychology Review, 26*, 466–485.

Seiffge-Krenke, I. (1998). Adolescents' health: A developmental perspective. Mahwah, NJ: Erlbaum.

Seiffge-Krenke, I. (2003). Testing theories of romantic development from adolescence to young adulthood: Evidence of a developmental sequence. *International Journal of Behavioral Development, 27*, 519–531.

Seiffge-Krenke, I. (2006). Leaving home or still in the nest? Parent–child relationships and psychological health as predictors of different leaving home patterns. *Developmental Psychology, 42*, 864–876.

Selby, J. M., & Bradley, B. S. (2003). Infants in groups: A paradigm for the study of early social experience. *Human Development, 46*, 197–221.

Seleen, D. R. (1982). The congruence between actual and desired use of time by older adults: A predictor of life satisfaction. *Gerontologist, 22,* 95–99.

Selikowitz, M. (2009). *ADHD: The facts,* 2nd ed. New York: Oxford.

Selkoe, D. J. (1997). Alzheimer's disease: From genes to pathogenesis. *American Journal of Psychiatry, 154,* 1198.

Selman, R. L. (1976). Social cognitive understanding: A guide to educational and clinical experience. In T. Lickona (Ed.), *Moral development and behavior: Theory, research and social issues.* New York: Holt, Rinehart & Winston.

Selman, R. L. (1980). *The growth of interpersonal understanding.* New York: Academic Press.

Seltzer, J. A. (2000). Families formed outside of marriage. *Journal of Marriage and the Family, 62,* 1247–1268.

Seltzer, M. M., & Li, L. W. (2000). The dynamics of caregiving: Transitions during a three-year prospective study, *Gerontologist, 40,* 165–178.

Semiz, S., Kurt, F., Kurt, D.T., Zencir, M., & Sevinç, O. (2008). Pubertal development of Turkish children. *Journal of Pediatric Endocrinology & Metabolism, 21,* 951–961.

Senter, M. S., & Senter, R. (1997). Student outcomes and the adult learner. *Continuing Higher Education Review, 61,* 75–87.

Sentse, M., Veenstra, R., Lindenberg, S., Verhulst, F. C., & Ormel, J. (2009). Buffers and risks in temperament and family for early adolescent psychopathology: Generic, conditional, or domain-specific effects? The Trails Study. *Developmental Psychology, 45,* 419–435.

Serafica, F. C., & Vargas, L. A. (2006). Cultural diversity in the development of child psychopathology. In D. Cicchetti & D. J. Cohen (Eds.), *Developmental psychopathology: Vol. 1. Theory and method* (2nd ed.). Hoboken, NJ: Wiley.

Serbin, L. A., Poulin-Dubois, D., & Eichstedt, J. A. (2002). Infants' response to gender-inconsistent events. *Infancy, 3,* 531–542.

Serbin, L. A., Powlishta, K. K., & Gulko, J. (1993). The development of sex typing in middle childhood. *Monographs of the Society for Research in Child Development, 58* (2, Serial No. 232).

Serbin, L. A., Tonick, I. J., & Sternglanz, S. H. (1977). Shaping cooperative cross-sex play. *Child Development, 48,* 924–929.

Sergeant, M. J. T., Davies, M. N. O., Dickins, T. E., & Griffiths, M. D. (2005). The self-reported importance of olfaction during human mate choice. *Sexualities, Evolution, and Gender, 7,* 199–213.

Servaty-Seib, H. L. (2009). Death of a friend during adolescence. In D. E. Balk & C. A. Corr (Eds.), *Adolescent encounters with death, bereavement, and coping.* New York: Springer.

Servin, A., Bohlin, G., & Berlin, L. (1999). Sex differences in 1-, 3-, and 5-year-olds' toy-choice in a structured play-session. *Scandinavian Journal of Psychology, 40,* 43–48.

Settersten, R. A., Jr. (1998). A time to leave home and a time never to return? Age constraints on the living arrangements of young adults. *Social Forces, 76,* 1373–1400.

Settersten, R. A., Jr. (2005). Linking the two ends of life: What gerontology can learn from childhood studies. *Journals of Gerontology: Social Sciences, 60B,* S173–S180.

Settersten, R. A., Jr., & Trauten, M. E. (2009). The new terrain of old age: Hallmarks, freedoms, and risks. In V. L. Bengtson, M. Silverstein, N. M. Putney, & D. Gans (Eds.), *Handbook of theories of aging* (2nd ed.). New York: Springer.

Shafer, V. L., & Garrido-Nag, K. (2009). The neurodevelopmental bases of language. In E. Hoff & M. Shatz (Eds.), *Blackwell Handbook of Language Development,* 21–45. Malden, MA: Wiley-Blackwell.

Shaffer, D., & Pfeffer, C. R. (2001). Practice parameters for the assessment and treatment of children and adolescents with suicidal behavior. *Journal of the American Academy of Child and Adolescent Psychiatry, 40,* 24S–51S.

Shaffer, D. R., Pegalis, L. J., & Cornell, D. P. (1992). Gender and self-disclosure revisited: Personal and contextual variations in self-disclosure to same-sex acquaintances. *Journal of Social Psychology, 132,* 307–315.

Shanahan, L., McHale, S. M., Osgood, D. W., & Crouter, A. C. (2004). Conflict frequency with mothers and fathers from middle childhood to late adolescence: Within- and between-families comparisons. *Developmental Psychology, 43,* 539–550.

Shanahan, M. J. (2000). Pathways to adulthood in changing societies: Variability and mechanisms in life course perspective. *Annual Review of Sociology, 26,* 667–692.

Shanahan, M. J., Erickson, L. D., & Bauer, D. J. (2005). One hundred years of knowing: The changing science of adolescence, 1904 and 2004. *Journal of Research on Adolescence, 15,* 383–394.

Shanahan, M. J., Finch, M. D., Mortimer, J. T., & Ryu, S. (1991). Adolescent work experience and depressive affect. *Social Psychology Quarterly, 54,* 299–317.

Shannon, J. B. (2006). *Death and dying sourcebook* (2nd ed.). Detroit, MI: Omnigraphics.

Shapiro, D. N., Peterson, C., & Stewart, A. J. (2009). Legal and social contexts and mental health among lesbian and heterosexual mothers. *Journal of Family Psychology, 23,* 255–262.

Shapiro, E. R. (2001). Grief in interpersonal perspective: Theories and their implications. In M. S. Stroebe, R. O. Hansson, W. Stroebe, & H. Schut (Eds.), *Handbook of bereavement research. Consequences, coping, and care.* Washington, DC: American Psychological Association.

Shapiro-Mendoza, C. K., Kimball, M., Tomashek, K. M., Anderson, R. N., & Blanding, S. (2009). U.S. infant mortality trends attributable to accidental suffocation and strangulation in bed from 1984 through 2004: Are rates increasing? *Pediatrics, 123,* 533–539.

Sharabany, R., Gershoni, R., & Hofman, J. E. (1981). Girlfriend, boyfriend: Age and sex differences in intimate friendship. *Developmental Psychology, 17,* 800–808.

Sharpe, P. A., Jackson, K. L., White, C., Vaca, V. L., Hickey, T., Gu, J., & Otterness, C. (1997). Effects of a one-year physical activity intervention for older adults at congregate nutrition sites. *Gerontologist, 37,* 208–215.

Sharpe, T. M., Killen, J. D., Bryson, S. W., Shisslak, C. M., Estes, L. S., Gray, N., Crago, M., & Taylor, C. G. (1998). Attachment style and weight concerns in preadolescent and adolescent girls. *International Journal of Eating Disorders, 23,* 39–44.

Shaver, P. R., & Fraley, R. C. (2008). Attachment, loss, and grief: Bowlby's views and current controversies. In J. Cassidy & P. R. Shaver (Eds.), *Handbook of attachment: Theory, research, and clinical applications* (2nd ed.). New York: Guilford.

Shaw, B. A., Krause, N., Chatters, L. M., Connell, C. M., & Ingersoll-Dayton, B. (2004). Emotional support from parents early in life, aging, and health. *Psychology and Aging, 19,* 4–12.

Shaywitz, B. A., Shaywitz, S. E., Pugh, K. R., Constable, R. T., Skudlarski, P., & Fulbright, R. K. (1995). Sex differences in the functional organization of the brain for language. *Nature, 373,* 607–609.

Shaywitz, B. A., Shaywitz, S. E., Pugh, K. R., Fulbright, R. K., Mencl, E., Bonstable, R. T., Skudlarski, P., Fletcher, J. J., Lyon, G. R., & Gore, J. C. (2001). The neurobiology of dyslexia. *Clinical Neuroscience, 1,* 291–299.

Shaywitz, S. E., Fletcher, J. M., Holahan, J. M., Shneider, A. E., Marchione, K. E., Stuebing, K. K., Francis, D. J., Pugh, K. R., & Shaywitz, B. A. (1999). Persistence of dyslexia: The Connecticut Longitudinal Study at Adolescence. *Pediatrics, 104,* 1351–1359.

Shea, C. H., Park, J. H., & Braden, H. W. (2006). Age-related effects in sequential motor learning. *Physical Therapy, 86,* 478–488.

Sheiner, E., Shoham-Vardi, I., Sheiner, E. K., Press, F., Hackmon-Ram, R., Mazor, M., & Katz, M. (2000). A comparison between the effectiveness of epidural analgesia and parenteral pethidine during labor. *Archives of Gynecology and Obstetrics, 263,* 95–98.

Shepard, R. J. (1997). Curricular physical activity and academic performance. *Pediatric Exercise Science, 9,* 113–126.

Shepard, R. N., & Metzler, J. (1971). Mental rotation of three-dimensional objects. *Science, 171,* 701–703.

Shepard, T. H. & Lemire, R. J. (2004). *Catalog of teratogenic agents* (11th ed.). Baltimore, MD: Johns Hopkins University Press.

Shih, M., Pittinsky, T. L., & Ambady, N. (1999). Stereotype susceptibility: Identity salience and shifts in quantitative performance. *Psychological Science, 10,* 80–83.

Shihadeh, A., & Al-Najdawi, W. (2001). Forceps or vacuum extraction: A comparison of maternal and neonatal morbidity. *Eastern Mediterranean Health, 7,* 106–114.

Shiner, R. (2006). Temperament and personality in childhood. In D. K. Mroczek & T. D. Little (Eds.), *Handbook of personality development.* Mahwah, NJ: Erlbaum.

Ship, J. A., Pearson, J. D., Cruise, L. J., Brant, L. J., & Metter, E. J. (1996). Longitudinal changes in smell identification. *Journals of Gerontology: Biological Sciences and Medical Sciences, 51,* M86–M91.

Ship, J. A., & Weiffenbach, J. M. (1993). Age, gender, medical treatment, and medication effects on smell identification. *Journal of Gerontology, 48,* M26–M32.

Shneidman, E. S. (1973). *Deaths of man.* New York: Quadrangle.

Shneidman, E. S. (1980). *Voices of death.* New York: Harper & Row.

Shoda, Y., & Mischel, W. (2000). Reconciling contextualism with the core assumptions of personality psychology. *European Journal of Personality, 14,* 407–428.

Shonk, S. M., & Cicchetti, D. (2001). Maltreatment, competency deficits, and risk for academic and behavioral maladjustment. *Developmental Psychology, 37,* 3–17.

Shringarpure, R., & Davies, K. J. A. (2009). Free radicals and oxidative stress in aging. In V. L. Bengtson, M. Silverstein, N. M. Putney, & D. Gans (Eds.), *Handbook of theories of aging* (2nd ed.). New York: Springer.

Shurkin, J. N. (1992). *Terman's kids: The groundbreaking study of how the gifted grow up.* Boston: Little, Brown.

Shute, N. (2001, January 15). Children in anguish. A call for better treatment of kids' mental ills. *U.S. News & World Report,* 42.

Shweder, R. A., Goodnow, J. J., Hatano, G., LeVine, R. A., Markus, H. R., & Miller, P. J. (2006). The cultural psychology of development: One mind, many mentalities. In W. Damon & R. M. Lerner (Eds. in Chief) & R. M. Lerner (Vol. Ed.), *Handbook of child psychology: Vol. 1. Theoretical models of human development* (6th ed.). Hoboken, NJ: Wiley.

Shweder, R. A., Mahapatra, M., & Miller, J. G. (1990). Culture and moral development. In J. W. Stigler, R. A. Shweder, & G. Herdt (Eds.), *Cultural psychology. Essays on comparative human development*. Cambridge, England: Cambridge University Press.

Sibulesky, L., Hayes, K. C., Pronczuk, A., Weigel-DiFranco, C., Rosner, B., & Berson, E. L. (1999). Safety of 7500 RE (25,000 IU) vitamin A daily in adults with retinitis pigmentosa. *American Journal of Clinical Nutrition, 69,* 656–663.

Siebenbruner, J., Zimmer-Gembeck, M. J., & Egeland, B. (2007). Sexual partners and contraceptive use: A 16-year prospective study predicting abstinence and risk behavior. *Journal of Research on Adolescence, 17,* 179–206.

Siebold, C. (1992). *The hospice movement. Easing death's pains.* New York: Twayne Publishers.

Siegler, I. C., & Brummett, B. H. (2000). Associations among NEO personality assessments and well-being at mid-life: Facet-level analyses. *Psychology and Aging, 15,* 710–714.

Siegler, R. (2006). Microgenetic analysis of learning. In D. Kuhn & R. Siegler (Vol. Eds.), *Handbook of child psychology: Cognition, perception, and language: Vol. 2.* Hoboken, NJ: Wiley and Sons.

Siegler, R. S. (1981). Developmental sequences within and between concepts. *Monographs of the Society for Research in Child Development, 46* (2, Serial No. 189).

Siegler, R. S. (1989). Hazards of mental chronometry: An example from children's subtraction. *Journal of Educational Psychology, 81,* 497–506.

Siegler, R. S. (1996). *Emerging minds: The process of change in children's thinking.* New York: Oxford University Press.

Siegler, R. S. (2000). The rebirth of children's learning. *Child Development, 71,* 26–35.

Siegler, R. S., & Svetina, M. (2006). What leads children to adopt new strategies? A microgenetic/cross sectional study of class inclusion. *Child Development, 77,* 997–1015.

Sigelman, C. K., Carr, M. B., & Begley, N. L. (1986). Developmental changes in the influence of sex-role stereotypes on person perception. *Child Study Journal, 16,* 191–205.

Sigman, M., & Capps, L. (1997). *Children with autism. A developmental perspective.* Cambridge, MA: Harvard University Press.

Signorielli, N., & Kahlenberg, S. (2001). Television's world of work in the nineties. *Journal of Broadcasting and Electronic Media, 45,* 4–22.

Signorielli, N., & Lears, M. (1992). Children, television, and conceptions about chores: Attitudes and behaviors. *Sex Roles, 27,* 157–170.

Silk, J. B., Brosnan, S. F., Vonk, J., Henrich, J., Povinelli, D. J., Richardson, A. S., Lambeth, S. P., Mascaro, J., & Schapiro, S. J. (2005). Chimpanzees are indifferent to the welfare of unrelated group members. *Nature, 437*(7063), 1357–1359.

Silva, H. P., & Padez, C. (2006). Secular trends in age at menarche among Caboclo populations from Pará, Amazonia, Brazil: 1930-1980. *American Journal of Human Biology, 18,* 83–92.

Silventoinen, K., Haukka, J., Dunkel, L., Tynelius, P., & Rasmussen, F. (2008). Genetics of pubertal timing and its associations with relative weight in childhood and adult height: The Swedish young male twins study. *Pediatrics, 121,* e885–e891.

Silverberg, S. B., & Steinberg, L. (1990). Psychological well-being of parents with early adolescent children. *Developmental Psychology, 26,* 658–666.

Silverman, I. W. (2003). Gender differences in resistance to temptation: Theories and evidence. *Developmental Review, 23,* 219–259.

Silverman, P. R. (2000). *Never too young to know. Death in children's lives.* New York: Oxford University Press.

Silverman, P. R., & Worden, J. W. (1993). Children's reactions to the death of a parent. In M. S. Stroebe, W. Stroebe, & R. O. Hansson (Eds.),

Handbook of bereavement. Theory, research, and intervention. Cambridge, England: Cambridge University Press.

Silverman, W. K., Allen, A., & Ortiz, C. D. (2010). Lessons learned from Katrina and other devastating hurricanes: Steps necessary for adequate preparedness, response, and intervention. In R. P. Kilmer, V. Gil-Rivas, R. G. Tedeschi, & L. G. Calhoun (Eds.), *Helping families and communities recover from disaster: Lessons learned from Hurricane Katrina and its aftermath.* Washington, DC: American Psychological Association.

Silverstein, M., & Ruiz, S. (2006). Breaking the chain: How grandparents moderate the transmission of maternal depression to their grandchildren. *Family Relations, 55,* 601–612.

Sim, L. A., Homme, J. H., Lteif, A. N., Vande Voort, J. L., Schak, K. M., & Ellingson, J. (2009). Family functioning and maternal distress in adolescent girls with anorexia nervosa. *International Journal of Eating Disorders, 42,* 531–539.

Simcock, G., & Hayne, H. (2002). Breaking the barrier? Children fail to translate their preverbal memories into language. *Psychological Science, 13,* 225–231.

Simcock, G., & Hayne, H. (2003). Age-related changes in verbal and nonverbal memory during early childhood. *Developmental Psychology, 39,* 805–814.

Simmons, R. G., & Blyth, D. A. (1987). *Moving into adolescence: The impact of pubertal change and school context.* New York: Hawthorne, Aldine de Gruyter.

Simmons, R. G., Burgeson, R., Carlton-Ford, S., & Blyth, D. A. (1987). The impact of cumulative change in early adolescence. *Child Development, 58,* 1220–1234.

Simon, H. A. (1995). The information-processing theory of mind. *American Psychologist, 50,* 507–508.

Simon, H. A. (2001). Creativity in the arts and sciences. *The Canyon Review and Stand, 23,* 203–220.

Simonton, D. K. (1984). *Genius, creativity, and leadership: Historiometric inquiries.* Cambridge, MA: Harvard University Press.

Simonton, D. K. (1990). Creativity in the later years: Optimistic prospects for achievement. *Gerontologist, 30,* 626–631.

Simonton, D. K. (1999). Creativity from a historiometric perspective. In R. J. Sternberg (Ed.), *Handbook of creativity.* New York: Cambridge University Press.

Simonton, D. K. (1999). *Origins of genius: Darwinian perspectives on creativity.* New York: Oxford University Press.

Simpson, J. A., Collins, W. A., Tran, S., & Haydon, K. C. (2007). Attachment and the experience and expression of emotions in romantic relationships: A developmental perspective. *Journal of Personality and Social Psychology, 92,* 355–367.

Simpson, J. A., Rholes, W. S., Campbell, L., Tran, S., & Wilson, C. L. (2003). Adult attachment, the transition to parenthood, and depressive symptoms. *Journal of Personality and Social Psychology, 84,* 1172–1187.

Simpson, J. L., & Elias, S. (2003). *Genetics in obstetrics and gynecology.* Philadelphia: Saunders.

Simpson, R., & Otten, K. (2005). Structuring behavior management strategies and building social competence. In D. Zager (Ed.), *Autism spectrum disorders. Identification, education, and treatment* (3rd ed.). Mahwah, NJ: Erlbaum.

Singer, D. G., Golinkoff, R. M., & Hirsh-Pasek, K. (Eds.) (2006). *Play 5 learning: How play motivates and enhances children's cognitive and social-emotional growth.* New York: Oxford University Press.

Singer, L. T., Arendt, R., Fagan, J., Minnes, S., Salvator, A., Bolek, T., & Becker, M. (1999). Neonatal visual information processing in cocaine-

exposed and non-exposed infants. *Infant Behavior and Development, 22,* 1–15.

Singer, T., Verhaeghen, P., Ghisletta, P., Lindenberger, U., & Baltes, P. B. (2003). The fate of cognition in very old age: Six-year longitudinal findings in the Berlin Aging Study (BASE). *Psychology and Aging, 18,* 318–331.

Singh, B., Berman, B. M., Simpson, R. L., & Annechild, A. (1998). Incidence of premenstrual syndrome and remedy usage: A national probability sample study. *Alternative Therapeutic Health Medicines, 4,* 75–79.

Singh, D., & Bronstad, P. M. (2001). Female body odour is a potential cue to ovulation. *Proceedings of Biological Science, 268,* 797–801.

Singh, K., & Ozturk, M. (2000). Effect of part-time work on high school mathematics and science course taking. *Journal of Educational Research, 94,* 67–74.

Sinnott, J. (1996). The developmental approach: Postformal thought as adaptive intelligence. In F. Blanchard-Fields & T. M. Hess (Eds.), *Perspectives on cognitive change in adulthood and aging.* New York: McGraw-Hill.

Sinnott, J. D. (1984). Postformal reasoning: The relativistic stage. In M. L. Commons, F. A. Richards & C. Armon (Eds.), *Beyond formal operations,* 298–325. New York: Praeger.

Skelton, J. A., Cook, S. R., Auinger, P., Klein, J. D., & Barlow, S. E. (2009). Prevalence and trends of severe obesity among U.S. children and adolescents. *Academic Pediatrics, 9,* 322–329.

Skinner, B. F. (1983). Intellectual self-management in old age. *American Psychologist, 38,* 239–244.

Skinner, E. A., & Zimmer-Gembeck, M. J. (2007). The development of coping. *Annual Review of Psychology, 58,* 119–144.

Skotko, B. G. (2009, June 15). With new prenatal testing, will babies with Down syndrome slowly disappear? *Archives of Disease in Childhood, 94,* 823–826.

Slaby, R. G., & Guerra, N. G. (1988). Cognitive mediators of aggression in adolescent offenders: 1. Assessment. *Developmental Psychology, 24,* 580–588.

Slater, A. (2004). Visual perception. In G. Bremner & A. Fogel (Eds.), *Blackwell handbook of infant development,* 5–34. Malden, MA: Blackwell Publishing.

Slater, C. L. (2003). Generativity versus stagnation: An elaboration of Erikson's adult stage of human development. *Journal of Adult Development, 10,* 53–65.

Slater, R., Cantarella, A., Gallella, S., Worley, A. Boyd, S., Meek, J., & Fitzgerald, M. (2006). Cortical pain responses in human infants. *The Journal of Neuroscience, 26,* 3662–3666.

Slaughter, V., Jaakkola, R., & Carey, S. (1999). Constructing a coherent theory: Children's biological understanding of life and death. In M. Siegal & C. C. Peterson (Eds.), *Children's understanding of biology and health.* Cambridge, UK: Cambridge University Press.

Slaughter, V., & Lyons, M. (2003). Learning about life and death in early childhood. *Cognitive Psychology, 46,* 1–30.

Slavkin, M., & Stright, A. D. (2000). Gender role differences in college students from one- and two-parent families. *Sex Roles, 42,* 23–37.

Sliwinski, M., & Buschke, H. (1999). Cross-sectional and longitudinal relationships among age, cognition, and processing speed. *Psychology and Aging, 14,* 18–33.

Sliwinski, M., Buschke, H., Kuslansky, G., Senior, G., & Scarisbrick, D. (1994). Proportional slowing and addition speed in old and young adults. *Psychology and Aging, 9,* 72–80.

Slobin, D. I. (1979). *Psycholinguistics* (2nd ed.). Glenview, IL: Scott, Foresman.

Sloboda, D. M., Hart, R., Doherty, D. A., Pennell, C. E., & Hickey, M. (2007). Age at menarche:

Influences of prenatal and postnatal growth. *Journal of Clinical Endocrinology and Metabolism, 92,* 46–50.

Sloboda, Z. (2009). School prevention. In C. G. Leukefeld, T. P. Gullotta, & M. Staton-Tindall (Eds.), *Adolescent substance abuse. Evidence-based approaches to prevention and treatment.* New York: Springer.

Slotkin, T. A. (1998). Fetal nicotine or cocaine exposure: Which one is worse? *Journal of Pharmacology and Experimental Therapy, 285,* 931–945.

Smagorinsky, P. (1995). The social construction of data: Methodological problems of investigating learning in the zone of proximal development. *Review of Educational Research, 65,* 191–212.

Smaldone, A., Honig, J. C., & Byrne, M. W. (2007). Sleepless in America: Inadequate sleep and relationships to health and well-being of our nation's children. *Pediatrics, 119,* S29–S37.

Small, M. (1999). *Our babies, ourselves: How biology and culture shape the way we parent.* New York: Anchor Publishing.

Small, S., & Memmo, M. (2004). Contemporary models of youth development and problem prevention: Toward an integration of terms, concepts, and models. *Family Relations, 53,* 3–11.

Smetana, J. G. (1981). Preschool children's conceptions of moral and social rules. *Child Development, 52,* 1333–1336.

Smetana, J. G. (2006). Social-cognitive domain theory: Consistencies and variations in children's moral and social judgments. In M. Killen & J. G. Smetana (Eds.), *Handbook of moral development.* Mahwah, NJ: Erlbaum.

Smetana, J. G., Campione-Barr, N., & Metzger, A. (2006). Adolescent development in interpersonal and societal contexts. *Annual Review of Psychology, 57,* 255–284.

Smith, A. D., & Earles, J. L. K. (1996). Memory changes in normal aging. In F. Blanchard-Fields & T. M. Hess (Eds.), *Perspectives on cognitive change in adulthood and aging.* New York: McGraw-Hill.

Smith, A. K., Mick, E., & Raraone, S. V. (2009). Advances in genetic studies of attention-deficit/hyperactivity disorder. *Current Psychiatry Reports, 11,* 143–148.

Smith, G. E., Petersen, R. C., Ivnik, R. J., Malec, J. F., & Tangalos, E. G. (1996). Subjective memory complaints, psychological distress, and longitudinal change in objective memory performance. *Psychology and Aging, 11,* 272–279.

Smith, G. J., & Carlsson, I. M. (1990). *The creative process: A functional model based on empirical studies from early childhood to middle age.* Madison, CT: International Universities Press.

Smith, G. J. W. (2005). How should creativity be defined? *Creativity Research Journal, 17,* 293–295.

Smith, J., & Baltes, P. B. (1990). Wisdom-related knowledge: Age/cohort differences in response to life-planning problems. *Developmental Psychology, 26,* 494–505.

Smith, K. E., Landry, S. H., & Swank, P. R. (2000). Does the content of mothers' verbal stimulation explain differences in children's development of verbal and nonverbal cognitive skills? *Journal of School Psychology, 38,* 27–49.

Smith, L. B., & Thelen, E. (1993). *A dynamic systems approach to development: Applications.* Cambridge, MA: MIT Press.

Smith, P. K. (1978). A longitudinal study of social participation in preschool children: Solitary and parallel play reexamined. *Developmental Psychology, 14,* 517–523.

Smith, P. K. (2005). Types and functions of play in human development. In B. J. Ellis & D. F. Bjorklund (Eds.), *Origins of the social mind.* New York: Guilford Press.

Smith, P. K., & Daglish, L. (1977). Sex differences in parent and infant behavior in the home. *Child Development, 48,* 1250–1254.

Smith, P. K., Mahdavi, J., Carvalho, M., Fisher, S., Russell, S., & Tippett, N. (2008). Cyberbullying: Its nature and impact in secondary school pupils. *Journal of Child Psychology and Psychiatry, 49,* 376–385.

Smith, T. W., Berg, C. A., Florsheim, P., Uchino, B. N., Pearce, G., Hawkins, M., Henry, N. J. M., Beveridge, R. M., Skinner, M. A., & Olsen-Cerny, C. (2009). Conflict and collaboration in middle-aged and older couples: I. Age differences in agency and communion during marital interaction. *Psychology and Aging, 24,* 259–273.

Smithmyer, C. M., Hubbard, J. A., & Simons, R. F. (2000). Proactive and reactive aggression in delinquent adolescents: Relations to aggression outcome expectancies. *Journal of Clinical Child Psychology, 29,* 86–93.

Smolak, L. (2009). Risk factors in the development of body image, eating problems, and obesity. In L. Smolak & J. K. Thompson (Eds.), *Body image, eating disorders, and obesity in youth.* Washington, DC: American Psychological Association.

Smyke, A. T., Dumitrescu, A., & Zeanah, C. H. (2002). Attachment disturbances in young children. I: The continuum of caretaking casualty. *Journal of the American Academy of Child and Adolescent Psychiatry, 41,* 972–982.

Snarey, J., & Samuelson, P. (2008). Moral education in the cognitive developmental tradition: Lawrence Kohlberg's revolutionary ideas. In L. P. Nucci & D. Narvaez (Eds.), *Handbook of moral and character education.* New York: Routledge.

Snarey, J. R. (1985). Cross-cultural universality of social–moral development: A critical review of Kohlbergian research. *Psychological Bulletin, 97,* 202–232.

Snow, C. E., Arlman-Rupp, A., Hassing, Y., Jobse, J., Joosken, J., & Vorster, J. (1976). Mother's speech in three social classes. *Journal of Psycholinguistic Research, 5,* 1–20.

Snow, D. (2006). Regression and reorganization of intonation between 6 and 23 months. *Child Development, 77,* 281–296.

Snowdon, D. (2002). *Aging with grace: What the Nun Study teaches us about leading longer, healthier, and more meaningful lives.* New York: Bantam Books.

Snowdon, D. A. (1997). Aging and Alzheimer's disease: Lessons from the Nun Study. *Gerontologist, 37,* 150–156.

Snyder, E. Y., & Loring, J. F. (2005). A role for stem cell biology in the physiological and pathological aspects of aging. *Journal of the American Geriatrics Society, 53,* S287–S291.

Sobolewski, J. M., & King, V. (2005). The importance of the coparental relationship for nonresident fathers' ties to children. *Journal of Marriage and Family, 67,* 1196–1212.

Sodian, B., & Thoermer, C. (2008). Precursors to a theory of mind in infancy: Perspectives for research on autism. *Quarterly Journal of Experimental Psychology, 61,* 27–39.

Son, L. K. (2004). Spacing one's study: Evidence for a metacognitive control strategy. *Journal of Experimental Psychology: Learning, Memory, and Cognition, 30,* 601–604.

Son, L. K., & Metcalfe, J. (2000). Metacognitive and control strategies in study-time allocation. *Journal of Experimental Psychology: Learning, Memory, and Cognition, 26,* 204–221.

Song, J., & Manchester, J. (2009). Revisiting the 1983 Social Security reforms, 25 years later. *Research on Aging, 31,* 233–260.

Soriano, F. I., Rivera, L. M., Williams, K. J., Daley, S. P., & Reznik, V. M. (2004). Navigating between cultures: The role of culture in youth violence. *Journal of Adolescent Health, 34,* 169–176.

Sostek, A. M., Vietze, P., Zaslow, M., Kreiss, L., van der Waals, F., & Rubinstein, D. (1981). Social context in caregiver-infant interaction: A film study of Fais and the United States. In T. M. Field, A. M. Sostek, P. Vietze, & P. H. Liederman (Eds.), *Culture and early interactions.* Hillsdale, NJ: Erlbaum.

Sotomi, O., Ryan, C. A., O'Connor, G., & Murphy, B. P. (2007). Have we stopped looking for a red reflex in newborn screening? *Irish Medical Journal, 100,* 398–400.

Span, P. (2000, August 27). Home alone. *The Washington Post Magazine,* 12–15, 24–25.

Spaniol, J., Madden, D. J., & Voss, A. (2006). A diffusion model analysis of adult age differences in episodic and semantic long-term memory retrieval. *Journal of Experimental Psychology: Learning, Memory, and Cognition, 32,* 101–117.

Sparling, P. B., O'Donnell, E. M., & Snow, T. K. (1998). The gender difference in distance running performance has plateaued: An analysis of world rankings from 1980 to 1996. *Medicine and Science in Sports and Exercise, 30,* 1725–1729.

Sparrow, S. S., & Davis, S. M. (2000). Recent advances in the assessment of intelligence and cognition. *Journal of Child Psychology and Psychiatry, 41,* 117–131.

Spear, L. P. (2000a). The adolescent brain and age-related behavioral manifestations. *Neuroscience and Biobehavioral Reviews, 24,* 417–463.

Spear, L. P. (2000b). Neurobehavioral changes in adolescence. *Current Directions in Psychological Science, 9,* 111–114.

Spear, L. P. (2010). *The behavioral neuroscience of adolescence.* New York: W. W. Norton.

Spearman, C. (1927). *The abilities of man.* New York: Macmillan.

Speece, M. W., & Brent, S. B. (1984). Children's understanding of death: A review of three components of a death concept. *Child Development, 55,* 1671–1686.

Speece, M. W., & Brent, S. B. (1992). The acquisition of a mature understanding of three components of the concept of death. *Death Studies, 16,* 211–229.

Spelke, E. S. (1990). Principles of object perception. *Cognitive Science, 14,* 29-56.

Spelke, E. S. (1994). Initial knowledge: Six suggestions. *Cognition, 50,* 431–445.

Spelke, E. S., Breinlinger, K., Macomber, J., & Jacobson, K. (1992). Origins of knowledge. *Psychological Review, 99,* 605–632.

Spelke, E. S., & Hermer, L. (1996). Early cognitive development: Objects and space. In R. Gelman & T. Fong (Eds.), *Handbook of perception and cognition* (2nd ed.). New York: Academic Press.

Spence, J. T. (1985). Achievement American style: The rewards and costs of individualism. *American Psychologist, 40,* 1285–1295.

Spence, J. T., & Buckner, C. E. (2000). Instrumental and expressive traits, trait stereotypes, and sexist attitudes. *Psychology of Women Quarterly, 24,* 44–62.

Spence, J. T., & Hall, S. K. (1996). Children's gender-related self-perceptions, activity preferences, and occupational stereotypes: A test of three models of gender constructs. *Sex Roles, 35,* 659–691.

Spence, J. T., & Helmreich, R. L. (1978). *Masculinity and femininity: Their psychological dimensions, correlates, and antecedents.* Austin: University of Texas Press.

Spence, J. T., Helmreich, R. L., & Stapp, J. (1973). The Personal Attributes Questionnaire: A Measure of sex-role stereotypes and masculinity-femininity. *JSAS Catalog of Selected Documents in Psychology, 4,* 43–44 (Ms. 617).

Spencer, J. P., Blumberg, M. S., McMurray, B., Robinson, S. R., Samuelson, L. K., & Tomblin, J. B. (2009). Short arms and talking eggs: Why we should no longer abide the nativist-empiricist debate. *Child Development Perspectives, 3,* 79–87.

Spencer, J. P., Corbetta, D., Buchanan, P., Clearfield, M., Ulrich, B., & Schoner, G. (2006). Moving toward a grand theory of development: In memory of Esther Thelen. *Child Development, 77,* 1521–1538.

Spencer, M. B. (2006). Phenomenology and ecological systems theory: Development of diverse groups. In W. Damon & R. M. Lerner (Eds. in Chief) & R. M. Lerner (Vol. Ed.), *Handbook of child psychology: Vol. 1. Theoretical models of human development* (6th ed.). Hoboken, NJ: Wiley.

Spencer, M. B., & Markstrom-Adams, C. (1990). Identity processes among racial and ethnic minority children in America. *Child Development, 61,* 290–310.

Spencer, P. E. (1996). The association between language and symbolic play at two years: Evidence from deaf toddlers. *Child Development, 67,* 867–876.

Spera, C. (2006). Adolescents' perceptions of parental goals, practices, and styles in relation to the motivation and achievement. *Journal of Early Adolescence, 26,* 456–490.

Sperry, S., Roehrig, M., & Thompson, J. K. (2009). Treatment of eating disorders in childhood and adolescence. In L. Smolak & J. K. Thompson (Eds.), *Body image, eating disorders, and obesity in youth.* Washington, DC: American Psychological Association.

Spiby, H., Henderson, B., Slade, P., Escott, D., & Fraser, R. B. (1999). Strategies for coping with labour: Does antenatal education translate into practice? *Journal of Advanced Nursing, 29,* 388–394.

Spieler, D. H., & Griffin, Z. M. (2006). The influence of age on the time course of word preparation in multiword utterances. *Language and Cognitive Processes, 21,* 291–321.

Spilich, G. J., Vesonder, G. T., Chiesi, H. L., & Voss, J. F. (1979). Text processing of domain-related information for individuals with high and low domain knowledge. *Journal of Verbal Learning and Verbal Behavior, 18,* 275–290.

Spinath, B., Spinath, F. M., Harlaar, N., & Plomin, R. (2006). Predicting school achievement from general cognitive ability, self-perceived ability, and intrinsic value. *Intelligence, 34,* 363–374.

Spirduso, W. W., & MacRae, P. G. (1990). Motor performance and aging. In J. E. Birren & K. W. Schaie (Eds.), *Handbook of the psychology of aging* (3rd ed.). San Diego: Academic Press.

Spitz, R. A. (1946). Anaclitic depression: An inquiry into the genesis of psychiatric conditions in early childhood, II. *Psychoanalytic Study of the Child, 2,* 313–342.

Spitze, G., & Trent, K. (2006). Gender differences in adult sibling relations in two-child families. *Journal of Marriage and Family, 68,* 977–992.

Spokane, A. R., Meir, E. I., & Catalano, M. (2000). Person-environment congruence and Holland's theory: A review and reconsideration. *Journal of Vocational Behavior, 57,* 137–187.

Spoth, R., Trudeau, L., Guyll, M., Shin, C., & Redmond, C. (2009). Universal intervention effects on substance use among young adults mediated by delayed adolescent substance initiation. *Journal of Consulting and Clinical Psychology, 77,* 620–632.

Springen, K. (2004, January 26). The ancient art of making babies. *Newsweek,* 51.

Springer, S., & Deutsch, G. (1997). *Left brain, right brain: Perspectives from cognitive neuroscience* (5th ed.). New York: W. H. Freeman.

Spruyt, K., Aitken, R., So, K., Charlton, M., Adamson, T., & Horne, R. (2008). Relationship between sleep/wake patterns, temperament and overall development in term infants over the first year of life. *Early Human Development, 84*(5), 289–296.

Sroufe, L. A. (1977). Wariness of strangers and the study of infant development. *Child Development, 48,* 1184–1199.

Sroufe, L. A. (1996). *Emotional development: The organization of emotional life in the early years.* Cambridge, England: University of Cambridge Press.

Sroufe, L. A. (1997). Psychopathology as an outcome of development. *Development and Psychopathology, 9,* 251–268.

Sroufe, L. A. (2009). The concept of development in developmental psychopathology. *Child Development Perspectives, 3,* 178–183.

Sroufe, L. A., Bennett, C., Englund, M., Urban, J., & Shulman, S. (1993). The significance of gender boundaries in preadolescence: Contemporary correlates and antecedents of boundary violation and maintenance. *Child Development, 64,* 455–466.

Sroufe, L. A., Egeland, B., Carlson, E., & Collins, W. A. (2005). Placing early attachment experiences in developmental context: The Minnesota Longitudinal Study. In K. E. Grossmann, K. Grossmann, & E. Waters (Eds.), *Attachment from infancy to adulthood: The major longitudinal studies.* New York: Guilford Press.

Sroufe, L. A., & Rutter, M. (1984). The domain of developmental psychopathology. *Child Development, 55,* 17–29.

Sroufe, L. A., Waters, E., & Matas, L. (1974). Contextual determinants of infant affectional response. In M. Lewis & L. A. Rosenblum (Eds.), *The origins of fear.* New York: Wiley.

St. Clair, D., Xu, M., Wang, P., Yu, Y., Fang, Y., Zhang, F., Zheng, X., Gu, N., Feng, G., Sham, P., & He, L. (2005). Rates of adult schizophrenia following prenatal exposure to the Chinese famine of 1959–1961. *Journal of the American Medical Association, 294,* 557–562.

St. George, D. (2001, June 8). A child's unheeded cry for help. *The Washington Post,* A1, A20–A21.

St. George, D. (2010, March 18). Households with little room for a generation gap. *The Washington Post,* p. B6.

St. John, W., Cameron, C., & McVeigh, C. (2005). Meeting the challenge of new fatherhood during the early weeks. *Obstetrics and Gynaecology, 34,* 180–189.

St. Petersburg–USA Orphanage Research Team (2008). The effects of early social-emotional and relationship experience on the development of young orphanage children. *Monographs of the Society for Research in Child Development, 73* (3, Serial No. 291).

Stambrook, M., & Parker, K. C. H. (1987). The development of the concept of death in childhood: A review of the literature. *Merrill-Palmer Quarterly, 33,* 133–157.

Stanley, S. M., Amato, P. R., Johnson, C. A., & Markman, H. J. (2006). Premarital education, marital quality, and marital stability: Findings from a large, random household survey. *Journal of Family Psychology, 20,* 117–126.

Stanovich, K. E. (1986). Matthew effects in reading: Some consequences of individual differences in the acquisition of literacy. *Reading Research Quarterly, 21,* 360–407.

Stanovich, K. E., & Stanovich, P. J. (1999). How research might inform the debate about early reading acquisition. In J. Oakhill & R. Beard (Eds.), *Reading development and the teaching of reading,* 12–41. Oxford: Blackwell.

Stanovich, K. E., & West, R. F. (1997). Reasoning independently of prior belief and individual differences in actively open-minded thinking. *Journal of Educational Psychology, 89,* 342–357.

Staudinger, U. M., & Baltes, P. B. (1996). Interactive minds: A facilitative setting for wisdom-related performance? *Journal of Personality and Social Psychology, 71,* 746–762.

Staudinger, U. M., Smith, J., & Baltes, P. B. (1992). Wisdom-related knowledge in a life review task: Age differences and the role of professional specialization. *Psychology and Aging, 7,* 271–281.

Steele, C. M. (1997). A threat in the air: How stereotypes shape intellectual identity and performance. *American Psychologist, 52,* 613–629.

Steele, C. M. (1999). Thin ice: "Stereotype threat" and black college students. *Atlantic, 284,* 44–54.

Steele, C. M., & Aronson, J. (1995). Stereotype threat and the intellectual test performance of African Americans. *Journal of Personality and Social Psychology, 69,* 797–811.

Steenari, M., Vuontela, V., Paavonen, E. J., Carlson, S., Fjallberg, M., & Aronen, E. T. (2003). Working memory and sleep in 6- to 13-year-old schoolchildren. *Journal of the American Academy of Child and Adolescent Psychiatry, 42,* 85–92.

Steenland, K., Henley, J., & Thun, M. (2002). All-cause and cause-specific death rates by educational status for two million people in two American Cancer Society cohorts, 1959–1999. *American Journal of Epidemiology, 156,* 11–21.

Steffen, L. M., Dai, S., Fulton, J. E., & Labarthe, D. R. (2009). Overweight in children and adolescents associated with TV viewing and parental weight: Project HeartBeat! *American Journal of Preventive Medicine, 37l,* S50–S55.

Stein, C. H. (2009). "I owe it to them": Understanding felt obligation toward parents in adulthood. In K. Shifren (Ed.), *How caregiving affects development. Psychological implications for child, adolescent, and adult caregivers.* Washington, DC: American Psychological Association.

Stein, J. H., & Reiser, L. W. (1994). A study of white middle-class adolescent boys' responses to "semenarche" (the first ejaculation). *Journal of Youth and Adolescence, 23,* 373–384.

Stein, L. (2009, July 8). Variants of "umami" taste receptor contribute to our individualized flavor worlds. *Eurekalert!* Available at: www.eurekalert.org/pub_releases?2009-07/mcsc-vo070809.php. Accessed: November 23, 2009.

Stein, Z. A., Susser, M. W., Saenger, G., & Marolla, F. (1975). *Famine and human development: The Dutch hunger winter of 1944–1945.* New York: Oxford University Press.

Steinberg, L. (1989). Pubertal maturation and parent–adolescent distance: An evolutionary perspective. In G. R. Adams, R. Montemayor, & T. P. Gullotta (Eds.), *Advances in adolescent behavior and development* (pp. 71–97). Newbury Park, CA: Sage.

Steinberg, L. (2001). We know some things: Parent–adolescent relationships in retrospect and prospect. *Journal of Research on Adolescence, 11,* 1–19.

Steinberg, L. (2007). Risk taking in adolescence: New perspectives from brain and behavioural science. *Current Directions in Psychological Sciences, 16,* 55–59.

Steinberg, L. (2008a). A social neuroscience perspective on adolescent risk-taking. *Developmental Review, 28,* 78–106.

Steinberg, L. (2008b). *Adolescence* (8th ed.). New York: McGraw-Hill.

Steinberg, L., Albert, D., Cauffman, E., Banich, M., Graham, S., & Woolard, J. (2008). Age differences in sensation seeking and impulsivity as indexed by behavior and self-report: evidence for a dual systems model. *Developmental Psychology, 44,* 1764–1778.

Steinberg, L., & Avenevoli, S. (2000). The role of context in the development of psychopathology: A conceptual framework and some speculative propositions. *Child Development, 71,* 66–74.

Steinberg, L., & Dornbusch, S. M. (1991). Negative correlates of part-time employment during adolescence: Replication and elaboration. *Developmental Psychology, 27,* 304–313.

Steinberg, L., Dornbusch, S. M., & Brown, B. B. (1992). Ethnic differences in adolescent achievement: An ecological perspective. *American Psychologist, 47,* 723–729.

Steinberg, L., Fegley, S., & Dornbusch, S. M. (1993). Negative impact of part-time work on adolescent adjustment: Evidence from a longitudinal study. *Developmental Psychology, 29,* 171–180.

Steiner, J. E. (1979). Human facial expressions in response to taste and smell stimulation. In H. W. Reese & L. P. Lipsitt (Eds.), *Advances in child development and behavior* (Vol. 13). New York: Academic Press.

Steinhausen, H.-C. (2007). Longitudinal perspectives, outcome and prognosis. In T. Jaffa & B. McDermott (Eds.), *Eating disorders in children and adolescents.* Cambridge, UK: Cambridge University Press.

Stemler, S. E., Grigorenko, E. L., Jarvin, L., & Sternberg, R. J. (2006). Using the theory of successful intelligence as a basis for augmenting AP exams in Psychology and Statistics. *Contemporary Educational Psychology, 31,* 344–376.

Stemp, P. S., Turner, J., & Noh, S. (1986). Psychological distress in the postpartum period: The significance of social support. *Journal of Marriage and the Family, 48,* 271–277.

Stene-Larsen, K., Borge, A. I., & Vollrath, M. E. (2009). Maternal smoking in pregnancy and externalizing behavior in 18-month-old children: Results from a population-based prospective study. *Journal of the American Academy of Child & Adolescent Psychiatry, 48,* 283–289.

Stephens, M. A., Townsend, A. L., Martire, L. M., & Druley, J. A. (2001). Balancing parent care with other roles: Interrole conflict of adult daughter caregivers. *Journal of Gerontology: Psychological Sciences, 56B,* P24–34.

Stephens, M. A. P., Franks, M. M., Martire, L. M., Norton, T. R., & Atienza, A. A. (2009). Women at midlife: Stress and rewards of balancing parent care with employment and other family roles. In K. Shifren (Ed.), *How caregiving affects development. Psychological implications for child, adolescent, and adult caregivers.* Washington, DC: American Psychological Association.

Stepp, L. S. (2001, November 2). Children's worries take new shape. *The Washington Post,* C1, C4.

Stern, D. (1977). *The first relationship: Infant and mother.* Cambridge, MA: Harvard University Press.

Stern, M., & Karraker, K. H. (1989). Sex stereotyping of infants: A review of gender labeling studies. *Sex Roles, 20,* 501–522.

Sternberg, R. J. (1985). *Beyond IQ: A triarchic theory of human intelligence.* Cambridge, MA: Cambridge University Press.

Sternberg, R. J. (1988a). *The triarchic mind: A new theory of human intelligence.* New York: Viking.

Sternberg, R. J. (1988b). Triangulating love. In R. J. Sternberg and M. L. Barnes (Eds.), *The psychology of love.* New Haven, CT: Yale University Press.

Sternberg, R. J. (1997). Educating intelligence: Infusing the triarchic theory into school instruction. In R. J. Sternberg & E.L. Grigorenko (Eds.), *Intelligence, heredity, and environment.* New York: Cambridge University Press.

Sternberg, R. J. (Ed.) (1999a). *Handbook of creativity.* New York: Cambridge University Press.

Sternberg, R. J. (1999b). The theory of successful intelligence. *Review of General Psychology, 3,* 292-316.

Sternberg, R. J. (2003). *Wisdom, intelligence, and creativity synthesized.* Cambridge, England: Cambridge University Press.

Sternberg, R. J. (2004). Culture and intelligence. *American Psychologist, 59,* 325–338.

Sternberg, R. J. (2006a). A duplex theory of love. In R. J. Sternberg & K. Weis (Eds.), *The new psychology of love.* New Haven, CT: Yale University Press.

Sternberg, R. J. (2006b). The nature of creativity. *Creativity Research Journal, 18,* 87–98.

Sternberg, R. J. (2009a). The Rainbow and Kaleidoscope projects: a new psychological approach to undergraduate admissions. *European Psychologist, 14,* 279-287.

Sternberg, R. J. (2009b). The theory of successful intelligence as a basis for new forms of ability testing at the high school, college, and graduate school levels. In J. C. Kaufman (Ed.), *Intelligent testing: Integrating psychological theory and clinical practice* (pp. 113-147). New York: Cambridge University Press.

Sternberg, R. J. (2010). Academic intelligence is not enough! WICS: An expanded model for effective practice in school and later life. In D. D. Preiss & R. J. Sternberg (Eds.), *Innovations in educational psychology: Perspectives on learning, teaching, and human development,* 403-440. New York: Springer.

Sternberg, R. J. (2010). WICS: A new model for cognitive education. *Journal of Cognitive Education and Psychology, 9,* 34-46.

Sternberg, R. J., Castejón, J. L., Prieto, J. D., Hautamäki, J., & Grigorenko, E. L. (2001). Confirmatory factor analysis of the Sternberg Triarchic Abilities Test in three international samples: An empirical test of the triarchic theory of intelligence. *European Journal of Psychological Assessment, 17,* 1–16.

Sternberg, R. J., Grigorenko, E. L., & Bundy, D. A. (2001). The predictive value of IQ. *Merrill-Palmer Quarterly, 47,* 1–41.

Stevens, D. P., & Truss, C. V. (1985). Stability and change in adult personality over 12 and 20 years. *Developmental Psychology, 21,* 568–584.

Stevens, G. (1999). Age at immigration and second language proficiency among foreign-born adults. *Language in Society, 28,* 555–578.

Stevens, M. M., & Dunsmore, J. C. (1996). Adolescents who are living with a life-threatening illness. In C. A. Corr & D. E. Balk (Eds.), *Handbook of adolescent death and bereavement.* New York: Springer.

Stevens, R. J., & Slavin, R. E. (1995). The cooperative elementary school: Effects on students' achievement, attitudes, and social relations. *American Educational Research Journal, 32,* 321–351.

Stevens, W. D., Hasher, L., Chiew, K. S., & Grady, C. L. (2008). A neural mechanism underlying memory failure in older adults. *Journal of Neuroscience, 28,* 12820–12824.

Stevenson, H. W., Chen, C., & Lee, S. (1993). Mathematics achievement of Chinese, Japanese, and American children: Ten years later. *Science, 259,* 53–58.

Stevenson, H. W., & Lee, S. Y. (1990). Contexts of achievement: A study of American, Chinese, and Japanese children. *Monographs of the Society for Research in Child Development, 55* (1–2, Serial No. 221).

Stevenson, H. W., Lee, S. Y., & Stigler, J. W. (1986). Mathematics achievement of Chinese, Japanese, and American children. *Science, 231,* 693–699.

Stevenson, H. W., Stigler, J. W., Lee, S., Lucker, G. W., Kitamura, S., & Hsu, C. (1985). Cognitive performance and academic achievement of Japanese, Chinese, and American children. *Child Development, 56,* 718–734.

Stevenson, R. J., Mahmut, M., & Sundqvist, N. (2007). Age related changes in odor discrimination. *Developmental Psychology, 43,* 253–260.

Stewart, P. W., Lonky, E., Reihman, J., Pagano, J., Gump, B. B., & Darvill, T. (2008). The Relationship between Prenatal PCB Exposure and Intelligence (IQ) in 9-Year-Old Children. *Environmental Health Perspectives, 116,* 1416–1422.

Stewart, R. B., & Marvin, R. S. (1984). Sibling relations: The role of conceptual perspective-taking in the ontogeny of sibling caregiving. *Child Development, 55,* 1322–1332.

Stewart, R. C. (2007). Maternal depression and infant growth: A review of recent evidence. *Maternal and Child Nutrition, 3,* 94–107.

Stice, E., & Presnell, K. (2007). *The Body Project: Promoting body acceptance and preventing eating disorders: Facilitator guide.* New York: Oxford University Press.

Stice, E., Rohde, P., Gau, J., & Shaw, H. (2009). An effectiveness trial of a dissonance-based eating disorder prevention program for high-risk adolescent girls. *Journal of Consulting and Clinical Psychology, 77,* 825–834.

Stifter, C. (2003). Child effects on the family: An example of the extreme case and a question of methodology. In A. C. Crouter & A. Booth (Eds.), *Children's influence on family dynamics. The neglected side of family relationships.* Mahwah, NJ: Erlbaum.

Stigler, J. W., Lee, S. Y., & Stevenson, H. W. (1987). Mathematics classrooms in Japan, Taiwan, and the United States. *Child Development, 58,* 1272–1285.

Stillion, J. M., & McDowell, E. E. (1996). *Suicide across the life span: Premature exits* (2nd ed.). Washington, DC: Taylor & Francis.

Stillion, J. M., & Papadatou, D. (2002). Suffer the children: An examination of psychosocial issues in children and adolescents with terminal illness. *American Behavioral Scientist, 46,* 299–315.

Stine, E. A. L., Soederberg, L. M., & Morrow, D. G. (1996). Language and discourse processing through adulthood. In F. Blanchard-Fields & T. M. Hess (Eds.), *Perspectives on cognitive change in adulthood and aging.* New York: McGraw-Hill.

Stine-Morrow, E. A. L., Loveless, M. K., & Soederberg, L. M. (1996). Resource allocation in on-line reading by younger and older adults. *Psychology and Aging, 11,* 475–486.

Stine-Morrow, E. A. L., Parisi, J. M., Morrow, D. G., Greene, J., & Park, D. C. (2007). An engagement model of cognitive optimization through adulthood. *Journals of Gerontology B: Psychological and Social Sciences, 62,* 62–69.

Stine-Morrow, E. A. L., Parisi, M. M., Morrow, D. G., & Park, D. C. (2008). The effects of an engaged lifestyle on cognitive vitality: A field experiment. *Psychology and Aging, 23,* 778–786.

Stipek, D., Gralinski, H., & Kopp, C. (1990). Self-concept development in the toddler years. *Developmental Psychology, 26,* 972–977.

Stipek, D., & Hakuta, K. (2007). Strategies to ensure that no child starts from behind. In J. L. Aber, S. J. Bishop-Josef, S. M. Jones, K. T. McLearn, & D. A. Phillips (Eds.), *Child development and social policy: Knowledge for action.* Washington, DC: American Psychology Association.

Stipek, D. J. (1984). The development of achievement motivation. In R. Ames & C. Ames (Eds.), *Research on motivation in education* (Vol. 1). Orlando, FL: Academic Press.

Stipek, D. J., Feiler, R., Daniels, D., & Milburn, S. (1995). Effects of different instructional approaches on young children's achievement and motivation. *Child Development, 66,* 209–223.

Stipek, D. J., & Gralinski, J. H. (1996). Children's beliefs about intelligence and school performance. *Journal of Educational Psychology, 88,* 397–407.

Stipek, D. J., & Mac Iver, D. J. (1989). Developmental change in children's assessment of intellectual competence. *Child Development, 60,* 521–538.

Stipek, D. J., Recchia, A., & McClintic, S. (1992). Self-evaluation in young children. *Monographs of the Society for Research in Child Development, 57* (1, Serial No. 226).

Stith, S. M., Rosen, K. H., Middleton, K. A., Busch, A. L., Lundeberg, K., & Carlton, R. P. (2000). The intergenerational transmission of spouse abuse: A meta-analysis. *Journal of Marriage and the Family, 62,* 640–654.

Stoddart, T., & Turiel, E. (1985). Children's concepts of cross-gender activities. *Child Development, 56,* 1241–1252.

Stone, R. (1992). Can a father's exposure lead to illness in his children? *Science, 258,* 31.

Stone, R. (2009). *A teenager talks about growing up with ADHD*. NYU Child Study Center. Available at: www.aboutourkids.org. Accessed: December 2, 2009.

Stones, M. J., & Kozma, A. (1985). Physical performance. In N. Charness (Ed.), *Aging and human performance*. Chichester, England & New York: Wiley.

Stoolmiller, M. (1999). Implications of the restricted range of family environments for estimates of heritability and nonshared environment in behavior-genetic adoption studies. *Psychological Bulletin, 125*, 392–409.

Storgaard, L., Bonde, J. P., Ernst, E., Spano, M., Andersen, C. Y., Frydenberg, M., & Olsen, J. (2003). Does smoking during pregnancy affect sons' sperm count? *Epidemiology, 14*, 278–286.

Story, M., Nanney, M. S., & Schwartz, M. B. (2009). Schools and obesity prevention: Creating school environments and policies to promote healthy eating and physical activity. *Milbank Quarterly, 87*, 71–100.

Straus, M. A., & Gelles, R. J. (1986). Societal change and change in family violence from 1975 to 1985 as revealed by two national surveys. *Journal of Marriage and the Family, 48*, 465–479.

Straus, M. A., & Gelles, R. J. (Edited with C. Smith) (1990). *Physical violence in American families. Risk factors and adaptations to violence in 8145 families*. New Brunswick, NJ: Transaction Publishers.

Streissguth, A. P., Barr, H. M., Bookstein, F. L., Sampson, P. D., & Olson, H. C. (1999). The long-term neurocognitive consequences of prenatal alcohol exposure: A 14-year study. *Psychological Science, 10*, 186–190.

Streissguth, A. P., & Dehaene, P. (1993). Fetal alcohol syndrome in twins of alcoholic mothers: Concordance of diagnosis and IQ. *American Journal of Medical Genetics, 47*, 857–861.

Streri, A. (2003). Cross-modal recognition of shape from hand to eyes in human newborns. *Somatosensory Motor Research, 20*, 13–18.

Streri, A., & Gentaz, E. (2004). Cross-modal recognition of shape from hand to eyes and handedness in human newborns. *Neuropsychologia, 42*, 1365–1369.

Streri, A., & Pecheux, M. (1986). Vision-to-touch and touch-to-vision transfer of form in 5-month-old infants. *British Journal of Developmental Psychology, 4*, 161–167.

Strigini, P., Sansone, R., Carobbi, S., & Pierluigi, M. (1990). Radiation and Down's syndrome. *Nature, 347*, 717.

Stringer, J. S., Sinkala, M., Goldenberg, R. L., Kumwenda, R., Acosta, E. P., Aldrovandi, G. M., Stout, J. P., & Vermund, S. H. (2004). Universal nevirapine upon presentation in labor to prevent mother-to-child HIV transmission in high prevalence settings. *AIDS, 18*, 939–943.

Strober, M., Freeman, R., Lampert, C., Diamond, J., & Kaye, W. (2000). Controlled family study of anorexia nervosa and bulimia nervosa: Evidence of shared liability and transmission of partial syndromes. *American Journal of Psychiatry, 157*, 393–401.

Stroebe, M. (2001a). Bereavement research and theory: Retrospective and prospective. *American Behavioral Scientist, 44*, 854–865.

Stroebe, M. (2001b). Gender differences in adjustment to bereavement: An empirical and theoretical review. *Review of General Psychology, 5*, 62–83.

Stroebe, M., Schut, H., & Boerner, K. (2010). Continuing bonds in adaptation to bereavement: Toward theoretical integration. *Clinical Psychology Review, 30*, 259–268.

Stroebe, M. S., & Schut, H. A. W. (1999). The dual process model of coping with bereavement: Rationale and description. *Death Studies, 23*, 197–224.

Strong, B., DeVault, C., & Cohen, T. F. (2008). *The marriage and family experience. Intimate relationships in a changing society* (10th ed.). Belmont, CA: Thomson Wadsworth.

Strough, J., Leszczynski, J. P., Neely, T. L., Flinn, J. A., & Margrett, J. (2007). From adolescence to later adulthood: Femininity, masculinity, and androgyny in six age groups. *Sex Roles, 57*, 385–396.

Substance Use and Mental Health Services Administration, Office of Applied Studies (2009, May 21). *The NSDUH Report: substance use among women during pregnancy and following childbirth*. Rockville, MD: SAMHSA.

Sudhalter, V., & Braine, M. D. S. (1985). How does comprehension of passives develop? A comparison of actional and experiential verbs. *Journal of Child Language, 12*, 455–470.

Suitor, J. J. (1991). Marital quality and satisfaction with the division of household labor across the family life cycle. *Journal of Marriage and the Family, 53*, 221–230.

Suitor, J. J., Sechrist, J., Plikuhn, M., Pardo, S. T., Gilligan, M., & Pillemer, K. (2009). The role of perceived maternal favoritism in sibling relations in midlife. *Journal of Marriage and Family, 71*, 1026–1038.

Suitor, J. J., Sechrist, J., Plikuhn, M., Pardo, S. T., & Pillemer, K. (2008). Within-family differences in parent-child relations across the life course. *Current Directions in Psychological Science, 17*, 334–338.

Sullivan, H. S. (1953). *The interpersonal theory of psychiatry*. New York: Norton.

Sullivan, S., & Ruffman, T. (2004). Social understanding: How does it fare with advancing years? *British Journal of Psychology, 95*, 1–18.

Sullivan/Anderson, A. (2009, March 30). How to end the war over sex ed. *Time*, 40–43.

Sulloway, F. J. (2007). Birth order and intelligence. *Science, 316*, 1711–1717.

Super, D. E., Savickas, M. L., & Super, C. M. (1996). The life-span, life-space approach to careers. In D. Brown, L. Brooks, & Associates (Eds.), *Career choice and development* (3rd ed.). San Francisco: Jossey-Bass.

Surdin, A. (2009, January 1). In several states, a push to stem cyber-bullying. *The Washington Post*, A3.

Susser, M., & Stein, Z. (1994). Timing in prenatal nutrition: A reprise of the Dutch Famine Study. *Nutrition Reviews, 52*, 84–94.

Sutton-Brown, M., & Suchowersky, O. (2003). Clinical and research advances in Huntington's disease. *Canadian Journal of Neurological Sciences, 30* (Suppl. 1), S45.

Swain, J. E., Tasgin, E., Mayes, L. C., Feldman, R., Constable, R. T., & Leckman, J. F. (2008). Maternal brain response to own baby-cry is affected by cesarean section delivery. *Journal of Child Psychology and Psychiatry, 49*, 1042–1052.

Swanson, H. L. (1999). What develops in working memory? A life span perspective. *Developmental Psychology, 35*, 986–1000.

Swarr, A. E., & Richards, M. H. (1996). Longitudinal effects of adolescent girls' pubertal development, perceptions of pubertal timing, and parental relations on eating problems. *Developmental Psychology, 32*, 636–646.

Symons, D. K., & Clark, S. E. (2000). A longitudinal study of mother–child relationships and theory of mind in the preschool period. *Social Development, 9*, 3–23.

Szinovacz, M. E., & Davey, A. (2005). Retirement and marital decision making: Effects on retirement satisfaction. *Journal of Marriage and the Family, 67*, 387–398.

Szinovacz, M. E., DeViney, S., & Atkinson, M. P. (1999). Effects of surrogate parenting on grandparents' well-being. *Journal of Gerontology: Social Sciences, 54B*, S376–S388.

Szoeke, C. E. I., Campbell, S., Chiu, E., & Ames, D. (2009) Vascular cognitive disorder. In M. F. Weiner & A. M. Lipton (Eds.), *The American Psychiatric Publishing Textbook of Alzheimer disease and other dementias*. Washington, DC: American Psychiatric Publishing.

T

Tabert, M. H., Manly, J. J., Liu, X., Pelton, G. H., Rosenblum, S., Jacobs, M., Zamora, D., Goodkind, M., Bell, K., Stern, Y., Devanand, D. P. (2006). Neuropsychological prediction of conversion to Alzheimer disease in patients with mild cognitive impairment. *Archives of General Psychiatry, 63*, 916–924.

Tach, L., & Halpern-Meekin, S. (2009). How does premarital cohabitation affect trajectories of marital quality? *Journal of Marriage and Family, 71*, 298–317.

Tackett, J. L., Krueger, R. F., Iacono, W. G., & McGue, M. (2008). Personality in middle childhood: A hierarchical structure and longitudinal connections with personality in late adolescence. *Journal of Research in Personality, 42*, 1456–1462.

Taddio, A. (2002). Conditioning and hyperalgesia in newborns exposed to repeated heel lances, *Journal of the American Medical Association, 288*, 857–861.

Taeymans, J., Clarys, P., Abidi, H., Hebbelinck, M., & Duquet, W. (2009). Developmental changes and predictability of static strength in individuals of different maturity: a 30-year longitudinal study. *Journal of Sports Science, 27*, 833–841.

Taeymans, J., Hebbelinck, M., Borms, J., Clarys, P., Abidi, H., & Duquet, W. (2008). Tracking of adult adiposity in early, average and late maturing children: a thirty year longitudinal growth study. *Journal of Sports Medicine and Physical Fitness. 48*, 326–334.

Tafarodi, R. W., Lo, C., Yamaguchi, S., Lee, W. W., & Katsura, H. (2004). The inner self in three countries. *Journal of Cross-Cultural Psychology, 35*, 97–117.

Tager-Flusberg, H. (2000). Language and understanding minds: Connections in autism. In S. Baron-Cohen, H. Tager-Flusberg, & D. J. Cohen (Eds.), *Understanding other minds. Perspectives from developmental cognitive neuroscience* (2nd ed.). Oxford: Oxford University Press.

Tager-Flusberg, H. (2005). Morphology and syntax in the preschool years. In J. B. Gleason (Ed.), *The development of language* (6th ed.). Boston: Allyn & Bacon.

Takahashi, K. (1990). Are the key assumptions of the "Strange Situation" procedure universal? A view from Japanese research. *Human Development, 33*, 23–30.

Tallal, P., Miller, S. L., Bedi, G., Byma, G., Wang, X., Nagarajan, S. S., Schreiner, C., Jenkins, W. M., & Merzenich, M. M. (1996). Language comprehension in language-learning impaired children improved with acoustically modified speech. *Science, 271*, 81–84.

Talpade, M. (2008). Hispanic versus African American girls: body image, nutrition, and puberty. *Adolescence, 43*, 119–127.

Talwar, V., & Lee, K. (2008). Social and cognitive correlates of children's lying behavior. *Child Development, 79*, 866–881.

Tam, C. S., de Zegher, R., Garnett, S. P., Baur, L. A., & Cowell, C. T. (2006). Opposing influences of prenatal and postnatal growth on the timing of menarche. *Journal of Clinical Endocrinology and Metabolism, 91*, 4369–4373.

Tamis-LeMonda, C. S., Adolph, K. E., Lobo, S. A., Karasik, L. B., Ishak, S., Dimitropoulou, K. A. (2008). When infants take mothers' advice: 18-month-olds integrate perceptual and social information to guide motor action. *Developmental Psychology, 44,* 734–746.

Tan, R. S., & Pu, S. J. (2004). Is it andropause? Recognizing androgen deficiency in aging men. *Postgraduate Medicine, 115,* 62–66.

Tan, U., & Tan, M. (1999). Incidences of asymmetries for the palmar grasp reflex in neonates and hand preference in adults. *Neuroreport: For Rapid Communication of Neuroscience Research, 10,* 3254–3256.

Tannen, D. (1991). *You just don't understand: women and men in conversation.* New York: Ballantine.

Tanner, J. L., Arnett, J. J., & Leis, J. A. (2009). Emerging adulthood. Learning and development during the first stage of adulthood. In M. C. Smith (Ed.) & N. DeFrates-Densch (Asst. Ed.), *Handbook of research on adult learning and development.* New York: Routledge.

Tanner, J. M. (1990). *Foetus into man: Physical growth from conception to maturity* (2nd ed.). Cambridge, MA: Harvard University Press.

Tanzi, R. E., & Parson, A. B. (2000). *Decoding darkness. The search for the genetic causes of Alzheimer's disease.* Cambridge, MA: Perseus Publishing.

Tardif, T., & Wellman, H. M. (2000). Acquisition of mental state language in Mandarin- and Cantonese-speaking children. *Developmental Psychology, 36,* 25–43.

Taste science (2010). The Taste Science Laboratory. Available at: www.tastescience.com. Accessed: February 10, 2010.

Taveras, E. M., Rifas-Shiman, S. L., Belfort, M. B., Kleinman, K. P., Oken, E. & Gillman, M. W. (2009). Weight status in the first 6 months of life and obesity at 3 years of age. *Pediatrics, 123,* 1177–1183.

Taylor, C. B., Bryson, S., Luce, K. H., Cunning, D., Doyle, A. C., Abascal, L. B., Rockwell, R., Dev, P., Winzelberg, A. J., & Wilfley, D. E. (2006). Prevention of eating disorders in at-risk college-age women. *Archives of General Psychiatry, 63,* 881–888.

Taylor, M., & Carlson, S. M. (1997). The relation between individual differences in fantasy and theory of mind. *Child Development, 68,* 436–455.

Taylor, M., Carlson, S. M., Maring, B. L., Gerow, L., & Charley, C. M. (2004). The characteristics and correlates of fantasy in school-age children: Imaginary companions, impersonation, and social understanding. *Developmental Psychology, 40,* 1173–1187.

Taylor, M. D., Frier, B. M., Gold, A. E., & Deary, I. J. (2003). Psychosocial factors and diabetes-related outcomes following diagnosis of Type 1 diabetes. *Diabetic Medicine, 20,* 135–146.

Taylor, M. G. (1996). The development of children's beliefs about social and biological aspects of gender differences. *Child Development, 67,* 1555–1571.

Taylor, M. R. (2003). Dealing with death: Western philosophical strategies. In C. D. Bryant (Ed.), *Handbook of death and dying.* Thousand Oaks, CA: Sage.

Taylor, R. D., Jacobson, L., Rodriquez, A. U., Dominguez, A., Cantic, R., Doney, J., Boccuti, A., Alejandro, J., & Tobon, C. (2000). Stressful experiences and the psychological functioning of African-American and Puerto Rican families and adolescents. In R. D. Taylor & M. C. Wang (Eds.), *Resilience across contexts: Family, work, culture, and community.* Mahwah, NJ: Erlbaum.

Taylor, R. E., & Richards, S. B. (1991). Patterns of intellectual differences of black, Hispanic, and white children. *Psychology in the Schools, 28,* 5–9.

Taylor, R. J., Chatters, L. M., & Jackson, J. S. (2007). Religious and spiritual involvement among older African Americans, Caribbean black, and non-Hispanic whites: Findings from the National Survey of American Life. *Journal of Gerontology: Social Sciences, 62B,* S238–S250.

Taylor, S. E., Saphire-Bernstein, S., & Seeman, T. E. (2010). Are plasma oxytocin in women and plasma vasopressin in men biomarkers of distressed pair-bond relationships? *Psychological Science, 21,* 3–7.

Teachman, B. A. (2006). Aging and negative affect: The rise and fall and rise of anxiety and depression symptoms. *Psychology and Aging, 21,* 201–207.

Teachman, J. D. (2000). Diversity of family structure: Economic and social influences. In D. H. Demo, K. R. Allen, & M. A. Fine (Eds.), *Handbook of family diversity.* New York: Oxford University Press.

Teachman, J. D. (2002). Stability across cohorts in divorce risk factors. *Demography, 39,* 331–351.

Teachman, J. D. (2003). Premarital sex, premarital cohabitation and the risk of subsequent marital dissolution among women. *Journal of Marriage and the Family, 65,* 444–455.

Teachman, J., & Tedrow, L. (2008). The demography of stepfamilies in the United States. In J. Pryor (Ed.), *The international handbook of stepfamilies: Policy and practice in legal, research, and clinical environments.* Hoboken, NJ: Wiley.

Tedeschi, R. G., & Calhoun, L. G. (2004). Post-traumatic growth: Conceptual foundations and empirical evidence. *Psychological Inquiry, 15,* 1–18.

Teeter, P. A. (1998). *Interventions for ADHD. Treatment in developmental context.* New York: Guilford.

Temple, E., Poldrack, R. A., Protopapas, A., Nagarajan, S., Salz, T., Tallal, P., Merzenich, M. M., & Gabrieli, J. D. (2000). Disruption of the neural response to rapid acoustic stimuli in dyslexia: Evidence from functional MRI. *Proceedings of the National Academy of Science, 97,* 13907–13912.

Tenenbaum, H. R., & Leaper, C. (2003). Parent–child conversations about science: The socialization of gender inequities. *Developmental Psychology, 39,* 34–47.

Tenenbaum, H. R., Poe, M. V., Snow, C. E., Tabors, P., & Ross, S. (2007). Maternal and child predictors of low-income children's educational attainment. *Journal of Applied Development Psychology, 28,* 227–238.

Teno, J. M., Clarridge, B. R., Casey, V., Welch, L. C., Wetle, T., Shield, R., & Mor, V. (2004). Family perspectives on end-of-life care at the last place of care. *Journal of the American Medical Association, 291,* 88–93.

Terman, L. M. (1954). The discovery and encouragement of exceptional talent. *American Psychologist, 9,* 221–238.

Testa, M., Hoffman, J.H., & Livingston, J.A. (2010). Alcohol and sexual risk behaviors as mediators of the sexual victimization-revictimization relationship. *Journal of Consulting and Clinical Psychology, 78,* 249–259.

Teti, D. M. (Ed.) (2005). *Handbook of research methods in developmental science.* Malden, MA: Blackwell Publishing.

Teti, D. M., Sakin, J. W., Kucera, E., & Corns, K. M. (1996). And baby makes four: Predictors of attachment security among preschool-age firstborns during the transition to siblinghood. *Child Development, 67,* 579–596.

Thapar, A. (2003). Attention deficit hyperactivity disorder: New genetic findings, new directions. In R. Plomin, J. C. DeFries, I. W. Craig, & P. McGuffin (Eds.), *Behavioral genetics in the postgenomic era.* Washington, DC: American Psychological Association.

Thapar, A., Harold, G., Rice, F., Ge, X., Boivin, J., Hay, D., van den Bree, M., & Lewis, A. (2007). Do intrauterine or genetic influences explain the foetal origins of chronic disease? A novel experimental method for disentangling effects. *BMC Medical Research Methodology, 7,* 25.

Tharinger, D. (1990). Impact of child sexual abuse on developing sexuality. *Professional Psychology: Research & Practice, 21,* 331–337.

Thelen, E. (1984). Learning to walk: Ecological demands and phylogenetic constraints. In L. P. Lipsitt & C. Rovee-Collier (Eds.), *Advances in infancy research* (Vol. 3). Norwood, NJ: Ablex.

Thelen, E. (1995). Motor development: A new synthesis. *American Psychologist, 50,* 79–95.

Thelen, E. (1996). The improvising infant: Learning about learning to move. In M. R. Merrens & G. G. Brannigan (Eds.). *The developmental psychologists: Research adventures across the life span* (pp. 21–35). McGraw-Hill.

Thelen, M. H., Powell, A. L., Lawrence, C., & Kuhnert, M. E. (1992). Eating and body image concerns among children. *Journal of Clinical Child Psychology, 21,* 41–46.

Thelen, E., & Smith, L. B. (1994). *A dynamic systems approach to the development of cognition and action.* Cambridge, MA: MIT Press.

Theodoridou, A., Rowe, A. C., Penton-Voak, I. S., & Rogers, P. J. (2009). Oxytocin and social perception: Oxytocin increases perceived facial trustworthiness and attractiveness. *Hormones and Behavior, 56,* 128–132.

Thibault, H., Contrand, B., Saubusse, E., Baine, M., & Maurice-Tison, S. (2009). Risk factors for overweight and obesity in French adolescents: Physical activity, sedentary behavior and parental characteristics. *Nutrition,* Epub ahead of print.

Thiede, K. W., & Dunlosky, J. (1999). Toward a general model of self-regulated study: An analysis of selection of items for study and self-paced study time. *Journal of Experimental Psychology: Learning, Memory, and Cognition, 25,* 1024–1037.

Thigpen, J. W. (2009). Early sexual behavior in a sample of low-income, African American children. *Journal of Sex Research, 46,* 67–79.

Thomas, A., & Chess, S. (1986). The New York Longitudinal Study: From infancy to early adult life. In R. Plomin & J. Dunn (Eds.), *The study of temperament: Changes, continuities, and challenges.* Hillsdale, NJ: Erlbaum.

Thomas, A. K., & Bulevich, J. B. (2006). Effective cue utilization reduces memory errors in older adults. *Psychological Aging, 21,* 379–389.

Thomas, F., Renaud, F., Benefice, E., de Meeus, T., & Guegan, J. (2001). International variability of ages at menarche and menopause: Patterns and main determinants. *Human Biology, 73,* 271.

Thomas, J. (1998, May 13). Concerns heighten as U.S. teens work increasing numbers of hours. *The New York Times.* Available at: http://mbhs.bergtraum.k12.ny.us/cybereng/opinion3/working-teens.html. Accessed: January 15, 2005.

Thomas, J. R., Yan, J. H., & Stelmach, G. E. (2000). Movement substructures change as a function of practice in children and adults. *Journal of Experimental Child Psychology, 75,* 228–244.

Thomas, O. N., Caldwell, C. H., Faison, N., & Jackson, J. S. (2009). Promoting academic achievement: The role of racial identity in buffering perceptions of teacher discrimination on academic achievement among African American and Caribbean Black adolescents. *Journal of Educational Psychology, 101,* 420–431.

Thompson, A. M., & Smart, J. L. (1993). A prospective study of the development of laterality: Neonatal laterality in relation to perinatal factors and maternal behavior. *Cortex, 29,* 649–659.

Thompson, D. (2009). A brief history of research and theory on adult learning and cognition. In M. C. Smith (Ed.) & N. DeFrates-Densch (Asst. Ed.), *Handbook of research on adult learning and development.* New York: Routledge.

Thompson, J. R., & Chapman, R. S. (1977). Who is "Daddy" revisited? The status of two-year-olds' overextended words in use and comprehension. *Journal of Child Language, 4,* 359–375.

Thompson, R. A. (1994). Emotion regulation: A theme in search of definition. In N. A. Fox (Ed.), The development of emotion regulation: Biological and behavioral considerations. *Monographs of the Society for Research in Child Development, 59* (Nos. 2–3, Serial No. 240).

Thompson, R. A. (2006). Conversation and developing understanding: Introduction to the special issue. *Merrill-Palmer Quarterly, 52,* 1–16.

Thompson, R. A. (2006). The development of the person: Social understanding, relationships, conscience, and self. In N. Eisenberg (Vol. Ed.), & W. Damon & R. M. Lerner (Eds. in Chief), *Handbook of child psychology: Vol. 3. Social, emotional, and personality development* (6th ed.). Hoboken, NJ: Wiley.

Thompson, R. A., & Amato, P. R. (1999). The post divorce family. An introduction to the issues. In R. A. Thompson & P. R. Amato (Eds.), *The post divorce family. Children, parenting, & society.* Thousand Oaks, CA: Sage.

Thompson, R. A., & Meyer, S. (2007). Socialization of emotion regulation in the family. In J. J. Gross (Ed.), *Handbook of emotion regulation.* New York: Guilford.

Thompson, R. A., Meyer, S., & McGinley, M. (2006). Understanding values in relationships: The development of conscience. In M. Killen & J. G. Smetana (Eds.), *Handbook of moral development.* Mahwah, NJ: Erlbaum.

Thompson, R. A., & Raikes, H. A. (2003). Toward the next quarter-century: Conceptual and methodological challenges for attachment theory. *Development and Psychopathology, 15,* 691–718.

Thompson, R. F. (1975). *Introduction to physiological psychology.* New York: Harper & Row.

Thompson, R. F. (2000). *The brain: An introduction to neuroscience* (3rd ed.). New York: Worth.

Thompson, S. B. N. (2006). *Dementia and memory: A handbook for students and professionals.* Hampshire, UK: Ashgate Publishing.

Thorndike, R. L. (1997). The early history of intelligence testing. In D. P. Flanagan, J. L. Genshaft, & P. L. Harrison (Eds.), *Contemporary intellectual assessment: Theories, tests, and issues.* New York: Guilford.

Thorne, B. (1993). *Gender play: Girls and boys in school.* New Brunswick, NJ: Rutgers University Press.

Thornton, R., & Light, L. L. (2006). Language comprehension and production in normal aging. In J. E. Birren & K. W. Schaie (Eds.), *Handbook of the psychology of aging.* Boston: Elsevier Academic Press.

Thulier, D., & Mercer, J. (2009). Variables associated with breastfeeding duration. *Journal of Obstetrics, Gynecology, and Neonatal Nursing, 38,* 259–268.

Thurber, C. A. (1995). The experience and expression of homesickness in preadolescent and adolescent boys. *Child Development, 66,* 1162–1178.

Thys-Jacobs, S. (2000). Micronutrients and the premenstrual syndrome: The case for calcium. *Journal of the American College of Nutrition, 19,* 220–227.

Tienari, P., Wynne, L. C., Sorri, A., Lahti, I., Laksy, K., Moring, J., Naarala, M., Nieminen, P., & Wahlberg, K. E. (2004). Genotype–environment interaction in schizophrenia-spectrum disorder. Long-term follow-up study of Finnish adoptees. *British Journal of Psychiatry, 184,* 216–222.

Tietjen, A. M., & Walker, L. J. (1985). Moral reasoning and leadership among men in a Papua New Guinea society. *Developmental Psychology, 21,* 982–992.

Tiggemann, M. & Lacey, C. (2009). Shopping for clothes: Body satisfaction, appearance investment, and functions of clothing among female shoppers. *Body Image, 6,* 285–291.

Timmer, E., Bode, C., & Dittmann-Kohli, F. (2003). Expectations of gains in the second half of life: A study of personal conceptions of enrichment in a lifespan perspective. *Ageing & Society, 23,* 3–24.

Tisak, M. S., & Tisak, J. (1990). Children's conceptions of parental authority, friendship, and sibling relations. *Merrill-Palmer Quarterly, 36,* 347–368.

Tita, A. T., Landon, M. B., Spong, C. Y., Lai, Y., Leveno, K. J., Varner, M. W., Moawad, A. H., Caritis, S. N., Meis, P. J., Wapner, R. J., Sorokin, Y., Miodovnik, M., Carpenter, M., Peaceman, A. M., O'Sullivan, M. J., Sibai, B. M., Langer, O., Thorp, J. M., Ramin, S. M., Mercer, B. M., & the Eunice Kennedy Shriver NICHD Maternal–Fetal Medicine Units Network (2009). Timing of elective repeat cesarean delivery at term and neonatal outcomes. *New England Journal of Medicine, 360,* 111–120.

Tither, J. M. & Ellis, B. J. (2008). Impact of fathers on daughters' age at menarche: A genetically and environmentally controlled sibling study. *Developmental Psychology, 44,* 1409–1420.

Tolan, P., Gorman-Smith, D., & Henry, D. (2006). Family violence. *Annual Review of Psychology, 57,* 557–583.

Tomasello, M. (2003) Constructing a language: A usage-based theory of language acquisition. Harvard University Press.

Tomasello, M. (2006). Acquiring linguistic constructions. In D. Kuhn & R. Siegler (Vol. Eds.), *Handbook of child psychology: Cognition, perception, and language: Vol. 2* (6th ed.). Hoboken, NJ: Wiley and Sons.

Tomasello, M. (2009). The usage-based theory of language acquisition. In E. L. Bavin (Ed.), *The Cambridge handbook of child language,* 69–87. New York: Cambridge University Press.

Tomasello, M., Call, J., & Hare, B. (2003). Chimpanzees understand psychological states: The question is which ones and to what extent. *Trends in Cognitive Sciences, 7,* 153–156.

Tomasello, M., with Dweck, C., Silk, J., Skyrms, B., & Spelke, E. (2009). *Why we cooperate.* Cambridge, MA: MIT Press.

Tomblin, J. B. (2009). Children with specific language impairment. In E. L. Bavin (Ed.), *The Cambridge handbook of child language,* 418–431. New York: Cambridge University Press.

Tomlinson-Keasey, C., & Keasey, C. B. (1974). The mediating role of cognitive development in moral judgment. *Child Development, 45,* 291–298.

Tomlinson-Keasey, C., & Little, T. D. (1990). Predicting educational attainment, occupational achievement, intellectual skill, and personal adjustment among gifted men and women. *Journal of Educational Psychology, 82,* 442–455.

Tomporowski, P. D., Davis, C. L., Miller, P. H., Naglieri, J. A. (2008). Exercise and children's intelligence, cognition, and academic achievement. *Educational Psychology Review, 20,* 111–131.

Tong, V. T., Jones, J. R., Dietz, P. M., D'Angelo, D., & Bombard, J. M. (2009, May 29). Trends in smoking before, during, and after pregnancy— Pregnancy Risk Assessment Monitoring System (PRAMS), United States, 31 sites, 2000–2005. *Morbidity and Mortality Weekly Report Surveillance Summary, 58,* 1–31.

Torges, C. M., Stewart, A. J., & Duncan, L. E. (2008). Achieving ego integrity: Personality development in late midlife. *Journal of Research in Personality, 42,* 1004–1019.

Torner, N., Valerio, L., Costa, J., Parron, I., Dominguez, A. (2006). Rubella outbreak in young adults of Brazilian origin in a Barcelona suburb, October-December 2005. *Euro Surveill, 11,* (2):E060223.3. Available at: http://www.eurosurveillance.org/ew/2006/060223.asp#3. Accessed: February 10, 2007.

Torrance, E. P. (1968). A longitudinal examination of the fourth grade slump in creativity. *Gifted Child Quarterly, 12,* 195–199.

Torrance, E. P. (1975). Creativity research in education: Still alive. In I. A. Taylor & J. W. Getzels (Eds.), *Perspectives in creativity.* Chicago: Aldine-Atherton.

Torrance, E. P. (1988). The nature of creativity as manifest in its testing. In R. J. Sternberg (Ed.), *The nature of creativity: Contemporary psychological perspectives.* Cambridge, England: Cambridge University Press.

Torres-Mejía, G., Cupul-Uicab, L. A., Allen, B., Galal, O., Salazar-Martínez, E., & Lazcano-Ponce, E. C. (2005). Comparative study of correlates of early age at menarche among Mexican and Egyptian adolescents. *American Journal of Human Biology, 17,* 654–658.

Toth, S. L., Rogosch, F. A., Sturge-Apple, M., & Cicchetti, D. (2009). Maternal depression, children's attachment security, and representational development: An organizational perspective. *Child Development, 80,* 192–208.

Tozzi, A. E., Bisiacchi, P., Tarantino, V., de Mei, B., D'Elia, L., Chiarotti, F., & Salmaso, S. (2009). Neuropsychological performance 10 years after immunization in infancy with thimerosal-containing vaccines. *Pediatrics, 123,* 475–482.

Trabasso, T. (1975). Representation, memory, and reasoning: How do we make transitive inferences? In A. D. Pick (Ed.), *Minnesota Symposia on Child Psychology (Vol. 9).* Minneapolis: University of Minnesota.

Trautner, H. M., Gervai, J., & Nemeth, R. (2003). Appearance-reality distinction and development of gender constancy understanding in children. *International Journal of Behavioral Development, 27,* 275–281.

Trautner, H. M., Ruble, D. N., Cyphers, L., Kirsten, B., Behrendt, R., & Hartmann, P. (2005). Rigidity and flexibility of gender stereotypes in childhood: Developmental or differential? *Infant and Child Development, 14,* 365–381.

Traylor, E. S., Hayslip, B. Jr., Kaminski, P. L., & York, C. (2003). Relationships between grief and family system characteristics: A cross lagged longitudinal analysis. *Death Studies, 27,* 575–601.

Treas, J. & Hill, T. (2009). Social trends and public policy in an aging society. In M. C. Smith (Ed.) & N. DeFrates-Densch (Asst. Ed.), *Handbook of research on adult learning and development.* New York: Routledge.

Treffert, D. A. (2000). *Extraordinary people: Understanding savant syndrome.* Available at: iUniverse.com.

Treiman, R. (2000). The foundations of literacy. *Current Directions in Psychological Science, 9,* 89–92.

Treiman, R., & Broderick, V. (1998). What's in a name? Children's knowledge about the letters in their own names. *Journal of Experimental Child Psychology, 70,* 97–116.

Tremblay, M. S., Inman, J. W., & Willms, J. D. (2000). The relationship between physical activity, self-esteem, and academic achievement in 12-year-old children. *Pediatric Exercise Science, 12,* 312–323.

Tremblay, R. E. (2000). The development of aggressive behaviour during childhood: What have we learned in the past century? *International Journal of Behavioral Development. 24,* 129–141.

Triandis, H. C. (1989). Self and social behavior in differing cultural contexts. *Psychological Review, 96,* 269–289.

Triandis, H. C. (1995). *Individualism and collectivism.* Boulder, CO: Westview Press.

Trickett, P. K., & Putnam, F. W. (1993). Impact of child sexual abuse on females: Toward a developmental, psychobiological integration. *Psychological Science, 4,* 81–87.

Tronick, E. Z. (1989). Emotions and emotional communication in infants. *American Psychologist, 44*, 112–119.

Trudel, G., Boyer, R., Villeneuve, V., Anderson, A., Pilon, G., & Bounader, J. (2008). The Marital Life and Aging Well Program: Effects of a group preventive intervention on the marital and sexual functioning of retired couples. *Sexual and Relationship Therapy, 23*, 5–23.

Trueheart, C. (1997, August 5). Champion of longevity ends her reign at 122. *The Washington Post*, A1, A12.

Tryon, R. C. (1940). Genetic differences in maze learning in rats. *Yearbook of the National Society for Studies in Education, 39*, 111–119.

Trzesniewski, K. H., Donnellan, M. B., Moffitt, T. E., Robins, R. W., Poulton, R., & Caspi, A. (2006). Low self-esteem during adolescence predicts poor health, criminal behavior, and limited economic prospects during adulthood. *Developmental Psychology, 42*, 381–390.

Tsai, Y.-M., Kunter, M., Ludtke, O., Trautwein, U., & Ryan, R. M. (2008). What makes lessons interesting? The role of situational and individual factors in three school subjects. *Journal of Educational Psychology, 100*, 460–472.

Tsuchiya, K. J., Takagai, S., Kawai, M., Matsumoto, H., Nakamura, K., Minabe, Y., Mori, N., & Takei, N. (2005). Advanced paternal age associated with an elevated risk for schizophrenia in offspring in a Japanese population. *Schizophrenia Research, 65*, 337–342.

Tucker, B. P. (1998). Deaf culture, cochlear implants, and elective disability. *Hastings Center Report, 28*, 6–14.

Tuckman, B. W. (1999). The effects of exercise on children and adolescents. In A. J. Goreczny & M. Hersen (Eds.), *Handbook of pediatric and adolescent health psychology*, 275–286. Boston: Allyn & Bacon.

Tullos, A., & Woolley, J. D. (2009). The development of children's ability to use evidence to infer reality status. *Child Development, 80*, 101–114.

Tun, P. A., McCoy, S., & Wingfield, A. (2009). Aging, hearing acuity, and the attentional costs of effortful listening. *Psychology and Aging, 24*, 761–766.

Turati, C. (2004). Why faces are not special to newborns: An alternative account of the face preference. *Current Directions in Psychological Science, 13*, 5–8.

Turiel, E. (1978). The development of concepts of social structure: Social convention. In J. Glick & A. Clarke-Stewart (Eds.), *The development of social understanding*. New York: Gardner Press.

Turiel, E. (1983). *The development of social knowledge. Morality and convention*. Cambridge, England: Cambridge University Press.

Turiel, E. (2006). The development of morality. In N. Eisenberg (Vol. Ed.), & W. Damon & R. M. Lerner (Eds. in Chief), *Handbook of child psychology: Vol. 3. Social, emotional, and personality development* (6th ed.). Hoboken, NJ: Wiley.

Turk-Charles, S., & Carstensen, L. L. (1999). The role of time in the setting of social goals across the life span. In T. M. Hess & F. Blanchard-Fields (Eds.), *Social cognition and aging*. San Diego: Academic Press.

Turkheimer, E. (2000). Three laws of behavior genetics and what they mean. *Current Directions in Psychological Science, 9*, 160–164.

Turner, P. J., & Gervai, J. (1995). A multidimensional study of gender typing in preschool children and their parents: Personality, attitudes, preferences, behavior, and cultural differences. *Developmental Psychology, 31*, 759–772.

Turner, R. J., & Lloyd, D. A. (2004). Stress burden and the lifetime incidence of psychiatric disorder in young adults racial and ethnic contrasts. *Archives of General Psychiatry, 61*, 481–488.

Turnpenny, P. D., & Ellard, S. (2005). *Emery's elements of medical genetics*. Edinburgh: Elsevier.

Twenge, J. M. (1997). Changes in masculine and feminine traits over time: A meta-analysis. *Sex Roles, 36*, 305–325.

Tyre, P. (2005, December 5). No one to blame. *Newsweek*, 50–59.

Tyson-Rawson, K. J. (1996). Adolescent responses to the death of a parent. In C. A. Corr & D. E. Balk (Eds.), *Handbook of adolescent death and bereavement*. New York: Springer.

U

U. S. Census Bureau (2006). *Statistical abstract of the United States 2007* (126th ed.). Washington, DC: U. S. Government Printing Office, 2006. Available at: www.census.gov/compendia/statab.

U. S. Census Bureau (2007). *Educational attainment in the United States: 2004. Detailed Tables: Table 8*. Washington, DC: Government Printing Office. Available at www.census.gov/population/socdemo/education/cps2004/tab08-1.pdf. Accessed: September 25, 2007.

U. S. Census Bureau (2009). *Statistical abstracts of the United States, 2010* (129th ed.). Washington, DC: U. S. Census Bureau. Available at: www.census.gov/statab/www/. Accessed: April 8, 2010.

U. S. Department of Education (1997). *Digest of Education Statistics, 1997*. Washington, DC: National Center for Education Statistics.

U. S. Department of Health and Human Services, Administration on Children, Youth, and Families. (2007). *Child maltreatment 2005*. Washington, DC: U. S. Government Printing Office. Available at: www.acf.hhs.gov/programs/cb/pubs/cm05/index.htm.

U. S. Department of Labor (2010). *20 Leading occupations of employed women—2009 annual averages*. Available at: www.dol.gov/wb/factsheets/20lead2009.htm. Accessed: April 22, 2010.

Uchida, N., Fujita, K., & Katayama, T. (1999). Detection of vehicles on the other crossing path at an intersection: Visual search performance of elderly drivers. *Japanese Society of Automotive Engineers Review, 20*, 381.

Uchino, B. N. (2009). Understanding the links between social support and physical health. A lifespan perspective with emphasis on the separation of perceived and received support. *Perspectives on Psychological Science. 4*, 236–255.

Uchronski, M. (2008). Agency and communion in spontaneous self-descriptions: Occurrence and situational malleability. *European Journal of Social Psychology, 38*, 1093–1102.

Ueno, K., & Adams, R. G. (2006). Adult friendship: A decade review. In P. Noller & J. A. Feeney (Eds.), *Close relationships: Functions, forms, and processes*. New York: Psychology Press.

Umaña-Taylor, A. J., & Alfaro, E. C. (2006). Ethnic identity among U. S. Latino adolescents: Theory, measurement, and implications for well-being. In F. A. Villarruel & T. Luster (Eds.), *The crisis in youth mental health: Critical issues and effective programs: Vol 2. Disorders in adolescence*. Westport, CT: Praeger.

Umaña-Taylor, A. J., Bhanot, R., & Shin, N. (2006). Ethnic identity formation during adolescence: The critical role of families. *Journal of Family Issues, 27*, 390–414.

Umaña-Taylor, A. J., Gonzales-Backen, M. A., & Guimond, A. B. (2009). Latino adolescents' ethnic identity: Is there a developmental progression and does growth in ethnic identity predict growth in self-esteem? *Child Development, 80*, 391–405.

Umberson, D. (1992). Relationships between adult children and their parents: Psychological consequences for both generations. *Journal of Marriage and the Family, 54*, 664–674.

Umberson, D. (2003). *Death of a parent: Transition to a new adult identity*. Cambridge, UK: Cambridge University Press.

Umberson, D., & Slaten, E. (2000). Gender and intergenerational relationships. In D. H. Demo, K. R. Allen, & M. A. Fine (Eds.), *Handbook of family diversity*. New York: Oxford University Press.

Underwood, A. (2004, January 19). Now, reduce your risk of Alzheimer's. *Newsweek*, 72–73.

Unger, J. B., Molina, G. B., & Teran, L. (2000). Perceived consequences of teenage childbearing among adolescent girls in an urban sample. *Journal of Adolescent Health, 26*, 205–212.

United Nations, Department of Economic and Social Affairs, Population Division (2007). *World population prospects: The 2006 revision, highlights*. Available at: www.un.org/esa/population/publications/wpp2006/WPP2006_Highlights_rev.pdf. Working Paper No. ESA/P/WP.202.

University of Copenhagen (2008, December 18). Girls have superior sense of taste to boys. *ScienceDaily*. Available at: www.sciencedaily.com/releases/2008/12/081216104035.htm. Accessed: February 10, 2010.

University of Exeter (2009, January 8). Lifelong gender difference in physical activity revealed. *ScienceDaily*. Available at: http://www.sciencedaily.com/releases/2009/01/090105190740.htm. Accessed: October 19, 2009.

Updegraff, K., & McHale, S. M., & Crouter, A. C. (1996). Gender roles in marriage: What do they mean for girls' and boys' school achievement? *Journal of Youth and Adolescence, 25*, 73–88.

Urdan, T., & Mestas, M. (2006). The goals behind performance goals. *Journal of Educational Psychology, 98*, 354–365.

Urofsky, M. I. (1993). *Letting go. Death, dying, and the law*. New York: Charles Scribner's Sons.

Usher, J. A., & Neisser, U. (1993). Childhood amnesia and the beginnings of memory for four early life events. *Journal of Experimental Psychology: General, 122*, 155–165.

Usher-Seriki, K. K., Bynum, M. S., & Callands, T. A. (2008). Mother-daughter communication about sex and sexual intercourse among middle- to upper-class African American girls. *Journal of Family Issues, 29*, 901–917.

V

Vaglio, S. (2009). Chemical communication and mother-infant recognition. *Communicative and Integrative Biology, 2*, 279–281.

Vaillant, G. E. (1977). *Adaptation to life*. Boston: Little, Brown.

Vaillant, G. E. (1983). Childhood environment and maturity of defense mechanisms. In D. Magnusson & V. L. Allen (Eds.), *Human development. An interactional perspective*. New York: Academic Press.

Vaillant, G. E., & Milofsky, E. (1980). Natural history of male psychological health. IX: Empirical evidence for Erikson's model of the life cycle. *American Journal of Psychiatry, 137*, 1348–1359.

Valente, T. W., Fujimoto, K., Chou, C. P., & Spruijt-Metz, D. (2009). Adolescent affiliations and adiposity: A social network analysis of friendships and obesity. *Journal of Adolescent Health, 45*, 202–204.

Valenza, E., Leo, I., Gava, L., & Simion, F. (2006). Perceptual completion in newborn human infants. *Child Development, 77*, 1810–1821.

Valian, V. (2009). Innateness and learnability. In E. L. Bavin (Ed.), *The Cambridge handbook of child language*, 15–34. New York: Cambridge University Press.

Valiente, C., Lemery-Chalfant, K., Swanson, J., & Reiser, M. (2008). Prediction of children's academic competence from their effortful control, relationships, and classroom participation. *Journal of Educational Psychology, 100*, 67–77.

Valkenberg, P. M., & Jochen, P. (2009). Social consequences of the internet for adolescents. *Current Directions in Psychological Sciences, 18*, 1–5.

Van Beurden, E., Zask, A., Barnett, L. M., & Dietrich, U. C. (2002). Fundamental movement skills—How do primary school children perform? The "Move it, Groove it" program in rural Australia. *Journal of Science and Medicine on Sport, 5*, 244–252.

Van Beveren, T. T., Little, B. B., & Spence, M. (2000). Effects of prenatal cocaine exposure and postnatal environment on child development. *American Journal of Human Biology, 12*, 417–428.

van den Boom, D. C. (1995). Do first-year intervention effects endure? Follow-up during toddlerhood of a sample of Dutch irritable infants. *Child Development, 66*, 1798–1816.

Van den Dries, L., Juffer, F., van IJzendoorn, M. H., & Bakermans-Kranenburg, M. J. (2009). Fostering security? A meta-analysis of attachment in adopted children. *Children and Youth Services Review, 31*, 410–421.

van der Maas, H., & Jansen, B. R. J. (2003). What response times tell of children's behavior on the balance scale task. *Journal of Experimental Child Psychology, 85*, 141–177.

Van Doesum, K. T. M., Riksen-Walraven, J. M., Hosman, C. M. H., & Hoefnagels, C. (2008). A randomized controlled trial of a home-visiting intervention aimed at preventing relationship problems in depressed mothers and their infants. *Child Development, 79*, 547–561.

Van Gaalen, R. I., & Dykstra, P. A. (2006). Solidarity and conflict between adult children and parents: A latent class analysis. *Journal of Marriage and Family, 68*, 947–960.

van Galen, G. P. (1993). Handwriting: A developmental perspective. In A. F. Kalverboer, B. Hopkins, & R. H. Geuze (Eds.), *Motor development in early and later childhood: Longitudinal approaches.* Cambridge, England: Cambridge University Press.

Van Hecke, A. V., Mundy, P. C., Acra, C. F., Block, J. J., Delgado, C. E. F., Parlade, M. V., Meyer, J. A., Neal, A. R., & Pomares, Y. B. (2007). Infant joint attention, temperament, and social competence in preschool children. *Child Development, 78*, 53–69.

van Hoeken, D., Seidell, J., & Hoek, H. (2003). Epidemiology. In J. Treasure, U. Schmidt, & E. van Furth (Eds.), *Handbook of eating disorders* (2nd ed.). Chicester, UK: Wiley.

van Hoof, A. (1999). The identity status field re-reviewed: An update of unresolved and neglected issues with a view on some alternative approaches. *Developmental Review, 19*, 497–556.

van IJzendoorn, M. H. (1992). Intergenerational transmission of parenting: A review of studies in non-clinical populations. *Developmental Review, 12*, 76–99.

van IJzendoorn, M. H. (1995). Adult attachment representations, parental responsiveness, and infant attachment: A meta-analysis on the predictive validity of the Adult Attachment Interview. *Psychological Bulletin, 117*, 387–403.

van IJzendoorn, M. H., & DeWolff, M. S. (1997). In search of the absent father: Meta-analyses of infant-father attachment: A rejoinder to our discussants. *Child Development, 68*, 604–609.

van IJzendoorn, M. H., & Juffer, F. (2005). Adoption is a successful natural intervention enhancing adopted children's IQ and school performance. *Current Directions in Psychological Science, 14*, 326–330.

van IJzendoorn, M. H., & Juffer, F. (2006). The Emanuel Miller Memorial Lecture 2006: Adoption as intervention: Meta-analytic evidence for massive catch-up and plasticity in physical, socio-emotional, and cognitive development. *Journal of Child Psychology and Psychiatry, 47*, 1228–1245.

van IJzendoorn, M. H., Rutgers, A. H., Bakermans-Kranenburg, M. J., Swinkels, S. H. N., van Daalen, E., Dietz, C., Naber, F. B. A., Buitelaar, J. K., & van Engeland, H. (2007). Parental sensitivity and attachment in children with autism spectrum disorder: Comparison with children with mental retardation, with language delays, and with typical development. *Child Development, 78*, 597–608.

van IJzendoorn, M. H., & Sagi, A. (1999). Cross-cultural patterns of attachment: Universal and contextual dimensions. In J. Cassidy & P. R. Shaver (Eds.), *Handbook of attachment.* New York: Guilford.

van IJzendoorn, M. H., & Sagi-Schwartz, A. (2008). Cross-cultural patterns of attachment. Universal and contextual dimensions. In J. Cassidy & P. R. Shaver (Eds.), *Handbook of attachment: Theory, research, and clinical applications* (2nd ed.). New York: Guilford.

van IJzendoorn, M. H., Schuengel, C., & Bakermans-Kranenburg, M. J. (1999). Disorganized attachment in early childhood: Meta-analysis of precursors, concomitants, and sequelae. *Development and Psychopathology, 11*, 225–249.

van Kleeck, A., Gillam, R. B., Hamilton, L., & McGrath, C. (1997). The relationship between middle-class parents' book-sharing discussion and their preschooler's abstract language development. *Journal of Speech, Language, and Hearing Research, 40*, 1261–1271.

Van Leeuwen, M., Van den Berg, S. M., & Boomsma, D. I. (2008). A twin-family study of general IQ. *Learning and Individual Differences, 18*, 76–88.

van Praag H. (2009). Exercise and the brain: something to chew on. *Trends in Neuroscience, 32*, 283–290.

Van Rossem, L., Oenema, A., Steegers, E. A., Moll, H. A., Jaddoe, V. W., Hofman, A., Mackenbach, J. P., & Raat, H. (2009). Are starting and continuing breastfeeding related to educational background? The generation R study. *Pediatrics, 123*, e1017–1027.

van Solinge, H., & Henkens, K. (2005). Couples' adjustment to retirement: A multi-actor study. *Journal of Gerontology: Psychological and Social Sciences, 60B*, S11–S20.

Van Solinge, H., & Henkens, K. (2008). Adjustment to and satisfaction with retirement: Two of a kind? *Psychology and Aging, 23*, 422–434.

Vandell, D. L., Wilson, K. S., & Buchanan, N. R. (1980). Peer interaction in the first year of life: An examination of its structure, content, and sensitivity to toys. *Child Development, 51*, 481–488.

Varea, C., Bernis, C., Montero, P., Arias, S., Barroso, A., & Gonzalez, B. (2000). Secular trend and intrapopulational variation in age of menopause in Spanish women. *Journal of Biosocial Science, 32*, 383–393.

Vargha-Khadem, F., Gadian, D. G., Watkins, K. E., Connelly, A., Van Paesschen, W., & Mishkin, M. (1997). Differential effects of early hippocampal pathology on episodic and semantic memory. *Science, 277*, 376–380.

Vargha-Khadem, F., Watkins, K., Alcock, K., Fletcher, P., Passingham, R. (1995). Praxic and nonverbal cognitive deficits in a large family with a genetically transmitted speech and language disorder. *Proceedings of the National Academy of Sciences of the United States of America, 92*, 930–933.

Vaughn, B. E., Azria, M. R., Krzysik, L., Caya, L. R., Bost, K. K., Newell, W., & Kazura, K. L. (2000). Friendship and social competence in a sample of preschool children attending head start. *Developmental Psychology, 36*, 326–338.

Vaughn, B. E., Lefever, G. B., Seifer, R., & Barglow, P. (1989). Attachment behavior, attachment security, and temperament during infancy. *Child Development, 60*, 728–737.

Vazsonyi, A. T., Hibbert, J. R., & Snider, J. B. (2003). Exotic enterprise no more? Adolescent reports of family and parenting processes from youth in four countries. *Journal of Research on Adolescence, 13*, 129–160.

Vedantam, S. (2006, December 14). Antidepressants a suicide risk for young adults. *The Washington Post*, A16.

Vedantam, S. (2007, June 10). Fight over vaccine–autism link hits court. *The Washington Post*, A6.

Veenstra-Vanderweele, J., & Cook, E. H. (2003). Genetics of childhood disorders: XLVI. Autism, part 5: Genetics of autism. *Journal of the American Academy of Child and Adolescent Psychiatry, 42*, 116–118.

Velderman, M.K., Bakermans-Kranenburg, M. J., Juffer, F., & van IJzendoorn, M. H. (2006). Effects of attachment-based interventions on maternal sensitivity and infant attachment: Differential susceptibility of highly reactive infants. *Journal of Family Psychology, 20*, 266–274.

Vellutino, F. R. (1991). Introduction to three studies on reading acquisition: Convergent findings on theoretical foundations of code-oriented versus whole language approaches to reading instruction. *Journal of Educational Psychology, 83*, 437–443.

Vellutino, F. R., Scanlon, D. M., Sipay, E. R., & Small, S. G. (1996). Cognitive profiles of difficult-to-remediate and readily remediated poor readers: Early intervention as a vehicle for distinguishing between cognitive and experiential deficits as basic causes of specific reading disability. *Journal of Educational Psychology, 88*, 601–638.

Verbeek, P. (2006). Everyone's monkey: Primate moral roots. In M. Killen & J. G. Smetana (Eds.), *Handbook of moral development.* Mahwah, NJ: Erlbaum.

Verghese, J., Lipton, R. B., Katz, M. J., Hall, C. B., Derby, C. A., Kuslansky, G., Ambrose, A. F., Sliwinski, M., & Buschke, H. (2003). Leisure activities and the risk of dementia in the elderly. *New England Journal of Medicine, 348*, 2508–2516.

Verhaak, C. M., Smeenk, J. M., van Minnen, A., Kremer, J. A., & Kraaimaat, F. W. (2005). A longitudinal, prospective study on emotional adjustment before, during, and after consecutive fertility treatment cycles. *Human Reproduction, 20*, 2253–2260.

Verhaeghen, P. (2003). Aging and vocabulary scores: A meta-analysis. *Psychology and Aging, 18*, 332–339.

Verma, S., & Larson, R. (Eds.) (2003). *Examining adolescent leisure time across cultures: New directions for child and adolescent development*, No. 99. San Francisco: Jossey-Bass.

Vermeulen, A. (2000). Andropause. *Maturitas, 15*, 5–15.

Veroff, J., Reuman, D., & Feld, S. (1984). Motives in American men and women across the adult life span. *Developmental Psychology, 20*, 1142–1158.

Véronneau, M-H., Vitaro, F., Pedersen, S., & Tremblay, R. E. (2008). Do peers contribute to the likelihood of secondary school graduation among disadvantaged boys? *Journal of Educational Psychology, 100*, 429–442.

Veroudea, K., Norrisa, D. G., Shumskayaa, E., Gullberg, M., & Indefrey, P. (2010). Functional connectivity between brain regions involved in learning words of a new language. *Brain and Language, 113*, 21–27.

Verquer, M. L., Beehr, T. A., & Wagner, S. H. (2003). A meta-analysis of relations between person-organization fit and work attitudes. *Journal of Vocational Behavior, 63*, 473–489.

Verrillo, R. T., & Verrillo, V. (1985). Sensory and perceptual performance. In N. Charness (Ed.), *Aging and human performance.* Chichester, England: Wiley.

Verschueren, K., Buyck, P., & Marcoen, A. (2001). Self-representations and socioemotional competence in young children: A 3-year longitudinal study. *Developmental Psychology, 37,* 126–134.

Vinden, P. G., & Astington, J. W. (2000). Culture and understanding other minds. In S. Baron-Cohen, H. Tager-Flusberg, & D. J. Cohen (Eds.), *Understanding other minds. Perspectives from developmental cognitive neuroscience* (2nd ed.). Oxford: Oxford University Press.

Vining, E. P. G., Freeman, J. M., Pillas, D. J., Uematsu, S., Carson, B. S., Brandt, J., Boatman, D., Pulsifer, M. B., & Zuckerberg, A., (1997). Why would you remove half a brain? The outcome of 58 children after hemispherectomy—the Johns Hopkins experience: 1968 to 1996. *Pediatrics, 100,* 163–171.

Vita, A. J., Terry, R. B., Hubert, H. B., & Fries, J. F. (1998). Aging, health risks, and cumulative disability. *New England Journal of Medicine, 338,* 1035–1041.

Vitario, F., Boivin, M., & Bukowski, W. M. (2009). The role of friendship in child and adolescent psychosocial development. In K. H. Rubin, W. M. Bukowski & B. Laursen (Eds.), *Handbook of peer interactions, relationships, and groups.* New York: Guilford.

Vitiello, B., Zuvekas, S. H., & Norquist, G. S. (2006). National estimates of antidepressant medication use among U.S. children. *Journal of the American Academy of Child and Adolescent Psychiatry, 45,* 271–279.

Vogler, G. P. (2006). Behavior genetics and aging. In J. E. Birren & K. W. Schaie (Eds.), *Handbook of the psychology of aging* (6th ed.). Burlington, MA: Elsevier Academic Press.

Vohr, B.R., Poindexter, B. B., Dusick, A. M., McKinely, L. T., Wright, L. L., Langer, J.C., & Poole, W. K. (2006). Beneficial effects of breast milk in the neonatal intensive care unit on the developmental outcome of extremely low birth weight infants at 18 months of age. *Pediatrics, 118,* 115–123.

Voight, B. F., Kudaravalli, S., Wen, X., & Pritchard, J. K. (2006). A map of recent positive selection in the human genome. *PLoS Biology, 4,* 0446–0458.

Volkmar, F. R. (2001). Pharmacological interventions in autism: Theoretical and practical issues. *Journal of Clinical Child Psychology, 30,* 80–87.

Volkmar, F. R., Lord, C., Bailey, A., Schultz, R. T., & Klin, A. (2004). Autism and pervasive developmental disorders. *Journal of Child Psychology and Psychiatry and Allied Disciplines, 45,* 135–170.

Volling, B. L. (2005). The transition to siblinghood: A developmental ecological systems perspective and directions for future research. *Journal of Family Psychology, 19,* 542–549.

von Hofsten, C. (1993). Studying the development of goal-directed behavior. In A. F. Kalverboer, B. Hopkins, & R. H. Geuze (Eds.), *Motor development in early and later childhood: Longitudinal approaches.* Cambridge, England: Cambridge University Press.

von Hofsten, C. (2007). Action in development. *Developmental Science, 10,* 54–60.

Vondra, J., & Belsky, J. (1993). Developmental origins of parenting: Personality and relationship factors. In T. Luster & L. Okagaki (Eds.), *Parenting. An ecological perspective.* Hillsdale, NJ: Erlbaum.

Vouloumanos, A., & Werker, J. F. (2007). Listening to language at birth: Evidence for a bias for speech in neonates. *Developmental Science, 10,* 159–171.

Voyer, D., Postma, A., Brake, B., & Imperato-McGinley, J. (2007). Gender differences in object location memory: A meta-analysis. *Psychonomic Bulletin and Review, 14,* 23–38.

Vuoksimaa, E., Koskenvuo, M., Rose, R. J., & Kaprio, J. (2009). Origins of handedness: A nationwide study of 30,161 adults. *Neuropsychologia, 47,* 1294–1301.

Vuorialho, A., Karinen, P., & Sorri, M. (2006). Effect of hearing aids on hearing disability and quality of life in the elderly. *International Journal of Audiology, 45,* 400–405.

Vurpillot, E. (1968). The development of scanning strategies and their relation to visual differentiation. *Journal of Experimental Child Psychology, 6,* 632–650.

Vygotsky, L. S. (1962). *Thought and language* (E. Hanfmann & G. Vakar, Eds. & Trans.). Cambridge, MA: MIT Press. (Original work published 1934).

Vygotsky, L. S. (1978). *Mind in society: The development of higher mental processes* (M. Cole, V. John-Steiner, S. Scribner, & E. Souberman, Eds.). Cambridge, MA: Harvard University Press. (Original work published 1930, 1933, 1935).

W

Wade, B., & Moore, M. (1998). An early start with books: Literacy and mathematical evidence from a longitudinal study. *Educational Review, 50,* 135–145.

Waechter, E. H. (1984). Dying children. Patterns of coping. In H. Wass & C. A. Corr (Eds.), *Childhood and death.* Washington, DC: Hemisphere.

Waite, L. J., & Gallagher, M. (2000). *The case for marriage. Why married people are happier, healthier, and better off financially.* New York: Doubleday.

Waldemar, G., & Burns, A. (Eds.). (2009). *Alzheimer's disease.* Oxford, UK: Oxford University Press.

Waldenström, U., Borg, I., Olsson, B., Sköld, M., & Wall, S. (1996). The childbirth experience: A study of 295 new mothers. *Birth, 23,* 144–153.

Waldman, I. D., & Gizer, I. R. (2006). The genetics of attention deficit hyperactivity disorder. *Clinical Psychology Review, 26,* 396–432.

Walford, R. L. (1983). *Maximum life span.* New York: Norton.

Walford, R. L., Mock, D., Verdery, R., & MacCallum, T. (2002). Calorie restriction in Biosphere 2: Alterations in the physiologic, hematologic, hormonal, and biochemical parameters in humans restricted for a 2-year period. *Journal of Gerontology, 57A,* B211–B224.

Walker, L. J. (1980). Cognitive and perspective-taking prerequisites of moral development. *Child Development, 51,* 131–139.

Walker, L. J. (2004). Gus in the gap: Bridging the judgment-action gap in moral reasoning. In D. K. Lapsley & D. Narvaez (Eds.), *Moral development, self, and identity.* Mahwah, NJ: Erlbaum.

Walker, L. J. (2006). Gender and morality. In M. Killen & J. G. Smetana (Eds.), *Handbook of moral development.* Mahwah, NJ: Erlbaum.

Walker, L. J., Hennig, K. H., & Krettenauer, T. (2000). Parent and peer contexts for children's moral reasoning development. *Child Development, 71,* 1033–1048.

Walker-Andrews, A. S. (1997). Infants' perception of expressive behaviors: Differentiation of multimodal information. *Psychological Bulletin, 121,* 437–456.

Wallace, J. E., & Young, M. C. (2008). Parenthood and productivity: A study of demands, resources and family-friendly firms. *Journal of Vocational Behavior, 72,* 110–122.

Wallace, P. S., & Whishaw, I. Q. (2003). Independent digit movements and precision grip patterns in 1–5-month-old human infants: Hand-babbling, including vacuous then self-directed hand and digit movements, precedes targeted reaching. *Neuropsychologia, 41,* 1912–1918.

Wallach, M. A. & Kogan, N. (1965). *Thinking in young children.* New York: Holt, Rinehart & Winston.

Wallen, K. (1996). Nature needs nurture: The interaction of hormonal and social influences on the development of behavioral sex differences in rhesus monkeys. *Hormones and Behavior, 30,* 364–378.

Wallis, C. (2008, July 7). The fragile X factor. *Time,* 46–48.

Walls, R. T. (2000). Vocational cognition: Accuracy of 3rd-, 6th-, 9th-, and 12th-grade students. *Journal of Vocational Behavior, 56,* 137–144.

Walsh, C. E. (2003). Gene therapy progress and prospects: Gene therapy for the hemophilias. *Gene Therapy, 10,* 999–1003.

Walsh, L. (2009). *Depression care across the lifespan.* Chichester, UK: Wiley-Blackwell.

Walster, E., Walster, G. W., & Berscheid, E. (1978). *Equity: Theory and research.* Boston: Allyn & Bacon.

Walter, C. A., & McCoyd, J. L. M. (2009). *Grief and loss across the lifespan. A biopsychosocial perspective.* New York: Springer.

Walton, G., & Spencer, S. (2009). Latent ability: Grades and test scores systematically underestimate the intellectual ability of negatively stereotyped students. *Psychological Science, 20,* 1132–1139.

Wang, H. Y., & Amato, P. R. (2000). Predictors of divorce adjustment: Stressors, resources, and definitions. *Journal of Marriage and the Family, 62,* 655–668.

Wang, J., Iannotti, R. J., & Nansel, T. R. (2009). School bullying among adolescents in the United States: Physical, verbal, relational, and cyber. *Journal of Adolescent Health, 45,* 323–325.

Wang, P. S., Berglund, P., Olfson, M., Pincus, H. A., Wells, K. B., & Kessler, R. C. (2005). Failure and delay in initial treatment contact after first onset of mental disorders in the National Comorbidity Survey Replication. *Archives of General Psychiatry, 62,* 603–613.

Wang, Q. (2004). Cultural self-constructions: Autobiographical memory and self-description in European American and Chinese children. *Developmental Psychology, 40,* 3–15.

Wang, Q. (2006). Culture and the development of self-knowledge. *Current Directions in Psychological Science, 15,* 182–187.

Wang, Q., & Conway, M. A. (2004). The stories we keep: Autobiographical memory in American and Chinese middle-aged adults. *Journal of Personality, 72,* 911–938.

Wang, S. H., Baillargeon, R., & Brueckner, L. (2004). Young infants' reasoning about hidden objects: Evidence from violation-of-expectation tasks with test trials only. *Cognition, 93,* 167–198.

Wang, S. S. (2010, March 30). Making cells live forever in quest for cures. *The Wall Street Journal,* D3.

Wang, S. Y., & Chen, C. H. (2006). Psychosocial health of Taiwanese postnatal husbands and wives. *Journal of Psychosomatic Research, 60,* 303–307.

Ward, C. D., & Cooper, R. P. (1999). A lack of evidence in 4-month-old human infants for paternal voice preference. *Developmental Psychobiology, 35,* 49–59.

Ward, H., Munro, E. R., & Dearden, C. (2006). *Babies and young children in care: Life pathways, decision-making and practice.* London: Jessica Kingsley.

Ward, R., & Spitze, G. (1992). Consequences of parent–adult child coresidence. *Journal of Family Issues, 13,* 533–572.

Ward, R., & Spitze, G. (2004). Marital implications of parent–adult child coresidence: A longitudinal view. *Journal of Gerontology: Social Sciences, 59B,* S2–S8.

Warin, J. (2000). The attainment of self-consistency through gender in young children. *Sex Roles, 42,* 209–231.

Warneken, F., Chen, F., & Tomasello, M. (2006). Cooperative activities in young children and chimpanzees. *Child Development, 77,* 640–663.

Warren, J. R., LePore, P. C., & Mare, R. D. (2000). Employment during high school: Consequences for students' grades in academic courses. *American Educational Research Journal, 37*, 943–970.

Waskowic, T. D., & Chartier, B. M. (2003). Attachment and the experience of grief following the loss of a spouse. *Omega: Journal of Death and Dying, 47*, 77–91.

Wass, H. (1991). Helping children cope with death. In D. Papadatou & C. Papadatos (Eds.), *Children and death*. New York: Hemisphere.

Wasserman, D. (2006). *Depression: The facts*. Oxford, UK: Oxford University Press.

Waterman, A. S. (1982). Identity development from adolescence to adulthood: An extension of theory and a review of research. *Developmental Psychology, 18*, 341–358.

Waterman, A. S. (1992). Identity as an aspect of optimal psychological functioning. In G. R. Adams, T. P. Gullotta, & R. Montemayor (Eds.), *Adolescent identity formation* (Advances in Adolescent Development, Vol. 4). Newbury Park, CA: Sage.

Waters, E., Wippman, J., & Sroufe, L. A. (1979). Attachment, positive affect, and competence in the peer group: Two studies in construct validation. *Child Development, 50*, 821–829.

Watson, J. B. (1913). Psychology as the behaviorist views it. *Psychological Review, 20*, 158–177.

Watson, J. B. (1925). *Behaviorism*. New York: Norton.

Waxman, S. R., & Hatch, T. (1992). Beyond the basics: Preschool children label objects flexibly at multiple hierarchical levels. *Journal of Child Language, 19*, 153–166.

Wayne, A. J., & Youngs, P. (2003). Teacher characteristics and student achievement gains: A review. *Review of Educational Research, 73*, 89–122.

Webster, J. D. (1998). Attachment styles, reminiscence functions, and happiness in young and elderly adults. *Journal of Aging Studies, 12*, 315–330.

Webster, J. D., & Haight, B. K. (Eds.) (2002). *Critical advances in reminiscence work: From theory to application*. New York: Springer.

Wechsler, D. (2002). *Wechsler Preschool and Primary Scale of Intelligence* (3rd ed.). The Psychological Corporation.

Wechsler, D. (2003). *Wechsler Intelligence Scale for Children* (4th ed.). (WISC–IV). San Antonio, TX: The Psychological Corporation.

Wechsler, D. (2008). *Wechsler Adult Intelligence Scale*, 4th ed. Toronto: Pearson.

Weiffenbach, J. M., Cowart, B. J., & Baum, B. J. (1986). Taste intensity perception in aging. *Journal of Gerontology, 41*, 460–468.

Weinberg, K. M., Olson, K. L., Beeghly, M., & Tronick, E. Z. (2006). Making up is hard to do, especially for mothers with high levels of depressive symptoms and their infant sons. *Journal of Child Psychology and Psychiatry and Allied Disciplines, 47*, 670–683.

Weinberg, R. A., Scarr, S., & Waldman, I. D. (1992). The Minnesota transracial adoption study: A follow-up of IQ test performance at adolescence. *Intelligence, 16*, 117–135.

Weiner, M. F., Garrett, R., & Bret, M. E. (2009). Neuropsychiatric assessment and diagnosis. In M. F. Weiner & A. M. Lipton (Eds.), *The American Psychiatric Publishing textbook of Alzheimer disease and other dementias*. Washington, DC: American Psychiatric Publishing.

Weinert, F. E., & Hany, E. A. (2003). The stability of individual differences in intellectual development: Empirical evidence, theoretical problems, and new research questions. In R. J. Sternberg, J. Lautrey, & T. I. Lubart (Eds.), *Models of intelligence: International perspectives* (pp. 169–181). Washington, DC: American Psychological Association.

Weinert, F. E., & Schneider, W. (1999). *Individual development from 3 to 12: Findings from the Munich*

Longitudinal Study. Cambridge, England: Cambridge University Press.

Weinfield, N. S., Sroufe, L. A., & Egeland, B. (2000). Attachment from infancy to early adulthood in a high-risk sample: Continuity, discontinuity, and their correlates. *Child Development, 71*, 695–702.

Weinraub, M., & Lewis, M. (1977). The determinants of children's responses to separation. *Monographs of the Society for Research in Child Development*, (4, Serial No. 172).

Weir, K. N. (2003). Adoptive family "leap-frogging" patterns. *Adoption Quarterly, 7*, 27–41.

Weisberg, P. (1963). Social and nonsocial conditioning of infant vocalization. *Child Development, 34*, 377–388.

Weisner, T. S., & Gallimore, R. (1977). My brother's keeper: Child and sibling caretaking. *Current Anthropology, 18*, 169–190.

Weiss, B., & Garber, J. (2003). Developmental differences in the phenomenology of depression. *Development and Psychopathology, 15*, 403–430.

Weiss, B., Tram, J. M., Weisz, J. R., Rescorla, L., & Achenbach, T. M. (2009). Differential symptom expression and somatization in Thai versus U. S. children. *Journal of Consulting and Clinical Psychology, 77*, 987–992.

Weiss, L. H., & Schwarz, J. C. (1996). The relationship between parenting types and older adolescents' personality, academic achievement, adjustment, and substance use. *Child Development, 67*, 2101–2114.

Weiss, R. (2003a, February 28). Dream unmet 50 years after DNA milestone. *The Washington Post*, A1, A10.

Weiss, R. (2003b, April 15). Genome Project completed. *The Washington Post*, A6.

Weiss, R. (2008, March 25). Genetic testing gets personal. Firms sell answers on health, even love. *The Washington Post*, A1, A6.

Weiss, R., & Gillis, J. (2000, June 27). DNA-mapping milestone heralded. *The Washington Post*, A1, A12–A13.

Weiss, S. (2008, April 1). Midlife. What crisis? *The Washington Post*, F1, F5.

Weisz, J. R., McCarty, C. A., Eastman, K. L., Chaiyasit, W., & Suwanlert, S. (1997). Developmental psychopathology and culture: Ten lessons from Thailand. In S. S. Luthar, J. A. Burack, D. Cicchetti, & J. R. Weisz (Eds.), *Developmental psychopathology: Perspectives on adjustment, risk and disorder*. Cambridge, England: Cambridge University Press.

Weisz, J. R., McCarty, C. A., & Valeri, S. M. (2006). Effects of psychotherapy for depression in children and adolescents: A meta-analysis. *Psychological Bulletin, 132*, 132–149.

Weizman, A. O., & Snow, C. E. (2001). Lexical input as related to children's vocabulary acquisition: Effects of sophisticated exposure and support for meaning. *Developmental Psychology, 37*, 265–279.

Wellbery, C. (2006). Intervention to increase breast-feeding rates. *American Family Physician, 73*, 2047.

Wellman, H. M. (1990). *The child's theory of mind*. Cambridge, MA: MIT Press.

Wellman, H. M., & Bartsch, K. (1994). Before belief: Children's early psychological theory. In C. Lewis & P. Mitchell (Eds.), *Children's early understanding of mind: Origins and development*. Hove, England: Erlbaum.

Wellman, H. M., Cross, D., & Watson, J. (2001). Meta-analysis of theory-of-mind development: The truth about false-belief. *Child Development, 72*, 655–684.

Wellman, H. M., & Gelman, S. A. (1992). Cognitive development: Foundational theories of core domains. *Annual Review of Psychology, 43*, 337–375.

Wellman, H. M., & Liu, D. (2004). Scaling of theory-of-mind-tasks. *Child Development, 75*, 523–541.

Wellman, H. M., Phillips, A. T., & Rodriguez, T. (2000). Young children's understanding of perception, desire, and emotion. *Child Development, 71*, 895–912.

Welsh, J. A., Nix, R. L., Blair, C., Bierman, K. L., & Nelson, K. E. (2010). The development of cognitive skills and gains in academic school readiness for children from low-income families. *Journal of Educational Psychology, 102*, 43–53.

Wenglinsky, H. (1998). Finance equalization and within-school equity: The relationship between education spending and the social distribution of achievement. *Educational Evaluation and Policy Analysis, 20*, 269–283.

Wentzel, K. R. (2003). Sociometric status and adjustment in middle school: A longitudinal study. *Journal of Early Adolescence, 23*, 5–28.

Werker, J. F., & Desjardins, R. N. (1995). Listening to speech in the first year of life: Experiential influences on phoneme perception. *Current Directions in Psychological Science, 4*, 76–81.

Werker, J. F., Gilbert, J. H. V., Humphrey, K., & Tees, R. C. (1981). Developmental aspects of cross-language speech perception. *Child Development, 52*, 349–355.

Werker, J. F., & Tees, R. C. (2005). Speech perception as a window for understanding plasticity and commitment in language systems of the brain. *Developmental Psychobiology, 46*, 233–234.

Werner, E. A., Myers, M. M., Fifer, W. P., Cheng, B., Fang, Y., Allen, R., & Monk, C. (2007). Prenatal predictors of infant temperament. *Developmental Psychobiology, 49*, 474–484.

Werner, E. E. (1989a). Children of the Garden Island. *Scientific American, 260*, 106–111.

Werner, E. E. (1989b). High-risk children in young adulthood: A longitudinal study from birth to 32 years. *American Journal of Orthopsychiatry, 59*, 72–81.

Werner, E. E., & Smith, R. S. (1982). *Vulnerable but invincible: A longitudinal study of resilient children and youth*. New York: McGraw-Hill.

Werner, E. E., & Smith, R. S. (1992). *Overcoming the odds: High risk children from birth to adulthood*. Ithaca, NY: Cornell University Press.

Werner, E. E., & Smith, R. S. (2001). *Journeys from childhood to midlife: Risk, resilience, and recovery*. Ithaca, NY: Cornell University Press.

Werner, H. (1957). The concept of development from a comparative and organismic point of view. In D. B. Harris (Ed.), *The concept of development: An issue in the study of human behavior*. Minneapolis: University of Minnesota Press.

Werth, J. L., Jr., Blevins, D., Toussaint, K. L., & Durham, M. R. (2002). The influence of cultural diversity on end-of-life care and decisions. *American Behavioral Scientist, 46*, 204–219.

West, D. S., Bursac, Z,, Quimby, D., Prewitt, T. E., Spatz, T., Nash, C., Mays, G., & Eddings, K. (2006). Self-reported sugar-sweetened beverage intake among college students. *Obesity, 14*, 1825–1831.

West, G. L., Anderson, A. A. K., & Pratt, J. (2009). Motivationally significant stimuli show visual prior entry: Evidence for attentional capture. *Journal of Experimental Psychology: Human Perception and Performance, 35*, 1032–1042.

Westen, D., Gabbard, G. O., & Ortigo, K. M. (2008). Psychoanalytic approaches to personality. In O. P. John, R. W. Robins, & L. A. Pervin (Eds.), *Handbook of personality theory and research* (3rd ed.). New York: Guilford.

Wethington, H. R., Hahn, R. A., Fuqua-Whitley, D. S., Crosby, A. E., Liberman, A. M., Price, L. N., Kalra, G., Chattopadhyay, S. K., Tuma, F. K., Moscicki, E., Johnson, R. L., & Sipe, T. A., Task Force on Community Preventive Services (2008). The effectiveness of interventions to reduce psychological harm from traumatic events among children and adolescents: A systematic review. *American Journal of Preventive Medicine, 35,* 287–313.

Weyandt, L. L. (2007). *An ADHD primer* (2nd ed.). Mahwah, NJ: Erlbaum.

Whalen, G., Griffin, M. R., Shintani, A., Mitchel, E., Cruz-Gervis, R., Forbes, B. L., & Hartet, T. V. (2006). Smoking rates among pregnant women in Tennessee, 1990–2001. *Preventive Medicine, 43,* 196–199.

Whipp, B. J., & Ward, S. A. (1992). Will women soon outrun men? *Nature, 355,* 25.

Whitbourne, S. K. (2008). *Adult development and aging: biopsychosocial perspectives* (3rd ed.). Hoboken, NJ: John Wiley & Sons.

Whitbourne, S. K., & Tesch, S. A. (1985). A comparison of identity and intimacy statuses in college students and alumni. *Developmental Psychology, 21,* 1039–1044.

Whitbourne, S. K., & Willis, S. L. (Eds.). (2006). *The baby boomers grow up: Contemporary perspectives on midlife.* Mahwah, NJ: Erlbaum.

White, L., & Edwards, J. N. (1990). Emptying the nest and parental well-being: An analysis of national panel data. *American Sociological Review, 55,* 235–242.

White, L., & Rogers, S. J. (1997). Strong support but uneasy relationships: Coresidence and adult children's relationships with their parents. *Journal of Marriage and the Family, 59,* 62–76.

White, L., & Rogers, S. J. (2000). Economic circumstances and family outcomes: A review of the 1990s. *Journal of Marriage and the Family, 62,* 1035–1051.

White, R. M. B., Roosa, M. W., Weaver, S. R., & Nair, R. L. (2009). Cultural and contextual influences on parenting in Mexican American families. *Journal of Marriage and Family, 71,* 61–79.

White, S., Hill, E., Happé, F., & Frith, U. (2009). Revisiting the Strange Stories: Revealing mentalizing impairments in autism. *Child Development, 80,* 1097–1117.

Whitebread, D. (1999). Interactions between children's metacognitive abilities, working memory capacity, strategies and performance during problem-solving. *European Journal of Psychology of Education, 14,* 489–507.

Whitehead, B. D., & Popenoe, D. (2003). *The state of the unions. The social health of marriage in America 2003. Essay: Marriage and children: Coming together again?* The National Marriage Project, Rutgers University. Available at: http:// marriage.rutgers.edu/Publications/Print/ PrintSOOU2003.htm.

Whitehurst, G. J., & Lonigan, C. J. (1998). Child development and emergent literacy. *Child Development, 69,* 848–872.

Whitehurst, G. J., & Valdez-Menchaca, M. C. (1988). What is the role of reinforcement in early language acquisition? *Child Development, 59,* 430–440.

Whiteman, S. D., McHale, S. M., & Crouter, A. C. (2007). Longitudinal changes in marital relationships: The role of offspring's pubertal development. *Journal of Marriage and Family, 69,* 1005–1020.

Whiting, B. B., & Edwards, C. P. (1988). *Children of different worlds: The formation of social behavior.* Cambridge, MA: Harvard University Press.

WHO Multicentre Growth Reference Study Group (2006). WHO Motor Development Study: Windows of achievement for six gross motor development milestones. *Acta Paediatric Supplement, 450,* 86–95.

Wickens, A. P. (1998). *The causes of aging.* Amsterdam: Harwood Academic Publishers.

Widaman, K. F. (2009). Phenylketonuria in children and mothers. Genes, environments, behavior. *Current Directions in Psychological Science, 18,* 48–52.

Widén, S. E., & Erlandsson, S. I. (2004). The influence of socio-economic status on adolescent attitude to social noise and hearing protection. *Noise Health, 7,* 59–70.

Widén, S. E., Holmes, A. E., Johnson, T., Bohlin, M., & Erlandsson, S. I. (2009). Hearing, use of hearing protection, and attitudes towards noise among young American adults. *International Journal of Audiology, 48,* 537–545.

Widmer, E. D., Giudici, F., Le Goff, J., & Pollien, A. (2009). From support to control: A configurational perspective on conjugal quality. *Journal of Marriage and Family, 71,* 437–448.

Widmer, E. D., Treas, J., & Newcomb, R. (1998). Attitudes toward nonmarital sex in 24 countries. *Journal of Sex Research, 35,* 349–358.

Wigfield, A., Eccles, J. S., Yoon, K. S., & Harold, R. D. (1997). Change in children's competence beliefs and subjective task values across the elementary school years: A 3-year study. *Journal of Educational Psychology, 89,* 451–469.

Wijngaards-de-Meij, L., Stroebe, M., Schut, H., Stroebe, W., van den Bout, J., van der Heijden, P., & Dijkstra, I. (2007). Neuroticism and attachment insecurity as predictors of bereavement outcome. *Journal of Research in Personality, 41,* 498–505.

Wijngaards-de Meij, L., Stroebe, M., Schut, H., Stroebe, W., van den Bout, J., van der Heijden, P., & Dijkstra, I. (2008). Parents grieving the loss of their child: Interdependence in coping. *Journal of Clinical Psychology, 47,* 31–42.

Wikan, U. (1988). Bereavement and loss in two Muslim communities: Egypt and Bali compared. *Social Science and Medicine, 27,* 451–460.

Wikan, U. (1991). *Managing turbulent hearts.* Chicago: University of Chicago Press.

Wilbur, J., Miller, A., & Montgomery, A. (1995). The influence of demographic characteristics, menopausal status, and symptoms on women's attitudes toward menopause. *Women and Health, 23,* 19–39.

Wilcock, A., Kobayashi, L., & Murray, I. (1997). Twenty-five years of obstetric patient satisfaction in North America: A review of the literature. *Journal of Perinatal and Neonatal Nursing, 10,* 36–47.

Wilcox, S., Evenson, K. R., Aragaki, A., Wassertheil-Smoller, S., Mouton, C. P., & Loevinger, B. L. (2003). The effects of widowhood on physical and mental health, health behaviors, and health outcomes: The Women's Health Initiative. *Health Psychology, 22,* 513–522.

Wilfond, B., & Ross, L. F. (2009). From genetics to genomics: Ethics, policy, and parental decision-making. *Journal of Pediatric Psychology, 34,* 639–647.

Wilkinson, D. (2009). Pharmacological treatment of Alzheimer's disease. In G. Waldemar & A. Burns (Eds.), *Alzheimer's disease.* Oxford: Oxford University Press.

Willats, P. (1990). Development of problem solving strategies in infancy. In D. F. Bjorklund (Ed.), *Children's strategies.* Hillsdale, NJ: Erlbaum.

Willcox, D. C., Willcox, B. J., Rosenbaum, M., Sokolovsky, J., & Suzuki, M. (2009). Exceptional longevity and the quest for healthy aging: Insights from the Okinawa Centenarian Study. In J. Sokolovsky (Ed.), *The cultural context of aging* (3rd ed.). Westport, CT: Praeger.

Williams, J. (2003). Dementia and genetics. In R. Plomin, J. C. DeFries, I. W. Craig, & P. McGuffin (Eds.), *Behavioral genetics in the postgenomic era.* Washington, DC: American Psychological Association.

Williams, J. E., & Best, D. L. (1990). *Measuring sex stereotypes: A multination study* (rev. ed.). Newbury Park, CA: Sage.

Williams, J. H., Waiter, G. D., Gilchrist, A., Perrett, D. I., Murray, A. D., & Whiten, A. (2006). Neural mechanisms of imitation and 'mirror neuron' functioning in autistic spectrum disorder. *Neuropsychologia, 44,* 610–621.

Williams, M. V., Baker, D. W., Parker, R. M., & Nurss, J. R. (1998). Relationship of functional health literacy to patients' knowledge of their chronic disease. *Archives of Internal Medicine, 158,* 166–172.

Williams, P. T. (1997). Evidence for the incompatibility of age-neutral overweight and age-neutral physical activity standards from runners. *American Journal of Clinical Nutrition, 65,* 1391–1396.

Williams, T., Connolly, J., & Cribbie, R. (2008). Light and heavy heterosexual activities of young Canadian adolescents: Normative patterns and differential predictors. *Journal of Research on Adolescence, 18,* 145–172.

Willis, S. L., & Schaie, K. W. (1986). Training the elderly on the ability factors of spatial orientation and inductive reasoning. *Psychology and aging, 1,* 239–247.

Willis, S. L., Tennstedt, S. L., Marsiske, M., Ball, K., Elias, J., Koepke, K. M., Morris, J. N., Rebok, G. W., Unverzagt, F. W., & Stoddard, A. M. for the ACTIVE Study Group (2006). Long-term effects of cognitive training on everyday functional outcomes in older adults. *Journal of the American Medical Association, 296,* 2805–2814.

Wilmoth, J. M., & Longino, C. F., Jr. (2006). Demographic trends that will shape U.S. policy in the twenty-first century. *Research on Aging, 28,* 269–288.

Wilson, A. E., Smith, M. D., Ross, H. S., & Ross, M. (2004). Young children's personal accounts of their sibling disputes. *Merrill-Palmer Quarterly, 50,* 39–60.

Wilson, G. T., Becker, C. B., & Heffernan, K. (2003). Eating disorders. In E. J. Mash & R. A. Barkley (Eds.), *Child psychopathology* (2nd ed.). New York: Guilford Press.

Wilson, R. (2003, December 5). How babies alter careers for academics. *The Chronicle of Higher Education,* A1, A6–A8.

Wilson, R. S. (1978). Synchronies in mental development: An epigenetic perspective. *Science, 202,* 939–948.

Wilson, R. S. (1983). The Louisville twin study: Developmental synchronies in behavior. *Child Development, 54,* 298–316.

Wilson, R. S., Arnold, S. E., Tang, Y. & Bennett, D. A. (2006). Odor identification and decline in different cognitive domains in old age, *Neuroepidemiology, 26,* 61–67.

Wilson, S. J., Lipsey, M. W., & Derzon, J. H. (2003). The effects of school-based intervention programs on aggressive behavior: A meta-analysis. *Journal of Consulting and Clinical Psychology, 71,* 136–149.

Wilson-Costello, D., Friedman, H., Minich, N., Siner, B., Taylor, G., Schluchter, M., & Hack, M. (2007). Improved neurodevelopmental outcomes for extremely low birth weight infants in 2000–2002. *Pediatrics, 119,* 37–45.

Wineberg, H., & Werth, J. L. Jr. (2003). Physician-assisted suicide in Oregon: What are the key factors? *Death Studies, 27,* 501–518.

Wingfield, A., Poon, L. W., Lombardi, L., & Lowe, D. (1985). Speed of processing in normal aging: Effects of speech rate, linguistic structure, and processing time. *Journal of Gerontology, 40,* 579–595.

Wink, P., Ciciolla, L., Dillon, M., & Tracy, A. (2007). Religiousness, spiritual seeking, and personality: Findings from a longitudinal study. *Journal of Personality, 75,* 1051–1070.

Wink, P., & Dillon, M. (2002). Spiritual development across the adult life course: Findings from a longitudinal study. *Journal of Adult Development, 9,* 79–94.

Wink, P., & Dillon, M. (2003). Religiousness, spirituality, and psychosocial functioning in late adulthood: findings from a longitudinal study. *Psychology and Aging, 18*, 916–924.

Wink, P., & Dillon, M. (2008). Religiousness, spirituality, and psychosocial functioning in late adulthood: Findings from a longitudinal study. *Psychology of Religion and Spirituality, S* (1), 102–115.

Wink, P., & Helson, R. (1993). Personality change in women and their partners. *Journal of Personality and Social Psychology, 65*, 597–605.

Winkler, I., Kushnerenko, E., Horvath, J., Ceponiene, R., Fellman, V., Huotilainen, M., Naatanen, R., & Sussman, E. (2003). Newborn infants can organize the auditory world. *Proceedings of the National Academy of Sciences, 100*, 11812–11815.

Winner, E. (1996). *Gifted children: Myths and realities.* New York: Basic Books.

Winsler, A., Carlton, M. P., & Barry, M. J. (2000). Age-related changes in preschool children's systematic use of private speech in a natural setting. *Journal of Child Language, 27*, 665–687.

Wismer Fries, A. B., Shirtcliff, E. A., & Pollak, S. D. (2008). Neuroendocrine dysregulation following early social deprivation in children. *Developmental Psychobiology, 50*, 588–599.

Witt, S. (1997). Parental influence on children's socialization to gender roles. *Adolescence, 32*, 253–259.

Witte, K. (2006, April 2). Untitled. *Washington Post*, p. D1.

Wlodkowski, R. J. (1999). *Enhancing adult motivation to learn: A comprehensive guide for teaching all adults.* San Francisco: Jossey-Bass Higher and Adult Education Series.

Wodrich, D. L. (2006). Sex chromosome anomalies. In L. Phelps (Ed.), *Chronic health–related disorders in children: Collaborative medical and psychoeducational interventions.* Washington, DC: American Psychological Association.

Wolchik, S. A., West, S. G., Sandler, I. N., Tein, J. Y., Coatsworth, D., Lengua, L., Weiss, L., Anderson, E. R., Greene, S. M., & Griffin, W. A. (2000). An experimental evaluation of theory-based mother and mother–child programs for children of divorce. *Journal of Consulting and Clinical Psychology, 68*, 843–856.

Wolfe, J., Grier, H. E., Klar, N., Levin, S. B., Ellenbogen, J. M., Salem-Schatz, S., Emanuel, E. J., & Weeks, J. C. (2000). Symptoms and suffering at the end of life in children with cancer. *New England Journal of Medicine, 342*, 326–333.

Wolff, P. H. (1963). Observations on the early development of smiling. In B. M. Foss (Ed.), *Determinants of infant behavior* (Vol. 2). London: Methuen.

Wolfner, G. D., & Gelles, R. J. (1993). A profile of violence toward children: A national study. *Child Abuse and Neglect, 17*, 197–212.

Wolfson, A. R., & Carskadon, M. A. (1998). Sleep schedules and daytime functioning in adolescents. *Child Development, 69*, 875–998.

Women's Health Initiative (2004). *The estrogen-plus-progestin study.* Available at: http://www.nhlbi.nih.gov/whi/estro_pro.htm. Accessed: September 9, 2004.

Wong, C. A., Eccles, J. S., & Sameroff, A. (2003). The influence of ethnic discrimination and ethnic identification on African American adolescents' school and socioemotional adjustment. *Journal of Personality, 71*, 1197–1232.

Wong, J. Y., & Earl, J. K. (2009). Towards an integrated model of individual, psychosocial, and organizational predictors of retirement adjustment. *Journal of Vocational Behavior, 75*, 1–13.

Wong, P. T. P., & Watt, L. M. (1991). What types of reminiscence are associated with successful aging? *Psychology and Aging, 6*, 272–279.

Woo, S. M., & Keatinge, C. (2008). *Diagnosis and treatment of mental disorders across the lifespan.* New York: Wiley.

Wood, E., Desmarais, S., & Gugula, S. (2002). The impact of parenting experience on gender stereotyped toy play of children. *Sex Roles, 47*, 39–49.

Woodhill, B. M., & Samuels, C. A. (2003). Positive and negative androgyny and their relationship with psychological health and well-being. *Sex Roles, 49*, 555–565.

Woodhill, B. M., & Samuels, C. A. (2004). Desirable and undesirable androgyny: A prescription for the twenty-first century. *Journal of Gender Studies, 13*, 15–28.

Woodward, A. L. (2009). Infants' grasp of others' intentions. *Current Directions in Psychological Science, 18*, 53–57.

Woodward, A. L., & Markman, E. M. (1998). Early word learning. In D. Kuhn & R. S. Siegler (Vol. Eds.), W. Damon (Editor-in-Chief), *Handbook of child psychology: Vol. 2. Cognition, perception, and language* (5th ed.), 371–420. New York: Wiley.

Woodward, L., Fergusson, D. M., & Belsky, J. (2000). Timing of parental separation and attachment to parents in adolescence: Results of a prospective study from birth to age 16. *Journal of Marriage and the Family, 62*, 162–174.

Woolley, J. D., Boerger, E. A., & Markman, A. B. (2004). A visit from the Candy Witch: Factors influencing young children's belief in a novel fantastical being. *Developmental Science, 7*, 456–468.

Worchel, F. F., Copeland, D. R., & Barker, D. G. (1987). Control-related coping strategies in pediatric oncology patients. *Journal of Pediatric Psychology, 12*, 25–38.

Worden, J. W., & Silverman, P. R. (1996). Parental death and the adjustment of school-age children. *Omega: Journal of Death and Dying, 33*, 91–102.

Worden, J. W., & Silverman, P. S. (1993). Grief and depression in newly widowed parents with school-age children. *Omega: Journal of Death and Dying, 27*, 251–261.

Worfolk, J. B. (2000). Heat waves: Their impact on the health of elders. *Geriatric Nursing, 21*, 70–77.

"World's Oldest Mother Gives Birth at 70 Years Old" (2009). Available at: www.incrediblebirths.com/Worlds-Oldest-Mother.html. Accessed: July 27, 2009.

Wortman, C. B., & Boerner, K. (2007). Beyond the myths of coping with loss: Prevailing assumptions versus scientific evidence. In H. S. Friedman & R. C. Silver (Eds.), *Foundations of health psychology.* New York: Oxford University Press.

Wortman, C. B., & Silver, R. C. (2001). The myths of coping with loss revisited. In M. S. Stroebe, R. O. Hansson, W. Stroebe, & H. Schut (Eds.), *Handbook of bereavement research. Consequences, coping, and care.* Washington, DC: American Psychological Association.

Wright, S. P., Horn, S. P., & Sanders, W. L. (1997). Teacher and classroom context effects on student achievement: Implications for teacher evaluation. *Journal of Personnel Evaluation in Education 11*, 57–67.

Wright, W. E., & Shay, J. W. (2005). Telomere biology in aging and cancer. *Journal of the American Geriatrics Society, 53*, S292–S294.

Wrosch, C., Bauer, I., & Scheier, M. F. (2005). Regret and quality of life across the adult life span: The influence of disengagement and available future goals. *Psychology and Aging, 20*, 657–670.

Wrosch, C., Schulz, R., & Heckhausen, J. (2004). Health stresses and depressive symptomatology in the elderly: A control-process approach. *Current Directions in Psychological Science, 13*, 17–20.

Wu, C. H., Cheng, Y., Ip, H. M., & McBride-Change, C. (2005). Age differences in creativity: Task structure and knowledge base. *Creativity Research Journal, 17*, 321–326.

Wu, C. Y., Yu, T. J., & Chen, M. J. (2000). Age related testosterone level changes and male andropause syndrome. *Changgeng Yi Xue Za Zhi [Chinese Medical Journal], 23*, 348–353.

Wu, P., & Chiou, W. (2008). Postformal thinking and creativity among late adolescents: A post-Piagetian approach. *Adolescence, 43*, 237–251.

Wu, S., Jia, M., Ruan, Y., Liu, J., Guo, Y., Shuang, M., Gong, X., Zhang, Y., Yang, X., & Zhang, D. (2005). Positive association of the oxytocin receptor gene (OXTR) with autism in the Chinese Han population. *Biological Psychiatry, 58*, 74–77.

Wu, T., Mendola, P., & Buck, G. M. (2002). Ethnic differences in the presence of secondary sex characteristics and menarche among US girls: The Third National Health and Nutrition Examination Survey, 1988–1994. *Pediatrics, 110*, 752–757.

Wurmser, H., Rieger, M., Domogalla, C., Kahnt, A., Buchwald, J., Kowatsch, M., Kuehnert, N., Buske-Kirschbaum, A., Papousek, M., Pirke, K. M., & von Voss, H. (2006). Association between life stress during pregnancy and infant crying in the first six months of postpartum: A prospective longitudinal study. *Early Human Development, 82*, 341–349.

Wysocki, C. J., Louie, J., Leyden, J. J., Blank, D., Gill, M., & Smith, L., McDermott, K, & Preti, G. (2009, April 7). Cross-adaptation of a model human stress-related odor with fragrance chemicals and ethyl esters of axillary odorants: Gender-specific effects. *Flavour and Fragrance Journal, 24* (5), 209–218.

Y

Yaffe, K., Barnes, D., Nevitt, M., Lui, L., & Covinsky, K. (2001). A prospective study of physical activity and cognitive decline in el-derly women. *Archives of Internal Medicine, 161*, 1703–1708.

Yamagata, S., Suzuki, A., Ando, J., Ono, Y., Kijima, N., Yoshimura, K., Ostendorf, F., Angleitner, A., Riemann, R., Spinath, F. M., Livesley, W. J., & Jang, K. L. (2006). Is the genetic structure of human personality universal? A cross-cultural twin study from North America, Europe, and Asia. *Journal of Personality and Social Psychology, 90*, 987–998.

Yamasue, H., Kuwabara, H., Kawakubo, Y., & Kasai, K. (2009). Oxytocin, sexually dimorphic features of the social brain, and autism. *Psychiatry and Clinical Neurosciences, 63*, 129–140.

Yan, A. F., Voorhees, C. C., Clifton, K, Burnier, C., Voorhees, C. C., Clifton, K, & Burnier, C. (2009). "Do you see what I see?"—Correlates of multidimensional measures of neighborhood types and perceived physical activity-related neighborhood barriers and facilitators for urban youth. *Preventive Medicine*, Epub ahead of print.

Yan, B., & Arlin, P. K. (1995). Nonabsolute/relativistic thinking: A common factor underlying models of postformal reasoning? *Journal of Adult Development, 2*, 223–240.

Yan, J. H., Thomas, J. R., & Stelmach, G. E. (1998). Aging and rapid aiming arm movement control. *Experimental Aging Research, 24*, 155–168.

Yan, J. H., Thomas, J. R., Stelmach, G. E., & Thomas, K. T. (2000). Developmental features of rapid aiming arm movements across the lifespan. *Journal of Motor Behavior, 32*, 121–140.

Yeates, K. O., & Selman, R. L. (1989). Social competence in the schools: Toward an integrative developmental model for intervention. *Developmental Review, 9*, 64–100.

Yeh, Y., & Wu, J. (2006). The cognitive processes of pupils' technological creativity. *Creativity Research Journal, 18*, 213–227.

Yendovitskaya, T. V. (1971). Development of attention. In A. V. Zaporozhets & D. B. Elkonin (Eds.),

The psychology of preschool children. Cambridge, MA: MIT Press.

Yeung, W. J., & Pfeiffer, K. M. (2009). The black-white test score gap and early home environment. *Social Science Research, 38*, 412–437.

Yilmaz, G., Hizli, S., Karacan, C., Yurdakök, K., Coskun, T., & Dilmen, U. (2009). Effect of passive smoking on growth and infection rates of breast-fed and non-breast-fed infants. *Pediatrics International, 51*, 352–358.

Yonkers, K. A., O'Brien, P.M., & Eriksson, E. (2008). Premenstrual syndrome. *Lancet, 371*, 1200–1210.

Youn, G. Y., Knight, B. G., Jeong, H. S., & Benton, D. (1999). Differences in familism values and caregiving outcomes among Korean, Korean American, and White American dementia caregivers. *Psychology and Aging, 14*, 355–364.

Young, W. C., Goy, R. W., & Phoenix, C. H. (1964). Hormones and sexual behavior. *Science, 143*, 212–218.

Youngblade, L. M., & Dunn, J. (1995). Individual differences in young children's pretend play with mother and sibling: Links to relationships and understanding of other people's feelings and beliefs. *Child Development, 66*, 1472–1492.

Youniss, J. (1980). *Parents and peers in social development. A Sullivan–Piaget perspective*. Chicago: University of Chicago Press.

Youth Risk Behavior Survey (2009). *National Trends in Risk Behaviors*. Available at: http://www.cdc.gov/HealthyYouth/yrbs/trends.htm. Accessed: October 27, 2009.

Yuill, N. (1993). Understanding of personality and dispositions. In M. Bennett (Ed.), *The development of social cognition: The child as psychologist*. New York: Guilford.

Z

Zahn-Waxler, C., Friedman, R. J., Cole, P. M., Mizuta, I., & Himura, N. (1996). Japanese and United States preschool children's responses to conflict and distress. *Child Development, 67*, 2462–2477.

Zahn-Waxler, C., Radke-Yarrow, M., Wagner, E., & Chapman, M. (1992). Development of concern for others. *Developmental Psychology, 28*, 126–136.

Zajac, R., & Hayne, H. (2003). I don't think that's what really happened: The effect of cross-examination on the accuracy of children's reports. *Journal of Experimental Psychology: Applied, 9*, 187–195.

Zajonc, R. B. (2001a). Birth order debate resolved? *American Psychologist, 56*, 522–523.

Zajonc, R. B. (2001b). The family dynamics of intellectual development. *American Psychologist, 56*, 490–496.

Zamrini, E., & Quiceno, M. (2009). Other causes of dementia. In M. F. Weiner & A. M. Lipton (Eds.), *The American Psychiatric Publishing textbook of Alzheimer disease and other dementias*. Washington, DC: American Psychiatric Publishing.

Zander, L., & Chamberlain, G. (1999). Place of birth. *British Medical Journal, 318*, 721.

Zanor, C. (2008). One way to handle grief: Just get over it. *The Washington Post*, F4.

Zaporozhets, A. V. (1965). The development of perception in the preschool child. *Monographs of the Society for Research in Child Development, 30* (2, Serial No. 100), 82–101.

Zarit, S. H. (2009). Empirically supported treatment for family caregivers. In S. H. Qualls & S. H. Zarit (Eds.), *Aging families and caregiving*. Hoboken, NJ: John Wiley.

Zaslow, M. (1980). Relationships among peers in kibbutz toddler groups. *Child Psychiatry and Human Development, 10*, 178–189.

Zeanah, C. H., & Smyke, A. T. (2008). Attachment disorders in family and social context. *Infant Mental Health Journal, 29*, 219–233.

Zemach, I., Chang, S., & Teller, D. Y. (2006). Infant color vision: Prediction of infants' spontaneous color preferences. *Vision Research, 47*, 1368–1381.

Zemel, B. (2002). Body composition during growth and development. In N. Cameron (Ed.), *Human growth and development*, 271–293. New York: Academic Press.

Zhang, H. (2009). The new realities of aging in contemporary China: Coping with the decline in family care. In J. Sokolovsky (Ed.), *The cultural context of aging* (3rd ed.). Westport, CT: Praeger.

Zhang, L. (2002). Thinking styles and cognitive development. *Journal of Genetic Psychology, 163*, 179–195.

Zhang, T., & Meaney, M. J. (2010). Epigenetics and the environmental regulation of the genome and its function. *Annual Review of Psychology, 61*, 439–466.

Zick, C. D., & Holden, K. (2000). An assessment of the wealth holdings of recent widows. *Journal of Gerontology: Social Sciences, 55*, S90–S97.

Zigler, E. (1995). Can we "cure" mild mental retardation among individuals in the lower socioeconomic stratum? *American Journal of Public Health, 85*, 302–304.

Zigler, E., Abelson, W. D., Trickett, P. K., & Seitz, V. (1982). Is an intervention program necessary to improve economically disadvantaged children's IQ scores? *Child Development, 53*, 340–348.

Zigler, E., & Hodapp, R. M. (1991). Behavioral functioning in individuals with mental retardation. *Annual Review of Psychology, 42*, 29–50.

Zimmerman, F. J., Christakis, D. A., & Meltzoff, A. N. (2007). Television and DVD/video viewing in children younger than 2 years. *Archives of Pediatrics & Adolescent Medicine, 161*, 473–479.

Zimmerman, F. J., Gilkerson, J., Richards, J. A., Christakis, D. A., Xu, D., Gray, S., & Yapanel, U. (2009). Teaching by listening: The importance of adult-child conversations to language development. *Pediatrics, 124*, 342–349.

Zimmermann, M. B. (2007). The adverse effects of mild-to-moderate iodine deficiency during pregnancy and childhood: a review. *Thyroid, 17*, 829–835.

Zimprich, D., & Martin, M. (2002). Can longitudinal changes in processing speed explain longitudinal age changes in fluid intelligence? *Psychology and Aging, 17*, 690–695.

Zisook, S., & Shuchter, S. R. (2001). Treatment of the depressions of bereavement. *American Behavioral Scientist, 44*, 782–797.

Zissimopoulos, J. M., & Karoly, L. A. (2009). Labor-force dynamics at older ages. Movements into self-employment for workers and nonworkers. *Research on Aging, 31*, 89–111.

Zorn, B., Auger, Velikonja, V., Kolbezen, M., Meden-Vrtovec, H. (2008). Psychological factors in male partners of infertile couples: Relationship with semen quality and early miscarriage. *International Journal of Andrology, 31*, 557–564.

Zosuls, K. M. Ruble, D. N., Bornstein, M. H., & Greulich, F. K. (2009). The acquisition of gender labels in infancy: Implications for gender-typed play. *Developmental Psychology, 45*, 688–701.

Zucker, A. N., Ostrove, J. M., & Stewart, A. J. (2002). College-educated women's personality development in adulthood: Perceptions and age differences. *Psychology and Aging, 17*, 236–244.

Zvoch, K., & Stevens, J. J. (2006). Longitudinal effects of school context and practice on middle school mathematics achievement. *The Journal of Educational Research, 99*, 347–356.

Zwaigenbaum, L., Bryson, S., Rogers, T., Roberts, W., Brian, J., & Szatmari, P. (2005). Behavioral manifestations of autism in the first year of life. *International Journal of Developmental Neuroscience, 23*, 143–152.

Name Index

Subject Index

later development and, 475
parenting styles and, 471
personality and, 472
relationship quality, 469–473
separations and, 474
social deprivation and, 473–474
types of, 467–469
Attachments
adolescent, 481
adult styles, 487–489
bereavement model, 570–572
contextual aspects, 472
dismissing style of, 487
disorganized-disoriented, 471
fears of, 469
later development and, 463–464
nature/nurture and, 462–463
oxytocin and, 463–464
parent–child, 476–477
parenting styles and, 471
quality of, 469–473
resistance, 469–470
secure, 469
theory of, 462
therapies, 490
true, 469
Attention
adult, 213
defined, 201
joint, 429
problems of, 202–205
selective, 201–202
systematic, 202
Attention deficit hyperactivity disorder (ADHD)
adults with, 203
causes, 203–205
development of, 203
onset age, 203
symptoms, 202
test for, 204
treatment, 205
Attention spans, 201, 206
Attitude, gender role in, 413
Authoritarian parents, 502
Authoritative parents, 502
Authority morality, 438, 448
Autism
causes, 536–537
characteristics, 536
Down syndrome and, 429
DSM-IV-TR criteria, 535
identification of, 534–535
outcomes, 537–539
prevalence of, 535–536
theory of mind and, 429
treatment, 537–539
Autism spectrum disorders (ASDS), 535
Autobiographical memory
adult, 274–275
beginning of, 267–268
Autonomy
adolescent achievement of, 508–509
development of, 53
shame and doubt *versus*, 382

B

Babbling, 326
Baby biographies, 23
Baby boom generation, 34
Bandura, Albert, theory of, 57–59
Bargaining, 569
Bayley Scales of Infant Development, 295–296
Behavior
antisocial, 448–453
exploratory, 469
gender role, 413
gender-typed, 401–402
inhibition, 364–365
neonate, 155
prosocial, 436, 442–444
school refusal, 53
sexual, 414–415, 418–421
Behavior rating scale, 296
Behavioral genetics studies. *See also* Nature/nurture
ADHD findings, 204–205
breeding, 91

controversies, 101, 103
intellectual ability findings, 94–95
molecular genetics and, 93–94
personality findings, 95–96
psychological disorder findings, 96–97
temperament findings, 95–96
twins and adoption, 91–93
Behaviorism, 54
Belief
desire and, 430
false, 430
Bereavement. *See also* Grief
attachment model of, 570–572
care during, 584–585
child, 575–576
defined, 570
dual-process model of, 572
family program, 585
human development and, 583
Beta-amyloid, 553
Bias
IQ tests, 312–313
moral reasoning and, 453–455
Bidirectional influences model, 65
Big-fish–little-pond effect, 369–370
Bioecological model
introduction of, 63
principles of, 20–22
Biological aging, 15
Biological sex, 394
Birthing practices, 128–129
Blood sampling. *See* Maternal blood sampling
BMI. *See* Body mass index (BMI)
Bodily-kinesthetic intelligence, 291
Body mass index (BMI), 166
Bonding, 463
Bones, 154, 180
Born to Learn, 336
Bottle feeding, 137
Brain
adolescent, 150
aging, 152–153
developmental stages, 111
early experience and, 199
fetal, 113
genetics and, 150–151
language and, 330
lateralization of, 151
neurogenesis in, 151–152
neurotransmitters, 544
plasticity of, 151
Brazelton training, 136
Breast feeding, 137
Bronfenbrenner, Urie, theory of, 21–22
Brown v. Board of Education, 346
Bulimia nervosa, 545

C

Caloric restriction, 567
Caregivers. *See* Parents
Carriers, 82
Cascade model of substance abuse, 548–549
Case studies
defined, 29
life-span development, 29
socialization, 446
Cataracts, 199
Catch-up growth, 147
Centenarians, 568
Centration, 229
Cephalocaudal principle, 153
Cesarean section, 129, 131
Characteristic adaptations, 360
Chemical senses
adolescent, 207–208
aging and, 215–216
infants, 196–197
Child abuse
attention given to, 522
perpetuator profile, 522–523
victim profile, 523–524
Child effects model, 505
Childbirth
anoxia and, 129–131
changes in, 128–129
complications, 131

cultural factors, 132–133
father's experience, 133–135
hazards in, 132
medications, 131–132
mother's experience, 132–133
postponing, 499
stages of, 129–130
Child-directed speech, 334
Childhood
amnesia, 267
changing views of, 17–19
gene expression in, 83
growth during, 163
growth patterns, 164
peers in, 464–465
psychological disorders in, 540
psychosexual development in, 49–50
psychosocial stages of, 52–54
sexuality, 414–416
Children
academic achievement by, 338–339
attention development, 201–205
bereavement by, 575–576
classification problems, 230, 232
concrete operations stage, 233–234
conservation by, 229–231, 233–234
continuity of, 541, 543
creativity of, 297–299
death concept of, 573–575
death of, 575, 579–580
depression in, 543–544
developing personality in, 368
discontinuity of, 541, 543
egocentrism of, 230
externalizing problems by, 540–543
friendships and, 480–481
gender differences in, 399–402
health of, 165–167
hearing-impaired, 194–195
Hurricane Katrina effects on, 542
inclusion problems, 232
intelligence of, 296–300
internalizing problems by, 540–543
moral development, 444–447
overweight, 166–167
parental attachments, 476–477
peer networks, 477
physical behavior, 163, 165
play by, 477–479
popularity of, 479–480
in poverty, 499
preoperational stage, 229–233
preschool, 232–233
psychological treatment for, 544
psychopathology in, 540–545
reaction time, 165
reading, learning to, 341–344
Santa Claus belief by, 230
self-esteem of, 367–368
sense of self, 366–367
seriation and, 234
sexual abuse of, 415–416
theory of mind and, 429–433
wellness of, 165–167
Chlamydia, 420
Chorion, 109
Chorionic villus sampling (CVS), 90
Chromosome abnormalities, 86–87
Chromosomes
characterization, 78
gender roles and, 403
Chronosystem, 22
Cigarette smoking. *See* Tobacco
Classical conditioning
defined, 54
phases in, 55
principles of, 54
strengths of, 59
weaknesses of, 59
Classification problems, 230, 232
Clinical method, 222
Cliques, 482
Cocaine, prenatal effects of, 120
Cochlear implants, 195
Coercive family environment theory, 450
Coercive family environments, 452

single head of household, 499
teens relationship with, 374
teens sexual activity and, 420–421
unmarried, 498
Parkes/Bowlby attachment model of bereavement, 570–572
Participants, rights of, 38–39
Passion, 486
Passive euthanasia, 561
Passive gene–environment correlations, 100–101
Pattern perception, 189–191
Patterson, Gerald, theory of, 450
Peers
acceptance, 479–480
childhood in, 464–465
dark side of, 473
infants, 475–476
networks, 477
Pendulum problem, 235
Perception
depth, 191–193
early influences, 198–201
factors influencing, 186–187
pattern, 189–191
speech, 194–196
Perceptual salience, 229
Perinatal environment. *See also* Childbirth
cultural aspects, 128–129
cultural factors, 132–133
defined, 128
father's experience, 133–135
mother's experience, 132–133
resilience in, 141
risks, 141
sibling adjustment, 135
Perinatologist, 129
Peripheral vision, 212
Permissive parents, 502
Permissiveness–restrictiveness parents, 502
Personal distress, 530
Personal fable, 240
Personality. *See also* Temperament
adolescent, 369–375
adult, 375–389
aging and, 389
attachment style and, 472
basic concepts of, 360
changing, factors for, 381
children, 366–369
continuity in, 379–381
defined, 360
dimensions of, 379
discontinuity in, 379–381
dying and, 570
Erikson view, 381–384
heredity and, 381
ranking changes, 379–381
scale for, 362
theories of, 360–363
traits, 360
vocational development, 385
Personality development theory, 361
Pesticide exposure, 124
Phallic stage, 49–50
Phenotypes, 81
Phenylketonuria (PKU), 88, 102
Phonemes, 194
Phonics, 343
Phonological awareness, 341
Physical behavior
adolescent, 171–172
children, 163, 165
infants, 157–162
Physiological measurements, 28–29
Piaget, Jean. *See also* Cognitive developmental theory
challenges to, 245–246
contributions of, 244
moral development theory, 437
theory of, 60–62, 222
Vygotsky *versus*, 250
Pincer grasp, 160
Pitocin. *See* Oxytocin
PKU. *See* Phenylketonuria (PKU)
Placenta, 109
Placental barrier, 109

Plasticity
brain and, 151
defined, 24
Play
characterization, 477
frequency of, 478
imaginative, 477–478
importance of, 478–479
rule-governed, 478
social aspects of, 477–478
Playmate selection, 401
PMS. *See* Premenstrual syndrome (PMS)
Pollutants. *See also specific substance*
prenatal effects of, 123–124
Polygenic inheritance, 85
Positive effect, 485
Positive punishment, 56
Positive reinforcement, 55
Postconventional reasoning, 448
Postformal thought, 242
Postpartum depression, 133
Post-traumatic stress disorder, 415–416
Poverty. *See* Socioeconomic status (SES)
Power assertion, 445
Practical component, 292
Practical intelligence, 292
Preconventional morality, 438, 448
Preferential looking, 187–188
Pregnancy. *See also* Childbirth
age at, 124–126
denial of, 134
emotional factors, 126
ethnic factors, 124–126
miscarriage, 109
nutritional factors, 126–128
prenatal screenings, 89–90
racial factors, 124–126
teen, 419–420
Preimplantation genetic diagnosis, 90
Premature infants, 138
Premenstrual syndrome (PMS), 176
Prenatal development
conception, 108–109
embryonic period, 109–111
fetal period, 111–114
germinal period, 109
screenings, 89–90
taste, 196–196
Prenatal environment
diseases and, 120–123
hearing in, 193
maternal factors, 124–127
overview of, 114
paternal factors, 128
pollutants and, 123–124
radiation and, 123
resilience in, 141
risks, 141
substance abuse and, 115–120
toxins and, 115
vulnerability of, 114–115
Preoccupied internal working model, 487
Preoperational stage, 61, 229
Presbyopia, 211
Preservation errors, 264
Pretend play, 429, 477
Primary circular reactions, 225
Private speech, 248
Proactive parenting strategies, 446
Problem solving
aging and, 280–282
children, 269–271
infant, 259
Procedural memory, 258
Production deficiency, 264
Progesterone, 148
Programmed theories, 565–566
Prosocial behavior, 436, 442–444
Prosody, 325
Proximodistal principle, 153
Prozac, 544
Psychoanalytic theory
defense mechanisms, 51
instincts and, 48–49
learning theories *versus*, 58–59

moral development, 436–437
neo-Freudian, 52–54
personality, 361
perspective of, 67
psychic energy and, 49
psychosexual development, 49–51
strengths of, 51–52
teen pregnancy and, 70–71
unconscious motives and, 49
weaknesses of, 51–52
Psychological development
adolescents, 169–170
adults, 175–186
defined, 15
Psychological disorders, 96–97
Psychometric approach, 289–291
Psychopathology. *See* Developmental psychopathology
Psychosexual development
anal stage, 49–50
defined, 49
latency period, 51
oral stage, 49
phallic stage, 49–50
Psychosocial theory
early adult intimacy concept, 382–383
early conflicts concept, 382
midlife generativity concept, 383
stages of, 52–54, 382
Puberty
anorexia onset and, 546
defined, 167
physical signs of, 167–168
psychological aspects, 169–170
Punishment. *See* Correctional method
Punishment–and–obedience orientation, 438
Pupil changes, 209–211

Q

Quantitative changes, 47
Quinlan, Karen Ann, 561

R

Race. *See also* Ethnicity
death and, 563
fetal health and, 124–126
IQ scores and, 312–314
school integration and, 346–347
sexual maturation and, 167–168
Radiation, 123
Random assignment, 30
Reaching, 160
Reactions
primary circular, 225
tertiary circular, 226
time, 165
Reactive attachment disorder, 490
Reading
achievement of, 341
advancement in, 342
alphabetic principles and, 341–342
difficulties, 342–343
literacy and, 342
teaching approaches, 343–344
Real self, 375–376
Reasoning, hypothetical–deductive, 236
Recall, memory and, 261–262
Reciprocal determinism, 58
Recognition
face, 191
memory, 258
recall *versus*, 277
Reconstituted families, 520–521
Reflex, defined, 155
Reinforcement
negative, 55–56
positive, 55
vicarious, 57
Relationships. *See also* Attachment
adolescent, 481–484
adult, 484–491
childhood peers, 464–465
children, 476–480
early emotional development, 465–466
emotions and, 466–467

SUMMARY OF PHYSICAL, COGNITIVE, PERSONAL, AND SOCIAL DEVELOPMENT ACROSS THE LIFE SPAN

Period	Physical Development	Cognitive Development
Infant (Birth to 2 years)	Brain rapidly grows and is pruned; physical growth is rapid. Reflexes are followed by more voluntary motor control; walking occurs at 1 year. Functioning senses are available at birth; there is an early ability to understand sensory information.	Sensorimotor period: Through senses and actions, infants acquire symbolic capacity and object-permanence concept. Cooing and babbling are followed by one-word and two-word sentences. Learning capacity and recognition memory are present from birth; recall improves with age.
Preschool child (2 to 5 years)	Rapid brain development continues. Coordination and fine motor skills improve. Perceptual abilities are good; attention span is short.	Preoperational stage: Thought is guided by perceptions rather than logic. Symbolic capacity (language acquisition and pretend play) blossoms. There are some limits in information-processing capacity, use of memory strategies, and reasoning.
School-age child (6 to 11 years)	Physical growth is slow; motor skills gradually improve. Children have increased ability to control attention and use the senses intelligently.	Concrete operations stage: Logical actions occur in the head; children master conservation. They also master fine points of language; memory strategies and problem solving with concrete objects improve. IQs begin to stabilize.
Adolescent (12 to 19 years)	Adolescents experience a brain spurt, a growth spurt, and attainment of sexual maturity. Physical functioning improves. Concern with body image is common.	Formal operations stage: Hypothetical and abstract thought emerge; scientific problem solving improves. Attention and information-processing skills continue to improve, linked to brain growth spurt.
Young adult (20 to 39 years)	This is the time of peak functioning, but a gradual decline in physical and perceptual capacities begins.	Intellectual functioning is mostly stable, and peak expertise and creative achievement often occur. Fluid intelligence may begin to decline, but crystallized knowledge is maintained well.
Middle-aged adult (40 to 64 years)	Physical declines become noticeable (e.g., some loss of endurance, need for reading glasses). Chronic illness increases. Menopause and male andropause occur.	Sophisticated cognitive skills develop, especially in areas of expertise. There is the possibility of growth beyond formal thought and gains in knowledge.
Older adult (65 years and older)	Physical decline continues; more chronic disease, disability, and sensory impairment are common; and reaction time slows. But there is also continued plasticity and reorganization of the brain in response to intellectual stimulation.	Declines in cognition are common but not inevitable. Slower learning, memory problems, declines in IQ and problem solving occur, especially if skills are rarely exercised, but crystallized intelligence survives longer than fluid.